Fodor's 06

HAWAI`I

**Where to Stay and Eat
for All Budgets**

**Must-See Sights
and Local Secrets**

Ratings You Can Trust

Fodor's Travel Publications   New York, Toronto, London, Sydney, Auckland
www.fodors.com

FODOR'S HAWAI'I 2006
Editors: Amanda Theunissen and Mary Beth Bohman

Editorial Production: David N. Downing
Editorial Contributors: Wanda Adams, Don Chapman, Andy Collins, Joan Conrow, Chad Pata, Peter Serafin, Kim Steutermann Rogers, Lance Tominaga, Amy Westervelt, Joana Varawa, Shannon Wianecki, Paul Wood, Maggie Wunsch, Katie Young
Maps: David Lindroth, *cartographer;* Rebecca Baer and Bob Blake, *map editors*
Design: Fabrizio La Rocca, *creative director;* Siobhan O'Hare, Chie Ushio, Tina Malaney, Brian Panto, Moon Sun Kim.
Photography: Melanie Marin, *senior picture editor;* Cover Photo (waterfall, Maui): Thinkstock/Creatas
Production/Manufacturing: Angela L. McLean

SPECIAL SALES
This book is available for special discounts for bulk purchases for sales promotions or premiums. Special editions, including personalized covers, excerpts of existing books, and corporate imprints, can be created in large quantities for special needs. For more information, write to Special Markets/Premium Sales, 1745 Broadway, MD 6-2, New York, New York 10019, or e-mail specialmarkets@randomhouse.com.

AN IMPORTANT TIP & AN INVITATION
Although all prices, opening times, and other details in this book are based on information supplied to us at press time, changes occur all the time in the travel world, and Fodor's cannot accept responsibility for facts that become outdated or for inadvertent errors or omissions. So **always confirm information when it matters,** especially if you're making a detour to visit a specific place. Your experiences—positive and negative—matter to us. If we have missed or misstated something, **please write to us.** We follow up on all suggestions. Contact the Hawai'i editor at editors@fodors.com or c/o Fodor's at 1745 Broadway, New York, NY 10019.

PRINTED IN THE UNITED STATES OF AMERICA

10 9 8 7 6 5 4 3 2 1

Be a Fodor's Correspondent

Your opinion matters. It matters to us. It matters to your fellow Fodor's travelers, too. And we'd like to hear it. In fact, we *need* to hear it.

When you share your experiences and opinions, you become an active member of the Fodor's community. That means we'll not only use your feedback to make our books better, but we'll publish your names and comments whenever possible. Throughout our guides, look for "Word of Mouth," excerpts of your unvarnished feedback.

Here's how you can help improve Fodor's for all of us.

Tell us when we're right. We rely on local writers to give you an insider's perspective. But our writers and staff editors—who are the best in the business—depend on you. Your positive feedback is a vote to renew our recommendations for the next edition.

Tell us when we're wrong. We're proud that we update most of our guides every year. But we're not perfect. Things change. Hotels cut services. Museums change hours. Charming cafés lose charm. If our writer didn't quite capture the essence of a place, tell us how you'd do it differently. If any of our descriptions are inaccurate or inadequate, we'll incorporate your changes in the next edition and will correct factual errors at fodors.com *immediately.*

Tell us what to include. You probably have had fantastic travel experiences that aren't yet in Fodor's. Why not share them with a community of like-minded travelers? Maybe you chanced upon a beach or bistro or B&B that you don't want to keep to yourself. Tell us why we should include it. And share your discoveries and experiences with everyone directly at fodors.com. Your input may lead us to add a new listing or highlight a place we cover with a "Highly Recommended" star or with our highest rating, "Fodor's Choice."

Give us your opinion instantly at our feedback center at www.fodors.com/feedback. You may also e-mail editors@fodors.com with the subject line "Hawai'i Editor." Or send your nominations, comments, and complaints by mail to Hawai'i Editor, Fodor's, 1745 Broadway, New York, NY 10019.

You and travelers like you are the heart of the Fodor's community. Make our community richer by sharing your experiences. Be a Fodor's correspondent.

Aloha!

Tim Jarrell, Publisher

CONTENTS

PLANNING YOUR TRIP

Be a Fodor's Correspondent F3
About This Book .F7
What's Where F8
Quintessential Hawai'i F10
If You Like F12
When to Go F14
Smart Travel Tips A to Z F18

THE FACE OF HAWAI'I

1 O'AHU 1
Beaches 7
Water Activities & Tours 15
Golf, Hiking & Outdoor Activities 27
Exploring O'ahu 35
Where to Stay 75
Where to Spa 95
Where to Eat 98
Entertainment & Nightlife 114
Shopping 123
O'ahu Essentials 129

2 MAUI 133
Beaches 139
Water Activities & Tours 145
Golf, Hiking & Outdoor Activities 160
Exploring Maui 171
Where to Stay 196
Where to Spa 228
Where to Eat 231
Entertainment & Nightlife 245
Shopping 249
Maui Essentials 254

3 MOLOKA'I 259
Beaches 263

Water Activities & Tours 265
Golf, Hiking & Outdoor Activities 269
Exploring Moloka'i 273
Where to Eat 280
Where to Stay 282
Entertainment & Nightlife 286
Shopping 286
Moloka'i Essentials 288

4 LĀNA'I 291
Beaches 295
Water Activities & Tours 296
Golf, Hiking & Outdoor Activities 298
Exploring Lāna'i 300
Where to Stay 306
Where to Spa 309
Where to Eat 309
Entertainment & Nightlife 311
Shopping 312
Lāna'i Essentials 313

5 THE BIG ISLAND OF HAWAI'I . .315
Beaches 321
Water Activities & Tours 329
Golf, Hiking & Outdoor Activities 338
Exploring the Big Island 347
Where to Stay 390
Where to Spa 412
Where to Eat 414
Entertainment & Nightlife 432
Shopping 435
Big Island Essentials 441

6 KAUA'I 447
Beaches 452
Water Activities & Tours 459
Golf, Hiking & Outdoor Activities 471
Exploring Kaua'i 485

Where to Stay 502
Where to Spa 516
Where to Eat 517
Entertainment & Nightlife 531
Shopping .535
Kaua'i Essentials 540

UNDERSTANDING HAWAI'I . . .545
The Aloha Shirt; A Colorful
  Swatch of Island History 546
These Volcanic Isles 548
Hawai'i at a Glance 552
Hawaiian Vocabulary 554

INDEX 557

ABOUT OUR WRITERS 566

HAWAI'I IN FOCUS

Pearl Harbor 55
North Shore Surfing & the Triple Crown . . .69
Haleakalā National Park 187
Road to Hāna 197
Hawai'i Volcanoes National Park 368
Hiking the Kalalau Trail 479

CLOSE UPS

Takeout 38
Chinatown 47
Izakaya 106
Beyond "Tiny Bubbles" 118
Diving 101 .151
The Humpback's Winter Home 159
Hawai'i's Flora & Fauna 167
The Boy Who Raised an Island 183
Maui Sightseeing Tours 195
Ironman & Friends 341
Graffiti 350

If Trees Could Talk 380
The Plate Lunch Tradition 422
Hawai'i's Hippy Hippy Shake 433
Seal-Spotting on the South Side 458
Kaua'i Sightseeing Tours 499
The Forbidden Isle 533

MAPS & CHARTS

The Hawaiian Islands F15
Welcome to O'ahu 2–3
Honolulu Including Waikīkī 36–37
Waikīkī 42–43
Downtown Honolulu 49
O'ahu 62–63
Pearl Harbor .56
North Shore .71
Where to Stay in Waikīkī & O'ahu 78–80
Where to Eat in Waikīkī 99
Where to Eat in Honolulu 105
Where to Eat on O'ahu 113
Welcome to Maui 134–135
Maui 174–175
Lahaina 176
Kahului-Wailuku 181
Haleakalā National Park 188–189
Road to Hāna 198–202
Where to Stay in West Maui 208–209
Where to Stay on the South Shore . . .216–217
Where to Stay around Maui 226
Where to Eat on Maui 234–235
Welcome to Moloka'i 260–261
Moloka'i 276
Welcome to Lāna'i 292–293
Lāna'i 303
Welcome to the Big Island 316–317
The Big Island of Hawai'i 348–349

The Kohala District 352
Kailua-Kona 357
South Kona & Ka'u 360
Hawai'i Volcanoes National Park 368
Kīlauea Caldera 370
Chain of Craters Road 373
Hilo Vicinity 379
Hāmākua Coast 383
Puna 387
Where to Stay on the
   Kohala Coast & in Waimea 392-393

Where to Stay on the
   Kona Coast & Upcountry 400-401
Where to Stay Hilo Side & in Volcano ...406
Where to Eat on the Big Island ...426-427
Welcome to Kaua'i 448-449
Kalalau Trail 480-481
Kaua'i 486-487
Where to Stay on Kaua'i 505-507
Where to Eat on Kaua'i 518-519

ABOUT THIS BOOK

Our Ratings

Sometimes you find terrific travel experiences and sometimes they just find you. But usually the burden is on you to select the right combination of experiences. That's where our ratings come in.

As travelers we've all discovered a place so wonderful that its worthiness is obvious. And sometimes that place is so experiential that superlatives don't do it justice: you just have to be there to know. These sights, properties, and experiences get our highest rating, Fodor's Choice, indicated by orange stars throughout this book.

Black stars highlight sights and properties we deem Highly Recommended, places that our writers, editors, and readers praise again and again for consistency and excellence.

By default, there's another category: any place we include in this book is by definition worth your time, unless we say otherwise. And we will.

Disagree with any of our choices? Care to nominate a place or suggest that we rate one more highly? Visit our feedback center at www.fodors.com/feedback.

Budget Well

Hotel and restaurant price categories from ¢ to $$$$ are defined in those sections of each chapter. For attractions, we always give standard adult admission fees; reductions are usually available for children, students, and senior citizens. Want to pay with plastic? AE, D, DC, MC, V following restaurant and hotel listings indicate if American Express, Discover, Diner's Club, MasterCard, and Visa are accepted.

Restaurants

Unless we state otherwise, restaurants are open for lunch and dinner daily. We mention dress only when there's a specific requirement and reservations only when they're essential or not accepted—it's always best to book ahead.

Hotels

Hotels have private bath, phone, TV, and air-conditioning. We always list facilities but not whether you'll be charged an extra fee to use them, so when pricing accommodations, find out what's included.

Many Listings
- ★ Fodor's Choice
- ★ Highly recommended
- ✉ Physical address
- ✛ Directions
- ⌖ Mailing address
- ☎ Telephone
- 🖷 Fax
- ⊕ On the Web
- ✐ E-mail
- 🎫 Admission fee
- 🕐 Open/closed times
- ► Start of walk/itinerary
- 🖃 Credit cards

Hotels & Restaurants
- 🏨 Hotel
- 🛏 Number of rooms
- ⚴ Facilities
- 🍴 Meal plans
- ✕ Restaurant
- ⚭ Reservations
- 👗 Dress code
- 🚭 Smoking
- 🍷 BYOB
- ✕🏨 Hotel with restaurant that warrants a visit

Outdoors
- 🏌 Golf
- ⛺ Camping

Other
- ♥ Family-friendly
- ⓘ Contact information
- ⇨ See also
- ✉ Branch address

WHAT'S
WHERE

O'AHU

O'ahu—where Honolulu and Waikīkī are—is a great big lū'au. If this is your first trip, O'ahu should definitely serve as your jumping-off point. Here, on the third largest island, you'll find 75% of the state's population. Waikīkī beach offers a gentle introduction to water-related pursuits, while the North Shore's monster winter surf challenges the nerves of professional surfers. The island's museums and historic and cultural sites will ground you, at least a bit, in Hawai'i history. The widest range of restaurants as well as the best nightlife scene are here, too. And the island, with its knife-edged mountain ranges, verdant green valleys, territorial-era architecture, and ring of white-sand beaches, is just the Hawai'i you came to see.

MAUI

Maui nō ka 'oi—Maui is the best, the most, the top of the heap. To those who know the island well, there's good reason for the superlatives. The second-largest in the Hawaiian chain, the Valley Isle has made a name for itself with its tropical allure, arts and cultural activities, and miles of perfect-tan beaches. Popularity and success have led to some modern-day problems: too many cars, for example. Still, from the chilly heights of Haleakalā to the below-sea-level taro beds of Ke'anae Peninsula, Maui continues to weave a spell over the more than 2 million people who visit its shores each year. Pursuits range from hiking in a crater to swimming under a waterfall to diving with sea turtles. This is without question the most diversified island, recommended for a family or group with divergent interests.

MOLOKA'I

Moloka'i is the least-changed, most laid-back of the islands. To Hawaiians, she is *Moloka'i-nui-a-Hina,* the great child of the moon goddess; some believe hula was born here. Today, Moloka'i offers only two struggling resorts and one tiny town. Its charms include the unforgettable mule ride down a cliff trail to Kalaupapa Peninsula; the rich Kamakou Preserve, a 2,774-acre wildlife refuge; world-class deep-sea fishing; and plenty of peace and quiet. The Visitors' Bureau dubs it "The Friendly Isle," but development-resistant residents would prefer it to be the forgotten isle. This is a place where you should expect to conform to the lifestyle, not the other way around.

LĀNA'I	
	Even many locals have never been to Lāna'i because, for years, there was nothing to see but mile upon mile of pineapple and red-dirt roads. Two upscale resorts offer the usual island mix of sun and sand, plus archery and shooting, four-wheel-drive excursions, and superb scuba diving. Both attract the well-heeled in search of privacy, but the luxe shine has worn a bit. Do stroll Dole Park, the town square; if there's a local event on, you'll meet the bulk of the population in minutes.
THE BIG ISLAND	
	Hawai'i, the Big Island, is a land with two faces, watched over by snow-capped Mauna Kea and steaming Mauna Loa. On the west, the sunny Kona side of the island has parched, lava-strewn lowlands and uplands blessed with misty mornings and sunny afternoons. Upscale resorts line the coast, with the touristy, trafficy town of Kailua-Kona serving as social and economic center. The uplands vary from the cowboy country of the northern ranches to southern hillsides planted in coffee, vanilla orchids, macadamia nuts, and tropical fruits. To the east, the rain- and mist-shrouded Hilo side is characterized by flower farms, a fishing fleet, waterfalls, and rainbows. Southwest of Hilo looms one of the world's most active volcanoes. Here, in Volcanoes National Park, lava has been flowing for more than a decade. The sheer size of the Big Island, larger than all of the other islands combined, can be its main drawback for the explorer—you can drive and drive and drive and drive between attractions. So alot your time accordingly.
KAUA'I	
	The oldest inhabited island in the chain, Kaua'i has always been one of a kind. These days, the counter culture is of the artsy and alternative sort with a dash of surfer insouciance. The island's geography contributes to its individuality: the remote, northwestern shore known as Nā Pali (The Cliffs) Coast boasts folding sea cliffs thousands of feet high; the island's center is occupied by impossibly wet and jagged mountains; and the shores feature more sandy beaches per mile of coastline than any other Hawaiian island. Driving the single highway that circles the island is a bit of an adventure, especially given the hordes of chickens who all seem to have heard the joke about crossing the road. Kayaking, hiking, and birding are world-class, and the first sight of Waimea Canyon will stop your heart.

QUINTESSENTIAL HAWAI‘I

Traveling to Hawai‘i is as close as an American can get to visiting another country while staying within the United States. There is much to learn and understand about the state's indigenous culture, the hundred years of immigration that resulted in today's blended society, and the tradition of aloha that has welcomed millions of visitors over the years.

Polynesian Paralysis

You may find that you suffer from "Polynesian paralysis" when you arrive—a pleasurable ennervation, an uncontrollable desire to lie down and sleeeeeeeep. Go with it. Besides the fact that it's an actual physical condition caused by abrupt changes in temperature, humidity, and time zones, it'll give you a feel of the old days in Hawai‘i, when a nap under a tree wasn't the rarity it is today.

Native Knowledge

An Iowan is from Iowa and a Californian is from California, but Hawaiians are members of an ethnic group. Use Hawaiian only when speaking of someone who *get koko* (has Hawaiian blood); otherwise, say Islanders or Hawai‘i people. *Kāma‘aina* (child of the land) are people who are born here, whatever their ethnicity. "Local" is the catch-all term for the melange of customs, foodways, beliefs, and cultural "secret handshakes" that define those who are deeply entrenched in the Island way of life.

When a visitor says "back in the states" or "stateside," it sets Islanders' teeth on edge—Hawai‘i has been the 50th state for almost 50 years.

Learn How to Holoholo

That's not a hula. Holoholo means to go out for the fun of it—an aimless stroll, ride, or drive. "Wheah you goin', braddah?"

"Oh, holoholo." It's local-speak for Sunday drive, no plan, it's not the destination but the journey. Try setting out without an itinerary.

Act Like a Local

You might never truly "pass"; Islanders can spot a fresh sunburn or tender feet at 1,000 paces. But adopting local customs is a first-hand introduction to the Islands' unique culture. So live in T-shirts and shorts. Wear cheap rubber zoris, but call them "slippers." Wave people into your lane on the highway, and, when someone lets you in, give them a wave of thanks in return. Never, ever blow your horn, even when the pickup truck in front of you is stopped for a long session of "talk story" right in the middle of the road. Learn to shaka: pinky and thumb extended, middle fingers curled in, waggle sideways. Eat white rice with everything. When someone says "Aloha!," answer "Aloha no!" ("and a real big aloha back to you"). And—as the locals say— "no make big body" (try not to act like you own the place).

Have a Hula

"Hula is the language of the heart, therefore the heartbeat of the Hawaiian people." Thousands—from tots to seniors—devote hours each week to hula classes. All these dancers need some place to show off their stuff. The result is a network of hula competitions (generally free or very inexpensive) and free performances in malls and other public spaces. Many resorts offer hula instruction or "hula-cise." To watch hula, especially in the ancient style, is to understand that this was a sophisticated culture—skilled in many arts, including not only poetry, chant, and dance but also in constructing instruments and fashioning adornments.

IF YOU LIKE . . .

Full Body Adventures

Ready for a workout with just enough risk to make things interesting? The Islands are your destination for adventures—paddling, hiking, biking, and surfing among them. One thing you can't do is rock-climb; formations are too crumbly and unstable. Get ready to earn that umbrella drink at sunset.

- **Kayaking the Nā Pali Coast, Kaua'i.** Experience the majesty of this stunning shoreline of sheer cliffs and deep-cut valleys from the water. This once-in-a-lifetime adventure is a summer-only jaunt.

- **Haleakalā Downhill, Maui.** Tour operators drive you and your rented bike literally into the clouds, then let you loose to pedal and coast, pedal and coast, down the long looping Haleakalā Highway. Don't let them talk you into this unless you've ridden a bike in traffic recently.

- **Surfing.** You can't learn to surf in a day, but with the proper instruction, you'll probably manage at least a ride or two—and the thrill is unforgettable. Upper body strength is a must. Beach boys offer quickie lessons; if you're serious, look for a reputable surfing school with multiday training sessions.

The Underwater World

Hawai'i is heaven for snorkelers and divers. Nearly 600 species of tropical fish inhabit the colorful coral reefs and lava tubes. Incredible spots are easy to reach; picking which ones to try is a matter of time, expense, and personal preference. Snorkeling is easy. Equipment rentals and excursions are inexpensive, and even fraidy-cats, first-timers, and people with claustrophobia can handle the relatively simple skill set required.

- **Molokini, Maui.** The tiny quarter-moon of Molokini, a half-sunken crater that forms a naturally sheltered bay, is a snorkeler's dream. Sometimes too many snorkelers have the same dream—go in the early morning for the least human company.

- **Tables & Shark's Cove, O'ahu.** Snorkelers *and* divers in your group? Tables, a series of onshore reefs, offers safe paddling, while neighboring Shark's Cove is the most popular cavern dive on the island. These are summer-only spots, however, as winter storms kick up that legendary North Shore surf.

- **Kealakekua Bay, the Big Island.** Dramatic cliffs shelter this marine reserve, where spinner dolphins and tropical fish greet snorkelers and kayakers.

- **Cathedrals & Sergeant Major Reef, Lāna'i.** If you want to avoid crowds, we've got one word for you: Lāna'i. Hulopo'e Beach has safe and interesting snorkeling, while Cathedrals and Sergeant Major Reef are legendary for diving.

Complete Indulgence

Hawai'i's resort hotels know how to pamper you. Their goal is to fulfill your every desire so completely that you never feel the need, or indeed the energy, to go "off property."

- **Halekulani Hotel, O'ahu.** What Waikīkī's venerable Halekulani lacks in size, it more than makes up for in service. There is quite simply nothing that is too much to ask. Expect the exceptional in the signature restaurant, La Mer.

- **Spa Grande at the Grand Wailea Hotel, Maui.** Dissolve your stress in the *termé*, a hydrotherapy circuit including baths from Roman to Japanese furo and Swiss-jet showers.

- **The Lodge at Kō'ele, Lāna'i.** As close to a county inn as Hawai'i gets, the Lodge combines period architecture with exceptional service, fine dining, and a slow pace exemplified by the koa rockers on the veranda. Golf, snorkeling, and even archery are available, but the best thing to do here is sit and contemplate the view.

- **Mauna Lani Bay Hotel & Bungalows, Big Island.** If you really want to indulge yourself, rent a lagoon-side bungalow the size of a small house, complete with butler service.

- **Hyatt Regency Kaua'i, Kaua'i.** This is another got-everything resort: it's family- and honeymooner-friendly with large rooms and beautiful views (whale-watching from the balcony, no less). Its best feature, however, is the Anara Spa, where treatment rooms open onto private gardens.

Lying Back at the Beach

No one ever gets as much beach time in Hawai'i as they planned to, it seems, but it's a problem of time, not beaches. Beaches of every size, color (even green), and description line the state's many shorelines. They have different strengths: some are great for sitting but not so great for swimming; some offer beach park amenities like lifeguards and showers, whereas others are more private and isolated. Read up before you head out.

- **Kailua & Lanikai Beaches, O'ahu.** Popular see- and be-seen spots, these slim, white-sand beaches draw sunbathers, walkers, swimmers, and kayakers to O'ahu's Windward shores.

- **Mākena (Big & Little) Beach, Maui.** Big Beach is just that—its wide expanse and impressive length can swallow up a lot of folks, so it never feels crowded. Little Beach, over the hill, is where the nude sunbathers hang out.

- **Hāpuna Beach, Big Island.** This wide white-sand beach has it all: space, parking, and, in summer when waters are calm, swimming, snorkeling, and body surfing.

- **Po'ipū Beach Park, Kaua'i.** Kaua'i has more beautiful and more isolated beaches, but, if you're looking to sunbathe, swim, picnic, and people-watch, this one is right up there.

- **Hulopo'e Beach, Lāna'i.** The protected half-circle of white sand fronting the Mānele Resort offers grassy areas for picnicking, clear waters for snorkeling and swimming, and tide pools for exploring.

WHEN TO GO

Long days of sunshine and fairly mild year-round temperatures make Hawai'i an all-season destination. Most resort areas are at sea level, with average afternoon temperatures of 75°F–80°F during the coldest months of December and January; during the hottest months of August and September the temperature often reaches 90°F. Only at high elevations does the temperature drop into the colder realms, and only at mountain summits does it reach freezing.

Most travelers head to the Islands in winter. From mid-December through mid-April, visitors from the mainland and other areas covered with snow find Hawai'i's sun-splashed beaches and balmy trade winds appealing. This high season means that fewer travel bargains are available; room rates average 10%–15% higher during this season than the rest of the year.

Rainfall can be high in winter, particularly on the north and east shores of each island. Generally speaking, you're guaranteed sun and warm temperatures on the west and south shores no matter what time of year. Kaua'i's and the Big Island's northern sections get more annual rainfall than the rest of Hawai'i, and so much rain falls on Kaua'i's Mount Wai'ale'ale (approximately 472 inches of rain, or 39 feet), that it's considered the wettest place on earth.

Climate

Moist trade winds drop their precipitation on the north and east sides of the islands, creating tropical climates, while the south and west sides remain hot and dry with desertlike conditions. Higher "Upcountry" elevations typically have cooler, and often misty conditions.

The following are average maximum and minimum temperatures for Honolulu; the temperatures throughout the Hawaiian Islands are similar.

Forecasts **Weather Channel Connection** ⊕ www.weather.com.

ONLY IN HAWAI'I HOLIDAYS

If you happen to be in the Islands on March 26 or June 11, you'll notice light traffic and busy beaches—these are state holidays not celebrated anywhere else. March 26 recognizes the birthday of Prince Jonah Kūhio Kalaniana'ole, a member of the royal line who served as a delegate to Congress and spearheaded the effort to set aside homelands for Hawaiian people. June 11 honors the first island-wide monarch, Kamehameha I; locals drape his statues with lei and stage elaborate parades. May 1 isn't an official holiday, but it's the day when schools and civic groups celebrate the quintessential Island gift, the flower lei, with leimaking contests and pageants. Statehood Day is celebrated on the third Friday in August (Admission Day was August 21, 1959). Another holiday much celebrated is Chinese New Year, in part because many Hawaiians married Chinese immigrants. Homes and businesses sprout bright red good luck mottoes, lions dance in the streets, and everybody eats *gau* (steamed pudding) and *jai* (vegetarian stew). The state also celebrates Good Friday as a spring holiday, a favorite for family picnics.

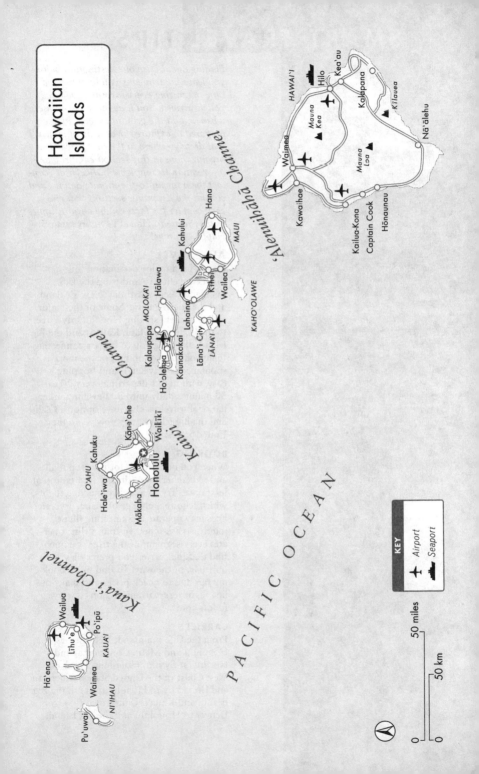

SMART TRAVEL TIPS

Air Travel

Airports

Boat & Ferry Travel

Bus Travel

Cameras & Photography

Car Rental

Car Travel

Children in Hawai'i

Consumer Protection

Cruise Travel

Customs & Duties

Disabilities & Accessibility

Discounts & Deals

Eating & Drinking

Ecotourism

Etiquette & Behavior

Gay & Lesbian Travel

Health

Insurance

For International Travelers

Language

Lei Greetings

Lodging

Media

Money Matters

National Parks & State Parks

Packing

Safety

Senior-Citizen Travel

Shopping

Students in Hawai'i

Taxes

Time

Tipping

Tours & Packages

Transportation around Hawai'i

Travel Agencies

Visitor Information

Web Sites

Finding out about your destination before you leave home means you won't spend time organizing everyday minutiae once you've arrived. You'll be more streetwise when you hit the ground as well, better prepared to explore the aspects of Hawai'i that drew you here in the first place. The organizations in this section can provide information to supplement this guide; contact them for up-to-the-minute details, and consult the Essentials sections that end each chapter for facts on the various topics as they relate to Hawai'i's many regions. Happy landings!

AIR TRAVEL

Hawai'i is a major destination link for flights traveling to and from the U.S. mainland, Asia, Australia, New Zealand, and the South Pacific. Some of the major airline carriers serving Honolulu fly direct to the islands of Maui, Kaua'i, and the Big Island, allowing you to bypass connecting flights out of Honolulu. For the more spontaneous traveler, island-hopping is easy, with flights departing every 20 to 30 minutes daily until mid-evening. International travelers also have options: O'ahu and the Big Island are gateways to the United States.

BOOKING

When you book, look for nonstop flights and remember that "direct" flights stop at least once. Try to avoid connecting flights, which require a change of plane. Two airlines may operate a connecting flight jointly, so ask whether your airline operates every segment of the trip; you may find that the carrier you prefer flies you only part of the way. To find more booking tips and to check prices and make online flight reservations, log on to www.fodors.com.

CARRIERS

From the U.S. mainland, Delta serves Honolulu and Maui. Continental and Northwest fly into Honolulu. From the West Coast of the United States, American and United fly to Honolulu, Maui, the Big Island, and Kaua'i. United also flies from Denver to Honolulu and the Big Island.

Aloha Airlines flies from California—Burbank, Oakland, Sacramento, San Diego, and Orange County—to Honolulu, Maui, and the Big Island. Aloha also flies from Vancouver, British Columbia, to Honolulu, and offers connecting services from Phoenix, AZ and Reno, NV. Hawaiian Airlines serves Honolulu and Maui from Las Vegas, Los Angeles, Ontario, Phoenix, Portland, Sacramento, San Diego, San Francisco, and Seattle. In addition to Aloha and Hawaiian, Island Air and Pacific Wings also provide interisland service. Paragon Airlines offers private charter service to all the Islands.

Major Airlines American ☎ 800/433-7300. **Continental** ☎ 800/523-3273. **Delta** ☎ 800/221-1212. **Northwest** ☎ 800/225-2525. **United** ☎ 800/241-6522.

Direct Flights from the U.K. Air New Zealand ☎ 0800/028-4149. **American** ☎ 0208/572-5555. **Continental** ☎ 0800/776-464. **Delta** ☎ 0800/414-767. **United** ☎ 0845/844-4777. **Trailfinders** ✉ 1 Threadneedle St., London EC2R 8JX ☎ 0207/628-7628 can arrange bargain flights.

Interisland Flights Aloha Airlines ☎ 800/367-5250. **Hawaiian Airlines** ☎ 800/367-5320. **Island Air** ☎ 800/323-3345. **Pacific Wings** ☎ 888/575-4546 **Paragon Airlines** ☎ 800/428-1231.

CHECK-IN & BOARDING
Always **find out your carrier's check-in policy.** Plan to arrive at the airport about two hours before your scheduled departure time for domestic flights and 2½ to 3 hours before international flights. You may need to arrive earlier if you're flying from one of the busier airports or during peak air-traffic times. Plan to **arrive at the airport 45 to 60 minutes before departure for interisland flights.**

Although the Neighbor Island airports are smaller and more casual than Honolulu International, during peak times they can also be quite busy. Allot extra travel time to all airports during morning and afternoon rush-hour traffic periods.

To avoid delays at airport-security checkpoints, try not to wear any metal. Jewelry, belt and other buckles, steel-toe shoes, barrettes, and underwire bras are among the items that can set off detectors.

Assuming that not everyone with a ticket will show up, airlines routinely overbook planes. When everyone does, airlines ask for volunteers to give up their seats. In return, these volunteers usually get a several hundred-dollar flight voucher, which can be used toward the purchase of another ticket, and are rebooked on the next available flight out. If there are not enough volunteers, the airline must choose who will be denied boarding. The first to get bumped are passengers who checked in late and those flying on discounted tickets, so get to the gate and check in as early as possible, especially during peak periods.

Always **bring a government-issued photo I.D.** to the airport; even when it's not required, a passport is best.

AGRICULTURAL INSPECTION
Plants and plant products are subject to regulation by the Department of Agriculture, both on entering and leaving Hawai'i. Upon leaving the Islands, you'll have to have your bags X-rayed and tagged at one of the airport's agricultural inspection stations before you proceed to check-in. Pineapples and coconuts with the packer's agricultural inspection stamp pass freely; papayas must be treated, inspected, and stamped. All other fruits are banned for export to the U.S. mainland. Flowers pass except for gardenia, rose leaves, jade vine, and mauna loa. Also banned are insects, snails, soil, cotton, cacti, sugarcane, and all berry plants.

You'll have to **leave dogs and other pets at home.** A 120-day quarantine is imposed to keep out rabies, which is nonexistent in Hawai'i. If specific pre- and post-arrival requirements are met, animals may qualify for a 30-day or 5-day-or-less quarantine.

U.S. Customs and Border Protection ✉ for inquiries and equipment registration, 1300 Pennsylvania Ave. NW, Washington, DC 20229 ⊕ www.cbp.gov ☎ 877/287-8667, 202/354-1000 ✉ for complaints, Customer Satisfaction Unit, 1300 Pennsylvania Ave. NW, Room 5.2C, Washington, DC 20229.

CUTTING COSTS
Check local and community newspapers when you're on the Islands for deals and coupons on interisland flights. Both

Hawaiian Airlines and Aloha Airlines have stopped offering the once-popular multi-island air passes, but there are other ways to save money on interisland fares. Sign up for either airlines' free frequent-flyer programs, and you'll be eligible for excellent online specials that aren't available by phone or elsewhere.

The least expensive airfares to Hawai'i are usually priced for round-trip travel and usually must be purchased in advance. Airlines generally allow you to change your return date for a fee; most low-fare tickets, however, are nonrefundable. It's smart to call a number of airlines and check the Internet; when you are quoted a good price, book it on the spot—the same fare may not be available the next day, or even the next hour. Always check different routings and look into using alternate airports. Also, price off-peak flights and red-eye, which may be significantly less expensive than others. Travel agents, especially low-fare specialists (⇨ Discounts & Deals), are helpful.

Consolidators are another good source. They buy tickets for scheduled flights at reduced rates from the airlines, then sell them at prices that beat the best fare available directly from the airlines. (Many also offer reduced car-rental and hotel rates.) Sometimes you can even get your money back if you need to return the ticket. Carefully read the fine print detailing penalties for changes and cancellations, purchase the ticket with a credit card, and confirm your consolidator reservation with the airline.

When you fly as a courier, you trade your checked-luggage space for a ticket deeply subsidized by a courier service. There are restrictions on when you can book and how long you can stay. Some courier companies list with membership organizations, such as the Air Courier Association and the International Association of Air Travel Couriers; these require you to become a member before you can book a flight.

Consolidators AirlineConsolidator.com ☎ 888/468-5385 ⊕ www.airlineconsolidator.com, for international tickets. **Best Fares** ☎ 800/880-1234 ⊕ www.bestfares.com; $59.90 annual membership. **Cheap Tickets** ☎ 800/377-1000 or 800/652-4327

⊕ www.cheaptickets.com. **Expedia** ☎ 800/397-3342 or 404/728-8787 ⊕ www.expedia.com. **Hotwire** ☎ 866/468-9473 or 920/330-9418 ⊕ www.hotwire.com. **Now Voyager Travel** ✉ 1717 Ave. M, Brooklyn, NY 11230 ☎ 212/459-1616 🖷 718/504-4762 ⊕ www.nowvoyagertravel.com. **One-travel.com** ⊕ www.onetravel.com. **Orbitz** ☎ 888/656-4546 ⊕ www.orbitz.com. **Priceline.com** ⊕ www.priceline.com. **Travelocity** ☎ 888/709-5983, 877/282-2925 in Canada, 0870/111-7061 in U.K. ⊕ www.travelocity.com.

Courier Resources Air Courier Association/Cheaptrips.com ☎ 800/211-5119 ⊕ www.aircourier.org or www.cheaptrips.com; $20 annual membership. **Courier Travel** ☎ 303/570-7586 🖷 313/625-6106 ⊕ www.couriertravel.org; $50 annual membership. **International Association of Air Travel Couriers** ☎ 308/632-3273 🖷 308/632-8267 ⊕ www.courier.org; $45 annual membership. **Now Voyager Travel** ✉ 1717 Ave. M, Brooklyn, NY 11230 ☎ 212/459-1616 🖷 718/504-4762 ⊕ www.nowvoyagertravel.com.

ENJOYING THE FLIGHT

State your seat preference when purchasing your ticket, and then repeat it when you confirm and when you check in. For more legroom, you can request one of the few emergency-aisle seats at check-in, if you're capable of moving obstacles comparable in weight to an airplane exit door (usually between 35 pounds and 60 pounds)—a Federal Aviation Administration requirement of passengers in these seats. Seats behind a bulkhead also offer more legroom, but they don't have under-seat storage. Don't sit in the row in front of the emergency aisle or in front of a bulkhead, where seats may not recline. SeatGuru.com has more information about specific seat configurations, which vary by aircraft.

Ask the airline whether a snack or meal is served on the flight. If you have dietary concerns, request special meals when booking. These can be vegetarian, low-cholesterol, or kosher, for example. It's a good idea to pack some healthful snacks and a small (plastic) bottle of water in your carry-on bag. On long flights, try to maintain a normal routine, to help fight jet lag. At night, get some sleep. By day, eat light meals, drink water (not alcohol), and move around the cabin to stretch your legs. For additional jet-lag tips consult *Fodor's FYI: Travel Fit & Healthy* (available at bookstores everywhere).

Smoking policies vary from carrier to carrier. Most airlines prohibit smoking on all of their flights; others allow smoking only on certain routes or certain departures. Ask your carrier about its policy.

FLYING TIMES
Flying time is about 10 hours from New York, 8 hours from Chicago, 5 hours from Los Angeles, and 15 hours from London, not including layovers.

HOW TO COMPLAIN
If your baggage goes astray or your flight goes awry, complain right away. Most carriers require that you **file a claim immediately.** The Aviation Consumer Protection Division of the Department of Transportation publishes *Fly-Rights,* which discusses airlines and consumer issues and is available online. You can also find articles and information on mytravelrights.com, the Web site of the nonprofit Consumer Travel Rights Center.

F Airline Complaints Aviation Consumer Protection Division ✉ U.S. Department of Transportation, Office of Aviation Enforcement and Proceedings, C-75, Room 4107, 400 7th St. SW, Washington, DC 20590 ☎ 202/366-2220 ⊕ airconsumer.ost.dot.gov. Federal Aviation Administration Consumer Hotline ✉ for inquiries: FAA, 800 Independence Ave. SW, Washington, DC 20591 ☎ 800/322-7873 ⊕ www.faa.gov.

RECONFIRMING
Check the status of your flight before you leave for the airport. You can do this on your carrier's Web site, by linking to a flight-status checker (many Web booking services offer these), or by calling your carrier or travel agent.

AIRPORTS
All of Hawai'i's major islands have their own airports, but Honolulu's International Airport is the main stopover for most flights both international and Mainland. From Honolulu, there are departing flights to the Neighbor Islands leaving almost

every half-hour from early morning until evening. In addition, some carriers now offer nonstop service directly from the Mainland to Maui and the Big Island on a limited basis. No matter the island, all of Hawai'i's airports are "open-air," meaning you can enjoy those tradewind breezes up until the moment you step on the plane.

HONOLULU/O'AHU AIRPORT
Hawai'i's major airport is Honolulu International, on O'ahu, 20 minutes (9 mi) west of Waikīkī. To travel interisland from Honolulu, you can depart from either the interisland terminal or the commuter-airline terminal, located in two separate structures adjacent to the main overseas terminal building. A free bus service, the Wiki Wiki Shuttle, operates between terminals.
F Honolulu International Airport (HNL) ☎ 808/836-6413.

MAUI AIRPORTS
Maui has two major airports. Kahului Airport handles major airlines and interisland flights; it is the only airport on Maui that has direct service from the mainland. Kapalua–West Maui Airport is served by Aloha Airlines and Pacific Wings. If you're staying in West Maui and you're flying in from another island, you can avoid an hour's drive from the Kahului Airport by flying into Kapalua–West Maui Airport. The tiny town of Hāna in East Maui also has an airstrip, served by commuter planes from Honolulu and charter flights from Kahului and Kapalua. Flying here is a great option if you want to avoid the long and windy drive to Hāna from one of the other airports.
F Kahului Airport (OGG) ☎ 808/872-3893; Kapalua-West Maui Airport (JHM) ☎ 808/669-0623; Hāna Airport (HNM) ☎ 808/248-8208.

BIG ISLAND AIRPORTS
Those flying to the Big Island of Hawai'i regularly land at one of two fields. Kona International Airport at Keāhole, on the west side, best serves Kailua-Kona, Keauhou, and the Kohala Coast. Hilo International Airport is more appropriate for those going to the east side. Waimea-Kohala Airport, called Kamuela Airport

by residents, is used primarily for commuting among the Islands.

F Hilo International Airport (ITO) ☎ 808/934-5838; Kona International Airport at Keāhole (KOA) ☎ 808/329-3423; Waimea-Kohala Airport (MUE) ☎ 808/887-8126.

KAUA'I, MOLOKA'I & LĀNA'I

On Kaua'i, visitors fly into Līhu'e Airport, on the east side of the island.

Moloka'i's Ho'olehua Airport is small and centrally located, as is Lāna'i Airport. Both rural airports handle a limited number of flights per day. Visitors coming from the mainland to these islands must first stop in O'ahu and change to an interisland flight.

F Kaua'i: Līhu'e Airport (LIH) ☎ 808/246-1448. Lāna'i: Lāna'i Airport (LNY) ☎ 808/565-6757. Moloka'i: Ho'olehua Airport (MKK) ☎ 808/567-6361.

BOAT & FERRY TRAVEL

For now, ferry travel in the Islands is limited to daily service between Lahaina, Maui, and Mānele Bay, Lāna'i. The 9-mi crossing costs $50 cash (or $52 if you pay with a credit card) round-trip per person and takes about 45 minutes or so, depending on ocean conditions (which can make this trip a rough one). Reservations are essential. There are talks of introducing high-speed interisland ferry service that would run among Honolulu, the Big Island, Maui, and Kauai, but as of this writing, the state legislature was still debating its prospects. If all goes well, this service could be introduced as early as late 2006.

F Boat & Ferry Information Expeditions Lāna'i Ferry ☎ 800/695-2624 ⊕ www.go-lanai.com.

BUS TRAVEL

Getting around by bus is an option on O'ahu, especially in urban Honolulu and Waikīkī, but on Neighbor Islands services are limited and car rental is recommended.

THEBUS IN HONOLULU/O'AHU

O'ahu's transportation system, known just as TheBus, is one of the island's best bargains. Fares per ride are $2, and with more than 70 bus routes you can even do an O'ahu circle-island tour. Taking TheBus in the Waikīkī and downtown Honolulu areas is especially convenient, with buses

making stops in Waikīkī every 15 minutes to take passengers to nearby shopping areas, such as Ala Moana Center.

F TheBus ☎ 808/848-5555 on O'ahu ⊕ www.thebus.org.

BUS TRAVEL ON MAUI

Maui has a limited bus system, run in conjunction with a private company, Roberts Hawai'i. Four routes deliver passengers between Wailuku, Kahului, Kīhei, Wailea, Ma'alaea, and Lahaina. Inexpensive one-way, round-trip, and all-day passes are available.

F Roberts Hawai'i ☎ 808/871-4838 ⊕ www.co.maui.hi.us/bus.

BUS TRAVEL ON THE BIG ISLAND

The Big Island's Hele-On Bus travels a Kailua-Kona–to–Hilo route once daily except Sunday for $6 each way. There are limited routes to other areas. Ali'i Shuttle operates a bus service in the Kona resort area between Keauhou Bay and Kailua-Kona town Monday through Saturday, 8:30 AM to 7 PM. The shuttle connects all major hotels, condos, attractions, and shopping centers along Ali'i Drive. Fares are $3 each way.

F Ali'i Shuttle ☎ 808/938-1112. Hele-On Bus ☎ 808/961-8744.

CAMERAS & PHOTOGRAPHY

Today's underwater "disposable" cameras can provide terrific photos for those once-in-a-lifetime underwater experiences. Film developing is available on all of the Islands. Many hotel–resort sundries stores offer the service, and larger department stores, such as Long's Drugs, have one-hour service for regular film developing and overnight service for panoramic film. The *Kodak Guide to Shooting Great Travel Pictures* (available at bookstores everywhere) is loaded with tips.

F Photo Help Kodak Information Center ☎ 800/242-2424 ⊕ www.kodak.com.

EQUIPMENT PRECAUTIONS

Don't pack film or equipment in checked luggage, where it is much more susceptible to damage. X-ray machines used to view checked luggage are extremely powerful and therefore are likely to ruin your film. Try to ask for hand inspection of film, which becomes clouded after repeated exposure to airport X-ray machines, and keep videotapes and computer disks away from metal detectors. Always keep film, tape, and computer disks out of the sun. Carry an extra supply of batteries, and be prepared to turn on your camera, camcorder, or laptop to prove to airport security personnel that the device is real.

CAR RENTAL

You can rent anything from a $26-a-day econobox to a $1,100-a-day Ferrari. It's wise to make reservations in advance, especially if visiting during peak seasons or for major conventions or sporting events.

Rates in Honolulu begin at $38 a day ($164 a week) for an economy car with air-conditioning, automatic transmission, and unlimited mileage. Rates on Maui begin at $35 a day ($144 a week) for the same. This does not include vehicle registration fee and weight tax, insurance, sales tax and a $3-per-day Hawai'i state surcharge.

7 Major Agencies **Alamo** ☎ 800/327-9633 ⊕ www.alamo.com. **Avis** ☎ 800/331-1212, 800/879-2847 or 800/272-5871 in Canada, 0870/606-0100 in U.K., 02/9353-9000 in Australia, 09/526-2847 in New Zealand ⊕ www.avis.com. **Budget** ☎ 800/527-0700 ⊕ www.budget.com. **Dollar** ☎ 800/800-4000, 0800/085-4578 in U.K. ⊕ www.dollar.com. **Hertz** ☎ 800/654-3131, 800/263-0600 in Canada, 0870/844-8844 in U.K., 02/9669-2444 in Australia, 09/256-8690 in New Zealand ⊕ www.hertz.com. **National Car Rental** ☎ 800/227-7368 ⊕ www.nationalcar.com.

CUTTING COSTS

Many rental companies in Hawai'i offer coupons for discounts at various attractions that could save you money later on in your trip.

For a good deal, book through a travel agent who will shop around. Also, price local car-rental companies—whose prices may be lower still, although their service and maintenance may not be as good as those of major rental agencies—and re search rates on the Internet. Consolidators that specialize in air travel can offer good rates on cars as well (⇨ Air Travel). Remember to ask about required deposits, cancellation penalties, and drop-off

charges if you're planning to pick up the car in one city and leave it in another. If you're traveling during a holiday period, also make sure that a confirmed reservation guarantees you a car.

Do look into wholesalers, companies that do not own fleets but rent in bulk from those that do and often offer better rates than traditional car-rental operations. Prices are best during off-peak periods. Rentals booked through wholesalers often must be paid for before you leave home.

7 Local Agencies **AA Aloha Cars-R-Us** ☎ 800/655-7989 ⊕ www.hawaiicarrental.com. **JN Car and Truck Rentals** ☎ 800/475-7522, 808/831-2724 on O'ahu ⊕ www.jnautomotive.com. **Ho'okipa Haven** ☎ 808/579-8282 or 800/398-6284 ⊕ www.hookipa.com on Maui. **VIP Car Rentals** ☎ 808/922-4605 on O'ahu.

INSURANCE

When driving a rented car you are generally responsible for any damage to or loss of the vehicle. You also may be liable for any property damage or personal injury that you may cause while driving. Before you rent, see what coverage you already have under the terms of your personal auto-insurance policy and credit cards.

For about $9 to $25 a day, rental companies sell protection, known as a collision- or loss-damage waiver (CDW or LDW), that eliminates your liability for damage to the car; it's always optional and should never be automatically added to your bill. In most states you don't need a CDW if you have personal auto insurance or other liability insurance. However, **make sure you have enough coverage to pay for the car.** If you do not have auto insurance or an umbrella policy that covers damage to third parties, purchasing liability insurance and a CDW or LDW is highly recommended.

REQUIREMENTS & RESTRICTIONS

In Hawai'i you must be 21 years of age to rent a car and you must have a valid driver's license and a major credit card. Those under 25 will pay a daily surcharge of $15–$25.

In Hawai'i your unexpired mainland driver's license is valid for rental for up to 90 days.

SURCHARGES

Before you pick up a car in one city and leave it in another, ask about drop-off charges or one-way service fees, which can be substantial. Also inquire about early-return policies; some rental agencies charge extra if you return the car before the time specified in your contract while others give you a refund for the days not used. Most agencies note the tank's fuel level on your contract; to avoid a hefty refueling fee, return the car with the same tank level. If the tank was full, refill it just before you turn in the car, but be aware that gas stations near the rental outlet may overcharge. It's almost never a deal to buy a tank of gas with the car when you rent it; the understanding is that you'll return it empty, but some fuel usually remains. Surcharges may apply if you're under 25 or if you take the car outside the area approved by the rental agency. You'll pay extra for child seats (about $8 a day), which are compulsory for children under five, and usually for additional drivers (up to $25 a day, depending on location).

CAR TRAVEL

Technically, the Big Island of Hawai'i is the only island you can completely circle by car, but each island offers plenty of sightseeing from its miles of roadways. O'ahu can be circled except for the road-less west-shore area around Ka'ena Point. Elsewhere, major highways follow the shoreline and traverse the island at two points. Rush-hour traffic (6:30 to 8:30 AM and 3:30 to 6 PM) can be frustrating around Honolulu and the outlying areas, as many thoroughfares allow no left turns due to contra-flow lanes. Traffic on Maui can be very bad branching out from Kahu-lui to and from Pā'ia, Kīhei and Lahaina. Drive here during peak hours and you'll know why local residents are calling for restrictions on development. Parking along many streets is curtailed during these times, and towing is strictly practiced. Read curbside parking signs before leaving your vehicle, even at a meter.

Your driver's license may not be recognized outside your home country. International driving permits (IDPs) are available from the American and Canadian automobile associations and, in the United Kingdom, from the Automobile Association and Royal Automobile Club. These international permits, valid only in conjunction with your regular driver's license, are universally recognized; having one may save you a problem with local authorities.

GASOLINE

Regardless of today's fluctuating gas prices, you can pretty much count on having to pay more at the pump for gasoline on the Islands than on the U.S. mainland.

ROAD CONDITIONS

It's difficult to get lost in most of Hawai'i. Roads and streets, although they may challenge the visitor's tongue, are well marked; just watch out for the many one-way streets in Waikīkī. **Keep an eye open for the Hawai'i Visitors and Convention Bureau's red-caped King Kamehameha signs,** which mark major attractions and scenic spots. Ask for a map at the car-rental counter. Free publications containing good-quality road maps can be found on all Islands.

The Big Island and O'ahu have well-maintained roads, which can be easily negotiated and do not require a four-wheel-drive vehicle. Kaua'i has a well-maintained highway running south from Līhu'e to Barking Sands Beach; a spur at Waimea takes you along Waimea Canyon to Kōke'e State Park. A northern route also winds its way from Līhu'e to end at Hā'ena, the beginning of the rugged and roadless Nā Pali Coast. Maui also has its share of impenetrable areas, although four-wheel-drive vehicles rarely run into problems on the island. Although Moloka'i and Lāna'i have fewer roadways, car rental is still worthwhile and will allow plenty of interesting sightseeing. **Opt for a four-wheel-drive vehicle** if dirt-road exploration holds any appeal.

RULES OF THE ROAD

Be sure to **buckle up.** Hawai'i has a strictly enforced seat-belt law for front-seat passengers. Children under four must be in a car seat (available from car-rental agencies). Children 18 and under, riding in the backseat, are also required by state law to use seat belts. The highway speed limit is usually 55 mph. In-town traffic moves from 25 to 40 mph. Jaywalking is very common, so be particularly watchful for pedestrians, especially in congested areas such as Waikīkī. Unauthorized use of a parking space reserved for persons with disabilities can net you a $150 fine.

Asking for directions will almost always produce a helpful explanation from the locals, but you should be prepared for an island term or two. Instead of using compass directions, remember that Hawai'i residents refer to places as being either *mauka* (toward the mountains) or *makai* (toward the ocean) from one another. Other directions depend on your location: in Honolulu, for example, people say to "go Diamond Head," which means toward that famous landmark, or to "go 'ewa," meaning in the opposite direction. A shop on the mauka–Diamond Head corner of a street is on the mountain side of the street on the corner closest to Diamond Head. It all makes perfect sense once you get the lay of the land.

CHILDREN IN HAWAI'I

Sunny beaches and many family-oriented cultural sites, activities, and attractions make Hawai'i a very *keiki-* (child-) friendly place. Here kids can swim with a dolphin, surf with a boogie board, check out an active volcano, or ride a sugarcane train. Parents should **use caution on beaches and during water sports.** Even waters that appear calm can harbor powerful rip currents. Be sure to **read any beach-warning guides your hotel may provide. Ask around for kid-friendly beaches** that might have shallow tide pools or are protected by reefs. And remember that the sun's rays are in operation full-force year-round here. Sunblock for children is essential.

Most major resort chains in Hawai'i offer children's activity programs for kids ages 5 to 12. These kid clubs provide opportunities to learn about local culture, make friends with children from around the world, and experience age-appropriate activities while giving moms and dads a

"time-out." Upon arrival, check out the daily local newspapers for children's events. The *Honolulu Advertiser's* "TGIF" section each Friday includes a section on keiki activities with a local flavor.

If you are renting a car, don't forget to arrange for a car seat when you reserve. For general advice about traveling with children, consult *Fodor's FYI: Travel with Your Baby* (available in bookstores everywhere).

FLYING

If your children are two or older, ask about children's airfares. As a general rule, infants under two not occupying a seat fly at greatly reduced fares or even for free. But if you want to guarantee a seat for an infant, you have to pay full fare. Consider flying during off-peak days and times; most airlines will grant an infant a seat without a ticket if there are available seats.

Experts agree that it's a good idea to use safety seats aloft for children weighing less than 40 pounds. Airlines set their own policies: if you use a safety seat, U.S. carriers usually require that the child be ticketed, even if he or she is young enough to ride free, because the seats must be strapped into regular seats. And even if you pay the full adult fare for the seat, it may be worth it, especially on longer trips. Do **check your airline's policy about using safety seats during takeoff and landing.** Safety seats are not allowed everywhere in the plane, so get your seat assignments as early as possible.

When reserving, request children's meals or a freestanding bassinet (not available at all airlines) if you need them. But note that bulkhead seats, where you must sit to use the bassinet, may lack an overhead bin or storage space on the floor.

LODGING

Families can't go wrong choosing resort locations that are part of larger hotel chains such as Hilton, Sheraton, Outrigger, and Westin. Many of these resorts are on the best beaches on each island, have activities created for children, and are centrally located. Outrigger's "Ohana" brand hotels are off the beachfront but provide great value at good prices. Many condominium resorts now also offer children's activities and amenities during holiday periods.

Most hotels in Hawai'i allow children under a certain age to stay in their parents' room at no extra charge, but others charge for them as extra adults; be sure to find out the cutoff age for children's discounts. Also **check for special seasonal programs,** such as "kids eat free" promotions.
⑦ Best Choices Aston Hotels Resort Quest International ☎ 800/922-7866 ⊕ www.aston-hotels. com. **Four Seasons Hotels and Resorts** ☎ 800/ 819-5053 ⊕ www.fourseasons.com. **Hilton** ☎ 800/ 774-1500 ⊕ www.hilton.com. **Hyatt Hotels & Resorts** ☎ 888/591-1234 ⊕ www.hyatt.com. **Marriott** ☎ 888/236-2427 ⊕ www.marriott.com. **Outrigger Hotels** ☎ 800/688-7444 ⊕ www.outrigger.com. **Starwood Hotels and Resorts** ☎ 888/625-5144 for Westin and Sheraton, 800/325-3589 for Luxury Collection, 877/946-8357 for W Hotels ⊕ www. starwood.com.

SIGHTS & ATTRACTIONS
Places that are especially appealing to children are indicated by a rubber-duckie icon (🐤) in the margin. Top picks for children run the gamut from natural attractions kids can enjoy for free to some fairly expensive amusements. On O'ahu, favorites include surfing lessons at Waikīkī Beach, hiking Diamond Head, snorkeling Hanauma Bay, learning about marine life at Sea Life Park, splashing about the 29-acre Hawaiian Waters Adventure Park, and touring through South Pacific cultures at the Polynesian Cultural Center. On Maui, kid favorites include the Sugarcane Train that runs between Lahaina and Kā'anapali, snorkeling to Molokini Island, and whale-watching after a visit to the Maui Ocean Center. Visiting Hawai'i Volcanoes National Park, star gazing atop Mauna Kea, touring the Mauna Loa Macadamia Factory near Hilo, swimming with dolphins at the Hilton Waikoloa, and horseback riding at Parker Ranch are fun things to do on the Big Island.

Kaua'i is where kids go to explore film locations such as Peter Pan's *Never-Never Land* and *Jurassic Park.* They can learn to water-ski on the Wailua River, visit Kōke'e National Park, or just spend the day swimming Po'ipū's sunny south shores. Lāna'i and Moloka'i are great islands for adventurous youngsters. At Sheraton Moloka'i Lodge and Beach Village, families can sleep in canvas bungalows and enjoy everything from star gazing and spear fishing to horseback riding with a paniolo (Hawaiian cowboy). On Lāna'i, four-wheel-drive off-road adventure tours take families to destinations such as Shipwreck Beach and Mānele Bay, where the dolphins sometimes come to play.

CONSUMER PROTECTION
Whether you're shopping for gifts or purchasing travel services, **pay with a major credit card** whenever possible, so you can cancel payment or get reimbursed if there's a problem (and you can provide documentation). If you're doing business with a particular company for the first time, contact your local Better Business Bureau and the attorney general's offices in your state and (for U.S. businesses) the company's home state as well. Have any complaints been filed? Finally, if you're buying a package or tour, always consider travel insurance that includes default coverage (⇨ Insurance).
⑦ BBBs Council of Better Business Bureaus ✉ 4200 Wilson Blvd., Suite 800, Arlington, VA 22203 ☎ 703/276-0100 🖶 703/525-8277 ⊕ www. bbb.org.

CRUISE TRAVEL
When Pan Am's amphibious *Hawai'i Clipper* touched down on Pearl Harbor's waters in 1936, it marked the beginning of the end of regular passenger-ship travel to the Islands. From that point on, the predominant means of transporting visitors would be by air, not by sea. Today, however, cruising to Hawai'i is making a comeback.

Norwegian Cruise Lines offers four "freestyle" cruises (no set meal times, less formal clothing, more nightlife choices) with Hawai'i itineraries. Norwegian's two new U.S.-flagged ships, *Pride of America* and *Pride of Aloha* sail interisland on three-, four-, and seven-day schedules. To get the best deal on a cruise, **consult a cruise-only travel agency.**

Even if you choose, as most travelers do, to travel by air to the Islands, you can get the flavor of what the luxury-cruise era in Hawai'i was like by checking out Aloha Tower Marketplace's Boat Day Celebrations in Honolulu. Vessels stopping here are met upon arrival by hula dancers and the kind of entertainment and floral festivities that once greeted travelers almost a century ago. Contact Aloha Tower Marketplace for a boat-day schedule upon arrival.

To learn how to plan, choose, and book a cruise-ship voyage, consult *Fodor's FYI: Plan & Enjoy Your Cruise* (available in bookstores everywhere).

7 Cruise Lines Aloha Tower Marketplace ⊠ 1 Aloha Tower Dr., at Piers 8, 9, and 10, Honolulu ☎ 808/528-5700 ⊕ www.alohatower.com. **Carnival** ☎ 888/227-6482 ⊕ www.carnival.com. **Celebrity** ☎ 800/722-5941 ⊕ www.celebritycruises. com. **Crystal Cruises** ☎ 800/804-1500 ⊕ www. crystalcruises.com. **Cunard** ☎ 800/728-6273 ⊕ www.cunard.com. **Holland America** ☎ 877/724-5425 ⊕ www.hollandamerica.com. **Norwegian Cruise Lines** ☎ 800/327-7030 ⊕ www. norwegiancruiselines.com. **Princess** ☎ 800/774-6237 ⊕ www.princess.com. **Royal Caribbean Cruise Line** ☎ 800/398-9819 ⊕ www.royalcaribbean.com. **Seabourn** ☎ 800/929-9391 ⊕ www.seabourn.com

CUSTOMS & DUTIES

IN AUSTRALIA

Australian residents who are 18 or older may bring home A$900 worth of souvenirs and gifts (including jewelry), 250 cigarettes or 250 grams of cigars or other tobacco products, and 2.25 liters of alcohol (including wine, beer, and spirits). Residents under 18 may bring back A$450 worth of goods. If any of these individual allowances are exceeded, you must pay duty for the entire amount (of the group of products in which the allowance was exceeded). Members of the same family traveling together may pool their allowances. Prohibited items include meat products. Seeds, plants, and fruits need to be declared upon arrival.

7 Australian Customs Service ⌂ Locked Bag 3000, Sydney International Airport, Sydney, NSW 2020 ☎ 02/6275-6666 or 1300/363263, 02/8334-7444 or 1800/020-504 quarantine-inquiry line ⌂ 02/8339-6714 ⊕ www.customs.gov.au.

IN CANADA

Canadian residents who have been out of Canada for at least seven days may bring in C$750 worth of goods duty-free. If you've been away fewer than seven days but more than 48 hours, the duty-free allowance drops to C$200. If your trip lasts 24 to 48 hours, the allowance is C$50; if the goods are worth more than C$50, you must pay full duty on all of the goods. You may not pool allowances with family members. Goods claimed under the C$750 exemption may follow you by mail; those claimed under the lesser exemptions must accompany you. Alcohol and tobacco products may be included in the seven-day and 48-hour exemptions but not in the 24-hour exemption. If you meet the age requirements of the province or territory through which you reenter Canada, you may bring in, duty-free, 1.5 liters of wine *or* 1.14 liters (40 imperial ounces) of liquor *or* 24 12-ounce cans or bottles of beer or ale. Also, if you meet the local age requirement for tobacco products, you may bring in, duty free, 200 cigarettes, 50 cigars or cigarillos, and 200 grams of tobacco. You may have to pay a minimum duty on tobacco products, regardless of whether or not you exceed your personal exemption. Check ahead of time with the Canada Border Services Agency or the Department of Agriculture for policies regarding meat products, seeds, plants, and fruits.

You may send an unlimited number of gifts (only one gift per recipient, however) worth up to C$60 each duty-free to Canada. Label the package UNSOLICITED GIFT—VALUE UNDER $60. Alcohol and tobacco are excluded.

7 Canada Border Services Agency ⊠ Customs Information Services, 191 Laurier Ave. W, 15th fl., Ottawa, Ontario K1A 0L5 ☎ 800/461-9999 in Canada, 204/983-3500, 506/636-5064 ⊕ www.cbsa.gc.ca.

IN NEW ZEALAND

All homeward-bound residents may bring back NZ$700 worth of souvenirs and gifts; passengers may not pool their allowances, and children can claim only the concession on goods intended for their own use. For those 17 or older, the duty-free allowance also includes 4.5 liters of wine or beer; one 1,125-ml bottle of spirits; and either 200 cigarettes, 250 grams of tobacco, 50 cigars, *or* a combination of the three up to 250 grams. Meat products, seeds, plants, and fruits must be declared upon arrival to the Agricultural Services Department.

🏴 **New Zealand Customs** ✉ Head office: The Customhouse, 17–21 Whitmore St., Box 2218, Wellington ☎ 09/300–5399 or 0800/428–786 ⊕ www.customs. govt.nz.

IN THE U.K.
If you are a U.K. resident and your journey was wholly within the European Union, you probably won't have to pass through customs when you return to the United Kingdom. If you plan to bring back large quantities of alcohol or tobacco, check EU limits beforehand. In most cases, if you bring back more than 200 cigars, 3,200 cigarettes, 400 cigarillos, 3 kilograms of tobacco, 10 liters of spirits, 110 liters of beer, 20 liters of fortified wine, and/or 90 liters of wine, you have to declare the goods upon return.

From countries outside the European Union, including the United States, you may bring home, duty-free, 200 cigarettes, 50 cigars, 100 cigarillos, or 250 grams of tobacco; 1 liter of spirits or 2 liters of fortified or sparkling wine or liqueurs; 2 liters of still table wine; 60 ml of perfume; 250 ml of toilet water; plus £145 worth of other goods, including gifts and souvenirs. Prohibited items include meat and dairy products, seeds, plants, and fruits.

🏴 **HM Customs and Excise** ✉ Portcullis House, 21 Cowbridge Rd. E, Cardiff CF11 9SS ☎ 0845/010– 9000 or 0208/929–0152 advice service, 0208/929– 6731 or 0208/910–3602 complaints ⊕ www.hmce. gov.uk.

DISABILITIES & ACCESSIBILITY
The Society for the Advancement of Travel for the Handicapped has named Hawai'i the most accessible vacation spot for people with disabilities. Ramped visitor areas and specially equipped lodgings are relatively common. Travelers with vision impairments who use a guide dog don't have to worry about quarantine restrictions. All you need to do is present documentation that the ani-

mal is a trained guide dog and has a current inoculation record for rabies. Access Aloha Travel is the state's only travel planner specializing in the needs of Hawai'i-bound travelers with disabilities. The company can arrange accessible accommodations, sightseeing, dining, activities, medical equipment rentals and personal care attendants. Access Aloha also rents wheelchairs and scooter vans on O'ahu and Maui.

🏴 **Local Resources Disability and Communication Access Board** ✉ 919 Ala Moana Blvd., Room 101, Honolulu 96814 ☎ 808/586–8121. **Access Aloha Travel** ✉ 414 Kuwili St., Suite 101, Honolulu 96817 ☎ 800/480–1143 or 808/545–1143 🖷 808/545–7657 ⊕ www.accessalohatravel.com.

LODGING
Despite the Americans with Disabilities Act, the definition of accessibility seems to differ from hotel to hotel. Some properties may be accessible by ADA standards for people with mobility problems but not for people with hearing or vision impairments, for example.

If you have mobility problems, ask for the lowest floor on which accessible services are offered. If you have a hearing impairment, check whether the hotel has devices to alert you visually to the ring of the telephone, a knock at the door, and a fire/ emergency alarm. Some hotels provide these devices without charge. Discuss your needs with hotel personnel if this equipment isn't available, so that a staff member can personally alert you in the event of an emergency.

If you're bringing a guide dog, get authorization ahead of time and write down the name of the person with whom you spoke.

Travelers with disabilities and people using wheelchairs find it easy to get around Hawai'i's resorts and hotels, with indoor-outdoor layouts that are easily navigated. If choosing a smaller hotel or a condo or apartment rental, inquire about ground-floor accommodations and **check to see if rooms will accommodate wheelchairs and if bathrooms are accessible.** Many hotels now offer special-needs rooms featuring larger living spaces and bathrooms equipped for guests who require additional assistance.

RESERVATIONS

When discussing accessibility with an operator or reservations agent, ask hard questions. Are there any stairs, inside *or* out? Are there grab bars next to the toilet and in the shower/tub? How wide is the doorway to the room? To the bathroom? For the most extensive facilities meeting the latest legal specifications, opt for newer accommodations. If you reserve through a toll-free number, consider also calling the hotel's local number to confirm the information from the central reservations office. Get confirmation in writing when you can.

SIGHTS & ATTRACTIONS

Many of Hawai'i's sights and attractions are accessible to travelers with disabilities. The Honolulu Department of Parks and Recreation provides "all-terrain" wheelchairs and beach mats at several beach parks on O'ahu. Accessible Vans of Hawaii rents wheelchairs and scooter vans on O'ahu, Maui, and the Big Island. In addition, the company can arrange accessible accommodations, sightseeing, dining, activities, medical-equipment rentals, and personal care attendants.

🚹 **Accessible Vans of Hawaii** ☏ 800/303-3750 ⊕ www.accessiblevanshawaii.com. **Therapeutic Recreation Unit of the Honolulu Department of Parks and Recreation** ☏ 808/692-5461 Therapeutic Recreation Unit ⊕ www.co.honolulu.hi.us/parks/programs/beach.

TRANSPORTATION

Paratransit Services (HandiVan) will take you to a specific destination on O'ahu—not on sightseeing outings—in vans with lifts and lock-downs. With a HandiVan Pass, one-way trips cost $2. Passes are free and can be obtained from the Department of Transportation Services, which is open weekdays 7:45–4:30; you'll need a doctor's written confirmation of your disability or a Paratransit ID card. Application forms also can be obtained in advance of your visit by calling the Department of Transportation Services or going online. Handi-Cabs of the Pacific also operates ramp-equipped vans with lock-downs in Honolulu. Fares are $9 plus $2 per mi for curbside service and $19 plus $2 per mile

for door-to-door service. Reservations at least 24 hours in advance are required by both companies, so plan ahead.

Those who prefer to do their own driving may rent hand-controlled cars from Alamo, Avis, Budget, Dollar, Hertz and National. You can use the windshield card from your own state to park in spaces reserved for people with disabilities. All require at least 48 hours notice.

The U.S. Department of Transportation Aviation Consumer Protection Division's online publication *New Horizons: Information for the Air Traveler with a Disability* offers advice for travelers with a disability, and outlines basic rights. Visit DisabilityInfo.gov for general information.

🚹 **Alamo** ☏ 800/651-1223. **Avis** ☏ 800/321-3712. **Budget** ☏ 800/526-6408. **Dollar** ☏ 800/367-5171. **Hertz** ☏ 800/654-3011. **National** ☏ 800/227-7368. **Department of Transportation Services** ✉ 650 S. King St., 2nd fl., Honolulu 96813 ☏ 808/523-4083. **Handi-Cabs of the Pacific** ☏ 808/524-3866. **Paratransit Services (HandiVan)** ☏ 808/456-5555.

🚹 **Complaints Aviation Consumer Protection Division** (⇨ Air Travel) for airline-related problems; ⊕ airconsumer.ost.dot.gov/publications/horizons.htm for airline travel advice and rights. **Departmental Office of Civil Rights** ✉ For general inquiries, U.S. Department of Transportation, S-30, 400 7th St. SW, Room 10215, Washington, DC 20590 ☏ 202/366-4648, 202/366-8538 TTY ☐ 202/366-9371 ⊕ www.dotcr.ost.dot.gov. **Disability Rights Section** ✉ NYAV, U.S. Department of Justice, Civil Rights Division, 950 Pennsylvania Ave. NW, Washington, DC 20530 ☏ ADA information line 202/514-0301, 800/514-0301, 202/514-0383 TTY, 800/514-0383 TTY ⊕ www.ada.gov. **U.S. Department of Transportation Hotline** ☏ For disability-related air-travel problems, 800/778-4838 or 800/455-9880 TTY.

TRAVEL AGENCIES

In the United States, the Americans with Disabilities Act requires that travel firms serve the needs of all travelers. Some agencies specialize in working with people with disabilities.

🚹 **Travelers with Mobility Problems Access Adventures/B. Roberts Travel** ✉ 1876 East Ave., Rochester, NY 14610 ☏ 800/444-6540 ⊕ www.brobertstravel.com, run by a former physical-rehabilitation counselor. **Access Aloha Travel** ✉ 414 Kuwili St., Suite 101, Honolulu, HI 96817 ☎ 800/480-1143 🖹 808/545-7657 ⊕ www.accessalohatravel.com. **Accessible Vans of America** ✉ 37 Daniel Rd. W, Fairfield, NJ 07004 ☎ 877/282-8267, 888/282-8267, 973/808-9709 reservations 🖹 973/808-9713 ⊕ www.accessiblevans.com. **Accessible Vans of Hawaii** ✉ 355 Hukulike St., Suite 121A, Kahului, HI 96732 ☎ 808/871-7785 or 800/303-3750 🖹 808/871-7536 ⊕ www.accessiblevanshawaii.com. **Care-Vacations** ✉ No. 5, 5110-50 Ave., Leduc, Alberta, Canada, T9E 6V4 ☎ 780/986-6404 or 877/478-7827 🖹 780/986-8332 ⊕ www.carevacations.com, for group tours and cruise vacations. **Flying Wheels Travel** ✉ 143 W. Bridge St., Box 382, Owatonna, MN 55060 ☎ 507/451-5005 🖹 507/451-1685 ⊕ www.flyingwheelstravel.com. 🚹 Travelers with Developmental Disabilities **New Directions** ✉ 5276 Hollister Ave., Suite 207, Santa Barbara, CA 93111 ☎ 805/967-2841 or 888/967-2841 🖹 805/964-7344 ⊕ www.newdirectionstravel.com. **Sprout** ✉ 893 Amsterdam Ave., New York, NY 10025 ☎ 212/222-9575 or 888/222-9575 🖹 212/222-9768 ⊕ www.gosprout.org.

DISCOUNTS & DEALS

Be a smart shopper and compare all your options before making decisions. A plane ticket bought with a promotional coupon from travel clubs, coupon books, and direct-mail offers or purchased on the Internet may not be cheaper than the least expensive fare from a discount ticket agency. And always keep in mind that what you get is just as important as what you save.

DISCOUNT RESERVATIONS

To save money, look into discount reservations services with Web sites and toll-free numbers, which use their buying power to get a better price on hotels, airline tickets (⇨ Air Travel), even car rentals. When booking a room, always **call the hotel's local toll-free number** (if one is available) rather than the central reservations number—you'll often get a better price. Always ask about special packages or corporate rates.
🚹 Hotel Rooms **Accommodations Express** ☎ 800/444-7666 or 800/277-1064. **Quikbook** ☎ 800/789-9887 ⊕ www.quikbook.com. **Steigenberger Reservation Service** ☎ 800/223-5652

⊕ www.srs-worldhotels.com. **Turbotrip.com** ☎ 800/473-7829 ⊕ w3.turbotrip.com.

PACKAGE DEALS

Don't confuse packages and guided tours. When you buy a package, you travel on your own, just as though you had planned the trip yourself. Fly–drive packages, which combine airfare and car rental, are often a good deal. In cities, ask the local visitor's bureau about hotel and local transportation packages that include tickets to major museum exhibits or other special events.

EATING & DRINKING

Food in Hawai'i is a reflection of the state's diverse cultural makeup and tropical location. Fresh seafood is the hallmark of Hawai'i regional cuisine, and its preparations are drawn from across the Pacific Rim, including Japan, the Philippines, Korea, and Thailand. But Hawaiian food is a cuisine in its own right. Meals in resort areas are costly but often excellent. In general, when you order a regular coffee, you get coffee with milk and sugar.

The restaurants we list are the cream of the crop in each price category.

CATEGORY	COST
$$$$	over $30
$$$	$20-$30
$$	$12-$20
$	$7-$12
¢	under $7

Prices are for one main course at dinner.

MEALTIMES

Unless otherwise noted, the restaurants listed in this guide are open daily for lunch and dinner.

RESERVATIONS & DRESS

Hawai'i is decidedly casual. Aloha shirts and shorts or long pants for men and island-style dresses or casual resort wear for women are standard attire for evenings in most hotel restaurants and local eateries. T-shirts and shorts will do the trick for breakfast and lunch.

Reservations are always a good idea; we mention them only when they're essential or not accepted. Book as far ahead as you can, and reconfirm as soon as you arrive. (Large parties should always call ahead to check the reservations policy.) We mention dress only when men are required to wear a jacket or a jacket and tie.

SPECIALTIES

Fish, fruit, and fresh island-grown produce are the base of Hawai'i regional cuisine. The "plate lunch" is the heart of most Hawaiians' days and usually consists of grilled teriyaki chicken, beef, or fish, served with two scoops of white rice and two side salads. *Poke,* marinated raw tuna, is a local hallmark.

WINE, BEER & SPIRITS

Hawai'i has a new generation of micro breweries, including on-site microbreweries at many restaurants. The drinking age in Hawai'i is 21 years of age, and a photo ID must be presented to purchase alcoholic beverages. Bars are open until 2 AM; venues with a cabaret license can stay open until 4 AM. No matter what you might see in the local parks, drinking alcohol in public parks or on the beaches is illegal. It is also illegal to have open containers of alcohol in motor vehicles.

ECOTOURISM

Hawai'i's connection to its environment is spiritual, cultural, and essential to its survival. You'll find a rainbow of natural attractions to explore, from the ribbons of beaches to volcanic peaks, where lava shows after dark are spectacular. There are 13 climatic regions in the world, and Maui and the Big Island offer ecotravelers a glimpse of 11 of them. Much of Kaua'i's natural beauty can be seen only on foot. Its Nā Pali Coast/Waimea Canyon/Kōke'e trail network includes 28 trails totaling some 45 mi rich in endemic species of flora and fauna. Maui offers the exhilaration of a rain-forest hike in Hāna, the cool Upcountry climes of Kula, and the awe-inspiring Haleakalā Crater. Moloka'i and Lāna'i, two of the least-developed islands, hold adventures best experienced on foot and by four-wheel-drive vehicle, or even by mule. Ecotouring in Hawai'i gives you the opportunity to learn from local guides who are familiar with the *aina* (land) and

Hawai'i's unique cultural heritage. Many of these tours take clients to locations less traveled, so it helps to be in good physical shape. The views at the ends of these roads are an exceedingly rich reward.

Nature and all its ornaments are sacred to Hawaiians, so before taking pieces of lava rock home for souvenirs, listen to what residents (and some vacationers) will tell you: don't touch! Hapless travelers who take "souvenir" rocks speak of "bad-luck" consequences in the form of stalled cars, travel delays, and bouts of illness. Park rangers spin tales about lava rocks mailed from around the world with attached tales of woe and pleas for the rocks to be put back. If nothing else, with millions of visitors a year, there aren't enough cool rocks to go around.

During the winter months, be sure to watch the beachfronts for endangered sea turtles, or recently laid nests. If you spot one, notify local authorities—they'll be thankful for your help in tracking these elusive creatures.

🇫 **Alternative-Hawai'i** ☎ 808/695-5113 ⊕ www. alternative-hawaii.com. **Hawai'i Ecotourism Association** 🖃 877/300-7058 ⊕ www. hawaiiecotourism.org.

ETIQUETTE & BEHAVIOR

Hawai'i was admitted to the Union in 1959, so residents can be pretty sensitive when visitors refer to their own hometowns as "back in the States." Remember, when in Hawai'i, refer to the contiguous 48 states as "the mainland" and not as the United States. When you do, you won't appear to be such a *malahini* (newcomer).

GAY & LESBIAN TRAVEL

A few small hotels and some bed-and-breakfasts in Hawai'i are favored by gay and lesbian visitors; Purple Roofs is a listing agent for gay-friendly accommodations in Hawai'i. Pacific Ocean Holidays specializes in prearranging package tours for independent gay travelers. The organization also publishes the *Pocket Guide to Hawai'i,* an online directory of gay and gay-friendly businesses and community resources on O'ahu, Maui, Kaua'i and the Big Island.

For details about the gay and lesbian scene, consult *Fodor's Gay Guide to the USA* (available in bookstores everywhere). ⬛ Local Resources **Pacific Ocean Holidays** 🏠 Box 88245, Honolulu 96830 ☎ 808/923-2400 or 800/735-6600 ⬛ www.gayHawaii.com. **Purple Roofs** ⬛ www.purpleroofs.com. ⬛ Gay- & Lesbian-Friendly Travel Agencies **Different Roads Travel** ✉ 1017 N. LaCienega Blvd., Suite 308, West Hollywood, CA 90069 ☎ 310/289-6000 or 800/429-8747 (Ext. 14 for both) 🖨 310/855-0323 ✉ lgernert@tzell.com. **Kennedy Travel** ✉ 130 W. 42nd St., Suite 401, New York, NY 10036 ☎ 800/237-7433 or 212/840-8659 🖨 212/730-2269 ⬛ www.kennedytravel.com. **Now, Voyager** ✉ 4406 18th St., San Francisco, CA 94114 ☎ 415/626-1169 or 800/255-6951 🖨 415/626-8626 ⬛ www. nowvoyager.com. **Skylink Travel and Tour/Flying Dutchmen Travel** ✉ 1455 N. Dutton Ave., Suite A, Santa Rosa, CA 95401 ☎ 707/546-9888 or 800/225-5759 🖨 707/636-0951; serving lesbian travelers.

HEALTH

Hawai'i is known as the Health State. The life expectancy here is 79 years, the longest in the nation. Balmy weather makes it easy to remain active year-round, and the low-stress aloha attitude certainly contributes to general well-being. When visiting the Islands, however, there are a few health issues to keep in mind.

The Hawai'i State Department of Health recommends that you drink 16 ounces of water per hour to avoid dehydration when hiking or spending time in the sun. **Use sunblock, wear UV-reflective sunglasses, and protect your head with a visor or hat for shade.** If you're not acclimated to warm, humid weather you should allow plenty of time for rest stops and refreshments. When visiting freshwater streams, be aware of the tropical disease leptospirosis, which is spread by animal urine and carried into streams and mud. Symptoms include fever, headache, nausea, and red eyes. If left untreated it can cause liver and kidney damage, respiratory failure, internal bleeding, and even death. To avoid this, don't swim or wade in freshwater streams or ponds if you have open sores and **don't drink from any freshwater streams or ponds.**

On the Islands, fog is a rare occurrence, but there can often be "vog," an airborne haze of gases released from volcanic vents on the Big Island. During certain weather conditions such as "Kona Winds," the vog can settle over the Islands and wreak havoc with respiratory and other health conditions, especially asthma or emphysema. If susceptible, stay indoors and get emergency assistance if needed.

PESTS & OTHER HAZARDS

The Islands have their share of bugs and insects that enjoy the tropical climate as much as visitors do. Most are harmless but annoying. When planning to spend time outdoors in hiking areas, **wear long-sleeved clothing and pants** and **use mosquito repellent containing deet.** In very damp places you may encounter the dreaded local centipede. On the Islands they usually come in two colors, brown and blue, and they range from the size of a worm to an 8-inch cigar. Their sting is very painful, and the reaction is similar to bee- and wasp-sting reactions. When camping, **shake out your sleeping bag before climbing in, and check your shoes in the morning,** as the centipedes like cozy places. If planning on hiking or traveling in remote areas, always carry a first-aid kit and appropriate medications for sting reactions.

INSURANCE

The most useful travel-insurance plan is a comprehensive policy that includes coverage for trip cancellation and interruption, default, trip delay, and medical expenses (with a waiver for preexisting conditions).

Without insurance you'll lose all or most of your money if you cancel your trip, regardless of the reason. Default insurance covers you if your tour operator, airline, or cruise line goes out of business—the chances of which have been increasing. Trip-delay covers expenses that arise because of bad weather or mechanical delays. Study the fine print when comparing policies.

U.K. residents can buy a travel-insurance policy valid for most vacations taken during the year in which it's purchased (but check preexisting-condition coverage).

Always **buy travel policies directly from the insurance company**; if you buy them from a cruise line, airline, or tour operator that goes out of business you probably won't be covered for the agency or operator's default, a major risk. Before making any purchase, review your existing health and home-owner's policies to find what they cover away from home.

🛈 **Travel Insurers In the U.S.: Access America** ✉ 2805 N. Parham Rd., Richmond, VA 23294 ☎ 800/284-8300 🖷 804/673-1469 or 800/346-9265 ⊕ www.accessamerica.com. **Travel Guard International** ✉ 1145 Clark St., Stevens Point, WI 54481 ☎ 800/826-1300 or 715/345-1041 🖷 800/955-8785 or 715/345-1990 ⊕ www.travelguard.com.

FOR INTERNATIONAL TRAVELERS

For information on customs restrictions, *see* Customs & Duties.

CAR RENTAL

When picking up a rental car, non-U.S. residents need a reservation voucher for any prepaid reservations that were made in the traveler's home country, a passport, a driver's license, and a travel policy that covers each driver.

CAR TRAVEL

Gas costs range from $2 to $2.50 a gallon. Stations are plentiful. Most stay open late (24 hours along large highways and in big cities), except in rural areas, where Sunday hours are limited and where you may drive long stretches without a refueling opportunity. Highways are well paved. Interstate highways—limited-access, multilane highways whose numbers are prefixed by "I–"—are the fastest routes. Interstates with three-digit numbers encircle urban areas, which may have other limited-access expressways, freeways, and parkways as well. Tolls may be levied on limited-access highways. So-called U.S. highways and state highways are not necessarily limited-access but may have several lanes.

Along larger highways, roadside stops with restrooms, fast-food restaurants, and sundries stores are well spaced. State police and tow trucks patrol major highways and lend assistance. If your car breaks down on an interstate, pull onto the shoulder and wait for help, or have your passengers wait while you walk to an emergency phone (available in most states). If you carry a cell phone, dial 911, noting your location on the small green roadside mileage markers.

Driving in the United States is on the right. Do obey speed limits posted along roads and highways. Watch for lower limits in small towns and on back roads. On weekdays between 6 and 10 AM and again between 4 and 7 PM expect heavy traffic. To encourage carpooling, some freeways have special lanes for so-called high-occupancy vehicles (HOV)—cars carrying more than one passenger.

Bookstores, gas stations, convenience stores, and rest stops sell maps (about $3) and multiregion road atlases (about $10).

CONSULATES & EMBASSIES

🛈 **Australia Australian Consulate** ✉ 1000 Bishop St., Honolulu 96813 ☎ 808/524-5050. 🛈 **Canada Canadian Consulate** ✉ 1000 Bishop St., Honolulu 96813 ☎ 808/524-5050. 🛈 **New Zealand New Zealand Consulate** ✉ 900 Richards St., Room 414, Honolulu 96813 ☎ 808/543-7900. 🛈 **United Kingdom British Consulate** ✉ 1000 Bishop St., Honolulu 96813 ☎ 808/524-5050.

CURRENCY

The dollar is the basic unit of U.S. currency. It has 100 cents. Coins are the copper penny (1¢); the silvery nickel (5¢), dime (10¢), quarter (25¢), and half-dollar (50¢); and the golden $1 coin, replacing a now-rare silver dollar. Bills are denominated $1, $5, $10, $20, $50, and $100, all mostly green and identical in size; designs and background tints vary. In addition, you may come across a $2 bill, but the chances are slim. The exchange rate at this writing is US$1.78 per British pound, .74¢ per Canadian dollar, .73¢ per Australian dollar, and .63¢ per New Zealand dollar.

ELECTRICITY

The U.S. standard is AC, 110 volts/60 cycles. Plugs have two flat pins set parallel to each other.

EMERGENCIES

For police, fire, or ambulance, **dial 911** (0 in rural areas).

INSURANCE

Britons and Australians need extra medical coverage when traveling overseas.

7 Insurance Information In the U.K.: **Association of British Insurers** ✉ 51 Gresham St., London EC2V 7HQ ☎ 020/7600-3333 🖷 020/7696-8999 ⊕ www.abi.org.uk. In Australia: **Insurance Council of Australia** ✉ Level 3, 56 Pitt St. Sydney, NSW 2000 ☎ 02/9253-5100 🖷 02/9253-5111 ⊕ www.ica.com.au. In Canada: **RBC Insurance** ✉ 6880 Financial Dr., Mississauga, Ontario L5N 7Y5 ☎ 800/387-4357 or 905/816-2559 🖷 888/298-6458 ⊕ www.rbcinsurance.com. In New Zealand: **Insurance Council of New Zealand** ✉ Level 7, 111-115 Customhouse Quay, Box 474, Wellington ☎ 04/472-5230 🖷 04/473-3011 ⊕ www.icnz.org.nz.

MAIL & SHIPPING

You can buy stamps and aerograms and send letters and parcels in post offices. Stamp-dispensing machines can occasionally be found in airports, bus and train stations, office buildings, drugstores, and the like. You can also deposit mail in the stout, dark blue, steel bins at strategic locations everywhere and in the mail chutes of large buildings; pickup schedules are posted. You can deposit packages at public collection boxes as long as the parcels are affixed with proper postage and weigh less than one pound. Packages weighing one or more pounds must be taken to a post office or handed to a postal carrier.

For mail sent within the United States, you need a 37¢ stamp for first-class letters weighing up to 1 ounce (23¢ for each additional ounce) and 23¢ for postcards. You pay 80¢ for 1-ounce airmail letters and 70¢ for airmail postcards to most other countries; to Canada and Mexico, you need a 60¢ stamp for a 1-ounce letter and 50¢ for a postcard. An aerogram—a single sheet of lightweight blue paper that folds into its own envelope, stamped for overseas airmail—costs 70¢.

To receive mail on the road, have it sent c/o General Delivery at your destination's main post office (use the correct five-digit ZIP code). You must pick up mail in person within 30 days and show a driver's license or passport.

PASSPORTS & VISAS

When traveling internationally, carry your passport even if you don't need one (it's always the best form of ID) and **make two photocopies of the data page** (one for someone at home and another for you, carried separately from your passport). If you lose your passport, promptly call the nearest embassy or consulate and the local police.

Visitor visas aren't necessary for Canadian or European Union citizens, or for citizens of Australia who are staying fewer than 90 days.

7 Australian Citizens Passports Australia ☎ 131-232 ⊕ www.passports.gov.au. **United States Consulate General** ✉ MLC Centre, Level 59, 19-29 Martin Pl., Sydney, NSW 2000 ☎ 02/9373-9200, 1902/941-641 fee-based visa-inquiry line ⊕ usembassy-australia.state.gov/sydney. **7 Canadian Citizens Passport Office** ✉ To mail in applications: 70 Cremazie St., Gatineau, Québec J8Y 3P2 ☎ 800/567-6868, 866/255-7655 TTY ⊕ www.ppt.gc.ca. **7 New Zealand Citizens New Zealand Passports Office** ✉ For applications and information, Level 3, Boulcott House, 47 Boulcott St., Wellington ☎ 0800/22-5050 or 04/474-8100 ⊕ www.passports.govt.nz. **Embassy of the United States** ✉ 29 Fitzherbert Terr., Thorndon, Wellington ☎ 04/462-6000 ⊕ usembassy.org.nz. **U.S. Consulate General** ✉ Citibank Bldg., 3rd floor, 23 Customs St. E, Auckland ☎ 09/303-2724 ⊕ usembassy.org.nz. **7 U.K. Citizens U.K. Passport Service** ☎ 0870/521-0410 ⊕ www.passport.gov.uk. **American Consulate General** ✉ Danesfort House, 223 Stranmillis Rd., Belfast, Northern Ireland BT9 5GR ☎ 028/9038-6100 🖷 028/9068-1301 ⊕ www.usembassy.org.uk. **American Embassy** ✉ For visa and immigration information or to submit a visa application via mail (enclose an SASE), Consular Information Unit, 24 Grosvenor Sq., London W1A 2LQ ☎ 090/5544-4546 or 090/6820-0290 for visa information (per-minute charges), 0207/499-9000 main switchboard ⊕ www.usembassy.org.uk.

TELEPHONES

All U.S. telephone numbers consist of a three-digit area code and a seven-digit local number. Within many local calling areas, you dial only the seven-digit number. Within some area codes, you must dial

"1" first for calls outside the local area. To call between area-code regions, dial "1" then all 10 digits; the same goes for calls to numbers prefixed by "800," "888," "866," and "877"—all toll-free. For calls to numbers preceded by "900" you must pay—usually dearly.

For international calls, dial "011" followed by the country code and the local number. For help, dial "0" and ask for an overseas operator. The country code is 61 for Australia, 64 for New Zealand, 44 for the United Kingdom. Calling Canada is the same as calling within the United States, although you might not be able to get through on some toll-free numbers. Most local phone books list country codes and U.S. area codes. The country code for the United States is 1.

For operator assistance, dial "0." To obtain someone's phone number, call directory assistance at 555–1212 or occasionally 411 (free at many public phones). To have the person you're calling foot the bill, phone collect; dial "0" instead of "1" before the 10-digit number.

At pay phones, instructions often are posted. Usually you insert coins in a slot (usually 25¢–50¢ for local calls) and wait for a steady tone before dialing. When you call long-distance, the operator tells you how much to insert; prepaid phone cards, widely available in various denominations, are easier. Call the number on the back, punch in the card's personal identification number when prompted, then dial your number.

LANGUAGE

English is the primary language on the Islands. Making the effort to learn some Hawaiian words can be rewarding, however. Despite the length of many Hawaiian words, the Hawaiian alphabet is actually one of the world's shortest, with only 12 letters: the five vowels, *a, e, i, o, u,* and seven consonants, *h, k, l, m, n, p, w.* Hawaiian words you are most likely to encounter during your visit to the Islands are *aloha, mahalo* (thank you), *keiki* (child), *haole* (Caucasian or foreigner), *mauka* (toward the mountains), *makai* (toward

the ocean), and *pau* (finished, all done). Hawaiian history includes waves of immigrants, each bringing their own language. To communicate with each other, they developed a sort of slang known as "pidgin." If you listen closely, you will know what is being said by the inflections and by the extensive use of body language. For example, when you know what you want to say but don't know how to say it, just say "you know, da kine." For an informative and somewhat-hilarious view of things Hawaiian, check out Jerry Hopkins's series of books titled *Pidgin to the Max* and *Fax to the Max,* available at most local bookstores in the Hawaiiana sections.

LEI GREETINGS

When you walk off a long flight, perhaps a bit groggy and stiff, nothing quite compares with a Hawaiian lei greeting. The casual ceremony ranks as one of the fastest ways to make the transition from the worries of home to the joys of your vacation. Though the tradition has created an expectation that everyone receives this floral garland when they step off the plane, the state of Hawai'i cannot greet each of its nearly 7 million annual visitors.

Still, it's easy to **arrange for a lei ceremony for yourself or your companions before you arrive.** Contact one of the following companies if you have not signed up with a tour company that provides it. If you really want to be wowed by the experience, request a lei of tuberoses, some of the most divine-smelling blossoms on the planet. Greeters of Hawai'i requires 48 hours' notice and charges $20.95 to $30.95 per person; add $10 for late notification. Kama'aina Leis, Flowers & Greeters requires two days' notice and charges $12.65 for a standard greeting on O'ahu and $15 on the Neighbor Islands.
🖪 **Greeters of Hawai'i** ☎ 800/366-8559 📠 800/926-2644 ⊕ www.greetersofhawaii.com. **Kama'aina Leis, Flowers & Greeters** ☎ 808/836-3246 or 800/367-5183 📠 808/836-1814.

LODGING

No matter what your budget, there is a place for you in Hawai'i. Large city-size resorts fill the Islands' most scenic shores.

Family-style condominiums have many of the amenities of fine hotels, and it's possible to find some at reasonable prices. Vacation rentals and B&Bs are becoming increasingly popular as visitors look for a real slice of Hawai'i away from the crowds. Often tucked into nooks of the Islands you would normally never see, they are competitively priced, highly personalized, and great for relaxing.

The lodgings we list are the cream of the crop in each price category. We always list the facilities that are available, but we don't specify whether they cost extra. When pricing accommodations, always ask what's included and what costs extra.

CATEGORY	COST
$$$$	over $200
$$$	$150–$200
$$	$100–$150
$	$60–$100
¢	under $60

Prices are for two people in a standard double room in high season, including tax and service.

APARTMENT & HOUSE RENTAL
If you want a home base that's roomy enough for a family and comes with cooking facilities, consider a furnished rental. These can save you money, especially if you're traveling with a group. Home-exchange directories sometimes list rentals as well as exchanges.

🔂 **International Agents Hideaways International** ✉ 767 Islington St., Portsmouth, NH 03801 ☎ 603/430-4433 or 800/843-4433 🖷 603/430-4444 ⊕ www.hideaways.com, annual membership $185. **Hometours International** ✉ 1108 Scottie La., Knoxville, TN 37919 ☎ 865/690-8484 or 866/367-4668 ✍ hometours@aol.com ⊕ thor.he.net/~hometour/. **Vacation Home Rentals Worldwide** ✉ 235 Kensington Ave., Norwood, NJ 07648 ☎ 201/767-9393 or 800/633-3284 🖷 201/767-5510 ⊕ www.vhrww.com. **Villas and Apartments Abroad** ✉ 183 Madison Ave., Suite 201, New York, NY 10016 ☎ 212/213-6435 or 800/433-3020 🖷 212/213-8252 ⊕ www.vaanyc.com.

🔂 **Exchange Clubs HomeLink USA** ✉ 2937 N.W. 9th Terrace, Wilton Manors, FL 33311 ☎ 954/566-2687 or 800/638-3841 🖷 954/566-2783 ⊕ www.

homelink.org; $75 yearly for a listing and online access; $45 additional to receive directories. **Intervac U.S.** ✉ 30 Corte San Fernando, Tiburon, CA 94920 ☎ 800/756-4663 🖷 415/435-7440 ⊕ www.intervacus.com; $128 yearly for a listing, online access, and a catalog; $68 without catalog.

HOSTELS
No matter what your age, you can save on lodging costs by staying at hostels. Most hostels in Hawai'i cater to a lively international crowd of backpackers, surfers, and windsurfers; those seeking intimacy or privacy should seek out a B&B.

In some 4,500 locations in more than 70 countries around the world, Hostelling International (HI), the umbrella group for a number of national youth-hostel associations, offers single-sex, dorm-style beds and, at many hostels, rooms for couples and family accommodations. Membership in any HI national hostel association, open to travelers of all ages, allows you to stay in HI-affiliated hostels at member rates; one-year membership is about $28 for adults (C$35 for a two-year minimum membership in Canada, £15 in the U.K., A$52 in Australia, and NZ$40 in New Zealand); hostels charge about $10–$30 per night. Members have priority if the hostel is full; they're also eligible for discounts around the world, even on rail and bus travel in some countries.

🔂 **Organizations Hostelling International–USA** ✉ 8401 Colesville Rd., Suite 600, Silver Spring, MD 20910 ☎ 301/495-1240 🖷 301/495-6697 ⊕ www.hiusa.org. **Hostelling International–Canada** ✉ 205 Catherine St., Suite 400, Ottawa, Ontario K2P 1C3 ☎ 613/237-7884 or 800/663-5777 🖷 613/237-7868 ⊕ www.hihostels.ca. **YHA England and Wales** ✉ Trevelyan House, Dimple Rd., Matlock, Derbyshire DE4 3YH, U.K. ☎ 0870/870-8808, 0870/770-8868, 0162/959-2600 🖷 0870/770-6127 ⊕ www.yha.org.uk. **YHA Australia** ✉ 422 Kent St., Sydney, NSW 2001 ☎ 02/9261-1111 🖷 02/9261-1969 ⊕ www.yha.com.au. **YHA New Zealand** ✉ Level 1, Moorhouse City, 166 Moorhouse Ave., Box 436, Christchurch ☎ 03/379-9970 or 0800/278-299 🖷 03/365-4476 ⊕ www.yha.org.nz.

HOTELS

All hotels listed have private bath unless otherwise noted.

7 Toll-Free Numbers Best Western ☎ 800/528-1234 ⊕ www.bestwestern.com. **Choice** ☎ 800/424-6423 ⊕ www.choicehotels.com. **Days Inn** ☎ 800/325-2525 ⊕ www.daysinn.com. **Doubletree Hotels** ☎ 800/222-8733 ⊕ www.doubletree.com. **Embassy Suites** ☎ 800/362-2779 ⊕ www.embassysuites.com. **Fairfield Inn** ☎ 800/228-2800 ⊕ www.marriott.com. **Four Seasons** ☎ 800/332-3442 ⊕ www.fourseasons.com. **Hilton** ☎ 800/445-8667 ⊕ www.hilton.com. **Holiday Inn** ☎ 800/465-4329 ⊕ www.ichotelsgroup.com. **Howard Johnson** ☎ 800/446-4656 ⊕ www.hojo.com. **Hyatt Hotels & Resorts** ☎ 800/233-1234 ⊕ www.hyatt.com. **La Quinta** ☎ 800/531-5900 ⊕ www.lq.com. **Marriott** ☎ 800/228-9290 ⊕ www.marriott.com. **Quality Inn** ☎ 800/424-6423 ⊕ www.choicehotels.com. **Radisson** ☎ 800/333-3333 ⊕ www.radisson.com. **Ramada** ☎ 800/228-2828, 800/854-7854 international reservations ⊕ www.ramada.com or www.ramadahotels.com. **Red Lion and WestCoast Hotels and Inns** ☎ 800/733-5466 ⊕ www.redlion.com. **Renaissance Hotels & Resorts** ☎ 800/468-3571 ⊕ www.marriott.com. **Ritz-Carlton** ☎ 800/241-3333 ⊕ www.ritzcarlton.com. **Sheraton** ☎ 800/325-3535 ⊕ www.starwood.com/sheraton. **Sleep Inn** ☎ 800/424-6423 ⊕ www.choicehotels.com. **Westin Hotels & Resorts** ☎ 800/228-3000 ⊕ www.starwood.com/westin.

MEDIA

Hawai'i is wired to a variety of media, including network television, cable television, Web-based media, newspapers, magazines, and radio. Many of the resorts and hotels throughout the Islands include an additional visitor-information channel on your in-room television. Consult your in-room directory to get channel and scheduling information and to find out the special activities or events that might be happening during your visit.

NEWSPAPERS & MAGAZINES

Each of the Islands has its own daily newspaper, available through many hotel bell desks; in sundry stores, restaurants, and cafés; and at newsstands. Many hotels will deliver one to your room upon request. The *Honolulu Advertiser* is O'ahu's morning and Sunday paper; the *Honolulu Star-Bulletin* is O'ahu's evening paper and also prints in the morning and on Sundays. *West Hawai'i Today* is the Big Island's Kona Coast newspaper, and the *Hawai'i Tribune-Herald* serves the Hilo side of the island. On Maui, it's the *Maui News*. On Kaua'i, it's the *Garden Island* and *Kaua'i Times*. The *Honolulu Weekly* is a great guide for arts and alternative events, and the *Pacific Business News* provides the latest in business news. The monthly *Honolulu Magazine* focuses on O'ahu issues and happenings. Check out local bookstores for Neighbor Island magazines, some of which publish on a quarterly schedule.

RADIO & TELEVISION

Radio airwaves on the Islands are affected by natural terrain, so don't expect to hear one radio station islandwide. For Hawaiian music, tune your FM radio dial to 98.5 KDNN (O'ahu), 100.3 KCCN (O'ahu), 99.5 KHUI (O'ahu), 105.1 KINE (O'ahu), 100.3 KAPA (East Hawai'i), 99.1 KAGB (West Hawai'i), 93.5 KPOA (Maui), and 95.9 KSRF (Kaua'i). News junkies can get their fill of news and talk by tuning to the AM radio dial and the following island stations: 590 KSSK (O'ahu), 650 KHNR (O'ahu), 830 KHVH (O'ahu), 990 KHBZ (O'ahu), 1080 KWAI (O'ahu), 670 KPUA (East Hawai'i), 620 KIPA (West Hawai'i), 1110 KAOI (Maui), 570 KQNG (Kaua'i). National Public Radio enthusiasts can tune to the FM dial for NPR programming on 88.1 KHPR (O'ahu), 89.3 KIPO (O'ahu) and 90.7 KKUA (Maui). On Kaua'i check out the only commercial-free public radio station on the Islands, KKCR, at 90.9 and 91.9 FM. It broadcasts Hawaiian music, jazz, blues, rock, and reggae, as well as talk shows on local issues.

On O'ahu, many residents wake up with Perry & Price on KSSK AM 59 or FM 92. The lively duo provides news, traffic updates, and weather reports between "easy-listening" music and phone calls from listeners from 5 to 10 AM.

Television channels on the Islands are plentiful between network and cable channels. Channel allocation varies by island and location. On Oʻahu, you can find the following network programming with its channel and local affiliate call sign: FOX (2) KHON, ABC (4) KITV, UPN/WB (5) KHVE, CBS (9) KGMB, PBS (10) KHET, and NBC (13) KHNL.

MONEY MATTERS

Prices throughout this guide are given for adults. Substantially reduced fees are almost always available for children, students, and senior citizens. For information on taxes, *see* Taxes.

ATMS

Automatic teller machines for easy access to cash are everywhere on the Islands. ATMs can be found in shopping centers, small convenience and grocery stores, inside hotels and resorts, as well as outside most bank branches. For a directory of locations, call 800/424–7787 for the Master-Card/Cirrus/Maestro network or 800/843–7587 for the Visa/Plus network.

CREDIT CARDS

Throughout this guide, the following abbreviations are used: **AE**, American Express; **D**, Discover; **DC**, Diners Club; **MC**, MasterCard; and **V**, Visa.

🛃 Reporting Lost Cards American Express ☎ 800/992–3404. **Diners Club** ☎ 800/234–6377. **Discover** ☎ 800/347–2683. **MasterCard** ☎ 800/622-7747. **Visa** ☎ 800/847–2911.

NATIONAL PARKS & STATE PARKS

Hawaiʻi has seven national parks. On the island of Oʻahu, the USS *Arizona* Memorial at Pearl Harbor is overseen by the National Park Service. On Maui is the summit and crater of the Haleakalā volcano, at Haleakalā National Park. Molokaʻi's Kalaupapa National Historical Park was once a leper colony where victims of Hansen's disease were sent into exile in the late 1800s and cared for by Father Damien, a Belgian missionary.

The Big Island, Hawaiʻi's largest island, has four national parks. Hawaiʻi Volcanoes National Park is the state's number one attraction, where vents have been spewing lava for nearly 20 years. The

other three are Puʻuhonua O Hōnaunau National Historical Park, Puʻukoholā Heiau National Historical Site, and Kaloko-Honokōhau National Historical Park, all of which give a glimpse into Hawaiʻi's rich cultural history.

Hawaiʻi's 52 state parks encompass more than 25,000 acres on five islands and include many of its most beautiful beaches and coastal areas. The State Parks Division of the Hawaiʻi State Department of Land and Natural Resources can provide information on state parks and historic areas.

Look into discount passes to save money on park entrance fees. For $50, the National Parks Pass admits you (and any passengers in your private vehicle) to all national parks, monuments, and recreation areas, as well as other sites run by the National Park Service, for a year. (In parks that charge per person, the pass admits you, your spouse and children, and your parents, when you arrive together.) Camping and parking are extra. The $15 Golden Eagle Pass, a hologram you affix to your National Parks Pass, functions as an upgrade, granting entry to all sites run by the NPS, the U.S. Fish and Wildlife Service, the U.S. Forest Service, and the Bureau of Land Management. The upgrade, which expires with the parks pass, is sold by most national-park, Fish-and-Wildlife, and BLM fee stations. A major percentage of the proceeds from pass sales funds National Parks projects.

Both the Golden Age Passport ($10), for U.S. citizens or permanent residents who are 62 and older, and the Golden Access Passport (free), for persons with disabilities, entitle holders (and any passengers in their private vehicles) to lifetime free entry to all national parks, plus 50% off fees for the use of many park facilities and services. (The discount doesn't always apply to companions.) To obtain them, you must show proof of age and of U.S. citizenship or permanent residency—such as a U.S. passport, driver's license, or birth certificate—and, if requesting Golden Access, proof of disability. The Golden Age and Golden Access passes are available only at NPS-run sites that charge an entrance fee.

The National Parks Pass is also available by mail and phone and via the Internet.

National Park Foundation ⊠ 11 Dupont Circle NW, Suite 600, Washington, DC 20036 ☎ 202/238-4200 ⊕ www.nationalparks.org. **National Park Service** ⊠ National Park Service/Department of Interior, 1849 C St. NW, Washington, DC 20240 ☎ 202/208-6843 ⊕ www.nps.gov. **National Parks Conservation Association** ⊠ 1300 19th St. NW, Suite 300, Washington, DC 20036 ☎ 202/223-6722 or 800/628-7275 ⊕ www.npca.org.

Passes by Mail & Online National Park Foundation ⊕ www.nationalparks.org. **National Parks Pass** National Park Foundation ⊠ Box 34108, Washington, DC 20043 ☎ 888/467-2757 ⊕ www.nationalparks.org; include a check or money order payable to the National Park Service, plus $3.95 for shipping and handling (allow 8 to 13 business days from date of receipt for pass delivery), or call for passes.

State Parks State Parks Division, Hawai'i State Department of Land and Natural Resources ⊠ 1151 Punchbowl St., Room 310, Honolulu 96813 ☎ 808/587-0300 ⊕ www.hawaii.gov.

PACKING

Hawai'i is casual: sandals, bathing suits, and comfortable, informal clothing are the norm. In summer synthetic slacks and shirts, although easy to care for, can be uncomfortably warm.

Probably the most important thing to tuck into your suitcase is sunscreen. This is the tropics, and the ultraviolet rays are powerful, even on overcast days. Doctors advise putting on sunscreen when you get up in the morning, whether it's cloudy or sunny. Don't forget to **reapply sunscreen periodically during the day,** since perspiration can wash it away. Consider using sunscreens with a sun protection factor (SPF) of 15 or higher. There are many tanning oils on the market in Hawai'i, including coconut and *kukui* (the nut from a local tree) oils, but they can cause severe burns. Too many Hawaiian vacations have been spoiled by sunburn and even sun poisoning. Hats and sunglasses offer important sun protection, too. Both are easy to find in island shops, but if you already have a favorite packable hat or sun visor, bring it with you, and don't forget to wear it. All major hotels in Hawai'i provide beach towels.

As for clothing in the Hawaiian Islands, there's a saying that when a man wears a suit during the day, he's either going for a loan or he's a lawyer trying a case. Only a few upscale restaurants require a jacket for dinner. The aloha shirt is accepted dress in Hawai'i for business and most social occasions. Shorts are acceptable daytime attire, along with a T-shirt or polo shirt. There's no need to buy expensive sandals on the mainland—here you can get flip-flops for a couple of dollars and off-brand sandals for $20. Golfers should remember that many courses have dress codes requiring a collared shirt; call courses you're interested in for details. If you're not prepared, you can pick up appropriate clothing at resort pro shops. If you're visiting in winter or planning to visit a high-altitude area, **bring a sweater or light- to medium-weight jacket.** A polar fleece pullover is ideal, and makes a great impromptu pillow.

In your carry-on luggage, pack an extra pair of eyeglasses or contact lenses and enough of any medication you take to last a few days longer than the entire trip. You may also ask your doctor to write a spare prescription using the drug's generic name, as brand names may vary from country to country. In luggage to be checked, **never pack prescription drugs, valuables, or undeveloped film.** And don't forget to carry with you the addresses of offices that handle refunds of lost traveler's checks. Check *Fodor's How to Pack* (available at online retailers and bookstores everywhere) for more tips.

To avoid customs and security delays, carry medications in their original packaging. Don't pack any sharp objects in your carry-on luggage, including knives of any size or material, scissors, nail clippers, and corkscrews, or anything else that might arouse suspicion.

To avoid having your checked luggage chosen for hand inspection, don't cram bags full. The U.S. Transportation Security Administration suggests packing shoes on top and placing personal items you don't want touched in clear plastic bags.

CHECKING LUGGAGE

You're allowed to carry aboard one bag and one personal article, such as a purse or a laptop computer. Make sure what you carry on fits under your seat or in the overhead bin. Get to the gate early, so you can board as soon as possible, before the overhead bins fill up.

Baggage allowances vary by carrier, destination, and ticket class. On international flights, you're usually allowed to check two bags weighing up to 70 pounds (32 kilograms) each, although a few airlines allow checked bags of up to 88 pounds (40 kilograms) in first class. Some international carriers don't allow more than 66 pounds (30 kilograms) per bag in business class and 44 pounds (20 kilograms) in economy. If you're flying to or through the United Kingdom, your luggage cannot exceed 70 pounds (32 kilograms) per bag. On domestic flights, the limit is usually 50 to 70 pounds (23 to 32 kilograms) per bag. In general, carry-on bags shouldn't exceed 40 pounds (18 kilograms). Most airlines won't accept bags that weigh more than 100 pounds (45 kilograms) on domestic or international flights. Expect to pay a fee for baggage that exceeds weight limits. Check baggage restrictions with your carrier before you pack.

Airline liability for baggage is limited to $2,500 per person on flights within the United States. On international flights it amounts to $9.07 per pound or $20 per kilogram for checked baggage (roughly $640 per 70-pound bag), with a maximum of $634.90 per piece, and $400 per passenger for unchecked baggage. You can buy additional coverage at check-in for about $10 per $1,000 of coverage, but it often excludes a rather extensive list of items, shown on your airline ticket.

Before departure, itemize your bags' contents and their worth, and label the bags with your name, address, and phone number. (If you use your home address, cover it so potential thieves can't see it readily.) Include a label inside each bag and **pack a copy of your itinerary.** At check-in, make sure each bag is correctly tagged with the destination airport's three-letter code. Because some checked bags will be opened for hand inspection, the U.S. Transportation Security Administration recommends

that you leave luggage unlocked or use the plastic locks offered at check-in. TSA screeners place an inspection notice inside searched bags, which are re-sealed with a special lock.

If your bag has been searched and contents are missing or damaged, file a claim with the TSA Consumer Response Center as soon as possible. If your bags arrive damaged or fail to arrive at all, file a written report with the airline before leaving the airport.

🔁 **Complaints U.S. Transportation Security Administration Contact Center** ☎ 866/289-9673 ⊕ www.tsa.gov.

SAFETY

Hawai'i is generally a safe tourist destination, but it's still wise to follow the same common sense safety precautions you would normally follow in your own hometown. Hotel and visitor-center staff can provide information should you decide to head out on your own to more remote areas. **Rental cars are magnets for break-ins, so don't leave any valuables in the car, not even in a locked trunk.** Avoid poorly lighted areas, beach parks, and isolated areas after dark as a precaution. When hiking, **stay on marked trails,** no matter how alluring the temptation might be to stray. Weather conditions can cause landscapes to become muddy, slippery, and tenuous, so staying on marked trails will lessen the possibility of a fall or getting lost. Ocean safety is of the utmost importance when visiting an island destination. **Don't swim alone, and follow the international signage posted at beaches** that alerts swimmers to strong currents, man-of-war jellyfish, sharp coral, high surf, sharks, and dangerous shore breaks. At coastal lookouts along cliff tops, heed the signs indicating that waves can climb over the ledges. Check with lifeguards at each beach for current conditions, and **if the red flags are up, indicating swimming and surfing are not allowed, don't go in.** Waters that look calm on the surface can harbor strong currents and undertows, and not a few people who were just wading have been dragged out to sea.

LOCAL SCAMS

Be wary of those hawking "too good to be true" prices on everything from car rentals to attractions. Many of these offers are just a lure to get you in the door for timeshare presentations. When handed a flyer, read the fine print before you make your decision to participate.

WOMEN IN HAWAI'I

Women traveling alone are generally safe on the Islands, but always follow the safety precautions you would use in any major destination. When booking hotels, **request rooms closest to the elevator,** and always keep your hotel-room door and balcony doors locked. Stay away from isolated areas after dark; camping and hiking solo are not advised. If you stay out late visiting nightclubs and bars, **use caution when exiting night spots** and returning to your lodging.

SENIOR-CITIZEN TRAVEL

Hawai'i is steeped in a tradition that gives great respect to elders, or *kupuna,* and considers them "keepers of the wisdom." Visitors may not be so esteemed, but senior citizens traveling in Hawai'i will find discounts, special senior citizen–oriented activities, and buildings with easy access. Many lodging facilities have discounts for members of the American Association of Retired Persons (AARP).

To qualify for age-related discounts, mention your senior-citizen status up front when booking hotel reservations (not when checking out) and before you're seated in restaurants (not when paying the bill). Be sure to have identification on hand. When renting a car, ask about promotional car-rental discounts, which can be cheaper than senior-citizen rates.

⁊ Educational Programs Elderhostel ⊠ 11 Ave. de Lafayette, Boston, MA 02111 ☎ 877/426–8056, 978/323–4141 international callers, 877/426–2167 TTY ⊞ 877/426–2166 ⊕ www.elderhostel.org. **Interhostel** ⊠ University of New Hampshire, 6 Garrison Ave., Durham, NH 03824 ☎ 603/862–1147 or 800/733–9753 ⊞ 603/862–1113 ⊕ www.learn.unh.edu.

SHOPPING

KEY DESTINATIONS

On O'ahu, Ala Moana Center is one of the largest shopping spots; it's within easy walking distance of the west end of Waikīkī. The Royal Hawaiian Shopping Center is centrally located in Waikīkī itself. Farther away, you'll find Ward Centers, Aloha Tower Marketplace, and the Kāhala Mall.

The Neighbor Islands offer more in the way of smaller strips of shops. Still, it's possible to find larger stores grouped in areas such as Kaua'i's Kukui Grove Center in Līhu'e, Maui's Ka'ahumanu Shopping Center and Maui Mall in Kahului, the Shops at Wailea and Whaler's Village in Kā'anapali, the Big Island's Prince Kūhiō Shopping Plaza in Hilo, King's Shops in Waikoloa, the Shops at Mauna Lani, and Keauhou Shopping Village and Lanihau Center in Kailua-Kona. Exclusive shops can often be found in the lobbies of luxury hotels.

SMART SOUVENIRS

Aloha shirts and resort wear, Hawaiian-music recordings, shell leis, coral jewelry, traditional quilts, island foods, Kona coffee, and koa-wood products are just a few of the gifts that visitors to Hawai'i treasure. For the more elegant gift items, check out the Hawaiian boutiques in major island shopping centers as well as those tucked away in smaller shopping areas in residential districts. Island crafts fairs and swap meets offer a bargain bazaar of standard items such as T-shirts and tiki statues as well as the original works of local artisans.

WATCH OUT

Souvenirs made from coral or tortoise shell may not have been harvested legally, so in the interest of preserving Hawai'i's environment, it's best to avoid these.

STUDENTS IN HAWAI'I

Hawai'i is a popular destination for exchange students from around the world, who mainly attend the University of Hawai'i in Honolulu. Contact your hometown university about study and internship possibilities. To check out the student scene on the Islands, stop by any of the University of Hawai'i campuses or community college campuses, and read the *Honolulu Weekly* upon arrival for club and event information. Be sure to ask about discounts for students at all museums and major attractions and be prepared to show ID to qualify.

IDs & Services STA Travel ✉ 10 Downing St., New York, NY 10014 ☎ 212/627-3111, 800/777-0112 24-hr service center 🖷 212/627-3387 ⊕ www.sta. com. **Travel Cuts** ✉ 187 College St., Toronto, Ontario M5T 1P7, Canada ☎ 800/592-2887 in the U.S., 416/979-2406 or 866/246-9762 in Canada 🖷 416/979-8167 ⊕ www.travelcuts.com.

TAXES

SALES TAX

There's a 4.16% state sales tax on all purchases, including food. A hotel room tax of 7.25%, combined with the sales tax of 4%, equals an 11.41% rate added onto your hotel bill. A $3-per-day road tax is also assessed on each rental vehicle.

TIME

Hawai'i is on Hawaiian Standard Time, 5 hours behind New York, 2 hours behind Los Angeles, and 10 hours behind London.

When the U.S. mainland is on daylight saving time, Hawai'i is not, so add an extra hour of time difference between the Islands and U.S. mainland destinations. You may also find that things generally move more slowly here. That has nothing to do with your watch—it's just the laid-back way called Hawaiian time.

TIPPING

Tip cab drivers 15% of the fare. Standard tips for restaurants and bar tabs run from 15% to 20% of the bill, depending on the standard of service. Bellhops at hotels usually receive $1 per bag, more if you have bulky items such as bicycles and surfboards. Tip the hotel room maid $1 per night, paid daily. Tip doormen $1 for assistance with taxis; tips for concierge vary depending on the service. For example, tip more for "hard-to-get" event tickets or dining reservations.

TOURS & PACKAGES

Because everything is prearranged on a prepackaged tour or independent vacation, you spend less time planning—and often get it all at a good price.

BOOKING WITH AN AGENT

Travel agents are excellent resources. But it's a good idea to collect brochures from several agencies, as some agents' suggestions may be influenced by relationships with tour and package firms that reward them for volume sales. If you have a special interest, find an agent with expertise in that area. The American Society of Travel Agents (ASTA) has a database of specialists worldwide; you can log on to the group's Web site to find one near you.

Make sure your travel agent knows the accommodations and other services of the place being recommended. Ask about the hotel's location, room size, beds, and whether it has a pool, room service, or programs for children, if you care about these. Has your agent been there in person or sent others whom you can contact?

Do some homework on your own, too: local tourism boards can provide information about lesser-known and small-niche operators, some of which may sell only direct.

BUYER BEWARE

Each year consumers are stranded or lose their money when tour operators—even large ones with excellent reputations—go out of business. So check out the operator. Ask several travel agents about its reputation, and try to **book with a company that has a consumer-protection program.** (Look for information in the company's brochure.) In the United States, members of the United States Tour Operators Association are required to set aside funds (up to $1 million) to help eligible customers cover payments and travel arrangements in the event that the company defaults. It's also a good idea to choose a company that participates in the American Society of Travel Agents' Tour Operator Program; ASTA will act as mediator in any disputes between you and your tour operator.

Remember that the more your package or tour includes, the better you can predict the ultimate cost of your vacation. Make sure you know exactly what is covered, and beware of hidden costs. Are taxes,

tips, and transfers included? Entertainment and excursions? These can add up.
🔢 **Tour-Operator Recommendations American Society of Travel Agents** (⇨ Travel Agencies). **CrossSphere–The Global Association for Packaged Travel** ✉ 546 E. Main St., Lexington, KY 40508 ☎ 859/226–4444 or 800/682–8886 📠 859/226–4414 ⊕ www.CrossSphere.com. **United States Tour Operators Association (USTOA)** ✉ 275 Madison Ave., Suite 2014, New York, NY 10016 ☎ 212/599–6599 📠 212/599–6744 ⊕ www.ustoa.com.

TRANSPORTATION AROUND HAWAI'I

Renting a car is definitely recommended for those who plan to move beyond their hotel lounge chair. With the exception of O'ahu, public transportation is extremely limited, and even if you are staying in Honolulu or Waikīkī you may want a car if you plan to do any exploring or if you're short on time. **Reserve your vehicle in advance,** particularly during peak travel times and on the smaller islands, where the car-rental fleets are limited. Most major companies have airport counters and complimentary transportation for pickup/drop-off back at the airport upon departure.

Taxis can also be found at island airports, through your hotel doorman, in the more popular resort areas, or by contacting local taxi companies by telephone. Flag-down fees are $2, and each additional mile is $1.70. Most companies will also provide a car and driver for half-day or daylong island tours if you absolutely don't want to rent a car, and a number of companies also offer personal guides. Remember, however, that rates are quite steep for these services, ranging from $100 to $200 or more per day.

TRAVEL AGENCIES

A good travel agent puts your needs first. Look for an agency that has been in business at least five years, emphasizes customer service, and has someone on staff who specializes in your destination. In addition, **make sure the agency belongs to a professional trade organization.** The American Society of Travel Agents (ASTA) has more than 10,000 members in some 140 countries, enforces a strict code of

ethics, and will step in to mediate agent-client disputes involving ASTA members. ASTA also maintains a directory of agents on its Web site; ASTA's TravelSense.org, a trip planning and travel advice site, can also help to locate a travel agent who caters to your needs. (If a travel agency is also acting as your tour operator, *see* Buyer Beware *in* Tours & Packages.)
🔢 **Local Agent Referrals American Society of Travel Agents (ASTA)** ✉ 1101 King St., Suite 200, Alexandria, VA 22314 ☎ 703/739–2782 or 800/965–2782 24-hr hotline 📠 703/684–8319 ⊕ www.astanet.com and www.travelsense.org. **Association of British Travel Agents** ✉ 68–71 Newman St., London W1T 3AH ☎ 020/7637–2444 📠 020/7637–0713 ⊕ www.abta.com. **Association of Canadian Travel Agencies** ✉ 130 Albert St., Suite 1705, Ottawa, Ontario K1P 5G4 ☎ 613/237–3657 📠 613/237–7052 ⊕ www.acta.ca.**Australian Federation of Travel Agents** ✉ Level 3, 309 Pitt St., Sydney, NSW 2000 ☎ 02/9264–3299 or 1300/363–416 📠 02/9264 1085 ⊕ www.afta.com.au. **Travel Agents' Association of New Zealand** ✉ Level 5, Tourism and Travel House, 79 Boulcott St., Box 1888, Wellington 6001 ☎ 04/499–0104 📠 04/499–0786 ⊕ www.taanz.org.nz.

VISITOR INFORMATION

Before you go, contact the Hawai'i Visitors & Convention Bureau (HVCB) for general information on each island, free brochures that include an accommodations and car-rental guide, and an entertainment and dining guide containing one-line descriptions of bureau members. Take a virtual visit to Hawai'i on the Web, which can be most helpful in planning many aspects of your vacation. The HVCB site has a calendar section that allows you to see what local events are in place during the time of your stay.
🔢 **Tourist Information Hawai'i Visitors & Convention Bureau** ✉ 2270 Kalakaua Ave., Suite 801, Honolulu 96817 ☎ 808/923–1811, 800/464–2924 for brochures ⊕ www.gohawaii.com. In the U.K. contact the **Hawai'i Visitors & Convention Bureau** 📮 Box 208, Sunbury, Middlesex TW16 5RJ ☎ 020/8941–4009 ⊕ www.gohawaii.com. Send a £2 check or postal order for an information pack.
🔢 **Government Advisories U.S. Department of State** ✉ Bureau of Consular Affairs, Overseas Citizens Services Office, 2201 C St. NW Washington, DC

20520 ☎ 202/647–5225 or 888/407–4747, 317/472–2328 for interactive hotline ⊕ www.travel.state.gov. **Consular Affairs Bureau of Canada** ☎ 800/267–6788 or 613/944–6788 ⊕ www.voyage.gc.ca. **U.K. Foreign and Commonwealth Office** ✉ Travel Advice Unit, Consular Directorate, Old Admiralty Bldg., London SW1A 2PA ☎ 0870/606–0290 or 020/7008–1500 ⊕ www.fco.gov.uk/travel. **Australian Department of Foreign Affairs and Trade** ☎ 300/139–281 travel advisories, 02/6261–1299 Consular Travel Advice ⊕ www.smartraveller.gov.au or www.dfat.gov.au. **New Zealand Ministry of Foreign Affairs and Trade** ☎ 04/439–8000 ⊕ www.mft.govt.nz.

WEB SITES

Do check out the World Wide Web when planning your trip. You'll find everything from weather forecasts to virtual tours of famous cities. Be sure to visit Fodors.com (⊕ www.fodors.com), a complete travel-planning site. You can research prices and book plane tickets, hotel rooms, rental cars, vacation packages, and more. In addition, you can post your pressing questions in the Travel Talk section. Other planning tools include a currency converter and weather reports, and there are loads of links to travel resources.

For more information on Hawai'i, visit ⊕ www.gohawaii.com, the official Web site of the Hawai'i Visitors & Convention Bureau.

Other sites to check out include ⊕ www.bigisland.org (Big Island Visitors Bureau); ⊕ www.visitmaui.com (Maui County Visitors Bureau); ⊕ www.visit-oahu.com (O'ahu Visitors Bureau); ⊕ www.kauaivisitorsbureau.org (Kaua'i Visitors Bureau); and ⊕ www.molokai-hawaii.com (Moloka'i Visitor Information).

The Web site ⊕ www.search-hawaii.com has an engine that can search all linked Hawaiian Web pages by topic or word.

Visit ⊕ www.hshawaii.com for the Hawai'i State vacation planner; ⊕ www.kauai-hawaii.com for Kaua'i visitor information; ⊕ www.honoluluweekly.com for a weekly guide to the arts, entertainment, and dining in Honolulu; and ⊕ www.hawaii.gov, the state's official Web site, for all information on the destination, including camping.

O'ahu

WORD OF MOUTH

"I love flying into Honolulu, especially at night, and seeing all the millions of tiny lights of Waikīkī reflecting against the Pacific and then waking up to a gorgeous view of turquoise waters and Diamond Head."

—ggartist

WELCOME TO O'AHU

Getting Oriented

O'ahu, the third largest of the Hawaiian Islands, is not just Honolulu and Waikīkī. It is looping mountain trails on the western Wai'anae and eastern Ko'olau ranges. It is monster waves breaking on the golden beaches of the North Shore. It is country stores and beaches where turtles are your swimming companions.

TOP 5 Reasons to Go

1 **Waves:** Boogie board or surf some of the best breaks on the planet.

2 **Diamond Head:** Scale the crater whose iconic profile looms over Waikīkī.

3 **A Sea Plane Flight:** The trip along the exact path used by the Japanese Zeros over Pearl Harbor in 1941 brings a chill to even the most stoic soul.

4 **Movies on Waikīkī Beach:** Sand, silver screen, and stars—it's a theater experience like no other.

5 **A Swim with the Turtles at Mokulē'ia Beach:** Dozens swim just yards from the shore where they shoot the TV show *Lost*.

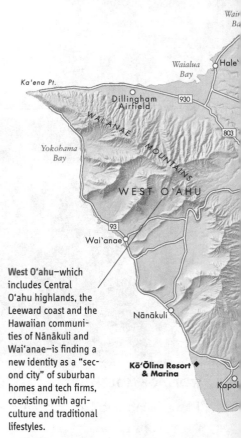

Wair
Ba

Waialua Bay   Hale'

Ka'ena Pt.

Dillingham Airfield   930

WAIANAE   803

Yokohama Bay

MOUNTAINS

WEST O'AHU

93

Wai'anae

West O'ahu–which includes Central O'ahu highlands, the Leeward coast and the Hawaiian communities of Nānākuli and Wai'anae–is finding a new identity as a "second city" of suburban homes and tech firms, coexisting with agriculture and traditional lifestyles.

Nānākuli

Kō'Ōlina Resort & Marina

Kapol

0   8 mi
0   8 km

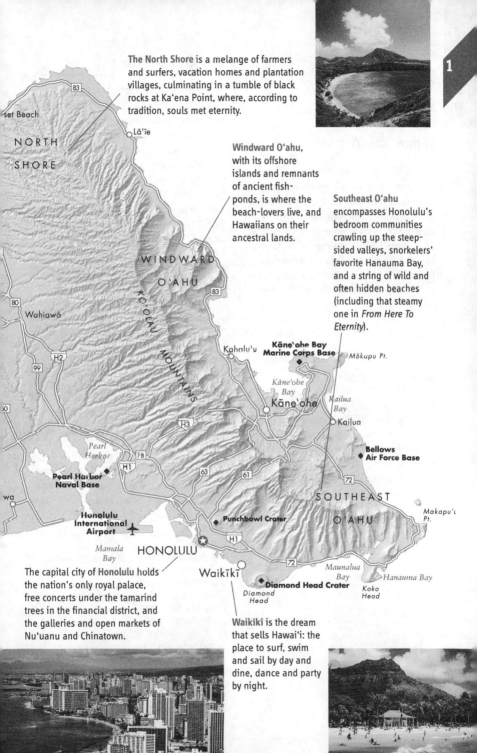

1

The North Shore is a melange of farmers and surfers, vacation homes and plantation villages, culminating in a tumble of black rocks at Ka'ena Point, where, according to tradition, souls met eternity.

NORTH SHORE

set Beach

Lā'ie

83

Windward O'ahu, with its offshore islands and remnants of ancient fish-ponds, is where the beach-lovers live, and Hawaiians on their ancestral lands.

Southeast O'ahu encompasses Honolulu's bedroom communities crawling up the steep-sided valleys, snorkelers' favorite Hanauma Bay, and a string of wild and often hidden beaches (including that steamy one in *From Here To Eternity*).

WINDWARD O'AHU

KO'OLAU MOUNTAINS

80

Wahiawā

H2

99

H3

Kahalu'u

Kāne'ohe Bay Marine Corps Base

Kāne'ohe Bay

Kāne'ohe

Mōkapu Pt.

Kailua Bay

Kailua

Bellows Air Force Base

Pearl Harbor

78

Pearl Harbor Naval Base

H1

63

61

72

SOUTHEAST O'AHU

Makapu'ı Pt.

Honolulu International Airport

Mamala Bay

HONOLULU

Punchbowl Crater

H1

72

Waikīkī

Diamond Head Crater

Diamond Head

Maunalua Bay

Hanauma Bay

Koko Head

The capital city of **Honolulu** holds the nation's only royal palace, free concerts under the tamarind trees in the financial district, and the galleries and open markets of Nu'uanu and Chinatown.

Waikīkī is the dream that sells Hawai'i: the place to surf, swim and sail by day and dine, dance and party by night.

wa

O'AHU PLANNER

When You Arrive

Honolulu International Airport is 20 minutes from Waikīkī (40 during rush hour). Car rental is across the street from baggage claim. A cumbersome and inefficient airport taxi system requires you to line up to a taxi wrangler who radios for cars (about $25 to Waikīkī). Other options: TheBus ($2, one lap-size bag allowed) or public airport shuttle ($8). ■ TIP→→ Ask the driver to take H1, not Nimitz Highway, at least as far as downtown, or your introduction to paradise will be Honolulu's industrial backside.

Buy that Board

There are more than 30 boogie board rental spots on Waikīkī Beach, all offering basically the same prices. But if you plan to hit the waves for more than just an hour, buy a board for $20 to $30 at an ABC convenience store and give it to a kid when you're preparing to end your vacation. It will be more cost-effective for you and will imbue you with the aloha spirit while making a kid's day.

Get Out of Town

They'll tell you, wrongly, that O'ahu means "the gathering place." But scholars agree that no one knows what this ancient word really means. In any case, the island is a literal gathering place—for 800,000-plus residents and several thousand more visitors every day. If noise, traffic and crowding in Waikīkī and Honolulu get to you, head in any direction—you'll soon see that O'ahu has a rural side of exceptional beauty and even tranquility.

Car Rentals

Waikīkī and Honolulu can realistically be done without a car. Public buses and free shuttles reach most important sites. If you want to see the North Shore or the Windward beaches, you'll need to rent a car.

TIPS→→

■ If you are staying in Waikīkī, rent a car only on the days when you wish to go farther afield. You don't need a car in Waikīkī itself, and inconveniently-located hotel parking garages charge everyone (even hotel guests) close to $20 a day, plus tips.

■ Renting a Mustang convertible is a sure sign that you're a tourist and practically begs "come burglarize me." A good rule of thumb: When the car is out of your sight even for a moment, it should be empty of anything you care about.

1

To Island-Hop or Stop?

Should you try to fit another island into your trip or stay put in O'ahu? Tough call. Although none of the islands is more than 30 minutes away from another by air, security hassles, transport and check-in all swallow up precious vacation hours. If you've got less than a week, do O'ahu well and leave the rest for the next trip. With a week, you can give three good tour days to O'ahu (Pearl Harbor, Honolulu, and one rural venture), then head to a Neighbor Island for some serious beach time and maybe an adventure or two. If you do decide to island-hop, book in advance; you'll get a better fare by packaging your travel. ■ TIP→→ If you want to get along on the Neighbor Islands, don't compare them to Honolulu and never call them "the outer islands"—that's insultingly O'ahu-centric.

Will it Rain?

There's a reason why Hawai'i's most-watched TV news show doesn't have a weather forecaster. Weather here is blissfully predictable: Mid to low 80s, morning showers at high elevations and in misty valleys, trade winds 5 to 15 miles per hour. The only reason anyone listens to the weather is to find out if the surf is up (especially in winter) and when low tide will be (for fishing).

Timing is Everything

When to visit? Winter is whales (November through March) and waves (surf competitions December through February). In fall, the Aloha Festivals celebrate island culture in September. In summer, the Islands honor the king who made them a nation, Kamehameha I, on June 11, with parades and events on all islands. O'ahu's one-of-a-kind Pan Pacific Festival backs up to the Kamehameha Day, bringing together hundreds of performers from Japan's seasonal celebrations.

Guided Activities

When it comes to surfing, you come to O'ahu. For a much less exhausting trip beyond the breaks, try a short sail on a beach catamaran from Waikīkī.

ACTIVITY	COST
Deep Sea Fishing	$100–$600
Golf	$40–$165
Helicopter & Seaplane Tours	$90–$185
Luau	$58–$110
Beach Catamaran Sails	$12–$20
Shark Tours	$120
Snorkel Cruises	$37–$75
Surfing Lessons	$50–$139
Whale Watching	$95–$120

1-Day Itineraries

To experience even a fraction of O'ahu's charms, you need a minimum of four days and a bus pass. Five days and a car is better: Waikīkī is at least a day, Honolulu and Chinatown another, Pearl Harbor the better part of another. Each of the rural sections can swallow a day each, just for driving, sight-seeing and stopping to eat. And that's before you've taken a surf lesson, hung from a parasail, hiked a loop trail, or visited a botanical garden. The following itineraries will take you to our favorite spots on the island.

First day in Waikīkī: You'll be up at dawn due to the time change and dead on your feet by afternoon due to jet lag. Have a dawn swim, change into walking gear, and head east along Kalākaua Avenue to Monsarrat Avenue, and climb Diamond Head. After lunch, nap in the shade (sunburn!), do some shopping, or visit the nearby East Honolulu neighborhoods of Mō'ili'ili and Kaimukī, rife with small shops and good, little restaurants. End the day with an early, interesting, and inexpensive dinner at one of these neighborhood spots.

Windward Exploring: For sand, sun, and surf, follow H1 east to keyhole-shaped Hanauma Bay for picture-perfect snorkeling, then round the southeast tip of the island with its wind-swept cliffs and the famous Hālona Blowhole. Fly a kite or watch body surfers at Sandy Beach. Take in Sea Life Park. In Waimānalo, stop for local-style plate lunch, or punch on through to Kailua, where there's intriguing shopping and good eating.

The North Shore: Hit H1 westbound and then H2 to get to the North Shore. You'll pass through pineapple country, then drop down a scenic winding road to Waialua and Hale'iwa. Stop in Hale'iwa town to shop, to experience shave ice, and to pick up a guided dive or snorkel trip. On winding Kamehameha Highway, stop at famous big-wave beaches, take a dip in a cove with a turtle, and buy fresh Island fruit at roadside stands.

Pearl Harbor: Pearl Harbor is an almost all-day investment. Be on the grounds by 7:30 AM to line up for *Arizona* Memorial tickets. Clamber all over the USS *Bowfin* submarine. Finally, take the free trolley to see the Mighty Mo battleship. If it's Wednesday or Saturday, make the 5-minute drive mauka (toward the mountains) for bargain-basement shopping at the sprawling Aloha Stadium Swap Meet.

Town time: If you are interested in history, devote a day to Honolulu's historic sites. Downtown, see 'Iolani Palace, the Kamehameha Statue, and Kawaiaha'o Church. A few blocks east, explore Chinatown, gilded Kuan Yin Temple, and artsy Nu'uanu with its galleries. On the water is the informative Hawai'i Maritime Center. Hop west on H1 to the Bishop Museum, the state's anthropological and archeological center. And a mile up Pali Highway is Queen Emma Summer Palace, whose shady grounds were a royal retreat. Worth a visit for plant lovers: Foster Botanical Garden.

■ For more details on any of the destinations mentioned in these itineraries, see Exploring O'ahu in this chapter.

BEACHES

1

By Wanda
Adams, Chad
Pata, Lance
Tominaga,
Maggie
Wunsch &
Katie Young

Many people save their whole lives to experience the beaches of Oʻahu—and with good reason. Tropical sun mixed with cooling trade winds and pristine waters make these shores a literal heaven on Earth. But contrary to many assumptions, the island is not one big beach. There are miles and miles of coastline without a grain of sand, so you need to know where you are going to fully enjoy the Hawaiian experience.

Many of the island's southern and eastern coasts are protected by inner reefs. The reefs provide still coastline water but not much as far as sand is concerned. However, where there are beaches on the south and east shores, they are mind-blowing. In West Oʻahu and on the North Shore you can find the wide expanses of sand you would expect for enjoying the sunset. Sandy bottoms and outside reefs make the water an adventure in the winter months. Most visitors assume the seasons don't change a thing in the Islands, and they would be right—except for the waves, which are big on the south shore in summer and placid in winter. It's exactly the opposite on the north side where winter storms bring in huge waves, but it goes to glass come May and June.

We start on the famed Waikīkī Beach and then work our way counterclockwise around the island to the epic waves of the North Shore. In the final section we head west, where the populations dwindle and the beauty expands.

Honolulu

The city of Honolulu only has one beach, the monstrous Ala Moana. It hosts everything from Dragon Boat competitions to the Aloha State Games.

★ ☺ **Ala Moana Beach Park.** Ala Moana has a protective reef, which makes it ostensibly a ½-mi wide saltwater swimming pool. After Waikīkī, this is the most popular beach among visitors. To the Waikīkī side is a peninsula called Magic Island, with shady trees and paved sidewalks ideal for jogging. Ala Moana also has playing fields, tennis courts, and a couple of small ponds for sailing toy boats. ⚠ **This beach is for everyone, but only in the daytime. It's a high-crime area after dark.** ✉ *Honolulu, near Ala Moana Shopping Center and Ala Moana Blvd. From Waikīkī take Bus 8 to shopping center and cross Ala Moana Blvd.* ♿ *Lifeguard, toilets, showers, food concession, picnic tables, grills, parking lot.*

Waikīkī

The 2½-mi strand called Waikīkī Beach extends from Hilton Hawaiian Village on one end to Kapiʻolani Park and Diamond Head on the other. Although it's one contiguous piece of beach, it's as varied as the people that inhabit the Islands. Whether you're an old-timer looking to enjoy the action from the shade or a sports nut wanting to do it all, you can find every beach activity here without ever jumping in the rental car.

If you're staying outside the area, our best advice is to park at either end of the beach and walk in. Plentiful parking exists on the west end at the Ala Wai Marina, where there are myriad free spots on the beach

Keep in Mind

Yes, the beaches are beautiful, but always be cognizant of the fact you are on a little rock in the middle of the Pacific Ocean. The current and waves will be stronger and bigger than any you may have experienced. Riptides can take you on a ride they call the "Moloka'i Express"—only problem is that it doesn't take you to the island of Moloka'i but rather out into the South Pacific. There are many safe spots, but always pay attention to the posted signs. If you have any doubts, ask a lifeguard for their assessment. They're professionals and can give you competent advice.

Also keep in mind that you are in the tropics. Although the sun may not feel that hot on your body due to the cool breezes, it's much more intense than you have likely experienced. Use sun screen early and often.

Finally, like anywhere in the world, there's a certain criminal element even in paradise. Keeping valuables in your hotel safe or in your possession will prevent your vacation from turning sour.

as well as metered stalls around the harbor. For parking on the east end, Kapi'olani Park and the Honolulu Zoo both have metered parking for $1 an hour—more affordable than the $10 per hour the resorts want.

We highlight the differences in this famous beach from west to east, letting you know not only where you may want to sunbathe but why.

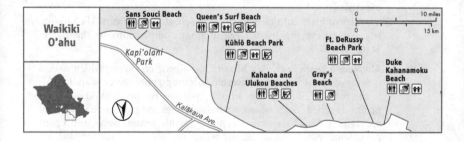

Duke Kahanamoku Beach. Named for Hawai'i's famous Olympic swimming champion, Duke Kahanamoku, this is a hard-packed beach with the only shade trees on the sand in Waikīkī. It's great for families with young children because of the shade and the calmest waters in Waikīkī, thanks to a rock wall that creates a semiprotected cove. The ocean clarity here is not as brilliant as most of Waikīkī because of the stillness of the surf, but it's a small price to pay for peace of mind about youngsters. ⊠ *In front of Hilton Hawaiian Village Beach Resort and Spa* ⚮ *Toilets, showers, food concession.*

★ **Fort DeRussy Beach Park.** Even before you take the two newly refurbished beach parks into account, this is one of the finest beaches on the south side of O'ahu. Wide, soft, ultrawhite beaches with gently lapping waves make it a family favorite for running/jumping/frolicking fun (this also

happens to be where the NFL holds their rookie sand football game every year). Add to that the new, heavily-shaded grass grilling area, sand volleyball courts, and aquatic rentals, making this a must for the active visitor. ☒ *In front of Fort DeRussy and Hale Koa Hotel ⅃ Lifeguard, toilets, showers, food concession, picnic tables, grills, playground.*
Gray's Beach. A little lodging house called Gray's-by-the-Sea stood here in the 1920s; now it's a gathering place for eclectic beach types from sailing pioneers like George Parsons to the bird men

	BEACHES KEY
🚻	Restroom
🚿	Shower
🏄	Surfing
🤿	Snorkel/Scuba
👪	Good for kids
P	Parking

of Waikīkī with their colorful parrots for rent. The tides often put sand space at a premium, but if you want a look back into old Waikīkī, have a mai tai at the Shorebird and check out a time gone by. ☒ *In front of Halekūlani ⅃ Lifeguard, toilets, showers, food concession.*

★ **Kahaloa and Ulukou Beaches.** The beach widens back out here, creating the "it" spot for the bikini crowd. Beautiful bodies abound, as do activities. This is where you find most of the sailing catamaran charters for a spectacular sail out to Diamond Head or surfboard and outrigger canoe rentals for a ride on "Hawai'i's Malibu" at **Canoe's** surf break. Great music and outdoor dancing beckon the sand-bound visitor to Duke's Bar and Grill, where shirt and shoes not only aren't required, they're discouraged. ☒ *In front of Royal Hawaiian Hotel and Sheraton Moana Surfrider ⅃ Lifeguard, toilets, showers, food concession.*

★ ☽ **Kūhiō Beach Park.** Due to recent renovations, this beach has seen a renaissance. Now bordered by a landscaped boardwalk, it's great for romantic walks any time of day. Check out the Kūhiō Beach hula mound nightly at 6:30 for free hula and Hawaiian-music performances; weekends there's a torch-lighting ceremony at sunset. Surf lessons for beginners are available from the beach center here every half hour. ☒ *Past Sheraton Moana Surfrider Hotel to Kapahulu Ave. pier ⅃ Lifeguard, toilets, showers, food concession.*

☽ **Queen's Surf.** So named as it was once the site of Queen Lili'uokalani's beach house. A mix of families and gay couples gathers here, and it seems as if someone is always playing a steel drum. Every weekend movie screens are set up on the sand, and major motion pictures are shown after the sun sets. Daytime there are banyan trees for shade and volleyball nets for pros and amateurs alike (this is where Misty May and Kerri Walsh play while in town). The water fronting Queen's Surf is an aquatic preserve, providing the best snorkeling in Waikīkī. ☒ *Across from entrance to Honolulu Zoo ⅃ Lifeguard, toilets, showers, picnic tables, grills.*

☽ **Sans Souci.** Nicknamed Dig-Me Beach because of its outlandish display of skimpy bathing suits, this small rectangle of sand is nonetheless a good sunning spot for all ages. Children enjoy its shallow, safe waters that are protected by the walls of the historic Natatorium, an Olympic-size saltwater swimming arena. Serious swimmers and triathletes also swim in the channel here, beyond the reef. Sans Souci is favored by locals wanting to avoid the crowds while still enjoying the convenience of Waikīkī. ☒ *Across from Kapi'olani Park, between New Otani Kaimana Beach*

Hotel and Waikīkī War Memorial Natatorium ⚐ *Lifeguard, toilets, showers, picnic tables.*

Diamond Head Beach. This is not for those who don't like hiking. If you don't mind the trek, you can find this beautiful, remote spot at the base of Diamond Head crater. It's a small strip of sand with lots of coral in the water. This said, the natural views looking out from the point are breathtaking and the windsurfers skimming along driven by the gusts off the point are amazing to watch. From the parking area, look for an opening in the wall where an unpaved trail leads down to the beach. Even for the unadventurous, a stop at the lookout point is well worth the time. ⊠ *At base of Diamond Head. Park at the crest of Diamond Head Rd. and walk down* ⚐ *Showers, parking lot.*

Southeast O'ahu

Much of this side of the island is surrounded by reef, making most of the coast uninviting to swimmers, but the spots where the reef opens up are true gems. The drive along this coast is amazing with its sheer lava-rock walls on one side and deep-blue ocean on the other. There are plenty of restaurants in the suburb of Hawai'i Kai on this side so feel free to make a day of it on this side and know that food isn't far away. Beaches are listed from south to north.

★ ☺ **Hanauma Bay Nature Preserve.** Picture this as the world's biggest open-air aquarium. You go here to see fish, and fish you'll see. Due to their exposure to thousands of visitors every week, these fish are more like family pets than the skittish marine life you might expect. An old volcanic crater has created a haven from the waves where the coral has thrived. There's an educational center where you must watch a nine-minute video about the nature preserve before being allowed down to the bay. ■ TIP➜➜ **The bay is best early in the morning (around 7), before the crowds arrive; it can be difficult to park later in the day.** No smoking is allowed, and the beach is closed on Tuesday. **Hanauma Bay Dive Tours** (☎ 808/256–8956), runs snorkeling, snuba, and scuba tours to Hanauma Bay with transportation from Waikīkī hotels. ⊠ *7455 Kalaniana'ole Hwy.* ☎ *808/396–4229* ⚐ *Lifeguard, toilets, showers, food concession, picnic tables, parking lot* 🖼 *Donation $5; parking $1; mask, snorkel, and fins rental $8; tram from parking lot down to beach $1.50* ☉ *Wed.–Mon. 6–7.*

★ **Hālona Cove.** Also known as "From Here to Eternity Beach" and "Pounders," this little beauty is never crowded due to the treacherous little climb down to the sand. But for the intrepid, what a treat this spot can be. It's in a break in the ocean cliffs, with the surrounding crags providing protection from the wind. Open-ocean waves roll up on the beach (thus the second nickname), but, unlike Sandy's, a gently sloping sand bottom takes much of the punch out of them before they hit the shore. Turtles frequent the small cove, seeking respite from the otherwise blustery coast. It's great for packing a lunch and holing up for the day. ⊠ *Below Halona Blow Hole Lookout parking lot* ⚐ *No facilities.*

Sandy Beach. Probably the most popular beach with locals on this side of O'ahu, the broad, sloping beach is covered with sunbathers there to watch **the Show** and soak up rays. The Show is a shore break that's like no other in the Islands. Monster ocean swells rolling into the beach combined with

1

the sudden rise in the floor causes waves to jack up and crash magnificently on the shore. Young and old brave this danger to get some of the biggest barrels you can find bodysurfing, but always keeping in mind the beach's other nickname, "Break Neck Beach." ⚠ **Use extreme caution when swimming here,** but feel free to kick back and watch the drama unfold from the comfort of your beach chair. ⊠ *Makai of Kalaniana'ole Hwy., 2 mi east of Hanauma Bay* ⚲ *Lifeguard, toilets, showers, picnic tables.*

Windward O'ahu

The Windward side lives up to its name with ideal spots for windsurfing and kiteboarding, or for the more intrepid, hang gliding. For the most part the waves are more mellow and the bottoms are all sand, making a nice spot to go with younger kids. The only drawback is that this side does tend to get more rain. But, as beautiful as the vistas are, a little sprinkling of "pineapple juice" shouldn't dampen your experience; plus it turns on the waterfalls that cascade down the Ko'olaus. Beaches are listed from north to south.

Fodor'sChoice **Makapu'u Beach.** A magnificent beach protected by Makapu'u Point welcomes you to the Windward side. Hang gliders circle above the beach, and the water is filled with body boarders. Just off the coast you can see Bird Island, a sanctuary for aquatic fowl, jutting out of the blue. ⚠ **The currents can be heavy, so check with a lifeguard if unsure.** Try not to not miss this spot for a dip; then take the prettiest (and coldest) outdoor shower available on the island. Being surrounded by tropical flowers and foliage while you rinse off that sand will be a memory you will cherish from this side of the rock. ⊠ *Across from Sea Life Park on Kalaniana'ole Hwy., 2 mi south of Waimānalo* ⚲ *Lifeguard, toilets, showers, picnic tables, grills.*

★ ☺ **Waimānalo Beach Park.** This is a "local" beach busy with picnicking families and active sports fields. It's a local area, so make sure you treat the beach with respect (read: don't litter) and lock your car. Those caveats aside, the beach is one of the island's most beautiful. Expect a wide stretch of sand; turquoise, emerald, and deep-blue seas; and gentle shore break waves that are fun for all ages to play in. ⊠ *South of Waimānalo town, look for signs on Kalaniana'ole Hwy.* ⚲ *Lifeguard, toilets, showers, picnic tables.*

Fodor'sChoice **Lanikai Beach Park.** Think of the beach you've been seeing in commercials: peaceful blue waters, perfect, soft-sand beach with families and dogs frolicking mindlessly. It's a perfect spot to camp out with a book, or for the nonreaders, there's plenty of action from wind- and kite surfers to keep the mind occupied. ⊠ *Past Kailua Beach Park; street parking on Mokulua Dr. for various public-access points to beach* ⚐ *Lifeguard, showers.*

Kailua Beach Park. This is like a big Lanikai Beach, but a little windier and a little wider. It's a better spot for a full day at the beach, though, with its palm-lining providing shade on the sand and a huge park boasting picnic pavilions to help escape the heat or feed the hordes. This is the "it" spot if you're looking to try your hand at windsurfing. ⊠ *Near Kailua town, turn right on Kailua Rd. at market, cross bridge, then turn left into beach parking lot* ⚐ *Lifeguard, toilets, showers, picnic tables, grills, playground, parking lot.*

Kualoa Regional Park. Grassy expanses border a long, narrow stretch of beach with spectacular views of Kāne'ohe Bay and the Ko'olau Mountains, making Kualoa one of the island's most beautiful picnic, camping, and beach areas. Dominating the view is an islet called Mokoli'i, better known as Chinaman's Hat, which rises 206 feet above the water. You can swim in the shallow areas year-round. The one drawback is that it's usually windy, but the wide open spaces are ideal for kite flying. ⊠ *North of Waiāhole, on Kamehameha Hwy.* ⚐ *Lifeguard, toilets, showers, picnic tables, grills.*

Mālaekahana Beach Park. The big attraction here is tiny Goat Island, a bird sanctuary just offshore. At low tide the water is shallow enough—never more than waist high—so that you can wade out to it. Wear sneakers so you don't cut yourself on the coral. Families love to camp in the groves of ironwood trees at Mālaekahana State Park. The beach itself is fairly narrow but long enough for a 20-minute stroll, one-way. The waves are never too big, and sometimes they're just right for the beginning bodysurfer. Note that the entrance gates are easy to miss because you can't see the beach from the road. Cabins are also available here, making a perfect rural getaway. ⊠ *Entrance gates are ½ mi north of Lā'ie on Kamehameha Hwy.* ⚐ *Toilets, showers, picnic tables, grills.*

North Shore

"North Shore, where the waves are mean, just like a washing machine" sing the Ka'au Crater Boys about this legendary side of the island. And in winter they are absolutely right. At times the waves overtake the road, stranding tourists and locals alike. When the surf is up, there will even be signs on the beach telling you how far to stay back so that you aren't swept out to sea. The most prestigious big-wave contest in the world, "The Eddie Aikau," is held at Waimea Bay on waves the size of a six-story building. The Triple Crown of Surfing (⇨ *See* North Shore Surfing and the Triple Crown *later in this chapter*) roams across three beaches in the winter months.

All this changes come summer when this tiger turns into a kitty with water smooth enough to water ski on and ideal for snorkeling. The fierce Banzai Pipeline surf break becomes a great dive area, allowing you to explore the deadly coral heads that have claimed so many on the ultrahollow tubes that are created here in winter. But even with the monster surf subsided, this is still a time for caution. Lifeguards become more scarce, and currents don't go away just because the waves do.

This all being said, it's a place like no other on earth and must be explored. From the turtles at Mokule'ia to the tunnels at Shark's Cove, you could spend your whole trip on this side and not be disappointed. Beaches are listed from east to west.

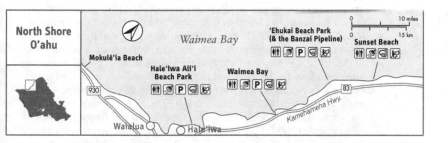

Sunset Beach. How this beach has not been awarded a "Best Beach" speaks not of its glory, but of a bad PR guy. It's popular for its gentle summer waves and crashing winter surf. The beach is broad, the sand is soft, and many love searching its shores for the puka shells that adorn the necklaces you see everywhere. ⚠ **Use caution in the water; at times the current can come ripping around the point.** Lining the adjacent highway there are usually carryout truck stands selling shaved ice, plate lunches, and sodas. ✉ *1 mi north of 'Ehukai Beach Park on Kamehameha Hwy.* ⚓ *Lifeguard, toilets, showers, picnic tables.*

'Ehukai Beach Park & the Banzai Pipeline. What sets 'Ehukai apart is the view of the famous **Banzai Pipeline**, where the winter waves curl into magnificent tubes, making it an experienced wave-rider's dream. ⚠ **It's also an inexperienced swimmer's nightmare, however. In spring and summer the waves are more accommodating to the average swimmer.** The joy of this beach is that, except when the surf contests are going on, there's no reason to stay on the central strip. Traveling either way on the beach the conditions remain the same, but the population thins out, leaving you with a magnificent stretch of sand all to yourself. ✉ *Small parking lot borders Kamehameha Hwy. 1 mi north of Foodland at Pūpūkea* ⚓ *Lifeguard, toilets, showers, parking lot.*

★ **Waimea Bay.** Made popular in that old Beach Boys song "Surfin' U.S.A.," Waimea Bay is a slice of big-wave heaven, home to king-size 25- to 30-foot winter waves. Summer is the time to swim and snorkel in the calm waters. The shore break is great for novice bodysurfers and for the thrill seeker, there's "Alligator Rock" off the west side of the beach where locals leap off. The sand bottoms make for easy landings whether you're riding the waves or jumping the rocks. Due to its popularity, the postage-stamp parking lot is quickly filled, but everyone parks along the side of the road and walks in. ⚠ **Use some caution whether jumping or swimming here as currents can get out of hand.** ✉ *Across from Waimea Valley, 3 mi north of Hale'iwa on Kamehameha Hwy.* ⚓ *Lifeguard, toilets, showers, picnic tables, parking lot.*

Hale'iwa Ali'i Beach Park. The winter waves are impressive here, but in summer the ocean is like a lake, ideal for family swimming. The beach itself is big and often full of locals. Its broad lawn off the highway invites volleyball and Frisbee games and groups of barbecuers. This is also the opening break for the Triple Crown of Surfing, and the grass is often filled with art festivals or carnivals. ⊠ *North of Hale'iwa town center and past harbor on Kamehameha Hwy.* ⚇ *Lifeguard, toilets, showers, picnic tables.*

★ **Mokulē'ia Beach Park.** There is a reason why the producers of the TV show *Lost* chose this beach for their set. On the remote northwest point of the island, it is about 10 mi from the closest store or public restroom; you could spend a day here and not see another living soul. And that is precisely its beauty—all the joy of being stranded on a deserted island without the trauma of the plane crash. The beach is wide and white, the waters bright blue (but a little choppy) and full of sea turtles and other marine life. Mokulē'ia is a great secret find, just remember to pack supplies. ⊠ *East of Hale'iwa town center, across from Dillingham Airfield.* ⚇ *No facilities.*

West O'ahu

While the North Shore is generally known as "Country," the West side is truly the rural area on O'ahu. There are commuters from this side to Honolulu, but many are born, live, and die on this side with scarcely a trip to town. For the most part, there's less hostility toward outsiders and more curiousity as to where they are from. Occasional problems have flared up, mostly due to drug abuse that has ravaged the fringes of the island. But this is generally in the car break-in realm, rather than violence toward visitors. So in short, lock your car, don't bring valuables to this side, and enjoy the amazing beaches.

The beaches on the west side are expansive and empty. Most O'ahu residents and tourists don't make it to this side simply because of the drive. In traffic it can take almost 90 minutes to make it to Ka'ena Point from Downtown Honolulu, but you'll be hard pressed to find a better sunset anywhere.

Mākaha Beach Park. This beach provides a slice of local life most visitors don't see. Families string up tarps for the day, fire up hibachis, set up lawn chairs, get out the fishing gear, and strum 'ukuleles while they "talk story" (chat). Legendary waterman Buffalo Kaeulana can be found in the shade of the palms playing with his grandkids and spinning yarns of yesteryear. In these waters Buffalo not only invented some of the most outrageous methods of surfing, but also raised his world champion son Rusty. He also made Mākaha the home of the world's first international surf meet in 1954 and still hosts his Big Board Surfing Classic. The swimming is generally decent in summer, but avoid the big winter waves. It's a great spot to try out long boarding with its long, slow building waves. ⊠ *1½ hrs west of Honolulu on H–1 Fwy. then Farrington Hwy.* ⚇ *Lifeguards, toilets, showers, picnic tables, grills.*

Yokohama Bay. You'll be one of the few outsiders at this Wai'anae Coast beach at the very end of the road. If not for the little strip of paved road, you'd feel like you're on a deserted isle. No stores, no houses, just a huge sloping stretch of beach and some of the darkest blue water off the island. Locals come here to fish and swim in waters that are calm enough for children in summer. Many like to camp right on the beach because early morning brings with it spinner dolphins by the dozens just offshore. Though Makua Beach up the road is the best spot to see these animals, it's not nearly as beautiful or sandy as "Yokes." ⊠ *Northern end of Farrington Hwy., about 7 mi north of Mākaha* ⚐ *Toilets, showers.*

WATER ACTIVITIES & TOURS

There's more to the beach than just lying on it. O'ahu is rife with every type of activity you can imagine. Most of the activities are offered in Waikīkī, right off the beach. But for the best experience sometimes it's best to get out and explore.

As with all sports, listen to the outfitter's advice—they're not just saying it for fun. Caution is always the best bet when dealing with "mother" ocean. She plays for keeps and forgives no indiscretions. That being said, she offers more entertainment than you can fit into a lifetime, much less a vacation. So try something new and enjoy.

A rule of thumb is that the ocean is much more wily and unpredictable on the north- and west-facing shores, but that's also why those sides have the most famous waves on Earth. So plan your activity side according to your skill level.

Boat Tours & Charters

Hawai'i Sailing Adventures. Looking to escape the "cattle-maran" experience? Providing rides on the largest private sailing yacht in the Islands, this charter, with its goal of exclusivity, is for you. They have capacity for up to 50 guests but prefer smaller crowds. They specialize in dinners catered to your specs. Not the place to go meet people, but that is exactly their point. When you want a sail for a romantic occasion or family reunion unfettered by crowds of people you don't know, try their yacht *Emeraude* and ask for Captain Roger. Rates begin at $119 a person, which includes unlimited super well drinks (drinks made with premium liquors like Tanquary Ten, Grey Goose). ⊠ *Kewalo Basin, Slip S, Honolulu* ☎ *808/596–9696.*

Paradise Cruises. One-stop shopping for specialty cruises, Paradise Cruises offers everything from day cruises around Diamond Head with snorkeling, kayaking, and windsurfing to fine dining night cruises with lobster and live entertainment. You can learn lei-making or coconut frond–weaving, or you can take a 'ukulele or hula lesson. They also offer seminars on Hawaiian history and culture through activities, videos, and artifact displays onboard the boat. In winter you can take a whale-watching cruise. ⊠ *Pier 5, Honolulu Harbor, Honolulu* ☎ *808/983–7700.*

Sashimi Fun Fishing. A combination trip suits those who can't commit to a dinner cruise and aren't ready for the open-ocean swells. Sashimi Fun Fishing runs a four-hour dinner cruise that features fishing and music. They keep close enough to shore that you can still see O'ahu and jig for a variety of reef fish (as opposed to trolling for big game). The cruise includes a local barbecue dinner, and you can also cook what you catch. Hotel transportation to the boat is included in the package, running $63 per person. ☎ *808/955–3474.*

Tradewind Charters. Tradewinds specializes in everything from weddings to funerals. They offer half-day private-charter tours for sailing, snorkeling, and whale-watching. Traveling on these luxury yachts not only gets you away from the crowds but also gives you the opportunity to "take the helm" if you wish. The cruise includes snorkeling at an exclusive anchorage as well as hands-on snorkeling and sailing instruction. Charter prices are approximately $495 for up to six passengers. ✉ *796 Kalanipuu St., Honolulu* ☎ *800/829–4899.*

Boogie Boarding & Bodysurfing

Boogie boarding (or sponging) has become a popular alternative to surfing for a couple of reasons. First, the start-up cost is much less—a usable board can be purchased for $30 to $40 or can be rented on the beach for $5 an hour. Second, it's a whole lot easier to ride a boogie board than to tame a surfboard. For beginner boogie boarding all you must do is paddle out to the waves, turn toward the beach, and kick like crazy when the wave comes.

Boogie boards can be purchased at most convenience and grocery stores. Though they do not rival what the pros use, with the smaller waves you'll be catching, you won't notice a difference in their handling. Another small investment you'll want to make is in surf fins. Most beach stands do not rent these with the boards, so if you want them you'll have to seek them out. These smaller, sturdier versions of dive fins sell for $25–$35 at surf and dive stores, sporting-goods stores, or even Wal-Mart. Though not necessary for boogie boarding, fins do

> **LOOK FIRST**
>
> With all water activities, check out your environment: are there rocks in the surf zone? Which way is the current pulling? Where are the closest lifeguard stands? It's always a good idea to spend at least 15 minutes on the beach watching the break you intend to surf. This allows you not only to check for dangerous areas and the size of the surf but also to see what spot is breaking cleanest and will therefore be the most fun.

give you a tremendous advantage while paddling into waves. If you plan to go out in bigger surf, we would also advise you to get fin leashes to prevent loss.

For bodysurfing, you definitely want to invest in fins. Check out the same spots as for boogie boarding. The art of bodysurfing is to get yourself ahead of the wave as it breaks, put down one hand on the wave in front of you to act as a ski, and try to stay ahead of the white water. If you start to feel yourself being sucked up the front of the wave, try to duck out the backside. If that isn't possible, curl up in a ball covering your head and experience firsthand what your jeans do in the washing machine.

If the direction of the current or dangers of the break are not readily apparent to you, don't hesitate to ask a lifeguard or a local for advice.

Best Spots

Boogie boarding and bodysurfing can be done anywhere there are waves, but, due to a paddling advantage surfers have over spongers, it's usually more fun to go to exclusively boogie-boarding spots.

The best spot on the island to boogie board is **Sandy Beach** (⊠ 2 mi east of Hanauma Bay on Kalaniana'ole Hwy.) on the Windward side. It's a short wave that goes right and left, but the barrels you get here are unparalleled for purely sponging. The ride is intense and breaks so sharply that you actually see the wave suck the bottom dry before it crashes on to it. That's the reason it's also called "Break Neck Beach." ⚠ **Awesome for the more advanced, but know its danger before enjoying the ride.**

For longer rides you may try **Makapu'u Beach** (⊠ Across from Sea Life Park, 2 mi south of Waimānalo on Kalaniana'ole Hwy.) on the Windward side; it's a sponger's dream beach with its extended waves and isolation from surfers. If you're a little more timid, go to the far end of the beach to **Keiki's** where the waves are mellowed by Makapu'u Point for an easier, if less thrilling, ride. ⚠ **Although the main break at Makapu'u is much less dangerous than Sandy's, check out the ocean floor—the sands are always shifting, sometimes exposing coral heads and rocks. Also always check the currents, they can get strong.** But for the most part, this is the ideal beach for both boogie boarding and bodysurfing.

Kūhiō Beach Park (⊠ Waikīkī, past Sheraton Moana Surfrider Hotel to Kapahulu Ave. pier) is an easy spot for the first timer to check out the action. Try **The Wall,** a break so named for the breakwall in front of the beach. It's a little crowded with kids, but it's close enough to shore to keep you at ease. There are dozens of breaks in Waikīkī:, but the Wall is the only one solely occupied by spongers. Start out here to get the hang of it before venturing out to Canoes or Kaiser Bowl's.

Equipment Rentals

There are more than 30 rental spots on Waikīkī Beach, all offering basically the same prices. But if you plan to do it for more than just an hour, we would suggest buying a board for $20 to $30 at an ABC convenience store and giving it to a kid when you're preparing to end your vacation. It will be more cost-effective for you and will imbue you with the Aloha spirit while making a kid's day.

Deep-Sea Fishing

The joy of fishing in Hawai'i is that there isn't really a season; it's good year-round. Sure, the bigger yellowfin tuna ('ahi) are generally caught in summer, and the coveted spearfish are more frequent in winter, but you can still catch them any day of the year. You can also find dolphin fish (mahimahi), wahoo (ono), skip jacks, and the king—Pacific blue marlin—ripe for the picking on any given day.

When choosing a fishing boat in the Islands, keep in mind the immensity of the surrounding ocean. Look for the older, grizzled captains who have been trolling these waters for half a century. All the fancy gizmos in the world can't match an old tar's knowledge of the waters.

The general rule on keeping the fish is an even split with the crew. Unfortunately, there are no "freeze-and-ship" providers here in the state, so, unless you plan to eat it while you're here, you'll probably want to leave it with the boat. Most boats do offer mounting services for trophy fish; ask your captain.

Besides the gift of fish, a gratuity of 10% to 20% is standard. It's up to the fisherman; use your own discretion depending on how you felt about the overall experience.

A final note—trying to get out on the cheap with half-day excursions can be a way to cut costs, but we suggest the full charter. It dramatically improves your odds of catching something, and that after all is why you're out there.

Boats & Charters

Inter-Island Sportfishing. The oldest running sportfishing company on O'ahu also boasts the largest landed Blue Marlin at more than 1,200 pounds. With two smaller boats and the 53-foot *Maggie Joe* (which can hold up to 25), they can manage pretty much any small party with air-conditioned cabins and cutting-edge fishing equipment. They also work with Grey's Taxidermy, the world's largest marine taxidermist, to mount the monster you reel in. ☎ 808/591–8888 ⊕ www.fish-hawaii.com.

Fodor'sChoice ★ Magic Sportfishing. When your direct competitors (who are docked right by you) are asked who has the best boat in the harbor and they say "Magic," we felt we need look no further. The awards Magic have garnered are too many to mention here, but we can tell you their magnificent 50-foot *Pacifica* fishing yacht is built for comfort, fishing, or otherwise. Unfortunately, Magic can accommodate only up to six. ☎ 808/596–2998 ⊕ www.magicsportfishing.com.

Monkey Biz. If you want a more intimate experience with a smaller company, the apes of the sea may be what you are looking for. Known for their reliable boats and friendly crews, these six-man charters can make your Hawaiian fishing experience a happy one. ☎ 808/591–2520 ⊕ www.monkeybizsportfishing.com.

Kayaking

Kayaking is quickly becoming a top choice for visitors to the Islands. Riding alone or with a partner on the open ocean in a kayak allows you a vantage point not afforded by swimming and surfing. Sitting upright and operating with a paddle allows even the amateur to travel long distances and to keep a lookout on what's going on around them.

This ability to travel long distances can also get you into trouble. Experts agree that rookies should stay on the Windward side. Their reasoning is simple: if you tire, break or lose an oar, or just plain pass out, the onshore winds will blow you back to the beach. The same cannot be said for the offshore breezes of the North Shore and West O'ahu.

Kayaks are now becoming specialized, and your outfitter can address your needs depending on your activities. Some kayaks are better suited for riding waves or traveling long distances. Expressing your plans with your outfitter can lead to a more enjoyable experience.

Best Spots

The hands-down winner for kayaking is **Lanikai Beach** (⊠ Past Kailua Beach Park; street parking on Mokulua Drive for various public-access points to beach) on the Windward side. This is perfect amateur territory with its still waters and onshore winds, but, if you're feeling more adventurous, it's a short paddle out to the Mokes. These are a pair of islands off the coast with beaches, surf breaks on the reef, and great picnicking areas. Due to the distance from shore (about a mile), the Mokes usually afford privacy from all but the intrepid kayakers. This spot is great year-round, and most kayak-rental companies have a store right up the street in Kailua.

For something a little different you may try **Kahana River** (⊠ Empties into Kahana Bay, 8 mi east of Kāne'ohe), also on the Windward side. The river does not inspire you with the blue water you can find while ocean kayaking, but the Ko'olau Mountains, with waterfalls aplenty when it's raining, are magnificent in the background. It's a short jaunt, about 2 mi round-trip, but is packed with rain-forest foliage and the other rain-forest denizen, mosquitos. Bring some repellent and enjoy this light workout.

> It's a short paddle out to the Mokes, a pair of islands with beaches, surf breaks on the reef, and great picnicking areas.

If you want to try your hand at surfing kayaks, **Bellows Beach** (⊠ Near Waimānalo town center, entrance on Kalaniana'ole Hwy.) on the Windward side and **Mokulē'ia Beach** (⊠ Across from Dillingham Airfield) on the North Shore are two great spots. Hard to-reach breaks, the ones that surfers exhaust themselves trying to reach, are easily accessed by kayak. The buoyancy of the kayak also allows you to catch the wave earlier and get out in front of the white wash. ⚠ One reminder on these spots, if you're a little green, stick to Bellows with those onshore winds. Generally speaking, you don't want to be catching waves where surfers are; in Waikīkī, however, pretty much anything goes.

Equipment Rentals & Tours

Go Bananas. At the only full-service store in Honolulu, staffers here really enjoy asking questions so they're able to outfit you with the right boat. It's a great spot to rent a variety of kayaks, with rates at $30 a day for a single or $42 for a double. ⊠ *799 Kapahulu Ave., Honolulu* ☎ *808/ 737–9514.*

Surf 'N Sea. Surf 'N Sea is the place to rent kayaks on the North Shore. Keep in mind that their yellow boats are great in summer when the ocean turns peaceful, but winter is a bit hazardous for even the hard-core fan. But from spring to fall, kayaks are great for getting to outside-reef-snorkeling spots or surfing the reduced waves of the summer months. ⊠ *62- 595 Kamehameha Hwy.* ☎ *808/637–9887.*

Twogood Kayaks Hawai'i. The one-stop shopping outfitter for kayaks on the Windward side offers rentals, lessons, guided kayak tours, and even weeklong camps if you want to immerse yourself in the sport. Although their prices are about $10 more than average, they do deliver the boats to the water for you and give you a crash course in ocean safety. It's a small price to pay for the convenience and peace of mind when entering new waters. ⌧ *345 Hahani St., Kailua* ☎ *808/262–5656* ⊕ *www. aloha.com/~twogood.*

Kiteboarding

⇨ *See* Wind Surfing & Kiteboarding

Sailing

For a sailing experience in O'ahu, you need go no farther than the beach in front of your hotel in Waikīkī. Strung along the sand are seven beach catamarans that will provide with one-hour rides during the day and 90-minute sunset sails. Pricewise look for $12 to $15 for day sails and $15 to $20 for sunset rides. ■ **TIP→→ They all have their little perks and they're known for bargaining so feel free to haggle, especially with the smaller boats.** Some provide drinks for free, some charge for them, and some let you pack your own, so keep that in mind when pricing the ride.

If you would like a fancier ride, ⇨ *see* Boat Tours & Charters.

Mai'Tai Catamaran. Taking off from in front of the Sheraton Hotel, this cat is the fastest and sleekest on the beach. If you have a need for speed and enjoy a little more upscale experience, this is the boat for you. ☎ *808/ 922–5665.*

★ **Na Hoku II Catamaran.** The diametric opposite of Mai'Tai, this is the Animal House of catamarans with reggae music and cheap booze. Their motto is "Cheap drinks, Easy Crew." They're beached right out in front of Duke's Barefoot Bar at the Outrigger Waikīkī Hotel and sail five times daily. ☎ *808/239–3900* ⊕ *www.nahokuii.com.*

Scuba Diving

All the great stuff to do atop the water sometimes leads us to forget the real beauty beneath the surface. Although snorkeling and snuba (more on that later) do give you access to this world, nothing gives you the freedom of scuba.

The diving on O'ahu is comparable with any you might do in the tropics, but its uniqueness comes from the isolated environment of the Islands. There are literally hundreds of species of fish and marine life that you can only find in this chain. Adding to the originality of diving here is the human history of the region. Military activities and tragedies of the 20th century filled the waters surrounding O'ahu with wreckage that the ocean creatures have since turned into their homes.

Although instructors certified to license you in scuba are plentiful in the Islands, we suggest that you get your PADI certification before coming as a week of classes may be a bit of a commitment on a short vacation. You can go on introductory dives without the certification, but the best dives require it.

Best Spots

The *Mahi Wai'anae,* a 165-foot minesweeper, was sunk in 1982 in the waters just south of Wai'anae on O'ahu's leeward coast to create an artificial reef. It's intact and penetrable, but you'll need a boat to access it. In the front resides an ancient moray eel who is so mellowed that you can pet his barnacled head without fearing for your hand's safety. Goatfish, tame lemon-butterfly fish, and blue-striped snapper hang out here, but the real stars are the patrols of spotted eagle rays that are always cruising by. It can be a longer dive as it's only 90 feet to the hull.

> **SHARK!**
>
> "You go inside the cage, cage goes in the water, you go in the water, shark's in the water . . ." You remember this line from *Jaws,* well now you get to play the role of Richard Dreyfus, as **North Shore Shark Adventures** provides you with an interactive experience out of your worst nightmare. The tour allows you to swim and snorkel in a cage as dozens of sharks lurk just feet from you in the open ocean off the North Shore, and all for just $120. ☎ *808/228–5900* ⊕ *sharktourshawaii.com.*

East of Diamond Head, **Maunalua Bay** has several boat-access sites, including Turtle Canyon, with lava-flow ridges and sandy canyons teeming with green sea turtles of all sizes; *Kāhala Barge,* a penetrable, 200-foot sunken vessel; Big Eel Reef, with many varieties of moray eels; and Fantasy Reef, a series of lava ledges and archways populated with barracuda and eels. There's also the sunken Corsair that doesn't boast much for sealife, but there's something about sitting in the cockpit of a plane 100 feet below the surface of the ocean.

The best shore dive available on O'ahu is **Shark's Cove** (⊠ Across from Foodland in Pūpūkea) on the North Shore, but unfortunately it's only accessible during the summer months. Novices can enjoy drifting along the outer wall, watching everything from turtles to eels. Veterans can explore the numerous lava tubes and tunnels where diffused sunlight from above creates a dreamlike effect in spacious caverns. It's 10- to 45-feet deep, ready-made for shore diving with a parking lot right next to the dive spot. **Three Tables** is just west of Shark's Cove, enabling you to have a second dive without moving your car or being redundant. Follow the three perpendicular rocks that break the surface out to this dive site, where you can find a variety of parrot fish and octopus, plus occasional shark and ray sightings at depths of 30 to 50 feet. It's not as exciting as Shark's Cove, but more accessible for the novice diver. ⚠ Be cautious the later in the year you go to either of these sights; the waves pick up strength in fall, and the reef can be turned into a washboard for you and your gear. Both are null and void during the winter surf sessions.

Charters, Lessons & Equipment

Captain Bruce's Hawai'i. Captain Bruce's focuses on the west and east shores, covering the *Mahi* and the Corsair. This full-service company has everything from refresher and introductory dives to more advanced drift and night dives. No equipment is needed; they provide it all. Two-tank boat dives range from $106 to $122. Most importantly, this is the only boat on O'ahu that offers hot showers onboard. ☎ *808/373–3590 or 800/535-2487* ⊕ *www.captainbruce.com.*

Hanauma Bay Dive Tours. You can guess the specialty here. They offer introductory dives in the federally protected reserve for those aged 12 ar.d above, with snuba available to 8 years old and up. The charge is $89 for the day plus a $5 fee for park entry. ☎ *808/256–8956.*

Reeftrekkers. The owners of the slickest dive Web site in Hawai'i are also the *Scuba Diving's* Reader's Choice winners for the past four years. Their thing is advance dive planning via the Internet. Using their dive descriptions and price quotes, you can plan your excursions before ever setting foot on the island. Two-tank dives range from $95 to $105. ☎ *808/943–0588* ⊕ *www.reeftrekkers.com.*

Surf'N Sea. The North Shore headquarters for all things water-related is great for diving that side as well. Everything from shore dives to night boat dives are covered. There is one interesting perk—the cameraman can shoot a video of you diving. It's hard to see facial expressions under the water, but it still might be fun for those that need documentation of all they do. Prices vary from $90 to $110 for two-tank dives. ☎ *808/ 637-3337* ⊕ *www.surfnsea.com.*

Snorkeling

One advantage that snorkeling has over scuba is that you never run out of air. That and the fact that anyone who can swim can also snorkel without any formal training. A favorite pastime in Hawai'i, snorkeling can be done anywhere there's enough water to stick your face in. Each spot will have its great days depending on the weather and time of year, so consult with the purveyor of your gear for tips on where the best viewing is that day. Keep in mind the North Shore should only be attempted when the waves are calm, namely the summertime.

■ **TIP→→** Think of buying a mask and snorkel as a prerequisite for your trip— they make any beach experience better. Just make sure you put plenty of sunblock on your back because once you start gazing below, your head may not come back up for hours.

Best Spots

As Waimea Bay is to surfing, **Hanauma Bay** (✉ 7455 Kalaniana'ole Hwy.) in Southeast O'ahu is to snorkeling. By midday it can appear like the mall at Christmas with all the bodies, but with over a half million fish to observe there's plenty to go around. Due to the protection you get from the narrow mouth of the cove and the prodigious reef, you will be hard pressed to find a place you will feel safer snorkeling.

Queen's Surf is a marine reserve right on the edge of Waikīkī, between the break wall and the Queen's pier. It's not as stocked full of fish as Hanauma, but it has its share of colorful reef fish and the occasional sea turtle just yards from shore. It's a great spot to escape to if you're stuck in Waikīkī and have grown weary of watching the surfers.

Great shallows right off the shore with huge reef protection make **Shark's Cove** (⊠ Across from Foodland in Pūpūkea) on the North Shore a great spot for youngsters. You can find a plethora of critters from crabs to octopus, all in waist-deep or shallower water. ⚠ The only cave at is that once the winter swell comes, this becomes a human pinball game rather than peaceful observation, so only try it in summer.

Directly across from the electric plant outside of Ko Olina resort, **Electric Beach** (⊠ 1 mi west of Ko Olina) in West Oʻahu has become a haven for tropical fish. The expulsion of hot water from the plant warms the ocean water, attracting all kinds of wildlife. Although the visibilty is not always the best, the crowds are thin, and the fish are guaranteed. Just park next to the old train tracks and enjoy this secret spot.

Cruises & Equipment Rental

Hanauma Bay Rental Stand. You can get masks, fins, and snorkels right at the park. ☎ *808/395–4725.*

Hanauma Bay Snorkeling Excursions. For those who are a little more timid about entering these waters, this outfitter provides a tour with a guide to help alleviate your fears. They'll even pick you up in Waikīkī and provide you with equipment and knowledge for around $30. ☎ *808/ 373–5060.*

Snorkel Bob's. We suggest buying your gear, unless it's going to be a one-day affair. Either way, Snorkel Bob's has all the stuff you'll need (and a bunch of stuff you don't) to make your water adventures enjoyable. Also feel free to ask the staff about the good spots at the moment, as the best spots can vary with weather and seasons. ⊠ *700 Kapahulu Ave.* ☎ *808/ 735–7944.*

Snuba

Snuba, the marriage of scuba and snorkeling, gives the nondiving set their first glimpse of the freedom of scuba. Snuba utilizes a raft with a standard airtank on it and a 20-foot air hose that hooks up to a regulator. Once attached to the hose, you can swim, unfettered by heavy tanks and weights, up to 15 feet down to chase fish and examine reef for as long as you fancy. If you ever get scared or need a rest, the raft is right there, ready to support you. Kids eight years and older can use the equipment. It can be pricey at about of $80 per dive. But, then again, how much is it worth to be able to sit face to face with a 6-foot-long sea turtle and not have to rush to the surface to get another breath? For Hanauma Bay snuba, contact **Hanauma Bay Snuba Dive** (☎ 808/256– 8956). **Dolphin Excursions** (☎ 808/239–5579) also offers snuba.

Submarine Tours

★ *Atlantis* **Submarines.** This is the underwater venture for the unadventurous. Not fond of swimming but want to see what you have been missing? Board this 64-passenger vessel for a ride down past ship wrecks, turtle breeding grounds, and coral reefs galore. Unlike a trip to the aquarium, this gives you a chance to see nature at work without the limitations of mankind. The tours, which leave from the pier at the Hilton Hawaiian Village, are available in several languages and run from $69 to $115. ✉ *Hilton Hawaiian Village Beach Resort and Spa, 2005 Kālia Rd., Waikīkī, Honolulu 96815* ☎ *808/973–1296.*

Surfing

Perhaps no word is more associated with Hawai'i than surfing. Every year the best of the best gather here to have their Super Bowl: the Triple Crown of Surfing (⇨ *See* North Shore Surfing and the Triple Crown *later in this chapter*). The pros dominate the waves for a month, but the rest of the year belongs to people like us, just trying to have fun and get a little exercise.

O'ahu is unique because it has so many famous spots: Banzai Pipeline, Waimea Bay, Kaiser Bowls, and Sunset Beach resonate in young surfers' hearts the world over. Their attraction comes with a price: competition for those waves. While the aloha spirit lives in many places, premium waves are not among those spots. If you're coming to visit and want to surf these world famous breaks, you need to go out with a healthy dose of respect and patience. As long as you follow the rules of the road and concede waves to local riders, you should not have problems. Just remember that locals view these waves as their property, and everything should be all right.

If you're nervous and don't want to run the risk of a confrontation, try some of the alternate spots listed below. They may not have the name recognition, but the waves can be just as great.

Best Spots

If you like to ride waves in all kinds of craft, try **Mākaha Beach** (✉ 1½ hrs west of Honolulu on H–1 Fwy. and Farrington Hwy.). It has interminable rights that allow riders to perform all manner of stunts: from six-man canoes with everyone doing headstands to bully boards (oversize boogie boards) with dad's whole family riding with him. Mainly known as a long-boarding spot, it's predominantly local but not overly

SURF SMART

A few things to remember when surfing in O'ahu:

1. The waves switch with the seasons—they're big in the south in summer, and they loom large in the north in winter. If you're not experienced, it's best to go where the waves are small. There will be fewer crowds, and your chances of injury dramatically decrease.

2. Always wear a leash. It may not look the coolest, but when your board gets swept away from you and you're swimming a half mile after it, you'll remember this advice.

3. Watch where you're going. Take a few minutes and watch the surf from the shore. Observe how big it is, where it's breaking, and how quickly the sets are coming. This knowledge will allow you to get in and out more easily and to spend more time riding waves and less time paddling.

aggressive to the respectful outsider. The only downside is that it's way out on the West shore. ⚠ Use caution in the wintertime as it can get huge.

White Plains Beach (⊠ In former Kolaeloa Military Installation) is a spot where trouble will not find you. Known among locals as "mini-Waikīkī," it breaks in numerous spots, preventing the logjam that happens with many of Oʻahu's more popular breaks. As part of a military base in West Oʻahu, the beach was closed to the public until a couple of years ago. It's now occupied by mostly novice to intermediate surfers, so egos are at a minimum, though you do have to keep a lookout for loose boards.

In town, try getting out to **Populars,** a break at **Ulukou Beach** (⊠ Waikīkī, in front of Royal Hawaiian Hotel). This is a nice easy right that never breaks too hard and is friendly to both the rookie and the veteran. The only downside here is the half-mile paddle out to the break, but no one ever said it was going to be easy, plus the long pull keeps it from getting overcrowded.

Finally, if you really need to go somewhere people have heard of, your safest bet on the North Shore is **Sunset Beach** (⊠ 1 mi north of ʻEhukai Beach Park on Kamehameha Hwy.). There are several breaks here including **Kammie's** on the west side of the strip and **Sunset Point,** which is inside of the main Sunset break. Both of these tend to be smaller and safer rides for the inexperienced. For the daring, Sunset is part of the Triple Crown for a reason. ⚠ Thick waves and long rides await, but you're going to want to have a thick board and a thicker skull. The main break is very local, so mind your Ps and Qs.

Surf Shops

★ **C&K Beach Service.** To rent a board in Waikīkī, visit the beach fronting the Hilton Hawaiian Village. Rentals cost $10 to $15 per hour, depending on the size of the board, and $18 for two hours. Small group lessons are $50 per hour with board, and trainers promise to have you riding the waves by lesson's end. ☎ *No phone.*

Surf 'N Sea. This is the Wal-Mart of water for the North Shore. Rent a short board for $5 an hour or a long board for $7 an hour ($24 and $30 for full-day rentals). Lessons cost $69 for two hours. Depending on how you want to attack your waves, you can also rent boogie boards or kayaks. ☎ *808/637–9887.*

Surfing Lessons

Hans Hedemann Surf Hawaii. Surfing and bodysurfing instruction from the staff of Hans Hedemann—who spent 17 years on the professional surfer World Tour circuit—is $50 per hour for group lessons and $115 for private lessons in Waikīkī. You can also attend surf camps on North Shore and in Waikīkī for four-day intensive training or fine-tuning courses with Hans himself. ☎ *808/924–7778* ⊕ *www.hhsurf.com.*

☾ **Hawaiian Fire, Inc.** Novice surfers can meet guaranteed success with lessons from some of Hawaiʻi's most knowledgeable water-safety experts— off-duty Honolulu firefighters—who man the boards at one of Hawaiʻi's hottest new surfing schools. Lessons ($97 for group lesson, $139 for private lesson) include equipment, safety and surfing instruction, and two hours of surfing time (with lunch break) at a secluded beach near Barbers Point. Transportation is available from Waikīkī. ☎ 808/384-8855.

North Shore Eco-Surf Tours. The only prerequisites here are "the ability to swim and the desire to surf." North Shore Eco-Surf has a more relaxed view of lessons, saying that the instruction will last somewhere between 90 minutes and four hours. There's also hiking and windsurfing instruction. ☎ 808/638-9503 ⊕ *www.ecosurf-hawaii.com.*

Whale-Watching

Hawai'i Sailing Adventures and Hawai'i Nautical (⇨ *See* Boat Tours & Charters) both run whale-watching charters during the winter months as well, but if you would like a more scientific view, try the Wild Side.

Wild Side Specialty Tours. Boasting a marine biologist crew, this west-side tour boat takes you to undisturbed snorkeling areas. Along the way you can view dolphins, turtles, and, in winter, whales. The tours leave early to catch the wildlife still active, so it's important to plan ahead as they're an hour outside Honolulu. Tours leave at 7 AM and cost approximately $95, including continental breakfast. ⊠ *Wai'anae Boat Harbor, Slip A11, Wai'anae Boat Harbor* ☎ 808/306-7273.

Windsurfing & Kiteboarding

Those who call windsurfing and kiteboarding cheating because they require no paddling have never tried hanging on to a sail or kite. It will turn your arms to spaghetti quicker than paddling ever could, and the speeds you generate . . . well, there's a reason why they're considered extreme sports.

Born here in the Islands, windsurfing is best practiced on the Windward side by amateurs as the onshore breezes will bring you back to land even if you don't know what you're doing. The new sport of kite surfing is tougher but more exhilirating as the kite will sometimes take you in the air for hundreds of feet. We suggest only those in top shape try the kites, but windsurfing is fun for all ages.

Equipment Rentals & Lessons

Kailua Sailboard and Kayaks Company. The appeal here is that they offer both beginner and high-performance gear. They also give lessons, either at $69 for a three-hour group lesson or $35 for a one-hour individual lesson (you must rent a board half-day at $39). Since both options are both around the same price, we suggest the one-hour individual lesson; then you have the rest of the day to practice what they preach. ⊠ *130 Kailua Rd., Kailua* ☎ 808/262-2555.

Naish Hawai'i. If you like to learn from the best, try out world-champion Robby Naish and his family services. Not only do they build and sell

> ### ON THE SIDELINES
>
> Watch the pros jump and spin on the waves during July's **Pan Am Hawaiian Windsurfing World Cup** (☎ 808/734-6999) off Kailua Beach. August's **Wahine Classic** (☎ 808/521-4322), held off Diamond Head point, features the world's best female boardsailors.

boards, rent equipment, provide accommodation referrals, but they also offer their windsurfing and kiteboarding expertise. A four-hour package, including 90 minutes of instruction, costs $55. ✉ *155A Hamakua Dr., Kailua* ☎ *808/261–6067* ⊕ *www.naish.com.*

GOLF, HIKING & OUTDOOR ACTIVITIES

Aerial Tours

An aerial tour of the Islands opens up a world of perspective. Looking down from the sky at the outline of the USS *Arizona* where it lays in its final resting place below the waters of Pearl Harbor or getting a glimpse of how Mother Nature carved a vast expanse of volcanic crater are the kind of views only seen by an "eye in the sky." If you go, don't forget your camera.

★ **The Original Glider Rides.** "Mr. Bill" has been offering piloted glider (sailplane) rides over the northwest end of Oʻahu's North Shore since 1970. These are piloted scenic rides for one or two passengers in sleek, bubble-top, motorless aircraft. You'll get aerial views of mountains, shoreline, coral pools, windsurfing sails, and, in winter, humpback whales. Reservations are recommended; 20- and 30-minute flights leave every 20 minutes daily 10–5. The charge for one passenger is $70; two people fly for $120 (ask about promotional pricing). ✉ *Dillingham Airfield, Mokulēʻia* ☎ *808/677–3404.*

★ **Island Seaplane Service.** Hailing back to the earliest air visitors to Hawaiʻi, the seaplane has always had a special spot in island lore. The only seaplane service still operating in Hawaiʻi takes off from Keʻehi Lagoon. Flight options are either a half-hour south and eastern Oʻahu shoreline tour or an hour island circle tour. The *Pan Am Clipper* may be gone, but you can revisit it for $89 to $139. ✉ *85 Lagoon Dr., Honolulu* ☎ *808/836–6273.*

Makani Kai Helicopters. This may be the best way to now see the infamous and now closed Sacred Falls park, where a rock slide killed 20 people and injured dozens more; Makani Kai dips their helicopter down to show you one of Hawaiʻi's former favorite hikes. There's also a Waikīkī by Night excursion that soars by the breathtaking Honolulu city lights. Tours range from $99 to $185, with customized charters available from $550 per hour. ✉ *110 Kapalulu Pl., Honolulu* ☎ *808/834–5813* ⊕ *www.makanikai.com.*

Biking

Oʻahu's coastal roads are flat and well paved. On the downside, roads are also awash in vehicular traffic. Frankly, biking is no fun in either Waikīkī or Honolulu, but things are a bit better outside the city. Be sure to take along a nylon jacket for the frequent showers on the windward side and remember that Hawaiʻi is "paradise after the fall": lock up your bike.

Honolulu City and County Bike Coordinator (☎ *808/527–5044*) can answer all your biking questions concerning trails, permits, and state laws.

Best Spots

Biking the North Shore may sound like a great idea, but the two-lane road is narrow and traffic heavy. We suggest you try the **West Kaunala Trail** (⊠ End of Pūpūkea Rd. This road is next to Foodland, the only grocery store on North Shore). It's a little tricky at times, but with the rain-forest surroundings and beautiful ocean vistas you'll hardly notice your legs burning on the steep ascent at the end. It's about 5.5 mi round-trip. Bring water because there's none on the trail unless it comes from the sky.

If going up a mountain is not your idea of mountain biking, then perhaps **Ka'ena Point Trail** (⊠ West O'ahu, end of Farrington Hwy.) is better suited to your needs. A longer ride (10 mi), but much flatter, takes you oceanside around the westernmost point on the Island. You pass sea arches and a mini-blowhole then finish up with some motocross jumps right before you turn around. There's no water on this ride either, but at least at the end you have the Yokohama beach showers to cool you off.

Fodor'sChoice Our favorite ride is in central O'ahu on the **'Aiea Loop Trail** (⊠ Central
★ O'ahu, just past Kea'iwa Heiau State Park, at end of 'Aiea Heights Dr.). There's a little bit of everything you expect to find in Hawai'i—wild pigs crossing your path, an ancient Hawaiian *heiau* (holy ground), and the remains of a World War II crashed airplane. Campsites and picnic tables are available along the way and, if you need a snack, strawberry guava trees abound. Enjoy the foliage change from bamboo to Norfolk pine in your climb along this 4.5 mi track.

Bike Shops & Clubs

Boca Hawai'i LLC. This is your shop if you want to do intense riding. There are full-suspension Trek 4500s for $35 a day and $25 for each additional day. We suggest you call ahead and reserve a bike as supplies are limited. ⊠ *330 Cooke St., next to Bike Factory, Waikīkī, Honolulu* ☎ *808/ 591–9839.*

Hawai'i Bicycling League. Not much for riding by yourself? Visit this shop online, and you can get connected with rides and contests. ☐ *Box 4403, Honolulu 96813* ☎ *808/735–5756* ⊕ *www.bikehawaii.com.*

Golf

Unlike those of the Neighbor Islands, the majority of O'ahu's golf courses are not associated with hotels and resorts. In fact, of the island's three-dozen-plus courses, only five are tied to lodging and none of them are in the tourist hub of Waikīkī.

★ **Coral Creek Golf Course.** On the 'Ewa Plain, 4 mi inland, Coral Creek is cut from ancient coral—left from when this area was still under water. Robin Nelson (1999) does some of his best work in making use of the coral, and of some dynamite, blasting out portions to create dramatic lakes and tee and green sites. They could just as easily call it Coral Cliffs, because of the 30- to 40-foot cliffs Nelson created. They include the par-3 10th green's grotto and waterfall, and the vertical drop-off on the right side of the par-4 18th green. An ancient creek meanders across the course but there's not much water, just enough to be a babbling nuisance. ⊠ *91-1111 Geiger Rd., 'Ewa Beach* ☎ *808/441–4653* ⊕ *www. coralcreekgolfhawaii.com* ⅄ *18 holes. 6818 yds. Par 72. Green Fee: $130* ↶ *Facilities: Driving range, putting green, golf carts, rental clubs, pro shop, lessons, restaurant, bar.*

Hawai'i Kai Golf Course. On the southeast tip of O'ahu, Hawai'i Kai offers a championship and an executive course. Hawai'i Kai Championship Golf Course (William F. Bell, 1973) winds through a Honolulu suburb at the foot of Koko Crater. Homes (and the liability of a broken window) come into play on many

> ### CARTS
>
> Unless you play a muni or certain daily fee courses, plan on taking a cart. Riding carts are mandatory at most courses and are included in the green fees.

holes, but that is offset by views of the nearby Pacific, and a crafty routing of holes. With several lakes, lots of trees, and bunkers in all the wrong places, Hawai'i Kai really is a "championship" golf course, especially when the trade winds howl. The Hawai'i Kai Executive Course (1962), a par-55 track, is the first of only three courses in Hawai'i built by Robert Trent Jones Sr. Although a few changes have been made to his original design, you can find the usual Jones attributes, including raised greens and lots of risk-reward options. ⊠ *8902 Kalaniana'ole Hwy., Hawai'i Kai* ☎ *808/ 395–2358* ⊕ *www.hawaiikaigolf.com* ⅄ *Championship Course: 18 holes. 6222 yds. Par 72. Green Fee: $80/$90. Executive Course: 18 holes. 2223 yds. Par 55. Green Fee: $37/$42* ↶ *Facilities: Driving range, putting green, golf carts, pull carts, rental clubs, pro shop, lessons, restaurant, bar.*

★ **Hawai'i Prince Golf Course.** Affiliated with the Hawai'i Prince Hotel in Waikīkī, the Hawai'i Prince Golf Course (not to be confused with the Prince Course at Princeville, Kaua'i) has a links feel to it, and it is popular with local charity fund-raiser golf tournaments. Arnold Palmer and Ed Seay (1991) took what had been flat, featureless sugarcane fields and sculpted 27 challenging, varied holes. Mounding breaks up the landscape, as do 10 lakes. Water comes into play on six holes of the A course, three of B, and seven of C. The most difficult combination is A and C (A and B from the forward tees). ⊠ *91-1200 Fort Weaver Rd., 'Ewa Beach* ☎ *808/944–4567* ⊕ *www.princeresortshawaii.com* ⅄ *A Course: 9 holes. 3138 yds. Par 36. B Course: 9 holes. 3099 yds. Par 36. C Course: 9 holes. 3076 yds. Par 36. Green Fee: $140* ↶ *Facilities: Driving range, putting green, golf carts, pull carts, rental clubs, pro shop, golf academy/ lessons, restaurant, bar.*

★ **Kapolei Golf Course.** This is a Ted Robinson water wonderland with waterfalls and four lakes—three so big they have names—coming into play on 10 holes. Set on rolling terrain, Kapolei is a serious golf course, especially when the wind blows. ⊠ *91-701 Farrington Hwy., Kapolei* ☎ *808/674–2227* ⅄ *18 holes. 7001 yds. Par 72. Green Fee: $130/$140* ↶ *Facilities: Driving range, putting green, golf carts, rental clubs, pro shop, lessons, restaurant, bar.*

Fodor'sChoice **Ko'olau Golf Club.** Ko'olau Golf Club is marketed as the toughest golf
★ course in Hawai'i and one of the most challenging in the country. Dick
Nugent and Jack Tuthill (1992) routed 10 holes over jungle ravines that
require at least a 110-yard carry. The par-4 18th may be the most difficult closing hole in golf. The tee shot from the regular tees must carry
200 yards of ravine, 250 from the blue tees. The approach shot is back
across the ravine, 200 yards to a well-bunkered green. Set at the windward base of the Ko'olau Mountains, the course is as much beauty as
beast. Kāne'ohe Bay is visible from most holes, orchids and yellow ginger bloom, the shama thrush (Hawai'i's best singer since Don Ho)
chirrups, and waterfalls flute down the sheer, green mountains above.
⊠ *45-550 Kionaole Rd., Kaneohe* ☎ *808/236–4653* ⊕ *www.
koolaugolfclub.com* ⚑ *18 holes. 7310 yds. Par 72. Green Fee: $125*
⚐ *Facilities: Driving range, putting green, golf carts, rental clubs, pro
shop, golf academy, restaurant, bar.*

★ **Ko Olina Golf Club.** Hawai'i's golden age of golf-course architecture
came to O'ahu when Ko Olina Golf Club opened in 1989. Ted Robinson, king of the water features, went splash-happy here, creating nine
lakes that come into play on eight holes, including the par-3 12th, where
you reach the tee by driving behind a Disney-like waterfall. Tactically,
though, the most dramatic is the par-4 18th, where the approach is a
minimum 120 yards across a lake to a two-tiered green guarded on the
left by a cascading waterfall. Today, Ko Olina, affiliated with the adjacent 'Ihilani Resort and Spa (guests receive discounted rates), has ma-
tured into one of Hawai'i's top courses. You can niggle about routing
issues—the first three holes play into the trade winds (and the morning
sun), and two consecutive par-5s on the back nine play into the trades—
but Robinson does enough solid design to make those of passing con-
cern. ⊠ *92-1220 Ali'inui Dr., Kapolei* ☎ *808/676–5300* ⊕ *www.
koolinagolf.com* ⚑ *18 holes. 6867 yds. Par 72. Green Fee: $160* ⚐ *Fa-
cilities: Driving range, putting green, golf carts, rental clubs, pro shop,
golf academy, restaurant, bar.*

MUNICIPAL GOLF COURSES

We don't have room to mention
every muni on O'ahu, so here are
three more you may want to consider.
Your best bet for a tee time is to call
the day-of and inquire about walk-
on availability. Green fees are standard at city courses, $42 walking
rate, riding cart $8 per person, pull
carts $4.

'Ewa Villages Golf Course Municipal.
⊠ *91-1760 Park Row St., 'Ewa Beach*
☎ *808/681–0220* ⚑ *18 holes.
6455yds. Par 73.*
Pali Golf Course Municipal. ⊠ *45-
050 Kamehameha Hwy., Kāne'ohe*
☎ *808/266–7612* ⚑ *18 holes.
6524 yds. Par 72.*
**Ted Makalena Golf Course Munic-
ipal.** ⊠ *93-059 Waipio Pt. Access
Rd., Waipahu* ☎ *808/675–6052*
⚑ *18 holes. 5946 yds. Par 71.*

Luana Hills Country Club. In windward Oʻahu's cool, lush Maunawili Valley, Pete and Perry Dye created what can only be called target jungle golf. In other words, the rough is usually dense jungle and you may not hit driver on three of the four par-5s, or several par-4s, including the perilous 18th that plays off a cliff to a narrow green protected by a creek. Mt. Olomana's twin peaks tower over Luana Hills, which opened in 1993 as Royal Hawaiian County Club. The back nine wanders deep into the valley, and includes an island green (par-3 11th) and perhaps the loveliest inland hole in Hawaiʻi (par-4 12th). ✉ *770 Auloa Rd., Kailua* ☎ *808/262–2139* ⊕ *www.luanahills.com* ⚑ *18 holes. 6164 yds. Par 72. Green Fee: $125* ☞ *Facilities: Driving range, putting green, golf carts, pull carts, rental clubs, pro shop, restaurant, bar.*

★ **Mākaha Resort Golf Club.** Known locally as Mākaha West, this William F. Bell classic design (1969) remains one of the island's true gems, and a serious golf course where subtle elevation changes, if not duly noted, can significantly affect scores. The back nine plays up into Mākaha Valley. Roving peacocks make Mākaha West one of the island's most colorful layouts. ✉ *84-626 Mākaha Valley Rd., Waiʻanae* ☎ *808/695–7519* ⊕ *www.makaharesort.com* ⚑ *18 holes. 7077 yds. Par 72. Green Fee: $110* ☞ *Facilities: Driving range, putting green, golf carts, rental clubs, pro shop, lessons, restaurant, bar.*

Mākaha Valley Country Club. This course (William F. Bell, 1968), known locally as Mākaha East, is indeed a valley course, taking great advantage of the steep valley walls and natural terrain. It's shorter than the nearby West course, but offers plenty of challenge from the back tees. The double-dogleg, downhill-uphill, par-5 18th is a doozy of a closer. ✉ *84-627 Mākaha Valley Rd., Waiʻanae* ☎ *808/695–9578* ⊕ *www.makahavalleycc.com* ⚑ *18 holes. 6091 yds. Par 71. Green Fee: $55* ☞ *Facilities: Driving range, putting green, golf carts, rental clubs, pro shop, restaurant, bar.*

Mililani Golf Course. Located on Oʻahu's central plain, Mililani is usually a few degrees cooler than downtown, 25 minutes away. The eucalyptus trees through which the course plays add to the cool factor and stands of Norfolk pines give Mililani a "mainland course" feel. Bob and Robert L. Baldock (1966) made good use of an old irrigation ditch reminiscent of a Scottish burn. ✉ *95-176 Kuahelani Ave., Mililani* ☎ *808/ 623–2222* ⊕ *www.mililanigolf.com* ⚑ *18 holes. 6455 yds. Par 72. Green Fee: $85* ☞ *Facilities: Driving range, putting green, golf carts, rental clubs, pro shop, lessons, restaurant, bar.*

New ʻEwa Beach Golf Club. A private course open to the public, New ʻEwa is one of the delightful products of the too brief collaboration of Robin Nelson and Rodney Wright (1992). Trees are very much part of the character here, but there are also elements of links golf, such as a double green shared by the 2nd and 16th holes. ✉ *91-050 Fort Weaver Rd., ʻEwa Beach* ☎ *808/689–8351* ⚑ *18 holes. 6124 yds. Par 72. Green Fee: $65* ☞ *Facilities: Putting green, golf carts, rental clubs, pro shop, restaurant.*

Pearl Harbor Country Club. Carved in the hillside high above Pearl Harbor, the 18 holes here are really two courses. The front nine rambles out along gently sloping terrain, while the back nine zig-zags up and down a steeper portion of the slope as it rises into the Ko'olau Mountains. The views of Pearl Harbor are breathtaking. ⊠ 98-535 Kaonohi St., 'Aiea ☎ 808/487–3802 ⊕ www.pearlcc.com ⚑ 18 holes. 6230 yds. Par 72. Green Fee: $100/$110 ⌖ Facilities: Driving range, putting green, golf carts, rental clubs, pro shop, lessons, restaurant, bar.

Fodor'sChoice
★ **Royal Kunia Country Club.** At one time the PGA Tour considered buying Royal Kunia Country Club and hosting the Sony Open there. It's that good. Every hole offers fabulous views from Diamond Head to Pearl Harbor to the nearby Wai'anae Mountains, and Robin Nelson's eye for natural sight lines and dexterity with water features adds to the visual pleasure. ⊠ 94-1509 Anonui St., Waipahu ☎ 808/688–9222 ⊕ www.royalkuniacc.com ⚑ 18 holes. 7007 yds. Par 72. Green Fee: $125/$135 ⌖ Facilities: Driving range, putting green, golf carts, rental clubs, pro shop, restaurant.

Fodor'sChoice
★ **Turtle Bay Resort & Spa.** When the Lazarus of golf courses, the Fazio Course at Turtle Bay (George Fazio, 1971), rose from the dead in 2002, Turtle Bay on O'ahu's rugged North Shore became a premier golf destination. Two holes had been plowed under when the Palmer Course at Turtle Bay (Arnold Palmer and Ed Seay, 1992) was built, while the other seven lay fallow, and the front nine remained open. Then new owners came along and re-created holes 13 and 14 using Fazio's original plans, and the Fazio became whole again. It's a terrific track with 90 bunkers. The gem at Turtle Bay, though, is the Palmer Course. The front nine is mostly open as it skirts Punaho'olapa Marsh, a nature sanctuary, while the back nine plunges into the wetlands and winds along the coast. The short par-4 17th runs along the rocky shore, with a diabolical string of bunkers cutting diagonally across the fairway from tee to green. ⊠ 57-049 Kuilima Dr., Kahuku ☎ 808/293–8574 ⊕ www.turtlebayresort.com ⚑ Fazio Course: 18 holes. 6535 yds. Par 72. Green Fee: $155. Palmer Course: 18 holes. 7199 yds. Par 72. Green Fee: $165 ⌖ Facilities: Driving range, putting green, golf carts, rental clubs, pro shop, lessons, restaurant, bar.

Waikele Golf Course. Outlet stores are not the only bargain at Waikele. The adjacent golf course is a daily fee course that offers a private club-like atmosphere and a terrific Ted Robinson (1992) layout. The target off the tee is Diamond Head, with Pearl Harbor to the right. Robinson's water features are less distinctive here, but define the short par-4 fourth hole, with a lake running down the left side of the fairway and guarding the green; and the par-3 17th, which plays across a lake. The par-4 18th is a terrific closing hole, with a lake lurking on the right side of the green. ⊠ 94-200 Paioa Pl., Waipahu ☎ 808/676–9000 ⊕ www.golfwaikele.com ⚑ 18 holes. 6261 yds. Par 72. Green Fee: $125 ⌖ Facilities: Driving range, putting green, golf carts, rental clubs, pro shop, lessons, restaurant, bar.

Hiking

For a free O'ahu recreation map that outlines the island's 33 major trails, contact the **Hawai'i State Department of Land and Natural Resources**

(⌂ 1151 Punchbowl St., Room 130, Honolulu 96813 ☎ 808/587–0300 ⊕ www.hawaii.gov). Contact the City and County of Honolulu's **Trails and Access Manager** (☎ 808/973–9782) for a free hiking-safety guide. Ask for a copy of "Hiking on O'ahu: The Official Guide."

Best Spots

Every vacation has requirements that must be fulfilled so that when your neighbors ask, you can say, "Yeah, did it." **Diamond Head Crater** (⊠ Enter on east of crater; there's limited parking inside, most park on street and walk in) is high on that list of things to do on O'ahu. It's a hike easy enough that even grandma can do it, as long as she takes a water bottle because it's hot and dry. Only a mile up, a clearly marked trail with handrails scales the inside of this extinct volcano. At the top, the fabled 99 steps take you up to the pill box overlooking the Pacific Ocean and Honolulu. It's a breathtaking view and a lot cheaper than taking a helicopter ride for the same photo op.

Fodor'sChoice Travel up into the valley beyond Honolulu to make the **Mānoa Falls** (⊠ Be-
★ hind Manoa Valley in Paradise Park. Take West Mānoa Rd. to end, park on side of road, and follow trail signs in) hike. Though only a mile long, this path passes through so many different ecosystems that you feel as if you're in an arboretum. Walk among the elephant ear ape plants, ruddy fir trees, and a bamboo forest straight out of China. At the top is a 150-foot waterfall with a small pool not quite suited for swimming but good for wading. This hike is more about the journey than the destination; make sure you bring some mosquito repellent because they grow 'em big up here.

Need more waterfall action that you can actually swim? Then **Maunawili Falls** (⊠ Take Pali Hwy., Rte. 61, from Honolulu, take 3rd right onto Auloa Rd., then take left fork immediately; at dead end, climb over vehicle gate for trailhead) after going through the tunnels is your trip. In fact, even if you don't want to get wet, you're going to have to cross Maunawili Stream several times to get to the falls. Along the way enjoy the ginger, vines, and heleconia before greeting fern-shrouded falls that are made for swimming. The water is not the clearest, but it's cool and refreshing after battling the bugs to get here.

Guided Hikes

Hawai'i Nature Center. A good choice for families, the center in upper Makiki Valley conducts a number of programs for both adults and children. There are guided hikes into tropical settings that reveal hidden waterfalls and protected forest reserves. ⊠ *2131 Makiki Heights Dr., Makiki Heights, Honolulu 96822* ☎ *808/955–0100.*

O'ahu Nature Tours. Guides explain the native flora and fauna that is your companion on glorious sunrise, hidden waterfall, mountain forest, rain forest, and volcanic walking tours. ☎ *808/924–2473* ⊕ *www.oahunaturetours.com.*

Horseback Riding

Kualoa Ranch. This ranch across from Kualoa Beach Park on the Windward side leads trail rides in Ka'a'awa, one of the most beautiful valleys

Honolulu Marathon

The **Honolulu Marathon** is a thrilling event to watch as well as to participate in. Join the throngs who cheer at the finish line at Kapiʻolani Park as internationally famous and local runners tackle the 26.2-mi challenge. It's held on the second Sunday in December and is sponsored by the **Honolulu Marathon Association** (☎ 808/734–7200 ⊕ www.honolulumarathon.org).

in all Hawaiʻi. Trail rides cost between $57 and $91. Kualoa has other activities such as windsurfing, jet skiing, all-terrain-vehicle trail rides, and children's activities, which may be combined for half- or full-day package rates. ⊠ *49-560 Kamehameha Hwy., Kaʻaʻawa* ☎ *808/237–8515* ⊕ *www.kualoa.com.*

Happy Trails Hawaiʻi. Take a guided horseback ride through the verdant Waimea Valley on trails that offer panoramic views from Kaena Point to the famous North Shore surfing spots. Rates vary depending on length of ride and skill level. ⊠ *1 mi mauka up Pupakea Rd. on right, Pupakea* ☎ *808/638–7433.*

Jogging

In Honolulu, the most popular places to jog are the two parks, **Kapiʻolani** and **Ala Moana,** at either end of Waikīkī. In both cases, the loop around the park is just under 2 mi. You can run a 4½-mi ring around **Diamond Head crater,** past scenic views, luxurious homes, and herds of other joggers.

Tennis

Oʻahu has 181 public tennis courts that are free and open for play on a first-come, first-served basis; you're limited to 45 minutes of court time if others are waiting to play. A complete listing is free of charge from the **Department of Parks and Recreation** (⊠ Tennis Unit, 650 S. King St., Honolulu 96813 ☎ 808/971–7150 ⊕ www.co.honolulu.hi.us).

Kapiʻolani Park, on the Diamond Head end of Waikīkī, has two tennis locations. The **Diamond Head Tennis Center** (⊠ 3908 Pākī Ave. ☎ 808/971–7150), near Kapiʻolani Park, has nine courts open to the public. There are more than a dozen courts for play at **Kapiʻolani Tennis Courts** (⊠ 2748 Kalākaua Ave. ☎ 808/971–2510). The closest public courts to the ʻewa end of Waikīkī are in **Ala Moana Park** (⊠ Ala Moana Blvd. ☎ 808/592–7031).

The **Pacific Beach Hotel** (⊠ 2490 Kalākaua Ave., Waikīkī ☎ 808/922–1233) has rooftop tennis courts that are open to nonguests for a fee.

Forty-five minutes from Waikīkī, on Oʻahu's ʻEwa Plain, are two championship tennis courts at the **Hawaiʻi Prince Golf Club** (⊠ 91-1200 Ft.

Weaver Rd., 'Ewa Beach ☏ 808/944–4567); shuttle service is available from the Hawai'i Prince Hotel Waikīkī for hotel guests.

EXPLORING O'AHU

Waikīkī

There's a good reason why Waikīkī is often referred to as O'ahu's playground: it's where the action is. It's been this way since the days of Hawai'i's kings and queens, who often retreated to Waikīkī to enjoy moonlight horseback rides, canoe races, and carefree romps in the ocean.

Since the Moana Hotel (now the Sheraton Moana Surfrider) opened its doors in 1901, visitors were invited to enjoy the sun, surf, and sand of Waikīkī as well. Once full of swamps and rivers (Waikīkī translates to "Spouting Water"), the area was effectively drained after the construction of the Ala Wai Canal, which borders most of Waikīkī's north end. The construction boom was in full force by the 1960s and '70s—some say the official state bird at the time was the crane—filling Waikīkī's 1.5 square mi with towering resorts and hotels. Today, however, Waikīkī, still just 3½ mi from downtown Honolulu, has enjoyed a renaissance of sorts. Sidewalks have been widened, the streets have been improved, and hotel workers have embraced a new appreciation for the Hawaiian culture and the propagating of Hawai'i's famous aloha spirit. From torchlighting ceremonies on the beach to the familiar croonings of Don Ho, Waikīkī continues to weave its alluring magic to millions of visitors each year.

a good walk

Begin at the **Ala Wai Yacht Harbor ❶** ☞, home to an armada of pleasure boats and two members-only yacht clubs. Routes 8 and 20 of TheBus stop in front of the Hawai'i Prince hotel, which is in front of the harbor.

From here head toward the main intersection of Ala Moana Boulevard and Kālia Road, and turn right at the large sculpture of hula dancers signaling the entry to the **Hilton Hawaiian Village Beach Resort and Spa ❷**, and wander through this 22-acre resort complex past gardens and waterfalls.

Continue makai on Kālia Road to Fort DeRussy, home of the **U.S. Army Museum ❸**. Across the street, on Saratoga Road, nestled snugly amid the commerce of Waikīkī, is an oasis of tranquillity: the teahouse at the **Urasenke Foundation ❹**, where the art of Hawaiian hospitality bows to the art of the centuries-old Japanese tea ceremony.

With a little taste of Asia and some Zen for the road, head mauka on Saratoga Road until you reach Kalākaua Avenue. Then turn right

WHICH WAY?

You may be confused by the way Hawaiians use *Diamond Head* and *'ewa*. These terms refer to both locations and directions. Diamond Head refers both to the iconic Waikīkī landmark peak and that direction (east, roughly speaking). 'Ewa is both a reference to the 'Ewa town on the leeward side of the island, and that direction (west, roughly speaking). And, of course, *makai* still means toward the ocean, while *mauka* is toward the mountains.

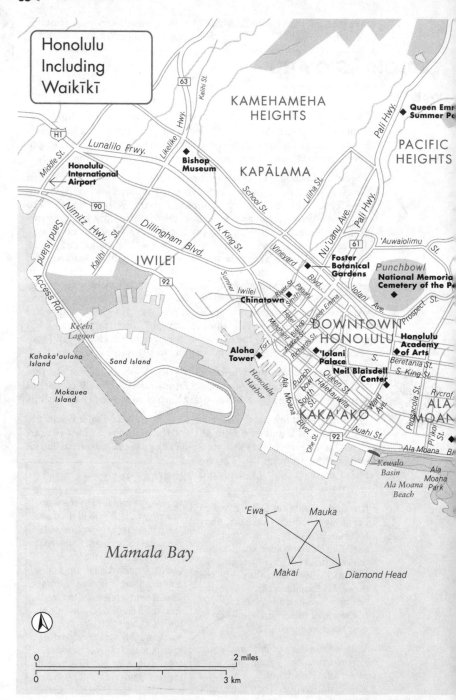

Honolulu Including Waikīkī

KAMEHAMEHA HEIGHTS

Queen Emma Summer Pa

PACIFIC HEIGHTS

Lunalilo Frwy.

Honolulu International Airport

Bishop Museum

KAPĀLAMA

Dillingham Blvd.

N. King St.

IWILEI

Foster Botanical Gardens

Punchbowl

National Memorial Cemetery of the Pa

Iwilei

Chinatown

Ke'ehi Lagoon

Kahaka'aulana Island

Sand Island

Aloha Tower

DOWNTOWN HONOLULU

Honolulu Academy of Arts

Mokauea Island

Honolulu Harbor

'Iolani Palace

Neil Blaisdell Center

Beretania St.

S. King St.

Rycrof

KAKA'AKO

Auahi St.

Ala Moana B

ALA MOAN

Kewalo Basin

Ala Moana Beach

Ala Moana Park

'Ewa — Mauka

Makai — Diamond Head

Māmala Bay

0   2 miles

0   3 km

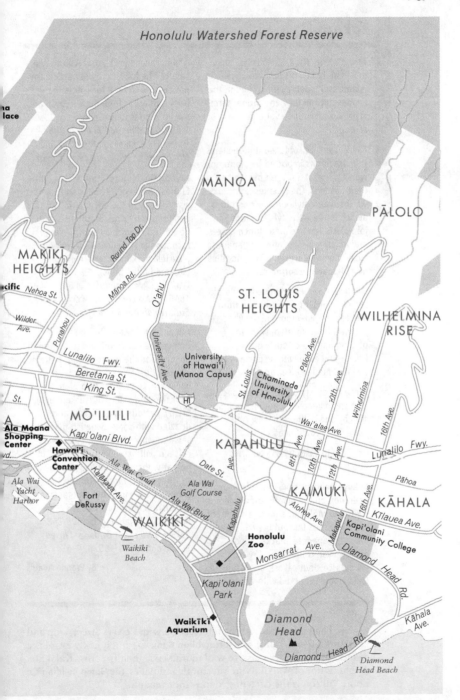

Honolulu Watershed Forest Reserve

MĀNOA

PĀLOLO

MAKĪKĪ
HEIGHTS

cific Nehoa St.

Wilder
Ave.

ST. LOUIS
HEIGHTS

WILHELMINA
RISE

Round Top Dr.

Mānoa Rd.

Punahou

Oʻahu

University Ave.

Lunalilo Fwy.

Beretania St.

King St.

University
of Hawaiʻi
(Manoa Capus)

Chaminade
University
of Honolulu

Pālolo Ave.

20th Ave.

Wilhelmina

16th Ave.

HI

St.

A
**Ala Moana
Shopping
Center**

MŌʻILIʻILI

Kapiʻolani Blvd.

Waiʻalae Ave.

KAPAHULU

8th Ave.

10th Ave.

12th Ave.

Lunalilo Fwy.

vd.

◆ **Hawaiʻi
Convention
Center**

Ala Wai Canal

Date St.

Ala Wai
Golf Course

Kapahulu Ave.

Pāhoa

*Ala Wai
Yacht
Harbor*

Kalākaua Ave.

Fort
DeRussy

Ala Wai Blvd.

WAIKĪKĪ

KAIMUKĪ

Aloha Ave.

Makapuʻu

16th Ave.

KĀHALA

Kīlauea Ave.

Kapiʻolani
Community College

**Honolulu
Zoo**

Monsarrat Ave.

*Waikīkī
Beach*

◆

*Kapiʻolani
Park*

Diamond   Head   Rd.

Kāhala
Ave.

**Waikīkī
Aquarium**

◆

*Diamond
Head*

▲

Diamond   Head   Rd.

*Diamond
Head Beach*

Takeout

FOR LUNCH AT THE BEACH, or a movie night in your hotel room, do as Islanders do: get takeout. (And in the Islands, incidentally, the proper term is always takeout, never take-away or to-go.)

The universality of takeout here stems from traditions imported by plantation workers from Asia. The Chinese had their bakeries, the Japanese, *okazu-ya*, the Asian-style delis. Honolulu is awash in Western-style fast food joints, island-style plate-lunch places, and Asian drive-ins offering Japanese sushi, Korean barbecue, Thai noodles, and Vietnamese spring rolls.

But locals particularly cherish the old-style businesses, now into the third and fourth generation, usually inconveniently located, with no parking and ridiculously quirky hours—and each with a specialty or two that no one else can quite match.

Buy a cheap Styrofoam cooler, pack it with ice to keep the goodies cool, and stop by one of these places. And remember: you'll need cash.

Here are three to try as you drive about O'ahu:

Fukuya Delicatessen. This family operation on the main thoroughfare in charming Mō'ili'ili, a mile or so out of Waikīkī, offers takeout breakfasts and lunches, Japanese snacks, noodle dishes, even confections. Try *mochi* (sweet rice-flour cakes), *chow fun* (silky noodles flecked with vegetables and barbecue pork), and Asian-style salads. The folks here are particularly patient and helpful to visitors; hang back and eavesdrop, then step up and ask your questions. Open 6 AM–2 PM. ⊠ *2710 S. King, Mō'ili'ili* ☎ *808/946-2073* ☉ *Closed Mon. and Tues. No dinner* ▭ *No credit cards $2–$6.*

Kwong On. Minutes from Waikīkī, this Chinese bakery and snack shop is best visited early in the day (open 7 AM to 3 PM Monday through Saturday, but the good stuff is gone by noon). We recommend the curried half-moon pastries, pork hash, and *manapua* (steamed filled buns). ⊠ *3620-A Wai'alae Ave., Kaimukī* ☎ *808/734-4666* ▭ *No credit cards* ☉ *Closed Sun. No dinner $1–$6.*

Mitsu-Ken. Trust us. Ignore the downscale neighborhood just north of the city and the unpromising, battered exterior. Just line up and order the garlic chicken (either as a plate lunch, with rice and salad, or chicken only). Crispy, profoundly garlickey, and drizzled with some sweetish glaze that sets the whole thing off, Mitsu-Ken chicken will haunt your dreams. But go early; they open at 4 AM and by 1 PM, they're washing down the sidewalks. It's in Kahili, not far from the Bishop Museum. ⊠ *1223 N. School St., Kapālama* ☎ *808/848-5573* ▭ *No credit cards* ☉ *Closed Sun. No dinner $1–$5.*

— By Wanda Adams

---

toward Diamond Head. At the intersection with Lewers Street, stop and peer into the lobby of the **First Hawaiian Bank ❺** for a quick view of the island's history in six massive wall murals. Diagonally across Kalākaua Avenue is one of Waikīkī's architectural landmarks, the **Gump Building ❻**; Louis Vuitton is the current ground-floor tenant.

Walk down Lewers Street toward the ocean. It dead-ends at the impressive **Halekūlani** ❼, one of Waikīkī's most prestigious hotels, famed for its elegant hospitality. From the Halekūlani stroll toward Diamond Head along the paved oceanside walkway. It leads past the Sheraton Waikīkī to the gracious, historic, and very pink **Royal Hawaiian Hotel** ❽. Return to Kalākaua Avenue and continue walking toward Diamond Head.

On the makai side of Kalākaua Avenue you can see the oldest hotel in Waikīkī, the venerable **Sheraton Moana Surfrider** ❾. Wander through the breezy lobby to the wide back porch, called the Banyan Veranda, or take a quick tour through tourism history in the Moana's second-floor historical room. From here, walk down the beach and head toward Diamond Head. Next to Kalākaua Avenue, just to the right of the Duke Kahanamoku Statue on the makai side, you can find the four **Kahuna (Wizard) Stones of Waikīkī** ❿. Legend has it that these stones hold magical powers. Sadly, however, the stones are often overlooked and, more often than not, irreverently draped with wet towels. The **Duke Kahanamoku Statue** ⓫ pays tribute to the memory of one of Hawai'i's most beloved surfers and swimmers. Every weekend evening at sunset, the torches along the beach are lighted from this statue to the stage one block 'ewa, where free hula entertainment kicks off Waikīkī after-dark celebrations.

Continue your walk four blocks farther down Kalākaua Avenue toward Diamond Head; then turn mauka onto 'Ōhua Avenue and you find the only church in Waikīkī with its own building, the Roman Catholic St. Augustine's. Sunday evening services include hymns sung by a Tongan choir. As you exit the front entrance of the Church, turn left on Kalākaua Avenue to the intersection of Kalākaua and Kapahulu avenues. On the makai side, you can see a 6-foot-tall bronze surfboard, which indicates the beginning of the **Waikīkī Historic Trail** ⓬. This 2-mi walk passes 20 bronze surfboard markers that feature photos and text highlighting Waikīkī's rich, historic past.

TIMING Allow yourself at least one full day for this walk, and time it so that you wind up on Waikīkī Beach at sunset. Many shops and attractions are open every day of the year from sunup to way past sundown to cater to the body clocks of tourists from around the world. Note, however, that the Urasenke Foundation tea ceremonies take place only on Wednesday and Friday mornings. Hawai'i's location near the equator can make the midday sun quite warm. Sunburns and dehydration are vacation spoilers, so be sure to pace yourself and drinks lots of water. There are plenty of air-conditioned places to rest along the way.

What to See

▶ ❶ **Ala Wai Yacht Harbor.** Every other summer the Trans-Pacific yacht race from Los Angeles makes its colorful finish here, complete with flags and onboard parties. The next Trans-Pac is estimated to arrive in July 2007. No matter when you visit Hawai'i, if you want a taste of what life on the water could be like, stroll around the docks and check out the variety of craft, from houseboats to luxury cruisers. Home to both the Waikīkī and Hawai'i Yacht Clubs, the waiting list for permanent boat slips here is at least a decade. ⊠ *1599 Ala Moana Blvd., across from Waikīkī Prince Hotel, Waikīkī.*

⓫ **Duke Kahanamoku Statue.** Known as the "father of modern surfing," Duke won his first gold medal for the 100-meter freestyle at the 1912 Olympics in Stockholm, Sweden. He later traveled the world to promote his beloved sport of wave riding. Duke passed away in 1968 at the age of 77. When the bronze statue was first placed here, it caused a wave of controversy because the Duke is standing with his back to the ocean, something no safety-conscious surfer would ever do. ⊠ *2 blocks Diamond Head of Sheraton Moana Surfrider on Kalākaua Ave., Waikīkī* ☞ *Free.*

> ## WHERE DO I PARK?
>
> Parking is at a premium in Waikīkī. The lot next to the Honolulu Zoo, at the Diamond Head end of the beach, is always the best place. There's also metered parking along the ocean side of Kapi'olani Park. At the other end of Waikīkī, try the Ala Wai Yacht Harbor. As for central Waikīkī, there's a parking structure on Seaside Avenue, just after the Waikīkī Shopping Plaza. It's $5 for the entire day and probably your best bet.

❺ **First Hawaiian Bank.** Get a glimpse of Hawaiian history kept safe in this Waikīkī bank, where half a dozen murals depict the evolution of Hawaiian culture. The impressive panels were painted between 1951 and 1952 by Jean Charlot (1898–1979), whose work is represented in Florence at the Uffizi Gallery and in New York at both the Metropolitan Museum and the Museum of Modern Art. The murals are beautifully lighted at night, with some panels visible from the street. ⊠ *2181 Kalākaua Ave., Waikīkī* ☎ *808/943–4670* ☞ *Free* ☉ *Mon.–Thurs. 8:30–4, Fri. 8:30–6.*

❻ **Gump Building.** Built in 1929 in Hawaiian-colonial style, with Asian architectural motifs and a blue-tile roof, this structure once housed Hawai'i's premier store, Gump's, which was known for high-quality Asian and Hawaiian objects. It's now home to a Louis Vuitton boutique. ⊠ *2200 Kalākaua Ave., Waikīkī.*

❼ **Halekūlani.** Maintaining an air of mystery within its tranquil setting, the modern Halekūlani hotel is centered on a portion of its original (1917) beachfront estate, immortalized as the setting for the 1925 Charlie Chan detective novel, *The House Without a Key.* For a view of an orchid blossom unlike any other, take a peek at the swimming pool with its huge orchid mosaic on the bottom. ⊠ *2199 Kālia Rd., Waikīkī* ☎ *808/923–2311.*

need a break? If it's lunchtime or close to sunset, linger at the Halekūlani and get a table at **House Without a Key** (⊠ 2199 Kālia Rd., Waikīkī ☎ 808/923–2311). The restaurant has a light lunch menu and serves wonderful tropical drinks and *pūpū* (appetizers) before dinner. Enjoy the view and the sounds of the Hawaiian steel guitar, and watch graceful hula performed nightly beneath the aged *kiawe* tree (kiawe is a mesquite-type wood).

② **Hilton Hawaiian Village Beach Resort and Spa.** Your first glimpse of the landmark Rainbow Tower, with its 31-story mosaic mural, might have been through a plane window; the mural was designed to be visible from the air corridor into Honolulu International. You certainly can't miss this 22-acre resort from the ground in Waikīkī. It dominates the 'ewa end of the beach, with its towers, shops, pools, and lush landscaping. **Bishop Museum Collection at the Hawaiian Arts & Culture Center** (◪ $7 ☉ Daily 10–5) in Kālia Tower displays Hawaiian art and historical artifacts from the holdings of the Bishop Museum. Historical photos, bird-feather cloaks of the Hawaiian nobility, and even Duke Kahanomoku's surfboard are assembled to tell the story of Waikīkī. *Atlantis* **Submarine** docks just offshore, at the only pier in Waikīkī. **Aloha Friday Fireworks** are a tradition. The King's Jubilee poolside revue (complete with fire-eaters and hula dancers) precedes the fireworks. You can either sit by the pool (one-drink minimum) or just spread a blanket on the sand for free. ✉ *2005 Kālia Rd., Waikīkī* ☎ *808/949–4321.*

⑩ **Kahuna (Wizard) Stones of Waikīkī.** According to legend, these boulders preserve the magnetic legacy of four Tahitian sorcerers—Kapaemahu, Kinohi, Kapuni, and Kahaloa. The stones are said to have healing powers for all who come here to honor these legendary figures. ✉ *Waikīkī Beach, just 'ewa of Duke Kahanamoku Statue, Waikīkī.*

⑧ **Royal Hawaiian Hotel.** Affectionately nicknamed the Pink Palace of the Pacific, this legendary hotel sticks out amid the high-rises on Waikīkī Beach like a pink confection. The Royal Hawaiian opened in 1927, and the lobby is reminiscent of an era when visitors to the Islands arrived on luxury liners. The coconut grove garden is another remnant of an earlier time. ✉ *2259 Kalākaua Ave., Waikīkī* ☎ *808/923–7311.*

★ **⑨** **Sheraton Moana Surfrider.** Listed on the National Register of Historic Places, this intricate beaux arts–style hotel was christened the First Lady of Waikīkī when she opened her doors at the turn of the 20th century. With period furnishings and historical exhibits, this landmark holds plenty of Hawai'i nostalgia. Visit the **Historical Room** in the rotunda above the main entrance to see the collection of old photographs and memorabilia dating from the opening of the hotel. ✉ *2365 Kalākaua Ave., Waikīkī* ☎ *808/922–3111.*

need a break? Since 1901, travelers to Waikīkī have sought respite in the shade of the **Moana's Banyan Veranda** (✉ 2365 Kalakaua Ave., Waikīkī ☎ 808/922–3111), where afternoon high tea has become tradition. Steps away from the ocean, you can close your eyes and linger over teas fragrant with the essence of tropical fruit like mango and papaya. Tea-time sandwiches and desserts are sweet additions and a reward for those who brave the rigors of surfing and swimming here in the waters of Waikīkī, once called the "playground of the kings."

④ **The Urasenke Foundation.** If you're looking for a slice of serenity in Waikīkī, this is a good place to find it. This authentic Japanese tearoom has been serving visitors here since 1977. The meditative ceremony re-

Waikīkī

Ala Wai Field & Park

Ala Wai Canal

Kapiolani Blvd.

Ala Wai Blvd.

Hawai'i Convention Center

Niu St.
Pau St.
Keoniana St.
Kuamo'o St.
Nāmāhana St.
Olohana St.
Kālaimoku St.
Launiu St.
Kai'olu St.
Lewers St.
Aloha Dr.
Manukai St.

Kalākaua Ave.

Kūhiō Ave.

Waikīkī Shopping Plaza

2100 Kalākaua

King Kalākaua Plaza

Fort DeRussy Military Reservation

Lau'ula St.

6

S DFS Galleria

S Seaside Ave.

P

Saratoga Rd.

Beach Walk

4

5

Lewers St.

Royal Hawaiian Ave.

Ena Rd.

Ala Wai Blvd.

Hobron La.

Ala Moana Blvd.

2

Helumoa Rd.

Kālia Rd.

Ala Moana Blvd.

Holomoana St.

Paoa Pl.

Kālia Rd.

Ala Wai Yacht Harbor

1

P

Duke Kahanamoku Beach

Ft. DeRussy Beach

3

7

Kal

Gray's Beach

Māmala Bay

Ala Wai Yacht Harbor . . . **1**

Diamond Head State Monument and Park . . .**18**

Duke Kahanamoku Statue **11**

First Hawaiian Bank **5**

Gump Building **6**

Halekūlani **7**

Hilton Hawaiian Village Beach Resort and Spa . . .**2**

Honolulu Zoo **13**

Kahuna (Wizard) Stones of Waikīkī **10**

Kapi'olani Bandstand **15**

Royal Hawaiian Hotel . . .**8**

Sheraton Moana Surfrider **9**

The Urasenke Foundation **4**

U.S. Army Museum **3**

Waikīkī Aquarium **16**

Waikīkī Historic Trail . . .**12**

Waikīkī Shell **14**

Waikīkī War Memorial Natatorium **17**

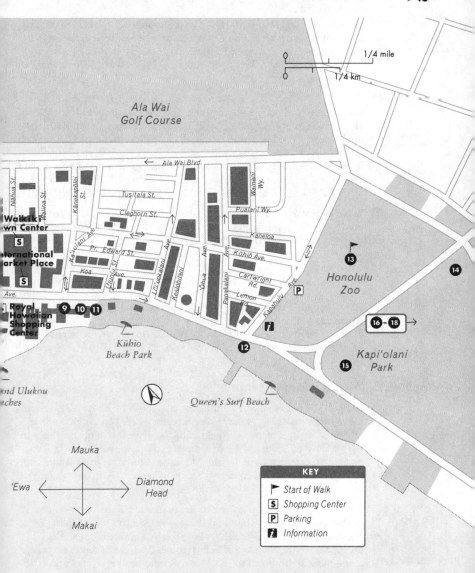

Ala Wai
Golf Course

1/4 mile

1/4 km

← Ala Wai Blvd.

Nahua St.

Walina St.

Kanekapolei St.

Tusitala St.

Cleghorn St.

Ka'iulani Ave.

Pr. Edward St.

K'oa Ave.

Uluniu Ave.

Lili'uokalani Ave.

Kealohilani Ave.

'Ohua Ave.

Ala Wai Blvd.

Walaiani Wy.

Pualani Wy.

Kaneloa

Kūhiō Ave.

Paoakalani Ave.

Cartwright Rd.

Lemon Rd.

Kapahulu Ave.

Waikiki
Town Center

S

International
Market Place

S

Ave.

Royal
Hawaiian
Shopping
Center

9 **10** **11**

Kūhio
Beach Park

12

and Ulukou
aches

Queen's Surf Beach

P

i

Honolulu
Zoo

13

14

16 – 18 →

15

Kapi'olani
Park

Mauka

'Ewa ←——→ Diamond
Head

Makai

KEY

⚑ Start of Walk

S Shopping Center

P Parking

i Information

flects the influences of centuries of Zen Buddhism. Each ceremony lasts approximately an hour; you can participate or just watch. Wear something comfortable enough for sitting on the floor (but no shorts, please). ✉ *245 Saratoga Rd., Waikīkī* ☎ *808/923–3059* ✉ *Minimum donation $3* ☯ *Wed. and Fri. 10–noon.*

❸ U.S. Army Museum. The museum at Fort DeRussy has an intimidating collection of war memorabilia. The major focus is on World War II, but exhibits range from ancient Hawaiian weaponry to displays relating to the Vietnam War. It's within Battery Randolph (Building 32), a bunker built in 1911 as a key to the defense of Pearl Harbor and Honolulu. Some of its walls are 22 feet thick. Guided group tours can be arranged; self-guided audio tours are also available. ✉ *Fort DeRussy, Bldg. 32, Kālia Rd., Waikīkī* ☎ *808/438–2822* ✉ *Free* ☯ *Tues.–Sun. 10–4:15.*

⑫ Waikīkī Historic Trail. Take a walk back in time to the Waikīkī of yesteryear along this scenic route. About a dozen "bronze surfboard" markers provide not only a written description of the sights along the way, but also include photography taken at those very same spots over the last 100 years. You get an intimate glance into Waikīkī's history as the playground of royalty, celebrities, and generations of tourists. Begin your tour of the trail at the standing bronze surfboard next to the Duke Kahanamoku statue. Free 90-minute guided walking tours begin at the Royal Hawaiian Shopping Center's entertainment stage at 9 AM on Tuesday, Thursday, and Saturday. ✉ *Waikīkī Beach, Diamond Head side of Sheraton Moana Surfrider, Waikīkī* ☎ *808/737–6442* ⊕ *www. waikikihistorictrail.com.*

Kapi'olani Park & Diamond Head

Kapi'olani Park, established during the late 1800s by King Kalākaua and named after his queen, is a 500-acre expanse where you can play all sorts of sports, enjoy a picnic, see wild animals, or hear live music. It lies in the shadow of Diamond Head Crater, perhaps Hawai'i's most recognizable natural landmark. Diamond Head got its name from sailors who thought they had found precious gems on its slopes. The diamonds proved to be volcanic refuse.

a good tour

This walk begins on the corner of Kalākaua and Kapahulu avenues, at the **Honolulu Zoo** ⑬ ▶. The zoo occupies the 'ewa end of Kapi'olani Park. Metered parking is available all along the makai side of the park and in the lot next to the zoo. Also, TheBus (routes 22 and 58) makes stops here along the way from and to Ala Moana Center and Sea Life Park.

■ **TIP→→** On weekends look for the Zoo Fence Art Mart, on Monsarrat Avenue outside the zoo, on the Diamond Head side, for affordable artwork by contemporary artists.

Across Monsarrat Avenue, between Kalākaua Avenue and Pākī Avenue in Kapi'olani Park, is the **Waikīkī Shell** ⑭, Honolulu's outdoor concert venue. Cut across the park toward the ocean to the **Kapi'olani Bandstand** ⑮, where you can hear more free island tunes on days when community events are taking place.

Cross Kalākaua Avenue toward the ocean to the **Waikīkī Aquarium** ⑯ and its neighbor, the **Waikīkī War Memorial Natatorium** ⑰, an open-air swimming stadium built in 1927 to commemorate lives lost in World War I.

As it leaves Kapiʻolani Park, Kalākaua Avenue forks into Diamond Head Road, a scenic 2-mi stretch popular with walkers and joggers, and winds around the base of Diamond Head alongside the ocean, passing handsome Diamond Head Lighthouse (not open to the public). Lookout areas offer views of the surfers and windsurfers below. The hike to the summit of **Diamond Head State Monument and Park** ⑱ requires strenuous walking. To save time and energy, drive, don't walk, along Kalakaua Avenue, turn left at Monsarrat Avenue, head a mile up the hill, and look for a sign on the right to the entrance to the crater. Drive through the tunnel to the inside of the crater. The trail begins at the parking lot.

TIMING Budget a full day to see Kapiʻolani Park and Diamond Head. If you want to hike up to the crater's summit, do it before breakfast. That way you beat not only the heat but the crowds. Hiking Diamond Head takes an hour round-trip, but factor in some extra time to enjoy the views from the top. Keep an eye on your watch if you're there at day's end, because the gates close promptly at 6. If you want to see the Honolulu Zoo, it's best to get there right when it opens, since the animals are livelier in the cool of the morning. Give the aquarium an hour, including 10 minutes in its Sea Visions Theater.

What to See

★ ⑱ **Diamond Head State Monument and Park.** Panoramas from this 760-foot extinct volcanic peak, once used as a military fortification, extend from Waikīkī and Honolulu in one direction and out to Koko Head in the other, with surfers and windsurfers scattered like confetti on the cresting waves below. This 360-degree perspective is a great orientation for first-time visitors of both this island, its neighbors, and this pyroclastic volcano. On a clear day you can even see the islands of Maui and Molokaʻi if you look to your left. The ¾-mi trail starts at the crater floor. New lighting inside the summit tunnel and spiral staircase eases the way to the top. Take bottled water with you on this hike to ensure that you stay hydrated under the tropical sun. ✉ *Diamond Head Rd. at 18th Ave., Waikīkī* ☎ *808/587–0285* ⊕ *www.state.hi.us/dlnr/dsp/oahu.html* ✉ *$1 per person, $5 per vehicle.* ☉ *Daily 6–6.*

🌀 ▶ ⑬ **Honolulu Zoo.** To get a glimpse of the endangered nēnē, the Hawaiʻi state bird, check out the Kipuka Nēnē Sanctuary. There are bigger and better zoos, but this one is lovely and has some great programs. Most notably, on Wednesday evenings in summer, the zoo puts on The Wildest Show in Town, a series of $1 admission concerts. The offerings for families are also appealing. Consider a family sleepover inside the zoo during "Snooze in the Zoo" events, which take place on a Friday or Saturday night every month. Or just head for the petting zoo, where kids can pet a llama and meet Abbey, the zoo's resident monitor lizard. ✉ *151 Kapahulu Ave., Waikīkī* ☎ *808/971–7171* ⊕ *www.honoluluzoo.org* ✉ *$6* ☉ *Daily 9–4:30.*

⓯ Kapi'olani Bandstand. A replica of the Victorian Kapi'olani Bandstand, which was originally built in the late 1890s, is Kapi'olani Park's centerpiece for community entertainment and concerts. The nation's only city-sponsored band, the Royal Hawaiian Band, performs free concerts on Sunday afternoons. Local newspapers list entertainment information. ✉ *'Ewa end of Kapi'olani Park, mauka side of Kalākaua Ave., Waikīkī.*

> ### UNDER THE STARS
>
> Waikīkī's entertainment scene isn't limited to dinner shows and lounge acts. There's plenty of free or nearly free offerings right on the beach and at Kapi'olani Park. Queen's Surf Beach hosts the popular Sunset on the Beach, which brings big-screen showings of recent Hollywood blockbusters to the great outdoors. Festivities get underway at 4 PM, and the movie usually begins right after sunset. Also, during the summer months, the Honolulu Zoo has weekly concerts, and admission is just $1. (⇨ See Entertainment & Nightlife *later in this chapter.*)

★ ☙ ⓰ **Waikīkī Aquarium.** This amazing little attraction harbors more than 2,500 organisms and 420 species of Hawaiian and South Pacific marine life, endangered Hawaiian monk seals, sharks, and the only chambered nautilus living in captivity. The Edge of the Reef exhibit showcases five different types of reef environments found along Hawai'i's shorelines. Check out the Sea Visions Theater, the biodiversity exhibit, and the self-guided audio tour, which is included with admission. Programs include Exploring the Reef at Night, Shark Nites, Stingray Tracking, and Aquarium After Dark activities. ✉ *2777 Kalākaua Ave., Waikīkī* ☎ *808/923–9741* ⊕ *www.waquarium. org* 🎟 *$9* ☉ *Daily 9–4:30.*

⓮ **Waikīkī Shell.** Local people bring a picnic and grab one of the 6,000 "grass seats" (lawn seating) for music under the stars. Here's a chance to enjoy some of Hawai'i's best musicians as well as visiting guest artists. Concerts are held May 1 to Labor Day, with a few winter dates, weather permitting. Check the newspapers to see who is performing. ✉ *2805 Monsarrat Ave., Waikīkī* ☎ *808/924–8934* ⊕ *www.blaisdellcenter.com.*

⓱ **Waikīkī War Memorial Natatorium.** This 1927 World War I monument, dedicated to the 102 Hawaiian servicemen who lost their lives in battle, stands proudly—its 20-foot archway, which was completely restored in 2002, is floodlighted at night. The 100-meter saltwater swimming pool, the training spot for Olympians Johnny Weissmuller and Buster Crabbe and the U.S. Army during World War II, is closed to the public. The future of the monument is currently up in the air, as plans for an $11-million renovation were scrapped in early 2005. ✉ *2777 Kalākaua Ave., Waikīkī.*

need a break? According to legend, Robert Louis Stevenson once sat beneath the eponymous *hau* tree in the courtyard of the **Hau Tree Lānai** (✉ 2863 Kalākaua Ave. ☎ 808/921–7066). You can enjoy the same shade, plus breakfast, lunch, or dinner, at this find in the New Otani Kaimana Beach Hotel, next to the Natatorium.

Chinatown

Honolulu's 15-Block Melting Pot

Honolulu's Chinatown was established in the late 1800s by laborers looking for a new life after their contracts with the sugar plantations ended. The neighborhood—bordered by North Beretania Street and North King Street to the north and south and Bethel Street and River Street to the east and west—has a tumultuous and fascinating history. It was twice destroyed by fire, first in 1886 and again in 1900 (the later fire was deliberately set to clear the area of the bubonic plague), but was lovingly rebuilt both times. By the 1930s it was a real center of influence, benefiting from a prime location just minutes from Honolulu Harbor. In the 1940s, however, the neighborhood became notorious as the seedy stomping ground of military personnel, who found their way here to sample the exotic food, as well as the bars, pool halls, tattoo parlors, and prostitution houses. For years after, Chinatown was crime-ridden and many of its historic buildings fell into disrepair. It wasn't until 1973, when the federal government declared the neighborhood a historic area, that Chinatown's slow upswing began. Since then new residential buildings and commercial space have been added and many cultural gems have been restored.

Today, visiting a revitalized Chinatown is like taking a two-hour tour throughout Asia. The neighborhood still retains much of its original architecture—notable are the Chinatown Police Station and the Hawai'i Theatre Center. At its heart is the **O'ahu Marketplace** (✉ N. King and Kekaulike Sts.), where everything a Chinese chef could desire is on display. Even amid the flurry of modern retail outlets, including the Maunakea Marketplace, Mahalo Antique Mall, and the more contemporary Chinese Cultural Plaza, are places of calm in the Taoist Lum Sai Ho Tong Society Temple, the Shinto Izumo Taisha Mission Cultural Hall, and the Kuan Yin Buddhist Temple. The wild orchid gardens at the **Foster Botanical Garden** (✉ N. Vineyard Blvd. at Nu'uanu Ave. ☎ 808/522-7060), open daily 9–4, are perfect for quiet contemplation.

The contemporary side of Chinatown is just as exciting. Though there's plenty of yesteryear to be found in the herb and antique shops, Chinatown is also a great place to shop for chic modern-day accoutrements. Additionally, Nu'uanu Avenue, north of Hotel Street known as "NOHO" is known for its smattering of trendy art galleries. Of course, one of the main reasons to visit this lively neighborhood is the food. Don't miss the *udon* noodles at the **Yat Hung Chow Noodle Factory** (✉ 150 N. King St. ☎ 808/531-7982). Equally delicious are the pastries at **Shung Chong Yuein** (✉ 1027 Maunakea St. ☎ 808/531-1983).

Downtown Honolulu: The Capitol District & Chinatown

Honolulu's past and present play a delightful counterpoint throughout the downtown sector. Modern skyscrapers stand directly across from the Aloha Tower, which was built in 1926 and was, until the early 1960s, the tallest structure in Honolulu. Buildings here tell the story of Hawai'i's history in architecture, from the Chinatown buildings of the late 1800s to the 21st-century design of the First Hawaiian Building. Washington Place, built in 1846, was the home of Queen Lili'uokalani until her death in 1917, and until 2003 it served as the residence for Hawai'i's governors. A new governor's residence has been built alongside Washington Place, and plans are under way to open Washington Place to the public as a historical museum.

a good walk

To reach Downtown Honolulu from Waikīkī by car, take Ala Moana Boulevard to Alakea Street. You can also take Route 19 or 20 of TheBus to the Aloha Tower Marketplace.

Begin at the **Hawai'i Maritime Center** ⑲ ☞ at the harborfront, across Ala Moana Boulevard from Alakea Street. Just 'ewa of the Hawai'i Maritime Center is **Aloha Tower Marketplace** ⑳, a complex of harborside shops and restaurants where you can also view the luxury cruise liners in port and the traditional Aloha Boat Days celebrations that greet each arrival.

Cross Ala Moana Boulevard, walk a block 'ewa, and turn mauka on Fort Street Mall, a pedestrian walkway, until you reach King Street. Turn left, and after a few blocks you reach **Chinatown** ㉑, the old section of Downtown Honolulu. Here you can find a Buddhist temple, a Japanese shrine, shops, art galleries, restaurants, and a big open market. The **Hawai'i Theater** ㉒ on Bethel Street is downtown's top entertainment venue.

From the theater, walk makai down to King Street, then head Diamond Head for two blocks until you reach Bishop Street. On the mauka side is lovely **Tamarind Park,** a popular lunchtime picnic spot for Honolulu office workers who gather under its shady plumeria, *kukui*, monkeypod—and one tamarind—trees. Continue down King Street and hang a left onto Richards Street. At the corner of Richards and Hotel streets

> ### WHERE DO I PARK?
>
> The best parking downtown is street parking along Punchbowl Street. There are also public parking lots (75¢ per half hour for the first two hours) in buildings along Alakea Street and Bethel Street (Gateway Plaza on Bethel Street is a good choice).

is the No. 1 Capitol District Building, which houses the **Hawai'i State Art Museum** ㉓. Walk back along Richards Street toward King Street until you reach **'Iolani Palace** ㉔, on the left-hand side. This graceful Victorian structure was built by King David Kalākaua in 1882. Also on the palace grounds is the Kalākaua Coronation Bandstand, where the Royal Hawaiian Band performs at noon most Fridays.

Across King Street from 'Iolani Palace is Ali'iōlani Hale, the judiciary building that once served as the parliament hall during the kingship era. In front of it is the gilded **Kamehameha I Statue** ㉕, which honors Hawai'i's

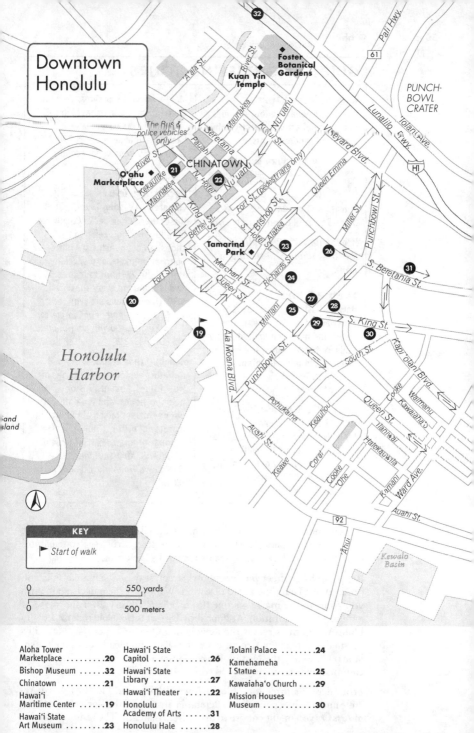

Downtown Honolulu

PUNCH-BOWL CRATER

Foster Botanical Gardens

Kuan Yin Temple

The BUS & police vehicles only

CHINATOWN

O'ahu Marketplace

Tamarind Park

Honolulu Harbor

...and ...sland

KEY

▶ *Start of walk*

0 ————— 550 yards
0 ————— 500 meters

Kewalo Basin

Aloha Tower
Marketplace **20**

Bishop Museum **32**

Chinatown **21**

Hawai'i
Maritime Center **19**

Hawai'i State
Art Museum **23**

Hawai'i State
Capitol **26**

Hawai'i State
Library **27**

Hawai'i Theater **22**

Honolulu
Academy of Arts **31**

Honolulu Hale **28**

'Iolani Palace **24**

Kamehameha
I Statue **25**

Kawaiaha'o Church **29**

Mission Houses
Museum **30**

GUIDED SIGHTSEEING TOURS

Bus & Van Tours

Ask exactly what the tour includes in the way of actual get-off-the-bus stops and window sights.

Polynesian Adventure Tours. ☎ 808/833–3000 ⊕ *www.polyad.com.*

Polynesian Hospitality. ☎ 808/526–3565 ⊕ *www.kobay.com.*

Roberts Hawai'i. ☎ 808/539–9400 ⊕ *www.robertshawaii.com.*

Theme Tours

Hawaiian Islands Eco-tours, Ltd.'s. Experienced guides take nature lovers and hikers on limited-access trails for tours ranging from hidden waterfalls to bird-watching. ☎ 808/236–7766 ⊕ *www.hikeoahu.com.*

Home of the Brave and Top Gun Tours. Perfect for military-history buffs. Narrated tours visit O'ahu's military bases and the National Memorial Cemetery of the Pacific. ☎ 808/396–8112 ⊕ *www.pearlharborhq.com.*

Mauka Makai Excursions. Visit the ancient Hawaiian archaeological, legendary, and nature sites that islanders hold sacred. ☎ 808/255–2206 ⊕ *www.hawaiianecotours.net.*

Walking Tours

Chinatown Walking Tour. Meet at the Chinese Chamber of Commerce for a fascinating peek into herbal shops, an acupuncturist's office, open-air markets, and specialty stores. The 2½-hour tour costs $5 and is available every Tuesday at 9:30. Reservations are required. ✉ *Chinese Chamber of Commerce, 42 N. King St., Downtown Honolulu* ☎ 808/533–3181.

Honolulu Time Walks. Costumed narrators explore the mysteries of Honolulu–its haunts, historic neighborhoods, and the different but not always talked about eras in its colorful history. Tour and seminar programs cost $7 to $45. ✉ *2634 S. King St., Suite 3, Downtown Honolulu* ☎ 808/943–0371.

greatest monarch. Walk one block mauka up Richards Street to tour the **Hawai'i State Capitol** ㉖. Almost across the street from the state capitol is Washington Place, the home of Hawai'i's governor.

Return to King Street via Punchbowl Street, stay on the mauka side, and proceed in a Diamond Head direction. Walk past the palace again until you come to the massive stone **Hawai'i State Library** ㉗, a showcase of architectural restoration. At Punchbowl Street is **Honolulu Hale** ㉘, or City Hall. Across the street is the **Kawaiaha'o Church** ㉙, perhaps Hawai'i's most famous religious structure. On the Diamond Head side of the Kawaiaha'o Church is the **Mission Houses Museum** ㉚, where the first American missionaries in Hawai'i lived.

From here it's three long blocks toward Diamond Head to Ward Avenue and one block mauka to Beretania Street and the **Honolulu Academy of Arts** ㉛ (you might choose to drive there instead). The museum houses

Western and Asian art. The **Bishop Museum** ③ is west of downtown, near the Likelike exit off H–1. You will need to drive to get there, but the spectacular collection of Hawaiian art and artifacts is more than worth the extra mileage.

TIMING Downtown Honolulu merits a full day of your time. Be sure to stop by the palace Tuesday through Saturday, the only days tours are offered. Remember that the Mission Houses Museum is closed Sunday and Monday and the Honolulu Academy of Arts is closed Monday. Saturday morning is the best time to walk through Chinatown; that's when the open-air markets do their biggest business with local families. A walk through Chinatown can take at least an hour, as can tours of the Mission Houses and 'Iolani Palace. Wrap up your day at sunset with refreshments or dinner back at the Aloha Tower Marketplace, which stays open late into the evening, with live entertainment on the harborfront.

What to See

☾ ② **Aloha Tower Marketplace.** Two stories of shops and kiosks sell island-inspired clothing, jewelry, art, and home furnishings. The Marketplace, located on the Honolulu Harborfront, also has indoor and outdoor restaurants, as well as live entertainment. For a bird's-eye view of this working harbor, take a free ride up to the observation deck of Aloha Tower, which anchors the market. The Marketplace's location makes it an ideal spot for watching the arrival of cruise ships. On Aloha Boat Days, the waterfront comes alive with entertainment and hula dancers who greet and send off the arriving and departing ships. ⊠ *1 Aloha Tower Dr., at Piers 8, 9, and 10, Downtown Honolulu* ☎ *808/528–5700, 808/566–2337 for entertainment info* ⊕ *www.alohatower.com* ☾ *Mon. Sat. 9–6, Sun. 9–6, restaurants 10 AM–2 AM.*

★ ③ **Bishop Museum.** Founded in 1889 by Charles R. Bishop as a memorial to his wife, Princess Bernice Pauahi, the museum began as a repository for the royal possessions of this last direct descendant of King Kamehameha the Great. Today it's the Hawai'i State Museum of Natural and Cultural History and houses more than 24.7 million items that tell the history of the Hawaiian Islands and their Pacific neighbors. The Hawaiian Hall houses world-famous displays of Polynesian artifacts: lustrous feather capes, the skeleton of a giant sperm whale, photography and crafts displays, and an authentic, well-preserved grass house inside a two-story 19th-century Victorian style gallery. Also check out the planetarium, daily hula and Hawaiian crafts demonstrations, special exhibits, and the Shop Pacifica. The building alone, with its huge Victorian turrets and immense stone walls, is worth seeing. ⊠ *1525 Bernice St.* ☎ *808/847–3511* ⊕ *www.bishopmuseum.org* ☒ *$14.95* ☾ *Daily 9–5.*

② **Chinatown.** Noodle factories and herb shops, lei stands and acupuncture studios, art galleries and Chinese and Thai restaurants make up this historic neighborhood. A major highlight is the colorful O'ahu Market, an open-air emporium with hanging pigs' heads, display cases of fresh fish, row after row of exotic fruits and vegetables, and vendors of all ethnic backgrounds. Check out the Chinese Cultural Plaza's Moongate stage for cultural events, especially around the Chinese New Year. A walking map of the area can be downloaded from the Web site. (See Chinatown CloseUp, p. 47.) ✉ *King St. between Smith and River Sts., Chinatown* ⊕ *www.chinatownhi.com.*

> **need a break?**
>
> For an exotic lunch stop by **Duk's Bistro** (✉ 1188 Maunakea St., Chinatown ☎ 808/531–6325), a tiny three-room eatery facing Chinatown's busiest street (near the intersection with Beretania Street) and featuring a French-Vietnamese menu. Spring for the shrimp, mushroom, and taro spring rolls or have a "Meal in a Bowl," brimming with rice noodles and fresh island vegetables.

🖐 ➤ ⑲ **Hawai'i Maritime Center.** The story of the Islands begins on the seas. The **Kalākaua Boat House** has interactive exhibits where you can learn about Hawai'i's whaling days, the history of Honolulu Harbor, the Clipper seaplane, and surfing and windsurfing in Hawai'i. Moored next to the Boat House is the *Falls of Clyde.* Built in 1778, this four-masted, square-rigged ship once brought tea from China to the U.S. West Coast and is now used as a museum. Self-guided audio tours are available in English, Japanese, and Korean. ✉ *Ala Moana Blvd. at Pier 7, Downtown Honolulu* ☎ *808/536–6373* ⊕ *www.bishopmuseum.org/exhibits/hmc/hmc.html* 🖭 *$7.50* ⊙ *Daily 8:30–5.*

㉓ **Hawai'i State Art Museum.** The second floor of the State Capitol District Building has 12,000 feet of gallery space dedicated to the art of Hawai'i in all its ethnic diversity. The Diamond Head Gallery features new acquisitions and thematic shows from the State Art Collection and the State Foundation on Culture and the Arts. The 'Ewa Gallery houses more than 150 works documenting Hawai'i's visual-arts history since becoming a state in 1959. Also included are a sculpture gallery as well as a café, a gift shop, and educational meeting rooms. ✉ *250 S. Hotel St., 2nd fl., Downtown Honolulu* ☎ *808/586–0300* ⊕ *www.hawaii.gov/sfca* 🖭 *Free* ⊙ *Tues.–Sat. 10–4.*

㉖ **Hawai'i State Capitol.** The capitol's architecture is richly symbolic: the columns look like palm trees, the legislative chambers are shaped like volcanic cinder cones, and the central court is open to the sky, representing Hawai'i's open society. Replicas of the Hawai'i state seal, each weighing 7,500 pounds, hang above both its entrances. The building, which in 1969 replaced 'Iolani Palace as the seat of government, is surrounded by reflecting pools, just as the Islands are embraced by water. ✉ *215 S. Beretania St., Downtown Honolulu* ☎ *808/586–0146* 🖭 *Free* ⊙ *Guided tours on request weekday afternoons.*

㉗ **Hawai'i State Library.** This beautifully renovated main library was originally built in 1913. Its Samuel M. Kamakau Reading Room, on the first floor in the mauka courtyard, houses an extensive Hawai'i and Pacific book collection and pays tribute to Kamakau, one of Hawai'i's noted historians. ✉ *478 King St., Downtown Honolulu* ☎ *808/586–3500* 🖭 *Free* ⊙ *Tues., Fri., and Sat. 9–5, Wed. 10–5, Thurs. 9–8.*

㉒ **Hawai'i Theatre.** Opened in 1922, this theater earned rave reviews for its neoclassical theme with Corinthian columns, marble statues, and plush carpeting and drapery. Nicknamed the "Pride of the Pacific," the facility was rescued from demolition in the early 1980s and underwent a $30-million renovation. Listed on both the State and National Register of Historic Places, it has become the centerpiece of revitalization efforts of Honolulu's downtown area. The 1,200-seat venue hosts concerts, theatrical productions, dance performances, and film screenings. ⊠ *1130 Bethel St., Downtown Honolulu* ☏ *808/528–0506* ⌨ *$5* ☉ *1-hr guided tours held every Tues.at 11.*

need a break?

In a vintage brick building at the corner of Nu'uanu Street, **Murphy's Bar & Grill** (⊠ 2 Merchant St., Downtown Honolulu ☏ 808/531–0422), is an old-fashioned Irish pub, sports bar, and kamā'aina-style family restaurant all rolled in one. Comfort food is the order of the day, from sizzling steaks and sandwiches to salads and local favorites.

㉛ Honolulu Academy of Arts. The academy dates to 1927 and has an impressive permanent collection that includes Hiroshige's *ukiyo-e* Japanese prints, donated by James Michener; Italian Renaissance paintings; and American and European art. Six open-air courtyards provide a casual counterpart to the more formal galleries. The Luce Pavilion complex has a traveling-exhibit gallery, a Hawaiian gallery, a café, and a gift shop. The Academy Theatre screens art films. There are select Islamic-art tours offered by the academy's art center that take you to the Doris Duke Foundation for Islamic Art, located within Duke's former Diamond Head estate, Shangri-La. Tours of this estate require reservations in advance. Guided tours of the academy are Tuesday–Saturday at 11 AM and Sunday at 1:15 PM. Call about special exhibits, concerts, and films. ⊠ *900 S. Beretania St., Downtown Honolulu* ☏ *808/532–8700* ⊕ *www.honoluluacademy. org* ⌨ *$7 Academy, free 1st Wed. of month, $25 Shangri-La Islamic Art Tours* ☉ *Tues.–Sat. 10–4:30, Sun. 1–5.*

㉘ Honolulu Hale. This Mediterranean Renaissance–style building was constructed in 1929 and serves as the center of city government. Stroll through the cool, open-ceiling lobby with exhibits of local artists, and time your visit to coincide with one of the free concerts sometimes offered in the evening, when the building stays open late. During the winter holiday season, the Hale becomes the focal point for the annual Honolulu City Lights program. ⊠ *530 S. King St., Downtown Honolulu* ☏ *808/523–4654* ⌨ *Free* ☉ *Weekdays 8–4:30.*

㉔ 'Iolani Palace. America's only royal residence was built in 1882 on the site of an earlier palace, and it contains the thrones of King Kalākaua and his successor (and sister) Queen Lili'uokalani. Bucking the stereotype of the primitive islander, the palace had electricity and telephone lines installed even before the White House did. Downstairs galleries showcase the royal jewelry, and kitchen and offices of the monarchy. The palace is open for guided tours only, and reservations are essential. Take a look at the gift shop, formerly the 'Iolani Barracks, built to house the Royal Guard. ⊠ *King and Richards Sts., Downtown Honolulu* ☏ *808/522–0832* ⊕ *www.iolanipalace.org* ⌨ *Grand Tour $20, downstairs galleries only $6* ☉ *Grand Tour Tues.–Sat. 9–2, with tours beginning on half-hr; Galleries tour, Tues.–Sat. 9–4.*

㉕ **Kamehameha I Statue.** This downtown landmark pays tribute to the Big Island chieftain who united all the warring Hawaiian Islands into one kingdom at the turn of the 18th century. The statue, which stands with one arm outstretched in welcome, is one of three originally cast in Paris, France, by American sculptor T. R. Gould; the original version is in Kapa'au, on the Big Island, near the king's birthplace. Each year on the king's birthday, June 11, the statue is draped in fresh lei that reach lengths of 18 feet and longer. ✉ *417 S. King St., outside Ali'iōlani Hale, Downtown Honolulu.*

㉙ **Kawaiaha'o Church.** Fancifully called Hawai'i's Westminster Abbey, this 14,000-coral-block house of worship witnessed the coronations, weddings, and funerals of generations of Hawaiian royalty. Each of the building's coral blocks was quarried from reefs offshore at depths of more than 20 feet and transported to this site. Interior woodwork was created from the forests of the Ko'olau Mountains. The upper gallery has an exhibit of paintings of the royal families. The graves of missionaries and of King Lunalilo are in the yard. Services in English and Hawaiian are held each Sunday. Although there are no guided tours, you can look around the church at no cost. ✉ *957 Punchbowl St., at King St., Downtown Honolulu* ☎ *808/522–1333* ⊠ *Free* ☯ *English service Sun. at 8* AM *and Wed. at 6* PM, *Hawaiian service Sun. at 10:30* AM.

㉚ **Mission Houses Museum.** The determined Hawai'i missionaries arrived in 1820, gaining royal favor and influencing every aspect of island life. Their descendants became leaders in government and business. You can walk through their original dwellings, including a white-frame house that was prefabricated in New England and shipped around the Horn—it's Hawai'i's oldest wooden structure. Certain areas of the museum may be seen only on a one-hour guided tour. ✉ *553 S. King St., Downtown Honolulu* ☎ *808/531–0481* ⊕ *www.lava.net/~mhm* ⊠ *$10* ☯ *Tues.–Sat. 10–6; guided tours at 11, 1, 2:45 and 4:30.*

Pearl Harbor   See Page 55

Southeast O'ahu

At once historic and contemporary, serene and active, the east end of O'ahu holds within its relatively small area remarkable variety and picture-perfect scenery of windswept cliffs and wave-dashed shores.

a good drive

From Waikīkī there are two routes to Lunalilo Freeway (H–1). On the Diamond Head end, go mauka on Kapahulu Avenue and follow the signs to the freeway. On the 'ewa end, take Ala Wai Boulevard and turn mauka at Kalākaua Avenue, staying on it until it ends at Beretania Street, which is one-way going left. Turn right off Beretania Street at Pi'ikoi Street, and the signs will direct you onto the freeway heading west.

Take the freeway exit marked Pali Highway (Route 61), one of three roads that cut through the Ko'olau Mountains. Heading toward Wind-

Continued on page 61

USS *West Virginia* (BB48), 7 December 1941

PEARL HARBOR

December 7, 1941. Every American then alive recalls exactly what he or she was doing when the news broke that the Japanese had bombed Pearl Harbor, the catalyst that brought the United States into World War II.

Although it was clear by late 1941 that war with Japan was inevitable, no one in authority seems to have expected the attack to come in just this way, at just this time. So when the Japanese bombers swept through a gap in Oʻahu's Koʻolau Mountains in the hazy light of morning, they found the bulk of America's Pacific fleet right where they hoped it would be: docked like giant stepping stones across the calm waters of the bay named for the pearl oysters that once prospered there. More than 2,000 people died that day, including 49 civilians. A dozen ships were sunk. And on the nearby air bases, virtually every American military aircraft was destroyed or damaged. The attack was a stunning success, but it lit a fire under America, which went to war with "Remember Pearl Harbor" as its battle cry. Here, in what is still a key Pacific naval base, the attack is remembered every day by thousands of visitors, including many curious Japanese, who for years heard little WWII history in their own country. In recent years, the Memorial has been the site of reconciliation ceremonies involving Pearl Harbor veterans from both sides.

GETTING AROUND

Pearl Harbor is both a working military base and also the most-visited O'ahu attraction. Three distinct destinations share a parking lot and are linked by footpath, shuttle, and ferry.

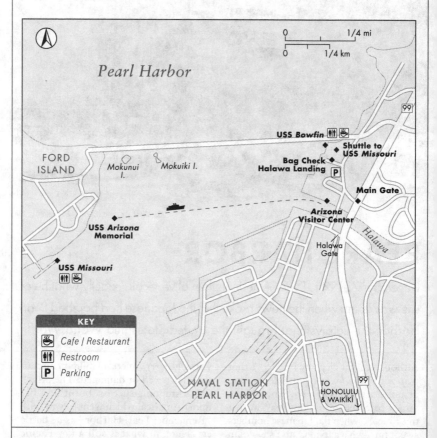

The USS *Arizona* Visitor Center is accessible from the parking lot. The *Arizona* Memorial itself is in the middle of the harbor; get tickets for the ferry ride at the Visitor center. The USS *Bowfin* is also reachable from the parking lot. The USS *Missouri* is docked at Ford Island, a restricted area of the naval base. Vehicular access is prohibited. To get there, take a shuttle bus from the station near the *Bowfin*.

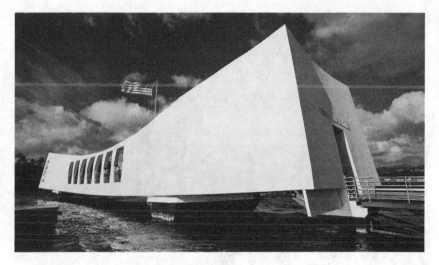

ARIZONA MEMORIAL

Snugged up tight in a row of seven battleships off Ford Island, the USS *Arizona* took a direct hit that December morning, exploded, and rests still on the shallow bottom where she settled.

A visit to the *Arizona* Memorial begins prosaically—a line, a ticket that assigns you to a group and tour time, a wait filled with shopping, visiting the museum, and strolling the grounds. When your number is called, you watch a 23-minute documentary film then board the ferry to the memorial. The swooping, stark-white memorial, which straddles the wreck of the USS *Arizona,* was designed by Honolulu architect Alfred Preis to represent both the depths of the low-spirited, early days of the war, and the uplift of victory. After the carnival-like courtyard, a somber, contemplative mood descends upon visitors during the ferry ride; this is a place where 1,777 people died. Gaze at the names of the dead carved into the wall of white marble. Scatter flowers (but no leis—the string is bad for the fish). Salute the flag. Remember Pearl Harbor.

808/422–0561 or 808/423–2263
www.nps.gov/usar

USS *MISSOURI* (BB63)

Together with the *Arizona* Memorial, the *Missouri's* presence in Pearl Harbor perfectly bookends America's WWII experience that began December 7, 1941, and ended on the "Mighty Mo's" starboard deck with the signing of the Terms of Surrender.

Surrender of Japan, USS *Missouri*, 2 September 1945

In the parking area behind the USS *Bowfin* Museum, board a jitney for a breezy, eight-minute ride to Ford Island and the teak decks and towering superstructure of the *Missouri,* docked for good in the very harbor from which she first went to war on January 2, 1945. The last battleship ever built, the *Missouri* famously hosted the final act of WWII, the signing of the Terms of Surrender. The commission that governs this floating museum has surrounded her with buildings tricked out in WWII style—a Canteen that serves as an orientation space for tours, a WACs and WAVEs Lounge with a flight simulator the kids will love ($5 for one person, $18 for four), Truman's Line restaurant serving Navy-style meals, and a Victory Store housing a souvenir shop and covered with period mottos ("Don't be a blabateur.").

■ TIP➔➔ Definitely hook up with a tour guide (additional charge) or purchase an audio tour ($2)—these add a great deal to the experience.

The *Missouri* is all about numbers: 209 feet tall, six 239,000-pound guns, capable of firing up to 23 mi away. Absorb these during the tour, then stop to take advantage of the view from the decks. The Mo is a work in progress, with only a handful of her hundreds of spaces open to view.

808/423–2263 or 888/877–6477 www.ussmissouri.com

USS *BOWFIN* (SS287)

1

PEARL HARBOR

SUBMARINE MUSEUM & PARK

Launched one year to the day after the Pearl Harbor attack, the USS *Bowfin* sank 44 enemy ships during WWII and now serves as the centerpiece of a museum honoring all submariners.

Although the *Bowfin* no less than the *Arizona* Memorial commemorates the lost, the mood here is lighter. Perhaps it's the child-like scale of the boat, a metal tube just 16 feet in diameter, packed with ladders, hatches, and other obstacles, like the naval version of a jungle gym. Perhaps it's the World War II-era music that plays in the covered patio. Or it might be the museum s touching displays—the penciled sailor's journal, the Vargas girlie posters. Aboard the boat nicknamed Pearl Harbor Avenger, compartments are fitted out as though "Sparky" was away from the radio room just for a moment, and "Cooky" might be right back to his pots and pans. The museum includes many artifacts to spark family conversations, among them a vintage dive suit that looks too big for

Shaquille O'Neal. A caution: The *Bowfin* could be hazardous for very young children; no one under four allowed.

808/423–1342
www.bowfin.org

CALL FOR ACTION

Pearl Harbor attractions operate with the aid of nonprofit organizations; the *Missouri* and *Bowfin* receive no government funds at all. A $34 million campaign has begun to rebuild the inadequate and aging *Arizona* Memorial Visitor's Center and create a series of mini-museums that do justice to the events that took place at Pearl Harbor. If fund-raising goes as planned, the center likely will close in 2007 during renovations.

Want to help?

Arizona Memorial
www.pearlharbormemorial.com, raising funds for a new visitor's center

USS *Missouri* Memorial Association
www.ussmissouri.com, membership program supports ongoing restoration

Bowfin
www.bowfin.org; no online giving, send check to USS *Bowfin*, 11 Arizona Memorial Dr., Honolulu, HI 96818

PLAN YOUR PEARL HARBOR DAY
LIKE A MILITARY CAMPAIGN

DIRECTIONS

Take H1 west from Waikīkī to Exit 15A and follow signs. Or take TheBus route 20 or 47 from Waikīkī. Beware high-priced private shuttles. It's a 30-minute drive from Waikīkī.

WHAT TO BRING

Picture ID is required during periods of high alert; bring it just in case.

You'll be standing, walking, and climbing all day. Wear something with lots of pockets and a pair of good walking shoes. Carry a light jacket, sunglasses, hat, and sunscreen.

No purses, packs, or bags are allowed. Take only what fits in your pockets. Cameras are okay but without bulky bags. A private bag storage booth is near the *Arizona* Memorial parking lot. Leave nothing in your car; theft is a problem despite bicycle security patrols.

HOURS

Hours are 8 AM to 5 PM for all attractions. However, the *Arizona* Memorial starts giving out tickets on a first-come, first-served basis at 7:30 AM; the last tickets are given out at 3 PM. Spring break, summer, and holidays are busiest, and tickets sometimes run out.

TICKETS

Arizona: Free. Add $5 for museum audio tours.

Missouri: $16 adults, $8 children. Add $6 for chief's guided tour or audio tour; add $33 for in-depth, behind-the-scenes tours.

Bowfin: $8 adults, $3 children. Add $2 for audio tours. Children under 4 may go into the museum but not aboard the *Bowfin*.

KIDS

This might be the day to enroll younger kids in the hotel children's program. Preschoolers chafe at long waits, and attractions involve some hazards for toddlers. Older kids enjoy the *Bowfin* and *Missouri,* especially.

MAKING THE MOST OF YOUR TIME

Expect to spend three hours minimum—that's if you hustle and skip audio tours. The better part of a day is better.

At the *Arizona* Memorial, you'll get a ticket, be given a tour time, and then have to wait — anywhere from 15 minutes to 3 hours. Everyone has to pick up their own ticket so you can't hold places. If you've got an hour or more, skip over to the *Bowfin* to fill the time.

SUGGESTED READING

Pearl Harbor and the USS Arizona Memorial, by Richard Wisniewski. $5.95. 64-page magazine-size quick history.

Bowfin, by Edwin P. Hoyt. $14.95. Dramatic story of undersea adventure.

The Last Battleship, by Scott C. S. Stone. $11.95. Story of the Mighty Mo.

ward Oʻahu via Pali Highway, pay a visit to the **National Memorial Cemetery of the Pacific (in Punchbowl Crater)** ㉝ ▶.

Take a few moments to honor the more than 44,000 war veterans who were laid to rest at this 112-acre cemetery. And while you're there, take in the sweeping views of Honolulu and Waikīkī—perhaps the finest on Oʻahu. Then head back up the Pali Highway to **Queen Emma Summer Palace** ㉞. The colonial-style white mansion, which once served as the summer retreat of King Kamehameha IV and his wife, Queen Emma, is now a museum.

As you drive toward the summit of the highway, the road is lined with sweet ginger in summer and red poinsettias in winter. If it's been raining, waterfalls will be tumbling down the chiseled cliffs of the Koʻolau. If it's windy, those waterfalls can look as if they're traveling up the cliffs, not down.

Watch for the turn to the **Nuʻuanu Pali Lookout** ㉟. There's a small parking lot and a lookout wall from which you can see all the way up and down the windward coast—a view that Mark Twain called the most beautiful in the world.

As you follow the highway down the other side of the mountain, continue straight along what becomes Kailua Road. If you're interested in Hawaiian history, look for the YMCA at the Castle Hospital junction of Kalanianaʻole Highway and Kailua Road. Behind it is **Ulupō Heiau** ㊱, an ancient outdoor shrine. Ready for a beach break? Head straight on Kailua Road to **Kailua Beach Park,** which many people consider the best on the island. The road twists and turns, so watch the signs.

Retracing your route back to Castle Junction, turn left at the intersection onto Kalanianaʻole Highway. Soon you come to the small town of **Waimānalo** ㊲. Waimānalo's two beaches are **Bellows Beach,** great for swimming and bodysurfing, and **Waimanalo Beach Park,** also safe for swimming.

Another mile along the highway, on the right, is **Sea Life Park** ㊳, home to the world's only "wholphin," the offspring of a whale and a dolphin. Across the highway from Sea Life Park is **Makapuʻu Beach,** a beautiful cove that's great for seasoned bodysurfers but treacherous for weak swimmers. The road winds up a hill, at the top of which is a turnoff on the makai side to **Makapuʻu Point** ㊴.

Next you see the inviting **Sandy Beach.** Tempting as this beach looks, it's not advisable to swim here because the waves are powerful and the rip currents more than tricky. From here the road twists and turns next to steep cliffs along the Koko Head shoreline. Offshore, the islands of Molokaʻi and Lānaʻi call like distant sirens, and every once in a while Maui is visible in blue silhouette. For the best photos, pull into the parking lot at **Hālona Blowhole** ㊵. At the top of the hill on the makai side of the road is the entrance to **Hanauma Bay Nature Preserve** ㊶, one of Oʻahu's most famous snorkeling destinations.

From here back to Waikīkī the highway passes several residential communities called Hawaiʻi Kai, Niu Valley, and ʻĀina Haina, each of which

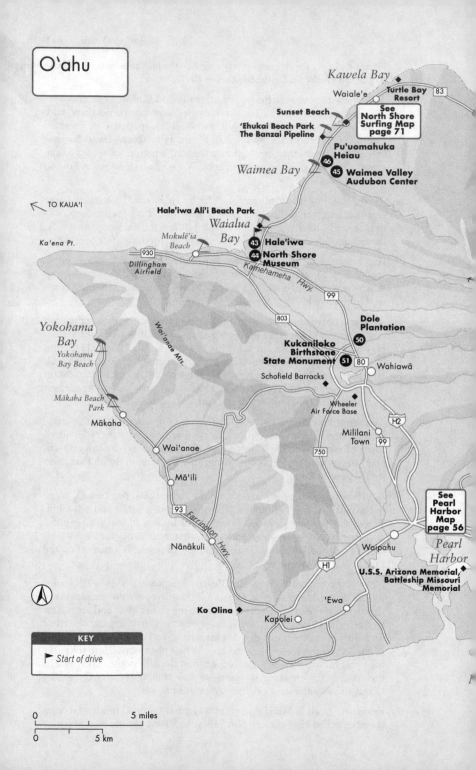

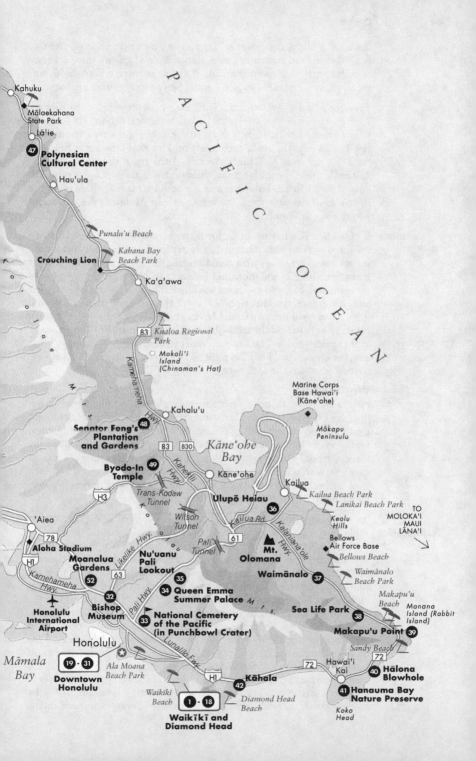

PACIFIC OCEAN

Kahuku

Mālaekahana
State Park

Lā'ie

47 Polynesian
Cultural Center

Hau'ula

Punalu'u Beach

Kahana Bay
Beach Park

Crouching Lion

Ka'a'awa

83 Kualoa Regional
Park

Mokoli'i
Island
(Chinaman's Hat)

Marine Corps
Base Hawai'i
(Kāne'ohe)

Kahalu'u

48

Senator Fong's
Plantation
and Gardens

83 830

Mōkapu
Peninsula

Kāne'ohe
Bay

Byodo-In
Temple

49

Kāne'ohe

Trans-Koʻolau
Tunnel

Kailua

Ulupō Heiau

Kailua Beach Park
Lanikai Beach Park

H3

Wilson
Tunnel

Kailua Rd.

36

TO
MOLOKA'I
MAUI
LĀNA'I

'Aiea

78

Keolu
Hills

Aloha Stadium

H1

Pali
Tunnel

61

Mt.
Olomana

Bellows
Air Force Base

Bellows Beach

Kamehameha Hwy.

Moanalua
Gardens

63

Nu'uanu
Pali
Lookout

52

Waimānalo

37

Waimānalo
Beach Park

32

35

Queen Emma
Summer Palace

34

Makapu'u
Beach

Honolulu
International
Airport

Bishop
Museum

33

National Cemetery
of the Pacific
(in Punchbowl Crater)

Sea Life Park

38

Manana
Island (Rabbit
Island)

Honolulu

Makapu'u Point

39

Sandy Beach

19 · 31

Lunalilo Hwy.

72

Hawai'i
Kai

72

Māmala
Bay

Downtown
Honolulu

Ala Moana
Beach Park

H1

Kāhala

40

Hālona
Blowhole

42

Waikīkī
Beach

1 · 18

Diamond Head
Beach

41

Hanauma Bay
Nature Preserve

Waikīkī and
Diamond Head

Koko
Head

has a small shopping center where you can pick up a soda or a snack. Right before you turn off from Kalaniana'ole Highway there's a long stretch of green on the makai side. This is the private Wai'alae Country Club, scene of the televised annual Sony Open golf tournament.

Take the Kīlauea Avenue exit. Turn left at the stoplight onto Kīlauea Avenue. Here you can see Kāhala Mall, an upscale shopping complex with yuppie eateries, high-fashion stores, and eight movie theaters. A few blocks past the mall, take a left on Hunakai Street and follow it until it dead-ends at Kāhala Avenue. Turn right and drive through **Kāhala** ❷, O'ahu's wealthiest neighborhood. Kāhala Avenue becomes Diamond Head Road. Follow it straight to Kapi'olani Park. Stay on the right side of the park until you hit Kapahulu Avenue. Take a left, and you're back in Waikīkī.

TIMING If Hanauma Bay is your main focus, remember that the park is closed on Tuesday. Also note that the bay is best in the early hours before the waters are churned up. You could reverse the above directions and get there first thing in the morning, before the crowds. Allow two hours for Hanauma Bay, two hours for Sea Life Park, and one for Queen Emma Summer Palace. Another tip: look up to the top of the mountains and, if it's clear, head directly to the Nu'uanu Pali Lookout. It's a shame to get there only to find the view obscured by clouds or fog. Temperatures at the summit are several degrees cooler than in warm Waikīkī, so bring a jacket along. And hang on tight to any loose possessions; it gets extremely windy at the lookout.

What to See

❹⓿ **Hālona Blowhole.** Below a scenic turnout along the Koko Head shoreline, this oft-photographed lava tube sucks the ocean in and spits it out. Don't get too close to the blowhole, as conditions can get dangerous. Look to your right to see the tiny beach below that was used to film the wave-washed love scene in *From Here to Eternity*. In winter it's a good spot to watch whales at play. Take your valuables with you and lock your car, because this scenic location is a hot spot for petty thieves. ⊠ *Kalaniana'ole Hwy., 1 mi east of Hanauma Bay.*

👆 ❹❶ **Hanauma Bay Nature Preserve.** This bay was created when the exterior
Fodor'sChoice wall of a volcanic crater collapsed, opening it to the sea and thereby giv-
★   ing birth to O'ahu's most famous snorkeling destination. Even from the overlook, the horseshoe-shape bay is a beauty, and you can easily see the reefs through the clear aqua waters. The wide beach is a great place for sunbathing and picnics. This is a marine conservation district, and regulations prohibit feeding the fish. Visitors are required to go through the Bay's Education Center before trekking down to the Bay. The center provides a cultural history of the area and exhibits about the importance of protecting its marine life. Check out the "Today at the Bay" exhibit for up-to-date information on daily tides, ocean safety warnings, and event activities. Food concessions and equipment rentals are also on-site. Come early to get parking, as the number of visitors allowed per day is limited. Call for current conditions. Weather permitting, Hanauma Bay by Starlight events are held on the second Saturday of every month, extending

1

the opening hours to 10 PM. ✉ *7455 Kalaniana'ole Hwy.* ☎ *808/396–4229* 🖹 *Donation $5; parking $1; mask, snorkel, and fins rental $8; tram from parking lot down to beach $1.50 round-trip* ⊙ *Wed.–Mon. 6–6.*

42 Kāhala. O'ahu's wealthiest neighborhood has streets lined with multimillion-dollar homes. At intervals along tree-lined Kāhala Avenue are narrow lanes that provide public access to Kāhala's magnificent coastal beaches. Kahala Mall is one of the island's largest indoor shopping centers. Kāhala is also the home of the private Wai'alae Golf Course, site of the annual Sony Open PGA golf tournament each January. ✉ *East of Diamond Head.*

★ **39 Makapu'u Point.** This spot has breathtaking views of the ocean, mountains, and the windward islands. The point of land jutting out in the distance is **Mōkapu Peninsula,** site of a U.S. Marine base. The spired mountain peak is **Mt. Olomana.** In front of you on the long pier is part of the **Makai Undersea Test Range,** a research facility that's closed to the public. Offshore is **Manana Island (Rabbit Island),** a picturesque cay said to resemble a swimming bunny with its ears pulled back. Ironically enough, Manana Island was once overrun with rabbits, thanks to a rancher who let a few hares run wild on the land. They were eradicated in 1994 by biologists who grew concerned that the rabbits were destroying the island's native plants.

Nestled in the cliff face is the **Makapu'u Lighthouse,** which became operational in 1909 and has the largest lighthouse lens in America. ■ TIP➔➔ The lighthouse is closed to the public, but near the Makapu'u Point turnout you can find the start of a mile-long paved road (closed to traffic). Hike up to the top of the 647-foot bluff for a closer view of the lighthouse and, in winter, a great whale-watching vantage point. ✉ *Kalaniana'ole Hwy., turnout above Makapu'u Beach.*

▶ **33 National Memorial Cemetery of the Pacific (in Punchbowl Crater).** Nestled in the bowl of Puowaina, or Punchbowl Crater, this 112-acre cemetery is the final resting place for more than 44,000 U.S. war veterans and family members. Among those buried here is Ernie Pyle, the famed World War II correspondent who was killed by a Japanese sniper off the northern coast of Okinawa. Puowaina, formed 75,000–100,000 years ago during a period of secondary volcanic activity, translates to "Hill of Sacrifice." Historians believe this site once served as an altar where ancient Hawaiians offered sacrifices to their gods. ■ TIP➔➔ The cemetery has unfettered views of Waikīkī and Honolulu. ✉ *2177 Puowaina Dr., Nu'uanu* ☎ *808/532–3720* ⊕ *www.cem.va.gov/nchp/nmcp.htm* 🖹 *Free* ⊙ *Mar.–Sept. daily 8–6:30, Oct.–Feb. daily 8–5:30.*

35 Nu'uanu Pali Lookout. This panoramic perch looks out to windward O'ahu. It was in this region that King Kamehameha I drove defending forces over the edges of the 1,000-foot-high cliffs, thus winning the decisive battle for control of O'ahu. From here you can see views that stretch from Kaneohe Bay to Chinaman's Hat, a small island off the coast, and beyond. It's a windy spot, so hang on to your hat. Lock your car if you get out, because break-ins have occurred here. ✉ *Top of Pali Hwy.* ⊙ *Daily 9–4.*

34 Queen Emma Summer Palace. Queen Emma and her family used this stately white home, built in 1848, as a retreat from the rigors of court life in hot and dusty Honolulu during the mid-1800s. It has an eclectic mix of European, Victorian, and Hawaiian furnishings and has excellent examples of Hawaiian quilts and koa-wood furniture as well as the queen's wedding dress and other memorabilia. ⊠ *2913 Pali Hwy.* ☎ *808/595–3167* ⊕ *www.daughtersofhawaii.org* ⊟ *$5* ⊘ *Guided tours daily 9–4.*

⚫ ❸❽ **Sea Life Park.** Dolphins leap and spin, penguins frolic, and a killer whale performs impressive tricks at this marine-life attraction 15 mi from Waikīkī at scenic Makapu'u Point. In addition to a 300,000-gallon Hawaiian reef aquarium, you can find the Pacific Whaling Museum, the Hawaiian Monk Seal Care Center, and a breeding sanctuary for Hawai'i's endangered *Honu* sea turtle. There are several interactive activities such as a stingray encounter, an underwater photo safari, and a "Splash University" dolphin-training session. Inquire about the park's behind-the-scenes tour for a glimpse of dolphin-training areas and the seabird rehabilitation center. The marine park was sold in early 2005, and its new owners were planning an extensive renovation to the facilities at this writing. ⊠ *41-202 Kalaniana'ole Hwy., Waimānalo* ☎ *808/259–7933 or 886/365–7446* ⊕ *www.sealifepark.com* ⊟ *$26* ⊘ *Daily 9:30–5.*

❸❻ **Ulupō Heiau.** Though they may look like piles of rocks to the uninitiated, *heiau* are sacred stone platforms for the worship of the gods and date from ancient times. *Ulupō* means "night inspiration," referring to the legendary *Menehune,* a mythical race of diminutive people who supposedly built the heiau under the cloak of darkness. ⊠ *Behind YMCA at Kalaniana'ole Hwy. and Kailua Rd.*

need a break? Generations of children have purchased their beach snacks and sodas at **Kalapawai Market** (⊠ 306 S. Kalāheo Ave.), near Kailua Beach. A windward landmark since 1932, the green-and-white market has distinctive charm. It's a good source for your carryout lunch, since there's no concession stand at the beach. At this writing, a new Kalapawai Cafe & Deli was set to open at the edge of Kailua Town.

❸❼ **Waimānalo.** This modest little seaside town flanked by chiseled cliffs is worth a visit. Its biggest draw is its beautiful beach, offering glorious views to the windward side. Down the side roads, as you head mauka, are little farms that grow a variety of fruits and flowers. Toward the back of the valley are small ranches with grazing horses. ■ **TIP→→** If you see any trucks selling corn and you're staying at a place where you can cook it, be sure to get some in Waimānalo. It may be the sweetest you'll ever eat, and the price is the lowest on O'ahu. ⊠ *Kalaniana'ole Hwy.*

The North Shore & Windward O'ahu

O'ahu's North Shore is about an hour's drive from Waikīkī, but it may as well be a world away. Here, bumper-to-bumper traffic and chorus lines of hotels give way to funky surf shops, country living, and some of the world's tallest winter waves. Similarly, Windward O'ahu is only a 15-minute drive from the hustle and bustle of Honolulu, but it's still been able to maintain a relatively low profile (just the way its residents like it). Both areas are worth a visit, especially if you desire to discover the "other" side of O'ahu.

a good drive

This tour begins in Haleʻiwa on Oʻahu's famed North Shore. It's about a 50-minute to an hour drive from Waikīkī. From Waikīkī, you can get onto Lunalilo Freeway (H–1) by either driving mauka on Kapahulu Avenue or taking Ala Wai Boulevard to Kalākaua Avenue, then turning right and driving to Beretania Street. Take a left (it's a one-way street) and then turn right at Piʻikoi Street. The signs will direct you to the freeway. From the H–1, drive ʻewa toward West Oʻahu past downtown Honolulu and Pearl City, then take the H–2 cutoff north and follow the signs to Haleʻiwa Town. The H–2 ends in Wahiawā, where you pick up Route 99 for the rest of the drive to Haleʻiwa.

Haleʻiwa ㊹ ▶ is a sleepy plantation town with fashion boutiques, surf shops, restaurants, and the best grilled mahimahi sandwich on the North Shore at Kua ʻAina Sandwich. For a nostalgic look at the history of surfing, drop by the **North Shore Surf and Cultural Museum** ㊽ in the North Shore Marketplace. Leave Haleʻiwa via the Kamehameha Highway (Route 83), you pass the famous North Shore beaches, where the winter surf comes in size extra large. The first of these is the famous big surf spot **Waimea Bay.** Across the street, on the mauka side of the road, is **Waimea Valley Audubon Center** ㊺, with its tempting waterfall and swimming hole. If you're interested in seeing a fine example of an ancient Hawaiian heiau, turn mauka at the Foodland store and take Pūpūkea Road up the steep climb, not quite a mile, to the dirt road on the right, leading to the **Puʻuomahuka Heiau** ㊻.

Continue along the coastal road past more **North Shore Surfing Beaches.** The trio of Haleʻiwa Beach, ʻEhukai (and the Banzai Pipeline) Beach, and Sunset Beach play host to the Triple Crown of Surfing every winter, when daring (some say crazy) surfers ride the towering waves with astounding grace. The only hotel of any consequence in these parts is your next landmark: the Turtle Bay Resort.

As you approach the town of Lāʻie, there's a long stretch of pine trees on the makai side. Look for the entrance to **Mālaekahana State Park;** on the mauka side is the sprawling **Polynesian Cultural Center** ㊼.

Continue driving east along Kamehameha Highway, you pass onto the Windward side of Oʻahu. As you approach the town of Kaʻaʻawa, take note of the **Crouching Lion** rock formation, a well-known landmark along the highway. Just past the town, look to the ocean and gaze at the uniquely shaped little island of **Mokoliʻi** (little lizard), a 206-foot-high sea stack also known as Chinaman's Hat. According to Hawaiian legend, the goddess Hiʻiaka, sister of Pele, slew the dragon Mokoliʻi and flung its tail into the sea, forming the distinct islet. Other dragon body parts—in the form of rocks, of course—were scattered along the base of nearby Kualoa Ridge.

In Kahaluʻu, turn right on Pulama Road to visit **Senator Fong's Plantation and Gardens** ㊽, a 725-acre wonderland of flora and gardens owned by the family of the late Senator Hiram Fong. Route 83 changes from the Kamehameha Highway to the Kahekili Highway in Kahaluʻu, at the point where Route 830 splits off to hug the coastline. Stay on 83 (the Kahekili Highway) to get to Kaneohe town. On the way, you might want to stop at the Valley of the Temples Memorial Park, site of the lovely **Byodo-In Temple** ㊾, a replica of a 900-year-old temple outside Uji, Japan.

Follow Kahekili Highway (Route 83) to Likelike Highway (Route 63), where you turn mauka and head back toward Honolulu through the Wilson Tunnel. The highway leads to Lunalilo Freeway going east. Exit at Pali Highway and go south through Downtown Honolulu on Bishop Street. Then turn left on Ala Moana Boulevard, which leads to Kalākaua Avenue in Waikīkī.

TIMING Hale'iwa is a half-day adventure, but you might want to factor in some extra North Shore time for hiking, relaxing on a beach, kayaking, taking a glider ride, and having a snack. Wear flip-flops but bring a pair of walking shoes as well. An excursion to Windward O'ahu, meanwhile, should last between two and three hours, affording you plenty of time to take in the scenery.

The weather is mercurial on the North Shore. It can be sunny and clear in Waikīkī and cloudy in the country. Bring along a light jacket, a hat, and sunscreen. Then you'll be ready for anything.

What to See

49 Byodo-In Temple. Tucked away in the back of the Valley of the Temples cemetery is a replica of the 11th-century Temple at Uji in Japan. A 2-ton carved wooden statue of the Buddha presides inside the main temple building. Next to the temple building are a meditation house and gardens set dramatically against the sheer, green cliffs of the Ko'olau Mountains. You can ring the 5-foot, 3-ton brass bell for good luck and feed some 10,000 carp that inhabit the garden's 2-acre pond. ⊠ *47-200 Kahekili Hwy., Kāne'ohe* ☎ *808/239–8811* 🎫 *$2* ⊙ *Daily 8:30–4:30.*

▶ **43 Hale'iwa.** During the 1920s this seaside hamlet was a trendy retreat at the end of a railroad line. During the 1960s hippies gathered here, followed by surfers. Today Hale'iwa is a fun mix, with old general stores and contemporary boutiques, galleries, and eateries. Be sure to stop in at **Lili'uokalani Protestant Church,** founded by missionaries in the 1830s. It's fronted by a large, stone archway built in 1910 and covered with night-blooming cereus. ⊠ *Follow H–1 west from Honolulu to H–2 north, exit at Wahiawā, follow Kamehameha Hwy. 6 mi, turn left at signaled intersection, then right into Hale'iwa* ⊕ *www.haleiwamainstreet.com.*

> **need a break?**

For a real slice of Hale'iwa life, stop at **Matsumoto's** (⊠ 66-087 Kamehameha Hwy. ⊕ www.matsumotoshaveice.com), a family-run business in a building dating from 1910, for shave ice in every flavor imaginable. For something different, order a shave ice with *adzuki* beans—the red beans are boiled until soft, mixed with sugar, and then placed in the cone with the ice on top.

> **North Shore Surfing**   **See Page 69**

44 North Shore Surf and Cultural Museum. Shop owner and curator Stephen Gould displays more than 30 vintage surfboards dating back to the 1930s, a shrine dedicated to legendary surfer Duke Kahanamoku, video pre-

Continued on page 73

Imagine picking your seat for free at the Super Bowl or wandering the grounds of Augusta National at no cost during The Masters, and you glimpse the opportunity you have when attending the Vans Triple Crown of Surfing on the North Shore.

NORTH SHORE SURFING & THE TRIPLE CROWN

10-FOOT WAVES.

10,000 FANS.

TOP 50 SURFERS.

Long considered the best stretch of surf breaks on Earth, the North Shore surf area encompasses six miles of coastline on the northwestern tip of O'ahu from Hale'iwa to Sunset Beach. There are over 20 major breaks within these six miles. Winter storms in the North Pacific send huge swells southward which don't break for thousands of miles until they hit the shallow reef of O'ahu's remote North Shore. This creates optimum surfing all winter long and was the inspiration for having surf competitions here each holiday season.

Every November and December the top 50 surfers in world rankings descend on "The Country" to decide who is the best all-around surfer in the world. Each of the three invitation-only contests that make up the Triple Crown has its own winner; competitors also win points based on the final standings. The surfer who excels in all three contests, racking up the most points overall, wins the Triple Crown title. The first contest is held at **Hale'iwa Beach,** the second at **Sunset Beach.** The season reaches its crescendo at the most famous surf break in the world, the **Banzai Pipeline.**

The best part is the cost to attend the events—nothing; your seat for the show—wherever you set down your beach towel. Just park your car, grab your stuff, and watch the best surfers in the world tame the best waves in the world.

> **The only surfing I understand involves a mouse.**
>
> The contests were created not only to fashion an overall champion, but to attract the casual fan to the sport. Announcers explain each ride over the loudspeakers, discussing the nuances and values being weighed by the judges. A scoreboard displays points and standings during the four days of each event.
>
> If this still seems incomprehensible to you, the action on the beach can also be exciting as some of the most beautiful people in the world are attracted to these contests.
>
> For more information, see www.triplecrownofsurfing.com

> **What should I bring?**
>
> Pack for a day at the Triple Crown the way you would for any day at the beach–sun block, beach towel, bottled water, and if you plan to make a day of it, food.
>
> These contest are held in rural neighborhoods (read: no stores), so pack anything you might need during the day. Also, binoculars are suggested, especially for the contest at Sunset. The pros will be riding huge outside ocean swells, and it can be hard to follow from the beach without binoculars. Hale'iwa's breaks and Pipeline are considerably closer to shore, but binoculars will let you see the intensity on the contestants' faces.

Hale'iwa Ali'i Beach Park
Triple Crown Contest #1: Vans Hawaiian Pro

The Triple Crown gets underway with high-performance waves (and the know-how to ride them) at Hale'iwa. Though lesser known than the other two breaks of the Triple Crown, it is the perfect wave for showing off: the contest here is full of sharp cutbacks (twisting the board dramatically off the top or bottom of the wave), occasional barrel rides, and a crescendo of floaters (balancing the board on the top of the cresting wave) before the wave is destroyed on the shallow table top reef called the Toilet Bowl. The rider who can pull off the most tricks will win this leg, evening the playing field for the other two contests, where knowledge of the break is the key. Also, the beach park is walking distance from historic Hale'iwa town, a mecca to surfers worldwide who make their pilgrimage here every winter to ride the waves. Even if you are not a fan, immersing yourself in their culture will make you one by nightfall.

Sunset Beach
Triple Crown Contest #2: O'Neill World Cup of Surfing

At Sunset, the most guts and bravado win the day. The competition is held when the swell is at 8 to 12 feet and from the northwest. Sunset gets the heaviest surf because it is the exposed point on the northern tip of O'ahu. Surfers describe the waves here as "moving mountains." The choice of waves is the key to this contest as only the perfect one will give the competitor a ride through the jigsaw-puzzle outer reef, which can kill a perfect wave instantly, all the way into the inner reef. Big bottom turns (riding all the way down the face of the wave before turning dramatically back onto the wave) and slipping into a super thick tube (slowing down to let the wave catch you and riding inside its vortex) are considered necessary to carry the day.

Banzai Pipeline
Triple Crown Contest #3: Rip Curl Pipeline Masters

It is breathtaking to watch the best surfers in the world disappear into a gaping maw of whitewash for a few seconds only to emerge from the other side unscathed. Surfing the Pipeline showcases their ability to specialize in surfing, to withstand the power and fury of a 10-foot wave from within its hollow tube.

How does the wave become hollow in the first place? When the deep ocean floor ascends steeply to the shore, the waves that meet it will pitch over themselves sharply, rather than rolling. This pitching causes a tube to form, and in most places in the world that tube is a mere couple of feet in diameter. In the case of Pipeline, however, its unique, extremely shallow reef causes the swells to open into 10-foot-high moving hallways that surfers can pass through. Only problem: a single slip puts them right into the raggedly sharp coral heads that caused the wave to pitch in the first place. Broken arms and boards are the rule rather than the exception for those who dare to ride and fail.

■ **TIP →→** The Banzai Pipeline is a surf break, not a beach. The best place to catch a glimpse of the break is from ʻEhukai Beach.

When Are the Contests?

The first contests at Haleʻiwa begin the second week of November, and the Triple Crown finishes up right before Christmas.

Surfing, more so than any other sport, relies on Mother Nature to allow competition. Each contest in the Triple Crown requires only four days of competition, but each is given a window of twelve days. Contest officials decide by 7 AM of each day whether the contest will be held or not, and they release the information to radio stations and via a hotline (whose number changes each year, unfortunately). By 7:15, you will know if it is on or not. Consult the local paper's sports section for the hotline number or listen to the radio announcement. The contests run from 8:30 to 4:30, featuring half-hour heats with four to six surfers each.

If big crowds bother you, go early on in the contests, within the first two days of each one. While the finale of the Pipeline Masters may draw about 10,000 fans, the earlier days have the same world class surfers with less than a thousand fans.

Sunset Beach

Banzai Pipeline

83 Waialeʻe

Waimea Bay   Waimea

**Waimea Bay
Beach Co. Park**

Haleʻiwa Beach

Kaunala Ridge

**Waimea Valley
Audubon Society**

83   Kawailoa
Beach

*Waiheʻe
(Waimea)
Falls 80*   Pupukea

Haleʻiwa
Beach
Co. Park

Kawailoa

Haleʻiwa

How Do I Get There?

If you hate dealing with parking and traffic, take TheBus. It will transport you from Waikīkī to the contest sites in an hour for two bucks and no hassle.

If you must drive, watch the news the night before. If they are expecting big waves that night, there is a very good chance the contest will be on in the morning. Leave by 6 AM to beat the crowd. When everybody else gets the news at 7:15 AM that the show is on, you will be parking your car and taking a snooze on the beach waiting for the surfing to commence.

Parking is limited so be prepared to park alongside Kamehameha Highway and trek it in.

But I'm not coming until Valentine's Day.

There doesn't need to be a contest underway for you to enjoy these spots from a spectator's perspective. The North Shore surf season begins in October and concludes at the end of March. Only the best can survive the wave at Pipeline. You may not be watching Kelly Slater or Andy Irons ripping, but, if the waves are up, you will still see surfing that will blow your mind. Also, there are surf contests year-round on all shores of O'ahu, so check the papers to see what is going on during your stay. A few other events to be on the lookout for:

Buffalo's Annual Big Board Surfing Classic

Generally held in March at legendary waterman "Buffalo" Keaulana's home beach of Mākaha, this is the Harlem Globetrotters of surfing contests. You'll see tandem riding, headstands, and outrigger canoe surfing. The contest is more about making the crowds cheer than beating your competitors, which makes it very accessible for the casual fan.

Converse Hawaiian Open

During the summer months, the waves switch to the south shore, where there are surf contests of one type or another each week. The Open is one of the biggest and is a part of the US Professional Longboard Surfing Championships. The best shoot it out every August on the waves Duke Kahanamoku made famous at Queen's Beach in Waikīkī.

Quiksilver in Memory of Eddie Aikau Big Wave Invitational

The granddaddy of them all is a one-day, winner-take-all contest in 25-foot surf at Waimea Bay. Because of the need for huge waves, it can be held only when there's a perfect storm. That could be at any time in the winter months, and there have even been a few years when it didn't happen at all. When Mother Nature does comply, however, it is not to be missed. You can hear the waves from the road, even before you can see the beach or the break.

sentations, surf memorabilia, and even a motorized surfboard that served as the forerunner to the Jet Ski. Donations accepted. ✉ 66-250 *Kamehameha Hwy., Hale'iwa* ☎ 808/637–8888 ☉ *Wed.–Mon. 11–5.*

☺ ㊸ **Polynesian Cultural Center.** Re-created, individual villages showcase the lifestyles and traditions of Hawai'i, Tahiti, Samoa, Fiji, the Marquesas Islands, New Zealand, and Tonga. This 45-acre center, 35 mi from Waikīkī, was founded in 1963 by the Church of Jesus Christ of Latter-day Saints. It houses restaurants, hosts lū'aus, and demonstrates cultural traditions such as tribal tattooing, fire dancing, and ancient customs and ceremonies. The expansive open-air shopping village carries Polynesian handicrafts. If you're staying in Honolulu, see the center as part of a van tour so you won't have to drive home late at night after the two-hour evening show. Various packages are available, from basic admission to an all-inclusive deal. Every May, the PCC hosts the World Fire Knife Dance Competition, an event that draws the top fire knife-dance performers from around the world. ✉ *55-370 Kamehameha Hwy., Lā'ie* ☎ *808/293–3333 or 800/367–7060* ⊕ *www.polynesia.com* ✉ *$50–$218* ☉ *Mon.–Sat. 12:30–9:30. Islands close at 6:30.*

㊻ **Pu'uomahuka Heiau.** Worth a stop for its spectacular views from a bluff high above the ocean overlooking Waimea Bay, this sacred spot was once the site of human sacrifices. It's now on the National Register of Historic Places. ✉ *½ mi north of Waimea Bay on Rte. 83, turn right on Pūpūkea Rd. and drive 1 mi uphill.*

㊽ **Senator Fong's Plantation and Gardens.** Hiram Fong, the first Asian-American to be elected to Congress, chose to share his love of Hawaiian flora and fauna by allowing tours of his 700-acre plantation estate. A 45-minute guided tram tour takes you through the estate's five lush valleys, each named for a U.S. president that Fong served under during his 17-year tenure in the Senate. The visitor center has a snack bar and gift shop. ✉ *47-285 Pūlama Rd., off Kahekili Hwy., 2 mi north of Byodo-In Temple, Kahalu'u* ☎ *808/239–6775* ⊕ *www.fonggarden.net* ✉ *$14.50* ☉ *Tram tours daily 10–4, the last tram tour begins at 3.*

need a break? The chocolate haupia pie at **Ted's Bakery** (✉ 59-024 Kamehameha Hwy., Waiale'e ☎ 808/638–8207) is legendary. Stop in for a takeout pie or for a quick plate lunch or sandwich.

★ ☺ ㊺ **Waimea Valley Audubon Center.** Waimea may get lots of press for the giant winter waves in the bay, but the valley itself is a newsmaker and an ecological treasure in its own right. The National Audubon Society is working to conserve and restore the natural habitat. Follow the Kamananui Stream up the valley through the 1,800-acres of gardens. The botanical collections here include over 5,000 species of tropical flora, including a superb gathering of Polynesian plants. It's the best place on the island to see native species, such as the endangered Hawaiian moorhen. You can also see the remains of the Hale O Lono heiau along with other ancient archaeological sites; evidence suggests that the area was an important spiritual center. At the back of the valley, **Waihī Falls** plunges 45-feet into swimming pond. ■ TIP➙➙ Bring your suit—a swim is the perfect way to end your hike. There's a lifeguard and changing room. Be sure to bring mosquito repellent, too; it gets buggy. ✉ *59-864 Kamehameha Hwy., Hale'iwa* ☎ *808/638–9199* ⊕ *www.audubon.org* 🅿 *$8, parking $2* ☉ *Daily 9:30–5.*

Central O'ahu

Nestled between the Ko'olau and Wai'anae mountain ranges is the central plain that stretches from Pearl Harbor to the residential towns of Mililani and Wahiawā. Central O'ahu is, appropriately enough, middle ground between Honolulu and the rugged North Shore. It's not as congested as Honolulu, but it's decidedly more developed than the North Shore. Once carpeted in pineapple and sugarcane plantations, the land is now home to ranches, banana farms, and fields of exotic flowers and coffee grown for export. Dole Plantation in Wahiawā welcomes nearly a million visitors every year, many of whom take on the challenge of escaping the famous Pineapple Garden Maze.

What to See

☺ ➎ **Dole Plantation.** Celebrate Hawai'i's famous golden fruit at this promotional, tourist-oriented center with exhibits, a huge gift shop, a snack concession, educational displays, and the world's largest maze. Although much more sophisticated than its original 1950 fruit stand, the Pavilion is filled with souvenir options galore, and kids love the 1.7-mi Pineapple Garden Maze, which is made up of 11,000 tropical plants and trees. Take a self-guided Garden Tour or hop aboard the Pineapple Express for a 20-minute train tour to learn a bit about life on a pineapple plantation.

It's about a 40-minute drive to Dole Plantation from Waikīkī. Take the H–1 freeway in the 'ewa direction, then take the H–2 North. Continue on to Kamehameha Highway (99). Dole will be on the right-hand side of the highway. Checking out the sights at Dole Plantation will take about 90 minutes, which includes enough time to enjoy a frosty Dole Whip to beat the heat. ✉ *64-1550 Kamehameha Hwy.* ☎ *808/621–8408* ⊕ *www.dole-plantation.com* 🅿 *Pavilion free, maze $5, train $7.50* ☉ *Daily 9–5:30; last train tour starts at 5.*

➎ **Kūkaniloko Birthstone State Monument.** The uplands of Wahiawā onced served as a place where *ali'i* or chiefs where born. Kūkaniloko was recognized as the royal birthsite on O'ahu; several distinguished chiefs were born here. One of the most significant cultural sites on the island, the lava rock stones here were believed to possess the power to ease the labor pains of childbirth. The site is marked by approximately 180 stones covering about a half-acre. It's about a 40–45 minute drive from Waikīkī. ✉ *Located in north side of Wahiawā at intersection of Kamehameha Hwy. and Whitmore Ave.*

➎ **Moanalua Gardens.** This lovely park is the site of the internationally acclaimed Prince Lot Hula Festival on the third weekend in July. Throughout the year, the Moanalua Gardens Foundation sponsors 3-mi guided walks into Kamananui Valley, usually on Sunday; call for specific times. Self-guided tour booklets ($5) are also available from the Moanalua Gardens Foundation office. To reach Moanalua Gardens, take the Moanalua Freeway westbound (78). Take the Tripler exit, then take a right on Mahiole Street. Pineapple Place is right after Moanalua Elementary School. ⊠ *1352 Pineapple Pl., Honolulu* ☏ *808/833–1944* ⊕ *www.mgf-hawaii. com* ✎ *Free, guided hikes $5* ⊘ *Weekdays 8–4:30.*

WHERE TO STAY

The 2½ mi stretch of sand known as Waikīkī Beach is a 24-hour playground and the heartbeat of Hawai'i's tourist industry. Waikīkī has a lot to offer—namely, the beach, shopping, restaurants, and nightlife, all within walking distance of your hotel. Business travelers stay on the western edge, near the Hawai'i Convention Center, Ala Moana, and downtown Honolulu. As you head east, Ala Moana Boulevard turns into Kalākaua Avenue, Waikīkī's main drag. This is hotel row (mid-Waikīkī), complete with historic boutique hotels, newer high rises, and megaresorts. Bigger chains like Sheraton, Outrigger, Aston, and Ohana have multiple properties along the strip, so it can get a little confusing. Surrounding the hotels and filling their lower levels is a flurry of shopping centers, restaurants, bars, and clubs. As you get closer to Diamond Head Crater, the strip opens up again, with the Honolulu Zoo and Kapi'olani Park providing green spaces. There's a handful of smaller hotels and condos at this end for those who like their Waikīkī with a "side of quiet."

Although Waikīkī is still the resort capital of this island, the continuing development of the Ko'Olina Resort and Marina, about 15 minutes from the airport in West O'ahu, looms large on the horizon. At this writing, the Grand I'hilani, a 1,000-room resort development, was scheduled to break ground.

Casual Windward and North Shore digs are shorter on amenities but have laid-back charms all their own. O'ahu offers a more limited list of B&Bs than other islands because the state stopped licensing them here in the 1980s; many of those operating here now do so under the radar. If you can't find your match below, contact a reservation service to make reservations at one of O'ahu's reputable B&Bs. The good news is, legislators on O'ahu are taking another look at this industry, and it's possible that B&Bs will flourish here again in the next decade.

Don't be intimidated by a hotel's published rates. There are always discounts to be had, be it through Internet sites, promotional specials, during the off season, combined hotel/car/air packages, special occasion rates, or by contacting the hotels directly on their toll-free lines for reservations. For a complete list of every hotel and condominium on the island, write or call the Hawai'i Visitors & Convention Bureau for a free *Accommodation Guide.*

■ TIP➔➔ **Keep in mind that most Waikīkī hotels charge $10 and up per day for parking.**

WHAT IT COSTS				
$$$$	$$$	$$	$	¢
over $200	$150–$200	$100–$150	$60–$100	under $60

Hotel prices are for two people in a standard double room in high season.

Waikīkī

Hotels & Resorts

$$$$
Fodor'sChoice
★

🔆 **Halekūlani.** Honeymooners and others seeking seclusion amidst the frenetic activity of the Waikīkī scene find it here, despite the proximity to the gigantic Sheraton Waikīkī convention hotel. Halekūlani exemplifies the translation of its name—the "house befitting heaven." From the moment you step inside the lobby, the attention to detail and service wraps you in luxury. It begins with private registration in your guest room and extends to the tiniest of details, such as complimentary tickets to the Honolulu Symphony, Contemporary Art Museum, and Honolulu Academy of Arts. The hotel's three restaurants—House Without a Key, La Mer, and Orchids—all have stellar reputations. Spacious guest rooms, artfully appointed in marble and wood, have ocean views. If you want to honeymoon in the ultimate style, we recommend the 2,125 square foot Vera Wang Suite, created by the noted wedding dress designer herself. It's entirely Vera, right down to the signature soft lavendar color scheme. Outside, the resort's freshwater pool has an orchid design created from more than 1½ million glass mosaic tiles. Gray's Beach, which fronts the hotel just beyond the pool, is small and has been known to disappear at high tide. ✉ *2199 Kālia Rd., Waikīkī 96815* ☎ *808/923–2311 or 800/367–2343* 🖷 *808/926–8004* 🌐 *www.halekulani.com* 🛏 *412 rooms, 44 suites* ♨ *3 restaurants, room service, A/C, in-room data ports, Wi-Fi, in-room safes, minibars, cable TV, pool, health club, hair salon, spa, beach, 3 bars, shops, dry cleaning, Internet room, business services, parking (fee), no-smoking rooms* ▱ *AE, DC, MC, V. $385–$660.*

$$$$
🔆 **Hawai'i Prince Hotel Waikīkī.** This slim high-rise fronts Ala Wai Yacht Harbor at the 'ewa edge of Waikīkī, close to Honolulu's downtown business districts, the convention center, and Ala Moana's outdoor mall. There's no beach here, but Ala Moana Beach Park is a 10-minute stroll away along the Harbor. It's the only resort in Waikīkī with a golf course—the 27-hole Arnold Palmer–designed golf course is in 'Ewa Beach, about a 45-minute ride from the hotel. The sleek, modern Prince looks to Asia both in its high-style decor and in such pampering touches as the traditional *oshiburi* (chilled hand towel) for refreshment upon check-in. Floor-to-ceiling windows overlooking the harbor sunsets make up for the lack of lānai. If you're planning to mix business with pleasure, inquire about the business room category, which features larger desks for work space and other amenities. The Prince Court prepares a subtle blend of Asian, European, and Hawaiian cuisines. ✉ *100 Holomoana St., Waikīkī 96815* ☎ *808/956–1111 or 800/321–6248* 🖷 *808/946–0811* 🌐 *www.hawaiiprincehotel.com* 🛏 *467 rooms, 57 suites* ♨ *3 restaurants,*

*room service, A/C, in-room data ports, in-room safes, minibars, cable
TV, 27-hole golf course, pool, gym, hair salon, spa, hot tub, bar, shops,
babysitting, business services, parking (fee), no-smoking rooms* ▤ *AE,
DC, MC, V. $325–$465.*

★ **$$$$** ▦ **Hilton Hawaiian Village Beach Resort and Spa.** Location, location, location. The HHV sprawls over 22 *acres* on Waikīkī's widest stretch of
beach. It has the perfect neighbor in Fort DeRussy, whose green lawns
create a buffer zone to the high-rise lineup of central Waikīkī. The
Hilton makes the most of its prime real estate—surrounding the five hotel
towers with lavish gardens, an aquatic playground of pools, a lagoon,
cascading waterfalls, koi ponds, penguins, and pink flamingos. Rainbow Tower, with its landmark 31-story mural, has knockout views of
Diamond Head. More of a city than a village, the HHV has an ABC, a
bookstore, Louis Vuitton, and a post office. Culture comes in the form
of an outpost of the Bishop Museum and the contemporary Hawaiian
art gracing the public spaces. It even has its own pier, docking point for
the Atlantis Submarine. The sheer volume of options, including free stuff
(lei-making, poolside hula shows, and fireworks), make the HHV a good
choice for families. This is a megaresort and a convention destination.
On the positive side, that means unique perks, like check-in kiosks
(complete with room keys) in the baggage claim area at the airport. On
the negative side, it means that there's usually big doings afoot on-site.
Be sure to try the family recipe Irish soda bread; it's in the bread baskets at the exclusive Bali by the Sea, but you can also get it at various
cafés. ✉ *2005 Kālia Rd., Waikīkī 96815* ☎ *808/949–4321 or 800/
221–2424* 🖷 *808/947–7898* ⊕ *www.hiltonhawaiianvillage.com* 🛏 *3,432
rooms, 365 suites, 264 condominiums* ⌕ *22 restaurants, room service,
A/C, in-room broadband, in-room safes, minibars, cable TV with movies,
5 pools, gym, spa, beach, snorkeling, 5 bars, shops, babysitting, children's programs (ages 5–12), dry cleaning, laundry service, Internet room,
business services, car rental, parking (fee), no-smoking rooms* ▤ *AE,
D, DC, MC, V. $199–$535.*

$$$$ ▦ **Hyatt Regency Waikīkī Resort and Spa.** Across the street from the Kūhiō
Beach section of Waikīkī, the Hyatt is actually "oceanfront," as there's
no resort between it and the Pacific Ocean. Renovations in 2004 added
a staircase leading directly from the pool deck to street level, for easy
beach access. An open-air atrium with a two-story waterfall, along with
free nightly live entertainment make this one of the liveliest lobbies anywhere. Check out the elevators, where an inlaid copper design evokes
the traditional little grass shack. An activity center offers kids' programs,
including lei-making lessons, 'ukulele lessons, and field trips to the
aquarium and zoo. ✉ *2424 Kalākaua Ave., Waikīkī 96815* ☎ *808/923–
1234 or 800/633–7313* 🖷 *808/923–7839* ⊕ *www.hyattwaikiki.com*
🛏 *1,212 rooms, 18 suites* ⌕ *5 restaurants, room service, A/C, in-room
data ports, in-room safes, minibars, cable TV with movies, pool, gym,
spa, 3 bars, shops, children's programs (ages 5–12), business services,
parking (fee), no-smoking rooms* ▤ *AE, D, DC, MC, V. $275–$425.*

$$$$ ▦ **Royal Hawaiian Hotel.** The high octane mai tai's at this resort's outdoor Mai Tai Bar made the drink famous. But the drinks aren't the only
thing that's legendary at the Pink Palace of the Pacific, so nicknamed

WHERE TO STAY IN WAIKĪKĪ & O'AHU

Hotels & Resorts

★ HOTEL NAME	Worth Noting	Cost $	Pools	Beach	Golf Course	Tennis Courts	Gym	Spa	Children Programs	Rooms	Restaurants	Other	Location
41 AAA Breck's Hostel	Near Sunset Beach	20–200								21			North Shore
36 Ala Moana Hotel	Near Ala Moana Shopping	135–235	1				yes			1,217	4		Honolulu
35 Aston, Executive Centre	Downtown, all suites	200–275	1				yes	yes		116	1	kitchens	Honolulu
30 Aston Waikīkī Beach Hotel	Beach across the street	153–410	1							657	1	shops	Waikīkī
26 ★ Aston Waikīkī Circle	Beach across the street	170–200								104	1		Waikīkī
42 Backpackers Vacation Inn	Near Waimea Bay	20–200								25		no A/C	North Shore
5 Doubletree Alana Waikīkī	Near Convention Center	120–175	1				yes			313	1	shops	Waikīkī
10 ★ Halekūlani	Great restaurants	385–660	1	yes			yes	yes		456	3	shops	Waikīkī
2 Hawai'i Prince Hotel	Near Convention Center	325–465	1		yes		yes	yes		524	3	shops	Waikīkī
4 ★ Hilton Hawaiian Village	Fabulous views, fireworks	219–520	5	yes			yes	yes	5–12	3,386	20	shops	Waikīkī
23 Hyatt Regency Waikīkī	Beach across the street	275–425	1				yes	yes	5–12	1,230	5	shops	Waikīkī
43 ★ J. W. Marriott 'Ihilani	Ko'Olina Resort, spa	354–549	2	yes	yes	6	yes	yes	5–12	450	4	shops	West O'ahu
37 ★ Kāhala Mandarin Oriental	Dolphin Quest	345–735	1	yes			yes	yes		370	5		Honolulu
1 Marc Hawai'i Polo	Near Ala Moana Shopping	98–148	1							106		kitchens	Waikīkī
22 Ohana East	2 blocks to beach	199–209	1				yes			445	4	kitchens	Waikīkī
7 Ohana Reef Lanai	1 block to beach	149–229								110		kitchens	Waikīkī
9 Outrigger Reef	Good value	148–360	1				yes		5–12	885	3		Waikīkī
19 ★ Outrigger Waikīkī	Duke's Canoe Club	180–600	1	yes			yes	yes	5–13	530	3	kitchens	Waikīkī
31 Queen Kapi'olani Hotel	1 block to beach	140–425	1							314	1	kitchens	Waikīkī
27 Radisson Waikīkī Prince K.	2 blocks to beach	129–225	1				yes			620	1		Waikīkī
3 Renaissance 'Ilikai Waikīkī	Short walk to beach	199–239	2			1	yes			779	3	kitchens	Waikīkī
25 Royal Grove Hotel	Good value	45–75	1							85			Waikīkī
15 Royal Hawaiian Hotel	Mai Tai Bar	395–680	1	yes				yes	5–12	525	2	shops	Waikīkī
20 Sheraton Moana Surfrider	Landmark historic wing	310–625	1	yes					5–12	839	2	shops	Waikīkī

# & Name	Notes	Price								Rooms			Region
21 Sheraton Princess K.	1 block to beach	175–700	1				yes		5-12	1,160	2		Waikīkī
14 Sheraton Waikīkī	30th Floor Cobalt Lounge	300–620	2	yes			yes		5-12	1,839	3	shops	Waikīkī
40 Turtle Bay Resort	Beach cottages, trails	350–780	2	yes	yes	10	yes	yes	5-12	455	4	shops	North Shore
33 W Honolulu–Diamond Head	1 block to beach, hip bar	280–355	1		yes					48	1		Waikīkī
★ 29 Waikīkī Beach Marriott	Spa Olakino, great sushi	189–329	2		yes		yes	yes		1,346	4		Waikīkī
18 Waikīkī Beachcomber Hotel	1 block to beach, 3 shows	245–295	1						5-12	507	1		Waikīkī
12 Waikīkī Joy (Aston)	2 blocks to beach, karaoke	164–295	1							94	1	kitchens	Waikīkī
★ 13 Waikīkī Parc	1 block to beach	229–339	1				yes			298	2		Waikīkī
24 Waikīkī Sand Villa	3 blocks to beach	109–190	1							212	1		Waikīkī
Condos													
6 Aloha Punawai	2 blocks to beach	105–135								19		kitchens	Waikīkī
28 Aston Waikīkī Beach Tower	1 block to beach	540–705	1			1				140		kitchens	Waikīkī
32 Aston Waikīkī Sunset	1 block to beach	240–460	1			1				307		kitchens	Waikīkī
11 The Breakers	1 block to beach	130–145	1							64	1	kitchens	Waikīkī
★ 8 Castle Waikīkī Shores	Great value	265–535		yes						168		kitchens	Waikīkī
16 Ilima Hotel	3 blocks to beach	189–285	1				yes			99		kitchens	Waikīkī
17 Pat Winston's Waikīkī Condos	2 blocks to beach	135–155	1					24				kitchens	Waikīkī
B&Bs & Vacation Rentals													
38 Ingrid's	Kailua, Japanese garden	150								2		kitchens	Windward
★ 34 Traditional Style B&B	Near Diamond Head Crater	130								2		no A/C	Waikīkī
39 Schrader's Windward Inn	On Kāneʻohe Bay	72–551	1							57		kitchens	Windward

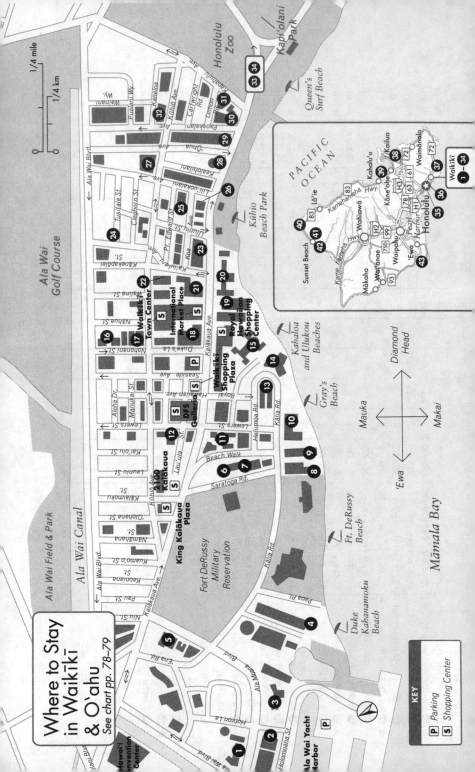

Where to Stay in Waikīkī & Oʻahu
See chart pp. 78–79

KEY

P Parking
S Shopping Center

for its cotton-candy color. The Royal was built in 1927 by Matson Navigation Company for its luxury-cruise passengers. A modern tower has since been added, but we're partial to the romance and architectural detailing of the Royal's historic wing with its canopy beds, Queen Anne–style desks, and the pinkest telephones on the planet. The only hotel in Waikīkī with its own coconut grove also has bragging rights to a private beach on some of the widest sands in central Waikīkī. The Royal's weekly lū'au—the only oceanfront lū'au in Waikīkī—is held Monday evenings underneath the stars on the Ocean Lawn. ⊠ *2259 Kalākaua Ave., Waikīkī 96815* ☎ *888/488–3535, 808/923–7311, or 866/500–8313* 🖷 *808/924–7098* ⊕ *www.royal-hawaiian.com* ➪ *472 rooms, 53 suites* ⟡ *2 restaurants, room service, A/C, in-room broadband, Web TV, minibars, cable TV, pool, hair salon, spa, beach, bar, children's programs (ages 5–12), business services, parking (fee), no-smoking rooms* ▭ *AE, DC, MC, V. $395–$680.*

$$$$ ⌂ **Sheraton Moana Surfrider.** Outrageous rates of $1.50 per night were the talk of the town when the "First Lady of Waikīkī" opened her doors in 1901. The *Hawai'i Calls* radio program was broadcast from the veranda during the 1940s and '50s. Today the Moana is still a wedding and honeymoon favorite with its sweeping main staircase and period furnishings in its historic main wing, the Moana. You can even renew your wedding vows during the Moana's weekly Promise Me Again ceremony held Saturday evenings underneath the stars of the Banyan Courtyard. In the late 1950s, the Diamond Head Tower was built. In the '70s, the Surfrider hotel went up next door—all three merged into one hotel in the 1980s. The newly refurbished Surfrider has oceanfront suites with two separate lānai, one for sunrise and one for sunset viewing. Relax on the private beach or in a cabana by the pool. ⊠ *2365 Kalākaua Ave., Waikīkī 96815* ☎ *888/488–3535, 808/922–3111, or 866/ 500–8313* 🖷 *808/923-0308* ⊕ *www.moana-surfrider.com* ➪ *793 rooms, 46 suites* ⟡ *2 restaurants, snack bar, room service, A/C, in-room data ports, in-room safes, cable TV, pool, beach, 3 bars, shops, children's programs (ages 5–12), parking (fee), no-smoking rooms* ▭ *AE, DC, MC, V. $310–$625.*

$$$$ ⌂ **Sheraton Waikīkī.** Towering over its neighbors on the prow of Waikīkī's famous sands, the Sheraton is center stage on Waikīkī Beach. Designed for the convention crowd, it's big and busy; the ballroom, one of O'ahu's largest, hosts convention expos, concerts, and boxing matches. A glass-wall elevator, with magnificent views of Waikīkī, ascends 30 stories to the Hano Hano Room's skyline Cobalt lounge and restaurant in the sky. Waikīkī's only beachfront nightclub, the Espirit, is jumping until the wee hours of the morning. The resort's best beach is on its Diamond Head side, fronting the Royal Hawaiian Hotel. If you don't shy away from crowds, this could be the place. The advantage here is that you have at your vacation fingertips a variety of amenities, venues, and programs, as well as a location smack dab in the middle of Waikīkī. Don't forget, we're talking living large here, so even the walk to your room could hike off a few of those calories consumed in Mai Tais. ⊠ *2255 Kalākaua Ave., Waikīkī 96815* ☎ *888/488–3535, 808/922–4422, or 866/ 500–8313* 🖷 *808/923–8785* ⊕ *www.sheratonwaikiki.com* ➪ *1,709* *rooms, 130 suites & 3 restaurants, room service, A/C, in-room broad-band, minibars, cable TV, 2 pools, health club, beach, 4 bars, dance club, shops, children's programs (ages 5–12), business services, parking (fee), no-smoking rooms ⊟ AE, DC, MC, V. $300–$620.*

$$$$ ▦ **W Honolulu—Diamond Head.** This link in the hip, modern chain adds Hawaiian warmth to the W's minimalist "whatever, whenever" service philosophy, with services like a tropical drink and chilled towel upon check-in and with a staff ready to cater to your every vacation wish, be it surfing the North Shore waves or creating an intimate dinner for two overlooking the Pacific Ocean. On the quiet end of Waikīkī, this 44-room boutique hotel has amenities like 250-count sheets, Balinese-inspired room furnishings and CD/DVD players. There's no beach, but it's a short half block to Sans Souci, known locally as Dig Me beach. The serpentine bar in the Wonder Lounge attracts O'ahu's young professionals. Don't look for your standard lobby here; it's vanished into the Living Room. Isn't that what you'd expect from a hotel with a bed in its bar? ✉ *2885 Kalākaua Ave., Waikīkī 96815* ☎ *808/922–1700 or 888/488–3535* 🖷 *808/923–2249* ⊕ *www.starwood.com* ⇥ *44 rooms, 4 suites & Restaurant, room service, A/C, in-room data ports, Web TV, minibars, cable TV, in-room DVD players/VCRs, 2 bars, dry cleaning, laundry service, business services, parking; no smoking ⊟ AE, D, DC, MC, V. $280–$355.*

$$$$ ▦ **Waikīkī Beachcomber Hotel.** This is pretty much showroom central, featuring the legendary Don Ho as well as the popular Blue Hawai'i and Magic of Polynesia revues. Set almost directly across from the Royal Hawaiian Shopping center and adjacent to the International Market-place (which is currently closed for a massive re-do), the hotel has a third-floor pool deck that offers the perk of front-row seating for any of Waikīkī's parades or Hoolaulea street party festivals that happen year-round. It's a family-friendly place, with cultural activities that include 'ukulele and hula lessons as well as arts and crafts. Rooms have private lānai and Polynesian motifs. On the hotel's ground level is an entrance to Macy's department store and a public beach accessway that opens up to the beach fronting the Royal Hawaiian hotel. ✉ *2300 Kalākaua Ave., Waikīkī 96815* ☎ *808/922–4646 or 800/622–4646* 🖷 *808/923–4889* ⊕ *www.waikikibeachcomber.com* ⇥ *500 rooms, 7 suites & Restaurant, snack bar, room service, A/C, minibars, refrigerators, cable TV, in-room data ports, pool, outdoor hot tub, bar, children's programs (ages 5–12), laundry facilities, Internet room, parking (fee), no-smoking rooms ⊟ AE, DC, MC, V. $245–$295.*

★ $$$$ ▦ **Waikīkī Parc.** One of the best-kept secrets in Waikīkī is this boutique hotel owned by the same group that manages the Halekūlani across the street. The Waikīkī Parc offers the same attention to detail in service and architectural design as the larger hotel but lacks the beachfront location and higher prices. Guests staying at the Parc have access to all the facilities of the Halekūlani and can sign charges there to their room at the Parc. Plus, a full breakfast buffet at the Parc Café, known for its bountiful island-style buffets, is included in the room rates. The pastel guest rooms in this high-rise complex have plantation-style shutters that open out to the lānai. Rooms have sitting areas, writing desks and a host of amenities including flat-screen TVs and high-speed Internet access. The hotel's pool and sundeck are eight floors up, affording a bit more privacy and peace for sunbathers. ⊠ *2233 Helumoa Rd., Waikīkī 96815* ☎ *808/921–7272 or 800/422–0450* 🖷 *808/931–6638* ⊕ *www.waikikiparc.com* ⇆ *298 rooms* ⚭ *2 restaurants, room service, A/C, in-room data ports, in-room safes, minibars, cable TV, in-room broadband, pool, gym, business services, parking (fee), no-smoking rooms* ▤ *AE, D, DC, MC, V. $229–$339.*

$$$–$$$$ 🏨 **Aston Waikīkī Beach Hotel.** A three-story volcano, backlighted in a faux eruption, crawls up the side of this Aston opposite Kuhio Beach and near Kapi'olani Park. Rooms in the main tower are hip to Hawaiiana, in colors ranging from neon pineapple yellow to hot lava tropical print red. The retro version of '60s island life continues with little touches like hand-painted bamboo curtains on the closets and surfboards used as entry signs. The Tiki Bar and Grill completes the retro experience. The hotel's Mauka Tower offers a very beige, very basic room for value rates. The third-floor pool deck is where all the action takes place. In the early mornings, there's an international food court where guests from the Main Tower can pick up their complimentary breakfast munchies in a takeout cooler bag and head to the beach across the street to catch some early morning wave action. In the evenings, the poolside bar breaks out with Hawaiian music that ranges from traditional to Jawaiian (Hawaiian sound with a reggae beat). There's also a Cold Stone Creamery and a Wolfgang Puck's Express, both on the street level. ⊠ *2570 Kalākaua Ave., Waikīkī 96815* ☎ *808/922–2511 or 877/997–6667* 🖷 *808/923–3656* ⊕ *www.aston-hotels.com* ⇆ *645 rooms, 12 suites* ⚭ *Restaurant, A/C, in-room safes, refrigerators, cable TV, in-room data ports, pool, shops, laundry facilities, parking (fee), no-smoking rooms* ▤ *AE, D, DC, MC, V. $153–$410.*

$$$–$$$$ 🏨 **Ohana East.** The flagship property for Ohana Hotels in Waikīkī is next to the Sheraton Princess Kaiulani on the corner of Kaiulani and Kūhiō avenues; it's only two blocks from the beach. Accommodations range from hotel rooms to suites with kitchenettes. Ohana East also offers 14 floors of no-smoking rooms as well as a fitness center and privileges at Outrigger's Serenity Spa in the Outrigger Reef on the Beach. ⊠ *150 Kaiulani Ave., Waikīkī 96815* ☎ *808/922–5353 or 800/462–6262* 🖷 *808/926–4334* ⊕ *www.ohanahotels.com* ⇆ *423 rooms, 22 suites* ⚭ *4 restaurants, room service, A/C, in-room broadband, in-room safes, some kitchenettes, refrigerators, cable TV with video games, pool, gym, hair salon, bar, laundry facilities, parking (fee), no-smoking floors* ▤ *AE, D, DC, MC, V. $199–$209.*

$$$–$$$$ 🏨 **Ohana Reef Lanai.** On Saratoga Road, this hotel faces the green expanse of 66-acre Fort DeRussy Park. The Reef offers studios and suites, many with kitchenettes and all with showers only. It's one block to the beach. Guests here receive a $4 dining credit for breakfast next door at Buzz's. ⊠ *225 Saratoga Rd., Waikīkī 96815* ☎ *808/923–3881 or 800/462–6262* 🖷 *808/923–3823* ⊕ *www.ohanahotels.com* ⇆ *110 studios and suites* ⚭ *A/C, in-room safes, in-room data ports, some kitchenettes, cable TV with movies and video games, bar, laundry facilities, parking (fee); no smoking* ▤ *AE, D, DC, MC, V. $149–$229.*

$$$-$$$$ 🏨 **Outrigger Reef on the Beach.** Value and a location right on the beach near to Fort DeRussy are the draw here—ideal if all you're looking for in a hotel room is a place to lay your head after a great day in the sun. If you're going to stay here, get an ocean view or oceanfront accommodation; the other rooms' view options include the less enchanting views of the walls of the Waikīkī Shores condominium next door. Most rooms have only showers. Kids who sign up for the Reef's Island Explorer program get their own backpack and binoculars at check-in. You can learn to surf or paddle an outrigger canoe or take an exercise class that uses the movements of hula for an aerobic workout. Hawai'i's celebration of culture—Aloha Fridays—finds this hotel brimming with lei makers, entertainers, and artisans willing to share their talents. For fun, cook your own meal inside the lively Shore Bird Oceanside Bar and Grill. ⊠ *2169 Kālia Rd., Waikīkī 96815* ☎ *808/923–3111 or 800/688–7444* 🖷 *808/924–4957* ⊕ *www.outrigger.com* 🛏 *846 rooms, 39 suites* ♿ *3 restaurants, room service, A/C, refrigerators, cable TV, pool, gym, beach, 4 bars, nightclub, laundry facilities, children's programs (ages 5–12), business services, parking (fee), no-smoking rooms* ☐ *AE, D, DC, MC, V. $148–$360.*

★ $$$-$$$$ 🏨 **Outrigger Waikīkī on the Beach.** The star jewel in the Outrigger Hotels & Resorts sits on one of the finest strands of Waikīkī beach, where throughout the year, the hotel plays host to canoe regattas, the World Ocean Games lifeguard competition, and the Honolulu Marathon. The 16-story resort's renovation in 2004 revived guest rooms in a tribute to plantation-style living with rich darkwood furnishings and Hawaiian artwork. For a night out on the town, look no further than the Outrigger's main showroom and the famous Society of Seven Las Vegas–style revue. Or, if you prefer to stay outside, the popular Duke's Canoe Club has beachfront concerts under the stars. ⊠ *2335 Kalākaua Ave., Waikīkī 96815* ☎ *808/923–0711 or 800/688–7444* 🖷 *808/921–9798* ⊕ *www. outrigger.com* 🛏 *500 rooms, 30 suites* ♿ *3 restaurants, room service, A/C, in-room data ports, in-room safes, some kitchenettes, minibars, cable TV, pool, gym, hot tub, beach, 6 bars, theater, shops, children's programs (ages 5–13), dry cleaning, laundry facilities, business services, parking (fee), no-smoking rooms* ☐ *AE, D, DC, MC, V. $180–$600.*

$$$-$$$$ 🏨 **Renaissance 'Ilikai Waikīkī.** At the 'ewa edge of Waikīkī overlooking the Ala Wai Harbor, this resort offers you the choice of either a spacious hotel room or a large kitchen room with a full kitchen, which can save you some bucks. The atmosphere here is casual with an open-air lobby, cascading waterfalls, and torchlighted walkways that are perfect for a romantic nightly stroll above the Harbor. There are two freshwater pools and a tennis court on property, but the nearest beach, at Ala Moana Beach Park, is a five-minute stroll away. For a sky-high view of Honolulu, book a table at Sarento's Top of the "I" where the Italian menu rivals the skyline. If while riding the glass elevator to the top of the "I", the uppermost balcony to the west looks vaguely familiar to you, here's a hint: it's on that balcony where Jack Lord's character Steve McGarrett turns to face the camera at the beginning of each episode of *Hawaii 5-0.* ⊠ *1777 Ala Moana Blvd., Waikīkī 96815* ☎ *808/949–3811 or 800/245–4524* 🖷 *808/947–0892* ⊕ *www.ilikaihotel.com* 🛏 *728*

rooms, 51 suites ♨ 3 restaurants, room service, A/C, in-room broadband, some kitchens, minibars, cable TV, tennis court, 2 pools, health club, outdoor hot tub, massage, 2 bars, video game room, shops, laundry facilities, business services, car rental, parking (fee), no-smoking rooms ☰ AE, D, DC, MC, V. $199–$239.

$$$–$$$$ 🏨 **Sheraton Princess Kaiulani.** This hotel sits across the street from its sister property, the Sheraton Moana Surfrider. You can sleep here, taking advantage of lower rates, and play at the oceanfront Sheratons, charging everything back to your room at the Princess Kaiulani. Kids who stay here can participate in the Keiki Aloha activity program, which is headquartered two blocks down the street at the Sheraton Waikīkī. Rooms are in two towers—some peer over the Moana's low-rise historic wing at the ocean. At night there's poolside hula and live Hawaiian music on the Lava Stage, while the hotel's showroom hosts the Creation: A Polynesian Odyssey revue. It's a two-minute stroll to the beach. The hotel's pool is street-side facing Kalākaua Avenue. ⊠ 120 Kaiulani Ave., Waikīkī 96815 ☎ 888/488–3535, 808/922–5811, or 866/500–8313 🖷 808/931–4577 ⊕ www.princesskaiulani.com ⇥ 1,150 rooms, 10 suites ♨ 2 restaurants, room service, A/C, in-room data ports, cable TV, pool, gym, bar, children's programs (ages 5–12), business services, no-smoking rooms ☰ AE, D, DC, MC, V. $175–$700.

★ **$$$–$$$$** 🏨 **Waikīkī Beach Marriott Resort.** On the eastern edge of Waikīkī, this hotel is across from Kūhiō Beach and close to Kapiʻolani Park, the zoo, and the aquarium. Deep Hawaiian woods and bold tropical colors fill the hotel's two towers, which have ample courtyards and public areas open to ocean breezes and sunlight. Rooms in the Kealohilani Tower are some of the largest in Waikīkī, and the Paokalani Tower's Diamond Head side rooms offer breathtaking views of Diamond Head crater and Kapiʻolani Park. The Marriott also offers a family-size room accommodation that sleeps six. Sushi lovers will be tempted by the menu at the Sansei Seafood, Sushi Bar and Steakhouse, whose executive chef, DK Kodama, is one of the original group of chefs responsible for creating and putting Hawaiʻi regional cuisine on the world's culinary map. The outdoor Moana Terrace, three floors up overlooking Waikīkī Beach features Hawaiian music in the early evenings. Check out the Thursday evening entertainment lineup on the Terrace, which features Hawaiʻi's legendary falsetto songstress Genoa Keawe. ⊠ 2552 Kalākaua Ave., Waikīkī 96815 ☎ 808/922–6611 or 800/367–5370 🖷 808/921–5222 ⊕ www.marriottwaikiki.com ⇥ 1,337 rooms, 9 suites ♨ 4 restaurants, room service, A/C, in-room data ports, Web TV, Wi-Fi, in-room safes, minibars, refrigerators, cable TV, 2 pools, gym, spa, 2 bars, business services, parking (fee) ☰ AE, D, MC, V. $189–$329.

$$$–$$$$ 🏨 **Waikīkī Joy (Aston).** In-room Jacuzzi tubs, deluxe stereo–entertainment systems, and lighting–sound control bedside panels are appealing perks at the Waikīkī Joy. Even more appealing is the soundproofing, which protects you when the guy in the next room cranks up the volume. One of the hotel's towers is standard rooms, while the other has suites. Request a room close to the top of the hotel's 11 stories if you want to see the ocean from your lānai. This intimate property is tucked away on a quiet side street next to the DFS Galleria and about a five-minute walk to Kalākaua Avenue and through one of the many public accessways to the beach, which can be a bit of a stroll if you are hauling beach chairs. Continental breakfast on the lobby veranda is included in the rate, and Cappucino's Cafe offers Internet access and takeout. They will also cater meals for you and your groupies if you're busy recording your first hit at the hotel's GS Karaoke Studio. ⊠ *320 Lewers St., Waikīkī 96815* ☎ *808/923–2300 or 877/997–6667* 🖷 *808/922–8785* ⊕ *www.aston-hotels.com* ⇘ *50 rooms, 44 suites* ⌂ *Restaurant, A/C, in-room data ports, in-room safes, kitchenettes, minibars, cable TV, pool, sauna, bar, parking (fee), no smoking rooms* ⊟ *AE, D, DC, MC, V. $164–$295.*

$$–$$$$ 🏨 **Queen Kapi'olani Hotel.** A half block from the shore on the Diamond Head end of Waikīkī, this hotel is across the street from the zoo and within walking distance of the aquarium, the Waikīkī Shell and Kapia'olani Park. The public Ala Wai Golf Course is three blocks up toward the mountains. Accommodations here are clean and basic and offer you a choice from standard hotel room to studios with kitchenettes and one-bedroom suites, all at rates that won't break the budget. ⊠ *150 Kapahulu Ave., Waikīkī 96815* ☎ *808/922–1941 or 800/367–2317* 🖷 *808/924–1982* ⊕ *www.queenkapiolani.com* ⇘ *307 rooms, 7 suites* ⌂ *Restaurant, room service, A/C, in-room data ports, kitchenettes, refrigerators, cable TV, pool, bar, laundry facilities* ⊟ *AE, D, DC, MC, V. $140–$425.*

$$–$$$$ 🏨 **Radisson Waikīkī Prince Kūhiō.** A $15 million redesign in 2004 and 2005 has given the Prince Kuhio a royal makeover. Radisson has made liberal use of rich wood detailing, contemporary fabrics and accented it all with magnificient displays of fresh tropical exotic flowers throughout the public spaces. If marriage is on your mind, a gazebo where weddings can be performed has been added to the hotel gardens. Two blocks from Kūhiō Beach and across the street from the Marriott Waikīkī, this 37-story high-rise is on the Diamond Head end of Waikīkī. The new Lobby Bar mixes up tropical cocktails, an island-style pūpū menu, wireless access and a wide-screen plasma TV for sports fans and news junkies. Book on an upper floor if you want to see the ocean from your lānai. ⊠ *2500 Kūhiō Ave., Waikīkī 96815* ☎ *808/922–8811 or 800/557–4422* 🖷 *808/923–0330* ⊕ *www.radisson.com/waikikihi* ⇘ *620 rooms* ⌂ *Restaurant, room service, A/C, cable TV, in-room broadband, in-room data ports, in-room safes, pool, gym, hot tub, bar, laundry facilities, business services, parking (fee), no-smoking rooms* ⊟ *AE, D, DC, MC, V. $129–$225.*

★ $$$ 🏨 **Aston Waikīkī Circle Hotel.** This unique 13-story circular hotel is a Waikīkī landmark. A charming interior-design scheme brings the Pacific inside, beginning at check-in beneath a seascape mural in the open-air lobby. The elevators are painted a bright sea blue–green, and hallway floors are textured to mimic the sandy beach, complete with appliqued sea shells and sea creatures dotting the circular walkways. We love that this is a hotel that never goes out of season. Rooms here are small, and every bit of space is utilized. Tiny bathrooms have showers only, but a sandpail and shovel sits on the counter, just begging you to go out and play. And you won't have far to walk—Waikīkī Beach is right down the front stairs and across the street. Honeymooners, snowbirds, and old-timers love this little hotel with a front-desk staff that takes the time to get to know you. Ginza Kia is a Tokyo-style noodle shop, perfect for refueling. ✉ *2464 Kalākaua Ave., Waikīkī 96815* ☎ *808/923–1571 or 877/997–6667* 🖷*808/926–8024* ⊕*www.aston-hotels.com* ⇗*104 rooms* 🍴 *Restaurant, in-room data ports, A/C, in-room safes, cable TV, laundry facilities, parking (fee), no-smoking floors* ▤ *AE, D, DC, MC, V. $170–$200.*

$$–$$$ 🏨 **Doubletree Alana Waikīkī.** The location (a five-minute walk from the Hawai'i Convention Center), three phones in each room, and the 24-hour business center meet the requirements of the Doubletree's global business clientele, but the smallness of the property, the staff's attention to detail, and the Japanese-style *furo* deep-soaking tubs have won it converts among vacationers. The modern lobby of this 19-story high-rise has rotating exhibits of local artists' work, and the gym is also open round-the-clock. It's on busy Ala Moana Boulevard across from Fort DeRussy. To get to the beach, you either cross Fort DeRussy or head through the Hilton Hawaiian Village. Padovani's Restaurant serves Mediterranean cuisine, and the Wine Bar has one of O'ahu's most extensive collections of wines by the glass. For a sweet ending to the evening, we recommend any of the desserts created by the Padovani brothers, especially their handmade chocolates. ✉ *1956 Ala Moana Blvd., Waikīkī 96815* ☎ *808/941–7275 or 800/222–8733* 🖷*808/949–0996* ⊕*www.alana-doubletree.com* ⇗*268 rooms, 45 suites* 🍴 *Restaurant, room service, A/C, in-room data ports, in-room safes, refrigerators, cable TV, pool, gym, bar, business services, parking (fee), no-smoking rooms* ▤ *AE, D, MC, V. $120–$175.*

$$–$$$ 🏨 **Waikīkī Sand Villa.** Families and others looking for an economical rate without sacrificing proximity to Waikīkī's beaches, dining and shopping return to the Waikīkī Sand Villa year after year. It's on the corner of Kaiulani Avenue and Ala Wai Boulevard, a three-block walk to restaurants and the beach. There's a high-rise tower and a three-story walk-up building of studio accommodations with kitchenettes. Corner deluxe units with lānai have the "golf view" overlooking the Ala Wai

> **PRIVATE BEACHES IN HAWAI'I?**
>
> The Royal Hawaiian Hotel and the Sheraton Moana Surfrider are the only hotels in Waikīkī with property lines that extend out into the sand. They have created "private roped off beach areas" that can only be accessed by hotel guests. The areas are adjacent to the hotel properties at the top of the beach.

canal and golf course. Complimentary breakfast is served poolside every morning beneath shady coconut trees, and the hotel's Sand Bar comes alive at happy hour with a great mix of hotel guests and locals who like to hang out and "talk story." The Sand Bar also has computers and Web cams, so that you can not only keep in touch with family by e-mail, you can taunt them with your developing tan. ✉ *2375 Ala Wai Blvd., Waikīkī 96815* ☎ *808/922–4744 or 800/247–1903* 🖷 *808/923–2541* ⊕ *www.sandvillahotel.com* ⇗ *212 rooms* 🍴 *Restaurant, in-room data ports, in-room safes, refrigerators, pool, hot tub, bar, shop, parking (fee), no-smoking rooms; no A/C in some rooms* ▤ *AE, D, DC, MC, V. $109–$190.*

$–$$ 🏨 **Marc Hawai'i Polo Inn and Tower.** This small hotel fronts busy Ala Moana Boulevard, one-block from Ala Moana Shopping Center and Ala Moana

Beach Park, on the 'ewa end of Waikīkī. While it doesn't offer too much in the way of views or room amenities, you do have the option of standard hotel rooms or studios with kitchenettes. If you're not about to spend your vacation slaving away in the kitchen but like the thought of having access to a microwave, reserve a room in the Bamboo category or a minisuite. The interior decor pays tribute to Hawai'i polo enthusiasts, and front-desk staff are happy to assist with driving directions to the playing fields at Mokuleia and Waimānalo, if you decide to take a picnic, and catch a match. ⊠ *1696 Ala Moana Blvd., 96815* ☎ *808/ 949–0061 or 800/535–0085* ⊕ *www.marcresorts.com* ⌁ *106 rooms* ♨ *A/C, in-room safes, some kitchenettes, some microwaves, cable TV, pool, shop, laundry facilities, parking (fee), no-smoking rooms* ▤ *AE, DC, MC, V. $98–$148.*

¢–$ ⊞ **Royal Grove Hotel.** Two generations of the Fong family have put their heart and soul into the operation of this tiny (by Waikīkī standards), six-story hotel, which offers clean, functional accommodations and a wealth of home-style Hawaiian hospitality to those on a shoestring budget. During the hot summer months, seriously consider splurging on the highest end accommodations, which feature air-conditioning, lānai, and small kitchens. The hotel's pool is its social center in the evenings, where you can usually find at least one or more members of the Fong family strumming a 'ukulele, dancing hula, and singing songs in the old Hawaiian style. On special occasions, the Fongs host a potluck dinner by the pool. Little touches that mean a lot include free use of boogie boards, surfboards, beach mats, and beach towels. The hotel is two blocks from Waikīkī's Kuhio Beach. On property are a tiny sushi bar, natural foods deli, and an authentic Korean barbeque plate-lunch place. For extra value, inquire about the Grove's weekly and monthly rates. ⊠ *151 Uluniu Ave., Waikīkī 96815* ☎ *808/923–7691* ⊕ *www.royalgrovehotel. com* 🖷 *808/922–7508* ⌁ *78 rooms, 7 suites* ♨ *Kitchenettes, pool; no A/C in some rooms, no parking* ▤ *AE, D, DC, MC, V. $45–$75.*

Condos

$$$$ ⊞ **Aston Waikīkī Beach Tower.** The elegance of a luxury condominium combined with the intimacy and service found in a boutique hotel resides at this Kalākaua Avenue address. Facing Kuhio Beach, this 39-story resort offers spacious (1,100–1,400 square feet) one- and two-bedroom suites with kitchens that would please a gourmet, twice-daily maid service, washer-dryers, and a private lānai. Valet parking is included in the rate. ⊠ *2470 Kalākaua Ave., Waikīkī 96815* ☎ *808/926–6400 or 877/997– 6667* 🖷 *808/926–7380* ⊕ *www.aston-hotels.com* ⌁ *140 suites* ♨ *Room service, A/C, kitchens, minibars, cable TV, tennis court, pool, sauna, billiards, paddle tennis, laundry facilities, parking, no-smoking rooms,* ▤ *AE, D, DC, MC, V. 1-bedroom $540–$585, 2-bedrooms $640–$705.*

$$$$ ⊞ **Aston Waikīkī Sunset.** This 38-story high-rise condominium resort is near Diamond Head, one block from Waikīkī Beach and TheBus line. Without leaving the property, you can swim, take a sauna break, throw some steaks on the outdoor grill, have access to a PC in the hospitality lounge, and make a racket after dark on the tennis court lit for night play. One- and two-bedroom suites have complete kitchens, daily maid ser-

vice, private lānai, and terrific views through floor-to-ceiling windows. The biggest complaint we've heard recently is about the elevators. The rides to the upper floors are smooth and quick enough, but the wait to get an elevator can be annoying slow. ⊠ *229 Paoakalani Ave., Waikīkī 96815* ☎ *808/922–0511 or 877/997–6667* 🖶 *808/922–8580* ⊕ *www.aston-hotels.com* 📇 *307 suites* ⚭ *BBQ, A/C, in-room data ports, kitchens, cable TV, tennis court, pool, sauna, shop, no-smoking rooms* ▤ *AE, D, DC, MC, V. 1-bedroom $240–$285, 2-bedroom $440–$460.*

★ **$$$$** ⊞ **Castle Waikīkī Shores.** Nestled between Fort DeRussy Beach Park and the Outrigger Reef on the Beach, this is only condo right on Waikīkī Beach. Units include studios and one- and two-bedroom suites with panoramic views of the Pacific Ocean. The beach directly fronting the building is nothing to write home about, but it's only a few steps to the large expanse of beach at Fort DeRussy. Many of these units have full kitchens, but some only have kitchenettes so be sure you inquire when booking. Families love this place for its spaciousness, while others love it for its quiet location on the 'ewa end of Waikīkī. ⊠ *2161 Kālia Rd., Waikīkī 96815* ☎ *808/952–4500 or 800/367–2353* 🖶 *808/952–4560* ⊕ *www.castleresorts.com* 📇 *168 units* ⚭ *A/C, in-room data ports, some kitchens, some kitchenettes, cable TV, beach, laundry facilities, parking (fee), no-smoking rooms* ▤ *AE, D, DC, MC, V. 1-bedroom $265–$340, 2-bedroom $425–$585.*

$$–$$$$ ⊞ **Ilima Hotel.** Tucked away on a residential side street near Waikīkī's Ala Wai Canal, this locally owned 17-story condominium-style hotel is a gem. The glass-wall lobby with koa-wood furnishings, original Hawaiian artwork, and friendly staff create a Hawaiian home-away-from-home. One of the selling points of this place is the decent rate for its spacious studios with kitchenettes, as well as its one- and two-bedroom suites with full kitchens, Jacuzzi baths, cable TV with free HBO and Disney channels, multiple phones, and spacious lānai. It's a three-block walk to Waikīkī Beach, shopping and Kalākala Avenue restaurants. The parking is free but limited. When the spots are full, you park on the street. ⊠ *445 Nohonani St., Waikīkī 96815* ☎ *808/923–1877 or 888/864–5462* 🖶 *808/924–2617* ⊕ *www.ilima.com* 📇 *99 units* ⚭ *A/C, in-room data ports, in-room safes, kitchens, cable TV, some in-room broadband, pool, gym, sauna, laundry facilities, parking, no-smoking rooms* ▤ *AE, DC, MC, V. 1-bedroom $189–$219, 2-bedrooms $265–$285.*

$–$$ ⊞ **Aloha Punawai.** Punawai provides all the basics for those on a budget. This family-operated apartment hotel is across Saratoga Road from Fort DeRussy Beach; Saratoga is a busy street, but this location can't be beat for its closeness to shopping, dining, and the beach. Each unit comes with a full kitchen, cable television, and a lānai. Studios have bathrooms with showers only. One-bedroom units have either two twins or a king-size bed, while one-bedroom deluxe units have one queen, one twin and a sofa bed. Furnishings are simple and spartan. You can opt for telephone service or forgo the distraction. ⊠ *305 Saratoga Rd., Waikīkī 96815* ☎ *808/923–5211 or 866/713–9694* 🖶 *808/923–5211* ⊕ *www.alternative-hawaii.com/alohapunawai* 📇 *19 units* ⚭ *A/C, kitchens, cable TV, laundry facilities; no phones in some rooms* ▤ *AE, DC, MC, V. 1-bedroom $105–$135.*

$-$$ ⊡ **The Breakers.** For a taste of Hawai'i in the '60s, right after Statehood, go retro at this low-rise hotel a mere half-block from Waikīkī Beach. The Breakers' six two-story buildings surround its pool and overlook gardens filled with tropical flowers. Taking a break from the sun means walking a few steps from the pool to the poolside bar where Tommy Turner, the Breaker's master of exotic cocktails, serves up a little attitude adjustment to complement one of the Breaker Cafe's legendary grilled hamburgers. Guest rooms have Japanese-style *shoji* doors that open to the lāai, kitchenettes, and bathrooms with showers only. Units 130, 132, and 134 have views of the Urasenke Teahouse. The toughest part of your visit just might be finding an available room as guests return here year after year. Parking is limited, but it's free. ⊠ *250 Beach Walk, Waikīkī 96815* ☎ *808/923–3181 or 800/426–0494* 🖷 *808/923–7174* ⊕ *www.breakers-hawaii.com* ↩ *64 units* ⚒ *Restaurant, A/C, kitchenettes, pool, bar, parking* ▤ *AE, DC, MC, V. 1-bedroom $130, 2-bedroom $145.*

> ## CONDO COMFORTS
>
> **Foodland** The local chain has two locations near Waikīkī: **Market City** (⊠ 2839 Harding Ave., near intersection with Kapahulu Ave. and highway overpass, Kaimukī ☎ 808/734-6303) and **Ala Moana Center** (⊠ 1450 Ala Moana Blvd., ground level, Ala Moana ☎ 808/949-5044)
>
> **Food Pantry** A smaller version of larger Foodland, Food Pantry also has apparel, beach stuff, and tourist-oriented items. (⊠ 2370 Kuhio Ave., across from Miramar hotel, Waikīkī ☎ 808/923-9831)
>
> **Blockbuster Video** (⊠ Ala Moana Shopping Center, 451 Piikoi St., Ala Moana ☎ 808/593-2595)
>
> **Pizza Hut** (☎ 808/643-1111 for delivery statewide)

$-$$ ⊡ **Pat Winston's Waikīkī Condos.** This five-story condominium complex is just off Kuhio Avenue near the International Marketplace and two blocks from Waikīkī Beach. All units have full kitchens, ceiling fans, sofa beds, and lānai. Interior designs vary, with units to accommodate families, honeymooners, business travelers, and nostalgia buffs (check out the Blue Hawaii or *Hawaii 5-0* theme suites). Owner Pat Winston provides everything from exercise equipment to rice cookers to tips on the best places to dine on the island. Limited parking is free. ⊠ *417 Nohonani St., Waikīkī 96815* ☎ *808/922–3894 or 800/545–1948* 🖷 *808/924–3332* ⊕ *www.winstonswaikikicondos.com* ↩ *24 units* ⚒ *A/C, in-room data ports, fans, kitchens, pool, exercise equipment, laundry facilities, parking* ▤ *AE, DC, MC, V. 1-bedroom $115–$135, 2-bedroom $135–$155.*

B&Bs & Vacation Rentals

$$ ⊡ **Traditional Style Bed and Breakfast.** Many a traveler and resident alike

Fodor'sChoice
★
would love to own a home like this art-filled B&B at the base of Waikīkī's famous Diamond Head crater. Each of the two guest rooms feature koa-wood furnishings, private bath, and open to a lānai and a big backyard filled with the sounds of birds and rustling trees. If you want to experience a bit of Hawaiian history, request the room that includes the extra-large hand-carved koa bed that once belonged to a Hawaiian princess. The closest beach is the intimate Sans Souci near the

Natatorium; it's hard to imagine that busy Waikīkī is a short stroll from the house. Reservations should be made three to four months in advance. ✉ *3240 Noela Dr., Waikīkī 96815* ⌂ *Reservations: Hawai'i's Best Bed and Breakfasts, Box 485, Laupahoehoe, 96767* ☎ *808/962–0100, 800/262–9912 reservations* 🖷 *808/962–6360* ⊕ *www.bestbnb.com* ⚐ *2 rooms* ⚬ *No A/C, no room phones, no smoking* ▭ *No credit cards. $130, 2-night minimum.*

Honolulu Beyond Waikīkī

$$$$ 🏨 **Aston at the Executive Centre Hotel.** Downtown Honolulu's only hotel is an all-suite high-rise in the center of the business district, within walking distance of the historic Capitol District and a 10-minute drive from Honolulu International Airport. Embarking on an interisland cruise? This hotel is three blocks from Aloha Tower Marketplace and the cruise ship terminal at Pier 10. This all suite hotel features accommodations on the top 10 floors of a 40-story glass-wall tower, providing magnificient views of downtown Honolulu and Honolulu Harbor by day or night. Many hotels offer their guests free continental breakfast each morning but here at the Executive Centre, it's served in the 40th Floor Executive Club with views so mesmerizing, you might linger over your morning coffee past sunset. Each spacious suite has a separate living area and kitchenette stocked with cold beverages. Some units have washer-dryers. The major disadvantage is that, after work hours, there are fewer dining options in the vicinity, so if you like to dine out, you might want to consider renting a car to explore after dark. ✉ *1088 Bishop St., Downtown Honolulu 96813* ☎ *808/539–3000 or 877/997– 6667* 🖷 *808/523–1088* ⊕ *www.aston-hotels.com* ⚐ *116 suites* ⚬ *Restaurant, A/C, in-room safes, kitchenettes, cable TV, in-room broadband, in-room data ports, pool, gym, spa, business services, parking (fee), no-smoking rooms* ▭ *AE, DC, MC, V. $200–$275.*

★ **$$$$** 🏨 **Kāhala Mandarin Oriental Hawai'i.** Hidden away in the wealthy residential neighborhood of Kāhala (on the other side of Diamond Head from Waikīkī), this elegant oceanfront hotel has played host to both presidents and princesses as one of Hawai'i's very first luxury resorts. The Kāhala is flanked by the exclusive Waialae Golf Links and the Pacific Ocean—surrounding it in a natural tranquillity in Waikīkī properties. Pathways meander out along a walkway with benches tucked into oceanfront nooks for lazy viewing or some seaside meditation. The reef not far from shore makes the waters here calm enough for young swimmers to try their water wings. You can also sign up for dolphin interactions in the 26,000-square-foot-lagoon. Rooms combine touches of Asia and old Hawai'i, with mahogany furniture, teak parquet floors, hand-loomed area rugs, local art, and grass-cloth wall coverings. Book a table at Hoku's for fantastic food and eye-popping views. If you plan to visit the second week of January and love the sport of golf, ask for a view of the course so you can have a bird's eye view of the PGA Sony Open from your lānai. ✉ *5000 Kāhala Ave., Kāhala 96816* ☎ *808/739– 8888 or 800/367–2525* 🖷 *808/739–8716* ⊕ *www.mandarinoriental.com/ kahala* ⚐ *341 rooms, 29 suites* ⚬ *5 restaurants, room service, A/C, in-room safes, minibars, cable TV, in-room data ports, pool, gym, spa, beach,* *dive shop, 2 bars, business services, no-smoking rooms* ⊟ *AE, D, DC, MC, V. $345–$735.*

$$–$$$$ 🏨 **Ala Moana Hotel.** Shoppers might wear out their Manolos here; the hotel is connected to O'ahu's biggest mall, the Ala Moana Shopping Center, by a pedestrian ramp, and it's a four-block stroll away from the Victoria Ward Centers. Business travelers are walking one block in the opposite direction to the Hawai'i Convention Center. Swimmers, surfers, and beachgoers make the two-minute walk to Ala Moana Beach Park across the street. Most rooms in the 36-story high-rise have a lānai with a view of Ala Moana Beach, the ocean, or the mountains; one-bedroom junior suites have a wall-to-wall Pacific Ocean view. Rooms on floors 29 to 35 have in-room whirlpool baths. The swimming pool has a chair lift for those with special needs. The hotel's nightclub, Rumours, is an after-work dance club favorite. ⊠ *410 Atkinson Dr., Ala Moana 96814* ☎ *808/955–4811 or 888/367–4811* 🖷 *808/944–6839* ⊕ *www. alamoanahotel.com* ⇆ *1,150 rooms, 67 suites* ♻ *4 restaurants, A/C, room service, in-room safes, minibars, cable TV, pool, gym, bar, 2 bars, dance club, nightclub, parking (fee), no-smoking rooms* ⊟ *AE, DC, MC, V. $135–$235.*

Windward O'ahu

$–$$$$ 🏨 **Schrader's Windward Country Inn.** If you're looking for an alternative to staying in Waikīkī and you aren't fussy about amenities, consider Schrader's. Though billed as "cottages by the sea," the setting is actually more roadside motel than resort. But Schrader's provides a moderately priced lodging option with amenities you won't find in Waikīkī, including complimentary biweekly ocean-reef tours that include snorkeling and kayaking the scenic windward coastline. One- to four-bedroom accommodations are available. Units feature microwaves and refrigerators, and some have full kitchens. Ask for the rooms that open onto Kāne'ohe Bay if you relish the possibility of fishing right off your lānai. ⊠ *47-039 Lihikai Dr., Kāne'ohe 96744* ☎ *808/239–5711 or 800/ 735–5711* 🖷 *808/239–6658* ⊕ *www.hawaiiscene.com/schrader* ⇆ *57 rooms* ♻ *BBQs, kitchenettes, pool* ⊟ *AE, D, DC, MC, V. 1-bedroom $72–$144, 2-bedroom $127–$215, 3-bedroom $226–$358, 4-bedroom $446–$551.*

$$ 🏨 **Ingrid's.** This B&B in the windward bedroom community of Kailua features a one-bedroom upstairs studio with decor that mimics those found in traditional Japanese inns, with *shoji* screen doors and black-tile counters. Ingrid is one of the island's most popular hosts, and she has created a little Zen of tranquillity in this unit that also features a kitchenette, deep soaking tub, and has its own private entrance through the home's Japanese-style garden. Guests have access to the pool, and Kailua Beach is less than 1 mi away. Three- to four-month advance reservations are required. ⊠ *Pauku St., Kailua 96734* ⒹReservations: *Hawai'i's Best Bed and Breakfasts, Box 485, Laupahoehoe, 96767* ☎ *808/962-0100, 800/262–9912 reservations* 🖷 *808/962-6360* ⊕ *www.bestbnb.com* ⇆ *2 rooms* ♻ *A/C, TV, kitchenettes; no room phones* ⊟ *No credit cards. $150, 4-night minimum.*

North Shore

$$$$ ☷ **Turtle Bay Resort.** A $35-million renovation in 2004 finally restored this resort to a grandeur worthy of its location on O'ahu's scenic North Shore. However, ongoing labor negotiations have proven to be a distraction for management and employees, causing the standard of service offered here to be inconsistant. If you decide to stay here, you might want to inquire about the status of those talks as the resort does have the potential to be one of O'ahu's jewels. The rooms are spacious, about 478 square feet, with lānai to showcase stunning peninsula views. In winter, when the big waves roll ashore, they provide a front row seat for watching the power of the surf. The oceanfront beach cottages are sumptuous retreats complete with Brazilian walnut floors, teak rockers on the lānai, and beds you can sink right into while listening to

> ## CHOOSING A VACATION RENTAL
>
> **Hawai'i's Best Bed and Breakfasts** (☎ 800/262-9912 ⊕ www.bestbnb.com) inspects and selects the top B&B's island-wide for its booking service inventory. You pay a $20 booking fee for your first reservation.
> **Pat's Kailua Beach Properties** (☎ 808/261-1653 or 808/262-4128 🖷 808/261-0893 ⊕ www.patskailua.com) books beachfront accommodations in the windward community of Kailua.
> **Team Real Estate** (☎ 808/637-3507 or 800/982-8602 🖷 808/637-8881 ⊕ www.teamrealestate.com) manages cottages, oceanfront homes, and condos on the North Shore.

the sounds of the surf right outside your cottage. Lei Lei's by the golf course is a resort favorite. Turtle Bay has 12 mi of nature trails, a Hans Heidemann Surf School, and the only 36-hole golf facility on O'ahu to keep you busy. A luxury home development is under construction in the resort area, adding a bit of construction noise to the resort's otherwise serene locale. ⊠ *57-091 Kamehameha Hwy., Box 187, Kahuku 96731* ☎ *808/293-8811 or 800/203-3650* 🖷 *808/293-9147* ⊕ *www.turtlebayresort.com* ➷ *373 rooms, 40 suites, 42 beach cottages* ⚒ *4 restaurants, room service, A/C, refrigerators, cable TV, 2 18-hole golf courses, 10 tennis courts, 2 pools, gym, spa, beach, horseback riding, 2 bars, shops, children's programs (ages 5–12), no-smoking rooms* ▤ *AE, D, DC, MC, V. $350–$780.*

¢–$$$$ ☷ **Backpackers Vacation Inn and Plantation Village.** Laid-back Hale'iwa surfer chic at its best. Spartan in furnishings, rustic in amenities, and definitely very casual in spirit, Backpackers is at Pūpūkea Beach Marine Sanctuary, otherwise known as Three Tables Beach. It's a short stroll to Waimea Bay. This is the place to catch z's between wave sets. Accommodation options include hostel-type dorm rooms, double rooms (some with a double bed, others with two single beds), cottages, and cabins. Some have kitchenettes; it's a three-minute walk to the supermarket. ⊠ *59-788 Kamehameha Hwy., Hale'iwa 96712* ☎ *808/638-7838* ⊕ *www.backpackers-hawaii.com* 🖷 *808/638-7515* ➷ *25 rooms* ⚒ *Some kitchenettes; no A/C, no phones in some rooms, no TV in some room* ▤ *MC, V. $20–$200.*

¢–$ 🖼 **AAA Breck's on the Beach Hostel.** Just north of Sunset Beach Park, Breck's offers convenient digs along the North Shore, with rooms ranging from basic dormitory to ocean-view balcony apartments that sleep eight people. Guests, usually surfer types from many continents, have access to free body boards and snorkeling equipment. Bicycles and surfboards are also available. Studio apartments have refrigerators and private baths, and the larger balcony apartments include kitchens. Airport pickup is available. ⊠ *59-043 Huelo St., Sunset Beach 96712* ☎ *808/638–7873* ⤴ *21 units* ⛵ *Some kitchens, airport shuttle; no A/C in some rooms* ⊟ *No credit cards. Hostel rates $20–$23, 1-bedroom $96–$114, cabins $132–$200, 3-night minimum.*

West O'ahu

★ $$$$ 🖼 **J. W. Marriott 'Ihilani Resort & Spa.** Forty-five minutes and a world away from the bustle of Waikīkī, this sleek, 17-story resort anchors the still-developing Ko'Olina Resort and Marina on O'ahu's leeward coastline. Honeymooners, NFL Pro Bowlers, and even local residents looking for a "neighbor island" experience without the hassle of catching a flight come to 'Ihilani for first-class R&R. The resort sits on one of Ko Olina's seven lagoons and features a lū'au cove and a Ted Robinson–designed 18-hole championship golf facility. Rooms here are spacious with 650 square feet, marble bathrooms with deep soaking tubs, private lānai, teak furnishings, in-room CD players, and high-tech control systems (lights, temperature controls). Most have ocean views. Dining options are increasing in the area, especially with the opening of Roy Yamaguchi's latest Hawaiian fusion eatery—Roy's at Ko Olina. A rental

> ### BUDGET-FRIENDLY HOTEL CHAINS
>
> The following local hotel chains specialize in hotel rooms and condo rentals for value prices. Buildings are older; amenities are limited; and the locations are rarely beachfront. However, you do get a clean place to toss your stuff and lay your head for the night. After all, you didn't come all the way here to stay in your hotel room, now did you?
>
> ■ **Aston Hotels** (☎ 877/997–6667 ⊕ www.aston-hotels.com).
> ■ **Castle Resorts** (☎ 800/367–5004 ⊕ www.castleresorts.com).
> ■ **Marc Resorts Hawaii** (☎ 800/535–0085 ⊕ www.marcresorts.com).
> ■ **Ohana Hotels** (☎ 800/462–6262 ⊕ www.ohanahotels.com).

car is pretty much a given if you choose to stay here; use it to shop at Waikele's Premium Outlets, to go to the movies in Kapolei, and to take the kids to the Hawaiian Waters Adventure Park (about a 10-minute drive). Just announced at this writing, Ko'Olina's next resort, the $1 billion, 1,000-room Grand 'Ilhilani, will include a world-class aquarium and should be under construction during 2006. ⊠ *92-1001 'Ōlani St., Kapolei 96707* ☎ *808/679–0079 or 800/626–4446* 🖷 *808/679–0080* ⊕ *www.ihilani.com* ⤴ *387 rooms, 63 suites* ⛵ *4 restaurants, room service, A/C, minibars, cable TV, 18-hole golf course, 6 tennis courts, 2 pools, health club, spa, beach, shops, babysitting, children's programs (ages 5–12), business services, no-smoking rooms* ⊟ *AE, DC, MC, V.*

WHERE TO SPA

Abhasa Spa. Natural organic skin and body treatments are the signature at this spa tucked away in the Royal Hawaiian Hotel's coconut grove. Thalasso therapy with seaweed, vegetarian lifestyle–spa therapies, color-light therapy, Ayurveda body treatments, acupuncture, and body cocooning are all available. You can choose to have your treatment in any of Abhasa's 12 indoor rooms or in one of their three garden cabanas. In the near future, look for an additional Abhasa Spa at the Sheraton Moana Surfrider Hotel, also in Waikīkī. ⊠ *Royal Hawaiian Hotel, 2259 Kalākaua Ave., Waikīkī* ☎ *808/922–8200* ⊕ *www.abhasa. com. $110, 50-minute lomi lomi massage.* ⚏ *Hair salon, indoor hot tub, sauna, showers. Services: massage, body cocoons and scrubs, hydrotherapy, waxing, facials.*

Ampy's European Facials and Body Spa. This 30-year-old spa has kept its prices reasonable over the years thanks to their "no frills" way of doing business. Just last year, Ampy's expanded their facilities to include two new facial rooms (all of Ampy's facials are 75-minutes) and manicure–pedicure stations. The spa has become famous for custom aromatherapy treatments. Call at least a week in advance because the appointment book fills up quickly here. It's in the Ala Moana Building, adjacent to the Ala Moana Shopping Center. ⊠ *1441 Kapi'olani Blvd., Suite 377, Ala Moana* ☎ *808/946–3838. $69, 60-min lomi lomi massage* ⚏ *Sauna. Services: Massage, body treatments, facials, hand and foot care.*

Aveda Salon and Spa. There are more than 3,000 independently owned Aveda spas in the world, but only one in Hawai'i. Aveda is the only spa on the island (and in the United States) to offer hydrotherm massage, where water-filled cushions cradle your body as a therapist works out your body's kinks. This spa has everything from Vichy showers to hydrotherapy rooms to customized aromatherapy. Ladies, they'll even touch-up your makeup for free before you leave. ⊠ *Ala Moana Shopping Center, 3rd fl., 1450 Ala Moana Blvd., Ala Moana* ☎ *808/ 947–6141* ⊕ *www.aveda.com. $110, 50-min lomi lomi massage* ⚏ *Hair salon, eucalyptus steam room. Services: massage, waxing, facials, body treatments.*

Hawaiian Rainforest Salon and Spa. This spa's most popular massage uses pressure and heat from natural Hawaiian lava rocks to rub your pain away. They also have Vichy showers, aromatherapy whirlpool baths, a Korean-style Akasuri body polish, and a wide selection of treatment packages. If you're sleepy from the long flight, try the jet-lag remedy, a 25-minute treatment that includes a neck massage, and scalp rub. ⊠ *Pacific Beach Hotel, 5th fl., 2490 Kalākaua Ave., Waikīkī* ☎ *808/441–4890* ⊕ *www.hawaiianrainforest.com. $85, 50-min lomi lomi massage* ⚏ *Hair salon, hot tubs, sauna. Services: massage, body wraps, body care, facials, makeup.*

J. W. Marriott 'Ihilani Resort & Spa. West O'ahu conceals a unique Hawaiian hydrotherapy spa that gives you the chance to soak in warm seawater among velvety orchid blossoms. Relax and rejuvenate in one of

18 treatment rooms with 'Ihilani spa's new Pua Kai line of natural aromatherapy products. These products include massage and body oil, bath crystals and body butter, which combine ingredients such as ginger, jasmine, rose petals, coconut and grape seed oil. The 'Ihilani spa also specializes in thalassotherapy treatments that may combine underwater jet massage with color therapy and essential oils. Specially designed treatment rooms have a hydrotherapy tub, a Vichy-style shower, and a needle shower with 12 heads. Bathing suits are optional in the women's only indoor Jacuzzi. ⊠ *J. W. Marriott 'Ihilani Resort & Spa, 92-1001 'Ōlani St., Kapolei* ☎ *808/679–0079* ⊕ *www.ihilani.com. $115, 50-min lomi lomi massage* ⚹ *Hair salon, hot tubs (indoor and outdoor), sauna, steam room. Gym with: cardiovascular machines, free weights, weight-training equipment. Services: aromatherapy, body wraps and scrubs, facials, massage, thalassotherapy. Classes and programs: aerobics, body sculpting, dance classes, fitness analysis, guided walks, personal training, Pilates, tai chi, yoga.*

★ **Mandara Spa at the Hilton Hawaiian Village.** From its perch in the Kalia Tower, the cosmopolitan Mandara Spa, an outpost of the chain that originated in Thailand, overlooks the high-rises of downtown Honolulu. Hawaiian ingredients and techniques headline an international roster of treatments. Choose a facial infused with vanilla and pīkake flowers or a scrub made from Kona coffee to follow your favorite massage. Exotic upgrades, like eye treatments using Japanese silk protein and reflexology, and Elemis products tempt you to turn indulgence into pure decadence. The delicately scented, candlelight waiting area can fill up quickly with robe-clad conventioneers, so be sure to make a reservation. Twenty-five treatment rooms keep appointments on schedule. The facility also includes spa suites for couples, a private infinity pool, and a café. ⊠ *Hilton Hawaiian Village Beach Resort and Spa, 2005 Kālia Rd., Waikīkī* ☎ *808/949–4321* ⊕ *www.hiltonhawaiianvillage.com. $115, 50-min lomi lomi massage* ⚹ *Hair salon, hot tubs (indoor and outdoor), sauna, steam room. Gym with: cardiovascular machines, free weights, weight-training equipment. Services: aromatherapy, body wraps and scrubs, facials, massage.*

Nā Hō'ola at the Hyatt Waikīkī. Nā Hō'ola is the largest spa in Waikīkī, sprawling across the fifth and sixth floors of the Hyatt, with 19 treatment rooms, jet baths, and Vichy showers. It's well worth it to arrive early for your treatment and sit to enjoy the view from the lounge, which has postcard views of Waikīkī beach. Four packages identified by Hawai'i's native healing plants—noni, kukui, awa, and kalo—span 2½–4 hours and combine various body, face, and hair treatments. If you're feeling adventurous, try the Champagne of the Sea body treatment, which will have you slathered in self-heating mud and wrapped in a snug cocoon to release tension and stress from your body. There's also a small exercise room with seven cardio machines for use by hotel guests only. ⊠ *Hyatt Regency Waikīkī Resort and Spa, 2424 Kalākaua Ave., Waikīkī* ☎ *808/921–6097* ⊕ *www.hyattwaikiki.com. $110, for a 50-min lomi lomi massage* ⚹ *Sauna, showers. Gym with: cardiovascular machines. Services: aromatherapy, body scrubs and wraps, facials, hydrotherapy, massage.*

Paul Brown Salon and Day Spa. This is one of the few salons where the principal owner still works the floor. Paul Brown's specialized treatments combat everything from cellulite to low energy to dry skin. There's even a facial designed especially for men. ⊠ *Ward Centre, 1200 Ala Moana Blvd., Ala Moana* ☎*808/591–1881* ⊕*www.paulbrownhawaii.com. $65, 50-min lomi lomi massage* ♿ *Hair and nail salon. Services: massage, body scrubs, body wraps, makeup, facials, waxing.*

Serenity Spa Hawai'i. Want to jump start your "just back from Hawai'i" tan without burning to a crisp? Consider the Golden Touch tanning massage, which combines a massage with tan accelerators, sunscreen, and scented oils. Only steps off the beach, this day spa provides aromatherapy treatments, massages, and facials. You can mix and match treatments from the menu to create a specialized package. ⊠ *Outrigger Reef on the Beach, 2169 Kālia Rd., Waikīkī* ☎ *808/926–2882* ⊕ *www. serenityspahawaii.com. $90, 55-min lomi lomi massage* ♿ *Showers, nail salon, hair station. Services: massage, facials, body treatments, waxing, makeup.*

SpaHalekulani. There's no common area or locker rooms, just seven individualized suites for personalized pampering. SpaHalekulani's signature treatments mine the healing traditions of the South Pacific Islands, including Hawai'i, Tahiti, Tonga, and Samoa. The exclusive Japanese Ton Ton Amma (pounders) is an invigorating massage. For a more relaxed experience try the popular Polynesian Nonu, which utilizes warm stones and healing nonu gel. SpaHalekulani has also created their own line of body products, all made in Hawai'i. Choose between relaxing lavender orchid, cleansing hibiscus, purifying limu seaweed, antiaging papaya-pineapple, nourishing coconut passion or invigorating Manoa mint. ⊠ *Halekūlani Hotel 2199 Kālia Rd., Waikīkī* ☎ *808/931–5322* ⊕ *www.halekulani.com. $180, 75-min lomi lomi massage* ♿ *Use of facilities is specific to treatment but may include Japanese furo bath, steam shower or whirlpool tub. Services: hair salon, nail care, massage, facials, body treatments.*

The Spa Luana at Turtle Bay Resort. Luxuriate at the ocean's edge at this serene spa, which offers custom massage treatments and beauty rituals, and includes a full-service hair and nail salon. To soothe sun-burned skin, try the Hawaiian Ti-leaf body wrap with kukui nut oil and coconut pulp or enjoy a relaxing Polynesian sea-salt scrub. In addition to in-spa treatments, there are private spa suites, an outdoor treatment cabana that overlooks the surf, a fitness center and outdoor exercise studio, and a lounge area and juice bar. ⊠ *Turtle Bay Resort, 57-091 Kamehameha Hwy., North Shore* ☎ *808/447–6868* ⊕ *www.turtlebayresort.com. $105, 50-min lomi lomi massage* ♿ *Hair and nail salon, showers, steam room, outdoor whirlpool. Gym with: free weights, cardio and weight-training machines. Services: facials, massages, body treatments, waxing. Classes and programs: hula aerobics, Pilates, yoga.*

★ **Spa Olakino at the Waikīkī Beach Marriott.** Paul Brown has created a spa facing Waikīkī Beach. Linger with a cup of tea between treatments and gaze through 75-foot windows at all the activity outside. Lush Hawaiian foliage, sleek Balinese teak furnishings, and a mist of ylang-ylang and nutmeg in the air inspire relaxation within. Paul Brown recently introduced a new Hapuna line of essential oils, as well as a thermal masking system using volcanic ash, which is incorporated into treatments. Spa Olakino's ultimate couples package is a four-hour experience that includes not only getting a massage but also learning how to give your partner a massage and ends with chocolate-covered strawberries at sunset. If you're going solo, try their signature Magic Island Massage, which fuses Thai, shiatsu, lomi lomi, and reflexology into one ultimate massage. ⊠ *Waikīkī Beach Marriott, 2552 Kalākaua Ave., Waikīkī* 🕾 *808/922–6611* ⊕ *www.marriottwaikiki.com. $100, 50-min lomi lomi massage* ♿ *Hair salon, nail care, steam showers. Services: massage, facials, body treatments, waxing.*

★ **Spa Suites at the Kāhala Mandarin Oriental.** At this spa, you'll feel like you're relaxing at home, and you're the only one there. The suites, which are really five renovated hotel rooms with wooden floors and hand-woven Hawaiian quilts, all have Jacuzzis, private vanity areas, and private gardens in which to relax between treatments. The therapist welcomes you with a foot bath ritual. Custom-designed treatments merge Hawaiian, Asian, and traditional therapies. ⊠ *Kāhala Mandarin Oriental, 5000 Kāhala Ave., Kāhala* 🕾 *808/739–8938. $165, 75-min lomi lomi massage* ♿ *Hair salon, hot tub, sauna, steam room. Services: facials, massage, body treatments.*

WHERE TO EAT

O'ahu, where the majority of the Islands' 2,000-plus restaurants are located, offers the best of all worlds: it's got the foreignness and excitement of Asia and Polynesia, but when the kids need McDonald's, or when you just have to have a Starbucks latte, they're here, too.

Budget for a $$$$ dining experience at the very top of the restaurant food chain, where chefs Alan Wong, Roy Yamaguchi, George Mavrothalassitis, and others you've read about in *Gourmet* put a sophisticated and unforgettable spin on local foods and flavors. Savor seared 'ahi tuna in sea urchin beurre blanc or steak marinated in Korean kim chee sauce.

Spend the rest of your food dollars where budget-conscious locals do: in plate-lunch places and small ethnic eateries, at roadside stands and lunchwagons, or at window-in-the-wall delis. Munch a musubi rice cake, slurp shave ice with red bean paste, order up Filipino pork adobo with two scoops of rice and macaroni salad.

In Waikīkī, where most visitors stay, you can find choices from gracious rooms with a view to surprisingly authentic Japanese noodle shops. But hop in the car, or on the trolley or bus, and travel just a few miles in any direction, and you can save your money and get in touch with the real food of Hawai'i.

Ka'imukī's Wai'alae Avenue, for example, offers one of the city's best espresso bars, a hugely popular Chinese bakery, a highly recommended patisserie, an exceptional Italian bistro, a dim sum restaurant, Mexican food (rare here), and a Hawai'i regional cuisine standout, 3660 on the Rise—all in three blocks and 10 minutes from Waikīkī. Chinatown, 10

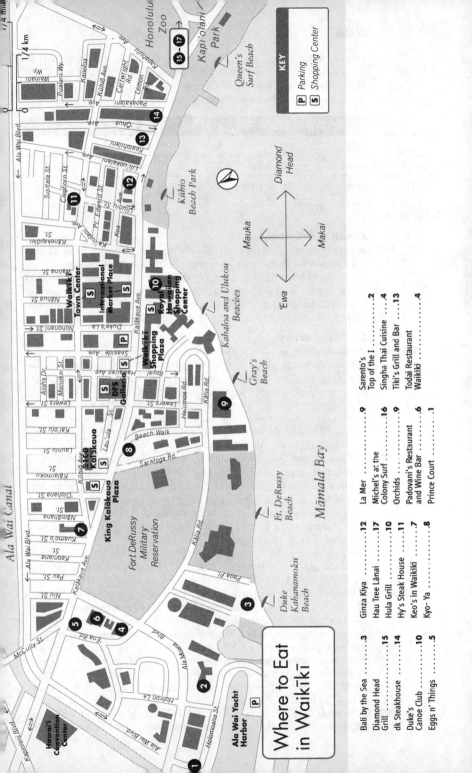

Where to Eat in Waikīkī

Bali by the Sea 3	Ginza Kiya 12
Diamond Head Grill 15	Hau Tree Lānai 17
dk Steakhouse 14	Hula Grill 10
Duke's Canoe Club 10	Hy's Steak House 11
Eggs n' Things 5	Keo's in Waikīkī 7
	Kyo-Ya 8

La Mer 12	Sarento's 9
Michel's at the Colony Surf 16	Top of the I 2
Orchids 9	Singha Thai Cuisine 4
Padovani's Restaurant and Wine Bar 6	Tiki's Grill and Bar 13
Prince Court 1	Todai Restaurant Waikīkī 4

KEY

P Parking
S Shopping Center

minutes in the other direction and easily reached by the Waikiki Trolley, is another dining (and shopping) treasure, not only for Chinese but also Vietnamese, Filipino, Malaysian, Indian, and Euro-Asian food, and even a chic little tea shop.

	WHAT IT COSTS				
	$$$$	**$$$**	**$$**	**$**	**¢**
RESTAURANTS	over $30	$20–$30	$12–$20	$7–$12	under $7

Restaurant prices are for one main course at dinner.

Waikīkī

American–Casual

$–$$ ✕ **Eggs 'n Things.** A favorite of Waikīkī hotel workers for its late hours (11 PM to 2 PM daily), this restaurant on the first floor of an obscure budget hotel has a hearty, country-style menu with a few island touches (tropical pancake syrups, fresh grilled fish) and a permanent line out front. ⊠ *Hawaiian Monarch Hotel, 1911–B Kalākaua Ave., Waikīkī* ☎ *808/949–0820* ▤ *No credit cards* ☉ *No dinner. $7–$14.*

Contemporary

$$$–$$$$ ✕ **Bali by the Sea.** This many-windowed, multilevel room takes delightful advantage of the restaurant's perch above the beach, facing Diamond Head. Chef Roberto Los Baños creates unfussy contemporary cuisine—grilled fish, steaks, and chops with fusion flavors predominating. The experienced staff, often called on to serve the VIPS who favor this hotel, extend unruffled and gracious service. ⊠ *Hilton Hawaiian Village, 2005 Kālia Rd., Waikīkī* ☎ *808/941–2254* ⚑ *Reservations essential* ▤ *AE, D, DC, MC, V* ☉ *Closed Sun. No lunch. $25–$43.*

$$$–$$$$ ✕ **Diamond Head Grill.** This beautifully appointed room, with its surprising view across Kapiʻolani Park and up the slopes of Diamond Head, has a split personality: quiet dinner house in the early evening, very happening bar in the late evening. The Hawaiʻi regional cuisine menu (Molokaʻi sweet potato gnocchi in marscarpone cream, macadamia-crusted lamb chops, lava cake with honey gelato) is seductive and well-prepared. A nice feature: you can pair half-orders of any two entrées if you just can't make up your mind ($40). ⊠ *W Hotel, 2nd fl., 2885 Kalākaua Ave. Waikīkī* ☎ *808/922–3734* ⚑ *Reservations essential* ▤ *AE, D, DC, MC, V. $23–$40.*

$$$–$$$$ ✕ **Prince Court.** Though little heralded, this restaurant overlooking Ala Wai Yacht Harbor is a multifaceted success, offering exceptional high-end lunches and dinners, daily one-price buffets at every meal, and sold-out weekend brunches. The style is contemporary island cuisine (portobello mushroom and crab hash napoleon, Pacific snapper with wild mushroom ragout) but with many Eastern touches, as this hotel is popular with Japanese nationals. ⊠ *Hawaiʻi Prince Hotel, 100 Holomoana St., Waikīkī* ☎ *808/944–4494* ⚑ *Reservations essential* ▤ *AE, D, DC, MC, V. $25–$42.*

$$–$$$$ ✕ **Hau Tree Lānai.** The many-branched, vinelike hau tree is ideal for sitting under, and it's said that the one that spreads itself over this beachside courtyard is the very one that shaded Robert Louis Stevenson as he mused and wrote about Hawai'i. In any case, diners are still enjoying the shade, though the view has changed—the gay-friendly beach over the low wall is paved with hunky sunbathers. The food is unremarkable island casual, but we like the place for late afternoon or early-evening drinks, pūpū, and people-watching. ⊠ *New Otani Kaimana Beach Hotel, 2863 Kalākaua Ave., Waikīkī* ☎ *808/921–7066* ⊕ *www.kaimana. com* ⅍ *Reservations essential* ⊟ *AE, D, DC, MC, V. $15–$32.*

$$–$$$ ✕ **Duke's Canoe Club.** Notorious as the spot where Jimmy Buffett did a free, impromptu concert that had people standing six-deep on the beach outside, Duke's is both an open-air bar and a very popular steak-and-seafood grill. It's known for its Big Island pork ribs, huli-huli (rotisserie) chicken, and grilled catch of the day, as well as for a simple and economical Sunday brunch. A drawback is that it's often loud and crowded, and the live contemporary Hawaiian music often stymies conversation. ⊠ *Outrigger Waikīkī on the Beach, 2335 Kalākaua Ave., Waikīkī* ☎ *808/922–2268* ⊕*www.hulapie.com* ⅍*Reservations essential* ⊟*AE, DC, MC, V. $12–$25.*

$–$$$ ✕ **Hula Grill.** The placid younger sister of boisterous Duke's downstairs, this restaurant and bar resembles a plantation-period summer home: open to the air, outfitted with kitschy decor, stone-flagged floors, warm wood, and floral prints. The food is carefully prepared and familiar—standard breakfast items, steaks and grilled seafood at dinner—but with local and Asian touches that add interest. There's a fabulous Diamond Head view. ⊠ *Outrigger Waikīkī on the Beach, 2335 Kalākaua Ave., Waikīkī* ☎ *808/923–4852* ⅍ *Reservations essential* ⊟ *AE, D, DC, MC, V* ⊘ *No lunch. $7–$26.*

$–$$$ ✕ **Tiki's Grill and Bar.** Tiki's, on the second floor of a busy hotel, is the kind of place people come to Waikīkī for: designed for fun, a retro–South Pacific spot with a back-of-the-bar faux volcano, an open-air lounge with live local-style music, indoor-outdoor dining, and a view of the beach across the street. The menu is—inevitably—contemporary island cuisine (Japanese seven-spice salmon, plate-lunch standards reinterpreted in a sophisticated way); exceptional desserts and a late-night bar menu. ⊠ *Aston Waikīkī Beach Hotel, 2570 Kalākaua Ave., Waikīkī* ☎ *808/ 923–8454* ⅍ *Reservations essential* ⊟ *AE, D, DC, MC, V. $10–$25.*

French

★ $$$$ ✕ **La Mer.** La Mer, like the hotel in which it's housed (Halekūlani, "House Befitting Heaven"), is pretty much heavenly. The softly lighted, low-ceiling room has its windows open to the breeze, the perfectly framed vista of Diamond Head, and the faint sound of music from a courtyard below. The food captures the rich and yet sunny flavors of the south of France in one tiny, exquisite course after another. We recommend the degustation menu; place yourself in the sommelier's hands for wine choices from the hotel's exceptional cellar. ⊠ *Halekūlani, 2199 Kālia Rd., Waikīkī* ☎ *808/923–2311* ⅍ *Reservations essential* ⅏ *Jacket required* ⊟ *AE, DC, MC, V* ⊘ *No lunch. $38–$48.*

$$$–$$$$ ✕ **Michel's at the Colony Surf.** With its wide-open windows so close to the water that you literally feel the soft mist at high tide, this is arguably the most romantic spot in Waikīkī for a sunset dinner for two. Venerable Michel's is synonymous with fine dining in the minds of Oahuans who have been coming here for 20 years. The menu is très, très French with both classic choices (escargot, foie gras) and more contemporary dishes (potato-crusted onaga fish). There's dinner nightly, and Sunday brunch. ⊠ *Colony Surf, 2895 Kalākaua Ave., Waikīkī* ☎ *808/923–6552* ⌖ *Reservations essential* ⊟ *AE, D, DC, MC, V* ⊘ *No lunch. $28–$40.*

$$–$$$$ ✕ **Padovani's Restaurant and Wine Bar.** Quiet (almost too quiet) and rather formal, Padovani's is composed of a second-floor wine bar—it was one of the first in the city, offering exceptional wines by the glass, as well as a single-malt scotch collection—and an elegant dining room. The menu ranges from simple bistro-style dishes (steak and fries, steamed clams) in the wine bar, to sophisticated Euro-Asian creations (melting salmon poached in olive oil, then served in a light lemongrass broth) in the dining room. We like the bar, which looks across the green lawns of Fort DeRussy, for a casual lunch or supper. In the dining room: slacks, collared shirts, closed shoes required for men; dresses, pantsuits for women. ⊠ *Doubletree Alana Waikīkī, 1956 Ala Moana Blvd., Waikīkī* ☎ *808/946–3456* ⌖ *Reservations essential* ⊟ *AE, D, DC, MC, V. $16–$35.*

Italian

$$–$$$$ ✕ **Sarento's Top of the 'I'.** Among the best view restaurants in the city, looking toward both the Ko'olau Mountains and the South Shore, 30th-floor Sarento's specializes in regional Italian cuisine and is an especially favored date-night venue. The lobster ravioli and osso buco are local favorites; the wine cellar contains some gems, and prices are reasonable for a fine-dining spot. ⊠ *Renaissance 'Ilikai Waikīkī Hotel, 1777 Ala Moana, top fl., Waikīkī* ☎ *808/955–5559* ⌖ *Reservations essential* ⊟ *AE, D, DC, MC, V* ⊘ *No lunch. $18–$36.*

Japanese

$$$–$$$$ ✕ **Kyo-Ya.** Tell an Islander that dinner is at Kyo-Ya, and you get a long drawn-out "Ooooh," acknowledging both the restaurant's reputation for quality, and its top-flight prices. As to authenticity, suffice it to say that you're likely to run into members of the Japanese consular staff. The menu is complete with *teishoku* (combination meals that include salad, soup, sides, and rice), very fresh sushi, noodles, grilled dishes, and hot pots prepared at table. Kyo-Ya occupies a striking building with a contemporary teahouse design fronted by an Asian garden. ⊠ *2057 Kalākaua Ave., Waikīkī* ☎ *808/947–3911* ⌖ *Reservations essential* ⊟ *AE, D, DC, MC, V* ⊘ *No lunch Sun. $20–$55.*

> **CHEAP EATS IN WAIKĪKĪ**
>
> Thanks to the many Japanese nationals who stay here, Waikīkī is blessed with lots of cheap, filling, authentic Japanese food, particularly noodles. Spots to try: Odoriko in King's Village, Menchanko-Tei in the Waikīkī Trade Center, Ezogiku at 2146 Kalākaua Avenue, or Gyu-Kaku at 307 Lewers Street. Plastic representations of food in the window are an indicator of authenticity and a help in ordering.

★ **$-$$$** ✕ **Sansei Seafood Restaurant & Sushi Bar.** D. K. Kodama's "Japanese-based Pacific Rim" cuisine is an experience not to be missed, from early-bird dinners (from 5 PM) to discounted late-night dining (until 1 AM, with karaoke). Specialty sushi ranges far beyond California rolls to mango-crab or foie gras nigiri sushi. We fantasize about the signature calamari salad with spicy Korean sauce and crisp-tender calamari. Cleverly named and beautifully prepared dishes come in big and small plates or in a $35 six-course tasting menu. Finish with tempura fried ice cream or Mama Kodama's brownies. ⊠ *Waikīkī Beach Marriott Resort and Spa, 2552 Kalākaua Ave., Waikīkī* ☎ *808/931–6286* ▭ *AE, D, MC, V. $4–$28.*

Japanese Noodle Shops

$-$$ ✕ **Ginza Kiya.** Distinctly unfancy, with linoleum floors and wooden tables, this Tokyo-style spot comes highly recommended for the only thing noodle fanciers care about: authentic, rich broth and fresh *udon* (wheat) and *soba* (buckweat) noodles. Hot noodle soup, cold noodles with dipping sauce, and *donburi* (rice bowls), are offered, plus such specialties as *hiya yakko* (cold tofu topped with ginger and soy sauce) and Western-style green salad on noodles with sesame dressing. Don't worry—there's an English-language menu and a fork will appear on your faux laqueur tray without your even having to ask. Portions are sizable; entrées are served with salad, pickles, and clear soup. The small bar stocks beer, sake, *shochu* (Japanese flavored liquor), and Japanese newspapers. ⊠ *Aston Waikiki Circle Hotel, 2464 Kalākaua Ave., Waikīkī* ☎ *808/ 923–8840* ⌂ *Reservations not accepted* ▭ *No credit cards. $7–$15.*

Seafood

$$$-$$$$ ✕ **Orchids.** Perched along the sea wall at historic Gray's Beach, Orchids is beloved of ladies who lunch, power breakfasters, and family groups celebrating at the elaborate Sunday brunch. La Mer, upstairs, is better known, but we were pleasantly surprised to find that dinner here is equally enjoyable, with the fold-back walls open to the breezes, the orchids adding splashes of color, the seafood perfectly prepared, and the wine list intriguing. Plus, Orchids is more casual and a bit less expensive. Whatever meal you have here, finish with the hotel's signature coconut layer cake, a longtime favorite of the local-born elite, who consider Halekūlani something of a private club. ⊠ *Halekūlani, 2199 Kālia Rd., Waikīkī* ☎ *808/923–2311* ⌂ *Reservations essential* ▭ *AE, D, DC, MC, V. $22–$40.*

$$-$$$ ✕ **Todai Restaurant WaikīkT.** Bountiful buffets and menus that feature seafood are Islanders' two favorites, so when this Japan-based restaurant opened some years ago, it was mobbed despite the difficulties of parking in Waikīkī. It continues to be popular with budget-conscious travelers for the wide range of hot dishes, sushi, and the 160-foot seafood spread, though the emphasis here is more on quantity than quality. Lunch is $14.95 weekdays, $15.95 weekends; dinner is $25.95–$26.95 daily. ⊠ *1910 Ala Moana Blvd., Waikīkī* ☎ *808/947–1000* ⌂ *Reservations essential* ▭ *AE, D, DC, MC, V. $15–$27.*

Steak

$$$-$$$$ ✕ **dk Steakhouse.** Around the country, the steak house has returned to prominent arts as dry-aging and preparing the perfect Bernaise sauce have been revived. D. K. Kodama's chic second-floor restaurant characterizes this trend with such presentations as the sybaritic 22-ounce bone-in rib eye aged 15 days in-house ($32.95) and Oscar of filet mignon with blue crab Bernaise ($29.95). The restaurant shares space, but not a menu, with Kodama's Sansei Seafood Restaurant & Sushi Bar; sit at the bar perched between the two and you can order from either menu. ⊠ *Waikīkī Beach Marriott Resort and Spa, 2552 Kalākaua Ave., Waikīkī* ☎ *808/ 931–6280* ⊟ *AE, D, MC, V* ☉ *No lunch. $19–$33.*

$$$–$$$$ ✕ **Hy's Steak House.** If the Rat Pack reconvened for big steaks and a bigger red, they'd feel right at home at Hy's, which has changed little in the last 30 years. The formula: prime grade beef, old-style service, a men's club atmosphere (but ladies very welcome), and a wine list recognized for excellence by *Wine Spectator.* Specialties: Beef Wellington, Caesar salad and those tableside flambéed desserts we see so rarely now. ⊠ *Waikīkī Park Heights Hotel, 2440 Kūhiō Ave., Waikīkī* ☎ *808/922– 5555* ⌖ *Reservations essential* ⊟ *AE, DC, MC, V* ☉ *No lunch. $20–$60.*

Thai

$$–$$$$ ✕ **Singha Thai Cuisine.** The Chaowasaree family's devotion to their native Thailand is evident in the gilt model of the Thai royal palace that graces the entryway of this tastefully decorated restaurant just below street level on a busy Waikīkī corner. This is also the only Thai restaurant in the city to showcase Thai dance each evening. We especially like Singha Thai's way with seafood—Siamese Fighting Fish, a whole fish sizzling in garlic-chili oil—and the contemporary additions to the menu masterminded by chef Chai—blackened 'ahi summer rolls. ⊠ *1910 Ala Moana Blvd., Waikīkī* ☎ *808/941–2898* ⊟ *AE, D, DC, MC, V* ☉ *No lunch. $13–$35.*

$–$$ ✕ **Keo's in Waikīkī.** Many Islanders—and many Hollywood stars—got their first taste of pad thai noodles, lemongrass, and coconut-milk curry at one of Keo Sananikone's restaurants. This one, perched right at the entrance to Waikīkī, characterizes his formula: a bright, clean space awash in flowers with intriguing menu titles and reasonable prices. Evil Jungle Prince, a stir-fry redolent of Thai basil, flecked with chilies and rich with coconut milk, is a classic. Also try the apple bananas in coconut milk. ⊠ *2028 Kūhiō Ave., Waikīkī* ☎ *808/951–9355* ⊟ *AE, D, DC, MC, V. $10–$18.*

Honolulu: Ala Moana, Downtown & Chinatown

American–Casual

★ **$–$$** ✕ **Side Street Inn.** Famous as the place where celebrity chefs gather after hours, local boy Colin Nishida's pub on an obscure side street near Ala Moana Shopping Center is worth searching for despite annoying smoke and sometimes surly staff because he makes the best darned pork chops and fried rice in the world. Local-style bar food comes in huge, share-plate portions here. This is a place to dress any way you like, nosh all night, watch sports on TV, and sing karaoke until they boot you out. Lunch is weekdays 10:30 AM to 1:30 PM. Pūpū (in portions so large as

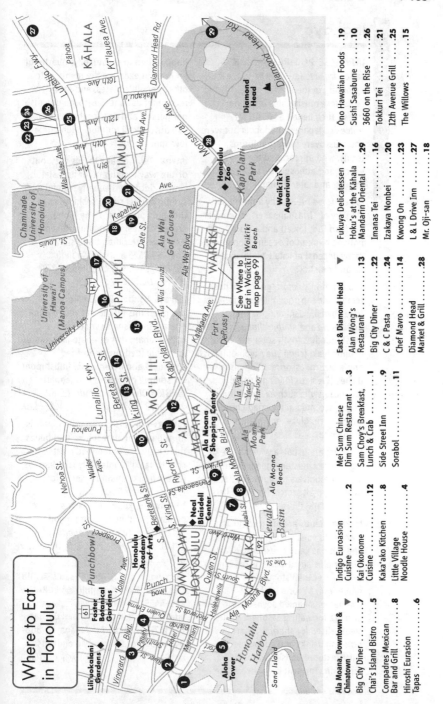

Where to Eat in Honolulu

Ala Moana, Downtown & Chinatown

Big City Diner **7**
Chai's Island Bistro **5**
Compadres Mexican Bar and Grill **8**
Hiroshi Eurasion Tapas **6**

Indigo Euroasion Cuisine **2**
Kai Okonome Cuisine **12**
Kaka'ako Kitchen **8**
Little Village Noodle House **4**

Mei Sum Chinese Dim Sum Restaurant ...**3**
Sam Choy's Breakfast, Lunch & Crab **1**
Side Street Inn **9**
Sorabol **11**

East & Diamond Head ▶

Alan Wong's Restaurant **13**
Big City Diner **22**
C & C Pasta **24**
Chef Mavro **14**
Diamond Head Market & Grill **28**

Fukuya Delicatessen ...**17**
Hoku's at the Kāhala Mandarin Oriental ...**29**
Imanas Tei **16**
Izakaya Nonbei **20**
Kwong On **23**
L & L Drive Inn **27**
Mr. Oji-san **18**

Ono Hawaiian Foods ...**19**
Sushi Sasabune **10**
3660 on the Rise **26**
Tokkuri Tei **21**
12th Avenue Grill **25**
The Willows **15**

Izakaya

JAPANESE PUB-RESTAURANTS, called *izakaya* (ee-ZAH-ka-ya), are sprouting in the Islands like *matsutake* mushrooms in a pine forest. They began as oases for homesick Japanese nationals but were soon discovered by adventurous locals, who appreciated the welcoming atmosphere, sprawling menus, and later dining hours.

Expect to be greeted by a merry, full-staff cry of "Irrashaimase!", offered an *oshibori* (hot towel) and a drink, and handed a menu of dozens (sometimes many dozens) of small-plate, made-to-order dishes.

You can find *yakitori* (grilled dishes), tempura (deep-fried dishes), *donburi* (rice bowls), sushi and sashimi, *nabemono* and *shabu-shabu* (hot pots), noodles (both soup and fried), okonomiyaki (chop suey-type omelets) and a bizarre assortment of *yoshoku* dishes (Western foods prepared in Japanese style, such as hamburgers in soy-accented gravy, fried chicken with a mirin glaze, odd gratins, and even pizza).

Full bars are usual; a wide choice of lager-type beers and good-to-great sakes are universal. Many specialize in single-malt scotch, but wine lists are generally short.

Izakaya menus are often confusing, many staff speak marginal English, and outings can get expensive fast (liquor plus small-plate prices equals eyes bigger than stomach). Prices range from $5 for a basket of edamame (steamed soybeans) to $20 or more for wafu (seasoned, grilled steak, sliced for sharing). Start by ordering drinks and edamame or silky-textured braised *kabocha* pumpkin. This will keep the waiter

happy. Then give yourself a quarter of an hour to examine the menu, ogle other people's plates, and seek recommendations. Start with one dish per person and one for the table; you can always call for more. Here are a few spots to try:

Imanas Tei. Go early to this cozy, out-of-the-way restaurant for its tasteful, simple decor and equally tasteful and simply perfect sushi, sashimi, *nabe* (hot pots prepared at the table), and grilled dishes; reservations taken from 5 to 7 PM; after that, there's always a line. ✉ *2626 S. King, Mō'ili'ili* ☎ *808/941-2626 or 808/934-2727* ▭ *AE, DC, MC, V $8-$25.*

Izakaya Nonbei. Teruaki Mori designed this pub to put you in mind of a northern inn in winter in his native Japan; dishes not to miss—*karei kara-age* (delicate deep-fried flounder) and *dobinmushi* (mushroom consommè presented in a teapot). ✉ *3108 Olu St., Kapahulu* ☎ *808/ 734-5573* ▭ *AE, D, DC, MC, V $7-$20.*

Tokkuri-Tei. This is a favorite of locals for the playful atmosphere that belies the excellence of the food created by chef Hideaki "Santa" Miyoshi, famous for his quirky menu names (Nick Jagger, Spider Poke); just say "Moriwase, kudasai" ("chef's choice, please"), and he'll order for you. ✉ *611 Kapahulu Ave., Kapahulu* ☎ *808/739-2800* ▭ *AE, D, DC, MC, V $13-$25.*

Also worth a visit: **Mr. Oji-san** (✉ 1018 Kapahulu Ave., Kapahulu ☎ 808/ 735-4455) for family-style izakaya specialties; and **Kai Okonomi Cuisine** (✉ 1427 Makaloa, Ala Moana ☎ 808/ 944-1555) for Osaka-style omelets.

– By Wanda Adams

to be dinner) is from 4 PM to 12:30 AM daily. Reservations are for large parties only. ⊠ *1225 Hopaka St., Ala Moana* ☎ *808/591–0253* ▤ *AE, D, DC, MC, V* ☺ *No lunch weekends. $8–$15.*

Chinese

$–$$ ✕ **Little Village Noodle House.** Unassuming and budget-friendly, Little Village sets a standard of friendly and attentive service to which every Chinese restaurant should aspire. We have roamed the large, pan-China menu and found a new favorite in everything we've tried: shredded beef, spinach with garlic, Shanghai noodles, honey-walnut shrimp, and orange chicken with actual oranges. Two words: go there. ⊠ *1113 Smith St., Chinatown* ☎ *808/545–3008* ▤ *AE, D, MC, V. $7–$15.*

Fodor'sChoice ★

¢–$ ✕ **Mei Sum Chinese Dim Sum Restaurant.** In contrast to the sprawling and noisy halls in which dim sum is generally served, Mei Sum is compact and shiny bright. It's open daily, serving nothing but small plates from 7:45 AM to 8:45 PM. Be ready to guess and point as not much English is spoken, but the delicate buns and tasty bits are exceptionally well-prepared. ⊠ *65 N. Pauahi St., Chinatown* ☎ *808/531–3268* ▤ *No credit cards. $3–$10.*

Contemporary

$$–$$$$ ✕ **Chai's Island Bistro.** Chai Chaowasaree's stylish, light-bathed and orchid-draped lunch and dinner restaurant expresses the sophisticated side of this Thai-born immigrant. He plays East against West on the plate in signature dishes such as *kataifi* (baked and shredded phyllo)–macadamia-crusted prawns, 'ahi *katsu* (tuna steaks dredged in crisp Japanese breadcrumbs and quickly deep-fried), crispy duck confetti spring rolls, and seafood risotto. Some of Hawai'i's best-known contemporary Hawaiian musicians play brief dinner shows here Wednesday through Sunday. ⊠ *Aloha Tower Marketplace, 1 Aloha Tower Dr., Downtown Honolulu* ☎ *808/585–0012* ▤ *AE, D, DC, MC, V* ☺ *No lunch Sat.–Mon. $18–$36.*

$$–$$$ ✕ **Indigo Euroasian Cuisine.** Owner Glenn Chu sets the mood for an evening out on the town: the walls are red brick, the ceilings are high, and from the restaurant's lounge next door comes the sultry sound of late-night jazz. Take a bite of goat cheese won tons with four-fruit sauce followed by rich Mongolian lamb chops. After dinner, duck into the hip Green Room lounge or Opium Den & Champagne Bar for a nightcap. If you're touring downtown at lunchtime, the Eurasian buffet is an especially good deal at $11 per person. ⊠ *1121 Nu'uanu Ave., Downtown Honolulu* ☎ *808/521–2900* ⊕ *www.indigo-hawaii.com* ▤ *AE, D, DC, MC, V. $16–$26.*

$–$$$ ✕ **Hiroshi Eurasion Tapas.** Built around chef Hiroshi Fukui's signature style of "west Japan" cuisine, this sleek dinner house focuses on small plates to share (enough for two servings each if you're friendly with your dining partner), with an exceptional choice of hard-to-find wines by the glass and in flights. Do not miss Hiroshi's red wine veal cheeks (he was doing them before everyone else), the delicately spiced tuna two ways, or the best *misoyaki* (marinated in a rich miso-soy blend, then grilled) butterfish ever. ⊠ *1341 Kapi'olani Blvd., Ala Moana* ☎ *808/955–0552* ▤ *AE, D, MC, V* ☺ *No lunch. $7–$22.*

★ **$-$$** ✕ **Kaka'ako Kitchen.** Russell Siu was the first of the local-boy fine-dining chefs to open a place of the sort he enjoys when he's off-duty, serving high-quality plate lunches (housemade sauce instead of from-a-mix-brown gravy, for example). Here you can get your "two scoops of rice" either white or brown and green salad instead of the usual macaroni salad; grilled fresh fish specials; and vegetarian options. Breakfast is especially good with combos like corned beef hash and eggs and exceptional goods such as *poi* bread. ⊠ *Ward Centre, 1200 Ala Moana Blvd., Kaka'ako* ☎ *808/596–7488* ⚖ *Reservations not accepted* ▤ *No credit cards. $7–$15.*

Korean

$-$$ ✕ **Sorabol.** The largest Korean restaurant in the city, this 24-hour eatery, with its impossibly tiny parking lot and maze of booths and private rooms, offers a vast menu encompassing the entirety of day-to-day Korean cuisine, plus sushi. English menu translations are cryptic at best. Still, we love it for wee hour "grinds": *bi bim bap* (veggies, meats, and eggs on steamed rice), *kal bi* and *bulgogi* (barbecued meats), and meat or fish *jun* (thin fillets fried in batter). ⊠ *805 Ke'eaumoku St., Ala Moana* ☎ *808/ 947–3113* ▤ *AE, DC, MC, V. $6–$20.*

Mexican

$-$$ ✕ **Compadres Mexican Bar and Grill.** The after-work crowd gathers here for potent margaritas and yummy pūpū. An outdoor terrace is best for cocktails only. Inside, the wooden floors, colorful photographs, and lively paintings create a festive setting. Compadres defines itself as "Western cooking with a Mexican accent": fajitas, baby back ribs, pork *carnitas* (slow-roasted shredded pork), and tortilla-encrusted chicken are specialties. There's a late-night appetizer menu available until midnight. ⊠ *Ward Centre, 1200 Ala Moana Blvd., Ala Moana* ☎ *808/591–8307* ▤ *D, MC, V. $8–$20.*

Seafood

$$$ ✕ **Sam Choy's Breakfast, Lunch and Crab & Big Aloha Brewery.** In this casual setting, great for families, diners can down crab and lobster—but since these come from elsewhere, we recommend the catch of the day, the *char siu* (Chinese barbecue), baby back ribs, or Sam's special fried *poke* (flash-fried tuna). This eatery's warehouse size sets the tone for its *bambucha* (huge) portions. An on-site microbrewery brews five varieties of Big Aloha beer. Sam Choy's is in Iwilei past Downtown Honolulu on the highway heading to Honolulu International Airport. ⊠ *580 Nimitz Hwy., Iwilei* ☎ *808/545–7979* ⊕ *www.samchoy.com* ▤ *AE, D, DC, MC, V. $19–$40.*

Honolulu: East & Diamond Head

American–Casual

$ ✕ **Big City Diner.** These unfussy retro diners offer a short course in local-style breakfasts—rice instead of potatoes, fish or Portuguese sausage instead of bacon, steaming bowls of noodles—with generous portions, low prices, and pronounced flavors. Breakfast is served all day. ⊠ *3569 Wai'alae Ave., Ka'imukī* ☎ *808/738–8855* ▤ *AE, D, MC, V. $5–$9.*

Contemporary

$$$$ ✕ **Chef Mavro.** George Mavrothalassitis, who took two hotel restaurants
Fodor'sChoice to the top of the ranks before founding this James Beard Award-
★ winning dinner house, admits he's "crazy." Crazy because the care he
takes to draw out the truest and most concentrated flavors, to track down
the freshest fish, to create one-of-a-kind wine pairings might strike
others as mad. But for this passionate Provençal transplant, there's no
other way. The menu changes quarterly, every dish (including dessert)
is matched with a select wine. We recommend multicourse tasting menus
($78–$137 with wines, depending on the number of dishes you mix and
match). Order anything with shrimp from the aquafarms of the Kahuku
area on the North Shore, Keahole lobster from the Big Island, lamb, or
fresh fish. Etched-glass windows black out the busy streetcorner scene
and all within is mellow and serene with starched white tablecloths, fresh
flowers, wood floors, and contemporary island art. ⊠ *1969 S. King St.,
Mōʻiliʻili* ☎ *808/944–4714* ⊕ *www.chefmavro.com* ⌖ *Reservations
essential* 🖃 *AE, DC, MC, V* ☺ *No lunch. $32–$42.*

$$$–$$$$ ✕ **Alan Wong's.** Alan Wong's is like that very rare shell you stumble upon
Fodor'sChoice on a perfect day at the beach—well polished and without a flaw. We've
★ never had a bad experience here, and we've never heard of anyone else
doing so, either. The "Wong Way," as it's not so jokingly called by his
staff, includes an ingrained understanding of the aloha spirit, evident
in the skilled but unstarched service, and creative and playful interpre-
tations of island cuisine. Try Da Bag (seafood steamed in a Mylar
pouch), Chinatown Roast Duck Nachos, and Poki Pines (rice-studded
seafood wonton appetizers). With a view of the Koʻolau Mountains, warm
tones of koa wood and lauhala grass weaving, you forget you're on the
third floor of an office building. Not to be missed. ⊠ *McCully Court,
1857 S. King St., 3rd fl., Mōʻiliʻili* ☎ *808/949–2526* ⊕ *www.alanwongs.
com* 🖃 *AE, MC, V* ☺ *No lunch. $25–$38.*

★ **$$$–$$$$** ✕ **Hoku's at the Kāhala Mandarin Oriental.** Everything about this room
speaks of quality and sophistication: the wall of windows with their beach
views, the avant-garde cutlery and dinnerware, the solicitous staff and
border-busting Pacific Rim cuisine. They do tend to get a bit architec-
tural (lots of edible stacks and towers), but the food invariably tastes
every bit as good as it looks. The international breads and the dessert
sampler in particular are noteworthy. ⊠ *Kāhala Mandarin Oriental, 5000
Kāhala Ave., Kāhala* ☎ *808/739–8780* 🖃 *AE, D, MC, V* ☺ *No lunch
Sat. $22–$39.*

★ **$–$$$** ✕ **3660 on the Rise.** This casually stylish eatery is a 10-minute drive from
Waikīkī in the up-and-coming culinary mecca of Kaimukī. Sample Chef
Russell Siu's New York Steak Alaea'a, the crab cakes, or the signature
'ahi katsu wrapped in nori and deep-fried with a wasabi-ginger butter
sauce. Siu combines a deep understanding of local flavors with a sophisticated palate, making this place especially popular with home-
grown gourmands. The dining room can feel a bit snug when it's full
(as it usually is); go early or later. ⊠ *3660 Waiʻalae Ave., Kaimukī*
☎ *808/737–1177* 🖃 *AE, DC, MC, V. $10–$30.*

$–$$$ ✕ **12th Avenue Grill.** Despite the maddening fact that there are no reser-
vations here, we love this clean, well-lighted place on a back street

where chef Kevin Hanney dishes up diner chic, including macaroni and cheese glazed with house-smoked cheddar and topped with savory breadcrumbs. The kimchee steak, a sort of teriyaki with kick, is a winner. Go early (5) or late (8:30) or do weekday lunch. Enjoy wonderful, homey desserts. ☒ *1145C 12th Ave., Kaimukī* ☎ *808/732-9469* ⚫ *Reservations not accepted* 🍴*BYOB* ☰*MC, V* ⊘ *Closed Sun. $8–$27.*

Delicatessens

¢–$$ ✗ **Diamond Head Market & Grill.** Kelvin Ro's one-stop spot is a plate-lunch place, a gourmet market, a deli, bakery, and espresso bar, too—and it's a five-minute hop from Waikīkī hotels. A takeout window offers grilled sandwiches or plates ranging from teriyaki beef to portobello mushrooms. The market's deli case is stocked with a range of heat-and-eat entrées from risotto cakes to lamb stew; specials change daily. There are packaged Japanese bento lunchboxes, giant scones, enticing desserts, even a small wine selection. ☒ *3158 Monsarrat Ave., Diamond Head* ☎ *808/ 732-0077* ⚫ *Reservations not accepted* ☰ *AE, D, MC, V. $5–$15.*

Fast Food

¢–$ ✗ **L&L Drive Inn.** On Monsarrat Avenue in Waikīkī and at more than 60 neighborhood locations throughout the island, the Drive Inn serves up an impressive mix of Asian-American and Hawaiian-style plate lunches. Chicken *katsu* (cutlet), shrimp curry, and seafood mix plates include two scoops of rice-and-macaroni salad. There are also "mini" versions of the large-portion plates that include just one scoop of starch. It's a quick takeout place to pick up lunch before heading to the nearest beach or park. ☒ *3045 Monsarrat Ave., Diamond Head* ☎ *808/735-1388* ⚫ *Reservations not accepted* ☰ *No credit cards. $5–$10.*

Hawaiian

$$–$$$ ✗ **The Willows.** The exterior of this garden restaurant gives little clue as to what awaits within. Man-made ponds are sprinkled among the thatched dining pavilions, and you can find a tiny wedding chapel and a gallery gift shop. The food, served buffet-style, includes the trademark Willows curry along with Hawaiian dishes such as *laulau* (a steamed bundle of ti leaves containing pork, butterfish, and taro tops) and local favorites such as Korean barbecue ribs. ☒ *901 Hausten St., Mō'ili'ili* ☎ *808/952-9200* ⚫ *Reservations essential* ☰ *AE, D, MC, V. $19–$28.*

¢–$ ✗ **'Ono Hawaiian Foods.** The adventurous in search of a real local-food experience should head to this no-frills hangout. You know it has to be good if residents are waiting in line to get in. Here you can sample *poi, lomi lomi* salmon (salmon massaged until tender and served with minced onions and tomatoes), laulau, *kālua* pork (roasted in an underground oven), and *haupia* (a light, gelatinlike dessert made from coconut). Appropriately enough, the Hawaiian word *'ono* means delicious. ☒ *726 Kapahulu Ave., Kapahulu* ☎ *808/737-2275* ⚫ *Reservations not accepted* ☰ *No credit cards* ⊘ *Closed Sun. $6–$14.*

Italian

$$–$$$ ✗ **C & C Pasta Co.** This cozy, relaxed restaurant tried to be a deli, but the deli case just kept getting pushed to the rear as folks from the neighborhood fell ever more in love with the osso buco, the Parmigiano gelato (intensely cheesy bruschetta spread), and the warm shrimp salad. Don't even try to drop in for dinner, especially on Friday when the locals own the place. Do lunch Tuesday to Saturday or reserve a spot early. ⊠ *3605 Wai'alae Ave., Kaimukī* ☎ *808/732–5999* ⌕ *Reservations essential* ▤ *MC, V* ⊗ *Closed Mon. $15–$28.*

Japanese

$$$$ ✕ **Sushi Sasabune.** You may find this restaurant's approach exasperating and a little condescending. Although it's possible to order from the menu, you're strongly encouraged to order omakase-style (oh-*mah*-ka-*say*, roughly, "trust me"), letting the chef send out his choices for the night. The waiters keep up a steady mantra: "Please, no shoyu on this one." "One piece, one bite." But then you take the first bite of California baby squid stuffed with Louisiana crab or unctuous *toro* ('ahi belly) smeared with a light soy reduction, washed down with a $20 glass of the smoothest sake you've ever tasted, and any trace of annoyance will vanish. Chef Seiji Kamagawa stands front and center at the counter, his hands—graceful as a conductor's, precise as a surgeon's—forming sushi or slicing sashimi, his eyes sternly examining the room. Caution: the courses come very rapidly; ask to be served every other time. Even bigger caution: the courses, generally two pieces of sushi or 6–8 slices of sashimi, add up fast. It's easy to spend more than $100 in a half hour, not counting drinks. Still, the meal will be as unforgettable as the tab. ⊠ *1419 S. King St., Mō'ili'ili* ☎ *808/947–3800* ⌕ *Reservations essential* ▤ *AE, D, DC, MC, V* ⊗ *Closed Sun. No lunch Sat. and Mon. $8–$20.*

Southeast O'ahu: Hawai'i Kai

Contemporary

$$–$$$$ ✕ **BluWater Grill.** Time your drive along Honolulu's South Shore to allow for a stop at this relaxed lunch and dinner restaurant on Kuapa Pond. The savvy chef-manager team left a popular chain restaurant to found this "American eclectic" eatery (wok-seared moi fish, mango and guava ribs, and lots of interesting small dishes $5–$10). They're open until 11 PM Monday through Thursday and on Sunday; until midnight Friday and Saturday. ⊠ *Hawai'i Kai Shopping Center, 377 Keahole St., Hawai'i Kai* ☎ *808/ 395–6224* ▤ *AE, DC, MC, V. $16–$30.*

★ **$$–$$$$** ✕ **Roy's.** Roy Yamaguchi's flagship restaurant across the highway from Maunalua Bay attracts food-savvy visitors like the North Shore attracts surfers. But it has a strong following among well-heeled Oahuans from surrounding neighborhoods who consider the place as an ex-

> ### ORDERING SUSHI
>
> In sushi restaurants two terms are helpful:
>
> *Moriwase* (moe-ree-*wa*-say) translates to "chef's choice" or "special of the day"—a one-price sushi spread that is supposed to showcase the best fish of the day. *Omakase* (oh-*mah*-ka-*say*) is a style of sushi dining in which the sushi chef sends out successive courses of his choosing, at the same time watching to note diner's preferences and eating pace.

tension of their homes and Roy's team their personal chefs. For this reason, Roy's is always busy and sometimes overly noisy. It's best to visit later in the evening if you're sensitive to pressure to turn the table. The wide-ranging and ever-interesting "Hawaiian fusion" menu changes daily except for such signature dishes as Szechuan Spiced BBQ Baby Back Ribs, Roy's Original Blackened 'Ahi with Soy Mustard Butter Sauce, and a legendary meat loaf. There's an exceptional wine list. ⊠ *Hawai'i Kai Corporate Plaza, 6600 Kalaniana'ole Hwy., Hawai'i Kai* ☎ *808/396–7697* ⚲ *Reservations essential* ▭ *AE, D, DC, MC, V. $17–$30.*

Windward O'ahu: Kailua & Kāne'ohe

American–Casual

$$–$$$ ✕ **Buzz's Original Steakhouse.** Virtually unchanged since it opened in 1967, this cozy maze of rooms opposite Kailua Beach Park is filled with the enticing aroma of grilling steaks. It doesn't matter if you're a bit sandy (but no bare feet). Stop at the salad bar, order up a steak, a burger, teri chicken, or the fresh fish special. If you sit at the bar, expect to make friends. ⊠ *413 Kawailoa Rd., Kailua* ☎ *808/261–4661* ▭ *No credit cards. $13–$23.*

$$–$$$ ✕ **Lucy's Grill and Bar.** This windward eatery offers outdoor seating and an open-air bar that shakes up a mean martini to go with its eclectic and innovative menu. (We prefer the lānai because the indoor seating, though attractive, gets very noisy.) Begin with the deep-fried kālua pig pastry triangles with a mandarin orange-plum dipping sauce. Seafood offerings include grilled mahimahi, and lemongrass-crusted scallops with a yellow Thai curry. For meat lovers, there are baby back ribs in sweet hoisin barbecue sauce. Desserts, such as the coconut-chocolate bar with vanilla gelato, are sinfully rich. There's brunch on Sunday. ⊠ *33 Aulike St., Kailua* ☎ *808/230–8188* ▭ *MC, V* ⊗ *No lunch. $15–$28.*

¢–$ ✕ **Big City Diner.** These unfussy retro diners offer a short course in local-style breakfasts—rice instead of potatoes, fish or Portuguese sausage instead of bacon, steaming bowls of noodles—with generous portions, low prices, and pronounced flavors. Breakfast is served all day. ⊠ *108 Hekuli St., Kailua* ☎ *808/263–8880* ▭ *AE, D, MC, V. $5–$9.*

¢–$ ✕ **Cinnamon's Restaurant.** Known for uncommon variations on common breakfast themes (pancakes, eggs Benedict, French toast, home

BEST BREAKFAST

Big City Diner (Ala Moana & Kailua). Start the day like a local: rice instead of toast, fish or Portuguese sausage instead of bacon, even noodles.

Cinnamon's Restaurant (Kailua). Voted best for breakfast in a local newspaper poll, Cinnamon's does all the breakfast standards.

Duke's Canoe Club and Hula Grill (Waikīkī). Duke's has an $11.95 buffet; Hula Grill has a pricier but carefully prepared à la carte breakfast.

Eggs 'n Things (Waikīkī). This is a longtime favorite for late hours and country-style food with island touches.

Big City Diner . . **5**

Blu Water
Grill **8**

Buzz's Original
Steakhouse **6**

Cinnamon's
Restaurant **7**

Hale'iwa
Joe's **1**

Kua'Aina
Sandwich
Shop **2**

Lucy's
Grill and Bar . . . **4**

Mitsu-Ken . . . **10**

Pah Ke's Chinese
Restaurant **3**

Roy's **9**

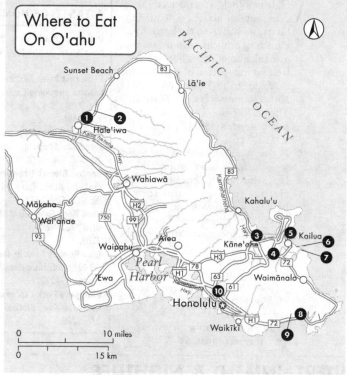

fries and eggs), this neighborhood favorite is tucked into a hard-to-find Kailua office park; call for directions. ⊠ *315 Uluniu, Kailua* ☎ *808/ 261–8724* ⊟ *D, DC, MC, V* ⊗ *7 AM–2 PM. $3–$10.*

Chinese

$$–$$$ ✕ **Pah Ke's Chinese Restaurant.** Chinese restaurants tend to be interchangeable but this one—named for the local pidgin term for Chinese—is worth the drive over from Honolulu for its focus on healthier cooking techniques, its seasonal specials such as cold soups and salads made from locally raised produce, and its exceptional East–West desserts. The menu offers all the usual suspects, but ask host Raymond Siu, a former hotel pastry chef, if he's got anything different and interesting in the kitchen, or call ahead to ask for a special menu. Reservations are recommended. ⊠ *46-018 Kamehameha Hwy., Kāne'ohe* ☎ *808/235–4505* ⊟ *AE, MC, V. $13–$23.*

The North Shore: Hale'iwa

American/Casual

$$ ✕ **Hale'iwa Joe's Seafood Grill.** After the long drive to the North Shore, we like to while away the afternoon on the covered open-air lānai at

Hale'iwa Joe's, scoring a couple of cute souvenir glasses, watching the boats and surfers in the harbor, and munching crunchy coconut shrimp, a mahi burger, or whatever's the freshest fish special. It's just past the Anahulu Stream Bridge. ⊠ 66-0011 *Kamehameha Hwy., Hale'iwa* ☎ 808/637–8005 ⚐ *Reservations not accepted* ⊟ *AE, DC, MC, V. $13–$20.*

¢ ✗ **Kua 'Aina Sandwich.** A must-stop spot during a drive around the island, this North Shore eatery specializes in large, hand-formed burgers heaped with bacon, cheese, salsa, and pineapple. The crispy shoestring fries alone are worth the trip. You can also check out Kua 'Aina's south-shore location across from the Ward Centre in Honolulu. ⊠ *66-160 Kamehameha Hwy., Hale'iwa* ☎ 808/637–6067 ⊠1116 *Auahi St., Ala Moana* ☎ 808/591–9133 ⚐ *Reservations not accepted* ⊟ *No credit cards. $4–$7.*

A TASTE OF HOME

It goes without saying that Starbuck's and Jamba Juice are everywhere.

California Pizza Kitchen. ⊠ *Ala Moana Shopping Center* ☎ *808/941–7715* ⊠ *Kāhala Mall* ☎ *808/737–9446.*

Cheesecake Factory. ⊠ *Royal Hawaiian Shopping Center* ☎ *808/924–5001.*

Gordon Biersch Brewery Restaurant. ⊠ *Aloha Tower MarketPl.* ☎ *808/599–4877.*

Hard Rock Cafe. ⊠ *1837 Kapi'olani Blvd., Ala Moana* ☎ *808/955–7383.*

Tony Roma's Famous for Ribs. ⊠ *1972 Kalākaua Ave., Waikīkī* ☎ *808/942–2121.*

Wolfgang Puck Express. ⊠ *2570 Kalākaua Ave., Waikīkī* ☎ *808/931–6226.*

ENTERTAINMENT & NIGHTLIFE

Many first-time visitors arrive in the Islands expecting to see scenic beauty and sandy beaches but not much at night. That might be true on some of the other Islands, but not in O'ahu. Honolulu sunsets herald the onset of the best nightlife scene in the Islands.

Local artists perform every night of the week along Waikīkī's Kalākaua and Kūhiō avenues and in Downtown Honolulu; the clubs dance to every beat from Top 40 to alternative to '80s.

The arts also thrive alongside the tourist industry. O'ahu has an established symphony, a thriving opera company, chamber music groups, and community theaters. Major Broadway shows, dance companies, and rock stars also make their way to Honolulu. Check the local newspapers— MidWeek the *Honolulu Advertiser,* the *Honolulu Star-Bulletin,* or the *Honolulu Weekly*—for the latest events.

Whether you make it an early night or stay up to watch that spectacular tropical sunrise, there's lots to do in paradise.

Entertainment

Lū'au

The lū'au is an experience that everyone, both local and tourist, should have. Today's lū'au still adhere to traditional foods and entertainment, but there's also a fun, contemporary flair. With most, you can even watch the roasted pig being carried out of its *'imu,* a hole in the ground used for cooking meat with heated stones.

Lū'au cost anywhere from $58 to $110. Most that are held outside of Waikīkī offer shuttle service so you don't have to drive. Reservations are essential.

Germaine's Lū'au. Billed as being "100 years away from Waikīkī," this lū'au is held on a private beach 35 minutes away from Waikīkī. Expect a lively crowd on the bus. The food is the usual multicourse, all-you-can-eat buffet, but it's very tasty. It's a good lū'au for first timers and at a reasonable price. ☎ *808/949–6626 or 800/367–5655* ⊙ *Daily at 6.*

★ **Paradise Cove Lū'au.** The scenery is the best here—the sunsets are unbelievable. Watch Mother Nature's special effects show on a remote beachfront estate beside a picturesque cove, a good 27 mi from the bustle of Waikīkī. The food isn't bad either, and the show features a fire-knife dancer, singing emcee, and both traditional and contemporary hula. Get your money's worth and also experience an array of traditional island games, arts and crafts and canoe rides in the cove. ☎ *808/842–5911* ⊕ *www.paradisecovehawaii.com* ⊙ *Daily at 5:30, doors open at 5.*

Fodor'sChoice **Polynesian Cultural Center Ali'i Lū'au.** The most traditional, and perhaps the
★ most elaborate, of all the lū'au is an hour's drive from Honolulu on the North Shore. It's set amid seven re-created Polynesian villages. We recommend a whole-day excursion; package deals include admission and dinner, which is an all-you-can-eat buffet with traditional lū'au food such as *kālua* pig and lomi lomi salmon. It's all followed by a revue. ☎ *808/293–3333 or 800/367–7060* ⊕ *www.polynesia.com* ⊙ *Mon.–Sat. center opens at noon; lū'au starts at 5.*

Royal Hawaiian Lū'au. For those who don't want to travel too far from the South shore, Waikīkī's only oceanfront lū'au is exotic and upscale. You won't get to see the 'imu ceremony here because Waikīkī law forbids it. You will, however, get a great view of the setting sun, Diamond Head, the Pacific Ocean, and the legendary Pink Palace as a backdrop. ☎ *808/923–7311* ⊙ *Mon. at 6.*

Cocktail & Dinner Cruises

Dinner cruises depart either from the piers adjacent to the Aloha Tower Marketplace in Downtown Honolulu or from Kewalo Basin, near Ala Moana Beach Park, and head along the coast toward Diamond Head. There's usually dinner, dancing, drinks, and a sensational sunset.
■ TIP→→ Get a good spot on deck early to enjoy the sunset, however, because everyone tends to pile outside at once. Except as noted, dinner cruises cost approximately $40–$110, cocktail cruises $25–$40. Most major credit cards are accepted.

Ali'i Kai **Catamaran.** Patterned after an ancient Polynesian vessel, this huge catamaran casts off from Aloha Tower with 1,000 passengers. The deluxe dinner cruise has two bars, a huge dinner, and an authentic Polynesian show with colorful hula music. The food is good, the after-dinner show loud and fun, and everyone dances on the way back to shore. ✉ *Pier 5, street level, Honolulu* ☎ *808/539–9400 Ext. 5.*

★ *Atlantis* **Cruises.** The sleekly high-tech *Navatek,* a revolutionary craft designed to sail smoothly in rough waters, powers farther along Waikīkī's coastline than its competitors, sometimes making it past Diamond Head and all the way to Hanauma Bay. Choose from sunset dinner buffet or moonlight cruises aboard the 300-passenger boat where you can feast on beef tenderloin and whole lobster or opt for the downstairs buffet. There's also the option of humpback whale-watch cruises December–mid-April. Tours leave from Pier 6, next to Aloha Tower Marketplace. ⊠ *Honolulu Harbor* ☎ *808/973–1311* ⊕ *www.atlantisadventures.com.*

Paradise Cruises. Prices vary depending on which deck you choose on the 1,600-passenger, four-deck *Star of Honolulu.* For instance, a seven-course French-style dinner and live jazz on the top deck costs $199. A steak-and-crab feast on level two costs $105. This ship also features daily Hawaiiana Lunch cruises that offer lei-making and 'ukulele and hula lessons starting at $42. Evening excursions also take place on the 340-passenger *Starlet I* and 230-passenger *Starlet II,* which offer three-course dinners beginning at $42. Also bring your bathing suits for a morning cruise for $60 complete with ocean fun on a water trampoline and slide, and feast on a BBQ lunch before heading back to shore. ⊠ *1540 S. King St., Honolulu* ☎ *808/983–7827* ⊕ *www.paradisecruises.com.*

Cocktail & Dinner Shows

Cocktail shows run $30 to $43, and the price usually includes one cocktail, tax, and tip. Dinner-show food is usually buffet-style with a definite local accent. Dinner shows are all in the $55 to $99 range. In all cases, reservations are essential. Artists tend to switch venues, so call in advance to check the evening's lineup.

Blue Hawai'i: The Show. The King loved the Islands. Jonathan Von Brana sings Elvis Presley tunes that showcase this affection. ⊠ *Waikīkī Beachcomber Hotel, 2300 Kalākaua Ave., Waikīkī* ☎ *808/923–1245* ۞ *Shows daily at 6:15.*

Creation: A Polynesian Odyssey. A daring Samoan fire-knife dancer is the highlight of this show that traces Hawai'i's culture and history, from its origins to statehood. ⊠ *'Āinahau Showroom, Sheraton Princess Ka'iulani Hotel, 120 Ka'iulani Ave., Waikīkī* ☎ *808/931–4660* ۞ *Dinner shows Tues.–Sun. at 6.*

Don Ho. Four decades ago, Don Ho put Waikīkī entertainment on the map, and his song "Tiny Bubbles" became a trademark. His show, a Polynesian revue (with a cast of young and attractive Hawaiian performers), has found the perfect home in this intimate club inside the Waikīkī Beachcomber Hotel. ⊠ *Waikīkī Beachcomber Hotel, 2300 Kalākaua Ave., Waikīkī* ☎ *808/923–3981* ۞ *Shows Sun., Tues., Thurs. at 8, with cocktail and dinner seatings.*

Magic of Polynesia. Hawai'i's top illusionist, John Hirokawa, displays mystifying sleight of hand in this highly entertaining show, which incorporates contemporary hula and island music into its acts. ⊠ *Waikīkī Beachcomber Hotel, 2300 Kalākaua Ave., Waikīkī* ☎ *808/971–4321* ۞ *Nightly at 8.*

۞ **Polynesian Cultural Center.** Easily one of the best on the Islands, this show has soaring moments and an "erupting volcano." The performers are students from Brigham Young University's Hawai'i campus. ⊠ *55-370*

Kamehameha Hwy., Lā'ie ☎ *808/293–3333 or 800/367–7060* ⊕ *www. polynesia.com* ☉ *Mon.–Sat. 12:30–9:30.*

Society of Seven. This lively, popular septet has great staying power and, after more than 25 years, continues to put on one of the best shows in Waikīkī. They sing, dance, do impersonations, play instruments, and, above all, entertain with their contemporary sound. ✉ *Outrigger Waikīkī on the Beach, 2335 Kalākaua Ave., Waikīkī* ☎ *808/922–6408* ☉ *Tues,–Sat. at 8·30*

Film

Hawai'i International Film Festival. It may not be Cannes, but this festival is unique and exciting. During the weeklong event from the end of November to early December, top films from the United States, Asia, and the Pacific are screened day and night at several theaters on O'ahu to packed crowds. It's a must-see for film adventurers. ☎ *808/528–3456.*

Honolulu Academy of Arts. Art, international, classic, and silent films are screened at the 280-seat Doris Duke theater. Though small, the theater is still classy and comfortable. It also has a great sound system. ✉ *900 S. Beretania St., Downtown Honolulu* ☎ *808/532–8768.*

★ **Sunset on the Beach.** It's like watching a movie at the drive-in, minus the car and the impossible speaker box. Think romantic and cozy; bring a blanket and find a spot on the sand to enjoy live entertainment, food from top local restaurants, and a movie feature on a 40-foot screen. Held twice a month on Waikīkī's Queens Surf Beach across from the Honolulu Zoo, Sunset on the Beach is a favorite event for both locals and tourists. If the weather is blustery, beware of flying sand. ☎ *808/923–1094* ⊕ *www.waikikiimprovement.com.*

Music

Hawai'i Opera Theater. Better known as "HOT," the Hawai'i Opera Theater has been known to turn the opera-challenged into opera lovers. HOT's season for 2006 runs February–March and features three Italian operas, *Rigoletto, Trittico,* and *Tosca,* performed by renowned international opera stars and guest conductors. All operas are sung in their original language with projected English translation. In July 2006, HOT will also put on a summer production of *The King and I.* Tickets range from $29 to $100. ✉ *Neil Blaisdell Center Concert Hall, Ward Ave. and King St., Downtown Honolulu* ☎ *808/596–7858* ⊕ *www.hawaiiopera.org.*

Honolulu Symphony Orchestra. In recent years, the Honolulu Symphony has worked hard to increase its appeal to all ages. The orchestra performs at the Neil Blaisdell Concert Hall under the direction of the young, dynamic Samuel Wong. The Honolulu Pops series, with performances under the summer stars at the Waikīkī Shell, features top local and national artists under the direction of talented conductor-composer Matt Cattingub. Tickets are $17–$59. ✉ *Dole Cannery, 650 Iwilei Rd., Suite 202, Iwilei* ☎ *808/792–2000* ⊕ *www.honolulusymphony.com.*

Honolulu Zoo Concerts. For almost two decades, the Honolulu Zoo Society has sponsored Wednesday evening concerts from June to August on the zoo's stage lawn. Listen to local legends play everything from Hawaiian to jazz to Latin music. At just $1 admission, this is one of the best deals in town. Take a brisk walk through the zoo exhibits before

Beyond "Tiny Bubbles"

ASK MOST VISITORS about Hawaiian music and they'll likely break into a lighthearted rendition of "Little Grass Shack." When they're finished, lead them directly to a stereo.

First, play them a recording of singer Kekuhi Kanahele, whose compositions combine ancient Hawaiian chants with modern melodies. Then ask them to listen to a CD by guitarist Keola Beamer, who loosens his strings and plays slack-key tunes dating to the 1830s. Amaze them with the 'ukulele stylings of young Jake Shimabukuro. Delight them with a sampling of Sean Na'auao's breezy, often-whimsical local ditties. Treat them to the traditional and contemporary Hawaiian sounds of Keali'i Reichel, a fixture on *Billboard* Magazine's World Music charts. Enthrall them with the soothing melodies of the Brothers Cazimero, still going strong after more than 30 years in the Hawaiian music industry. Share a recording by falsetto virtuoso Amy Hanaiali'i Gilliom, or play the late Israel Kamakawiwo'ole's version of "What a Wonderful World," which has appeared on scores of feature films and national television series. "Brother Iz," who died in 1997, was a native Hawaiian with a voice so pure, most of his songs were recorded simply with voice and 'ukulele.

These artists, like many others, are unearthing their island roots in the form of revered songs and chants, and they're reinterpreting them for today's audiences.

Granted, "Little Grass Shack" does have its place in the history books. After Hawai'i became a U.S. territory in 1900, the world discovered its music thanks to touring ensembles who turned heads with swaying hips, steel guitars, and pseudo-Hawaiian lyrics. Once radio and movies got into the act, dreams of Hawai'i came with a saccharine Hollywood sound track.

But Hawaiian music is far more complex. It harks back to the ancient islanders who beat rough-hewn drums, blew haunting calls on conch shells, and intoned chants for their gods. It recalls the voices of 19th-century Christian missionaries who taught islanders to sing in four-part harmony, a style that's still popular today.

The music takes on international overtones thanks to gifts from foreign immigrants: the 'ukulele from Portuguese laborers, for instance, and the guitar from Mexican traders. And it's enlivened by a million renderings of "Tiny Bubbles," as entertainers such as Don Ho croon Hawaiian-pop hits for Waikīkī tourists.

Island music came full circle in the late 1960s and '70s, when a few dedicated artists began giving voice to a resurgence of interest in Hawaiian culture, history, and traditions.

Today's artistic trailblazers are digging deep to explore their heritage, and their music reflects that thoughtful search. Musicians go one step further by incorporating such time-honored instruments as nose flutes and gourds, helping them keep pace with the past.

Check ads and listings in local papers for information on concerts, which take place in indoor and outdoor theaters, hotel ballrooms, and cozy nightclubs. When you hear the sound, you'll know it's Hawaiian because it'll make you feel right at home.

they close at 5:30 PM or join in the family activities; bring your own picnic for the concert, which starts at 6 PM. It's an alcohol-free event, and there's a food concession for those who come unprepared. ⊠ *151 Kapahulu Ave., Waikīkī* ☏ *808/926–3191* ⊕ *www.honoluluzoo.org* 🖃 *$1* ⊙ *Gates open at 4:30.*

Bars & Clubs

The locals call it "pau hana" but you might call it "off the clock and ready for a cocktail." The literal translation of the Hawaiian phrase means "done with work." On weeknights, it's likely that you'll find the working crowd still in their casual business attire sipping a few gin and tonics even before the sun goes down. Those who don't have to wake up in the early morning change into a fresh outfit and start the evening closer to 10 PM.

On the weekends, it's typical to have dinner at a restaurant before hitting the clubs around 9:30. Some bar hoppers start as early as 7, but partygoers typically don't patronize more than two establishments a night. That's because getting from one Oʻahu nightspot to the next usually requires packing your friends in the car and driving.

You can find a bar in just about any area on Oʻahu. Most of the clubs, however, are centralized to Waikīkī, Ala Moana, and Downtown Honolulu. The drinking age is 21 on Oʻahu and throughout Hawaiʻi. Many bars will admit younger people but will not serve them alcohol. By law, all establishments that serve alcoholic beverages must close by 2 AM. The only exceptions are those with a cabaret license, which have a 4 AM curfew. Most places have a cover charge of $5 to $10, but with some establishments, getting there early means you don't have to pay.

Waikīkī

Banyan Veranda. The Banyan Veranda is steeped in history. From this location the radio program *Hawaiʻi Calls* first broadcast the sounds of Hawaiian music and the rolling surf to a U.S. mainland audience in 1935. Today, a variety of Hawaiian entertainment continues to provide the perfect accompaniment to the sounds of the waves. ⊠ *Sheraton Moana Surfrider, 2365 Kalākaua Ave., Waikīkī* ☏ *808/922–3111.*

Fodor'sChoice **Cobalt Lounge.** Take the glass elevator up 30 stories to enjoy the sunset.
★ Floor-to-ceiling windows offer breathtaking views of Diamond Head and the Waikīkī shoreline. Leather sofas and cobalt-blue lighting set the "blue" Hawaiʻi mood. After darkness falls, you can find soft lights, starlight, and dancing in this lounge in the center of the Hanohano Room. ⊠ *Sheraton Waikīkī, 2255 Kalākaua Ave., Waikīkī* ☏ *808/922–4422* ⊙ *1st and 3rd Sat. of month.*

★ **Duke's Canoe Club.** Making the most of its oceanfront spot on Waikīkī Beach, Duke's presents "Concerts on the Beach" every Friday, Saturday, and Sunday with contemporary Hawaiian musicians like Henry Kapono. National musicians like Jimmy Buffett have also performed here. At Duke's Barefoot Bar, solo Hawaiian musicians take the stage nightly, and it's not unusual for surfers to leave their boards outside to step in for a casual drink after a long day on the waves. ⊠ *Outrigger Waikīkī, 2335 Kalākaua Ave., Waikīkī* ☎ *808/922–2268.*

Feng Shui Ultralounge. This once-a-week club event is the creation of party-master Justin Yoshino. After the dinner rush leaves Ciao Mein restaurant, the spacious venue is transformed into the only indoor–outdoor nightlife experience in Honolulu. There are complimentary appetizers and two dance floors featuring everything from deep house to hip-hop. With five bars, it's easy to get a drink; there's also ample space to get away from the booming music and lounge on a pool chair. Dress code–no slippers, shorts, headwear, jerseys, or T-shirts–is strictly enforced. ⊠ *Hyatt Regency Waikīkī Resort and Spa, 2424 Kalākaua Ave., Waikīkī* ☎ *808/957–0303* ☉ *Sat. at 9:30 PM.*

Formaggio Wine and Cheese Bar. Only people in the know, know where Formaggio is. There's no flashy signage for this establishment on the outskirts of Waikīkī—only the word "Formaggio" painted on the door. This tinted door cloaks a dimly-lighted bar, where young professionals and baby boomers enjoy live jazz nightly. There are more than 40 wines by the glass or taste and a Mediterranean menu with everything from pizzas to paninis. ⊠ *Market City Shopping Center, 2919 Kapi'olani Blvd., lower level, Waikīkī* ☎ *808/739–7719* ☉ *Tues.–Sun.*

Hula's Bar and Lei Stand. Hawai'i's oldest and best-known gay-friendly nightspot offers calming panoramic outdoor views of Diamond Head and the Pacific Ocean by day and a high-energy club scene by night. Check out the soundproof, glassed-in dance floor. ⊠ *Waikīkī Grand Hotel, 134 Kapahulu Ave., 2nd fl., Waikīkī* ☎ *808/923–0669.*

★ **Mai Tai Bar at the Royal Hawaiian.** The bartenders sure know how to make one killer mai tai. Just one could do the trick! This is, after all, the establishment that came up with the famous drink in the first place. The pink, umbrella-covered tables at the outdoor bar are front-row seating for Waikīkī sunsets and an unobstructed view of Diamond Head. Contemporary Hawaiian music is usually on stage, and the staff is extremely friendly. ⊠ *Royal Hawaiian Hotel, 2259 Kalākaua Ave., Waikīkī* ☎ *808/923–7311.*

Moana Terrace. Three floors up from Waikīkī Beach, this open-air terrace is the home of Aunty Genoa Keawe, the "First Lady of Hawaiian Music." Her falsetto sessions include jams with the finest of Hawai'i's musicians. ⊠ *Waikīkī Beach Marriott Resort, 2552 Kalākaua Ave., Waikīkī* ☎ *808/922–6611.*

Moose McGillycuddy's Pub and Cafe. Loud bands play for the beach-and-beer gang in a blue-jeans-and-T-shirt setting. Bikini contests are the thrill on Sunday nights; live bands play late '80s and '90s music the rest of the week. ⊠ *310 Lewers St., Waikīkī* ☎ *808/923–0751.*

Nashville Waikīkī. Country music in the tropics? You bet! Put on your *paniolo* (Hawaiian cowboy) duds and mosey on out to the giant dance floor. There are pool tables, dartboards, line dancing, and free dance lessons (Wednesday at 6:30 PM) to boot. Look for wall-to-wall crowds on the weekend. ⊠ *Ohana Waikīkī West Hotel, 2330 Kūhiō Ave., Waikīkī* ☎ *808/926–7911.*

Scruples Beach Club. After the sun goes down, the beach party moves from the sand to this discotheque right off Waikīkī's strip. Dance to the latest alternative, house, and Top 40 music with a clientele that is as diverse as all Hawai'i. Casual attire is welcome. ⊠ *2310 Kuhio Ave., at Nahua St., Waikīkī* ☎ 808/923–9530.

Shore Bird Oceanside Bar and Grill. This Waikīkī beachfront bar spills right out onto the sand. Local bands play nightly until 1 AM. ⊠ *Outrigger Reef on the Beach hotel, 2169 Kālia Rd., Waikīkī* ☎ 808/922–2887.

Tiki's Grill and Bar. Get in touch with your primal side at this restaurant–bar overlooking Kuhio Beach. Tiki torches, tiki statues, and other South Pacific art set the mood. There's nightly entertainment featuring contemporary Hawaiian musicians. Don't leave without sipping on a "lava flow." It's served in a whole coconut, which is yours to keep at the end of the night. ⊠ *Aston Waikīkī Beach Hotel, 2570 Kalākaua Ave., Waikīkī* ☎ 808/923–8454.

Wave Waikīkī. This venue has stood the test of time, anchoring the Waikīkī entertainment scene for more than two decades. Dance to live rock and roll until 1:30 AM and recorded music after that. It can be a rough scene (the place has seen more than its fair share of drunken fisticuffs), but the bands are tops. Late nights, the music here definitely goes "underground." ⊠ *1877 Kalākaua Ave., Waikīkī* ☎ 808/941–0424.

Wonder Lounge at the W Diamond Head. The hotel's Diamond Head Grill restaurant is also after-hours nightclub, full of hip, young professionals who enjoy martinis and the chance to do some not-so-serious networking. Look for a younger group on Saturday. Enjoy some fantastic (though pricey) eats until midnight, and keep dancing until 2 AM. ⊠ *W Honolulu— Diamond Head, 2885 Kalākaua Ave., Waikīkī* ☎ 808/922–1700 ⊙ *Fri. and Sat. at 9 PM.*

> The locals call it "pau hana" but you might call it "off the clock and ready for a cocktail."

Zanzabar. Traverse a winding staircase and make an entrance at Zanzabar where DJs spin top hits, from hip-hop to soul and techno to trance. It's easy to find a drink at this high-energy nightspot with its three bars. Not exactly sure how to get your groove on? Zanzabar offers free Latin dance lessons every Tuesday at 8 PM. Most nights are 21 and over, Sunday, Tuesday, Wednesday, and Thursday allow 18 and over in for $15. ⊠ *Waikīkī Trade Center, 2255 Kūhiō Ave., Waikīkī* ☎ 808/924–3939.

Elsewhere in Honolulu

Anna Bannana's. Generations of Hawai'i college students have spent more than an evening or two at this legendary two-story, smoky dive. A living-room atmosphere makes it a comfortable place to hang out. Here, the music is fresh, loud, and sometimes experimental. Live music happens Friday and Saturday, starting at 9 PM. There's also open mike night for amateurs on Monday. ⊠ *2440 S. Beretania St., Mō'ili'ili* ☎ 808/946–5190.

Blue Tropix. This nightclub features DJs mixing hip-hop and house for the 18-plus crowd. Upstairs is the Skybox Sports Lounge featuring plenty of pool tables, dart boards, and TVs to watch the big game. The two establishments, though owned by the same person, have separate entrances. ⊠ *1700 Kapi'olani Blvd., Ala Moana* ☎ 808/944–0001.

Chai's Island Bistro. Chai's welcomes some of Hawai'i's top entertainers, such as the Brothers Cazimero (on Wednesday evening), Hapa, and Jake Shimabukuro. Chai's is the perfect place if you're looking to enjoy the signature sounds of Hawai'i while dining on Pacific Rim cuisine. ⊠ *Aloha Tower Marketplace, 1 Aloha Tower Dr., Downtown Honolulu* ☎ *808/585–0011.*

Don Ho's Grill. This popular waterfront restaurant in the Aloha Tower Marketplace houses the Tiny Bubbles Bar, famous for its "suck 'em up" mai tai, a Don Ho classic. The dinner hour features Hawaiian musicians like Jerry Santos and Robert Cazimero. If you're lucky, you might catch a glimpse of the famous Ho, who frequents the restaurant. On the weekend, live bands play reggae music from 10 PM to 2 AM. ⊠ *Aloha Tower Marketplace, 1 Aloha Tower Dr., Downtown Honolulu* ☎ *808/ 528–0807.*

Kapono's. Owned and operated by legendary local musician Henry Kapono, this is one of the few places in Honolulu where you can hear live music outdoors and dance under the stars. There's enough room here to find your space if you need it. Call ahead to find out who's playing. ⊠ *Aloha Tower Marketplace, 1 Aloha Tower Dr., Downtown Honolulu* ☎ *808/536–2100.*

Little Vino. Step inside this small wine bar, and you'd think you have just arrived in Italy. The walls are painted to look like a rustic countryside with beautiful vineyards. Relax on one of the leather couches or at a table and enjoy wines hand-selected by the restaurant's master sommelier and Italian tapas (small plates) if you're hungry. ⊠ *Restaurant Row, 500 Ala Moana Blvd., Kaka'ako* ☎ *808/524–8466* ☉ *Wed.and Thurs. 5:30–9:30 PM, Fri. and Sat. 5:30–10:30 PM.*

Fodor'sChoice ★ **Mai Tai Bar at Ala Moana Center.** After a long day of shopping, the Mai Tai Bar on the third floor of Ala Moana Center is a perfect spot to relax. There's live entertainment and two nightly happy hours: one for food items and another strictly for specialty drinks. There's never a cover charge and no dress code, but to avoid waiting in line, get there before 9 PM. ⊠ *1450 Ala Moana Blvd., Ala Moana* ☎ *808/947–2900.*

Fodor'sChoice ★ **The Ocean Club.** The Ocean Club has withstood the test of time while other local nightclubs have failed. The indoor venue plays mostly Top 40 and hip-hop music. Tuesday is "Ladies' Night" featuring $2 drinks. Thursday is "Paddler's Night" so wear aloha print attire and avoid the cover charge. The last Saturday of every month is the "Piranha Room," where the club is decorated according to various themes, go-go dancers mesmerize, and the place is packed. Half-price pūpū until 8 PM. All nights are 23 and over except Thursday; dress code—no beach or athletic wear—is strictly enforced. ⊠ *Restaurant Row, 500 Ala Moana Blvd., Kaka'ako* ☎ *808/ 531–8444* ☉ *Tues., Thurs., Fri. at 4:30 PM, Sat. at 7 PM.*

★ **Opium Den & Champagne Bar at Indigo's.** This bar at the edge of Chinatown resembles a joint right out of a film noir. Jazz plays early in the evening on Tuesday; late-night DJs spin trance, Top 40, funk, disco, and rock on weekends. In addition to champagne, happy hour features sake martinis and complimentary pūpū buffet. ⊠ *Indigo Euroasian Cuisine, 1121 Nu'uanu Ave., Downtown Honolulu* ☎ *808/521–2900.*

Pipeline Cafe and Sports Bar. This is two stories of fun with pool, darts, and more. The upstairs sports bar has TVs galore and a skybox view of the dancing below. Music includes both live acts and seasoned DJs. ✉ *805 Pohukaina St., Kaka'ako* ☎ *808/589–1999.*

Rumours. The after-work crowd loves this spot, which has dance videos, disco, and throbbing lights. On Saturday "Little Chill" nights, the club plays oldies from the '70s, '80s, and '90s and serves free pūpū. ✉ *Ala Moana Hotel, 410 Atkinson St., Ala Moana* ☎ *808/955–4811.*

Venus Nightclub. This high-energy social bar, with leather couches ideal for a night of people-watching, features hip-hop, trance, and reggae with guest DJs five nights a week. Attention, ladies: there's a male dance revue Saturday evenings. ✉ *1349 Kapi'olani Blvd., Ala Moana* ☎ *808/951–8671.*

Southeast O'ahu

The Shack. This sports bar and restaurant is about the only late night spot you can find in Southeast O'ahu. After a day of snorkling at Hanauma Bay, stop by to kick back, have a beer, eat a burger, watch some sports or play a game of pool. It's open until 2 AM nightly. ✉ *Hawai'i Kai Shopping Center, 377 Keahole St., Hawai'i Kai,* ☎ *808/ 396–1919* ⊙ *Nightly until 2 AM.*

SHOPPING

Honolulu is the number-one shopping spot on the Islands and an international crossroads of the shopping scene. In Waikīkī and at Ala Moana Center, designer stores such as Louis Vuitton, Tiffany's, and Gucci line the streets like so many palm trees. Japanese visitors find that Hawai'i is the best place to shop for the latest styles at reasonable prices.

O'ahu has sprawling shopping malls, unique boutiques, neighborhood businesses, and a variety of other enterprises. Major shopping malls are generally open daily 10–9; smaller neighborhood boutiques are usually 9 to-5 operations.

Waikīkī

Shopping Centers

DFS Galleria Waikīkī. Hermès, Cartier, and Calvin Klein are among the shops at this enclosed mall, as well as Hawai'i's largest beauty and cosmetic store. An exclusive boutique floor caters to duty-free shoppers only. The Waikīkī Walk offers authentic fashions, arts and crafts, and gifts of the Hawaiian Islands. The Kālia Grill and Starbucks offer a respite for weary shoppers. ✉ *Kalākaua and Royal Hawaiian Aves., Waikīkī* ☎ *808/931–2655.*

King Kalākaua Plaza. Fashionable and relatively new, the open-air King Kalākaua Plaza has flagship Banana Republic and Nike Town stores. ✉ *2080 Kalākaua Ave., Waikīkī* ☎ *808/955–2878.*

King's Village. It looks like a Hollywood stage set of monarchy-era Honolulu, complete with a changing-of-the-guard ceremony every evening at 6:15; shops include Hawaiian Island Creations Jewelry, Swim City USA Swimwear, and Island Motor Sports. ✉ *131 Ka'iulani Ave., Waikīkī* ☎ *808/944–6855.*

Royal Hawaiian Shopping Center. Fronting the Royal Hawaiian and Sheraton Waikīkī hotels, the center is three blocks long and contains more than 100 stores on four airy levels. Browse through the Hawaiian Heirloom Jewelry Collection by Philip Rickard, which also has a museum with Victorian jewelry pieces. Bike buffs can check out the Harley-Davidson Motor Clothes and Collectibles Boutique. There are 15 restaurants, including the Paradiso Seafood Grill, the Cheesecake Factory, and Villa Paradiso. It even has a post office. ⊠ *2201 Kalākaua Ave., Waikīkī* ☏ *808/922–0588* ⊕ *www.shopwaikiki.com.*

2100 Kalākaua. The bronze statue fronting the newest addition to O'ahu's retail scene was created by Japanese artist Shige Yamada. Tenants of this unique, three-story, town-house-style center include Chanel, Coach, Tiffany & Co., Yves Saint Laurent, Gucci, and Tod and Bocheron. ⊠ *2100 Kalākaua Ave., Waikīkī* ☏ *808/550–4449* ⊕ *www.2100kalakaua.com.*

Waikīkī Shopping Plaza. This five-floor shopping center is across the street from the Royal Hawaiian Shopping Center. Walden Books, Guess, Clio Blue jewelers, and Tanaka of Tokyo Restaurant are some of its 50 shops and restaurants. There's also a downstairs food court and Hawaiian cultural classes are offered daily. ⊠ *2270 Kalākaua Ave., Waikīkī* ☏ *808/923–1191.*

Books

Bestsellers. This shop in the Hilton's Rainbow Bazaar is a branch of the local independent bookstore chain. They stock novelty Hawai'i memorabilia as well as books on Hawaiian history, local maps, and travel guides, and even Hawaiian music. ⊠ *Hilton Hawaiian Village Beach Resort and Spa, 2005 Kālia Rd. Waikīkī* ☏ *808/953–2378.*

Clothing

Bailey's Antique Clothing and Thrift Shop. The source for vintage aloha shirts. ⊠ *517 Kapahulu Ave., Waikīkī* ☏ *808/734–7628.*

Local Motion. If you plan on surfing or just want to look like a surfer, check out this outfitter's flagship store. They have it all—from surfboards to surf wear. ⊠ *1958 Kalākaua Ave., Waikīkī* ☏ *808/979–7873.*

Reyn's. Reyn's is a good place to buy the aloha-print fashions locals wear. This company manufacturers their own label in the islands and also carries aloha wear by other labels. Reyn's has 13 locations statewide and offers styles for men, women and children. ⊠ *Sheraton Waikīkī, 2255 Kalākaua Ave., Waikīkī* ☏ *808/923–0331.*

Gifts

Norma Kress Gallery. Emerging native Hawaiian and Pacific Island artists are the focus at Norma Kress. Works are in all mediums, including pottery, sculpture, paintings and drawings, and photography. ⊠ *Hawai'i Prince Hotel, 100 Holomana St., Waikīkī* ☏ *808/952–4761.*

Gallery Tokusa. Netsuke are the toggles used to fasten containers to kimonos. Gallery Tokusa specializes in intricately carved netsuke, both antique and contemporary, and one-of-a-kind necklaces. ⊠ *Halekūlani, 2199 Kālia Rd., Waikīkī* ☏ *808/923–2311.*

Jewelry

Haimoff & Haimoff Creations in Gold. Jewelry designer Harry Haimoff's pieces are sold at this shop. ⊠ *Halekūlani, 2199 Kālia Rd., Waikīkī* ☏ *808/923–8777.*

Philip Rickard. The heirloom design collection of this famed jeweler features custom Hawaiian wedding jewelry. ⊠ *Royal Hawaiian Shopping Center, 2201 Kalākaua Ave., Waikīkī* ☎ *808/924–7972.*

Tropical Flowers & Fruit

Tropical Fruits Distributors of Hawai'i. Avoid the hassle of airport inspections. This company specializes in packing inspected pineapple and papaya; they will deliver to your hotel and to the airport check-in counter or ship to the mainland United States and Canada. ⊕ *651 Ilalo St., Honolulu* ☎ *808/847–3224 or 800/697–9100* ⊕ *www.dolefruithawaii.com.*

Honolulu: Ala Moana & Downtown

Shopping Centers

Getting to the Ala Moana and Downtown Honolulu shopping centers from Waikīkī is quick and inexpensive thanks to **TheBus** and the **Waikīkī Trolley.**

★ **Ala Moana Shopping Center.** One of the nation's largest open-air malls is five minutes from Waikīkī by bus. Designer shops in residence include Gucci, Louis Vuitton, Gianni Versace, and Emporio Armani. All of Hawai'i's major department stores are here, including Neiman Marcus, Sears, and Macy's. More than 240 stores and 60 restaurants make up this 50-acre complex. To get there from Waikīkī, catch TheBus lines 8, 19, or 20 or hop aboard the Waikīkī Trolley's pink line, which comes through the area every half-hour. A one-way ride is $2. ⊠ *1450 Ala Moana Blvd., Ala Moana* ☎ *808/955–9517 special events and shuttle service.*

Aloha Tower Marketplace. Billing itself as a festival marketplace, Aloha Tower cozies up to Honolulu Harbor. Along with restaurants and entertainment venues, it has 80 shops and kiosks selling mostly visitor-oriented merchandise, from expensive sunglasses, to exceptional local artwork to souvenir refrigerator magnets. To get there from Waikīkī take the E-Transit Bus, which goes along TheBus routes every 15 minutes. ⊠ *1 Aloha Tower Dr., at Piers 8, 9, and 10, Downtown Honolulu* ☎ *808/566–2337* ⊕ *www.alohatower.com.*

★ **Victoria Ward Centers.** Heading west from Waikīkī toward Downtown Honolulu, you'll run into a section of town with five distinct shopping-complex areas; there are more than 120 specialty shops and 20 restaurants here. The Ward 16 Entertainment Complex features 16 movie theaters. A "shopping concierge" can assist you in navigating your way through the center's five complexes, which span four city blocks. Two of the largest and most popular complexes are the **Ward Warehouse** and the **Ward Centre.** Take TheBus routes 19 or 20; or follow The Waikīkī

GOOD ENOUGH TO EAT

Bring home fresh pineapple, papaya, or coconut to savor or share with friends and family. Jam comes in flavors such as pohā, passion fruit, and guava. Kona- and O'ahu-grown Waialua coffee beans have an international following. There are dried-food products such as saimin, haupia, and teriyaki barbecue sauce. All kinds of cookies are available, as well as exotic teas, drink mixes, and pancake syrups. And don't forget the macadamia nuts, from plain to chocolate-covered and brittled. By law, all fresh-fruit products must be inspected by the Department of Agriculture before export.

Trolley yellow line, which comes through the area every 45 minutes. Fare is $2 one way. ✉ *1050–1200 Ala Moana Blvd., Ala Moana.*

Books

Bestsellers. Hawai'i's largest independent bookstore has its flagship store in Downtown Honolulu on Bishop Square. They carry books by both local and national authors. There are also locations of Bestsellers at the Honolulu International Airport and in Waikīkī at the Hilton Hawaiian Village. ✉ *1001 Bishop St., Downtown Honolulu* ☎ *808/528–2378.*

> ### KOA KEEPSAKES
>
> Items handcrafted from native Hawaiian wood make beautiful gifts. Koa and milo have a beautiful color and grain. The great koa forests are disappearing because of environmental factors, so the wood is becoming valuable; most koa products you encounter are produced from wood grown on commercial farms.

Native Books/Na Mea Hawai'i. The book selection at this emporium covers subjects of local interest, including history, language, travel literature, novels, children's books, and street maps. ✉ *Ward Warehouse 1050 Ala Moana Blvd.* ☎ *808/596–8885.*

Clothing

★ **Anne Namba Designs.** Anne Namba brings the beauty of classic kimonos to the most contemporary of fashions. In addition to women's apparel, she also features a men's line and a stunningly beautiful wedding couture line. ✉ *324 Kamani St., Downtown Honolulu* ☎ *808/589–1135.*

Hilo Hattie. This is the world's largest manufacturer of Hawaiian and tropical aloha wear. It's also a good source for island souvenirs. Free shuttle service is available from Waikīkī. ✉ *700 N. Nimitz Hwy., Iwilei* ☎ *808/535–6500.*

Locals Only. Looking for a Hawaiian shirt? This shop carries an exclusive line of rayon aloha shirts in vintage-style patterns by Pineapple Juice and Locals Only sportswear. ✉ *Ala Moana Shopping Center, Ala Moana* ☎ *808/942–1555.*

Native Books/Na Mea Hawai'i. Don't miss this store for a unique view on Hawai'i's culture. They carry over 100 local artists' products from all the islands in the state. There are art pieces, wood work, original prints, jewelry, local food products, books, and clothing for adults and children. ✉ *Ward Warehouse 1050 Ala Moana Blvd.* ☎ *808/596–8885.*

Reyn's. Reyn's is a good place to buy the aloha print fashions locals wear. This company manufacturers their own label in the Islands and also carries aloha wear by other labels. Reyn's has 13 locations statewide and offers styles for men, women and children. ✉ *Ala Moana Shopping Center, 1450 Ala Moana Blvd., Ala Moana* ☎ *808/949–5929* ✉ *Kāhala Mall, 4211 Wai'alae Ave., Kāhala* ☎ *808/737–8313.*

Shanghai Tang. First opened in Hong Kong, Shanghai Tang now has its 11th branch at Ala Moana. An emphasis on workmanship and the luxury of fine fabrics upholds the tradition of old-Shanghai tailoring. They do custom work for men, women, and children. ✉ *Ala Moana Shopping Center, Ala Moana* ☎ *808/942–9800.*

1

Food

Honolulu Chocolate Company. To really impress those back home, pick up a box of gourmet chocolates here. They dip the flavors of Hawai'i, from Kona coffee to macadamia nuts, in fine chocolate. ⊠ *Ward Centre, 1200 Ala Moana Blvd., Ala Moana* ☎ *808/591–2997.*

Longs Drugs. Looking for local delicacies at locals prices? Try one of the many outposts of Longs. ⊠ *Ala Moana Shopping Center, 1450 Ala Moana Blvd., 2nd level, Ala Moana* ☎ *808/941–4433* ⊠ *Kāhala Mall, 4211 Wai'alae Ave., Kāhala* ☎ *808/732–0784.*

Gifts

Robyn Buntin Galleries. Chinese nephrite-jade carvings, Japanese lacquer and screens, and Buddhist sculptures are among the international pieces displayed here. ⊠ *820 S. Beretania St., Downtown Honolulu* ☎ *808/545–5572.*

Hawaiian Arts & Crafts

Hawaiian Quilt Collection. Traditional island comforters, wall hangings, pillows, and other Hawaiian-print quilt items are the specialty here. ⊠ *Ala Moana Center, 1450 Ala Moana Blvd., Ala Moana* ☎ *808/946–2233.*

Indich Collection. Bring home some aloha you can sink your bare feet into. Designs from this exclusive Hawaiian rug collection depict Hawaiian petroglyphs, banana leafs, and heliconia. ⊠ *Gentry Pacific Design Center, 560 N. Nimitz Hwy., Downtown Honolulu* ☎ *808/524–7769.*

Na Hoku. If you look at the wrists of local women, you are apt to see Hawaiian heirloom bracelets fashioned in either gold or silver in a number of island-inspired designs. Na Hoku sells jewelry in designs, such as these bracelets, that captures the heart of the Hawaiian lifestyle in all its elegant diversity. ⊠ *Ala Moana Center, 1450 Ala Moana, Ala Moana* ☎ *808/946–2100.*

Leis

Maunakea Street is lined with shop after shop displaying hanging lei. Most of these are family-run businesses that have been around for decades. Prices range from $3 to $30. With most of the shops on this street, you can pull up right outside the front door, jump out of the car, and buy a beautiful, fragrant memento of your vacation.

Cindy's Lei and Flower Shop. A local favorite with a good reputation, Cindy's will pack and mail your purchases to the mainland. ⊠ *1034 Maunakea St., Chinatown* ☎ *808/536–6538.*

Sweetheart's Lei. Everyone in the family helps out at this shop, where you can sometimes see them stringing fresh lei in the back. They're

BUYING LEIS

Airport lei are highly overpriced, so head to Chinatown as the locals do for the best deals. For the best smelling flowers, try pīkake, ginger, or pua kenikeni. The green pakalana flower and bright orange 'ilima blossom are beautiful but shrink quickly in the heat. If you want a lei that will last you a few days, try crown flower or a woven Thailand jumbo orchid lei. For something really special, get a colorful *haku* (head) lei, which is made from flowers, ferns, and native foliage—they're available year-round.

also very skilled at helping you pick the perfect lei. ✉ *69 North Beretania St., Chinatown* ☎ *808/537-3011*.

Honolulu: East

Shopping Center

Kāhala Mall. The upscale residential neighborhood of Kāhala, near the slopes of Diamond Head, is 10 minutes by car from Waikīkī. This indoor mall has 90 stores, including Macy's, Gap, Reyn's Aloha Wear, and Barnes & Noble. The Main Stage hosts arts performances, such as local ballet and contemporary Hawaiian music concerts. Eight **movie theaters** (☎ 808/733–6233) provide post-shopping entertainment. ✉ *4211 Wai'alae Ave., Kāhala* ☎ *808/732–7736.*

Specialty Stores

Hula Supply Center. This family-run business has been around since 1946 and sells everything from hand-crafted Hawaiian implements to lau hala bags, T-shirts, and Hawaiian music. Look for lei that will last a lifetime, made out of silk, shell or nuts, or get your own hula costume. ✉ *2346 S. King St., Mō'ili'ili* ☎ *808/941–5379.*

★ **Island Treasures.** Local residents come here to shop for gifts that are both unique and within reach of almost every budget. From koa accessories to original artwork, jewelry, beauty products, and home accessories, the quality and creativity displayed here are outstanding. ✉ *Koko Marina Center, 7192 Kalaniana'ole Hwy. Hawai'i Kai* ☎ *808/396–8827.*

Maui Divers Jewelry Design Center. Coral and pearl jewelry is popular, stunning, and fairly affordable. Take a tour at Maui Divers to see where it comes from and how the jewelry is designed. ✉ *1520 Liona St., Mō'ili'ili* ☎ *808/946–7979.*

Windward O'ahu & the North Shore

Adasa. Tucked away on the windward side in Kailua, this shop carries such designers as Flavio Olivera and Marc Jacobs. ✉ *25 Maluniu Ave., Kailua* ☎ *808/263–8500.*

North Shore Marketplace. While playing on the North Shore, check out this open-air plaza for boutiques like the Silver Moon Emporium for vintage clothing, Patagonia for adventure wear, and North Shore Custom and Design Swimwear for mix-and-match bikinis off the rack. ✉ *66-250 Kamehameha Hwy., Hale'iwa* ☎ *808/637–7000.*

Matsumoto Shave Ice. Actor Tom Hanks, sumo wrestler Konishiki, and ice skater Kristi Yamaguchi have all stopped in for a cold flavored cone at Mastumoto's. If you're going to the North Shore, it's a must to stop by this legendary local joint that was established in 1951. On average, they produce 1,000 shave ices a day. Mastumoto's also has T-shirts and souvenirs. ✉ *66-087 Kamehameha Hwy., Hale'iwa* ☎ *808/637–4827* ⊕ *www.matsumotoshaveice.com.*

West O'ahu

Aloha Stadium Swap Meet. This thrice-weekly outdoor bazaar attracts hundreds of vendors and even more bargain hunters. Every Hawaiian souvenir imaginable can be found here, from coral-shell necklaces to bikinis, as well as a variety of ethnic wares, from Chinese brocade dresses to Japanese pottery. There are also ethnic foods, silk flowers, and luggage in aloha floral prints. Wear comfortable shoes, use sunscreen, and bring bottled water. The flea market takes place in the Aloha Stadium parking lot Wednesday and weekends from 6 to 3; the $6 admission fee includes round-trip shuttle service from Waikīkī. ⊠ *99-500 Salt Lake Blvd., 'Aiea* ☎ *808/486–6704.*

★ **Waikele Premium Outlets.** Anne Klein Factory, Donna Karan Company Store, Kenneth Cole, and Saks Fifth Avenue Outlet anchor this discount destination. ✢ *H-1 Fwy., 30 min west of Downtown Honolulu* ⊠ *Waikele* ☎ *808/676–5656.*

O'AHU ESSENTIALS

Transportation

BY AIR

Most nonstop flights to Honolulu International originate in Los Angeles or San Francisco. Flying time from the West Coast is 4½ to 5 hours.

CARRIERS   Carriers flying into Honolulu from the mainland United States include Aloha, American, Continental, Delta, Hawaiian, Northwest, and United. Carriers flying from the United Kingdom to Honolulu include Air New Zealand, American, Continental, Delta, and United.

Charter flights are the least expensive and the least reliable—with chronically late departures and occasional cancellations. They also tend to depart less frequently (usually once a week) than do regularly scheduled flights. The savings may be worth the potential annoyance, however. Charter flights serving Honolulu International Airport are available from American Trans Air and Hawaiian Airlines. ⇨ *See* Smart Travel Tips A to Z.

AIRPORTS   More direct flights, by more domestic and international air carriers, arrive at and depart from Honolulu International Airport (HNL) than at any other airport in Hawai'i. If you find yourself waiting at the airport with extra time on your hands, kill some time at the Pacific Aerospace Museum, open daily, in the main terminal. It includes a 1,700-square-foot, three-dimensional, multimedia theater presenting the history of flight in Hawai'i, and a full-scale space-shuttle flight deck. Hands-on exhibits include a mission-control computer program tracing flights in the Pacific.
✈ **Honolulu International Airport (HNL)** ☎ 808/836–6411 ⊕ www.ehawaiigov.org.

TO & FROM THE AIRPORT   Some hotels have their own pickup service. Check when you book.

There are taxis right at the airport baggage-claim exit. At $1.50 startup plus $2.50 for each mile, the fare to Waikīkī will run approximately $23, plus tip. Drivers are also allowed to charge 30¢ per suitcase.

Roberts Hawai'i runs an airport shuttle service to and from Waikīkī. The fare is $8 one-way, $14 round-trip. Look for a representative at the baggage claim. Call for return reservations only. TheBus, the municipal bus, will take you into Waikīkī for only $1.50, but you are allowed only one bag, which must fit on your lap.

🚍 **Roberts Hawai'i** ☎ 808/523-7750. **TheBus** ☎ 808/848-5555 ⊕ www.thebus.org.

BY BUS

In Waikīkī, in addition to TheBus and the Waikīkī Trolley, there are also a number of brightly painted private buses, many free, that will take you to such commercial attractions as dinner cruises, garment factories, and the like.

THEBUS   You can go all around the island or just down Kalākaua Avenue for $2 on Honolulu's municipal transportation system, affectionately known as TheBus. You're entitled to one free transfer per fare if you ask for it when boarding. Exact change is required, and dollar bills are accepted. A four-day pass for visitors costs $20 and is available at ABC convenience stores in Waikīkī. Monthly passes cost $40.

There are no official bus-route maps, but you can find privately published booklets at most drugstores and other convenience outlets. The important route numbers for Waikīkī are 2, 4, 8, 19, 20, and 58. If you venture afield, you can always get back on one of these.

🚍 **TheBus** ☎ 808/848-5555 ⊕ www.thebus.org.

WAIKĪKĪ TROLLEY   The Waikīkī Trolley has three lines and 40 stops that allow you to design your own itinerary. The Red Line cruises around Waikīkī, Ala Moana, and Downtown Honolulu. The Yellow Line hits major shopping centers and restaurant locations. The Blue Line provides a tour of O'ahu's southeastern coastline, including Hanauma Bay and Sea Life Park. The trolleys depart from the Royal Hawaiian Shopping Center in Waikīkī every 15 minutes daily from 8 to 4:30. Fares range from $18–$25. At press time, there were reports that trolley service may be discontinued; please call ahead to see if trolleys are running.

🚍 **Waikīkī Trolley** ☎ 808/591-2561 or 800/824-8804 ⊕ www.waikikitrolley.com.

BY CAR

Waikīkī is only 2½ mi long and ½ mi wide, which means you can usually walk to where you are going. However, if you plan to venture outside of Waikīkī, a car is essential.

Roads and streets, although perhaps unpronounceable to visitors, are at least well marked. Bear in mind that many streets in Honolulu are one-way. Major attractions and scenic spots are marked by the distinctive HVCB sign with its red-caped warrior.

Driving in rush-hour traffic (6:30–8:30 AM and 3:30–5:30 PM) in Honolulu can be exasperating, because left turns are prohibited at many intersections and many roads turn into contra-flow lanes. Parking along many streets is curtailed during these hours, and towing is strictly enforced. Read the curbside parking signs before leaving your vehicle, even at a meter. Remember not to leave valuables in your car. Rental cars are often targets for thieves.

O'ahu's drivers are generally courteous, and you rarely hear a horn. People will slow down and let you into traffic with a wave of the hand. A friendly wave back is customary. If a driver sticks a hand out the window in a fist with the thumb and pinky sticking straight out, this is a good thing: it's the *shaka,* the Hawaiian symbol for "hang loose," and is often used to say "thanks," as well.

Hawai'i has a seat-belt law for front-seat passengers and those under the age of 18 in the back seats. Children under 40 pounds must be in a car seat, available from your car-rental agency.

CAR RENTAL During peak seasons—summer, Christmas vacations, and February—reservations are necessary. Rental agencies abound in and around the Honolulu International Airport and in Waikīkī. Avis, Budget, Dollar, Enterprise, Hertz, National, and Thrifty rent in O'ahu. ⇨ *See* Smart Travel Tips A to Z

🚗 Local Agencies: **JN Car and Truck Rentals** ☎ 808/831-2724 ⊕ www.jnag.com. **Paradise Rent A Car** ☎ 808/946-7777 or 888/882-2277 ⊕ www.paradiserentacar.com. **VIP** ☎ 808/922-4605.

LIMO RENTAL Cloud Nine Limousine Service provides red-carpet treatment in its chauffeur-driven super-stretch limousines. Rates begin at $50 an hour, plus tax and tip, with a two-hour minimum. Duke's Limousine, Inc. offers a choice of luxury super-stretches, sedans, or SUV limousines, with rates that begin at $50 per hour, with a two-hour minimum.

🚗 Local Agencies: **Cloud Nine Limousine Service** ☎ 808/524-7999 or 800/524-7999 ⊕ www.cloudninelimos. **Duke's Limousine, Inc.** ☎ 808/738-1878 ⊕ www.dukeslimo.com.

BY MOTORCYCLE & MOPED

Be aware of the traffic in Honolulu, as you would in any large city. Be especially careful in Waikīkī, where a lot of tourists are looking around at the sights and not keeping an eye on the street. Mopeds are good for getting around Waikīkī and Ala Moana, but you can't take them on the freeway. A motorcycle makes for a fun ride out to the North Shore, with the wind in your hair.

MOTORCYCLE & Big Kahuna Motorcycle Tours and Rentals rents a variety of motorcy-
MOPED RENTAL cles for $100–$175 a day. Blue Sky Rentals & Sports Center rents mopeds for $35 a day (8–6) and $40 for 24 hours. Mountain bikes from Blue Sky Rentals cost $20 a day, $25 for 24 hours, and $100 for the week, plus a $100 deposit.

🚗 Local Agencies: **Big Kahuna Motorcycle Tours and Rentals** ✉ 404 Seaside Ave., Waikīkī ☎ 808/924-2736. **Blue Sky Rentals & Sports Center** ✉ 1920 Ala Moana Blvd., across from Hilton Hawaiian Village, Waikīkī ☎ 808/947-0101.

BY TAXI

You can usually get a taxi right outside your hotel. Most restaurants will call a taxi for you. Rates are $1.50 at the drop of the flag, plus $2.50 per mile. Flat fees can also be negotiated for many destinations—just ask your driver. Drivers are generally courteous, and the cars are in good condition, many of them air-conditioned. For transportation throughout the

island, try Charley's Taxi & Tours. SIDA of Hawai'i Taxis, Inc., offers 24-hour island-wide transportation service and multilingual drivers.
🚕 Charley's Taxi & Tours ☎ 808/531-1333. SIDA of Hawai'i Taxis, Inc. ☎ 808/836-0011.

Contacts & Resources

EMERGENCIES
To reach the police, fire department, or an ambulance in an emergency, dial **911**.

A doctor, laboratory-radiology technician, and nurses are always on duty at Doctors on Call. Appointments are recommended but not necessary. Dozens of kinds of medical insurance are accepted, including Medicare, Medicaid, and most kinds of travel insurance.

Kūhiō Pharmacy is Waikīkī's only pharmacy and handles prescription requests only until 4:30 PM. Longs Drugs is open evenings at its Ala Moana location and 24 hours at its South King Street location (15 minutes from Waikīkī by car). Pillbox Pharmacy, located in Kaimukī, will deliver prescription medications for a small fee.

🚕 **Doctors & Dentists: Doctors on Call** ✉ Sheraton Princess Kaiulani Hotel, 120 Kaiulani Ave., Waikīkī ☎ 808/971-6000.

🚕 **Emergency Services: Coast Guard Rescue Center** ☎ 808/541-2450.

🚕 **Hospitals: Castle Medical Center** ✉ 640 Ulukahiki, Kailua ☎ 808/263-5500. **Kapiolani Medical Center for Women and Children** ✉ 1319 Punahou St., Makiki Heights, Honolulu ☎ 808/983-6000. **Queen's Medical Center** ✉ 1301 Punchbowl St., Downtown Honolulu, Honolulu ☎ 808/538-9011. **Saint Francis Medical Center-West** ✉ 91-2141 Ft. Weaver Rd., 'Ewa Beach ☎ 808/678-7000. **Straub Clinic** ✉ 888 S. King St., Downtown Honolulu, Honolulu ☎ 808/522-4000.

🚕 **Pharmacies: Kūhiō Pharmacy** ✉ Outrigger West Hotel, 2330 Kūhiō Ave., Waikīkī ☎ 808/923-4466. **Longs Drugs** ✉ Ala Moana Shopping Center, 1450 Ala Moana Blvd., 2nd level, Ala Moana ☎ 808/949-4010 ✉ 2220 S. King St., Mō'ili'ili ☎ 808/947-2651. **Pillbox Pharmacy** ✉ 1133 11th Ave., Kaimukī ☎ 808/737-1777.

VISITOR INFORMATION
🚕 **Activities & Attractions Association of Hawai'i** ☎ 808/871-7947 or 800/398-9698 ⊕ www.HawaiiFun.org. **Hawai'i Visitors & Convention Bureau** ✉ Waikīkī Business Plaza, 2270 Kalākaua Ave., Suite 801, Honolulu 96815 ☎ 808/923-1811 or 800/464-2924 ⊕ www.gohawaii.com. **O'ahu Visitor Bureau** ☎ 877/525-6248 ⊕ www.visit-oahu.com. **Surf Report** ☎ 808/973-4383. **Weather** ☎ 808/973-4381.

Maui

Adult Green Sea Turtle (Chelonia mydas).

WORD OF MOUTH

"People talk about how 'commercialized' Maui has become, but there are still so many places to visit on the island that give you the feeling you are the only person on the face of the Earth."   —Crazy4Hawaii

"My favorite Maui memory—being in a 28-foot boat and having a 45-foot-long humpback whale surface three feet from our side of the boat, exhale, and create a rainbow in her spray."
                                        —Dorothy01

www.fodors.com/forums

WELCOME TO MAUI

TOP 5
Reasons to Go

1 **The Road to Hāna:** Each curve of this legendary cliff-side road pulls you deeper into the lush green rain forest of Maui's eastern shore.

2 **Haleakalā National Park:** Explore the lava bombs, cinder cones, and silverswords at the gasp-inducing, volcanic summit of Haleakalā, the House of the Sun.

3 **Ho'okipa Beach:** The world's top windsurfers will dazzle you as they maneuver above the waves like butterflies shot from cannons.

4 **Wai'ānapanapa State Park:** Take a dip at the stunning black-sand beach or in the cave pool where an ancient princess once hid.

5 **Resorts, Resorts, Resorts:** Opulent gardens, pools, restaurants, and golf courses make Maui's resorts some of the best in the Islands.

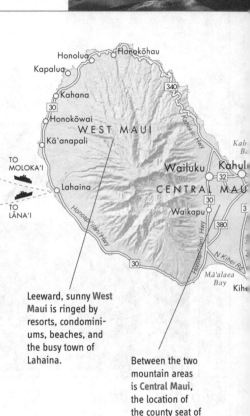

Leeward, sunny **West Maui** is ringed by resorts, condominiums, beaches, and the busy town of Lahaina.

Between the two mountain areas is **Central Maui**, the location of the county seat of Wailuku. Kahului Airport is also here.

Getting Oriented

Maui, the second largest island in the Hawaiian chain, is made up of two distinct circular landmasses. The smaller landmass, on the western part of the island, consists of 5,788-foot Pu'u Kukui and the rain-chiseled West Maui Mountains. The large landmass composing the eastern half of Maui is Haleakalā, with its cloud-wreathed volcanic peak.

The island's northeastern, windward side is largely one great rain forest, traversed by the **Road to Hāna.**

Island residents affectionately call the regions climbing up the slope of Haleakalā crater Upcountry.

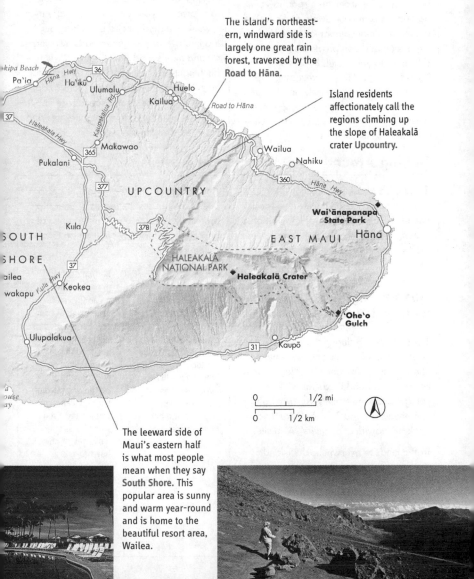

The leeward side of Maui's eastern half is what most people mean when they say **South Shore.** This popular area is sunny and warm year-round and is home to the beautiful resort area, Wailea.

MAUI PLANNER

When You Arrive

Most visitors arrive at Kahului Airport. The best way to get from the airport to your destination is in your own rental car. The major car-rental companies have desks at the airport and can provide a map and directions to your hotel. ■ TIP→→ Arriving flights in Maui tend to land around the same time. This can lead to extremely long lines at the car rental windows. If possible, send one member of your group to pick up the car while the others wait for the baggage.

Getting Around

If you need to ask for directions, try your best to pronounce the multi-vowel road names. Locals don't use (or know) highway route numbers and will respond with looks as lost as yours.

Tips for High Season Travelers

If you're coming during the peak season, be sure to book hotels and car rentals ahead of time. Advance booking of activities is also a good idea. This will ensure you get to do the activity you want and can often save you 10% or more if you book on individual outfitters' Web sites.

Traffic tends to overwhelm the island's simple infrastructure during these busy times. Try to avoid driving during typical commuter hours, and always allow extra travel time to reach your destination.

Where to Stay

Deciding where to stay is difficult, especially if you're a first-time visitor. To help narrow your choices, consider what type of property you'd like to stay at (big, flashy resort or private vacation rental) and what type of island climate you're looking for (beachfront strand or remote rain forest). If you're staying for more than a week, we recommend breaking your trip into two or even three parts. Moving around may sound daunting, and will rule out longer-stay discounts, but remember: each area of the island offers tons to do. If you stay in one spot, chances are you'll spend a lot of time driving to the sites and activities elsewhere.

Car Rentals

A rental car is a must on Maui. It's also one of the biggest expenses of your trip, especially when you add in the price of gasoline—higher on Maui than on O'ahu or the mainland.

■ TIPS→→

■ Soft-top jeeps are a popular option, but they don't have much space for baggage and it's impossible to lock anything into them. Four-wheel-drive vehicles are the most expensive options and not really necessary.

■ Don't be surprised if there is an additional fee for parking at your hotel or resort, parking is not always included in your room rate or resort fee. Booking a car-hotel or airfare package can save you money. Even some B&Bs offer packages—it never hurts to ask.

Island Hopping

If you have a week or more on Maui you may want to set aside a day or two for a trip to Moloka'i or Lāna'i. Tour operators such as Trilogy offer day-trip packages to Lāna'i which include snorkeling and a van tour of the island. Ferries are available to both islands. (The Moloka'i channel can be rough, so avoid ferry travel on a blustery day.)

Now that airport security checks and high prices have made island-hopping more of a challenge, your best bet for quick, scenic travel is a small air taxi. If you're not averse to flying on four- to 12-seaters, book with Pacific Wings or Hawai'i Air Taxi (*see* Maui Essentials *at the end of this chapter*). Pacific Wings flies to several

small airports—Hāna, Maui, and Kalaupapa, Moloka'i, for instance—in addition to the main airports. Hawai'i Air Taxi provides service only between Maui and Kailua-Kona on the Big Island.

■ **TIP→** Most inter-island flights on Hawaiian or Aloha are routed through O'ahu, even when it's out of the way.

Will it Rain?

Typically the weather on Maui is drier in summer (more guaranteed beach days) and rainier in winter (greener foliage, better waterfalls). Throughout the year, West Maui and the South Shore (the Leeward areas) are the driest, sunniest areas on the island—hence all the resorts here. East Maui and Hāna (the Windward areas) get the most rain, are densely forested, and abound with waterfalls and rainbows.

Timing is Everything

Each season brings its own highlights to Maui. The humpback whales start arriving in November, are in full force by February, and are gone by April. The biggest North Shore waves also show up in winter, whereas kite boarders and windsurfers enjoy the windy, late summer months. Jacarandas shower Upcountry roads in lilac-color blossoms in spring, and the truly astounding silverswords burst forth their blooms in summer. Fall is the quietest time on the island, a good time for a getaway. And, of course, there's what's known as high season—June through August, Christmas, and spring break—when the island is jam-packed with visitors.

Guided Activities

In winter, Maui is *the* spot for whale-watching. Sure, you can see whales on other islands, but they're just passing through to get to their real hang-out. The same could be said for windsurfers and kite boarders, Maui's North Shore is their mecca. This chart lists rough prices for Maui's most popular guided activities.

ACTIVITY	COST
Deep Sea Fishing	$80–$180
Golf	$50–$300
Helicopter Tours	$125–$350
Lū'au	$50–$95
Parasailing	$48–$55
Kayaking Tours	$65–$140
Snorkel Cruises	$80–$180
Surfing Lessons	$55–$325
Windsurfing	$80–$120
Whale-Watching	$20–$40

1-Day Itineraries

Maui's landscape is incredibly diverse, offering everything from underwater encounters with eagle rays to treks across moonlike terrain. Although daydreaming at the pool or on the beach may fulfill your initial island fantasy, Maui has much more to offer. The following one-day itineraries will take you to our favorite spots on the island.

A Day at the Beach in West Maui.
West Maui has some of the island's most beautiful beaches, though many of them are hidden by megaresorts. If you get an early start, you can begin your day snorkeling at Slaughterhouse Beach (in winter, D. T. Fleming Beach is a better option as it's less rough). Then spend the day beach-hopping through Kapalua, Nāpili, and Kāʻanapali as you make your way south. You'll want to get to Lahaina before dark so you can spend some time exploring the historic whaling town before choosing a restaurant for a sunset dinner.

Focus on Marine Life on the South Shore.
Start your South Shore trip early in the morning, and head out past Mākena into the rough lava fields of rugged La Pérouse Bay. At the road's end, the ʻĀhihi-Kīnaʻu Marine Preserve has no beach, but it's a rich spot for snorkeling and getting to know Maui's spectacular underwater world. Head to Kīhei for lunch then enjoy the afternoon learning more about Maui's marine life at the Maui Ocean Center at Māʻalaea.

The Road to Hāna.
This cliff-side driving tour through rain-forest canopy reveals Maui's lushest and most tropical terrain. It will take a full day, especially if you plan to make it all the way to ʻOheʻo Gulch. You'll pass through communities where old Hawaiʻi still thrives, and where the forest runs unchecked from the sea to the summit. You'll want to make frequent exploratory stops. To really soak in the magic of this place, consider staying overnight in Hāna town. That way you can spend a full day winding toward Hāna, hiking and exploring along the way, and the next day traveling leisurely back to civilization.

Haleakalā National Park, Upcountry & the North Shore.
If you don't plan to spend an entire day hiking in Haleakalā National Park, this itinerary will at least allow you to take a peek at it. Get up early and head straight for the summit of Haleakalā (if you're jetlagged and waking up in the middle of the night, you may want to get there in time for sunrise). Plan to spend a couple of hours exploring the various look-out points in the park. On your way down the mountain, turn right on Makawao Avenue and head into the little town of Makawao. You can have lunch here, or make a left on Baldwin Avenue and head downhill to the town of Pāʻia, where there are a number of great lunch spots and shops to explore. Spend the rest of your afternoon at Pāʻia's main strip of sand, Hoʻokipa Beach.

■ *For details on any of the destinations mentioned in these itineraries, see* Exploring Maui *in this chapter.*

BEACHES

By Shannon
Wianecki

On Maui, you can bury your toes in golden, sugary-white, black, or even red sand beaches. All of Hawai'i's beaches are free and open to the public—even those that grace the front yards of fancy hotels—so you can make yourself at home on any one of them. Some of the prettiest beaches are often hidden by buildings; look for the blue, beach-access signs that indicate rights-of-way through condominiums, resorts, and other private properties.

The island's leeward shores (the South Shore and West Side) have the calmest, sunniest beaches. Hit the beach early, when the aquamarine waters are as accommodating as bathwater. In summer, afternoon winds can be a sandblasting force, which can chase even the most dedicated sun worshippers away.

Windward shores (the North Shore and East Maui) offer more adventurous beachgoing. Beaches face the open ocean (rather than other islands) and tend to be rockier and more prone to surging swells. This is particularly true in winter, when the legendary North Shore becomes a playground for experienced big wave riders. Don't let this keep you away completely, however, some of the island's best beaches are those remote slivers of red-and-black volcanic sand found on the wild windward shore. And there's little better proof of relaxation than a few grains of sand—whatever its color—clinging to your ankles after a day spent on a Maui beach.

West Maui

West Maui beaches are the stuff of legend—glittering aquamarine waters banked by long stretches of golden sand. Reef fronts much of the western shore, making the underwater panorama something to behold. The beaches listed here start in the north at Kapalua and head south to Kā'anapali.

"Slaughterhouse" (Mokuleia) Beach. The island's northernmost beach is part of the Honolua-Mokuleia Marine Life Conservation District. "Slaughterhouse" is the surfers' nickname for what is officially Mokuleia. When the weather permits, this is a great place for bodysurfing and sunbathing. Concrete steps and a green railing help you get down the sheer cliff to the sand. The next bay over, Honolua, has no beach but offers one of the best surf breaks in Hawai'i. Often you can see competitions happening there, with cars pulled off the road and parked in the pineapple field. ⊠ *Mile marker 32 on Rte. 30 past Kapalua* ⚭ *No facilities.*

D. T. Fleming Beach. Because the current can be quite strong, this charming, mile-long sandy cove is better for sunbathing than for swimming. Still it's one of the island's most popular beaches. Part of the beach runs along the front of the Ritz-Carlton's Beachhouse Bar & Grill—a good place to grab a cocktail and enjoy the view. ⊠ *Rte. 30, 1 mi north of Kapalua* ⚭ *Toilets, showers, picnic tables, grills/firepits, parking lot.*

Kapalua Beach. Walk through the tunnel at the end of Kapalua Place and you find gorgeous Kapalua Beach—a pristine bay good for snorkeling, swimming, and general lazing. Located just north of Nāpili Bay, this lovely,

KEEP IN MIND

The ocean is an amazing but formidable playground. Conditions can change quickly throughout the day. Pay attention to any signs or flags warning of high surf, rough currents, or jellyfish. It's best to watch the surf for a while before entering. Notice where other people are swimming and how often swells come in. Swells arrive in sets of five or six. If you should get caught in a largish swell, don't panic. Take a deep breath and dive beneath each oncoming wave. When you feel comfortable, you can swim back to shore with the swell.

Remember the ocean is also home to an array of fragile marine life. **Never stand on coral reefs.** Hefty fines apply to anyone who chases or grabs at turtles, dolphins, and other federally protected animals. Hawai'i's sharks are generally harmless, but it's wise to avoid swimming at dawn, dusk, or in murky waters.

sheltered beach often remains calm late into the afternoon. You may have to share sand space with a number of other beachgoers, however, as the area is quite popular. ⊠ *From Rte. 30, turn onto Kapalua Pl., walk through tunnel* ⚒ *Toilets, showers, parking lot.*

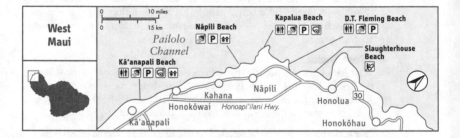

🗘 **Nāpili Beach.** Surrounded by sleepy condos, this
Fodor'sChoice round bay is a turtle-filled pool lined with a
★ sparkling white crescent of sand. Sunbathers love this beach. The shorebreak is steep but gentle and it's easy to keep an eye on kids here as the entire bay is visible from any point in the water. The beach is right outside the Nāpili Kai Beach Club, a popular little resort for honeymooners, only a few miles south of Kapalua. It's also a terrific sunset spot. ⊠ *5900 Lower Honoapi'ilani Hwy., look for Nāpili Pl. or Hui Dr.* ⚒ *Showers, parking lot.*

BEACHES KEY

🚻	Restroom
🚿	Shower
🏄	Surfing
🤿	Snorkel/Scuba
🧒	Good for kids
P	Parking

★ 🗘 **Kā'anapali Beach.** Stretching from the Sheraton Maui at its northernmost end to the Hyatt Regency Maui at its southern tip, Kā'anapali Beach is lined with resorts, condominiums, restaurants, and shops. If you're looking for quiet and seclusion, this is not the beach for you. But if you want lots of action, lay out your towel here. Also called "Dig Me Beach," this is one of Maui's best people-watching spots: catamarans, windsurfers, and parasailers head out from here while the beautiful people take in the scenery. A cement pathway weaves along the length of this 3-mi-long beach, leading from one astounding resort to the next.

The drop-off from Kā'anapali Beach's soft, sugary sand is steep, but waves hit the shore with barely a rippling slap. The area at the northernmost end (in front of the Sheraton Maui), known as Black Rock, has prime snorkeling. The bravest of the brave dive off the imposing rock into the

> ## THE SUN
>
> By far the biggest danger on the island is **sunburn**. The tropical sun is strong. Even at 9 AM, high SPF sunscreen—we recommend 30 SPF or higher—is a must. Rash guards, those clingy-looking lycra swim shirts, offer the best protection. Before seeking shade under a coconut palm, be aware that winds can be strong enough to knock fruit off the trees and onto your head (go ahead and giggle but this really can and does happen).

calm water below. ⊠ *Follow any of 3 Kā'anapali exits from Honoapi'ilani Hwy. and park at any hotel* ⛊ *Toilets, showers, parking lot.*

The South Shore

Sandy beach fronts nearly the entire southern coastline from Kīhei at the northern end to Mākena at the southern tip. The farther south you go, the better the beaches get. Kīhei has excellent beach parks right in town, with white sand, showers, restrooms, picnic tables, and BBQs. Good snorkeling can be done along the beaches' rocky borders. If Kīhei is excellent, though, Wailea is even better. Wailea's beaches are cleaner, facilities tidier, and views even more impressive. ⚠ Note that break-ins have been reported at many of these beach parking lots. As you head out to Mākena, the terrain gets wilder. Bring lunch and water with you. The following South Shore beaches are listed from north Kīhei southeast to Mākena.

ᄋ **Kama'ole I, II, and III.** Three steps from South Kīhei Road, you can find three golden stretches of sand separated by outcroppings of dark, jagged lava rocks. You can walk the length of all three beaches if you're willing to get your feet wet. The northernmost of the trio, Kama'ole I, offers perfect swimming with a sandy bottom a long way out and an active volleyball court. If you're one of those people who likes your beach sans the sand, there's also a great lawn for you to spread out on at the south end of the beach. Kama'ole II is nearly identical minus the lawn. The last beach, the one with all the people on it, is Kama'ole III. This is a great family beach, complete with a playground, volleyball net, BBQs, kite flying, and frequently, rented inflatable castles—a birthday-party must for every cool kid living on the island.

Locally known as "Kam" I, II, and III, all three beaches have great swimming and lifeguards. In the morning, the water can be as still as a lap pool. Kam III offers terrific breaks for beginning bodysurfers. ■ TIP→→ The public restrooms have seen better days; decent facilities are found at convenience stores and eateries across the street. ⊠ *S. Kīhei Rd., between Ke Ali'i Alanui Rd. and Keonekai Rd.* ⛊ *Lifeguard, toilets, showers, picnic tables, grills/firepits, playground, parking lot.*

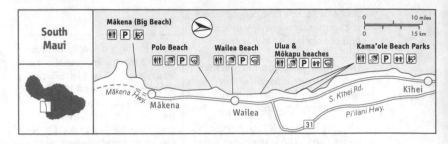

⏺ **Mōkapu & Ulua.** Look for a little road and public parking lot wedged between the first two big Wailea resorts—the Renaissance and the Marriott. This gets you to Mōkapu and Ulua beaches. Though there are no lifeguards, families love this place. Reef formations create tons of tide pools for kids to explore and the beaches are protected from major swells. Snorkeling is excellent at Ulua, the beach to the left of the entrance. Mōkapu, to the right, tends to be less crowded. ⊠ *Wailea Alanui Dr., south of Renaissance resort entrance* ⚴ *Toilets, showers, parking lot.*

Wailea Beach. A road just after the Grand Wailea resort takes you to Wailea Beach, a wide, sandy stretch with snorkeling, swimming, and, if you're a guest of the Four Seasons resort, Evian spritzes! If you're not a guest at the Grand Wailea or Four Seasons, the private cabanas and chaise-lounges can be a little annoying. But any complaint is more than made up for by the calm, unclouded waters and soft, white sand. ⊠ *Wailea Alanui Dr., south of Grand Wailea resort entrance* ⚴ *Toilets, showers, parking lot.*

Polo Beach. From Wailea Beach you can walk to this small, uncrowded crescent fronting the Fairmont Kea Lani resort. Swimming and snorkeling are great here and it's a good place to whale-watch. Similiar to Wailea Beach, private cabanas occupy prime sandy real estate, but there's plenty of room for you and your towel, and even a nice grass picnic area. The pathway connecting the two beaches is a great spot to jog or leisurely take in awesome views of nearby Molokini and Kahoʻolawe. Rare native plants grow along the ocean, or *makai,* side of the path; the honey-sweet smelling one is *naio,* or false sandalwood. ⊠ *Wailea Alanui Dr., south of Fairmont Kea Lani resort entrance* ⚴ *Toilets, showers, picnic tables, grills/firepits, parking lot.*

Fodor's Choice
★ **Mākena (Big Beach).** Locals successfully fought to give Mākena—one of Hawaiʻi's most breathtaking beaches—state park protection. Also known as "Big Beach," this stretch of deep-golden sand abutting sparkling aqua water is 3,000-feet-long and 100-feet-wide. It's never crowded, no matter how many cars cram into the lots. The water is fine for swimming, but use caution. ⚠ **The shore dropoff is steep and swells can get deceptively big.** Despite the infamous "Makena cloud," a blanket that rolls in during the early afternoon and obscures the sun, it rarely rains here. For a dramatic view of Big Beach, climb Puʻu Ōlaʻi, the steep cinder cone near the first entrance. Continue over the cinder cone's side

and you can discover "Little Beach"—clothing-optional by popular practice. (Officially, nude sunbathing is illegal in Hawai'i.) On Sunday, free spirits of all kinds crowd Little Beach's tiny shoreline for a drumming circle and bonfire. Little Beach has the island's best bodysurfing (no pun intended). Skimboarders catch air at Big Beach's third entrance. Each of the three paved entrances has portable toilets. ⊠ *Off Wailea Alanui Dr.* ⚐ *Toilets, parking lots.*

The North Shore

Many of the folks you see jaywalking in Pā'ia sold everything they owned to come to Maui and live a beach bum's life. Beach culture abounds on the North Shore. But these folks aren't sunbathers, they're big-wave riders, windsurfers, or kite boarders. The North Shore is their challenging sports arena. Beaches here face the open ocean and tend to be rougher and windier than beaches elsewhere on Maui—but don't let that scare you off. On calm days, the reef-speckled waters are truly beautiful and offer a beach-going experience quieter and less commercial than the leeward shore. Beaches below are listed from Kahului (near the airport) eastward to Ho'okipa.

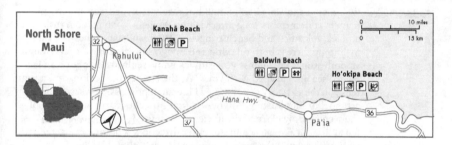

Kanahā Beach. Local folk and windsurfers like this long, golden strip of sand bordered by a wide grassy area and lots of shade. Though it typically gets windy in the early afternoon, this is a popular Kahului spot for joggers and picnicking families. At the far left end of the beach, you can watch kite boarders launch high into the breeze. ⊠ *Drive through airport and back out to car-rental road, Koeheke, turn right, and keep going* ⚐ *Toilets, showers, picnic tables, grills/firepits, parking lot.*

★ ☾ **Baldwin Beach.** Another local favorite, just west of Pā'ia town, Baldwin beach is a big body of comfortable white sand. This is a good place to stretch out, jog, or swim, though the waves can sometimes be choppy and the undertow strong. Don't be afraid of those big brown blobs floating beneath the surface, they're just pieces of alien seaweed awash in the surf. You can find shade along the beach beneath the ironwood trees, or in the large pavilion, a spot regularly overtaken by local parties and community events.

The long, shallow pool at the Kahului end of the beach is known as "Baby Beach." Separated from the surf by a flat reef wall, this is where ocean-loving families bring their kids (and sometimes puppies) to practice a few laps. The view of the West Maui Mountains is hauntingly beautiful from here. ✉ *Hāna Hwy., 1 mi west of Baldwin Ave.* ⚐ *Lifeguard, toilets, showers, picnic tables, grills/firepits, parking lot.*

★ **Hoʻokipa Beach.** If you want to see some of the world's finest windsurfers in action, hit this beach along Hāna Highway. The sport was largely developed right at Hoʻokipa and has become an art and a career to some. This beach is also one of Maui's hottest surfing spots, with waves as high as 20 feet. This is not a good swimming beach, nor the place to learn windsurfing, but plenty of picnic tables and BBQs are available for hanging out and watching the pros. Bust out your telephoto lens at the cliffside lookout. ✉ *2 mi past Pāʻia on Rte. 36* ⚐ *Toilets, showers, picnic tables, grills/firepits, parking lot.*

East Maui

Hāna's beaches will literally stop you in your tracks, they're that beautiful. Black-and-red sands stand out against pewter skies and lush tropical foliage creating picture-perfect scenes, which seem too breathtaking to be real. Rough conditions often preclude swimming, but don't let that stop you from exploring the shoreline. Beaches below are listed in order from the west end of Hāna town eastward.

Fodor'sChoice **Waiʻānapanapa State Park.** Small but rarely crowded, this beach will remain in your memory long after visiting. Fingers of white foam rush onto
★ a black volcanic-sand beach fringed with green beach vines and palms. Swimming here is both relaxing and invigorating: strong currents bump smooth stones up against your ankles while seabirds flit above a black, jagged sea arch draped with vines. At the edge of the parking lot, a sign tells you the sad story of a doomed Hawaiian princess. Stairs lead through a tunnel of interlocking Polynesian *hau* branches to an icy cave pool— the secret hiding place of the ancient princess. ⚠ **You can swim in this pool, but be wary of mosquitoes!** In the other direction, a dramatic coastal path continues beyond the campground, past sea arches, blowholes, and cultural sites all the way to Hāna town. ✉ *Hāna Hwy. near mile marker 32* ⚐ *Toilets, showers, picnic tables, girlls/firepits, parking lot.*

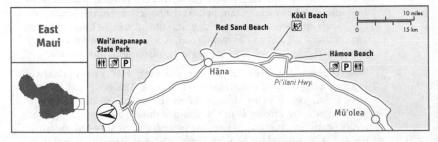

★ **Red Sand Beach.** This startlingly beautiful beach is not easy to find but when you round the last corner of the trail and are confronted with the sight of it, your jaw is bound to drop. Earthy red cliffs tower above the deep maroon sand beach and swimmers bob about in an arctic-blue-color lagoon formed by volcanic boulders just offshore (it's like floating around in a giant natural bath tub). It's worth spending a night in

2

Hāna just to make sure you can get here early and have some time to enjoy it before anyone else shows up.

Keep in mind, getting here is not easy and you have to pass through private property along the way—do so at your own risk. You need to tread carefully up and around Kaʻuiki (the red cinder hill); the cliff-side cinder path is slippery and constantly eroding. Travel is a gamble, and not recommended in shoes without traction, or in bad weather. By popular practice, clothing on the beach is optional. ⊠ *At end of Uākea Rd. past baseball field. Park near community center, walk through grass lot to trail below cemetery* ⛭ *No facilities.*

Kōkī Beach. You can tell from the trucks parked every which way alongside the road that this is a favorite local surf spot. ⚠ **Watch conditions before swimming or bodysurfing, because the riptides here can be mean.** *Iwa,* or white-throated frigate birds, dart like pterodactyls over Alau islet offshore. ⊠ *Haneoʻo Loop Rd., 2 mi east of Hāna town* ⛭ *No facilities.*

Hāmoa Beach. Why did James Michener describe this stretch of salt-and-pepper sand as the most "South Pacific" beach he'd come across, even though it's located in the North Pacific? Maybe it was the perfect half-moon shape, speckled with the shade of palm trees. Perhaps he was intrigued by the jutting black coastline, often outlined by rain showers out at sea, or the pervasive lack of hurry he felt once settled in here. Whatever it was, many still feel the lure. The beach is uncrowded and relaxing, despite a few chaise lounges and a guest-only picnic area set up by the Hotel Hāna-Maui. At times, the churning surf might intimidate beginning swimmers, but bodysurfing can be great here. ⊠ *½ mi past Kōki Beach on Haneoʻo Loop Rd., 2 mi east of Hāna town* ⛭ *Toilets, showers, picnic tables, parking lot.*

WATER ACTIVITIES & TOURS

Getting into (or onto) the water can be the highlight of a trip to Maui. At Lahaina and Māʻalaea harbors you can board boats for snorkeling, scuba diving, deep-sea fishing, whale-watching, parasailing, and sunset cocktail adventures. You can learn to surf, catch a ferry to Lānaʻi, or grab a seat on a fast inflatable. Along the leeward coastline, from Kāʻanapali on the West Shore all the way down to the tip of ʻĀhihi-Kīnaʻu on the South Shore, you can discover great snorkeling and swimming. If you're a thrill seeker, head out to the North Shore and Hoʻokipa, where surfers, kite boarders, and windsurfers catch big waves and big air.

Boogie Boarding & Bodysurfing

Bodysurfing and "sponging" (as boogie boarding is called by the regulars) are great ways to catch some waves without having to master surfing. You don't need balance or coordination to have fun. And you don't have to swim too far out—the best boogie boarding and bodysurfing waves are usually close to shore. Shorebreak (if it isn't too steep) can be exhilarating to ride. You'll know it's too steep if you hear the sound of slapping when the waves hit the sand. You're looking for waves that curl over and break further out, then roll, not slap onto the sand.

The technique for catching waves is the same with or without a board. Swim out to where the swell is just beginning to break, and position yourself toward shore. When the next wave comes, lie on your board (if you have one), kick like crazy, and catch it! You'll be carried along, bumping above the tumbling, foamy surf. The "sponge," or boogie board, is so called because it's soft—softer than a fiberglass surfboard that is. This allows you to safely ride in the rough-and-tumble surf zone; if you get tossed around (which is half the fun) you don't have a heavy, pointed surfboard to worry about, but you do have something to hang onto and glide along on. When bodysurfing, stiffen your body somewhat like a board to achieve the same effect. Real spongers invest in a single short, clipped fin that helps propel them further into the action. You only need one because you're standing half the time.

Best Spots

If you don't mind nudity (officially illegal, but practiced nonetheless), **Little Beach** (⊠ On Mākena Rd., first entrance to Mākena State Beach Park; climb rock wall at north end of beach) is the best break on the island for boogie boarding and bodysurfing. The shape of the sandy shoreline creates waves that break a ways out and tumble on into shore. Because it's sandy, you only risk stubbing a toe on the few submerged rocks, not a reef floor. Don't boogie board at neighboring Big Beach— you'll be unceremoniously slapped like a flapjack onto the steep shore. **Kamaʻole III** (⊠ S. Kīhei Rd.) is another good spot for bodysurfing and boogie boarding. It too has a sandy floor, with 1- to 3-foot waves breaking not too far out. It's often crowded late into the day, especially on weekends when local kids are out of school. Don't let that chase you away, the waves are wide enough for everyone. On the North Shore, **Pāia Bay** (⊠ Just before Pāia town, beyond large community building and grass field) has waves suitable for spongers and bodysurfers. ■ TIP→→ Park in the public lot across the street, as the beach lot is known for break-ins.

Equipment Rentals

Most condos and hotels have boogie boards available to guests—some in better condition than others (but beat-up boogies work just as well for beginners). You can also pick up a boogie board from any discount shop, such as K-mart, for upward of $30.

Auntie Snorkel. You can rent decent boogie boards here for $5 a day, or $15 a week. ⊠ 2439 S. Kīhei Rd. Kīhei ☎ 808/879–6263.

Honolua Surf. "Waverider" boogie boards with smooth undersides (superior to the bumpy kind) can be rented from this surf shop for $8 a day, or $35 a week. ⊠ 2411 S. Kīhei Rd., Kīhei ☎ 808/874–0999 ⊠ 845 Front St., Lahaina ☎ 808/661–8848.

Deep-Sea Fishing

If fishing is your sport, Maui is your island. You can throw in hook and bait for fish such as ʻahi, *aku* (skipjack tuna), barracuda, bonefish, *kawakawa* (bonito), mahimahi, Pacific blue marlin, ono, and *ulua* (jack crevalle). You can fish year-round and you don't need a license. ■ TIP→→ Because boats fill up fast during busy seasons (Christmas, spring break, tournament weeks), consider booking reservations before leaving for Maui.

2

Plenty of fishing boats run out of Lahaina and Māʻalaea harbors. If you charter a private boat, expect to spend in the neighborhood of $600 for a thrilling half-day in the swivel seat. You can share a boat for much cheaper if you don't mind close quarters with a stranger who may get seasick, drunk, or worse . . . lucky! Before you sign up, you should know that—as unfair as it may seem—the captain and crew keep the catch. They will, however, fillet a nice piece for you to take home. And if you catch a real beauty, you can have it professionally mounted.

■ TIP→→ Don't go out with a boater who charges for the fish you catch—that's harbor robbery. You're expected to bring your own lunch and nonglass beverages. (Shop the night before, it's hard to find snacks at 6 AM.) Boats supply coolers and bait. 10–20% tips are suggested.

Boats & Charters

★ **Finest Kind Inc.** A record 1,118-pound Blue Marlin was reeled in by the crew aboard *Finest Kind,* a lovely 37-foot Merritt kept so clean you'd never guess at the action it's seen. Ask Captain Dave about his pet frigate bird—he's been around these waters long enough to befriend other expert fishers. This family-run company operates four boats and specializes in live bait. ⊠ *Lahaina Harbor, Slip 7* ☎ *808/661–0338* ⊕ *www. finestkindsportfishing.com.*

Hinatea Sportfishing. The active crew aboard this first-class, 41-foot Hatteras has the motto, "No boat rides here—we go to catch fish!" Aside from sportfishing, they also offer private sunset and whale-watching cruises, and two-hour bottom fishing trips (unusual in these waters). If you're dying to take your kid out fishing, these less-intensive adventures are a good choice. ⊠ *Lahaina Harbor, Slip 27* ☎ *808/667–7548* ⊕ *www. fishmaui.com/hinatea.*

Ocean Activities Center. If you'd like to catch fish and drink mai tais, book a "family party boat" trip aboard the *Maka Kai,* or the *Wailea Kai,* two 65-foot Power Cats. For $80, lunch and beverages are provided and you can try your hand at angling. The center also offers full-day tours from Māʻalaea Harbor on a 37-foot Tolleycraft for $135 per person. Another option is the popular bottom-fishing tour on which you can keep your catch! Running from 4 to 8 PM, this tour costs $110 per pole, and includes a steak-and-chicken barbecue, and beverages. Spectators ride along for $50. ⊠ *1847 S. Kīhei Rd., Suite 205, Kīhei* ☎ *808/879–4485 or 800/ 798–0652.*

Kayaking

Kayaking is a fantastic way to experience Maui's coastal world. Floating aboard a plastic popsicle stick is easier than you might think, and allows you to cruise out to vibrant, living coral reefs and waters where dolphins and even whales roam. Be aware, however, kayaking can be a leisurely paddle or a challenge of heroic proportion, depending on your location, your inclination, and the weather. You can rent kayaks independently, but we recommend taking a guide. An apparently calm surface can hide extremely strong ocean currents—and you don't *really* want to take an unplanned trip to Tahiti! A good guide will steer you away from surging surf, lead you to pristine reefs, and point out camouflaged fish, like the stalking hawkfish. Not having to schlep your gear on top of your rental car is a bonus. A half-day tour runs around $75. Custom tours can be arranged.

> **TAKE NOTE**
>
> The 'Āhihi-Kīna'u Natural Area Reserve at the southernmost point of South Maui is closed to commercial traffic and you may not take rented kayaks into the reserve.

That said, tour companies will rent kayaks for the day with paddles, life vests, and roof racks, and many will meet you near your chosen location. Ask for a map of good entries and plan to avoid paddling back to shore against the wind (schedule extra time for the return trip regardless). When you're ready to snorkel, secure your belongings in a dry pack onboard and drag your boat by its bowline behind you. (This is not as much of a pain as it sounds).

Best Spots

On the West Side, past the steep cliffs on the Honoapi'ilani Highway and before you hit Lahaina, you can find a long stretch of inviting coastline, including **Ukumehame** and **Olowalu** beaches (⊠ Between mile markers 12 and 14 on Rte. 30). This is a good spot for beginners; entry is easy and there's much to see in every direction. If you want to snorkel, the best visibility is further out, at about 25 feet depth. ⚠ Watch for sharp *kiawe* thorns buried in the sand on the way into the water.

Makena Landing (⊠ Off Makena Rd.) is an excellent taking-off point for a South Maui adventure. Enter from the paved parking lot or the small sandy beach a little south. The bay itself is virtually empty, but the right edge is flanked with brilliant coral heads and juvenile turtles. If you round the point on the right, you come across **Five Caves,** a system of enticing underwater arches. In the morning you may see dolphins, and the arches are havens for lobsters, eels, and spectacularly hued butterfly fish. Check out the million-dollar mansions lining the shoreline and guess which celebrity lives where.

Equipment Rentals & Tours

Maui Sea Kayaking. This company guides small parties to secret spots and takes great care in customizing its outings. For example, the guides accommodate kayakers with disabilities as well as senior kayakers, and they also offer kid-size gear. Among their more unusual programs are kayak surfing and wedding-vow renewal. Trips leave from various locations, depending upon the weather. ☎ 808/572–6299 ⊕ *www.maui.net/~kayaking.*

FodorsChoice ★ **South Pacific Kayaks.** These guys pioneered recreational kayaking on Maui—they know their stuff. Guides are friendly, informative, and eager to help you get the most out of your experience; we're talking true, fun-loving, kayak geeks. Some activity companies show a strange lack of care for the marine environment; South Pacific stands out as adventurous *and* responsible. They offer a variety of trips leaving from both West Side and South Shore locations, including an advanced "Molokini Challenge." ☎ 800/776–2326 or 808/875–4848 ⊕ *www.southpacifickayaks.com.*

Kite Boarding

Catapulting up to 100 feet in the air above the breaking surf, the pioneers of kite boarding hardly seem of this world. Silken kites hold the athletes aloft for precious seconds—long enough for the execution of mind-boggling tricks—then deposit them back in the sea. This new sport is not for the weak-kneed. Injury is so likely, in fact, companies are not allowed to rent equipment. Beginners must take lessons, then purchase their own gear. Devotees swear after your first few lessons, committing to buying your kite is easy.

Kiteboarding School Maui. Call KSM, one of the world's first kite-boarding schools, for one-on-one "flight lessons." Pro kite boarders will induct you at "Kite Beach," providing instruction, equipment, snacks, and FAA guidelines. (Seriously, there are rules about avoiding airplanes at nearby Kahului Airport). ⊠ *22 Hāna Hwy., Kahului* ☎ *808/873–0015* ⊕ *www.ksmaui.com.*

> **ON THE SIDELINES**
>
> If you're not inclined to take to the air yourself, live vicariously at **Red Bull's King of the Air** (⊠ Ho'okipa Beach Park ☎ 808/573–3222 ⊕ www.redbullkingoftheair.com) showcase contest each fall. Contenders travel from as far as Poland and Norway for the chance to be crowned king or queen of the air.

Parasailing

Parasailing is an easy, exhilarating way to earn your wings: just strap on a harness attached to a parachute, and a powerboat pulls you up and over the ocean from a launching dock or a boat's platform. ■ **TIP→→** Keep in mind, parasailing is limited to Maui's West Side, and "thrill craft"—including parasails—are restricted in Maui waters during Humpback whale calving season, December 15 to April 15.

West Maui Para-Sail. Launch 400 feet above the ocean for a bird's eye view of Lahaina. The more daring 800-foot flights are smoother with better views. The captain will be glad to let you experience a "toe dip" or "freefall" if you request it. For safety reasons, passengers weighing less than 100 pounds must be strapped together in tandem. Hour-long trips departing from Lahaina Harbor include 10-minute flights and run from $48 to $55. Early-bird (8–9 AM) flights are cheapest. ☎ *808/661–4060* ⊕ *www.maui.net/~parasail.*

Sailing

With the islands of Moloka'i, Lāna'i, Kaho'olawe, and Molokini a stone's throw away, Maui waters offer visually arresting backdrops for sailing adventures. Sailing conditions can be fickle, so some operations throw in snorkeling or whale-watching, and others offer sunset cruises. Generally, afternoons are windier especially in summer. Prices range from around $35 for two-hour trips to $75 for half-day excursions. ■ **TIP→→** You won't be sheltered from the elements on the trim racing boats, so be sure to bring a hat (one that won't blow away), a light jacket or coverup, and extra sunscreen.

Boats & Charters

America II. This one-time America's Cup contender offers an exciting, intimate alternative to crowded catamarans. For fast action, try a tradewind sail. Sunset sails are generally calmer—a good choice if you don't want to spend two hours fully exposed to the sun. ⊠ *Harbor Slip #5, Lahaina* ☎ *808/667–2195.*

Paragon. If you want to snorkel and sail, this is your boat. Many snorkel cruises claim to sail but actually motor most of the way, Paragon is an exception. Both Paragon vessels (one catamaran in Lahaina, the other in Māʻalaea) are ship-shape and crews are competent and friendly. Their mooring in Molokini Crater is particularly good, and they often stay after the masses have left. Extras on their trips to Lānaʻi include mai tais, champagne, and blue-water swims. ⊠ *Lahaina and Māʻalaea Harbors* ☎ *808/244–2087* ⊕ *www.sailmaui.com.*

Scotch Mist Charters. Follow the wind aboard this 50-foot Santa Cruz sailing yacht. Two-hour snorkeling, sunset, or whale-watching trips emphasize sailing and usually carry less than 25 passengers. ⊠ *Lahaina Harbor Slip #2* ☎ *877/464–6284 or 808/661–0386* ⊕ *www.scotchmistsailingcharters.com.*

Rafting

The high-speed, inflatable rafts you find on Maui are nothing like the raft that Huck Finn used to drift down the Mississippi. While passengers grip straps, these rafts fly, skimming and bouncing across the sea. Because they're so maneuverable, they go where the big boats can't—secret coves, sea caves, and unvisited beaches. Two-hour trips run around $50, half-day trips upward of $100. ⚠ While safe, these trips are not for the faint of heart. If you have back or neck problems or are pregnant, you should reconsider this activity.

Blue Water Rafting. One of the only ways to get to the exciting Kenaio coast (the roadless southern coastline beyond ʻĀhihi-Kīnaʻu), this rafting tour begins trips conveniently at the Kīhei Boat ramp. Dolphins, turtles, and other marine life are the highlight of this adventure. ⊠ *Kīhei* ☎ *808/879–7238* ⊕ *www.bluewaterrafting.com.*

Ocean Riders. This West Side tour takes people all the way around the island of Lānaʻi. For snorkeling or gawking, the "back side" of Lānaʻi is one of Hawaiʻi's unsung marvels. Tours depart from Mala Wharf, at the northern end of Front Street. ⊠ *Lahaina* ☎ *808/661–3586* ⊕ *www.mauioceanriders.com.*

Scuba Diving

Maui is just as scenic underwater as it is on dry land. In fact, some of the finest diving spots in all of Hawaiʻi lie along the Valley Isle's western and southwestern shores. If you're a certified diver, you can rent gear at any Maui dive shop simply by showing your PADI or NAUI card. Unless you're familiar with the area, however, it's probably best to hook up with a dive shop for an underwater tour. Tours include tanks and weights

CLOSE UP	# Diving 101

IF YOU'VE ALWAYS WANTED GILLS, Hawai'i is a good place to get them. Although the bulky, heavy equipment seems freakish on shore, underwater it allows you to move about freely, almost weightlessly. As you descend into another world, you slowly grow used to the sound of your own breathing and the strangeness of being able to do so 30-plus feet down.

Most resorts offer introductory dive lessons in their pools, which allow you to acclimate to the awkward breathing apparatus before venturing out into the great blue. If you aren't starting from a resort pool, no worries. Most intro dives take off from calm, sandy beaches, such as Ulua or Kā'anapali. If you're bitten by the deep-sea bug and want to continue diving, you should get certified. Only

certified divers can rent equipment or go on more adventurous dives, such as night dives, open-ocean dives, and cave dives.

There are several certification companies, including PADI, NAUI, and SSI. PADI, the largest, is the most comprehensive. Once you begin your certification process, stick with the same company. The dives you log will not apply to another company's certification. (Dives with a PADI instructor, for instance, will not count toward SSI certification). Remember that you will not be able to fly or go to the airy summit of Haleakalā within eight hours of diving. An Open Water certification will take three to four days and cost around $300. From that point on, the sky . . . or rather, the sea's the limit!

---

and start around $120. Wetsuits and BCs are rented separately, for an additional $15 to $30. Shops also offer introductory dives ($100–$160) for those who aren't certified. ■ TIP→ Before signing on with any of these outfitters, it's a good idea to ask a few pointed questions about your guide's experience, the weather outlook, and the condition of the equipment.

Best Spots

Honolua Bay (⊠ Between mile markers 32 and 33 on Rte. 30, dirt road to left) has beach entry. This West Maui marine preserve is alive with many varieties of coral and tame tropical fish, including large *ulua, kāhala,* barracuda, and manta rays. With depths of 20 to 50 feet, this is a popular summer dive spot. ⚠ High surf often prohibits winter dives.

A crescent-shape islet formed by the eroding top of a volcano, **Molokini Crater** (accessible by boat only) is a marine preserve ranging 10 to 80 feet in depth. The numerous tame fish and brilliant coral dwelling within the crater make it a popular introductory dive site. On calm days, exploring the back side of Molokini is an exciting boat dive for advanced divers. The enormous dropoff into the 'Alalākeiki Channel (to 350 feet) offers dramatic seascapes and chance sightings of larger pelagic fish and sharks.

Equipment Rental & Dive Tours

★ **Ed Robinson's Diving Adventures.** Ed wrote the book, literally, on Molokini. An expert marine photographer, he offers diving instruction and boat charters to South Maui, the backside of Molokini, and Lāna'i. Weekly night dives are available. ✉ *50 Koki St., Kīhei* ☎ *808/879–3584 or 800/ 635–1273* ⊕ *www.maui-scuba.com.*

Lahaina Divers. This West Side shop offers tours of Maui, Molokini, and Lānaʻi; boats are accessible for passengers with disabilities. ✉ *143 Dickenson St., Lahaina* ☎ *808/667–7496 or 800/998–3483* ⊕ *www. lahainadivers.com.*

Maui Dive Shop. With six locations island-wide, Maui Dive Shop offers scuba charters, diving instruction, and equipment rental. Its main office is in Kīhei. ✉ *1455 S. Kīhei Rd., Kīhei* ☎ *808/879–3388* ⊕ *www. mauidiveshop.com.*

Snorkeling

No one should leave Maui without ducking underwater to meet a sea turtle, moray eel, or Humuhumunukunukuāpuaʻa—the state fish. Visibility is best in the morning, before the wind picks up.

There are two ways to approach snorkeling—by land or by sea. Daily around 7 AM, a parade of boats heads out to Molokini Crater, that little bowl of land off the coast of Wailea. Boat trips offer some advantages—deeper water, seasonal whale-watching, crew assistance, lunch, and gear. But you don't need a boat; much of Maui's best snorkeling is found just steps from the road. Nearly the entire leeward coastline from Kapalua south to ʻĀhihi-Kīnaʻu offers prime opportunities to ogle

> ### OCEAN ETIQUETTE & SAFETY
>
> "Look, don't touch, " is a good motto in the ocean where many creatures don't mind company, but reveal hidden stingers if threatened. Never stand on coral. Touching it—even briefly—can kill the delicate creatures residing within the hard shell. Remember that ocean conditions change throughout the day. Pop your head above the water periodically to ensure you aren't drifting too far out, or too close to rocks. And remember to wear a rash guard, it will keep you from being fried by the sun.

fish and turtles. If you're patient and sharp-eyed, you may glimpse eels, octopi, lobsters, eagle rays, and even a rare shark or monk seal.

Best Spots

Snorkel sites here are listed from north to south, starting at the northwest corner of the island.

On the west side of the island, just past Kapalua, **Honolua Bay** Marine Life Conservation District (✉ Between mile markers 32 and 33 on Rte. 30, dirt road to left), has a superb reef for snorkeling. When conditions are calm, it's one of the island's best spots with tons of fish and colorful corals to observe. ■ **TIP→→ Make sure to bring a fish key with you here, you're sure to see many species of triggerfish, filefish, and wrasses.** The coral formations on the right side of the bay are particularly dramatic and feature pink, aqua, and orange varieties. Take care entering the water, there's no beach here and the rocks and concrete ramp can be slippery.

2

The northeast corner of this windward-facing bay periodically gets hammered by big waves in winter and high-profile surf contests are held here. Avoid the bay then, and after a heavy rain (you'll know because Honolua stream will be running across the access path).

Just minutes south of Honolua, dependable **Kapalua Bay** (✉ From Rte. 30, turn onto Kapalua Pl., and walk through tunnel) beckons. As beautiful above the water as it is below, Kapalua is exceptionally calm, even when other spots get testy. Needle and butterfly fish dart just past the sandy beach, which is why it's sometimes crowded. ⚠ Sand can be particularly hot here, watch your toes!

Fodor'sChoice
★ We think **Black Rock** (✉ In front of Kā'anapali Sheraton Maui, Kā'anapali Pkwy.), at the northernmost tip of Kā'anapali Beach, is tops for snorkelers of any skill. The entry couldn't be easier—dump your towel on the sand in front of the Sheraton Maui resort and in you go. Beginners can stick close to shore and still see lots of action. Advanced snorkelers can swim beyond the sand to the tip of Black Rock, or Keka'a Point, to see larger fish and eagle rays. One of the underwater residents, a turtle named "Volkswagen" for its hefty size, can be found here. He sits very still; you must look closely. Equipment can be rented on-site. Parking, in a small lot adjoining the hotel, is the only hassle.

Along Honoapi'ilani Highway (Route 30) there are several favorite snorkel sites including the area just out from the cemetery at **Hanakao'o Beach Park** (✉ Near mile marker 23 on Rte. 30). At depths of 5 and 10 feet, you can see a variety of corals, especially as you head south toward **Waihikuli Wayside Park**. Farther down the highway, the shallow coral reef at **Olowalu** (✉ South of Olowalu General Store on Rte. 30) is good for a quick underwater tour, though the best spot is a ways out, at depths of 25 feet or more, and is better accessed by kayak. Boats sometimes stop nearby (they refer to this site as "Coral Gardens") on their return trip from Molokini.

Excellent snorkeling is found down the coastline between Kīhei and Mākena. The best spots are along the rocky fringes of Wailea's **Mōkapu, Ulua, Wailea,** and **Polo** beaches (✉ Off Wailea Alanui Rd.). Find one of the public parking lots sandwiched between Wailea's luxury resorts, and enjoy these beaches' sandy entries, calm waters with relatively good visibility, and variety of fish species. Of the four beaches, Ulua has the best reef. You can glimpse a box-shape pufferfish here, and listen to snapping shrimp and parrot fish nibbling on coral.

At the very southernmost tip of paved road in South Maui lies **'Āhihi-Kīna'u** Natural Area Reserve (✉ Just before end of Mākena Alanui Rd., follow marked trails through trees), also referred to as La Pérouse Bay. Despite its barren, lava-scorched landscape, the area recently gained such popularity with adventurers and activity purveyors that it had to be closed to commercial traffic. A ranger is stationed at the parking lot to assist visitors. It's difficult terrain and sometimes crowded, but if you make use of the rangers' suggestions (stay on marked paths, wear sturdy shoes to hike in and out), you can experience some of the reserve's outstanding treasures, such as the sheltered cove known as the "fishpond." ■ TIP→→ Be sure to bring water, this is a hot and unforgiving wilderness.

Snorkel Cruises

The same boats that offer whale-watching, sailing, and diving also offer snorkeling excurions. Trips usually include visits to two locales, lunch, gear, instruction, and possible whale or dolphin sightings. Some captains troll for fish along the way, which adds excitement.

Molokini Crater, a moon-shape crescent about 3 mi off the shore of Wailea, is the most popular snorkel cruise destination. You can spend half a day floating above the fish-filled crater for about $80. Some say it's not as good as it's made out to be, and that it's too crowded, but others consider it to be one of the best spots in Hawai'i. Visibility is generally outstanding and fish are incredibly tame. Your second stop will be somewhere along the leeward coast, either "Turtle Town" near Mākena or "Coral Gardens" toward Lahaina. ⚠ Be aware that on blustery mornings, there's a good chance the waters will be too rough to moor in Molokini and you'll end up snorkeling some place off the shore, which you could have driven to for free. For the safety of everyone on the boat, it's the captain's prerogative to choose the best spot for the day.

Snorkel cruises vary slightly—some serve mai tais and steaks while others offer beer and cold cuts. You might prefer a large ferry boat to a smaller sailboat, or vice versa. Whatever trip you choose, be sure you know where to go to board your vessel, getting lost in the harbor at 6 AM is a lousy start to a good day. ■ TIP➜➜ Bring sunscreen, an underwater camera (they're double the price onboard), a towel, and a cover-up for the windy return trip. Even tropical waters get chilly after hours of swimming so consider wearing a rash guard. Wetsuits can usually be rented for a fee. Hats without straps will blow away, and valuables should be left at home.

★ **Ann Fielding's Snorkel Maui.** For a personal introduction to Maui's undersea universe, this is the indisputable authority. A marine biologist, Fielding—formerly with the University of Hawai'i, Waikīkī Aquarium, and the Bishop Museum and the author of several guides to island sea life—is the Carl Sagan of Hawai'i's reef cosmos. She'll not only show you fish, but she'll also introduce you to *individual* fish. This is a good first experience for dry-behind-the-ears types. Snorkel trips include lunch and equipment. ☎ *808/572-8437* ⊕ *www.maui.net/~annf.*

Mahana Na'ia. This comfortable catamaran offers a good value snorkel trip to Molokini. The staff provides decent service and food on its cruise. Marketed as a sailboat, it rarely hoists it's canvas, but does fish while en route. Coffee and continental breakfast greet you at the dock, and beer and wine are served with barbecue chicken and salad for lunch. ✉ *Mā'alaea Harbor Slip #47* ☎ *808/871-8636* ⊕ *www.maui-snorkeling-adventures.com.*

Maui–Moloka'i Sea Cruises. If you're a landlubber who'd still like to see the sea, book a passage on the 92-foot *Prince Kuhio,* one of the largest air-conditioned cruise vessels in Maui waters. In addition to a deli-style lunch and open bar, they offer complimentary transportation to the harbor, which relieves you from parking and searching for the boat's slip at 7 AM. ✉ *Mā'alaea Harbor* ☎ *808/242-8777* ⊕ *www.mvprince.com.*

★ ⚲ **Pacific Whale Foundation.** The knowledgeable folks here will treat you to Molokini adventure like the others, only with a more ecological bent. Accordingly, they serve gardenburgers alongside the requisite barbecue chicken and their fleet runs on bona-fide biodiesel fuel. This is an A-plus trip for kids, the crew assists with an onboard junior naturalist program and throws in a free wildlife guide and poster. The multihulled boats are smooth and some have swim on–off platforms. Best of all, profits go to protecting the very treasures you're paying to enjoy. ✉ *Māʻalaea Harbor Slip* ☎ *800/942–5311 or 808/249–8811* ⊕ *www.pacificwhale.org.*

Trilogy Excursions. The longest-running operation on Maui is the Coon family's Trilogy Excursions. They have six beautiful multihulled sailing craft (though they usually only sail for a brief portion of the trip), manned by energetic crews who will keep you entertained with stories of the islands and plenty of corny jokes. A full-day catamaran cruise to Lānaʻi includes continental breakfast and a deli lunch onboard; a guided van tour of the island; a "Snorkeling 101" class and time to snorkel in the waters of Lānaʻi's Hulopoʻe Marine Preserve (Trilogy has exclusive commercial access); and a barbecue dinner on Lānaʻi. Many people consider this the highlight of their trip, but if you're not a good "group activity" person, this may not be for you. The company also offers a Molokini snorkel cruise. ✉ *Māʻalaea Harbor Slip #99, or Lahaina Harbor* ☎ *808/661–4743 or 800/874–2666* ⊕ *www.sailtrilogy.com.*

Snorkel Equipment Rental

Most hotels and vacation rentals offer free use of snorkel gear. Beachside stands fronting the major resort areas rent equipment by the hour or day. ■ TIP→ **Don't shy away from asking for instructions, a snug fit makes all the difference in the world. A mask fits if it sticks to your face when you inhale deeply through your nose. Fins should cover your entire foot (unlike diving fins, which strap around your heel).** If you're squeamish about using someone else's gear, (or need a prescription lens) pick up your own at any discount shop. Costco and Longs have better prices than ABC stores; dive shops have superior equipment.

Maui Dive Shop. You can rent pro gear (including optical masks, boogie boards, and wet suits) from six locations island-wide. Pump these guys for weather info before heading out, they'll know better than last night's news forecaster. ✉ *1455 S. Kīhei Rd., Kīhei* ☎ *808/873–3388* ⊕ *www. mauidiveshop.com.*

Snorkel Bob's. If you need gear, Snorkel Bob's will rent you a mask, fins, and a snorkel and throw in a carrying bag, map, and snorkel tips for as little as $9 per week. Avoid the circle masks and go for the split-level, it's worth the extra cash. ✉ *Nāpili Village Hotel, 5425 Lower Honoapiʻilani Hwy., Nāpili* ☎ *808/669–9603* ✉ *1217 Front St., Lahaina* ☎ *808/661–4421* ✉ *1279 S. Kīhei Rd., Kīhei* ☎ *808/875–6188* ✉ *2411 S. Kīhei Rd., Kīhei* ☎ *808/879–7449* ⊕ *www.snorkelbob.com.*

Surfing

Maui's diverse coastline has surf for every level of waterman or woman. Waves on leeward-facing shores (West and South Maui) tend to break in gentle sets all summer long. Surf instructors in Kīhei and Lahaina can rent you boards, give you onshore instruction, and then lead you out through the channel, where it's safe to enter the surf. They'll shout encouragement while you paddle like mad for the thrill of standing on water—some will even give you a helpful shove. These areas are great for beginners, the only danger is whacking a stranger with your board or stubbing your toe against the reef.

The North Shore is another story. Winter waves pound the windward coast, attracting water champions from every corner of the world. Adrenaline addicts are towed in by Jet Ski to a legendary, deep-sea break

> **ON THE SIDELINES**
>
> Even if you aren't a surfer, watching can be exhilarating. **Ho'okipa Beach Park** (⊠ 2 mi past Pā'ia on Hāna Hwy.) is an easy place to view the action. Near-perfect waves can be seen at **Honolua Bay**, on the northern tip of West Maui. To get there, continue 2 mi north of D. T. Fleming Park on Route 30 and take a left onto the dirt road next to a pineapple field; a path leads down the cliff to the beach. In December, the **Billabong Pro** invites female wave riders to compete at Honolua Bay.

called *Jaws*. Waves here periodically tower upward of 40 feet, dwarfing the helicopters seeking to capture unbelievable photos. The only spot for viewing this phenomenon (which happens just a few times a year) is on private property. So, if you hear the surfers next to you crowing about Jaws "going off," cozy up and get them to take you with them.

Whatever your skill, there's a board, a break, and even a surf guru to accommodate you. A two-hour lesson is a good intro to surf culture. Surf camps are becoming increasingly popular, especially with women. One- or two-week camps offer a terrific way to build muscle and self-esteem simultaneously. **Maui Surfer Girls** (⊕ www.mauisurfergirls.com) immerses adventurous young ladies in wave-riding wisdom during two-week camps. Coed camps are sponsored by **Action Sports Maui** (⊕ www.actionsportsmaui.com).

Best Spots

Beginners can hang 10 at Kīhei's **Cove Park** (⊠ S. Kīhei Rd., Kīhei), a sometimes crowded but reliable 1- to 2-foot break. Boards can easily be rented across the street, or in neighboring Kalama Park parking lot. The only bummer is having to balance the 9-plus-foot board on your head while crossing busy South Kīhei Road. But hey, that wouldn't stop world-famous longboarder Eddie Aikau, now would it?

Long- or short-boarders can paddle out anywhere along Lahaina's coastline. One option is at **Launiupoko State Wayside** (⊠ Honoapi'ilani Hwy. near mile marker 18). The east end of the park has an easy break, good for beginners. Even better is **Ukumehame** (⊠ Honoapi'ilani Hwy. near mile marker 12), also called "Thousand Peaks." You'll soon see how the spot got it's name, the waves here break again and again in wide and consistent rows, giving lots of room to beginning surfers.

For advanced wave riders, **Ho'okipa Beach Park** (⊠ 2 mi past Pā'ia on Ha'na Hwy.) boasts several well-loved breaks, including "Pavilions,"

"Lanes," "the Point," and "Middles." Surfers have priority until 11 AM, when windsurfers move in on the action. ⚠ Competition is stiff here; be prepared to be hassled if you don't know what you're doing.

Surf Shops & Lessons

Big Kahuna. Rent surfboards (soft-top longboards) here for $15 for two hours, or $20 for the day. The shop also rents kayaks and snorkel gear, and is across from Cove Park. ⊠ *Island Surf Bldg., 1993 S. Kīhei Rd. #2, Kīhei* ☎ *808/875–6395.*

★ **Goofy Foot.** Call us goofy, but we like the right-footed gurus here. Their safari shop is just plain cool and only steps away from "Breakwall," a great beginner's spot in Lahaina. Two-hour classes with five or fewer students are $55, and six-hour classes with lunch and an ocean-safety course are $250. ⊠ *505 Front St., Lahaina* ☎ *808/244–9283* ⊕ *www. goofyfootsurfschool.com.*

Hāna Highway Surf. If you're heading out to the North Shore surf, you can pick up boards ranging from beginner's soft-tops to high-performance shortboards here for $20 per day. ⊠ *69 Hāna Hwy., Pā'ia* ☎ *808/579–8999.*

Nancy Emerson School of Surfing. Instructors here will get even the most shaky novice riding with its pioneering "Learn to Surf in One Lesson" program. A private lesson with Nancy herself—a pro surfer and occasional stunt double—costs $215 for one hour or $325 for two; lessons with her equally qualified instructors are $100 for one hour and $165 for two. Group lessons are $75 for two hours. ⊠ *358 Papa Pl., Suite F, Kahului* ☎ *808/244–7873* ⊕ *www.surfclinics.com.*

Second Wind. Surfboard rentals at this centrally located shop are a deal—good boards go for $18 per day or $90 per week. ⊠ *111 Hāna Hwy., Kahului* ☎ *808/877–7467.*

Windsurfing

Something about Maui's wind and water stirs the spirit of innovation. Windsurfing, invented in the 1950s, found its true home at Ho'okipa in 1980. Seemingly overnight, windsurfing pioneers from around the world flooded Maui's north shore. Equipment evolved, amazing film footage was captured, and a new sport was born.

If you're new to the action, you can get lessons from the experts island-wide. For a beginner, the best thing about windsurfing is that, unlike surfing, you don't have to paddle. Unfortunately, you still need coordination and balance. You can learn standing still on a windless resort beach, but its way more fun at Kanahā, where the big boys go. Lessons range from two-hour introductory classes to five-day advanced "flight school." If you're an old salt, pick up tips and equipment from the companies below.

Best Spots

After **Ho'okipa Bay** (⊠ 2 mi past Pā'ia on Hāna Hwy.) was discovered by windsurfers three decades ago, this windy beach 10 mi east of Kahului gained an international reputation. The spot is blessed with optimal wave-sailing wind and sea conditions and can offer the ultimate aerial experience.

In summer the windsurfing crowd heads south to **Kalepolepo Beach.** (⊠ S. Kīhei Rd. near Ohukai St.). Tradewinds build in strength and by afternoon a swarm of butterfly-like sails can be seen skimming the whitecaps with the West Maui mountains as a backdrop.

A great site for speed, **Kanahā Beach Park** (⊠ Behind Kahului Airport) is dedicated to beginners in the morning hours, before the waves and wind really get roaring. After 11 AM, the professionals choose from

> ## ON THE SIDELINES
>
> Few places lay claim to as many windsurfing tournaments as Maui. In March the Hawaiian Pro Am Windsurfing competition gets under way. In April the Da Kine Hawaiian Pro Am lures top windsurfers, and in October the Aloha Classic World Wave Sailing Championships takes place. All are held at Hoʻokipa Bay, right outside the town of Pāʻia. For competitions featuring amateurs as well as professionals, check out the Maui Race Series (☎ 808/877–2111), six events held at Kanahā Beach in Kahului in summer.

their quiver of sails the size and shape best suited for the day's demands. This beach tends to have smallish waves and forceful winds—sometimes sending sailors flying along at 40 knots.

Equipment Rental & Lessons

Action Sports Maui. The quirky, friendly professionals here will meet you at Kanahā, outfit you with a "quiver" of sails, and guide you through your first "jibe" or turn. Don't be afraid to ask lots of questions. ⊠ 6 E. Waipulani Rd., Kīhei ☎ 808/871–5857 ⊕ www.actionsportsmaui.com.

Hi Tech. This large warehouse store offers excellent equipment rentals; $45 gets you a board, two sails, a mast, and roof racks for 24 hours. ⊠ 425 Koloa, Kahului ☎ 808/877–2111.

Maui Windsurfari. This company specializes in windsurfing vacation packages, offering a full range of services including accommodation bookings and high-tech-gear rental. ⊠ 360 Papa Pl. #205, Kahului ☎ 808/ 871–7766 or 800/736–6284 ⊕ www.windsurfari.com.

Second Wind. Located in Kahului, this company rents boards with two sails for $43 per day. Boards with three sails go for $48 per day. ⊠ 11 Hāna Hwy., Kahului ☎ 808/877–7467.

Whale-Watching

From November through April, whale-watching becomes one of the most popular activities on Maui. Boats leave the wharves at Lahaina and Māʻalaea in search of Humpback whales, merely to enjoy their awe-inspiring size in closer proximity. As it's almost impossible *not* to see whales in winter on Maui, you'll want to prioritize: is adventure or comfort your aim? If close encounters with the giants of the deep are your desire, pick a smaller boat that guarantees sightings. If an impromptu ma-

CLOSE UP

The Humpback's Winter Home

THE HUMPBACK WHALES' attraction to Maui is legendary. More than half the Pacific's humpback population winters in Hawai'i, especially in the waters around the Valley Isle, where mothers can be seen just a few hundred feet offshore training their young calves in the fine points of whale etiquette. Watching from shore it's easy to catch sight of whales spouting, or even breaching—when they leap almost entirely out of the sea, slapping back onto the water with a huge splash.

At one time there were thousands of the huge mammals, but a history of overhunting and marine pollution dwindled the world population to about 1,500. In 1966 humpbacks were put on the endangered species list. Hunting or harassing whales is illegal in the waters of most nations, and in the United States, boats and airplanes are restricted from getting too close. The word is still out, however, on the effects military sonar testing has on the marine mammals.

Marine biologists believe the humpbacks (much like the humans) keep returning to Hawai'i because of its warmth. Having fattened themselves in subarctic waters all summer, the whales migrate south in the winter to breed, and a rebounding population of thousands cruise Maui waters. Winter is calving time, and the young whales, born with little blubber, probably couldn't survive in the frigid Alaskan waters. No one has ever seen a whale give birth here, but experts know that calving is their main winter activity, since the 1- and 2-ton youngsters suddenly appear while the whales are in residence.

The first sighting of a humpback whale spout each season is exciting and reassuring for locals on Maui. A collective sigh of relief can be heard, "Ah, they've returned." In the not-so-far distance, flukes and flippers can be seen rising above the ocean's surface. It's hard not to anthropomorphize the tail-waving, it looks like such an amiable, human gesture. Each fluke is uniquely patterned, like a human's fingerprint, and used to identify the giants as they travel halfway around the globe and back.

2

---

rine-biology lesson sounds fun, go with the Pacific Whale Foundation. Two-hour forays into the whales' world cost $20. For those wanting to sip mai tais as whales cruise calmly by, stick with a sunset cruise on a boat with a full bar and buffet ($40 and up). ■ TIP→→ Afternoon trips are generally rougher because the wind picks up, but some say this is when the most surface action occurs.

Every captain aims to please during whale season, getting as close as legally possible (100 yards). Crew members know when a whale is about to dive (after several waves of its heart-shape tail) but rarely can predict breaches (when the whale hurls itself up and almost entirely out of the water). Prime viewing space (on the upper and lower decks, around the railings) is limited, so boats can feel crowded even when half-full. If you don't want to squeeze in beside strangers, opt for a smaller boat with less bookings. Don't forget to bring sunscreen, light long sleeves, and a hat you can secure. Weather can be extreme at sea, especially as the wind picks up. Arrive early to find parking.

Best Spots

From December 15 to May 1 the Pacific Whale Foundation has naturalists stationed in two places—on the rooftop of their headquarters and at the scenic viewpoint at **McGregor Point Lookout** (⊠ Between mile markers 7 and 8 on Honoapiʻilani Hwy., Rte. 30). Just like the commuting traffic, whales cruise along the *pali*, or cliff-side, of West Maui's Honoapiʻilani highway all day long. ⚠ Make sure to park safely before craning your neck out to see them.

The northern end of **Keawakapu Beach** (⊠ S. Kīhei Rd. near Kilohana Dr.) seems to be a whale magnet. Situate yourself on the sand or at the nearby restaurant, and you're bound to see a mama whale patiently teaching her calf the exact technique of flipper-waving.

Boats & Charters

Kiele V. The Hyatt Regency Maui's *Kiele V,* a 55-foot luxury catamaran, does seasonal whale-watching excursions as well as daily snorkel trips, and afternoon cocktail sails. A comfortable ride, the cat leaves from Kāʻanapali Beach, which is more fun than the harbor. ⊠ *200 Nohea Kai Dr., Lahaina* ☎ *808/661–1234.*

★ ♻ **Pacific Whale Foundation.** This nonprofit organization pioneered whale-watching back in 1979 and now runs four boats, with 15 trips daily. The crew offers insights into whale behavior (do they *really* know what those tail flicks mean?) and suggests ways for you to help save marine life worldwide. Trips meet at the Foundation's store, where you can buy whale paraphernalia, snacks, and coffee—a real bonus for 8 AM trips. Passengers are then herded much like migrating whales down to the harbor. Once you catch sight of the wildlife up-close, you can't help but be thrilled. ⊠ *Kealia Beach Plaza, 101 N. Kīhei Rd., Kīhei* ☎ *808/879–8811* ⊕ *www.pacificwhale.org.*

Pride Charters. Two-hour cruises narrated by a naturalist are offered aboard *Leilani.* This small, maneuverable boat offers good viewing opportunities. ⊠ *208 Kenolio Rd. Kīhei* ☎ *808/874–8835* ⊕ *www.prideofmaui.com.*

GOLF, HIKING & OUTDOOR ACTIVITIES

ATV Tours

Haleakalā ATV Tours. Haleakalā ATV Tours explore the mountainside in their own unique way: propelled through the forest on 350 cc, four-wheel-drive, Honda Rancher all-terrain vehicles. The adventures begin at Haleakalā Ranch and rev right up to the pristine Waikamoi rain-forest preserve. Kids under 15 ride alongside in the exciting Argo Conquest, an eight-wheel amphibious vehicle. Two-hour trips go for $90, and 3½-hour trips are $139. ☎ *808/661–0288* ⊕ *www.atvmaui.com.*

Biking

Maui County biking is safer and more convenient than in the past, but long distances and mountainous terrain keep it from being a practical mode of travel. Still, painted bike lanes enable riders to travel all the way from Mākena to Kapalua, and you'll see hardy souls pedaling under the hot Maui sun.

Several companies offer downhill bike tours from the top of Haleakalā all the way to the coast. ⚠ Be aware that this activity can be truly hazardous. Bikers have experienced serious injuries on the winding, heavily trafficked roadways. Most companies do not cancel in inclement weather. If you're not a confident rider, avoid this excursion.

Best Spots

Though it's changing, at present there are few truly good spots to ride on Maui. Street bikers will want to head out to scenic **Thompson Road** (⊠ Off Rte. 37, Kula Hwy., Keokea). It's quiet, gently curvy, and flanked by gorgeous views on both sides. Plus, because it's at a higher elevation, the air temperature is cooler. Mountain bikers can head up to **Polipoli Forest** (⊠ Off Rte. 377, end of Waipoli Rd.). A bumpy trail leads through an unlikely forest of conifers.

Bike Rentals & Guided Tours

Island Biker. This bike shop rents standard front-shock bikes and road bikes for $29 a day or $95 per week; helmets are included. ⊠ *415 Dairy Rd., Kahului* ☎ *808/877–7744.*

Maui Downhill. If biking down the side of Haleakalā sounds like fun, several companies are ready to assist you. Maui Downhill vans will shuttle you to the mountaintop, help you onto a bike, and follow you as you coast down through clouds and gorgeous scenery. Lunch or breakfast is included, depending on your trip's start time; treks cost $150. ⊠ *199 Dairy Rd., Kahului 96732* ☎ *808/871–2155 or 800/535–2453* ⊕ *www.mauidownhill.net.*

Maui Mountain Cruisers. Bike trips "cruise" down Haleakalā and are $125 including lunch; nonbikers can ride down in a van for $55. ⊠ *Box 1356, Makawao* ☎ *808/871–6014* ⊕ *www.mauimountaincruisers.com.*

West Maui Cycles. An assortment of cycles are offered here, including front-suspension bikes for $40 per day, full-suspension bikes for $50 per day, and standard hybrid bikes for $20 per day. ⊠ *1087 Limahana St., Lahaina* ☎ *808/661–9005.*

Golf

Maui's golf courses offer jaw-dropping vistas just about everywhere you look. Holes run across small bays, past craggy lava outcrops, and up into cool, forested mountains. Whether it's an elevated view of a whale leaping just offshore or a red cardinal flitting through a guava tree just off the fairway, nature and the beauty of Maui are a part of every shot. Most courses are affiliated with resorts, but there are also a few daily fee courses and a fun little muni.

Fodor'sChoice **The Dunes at Maui Lani.** This is Robin Nelson (1999) at his minimalist
★ best, a bit of British links in the middle of the Pacific. Some raters put
it among Hawai'i's top 10. Holes run through ancient, lightly wooded
sand dunes, 5 mi inland from Kahului Harbor. Thanks to the natural
humps and slopes of the dunes, Nelson had to move very little dirt and
created a natural beauty. During the design phase he visited Ireland, and
not so coincidentally the par-3 third looks a lot like the Dell at Lahinch:
a white dune on the right sloping down into a deep bunker and partially obscuring the right side of the green—just one of several blind to
semi-blind shots here. ⊠ *1333 Maui Lani Pkwy., Kahului* ☎ *808/
873–0422* ⊕ *www.dunesatmauilani.com* ⚐ *18 holes. 6841 yds. Par 72.
Green Fee: $110* ☞ *Facilities: Driving range, putting green, golf carts,
rental clubs, pro shop, golf academy/lessons, restaurant, bar.*

Elleaire Golf Course. Formerly known as Silversword (1987), Elleaire is
an exacting test. Fairways tend to be narrow, especially in landing areas,
and can be quite a challenge when the trade winds come up in the afternoon. The course is lined with enough coconut trees to make them
a collective hazard, not just a nutty nuisance. ⊠ *1345 Pi'ilani Hwy.,
Kīhei* ☎ *808/874–0777* ⚐ *18 holes. 6404 yds. Par 71. Green Fee:
$100* ☞ *Facilities: Driving range, putting green, rental clubs, golf carts,
lessons, restaurant.*

★ **Kā'anapali Resort.** The Kā'anapali
North Course (1963) is one of three
in Hawai'i designed by Robert Trent
Jones Sr., the godfather of modern
golf architecture. The greens average a whopping 10,000 square feet,
necessary because of the often severe
undulation. The par-4 18th hole
(into the prevailing trade breezes,
with out-of-bounds on the left, and
a lake on the right) is notoriously
tough. The South Course (Arthur

> **TIP!**
>
> Resort courses, in particular, offer
> more than the usual three sets of
> tees, sometimes four or five. So
> bite off as much or little challenge
> as you like. Tee it up from the tips
> and you'll end up playing a few
> 600-yard par-5s and see a few
> 250-yard forced carries.

Jack Snyder, 1976) shares similar seaside-into-the-hills terrain, but is rated
a couple of strokes easier, mostly because putts are less treacherous.
⊠ *2290 Kā'anapali Pkwy., Lahaina* ☎ *808/661–3691* ⊕ *www.kaanapali-
golf.com* ⚐ *North Course: 18 holes. 6136 yds. Par 71. Green Fee: $160.
South Course: 18 holes. 6067 yds. Par 71. Green Fee: $130* ☞ *Facili-
ties: Driving range, putting green, rental clubs, golf carts, lessons, restaurant, bar.*

Fodor'sChoice **Kapalua Resort.** Perhaps Hawai'i's best known golf resort, Kapalua hosts
★ the PGA Tour's first event each January, the Mercedes Championships
at the Plantation Course at Kapalua. Ben Crenshaw and Bill Coore
(1991) tried to incorporate traditional shot values in a very nontra-
ditional site, taking into account slope, gravity, and the prevailing trade
winds. The par-5 18th, for instance, plays 663 yards from the back
tees (600 from the resort tees). The fairway drops 170 feet from tee
to green, narrowing as it goes, and plays downwind and down-grain.
Despite the longer-than-usual distance, the slope is great enough and

the wind at your back usually brisk enough to reach the green with two well-struck shots.

The Bay Course (Arnold Palmer and Francis Duane, 1975) is the most traditional of Kapalua's triad. The most memorable hole is the par-3 fifth, playing across a turquoise finger of Onelua Bay. The Village Course at Kapalua (Palmer and Ed Seay, 1980) winds high into the West Maui Mountains through historic stands of Cook pines and eucalyptus, then out through pineapple fields and tall native grasses. The sixth hole is particularly dramatic: the tee is 100 feet above the fairway, with a dense stand of pines to the left and a lake to the right. **The Kapalua Golf Academy** (✉ 1000 Office Rd. ☎ 808/669–6500) offers 23 acres of practice turf and 11 teeing areas, a special golf fitness gym, and an instructional bay with video analysis. Each of the three courses has a separate clubhouse. **The Bay Course:** *✉ 300 Kapalua Dr., Kapalua ☎ 808/669–8820 ⊕ www.kapaluamaui.com/golf ⅄ 18 holes. 6600 yds. Par 72. Green Fee: $200 ☞ Facilities: Driving range, putting green, rental clubs, pro shop, lessons, restaurant, bar.* **The Plantation Course:** *✉ 2000 Plantation Club Dr., Kapalua ☎ 808/669–8877 ⊕ www.kapaluamaui.com/golf ⅄ 18 holes. 7269 yds. Par 73. Green Fee: $250 ☞ Facilities: Driving range, putting green, golf carts, pull carts, rental clubs, pro shop, golf academy/lessons, restaurant, bar.* **The Village Course:** *✉ 2000 Village Rd., Kapalua ☎ 808/669–8835 ⊕ www.kapaluamaui.com/golf ⅄ 18 holes. 6317 yds. Par 70. Green Fee: $185 ☞ Facilities: Driving range, putting green, golf carts, pull carts, rental clubs, pro shop, golf academy/lessons, restaurant, bar.*

King Kamehameha Golf Club. The former Sandalwood Course (Robin Nelson, 1991) is back as the Kahili Course. After four years of lying fallow due to financial problems, Sandalwood came back nine holes at a time and reopened as an 18-hole course in mid 2005. Nelson was invited back to tweak his design. Holes play along the flanks of the West Maui Mountains, overlooking Maui's central plain, with ocean views of both sides of the island. *✉ 2500 Honoapi'ilani Hwy., Wailuku ☎ 808/242–7090 ⅄ 18 holes. 6200 yds. Par 72. Green Fee: $95 ☞ Facilities: Driving range, putting green, rental clubs, golf carts, pro shop, lessons, restaurant, bar.*

Fodor'sChoice ★ **Makena Resort.** Robert Trent Jones Jr. and Don Knotts (not the Barney Fife actor) built the first course at Makena in 1981. A decade later Jones was asked to create 18 totally new holes and blend them with the existing course to form the North and South courses, which opened in 1994. Both courses—sculpted on the western seaside flank of Haleakalā—offer quick greens with lots of breaks, and plenty of scenic distractions. On the North Course, the fourth is one of the most picturesque inland par-3s in Hawai'i, with the green guarded on the right by a pond. The sixth is an excellent example of option golf: the fairway is sliced up the middle by a gaping ravine, which must sooner or later be crossed to reach the green. While trees frame most holes on the North, the South Course is more open. This means it plays somewhat easier off the tee, but the greens are trickier. The view from the elevated tee of the par-5 10th is lovely with the lake in the foreground mirroring the ocean in the dis-

ON THE SIDELINES

Maui has a number of golf tournaments, most of which are of professional caliber and worth watching. Many are also televised nationally. One attention-getter is the **Mercedes Championships** (☎ 808/669–2440) held in January. This is the first official PGA tour event, held on Kapalua's Plantation Course. The Aloha Section of the Professional Golfers Association of America hosts the **Verizon Hall of Fame** (☎ 808/669–8877) championship at the Plantation Course in May. A clambake

feast on the beach tops off the **Kapalua Clambake Pro-Am** (☎ 808/669–8812) in July.

Over in Wailea, in June, on the longest day of the year, self-proclaimed "lunatic" golfers start out at first light to play 100 holes of golf in the annual **Ka Lima O Maui** (☎ 808/875–5111), a fundraiser for local charities. The nationally televised **Senior Skins** (☎ 808/875–5111) in January pits four of the most respected Senior PGA players against one another.

tance. The par-4 16th is another looker, with the Pacific running along the left side. ⊠ *5415 Makena Alanui, Makena* ☎ *808/879–3344* ⊕ *www.mauiprincehotel.com* ℣ *North Course: 18 holes. 6567 yds. Par 72. Green Fee: $170. South Course: 18 holes. 6629 yds. Par 72. Green Fee: $180* ☞ *Facilities: Driving range, putting green, golf carts, rental clubs, pro shop, golf academy/lessons, restaurant, bar.*

Waiehu Golf Course. Maui's lone municipal course, Waiehu is really two courses in one. The front nine, authentic seaside links that run along Kahului Bay, opened in 1930, a plantation-era gem. The back nine, which climbs up into the lower reaches of the West Maui Mountains through macadamia orchards, opened in 1963 (Arthur Jack Snyder). ⊠ *200A Halewaiu Rd., Wailuku* ☎ *808/270–7400* ℣ *18 holes. 6330 yds. Par 72. Green Fee: $26/$30* ☞ *Facilities: Driving range, putting green, golf carts, pull carts, rental clubs, pro shop, restaurant, bar.*

Fodor'sChoice ★ **Wailea.** Wailea is one of just two Hawai'i resorts to offer three different courses: Gold, Emerald, and Blue. Designed by Robert Trent Jones Jr., these courses share similar terrain, carved into the leeward flank of Haleakalā. Although the ocean does not come into play, it's so close you can hear it breaking on the shore. And it comes into visual play on every hole. The Haleakalā effect comes into play on putts—they break toward the ocean.

Jones refers to the Gold Course at Wailea (1993) as the "masculine" course. It's all trees and lava. The trick here is to note even subtle changes in elevation. Jones takes advantage of the Technicolor beauty of Maui by creating fantastic sight lines. For example, the par-3 eighth plays from an elevated tee across a lava ravine to a large, well-bunkered green framed by palm trees, the blue sea, and tiny Molokini. The Emerald Course at Wailea (1994) is the "feminine" layout with lots of flowers and bunkering away from greens. Although this may seem to render the bunker benign, the opposite is true. A bunker well in front of a green disguises the distance to the holes. Likewise, the Emerald's extensive flower beds are designed to be dangerous distractions because of their beauty. The Gold and Emerald share a clubhouse, practice facility, and 19th hole. Judging elevation change is also the key at the Blue Course at Wailea (Arthur Jack Snyder, 1971). Fairways tend to be wider than on the Gold or Emerald, and run through colorful flora that includes hibiscus, wiliwili, bougainvillea and plumeria, as well as past million-dollar homes and luxury condominiums. **Blue Course:** ✉ *120 Kaukahi St,, Wailea* ☎ *808/875-5155* ⊕ *www.waileagolf.com* ⅄ *18 holes. 6797 yds. Par 72. Emerald Course: 18 holes. 6407 yds. Par 72. Green Fee: $175* ☞ *Facilities: Driving range, putting green, golf carts, rental clubs, pro shop, golf academy/lessons, restaurant, bar.* **Gold and Emerald Courses:** ✉ *100 Wailea Golf Club Dr., Wailea* ☎ *808/875-7450* ⊕ *www.waileagolf.com* ⅄ *Gold Course: 18 holes. 6653 yds. Par 72. Green Fee: $185. Emerald Course: 18 holes. 6407 yds. Par 72. Green Fee: $185* ☞ *Facilities: Driving range, putting green, golf carts, rental clubs, pro shop, golf academy/lessons, restaurant, bar.*

Hiking

Hikes on Maui range from coastal seashore to verdant rain forest to alpine desert. Orchids, hibiscus, ginger, heliconia, and anthuriums grow wild on many trails, and exotic fruits like mountain apple, lilikoi, thimbleberry, and strawberry guava provide refreshing snacks for hikers. Ironically, much of what you see in lower altitude forests is alien, brought to Hawai'i at one time or another by someone hoping to improve upon nature. Plants like strawberry guava and ginger may be tasty, but they outcompete native forest plants and have become serious, problematic weeds.

The best hikes get you out of the imported landscaping and into the truly exotic wilderness. Hawai'i possesses some of the world's rarest plants, insects, and birds. Pocket field guides are available at most grocery or drug stores and can really illuminate your walk. Before you know it you'll be

KEEP IN MIND

Wear sturdy shoes while hiking; you'll want to spare your ankles from a crash course in loose lava rock. When hiking near streams or waterfalls, be extremely cautious, flash floods can occur at any time. Do not drink stream water or swim in streams if you have open cuts; bacteria and parasites are not the souvenir you want to take home with you. As with most outdoor activities, exposure poses the main danger. Wear sunscreen, a hat, and layered clothing. At upper elevations, the weather is only guaranteed to be extreme—alternately chilly or blazing.

nudging your companion and pointing out trees that look like something out of a Dr. Suess book. If you watch the right branches quietly you can spot the same Honeycreepers or Happy-faced Spiders scientists have spent their lives studying.

Best Spots

Fodor'sChoice ★ Hiking **Haleakalā Crater** in Haleakalā National Park is undoubtedly the best hiking on the island. ⇨ *For more information see* Haleakalā National Park *later in this chapter.*

'Ohe'o Gulch (⊠ Rte. 31, 10 mi past Hāna town) is a branch of Haleakalā National Park. Famous for its "sacred" pools (the area is sometimes called the "Seven Sacred Pools"), the cascading gulch is the starting point of one of Maui's best hikes—the 2-mi trek upstream to the 400-foot **Waimoku Falls**. Follow signs from the parking lot up the road, past the bridge overlook, and uphill into the forest. Along the way you can take side trips and swim in the stream's basalt-lined pools. The trail bridges a sensational gorge and passes onto a boardwalk through a mystifying forest of giant bamboo. This stomp through muddy and rocky terrain takes around three hours to fully enjoy. It's best done early in the morning, before the touring crowds arrive (though it can never truly be called crowded). A $10 national park fee applies, which is valid for one week and can be used at Haleakalā's summit as well. Down at the grassy sea cliffs, you can camp, no permit required, although you can stay only three nights. Toilets, grills, and tables are available here, but there's no water and open fires aren't allowed.

A good hiking spot—and something totally unexpected on a tropical island—is **Polipoli Forest**. During the Great Depression the government began a program to reforest the mountain, and soon cedar, pine, cypress, and even redwood took hold. It's cold and foggy here, and often wet or at least misty. To reach the forest, take Route 37 all the way out to the far end of Kula. Then turn left at Route 377. After about a half mile, turn right at Waipoli Road. First you'll encounter switchbacks; after that the road is just plain bad, but passable. There are wonderful trails, a small campground, and a cabin that you can rent from the Division of State Parks. Write far in advance for the **cabin** (✑ Box 1049, Wailuku 96793 ☎ 808/244–4354); for the campground, you can wait until you arrive in Wailuku and visit the **Division of State Parks** (⊠ 54 High St. ☎ 808/984–8109).

A much neglected hike is the coastal **Hoapili Trail** (⊠ Follow Mākena Alanui to end of paved road, walk through parking lot along dirt road, follow signs) beyond the 'Āhihi-Kīn'au Natural Area Reserve. Named after a bygone Hawaiian king, it follows the shoreline, threading through the remains of ancient Hawaiian villages. The once-thriving community was displaced by one of Maui's last lava flows. Later, King Hoapili was responsible for overseeing the creation of an island-wide highway. This remaining section, a wide path of stacked lava rocks, is a marvel to look at and walk on, though it's not the easiest surface for the ankles. (It's rumored to have once been covered in grass.) You can wander over to the Hanamanioa lighthouse, or quietly ponder the rough life of the ancients. ⚠ Wear sturdy shoes and bring extra water. This is brutal territory with little shade and no facilities. Beautiful, yes. Accommodating, no.

★ You can take one of several easy hikes from the parking lot at **'Īao Valley State Park** (⊠ Western end of Rte. 32, Wailuku). Cross 'Īao Stream and explore the junglelike area past the curious **'Īao Needle**, a spire that rises more than 2,000 feet from the valley floor. This park has a beautiful network of trails that snake through the deep valley. You can pause

Hawai'i's Flora and Fauna

HAWAI'I BOASTS EVERY CLIMATE ON THE PLANET, excluding the two most extreme: arctic tundra and arid desert. The Islands have wine-growing regions, cactus-speckled ranchlands, icy mountaintops, and the rainiest forests on earth. The Galapagos has *nothing* on Hawai'i's biodiversity—more than 90% of Hawaiian plants and animals are endemic, meaning they exist nowhere else on earth. Most of the plants you see while walking around, however, aren't Hawaiian at all. Tropical flowers such as plumeria, orchids, red ginger, heliconia, and anthuriums are Asian or South American imports now growing wild on all the Islands.

Native Hawaiian plants are weird-looking, in the best sense. Take the silversword, for example. A giant, furry firework of a plant, it grows in one of the world's harshest climates: the summits of Haleakalā and Mauna Kea. Its 7-foot stalk, brimming with red or pale yellow flowers, blooms once and then dies. 'Ōhi'a trees—thought to be the favorite of Pele, the volcano goddess—bury their roots in fields of once-molten lava and sprout ruby pom-pom-like lehua blossoms. The deep yellow petals of 'ilima (once reserved for royalty) are tiny discs, which make the most elegant leis.

To match Hawai'i's unique flora, fantastic birds and insects evolved. Honeycreepers, distant relatives of the finch, have fabulously long, curved bills perfect for sipping nectar from lehua blossoms. The world's only carnivorous caterpillar can snatch a Hawaiian picture-wing fly from the air in less than a second. Hawai'i's state bird, the nēnē goose, is making a comeback from its former endangered status. It roams freely in parts of Maui, Kaua'i, and the Big Island. Pairs who mate for life are often spotted ambling across roads in Haleakalā or Hawai'i Volcanoes national park.

At the Kīlauea Point National Wildlife Refuge on Kaua'i, hundreds of Laysan albatross, wedge-tail shearwaters, red-footed boobies, and other marine birds glide and soar within photo-op distance of visitors to Kīlauea Lighthouse. Boobie chicks hatch in the fall and emerge from nests burrowed into cliff-side dirt banks and even under stairs—any launching pad from which the fledgling flyer can catch the nearest air current.

Hawai'i's two native mammals are rare sights. Doe-eyed Hawaiian monk seals breed in the northwestern Islands. With only 1,500 left in the wild, you probably won't catch many lounging on the beaches of Hawai'i's populated islands, though they have been spotted on the shores of Kaua'i in recent years. You can see rescued pups and adults along with Hawaiian green sea turtles at Sea Life Park and the Waikīkī Aquarium on O'ahu. The shy Hawaiian bat hangs out primarily at Kealakekua Bay on the Big Island.

in the garden of Hawaiian heritage plants and marvel at the local young-sters hurling themselves from the bridge into the chilly stream water with yelps of delight. Mist occasionally rises after a rainfall, which makes being here even more magical.

Guided Hikes

Hawai'i Nature Center. In 'Īao Valley, the Hawai'i Nature Center leads easy, interpretive hikes for children and their families. ✉ *875 'Īao Valley Rd., Wailuku 96793* ☎ *808/244–6500.*

Fodor'sChoice **Hike Maui.** Hike Maui is the oldest hiking company on the Islands, and
★   its rain-forest, mountain-ridge, crater, coastline, and archaeological-snorkel hikes are led by such knowledgeable folk as ethnobotanists and marine biologists. Prices range from $59 to $135 for hikes of 5 to 10 hours, including lunch. Hike Maui supplies waterproof day packs, rain ponchos, first-aid gear, water bottles, and transportation to the site. ☎ *808/879–5270* ⊕ *www.hikemaui.com.*

Maui Eco Adventures. For excursions into remote areas, contact Maui Eco Adventures. The ecologically minded company leads hikes into private or otherwise inaccessible areas. Hikes, which can be combined with kayak-ing, mountain biking, or sailing trips, explore botanically rich valleys in Kahakuloa and East Maui. ✉ *180 Dickenson St., Suite 101, Lahaina* ☎ *808/661–7720 or 877/661–7720.*

Paths in Paradise. Paths in Paradise is a small company offering spe-cialized hikes into wetlands, rain-forest areas, and the crater. The owner, Renate Gassman-Duvall, is an expert birder and biologist. She helps hikers spot native honeycreepers feeding on lehua blossoms and supplies them with bird and plant check cards. Half-day hikes run $110, and full-day hikes are $135, with lunch and gear provided. ☎ *808/579–9294.*

★ **Sierra Club.** A great avenue into the island's untrammeled wilderness is Maui's chapter of the Sierra Club. Rather than venturing out on your own, join one of the club's hikes into pristine forests and valley isle wa-tersheds, or along ancient coastal paths. Several hikes a month are led by informative naturalists who carry first aid kits and arrange waivers to access private land. Some outings include volunteer service, but most are just for fun. Bring your own food and water, sturdy shoes, and a suggested donation of $5—a true bargain. ✉ *71 Baldwin Ave., Pā'ia* ☎ *808/579–9802* ⊕ *www.hi.sierraclub.org/maui.*

Hang Gliding

Hang Gliding Maui. Armin Engert will take you on an instructional pow-ered hang-gliding trip out of Hāna Airport. A 25- to 30-minute flight lesson costs $95, and a 50- to 60-minute lesson is $165. Snapshots of your flight from a wing-mounted camera cost an additional $25. ☎ *808/572–6557* ⊕ *www.hanglidingmaui.com.*

Maluhialani. The name means "beautiful serenity" in Hawaiian, which is appropriate for an airborne trip taking off from Kula, and soaring

SPECTATOR SPORTS

POLO

Polo is popular on Maui. From April through June Haleakalā Ranch hosts "indoor" contests on a field flanked by side boards. The field is on Route 377, 1 mi from Route 37. During the "outdoor" polo season, mid-August to the end of October, matches are held at Olinda Field, 1 mi above Makawao on Olinda Road. There's a $5 admission charge for most games, which start at 1:30 PM on Sunday. The sport has two special events. The **Oskie Rice Memorial Tournament** occurs on Memorial Day. The **High Goal Benefit,** held on the last Sunday in October, draws challengers from Argentina, England, South Africa, New Zealand, and Australia. For information, contact ☎ 808/877–7744.

RODEOS

With dozens of working cattle ranches throughout the Islands, many youngsters learn to ride a horse before they can drive a car. Mauians love their rodeos and put on several for students at local high schools. Paniolos get in on the action, too, at three major annual events: the **Oskie Rice Memorial Rodeo,** usually staged the weekend after Labor Day; the **Cancer Benefit Rodeo** in April; and Maui's biggest event, drawing competitors from all the Islands as well as the U.S. mainland; the **4th of July Rodeo,** which comes with a full parade and other festivities that last for days. Cowboys are a tough bunch to tie down to a phone, but you can try calling the **Maui Roping Club** (☎ 808/572–2076) for information.

as far as the West Maui Mountains. Dwight Mounts, your pilot, built a grass runway on his scenic Upcountry property. ☎ *808/280–3307* ⊕ *www.maluhialani.com.*

Helicopter Tours

Helicopter flight-seeing excursions can take you over the West Maui Mountains, Hāna, and Haleakalā. This is a beautiful, exciting way to see the island, and the *only* way to see some of its most dramatic areas. Tour prices usually include a videotape of your trip so you can relive the experience at home. Prices run from about $125 for a half-hour rainforest tour to $340 for a two-hour mega-experience that includes a champagne toast on landing.

It takes about 90 minutes to travel inside the volcano, then down to the village of Hāna. Some companies stop in secluded areas for refreshments. Helicopter-tour operators throughout the state come under sharp scrutiny for passenger safety and equipment maintenance. Don't be afraid to ask about a company's safety record, flight paths, age of equipment, and level of operator experience.

Blue Hawaiian Helicopters. Blue Hawaiian has provided aerial adventures in Hawai'i since 1985, and it has the best service and safety record. Its AStar helicopters are air-conditioned and have noise-blocking headsets for all passengers. ⊠ *Kahului Heliport, Hangar 105, Kahului* ☎ *808/ 871–8844* ⊕ *www.bluehawaiian.com.*

Sunshine Helicopters. Sunshine offers tours of Maui and Moloka'i in its *Black Beauty* aircraft. ⊠ *Kahului Heliport, Hangar 107, Kahului* ☎ *808/ 871–0722 or 800/544–2520* ⊕ *www.sunshinehelicopters.com.*

Horseback Riding

Several companies on Maui offer horseback riding that's far more appealing than the typical hour-long trudge over a dull trail with 50 other horses.

Charley's Trail Rides & Pack Trips. Rides with this company require a stout physical nature (but not a stout physique: riders must weigh less than 200 pounds). Overnight trips go from Kaupō, a *tiny* village nearly 20 mi past Hāna, up the slopes of Haleakalā, where you spend the night in the crater. Charley is a bona fide *paniolo* (Hawaiian cowboy), and tours with him include meals, park fees, and camping supplies for $250 per person. Book several weeks in advance if you'd prefer a cabin instead of a tent. ☎ 808/248–8209.

Fodor'sChoice ★ **Maui Stables.** Hawaiian owned and run, this company provides a trip back in time, to an era when life moved more slowly and reverantly— though galloping is allowed, if you're able to handle your horse! Educational tours begin at the stable in remote Kipahulu, and pass through several historic Hawaiian sites. Before heading up into the forest, your guides intone the words to a traditional *oli*, or chant, asking for permission to enter. By the time you reach the mountain pasture overlooking Waimoku Falls, you'll feel lucky to have been a part of the tradition. ⊠ *Between mile markers 40 and 41 on Hwy. 37, Hāna* ☎ *808/248– 7799* ⊕ *www.mauistables.com.*

Pi'iholo Ranch. The wranglers here will lead you on a rousing ride through family ranchlands—up hillside pastures, beneath a eucalyptus canopy, and past many native trees. Morning picnic rides are 3½ hours and include lunch. Afternoon rides are two hours. Their well-kept horses navigate the challenging terrain easily, but hold on when deer pass by! ⊠ *End of Waiahiwi Rd., Makawao* ☎ *808/357–5544 or 866/572– 5544* ⊕ *www.piiholo.com.*

Pony Express Tours. Pony Express Tours will take you on horseback into Haleakalā Crater. The half-day ride goes down to the crater floor for a picnic lunch. The full-day excursion covers 12 mi of terrain and visits some of the crater's unusual formations. You don't need to be an experienced rider, but the longer ride can be tough if you're unathletic. The company also offers one- and two-hour rides on Haleakalā Ranch for $55 to $155. ☎ *808/667–2200 or 808/878–6698* ⊕ *www. ponyexpresstours.com.*

Tennis

Most courts charge by the hour but will let players continue after their initial hour for free, provided no one is waiting. In addition to the facilities listed below, many hotels and condos have courts open to nonguests for a fee. The best free courts are the five at the **Lahaina Civic Center** (⊠ 1840 Honoapiʻilani Hwy., Lahaina ☎ 808/661–4685), near Wahikuli State Park. They're available on a first-come, first-served basis.

Kapalua Tennis Garden. This complex, home to the Kapalua Tennis Club, serves the Kapalua Resort with 10 courts, four lighted for night play, and a pro shop. You'll pay $10 an hour if you're a guest, $12 if you're not. ⊠ 100 Kapalua Dr., Kapalua ☎ 808/669–5677.

Wailea Tennis Club. The club has 11 Plexipave courts (its famed grass courts are, sadly, a thing of the past), lessons, rentals, and ball machines. On weekday mornings clinics are given to help you improve your ground strokes, serve, volley, or doubles strategy. Rates are $27 per hour per court. ⊠ 131 Wailea Ike Pl., Kīhei ☎ 808/879–1958 or 800/ 332–1614.

ON THE SIDELINES

At the **Kapalua Jr. Vet/Sr. Tennis Championships** in May, players compete in singles and doubles events. On Labor Day, the **Wilson Kapalua Open Tennis Tournament** calls Hawaiʻi's hottest hitters to Kapalua's Tennis Garden and Village Tennis Center. Also at the Tennis Center, Women's International Tennis Association professionals rally with amateurs in a week of pro-am and pro-doubles competition during the **Kapalua Betsy Nagelsen Tennis Invitational** in December. All events are put on by the **Kapalua Tennis Club** (☎ 808/669–5677). The Wailea Open Tennis Championship is held in spring or summer at the **Wailea Tennis Club** (☎ 808/879-1958).

EXPLORING MAUI

Maui is more than a sandy beach with palm trees. Puʻu Kukui, the 5,788-foot interior of the West Maui Mountains, is one of the earth's wettest spots. Annual rainfall of 400 inches has sliced the land into impassable gorges and razor-sharp ridges. On the opposite side of the island, the blistering lava fields at ʻĀhihi-Kīnʻau receive scant rain. And just above this desert, *paniolo,* Hawaiian cowboys, herd cattle on rolling, fertile ranchlands reminiscent of Northern California. The natural bounty of this place is impressive. But nature isn't all Maui has to offer— it's also home to a rich and vivid culture. In small towns like Pāʻia and Hāna you can see remnants of the past mingling with modern-day life. Ancient *heiau* (ancient Hawaiian stone platforms once used as places of worship) line busy roadways. Old coral and brick missionary homes house broadcasting networks. The antique smokestacks of sugar mills tower above communities where the children blend English, Hawaiian, Japanese, Chinese, Portugese, Filipino, and more into one colorful language. Hawaiʻi is a melting pot like no other. Visiting an eclectic mom-and-pop shop (like Komoda's Bakery) can feel like stepping into another country, or back in time. The more you look here, the more you will find.

West Maui

West Maui, anchored by the amusing old whaling town of Lahaina, was the focus of development when Maui set out to become a premier tourist destination in the 1960s. The condo-filled beach towns of Nāpili, Kahana, and Honokōwai are arrayed between the stunning resorts of Kapalua and Kā'anapali, north of Lahaina.

Lahaina itself has a notorious past. There are stories of lusty whalers who met head-on with missionaries bent on saving souls. Both groups journeyed to Lahaina from New England in the early 1800s. At first, Lahaina might look touristy, but there's a lot that's genuine here as well. The town has renovated most of its old buildings, which date from the time when it was Hawai'i's capital. Much of the town has been designated a National Historic Landmark, and any new buildings must conform in style to those built before 1920.

a good tour

Begin the tour in **Kapalua ❶** ▶. Even if you re not staying there, have a look around the renowned Ritz-Carlton Hotel and enjoy a meal or snack at Honolua Store before you begin exploring. From Kapalua, drive north on the Honoapi'ilani Highway (Route 30). This road is paved, but storms now and then make it partly impassable, especially on the winding 8-mi stretch that's only one-lane wide, with no shoulder and a sheer drop-off into the ocean. You'll discover some gorgeous photo opportunities along the road, and if you go far enough, you'll come to **Kahakuloa ❷**, a sleepy fishing village tucked into a cleft in the mountain. The road pushes on to Wailuku, but you may be tired of the narrow and precipitously winding course you have to take.

From Kahakuloa turn around and go back in the direction from which you came—south toward Kā'anapali and Lahaina, past the beach towns of Nāpili, Kahana, and Honokōwai. If you wish to explore these towns, get off the Upper Honoapi'ilani Highway and drive closer to the water. If you're not staying in the planned resort community of **Kā'anapali ❸**, you may want to stop to see some of the luxury hotel complexes here. To reach them, turn right onto Kā'anapali Parkway. Next, head for Lahaina. Before you start your Lahaina trek, take a short detour by turning left from Honoapi'ilani Highway onto Lahainaluna Road, and stop at the **Hale Pa'i ❹**, the printing shop built by Protestant missionaries in 1837. Return down Lahainaluna Road, crossing Honoapi'ilani Highway, until you reach Front Street and turn left.

Since Lahaina is best explored on foot, use the drive along Front Street to get oriented and then park at or near **505 Front Street ❺**, at the south end of the town's historic and colorful commercial area. Walking back into town, turn right onto Prison Street and you come to **Hale Pa'ahao ❻**, which was built from coral blocks. Return to Front Street, and continue

ART NIGHT

If you arrange to spend a Friday afternoon exploring Front Street, you can dine in town and hang around for Art Night, when the galleries stay open into the evening and entertainment fills the streets.

north to the **Banyan Tree** ❼, one of the town's best-known landmarks. Behind it stands the old **Court House** ❽. Next door, also in Banyan Park, stand the reconstructed remains of the waterfront **Fort** ❾. About a half block northwest, you can find the site of Kamehameha's **Brick Palace** ❿. If you walk to the corner of Front and Dickenson streets, you can find the **Baldwin Home** ⓫, restored to reflect an early-19th-century house. Next door is the **Master's Reading Room** ⓬, Maui's oldest building.

Wander north or south on Front Street to explore Lahaina's commercial side. If you head north on Front Street, you come to the **Wo Hing Museum** ⓭ on the right. Walk another several blocks north and you find the **Seamen's Hospital** ⓮. If it's before dusk and you still have a hankering for just one more stop, try the **Waiola Church and Cemetery** ⓯. Walk south down Front Street, make a left onto Dickenson Street, and then make a right onto Waineʻe Street and walk another few blocks to reach the church.

TIMING You can walk the length of Lahaina's Front Street in less than 30 minutes if you don't stop along the way. Just *try* not to be intrigued by the town's colorful shops and historic sites. Realistically, you need at least a half day—if not a full day—to check out the area's coastal beaches, towns, and resorts. The Banyan Tree in Lahaina is a terrific spot to be when the sun sets— mynah birds settle in here for a screeching symphony, which can be an event in itself.

> The Banyan Tree is a popular and hard-to-miss meeting place if your party splits up for independent exploring.

What to See

★ ⓫ **Baldwin Home.** In 1835 an early missionary to Lahaina, Ephraim Spaulding, built this attractive thick-wall house of coral and stone. In 1836 Dr. Dwight Baldwin—also a missionary—moved in with his family. The home has been restored and furnished to reflect the period. You can view the living room, with the family's grand piano; the dining room; and Dr. Baldwin's dispensary. The Lahaina Restoration Foundation occupies the building, and its knowledgeable staff is here to answer almost any question about historic sites in town. Ask for its walking-tour brochure, a comprehensive map to historic sites around Lahaina. ✉ *696 Front St., Lahaina* ☎ *808/661–3262* ⊕ *www.lahainarestoration.org* 🖃 *$3* ⊙ *Daily 10–4.*

❼ **Banyan Tree.** This massive tree, was planted in 1873. It's the largest of its kind in the state and provides a welcome retreat for the weary who come to sit under its awesome branches. ✉ *Front St., between Hotel and Canal Sts., Lahaina.*

❿ **Brick Palace.** All that's left of the palace built by King Kamehameha I to welcome the captains of visiting ships are the excavated cornerstones and foundation in front of the Pioneer Inn. Hawaiʻi's first king lived only one year in the palace because his favorite wife, Kaʻahumanu, refused to stay here. It was then used as a warehouse, storeroom, and meeting house for 70 years, until it collapsed. ✉ *Makai end of Market St., Lahaina.*

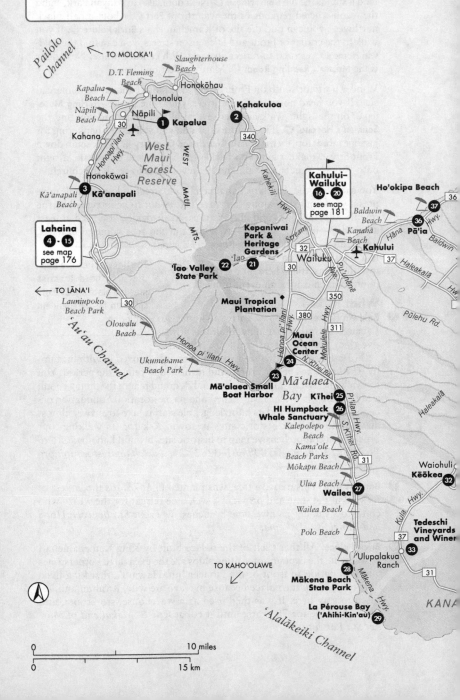

Maui

TO MOLOKA'I →

Pailolo Channel

Slaughterhouse Beach

D.T. Fleming Beach

Kapalua Beach

Honokōhau

Honolua

Nāpili Beach

Nāpili

1 Kapalua

2 Kahakuloa

Kahana

340

West Maui Forest Reserve

Honokōwai

3 Kā'anapali

Kā'anapali Beach

WEST MAUI MTS.

Kahekili Hwy.

'Īao Stream

Kahului-Wailuku
16 - 20
see map
page 181

Ho'okipa Beach

36

37

Baldwin Beach

36 Pā'ia

Hwy.

Baldwin

Kanahā Beach

Kahului

Haleakalā Hwy.

Lahaina
4 - 15
see map
page 176

Pu'uhene Ave.

Wailuku

32

30

37

Kepaniwai Park & Heritage Gardens

22 'Īao **21**

'Īao Valley State Park

← TO LĀNA'I

'Au'au Channel

Launiupoko Beach Park

30

Olowalu Beach

Maui Tropical Plantation

350

380

Honoa pi'ilani Hwy.

311

Pūlehu Rd.

Haleakalā Hwy.

Ukumehame Beach Park

Maui Ocean Center

24

Honoa pi'ilani Hwy.

N. Kīhei Rd.

Mokulele Hwy.

23

Mā'alaea Small Boat Harbor

Mā'alaea Bay

25 Kīhei

26

HI Humpback Whale Sanctuary

Kalepolepo Beach

Kama'ole Beach Parks

Mōkapu Beach

S. Kīhei Rd.

Pi'ilani Hwy.

Haleakalā

31

Waiohuli

Kēōkea 32

Ulua Beach

27 Wailea

Wailea Beach

Kula Hwy.

33

Tedeschi Vineyards and Winer

Polo Beach

37

TO KAHO'OLAWE →

Ulupalakua Ranch

28

Mākena Beach State Park

Mākena Hwy.

31

La Pérouse Bay ('Ahihi-Kin'au) 29

'Alalākeiki Channel

KANA

0 ___ 10 miles

0 ___ 15 km

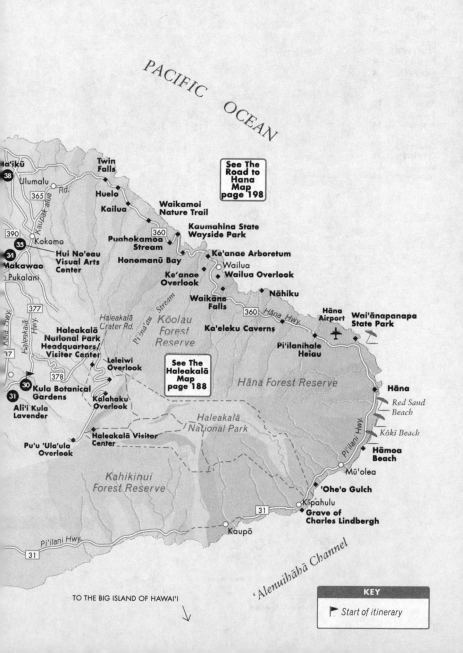

PACIFIC

OCEAN

See The
Road to
Hana
Map
page 198

Ha'ikū

38

Twin
Falls

Ulumalu

365

Kaupakalua Rd.

Huelo

Kailua

Waikamoi
Nature Trail

390

Kokomo

360

Kaumahina State
Wayside Park

34

Makawao

Pukalani

Hui No'eau
Visual Arts
Center

Puahokamoa
Stream

Honomanū Bay

Ke'anae Arboretum

Wailua

Ke'anae
Overlook

Wailua Overlook

377

Waikāne
Falls

Nāhiku

Hāna Hwy.

360

Haleakalā
Crater Rd.

Kōolau
Forest
Reserve

Pī'īna'au Stream

Ka'eleku Caverns

Hāna
Airport

Wai'ānapanapa
State Park

37

Haleakalā
National Park
Headquarters/
Visitor Center

378

Leleiwi
Overlook

See The
Haleakalā
Map
page 188

Pi'ilanihale
Heiau

Hāna Forest Reserve

Hāna

Red Sand
Beach

30

Kula Botanical
Gardens

Kalahaku
Overlook

Haleakalā
National Park

Kōkī Beach

31

Ali'i Kula
Lavender

Haleakalā Visitor
Center

Hāmoa
Beach

Pu'u 'Ula'ula
Overlook

Mū'olea

Pi'ilani Hwy.

Kahikinui
Forest
Reserve

'Ohe'o Gulch

Kīpahulu

Grave of
Charles Lindbergh

31

Kaupō

Pi'ilani Hwy.

31

'Alenuihāhā Channel

TO THE BIG ISLAND OF HAWAI'I

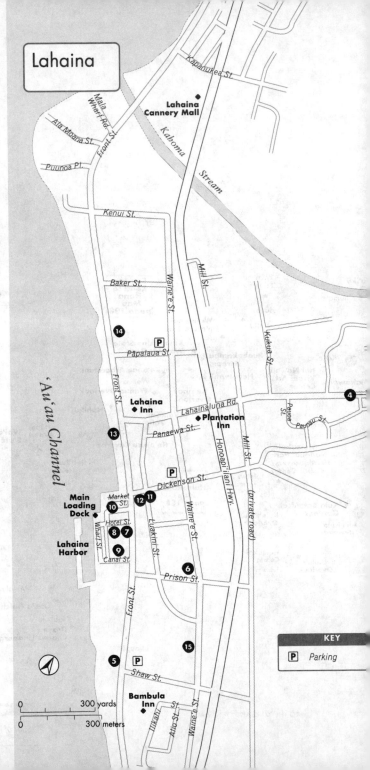

Lahaina

Baldwin Home 11

Banyan Tree . . .7

Brick Palace . .10

Court House . . .8

505 Front Street 5

Fort 9

Hale Pa'ahao (Old Prison) 6

Hale Pa'i 4

Master's Reading Room 12

Seamen's Hospital 14

Waiola Church and Cemetery 15

Wo Hing Museum 13

2

★ ❽ **Court House.** This old civic building was erected in 1859, rebuilt in 1925, and restored to its 1925 condition in 1999. At one time or another it served as a customhouse, post office, vault and collector's office, governor's office, police court, and courtroom. Now it houses terrific museum displays, the active Lahaina Arts Society, an art gallery, a visitor center, and, perhaps in greatest demand, ■ **TIP➔➔** a water cooler. ✉ *649 Wharf St., Lahaina* ☎ *808/661–0111* ⊒ *Free* ☉ *Daily 9–5.*

❺ **505 Front Street.** The quaint, New England–style mall on this quiet stretch of Front Street has many treasures, notably a resident endangered sea turtle. Year after year, turtle 5690 awes researchers and tourists alike by laying a record eight nests in the sand just steps from the mall. Catching sight of a nestling is rare, but 505's superb restaurants, galleries, surf shack, day spa, and local designer's boutique are much more accessible. ✉ *South end of Front St. near Shaw St., Lahaina.*

❾ **Fort.** Used mostly as a prison, this fortress was positioned so that it could police the whaling ships that crowded the harbor. It was built from 1831 to 1832 after sailors, angered by a law forbidding local women from swimming out to ships, lobbed cannonballs at the town. Cannons raised from the wreck of a warship in Honolulu Harbor were brought to Lahaina and placed in front of the fort, where they still sit today. The building itself is an eloquent ruin. ✉ *Canal and Wharf Sts., Lahaina.*

❻ **Hale Pa'ahao (Old Prison).** This jailhouse dates to rowdy whaling days. Its name literally means "stuck-in-irons house," referring to the wall shackles and ball-and-chain restraints. The compound was built in the 1850s by convict laborers out of blocks of coral that had been salvaged from the demolished waterfront Fort. Most prisoners were sent here for desertion, drunkenness, or reckless horse riding. Today, a wax figure representing an imprisoned old sailor tells his recorded tale of woe. ✉ *Waine'e and Prison Sts., Lahaina* ⊒ *Free* ☉ *Daily 8–5.*

❹ **Hale Pa'i.** Protestant missionaries established Lahainaluna Seminary as a center of learning and enlightenment in 1831. Six years later, they built this printing shop. Here at the press, they and their young Hawaiian scholars created a written Hawaiian language and used it to produce a Bible, history texts, and a newspaper. An exhibit displays a replica of the original Rampage press and facsimiles of early printing. The oldest U.S. educational institution west of the Rockies, the seminary now serves as Lahaina's public high school. ✉ *980 Lahainaluna Rd., Lahaina* ☎ *808/661–3262* ⊒ *Donations accepted* ☉ *Weekdays 10–3.*

❸ **Kā'anapali.** The theatrical look of Hawai'i tourism—planned resort communities where luxury homes mix with high-rise hotels, fantasy swimming pools, and a theme-park landscape—all began right here in the 1960s. Three miles of uninterrupted white beach and placid water form the front yard for this artificial utopia, with its 40 tennis courts and two championship golf courses. The six major hotels here are all worth visiting just for a look around, especially the Hyatt Regency Maui, which has a multimillion-dollar art collection. At the Whalers Village shopping complex, a small **Whaling Museum** (✉ Kā'anapali Pkwy., Suite H16

☎ 808/661–5992 ⊠ Donations accepted) tells the story of the 19th-century *Moby-Dick* era; it's open daily from 9:30 AM to 9:30 PM. ⊠ *2435 Kā'anapali Pkwy.*

2 **Kahakuloa.** Untouched by progress, this tiny village is a relic of pre–jet travel Maui. Remote villages similar to Kahakuloa used to be tucked away in several valleys of this area. Many residents still grow taro and live in the old Hawaiian way. This is the wild side of West Maui. True adventurers will find terrific snorkeling and swimming along this coast, as well as some good hiking trails. ⊠ *North end of Honoapi'ilani Hwy.*

⚑ 1 **Kapalua.** Set in a beautiful secluded spot surrounded by pineapple fields, this resort got its first big boost in 1978, when the Maui Land & Pineapple Company built the luxurious Kapalua Bay Hotel. The hotels host dedicated golfers, celebrities who want to be left alone, and some of the world's richest folks. Kapalua's shops and restaurants are among Maui's finest, but expect to pay high prices. By contrast, the old **Honolua Store,** just above the Ritz-Carlton, serves informal plate lunches popular with locals. ⊠ *Bay Dr., Kapalua.*

☺ **Lahaina–Kā'anapali & Pacific Railroad.** Affectionately called the Sugarcane Train, this is Maui's only passenger train. It's an 1890s-vintage railway that once shuttled sugar but now moves sightseers between Kā'anapali and Lahaina. This quaint little attraction with its singing conductor is a big deal for Hawai'i but probably not much of a thrill for those more accustomed to trains (though children like it no matter where they grew up). A barbecue dinner with entertainment is offered on Thursday at 5 PM. ⊠ *1½ blocks north of Lahainaluna Rd. stoplight, at Hinau St., on Honoapi'ilani Hwy., Lahaina* ☎ *808/661–0080* ⊠ *Round-trip $15.75, one-way $11.50, dinner train $65* ☾ *Daily 10:15–4.*

⑫ **Master's Reading Room.** This could be Maui's oldest residential building, constructed in 1834. In those days the ground floor was a mission's storeroom, and the reading room upstairs was for sailors. Today it houses local art and crafts for sale. ⊠ *Front and Dickenson Sts., Lahaina* ☎ *808/661–3262.*

⑭ **Seamen's Hospital.** Built in the 1830s to house King Kamehameha III's royal court, this property was later turned over to the U.S. government, which used it as a hospital for whalers. You can only view the outside of the building, as it now houses Channel 7. Just as well, rumor has it the place is haunted, perhaps by one of those whalers who can't bear to leave. Next door is a typical, circa 1900 **sugar plantation camp residence** where an enormous, experimental anchor decorates the lawn. ⊠ *1024 Front St., Lahaina* ☎ *808/661–3262.*

> **need a break?**
>
> The sandwiches have real Gruyère and Emmentaler cheese at **Maui Swiss Cafe** (⊠ 640 Front St., Lahaina ☎ 808/661–6776)—expensive ingredients with affordable results. The friendly owner scoops the best and cheapest locally made ice cream in Lahaina. Daily lunch specials are less than $6.

2

🅕 **Waiola Church and Cemetery.** The Waiola Cemetery is actually older than the neighboring church; it dates from the time when Kamehameha's sacred wife, Queen Keōpūolani, died and was buried here in 1823. The first church here was erected in 1832 by Hawaiian chiefs and was originally named Ebenezer by the queen's second husband and widower, Governor Hoapili. Aptly immortalized in James Michener's *Hawai'i* as the church that wouldn't stand, it was burned down twice and demolished in two windstorms. The present structure was put up in 1953 and named Waiola (water of life). ⊠ *535 Waine'e St., Lahaina* ☎ *808/661–4349.*

🅑 **Wo Hing Museum.** Built by the Wo Hing Society in 1912 as a fraternal society for Chinese residents, this eye-catching building now contains Chinese artifacts and a historic theater that shows Thomas Edison's films of Hawai'i, circa 1898. Upstairs is the only public Taoist altar on Maui. ⊠ *858 Front St., Lahaina* ☎ *808/661–5553* 🎫 *Donations accepted* 🕐 *Daily 10–4.*

Central Maui

Kahului, an industrial and commercial town in the center of the island, is home to many of Maui's permanent residents who find their jobs close by. The area was developed in the early '50s to meet the housing needs of workers for the large sugarcane interests here, specifically those of Alexander & Baldwin. The company was tired of playing landlord to its many plantation workers and sold land to a developer who promised to create affordable housing. The scheme worked, and Kahului became the first planned city in Hawai'i. Ka'ahumanu Avenue (Route 32), Kahului's main street, runs from the harbor to the hills. It's the logical place to begin your exploration of Central Maui.

West of Kahului, Wailuku, the county seat since 1950, is certainly the most charming town in Central Maui. Its name means "Water of Destruction," after a battle that pitted King Kamehameha I against Maui warriors in the 'Iao Valley. Wailuku was a politically important town until the sugar industry began to decline in the 1960s and tourism took hold. Businesses left the cradle of the West Maui Mountains and followed the new market to the shore, where tourists arrived by the boatload. Wailuku still houses the County government, but has the feel of a town that's been asleep for several decades. The charming boutiques and salons now inhabiting Main Street's plantation-style buildings serve as reminders of a bygone era.

a good tour

Begin at the **Alexander & Baldwin Sugar Museum** 🆖 ▶ in Pu'unēnē, directly across from the HC&S sugar mill.

From here, head northwest on Pu'unēnē Avenue all the way to its end at Ka'ahumanu Avenue and turn left. This is Kahului, which looks nothing like the lush, tropical paradise most people envision as Hawai'i. Three blocks ahead you can see the Sputnik-like canvas domes of Ka'ahumanu Center, Maui's largest shopping center. If you turn right at the signal just before that, you can follow the curve of Kahului Beach Road and see many ships in port at Kahului Harbor. On your left are the cream-and-brown buildings of the **Maui Arts & Cultural Center ⑰**. Continue past the harbor, turn right at Waiehu Beach Road, and about a mile later as you cross the 'Iao Stream you can see **Haleki'i-Pihana Heiau State Monument ⑱** on the hilltop to your left. Return along the harbor road and make a right turn at Kanaloa Avenue. Return to Ka'ahumanu Avenue on this road. Turn right to reach Wailuku (Ka'ahumanu Avenue eventually becomes Wailuku's Main Street). 'Iao Theater and several amusing shops line **Market Street ⑲**, between Vineyard and Main streets where you may want to stop for a stroll. Retrieve your car and turn right onto Main Street. After a few blocks, you can see **Bailey House ⑳**, on your left.

Continue driving uphill, into the mountains. Main Street turns into 'Iao Valley Road, the air cools, and the hilly terrain gets more lush. Soon you come to **Kepaniwai Park & Heritage Gardens ㉑** and '**Iao Valley State Park ㉒**. 'Iao Valley Road ends at the erosion-formed gray and moss-green rock called 'Iao Needle. This is a great place to picnic, wade in the stream, and explore the paths.

TIMING   You can explore Central Maui comfortably in little more than a half day. These are good sights to squeeze in on the way to the airport, or if you want to combine sightseeing with shopping. Hikers may want to expand their outing to a full day to explore 'Iao Valley State Park.

What to See

★ ▶ ⑯   **Alexander & Baldwin Sugar Museum.** "A&B," Maui's largest landowner, was one of the "Big Five" companies that spearheaded the planting, harvesting, and processing of sugarcane. Although Hawaiian cane sugar is now being supplanted by cheaper foreign versions—as well as by sugar derived from inexpensive sugar beets—the crop was for many years the mainstay of the Hawaiian economy. You can find the museum in a small, restored plantation manager's house next to the post office and the still-operating sugar refinery (black smoke billows up when cane is burning). Historic photos, artifacts, and documents explain the introduction of sugarcane to Hawai'i and how plantation managers brought in laborers from other countries, thereby changing the Islands' ethnic mix. Exhibits also describe the sugar-making process. ⊠ *3957 Hansen Rd., Pu'unēnē* ☎ *808/871–8058* ⊞ *$5* ☉ *Mon.–Sat. 9:30–4:30; last admission at 4.*

★ ⑳   **Bailey House.** This was the home of Edward and Caroline Bailey, two prominent missionaries who came to Wailuku to run the first Hawaiian girls' school on the island, the Wailuku Female Seminary. The school's main function was to train the girls in the "feminine arts." It once stood next door to the Baileys' home, which they called Halehō'ike'ike (House of Display), but locals always called it the Bailey House, and the sign painters eventually gave in. Construction of the house, between 1833 and 1850, was supervised by Edward Bailey himself. The Maui Historical Society runs a museum in the plastered stone house, with a small collection of artifacts from before and after

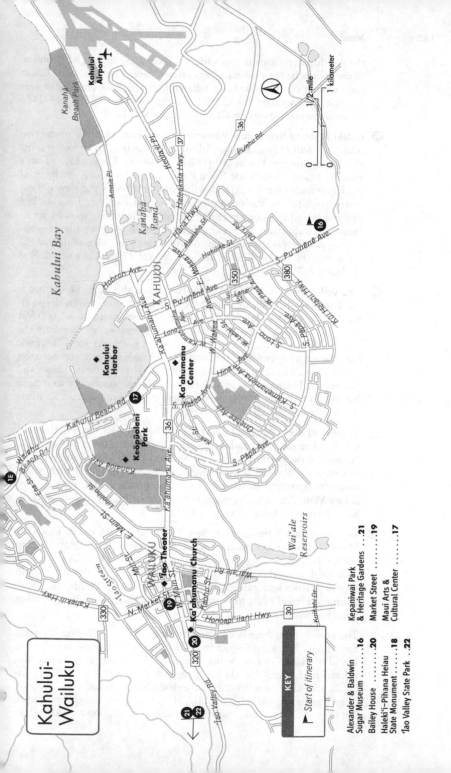

Kahului-Wailuku

Kahului Bay

Kahului Airport

Kanahā Beach Park

Kanahā Pond

Kahului Harbor

Keōpūolani Park

Kahului Beach Rd.

KAHULUI

Ka'ahumanu Center

WAILUKU

'Īao Theater

Ka'ahumanu Church

'Īao Stream

Wai'ale Reservoirs

KEY

▶ Start of itinerary

Alexander & Baldwin
Sugar Museum **16**

Bailey House **20**

Haleki'i-Pihana Heiau
State Monument **18**

'Īao Valley State Park ..**22**

Kepaniwai Park
& Heritage Gardens ..**21**

Market Street **19**

Maui Arts &
Cultural Center **17**

0   1/2 mile

0   1 kilometer

the missionaries' arrival and with Mr. Bailey's paintings of Wailuku. Some rooms have missionary-period furniture. The Hawaiian Room has exhibits on the making of tapa cloth, as well as samples of pre-Captain Cook weaponry. ⊠ *2375A Main St., Wailuku* ☎ *808/244–3326* ⊕ *www.mauimuseum.org* ⊠ *$5* ⊙ *Mon.–Sat. 10–4.*

⑱ Haleki'i-Pihana Heiau State Monument. Stand here at either of the two *heiau* (ancient Hawaiian stone platforms once used as places of worship) and imagine the king of Maui surveying his domain. That's what Kahekili, Maui's last fierce king, did, and so did Kamehameha the Great after he defeated Kahekili's soldiers. Today the view is most instructive. Below, the once-powerful 'Iao Stream has been sucked dry and boxed in by concrete. Before you is the urban heart of the island. The suburban community behind you is all Hawaiian Homelands—property owned solely by native Hawaiians. ⊠ *End of Hea Pl., off Kuhio Pl. from Waiehu Beach Rd., Rte. 340, Kahului* ⊠ *Free* ⊙ *Daily 7–7.*

★ ㉒ 'Iao Valley State Park. When Mark Twain saw this park, he dubbed it the Yosemite of the Pacific. Yosemite it's not, but it is a lovely deep valley with the curious 'Iao Needle, a spire that rises more than 2,000 feet from the valley floor. You can take one of several easy hikes from the parking lot across 'Iao Stream and explore the junglelike area. This park has a beautiful network of well-maintained walks, where you can stop and meditate by the edge of a stream or marvel at the native plants and flowers (*see* Hiking *earlier in this chapter*). Mist occasionally rises if there has been a rain, which makes being here even more magical. ⊠ *Western end of Rte. 32* ⊠ *Free* ⊙ *Daily 7–7.*

Ⓒ Keōpūolani Park. Maui's "Central Park" covers 101 acres, and—reflecting Maui residents' traditional love of sports—has seven playing fields. Named for the great Maui queen who was born near here and is buried in Lahaina's Waiola Church cemetery, the park is planted with native species that are still growing to reach their potential. The park also includes Maui Nui, a native-plant botanical garden, and a 3-mi walking path. ⊠ *Kanaloa Ave. next to YMCA.*

Ⓒ ㉑ Kepaniwai Park & Heritage Gardens. This county park is a memorial to Maui's cultural roots, with picnic facilities and ethnic displays dotting the landscape. Among the displays are an early-Hawaiian shack, a New England–style saltbox, a Portuguese-style villa with gardens, and dwellings from such other cultures as China and the Philippines. Next door, the Hawai'i Nature Center has an interactive exhibit and hikes good for children.

The peacefulness here belies the history of the area. During his quest for domination, King Kamehameha I brought his troops from the Big Island of Hawai'i to the Valley Isle in 1790 and engaged in a successful and particularly bloody battle against the son of Maui's chief, Kahekili, near Kepaniwai Park. An earlier battle at the site had pitted Kahekili himself against an older Big Island chief, Kalani'ōpu'u. Kahekili prevailed, but the carnage was so great that the nearby stream became known as

Waikīkī Beach, Oʻahu.

(*top*) Catching a wave. (*bottom*) Garden of the Gods, Lāna'i. (*opposite page, top*) Fire eater.
(*opposite page, bottom*) Children with haku (head) lei.

(*top*) Waikīkī, Oʻahu. (*bottom left*) Hula dancers. (*bottom right*) Hawaiʻi Volcanoes National Park, Big Island. (*opposite page*) Waiʻānapanapa State Park, Maui.

(*top*) Surfers, North Shore, O'ahu. (*bottom*) Lava flow, Hawai'i Volcanoes National Park, Big Island.

(*top left*) Golf Course at Mauna Lani Resort, Big Island. (*top right*) Haleakalā National Park, Maui. (*bottom*) Nā Pali Coast, Kaua'i.

(*top left*) Coffee picking contest, Kona, Big Island. (*top right*) Cyclists, North Shore sea cliffs overlooking Kalaupapa peninsula, Moloka'i. (*bottom*) Green Sea Turtles.

CLOSE UP

The Boy Who Raised an Island

ACCORDING TO LEGEND, the island of Maui was named after a demigod whose father, Akalana, kept the heavens aloft and whose mother, Hina, guarded the path to the netherworld. Of their children, Maui was the only one who possessed magic powers, though he wasn't a good fisherman and was teased mercilessly by his brothers for it. Eventually, the cunning young Maui devised a way to catch his own fish: he distracted his brothers and pulled his line across theirs, switching the hooks and stealing the fish they had caught.

When Maui's brothers caught on to his deception, they refused to take him fishing. To console Maui, his father gave him a magic hook, the Manaiakalani. Akalana said that the hook was fastened to the heavens and

when it caught land a new continent would be born. Maui was able to convince his brothers to take him out one more time. As they paddled deep into the ocean, he chanted a powerful spell, commanding the hook to catch "the Great Fish." The hook caught more than a fish—as they paddled along, mountain peaks were lifted out of the water's depths.

As the mountains began to rise, Maui told his brothers to paddle quickly without looking back. They did so for two days, at which point their curiosity proved too much. One of the brothers looked back, and as he stopped paddling, Maui's magic line snapped. Maui had intended to raise an entire continent, but had only an island to show for his efforts.

2

Wailuku (water of destruction) and the place where fallen warriors choked the stream's flow was called Kepaniwai (the water dam). ⊠ *Ţao Valley Rd., Wailuku* ⛱ *Free* ☉ *Daily 7–7.*

⑲ Market Street. An idiosyncratic assortment of shops makes Wailuku's Market Street a delightful place for a stroll. The Good Fortune Trading Company and Brown-Kobayashi carry interesting antiques and furnishings, while Gallerie Ha and the Sig Zane are sophisticated studio gift shops. Cafe Marc Aurel brews excellent espresso, which you can enjoy while sampling the selection of new and used CDs at the corner music shop. ⊠ *Wailuku.*

★ **⑰ Maui Arts & Cultural Center.** An epic fund drive by the citizens of Maui led to the creation of this $32 million facility. The top-of-the-line Castle Theater seats 1,200 people on orchestra, mezzanine, and balcony levels; rock stars play the A&B Amphitheater. The MACC (as it's called) also includes a small black box theater, an art gallery with interesting exhibits, and classrooms. The building itself is worth a visit: it incorporates work by Maui artists, and its signature lava-rock wall pays tribute to the skills of the Hawaiians. But the real draw is the Schaeffer International Gallery, which houses superb rotating exhibits. ⊠ *Above harbor on Kahului Beach Rd.* ☏ *808/242–2787, 808/242–7469 box office* ⊕ *www.mauiarts.org* ☉ *Weekdays 9–5.*

🖐 **Maui Tropical Plantation & Country Store.** When Maui's once-paramount crop declined in importance, a group of visionaries decided to open an agricultural theme park on the site of this former sugarcane field. The 60-acre preserve, on Route 30 just outside Wailuku, offers a 30-minute tram ride through its fields with an informative narration covering growing processes and plant types. Children will probably enjoy the historical-characters exhibit as well as fruit-tasting, coconut-husking, and lei-making demonstrations, not to mention some entertaining spider monkeys. There's a restaurant on the property and a "country store" specializing in Made in Maui products. ⊠ *Honoapiʻilani Hwy., Rte. 30, Waikapu* 🕿 *808/244–7643* 🖃 *Free; tram ride with narrated tour $9.50* ☼ *Daily 9–5.*

The South Shore

Twenty-five years ago a scant few adventurers lived in Kīhei. Now about one-third of the Maui population lives here in what was one of the fastest-growing towns in America. Traffic lights and mini-malls may not fit your notion of paradise, but Kīhei does offer sun, heat, and excellent beaches. Besides that, the town's relatively inexpensive condos and small hotels make this a home base for many Maui visitors. Great restaurants are easy to find in any price range. At the north end of this populous strip, you have Māʻalaea Small Boat Harbor and the Maui Ocean Center, a world-class seawater aquarium. At the south end, lovely Wailea—a resort community to rival those on West Maui—gives way to truly unspoiled coastline.

a good drive

Start with a look at **Māʻalaea Small Boat Harbor** ㉓ ➤, the departure point for many whale-watching trips, snorkel excursions (often out to the tiny crescent island Molokini), and sunset dinner cruises. Then tour the **Maui Ocean Center** ㉔, an aquarium dedicated to the sea life of the North Pacific. When you leave the aquarium, turn right onto Route 30 and then turn right again at the first traffic signal onto North Kīhei Road (Route 31). You're headed toward the town of **Kīhei** ㉕ on a straight road following the long, sandy coastline of Māʻalaea Bay. On your left is marshy Keālia Pond, a state-managed wildlife sanctuary. On your right, ecologically fragile dunes run between the road and the sea. A turnout provides some parking stalls, information about the dunes, and a boardwalk so you can cross the dunes and use the beach. When you get to the long, thin town of Kīhei, turn right at the fork in the road and experience the colorful stop-and-go beach route of South Kīhei Road, where you can find the **HI Humpback Whale Sanctuary** ㉖. If you're looking for the best beach, you might as well flip a coin. There are great beaches all along this coast. As you continue on, you hit the resort community of **Wailea** ㉗. Grand resorts interspersed with stretches of golf courses have access roads leading down to small but excellent beaches. Heading south on Wailea Alanui Drive, the manicured look of Wailea gives way to wildness and, after a couple of miles, to **Mākena Beach State Park** ㉘. Mākena is such a big beach that it has two paved parking areas. Beyond this point the land-

2

scape gets wilder and the road gradually fades away in black fields of cracked lava. This is **La Pérouse Bay** ㉙.

TIMING Because it includes so many fine beach choices, this is definitely an all-day excursion—especially if you include a visit to the aquarium. A good way to do this trip is to get active in the morning with exploring and snorkeling, then shower in a beach park, dress up a little, and enjoy the cool luxury of the Wailea resorts. At sunset, settle in for dinner at one of the area's many fine restaurants.

What to See

★ ✋ ㉖ **HI Humpback Whale Sanctuary.** The Sanctuary Education Center is beside a restored ancient Hawaiian fishpond, in prime humpback-viewing territory. Whether the whales are here or not, the center is a great stop for youngsters curious to know how things work underwater. Interactive displays and informative naturalists will explain it all. Throughout the year, the center hosts intriguing activities, ranging from moonlight tidal-pool explorations to "Two-ton talks." ✉ *726 S. Kīhei Rd., Kīhei* ☎ *808/879–2818 or 800/831–4888* ⊕ *www.hawaiihumpbackwhale.noaa.gov* ✉ *Free* ☉ *Daily 10–3.*

㉕ **Kīhei.** This is a community that's still discovering itself. A greenway for bikers and pedestrians is under construction, as is an unchecked surplus of new homes and properties. Moderately priced hotels, condos, and restaurants make the town convenient for visitors. The beaches and the reliably sunny weather are added attractions. The county beach parks such as Kamaʻole I, II, and III have lawns, showers, and picnic tables. Remember: beach park or no beach park, the public has a right to the entire coastal strand, and this one in Kīhei has many off-road delights.

㉙ **La Pérouse Bay.** Beyond Mākena Beach, the road fades away into a vast territory of black lava flows, the result of Haleakalā's last eruption some 200 years ago. This is where Maui received its first official visit by a European explorer—the French admiral Jean-François de Galaup, Comte de La Pérouse, in 1786. Before it ends, the road passes through ʻĀhihi-Kīnaʻu Marine Preserve, an excellent place for morning snorkel adventures.

⚑ ㉓ **Māʻalaea Small Boat Harbor.** With only 89 slips and so many good reasons to take people out on the water, this active little harbor needs to be expanded. The Army Corps of Engineers has a plan to do so, but harbor users are fighting it—particularly the surfers, who say the plan would destroy their surf breaks. In fact, the surf here is world renowned, especially the break to the left of the harbor called "freight train," said to be the fastest anywhere. ✉ *Off Honoapiʻilani Hwy., Rte. 30.*

★ ㉘ **Mākena Beach State Park.** "Big Beach" they call it—a huge stretch of coarse golden sand without a house or hotel for miles. A decade ago, Maui citizens campaigned successfully to preserve this beloved beach from development. At the right-hand end of the beach rises the beautiful hill called Puʻu Ōlaʻi, a perfect cinder cone. A climb over the rocks at this end leads to "Little Beach," where the (technically illegal) clothing-optional attitude prevails.

24 Maui Ocean Center. You'll feel as though you're walking from the seashore down to the bottom of the reef, and then through an acrylic tunnel in the middle of the sea at this aquarium, which focuses on Hawai'i and the Pacific. Special tanks get you close up with turtles, rays, and the unusual creatures of the tide pools. The center is part of a growing complex of retail shops and restaurants overlooking the harbor. ⊠ *Enter from Honoapi'ilani Hwy., Rte. 30, as it curves past Mā'alaea Harbor, Mā'alaea* ☎ *808/270–7000* ⊕ *www.mauioceancenter.com* ☎ *$20* ☉ *Daily 9–5.*

★ 27 Wailea. Wailea, the South Shore's resort community, is slightly quieter and drier than its West Side sister, Kā'anapali. Most visitors cannot pick a favorite and stay at both. The luxury of the resorts (edging on overindulgence) and the simple grandeur of the Shops at Wailea make the otherwise stark coast a worthy destination. A handful of perfect little beaches all have public access, and a paved beach walk allows you to stroll among all the properties, restaurants, and sandy coves. A great place to watch whales in the winter, the makai, or ocean, side of the beach walk is landscaped with exceptionally rare native plants.

Haleakalā National Park   See Page 187

Upcountry Maui & the North Shore

The west-facing upper slopes of Haleakalā are locally called "Upcountry." This region is responsible for much of Hawai'i's produce—lettuce, tomatoes, and sweet Maui onions—and the area is also a flower producer. As you drive along you'll notice cactus thickets mingled with purple jacaranda, wild hibiscus, and towering eucalyptus trees. Upcountry is also fertile ranch land, with such spreads as the historic 20,000-acre 'Ulupalakua Ranch and 32,000-acre Haleakalā Ranch. The North Shore centers around the colorful town of Pā'ia and the windsurfing mecca, Ho'okipa Beach.

a good drive

Drive toward the summit of Haleakalā on the Haleakalā Highway (Route 37) until you reach the intersection of Haleakalā Highway and—believe it or not—Haleakalā Highway. If you continue straight the road's name changes to Kula Highway (still Route 37). Instead, turn left onto Haleakalā Highway—this is now Route 377. About 2 mi past the turnoff for Haleakalā National Park you come to **Kula Botanical Gardens** 30 on your left. Stop here to admire the abundant tropical flora. Continue south. If you have reservations for tea, turn left up Waipoli Road. Follow the road to the cattle guard, and you see the driveway of **Ali'i Kula Lavender** 31 on the right, where you can munch on lavender scones and survey the scented view. If tea isn't your thing, continue south and you'll join Kula Highway (Route 37) again. Turn left and soak in

Continued on page 193

HALEAKALĀ NATIONAL PARK

HALEAKALA CRATER

From Tropics to the Moon! Two hours, 38 mi, 10,023 feet—those are the unlikely numbers involved in reaching Maui's highest point, the summit of Haleakalā. No where else on earth can you drive from sea level (Kahului) to 10,023 feet (the summit) in only 38 mi. And what's more shocking—in that short vertical ascent, you'll journey from lush, tropical-island landscape to the stark, moonlike basin of the volcano's enormous, otherworldly crater.

Established in 1916, Haleakalā National Park covers an astonishing 27,284 acres. Haleakalā Crater is the centerpiece of the park though it's not actually a crater. Technically, it's an erosional valley, flushed out by water pouring from the summit through two enormous gaps. The mountain has terrific camping and hiking, including a trail that loops through the crater, but the chance to witness this unearthly landscape is reason enough for a visit.

THE CLIMB TO THE SUMMIT

To reach Haleakalā National Park and the mountain's breathtaking summit, take Route 36 east of Kahului to the Haleakalā Highway (Route 37). Head east, up the mountain to the unlikely intersection of Haleakalā Highway and Haleakalā Highway. If you continue straight the road's name changes to Kula Highway (still Route 37). Instead, turn left onto Haleakalā Highway—this is now Route 377. After about 6 mi, make a left onto

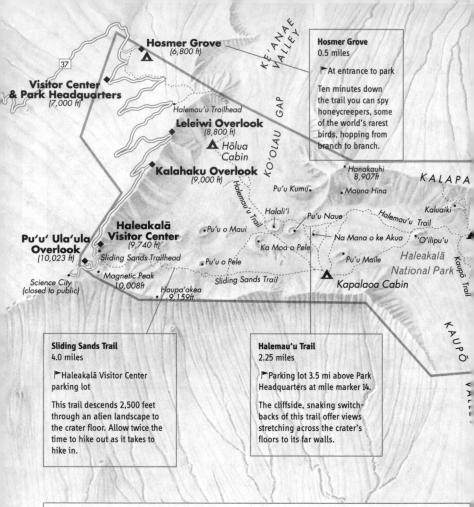

Hosmer Grove (6,800 ft)

Visitor Center & Park Headquarters (7,000 ft)

37

KE'ANAE VALLEY

Hosmer Grove
0.5 miles

► At entrance to park

Ten minutes down the trail you can spy honeycreepers, some of the world's rarest birds, hopping from branch to branch.

Halemau'u Trailhead

Leleiwi Overlook (8,800 ft)

Hōlua Cabin

KO'OLAU GAP

Kalahaku Overlook (9,000 ft)

Hanakauhi 8,907 ft

KALAPA

Pu'u Kumu

Mauna Hina

Halemau'u Trail

Halali'i

Pu'u Naue

Kaluaiki

Halemau'u Trail

Haleakalā Visitor Center (9,740 ft)

Pu'u o Maui

Na Mana o ke Akua

'O'ilipu'u

Pu'u' Ula'ula Overlook (10,023 ft)

Sliding Sands Trailhead

Ka Moa o Pele

Haleakalā National Park

Kaupō Trail

Science City (closed to public)

Magnetic Peak 10,008 ft

Pu'u o Pele

Pu'u Maile

Haupa'akea 9,159 ft

Sliding Sands Trail

Kapalaoa Cabin

KAUPŌ VALLEY

Sliding Sands Trail
4.0 miles

► Haleakalā Visitor Center parking lot

This trail descends 2,500 feet through an alien landscape to the crater floor. Allow twice the time to hike out as it takes to hike in.

Halemau'u Trail
2.25 miles

► Parking lot 3.5 mi above Park Headquarters at mile marker 14.

The cliffside, snaking switchbacks of this trail offer views stretching across the crater's floors to its far walls.

Crater Road (Route 378). After several long switchbacks (look out for downhill bikers!) you'll come to the park entrance.

■ **TIP→→** Before you head up Haleakalā, call for the latest **park weather conditions** (☎ 808/877–5111). Extreme gusty winds, heavy rain, and even snow in winter are not uncommon. Because of the high altitude, the mountaintop temperature is often as much as 30 degrees cooler than that at sea level. Be sure to bring a jacket. Also make sure you have a full tank of gas. No service stations exist beyond Kula.■

There's a $10 parking fee to enter the park; but it's good for one week and can be used at 'Ohe'o Gulch (Seven Sacred Pools), so save your receipt.

6,800 feet, Hosmer Grove. Just as you enter the park, Hosmer Grove has campsites and interpretive trails (*see* Hiking & Camping *on page 190*). Park rangers maintain a changing schedule of talks and hikes both here and at the top of the mountain. Call the park for current schedules.

7,000 feet, Park Headquarters/Visitor Center. Not far from Hosmer Grove, the Park Headquarters/Visitor Center (open daily from 8 to 4) has trail maps

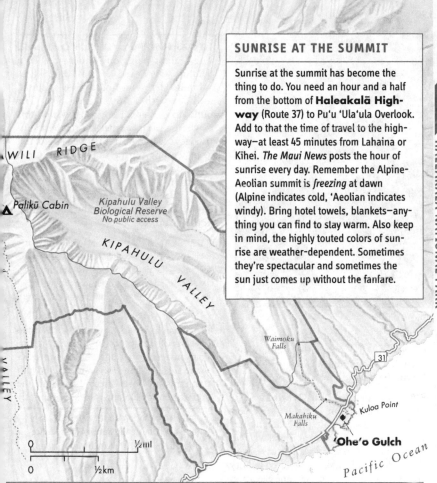

Sunrise at the summit has become the thing to do. You need an hour and a half from the bottom of **Haleakalā Highway** (Route 37) to Pu'u 'Ula'ula Overlook. Add to that the time of travel to the highway—at least 45 minutes from Lahaina or Kīhei. *The Maui News* posts the hour of sunrise every day. Remember the Alpine-Aeolian summit is *freezing* at dawn (Alpine indicates cold, 'Aeolian indicates windy). Bring hotel towels, blankets—anything you can find to stay warm. Also keep in mind, the highly touted colors of sunrise are weather-dependent. Sometimes they're spectacular and sometimes the sun just comes up without the fanfare.

and displays about the volcano's origins and eruption history. Hikers and campers should check-in here before heading up the mountain. Maps, posters, and other memorabilia are available at the gift shop.

8,800 feet, Leleiwi Overlook. Continuing up the mountain, you come to Leleiwi Overlook. A short walk to the end of the parking lot reveals your first awe-inspiring view of the crater. The small hills in the basin are volcanic cinder cones (called *pu'u* in Hawaiian), each with a small crater at its top, and each the site of a former eruption.

WHERE TO EAT

KULA LODGE (✉ Haleakalā Hwy., Kula ☎ 808/878-2517) serves hearty breakfasts from 7 to 11 AM, a favorite with hikers coming down from a sunrise visit to Haleakalā's summit, as well as those on their way up for a late-morning tramp in the crater. Spectacular ocean views fill the windows of this mountainside lodge.

If you're here in the late afternoon, it's possible you'll experience a phenomenon called the Brocken Specter. Named after a similar occurrence in East Germany's

Silversword

10,023 feet, Puʻu ʻUlaʻula Overlook.
The highest point on Maui is the Puʻu ʻUlaʻula Overlook, at the 10,023-foot summit. Here you find a glass-enclosed lookout with a 360-degree view. The building is open 24 hours a day, and this is where visitors gather for the best sunrise view. Dawn begins between 5:45 and 7, depending on the time of year. On a clear day you can see the islands of Molokaʻi, Lānaʻi, Kahoʻolawe, and Hawaiʻi (the Big Island). On a *really* clear day you can even spot Oʻahu glimmering in the distance.

■ **TIP→→**   The air is very thin at 10,000 feet. Don't be surprised if you feel a little breathless while walking around the summit. Take it easy and drink lots of water. Anyone who has been scuba diving within the last 24 hours should not make the trip up Haleakalā.■

On a small hill nearby, you can see **Science City**, an off-limits research and communications center straight out of an espionage thriller. The University of Hawaiʻi maintains an observatory here, and the Department of Defense tracks satellites.

For more information about Haleakalā National Park, contact the **National Park Service** (☎ 808/572–4400, ⊕ www.nps.gov/hale).

HIKING & CAMPING

Exploring Haleakalā Crater is one of the best hiking experiences on Maui. The volcanic terrain offers an impressive diversity of colors, textures, and shapes—almost as if the lava has been artfully sculpted. The barren landscape is home to many plants, insects, and birds that exist nowhere else on earth and have developed intriguing survival mechanisms, such as the sun-reflecting, hairy leaves of the silversword, which allow it to survive the intense climate.

Stop at park headquarters to register and pick up trail maps on your way into the park.

Harz Mountains, the specter allows you to see yourself reflected on the clouds and encircled by a rainbow. Don't wait all day for this because it's not a daily occurrence.

9,000 feet, Kalahaku Overlook. The next stopping point is Kalahaku Overlook. The view here offers a different perspective of the crater and at this elevation, the famous silversword plant grows amid the cinders. This odd, endangered beauty grows only here, and at the same elevation on the Big Island's two peaks. It begins life as a silver, spiny-leaf rosette and is the sole home of a variety of native insects (it's the only shelter around). The silversword reaches maturity between 7 and 17 years, when it sends forth a 3- to 8-foot-tall stalk with several hundred tiny sunflowers. It blooms once, then dies.

9,740 feet, Haleakalā Visitor Center.
Another mile up is the Haleakalā Visitor Center (open daily from sunrise to 3 PM). There are exhibits inside, and a trail from here leads to White Hill—a short easy walk that will give you an even better view of the valley.

2

1-Hour Hike. Just as you enter Haleakalā National Park, **Hosmer Grove** offers a short 10-minute hike, and an hour-long, ¹/₂-mi loop trail into the Waikamoi Cloud Forest that will give you insight into Hawai'i's fragile ecology. Anyone can go on the short hike, whereas the longer trail through the cloud forest is accessible only with park ranger-guided hikes. Call park headquarters for the schedule. Facilities here include six campsites (no permit needed, available on a first-come first-served basis), pit toilets, drinking water, and cooking shelters.

4 Hour Hikes. Two half-day hikes involve descending into the crater and returning the way you came. The first, **Halemau'u Trail** (trailhead is between mile markers 14 and 15), is 2 mi round-trip. The cliffside, snaking switchbacks of this trail offer views stretching across the crater's pu'u-speckled floor to its far walls. On clear days you can peer through the Ko'olau Gap to Hāna. Native flowers and shrubs grow along the trail, which is typically misty and cool (though still exposed to the sun). When you reach the gate at the bottom, head back up.

The other hike, which is 5 mi round-trip, descends down **Sliding Sands Trail** (trailhead is at the Haleakalā Visitor Center) into an alien landscape of reddish black cinders, lava bombs, and silverswords. It's easy to imagine life before humans in the solitude and silence of this place. Turn back when you hit the crater floor.

■ **TIP→→** Bring water, sunscreen, and a reliable jacket. These can be demanding hikes if you're unused to the altitude. Take it slowly to acclimate, and give yourself additional time for the uphill return trip.■

8-Hour Hike. The recommended way to explore the crater in a single, but full day is to go in two cars and ferry yourselves back and forth between the head of **Halemau'u Trail** and the summit. This way, you can hike from the summit down **Sliding Sands Trail**, cross the crater's floor, investigate the **Bottomless Pit** and **Pele's Paint Pot**, then climb out on the **switchback trail (Halemau'u)**. When you emerge, the shelter of your waiting car will be very welcome (this is an 11.2-mi hike). If you don't have two cars, hitching a ride from Halemau'u back to the summit should be relatively safe and easy.

■ **TIP→→** Take a backpack with lunch, water, sunscreen, and a reliable jacket for the beginning and end of the 8-hour hike. This is a demanding trip, but you will never regret or forget it.■

Overnight Hike. Staying overnight in one of Haleakalā's three cabins or two wilderness campgrounds is an experience like no other. You'll feel like the only person on earth when you wake up inside this enchanted, strange landscape. Nēnē and 'u'au (endangered storm petrels) make charming neighbors. The cabins, each tucked in a different corner of the crater's floor, are equipped with 12 bunk beds, wood-burning stoves, fake logs, and kitchen gear.

Hōlua cabin is the shortest hike, less than 4 hours (3.7 mi) from Halemau'u Trail. **Kapala'oa** is about 5 hours (5.5 mi) down Sliding Sands Trail. The most cherished cabin is **Palikū**, a solid eight-hour (9.3-mi) hike starting from either trail. It's nestled against the rain-forested cliffs above the Kaupō Gap. To reserve a cabin you have to apply to the National Park Service at least 90 days in advance and hope the lottery system is kind to you. Tent campsites at Hōlua and Palikū are free and easy to reserve on a first-come, first-served basis.

■ **TIP→→** Toilets and nonpotable water are available—bring iodine tablets to purify the water. Open fires are not allowed and packing out your trash is mandatory.■

For more information on hiking or camping, or to reserve a cabin, contact the National Park Service (✉ Box 369, Makawao 96768 ☎ 808/572-9306 ⊕ www.nps.gov/hale).

OPTIONS FOR EXPLORING

If you're short on time you can drive to the summit, take a peek inside, and drive back down. But the "House of the Sun" is really worth a day of your vacation time. There are lots of ways to experience the crater: by foot, bicycle, horseback, or helicopter.

BIKING

You cannot bike within the crater, but you can cruise the 38 mi from the summit down the outside of the mountain all the way to Pā'ia at sea level. The views along the way are exquisite, but dodging traffic can be a headache. If you rent bikes on your own, you'll need someone to ferry you up. Tours provide shuttle service and equipment.

HELICOPTER TOURS

Viewing Haleakalā from above can be a mind-altering experience, if you don't mind dropping $200 per person for a few blissful moments above the crater. Most tours buzz Haleakalā, where airspace is regulated, then head over to Hanā in search of waterfalls.

HORSEBACK RIDING

Several companies offer half-day, full-day, and even overnight rides into the crater. Advanced or at least confident riders can travel up the stunning Kaupō Gap with Charley's Trail Rides and stay overnight at Palikū.

For complete information on any of these activities, see Hiking & Outdoor Activities *earlier in this chapter* the slow pace of life when you stumble upon little **Kēōkea ③**. Follow the road coastward and you reach 'Ulupalakua Ranch headquarters and **Tedeschi Vineyards and Winery ③**, where Maui's only island wines can be sampled.

Return toward Kahului on Route 37, the Kula Highway. If you're pressed for time head downhill back to Kahului. Otherwise, turn north on Makawao Avenue (Route 365) toward **Makawao ③**, a classic old Hawaiian town. The **Hui No'eau Visual Arts Center ③** is about a mile from Makawao down Baldwin Avenue. From here it's a 7-mi drive down toward the ocean to the Hāna Highway at the town of **Pā'ia ③**. Make a right on the Hāna Highway to reach **Ho'okipa Beach ③**, arguably the windsurfing capital of the world. Two miles later, the bottom of Ha'ikū Road offers a right-turn side trip to **Ha'ikū ③**, a quiet pastoral town. Return to the Hāna Highway and make a left to head back to Kahului.

TIMING This can be an all-day outing with the detours to Tedeschi Vineyards and Makawao. You may want to cut these sidetrips short and combine your Upcountry tour with a visit to Haleakalā National Park (⇨ *see* Haleakalā National Park *earlier in this chapter*). If you leave early enough to catch the sunrise from the summit, you'll have plenty of time to explore the mountain, have lunch in Kula or at 'Ulupalakua Ranch, and end your day with dinner in Makawao, Pā'ia, or Ha'ikū.

What to See

★ **③** **Ali'i Kula Lavender.** Reserve a spot for tea or lunch at this lavender farm with a falcon's view. It's *the* relaxing remedy for those suffering from too much sun, shopping, or golf. Owners Ali'i and Lani lead tours through winding paths of therapeutic lavender varieties, proteas, succulents, and rare Maui wormwood. Their logo, a larger-than-life dragonfly, darts above chefs who are cooking up lavender-infused shrimp appetizers out on the lānai. The gift shop abounds with the farm's own innovative lavender products. ⊠ *1100 Waipoli Rd. Kula* ☎ *808/878–3004* ⊕ *www.mauikulalavender.com* 🖃 *$25* ⚘ *Reservations essential* ☉ *Daily 9–4, tours at 11 AM.*

③ **Ha'ikū.** At one time this town vibrated around a couple of enormous pineapple canneries. Now the place is reawakening and becoming a self-reliant community. At the town center, the old cannery has been turned into a rustic mall. Nearby warehouses are following suit. Continue 2 mi up Kokomo Road to see a large pu'u capped with a grove of columnar pines, and the 4th Marine Division Memorial Park. During World War II American GIs trained here for battles on Iwo Jima and Saipan. Locals have nicknamed the cinder cone Giggle Hill because it was a popular hangout for Maui women and their favorite servicemen. ⊠ *Intersection of Ha'ikū and Kokomo Rds.*

★ **③** **Ho'okipa Beach.** There is no better place on this or any other island to watch the world's best windsurfers in action. The surfers know five different surf breaks here by name. Unless it's a rare day without wind or waves, you're sure to get a show. ■ TIP➔➔ It's not safe to park on the shoulder. Use the ample parking lot at the county park entrance. ⊠ *2 mi past Pā'ia on Rte. 36.*

③⑤ **Hui No'eau Visual Arts Center.** The main house of this nonprofit cultural center on the old Baldwin estate, just outside the town of Makawao, is an elegant two-story Mediterranean-style villa designed in the 1920s by the defining Hawai'i architect C. W. Dickey. "The Hui" is the grande dame of Maui's well-known arts scene. The exhibits are always satisfying, and the grounds might as well be a botanical garden. The Hui also offers classes and maintains working artists' studios. ⊠ *2841 Baldwin Ave., Makawao* ☎ *808/572–6560* 🖃 *Free* ☉ *Daily 10–4.*

③② **Keōkea.** More of a friendly gesture than a town, this is the last outpost for Maui's cowboys on their way to work at 'Ulupalakua or Kaupō ranch. A coffee tree pushes through the sunny deck at Grandma's Coffee Shop, and tiny Keōkea Gallery sells some of the most original artwork on the island. ■ **TIP→→ The only restroom for miles is across the street at the public park, and the view makes stretching your legs worth it.**

③⓪ **Kula Botanical Gardens.** This well-kept garden has assimilated itself naturally into its craggy 6-acre habitat. There are beautiful trees here, including native koa (prized by woodworkers) and *kukui* (the state tree, a symbol of enlightenment). There's also a good selection of proteas, the flowering shrubs that have become a signature flower crop of Upcountry Maui. A natural stream feeds into a koi pond, which is also home to a pair of African cranes. ⊠ *638 Kekaulike Hwy., Kula* ☎ *808/878– 1715* 🖃 *$5* ☉ *Daily 9–4.*

> **need a break?**
>
> One of Makawao's most famous landmarks is **Komoda Store & Bakery** (⊠ 3674 Baldwin Ave. ☎ 808/572–7261)—a classic mom-and-pop store that has changed little in three-quarters of a century—where you can get a delicious cream puff if you arrive early enough. They make hundreds but sell out each day.

③④ **Makawao.** This once-tiny town has managed to hang on to its country charm (and eccentricity) as it has grown in popularity. The district was originally settled by Portuguese and Japanese immigrants who came to Maui to work the sugar plantations and then moved Upcountry to establish small farms, ranches, and stores. Descendants now work the neighboring Haleakalā and 'Ulupalakua ranches. Every July 4 the *paniolo* (Hawaiian cowboy) set comes out in force for the Makawao Rodeo. The crossroads of town—lined with chic shops and down-home eateries—reflects a growing population of people who came here just because they liked it. ⊠ *Intersection of Baldwin and Makawao Aves.*

★ ③⑥ **Pā'ia.** This little town on Maui's north shore was once a sugarcane enclave, with a mill, plantation camps, and shops to serve the workers. The town boomed during World War II when the marines set up camp in nearby Ha'ikū. The old HC&S sugar mill finally closed and no sign of the military remains, but the town continues to thrive. In the '70s Pā'ia became a hippie town as dropouts headed for Maui to open boutiques, galleries, and unusual eateries. In the '80s windsurfers discovered nearby Ho'okipa Beach and brought an international flavor to Pā'ia (to the benefit of the unusual eateries). Hāna Highway is the main street in town and budget inns have cropped up to accommodate eclectic travelers. Whether you're

Maui Sightseeing Tours

THIS IS A BIG ISLAND TO SEE IN ONE DAY, so tour companies tend to offer specialized tours, visiting either Haleakalā or Hāna and its environs. A tour of Haleakalā and Upcountry is usually a half-day excursion and is offered in several versions by different companies for about $60 and up. The trip often includes stops at a protea farm and at Tedeschi Vineyards, the only place in Maui where wine is made. A Haleakalā sunrise tour starts before dawn so that you can get to the top of the dormant volcano before the sun peeks over the horizon. Because they offer island-wide hotel pickup, many sunrise trips leave around 2:30 AM.

A tour of Hāna is almost always done in a van, since the winding road to Hāna just doesn't provide a comfortable ride in bigger buses. Of late, Hāna has so many of these one-day tours that it seems as if there are more vans than cars on the road. Still, to many it's a more relaxing way to do the drive than behind the wheel of a car. Guides decide where you stop for photos. Tours run from $80 to $120.

When booking a tour, remember that some tour companies use air-conditioned buses, whereas others prefer small vans. Then you've got your minivans, your microbuses, and your minicoaches. The key is to ask how many stops you get and how many other passengers will be onboard—otherwise you could end up on a packed bus, sightseeing through a window.

Most of the tour guides have been in the business for years. Some were born in the Islands and have taken special classes to learn more about their culture and lore. They expect a

tip ($1 per person at least), but they're just as cordial without one.

Maui Pineapple Plantation Tour. Explore one of Maui's pineapple plantations on this tour that takes you right into the fields in a company van. The 2½-hour, $26 trip gives you first-hand experience of the operation and its history, some incredible views of the island, and the chance to pick a fresh pineapple for yourself. Tours depart weekday mornings and afternoons from the Kapalua Logo Shop. ⊠ *Kapalua Resort Activity Desk, 500 Office Rd., Kapalua* ☎ *808/669-8088.*

Polynesian Adventure Tours. This company uses large buses with floor-to-ceiling windows. The drivers are fun and really know the island. ☎ *808/877-4242 or 800/622-3011* ⊕ *www.polyad.com.*

Roberts Hawai'i Tours. This is one of the state's largest tour companies, and its staff can arrange tours with bilingual guides if asked ahead of time. Eleven-hour trips venture out to Kaupō, the wild area past Hāna. ☎ *808/871-6226 or 800/767-7551* ⊕ *www.roberts-hawaii.com.*

Temptation Tours. Temptation Tours has targeted members of the affluent older crowd (though almost anyone would enjoy these tours) who don't want to be herded onto a crowded bus. Tours in plush six-passenger limovans explore Haleakalā and Hāna, and range from $110 to $249 per person. The "Hāna Sky-Trek" includes a return trip via helicopter—perfect for those leery of spending the entire day in a van. ☎ *808/877-8888* ⊕ *www.mauitours.us.*

looking for yoga pants or pumpkin soup, Pā'ia is sure to deliver. ⊠ *Intersection of Hāna Hwy. (Hwy. 36) and Baldwin Ave.*

need a break?

Pā'ia is a great place to find food. A French-Caribbean bistro with a sushi bar in back, a French-Indian creperie, a neo-Mexican gourmet restaurant, and a fish market all compete for your patronage near the intersection of Baldwin Avenue and Hāna Highway. This abundance is helpful because Pā'ia is the last place to snack before the pilgrimage to Hāna and the first stop for the famished on the return trip.

Anthony's Coffee Company (⊠ 90 Hāna Hwy. ☎ 808/579–8340) roasts its own beans, sells ice cream and picnic lunches, and is a great place to eavesdrop on the local windsurfing crowd. **Charley's Restaurant** (⊠ 142 Hāna Hwy. ☎ 808/579–9453) is an easygoing saloon-type hangout with pool tables. **Mana Foods** (⊠ 49 Baldwin Ave. ☎ 808/579–8078), the North Shore's natural-foods store, has an inspired deli with wholesome hot-and-cold items. The long line at **Pā'ia Fishmarket Restaurant** (⊠ 2A Baldwin Ave. ☎ 808/579–8030) attests to the popularity of their tasty mahi sandwiches. Fresh fish can also be bought by the pound. Pā'ia has an excellent wine store, the **Wine Corner** (⊠ 113 Hāna Hwy. ☎ 808/579–8904), which can be helpful because two good eateries nearby are BYOB.

★ ㉝ **Tedeschi Vineyards and Winery.** You can tour the winery and its historic grounds, the former Rose Ranch, and sample the island's only wines: a pleasant Maui Blush, Maui Champagne, and Tedeschi's annual Maui Nouveau. The top-seller, naturally, is the pineapple wine. The tasting room is a cottage built in the late 1800s for the frequent visits of King Kalākaua. The cottage also contains the **'Ulupalakua Ranch History Room,** which tells colorful stories of the ranch's owners, the paniolo tradition that developed here, and Maui's polo teams. The old General Store may look like a museum, but in fact it's an excellent pit stop. ⊠ *Kula Hwy., 'Ulupalakua Ranch* ☎ 808/878–6058 ⊕ *www.mauiwine.com* ☒ *Free* ⊙ *Daily 9–5, tours at 10:30 and 1:30.*

The Road to Hāna   See Page 197

BOOKS TO READ

Paul Wood's essays, collected in *Four Wheels, Five Corners: Facts of Life in Upcountry Maui,* are quirky tales of life on a rock in the middle of the Pacific.

Writers Paul Theroux, Barbara Kingsolver, and Maxine Hong Kingston are among those who share stories about the Islands in *Hawai'i: True Stories of the Island Spirit,* a collection edited by Rick and Marcie Carroll. *Call for Hawaiian Sovereignty,* by Michael Kioni Dudley, traces the growing movement for sovereignty.

ROAD TO HĀNA

As you round the impossibly tight turn, a one-lane bridge comes into view. Beneath its worn surface, a lush forested gulch plummets toward the coast. The sound of rushing water fills the air, compelling you to search the overgrown hillside for waterfalls. This is the Road to Hāna, a 55-mi journey into the unspoiled heart of Maui. Tracing a centuries-old path, the road begins as a well-paved highway in Kahului and ends in the tiny town of Hāna on the islands' rain-gouged windward side.

★ **Fodor's Choice** Despite the twists and turns, the road to Hāna is not as frightening as it may sound. You're bound to be a little nervous approaching it the first time; but afterwards you'll wonder if somebody out there is making it sound tough just to keep out the hordes. The challenging part of the road takes only an hour and a half, but you'll want to stop often and let the driver enjoy the view, too. Don't expect a booming city when you get to Hāna. Its lure is its quiet timelessness. Like the adage says, the journey *is* the destination.

During high season, the road to Hāna tends to clog—well, not clog exactly, but develop little choo-choo trains of cars, with everyone in a line of six or a dozen driving as slowly as the first car. The solution: leave early (dawn) and return late (dusk). And if you find yourself playing the role of locomotive, pull over and let the other drivers pass. You can also let someone else take the turns for you—several companies offer van tours, which make stops all along the way (*see* Sightseeing Tours *earlier in this chapter*).

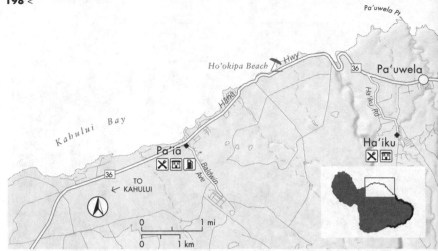

DRIVING THE ROAD TO HĀNA

Begin your journey in Pāʻia, the little town on Maui's North Shore. Be sure to fill up your gas tank here. There are no gas stations along Hāna Highway, and the station in Hāna closes by 6 PM. You should also pick up a picnic lunch. Lunch and snack choices along the way are limited to rustic fruit stands.

About 10 mi past Pāʻia, at the bottom of Kaupakalua Road, the roadside mileposts begin measuring the 36 mi to Hāna town. The road's trademark noodling starts about 3 mi after that. Once the road gets twisty, remember that many residents make this trip frequently. You'll recognize them because they're the ones zipping around every curve. They've seen this so many times before they don't care to linger. Pull over to let them pass.

All along this stretch of road, waterfalls are abundant. Roll down your windows. Breathe in the scent of guava and ginger. You can almost hear the bamboo growing. There are plenty of places to pull completely off the road and park safely. Do this often, since the road's curves make driving without a break difficult.

❶ Twin Falls. Keep an eye out for the fruit stand just after mile marker 2. Stop here and treat yourself to some fresh sugarcane juice. If you're feeling adventurous, follow the path beyond the stand to the paradisiacal waterfalls known as Twin Falls. Once a rough trail plastered with no trespassing signs, this treasured spot is now easily accessible. In fact, there's usually a mass of cars surrounding the fruit stand at the trail head. Several deep, emerald pools sparkle beneath waterfalls and offer excellent swimming and photo opportunities.

While it's still private property, the no trespassing signs have been replaced by colorfully painted arrows pointing away from residences and toward the falls. ■ TIP➔➔ **Bring water shoes for crossing streams along the way. Swim at your own risk and beware: flash floods here and in all East Maui stream areas can be sudden and deadly. Check the weather before you go.**

❷ Huelo & Kailua. Dry off and drive on past the sleepy country villages of Huelo (near mile marker 5) and Kailua (near mile marker 6). The little farm town of Huelo has two quaint churches and several lovely B&Bs. It's a good place to stay if you value privacy, but it also provides an opportunity to meet local residents and learn about a rural lifestyle you might not expect to find on the Islands. The same can

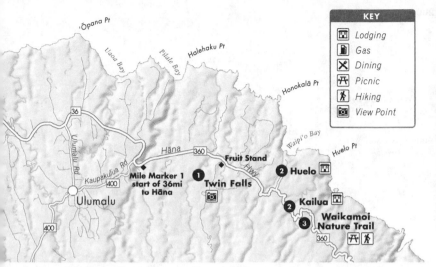

KEY

🏨	Lodging
⛽	Gas
✖	Dining
🪑	Picnic
🥾	Hiking
📷	View Point

be said for nearby Kailua, home to Alexander & Baldwin's irrigation employees.

③ Waikamoi Nature Trail. Between mile markers 9 and 10, the Waikamoi Nature Trail sign beckons you to stretch your car-weary limbs. A short (if muddy) trail leads through tall eucalyptus trees to a coastal vantage point with a picnic table and barbecue. Signage reminds visitors QUIET, TREES AT WORK and BAMBOO PICKING PERMIT REQUIRED. Awapuhi, or Hawaiian shampoo ginger, sends up fragrant shoots along the trail.

④ Puahokamoa Stream. About a mile farther, near mile marker 11, you can stop at the bridge over Puahokamoa Stream. This is one of many bridges you cross en route from Pā'ia to Hāna. It spans pools and waterfalls. Picnic tables are available, but there are no restrooms.

⑤ Kaumahina State Wayside Park. If you'd rather stretch your legs and use a flush toilet, continue another mile to Kaumahina State Wayside Park (at mile marker 12). The park has a picnic area, restrooms, and a lovely overlook to the Ke'anae Peninsula. Hardier souls can camp here, with a permit. The park is open from 8 AM to 4 PM and admission is free. ☎ 808/984–8109

🕐 | **TIMING TIPS**

With short stops, the drive from Pā'ia to Hāna should take you between two and three hours one-way. Lunching in Hāna, hiking, and swimming can easily turn the round-trip into a full-day outing. Since there's so much scenery to take in, we recommend staying overnight in Hāna. It's worth taking time to enjoy the waterfalls and beaches without being in a hurry. Try to plan your trip for a day that promises fair, sunny weather— though the drive can be even more beautiful when it's raining. ■ TIP→→ If you decide to spend a night or two in Hāna, you may want to check any valuable luggage with the valet at your previous hotel. That way, you won't have to leave it in your car unattended when you stop to see the sights on your way to Hāna.

Ke'anae Peninsula

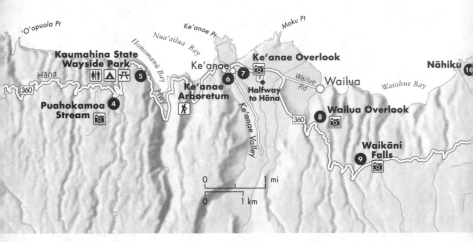

Near mile marker 14, before Keʻanae, you find yourself driving along a cliff side down into deep, lush Honomanū Bay, an enormous valley, with a rocky black-sand beach.

The Honomanū Valley was carved by erosion during Haleakalā's first dormant period. At the canyon's head there are 3,000-foot cliffs and a 1,000-foot waterfall, but don't try to reach them. There's not much of a trail, and what does exist is practically impassable.

6 Keʻanae Arboretum. Another 4 mi brings you to mile marker 17 and the Keʻanae Arboretum where you can add to your botanical education or enjoy a challenging hike into a forest. Signs help you learn the names of the many plants and trees now considered native to Hawaiʻi. The meandering Piʻinaʻau Stream adds a graceful touch to the arbor-etum and provides a swimming pond.

You can take a fairly rigorous hike from the arboretum if you can find the trail at one side of the large taro patch. Be careful not to lose the trail once you're on it. A lovely forest waits at the end of the 25-minute hike. Access to the arboretum is free.

7 Keʻanae Overlook. A half mile farther down Hāna Highway you can stop at the Keʻanae Overlook. From this obser-vation point, you can take in the patch-work-quilt effect the taro farms create below. The people of Keʻanae are working hard to revive this Hawaiian agricultural art and the traditional cultural values that the crop represents. The ocean provides a dramatic backdrop for the farms. In the other direction there are awesome views of Haleakalā through the foliage. This is a great spot for photos.

■ **TIP→→** Coming up is the halfway mark to Hāna. If you've had enough scenery, this is as good a time as any to turn around and head back to civilization.

8 Wailua Overlook. Between mile markers 20 and 21 you find Wailua Overlook. From the parking lot you can see Wailua Canyon, but you have to walk up steps to get a view

Taro Farm viewed from Hāna Highway

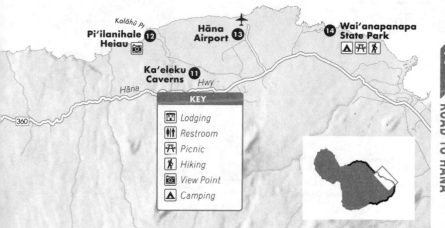

of Wailua Village. The landmark in Wailua Village is a church made of coral, built in 1860. Once called St. Gabriel's Catholic Church, the current Our Lady of Fatima Shrine has an interesting legend surrounding it. As the story goes, a storm washed enough coral up onto shore to build the church and then took any extra coral back to sea.

9 Waikāni Falls. After another ¹/₂ mi, past mile marker 21, you hit the best falls on the entire drive to Hāna, Waikāni Falls. Though not necessarily bigger or taller than the other falls, these are the most dramatic falls you'll find in East Maui. That's partly because the water is not diverted for sugar irrigation; the taro farmers in Wailua need all the runoff. This is a particularly good spot for photos.

10 Nahiku. At about mile marker 25 you see a road that heads down toward the ocean and the village of Nahiku. In ancient times this was a busy settlement with hundreds of residents. Now only about 80 people live in Nahiku, mostly native Hawaiians and some back-to-the-land types. A rubber grower planted trees here in the early 1900s, but the experiment didn't work out, and Nahiku was essentially abandoned. The road ends at the sea in a pretty landing. This is the rainiest, densest part of the East Maui rain forest.

Coffee Break. Back on the Hāna Highway, about 10 minutes before Hāna town, you can stop for—of all things—espresso. The tiny, colorful **Nahiku Ti Gallery and Coffee Shop** (between mile markers 27 and 28) sells local coffee, dried fruits and candies, and delicious (if pricey) banana bread. Sometimes the barbecue is fired up and you can try fish skewers or baked breadfruit (an island favorite nearly impossible to find elsewhere). The Ti Gallery sells Hawaiian crafts.

11 Ka'eleku Caverns. If you're interested in exploring underground turn left onto 'Ula'ino Road, just after mile marker 31, and follow the signs to Ka'eleku Caverns. **Maui Cave Adventures** leads amateur spelunkers into a system of gigantic lava tubes, accentuated by colorful underworld formations.

Monday through Thursday, from 10:30 to 3:30, you can take a self-guided, 30- to 45-minute tour for $11.95 per person. Friday and Saturday, choose either the 75-minute walking tour (at 11:15 AM; $29 per person) or the two-and-a-half-hour adventure tour (at 1:15 PM; $79 per person). Gear—gloves, flashlight, and hard hat—is provided, and visitors must be at least six years of age (15 years of age for the adventure tour). Call ahead to reserve a spot on the guided tours. ☎ 808/248–7308, ⊕ www.mauicave.com

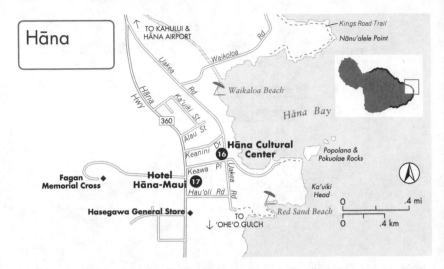

Hāna

TO KAHULUI &
HĀNA AIRPORT

Kings Road Trail
Nānu'alele Point

Waikoloa Beach

Hāna Bay

Hāna Cultural Center ⑯

Popolana &
Pokuolae Rocks

Fagan
Memorial Cross ◆

Hotel
Hāna-Maui ⑰

Ka'uiki
Head

Hasegawa General Store ◆

TO
↓ 'OHE'O GULCH

Red Sand Beach

0   .4 mi

0   .4 km

★ ⑫ Pi'ilanihale Heiau. Continue on 'Ula'ino Road, which doubles back for a mile, loses its pavement, and even crosses a stream before reaching Kahanu Garden and Pi'ilanihale Heiau, the largest prehistoric monument in Hawai'i. This temple platform was built for a great 16th-century Maui king named Pi'ilani and his heirs. This king also supervised the construction of a 10-foot-wide road that completely encircled the island. (That's why his name is part of most of Maui's highway titles.)

Hawaiian families continue to maintain and protect this sacred site as they have for centuries, and they have not been eager to turn it into a tourist attraction. However, they now offer a brochure so you can tour the property yourself for $5 per person. Parties of four or more can reserve a guided tour, for $10 per person, by calling 48 hours in advance. Tours include the 122-acre **Kahanu Garden**, a federally funded research center focusing on the ethno botany of the Pacific. The heiau and garden are open weekdays from 10 AM to 2 PM. ☎ 808/248–8912

⓭ Hāna Airport. Back on the Hāna Highway, and less than $^{1}/_{2}$ mi farther, is the turnoff for the Hāna Airport. Think of Amelia Earhart. Think of Waldo Pepper. If these picket-fence runways don't turn your thoughts to the derring-do of barnstorming pilots, you haven't seen enough old movies. Only the smallest planes can land and depart here, and when none of them happens to be around, the lonely wind sock is the only evidence that this is a working airfield. ☎ 808/248–8208

★ ⓮ Wai'anapanapa State Park. Just beyond mile marker 32 you reach Wai'anapanapa State Park, home to one of Maui's only volcanic-sand beaches and some freshwater caves for adventurous swimmers to explore. The park is right on the ocean, and it's a lovely spot to picnic, camp, hike, or swim. To the left you'll find the black-sand beach, picnic tables, and cave pools. To the right you'll find cabins and an ancient trail which snakes along the ocean past blowholes, sea arches, and archaeological sites.

The tide pools here turn red several times a year. Scientists say it's explained by the arrival of small shrimp, but legend claims the color represents the blood of Popoalaea, a princess said to have been murdered in one of the caves by her husband, Chief Kaakea. Whichever you choose to believe, the drama of the landscape itself—black sand, green beach vines, azure water—is bound to leave a lasting impression.

With a permit you can stay in state-run cabins here for less than $45 a night—the price varies depending on the number of people—but reserve early. They often book up a year in advance. ☎ 808/984–8109.

⓯ **Hāna.** By now the relaxed pace of life that Hāna residents enjoy should have you in its grasp, so you won't be discouraged to learn that town is little more than a gas station, a post office, and a ramshackle grocery.

Hāna, in many ways, is the heart of Maui. It's one of the few places where the slow pulse of island life is still strong. The town centers on its lovely circular bay, dominated on the right-hand shore by a pu'u called Ka'uiki. A short trail here leads to a cave, the birthplace of Queen Kā'ahumanu. This area is rich in Hawaiian history and legend. Two miles beyond town another pu'u presides over a loop road that passes two of Hāna's best beaches—Koki and Hāmoa. The hill is called Ka Iwi O Pele (Pele's Bone). Offshore here, at tiny 'Alau Island, the demigod Maui supposedly fished up the Hawaiian islands.

Sugar was once the mainstay of Hāna's economy; the last plantation shut down in the '40s. In 1946 rancher Paul Fagan built the **Hotel Hāna-Maui** and stocked the surrounding pastureland with cattle. The cross you see on the hill above the hotel was put

there in memory of Fagan. Now it's the ranch and hotel that put food on most tables, though many families still farm, fish, and hunt as in the old days. Houses around town are decorated with glass balls and nets, which indicate a fisherman's lodging.

⓰ **Hāna Cultural Center Museum.** If you're determined to spend some time and money in Hāna after the long drive, a single turn off the highway onto Ukea Street, in the center of town, will take you to the Hāna Cultural Center Museum. Besides operating a well-stocked gift shop, it displays artifacts, quilts, a replica of an authentic *kauhale* (an ancient Hawaiian living complex, with thatch huts and food gardens), and other Hawaiiana. The knowledgeable staff can explain it all to you. ☎808/248–8622

⓱ **Hotel Hāna-Maui.** With its surrounding ranch, the upscale hotel is the mainstay of Hāna's economy. It's pleasant to stroll around this beautifully rustic property. The library houses interesting, authentic Hawaiian artifacts. In the evening, while local musicians play in the casual lobby bar, their friends jump up to dance hula. The Sea Ranch cottages across the road, built to look like authentic plantation housing from the outside, are also part of the hotel. *See* Where to Stay *later in this chapter for more information.*

Hala Trees, Wai'anapanapa State Park

Hāna

Don't be suprised if the mile markers suddenly start descending as you head past Hāna. Technically, Hāna Highway (Route 360) ends at the Hāna Bay. The road that continues south is Pi'ilani Highway (Route 31)—though everyone still refers to it as the Hāna Highway.

⑱ Hāmoa Beach. Just outside Hāna, take a left on Haneo'o Loop to explore lovely Hāmoa. Indulge in swimming or bodysurfing at this beautiful salt-and-pepper beach. Picnic tables, restrooms, and showers beneath the idyllic shade of coconut trees offer a more than comfortable rest stop.

The road leading to Hāmoa also takes you to **Kōkī Beach**, where you can watch the Hāna surfers mastering the swells and strong currents, and the seabirds darting over **Ālau**, the palm-fringed islet off the coast. The swimming is safer at Hāmoa.

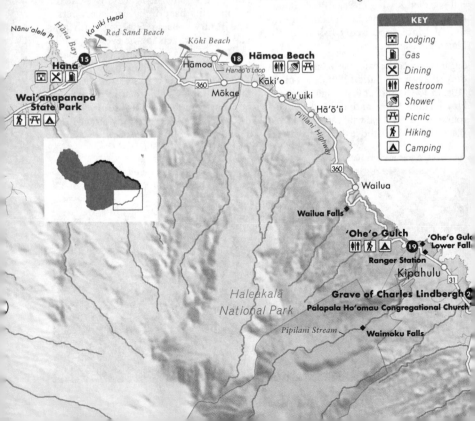

★ **⑲ 'Ohe'o Gulch.** Ten miles past town, at mile marker 42, you'll find the pools at 'Ohe'o Gulch. One branch of Haleakalā National Park runs down the mountain from the crater and reaches the sea here, where a basalt-lined stream cascades from one pool to the next. Some tour guides still call this area Seven Sacred Pools, but in truth there are more than seven, and they've never been considered sacred. You can park here—for a $10 fee—and walk to the lowest pools for a cool swim. The place gets crowded, since most people who drive the Hāna Highway make this their last stop.

If you enjoy hiking, go up the stream on the 2-mi hike to **Waimoku Falls.** The trail crosses a spectacular gorge, then turns into a boardwalk that takes you through an amazing bamboo forest. You can pitch a tent in the grassy campground down by the sea. *See* Hiking *earlier in this chapter for more information.*

⑳ Grave of Charles Lindbergh. Many people travel the mile past 'Ohe'o Gulch to see the Grave of Charles Lindbergh. You see a ruined sugar mill with a big chimney on the right side of the road and then, on the left, a rutted track leading to Palapala Ho'omau Congregational Church. The simple one-room church sits on a bluff over the sea, with the small graveyard on the ocean side. The world-renowned aviator chose to be buried here because he and his wife, writer Anne Morrow Lindbergh, spent a lot of time living in the area. He was buried here in 1974. Since this is a churchyard, be considerate and leave everything exactly as you found it. Next to the churchyard on the ocean side is a small county park, a good place for a peaceful picnic.

Kaupō Road. The road to Hāna continues all the way around Haleakalā's back side through 'Ulupalakua Ranch and into Kula. The desertlike area, with its grand vistas, is unlike anything else on the island, but the road itself is bad, some-

---

TROPICAL DELIGHTS

The drive to Hāna wouldn't be as enchanting without a stop or two at one of the countless fruit and flower stands alongside the highway. Every ¹/₂ mi or so a thatched hut tempts passersby with apple bananas, liliko'i (passion fruit), avocados, or starfruit just plucked from the tree. Leave 50¢ or $1 in the can for the folks who live off the land. Huge bouquets of tropical flowers are available for a handful of change, and some farms will ship.

---

times impassable in winter. Car-rental agencies call it off-limits to their passenger cars and there is no emergency assistance available. The danger and dust from increasing numbers of speeding jeep drivers are making life tough for the residents, especially in Kaupō, with its 4 mi of unpaved road. The small communities around East Maui cling tenuously to the old ways. Please keep them in mind if you do pass this way. If you can't resist the adventure, try to make the drive just before sunset. The light slanting across the mountain is incredible. At night, giant potholes, owls, and loose cattle can make for some difficult driving.

WHERE TO STAY

Maui's accommodations come in three sizes: small, medium, and gargantuan. Small B&Bs are personal and charming—often a few rooms or a cottage beside the owner's own home. They open a window into authentic island life. Medium-size condominiums are less personal (you won't see the owner out trimming the bougainvillaea) but highly functional—great for longer stays or families who want no-fuss digs. The resorts are out of this world. They do their best to improve on nature, trying to re-create what is beautiful about Maui. And their best is pretty amazing. Opulent gardens, fantasy swimming pools with slides (some with swim-up bars), waterfalls, spas, and championship golf courses make it hard to work up the willpower to leave the resort and go see the real thing.

So, where to go for what? The resorts are clustered along the leeward (west and south) shores, meaning they are hot and sunny in summer and hot and sunny in winter, with periodic downpours. Kāʻanapali (in West Maui), the grande dame, is the original resort community and has the most action, feeding off the old whaler's haunt, Lahaina town. Kapalua, farther north, is more private and serene, and catches a bit more wind and rain. On the South Shore, posh Wailea has excellent beaches and designer golf courses, each with a distinct personality.

If you're willing to compromise on luxury, you can find convenient condos on the West Side, (in Nāpili or Kahana) or on the South Shore (in Kīhei). Many are oceanfront and offer the amenities of a hotel suite without the cost. Furnishings can be a little scruffy, however, and rarely do condos have central air-conditioning—something to consider if you aren't used to sleeping in humidity.

Most of the accommodations elsewhere on the island—say, Upcountry or in Hāna—are B&Bs or vacation rentals. Few offer breakfast, but most deliver ample seclusion and a countryside experience. Some are extravagant, million-dollar ocean-view properties that you can really write home about. Others are humble guest rooms with cozy furnishings that make you feel right at home. ■ TIP→→ If you're booking off the Internet, it pays to fact-check. Questions to ask before making the deposit: how far from the airport/beach/shops is it? Will I have a private bathroom and kitchen? Is there a phone and TV in the room? Every owner thinks their vacation rental is a slice of heaven; whether you agree depends on your expectations.

> **MONEY MATTERS**
>
> Keep in mind that the prices listed in this guide are the rack rates given by the hotels at this writing. Always ask about special packages and discounts when making your reservations. The Web is also a great resource for discount rooms. Also note that in Hawaiʻi room prices can vary dramatically depending on whether or not a room has an ocean view. If you want to save money, ask for a garden or mountain view.

	WHAT IT COSTS				
	$$$$	**$$$**	**$$**	**$**	**¢**
HOTELS	over $200	$150–$200	$100–$150	$60–$100	under $60

Hotel prices are for two people in a double room in high season, including tax and service.

West Maui

West Maui is a long string of small communities, beginning with Lahaina at the south end and meandering into Kā'anapali, Honokowai, Kahana, Nāpili, and Kapalua. Here's the breakdown on what's where: Lahaina is the business district with all the shops, shows, restaurants, historic buildings, churches, and rowdy side streets. Ka'anapali is all glitz: fancy resorts set on Kā'anapali beach. Honokowai, Kahana, and Nāpili are quiet little nooks characterized by comfortable condos built in the late 1960s. All face the same direction, and get the same consistently hot, humid weather. Kapalua, at the northern tip, is slightly more windward and has a cooler climate.

Hotels & Resorts

$$$$ ⊞ **Hyatt Regency Maui.** Fantasy landscaping with splashing waterfalls, swim-through grottoes, a lagoonlike swimming pool, and a 130-foot water slide wows guests of all ages at this active Kā'anapali resort. Stroll through the lobby past museum-quality art, brilliant parrots, and . . . South African penguins (like we said, fantasy). It's not necessarily Hawaiian, but it is photogenic. At the southern end of Kā'anapali Beach, this resort is in the midst of the action. Also on the premises is Spa Moana, an oceanfront, full-service facility. ⊠ *200 Nohea Kai Dr., Kā'anapali 96761* ☎ *808/661–1234 or 800/233–1234* 🖷 *808/667–4199* ⊕ *www.maui. hyatt.com* ⤲ *815 rooms* ⅃ *4 restaurants, A/C, in-room data ports, in-room safes, cable TV with movies and video games, 2 18-hole golf courses, 6 tennis courts, pool, health club, spa, beach, 6 bars, library, children's programs (ages 3–12), no-smoking floors* ⊟ *AE, D, DC, MC, V.* *$275–$660.*

$$$$ ⊞ **Ritz-Carlton, Kapalua.** If butler-drawn baths and brocade drapery are ★ your cup of tea, book a room at this elegant hillside property. Not set immediately on the beach, the resort does command views of D. T. Fleming Beach, and Honolua Bay, and the three-level pool and two hot tubs are open 24 hours. The grounds have a private feel despite being in the midst of Kapalua's collection of hotels, shops, restaurants, and golf courses. A full-time cultural adviser, Clifford Nae'ole, educates employees and guests alike in Hawaiian traditions. Tuesday night Slack-key guitar performances are not to be missed. This is a great jumping-off point for golfers—privileges are available at three championship courses, and the island of Lāna'i with its two renowned courses is a quick ferry ride away. The dining is outstanding here; the decor needs some attention. ⊠ *1 Ritz-Carlton Dr., Kapalua 96761* ☎ *808/669–6200 or 800/262–*

WHERE TO STAY IN WEST MAUI

HOTEL NAME	Worth Noting	Cost $	Pools	Beach	Golf Course	Tennis Courts	Gym	Spa	Children Programs	Rooms	Restaurants	Other	Location
Hotels & Resorts													
5 Hyatt Regency Maui	130-ft water slide	275–660	1	yes	yes	6	yes	yes	3-12	815	4		Kā'anapali
8 Kā'anapali Beach Hotel	Hula & lei-making classes	185–610	1	yes	priv.					430	3		Kā'anapali
★ 1 Lahaina Inn	Historic property	125–175								12		no TVs	Lahaina
12 Mauian Hotel	On Nāpili Bay	145–195	1	yes						44		no TVs	Nāpili
★ 2 Plantation Inn	Gerard's restaurant	170–265	1							18	1		Lahaina
★ 14 Ritz-Carlton, Kapalua	Banyan Tree restaurant	395–705	1	yes	yes	10	yes	yes	5-12	548	3	shops	Kapalua
10 Royal Lahaina Resort	Cottage units available	280–790	3	yes	yes	11				592	3		Kā'anapali
★ 9 Sheraton Maui	Nightly torch-lighting ritual	360–640	1	yes		3	yes	yes	5-12	510	2		Kā'anapali
7 Westin Maui Resort	The Heavenly Spa	360–700	5	yes	priv.		yes	yes	0-12	761	3		Kā'anapali
Condos													
11 Aston at Papakea Resort	Cultural classes	200–600	2			4			5-12	364		kitchen	Honokowai
6 Kā'anapali Ali'i	Great location	360–760	2	yes	yes	6				264		kitchen	Kā'anapali
★ 13 Nāpili Kai Beach Club	Outstanding beach	200–700	4	yes					6-12	162		kitchen	Nāpili
B&Bs & Vacation Rentals													
3 Bambula Inn	Studio apartments	85–125								2		kitchen	Lahaina
★ 4 Ho'oilo House	Private outdoor showers	245	1							5		no kids	Lahaina

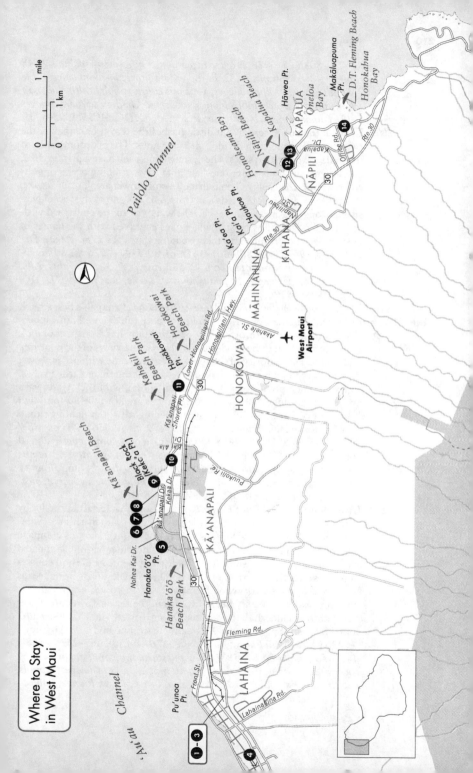

8440 ⌂ *808/665–0026* ⊕ *www.ritzcarlton.com/resorts/kapalua* ⏻ *548 rooms* ⌕ *3 restaurants, A/C, in-room data ports, in-room safes, cable TV with movies, golf privileges, 10 tennis courts, pool, health club, hair salon, massage, beach, lobby lounge, shops, spa, children's programs (ages 5–12), laundry service, business services* ⊟ *AE, D, DC, MC, V.* $395–$705.

$$$$ ⊞ **Royal Lahaina Resort.** What distinguishes the Royal Lahaina are the two-story cottages, each divided into four units. The bedrooms open to the trade winds on two sides. The upstairs units each have a private lānai, and downstairs units share one—all lānai have stunning ocean or golf-course views. The "deluxe" units in the 12-story tower aren't really deluxe; the property as a whole needs a revamp, but it's one of the less-expensive options on Kā'anapali Beach. The walkway to the courtyard wedding gazebo is lined with stepping-stones engraved with the names of past brides and grooms and their wedding dates. ⊠ *2780 Keka'a Dr., Kā'anapali 96761* ☎ *808/661–3611 or 800/447–6925* ⌂ *808/661–3538* ⊕ *www.hawaiihotels.com* ⏻ *592 rooms* ⌕ *3 restaurants, A/C, cable TV, golf privileges, 11 tennis courts, 3 pools, beach* ⊟ *AE, D, DC, MC, V.* $280–$790.

$$$$ ⊞ **Sheraton Maui.** Set among dense gardens on Kā'anapali's best stretch
Fodor'sChoice   of beach, the Sheraton offers a quieter, more understated atmosphere
★   than its neighboring resorts. The open-air lobby has a crisp, cool look with minimal furnishings and decor, and sweeping views of the pool area and beach. The majority of the spacious rooms come with ocean views; only one of the six buildings has rooms with mountain or garden views. The swimming pool looks like a natural lagoon, with rock waterways and wooden bridges. Best of all, the hotel sits next to the 80-foot-high "Black Rock," from which divers leap in a nightly torch-lighting ritual. ⊠ *2605 Kā'anapali Pkwy., Kā'anapali 97671* ☎ *808/661–0031 or 888/488–3535* ⌂ *808/661–0458* ⊕ *www.starwood.com/hawaii* ⏻ *510 rooms* ⌕ *2 restaurants, A/C, in-room safes, refrigerators, 3 tennis courts, pool, health club, hair salon, hot tub, spa, beach, lobby lounge, children's programs (ages 5–12), laundry facilities, Internet room, business services* ⊟ *AE, D, DC, MC, V.* $360–$640.

$$$$ ⊞ **The Westin Maui Resort & Spa.** The cascading waterfall in the lobby of this hotel gives way to an "aquatic playground" with five heated swimming pools, abundant waterfalls (15 at last count), lagoons complete with pink flamingos, and a premier beach. The water features combined with a spa and fitness center, and privileges at two 18-hole golf courses make this an active resort—great for families. Relaxation is by no means forgotten. Elegant dark-wood furnishings in the rooms accentuate the crisp linens of "Heavenly Beds." Rooms in the Beach Tower are newer but slightly smaller than those in the Ocean Tower. The 13,000-square-foot Heavenly Spa features 11 treatment rooms and a yoga studio. ⊠ *2365 Kā'anapali Pkwy., Kā'anapali 96761* ☎ *808/667–2525 or 888/488–3535* ⌂ *808/661–5831* ⊕ *www.starwood.com/hawaii* ⏻ *761 rooms* ⌕ *3 restaurants, cable TV with movies, golf privileges, 5 pools, health club, hair salon, 3 hot tubs, spa, beach, lobby lounge, babysit-*

ting, children's programs (infant–12), Internet, meeting rooms ⊟ AE, D, DC, MC, V. $360–$700.

$$$–$$$$ ⊞ **Kā'anapali Beach Hotel.** This attractive, old-fashioned hotel is full of aloha. Locals say that it's one of the few resorts on the island where visitors can get a true Hawaiian experience. The vintage-style Mixed Plate restaurant, known locally for its native cuisine program, has displays honoring the many cultural traditions represented by the staff: the employees themselves contributed the artifacts. The spacious rooms are simply decorated in wicker and rattan and face the beach beyond the courtyard. There are complimentary classes in authentic hula dancing, lei-making, and 'ukulele playing. ⊠ 2525 Kā'anapali Pkwy., Kā'anapali 96761 ☎ 808/661–0011 or 800/262–8450 ☏ 808/667–5978 ⊕ www. kbhmaui.com ⇨ 430 rooms ↺ 3 restaurants, A/C, in-room safes, cable TV with movies, golf privileges, pool, beach, lobby lounge ⊟ AE, D, DC, MC, V. $185–$610.

★ **$$$–$$$$** ⊞ **Plantation Inn.** Charm sets this inn apart, tucked into a corner of a busy street in the heart of Lahaina. Filled with Victorian and Asian furnishings, it's reminiscent of a southern plantation home. Secluded lānai draped with hanging plants face a central courtyard, pool, and a garden pavilion perfect for morning coffee. Each guest room or suite is decorated differently, with hardwood floors, French doors, slightly dowdy antiques, and four-poster beds. (We think number 10 is nicest.) Suites have kitchenettes and whirlpool baths. A generous breakfast is included in the room rate, and one of Hawai'i's best French restaurants, Gerard's, is on-site. Breakfast, coupled with free parking in downtown Lahaina makes this a truly great value, even if it's 10-minutes from the beach. ⊠ 174 Lahainaluna Rd., Lahaina 96761 ☎ 808/667–9225 or 800/ 433–6815 ☏ 808/667–9293 ⊕ www.theplantationinn.com ⇨ 18 rooms ↺ Restaurant, A/C, fans, refrigerators, cable TV, pool, hot tub ⊟ AE, MC, V. $170–$265.

★ **$$–$$$** ⊞ **Lahaina Inn.** This antique jewel right in the heart of town is classic Lahaina—a two-story wooden building that will transport you back to the turn of the 20th century. The nine small rooms and three suites shine with authentic period furnishings, including quilted bedcovers, antique lamps, and Oriental carpets. You can while away the hours in a wicker chair on your balcony, sipping coffee and watching Old Lahaina town come to life. An excellent continental breakfast is served in the parlor and the renowned restaurant, David Paul's, is downstairs. ⊠ 127 Lahainaluna Rd., Lahaina 96761 ☎ 808/661–0577 or 800/669–3444 ☏ 808/667–9480 ⊕ www.lahainainn.com ⇨ 9 rooms, 3 suites ↺ A/C, Internet room; no room TVs, no smoking, ⊟ AE, D, MC, V. $125–$175.

$$–$$$ ⊞ **Mauian Hotel.** If you're looking for a quiet place to stay, this nostalgic hotel way out in Napīli may be for you. The rooms have neither TVs nor phones—such noisy devices are relegated to the 'Ohana Room, where a continental breakfast is served daily. The simple two-story buildings date from 1959, but have been renovated with bright islander furnishings, including conveniently equipped kitchens. Best of all, the 2-acre property opens out onto lovely Napili Bay. ⊠ *5441 Lower Honoapi'ilani Hwy., Napili 96761* ☎ *808/669–6205 or 800/367–5034* 🖨 *808/669–0129* ⊕ *www.mauian.com* ➣ *44 rooms* ♿ *A/C, kitchens, pool, beach, hair salon, shuffleboard, laundry facilities, Internet; no room phones, no room TVs* 🖃 *AE, D, MC, V. $145–$195.*

Condos

$$$$ ⊞ **Kā'anapali Ali'i.** Yes, this is a condominium, but you'd never know it: the four 11-story buildings are put together so well you still have the feeling of seclusion. Instead of tiny rooms you can choose between ample one- and two-bedroom apartments. Each has great amenities: a chaise in an alcove, a bidet, a sunken living room, a whirlpool, and a separate dining room—though some of the furnishings are dated. The Kā'anapali Ali'i is maintained like a hotel, with daily maid service, an activities desk, and a 24-hour front desk. ⊠ *50 Nohea Kai Dr., Kā'anapali 96761* ☎ *808/667–1400 or 800/642–6284* 🖨 *808/661–1025* ⊕ *www.classicresorts.com* ➣ *264 units* ♿ *A/C, in-room safes, kitchens, 18-hole golf course, 6 tennis courts, 2 pools, sauna, beach, laundry facilities* 🖃 *AE, D, DC, MC, V. 1-bedroom $360–$540, 2-bedroom $490–$760.*

$$$–$$$$ ⊞ **Aston at Papakea Resort.** Although this oceanfront condominium has no beach, there are several close by. And with classes on swimming, snorkeling, pineapple cutting, and more, you'll have plenty to keep you busy. Papakea has built-in privacy because its units are spread out among 11 low-rise buildings on some 13 acres of land; bamboo-lined walkways between buildings and fish-stocked ponds add to the serenity. Fully equipped kitchens and laundry facilities make longer stays easy here. ⊠ *3543 Lower Honoapi'ilani Hwy., Honokowai 96761* ☎ *808/669–4848 or 800/922–7866* 🖨 *808/922–8785* ⊕ *www.aston-hotels.com* ➣ *364 units* ♿ *A/C, kitchens, putting green, 4 tennis courts, 2 pools, hot tub, sauna, children's programs (ages 5–12), laundry facilities* 🖃 *AE, MC, V. Studios $200–$225, 1-bedroom $245–$290, 2-bedroom $450–$550.*

★ $$$–$$$$ ⊞ **Nāpili Kai Beach Club.** On 10 beautiful beachfront acres—the beach here is one of the best on the West Side for swimming and snorkeling— the Nāpili Kai draws a loyal following. Hawaiian-style rooms are done in sea-foam green, mauve, and

---

GROCERIES & TAKEOUT

Foodland. This large grocery store should have everything you need, including video rentals and a Starbucks. ⊠ *Old Lahaina Center, 845 Waine'e St., Lahaina* ☎ *808/661–0975.*

Gaby's Pizzeria and Deli. The friendly folks here will toss a pie for takeout. ⊠ *505 Front St., Lahaina* ☎ *808/661-8112.*

The Maui Fish Market. It's worth stopping by this little fish market for an oyster or a cup of fresh fish chowder. You can also get live lobsters and fillets marinated for your barbecue. ⊠ *4405 Lwr. Honoapi'ilani Hwy., Honokowai* ☎ *808/665-9895.*

rattan; shoji doors open onto your lānai, with the beach and ocean right outside. The rooms closest to the beach have no air-conditioning, but ceiling fans usually suffice. "Hotel" rooms have only mini-refrigerators and coffeemakers, while studios and suites have fully equipped kitchenettes. This is a family-friendly place, with children's programs and free classes in hula and lei-making. Packages that include a car, breakfast, and other extras are available if you stay five nights or longer. ✉ *5900 Lower Honoapi'ilani Hwy., Nāpili 96761* ☎ *808/669–6271 or 800/367–5030* 🖷 *808/669–5740* ⊕ *www.napilikai.com* 🛏 *162 units* ⚒ *A/C in some rooms, in-room data ports, fans, kitchenettes, cable TV, 2 putting greens, 4 pools, exercise equipment, hot tub, beach, shuffleboard, children's programs (ages 6–12), dry cleaning, concierge* ☰ *AE, MC, V. Hotel Room $200–$290, Studios $250–$325, 1-bedroom $385–$450, 2-bedroom $555–$700.*

B&Bs & Vacation Rentals

$$$$
Fodor'sChoice
★

🖾 **Ho'oilo House.** If you really want to treat yourself to a luxurious getaway, spend a few nights at this Bali-inspired B&B. In the foothills of the West Maui Mountains, just south of Lahaina town, this stunning property brings the words "quiet perfection" to mind. As you enter the house your eye is immediately drawn to the immense glass doors that open up onto a small but sparkling pool and a breathtaking view of the Pacific. Almost all of the furnishings and the materials used to build the house were imported from Bali, giving the house a peaceful, Zen-like quality. Two "conversation tables" in the common area are filled with Balinese cushions, providing great spots to snack, chat, or just relax. Each room is uniquely decorated and features traditional Balinese doors with Mother of Pearl inlay, a custom bed, a private lānai, a huge bathroom with a giant bathtub, and best of all—a private outdoor shower. ✉ *138 Awaiku St., Lahaina 96761* ☎ *808/667–6669* 🖷 *808/661–7857* ⊕ *www.hooilohouse.com* 🛏 *5 rooms* ⚒ *A/C, fans, Wi-Fi, in-room safes, cable TV, pool, massage; no kids, no smoking* ☰ *AE, MC, V. $245, 3-night minimum.*

$–$$
🖾 **Bambula Inn.** This casual sprawling house in a quiet Lahaina residential area has two studio apartments, one attached to the house and one freestanding. No breakfast is served; this is a move-in-and-hang-out beach house. Just across the street is a small beach, and moored just offshore is a sailboat hand-built by the owner. He likes to take his guests out for whale-watching and sunset sails, no charge. He also provides snorkel equipment. This is a friendly, easygoing way to visit Lahaina. ✉ *518 Ilikahi St., Lahaina 96761* ☎ *808/667–6753 or 800/544–5524* 🖷 *808/667–0979* ⊕ *www.bambula.com* 🛏 *2 studios* ⚒ *A/C in some rooms, fans, kitchens, kitchenettes, cable TV* ☰ *AE, D, MC, V. $85–$125.*

he South Shore

The South Shore is composed of two main communities: resort-filled Wailea and down-to-earth Kīhei. In general, the farther south you go, the fancier the accommodations get. ■ **TIP→→ North Kīhei tends to have great prices but north-end beaches are typically windy and scattered with seaweed. (Not a problem if you don't mind driving 5 to 10 minutes to save a few bucks.) As you** travel down South Kīhei Road, you can find condos both on and off inviting beach parks, and close to shops and restaurants. Once you hit Wailea, the opulence quotient takes a giant leap—perfectly groomed resorts gather around Wailea and Polo beaches. This resort wonderland mimics (some say improves upon) Kāʻanapali. The two communities continuously compete over which is more exclusive and which has better weather—in our opinion it's a definite draw.

Hotels & Resorts

$$$$
FodorsChoice
★

Fairmont Kea Lani Hotel Suites & Villas. Gleaming white spires and tiled archways are the hallmark of this stunning resort. Spacious suites have microwaves, stereos, and marble bathrooms. But the villas are the real lure. Each is two-story, has a private plunge pool, two (or three) large bedrooms, a laundry room, and a fully equipped kitchen—BBQ and margarita blender included. Best of all, maid service does the dishes. A fantastic haven for families, the villas are side by side in a sort of miniature neighborhood. Request one on the end, with an upstairs sundeck. The resort offers good dining choices, a gourmet deli, and a small, almost private beach. ⊠ *4100 Wailea Alanui Dr., Wailea 96753* ☎ *808/875–4100 or 800/882–4100* ⊟ *808/875–1200* ⊕ *www.kealani.com* ⇆ *413 suites, 37 villas* △ *3 restaurants, A/C, in-room data ports, microwaves, refrigerators, in-room VCRs, golf privileges, 3 pools, health club, hair salon, 2 hot tubs, spa, beach, lobby lounge, shops, children's programs (ages 5–12)* ⊟ *AE, D, DC, MC, V. Suites $385–$665, villas $1,600–$,2800.*

$$$$
FodorsChoice
★

Four Seasons Resort. Impeccably stylish, subdued, and relaxing describe most Four Seasons properties; this one fronting award-winning Wailea beach is no exception. Thoughtful luxuries—like Evian spritzers poolside and room-service attendants who toast your bread in-room—earned this Maui favorite its reputation. The property has an understated elegance, with beautiful floral arrangements, courtyards, and private cabanas. Most rooms have an ocean view (avoid those over the parking lot in the North Tower) and you can find terry robes and whole-bean coffee grinders in each. Choose between three excellent restaurants, including Wolfgang Puck's Spago. The recently renovated spa is small but expertly staffed. Honeymooners: request Suite 301, with it's round tub and private lawn. ⊠ *3900 Wailea Alanui Dr., Wailea 96753* ☎ *808/874–8000 or 800/334–6284* ⊟ *808/874–6449* ⊕ *www.fourseasons.com/maui* ⇆ *380 rooms* △ *3 restaurants, A/C, in-room data ports, in-room safes, refrigerators, cable TV with movies and video games, golf privileges, 2 tennis courts, pool, health club, spa, beach, bicycles, badminton, croquet, volleyball, 3 bars, recreation room, children's programs (ages 5–12)* ⊟ *AE, D, DC, MC, V. $365–$890.*

$$$$

Grand Wailea. "Grand" is no exaggeration for this opulent sunny, 40-acre resort. Elaborate water features include a "canyon riverpool" with slides, caves, a tarzan swing, and a water elevator. Tropical garden paths meander past artwork by Léger, Warhol, Picasso, Botero, and noted Hawaiian artists—sculptures even hide in waterfalls. Spacious ocean-view rooms are outfitted with stuffed chaises, comfortable desks, and oversize marble bathrooms. Spa Grande, the island's most comprehensive spa facility, offers you everything from mineral baths to massage. For kids, Camp Grande has a full-size soda fountain, game room, and movie theater. Although not the place to go for quiet or especially attentive service, the property is astounding. ✉ *3850 Wailea Alanui Dr., Wailea 96753* ☎ *808/875–1234 or 800/888–6100* 🖷 *808/ 874–2442* ⊕ *www.grandwailea.com* ⤳ *779 rooms* ☖ *5 restaurants, A/C, in-room data ports, in-room safes, cable TV with movies, golf privileges, 3 pools, health club, hair salon, indoor and outdoor hot tubs, spa, beach, racquetball, 6 bars, nightclub, recreation room, shops, children's programs (ages 5–12)* ▱ *AE, D, DC, MC, V. $485–$805.*

$$$$ 🏨 **Marriott Wailea Resort.** The Marriott (formerly the Outrigger) was built before current construction laws were put in place, so rooms sit much closer to the crashing surf than at most resorts. Wailea Beach is a few steps away, as are the Shops at Wailea. The tropical lobby and interior spaces showcase a remarkable collection of Hawaiian and Pacific Rim artifacts. All of the spacious rooms have private lānai and are styled with a tropical theme. There are golf privileges at three nearby courses, as well as tennis privileges at the Wailea Tennis Club. The Mandara Spa provides beauty and relaxation treatments as well as massage. Although not as fancy as its neighbors, this resort is a solid deal for Wailea—especially if you take advantage of package deals. ✉ *3700 Wailea Alanui Dr., Wailea 96753* ☎ *808/879–1922 or 800/922–7866* 🖷 *808/874–8331* ⊕ *www.marriotthawaii.com* ⤳ *516 rooms* ☖ *3 restaurants, A/C, in-room data ports, in-room safes, cable TV with video games, golf privileges, 3 pools, hair salon, 2 hot tubs, spa, beach, children's programs (ages 5–12), dry cleaning, laundry service, business services* ▱ *AE, D, DC, MC, V. $319–$379.*

★ $$$$ 🏨 **Maui Prince.** This isn't the most luxurious resort on the South Shore— it could actually use a face lift—but it has many pluses that more than make up for the somewhat dated decor. The location is superb. Just south of Makena, the hotel is on a secluded piece of land surrounded by two magnificent golf courses and abuts a beautiful, near-private beach. The pool area is simple (two round pools), but surrounded by beautiful gardens that are quiet and understated compared to the other big resorts. The attention given to service is apparent from the minute you walk into the open-air lobby—the staff is excellent. Rooms on five levels all have ocean views (in varying degrees) and surround the courtyard, which has a Japanese garden with a bubbling stream. ✉ *5400 Mākena Alanui Rd., Mākena 96753* ☎ *808/874–1111 or 800/321–6284* 🖷 *808/879–8763* ⊕ *www.princeresortshawaii.com* ⤳ *310 rooms* ☖ *4 restaurants, A/C, in-room safes, some in-room VCRs, 2 18-hole golf courses, 6 tennis courts, 2 pools, exercise equipment, hot tub, beach, badminton, croquet, shuffleboard, children's programs (ages 5–12), business services, meeting rooms* ▱ *AE, DC, MC, V. $335–$525.*

$$$$ 🏨 **Renaissance Wailea Beach Resort.** Most of the rooms here are positioned on fantastic Mōkapu Beach. A giant ceremonial canoe enhances the lobby area. Outside, you can find exotic gardens, waterfalls, and reflecting ponds. A decent value package offers discounts at the restaurants and the hotel's own lūʻau, performed on-site three nights a week. The VIP Mōkapu Beach Club building has 26 luxury accommodations closest to the beach, and its own concierge, pool, and beach cabanas.

WHERE TO STAY ON THE SOUTH SHORE

HOTEL NAME	Worth Noting	Cost $	Pools	Beach	Golf Course	Tennis Courts	Gym	Spa	Children Programs	Rooms	Restaurants	Other	Location
Hotels & Resorts													
★ ❷ Fairmont Kea Lani Hotel	Villas available	385–665	3	yes	priv.		yes	yes	5–12	450	3	shops	Wailea
★ ❸ Four Seasons Resort	Luxurious	365–890	1	yes	priv.	2	yes	yes	5–12	380	3		Wailea
❹ Grand Wailea	Spa Grande	485–805	3	yes	priv.		yes	yes	5–12	779	5	shops	Wailea
★ ❿ Mana Kai Maui	Great prices	100–310	1	yes						98	1		Kihei
❺ Marriott Wailea Resort	Package deals avail.	319–379	3	yes	priv.			yes	5–12	516	3		Wailea
⓬ Maui Coast Hotel	Beach across the street	145–235	1			2				379	2		Kihei
⓮ Maui Lu Resort	50 rooms on beach	139–225	1	yes		2				120			Kihei
★ ❶ Maui Prince	Secluded beach	335–525	2	yes	yes	6			5–12	310	4		Mākena
❻ Renaissance Wailea	VIP club available	309–419	2	yes			yes		5–12	345	3		Wailea
Condos													
⓫ Kama'ole Sands	Beach across the street	195–485	1			4				309	1	kitchen	Kihei
⓭ Luana Kai	Poolside BBQs	99–269	1			4				113		no A/C	Kihei
⓯ Maui Sunseeker Resort	Beach across the street	115–165								4		kitchen	Kihei
★ ❼ Wailea Villas	6 resort villages available	200–730	6	yes	priv.	4				270		kitchen	Wailea
B&Bs & Vacation Rentals													
❽ Amanda and George's	1-BR suite	120	2			4				1		kitchen	Wailea
❾ Eva Villa	360° views from rooftop	130–150	1							3		kitchen	Wailea

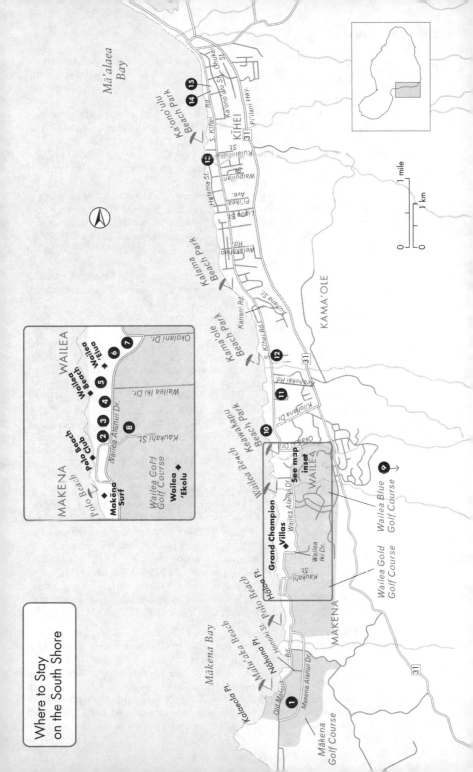

Where to Stay
on the South Shore

Mōkapu Beach Club guests also have access to nearby golf and tennis facilities. ⊠ *3550 Wailea Alanui Dr., Wailea 96753* ☎ *808/879–4900 or 800/992–4532* 🖷 *808/874–6128* ⊕ *www.renaissancehotels.com* ⏎ *345 rooms* ⚫ *3 restaurants, A/C, in-room data ports, refrigerators, cable TV with movies and video games, 2 pools, health club, hot tub, beach, basketball, Ping-Pong, shuffleboard, lobby lounge, children's programs (ages 5–12)* ▭ *AE, D, DC, MC, V. $309–$419.*

$$–$$$$ 🏨 **Maui Coast Hotel.** You might never notice this elegant hotel because it's set back off the street. The standard rooms are fine—very clean and modern—but the best deal is to pay a little more for one of the suites. In these you'll get an enjoyable amount of space and jet nozzles in the bathtub. You can sample nightly entertainment by the large, heated pool or workout in the new fitness center until 10 PM. The 6-mi-long stretch of Kamaʻole Beach I, II, and III is across the street. ⊠ *2259 S. Kīhei Rd., Kīhei 96753* ☎ *808/874–6284, 800/895–6284, or 800/426–0670* 🖷 *808/ 875–4731* ⊕ *www.westcoasthotels.com* ⏎ *265 rooms, 114 suites* ⚫ *2 restaurants, A/C, in-room safes, refrigerators, cable TV with movies, 2 tennis courts, pool, exercise equipment, 2 hot tubs, dry cleaning, laundry service* ▭ *AE, D, DC, MC, V. $145–$235.*

$–$$$$ 🏨 **Mana Kai Maui.** This unsung hero of South Maui hotels may be older,
Fodor'sChoice   but that only means it's closer to the beach—beautiful Keawakapu.
★   Hotel rooms with air-conditioning are remarkably affordable for the location. Two-room condos with private lānais benefit from the hotel amenities, such as daily maid service and discounts at the oceanfront restaurant downstairs. Shoji screens and bamboo furniture complement the marvelous ocean views, which in winter are punctuated by the visiting humpback whales. ⊠ *2960 S. Kīhei Rd., Kīhei 96753* ☎ *808/ 879–2778 or 800/367–5242* 🖷 *808/879–7825* ⊕ *www.crhmaui.com* ⏎ *49 hotel rooms, 49 1-bedroom condos* ⚫ *Restaurant, in-room safes, refrigerators, cable TV, pool, hair salon, hot tub, beach, meeting rooms* ▭ *AE, D, DC, MC, V. Hotel rooms $100–$135, condos $180–$310.*

$$–$$$$ 🏨 **Maui Lu Resort.** This was the first hotel in Kīhei; the main lobby was the summer home of the original owner, a Canadian logger. Over the years the Maui Lu has added numerous wooden buildings and cottages to its 28 acres. It's a little reminiscent of a rustic lodge and shows wear, but the rooms are comfortable and some face a relatively private North Kīhei beach. Of the 120 rooms, 50 are on the beach. The rest are across South Kīhei Road on the main property. ⊠ *575 S. Kīhei Rd., Kīhei 96753* ☎ *808/879–5881 or 800/922–7866* 🖷 *808/879–4627* ⊕ *www.aston-hotels.com* ⏎ *120 rooms* ⚫ *A/C, in-room safes, refrigerators, 2 tennis courts, pool, beach* ▭ *AE, D, DC, MC, V. $139–$225.*

Condos

$$$–$$$$ 🏨 **Kamaʻole Sands.** "Kam" Sands is a good choice for the active traveler; there are tennis and volleyball courts to keep you in shape, and the ideal family beach (Kamaʻole III) waits across the street. Eleven four-story buildings wrap around 15 acres of grassy slopes with swimming pools, a small waterfall, and BBQs. Condos are equipped with modern conveniences, but there's a relaxed, almost retro feel to the place. All units have kitchens, laundry facilities, and private lānai. The property has a 24-hour front desk and an activities desk. ■ TIP→→ (**Attention homeowners:** privately owned house-trade options are available at www.kamaole-sands.com.) ⊠ *2695 S. Kīhei Rd., Kīhei 96753* ☎ *808/874–8700 or 800/367–5004* 🖷 *808/879–3273* ⊕ *www.castleresorts.com/KSM* ↻ *309 units* ♨ *Restaurant, A/C in some rooms, fans, in-room data ports, kitchens, some cable TV, some in-room VCRs, 4 tennis courts, pool, 2 hot tubs, wading pool, volleyball* ⊟ *AE, D, DC, MC, V. 1-bedroom $195–$275, 2-bedroom $275–$375, 3-bedroom $485.*

★ **$$$–$$$$** ▥ **Wailea Villas.** The Wailea Resort started out with three fine condominiums named, appropriately, Wailea ʻEkahi, Wailea ʻElua, and Wailea ʻEkolu (Wailea One, Two, and Three). Since then, Wailea has added the Grand Champions Villas, and the adjoining Mākena Resort has built Mākena Surf and Polo Beach Club. All have large units (ranging from studios to three-bedroom apartments) with exceptional views and access to five of the island's best beaches. The Wailea ʻElua Village, Polo Beach Club, and Mākena Surf are the more luxurious properties, with rates to match. ⊠ *3750 Wailea Alanui Dr., Wailea 96753* ☎ *808/879–1595 or 800/367–5246* 🖷 *808/874–3554* ⊕ *www.drhmaui.com* ↻ *270 units* ♨ *A/C, fans, kitchens, cable TV, some in-room VCRs, 6 pools, 2 hot tubs, 4 tennis courts, beach, golf privileges, laundry facilities* ⊟ *AE, MC, V. Studios $200, 1-bedroom $185–$455, 2-bedroom $235–$730.*

$–$$$$ ▥ **Luana Kai.** Here's a prime example of a condominium-by-the-sea, perfect for setting up house for at least four nights (the required minimum). There are three different room plans, suited for couples, families, or friends traveling together. Each one comes with everything you need to make yourself at home—a fully equipped kitchen, dishwasher, laundry, TV, VCR, and stereo equipment. The pool area is a social place, with five gas grills, a full outdoor kitchen, and Jacuzzis. The beach is a ways down the road, but the property adjoins a grassy county park with tennis courts. ⊠ *940 S. Kīhei Rd., Kīhei 96753* ☎ *808/879–1268 or 800/669–1127* 🖷 *808/879–1455* ⊕ *www.luanakai.com* ↻ *113 units* ♨ *BBQs, fans, kitchens, in-room VCRs, putting green, 4 tennis courts, pool, hot tub, shuffleboard; no A/C* ⊟ *AE, DC, MC, V. 1-bedroom $99–$129, 2-bedroom $119–$169, 3-bedroom $219–$269; 4-night minimum.*

$$–$$$ ▥ **Maui Sunseeker Resort.** This small North Kīhei hotel is a great value for the area and is private and relaxed. You can opt for a simple but attractively furnished studio, one-bedroom, or two-bedroom penthouse; all have kitchenettes and full baths, as well as BBQs. The 4-mi stretch of

---

APARTMENT RENTALS

Besides the condos listed here, which operate like hotels and offer hotel-like amenities, Maui has condos you can rent through central booking agents. Most agents represent more than one condo complex (some handle single-family homes as well), so be specific about what kind of price, space, facilities, and amenities you want. The following are multiproperty agents: **Destination Resorts** (⊠ 3750 Wailea Alanui Dr., Wailea 96753 ☎ 800/367–5246 ⊕ www.drhmaui.com). **Maui Windsurfari** (⊠ 425 Koloa St., Kahului 96732 ☎ 808/871-7766 or 800/736-6284 ⊕ www.windsurfari.com).

beach across the street isn't the best for swimming, but it's great for strolling and watching windsurfers, whales (in winter), and sunsets. ⊠ *551 S. Kīhei Rd., Kīhei 96753* ☎ *808/879–1261 or 800/532–6284* 🖷 *808/874–3877* ⊕ *www.mauisunseeker.com* 🛏 *4 units* ☒ *A/C, kitchenettes, cable TV, some in-room VCRs, hot tub, laundry facilities, Internet room* ⊟ *MC, V. Studios $115, 1-bedroom $135, 2-bedroom $165; 3-night minimum.*

B&Bs & Vacation Rentals

$$ 🏠 **Amanda and George's Wonderful Wailea Condominium.** Exceptionally tasteful decor (king-size bed, leather couch, lovely artwork) makes this one-bedroom suite feel like royal accommodations. The views are nice, but the location is outstanding—on the Blue golf course, it's a quick drive (or 7-minute jog) to South Maui's best beaches, restaurants, and shops. The kitchen and bathroom are luxuriously supplied and spotless. Amenities include use of the two pools and Jacuzzis and access to the famed Wailea Tennis Club. ⊠ *At Grand Champions, Wailea Ike Pl. #25, Wailea 96753* ☎ *808/891–2214* ⊕ *www.travelmaui.com/condo rental/wailea* 🛏 *1 suite* ☒ *A/C, fans, kitchen, cable TV, 2 pools, 2 hot tubs, 4 tennis courts, BBQ, laundry facilities; no smoking* ⊟ *No credit cards. $120, 5-night minimum.*

$$ 🏠 **Eva Villa.** The waterfall and lilies at this elegant B&B's entrance instantly remind you that you're on vacation. In the residential neighborhood above Wailea, Eva Villa is both quiet and welcoming. Three modern, 600-square-foot suites come furnished with queen-size beds and sleeper sofas, kitchens stocked with continental breakfasts, and access to the pool and Jacuzzi. Rick and Dale Pounds, the congenial owners who live on-property, even provide guests with a farewell CD of island photos and music. The real treasure, however, is the 360-degree ocean and mountain view from the rooftop patio, accompanied by a telescope. ⊠ *815 Kumulani Dr., Wailea 96753* ☎ *808/874–6407* ⊕ *www.mauibnb.com* 🛏 *3 suites* ☒ *BBQ, fans, kitchens, cable TV, pool, hot tub, laundry facilities, Internet room. $130–$150.*

> ### GROCERIES & VIDEO RENTALS
>
> **Eskimo Candy.** Stop here for fresh fish or fish-and-chips. ⊠ *2665 Wai Wai Pl., Kīhei* ☎ *808/879–5686.*
>
> **Premiere Video.** With two locations, this is the best video store around. ⊠ *North Kīhei, 357 Huku Lii Pl.* ☎ *808/875–0500* ☒ *South Kīhei, 2439 S. Kīhei Rd.* ☎ *808/875–1113.*
>
> **Safeway.** Find every variety of grocery at this giant superstore. ⊠ *277 Piikea Ave., Kīhei* ☎ *808/891–9120.*
>
> **Who Cut the Cheese.** This shop has great party foods: *fromage,* fancy balsamics, and wines. ⊠ *Azeka Marketplace, 1279 S. Kīhei Rd., Suite 309* ☎ *808/874–3930.*

Central Maui

Kahului and Wailuku, the industrial centers that make up Central Maui, are not known for their lavish accommodations. The exceptions, of course, make the rule, and the few listed below meet some travelers' needs perfectly.

FAMILY REUNION HEADQUARTERS

For adventurous families, the lovely cottage at **Peace of Maui** (✉ 1290 Hali'imaile Rd., Hali'imaile ☎ 808/572–5045 or 888/475–5045 ⊕ www.peaceofmaui.com) makes a great HQ, while extended family members can stay in the main house, or "lodge." The casual digs are affordable and less than 15 minutes from most everything (on the North Shore, that is). We can't say enough about the friendliness of the owners here—you'll want to adopt them into your family. Call far in advance to make sure you can rent the whole shebang.

Kama'ole Sands (✉ 2695 S. Kīhei Rd., Kīhei 96753 ☎ 808/874–8700 or 800/367–5004 ⊕ www.castleresorts.com/KSM) is an easy spot for launching family activities. Two-bedroom units have everything a family needs: kitchens, laundry facilities, and pool access. The complex is across the street from Kam III beach park to boot—a great place for family barbecues, Frisbee championships, or kite-flying contests.

On the other end of the spectrum there are the villas at the **Fairmont Kea Lani** (✉ 4100 Wailea Alanui Dr., Wailea ☎ 808/875–4100 or 800/882–4100 ⊕ www.kealani.com). Twice as luxurious (and about six times more costly), a two-story villa is a posh hang out zone for the family. In-laws and cousins can book suites, while activities focus around the villa with its fully equipped kitchen, plunge pool, and BBQ.

B&Bs & Vacation Rentals

$$–$$$
Fodor'sChoice
★
Old Wailuku Inn. This historic home, built in 1924, may be the ultimate Hawaiian B&B. Each room is decorated with the theme of a Hawaiian flower, and the flower motif is worked into the heirloom Hawaiian quilt on each bed. Other features include 10-foot ceilings, floors of native hardwoods, and (depending on the room) some delightful bathtubs. The first-floor rooms have private gardens. A hearty breakfast is included. ✉ 2199 Kaho'okele St., Wailuku 96793 ☎ 808/244–5897 or 800/305–4899 ⊕ www.mauiinn.com ➫ 7 rooms ᏛA/C, in-room data ports, some cable TV, in-room VCRs, library, business services ⊟AE, D, DC, MC, V. $120–$180.

¢
Banana Bungalow Maui Hostel. A typical lively and cosmopolitan hostel, Banana Bungalow offers the cheapest accommodations on the island. Private rooms have one queen or two single beds; bathrooms are down the hall. Dorm rooms are available for $22 per night. Free daily tours to waterfalls, beaches, and Haleakalā Crater make this a stellar deal. (Yes, the tours are *free*.) The property's amenities include free high-speed Internet access in the common room, kitchen privileges, a Jacuzzi, and banana trees ripe for the picking. Tucked in an out-of-the-way corner of Wailuku, the old building has splendid mountain views. ✉ 310 N. Market St., Wailuku 96793 ☎ 808/244–5090 or 800/846–7835 ⊕ www.mauihostel.com ➫ 38 rooms ᏛBBQ, kitchen, laundry facilities, Internet; no A/C ⊟MC, V. Dorm rooms $22, private rooms $44–$66.

Upcountry

Upcountry accommodations (those in Kula, Makawao, and Hali'imaile) are on country estates and are generally small, privately owned vacation rentals, or B&Bs. At high elevation, these lodgings offer splendid views of the island, temperate weather, and a "getting away from it all" feel. Which is actually the case—most shops and restaurants are a fair drive away, and beaches even farther. You will definitely need a car here.

Hotels & Resorts

$$–$$$ ☷ **Kula Lodge.** This hotel isn't exactly typical for Hawai'i: the lodge inexplicably resembles a chalet in the Swiss Alps, and two units even have gas fireplaces. Charming and cozy in spite of the nontropical ambience, it's a good spot for a romantic stay. Units are in two wooden cabins; four have lofts in addition to the ample bed space downstairs. On 3 acres, the lodge has startling views of Haleakalā and two coasts, enhanced by the surrounding tropical gardens. The property has an art gallery and a protea store that will pack flowers for you to take home. ⊠ *Haleakalā Hwy., Rte. 377 ⬦ R.R. 1, Box 475, Kula 96790 ☎ 808/878–2517 or 800/233–1535 ᕊ 808/878–2518 ⊕ www.kulalodge.com ➾ 5 units ⚬ Restaurant, shop; no A/C, no room phones, no room TVs ⊟ AE, MC, V. $110–$165.*

B&Bs & Vacation Rentals

★ $$$$ ☷ **Aloha Cottages.** The two secluded cottages on this property, the Bali Bungalow and the Thai Treehouse, are perfect for honeymooners or anyone else seeking a romantic getaway. The property abounds with lush tropical greenery allowing each cottage complete privacy. Intricate woodwork and furnishings, all imported from Bali, give the interiors an exotic feel. Each cottage has a large comfortable bed, fully equipped kitchen, and outdoor hot tub on a private lānai. Ranjana, your hostess, is happy to assist you with planning activities and booking restaurants. She can also arrange for a private massage, yoga lessons, or even a candlelight dinner in the "Lotus House" on the property. The restaurants and shops of Makawao are a short drive away. ⊠ *1879 Olinda Rd., Makawao 96768 ☎ 808/573–8500 ⊕ www.alohacottage.com ➾ 2 rooms ⚬ Fans, kitchens, in-room data ports, cable TV, in-room VCRs, outdoor hot tubs; no A/C, no kids, no smoking ⊟ MC, V ☞ $245–$275, 3-night minimum.*

$$–$$$$ ☷ **Olinda Country Cottages & Inn.** This restored Tudor home and adjacent cottages are so far up Olinda Road above Makawao you'll keep thinking you must have passed them. The Inn, which sits amid an 8½-acre protea farm surrounded by forest and some wonderful hiking trails, has five accommodations: two upstairs bedrooms with private baths; the downstairs Pineapple Sweet; a romantic cottage, which looks like a dollhouse from the outside; and best of all, Hidden Cottage, which has a private hot tub. Bring warm clothes—the mountain air can be chilly. Breakfast is served in the common living room. ⊠ *2660 Olinda Rd., Olinda 96768 ☎☎ 808/572–1453 ᕊ 800/932–3435 ⊕ www.mauibnbcottages.com ➾ 3 rooms, 2 cottages ⚬ Some cable TV; no A/C, no smoking ⊟ No credit cards. $140–$245, 2- to 3-night minimum.*

$$$ ⌂ **The Star Lookout.** Hidden away halfway up Haleakalā, this charming 100 year-old perch is an ideal getaway. With a view of most of the Valley Isle, this retreat is remote, serene, and deliciously temperate—you'll want to snuggle up, rather than blast the A/C. Up to six people can be accommodated in this inventively designed house, but four is more comfortable, and two is downright romantic. Snipping a few fresh herbs from the garden will make cooking while on vacation all the more fun. ⊠ *622 Thompson Rd., Keokea* ☎ *907/346–8028* ⊕ *www.starlookout. com* ⌕ *1 house* ⚲ *Kitchen, cable TV, in-room VCR, hot tub; no A/C* ☰ *No credit cards. $200.*

> **GROCERIES & VIDEO RENTALS**
>
> Head to **Pukalani Terrace Center** (⊠ 55 Pukalani St., Pukalani) for pizza, a bank, post office, hardware store, and Starbucks. There's also a **Foodland** (☎ 808/572-0674), which has fresh sushi and a good seafood section in addition to the usual grocery store fare, and **Paradise Video** (☎ 808/572-6200).

$$–$$$ ⌂ **Bloom Cottage.** The name comes from the abundance of roses and other flowers that surround this well-run, classic B&B. The property consists of a main house and separate cottage. This is life in the slow lane, with quiet, privacy, and a living room fireplace for when the evenings are nippy. The furnishings are very Ralph Lauren, with a cowhide flourish suited to this ranch-country locale. The 1906 house has three rooms and is good for four to six people willing to share a single bathroom. The cottage is ideal for a couple. ⊠ *229 Kula Hwy., Kula 96790* ☎ *808/579–8282* ☏ *661/393–5015* ⊕ *www.hookipa. com/bloom_cottage.html* ⌕ *1 house, 1 cottage* ⚲ *Kitchens, cable TV, in-room VCRs, laundry facilities; no A/C, no smoking* ☰ *AE, D, MC, V. $125–$165, 3-night minimum.*

$–$$ ⌂ **Hale Ho'okipa Inn.** This handsome 1924 Craftsman-style house in the heart of Makawao town is a good base for excursions to the crater or to Hāna. The owner has furnished it with antiques and fine art, and allows guests to peruse her voluminous library of Hawai'i-related books. The house is divided into three single rooms, each prettier than the next, and the South Wing, which sleeps four and includes the kitchen. There's also a separate cottage on the property, which sleeps two to four. All rooms have private claw-foot baths. This inn has a distinct plantation-era feel with squeaky wooden floors and period furnishings to boot. ⊠ *32 Pakani Pl., Makawao 96768* ☎ *808/572–6698* ☏ *808/572–2580* ⊕ *www. maui-bed-and-breakfast.com* ⌕ *3 rooms, 1 2-bedroom suite, 1 cottage* ⚲ *A/C in some rooms, cable TV, library* ☰ *No credit cards. $95–$145.*

$ ⌂ **Kula View.** This affordable home-away-from-home sits in peaceful, rural Kula. At an elevation of 2,000 feet, the climate is pleasantly temperate. Guests stay in the entire upper floor of a tastefully decorated house with a private entrance, deck, and gardens. A commanding view of Haleakalā stretches beyond the French doors. The hostess provides an "amenity basket," a very popular continental breakfast, advice on touring, and even beach towels or warm clothes for your crater trip. ⊠ *600 Holopuni Rd., Kula 96790* ☎ *808/878–6736* ⊕ *www.kulaview.com* ⌕ *1 room* ⚲ *Kitchenette; no A/C* ☰ *No credit cards. $95.*

¢–$ 🏠 **Peace of Maui.** This Upcountry getaway is ideal for budget-minded travelers who want to be out and active all day. Well situated for accessing the rest of the island, it's only 15 minutes from Kahului and less than 10 from Pā'ia, Ha'ikū, and Makawao. Six modest double rooms in a "lodge" have pantries and mini-refrigerators. The kitchen, two bathrooms, and living room are shared. An amply equipped separate cottage (including fresh-cut flowers) sleeps four to six and overlooks the North Shore and the West Maui Mountains. You'll have sweeping views of rainbow-washed pineapple fields here. If you're lucky, the family dog will sit near the Jacuzzi while you relax after a hard day's adventuring. ✉ 1290 Hali'imaile Rd., Hali'imaile 96768 ☎ 808/572–5045 or 888/475–5045 ⊕ www.peaceofmaui.com ➥ 6 rooms with shared bath, 1 cottage ⚬ Refrigerators, cable TV, hot tub, Internet room; no A/C ⊟ No credit cards. $55–$100.

The North Shore

North Shore accomodations (in Pāia, Hā'iku, or Huelo) are at sea-level. Many are oceanfront—not necessarily beachfront—with tropical gardens overflowing with gingers, bananas, and papayas. It rains frequently here, especially in Hā'iku and Huelo. You'll need a car to enjoy staying on the North Shore.

B&Bs & Vacation Rentals

$$$–$$$$ 🏠 **Huelo Point Flower Farm.** Perched on a 300-foot cliff overlooking Waipio Bay, this 2-acre estate—with four vacation rental homes—has verdant foliage and views. Sometimes you can even spot turtles swimming down below. The **Main House**, with 22-foot cathedral ceilings, a sunken tub in the master bath, and a large patio with a private hot tub, can accommodate up to eight. The two-bedroom **Guesthouse** has floor-to-ceiling glass windows, a spacious patio, and a private hot tub facing the ocean. The **Carriage House** has cathedral ceilings, a loft bedroom with a queen-size bed, a den with a double bed, and two spacious decks. The **Gazebo Cottage** is small with a half bath, kitchenette, and an outdoor shower. The orchard and ozonated pool are special treats. Don't try to find this secluded rental at night. ✉ Door of Faith Rd. off Hāna Hwy. ✉ Box 1195, Pa'ia 96779 ☎ 808/572–1850 ⊕ www.maui.net/~huelopt ➥ 4 units ⚬ In-room VCRs, pool, hot tub; no A/C ⊟ No credit cards. $170–$425.

$ 🏠 **Halfway to Hāna House.** A private studio on Maui's lush rural north coast, this serene retreat includes a two-person hammock, surrounding organic gardens, and great ocean views. It's a short walk from here to natural pools, waterfalls, and hiking areas. The room comes

---

GROCERIES & VIDEO RENTALS

The **Hā'iku Cannery** (✉ 810 Hā'iku Rd., Hā'iku) is home to **Hā'iku Grocery** (☎ 808/575-9291), a somewhat limited grocery store where you can find the basics: veggies, meats, wine, snacks, and ice cream. **88-Cent Video** (☎ 808/575-2723) is also here, along with a laundromat, bakery, and hardware store. The post office is across the street.

with optional continental breakfast and a well-supplied kitchenette—all the equipment you need to do your own thing. ⊠ *Hāna Hwy. ⊕ Box 675, Ha'ikū 96708* ☎ *808/572–1176* 🖶 *808/572–3609* ⊕ *www.halfwaytohana.com/paradise.html* 🛏 *1 room* ⚬ *Kitchenette; no A/C* ⊟ *No credit cards. $85–$105, 3-night minimum.*

Hāna

Why stay in Hāna when it's so far from everything? For precisely that—its seclusion. In a world where everything moves at high-speed, Hāna still travels on horseback, ambling along slowly enough to smell the fragrant vines hanging from the trees. But old-fashioned and remote does not mean tame—this is a wild coast, known for heart-stopping scenery and passionate downpours. Leave city expectations behind, the single grocery may run out of milk and the only videos to rent may be several seasons old. The dining options are slim. ■ TIP→→ If you're staying for several days, or at a vacation rental, stock up on groceries before you head out to Hāna. Even with these inconveniences, Hāna is a place you won't want to miss.

> ### SHOPPING IN HĀNA
>
> **Hasegawa General Store.** The one-stop shopping option in Hāna is charming, old, ramshackle Hasegawa's. Buy fishing tackle, hot dogs, ice cream, and eggs here. You can rent videos and buy the newspaper, which isn't always delivered on time. Check out the bulletin board for local events and interesting services. Be sure to take a Hasegawa T-shirt home with you as proof of your stay out in heavenly Hāna. ⊠ *5165 Hāna Hwy.* ☎ *808/248–8231.*

Hotels & Resorts

$$$$
Fodor'sChoice
★

🏨 **Hotel Hāna-Maui.** Tranquillity envelops Hotel Hāna's ranch setting, with its unobstructed views of the Pacific. Small, secluded, and quietly luxurious, this property is a departure from the usual resort destinations. Spacious rooms (680 to 830 square feet) have bleached-wood floors, authentic kapa-print fabric furnishings, and sumptuously stocked minibars at no extra cost. Spa suites and a heated *watsu* pool complement a state-of-the-art spa and fitness center. The Sea Ranch Cottages with individual hot tubs are the best value. Horses nibble wild grass on the sea-cliff nearby. A shuttle takes you to beautiful Hāmoa Beach. ⊠ *Hāna Hwy.* ⊕ *Box 9, Hāna 96713* ☎ *808/248–8211 or 800/321–4262* 🖶 *808/248–7264* ⊕ *www.hotelhanamaui.com* 🛏 *19 rooms, 47 cottages, 1 house* ⚬ *A/C, 2 restaurants, 2 tennis courts, 2 pools, gym, hot tub, spa, beach, horseback riding, bar, library, Internet room; no room TVs* ⊟ *AE, D, DC, MC, V. $295–$725.*

B&Bs & Vacation Rentals

$$$–$$$$

🏨 **Ekena.** "Ekena" means Garden of Eden, and the grounds here are full of tropical fruit trees and exotic flowers. A hillside location makes for commanding views of the ocean. There are two houses, each with a fully equipped kitchen. Jasmine, the smaller of the two, is suited to parties of two. The main house, Sea Breeze, is huge (2,600 square feet), with two large suites, but occupancy is restricted to a maximum of four people. ⊠ *Off Hāna Hwy.* ⊕ *Box 728, Hāna 96713* 🖶🖶 *808/248–7047*

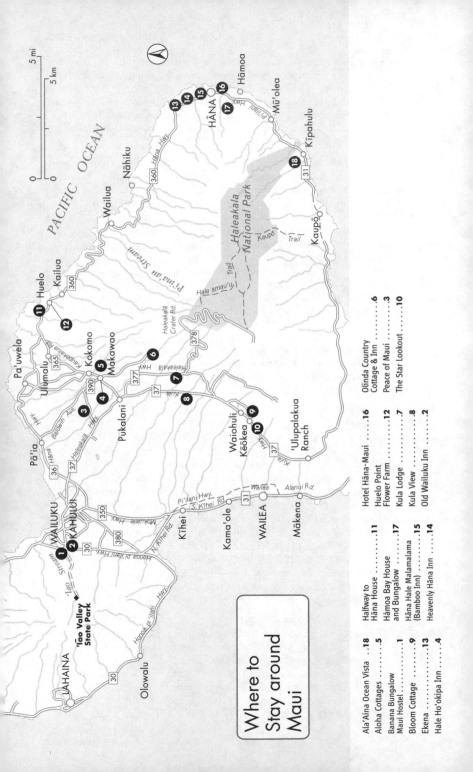

Where to Stay around Maui

Ala'Aina Ocean Vista ..**18**
Aloha Cottages **5**
Banana Bungalow
Maui Hostel **1**
Bloom Cottage **9**
Ekena **13**
Hale Ho'okipa Inn **4**

Halfway to
Hāna House **11**
Hāmoa Bay House
and Bungalow **17**
Hāna Hale Malamalama
(Bamboo Inn) **15**
Heavenly Hāna Inn **14**

Hotel Hāna-Maui **16**
Huelo Point
Flower Farm **12**
Kula Lodge **7**
Kula View **8**
Old Wailuku Inn **2**

Olinda Country
Cottage & Inn **6**
Peace of Maui **3**
The Star Lookout **10**

⊕ *www.ekenamaui.com* ⊅ *2 houses* ⚬ *Fans, kitchens, cable TV, in-room VCRs, laundry facilities; no A/C, no kids under 14* ⊟ *No credit cards. $185–$350, 3-night minimum.*

★ **$$$–$$$$** ⊞ **Hamoa Bay House & Bungalow.** This Balinese-inspired property is sensuous and secluded—a private sanctuary in a fragrant jungle. There are two buildings: the main house is 1,300 square feet and contains two bedrooms; one of them is a suite set apart by a breezeway. There's a screened veranda with an ocean view and an outdoor lava-rock shower accessible to all guests. The 600-square-foot bungalow is a treetop perch with a giant bamboo bed and a hot tub on the veranda. Hamoa Beach is a short walk away. ⊠ *Hāna Hwy.* ⊕ *Box 773, Hāna 96713* ☎ *808/248–7884* ⊟ *808/248–7047* ⊕ *www.hamoabay.com* ⊅ *1 house, 1 bungalow* ⚬ *Kitchen, in-room VCRs, laundry facilities; no kids under 14, no smoking* ⊟ *No credit cards. $195–$350, 3-night minimum.*

$$$–$$$$ ⊞ **Heavenly Hāna Inn.** An impressive Japanese gate, just as you enter Hāna town, marks the entrance to this small upscale inn. Lush gardens surround the three suites, all under one roof, but each with a separate entrance. Rooms are lovingly spare, with Japanese overtones, and the furniture was built with exotic woods by Hāna residents. There's also a traditional Japanese tearoom. ⊠ *Hāna Hwy. near mile marker 32* ⊕ *Box 790, Hāna 96713* ☎ *808/248–8442* ⊕ *www.heavenlyhanainn.com* ⊅ *3 suites* ⚬ *Fans; no A/C, no room phones, no kids under 15, no smoking* ⊟ *AE, D, MC, V. $185–$250.*

★ **$$–$$$$** ⊞ **Hāna Hale Malamalama (Bamboo Inn).** If you're looking for the amenities and activities of a resort, you won't be happy here. But if you want lots of nature and little distraction, this place is perfect. The two duplexes and three cottages overlook a natural spring-fed fish pond and the remains of a *heiau* (an ancient Hawaiian stone platform once used as a place of worship). A black-sand beach, surrounded by lush tropical forest is steps away. Accommodations are simple but clean with rustic bamboo furniture, full kitchens, large bathrooms, and private lānai. Don't be surprised to find a few ants, they come with all the scenery. A continental breakfast is served in the "lobby," a Polynesian-style, open-air hut. The roar of the ocean and the rustling of palm trees adds a soothing backdrop to the stunning setting. This is paradise as nature meant it to be. ⊕ *Box 374, Hana 96713* ☎ *808/248–8211* ⊕ *www.hanahale.com* ⊅ *4 rooms, 3 cottages* ⚬ *BBQs, fans, in-room data ports, kitchens, cable TV, in-room DVDs, Internet, no-smoking rooms; no A/C* ⊟ *MC, V. $135–$250.*

> **BED-AND-BREAKFASTS**
>
> Additional Bed & Breakfasts on Maui can be found by contacting **Bed & Breakfast Hawai'i** (☎ 808/733–1632 ⊕ www.bandb-hawaii.com), or **Bed and Breakfast Honolulu** (☎ 808/595–7533 or 800/288–4666 ⊕ www.hawaiibnb.com).

$$$ ⊞ **Ala'Aina Ocean Vista.** Located past 'Ohe'o Gulch (about a 40-minute drive from Hana), this B&B is on the grounds of an old banana plantation. Banana trees still populate the property alongside mango, papaya, and avocado trees. A Balinese garden, complete with lotus-shape pond, adds to the Zen-like atmosphere. The single room has a private lānai with an outdoor kitchenette, outdoor shower (there's a regular bath–shower in the room's bathroom as well), and astonishing views of the coastline. Sam and Mercury, a mother-daughter team, live in the main house on-site and are available to give tips and advice about exploring the area. This is a simple, back-to-nature kind of spot, perfect for a couple who wants to have a camping-type experience without the tent. ⊠ *Off Hwy. 31, 10 mi past Hāna* ⌀ *SR 184-A, Hāna 96713* ☏ *808/ 248–7824 or 877/216–1733* ⊕ *www.hanabedandbreakfast.com* ⌗ *1 room* ⌑ *BBQ, kitchenette, in-room TV/VCR with movies; no A/C* ⊟ *No credit cards. $165, 2-night minimum.*

WHERE TO SPA

Maui has recently become a spa paradise. Nearly every resort has jumped aboard the fitness–beauty bandwagon, giving spa goers more choices than ever before.

Traditional Swedish massage and European facials anchor most spa menus, though you'll also find shiatsu, ayurvedic, aromatherapy, and other body treatments drawn from cultures across the globe. *Lomi Lomi,* traditional Hawaiian massage involving powerful strokes down the length of the body, is a regional specialty passed down through generations. Many treatments incorporate local plants and flowers. *Awapuhi,* or Hawaiian ginger, and *noni,* a pungent-smelling fruit, are regularly used for their therapeutic benefits. *Limu,* or seaweed, and even coffee is employed in rousing salt scrubs and soaks. And this is just the beginning. The more extravagant the treatment, the weightier the price. But at least with resort spas, services are usually paired with all-day use of a resplendent facility, and a whole host of health-inspired activities—everything from Spinning to watercolor lessons.

And for those who don't want a fuss made over them with fancy products (guys, you know who you are), you can still enjoy a simple beachside massage. More and more men are discovering what women have long known—a little pampering can go a long way.

In spas on Maui, the emphasis is definitely on relaxation. But if you're craving your fitness routine, there should be no trouble continuing it here—or even ramping it up on the advanced equipment available to most resort guests. Complementing sightseeing with early-morning walks, meditation, fitness classes, treatments, and beauty services can deepen the relaxing effects of your vacation.

The Spa at Four Seasons Resort. The Four Seasons' hawklike attention to detail is reflected here. Thoughtful gestures like fresh flowers beneath the massage table (to give you something to stare at) and a choice of music relax you before your treatment even begins. The spa is genuinely stylish and serene, and the therapists are among the best. If you're looking to lounge all day here though, it's a bit small. For a private, outdoor experience, the oceanfront massage *hales* (structures) are particularly charming and well worth the extra $25. ⊠ *3900 Wailea Alanui Dr., Wailea* ☏ *808/ 874–8000 or 800/334–6284* ⊕ *www.fourseasons.com* ⌗ *$125 50-minute* massage, $370 3-treatment packages ♿ Hair salon, steam room. Gym with: cardiovascular machines, free weights, weight-training equipment. Services: aromatherapy, body wraps, facials, hydrotherapy, massage. Classes and programs: aquaerobics, meditation, personal training, Pilates, Spinning, tai chi, yoga.

Fodor's Choice ★ **Spa Grande, Grand Wailea.** Built to satisfy an indulgent Japanese billionaire, this 50,000-square-foot spa makes others seem like well-appointed closets. Slathered in honey and wrapped up in the steam room (if you go for the Ali'i honey steam wrap), you'll feel like royalty. All treatments include a loofah scrub and a trip to the *termé*, a hydrotherapy circuit including a Roman Jacuzzi, furo bath, plunge pool, powerful waterfall and Swiss jet showers, and five therapeutic baths. (Soak for 10 minutes in the moor mud to relieve sunburn or jellyfish stings.) Plan to arrive an hour before your treatment to fully enjoy the baths. The termé is available separately for $55 ($80 for non-hotel guests). At times—especially during the holidays—this wonderland can be crowded. ✉ 3850 Wailea Alanui Dr., Wailea ☎ 808/875–1234 or 800/888–6100 ⊕ www.grandwailea.com ✆ $145 50-minute massage, $325 half-day spa packages ♿ Hair salon, hot tub, sauna, steam room. Gym with: cardiovascular machines, free weights, racquetball, weight-training equipment. Services: aromatherapy, body wraps, facials, hydrotherapy, massage, Vichy shower. Classes and programs: aquaerobics, cycling, Pilates, qigong, yoga.

Fodor's Choice ★ **The Spa at Hotel Hāna Maui.** A bamboo gate opens into an outdoor sanctuary with a lava-rock pool and hot tub; at first glimpse this spa makes you think it must have been organically grown, not built. The decor here can hardly be called decor—it's an abundant, living garden. Taro varieties, orchids, and ferns still wet from Hāna's frequent downpours nourish the spirit as you rest with a cup of jasmine tea, or take an invigorating dip in the plunge pool. Signature aromatherapy treatments utilize *Honua*, the spa's own sumptuous blend of sandalwood, coconut, ginger, and vanilla orchid essences. Daily yoga classes round out a perfectly relaxing experience. ✉ 3850 Wailea Alanui Dr., Wailea ☎ 808/875–1234 or 800/888–6100 ⊕ www.hotelhanamaui.com ✆ $125 60-minute massage, $250 spa packages ♿ Hair salon, hot tubs (indoor and outdoor), sauna, steam room. Gym with: cardiovascular machines, free weights, weight-training equipment. Services: aromatherapy, body wraps, facials, hydrotherapy, massage. Classes and programs: meditation, Pilates, yoga.

SPA TIPS

- Arrive early for your treatment, so that you can enjoy the steam room and other amenities.

- Bring a comfortable change of clothing and remove your jewelry.

- Most spas are clothing-optional. If a swimsuit is required for a hydrotherapy treatment, you will be notified.

- If you're pregnant, or have allergies, inform the receptionist before booking a treatment.

- Your therapist should be able to explain the ingredients of all products being used in your treatment. If anything stings or burns, say so immediately.

- Fifteen to 20% gratuities are suggested.

Spa Kea Lani, Fairmont Kea Lani Hotel Suites & Villas. Once one of the island's nicest, this tiny spa now lags behind the others. Treatments are still superb, but the facility is small, even cramped. You can overcome this by opting for a poolside massage—treatments by the divinely serene adult pool can be reserved on the spot. If the pool feels too exposed, we recommend opting for the spa's Citrus Glow treatment: a private hydrotherapy tub treatment prepares you for an exfoliating massage. ✉ *4100 Wailea Alanui Dr., Wailea* ☎ *808/875–4100 or 800/659–4100* ⊕ *www.kealani.com* ✆ *$120 55-minute massage, $295 spa packages* ⚥ *Hair salon, steam room. Gym with: cardiovascular machines, free weights, weight-training equipment. Services: aromatherapy, body wraps, facials, hydrotherapy, massage, Vichy shower. Classes and programs: aquaerobics, yoga.*

Spa Moana, Hyatt Regency Maui. Spa Moana's oceanfront salon has a million-dollar view; it's a perfect place to beautify before your wedding or special anniversary. An older facility, it's still spacious and well-appointed,

> ### BUDGET-FRIENDLY SPAS
>
> If hotel spa prices are a little intimidating, try **Spa Luna** (✉ 810 Hā'iku Rd., Hā'iku ☎ 808/575–2440), a day spa, which is also an aesthetician's school. In the former Hā'iku Cannery, it offers services ranging from massage to microdermabrasion. You can opt for professional services, but the student clinics are the real story here. The students are subject to rigorous training, and their services are offered at a fraction of the regular cost ($25 for a 50-minute massage).

offering numerous innovative treatments such as the Ka'anapali Coffee Scrub or the Maui Sugar Scrub, in addition to traditional Swedish and Thai massage, reiki, and shiatsu. For body treatments, the oceanfront rooms are a tad too warm—request one in back. In conjunction with Spa Moana, the Maui Wellness Institute offers two-day programs including workshops on kinesiology, feng shui, sex, and chocolate. Er . . . yum. ✉*200 Nohea Kai Dr., Lahaina* ☎ *808/661–1234 or 800/233–1234* ⊕ *www. hyatt.com* ✆ *$150 50-minute massage, $420 all-day spa packages* ⚥ *Hair salon, hot tub, sauna, steam room. Gym with: cardiovascular machines, free weights, weight-training equipment. Services: aromatherapy, body wraps, facials, hydrotherapy, massage, Vichy shower. Classes and programs: aquaerobics, Pilates, tai chi, yoga.*

Waihua, Ritz-Carlton, Kapalua. If the stress of traveling has riled your nerves (or even if if hasn't) book a Waihua signature treatment such as "Harmony" or "Family Relations," which employs aromatherapy, hot stones, and massage. High-quality, handcrafted products enhance treatments inspired by Hawaiian culture, such as the *lomi lomi* massage with healing plant essences followed by a salt foot scrub. The newly refurbished facility lacks some of the other spas' amenities (what! no *oshibori* towels?) but does offer superb services and a well-stocked boutique. Attention fitness junkies: personal DVDs are attached to the state-of-the-art cardiovascular machines. ✉ *1 Ritz-Carlton Dr., Kapalua* ☎ *808/669–6200 or 800/262–8440* ⊕ *www.ritzcarlton.com* ✆ *$120 60-minute massage, $320 half-day spa packages* ⚥ *Hair salon, sauna, steam room. Gym with: cardiovascular machines, free weights, weight-training equip-*

ment. Services: aromatherapy, body wraps, facials, massage. Classes and programs: aquaerobics, nutrition, yoga.

★ **The Spa at the Westin Maui.** An exquisite 80-minute Lavender Body Butter treatment is the star of this spa's menu, thanks to a partnership with a local lavender farm. Other options include cabana massage (for couples, too) and water lily sunburn relief with green tea. The brand-new facility is flawless, and it's worth getting a treatment just to sip lavender lemonade in the posh ocean-view waiting room (it's coed, so keep your robe tightly tied). The open-air yoga studio and "reebok-powered" gym offer energizing workouts. Bridal parties can request a private area within the salon. ⊠ *Westin Káanapali, 2365 Ka'anapali Pkwy., Ka'anapali* ☎ *808/667–2525* ⊕ *www.westinmaui.com* ☞ *$115 50-minute massage, $137–$411 day spa packages* ⚒ *Hair salon, hot tub, sauna, steam room. Gym with: cardiovascular machines, free weights, weight-training equipment. Services: aromatherapy, body wraps, facials, hydrotherapy, massage, Vichy shower. Classes and programs: aquaerobics, yoga.*

WHERE TO EAT

A history of innovative Pacific Rim cuisine has supplied Maui with many outstanding restaurants. Island chefs use fruits and vegetables unique to Hawai'i in classic European or Asian ways—spawning such dishes as *'ahi* (yellowfin tuna) carpaccio, breadfruit soufflé, and *lilikoi* (passion fruit) cheesecake. Fresh fish, island-grown produce, and simple, stylized presentations characterize the very best.

You can find ethnic and local-style cooking here and there—particularly if you wander into the less-touristy areas of Wailuku or Kahului, for example. A good Hawaiian "plate lunch" will fulfill your daily requirement of carbohydrates: macaroni salad, two scoops of rice, and an entrée of, say, curry stew, teriyaki beef, or *kālua* (roasted in an underground oven) pig and cabbage.

■ TIP→→ Unless a resort is noted for its culinary department (such as the Ritz-Carlton, or Four Seasons), you may find hotel restaurants somewhat overpriced and underwhelming. Head out to a free-standing restaurant with a menu more varied and less astronomically priced.

Reservations are usually unnecessary, but it's never a bad idea to phone ahead to book a table. Restaurants are open daily unless otherwise specified. Generally, dinner is served from 5 to 9 PM. Casual dress—an aloha shirt and pants for men and a simple dress or pants for women—are acceptable in all establishments.

WHAT IT COSTS					
	$$$$	**$$$**	**$$**	**$**	**¢**
RESTAURANTS	over $30	$20–$30	$12–$20	$7–$12	under $7

Restaurant prices are for one main course at dinner.

West Maui

American

★ $–$$$ ✕ **Lahaina Coolers.** This breezy little café with a surfboard hanging from its ceiling serves such tantalizing fare as Evil Jungle Pasta (pasta with grilled chicken in spicy Thai peanut sauce) and linguine with prawns, basil, garlic, and cream. It also has pizzas, steaks, burgers, and desserts such as a chocolate taco filled with tropical fruit and berry salsa. Pastas are made fresh in-house. Don't be surprised to see a local fisherman walk through or a harbor captain reeling in a hearty breakfast. ✉ *180 Dickenson St., Lahaina* ☎ *808/661–7082* ▱ *AE, MC, V. $11–$26.*

¢–$ ✕ **The Gazebo Restaurant.** Even locals will stand in line up to a half hour for a table overlooking the beach at this restaurant, an actual open-air gazebo. The food is standard diner fare, but it's thoughtfully prepared. Breakfast choices include macadamia-nut pancakes and Portuguese-sausage omelets. There are satisfying burgers and salads at lunch. The friendly hotel staff puts out coffee for those waiting in line. ✉ *Nāpili Shores Resort, 5315 Lower Honoapi'ilani Hwy., Nāpili* ☎ *808/669–5621* ▱ *No credit cards* ◷ *No dinner. $3–$9.*

Continental

$$$–$$$$ ✕ **Swan Court.** A grand staircase leads down into a cathedral-ceiling ballroom, and black and white swans glide across a waterfall-fed lagoon at this elegant eatery. Try the crispy scallop dim sum in plum sauce; creamy lobster-coconut bisque brimming with chunks of fish, lobster, shrimp, and button mushrooms; or charbroiled lamb chops in macadamia satay sauce. Arrive early and ask for a table on the left side, where the swans linger in the evening. The restaurant also serves a breakfast buffet. ✉ *Hyatt Regency Maui, Kā'anapali Beach Resort, 200 Nohea Kai Dr., Kā'anapali* ☎ *808/661–1234* ▱ *AE, D, DC, MC, V. $28–$45.*

Eclectic

$$–$$$ ✕ **Café Sauvage.** This eclectic little restaurant is in a courtyard on Front Street. The atmosphere is not as intimate or elegant as some of its neighboring, oceanfront restaurants, but the food is excellent and the prices are surprisingly low. Specialties include peppered ahi tuna, cajun seared scallops, and a petite filet mignon wrapped in bacon and served with truffle butter and red-wine sauce. The Seafood Sampler, which includes the fish of the day, tempura prawns, lobster ravioli, soup or salad, dessert and coffee, is a great deal. ✉ *844 Front St., Lahaina* ☎ *808/ 661–7600* ▱ *AE, MC, V. $16–$27.*

French

★ $$$–$$$$ ✕ **Chez Paul.** Since 1975 this tiny roadside restaurant between Lahaina and Mā'alaea in Olowalu has been serving excellent French cuisine to a packed house of repeat customers. Such dishes as fresh local fish poached in white wine with shallots, cream, and capers typify the classical menu. The restaurant's nondescript exterior belies the fine art, linen-draped tables, and wine cellar. Don't blink or you'll miss this small group of buildings huddled in the middle of nowhere. ✉ *Honoapi'ilani Hwy., 4 mi south of Lahaina, Olowalu* ☎ *808/661–3843* ◿ *Reservations essential* ▱ *AE, D, MC, V* ◷ *No lunch. $29–$45.*

$$$–$$$$ ✕ **Gerard's.** Owner and celebrated chef Gerard Reversade started cook-
Fodor'sChoice ing at the age of 10, and at 12 he was baking croissants. He honors the
★ French tradition with such exquisitely prepared dishes as rack of lamb
in mint crust with thyme jus, and venison cutlets in a port sauce with
confit of chestnuts, walnuts, fennel, and pearl onions. The menu changes
once a year, but many favorites—such as the sinfully good crème brûlée—
remain. A first-class wine list, a lovely room, and celebrity-spotting round
out the experience. ✉ *Plantation Inn, 174 Lahainaluna Rd., Lahaina*
☎ *808/661–8939* ▭ *AE, D, DC, MC, V* ☯ *No lunch. $28–$47.*

Hawaiian–Pacific Rim

★ **$$$$** ✕ **The Banyan Tree.** If you've never tried foie gras ice cream, don't be
shy. Australian Chef Antony Scholtmeyer's menu is daring but delectable.
Nothing is prepared as it should be: the priciest dish, lobster and scal-
lops, is a salad, and the fish of Hawai'ian royalty, *moi,* is served atop
Indian-spice lentils with a yogurt sauce. We recommend placing your
evening's fate in the care of the chef. The tasting menus and wine pair-
ings provide an epicurean experience to be savored long afterward in
memory. The open-beam restaurant's subdued atmosphere is charged
with the sounds of live world music. ✉ *Ritz-Carlton, Kapalua, 1 Ritz-
Carlton Dr., Kapalua* ☎ *808/669–6200* ▭ *AE, D, DC, MC, V. $32–$48.*

$$$–$$$$ ✕ **David Paul's Lahaina Grill.** Though the restaurant's namesake is only
Fodor'sChoice a consultant now, David Paul's is still a favorite of both locals and tourists
★ alike. Beautifully designed, it's adjacent to the elegant Lahaina Inn in a
historic building on Lahainaluna Road. The celebrated menu is revised
seasonally, but you can count on finding the signature tequila shrimp
and firecracker rice along with such scrumptious desserts as triple-berry
pie. The restaurant has an extensive wine cellar, an in-house bakery, and
splashy artwork decorating the walls. ✉ *127 Lahainaluna Rd., La-
haina* ☎ *808/667–5117* ▭ *AE, DC, MC, V. $26–$42.*

★ **$$$–$$$$** ✕ **I'o.** From its opening, this restaurant established itself as cutting edge
in Lahaina, both for its theatrical interior designed by the artist Dado
and for its contemporary Pacific Rim menu. A prized appetizer is the Silken
Purse—steamed wontons stuffed with roasted peppers, mushrooms,
macadamia nuts, and tofu. Favorite dinners include lemongrass-coconut
fish and nori-wrapped rare tuna, served with green-papaya salad. Desserts
to savor are the Hawaiian Vintage Chocolate Mousse and the chocolate
pâté with Kula strawberries. ✉ *505 Front St., Lahaina* ☎ *808/661–
8422* ▭ *AE, D, DC, MC, V* ☯ *No lunch. $28–$32.*

★ **$$$–$$$$** ✕ **Roy's Kahana Bar & Grill.** Roy Yamaguchi's own sake brand ("Y") and
Hawaiian fusion specialties, such as shrimp with sweet-and-spicy chili
sauce, keep regulars returning for more. Locals know to order the in-
comparable chocolate soufflé immediately after being seated. Next door,
Roy's somewhat quieter restaurant, Nicolina, caters to a spice-loving
crowd. Grilled Southwestern chicken with chili hash, and smoked-and-
peppered duck with gingered sweet potatoes are favorites. All three restau-
rants, two in Kahana and one in Kīhei, are in supermarket parking
lots—it's not the view that excites, it's the food. ✉ *Kahana Gateway
Shopping Center, 4405 Honoapi'ilani Hwy., Kahana* ☎ *808/669–6999
for Roy's, 808/669–5000 for Nicolina* ✉ *Safeway Shopping Center, 303
Piikea Ave., Kīhei* ☎ *808/891–1120* ▭ *AE, D, DC, MC, V. $25–$31.*

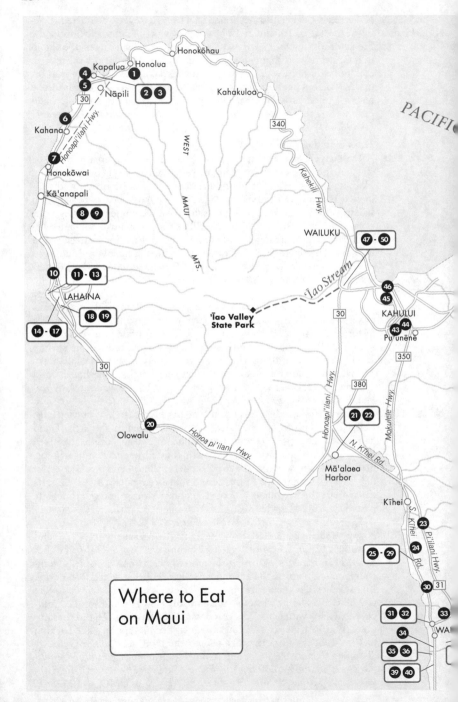

Where to Eat
on Maui

OCEAN

0 _____ 5 miles

0 _____ 5 km

51 · 53 55
Pa'uwela
Hāna Hwy.
Pā'ia 54 Ha'ikū
Ulumalu
36 365
Baldwin Ave. Kaupakalua Rd.
37 Haleakala Hāli'imaile Rd.
56 390 Kokomo
57 - 60
Makawao
Pukalani
61
377
Kula Hwy. Haleakalā Hwy.
37
378
Waiohuli
Kēōkea
37 38
Kula Hwy.

A.K's Café **50**
A Saigon Café **47**
Aloha Mixed Plate **10**
Ba Le **43**
The Banyan Tree **2**
Blue Marlin
Harborfront
Grill & Bar **22**
Cafe Des Amis **53**
Café Sauvage **12**
Caffe Ciao **40**
Capische **38**
Casanova Italian
Restaurant & Deli **58**
Chez Paul **20**
David Paul's
Lahaina Grill **14**
Dragon Dragon **46**
Garden Café **60**
The Gazebo
Restaurant **4**
Gerard's **15**
Hāli'imaile
General Store **56**
Hakone **42**
Hirohachi **27**
Honokowai Okazuya **7**
Hula Grill **9**
Hula Moons **32**
Humuhumunu-
kunukuāpua'a **35**
I'o **18**
Jacque's **51**
Joe's Bar & Grill **33**
Kai **3**
Kihei Caffe **29**
Kimo's **13**
Lahaina Coolers **16**
Longhi's **11,34**
Mā'alaea Waterfront
Restaurant **21**
Makawao
Steak House **57**
Mama's Fish House . . . **54**
Mañana Garage **45**
Marco's
Grill & Deli **24, 44**

Maui Bake Shop **49**
Maui's Best Tamales . . . **61**
Maui Onion **31**
Milagro's **52**
Mulligan's
on the Blue **37**
Nick's Fishmarket
Maui **39**
Pacific'O **19**
Pauwela Café **55**
Penne Pasta **17**
Plantation House
Restaurant **1**
Polli's **59**
Roy's Kahana
Bar & Grill **6, 23**
Saeng's
Thai Cuisine **48**
Sansei **5, 26**
Sarento's on the
Beach **30**
Seawatch **41**
Spago **36**
Swan Court **9**
Tastings **28**
Thai Cuisine **25**

$$–$$$$ ✕ **Hula Grill.** Genial chef-restaurateur Peter Merriman's bustling, family-oriented restaurant is in a re-created 1930s Hawaiian beach house, and every table has an ocean view. You can also dine on the beach, toes in the sand, at the Barefoot Bar, where Hawaiian entertainment is presented every evening. South Pacific snapper is baked with tomato, chili, and cumin aioli and served with a black bean, Maui onion, and avocado relish. Spareribs are steamed in banana leaves, then grilled with mango barbecue sauce over mesquitelike *kiawe* wood. ⊠ *Whalers Village, 2435 Kā'anapali Pkwy., Kā'anapali* ☎ *808/667–6636* ▭ *AE, DC, MC, V. $17–$32.*

$$–$$$$ ✕ **Plantation House Restaurant.** It's hard to decide which is better here, the food or the view. Hills, grassy volcanic ridges lined with pine trees, and fairways that appear to drop off into the ocean provide an idyllic setting. The specialty is fresh island fish prepared according to different "tastes"—Upcountry Maui, Asian-Pacific, Provence, and others. The breeze through the large shuttered windows can be cool, so you may want to bring a sweater or sit by the fireplace. Breakfast here is a luxurious way to start your day. ⊠ *Plantation Course Clubhouse, 2000 Plantation Club Dr., past Kapalua* ☎ *808/669–6299* ▭ *AE, MC, V. $18–$32.*

¢–$$ ✕ **Aloha Mixed Plate.** Set right on the ocean, this funky open-air bar and restaurant is a great place for "ono grinds"—good food in Hawaiian slang. Crispy coconut prawns, taro burgers, shoyu chicken, and kahlua pork are favorite island comfort foods (these are the things local kids daydream about when they're sent away to college). You too can indulge in these Hawaiian treats at this awesome outdoor location. ⊠ *1286 Front St., Lahaina* ☎ *808/661–3322* ▭ *AE, D, DC, MC, V. $5–$13.*

¢–$ ✕ **Honokowai Okazuya.** Don't expect to sit down at this miniature restaurant sandwiched between a dive shop and a salon—this is strictly a take-out joint. You can order local plate lunches, Chinese, vegetarian, or sandwiches. The spicy eggplant is delicious, and the fresh chow fun noodles are bought up quickly. ⊠ *3600-D Lower Honoapi'ilani Hwy., Lahaina* ☎ *808/665–0512* ▭ *No credit cards* ☉ *Closed Sun. and daily 2:30–4:30. $7–$11.*

Italian

$$$–$$$$ ✕ **Longhi's.** A Lahaina establishment, Longhi's has been around since 1976, serving great Italian pasta as well as sandwiches, seafood, beef, and chicken dishes. The pasta is homemade, and the in-house bakery turns out breakfast pastries, desserts, and fresh bread. Even on a warm day, you won't need air-conditioning with two spacious, breezy, open-air levels to choose from. The black-and-white tile floors are a nice touch. There's a second restaurant on the South Shore, at the Shops at Wailea. ⊠ *888 Front St., Lahaina* ☎ *808/667–2288* ⊠ *The Shops at Wailea, 3750 Wailea Alanui Dr., Wailea* ☎ *808/891–8883* ▭ *AE, D, DC, MC, V. $25–$35.*

$–$$ ✕ **Penne Pasta.** Heaping plates of flavorful pasta and low-key, unintrusive service make this restaurant the perfect alternative to an expensive night out in Lahaina. The osso buco (Thursday's special) is sumptuous, and the traditional salad niçoise overflows with generous portions of olives, peppers, garlic 'ahi, and potatoes. Couples should split a salad and entrée, as portions are large. ☒ *180 Dickenson St., Lahaina* ☎ *808/ 661–6633* ⊟ *AE, D, DC, MC, V* ☺ *No lunch weekends. $7–$15.*

Japanese

★ **$–$$$$** ✕ **Kai.** Master sushi chef Tadashi Yoshino sits at the helm of this intimate, ocean-view sushi bar, hidden behind the Lobby bar at the Ritz-Carlton, Kapalua. The menu includes sushi and hot Japanese entrées, but your best bet is to let Chef Yoshino design the meal. He might have yellowtail cheeks, fresh sea urchin, and raw lobster. He also makes lobster-head soup, a Japanese comfort food. ☒ *Ritz-Carlton, Kapalua, 1 Ritz-Carlton Dr., Kapalua* ☎ *808/669–6200* ⊟ *AE, D, DC, MC, V. $10–$50.*

$–$$$
Fodor'sChoice
★
✕ **Sansei.** One of the best-loved restaurants on the island, Sansei is Japanese with a Hawaiian twist. Inspired dishes include *panko*-crusted 'ahi (panko are Japanese bread crumbs), spicy fried calamari, mango-and-crab-salad roll, and a decadent foie gras *nigiri* (served on rice without seaweed) sushi. Desserts often use local fruit; the Kula-persimmon crème brûlée is stunning. Both locations are now popular karaoke hangouts, serving late-night sushi at half price. ☒ *Kapalua Shops, 115 Bay Dr., Kapalua* ☎ *808/666–6286* ☒ *Kihei Town Center, 1881 S. Kihei Rd., Kihei* ☎ *808/879–0004* ⊟ *AE, D, MC, V* ☺ *No lunch. $8–$30.*

Seafood

★ **$$$–$$$$** ✕ **Pacific'O.** You can sit outdoors at umbrella-shaded tables near the water's edge, or find a spot in the breezy, marble-floor interior. The exciting menu features fresh 'ahi-and-ono tempura, in which the two kinds of fish are wrapped around *tobiko* (flying-fish roe), then wrapped in nori, and wok-fried. There's a great lamb dish, too—a whole rack of sweet New Zealand lamb, sesame-crusted and served with roasted macadamia sauce and Hawaiian chutney. Live jazz is played Thursday through Saturday from 9 to midnight. ☒ *505 Front St., Lahaina* ☎ *808/667–4341* ⊟ *AE, D, DC, MC, V.*

$$–$$$$ ✕ **Kimo's.** On a warm Lahaina day, it's a treat to relax at an umbrella-shaded table on this restaurant's lānai, sip a mai tai, and watch sailboats glide in and out of the harbor. Outstanding seafood is just one of the options here; also good are Hawaiian-style chicken and pork dishes, and burgers. Try the signature dessert, Hula Pie: vanilla-macadamia nut ice cream topped with chocolate fudge and whipped cream in an Oreo-cookie crust. ☒ *845 Front St., Lahaina* ☎ *808/661–4811* ⊟ *AE, DC, MC, V. $17–$37.*

Central Maui

American

¢–$ ✕ **Maui Bake Shop.** Wonderful breads baked in old brick ovens (dating to 1935), hearty lunch fare, and irresistible desserts make this a popular spot in Central Maui. Baker José Krall was trained in France, and his wife, Claire, is a Maui native whose friendly face you can often see when you walk in. Standouts include the focaccia and homemade soups. ☒ *2092 Vineyard St., Wailuku* ☎ *808/242–0064* ⊟ *AE, D, MC, V* ☺ *Closed Sun. No dinner. $4–$8.*

Chinese

¢–$$ ✕ **Dragon Dragon.** Whether you're a party of 10 or 2, this is the place to share seafood-tofu soup, spareribs with garlic sauce, or fresh Dungeness crab with four sauces. Tasteful, simple decor complements the solid menu. The restaurant shares parking with the Maui Megaplex and makes a great pre- or post-movie stop. ⊠ *In Maui Mall, 70 E. Kaahumanu Ave., Kahului* ☎ *808/893–1628* ⊟ *AE, D, MC, V. $6–$17.*

Hawaiian

¢–$$ ✕ **A.K.'s Café.** Nearly hidden between auto-body shops and karaoke bars is this wonderful, bright café. Affordable, tasty entrées such as grilled tenderloin with wild mushrooms or garlic-crusted ono with ginger relish come with a choice of two sides. The flavorful dishes are healthy, too—Chef Elaine Rothermal previously instructed island nutritionists on how to prepare health-conscious versions of local favorites. Try the Hawaiian french-fried sweet potatoes, the steamed *ulu* (breadfruit), or the poi. ⊠ *1237 Lower Main, Wailuku* ☎ *808/244–8774* ⊟ *D, MC, V* ⊗ *Closed Sun. $4–$14.*

Italian

$–$$$ ✕ **Marco's Grill & Deli.** This convenient eatery outside Kahului Airport (look for the green awning) serves reliable Italian food that's slightly overpriced. Homemade pastas appear on the extensive menu, along with an unforgettably good Reuben sandwich and the best tiramisu on the island. The local business crowd fills the place for breakfast, lunch, and dinner. The Kīhei branch is in a gorgeous new building with a grand piano. ⊠ *444 Hāna Hwy., Kahului* ☎ *808/877–4446* ⊠ *1445 S. Kīhei Rd., Kīhei* ☎ *808/874–4041* ⊟ *AE, D, DC, MC, V. $7–$27.*

Latin

$$–$$$ ✕ **Mañana Garage.** Parked in downtown Kahului is this restaurant, which makes the most of its automobile theme—it's probably the only place you can have your wine served out of buckets with crankshaft stems. Chef Tom Lelli's cuisine ranges from Cuban to Brazilian to Mexican, with a few Hawaiian touches thrown in for good measure. The best dishes include ceviche marinated in coconut milk and lime, 'ahi sashimi, and quesadillas made with homemade corn tortillas. For dessert, the pound-cake ice-cream sandwich with sweet potato and praline is a must. There's lively music on the weekends. ⊠ *33 Lono Ave., Kahului* ☎ *808/ 873–0220* ⊟ *AE, D, MC, V* ⊗ *No lunch weekends. $16–$29.*

Thai

$–$$ ✕ **Saeng's Thai Cuisine.** Choosing a dish from the six-page menu here requires determination, but the food is worth the effort, and most dishes can be tailored to your taste buds: hot, medium, or mild. Begin with spring rolls and a dipping sauce, move on to such entrées as Evil Prince Chicken (cooked in coconut sauce with Thai herbs), or red-curry shrimp, and finish up with tea and tapioca pudding. Asian artifacts, flowers, and a waterfall decorate the dining room, and tables on a veranda satisfy lovers of the outdoors. ⊠ *2119 Vineyard St., Wailuku* ☎ *808/244–1567* ⊟ *AE, MC, V. $8–$13.*

Vietnamese

★ $-$$ ✕ **A Saigon Café.** The only storefront sign announcing this small, delightful hideaway is one reading OPEN. Once you find it, treat yourself to *banh hoi chao tom*, more commonly known as "shrimp pops burritos" (ground marinated shrimp, steamed and grilled on a stick of sugarcane). Fresh island fish is always available and vegetarian fare is well represented—try the green-papaya salad. The white interior serves as a backdrop for Vietnamese carvings in this otherwise unadorned space. Background music includes one-hit wonders from the early '70s. ✉ *1792 Main St., Wailuku* ☎ *808/243–9560* ▭ *D, MC, V. $9–$19.*

★ ¢-$ ✕ **Ba Le.** Tucked into the mall's food court is the best, cheapest fast food on the island. The famous soups, or *pho*, come laden with seafood or rare beef, fresh basil, bean sprouts, and lime. Tasty sandwiches are served on crisp French rolls—lemongrass chicken is a favorite. The word is out, so the place gets busy at lunchtime, though the wait is never long. ✉ *Kau Kau Corner food court, Maui Marketplace, 270 Dairy Rd., Kahului* ☎ *808/877–2400* ▭ *AE, D, DC, MC, V. $4–$8.*

The South Shore

American

$$$-$$$$ ✕ **Joe's Bar & Grill.** With friendly service, a great view of Lāna'i, and such dishes as New York strip steak with caramelized onions, wild mushrooms, and Gorgonzola cheese crumble, there are lots of reasons to stop in at this spacious, breezy spot. Owners Joe and Bev Gannon, who run the immensely popular Hāli'imaile General Store, have brought their flair for food home to roost in this comfortable treetop-level restaurant at the Wailea Tennis Club, where you can dine while watching court action from a balcony seat. ✉ *131 Wailea Ike Pl., Wailea* ☎ *808/875–7767* ▭ *AE, MC, V. $20–$38.*

$$-$$$ ✕ **Seawatch.** The Plantation House's South Shore sister restaurant has an equally good view, and almost as delicious a menu. Breakfast is especially nice here—the outdoor seating is cool in the morning, overlooking the parade of boats heading out to Molokini. The crab-cake Benedicts are a well-loved standard. ✉ *100 Golf Club Dr., Wailea* ☎ *808/875–8080* ▭ *AE, D, DC, MC, V. $16–$28.*

★ $-$$$ ✕ **Maui Onion.** Forget the overrated Cheeseburger in Paradise in Lahaina—Maui Onion has the best burgers on the island, hands down, and phenomenal onion rings as well. They coat the onions in pancake

---

BEST BETS FOR BREAKFAST

Gazebo Restaurant (West Maui). If you're a sucker for coconut syrup, "nene" eggs, and a view of the Pacific, this place is worth the wait.

Plantation House (West Maui). Good luck deciding which is more delicious, the crab cake Benedict or the view of Molokāi.

Kihei Caffe (South Shore). Hearty, affordable portions will prepare you for a day of surfing across the street at Kalama Park.

Seawatch (South Shore). Your debate can grow even more finicky at the Plantation House's sister restaurant—are the Benedicts better here, with this view?

---

batter, dip them in panko, then fry them until they're golden brown. ⊠ *Renaissance Wailea, 3550 Wailea Alanui Dr., Wailea* ☎ *808/879–4900* ⊟ *AE, D, DC, MC, V. $10–$24.*

★ **$–$$$** ✕ **Tastings.** A wedge of a restaurant, this tiny epicurean mecca is tucked in behind a number of rowdy bars on South Kīhei Road. The owner-chef hails from Healdsburg, California, and he brought his highly regarded restaurant with him. The menu features "tastings" of oysters, risotto, lamb chops, and seared *opakapaka* (Hawaiian pink snapper) with a number of well-chosen wines by the bottle or glass. At the bar you can rub elbows with chefs and waiters from the island's best restaurants who come to spend their hard-earned tips here. ⊠ *1913 S. Kīhei Rd., Kīhei* ☎ *808/879–8711* ⊕ *www.tastingsrestaurant.com* ⊟ *AE, D, DC, MC, V. $8–$27.*

¢–$ ✕ **Kihei Caffe.** People-watching is fun over a cup of coffee at this casual breakfast and lunch joint. Hearty, affordable portions will prepare you for a day of surfing across the street at Kalama Park. The bowl-shape egg scramble is tasty and almost enough for two. ⊠ *1945 S. Kīhei Rd., Kīhei* ☎ *808/879–2230* ⊟ *MC, V. $6–$10.*

Hawaiian–Pacific Rim

$$$–$$$$ ✕ **Humuhumunukunukuāpua'a.** Wrestle with the restaurant's formidable name—the name of the state fish—or simply watch the fish swim by in the 2,100-gallon tank at the bar. The thatch-roof building actually floats on a lagoon, creating an atmosphere that tends to outshine the food. Sweet corn and lobster soup with poached rock shrimp and basil puree is a standout, as is the sesame-crusted mahimahi with coconut rice, baby bok choy, and black-bean miso sauce. You can fetch your own spiny lobster (which is best simply grilled) from a cage below the water's surface. You may have to fetch your own drinks as well; the service is notoriously slow. ⊠ *Grand Wailea Resort, 3850 Wailea Alanui Dr., Wailea* ☎ *808/875–1234* ⊟ *AE, D, DC, MC, V. $28–$38.*

★ **$$$–$$$$** ✕ **Spago.** Celebrity chef and owner Wolfgang Puck wisely brought his fame to this gorgeous locale. Giant sea-anemone prints, modern-art-inspired lamps, and views of the shoreline give diners something to look at while waiting. The solid menu delivers with dishes like seared scallops with asparagus and *pohole* (fiddlehead fern) shoots, and "chinois" lamb chops with Hunan eggplant. The beef dish, with braised celery, Armagnac, and horseradish potatoes, may be the island's priciest—but devotees swear it's worth every cent. ⊠ *Four Seasons Resort, 3900 Wailea Alanui Dr., Wailea* ☎ *808/879–2999* ⊟ *AE, D, DC, MC, V* ☾ *No lunch. $29–$57.*

$$–$$$$ ✕ **Hula Moons.** This delightful oceanside spot is full of memorabilia chronicling the life of Don Blanding, an artist and poet who became Hawai'i's unofficial ambassador of aloha in the 1930s. The vegetarian appetizer of fresh pohole ferns, Hāna tomatoes, and Kula onions is fabulous. Try the bamboo-steamed whole *moi*, a fish once reserved for Hawaiian royalty, or the tangy braised short ribs. Sunday brunch is one of the most lavish on the island, and the wine list is extensive. You can dine inside, poolside, or on the terrace. ⊠ *Marriott Wailea Resort, 3700 Wailea Alanui Dr., Wailea* ☎ *808/879–1922* ⊟ *AE, D, DC, MC, V. $15–$39.*

WHERE TO WINE

DON'T LET THE PINEAPPLE WINE FOOL YOU, Maui residents can sip syrah with the best of them. At **Tastings** (✉ 1913 S. Kīhei Rd. ☎ 808/879–8711) on the South Shore, you can sample oysters, risotto, and steak with a number of wines by the bottle or glass. Small and smartly designed, this epicurean mecca is tucked in between a number of rowdy bars in Kīhei. **Marc Aurel's Espresso & Wine Bar** (✉ 28 Market St., Wailuku ☎ 808/244–0852) has an even wider selection of wines by the glass. The impressive five-page wine menu reads like a novel and is complemented by Marc's own *tzatziki* (fresh cucumber dip) and a terrific assortment of cheeses. This favorite Wailuku watering hole is popular for *pau hanas*, or after-work drinks, so be sure to stop by before 9 PM.

On the West Side, try **Vino** (✉ 2000 Village Rd., Kapalua ☎ 808/661–8466). Beloved island chef–restaurateur, D. K. Kodama (the force behind Sansei), opened this eclectic dining experience on the golf course, tweaking some of his favorite recipes and creating new ones to match his Master Sommelier's recommendations.

True connoisseurs might wrap their vacation around the **Kapalua Wine & Food Festival** (☎ 800/527–2782 ⊕ www.kapaluamaui.com). Well into its 25th year, this extravaganza sponsored by Kapalua Resort pairs many of the island's top chefs with great wines from around the world. It kicks off in mid-July and events are spread out over four days.

Irish

¢–$$ ✕ **Mulligan's on the Blue.** If you're hankering for bangers and mash or shepherd's pie, stop in at this pub on Wailea's Blue golf course. You'll be greeted by a nearly all-Irish staff, and before you know it, you'll be sipping a heady pint of Guinness. Breakfast is a good value for the area, and the view is one of the best. Live music makes evenings fun. ✉ *100 Kaukahi St., Wailea* ☎ *808/874–1131* ▭ *AE, D, DC, MC, V. $6–$18.*

Italian

$$$–$$$$ ✕ **Capische.** Hidden up at the quiet Blue Diamond Resort, this restau-
Fodor's Choice rant is one local patrons would like kept secret. A circular stone atrium
★ gives way to a small piano lounge, where you can find the best sunset view on the island. You can count on the freshness of the ingredients in superb dishes like the quail saltimbocca, and the saffron *vongole*—a colorful affair of squid-ink pasta and spicy saffron broth. Intimate and well conceived, Capische, with its seductive flavors and ambience, makes for a romantic night out. ✉ *Blue Diamond Resort, 555 Kaukahi St., Wailea* ☎ *808/879–2224* ▭ *AE, D, DC, MC, V* ☉ *No lunch. $26–$45.*

$$$–$$$$ ✕ **Sarento's on the Beach.** Chef George Gomes, formerly of A Pacific Café, heads the kitchen at South Maui's newest Italian restaurant. The beachfront setting is irresistible, and the menu features both traditional Italian dishes—like penne Calabrese and seafood *fra diavolo*—as well as inventions such as swordfish saltimbocca, a strangely successful entrée with a prosciutto, Bel Paese cheese, radicchio, and porcini-mushroom sauce.

The wine list includes some affordable finds. ⊠ *2980 S. Kīhei Rd., Kīhei* ☎ *808/875–7555* ⊟ *AE, D, DC, MC, V* ⊙ *No lunch. $27–$41.*

$$–$$$$ ✕ **Caffe Ciao.** Caffe Ciao brings Italy to the Fairmont Kea Lani. Authentic, fresh gnocchi and lobster risotto taste especially delicious in the open-air café, which overlooks the swimming pool. For casual European fare, try the poached-tuna salad, grilled panini, or pizza from the wood-burning oven. Locals have long known Caffe Ciao's sister deli as the sole source for discerning palates: delectable pastries, tapenades, mustards, and even $50 bottles of truffle oil. ⊠ *Fairmont Kea Lani, 4100 Wailea Alanui Dr., Wailea* ☎ *808/875–4100* ⊟ *AE, D, DC, MC, V. $13–$32.*

Japanese

$$$–$$$$ ✕ **Hakone.** The Japanese food served at this restaurant in the Maui Prince hotel has a great reputation. Each night, a different "Special Attraction Buffet" is served: Crazy Crab, Sake Sampler, or the Japanese buffet with numerous dishes of raw, cooked, hot, cold, sweet, and savory items. At $44, it's a good value for the quality of food presented. Impeccably fresh sushi, traditional cooked dishes, and an impressive sake list round out the menu. ⊠ *Maui Prince, 5400 Mākena Alanui Rd., Mākena* ☎ *808/874–1111* ⊟ *AE, MC, V* ⊙ *No lunch. $20–$44.*

★ ¢–$$ ✕ **Hirohachi.** A stone's throw from the flashier Sansei, Hirohachi has been serving authentic Japanese fare for years. Owner Hiro has discerning taste, he buys only the best from local fishermen and imports many ingredients from Japan. Order with confidence even if you can't read the Japanese specials posted on the wall, everything on the menu is high quality. ⊠ *1881 S. Kīhei Rd., Kīhei* ☎ *808/875–7474* ⊟ *AE, MC, V* ⊙ *Closed Mon. $6–$18.*

Seafood

$$$–$$$$ ✕ **Nick's Fishmarket Maui.** This romantic spot serves fresh seafood using the simplest preparations: mahimahi with Kula-corn relish, 'ahi pepper fillet, and *opakapaka* (Hawaiian pink snapper) with rock shrimp in a lemon-butter-caper sauce, to name a few. Everyone seems to love the Greek Maui Wowie salad made with local onions, tomatoes, avocado, feta cheese, and bay shrimp. Service is somewhat formal, but it befits the beautiful food presentations and extensive wine list. ⊠ *Fairmont Kea Lani, 4100 Wailea Alanui Dr., Wailea* ☎ *808/879–7224* ⊟ *AE, D, DC, MC, V* ⊙ *No lunch. $27–$49.*

$$–$$$$ ✕ **Waterfront Restaurant.** At this harborside establishment, fresh fish is prepared in a host of sumptuous ways: baked in buttered parchment paper; imprisoned in ribbons of angel-hair potato; or topped with tomato salsa, smoked chili pepper, and avocado. The varied menu also lists an outstanding rack of lamb and veal scallopini. Visitors like to come early to dine at sunset on the outdoor patio. Enter Mā'alaea at the Maui Ocean Center and then follow the blue WATERFRONT RESTAURANT signs to the third condominium. ⊠ *50 Hau'oli St., Mā'alaea* ☎ *808/244–9028* ⊟ *AE, D, DC, MC, V* ⊙ *No lunch. $19–$53.*

$–$$$ ✕ **Blue Marlin Harborfront Grill & Bar.** This is a casual, less expensive alternative to the Waterfront Restaurant. It's as much a bar as it is a grill, but the kitchen nonetheless sends out well-prepared, substantial servings of fresh fish, burgers, and salads. The sidewalk tables have a lovely view of the harbor. ⊠ *Māʻalaea Harbor Village, at Old Māʻalaea Rd. and Honoapiʻilani Hwy., next to Maui Ocean Center, Māʻalaea* ☎ *808/244–8844* ☰ *AE, MC, V. $10–$28.*

Thai

★ **$–$$** ✕ **Thai Cuisine.** Fragrant tea and coconut-ginger chicken soup begin a satisfying meal at this excellent Thai restaurant. The care that goes into the decor here (reflected in the glittering Buddhist shrines, fancy napkin folds, and matching blue china) also applies to the cuisine. The lean and moist meat of the red-curry duck rivals similar dishes at resort restaurants, and the fried bananas with ice cream are wonderful. ⊠ *In Kukui Mall, 1819 S. Kīhei Rd., Kīhei* ☎ *808/875–0839* ☰ *AE, D, DC, MC, V. $8–$17.*

Upcountry

American

¢–$ ✕ **Garden Café.** A good bet for casual lunch in Makawao, this small restaurant is squeezed in between clothing shops, art galleries, and holistic healers. Especially recommended is the snowcrab-and-avocado sandwich on focaccia. Seating is outdoors only. ⊠ *Paniolo Courtyard, 3673 Baldwin Ave., Makawao* ☎ *808/573–9065* ☰ *No credit cards* ☺ *Closed Sun. No dinner. $5–$7.*

Italian

$$–$$$$ ✕ **Casanova Italian Restaurant & Deli.** This family-owned Italian dinner house is an Upcountry institution. The pizzas, baked in a brick woodburning oven imported from Italy, are the best on the island, especially the *tartufo*, or truffle oil pizza. The daytime deli serves outstanding sandwiches and espresso. After dining hours, local and visiting entertainers heat up the dance floor. ⊠ *1188 Makawao Ave., Makawao* ☎ *808/572–0220* ☰ *D, DC, MC, V. $13–$33.*

Mexican

$–$$ ✕ **Polli's.** This Mexican restaurant not only offers standards such as enchiladas, chimichangas, and fajitas but will also prepare any item on the menu with seasoned tofu or vegetarian taco mix—and the meatless dishes are just as good as the real thing. A special treat are the *bunuelos*—light pastries topped with cinnamon, maple syrup, and ice cream. The intimate interior is plastered with colorful sombreros and other cantina knickknacks. ⊠ *1202 Makawao Ave., Makawao* ☎ *808/572–7808* ☰ *AE, D, DC, MC, V. $8–$18.*

★ ¢ ✕ **Maui's Best Tamales.** The owner of this tiny tamale haven can sometimes be seen surrounded by towers of fresh Kula corn. From these she makes indisputably "Maui's best tamales." Her daily specials—chipotle pork or chicken mole—are divine. This is a great spot to grab a bite to eat while touring Upcountry. ⊠ *In Pukalani Sq., 81 Makawao Ave., Pukalani* ☎ *808/573–2998* ☺ *Closes at 6 PM. $3–$7.*

Steak

$$–$$$ ✕ **Makawao Steak House.** A restored 1927 house on the slopes of Haleakalā is the setting for this *paniolo* restaurant, which serves consistently good prime rib, rack of lamb, and fresh fish. Three fireplaces, friendly service, and an intimate lounge create a cozy, welcoming atmosphere. ⊠ *3612 Baldwin Ave., Makawao* ☎ *808/572–8711* ▭ *D, DC, MC, V* ⊙ *No lunch. $18–$28.*

The North Shore

American

¢–$ ✕ **Pauwela Café.** Ultracasual and ultrafriendly, this spot just off Hāna Highway is worth the detour. Order a kālua-pork sandwich and a piece of coffee cake and pass the afternoon. The large breakfast burritos and homemade soups are also good. ⊠ *375 W. Kuiaha Rd., off Hāna Hwy. past Ha'ikū Rd., Ha'ikū* ☎ *808/575–9242* ⊙ *No dinner. $3–$7.*

Eclectic

$–$$$ ✕ **Jacque's.** Jacque, an amiable French chef, won the hearts of the windsurfing crowd when he opened this hip, ramshackle bar and restaurant. French-Caribbean dishes like *Jacque's Crispy Little Poulet* (chicken) reveal the owner's expertise. The outdoor seating can be a little chilly at times; coveted spots at the sushi bar inside are snatched up quickly. ⊠ *120 Hāna Hwy., Pā'ia* ☎ *808/579–8844* ▭ *AE, D, MC, V. $11–$22.*

¢–$ ✕ **Cafe Des Amis.** Papier-mâché wrestlers pop out from the walls at this small creperie. French crêpes with Gruyère, and Indian wraps with lentil curry are among the choices, all served with wild greens and sour cream or chutney on the side. For dessert there are crêpes, of course, filled with chocolate, Nutella, cane sugar, or banana. ⊠ *42 Baldwin Ave., Pā'ia* ☎ *808/579–6373* ▭ *AE, D, MC, V. $6–$11.*

Hawaiian–Pacific Rim

★ $$–$$$$ ✕ **Hāli'imaile General Store.** What do you do with a lofty wooden building surrounded by sugarcane and pineapple fields that was a tiny town's camp store in the 1920s? If you're Bev and Joe Gannon, you invent a legendary restaurant. The Szechuan barbecued salmon and Hunan-style rack of lamb are classics, as is the sashimi napoleon appetizer: a tower of crispy wontons layered with 'ahi and salmon. Pastry chef Teresa Gannon makes an unbelievable pineapple upside-down cake. The restaurant even has its own cookbook. ⊠ *900 Hāli'imaile Rd., left at exit off Rte. 37, 5 mi from Hāna Hwy., Hāli'imaile* ☎ *808/572–2666* ▭ *MC, V. $15–$35.*

Mexican

$–$$$ ✕ **Milagro's.** Delicious fish tacos are found at this corner hangout, along with a selection of fine tequilas. Latin fusion recipes ignite fresh fish and vegetables. The location at the junction of Baldwin Avenue and Hāna Highway makes people-watching under the awning shade a lot of fun. Lunch and happy hour (3–5) are the best values; the prices jump at dinnertime. ⊠ *3 Baldwin Ave., Pā'ia* ☎ *808/579–8755* ▭ *AE, D, DC, MC, V. $8–$29.*

Seafood

★ $$$$ ✕ **Mama's Fish House.** For years Mama's has been *the* destination for special occasions. A stone- and shell-engraved path leads you up to what would be, in an ideal world, a good friend's house. The Hawaiian nau-

2

tical theme is hospitable and fun—the menu even names which boat reeled in your fish. But, sadly, fame has gone to this restaurant's head. Prices bulged while portions shrank. If you're willing to fork over the cash, the daily catch baked in a creamy caper sauce or steamed in traditional lū'au leaves is still worth trying. Mama's is marked by a tiny fishing boat perched above the entrance about 1½ mi east of Pa'ia on Hāna Highway. ⊠ *799 Poho Pl., Kū'au* ☎ *808/579–8488* ⌖ *Reservations essential* ⊟ *AE, D, DC, MC, V. $32–$48.*

ENTERTAINMENT & NIGHTLIFE

Nightlife on Maui might be better labeled "evening life." The quiet island has little of Waikīkī's after-hours decadence. But before 10 PM there's a lot on offer, from lū'au shows and dinner cruises to concerts. Lahaina still tries to uphold its reputation as a party town and succeeds wildly every Halloween when thousands converge on Front Street.

★ The **Maui Arts & Cultural Center** (⊠ Above the harbor on Kahului Beach Rd. ☎ 808/242–2787) is the backbone of Maui's arts and entertainment. The complex includes the 1,200-seat Castle Theater, which hosts international performances and weekly film showings; a 4,000-seat amphitheater for large outdoor concerts; and the 350-seat McCoy Theater for plays and recitals. For information on current programs, check the Events Box Office (☎ 808/242–7469) or the *Maui News.*

Entertainment

Lū'au

★ **The Feast at Lele.** "Lele" is an older, more traditional name for Lahaina. This "feast" is redefining the lū'au by crossing it with island-style fine dining in an intimate beach setting. Both the show and the five-course meal express the spirit of a specific island culture—Hawaiian, Samoan, Tongan, or Tahitian. The wine list and liquor selections are excellent. ⊠ *505 Front St., Lahaina* ☎ *808/ 667–5353* ⌖ *Reservations essential* ☲ *$95* ⊙ *Mon.–Sat. at 5:30 in winter, 6:30 in summer.*

Nāpili Kai Beach Club Keiki Hula Show. Expect to be charmed as well as entertained when 30 children ages 6 to 17 take you on a dance tour of Hawai'i, New Zealand, Tahiti, Samoa, and other Polynesian islands. The talented youngsters make their own ti-leaf skirts and fresh-flower leis. They give the leis to the audience at the end of the show. This is a nonprofessional but delightfully engaging review, and the 80-seat

> **STARGAZING**
>
> For nightlife of a different sort, children and astronomy buffs should try stargazing at **Tour of the Stars,** a one-hour program held nightly on the roof of the Hyatt Regency Maui. A romantic program for couples, with roses and chocolate, is held on Friday and Saturday nights at 11. Check in at the hotel lobby 15 minutes prior to starting time. ⊠ *Lahaina Tower, Hyatt Regency Maui, 200 Nohea Kai Dr., Kā'anapali* ☎ *808/661– 1234 Ext. 4727* ☲ *$25* ⊙ *Nightly at 8, 9, and 10; Fri. and Sat. romantic program at 11.*

oceanfront room is usually sold out. ⊠ *Nāpili Kai Beach Club, 5900 Lower Honoapi'ilani Hwy., Nāpili* ☎ *808/669–6271* ⊕ *$50* ☉ *Dinner Fri. at 6, show at 7:30.*

FodorsChoice **Old Lahaina Lū'au.** We can't think of a better way to get into the Hawaiian swing of things—this is the best lū'au on Maui. Even cynical, tough-guy husbands who initially have to be dragged here usually leave with a newfound respect for the aloha spirit. The Old Lahaina Lū'au is small, personal, and authentic and is performed in an outdoor theater designed specifically for traditional Hawaiian entertainment. The setting feels like an old seaside village. In addition to fresh fish and grilled steak and chicken, you'll get all-you-can-eat traditional lū'au fare: kālua pig, chicken long rice, *lomi lomi* salmon (massaged until tender and served with minced onions and tomatoes), *haupia* (coconut pudding), and other treats. Limitless drinks are also included. Guests sit on tatami mats or at tables. Then there's the entertainment: a musical journey from old Hawai'i to the present with hula dancing, chanting, and singing. ■ TIP→→ Though it's performed nightly, this lū'au is known to sell out weeks in advance. Try to make reservations when you're planning your trip to Maui. You can cancel without a penalty up to 24 hours in advance. ⊠ *1251 Front St., makai of Lahaina Cannery Mall, Lahaina* ☎ *808/667–1998* ⊜ *Reservations essential* ⊕ *www. oldlahainaluau.com* ⊕ *$79* ☉ *Nightly at 5:45.*

Dinner & Sunset Cruises

***America II* Sunset Sail.** The star of this two-hour cruise is the craft itself—a 1987 America's Cup 12-meter class contender that is exceptionally smooth and steady. ⊠ *Lahaina Harbor, Lahaina* ☎ *808/667–2195* ⊕ *$39.*

***Kaulana* Cocktail Cruise.** This two-hour sunset cruise (with a bit of whale-watching in season) serves *pūpūs* (appetizers) and has an open bar and live music. ⊠ *Lahaina Harbor, Lahaina* ☎ *808/871–1144* ⊕ *$39.*

Pride Charters. A 65-foot catamaran built specifically for Maui's waters, the *Pride of Maui* has a large cabin, a large upper sundeck for unobstructed viewing, and a stable, comfortable ride. Evening cruises include cocktails and *pūpūs* such as wontons and chicken teriyaki sticks. Daytime sailing and snorkeling trips are also available. ⊠ *Mā'alaea Harbor, Mā'alaea* ☎ *808/242–0955* ⊕ *$47.*

Scotch Mist Charters. A two-hour champagne sunset sail is offered on the 25-passenger Santa Cruz 50 sloop *Scotch Mist II.* ⊠ *Lahaina Harbor, Lahaina* ☎ *808/661–0386* ⊕ *$45.*

Film

There are megaplexes showing first-run movies in Kukui Mall, Lahaina Center, Maui Mall, and Ka'ahumanu Shopping Center. Check local papers for showtimes.

★ **Maui Film Festival.** In this ongoing celebration, quality films that may not show up at the local megaplex are screened every Wednesday evening. Screenings in Maui's most luxurious movie house—Castle Theater at Maui Arts & Cultural Center—are accompanied by live music and poetry readings in the Candlelight Cafe. In summer, a special weeklong festival attracts big-name celebrities to Wailea for cinema under the stars. This annual "Celestial Cinema" includes music, hula, and Hawaiian storytelling. ☎ 808/572–3456 *recorded program information* ⊕ *www. mauifilmfestival.com.*

Theater

Maui Academy of Performing Arts. For a quarter-century this group has offered fine performances as well as dance and drama classes for children and adults. It has presented such plays as *Peter Pan, Jesus Christ Superstar,* and *The Nutcracker.* Call ahead for performance venue. ✉ *81 N. Church St., Wailuku* ☎ *808/244–8760* ✍ *$10–$12.*

Maui Community Theatre. The oldest dramatic group on the island—it was started in the early 1900s—is now staging about six plays a year. Each July the group also holds a fund-raising variety show, which can be a hoot. ✉ *'Iao Theatre, 68 N. Market St., Wailuku* ☎ *808/242–6969* ✍ *Musicals $10–$15, nonmusicals $8–$13.*

★ ☺ **"'Ulalena" at Maui Theater.** One of Maui's hottest tickets, "'Ulalena" is a 75-minute musical extravaganza that is well received by audiences and Hawaiian-culture experts alike. Cirque de Soleil–inspired, the ensemble cast (20 singer-dancers and a five-musician orchestra) mixes native rhythms and stories with acrobatic performance. High-tech stage wizardry gives an inspiring introduction to island culture. It has auditorium seating, and beer and wine are for sale at the concession stand. There are dinner-theater packages in conjunction with top Lahaina restaurants. ✉ *878 Front St., Lahaina* ☎ *808/661–9913 or 877/688–4800* ⚓ *Reservations essential* ✍ *$48–$68* ☉ *Tues.–Sat. at 6 PM.*

Warren & Annabelle's. Magician Warren Gibson entices his guests into a swank nightclub with red carpets and a gleaming mahogany bar, and plies them with appetizers (coconut shrimp, crab cakes), desserts (rum cake, crème brûlée), and "smoking cocktails." Then he performs tableside magic while his ghostly assistant, Annabelle, tickles the ivories. The show is fun, and all the better for not being too slick. Note that this is a nightclub, so no one under 21 is allowed. ✉ *Lahaina Center, 900 Front St.* ☎ *808/ 667–6244* ⚓ *Reservations essential* ✍ *$39.95* ☉ *Mon.–Sat. at 5.*

Bars & Clubs

With a little homework, good music and high times can be had on Maui. *Maui Times Magazine,* a free publication found at most stores and restaurants, will help you find out who's playing where. The *Maui News* also publishes an entertainment schedule in its Thursday edition of "Maui Scene."

West Maui

Cheeseburger in Paradise. This Front Street joint is known for—what else?—big beefy cheeseburgers (not to mention a great spinach-nut burger). Locals also know it as a great place to tune in to live bands playing rock and roll, Top 40, and oldies from 4:30 PM to closing. There's no dance floor, but the second-floor balcony is a good place to watch Lahaina's Front Street action. ✉ *811 Front St., Lahaina* ☎ *808/ 661–4855.*

Hard Rock Cafe. Maui's version of the Hard Rock is popular with young locals as well as visitors who like their music *loud.* ✉ *Lahaina Center, 900 Front St., Lahaina* ☎ *808/667–7400.*

Moose McGillycuddy's. The Moose offers no-cover live music on Tuesday and Thursday and draws a young crowd that comes to enjoy the burgers and beer, dancing and mingling. ⊠ *844 Front St., Lahaina* ☎ *808/667–7758.*

Pacific'O. This highly recommended restaurant is also a reliable place to hear live jazz on the beach. It's a mellow, Pacific sort of jazz—naturally—and it plays from 9 until midnight Thursday through Saturday. Guest musicians—George Benson, for example—often sit in. ⊠ *505 Front St., Lahaina* ☎ *808/667–4341.*

★ **Paradice Bluz.** Live local bands and comedians frequent the stage at this highly popular, underground West Side hangout. Busy weekend nights usually involve a cover charge. ⊠ *744 Front St., Lahaina* ☎ *808/667–5299.*

The Sly Mongoose. Off the beaten tourist path, the Sly Mongoose is the seediest dive bar in town, and one of the friendliest. The bartender will know your name and half your life history inside of 10 minutes, and she makes the strongest mai tai on the island. ⊠ *1036 Limahana Pl., Lahaina* ☎ *808/661–8097.*

The South Shore

Hapa's Brewhaus & Restaurant. Well-loved local performer Willi K. owns Monday nights at this club, which has a large stage, a roomy dance floor, state-of-the-art light-and-sound systems, and tier seating. Crowds pile in on this and other nights for live music, televised sports, and fine brews. ⊠ *Lipoa Center, 41 E. Lipoa St., Kīhei* ☎ *808/879–9001.*

Kahale's Beach Club. A friendly, informal hangout, Kahale's offers live music (usually Hawaiian), drinks, and burgers every day from 10 AM until 2 in the morning. ⊠ *36 Keala Pl., Kīhei* ☎ *808/875–7711.*

Lobby Lounge. In the comfortable Four Seasons lobby, you can listen to contemporary and Hawaiian music played by some of the island's best musicians. A hula dancer performs at sunset. The superior menu offers selections from all of the resort's restaurants. ⊠ *Four Seasons Resort, 3900 Wailea Alanui Dr., Wailea* ☎ *808/874–8000.*

★ **Mulligan's on the Blue.** Perfect pints of Guinness and late-night fish-and-chips—who could ask for more? Add to that live entertainment (including Sunday-evening Irish jams), gorgeous sunset views, an optimal resort location, and a dance floor, and you've got one of Maui's busiest nighttime hangouts. Don't miss *Wailea Nights,* an inspired dinner show performed twice weekly by members of the band "Hapa." ⊠ *Blue Golf Course, 100 Kaukahi St., Wailea* ☎ *808/874–1131.*

Tsunami's. You can dance to hip-hop, house, techno, reggae, and Top 40 hits in this sophisticated, high-tech disco, where laser beams zigzag high above a futuristic dance floor. The music plays from 9 to 1 on Friday and Saturday nights. Expect a dress code—no jeans or T-shirts—and a $10 cover charge. ⊠ *Grand Wailea, 3850 Wailea Alanui Dr., Wailea* ☎ *808/875–1234.*

Upcountry & the North Shore

Casanova Italian Restaurant & Deli. Popular Casanova claims to be the best place on the island for singles. When a DJ isn't spinning, contemporary musicians play blues, country and western, rock and roll, and reggae. Past favorites have included Kool and the Gang, Los Lobos, and

Taj Mahal. Expect a cover charge on nights featuring live entertainment. ⊠ *1188 Makawao Ave., Makawao* ☎ *808/572–0220.*

Moana Bakery and Cafe. While its name doesn't lend itself to visions of late nights on the town, this popular North Shore restaurant is an intimate venue for jazz and blues duos, and the occasional flamenco guitarist. The menu is good, too. ⊠ *71 Baldwin Ave., Pa'ia* ☎ *808/579–9999.*

Sandbar & Grill. In Pā'ia, you can catch local musicians and DJs at this popular, casual bar—frequently without having to pay a cover. ⊠ *89 Hāna Hwy., Pā'ia* ☎ *808/579–8742.*

SHOPPING

Shopping is, of course, abundant in the resort areas. Whether you're searching for a dashboard hula dancer or something a little more upmarket, you can probably buy it on Front Street in Lahaina or South Kīhei Road in Kīhei. But don't miss the great boutiques lining the streets of small towns like Pā'ia and Makawao. You can purchase upscale fashions and art while strolling through these charming, quieter communities.

Local artisans turn out gorgeous work in a range of prices. Special souvenirs include rare hardwood bowls and boxes, prints of sea life, Hawaiian quilts, and specialty food products like Kona coffee. A group that calls itself Made on Maui exists solely to promote the products of its members—items ranging from pottery and paintings to Hawaiian teas and macadamia caramel corn. You can identify the group by its distinctive Haleakalā logo.

Local produce—pineapples, papayas, coconuts, or Maui onions—and Made in Maui jams and jellies make great souvenirs. Cook Kwee's Maui Cookies have gained quite a following, as have Maui Potato Chips. Both are available in most Valley Isle grocery stores. Coffee sellers now have

> **SIMPLE SOUVENIRS**
>
> **Take Home Maui.** The folks at this colorful grocery and deli will supply, pack, and deliver produce to the airport or your hotel. ⊠ *121 Dickenson St., Lahaina* ☎ *808/661–8067 or 800/545–6284.*

Maui-grown-and-roasted beans alongside the better-known Kona varieties. Remember that fresh fruit must be inspected by the U.S. Department of Agriculture before it can leave the state, so it's safest to buy a box that has already passed muster.

Business hours for individual shops on the island are usually 9 to 5, seven days a week. Shopping centers tend to stay open later (until 9 or 10 at least one night of the week).

West Maui

Shopping Centers

Lahaina Cannery Mall. Set in a building reminiscent of an old pineapple cannery are 50 shops and an active stage. The mall hosts fabulous free events year-round (like the International Jazz Festival). Recommended stops include Na Hoku, purveyor of striking Hawaiian heirloom jewelry and pearls; Totally Hawaiian Gift Gallery; and Kite Fantasy, one of the best kite shops on Maui. An events schedule is available on the Web site. ✉ *1221 Honoapi'ilani Hwy., Lahaina* ☎ *808/661–5304* ⊕ *www.lahainacannery.com.*

Lahaina Center. Island department store Hilo Hattie Fashion Center anchors the complex and puts on a free hula show at 2 PM every Wednesday and Friday. In addition to Hard Rock Cafe, Banana Republic, and a four-screen cinema, you can find a replica of an ancient Hawaiian village complete with three full-size thatch huts built with 10,000 feet of Big Island 'ōhi'a wood, 20 tons of *pili* grass, and more than 4 mi of hand-woven coconut *senit* (twine). There's all that *and* validated parking. ✉ *900 Front St., Lahaina* ☎ *808/667–9216.*

Whalers Village. Chic Whalers Village has a whaling museum and more than 50 restaurants and shops. Upscale haunts include Louis Vuitton, Ferragamo, Versace, and Chanel Boutique. The complex also offers some interesting diversions: Hawaiian artisans display their crafts daily; hula dancers perform on an outdoor stage weeknights from 7 to 8; and three films spotlighting whales and marine history are shown daily for free at the Whale Center of the Pacific. ✉ *2435 Kā'anapali Pkwy., Kā'anapali* ☎ *808/661–4567.*

Clothing

Hilo Hattie Fashion Center. Hawai'i's largest manufacturer of aloha shirts and mu'umu'u also carries brightly colored blouses, skirts, and children's clothing. ✉ *Lahaina Center, 900 Front St., Lahaina* ☎ *808/661–8457.*

Honolua Surf Company. If you're not in the mood for a matching aloha shirt and mu'umu'u ensemble, check out this surf shop—popular with young men and women for surf trunks, casual clothing, and accessories. ✉ *845 Front St., Lahaina* ☎ *808/661–8848.*

Maggie Coulombe. Maggie Coulombe's cutting-edge fashions have the style of SoHo and the heat of the Islands. The designs here are unique and definitely worth a look. ✉ *505 Front St., Lahaina* ☎ *808/662–0696.*

Jewelry

Haimoff & Haimoff Creations in Gold. This shop carries the original work of several jewelry designers, including the renowned Harry Haimoff. ✉ *Kapalua Resort* ☎ *808/669–5213.*

Jessica's Gems. Jessica's has a good selection of Hawaiian heirloom jewelry, and its Lahaina store specializes in black pearls. ✉ *Whalers Village, 2435 Kā'anapali Pkwy., Kā'anapali* ☎ *808/661–4223* ✉ *858 Front St., Lahaina* ☎ *808/661–9200.*

Lahaina Scrimshaw. Here you can buy brooches, rings, pendants, cuff links, tie tacks, and collector's items adorned with intricately carved sailors' art. ✉ *845A Front St., Lahaina* ☎ *808/661–8820* ✉ *Whalers Village, 2435 Kā'anapali Pkwy., Kā'anapali* ☎ *808/661–4034.*

Maui Divers. This company has been crafting gold and coral into jewelry for more than 20 years. ✉ *640 Front St., Lahaina* ☎ *808/661–0988.*

Galleries

Lahaina Galleries. Works of both national and international artists are displayed at the gallery's two locations in West Maui. ✉ *828 Front St., Lahaina* ☎ *808/667–2152* ✉ *Kapalua Resort, Bay Dr., Kapalua* ☎ *808/ 669–0202.*

Lahaina Printsellers Ltd. Hawai'i's largest selection of original antique maps and prints pertaining to Hawai'i and the Pacific is available here. It also sells museum-quality reproductions and original oil paintings from the Pacific Artists Guild. A second, smaller shop is open at 505 Front Street. ⊠ *Whalers Village, 2435 Kā'anapali Pkwy., Kā'anapali* ☎ 808/667–7617.

Martin Lawrence Galleries. Martin Lawrence displays the works of noted mainland artists, including Andy Warhol and Keith Haring, in a bright and friendly gallery. ⊠ *Lahaina Market Pl., At Front St. and Lahainaluna Rd., Lahaina* ☎ *808/661–1788.*

Village Gallery. This gallery, with two locations on the island, showcases the works of such popular local artists as Betty Hay Freeland, Wailehua Gray, Margaret Bedell, George Allen, Joyce Clark, Pamela Andelin, Stephen Burr, and Macario Pascual. ⊠ *120 Dickenson St., Lahaina* ☎ *808/661–4402* ⊠ *Ritz-Carlton, 1 Ritz-Carlton Dr., Kapalua* ☎ *808/669–1800.*

Central Maui

Shopping Centers

Ka'ahumanu Center. This is Maui's largest mall with more than 75 stores, movie theaters, an active stage, and a food court. The mall's impressive rooftop, composed of a series of manta ray–like umbrella shades, is easily spotted. Stop at Camellia Seed Shop for what the locals call "crack seed," a delicacy made from dried fruits, nuts, and lots of sugar. Other stops here include mall standards such as Macy's, Gap, and American Eagle Outfitters. ⊠ *275 Ka'ahumanu Ave., Kahului* ☎ *808/877–3369.*

Maui Mall. The anchor stores here are Longs Drugs and Star Market, and there's a good Chinese restaurant, Dragon Dragon. The Tasaka Guri Guri Shop is an oddity. It's been around for nearly a hundred years, selling an ice-cream–like confection called "guri guri." The mall also has a whimsically designed 12-screen megaplex. ⊠ *70 Ka'ahumanu Ave., Kahului* ☎ *808/877–7559.*

Maui Marketplace. On the busy stretch of Dairy Road, just outside the Kahului Airport, this behemoth marketplace couldn't be more conveniently located. The 20-acre complex houses several outlet stores and big retailers, such as Pier One Imports, Sports Authority, and Borders Books & Music. Sample local food at the Kau Kau Corner food court. ⊠ *270 Dairy Rd., Kahului* ☎ *808/873–0400.*

> ### FLEA MARKETS
>
> **Maui Swap Meet.** This Saturday flea market is the biggest bargain on Maui, with crafts, gifts, souvenirs, fruit, flowers, jewelry, antiques, art, shells, and lots more. ⊠ *Rte. 350, off S. Pu'unēnē Ave., Kahului* ☲ 50¢ ☉ *Sat. 5:30 AM–noon.*

Food Specialties

Maui Coffee Roasters. This café and roasting house near Kahului Airport is the best stop for Kona and Island coffees. The salespeople give good advice and will ship items. You even get a free cup of joe in a signature to-go cup when you buy a pound of coffee. ⊠ *444 Hāna Hwy., Unit B, Kahului* ☎ *808/877–2877* ⊕ *www.hawaiiancoffee.com.*

The South Shore

Shopping Centers

Azeka Place Shopping Center. Azeka II, on the *mauka* (towards the mountains) side of S. Kīhei Road, has Longs Drugs (the place for slippers), The Coffee Store (the place for iced mochas), Who Cut the Cheese (the place for aged gouda), and the Nail Shop (the place for shaping, waxing, and tweezing). Azeka I, the older half on the makai side of the street, has a decent Vietnamese restaurant and Kīhei's post office. ✉ *1280 S. Kīhei Rd., Kīhei.*

Rainbow Mall. This mall is one-stop shopping for condo guests—it offers video rentals, Hawaiian gifts, plate lunches, and a liquor store. ✉ *2439 S. Kīhei Rd., Kīhei.*

The Shops at Wailea. Stylish, upscale, and close to most of the resorts, this mall brings high fashion to Wailea. Luxury boutiques such as Gucci, Fendi, Cos Bar, and Tiffany & Co. have shops, as do less-expensive chains like Gap, Guess, and Tommy Bahama's. Several good restaurants face the ocean, and regular Wednesday-night events include live entertainment, art exhibits, and fashion shows. ✉ *3750 Wailea Alanui Dr., Wailea* ☎ *808/891–6770.*

Kīhei Kalama Village Marketplace. This is a fun place to investigate. Shaded outdoor stalls sell everything from printed and hand-painted T-shirts and sundresses to jewelry, pottery, wood carvings, fruit, and gaudily painted coconut husks—some, but not all, made by local craftspeople. ✉ *1941 S. Kīhei Rd., Kīhei* ☎ *808/879–6610.*

Clothing

Hilo Hattie Fashion Center. Hawai'i's largest manufacturer of aloha shirts and mu'umu'u also carries brightly colored blouses, skirts, and children's clothing. ✉ *297 Pi'ikea Ave., Kīhei* ☎ *808/875–4545.*

Honolua Surf Company. If you're in the mood for colorful print tees and sundresses, check out this surf shop. It's popular with young men and women for surf trunks, casual clothing, and accessories. ✉ *2411 S. Kīhei Rd., Kīhei* ☎ *808/874–0999.*

Nell. Far better than typical resort boutiques, this expansive shop at the Fairmont Kea Lani carries truly stylish resort clothing for women. If you've recently spied a pretty bracelet on a celebrity in a magazine, there's a good chance you can find it here. ✉ *Fairmont Kea Lani, 4100 Wailea Alanui Dr., Wailea* ☎ *808/875–4100.*

Sisters & Company. Opened by four sisters, this little shop has a lot to offer—current brand-name clothing such as Tamara Katz and ener-chi, locally made jewelry, beach sandals, and gifts. Sister No. 3, Rhonda, runs a tiny, ultrahip hair salon in back. ✉ *1913 S. Kīhei Rd., Kīhei* ☎ *808/875–9888.*

Tommy Bahama's. It's hard to find a man on Maui who *isn't* wearing a TB-logo aloha shirt. For better or worse, here's where you can get yours. Make sure to grab a Barbados Brownie on the way out at the restaurant, which is attached to the shop. ✉ *The Shops at Wailea, 3750 Wailea Alanui Dr., Wailea* ☎ *808/879–7828.*

Upcountry, the North Shore & Hāna

Swimwear

★ **Maui Girl.** This is *the* place for swimwear, cover-ups, beach hats, and sandals. Maui Girl designs its own suits and imports teenier versions from Brazil as well. Whatever your size, tops and bottoms can be purchased separately. ⊠ *13 Baldwin Ave., Pā'ia* ☎ *808/579–9266.*

Fashion & Jewelry

Collections. This eclectic boutique is brimming with women's fashions, jewelry, gift cards, and more. ⊠ *Baldwin Ave., Makawao* ☎ *808/572–0781.*

Master Touch Gallery. The exterior of this shop is as rustic as all the old buildings of Makawao, so there's no way to prepare yourself for the elegance of the handcrafted jewelry displayed within. Owner David Sacco truly has the "master touch." ⊠ *3655 Baldwin Ave., Makawao* ☎ *808/ 572–6000.*

Galleries

Hot Island Glassblowing Studio & Gallery. With the glass-melting furnaces glowing bright orange and the shop loaded with mesmerizing sculptures and functional pieces, this is an exciting place to visit. The working studio, set back from Makawao's main street in "The Courtyard," is owned by a family of glassblowers. ⊠ *3620 Baldwin Ave., Makawao* ☎ *808/572–4527.*

Maui Crafts Guild. This is one of the most interesting galleries on Maui. Set in a two-story wooden building alongside the highway, the Guild is crammed with treasures. Resident artists craft everything in the store— from Norfolk-pine bowls to *raku* (Japanese lead-glazed) pottery to original sculpture. The prices are surprisingly low. Upstairs, gorgeous pieces of handcrafted hardwood furniture are on display. ⊠ *43 Hāna Hwy., Pā'ia* ☎ *808/579–9697.*

Maui Hands. This gallery shows work by dozens of local artists, including *paniolo*-theme lithographs by Sharon Shigekawa, who knows whereof she paints: she rides each year in the Kaupō Roundup. ⊠ *3620 Baldwin Ave., Makawao* ☎ *808/572–5194.*

Hāna Coast Gallery. One of the best places to shop on the island, this 3,000-square-foot gallery has fine art and jewelry on consignment from local artists. ⊠ *Hotel Hāna-Maui, Hāna Hwy., Hāna* ☎ *808/248–8636 or 800/637–0188.*

Hāna Cultural Center. The center sells distinctive island quilts and other Hawaiian crafts. ⊠ *4974 Uakea St., Hāna* ☎ *808/248–8622.*

Grocery Stores on Maui

Foodland. In Kīhei town center, this is the most convenient supermarket for those staying in Wailea. It's open round-the-clock. ⊠ *1881 S. Kīhei Rd., Kīhei* ☎ *808/879–9350.*

Lahaina Square Shopping Center Foodland. This Foodland serves West Maui and is open daily from 6 AM to midnight. ⊠ *840 Waine'e St., Lahaina* ☎ *808/661–0975.*

Mana Foods. Stock up on local fish and grass-fed beef for your barbecue here. You can find the best selection of organic produce on the island, as well as a great bakery and deli at this typically crowded health-food store. ⊠ *49 Baldwin Ave., Pā'ia* ☎ *808/579–8078.*

Safeway. Safeway has three stores on the island open 24 hours daily. ⊠ *La-haina Cannery Mall, 1221 Honoapi'ilani Hwy., Lahaina* ☎ *808/667–4392* ⊠ *170 E. Kamehameha Ave., Kahului* ☎ *808/877–3377* ⊠ *277 Piikea Ave., Kihei* ☎ *808/891–9120.*

MAUI ESSENTIALS

Transportation

BY AIR

You can fly to Maui from the mainland United States or from Honolulu. Flight time from the West Coast to Maui is about 5 hours; from the Midwest, expect about an 8-hour flight; and coming from the East Coast will take about 10 hours, not including layovers. Maui is the most visited of the Neighbor Islands and therefore the easiest to connect to on an interisland flight. Honolulu–Kahului is one of the most heavily traveled air routes in the nation.

CARRIERS   United flies nonstop to Kahului from Los Angeles and San Francisco. American also flies into Kahului, with one stop in Honolulu, from Chicago, and nonstop from Los Angeles and Dallas. Delta has connecting service to Maui daily from Salt Lake City, Atlanta, and Los Angeles and one nonstop flight daily from Los Angeles. Continental flies nonstop to Kahului from Houston. Hawaiian Airlines has direct flights to Kahului from the U.S. West Coast.

Continental, Hawaiian, and Northwest fly from the mainland to Honolulu, where Maui-bound passengers can connect with a 40-minute interisland flight. Flights generally run about $75 one-way between Honolulu and Maui and are available from Hawaiian Airlines, Aloha Airlines, and Island Air. ⇨ *See* Smart Travel Tips *at the front of this guide for airline contact information.*

AIRPORTS   The Kahului Airport is efficient and remarkably easy to navigate. Its main disadvantage is its distance from the major resort destinations in West Maui. Kahului is the only airport on Maui that has direct service from the mainland.

If you're staying in West Maui, you might be better off flying into the **Kapalua–West Maui Airport** (808/669–0623). The only way to get to the Kapalua–West Maui Airport is on an interisland flight from Honolulu because the short runway accommodates only small planes. Set in the midst of a pineapple field with a terrific view of the ocean far below, the little airport provides one of the most pleasant ways to arrive on the Valley Isle.

Hāna Airport isn't much more than a landing strip. Only commuter Aloha Island Air flies here, landing twice a day from Honolulu (via Moloka'i and Kahului) and departing 10 minutes later. The morning flight originates in Princeville, Kaua'i. When there's no flight, the tiny terminal usually stands eerily empty, with no gate agents, ticket takers, or other people in sight.

🔒 **Hāna Airport** ☎ 808/248-8208. **Kahului Airport** ☎ 808/872-3800 or 808/872-3830. **Kapalua-West Maui Airport** ☎ 808/669-0623.

TO & FROM THE AIRPORTS The best way to get from the airport to your destination—and to see the island itself—is in your own rental car. Most major car-rental companies have desks or courtesy phones at each airport. They also can provide a map and directions to your hotel from the airport.

It will take you about an hour, with traffic in your favor, to get from Kahului Airport to a hotel in Kapalua or Kāʻanapali and 30 to 40 minutes to go to Kīhei or Wailea.

Shuttles also run between the airport and the Kāʻanapali and Kapalua resorts during daylight hours at regular intervals.

Maui has more than two-dozen taxi companies, and they make frequent passes through the Kahului and Kapalua-West Maui airports. If you don't see a cab, you can call La Bella Taxi (808/242-8011) for island-wide service from the airport. Call Kīhei Taxi (808/879-3000) if you're staying in the Kīhei, Wailea, or Mākena area. Charges from Kahului Airport to Kāʻanapali run about $57; to Wailea, about $36; and to Lahaina, about $50.

If you're flying into Hāna Airport and staying at the Hotel Hāna-Maui, your flight will be met by a 1932 Packard. If you have reserved a rental car, the agent will usually know your arrival time and meet you. Otherwise you can call Dollar Rent A Car (☎ 800/800-4000) to pick you up.

BY BUS

Maui has a limited bus system, run in conjunction with a private company, Roberts Hawaiʻi. Four routes deliver passengers between Wailuku, Kahului, Kīhei, Wailea, Maʻalaea, and Lahaina. Inexpensive one-way, round-trip, and all-day passes are available. Schedules are available online.

🔒 **Roberts Hawaiʻi** ☎ 808/871-4838 ⊕ www.co.maui.hi.us/bus.

BY CAR

To see the island, your best bet is a car. Maui has bad roads in beautiful places. Roads generally have two lanes, sometimes four, and sometimes only one—ancient highways that bridge staggering valleys in testimony to their bygone engineers. Maui's landscape is extraordinarily diverse for such a small island. Your sense of place (and the weather) will seem to change every few miles. If you drive to the summit of Haleakalā, you can rise from palm-lined beaches to the rare world inhabited by silverswords in less than two hours. The Road to Hāna winds through tropical rain forest, testing your reflexes behind the wheel on the rain-gouged windward side. Upcountry—around Makawao and Haʻikū—you can drive into and out of the rain, with rainbows that seem to land on the hood of your car.

The two difficult roads on Maui are Hāna Highway (Rte. 36) and an 8-mi scenic stretch between Kapalua and Wailuku. If you're going to attempt the partially paved, patched, and bumpy road between Hāna and 'Ulupalakua, take a four-wheel-drive vehicle. Be forewarned: rental-car companies prohibit travel on roads they've determined might damage the car. If you break down, you're on your own for repairs.

CAR RENTAL   During peak seasons—summer, and Christmas through Easter—be sure to reserve your car well ahead of time. Expect to pay about $35–$40 a day—before taxes, insurance, and extras—for a compact car from one of the major companies. You can get a less-expensive deal from one of the locally owned budget companies. There's a $3 daily road tax on all rental cars in Hawai'i.

Budget, Dollar, and National have courtesy phones at the Kapalua–West Maui Airport; Hertz and Alamo are nearby. All of the above, plus Avis, have desks at or near Maui's major airport in Kahului. Quite a few locally owned companies rent cars on Maui, including Aloha Rent-A-Car (808/877–4477 or 877/452–5642), which will pick you up at Kahului Airport or leave a vehicle for you if your flight comes in after-hours.

MOPED RENTAL   To rent a moped, you need to be 18 years of age, and have a driver's licence and credit card. Be especially careful navigating roads where there are no designated bicycle lanes. Note that helmets are optional on Maui, but eye protection is not.

Hawaiian Riders specializes in exotic auto rentals, including Jeeps, Harleys, and mopeds. Aloha Toys Exotic Cars, in West Maui, can outfit you with a moped.

🚗 **Hawaiian Riders** ✉ 196 Lahainaluna Rd., Lahaina ☎ 808/662-4386 ✉ S. Kīhei Rd., Kīhei ☎ 808/891-0889. **Aloha Toys Exotic Cars** ✉ 640 Front St., Lahaina ☎ 808/891-0888.

BY FERRY

The quieter islands of Lāna'i and Moloka'i can be visited by ferry from Lahaina. The *Maui Princess,* a 118-foot luxury yacht will bear you to the "friendly isle" of Moloka'i for $40 one-way, leaving early and returning late once daily. The crossing takes 90 minutes. Ferries to Mānele Bay Harbor on Lāna'i cross the channel five times daily. Trips take 45 minutes and cost $25 each way.

🚢 *Maui Princess* ☎ 808/662-3355 ⊕ www.molokaiferry.com. **Lāna'i Ferry** ☎ 808/661-3756 or 800/695-2624 ⊕ www.go-lanai.com.

BY SHUTTLE

If you're staying in the right hotel or condo, there are a few shuttles that can get you around the area. Akina Bus Service has a double-decker West Maui Shopping Express that ferries passengers to and from Kā'anapali, Kapalua, Honokōwai, and Lahaina from 8 AM to 10 PM. The fare is $1 per person each way, and schedules are available at most hotels.

The free Kā'anapali Trolley Shuttle runs within the resort area between 9 AM and 11 PM and stops automatically at all hotels and at condos when requested. All Kā'anapali hotels have copies of schedules.

2

The Wailea Shuttle and the Kapalua Shuttle run within their respective resort areas and are free. Schedules are available throughout each resort area.

🚍 **Akina Bus Service** ☎ 808/870-2828 ⊕ www.akinatours.com. **Kā'anapali Trolley Shuttle** ☎ 808/661-7370, the Kā'anapali Operation Assoc.

BY TAXI

For short hops between hotels and restaurants, taxis can be a convenient way to go, but you'll have to call ahead. Even busy West Maui doesn't have curbside taxi service. Long distances between towns spike the prices; you'd be smart to use taxis just for the areas in which they're located.

Ali'i Cab covers West Maui. Arthur's Limousine Service offers a chauffeured super-stretch Lincoln complete with bar and two TVs for $88 per hour. Arthur's fleet also includes less grandiose Lincoln Town Cars for $65 per hour with a two-hour minimum. Classy Taxi offers limos, convertibles, and a 1929 Model A Ford Phaeton for a regular cab's fare. Kīhei Taxi serves Central Maui. Wailea Limousine Service provides limousines on the South Shore. Despite the name, they also provide limousines to the Lahaina area.

🚕 **Ali'i Cab** ☎ 808/661-3688. **Arthur's Limousine Service** ☎ 808/871-5555 or 877/408-9559. **Classy Taxi** ☎ 808/665-0003. **Kīhei Taxi** ☎ 808/879-3000. **Wailea Limousine Service** ☎ 808/875-4114, 808/661-4114 in Lahaina.

Contacts & Resources

EMERGENCIES

In an emergency, dial **911** to reach an ambulance, the police, or the fire department.

For emergency road service, there's a Honolulu-based AAA. A dispatcher will send a tow truck, but you will need to tell the driver where to take your car. Don't forget to carry your membership card with you.

For medical assistance in West Maui, call Doctors on Call. Or try West Maui Health Care Center, a walk-in clinic at Whalers Village. It's open daily from 8 AM to 10 PM. Kīhei Clinic Medical Services is in South Maui and is geared to working with visitors in Kīhei and Wailea.

🚑 **Doctors Doctors on Call** ✉ Hyatt Regency Maui, Nāpili Tower, Suite 100, 200 Nohea Kai Dr., Lahaina ☎ 808/667-7676. **Kīhei Clinic Medical Services** ✉ 2349 S. Kīhei Rd., Suite D, Kīhei ☎808/879-1440. **West Maui Health Care Center** ✉2435 Kā'anapali Pkwy., Suite H-7, Kā'anapali ☎ 808/667-9721.

🚑 **Emergency Services AAA** ☎ 800/222-4357. **Coast Guard Rescue Center** ☎ 800/552-6458.

🚑 **Hospitals Hāna Medical Center** ✉ Hāna Hwy., Hāna ☎ 808/248-8294. **Kula Hospital** ✉ 204 Kula Hwy., Kula ☎ 808/878-1221. **Maui Memorial Hospital** ✉ 221 Mahalani St., Wailuku ☎ 808/244-9056.

🚑 **Pharmacies Kīhei Professional Pharmacy** ✉ 41 E. Lipoa Kīhei ☎ 808/879-8499. **Kmart Stores** ✉ 424 Dairy Rd., Kahului ☎ 808/871-5677. **Valley Isle Pharmacy** ✉ 130 Prison St., Lahaina ☎ 808/661-4747.

VISITOR INFORMATION

The Maui Visitors Bureau can provide you with brochures and information. Visitor Channel 7 televises visitor information 24 hours a day, including video tours, restaurant previews, and activities information. The National Weather Service/Maui Forecast covers the islands of Maui, Moloka'i, and Lāna'i.

⑦ Maui Visitors Bureau ✉ 1727 Wili Pā Loop, Wailuku 96793 ☎ 800/525-6284 🖷 808/244-1337 ⊕ www.visitmaui.com. **National Weather Service/Maui Forecast** ☎ 808/877-5111.

Moloka'i

Biking on Moloka'i Ranch, top of Maunaloa

WORD OF MOUTH

"We took the 10-minute flight to Kalaupapa . . . we were surrounded by immense beauty, including views of the towering sea cliffs."
—Lorraine

"Moloka'i was a unique place . . . like being in Colorado with an ocean view. Wild turkeys, horses grazing in the pastures. Very Cowboy."

—Nancy03

WELCOME TO MOLOKA'I

TOP 5
Reasons to Go

1 **Kalaupapa Peninsula:** Hike or take a mule ride down the world's tallest sea cliffs to a fascinating, historic community.

2 **Biking Single-Track Trails at Moloka'i Ranch:** A complex network of trails offers some of the best mountain-bike experiences in the world.

3 **Deep-Sea Fishing:** Big sport fish are plentiful in these waters, as are gorgeous views of several islands.

4 **Nature:** Deep valleys, sheer cliffs, and the untamed ocean are the main attractions on Moloka'i.

5 **Pāpōhaku Beach:** This 3-mile stretch of sand is one of the most sensational beaches in all of Hawai'i.

■ TIP→→ Directions on the island are often given as *mauka* (toward the mountains) and *makai* (toward the ocean).

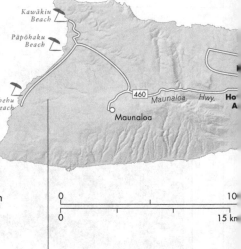

The most arid part of the island, the West End has two inhabited areas: the coastal stretch includes a few condos and luxury homes, and the largest beaches on the island. Nearby, the hilltop hamlet of Maunaloa boasts the finest accommodation on the island, the Lodge at Moloka'i Ranch.

Getting Oriented

Shaped like a long bone, Moloka'i is only about ten miles wide on average, and four times that long. The North Shore thrusts up from the sea to form the tallest sea-cliffs on Earth, while the South Shore slides almost flat into the water, then fans out to form the largest shallow-water reef system in the United States. Surprisingly, the highest point on Moloka'i rises only to about 4,000 feet.

The island's only true town, Kaunakakai, with its mile-long wharf, lies in **Central Moloka'i**. Nearly all the island's eateries and stores are in or close to Kaunakakai. Highway 470 crosses the center of the island, rising to the top of the sea-cliffs and the Kalaupapa overlook.

The scenic drive around the **East End** passes through the green pastures of Pu'u O Hoku Ranch and climaxes with a descent into Hālawa Valley. The farther east you go, the lusher the island gets.

MOLOKA'I PLANNER

What You Won't Find on Moloka'i

Moloka'i is a great place to be outdoors. And that's a good thing, because with only about 7,000 residents Moloka'i has very little of what you would call "indoors." There are no tall buildings, no traffic lights, no street lights, no stores bearing the names of national chains, and almost nothing at all like a resort. Among the Hawaiian Islands, Moloka'i has distinguished itself as the one least interested in attracting tourists. At night the whole island grows dark, creating a velvety blackness and a wonderful, rare thing called silence.

Where to Stay

Moloka'i appeals most to travelers who appreciate genuine Hawaiian hospitality rather than swanky digs. Aside from the upscale Lodge at Moloka'i Ranch, most hotel and condominium properties range from adequate to funky. Visitors who want to lollygag on the beach should choose one of the condos or home rentals at the West End. Locals tend to choose Hotel Moloka'i, located seaside just 2 mi from Kaunakakai, with its on-site restaurant, bar, and live music. Travelers who want to immerse themselves in the spirit of the island should seek out a bed-and-breakfast or cottage, the closer to the East End the better.

Additional planning details are listed in Moloka'i Essentials at the end of this chapter.

Timing is Everything

If you're keen to explore Moloka'i's beaches, coral beds, or fishponds, summer is your best bet for non-stop calm seas and sunny skies. For a real taste of Hawaiian culture, plan your visit around a festival. In January, islanders and visitors compete in ancient Hawaiian games at the Ka Moloka'i Makahiki Festival. The Moloka'i Ka Hula Piko, an annual daylong event in May, draws the state's premiere hula troupes, musicians, and storytellers to perform. The Festival of Lights includes an Electric Light Parade down the main street of Kaunakakai in December. While never crowded, the island is busier during these events—book accommodations and transportation six months in advance.

Will it Rain?

Moloka'i's weather mimics that of the other islands: mid to low 80s year-round, slightly rainier during winter. Because the island's accommodations are clustered at low elevation or along the leeward coast, warm weather is a dependable constant for visitors (only 15 to 20 inches of rain fall each year on the coastal plain). As you travel up the mountainside, the weather changes with bursts of forest-building downpours.

Cell Phones and the Internet

Communication with the outside world is a real challenge on Moloka'i. Most of the island lies outside the range of cell-phone service. Even regular telephone service, at Hotel Moloka'i for example, can be unreliable. Travelers who absolutely need to stay in touch with home or the office should get a room at the Lodge at Moloka'i Ranch.

BEACHES

By Paul Wood

Moloka'i's strange geography gives the island plenty of drama and spectacle along the shorelines but not so many places for seaside basking and bathing. The long North Shore consists mostly of towering cliffs that plunge directly into the sea. Much of the South Shore is enclosed by a huge reef that stands as far as a mile offshore and blunts the action of the waves. Within this reef you will find a thin strip of sand, but the water here is flat, shallow, and clouded with silt. This reef area is best suited to kayaking or learning how to windsurf.

The big, fat, sandy beaches lie along the West End. The largest of these—one of the largest in the Islands—is Pāpōhaku Beach, which adjoins a grassy park shaded by a grove of *kiawe* (mesquite) trees. These stretches of West-End sand are generally unpopulated. ⚠ The solitude can be a delight, but it should also be a caution; the sea here can be treacherous. At the East End, where the road hugs the sinuous shoreline, you encounter a number of pocket-size beaches in rocky coves, good for snorkeling. The road ends at Hālawa Valley with its unique double bay.

If you need beach gear, head to Moloka'i Fish & Dive at the west end of Kaunakakai's one commercial strip. You can rent equipment (snorkels, boogie boards, kayaks) from Moloka'i Outdoors, in the lobby of Hotel Moloka'i.

All of Hawai'i's beaches are free and open to the public. None of the beaches on Moloka'i have telephones or lifeguards and they're all under the jurisdiction of the **Department of Parks, Land and Natural Resources** (🖂 Box 153, Kaunakakai 96746 ☎ 808/567–6083).

West Moloka'i

Moloka'i's West End looks across a channel to the island of O'ahu. Crescent-shaped, this cup of coastline holds the island's best sandy beaches as well as the most arid and sunny weather. Developers have envisioned resorts here and a few signs of this development dream mark the coast—good-looking condos, the Kaluako'i Resort (now closed), and some expensive ocean-view homes. Remember: all beaches are public property, even those that front these developments. Beaches below are listed from north to south.

Kawākiu Beach. Seclusion is the reason to come to this remote beach, accessible only by four-wheel drive or a 45-minute walk. The white-sand beach is beautiful, but ⚠ rocks and undertow can make swimming extremely dangerous at times, so use caution. 🖂 *Past Ke Nani Kai condos on Kaluako'i Rd., look for dirt road off to right. Park here and hike in or, with 4WD, drive along dirt road to beach.* ⚑ *No facilities.*

Kepuhi Beach. Kaluako'i Hotel is closed but nine holes of its golf course are open, and so is this half-mile of ivory white sand. The beach shines beautifully against the turquoise sea, black outcroppings of lava, and magenta bougainvillea flowers of the resort's landscaping. When the water is perfectly calm, lava ridges in the water make good snorkeling spots. With any surf at all, however, the water around these rocky places churns and foams, wiping out visibility and making it difficult to avoid being slammed into the jagged rocks. ⊠ *Kaluako'i Hotel and Golf Club, Kaluako'i Rd.* ⚹ *Toilets, showers.*

Fodor'sChoice
★

Pāpōhaku Beach. One of the most sensational beaches in Hawai'i, Pāpōhaku is a 3-mi-long strip of light golden sand, the longest of its kind on the island. ⚠ **Some places are too rocky for swimming, so look carefully before entering the water and go in only when the waves are small (generally in summer).** There's so much sand here that Honolulu once purchased barge-loads in order to replenish Waikiki Beach. Moloka'i people laugh about the fact that gradually, year by year, the sea is returning all that sand to the place it's meant to be. A shady beach park just inland is the site of the Ka Hula Piko Festival of Hawaiian Music and Dance, held each year in May. The park is also a great sunset-facing spot for a rustic afternoon barbecue. ⊠ *Kaluako'i Rd.; 2 mi south of Kaluako'i Hotel and Golf Club* ⚹ *Toilets, showers, picnic tables, grills/firepits.*

Kapukahehu Bay. Locals like to surf just out from this bay in a break called Dixie's or Dixie Maru. The sandy protected cove is usually completely deserted during the weekdays but can fill up when the surf is up. The water in the cove is clear and shallow with plenty of well-worn rocky areas. These conditions make for excellent snorkeling, swimming, and boogie-boarding on calm days. ⊠ *Drive about 3½ mi south of Pāpōhaku Beach to end of Kaluako'i Rd.; beach-access sign points to parking lot* ⚹ *No facilities.*

Central Moloka'i

The South Shore is mostly a huge, reef-walled pool of flat saltwater edged with a thin strip of gritty sand and stones, mangrove swamps, and the amazing system of fishponds constructed by the residents of ancient Moloka'i. From this shore you can look out across glassy water to see people standing on top of the sea—actually, way out on top of the reef—casting fishing lines into the distant waves. This is not a great area for beaches, but is interesting in its own right.

One Ali'i Beach Park. Clear, close views of Maui and Lāna'i across the Pailolo Channel dominate One Ali'i Beach Park (*One* is pronounced *o-nay*, not *won*), the only decent beach park on the island's south-central shore. Moloka'i folks gather here for family reunions and community celebrations; the park's tightly trimmed expanse of lawn could accommodate the entire island population. Swimming within the reef is perfectly safe, but don't expect to catch any waves. ⊠ *Rte. 450, east of Hotel Moloka'i* ⚹ *Toilets, showers, picnic tables.*

> **KEEP IN MIND!**
>
> Unlike protected shorelines such as Kā'anapali on Maui, the coasts of Moloka'i are exposed to rough sea channels and dangerous rip currents. The ocean tends to be calmer in the morning and in summer. No matter what the time, however, always study the sea before entering. Unless the water is placid and the wave action minimal, it's best to simply stay on shore or keep within touch of solid ground. And don't forget to protect yourself with sunblock. Cool breezes make it easy to underestimate the power of the sun.

East Moloka'i

The East End unfolds as a coastal drive with turn-outs for tiny cove beaches—good places for snorkeling, shore-fishing, or scuba exploring. Rocky little Mokuho'oniki Island marks the eastern point of the island and serves as a nursery for humpback whales in the winter. The road loops around the East End, then descends and ends at Hālawa Valley.

Waialua Beach Park. This arched strip of golden sand, a roadside pull-off near mile marker 20, also goes by the name Twenty Mile Beach. The water here, protected by the flanks of the little bay, is often so clear and shallow (sometimes too shallow) that even from land you can watch fish swimming among the coral heads. ■ TIP→→ This is the most popular snorkeling spot on the island, a pleasant place to stop on the drive around the East End. ⊠ *Drive east on Rte. 450 to mile marker 20* ᐸ *No facilities.*

Hālawa Beach Park. The vigorous water that gouged the steep, spectacular Hālawa Valley, also carved out two bays side by side. Coarse sand and river rock has built up against the sea along the wide valley mouth, creating some protected pool areas that are good for wading or floating around. Most people come here just to hang out and absorb the beauty of this remote valley. Sometimes you will see people surfing, but it's not wise to entrust your safety to the turbulent open sea along this coast, except on the calmest summer days. ⊠ *Drive east on Rte. 450 to dead end* ᐸ *Toilets.*

WATER ACTIVITIES & TOURS

Moloka'i's unique shoreline topography limits opportunities for water sports. The North Shore is all seacliffs; the South Shore is largely encased by a huge, taming reef. ⚠ Open-sea access at West End and East End beaches should be used with caution because seas are rough, especially in winter. Generally speaking, there's no one around—certainly not lifeguards—if you get into trouble. For this reason alone, guided excursions are recommended. At least be sure to ask for advice from outfitters or residents. Two kinds of water activities predominate: kayaking within the reef area, and open-sea excursions on charter boats, most of which tie up at Kaunakakai Wharf.

Boogie Boarding, Bodysurfing & Surfing

You rarely see people boogie boarding or body surfing on Moloka'i and the only sufing is for advanced wave riders only. One outfitter, **Moloka'i Outdoors** (⊠ Hotel Moloka'i lobby ☎ 808/553–4227) rents boogie boards for $5 a day, $20 a week. The best spots for boogie boarding, when conditions are safe (occasional summer mornings), are the West End beaches, especially Kepuhi Beach at the old Kaluako'i Hotel. Or seek out waves at the East End around mile marker 20.

Two companies offer good surf/snorkel excursions—for advanced surfers only—with guides. One is **Moloka'i Fish and Dive** (⊠ 61 Ala Mālama St., Kaunakakai ☎ 808/553–5926), the island's main resource for all outdoor activities. The other is **Fun Hogs Hawai'i** (⊠ Kaunakakai Wharf ☎ 808/567–6789), which takes people to good wave action on its charter boat *Ahi*.

Fishing

For Moloka'i people, as in days of yore, the ocean is more of a larder than a playground. It's common most any day to see residents fishing along the shoreline or atop the South-Shore reef, using poles or lines. If you'd like to try your hand at this form of local industry, go to **Moloka'i Fish and Dive** (⊠ 61 Ala Mālama St., Kaunakakai ☎ 808/553–5926) for gear and advice. You can also rent poles from **Moloka'i Outdoors** (⊠ Hotel Moloka'i lobby ☎ 808/553–4227) for $5 a day.

Deep-sea fishing by charter boat is a great Moloka'i adventure. The sea channels here, though often rough and windy, provide gorgeous views of several islands. The big sport fish are plentiful in these waters, especially mahimahi, small marlin, and various kinds of tuna. Generally speaking, boat captains will customize the outing to your interests, share a lot of information about the island, and let you keep some or all of your catch. That's Moloka'i style—personal and friendly.

BOATS & CHARTERS
Alyce C. The six-passenger, 31-foot cruiser runs excellent sportfishing excursions. The cost is $400 for a nine-hour trip, $300 for five to six hours. Shared charters are available. Gear is provided. In the fish-rich waters of Moloka'i, it's a rare day when you don't snag at least one mahimahi. ⊠ *Kaunakakai Wharf* ☎ *808/558–8377.*

Fun Hogs Hawai'i. Trim and speedy, the 27-foot flybridge sport-fishing boat named *Ahi* takes people out for half-day ($350), six-hour ($400), and full-day ($450) sportfishing excursions. Full-day bottom-fishing trips, all equipment furnished, are $500. Skipper Mike Holmes also provides one-way or round-trip journeys to Lāna'i, as well as (in winter only) sunset cruises. ⊠ *Kaunakakai Wharf* ☎ *808/567–6789.*

Moloka'i Action Adventures. Walter Naki's Moloka'i roots go back forever, and he knows the island intimately. What's more, he has traveled (and fished) all over the globe, and he's a great talker. He will create customized fishing and hunting expeditions and gladly share his wealth of experience. His 21-foot Boston Whaler is usually to be seen at the mouth of Hālawa Valley, in the East End. ☎ *808/558–8184.*

Kayaking

Moloka'i's South Shore is enclosed and tamed by the largest reef system in the United States—an area of shallow, protected sea that stretches over 30 mi. This reef gives inexperienced kayakers an unusually safe, calm environment for shoreline exploring. ⚠ **Outside the reef, Moloka'i waters are often rough and treacherous. Kayakers out here should be strong, experienced, and cautious.**

Best Spots

The **South Shore Reef** area is superb for flat-water kayaking any day of the year. It's best to rent a kayak at Hotel Moloka'i and slide into the water right there, though another easy entry spot is Kaunakakai Wharf, either side. Get out in the morning before the wind picks up and paddle east, exploring the ancient Hawaiian fishponds. When you turn around to return, you'll usually get a push home by the wind, which blows strong and westerly along this shore in the afternoon.

Independent kayakers who are confident about testing their skills in rougher seas can launch at the West End of the island from **Hale O Lono Harbor,** (at the end of a long dirt road from Maunaloa town). At the East End of the island, enter the water near mile marker 20 or beyond and explore in the direction of Mokuhoʻoniki Island. ⚠ Kayaking anywhere outside the South Shore Reef is only safe on calm days in summer.

LESSONS & EQUIPMENT RENTALS

Molokaʻi Fish and Dive. At the west end of Kaunakakai's commercial strip, this all-around outfitter provides guided kayak excursions inside the South Shore Reef. One excursion paddles through a dense mangrove forest and explores a huge, hidden ancient fishpond. One bonus of going with guides: if the wind starts blowing hard, they can tow you back with their boat. The fee is $80 for the half-day trip. Check at the store (on Ala Mālama Street) for numerous other outdoor activities. ⊠ *61 Ala Mālama St., Kaunakakai* ☎ *808/553–5926.*

Molokaʻi Outdoors. This is the place to rent a kayak for exploring on your own—right on the shoreline in Central Molokaʻi, 2 mi east of Kaunakai. Kayaks rent for $12 to $15 an hour. Car racks and extra paddles are also available. ⊠ *Hotel Molokaʻi lobby* ☎ *808/553–4227.*

Sailing

Molokaʻi is a place of strong predictable winds that make for good and sometimes rowdy sailing. The island views in every direction are stunning. Kaunakakai Wharf is the home base for all of the island's charter sailboats.

Molokaʻi Charters. The 42-foot Cascade sloop *Satan's Doll* is your craft with Molokaʻi Charters. The company arranges two-hour sails for $40 per person. Half-day sailing trips cost $50 per person, including soft drinks and snacks. One commendable trip is the sail to Lānaʻi with stops for snorkeling. A minimum of four people is required, but shared charters can be arranged. ⊠ *Kaunakakai Wharf* ☎ *808/553–5852.*

Gypsy Sailing Adventures. The 33-plus-foot ocean-going catamaran *Star Gypsy* has a large salon, three staterooms, and a fully equipped galley. They do any kind of sailing you want—"any kind of adventure that's prudent and safe"—from two-hour explorations of Molokaʻi's huge reef (stopping at otherwise inaccessible coves and beaches) to interisland cruising (Maui and Lānaʻi). In summer, this company does two-day trips that explore the island's North Shore. Full days cost $500 to $750, depending on the amount of catering involved. Half days are $300. ⊠ *Kaunakakai Wharf* ☎ *808/553–5852.*

Scuba Diving

Molokaʻi Fish and Dive is the only PADI-certified purveyor of scuba gear, training, and dive trips on Molokaʻi. Shoreline access for divers is extremely limited, even nonexistent in winter. Boat diving is the way to go. Without guidance, visiting divers can easily find themselves in risky situations with wicked currents. Proper guidance, though, opens an undersea world rarely seen.

Moloka'i Fish and Dive. Tim and Susan Forsberg, owners, can fill you in on how to find dive sites, rent you the gear, or hook you up with one of their PADI-certified dive guides to take you to the island's best underwater spots. (They work with Fun Hogs Hawai'i's 27-foot power boat called *Ahi*.) They know the island's best blue holes and underwater cave systems, and they can take you swimming with hammerhead sharks. ⊠ *61 Ala Mālama St., Kaunakakai* ☎ *808/553–5926.*

Snorkeling

During the times when swimming is safe—mainly in summer, just about every beach on Moloka'i offers good snorkeling along the lava outcroppings in the island's clean and pristine waters.

Best Spots

Kepuhi Beach. In winter, the sea here is deadly. But in summer, this half-mile-long beach offers plenty of rocky nooks that swirl with sea life. The presence of outdoor showers is a bonus. Take Kaluako'i Road all the way to the West End. Park at Kaluako'i Resort (it's presently closed) and walk through the lobby area to the beach.

Waialua Beach Park. A thin curve of sand rims a sheltered little bay loaded with coral heads and aquatic life. The water here is shallow—sometimes so shallow that you bump into the underwater landscape—and it's crystal clear. To find this spot, head to the East End on Route 450, and pull off near mile marker 20. When the sea is calm, you'll find several other good snorkeling spots along this stretch of road.

DIVE TOURS & EQUIPMENT RENTAL Rent snorkel sets from either of the two outfitters previously mentioned—Moloka'i Outdoors in the lobby of Hotel Moloka'i, or Moloka'i Fish and Dive in Kaunakakai. Rental fees are nominal—$6 a day. All the charter boats carry snorkel gear and include dive stops as part of the expedition.

Fun Hogs Hawai'i. Mike Holmes, captain of the 27-foot power boat *Ahi*, knows the island waters intimately, likes to have fun, and is willing to arrange any type of excursion—for example, one dedicated entirely to snorkeling. His 2½-hour snorkel trips leave early in the morning and explore rarely seen fish and turtle posts outside the reef west of the wharf. Bring your own food and drinks; the trips cost $65 per person. ⊠ *Kaunakakai Wharf* ☎ *808/567–6789.*

Moloka'i Charters. The 42-foot sloop *Satan's Doll* harnesses the power of wind to seek the island's best snorkel spots. The full-day snorkeling excursion to the island of Lāna'i costs $90 per person. Four passengers are the minimum they will carry. Soft drinks and a picnic lunch are included. ⚠ **You can generally count on rough seas for the afternoon return channel crossing.** ⊠ *Kaunakakai Wharf* ☎ *808/553–5852.*

Whale-Watching

Maui gets all the credit for the local wintering humpback whale population. Most people don't realize that the beautiful big cetaceans also come to Moloka'i. Mokuho'oniki Island at the East End serves as a whale nursery and playground, and the whales pass back and forth along the South Shore. This being Moloka'i, whale-watching here will never involve floating amid a group of boats all ogling the same whale.

Alyce C. Although this six-passenger sportfishing boat is usually busy hooking mahimahi and marlin, the captain gladly takes three-hour excursions to admire the humpback whales. The price is about $65 per person, depending on the number of passengers in the group. ⊠ *Kaunakakai Wharf* ☎ *808/558–8377.*

Fun Hogs Hawai'i. The *Ahi*, a flybridge sportfishing boat, takes 2½-hour whale-watching trips in the morning from December to April. The cost is $65 per person. Bring your own snacks and drinks. ⊠ *Kaunakakai Wharf* ☎ *808/567–6789.*

Gypsy Sailing Adventures. Being a catamaran, the *Star Gypsy* can drift silently under sail and follow the whales without disturbing them. Captain Richard Messina and crew share a lot of knowledge about the whales and pride themselves on being ecologically-minded. The 2½-hour trip costs $75 and includes soft drinks and water. ⊠ *Kaunakakai Wharf* ☎ *808/553–5852.*

GOLF, HIKING & OUTDOOR ACTIVITIES

Biking

Single-Track Trails at Moloka'i Ranch. Moloka'i Ranch, headquartered in the small town of Maunaloa, has developed some of the best mountain-bike experiences in the world, compared favorably by enthusiasts to Moab and Hood River. Moloka'i Fish and Dive runs the activity desk at the Ranch, and has a well-stocked rental shop for mountain bikes and related two-wheel gear. With or without guides, you can head out from here to a complex network of trails that are rated like ski slopes according to their difficulty. Excursions can be super-challenging or as easy as a mild gravity ride over miles of twisty terrain down to the coast, with van transport back. ⊠ *61 Ala Mālama St., Kaunakakai* ☎ *808/553–5926.*

Na'iwa Mountain Trails. Guides from Moloka'i Fish and Dive take biking extremists on a gorgeous but challenging adventure in Na'iwa—the remote central mountains—for convoluted forest courses, daredevil verticals (if you want), and exhilarating miles at the brink of the world's tallest sea cliffs. ⊠ *61 Ala Mālama St., Kaunakakai* ☎ *808/553–5926.*

East End Trails. Moloka'i Bicycle will take mountain-bikers out to two-wheel the expansive East End spread of Pu'u O Hoku Ranch. You might ride along an eastern ridge rimming Hālawa Valley to four waterfalls and a remote pool for swimming, or pedal on sea cliffs to a secluded beach. Daily tours for a minimum of two people cost $45 per person for a half day and $65 for a full day, including lunch. ☎ 808/553–3931.

Street biking on this island is a dream for peddlers who like to eat up the miles. Moloka'i's few roads are long, straight, and extremely rural. You can really stretch out and go for it—no traffic lights and most of the time no traffic.

If you don't happen to be one of those athletes who always travels with your own customized cycling tool, you can rent something from **Moloka'i Bicycle** (☎ 808/553–3931) in Kaunakakai. Another place to rent bikes is **Moloka'i Outdoors** (☎ 808/553–4227), based in the lobby of Hotel Moloka'i.

Golf

While the golf is good on Moloka'i, there isn't much of it—just two courses and a total of 27 holes.

Ironwood Hills Golf Course. Like the other 9-hole plantation era courses with which it shares lineage, Ironwood Hills is not for everyone. It helps if you like a bit of rugged history with your golf, and can handle the occasionally rugged conditions. On the plus side, most holes here offer lovely views of the ocean and the island of Lāna'i. Fairways are kukuya grass and run through pine, ironwood, and eucalyptus trees. Carts are rented, but there's not always someone there to rent you a cart—in which case, there's a wooden box for your green fee (honor system), and happy walking. ⊠ *Kala'e Hwy., Kualapu'u* ☎ *808/567–6000* 🏌 *9 holes. 3088 yds. Par 35. Green Fee: $20 Facilities: Putting green, golf carts, pull carts.*

★ **Kaluakoi Golf Course.** Kaluakoi Golf Course, associated with the Lodge at Moloka'i Ranch, has more ocean frontage than any other Hawai'i course. Ted Robinson (1976) was given a fantastic site and created some excellent holes, starting with the par-5 first, with the beach on the right from tee to green. The course, closed by former owners for financial reasons, reopened in 2002 after substantial refurbishing. The front nine is generally flat, never running far from the sea, and providing dramatic views of the island of O'ahu. The back nine winds through rolling hills and dense forest. ⊠ *Box 259, Maunaloa* ☎ *808/552–0255* ⊕ *www.molokairanch.com* 🏌 *18 holes. 6200 yds. Par 72. Green Fee: $70 Facilities: Driving range, putting green, golf carts, rental clubs.*

Hiking

Rural and rugged, Moloka'i is an excellent place for hiking. Roads and developments are few, so the outdoors is always beckoning. The island is steep, so hikes often combine spectacular views with hearty physical exertion. Because the island is small, you can traverse quite a bit of it on foot and come away with the feeling of really knowing the place. And you won't see many other people around. Most of the time, it's just you and the *'aina* (the land).

'Ili'ili'ōpae Heiau Hike. Here's an easy one with a thought-provoking pay-off. Walk less than half a mile under tree shade, cut left across a small stream bed, and then confront one of the most beautifully constructed *heiau* (ancient temple platform), in Hawai'i. Selected lava boulders arranged with architectural precision form a rectilinear plateau big enough to host the Superbowl. Scramble up the steep path to view the heiau in the lay of the land. Call first as a courtesy to the neighbors whose private property you must cross to reach the heiau. If you forget to call, be sure to say aloha and ask permission of anyone you see. ⊠ *Park roadside at historical marker on Rte. 450, near mile marker 15* ☎ *808/558–8380.*

Kalaupapa Trail. You can make a day of hiking down to Kalaupapa Peninsula and back by means of a 3-mi, 26-switchback trail. The trail is nearly vertical, traversing the face of some of the highest sea cliffs in the world. From a distance, the route looks as though it would paralyze anyone who's phobic about heights; in fact, the trail is lined with forest and engineered into giant steps. The trek feels very safe and takes about 1½ hours each way.

> **TIP!**
>
> The alternative to hiking to Kalaupapa is to ride a mule (*see* Moloka'i Mule Ride *under* Exploring Moloka'i). The mules go down once a day, hitting the trail at about 8:30 AM and returning to the top around 3. Hikers should keep that schedule in mind and hit the trail before the mules do. The reason: the trail has virtually no shoulder, so passing or being passed by a mule is difficult, to say the least.

The trail and peninsula below are all part of **Kalaupapa National Historical Park** (☎ 808/567–6802 ⊕ www.nps.gov/kala/), which is open every day but Sunday. Nature here is intensely beautiful and includes some rare native habitat for endangered endemic plants and birds. The park also tells a poignant human story. The Kalaupapa Peninsula was once a community of about 1,000 victims of Hansen's disease (leprosy) who were banished from other parts of Hawai'i. There are about 40 patients still living in Kalaupapa—now by choice, as the disease is controlled by drugs and patients are no longer carriers. Out of respect to these people, visitors must be at least 16 years old, cannot stay overnight, and must be on a guided tour or invited by a resident. Guided tours of the community are available by reservation through **Damien Tours** (☎ 808/567–6171). Hikers need to start walking by 8 AM to connect with the 10 AM tour and reservations are a must. ■ **TIP➜➜ Keep in mind that there are no public facilities (except an occasional restroom) anywhere in the park. Pack your own food and water, as well as light rain gear, sunscreen, and bug repellent.** ⊠ *Trailhead is clearly marked with ample parking near end of Kala'e Hwy., Hwy. 470.*

Kamakou Preserve. Four-wheel drive is essential for this half-day (minimum) journey into the Moloka'i highlands. The Nature Conservancy of Hawai'i manages the 2,774-acre Kamakou Preserve, one of the last stands of Hawai'i's native plants and birds. A long, rough dirt road, that begins not far from Kaunakakai town, leads to the preserve. The road is not marked, so you must check in with the **Nature Conservancy's Moloka'i office** (⊠ At Moloka'i Industrial Park about 3 mi west of

Kaunkakai, 23 Pueo Pl. ☎ 808/553–5236 ⊕ www.nature.org), for directions. Let them know that you plan to visit the preserve, and pick up the informative 24-page brochure with trail maps.

On your way up to the preserve, be sure to stop at Waikolu Overlook, which gives a head-spinning view into a precipitous North-Shore canyon. Once inside the preserve, various trails are clearly marked. The trail of choice—and you can drive right to it—is the 1½-mi boardwalk trail through Pēpē'ōpae Bog, an ecological treasure-trove. Organic deposits here date back at least 10,000 years, and the plants are undisturbed natives. This is the true landscape of prediscovery Hawai'i. It's a mean trek; you have to be tough, nimble, and reverential all at the same time. ■ TIP→→ **Wear long pants and bring rain gear. Your shoes ought to provide good traction on a slippery, narrow boardwalk.**

Kawela Cul-de-Sacs. Just east of Kaunakakai, three streets—Kawela One, Two, and Three—jut up the mountainside from the Kamehameha V Highway. These roads end in cul-de-sacs that are also informal trailheads. Rough dirt roads work their way from here to the top of the mountain. The lower slopes are dry, rocky, steep, and austere. (It's good to start in the cool of the early morning.) A hiker in good condition can get all the way up into the high forest in two or three hours. There's no park ranger and no water fountain—these are not for the casual stroller. But if you're prepared for the challenge, you will be well rewarded.

GUIDED HIKES   **Historical Hikes of West Moloka'i.** This company has six guided hikes, ranging from two to six hours. The outings focus on Moloka'i's cultural past taking you to sites such as an ancient quarry, an early fishing village, or high sea cliffs where Hawaiian chiefs played games during the traditional *Makahiki* (harvest festival) season. Backpacks are provided, as is lunch on intermediate and advanced hikes. Guides Lawrence and Catherine Aki also run A Hawaiian Getaway vacation rental. ⊠ *The Lodge at Moloka'i Ranch Activity Desk, Maunaloa Hwy., Maunaloa* ☎ *808/552–2797, 808/553–9803, or 800/274–9303* ⊕ *www.molokai-aloha.com/hikes* ☜ *$45–$125.*

Hālawa Valley Cultural Waterfall Hike. Hālawa is a gorgeous, steep-walled valley carved by two rivers and rich in history. Site of what could be the earliest Polynesian settlement in Hawai'i, Hālawa sustained island culture with its ingeniously designed *lo'i,* or taro fields. In the 1960s the valley became derelict and increasingly mysterious. Now Hawaiian families are restoring the lo'i and walking people through the valley, which includes two-thirds of Moloka'i's *luakini heiau* (sacred temples). Half-day visits, morning or afternoon, cost $75 (less for children) and support the work of restoration. Call ahead to visit any day at 9:30 AM or 2 PM. Bring water, food, and insect repellent. ☎ *808/553–9803 or 808/274–9303* ⊕ *www.molokai-aloha.com/hikes* ☜ *$75.*

Horseback Riding

Pu'u O Hoku Ranch. Set on the prow of the island's Maui-facing east end, this ranch keeps a stable of magnificent, amiable horses that are available for trail rides starting at $55 an hour. The peak experience is a four-hour beach ride ($120) that culminates at a secluded cove where the horses are happy to swim, rider and all. Bring your own lunch. This is a good experience for people with little or no horse skills. They match skill-levels with appropriate steeds. ⊠ *Rte. 450, 20 mi east of Kaunakakai* ☎ *808/ 558–8109* ⊕ *www.puuohoku.com.*

EXPLORING MOLOKA'I

The first thing to do on Moloka'i is to drive everywhere. It's a feat you can accomplish in less than a day. Basically you have one 40-mi west-to-east highway (two lanes, no stop lights) with three side trips: the little West End town of Maunaloa; the Highway 470 drive (just a few miles) to the top of the North Shore and the overlook of Kalaupapa Peninsula; and the short stretch of shops in Kaunakakai town. After you learn the general lay of the land, you can return for in-depth experiences on foot.

West Moloka'i

The region is largely made up of the 53,000-acre Moloka'i Ranch. The rolling pastures and farmlands are presided over by Maunaloa, a sleepy little plantation town with a dormant volcano of the same name. West Moloka'i has another claim to fame: Pāpōhaku, the island's best beach.

a good drive

This driving tour focuses on two of Moloka'i's tourist areas. If you're approaching the west end from Kaunakakai on Route 460 (also called Maunaloa Highway), turn right at mile marker 15 down Kaluako'i Road and right again at the sign for **Kaluako'i Hotel and Golf Club ❶** ▷. Take time to enjoy the grounds and the beach.

Back behind the wheel, turn right out of Kaluako'i Hotel and Golf Club and follow Kaluako'i Road 2 mi west until it dead-ends. This shore-

> ### GUIDED TOURS
>
> **Moloka'i Off-Road Tours and Taxi.** Visit Hālawa Valley, Kalaupapa Lookout, Maunaloa town, and other points of interest in the comfort of an air-conditioned van on four- or six-hour tours. Pat and Alex Pua'a, your personal guides, will even help you mail a coconut back home. Tours cost $36 to $49 and begin at 9 AM. Charters are also available. ☎ *808/553–3369.*

line drive takes you past a number of lovely parks, including **Pāpōhaku Beach ❷**, the largest white-sand beach on the island. Look for a big sign on the side of the road.

Turn around and follow Kaluako'i Road back past the resort entrance, and continue uphill to the intersection with Route 460. Turn right and drive 2 mi on Route 460 (Maunaloa Highway) to **Maunaloa ❸**, a former plantation town that was torn down and replaced with—guess what—buildings resembling a plantation town. This hamlet is headquarters for Moloka'i Ranch, site of the island's one movie theater and its one resortlike accommodation, the rustic-elegant Lodge at Moloka'i Ranch. The Lodge is home to a colorful kite factory; it's the starting point for some of Hawaii's best mountain-bike trails; and it's the portal to luxurious Kaupoa Campground and beautifully derelict Hale O Lono Harbor. Food and gas is available here, too.

TIMING If you follow this excursion at a leisurely Moloka'i pace, it will take you the better part of a day, particularly if your accommodations are not on the West End. A walk around Kaluako'i Hotel and Golf Club can take an hour or more.

Another hour can fly by at Pāpōhaku Beach as you dig your toes in its sands and picnic on its shady grassy area. Allow one hour for exploring Maunaloa's main street to shop for souvenirs and chat with local shop owners. Don't try to do your shopping on Sunday, or you may find many CLOSED signs on the doors.

What to See

► ❶ **Kaluako'i Hotel and Golf Club.** This late-1960s resort passed through several owners, and the hotel itself is now closed, awaiting its next incarnation. Some very nice condos are still operating here, however. Stroll the grounds—an impressive 6,700 acres of beachfront property, including the newly revived golf course and 5 mi of coastline. ⊠ *Kaluako'i Rd., Maunaloa* ☎ *808/552–2555 or 888/552–2550.*

★ ❸ **Maunaloa.** This sleepy town was developed in 1923 to support the island's pineapple plantation. Although the fields of golden fruit have gone fallow, some of the workers' dwellings still stand, anchoring the west end of Moloka'i. Colorful local characters run the half-dozen businesses (including a kite shop and an eclectic old market) along the town's short main street. This is also the headquarters for Moloka'i Ranch. ⊠ *Western end of Maunaloa Hwy., Rte. 460.*

❷ **Pāpōhaku Beach.** The most splendid stretch of white sand on Moloka'i, Pāpōhaku is also the island's largest beach—it stretches 3 mi along the western shore. Even on busier days you're likely to see only a handful of other people. If the waves are up, swimming is dangerous. ⊠ *Kaluako'i Rd.; 2 mi beyond Kaluako'i Hotel and Golf Club.*

Central Moloka'i

Most residents live central, near the island's one and only true town Kaunakakai. It's just about the only place on island to get food and supplies. It *is* Moloka'i. Go into the shops along and around Ala Mālama Street. Buy stuff. Talk with people. You'll learn the difference between being a tourist and being a visitor.

a good drive

If you have reserved the **Moloka'i Mule Ride** ❹, go directly to Kala'e, north on Route 470. Otherwise, drive north on Route 470 until it ends at **Pālā'au State Park** ❺ ►, where you can admire knockout views of **Kalaupapa** ❻ and the Kalaupapa Peninsula. Bring along a light jacket for cooler upland weather in fall and winter.

On the way back down the hill on Route 470, stop at the **R. W. Meyer Sugar Mill and Moloka'i Museum** ❼ to see photos and machinery from earlier times. Then turn right on Farrington Highway to visit the little town of Kualapu'u, where **Friendly Isle Coffee** ❽ has a plantation store and espresso bar and offers tours of its coffee fields and processing plant. A five-minute drive west takes you to **Purdy's Macadamia Nut Farm** ❾ in Ho'olehua.

Head back on Farrington Highway, and then take a right onto Route 470; go down the rest of the hill and turn left on Route 460. Near the ocean on Route 460 are two stops of note that are practically right across the road from each other: **Kapuāiwa Coconut Grove** ⑩ and **Church Row** ⑪. Follow Route 460 east to reach **Kaunakakai** ⑫, Moloka'i's "big city." **Kaunakakai Wharf** ⑬ is the home base for deep-sea fishing excursions and other aqua adventures.

TIMING Get into the Moloka'i rhythm and take a full day to explore the highlands and the town. Drive up to the top of the road and walk the easy forest trails to the Kalaupapa Lookout and the phallic stone. On the way down the hill stop for an hour each at the historic sugar mill, the macadamia farm, and the coffee plantation. Then hit Kaunakakai and indulge yourself. ■ TIP→→ Don't forget that Central Moloka'i (except for a few restaurants) closes at sunset and all day Sunday.

If you take the mule ride to Kalaupapa, you should still have the time (if not the grit) to stop at some interesting sites listed in the tour after you dismount.

What to See

⑪ **Church Row.** Standing together along the highway are several houses of worship with primarily native Hawaiian congregations. Notice the unadorned, boxlike style of architecture so similar to missionary homes. ⊠ *Mauka (toward the mountains) side of Rte. 460, 5½ mi southwest of airport.*

⑥ **Kalaupapa.** The Kalaupapa Peninsula was once a community of about
FodorśChoice 1,000 victims of Hansen's disease (leprosy) who were banished from
★ other parts of Hawai'i. Father Damien committed himself to the care of the afflicted until he died here of the same disease in 1889. There are about 40 patients still living in Kalaupapa—now by choice, as the disease is controlled by drugs and patients are no longer carriers. You will probably not see any patients other than perhaps the tour guide. The history of the community is fascinating and heart wrenching. Views of the peninsula from Kalaupapa Lookout in Pālā'au State Park are a standout. Note that no one under the age of 16 is allowed to visit Kalaupapa. Whether you hike down, take a mule ride down, or fly in, you must be part of a tour to visit. You can book through Moloka'i Mule Ride (see below), or through **Damien Tours** (☎ 808/567–6171) if you want to hike or fly in. Book before getting to the island. Hikers need to start walking by 8 AM to connect with a tour. ⊠ *North end of Rte. 470.*

⑩ **Kapuāiwa Coconut Grove.** At first glance this looks like a sea of coconut trees. Close-up you can see that the tall, stately palms are planted in long rows leading down to the sea. This is one of the last surviving royal groves planted by Prince Lot, who ruled Hawai'i as King Kamehameha V from 1863 until his death in 1872. Watch for falling coconuts; protect your head and your car. ⊠ *Makai side of Rte. 460, 5½ mi south of airport.*

★ ⑫ **Kaunakakai.** Kaunakakai looks like an Old West movie set. Along the one-block main drag is a cultural grab bag of restaurants and shops. People are friendly and willing to supply directions. The preferred dress is

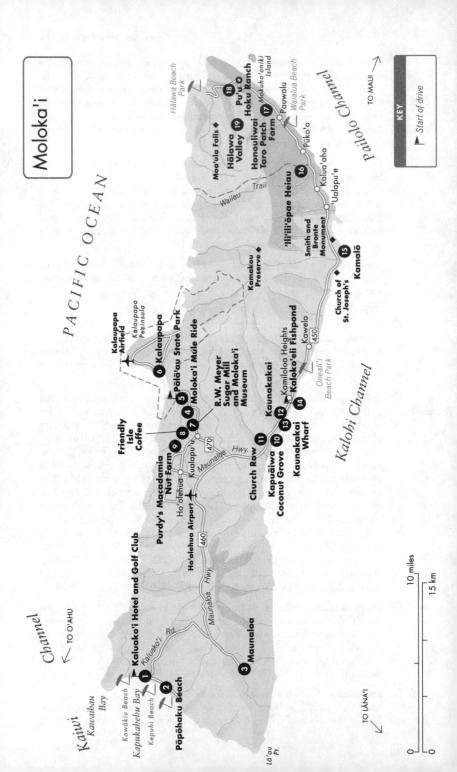

shorts and a tank top, and no one wears anything fancier than a mu'umu'u or aloha shirt. ⊠ *Rte. 460, about 3 blocks north of Kaunakakai Wharf.*

⓭ **Kaunakakai Wharf.** Docks, once bustling with watercraft exporting pineapples, now host boats shipping out potatoes, tomatoes, baby corn, herbs, and other produce. The wharf is also the starting point for excursions, including deep-sea fishing, sailing, snorkeling, whale-watching, and scuba diving. ⊠ *Rte. 450 and Ala Mālama St.; drive makai on Kaunakakai Pl., which dead-ends at wharf.*

❽ **Friendly Isle Coffee.** Visit the headquarters of a 500-acre plantation of Moloka'i coffee. The espresso bar serves java in artful ways, sand-wiches, and *liliko'i* (passion fruit) cheesecake. The gift shop offers a wide range of Moloka'i handicrafts and memorabilia, and, of course, coffee. ⊠ *Farrington Hwy., off Rte. 470, Kualapu'u* ☎ *800/709–2326 or 808/567–9023* ⊕ *www.molokaicoffee.com.*

❹ **Moloka'i Mule Ride.** Mount a friendly mule and wind along a 3-mi, 26-switchback trail to reach the town of Kalaupapa. The path was built in 1886 as a supply route for the settlement below. Once in Kalaupapa, you can take a guided tour of the town and have a picnic lunch. The trail is very steep, down some of the highest sea cliffs in the world. Only those in good shape should attempt the ride, as two hours each way on a mule can take its toll. The entire event takes seven hours. It's wise to make reservations ahead of time, as spots are limited. The same outfit can also arrange for you to hike down or fly in, or some combination of a hike in and fly out. ⊠ *100 Kala'e Hwy., Rte. 470, Kualapu'u* ☎ *808/567–6088* ⊕ *www.muleride.com* ⊇ *$150* ☉ *Mon.–Sat. 8–3:30.*

Fodor'sChoice ★

★ ▶ ❺ Pālā'au State Park. One of the island's few formal recreation areas, this cool retreat covers 233 acres at a 1,000-foot elevation. A short path through a heady pine forest leads to **Kalaupapa Lookout,** a magnificent overlook with views of the town of Kalaupapa and the 1,664-foot-high sea cliffs protecting it. Informative plaques have facts about leprosy, Father Damien, and the colony itself. The park is also the site of **Phallic Rock,** known as Kauleonānāhoa to the ancient Hawaiians. It's said that if women sit by this large rock formation they will become more fertile. The park is well maintained, with camping facilities, restrooms, and picnic tables. ⊠ *Take Rte. 460 west from Kaunakakai and then head mauka on Rte. 470, which ends at park* ☎ *No phone* ⊇ *Free* ☉ *Daily dawn–dusk.*

❾ **Purdy's Macadamia Nut Farm.** Moloka'i's only working macadamia-nut farm is open for educational tours hosted by the knowledgeable and en-tertaining owner. A family business on Hawaiian homestead land in Ho'olehua, the farm takes up 1½ acres with a flourishing grove of some 50 trees more than 70 years old. Taste a delicious nut right out of its shell, or fresh macadamia-blossom honey; then buy some at the shop on the way out. Look for Purdy's sign behind Moloka'i High School. ⊠ *Lihipali Ave., Ho'olehua* ☎ *808/567–6601* ⊇ *Free* ☉ *Weekdays 9:30–3:30, Sat. 10–2.*

❼ **R. W. Meyer Sugar Mill and Moloka'i Museum.** Built in 1877, this old mill has been reconstructed as a testament to Moloka'i's agricultural history.

The equipment is still in working order, including a mule-driven cane crusher, redwood evaporating pans, some copper clarifiers, and a steam engine. A museum with changing exhibits on the island's early history and a gift shop are on-site as well. The facility serves as a campus for Elderhostel programs. ✉ *Rte. 470, 2 mi southwest of Pālā'au State Park, Kala'e* ☎ *808/567–6436* 💲 *$2.50* 🕙 *Mon.–Sat. 10–2.*

East Moloka'i

On the beautifully undeveloped East End of Moloka'i, you can find ancient fishponds, a magnificent coastline, splendid ocean views, and a gaping valley that's been inhabited for centuries. The east is flanked by Mt. Kamakou, the island's highest point at 4,961 feet, and home to The Nature Conservancy's Kamakou Preserve. Mist hangs over waterfall-filled valleys, and ancient lava cliffs jut out from the sea.

a good drive

On Route 450, the farther east you drive, the wilder the coastline, changing from white sandy beaches to rocky shores. Much of the road hugs the shore as it twists and turns. Be forewarned: it's fraught with bumps, blind curves, and potholes. There are, however, several turnouts along the way next to coves and small stretches of sand. There's very little traffic out here, so no need to hurry. Keep your eyes open for mile markers: at times, they're the only references for locating sights.

Six miles east of Kaunakakai, look offshore to see **Kaloko'eli Fishpond** ⑭ ►, surrounded by the most picturesque of Moloka'i's historic rock walls. After another 5 mi you reach the natural harbor of **Kamalō** ⑮. En route is the stark white Church of St. Joseph's, built in 1876. It's one of four houses of worship built by Father Damien. The statue of him here is frequently adorned with flower lei. At mile marker 15, a hidden trail leads to the enormous **'Ili'ili'ōpae Heiau** ⑯. Close to mile marker 20 at a small but deeply curved bay, an unpaved road leads a short distance off the highway to **Honouliwai Taro Patch Farm** ⑰. After that the road climbs and winds through **Pu'u O Hoku Ranch** ⑱, a vast Upcountry expanse with sparkling ocean panoramas. Route 450 dead-ends at the beach in the lush **Hālawa Valley** ⑲, the site of a courageous new effort to restore an ancient Hawaiian way of life.

TIMING   If you include the tour of Hālawa Valley (which you should) plan on spending a full day in this meandering expedition. If you take it as a scenic drive with occasional stops, half a day is plenty.

What to See

⑲ **Hālawa Valley.** As far back as AD 650 a busy community lived in this valley, one of the oldest recorded habitations in Hawai'i. Hawaiians lived in a perfectly sustainable relationship with the valley's resources, growing taro and fishing, until the 1960s, when pressures of the modern economy forced the old-timers to abandon their traditional lifestyle. Now a new generation of Hawaiians has returned to the valley and begun the challenging work of clearing trees and restoring the taro fields. Much of this work involves rerouting stream water to flow through carefully engineered level ponds called lo'i. The taro plants with their big dancing leaves grow in the submerged mud of the lo'i, where the water is always cool and flowing. The Hālawa Valley Cooperative gives tours of this restoration project and leads hikes through the valley, which is home to many historic sites and the 3-mi trail to Moa'ula Falls, a 250-foot cascade. The $75 fee ($45 for children) goes to support the restoration work. ⊠ *Eastern end of Rte. 450* ☎ *800/274–9303 or 808/553–9803* ⊕ *www.molokai-aloha.com/hikes.*

⑰ Honouliwai Taro Patch Farm. While they are not reviving an entire valley and lifestyle, like the folks in Hālawa, Jim and Lee Callahan are reviving taro cultivation on their small East End farm watered by a year-round spring. The owners provide 1½-hour educational tours so visitors can experience all phases of taro farming, from planting to eating. Lee was born and raised in Thailand, so she uses a traditional southeast Asian farm device—a docile, plow-pulling water buffalo named Bigfoot. Tours are available every day, but you must call for an appointment. ⊠ *East of mile marker 20, mauka side, where the sign says "Honouliwai Is a Beautiful Place to Be"* ☎ *808/558–8922* ⊕ *www.angelfire.com/film/chiangmai/index.html* ⌑ *$20.*

⑯ 'Ili'ili'ōpae Heiau. Human sacrifices once took place at this hidden *heiau*. As long as a football field, it's a well-preserved example of Hawai'i's ancient outdoor shrines. This revered site is still said to hold great power. Please act with respect by speaking in a soft voice. The sacrifices were introduced by Tahitian immigrants who came between AD 1090 and 1240, but the heiau could have existed before then—as early as AD 650, the time of the first island habitation. The trail is on private property, but the owners don't object to people simply visiting the heiau. Permission should be requested by phone. ⊠ *15 mi east of Kaunakakai and ½ mi inland of Rte. 450; park on side of road, look for Wailau Trail sign, and walk about 10 min mauka until you see sign on left for heiau* ☎ *808/558–8380.*

★ ▶ ⑭ Kaloko'eli Fishpond. With its narrow rock walls connecting two points of the shore, Kaloko'eli is typical of the numerous fishponds that define southern Moloka'i. Many of them were built around the 13th century. This early type of aquaculture, particular to Hawai'i, exemplifies the ingenuity of precontact Hawaiians. One or more openings were left in the wall, where gates called *makaha* were installed. These gates allowed seawater and tiny fish to enter the enclosed pond but kept larger predators out. The tiny fish would then grow too big to get out. At one time there were 62 fishponds around Moloka'i's coast. ⊠ *Rte. 450, about 6 mi east of Kaunakakai.*

off the beaten path

KAMAKOU PRESERVE – Tucked away on the slopes of Mt. Kamakou, Moloka'i's highest peak, the 2,774-acre preserve is a dazzling wonderland full of wet 'ōhi'a (hardwood trees of the myrtle family, with red blossoms called lehua flowers) forests, rare bogs, and native trees and wildlife. Guided hikes, limited to eight people, are held on the first Saturday of each month. Reservations are required well in advance. You can visit the park without a tour, but you need a good four-wheel-drive vehicle, and the Nature Conservancy requests that you sign in at the office and get directions first. ⊠ *The Nature Conservancy, 23 Pueo Pl., Kualapu'u* ☎ *808/553-5236* ⊕ *www. nature.org* ☞ *Free; donation suggested for guided hike, $10 members, $25 nonmembers, includes 1-yr membership.*

⑮ Kamalō. A natural harbor used by small cargo ships during the 19th century, this is also the site of the **Church of St. Joseph's,** a tiny white church built by Father Damien in the 1880s. The door is always unlocked. Slip inside and sign the guestbook. The congregation keeps this church in beautiful condition. ⊠ *Rte. 450, about 11 mi east of Kaunakakai, on makai side.*

> **need a break?**
>
> The best place to grab a snack or stock up on picnic supplies is the **Neighborhood Store 'N Counter** (⊠ Rte. 450, 16 mi east of Kaunakakai, Puko'o ☎ 808/558-8498). It's the only place on the East End where you can find essentials such as ice and bread, and not-so-essentials such as burgers and shakes.

⑱ Pu'u O Hoku Ranch. A 14,000-acre private spread in the highlands of East Moloka'i, Pu'u O Hoku was developed in the '30s by wealthy industrialist Paul Fagan. Route 450 cuts right through this rural gem with its green pastures and grazing horses and cattle. As you drive along, enjoy the splendid views of Maui and Lāna'i. The small island off the coast is Mokuho'oniki, a humpback whale nursery where the military practiced bombing techniques during World War II. The ranch offers horseback trail rides, two large guest cottages, and a retreat facility for groups. ⊠ *Rte. 450 about 20 mi east of Kaunakakai* ⊕ *www.puuohoku.com.*

WHERE TO EAT

During a week's stay, you might easily hit all the dining spots worth a visit, then return to your favorites for a second round. The dining scene is fun because it's a microcosm of Hawai'i's diverse cultures. You can find locally grown vegetarian foods, spicy Filipino cuisine, and Hawaiian fish with a Japanese influence—such as 'ahi or *aku* (types of tuna), mullet, and moonfish grilled, sautéed, or mixed with seaweed and eaten raw as *poke* (marinated raw fish). Most eating establishments are on Ala Mālama Street in Kaunakakai, with pizza, pasta, and ribs only a block away. What's more, the price is right.

WHAT IT COSTS				
$$$$	**$$$**	**$$**	**$**	**¢**
RESTAURANTS over $30	$20–$30	$12–$20	$7–$12	under $7

Restaurant prices are for one main course at dinner.

West Moloka'i

★ **$$-$$$$** ✕ **Maunaloa Room.** Order haute cuisine appetizers such as coconut-crusted shrimp, Moloka'i *'opihi* (a crunchy limpet), or *lumpia* (egg roll) stuffed with *kālua* duck (roasted in an underground oven). Entrées follow a steak-and-seafood theme, and the catch of the day can be prepared with *alae* (a pale-orange salt found in Moloka'i and Kaua'i). Inside, wagon-wheel chandeliers with electric candles typify the hotel restaurant's ranch fixtures. A dinner on the outside deck can't be beat. ⊠ *The Lodge at Moloka'i Ranch, 8 Maunaloa Hwy., Maunaloa* ☎ *808/660–2725* ▭ *AE, MC, V $14–$31.*

¢ ✕ **Paniolo Cafe.** The only other restaurant in Maunaloa town is this casual place that specializes in "plate lunches"—hearty fare with scoops of rice and macaroni salad accompanying an island-style main dish such as chicken *katsu* (breaded cutlet), kālua pork, or teriyaki beef. The servings are generous. Technically the café doesn't serve dinner. But they stay open until 7:30, so if you find yourself wondering where to dine, especially at the West End, come here for takeout boxes. ⊠ *Maunaloa town right next to movie theater* ☎ *808/552–2625* ▭ *No credit cards $4–$7.*

Central Moloka'i

$$ ✕ **Oceanfront Dining Room.** This is *the* place to hang out on Moloka'i. Locals relax at the bar listening to live music on weekends, or they come in for theme-night dinners (posters around town tell you what's in store for the week). Prime-rib specials on Friday and Saturday nights draw a crowd. Try the broiled baby back ribs smothered in barbecue sauce. Every Friday from 4 to 6 PM Moloka'i's *kūpuna* (old-timers) bring their instruments here for a lively Hawaiian jam session, a wonderful experience of grassroots aloha spirit. ⊠ *Hotel Moloka'i, Kamehameha V Hwy., Kaunakakai* ☎ *808/553–5347* ▭ *AE, D, DC, MC, V $12–$18.*

$–$$ ✕ **Moloka'i Pizza Cafe.** A cheerful, busy restaurant, Moloka'i Pizza is a popular gathering spot for families. Pizza, sandwiches, salads, pasta, fresh fish, and homemade pies are simply prepared and tasty. Kids keep busy on a few little coin-operated rides. ⊠ *Kaunakakai Pl. on Wharf Rd., Kaunakakai* ☎ *808/553–3288* ▭ *No credit cards $8–$19.*

$ ✕ **Oviedo's.** This modest lunch counter specializes in *adobos* (stews) with traditional Filipino spices and sauces. Try the tripe, pork, or beef adobo for a real taste of tradition. The locals say that Oviedo's makes the best roast pork in the state. You can eat in or takeout. ⊠ *145 Ala Mālama St., Kaunakakai* ☎ *808/553–5014* ▭ *No credit cards* ☉ *No dinner $8–$9.*

¢–$ ✕ **Paddler's Inn.** A roomy, comfortable restaurant with an extensive menu, Paddler's Inn is right in Kaunakakai town but on the ocean side of Kamehameha V Highway. There are three eating areas—standard restaurant seating, a shady cool bar, and an open-air courtyard where you can sit at a counter eating raw fish and drinking beer while getting cooled with spray from an overhead misting system. The food is a blend of island-style and standard American fare (fresh poke every day; a prime rib special every Friday night). There's live entertainment every night; it's open until midnight on weekdays, 2 AM on weekends. ⊠ *10 Mohala St., Kaunakakai* ☎ *808/553–5256* ▭ *AE, D, DC, MC, V $5–$14.*

$–$$　✕ **Kamuela's Cookhouse.** Kamuela's is the only eatery in rural Kualapu'u. From the outside, this laid-back diner looks like a little plantation house; inside, paintings of hula dancers and island scenes enhance the green-and-white furnishings. Typical fare is a plate of chicken or pork *katsu* served with rice. They shut down the grill by 6 PM, so unless you order takeout ahead of time, this is not a dinner option. It's across the street from the Kualapu'u Market. ✉ *Farrington Hwy., 1 block west of Rte. 470, Kulapūu* ☎ *808/567–9655* ▭ *No credit cards* ☼ *Closed Mon. No dinner $8–$20.*

¢–$
Fodors'Choice
★　✕ **Kanemitsu Bakery and Restaurant.** Come here for a taste of *lavosh*, a pricey flatbread flavored with sesame, taro, Maui onion, Parmesan cheese, or jalapeño. Or try the round Moloka'i bread—a sweet, pan-style white loaf that makes excellent cinnamon toast. ✉ *79 Ala Mālama St., Kaunakakai* ☎ *808/553–5855* ▭ *No credit cards* ☼ *Closed Tues. $4–$8.*

¢–$　✕ **Moloka'i Drive Inn.** Fast food Moloka'i-style is served at a walk-up counter. Hot dogs, fries, and sundaes are on the menu, but residents usually choose the foods they grew up on, such as saimin, plate lunches, shaved ice (snow cone), and the beloved *loco moco* (rice topped with a hamburger and a fried egg, covered in gravy). ✉ *857 Ala Mālama St., Kaunakakai* ☎ *808/553–5655* ▭ *No credit cards $3–$9.*

¢–$　✕ **Sundown Deli.** This clean little rose-color deli focuses on freshly made takeout food. Sandwiches come on half a dozen types of bread, and the Portuguese bean soup and chowders are rich and filling. Specials, such as vegetarian quiche, change daily. The deli also sells vitamins and local-theme T-shirts. ✉ *145 Ala Mālama St., Kaunakakai* ☎ *808/553–3713* ▭ *AE, MC, V* ☼ *Closed Sun. No dinner $4–$8.*

¢　✕ **Outpost Natural Foods.** A well-stocked store, Outpost is the heart of Moloka'i's health-food community. At the counter you can get fresh juices and delicious sandwiches geared toward the vegetarian palate. It's a great place to pick up local produce and all the ingredients you need for a picnic lunch. ✉ *70 Makaena St., Kaunakakai* ☎ *808/553–3377* ▭ *No credit cards* ☼ *Closed Sat. No dinner $3–$5.*

WHERE TO STAY

The coastline along the West End has ocean-view condominium units and luxury homes available as vacation rentals. In the hills above, little Maunaloa town offers the superb Lodge at Moloka'i Ranch and the oddly luxurious seaside tents at Kaupoa Beach Village. Central Moloka'i has B&Bs with extremely helpful owners, two seaside condominiums, and the icon of the island—Hotel Moloka'i. The only lodgings on the East End are some guest cottages in magical settings.

WHAT IT COSTS				
$$$$	**$$$**	**$$**	**$**	**¢**
HOTELS　over $200	$150–$200	$100–$150	$60–$100	under $60

Hotel prices are for two people in a standard double room in high season, including tax and service.

West Moloka'i

Hotels & Resorts

$$$$ ⌂ **The Lodge at Moloka'i Ranch.** Moloka'i's plushest accommodation is
Fodor'sChoice   this Old West–style lodge. Ranching memorabilia and local artwork
★   adorn guest-room walls, with each of the 22 suites individually decorated.
All rooms have private lānai and some have skylights. An impressive stone
fireplace warms up the central Great Room, and there's a games room
for pleasant socializing during cool Moloka'i evenings. Pathways and a
greenhouse delineate the grounds. Spa facilities include massage rooms,
a juice bar, and men's and women's saunas. ⌂ *Maunaloa Hwy., Box 259,
Maunaloa 96770* ☎ *888/627–8082* ⊕ *www.molokairanch.com* ⋑ *22
rooms* ⌂ *Restaurant, in-room safes, refrigerators, in-room data ports,
pool, gym, massage, sauna, spa, beach, boating, fishing, mountain bikes,
billiards, hiking, horseback riding, horseshoes, bar, lounge, library, recreation room, children's programs (ages 5–12)* ⊟ *AE, D, MC, V $305–$355.*

★ **$$$–$$$$**   ⌂ **Kaupoa Beach Village.** This dream-come-true campground consists of
one- and two-unit canvas bungalows, mounted on wooden platforms.
Don't let the presence of ecotravelers fool you—the rooms are unex-
pectedly luxurious, with queen-size beds, self-composting flush toilets,
and private outdoor showers. Breakfast, lunch, and dinner are served
family-style in an open-air pavilion (price not included in room rate).
Extensive activities, including snorkeling, kayaking, clay shooting, and
mountain biking, are available. ⌂ *Maunaloa Hwy., Box 259, Maunaloa
96770* ☎ *888/627–8082* ⊕ *www.molokairanch.com* ⋑ *100 tents*
⌂ *Restaurant, fans, beach, snorkeling, boating, mountain bikes, hik-
ing, horseback riding, airport shuttle; no A/C, no room phones, no
room TVs* ⊟ *AE, D, MC, V $185–$255.*

Condos & Vacation Rentals

$$$$ ⌂ **Hale Aloha.** This spacious four-bedroom, three-bath vacation rental
is on 12 secluded acres, has ocean views, and is surrounded by wood-
lands and an orchard. Wood floors stretch the length of the house, con-
necting the two kitchens. A wraparound porch leads to a gazebo-covered
hot tub. Rooms are open and simple, with wood-beam ceilings. The man-
agers of this property, 1-800-Molokai, also handle a number of other
West-End condos for as little as $100 a night. ⌂ *Kaluako'i Rd., Box
20, Maunaloa 96770* ☎ *800/665–6524 or 808/552–2222* ⊕ *www.1-
800-molokai.com* ⋑ *1 house* ⌂ *Fans, kitchen, cable TV, in-room
VCRs, pool, hot tub; no A/C* ⊟ *AE, MC, V $214–$500.*

★ **$$–$$$$**   ⌂ **Paniolo Hale.** Perched high on a ledge overlooking the beach, Paniolo Hale is one of Moloka'i's best condominium properties. Some units
have spectacular ocean views. Studios and one- or two-bedroom units
all have beautiful screened lānai and kitchens; some have hot tubs for
an additional charge. Kitchens are well equipped, and the rooms are tidy
and simple. The property is adjacent to the Kaluako'i Golf Course and
a stone's throw from the Kaluako'i Hotel and Golf Club. ⌂ *Lio Pl.,
Box 190, Maunaloa 96770* ☎ *808/553–8334 or 800/367–2984* ☐ *808/
553–3784* ⊕ *www.molokai-vacation-rental.com* ⋑ *77 condominiums*
⌂ *Kitchens, microwaves, 18-hole golf course, golf privileges, pool, paddle tennis* ⊟ *AE, MC, V $105–$275.*

$-$$$ 🏨 **Kaluako'i Villas.** Studios and one-bedroom ocean-view suites are decorated in blue and mauve, with island-style art, rattan furnishings, and private lānai. Units are spread out in 21 two-story buildings covering 29 acres, adjacent to the now defunct Kaluako'i Resort. The view toward the ocean looks across the newly revived golf course. The seclusion and sunsets make this a great find. ⊠ *1131 Kaluako'i Rd., Box 200, Maunaloa 96770* ☎ *808/552–2721 or 800/367–5004* 📠 *808/552–2201* ⊕ *www.castleresorts.com* ⇨ *47 units, 2 cottages* ♿ *Fans, kitchens, in-room VCRs, 18-hole golf course, pool, beach, shops; no A/C* ⊟ *AE, MC, V $75–$200.*

$-$$ 🏨 **Ke Nani Kai.** These pleasant one- and two-bedroom condo units have ocean views and use of the facilities at the former Kaluako'i Hotel and Golf Club. Furnished lānai have flower-laden trellises, and the spacious interiors are decorated with rattans and pastels. Each unit has a washer-dryer unit and a fully equipped kitchen. The beach is a five-minute walk away. ⊠ *Kaluako'i Rd., Box 289, Maunaloa 96770* ☎ *808/553–8334 or 800/367–2984* 📠 *808/553–3784* ⊕ *www.molokai-vacation-rental. com* ⇨ *120 condominiums (22 rentals)* ♿ *Fans, kitchens, cable TV, 18-hole golf course, 2 tennis courts, pool, laundry facilities; no A/C* ⊟ *AE, D, DC, MC, V $95–$150.*

Central Moloka'i

Hotels & Resorts

$-$$ 🏨 **Hotel Moloka'i.** Friendly staff members here embody the aloha spirit.
Fodor'sChoice Low-slung Polynesian-style buildings with wood roof shingles are set
★ waterside. Simple, tropical furnishings with white rattan accents fill the rooms, and a basket swing awaits on the lānai. The Oceanfront Dining Room serves breakfast, lunch, dinner, and libations—with entertainment on weekend nights. Ask about deals in conjunction with airlines and rental-car companies when you make your reservation. ⊠ *Kamehameha V Hwy., Box 1020, Kaunakakai 96748* ☎ *808/553–5347 or 800/367–5004* 📠 *808/553–5047* ⊕ *www.hotelmolokai.com* ⇨ *45 rooms* ♿ *Restaurant, fans, some kitchenettes, cable TV, pool, lounge, laundry facilities; no A/C* ⊟ *AE, D, DC, MC, V $80–$135.*

Condos & B&Bs

$$ 🏨 **Moloka'i Shores.** Every room in this oceanfront, three-story condominium complex has a view of the water. One-bedroom, one-bath units or two-bedroom, two-bath units all have full kitchens and furnished lānai, which look out on 4 acres of manicured lawns with picnic tables. There's a great view of Lāna'i in the distance. ⊠ *1000 Kamehameha V Hwy., Box 1887, Kaunakakai 96748* ☎ *808/553–5954 or 800/535–0085* ⊕ *www.marcresorts.com* 📠 *800/633–5085* ⇨ *100 units* ♿ *Fans, kitchens, cable TV, pool, shuffleboard; no A/C* ⊟ *AE, D, MC, V $129.*

$-$$ 🏨 **Wavecrest.** This oceanfront condominium complex is convenient if you want to explore the east side of the island—it's 3 mi east of Kaunakakai. Individually decorated one- and two-bedroom units have full kitchens. Each has a furnished lānai, some with views of Maui and Lāna'i. Be sure to ask for an updated unit when you make your reservation. The shallow water here is bad for swimming but good for fishing. ⊠ *Rte. 450 near mile marker 13* 🏢 *Friendly Isle Realty, 75 Ala Mālama,*

Kaunakakai 96748 ☎ *808/553–3666 or 800/600–4158* 🖷*808/553–3867* ⊕ *www.molokairesorts.com* 🖙 *126 units* ⚲ *Fans, kitchens, 2 tennis courts, pool, beach, shuffleboard; no A/C* ➡ *V $85–$125.*

¢–$ 🏠 **A Hawaiian Getaway.** If you want to learn about Moloka'i's history and culture, consider staying here: gracious hosts Lawrence and Catherine Aki have an extensive library and also conduct cultural hikes through their company, Historical Hikes of West Moloka'i (*see* Hiking *earlier in this chapter*). Two rooms in the home are available. Small and simply decorated, both have double beds and one has a TV and VCR. Guests use the same entrance, bathroom, and living room as the proprietors. It's within walking distance of Kaunakakai town. ✉ *270 Kaiwi St., Kaunakakai 96748* ☎ *808/553–9803 or 800/274–9303* 📧 *mcai@aloha.net* 🖙 *2 rooms with shared bath* ⚲ *Fans, some cable TV, some in-room VCRs, hair salon, library, laundry facilities; no A/C* ➡ *No credit cards $50–$75.*

> ## GROCERY STORES
>
> **Friendly Market Center** (✉ 93 Ala Mālama St., Kaunakakai ☎ 808/553–5595) is the best-stocked supermarket on the island. **Misaki's Inc.** (✉ 78 Ala Mālama St., Kaunakakai ☎ 808/553–5505) is a good spot for housewares, beverages, and food staples. **Moloka'i Wines 'n' Spirits** (✉ 77 Ala Mālama St., Kaunakakai ☎ 808/553–5009) carries a good selection of fine wines and liquors, as well as gourmet cheese and snacks.

East Moloka'i

B&Bs & Vacation Rentals

$$$ 🏠 **Dunbar Beachfront Cottages.** These two spotlessly clean two-bedroom, one-bath cottages with complete kitchens—each with its own secluded beach—are set about ¼ mi apart. The beach is good for swimming and snorkeling during the summer months and great for whale-watching in winter. Covered lānai have panoramic vistas of Maui, Lāna'i, and Kaho'olawe across the ocean. ✉ *King Kamehameha V Hwy., mile marker 18, HC01, Box 901, Kaunakakai 96748* ☎ *808/558–8153 or 800/673–0520* 🖷 *808/558–8153* ⊕ *www.molokai-beachfront-cottages.com* 🖙 *2 cottages* ⚲ *BBQ, fans, kitchens, in-room VCRs, beach; no A/C, no smoking* ➡ *No credit cards $170, 3-night min.*

$$ 🏠 **Pu'u O Hoku Ranch.** At the east end of Moloka'i, near mile marker 25, lie these three ocean-view accommodations, on 14,000 isolated acres of pastures and forest. One country cottage has two bedrooms, basic wicker furnishings, and *lau hala* (natural fiber) woven matting on the floors. An airy four-bedroom cottage has a small deck and a somewhat Balinese air. For large groups—family reunions, for example—the Ranch has a lodge with 11 rooms, nine bathrooms, and a large kitchen. The full lodge goes for $1,250 nightly (rooms are not available on an individual basis). Inquire about horseback riding on the property. ✉ *Rte. 450, Box 1889, Kaunakakai 96748* ☎ *808/558–8109* 🖷 *808/558–8100* ⊕ *www.puuohoku.com* 🖙 *1 2-bedroom cottage, 1 4-bedroom cottage, 11 rooms in lodge* ⚲ *Kitchens, pool, hiking, horseback riding; no A/C* ➡ *MC, V $140.*

$–$$ ⌂ **Kamalō Plantation Cottage and Moanui Beach House.** Both of these Polynesian-style cottages have a fully equipped kitchen, living room, dining room, and deck. Kamalō is at the base of a mountain and sleeps two. Moanui sleeps four and has a TV and VCR. It's on a good snorkeling beach and has great views from its huge deck. Homegrown fruit and fresh-baked bread are provided for breakfast at both cottages. ⊠ *East of Kaunakakai off Rte. 450* ⌂ *HC 01, Box 300, Kaunakakai 96748* ☎ *808/558–8236* ⊕ *www.molokai.com/kamalo* ⌂ *2 cottages* ⌂ *Fans, kitchens; no A/C* ⊟ *No credit cards $95–$150.*

$ ⌂ **Honomuni House.** This cottage sits on an acre of tropical gardens that are complemented by waterfalls and a freshwater stream. The rental can sleep up to four and includes one bedroom, one bath, a large living-dining room with pullout couch, and a kitchen. An outdoor shower with hot water is an added bonus. It's 17 mi east of Kaunakakai on Route 450. ⊠ *Rte. 450, HC 1, Box 700, Kaunakakai 96748* ☎ *808/558–8383* ⊕ *www.molokai-aloha.com/honomuni* ⌂ *1 house* ⌂ *Kitchen; no A/C, no room TVs* ⊟ *No credit cards $85.*

> ## WHERE TO SPA
>
> **Turning Point Therapeutic Massage** has herbal remedies, and the staff offers nutritional advice to keep you at the top of your form. Allana Noury has been studying natural medicine for more than 30 years and is a licensed massage therapist, herbalist, and naturopathic physician. Ask for a traditional Hawaiian *lomi lomi* treatment. A 30-minute massage is $30; one hour is $50. It's just across the street from the Friendly Market in Kaunakakai. ⊠ *107 Ala Mālama, Kaunakakai* ☎ *808/553–8034.*

ENTERTAINMENT & NIGHTLIFE

Local nightlife consists mainly of gathering with friends and family, sipping a few cold ones, strumming 'ukuleles and guitars, singing old songs, and talking story. Still, there are a few ways to kick up your heels for a festive night out. Pick up a copy of the weekly *Moloka'i Dispatch*—and see if there's a church supper or square dance. The bar at the Hotel Moloka'i is always a good place to drink by the tiki torches. Most nights they have some kind of live music by island performers. The "Aloha Friday" weekly gathering here, 4 to 6 PM, always attracts a couple dozen old-timers with guitars and 'ukuleles. This impromptu, feel-good event is a peak experience for any Moloka'i trip. The Paddler's Inn in Kaunakakai has live music every night. The bar stays open until 2 AM on the weekends.

Movie fans can head to **Maunaloa Town Cinemas** (⊠ Maunaloa Hwy., Maunaloa ☎ 808/552–2707). Folks from all around Moloka'i come here nightly for current blockbusters.

SHOPPING

Moloka'i has one main commercial area: Ala Mālama Street in Kaunakakai. There are no department stores or shopping malls, and the clothing available is typical island wear. A handful of family-run businesses line the main drag of Maunaloa, a rural plantation town.

Most stores in Kaunakakai are open Monday through Saturday between 9 and 6. In Maunaloa most shops close by 4 in the afternoon and all day Sunday.

Arts & Crafts

The **Big Wind Kite Factory and Plantation Gallery** (✉ 120 Maunaloa Hwy., Maunaloa ☎ 808/552–2364) has custom-made appliquéd kites you can fly or display. Designs range from hula girls to tropical fish. Also in stock are kite-making kits, paper kites, minikites, and wind socks. Ask to go on the factory tour, or take a free kite-flying lesson. The gallery is intermingled with the kite shop and carries everything from locally made crafts to Hawaiian books and CDs, sunglasses, and incense.

Kamakana Fine Arts Gallery (✉ 110 Ala Mālama St., Kaunakakai ☎ 808/553–8520) only represents artists who live on the island, including world-class talent in photography, wood carving, ceramics, and Hawaiian musical instruments. This business actively supports the local community by showcasing talents that might otherwise go undiscovered. It's above American Savings Bank.

Clothing

Casual, knockabout island wear is sold at **Imports Gift Shop** (✉ 82 Ala Mālama St., Kaunakakai ☎ 808/553–5734), across from Kanemitsu Bakery. **Moloka'i Island Creations** (✉ 62 Ala Mālama St., Kaunakakai ☎ 808/553–5926) carries exclusive swimwear, beach cover-ups, sun hats, and tank tops. **Moloka'i Surf** (✉ 130 Kamehameha V Hwy., Kaunakakai ☎ 808/553–5093) is known for its wide selection of Moloka'i T-shirts, swimwear, and sports clothing.

Grocery Stores

Friendly Market Center (✉ 93 Ala Mālama St., Kaunakakai ☎ 808/553–5595) is the best-stocked supermarket on the island. Its slogan—"Your family store on Moloka'i"—is truly credible: hats, T-shirts, and sun-and-surf essentials keep company with fresh produce, meat, groceries, liquor, and sundries. Locals say the food is fresher here than at the other major supermarket in town. It's open weekdays 8:30–8:30 and Saturday 8:30–6:30.

Victuals and travel essentials are available at the **Maunaloa General Store** (✉ 200 Maunaloa Hwy., Maunaloa ☎ 808/552–2346). Open Monday–Saturday 8 to 6, it's convenient for guests staying at the nearby condos of the Kaluako'i Resort area. The store sells meat, produce, dry goods, drinks, and all the little things you find in a general store.

Misaki's Inc. (✉ 78 Ala Mālama St., Kaunakakai ☎ 808/553–5505) is a grocery with authentic island allure. It has been in business since 1922. Pick up housewares and beverages here, as well as your food staples, Monday through Saturday 8:30 to 8:30, and Sunday 9 to noon.

Don't let the name **Moloka'i Wines 'n' Spirits** (✉ 77 Ala Mālama St., Kaunakakai ☎ 808/553–5009) fool you. Along with a surprisingly good selection of fine wines and liquors, the store also carries gourmet cheeses and snacks. It's open Sunday through Thursday 9 AM to 10 PM, Friday and Saturday until 10:30.

Island Goods

The **Plantation Store** (✉ Kualapu'u Base Yard, Farrington Hwy., Ho'olehua ☎ 808/567–9023) has Moloka'i-made products, including Moloka'i-grown coffee, local artwork, jewelry, homemade jellies and jams, island soaps, pen-and-ink drawings of Moloka'i landscapes, and handcrafted pottery.

Jewelry

Imports Gift Shop (✉ 82 Ala Mālama St., Kaunakakai ☎ 808/553–5734) sells a decent collection of 14-karat-gold chains, rings, earrings, and bracelets, plus a jumble of Hawaiian quilts, pillows, books, and postcards. It also carries Hawaiian heirloom jewelry, a unique style of jewelry, inspired by popular Victorian pieces, that has been crafted in Hawai'i since the late 1800s. These stunning gold pieces are made to order with your Hawaiian name inscribed on them.

Moloka'i Island Creations (✉ 62 Ala Mālama St., Kaunakakai ☎ 808/553–5926) carries its own unique line of jewelry, including sea opal, coral, and sterling silver, as well as other gifts and resort wear.

Sporting Goods

Moloka'i Bicycle (✉ 80 Mohala St., Kaunakakai ☎ 808/553–5740 or 800/709–2453 ⊕ www.bikehawaii.com/molokaibicycle) rents and sells mountain and road bikes as well as jogging strollers, kids' trailers, helmets, and racks. It supplies maps and information on biking and hiking and will drop off and pick up equipment for a fee nearly anywhere on the island. Call or stop by to arrange what you need.

Moloka'i Fish and Dive (✉ 61 Ala Mālama St., Kaunakakai ☎ 808/553–5926) is *the* source for sporting needs, from snorkel rentals to free and friendly advice. These folks handle all activities for The Lodge at Moloka'i Ranch. This is also a good place to pick up original-design Moloka'i T-shirts and gifts.

MOLOKA'I ESSENTIALS

Transportation

BY AIR

If you're flying in from the mainland United States, you must first make a stop in Honolulu. From there, it's a 25-minute trip to the Friendly Isle.

CARRIERS Island Air, the puddle-jumper arm of Aloha Airlines, provides daily flights between Moloka'i and O'ahu or Maui on its 37-passenger de Haviland

3

Dash-8 aircrafts. Pacific Wings operates chartered flights of its nine-passenger Cessna between O'ahu and Moloka'i.

If you fly into the airstrip at Kalaupapa, your arrival should coincide with one of the authorized ground tours of the area. Otherwise you'll be asked to leave. Pacific Wings and Moloka'i Air Shuttle fly from Honolulu to Kalaupapa. Paragon Air runs charter flights from Maui to Kalaupapa.

🚹 **Island Air** ☎ 800/323-3345 ⊕ www.islandair.com. **Moloka'i Air Shuttle** ☎ 808/567-6847 in Honolulu. **Pacific Wings** ☎ 808/873-0877 or 888/575-4546 ⊕ www.pacificwings.com. **Paragon Air** ☎ 808/244-3356 or 800/428-1231 ⊕ www.paragon-air.com.

AIRPORTS Moloka'i's transportation hub is Ho'olehua Airport, a tiny airstrip 8 mi west of Kaunakakai and about 18 mi east of Maunaloa. An even smaller airstrip serves the little community of Kalaupapa on the North Shore.

🚹 **Ho'olehua Airport** ☎ 808/567-6140. **Kalaupapa Airfield** ☎ 808/567-6331.

TO & FROM THE AIRPORT From Ho'olehua Airport, it takes about 10 minutes to reach Kaunakakai and 25 minutes to reach the West End of the island by car. Since there's no rush hour, traffic won't be a problem. There's no public bus.

Shuttle service for two passengers costs about $18 from Ho'olehua Airport to Kaunakakai. A trip to Moloka'i Ranch costs $28, divided by the number of passengers. For shuttle service, call Moloka'i Off-Road Tours and Taxi or Molokai Outdoors.

🚹 **Moloka'i Off-Road Tours and Taxi** ☎ 808/553-3369. **Moloka'i Outdoors** ☎ 808/553-4227 ⊕ www.molokai-outdoors.com.

BY CAR

If you want to explore Moloka'i from one end to the other, it's best to rent a car. With just a few main roads to choose from, it's a snap to drive around here.

The gas stations are in Kaunakakai and Maunaloa. When you park your car, be sure to lock it—thefts do occur. Drivers must wear seat belts or risk a $42 fine. Children under three must ride in a federally approved child passenger restraint device, easily leased at the rental agency. Ask your rental agent for a free *Moloka'i Drive Guide*.

CAR RENTAL Budget maintains a counter near the baggage claim area at the airport. Dollar also has offices at Ho'olehua Airport, and your rental car can be picked up in the parking lot. Expect to pay from $40 to $50 per day for a standard compact and from $50 to $70 for a midsize car. Rates are seasonal and may run higher during the peak winter months. It's best to make arrangements in advance. If you're flying on Island Air or Hawaiian Airlines, see whether fly-drive package deals are available—you might luck out on a less-expensive rate. Hotels and outfitters might also offer packages.

Locally owned Island Kine Rent-a-Car offers airport or hotel pickup and sticks to one rate year-round for vehicles in a broad spectrum from two- and four-wheel drives to 15-passenger vans. The same is true for Moloka'i Rentacar, located right on the main street in Kaunakakai.

🚹 **Major Agencies Budget** ☎ 808/451-3600 or 800/527-7000 ⊕ www.budget.com. **Dollar** ☎ 808/567-6156 or 800/367-7006 ⊕ www.dollar.com.

⌗ Local Agencies Island Kine Rent-a-Car ☎ 808/553-5242 ⊕ www.molokai-car-rental.com. **Moloka'i Rentacar** ⊠ 82 Ala Mālama, Kaunakakai ☎ 808/553-3929 ⎙ 808/553-9808.

BY FERRY
The Moloka'i Ferry crosses the channel every day between Lahaina (Maui) and Kaunakakai, making it easy for West Maui visitors to put Moloka'i on their itineraries. The 1½-hour trip takes passengers but not cars, so arrange ahead of time for a car rental or tour at the arrival point. The easiest way to do this is to contact Moloka'i Outdoors, who will arrange your transportation and lodgings. Tack this trek onto the end of a vacation in West Maui.

⌗ Moloka'i Ferry ☎ 808/667-2585 ⊕ www.molokaiferry.com.

Contacts & Resources

EMERGENCIES
Round-the-clock medical attention is available at Moloka'i General Hospital. Severe cases or emergencies are often airlifted to Honolulu.

⌗ Emergency Services Ambulance and general emergencies ☎ 911. **Coast Guard** ☎ 808/552-6458 on O'ahu. **Fire** ☎ 808/553-5601 in Kaunakakai, 808/567-6525 at Ho'olehua Airport. **Police** ☎ 808/553-5355.

⌗ Hospital Moloka'i General Hospital ⊠ 280A Puali St., Kaunakakai ☎ 808/553-5331.

VISITOR INFORMATION
There's tourist information available in kiosks and stands at the airport in Ho'olehua or at the Moloka'i Visitors Association. The Maui Visitors Bureau has travel information for Maui County, of which Moloka'i is a part.

Molokaievents.com, Inc., has information on island events and can help you plan your own events on the island.

Car-rental agencies distribute the free *Moloka'i Drive Guide* along with maps and other up-to-date information.

⌗ Maui Visitors Bureau ⌂ On Maui: Box 580, Wailuku 96793 ☎ 808/244-3530 ⊕ www.visitmaui.com. **Molokaievents.com, Inc.** ☎ 808/567-6789 ⊕ www.molokaievents.com. **Moloka'i Visitors Association** ⊠ 10 Kamehameha V Hwy. (Box 960), Kaunakakai ☎ 808/553-3876 or 800/800-6367 ⊕ molokai-hawaii.com.

Lāna'i

Polihua Beach

WORD OF MOUTH

"Lāna'i is one funky-looking island. There are places like the Garden of the Gods, where it looks like you are on another planet. . . . We also drove the Munro Trail which takes you up to the highest part of the island. Spectacular scenery. On a clear day, you can see all of the Islands except Kaua'i and Ni'ihau."

—Alex

WELCOME TO LĀNAʻI

Polihua Beach

TOP 5
Reasons to Go

1 **Seclusion & Serenity:** Lānaʻi is small: local motion is slow motion. Go home rested instead of exhausted.

2 **Garden of the Gods:** Walk amid the eerie red rock spires that ancient Hawaiians believed to be the home of the spirits.

3 **A Dive at Cathedrals:** Explore underwater pinnacle formations and mysterious caverns lit by shimmering rays of light.

4 **Dole Square:** Hang out in the shade of the Cook Pines and talk story with the locals.

5 **Lānaʻi Pine Sporting Clays & Archery Range:** Play a Pacific William Tell, aiming your arrow at a pineapple.

■ **TIP**➜➜ Directions on the island are often given as *mauka* (toward the mountains) and *makai* (toward the ocean).

Kaʻena Pt.

Garden of the Gods

440

Kaumalapau Harbor

Lā
Air

Kai

Hulopoʻe Beach   *Garden of the Gods*

Getting Oriented

Unlike the other Hawaiian islands with their tropical splendors, Lāna'i looks like a desert; kiawe trees right out of Africa, red dirt roads that glow molten at sunset, and a deep blue sea that literally leads to Tahiti. Lāna'ihale (house of Lāna'i), the mountain that bisects the island, is carved into deep canyons by rain and wind on the windward side, and the dryer leeward side slopes gently to the sea, where waves pound against surf-carved cliffs.

Spinner Dolphins

4

Windward Lāna'i is the long white sand beach at the base of Lāna'ihale. Now uninhabited, it was once occupied by thriving Hawaiian fishing villages and a sugar cane plantation.

Lāna'i City is really a tiny plantation village. Locals hold conversations in front of Dole Park shops and from their pickups on the road, and kids ride bikes in colorful impromptu parades while cars wait for them.

Cool and serene, Upcountry is graced by Lāna'i City, towering Cook Pine trees, and misty mountain vistas.

The more developed beach side of the island, Mānele Bay and harbor are where it's happening: swimming, picnicking, off-island excursions, and boating are all concentrated in this very accessible area.

Mānele Bay Hotel   Lāna'i Pine Archery

LĀNAʻI PLANNER

Sunsets and Moonrises

One of the best ways to tap into Lānaʻi's Pacific Island pace is to take the time not just to watch the sun set but also to watch the moon rise. The best sunset-viewing spots are the veranda at The Lodge, the grassy field past the Lodge's tennis courts, Hulopoʻe Beach, and the Challenge at Mānele clubhouse. For full moons, nothing beats the trail that leads to Puʻu Pehe or the many stopping places along Keōmoko Road.

Navigating Without Signs

Lānaʻi has no traffic, no traffic lights, and only three paved roads. Bring along a good topographical map, study it, and keep in mind your directions. Stop from time to time and re-find landmarks and gauge your progress. Distance is better measured in the condition of the road than in miles. Watch out for other jeep drivers who also don't know where they are. Never drive to the edge of lava cliffs, as rock can give way under you.

Timing is Everything

Whales are seen off Lānaʻi's shores from December through April. A Pineapple Festival on the 4th of July Saturday in Dole Park features local food, Hawaiian entertainment, a pineapple eating and cooking contest and fireworks. Buddhists hold their annual outdoor Obon Festival honoring departed ancestors with joyous dancing, food booths, and taiko drumming in early July. Lānaʻi celebrates the state-wide Aloha Festivals in mid October with a hometown parade, car contests, more food, and more music. Beware hunting season weekends—from mid February through mid May, and mid July through mid October. Most of the private lodging properties are booked way in advance.

A Special Island

Castle & Cooke Resorts, LLC, which is owned by David H. Murdock, owns 98% of the land on Lānaʻi—resorts, luxury developments, commercial properties, and stores. The exceptions are private residences, the school, the police station, the airport, and county highways. As Castle & Cooke allows the public to use its land without compensation, the company has no liability or legal responsibility under Hawaiian law for your safety. So be careful.

Will it Rain?

As higher mountains on Maui capture the trade wind clouds, Lānaʻi receives little rainfall and has a desert ecology. It's always warmer at the beach and can get cool or even cold (by Hawaiian standards) upcountry. Consider the wind direction when planning your day. If it's blowing a gale on the windward beaches, head for the lee at Hulopoʻe or check out Garden of The Gods. Overcast days, when the wind stops or comes lightly from the southwest, are common in whale season. Try a whale watching trip or the windward beaches.

BEACHES

By Joana
Varawa

Lāna'i offers miles of secluded white-sand beaches on its windward side, and a moderately developed Hulopo'e Beach adjacent to the Mānele Bay Hotel. Hulopo'e is accessible by car or hotel shuttle bus; to reach the windward beaches you need a four-wheel-drive vehicle. An offshore reef, rocks, and coral make swimming on the windward side problematic, but it's fun to splash around in the shallow water. Driving on the beach itself is illegal and can be dangerous. Beaches are listed alphabetically.

Hulopo'e Beach. A short stroll from the Mānele Bay Hotel, Hulopo'e is considered one of the best beaches in all Hawai'i. The sparkling crescent of this Marine Life Conservation District beckons with calm waters safe for swimming almost all year round: great snorkeling reefs, tide pools, and, sometimes, spinner dolphins. A shady, grassy beach park is perfect for picnics. If the shore break is pounding, or if you see surfers riding big waves, stay out of the water. ✉ *From Lāna'i City follow Hwy. 440 (Mānele Rd.) south to bottom of hill; road dead-ends at beach's parking lot* ♿ *Toilets, showers, picnic tables, grills, parking lot.*

Lōpā Beach. A popular surfing spot for locals, Lōpā is also an ancient fishpond. With majestic views of West Maui and Kaho'olawe, this remote, white-sand beach is a great place for a picnic. ⚠ **Don't let the sight of surfers fool you: the channel's currents are too strong for swimming.** ✉ *East side of Lāna'i, 7 mi down dirt road that runs from end of Keōmuku Hwy. along eastern shore* ♿ *No facilities.*

Polihua Beach. This often-deserted beach should get a star for beauty

THE COASTAL ROAD

Many of the spur roads leading to the windward beaches from the coastal dirt road cross private property and are closed off by chains. Look for open spur roads with recent tire marks (a fairly good sign that they are safe to drive on). It's best to park on firm ground and walk in to avoid getting your car mired in the sand.

with its long, wide stretch of white sand and the clear views of Moloka'i. The dirt road to get here is often bad, however, and frequent high winds whip up sand and waves. ⚠ **Strong currents and a sudden drop in the ocean floor make swimming extremely dangerous.** On the northern end, the beach ends at a rocky lava cliff with some interesting tide pools. Polihua is named after the sea turtles that lay their eggs in the sand. Do not drive on the beach and endanger their nests. Curiously, wild bees sometimes gather around your car for water at this beach. To get rid of them, put out water some place away from the car and wait a bit. ✉ *Windward Lāna'i, 11 mi from Lāna'i City, past Garden of the Gods* ♿ *No facilities.*

Shipwreck Beach. Beachcombers come to this fairly accessible beach for shells and washed-up treasures; photographers for great shots of Moloka'i, just across the 9-mi wide Kalohi Channel; and walkers for the long stretch of sand. It may still be possible to find glass ball fishing floats but more common is water-born debris from the Moloka'i channel. Kaiolohia, its Hawaiian name, is a favorite local diving spot. ⚠ **An offshore reef and rocks in the water mean that it's not for swimmers, though you can play in the**

shallow water on the shoreline. ⊠ *North shore, 10 mi north of Lāna'i City at end of Keōmuku Hwy.* ⚬ *No facilities.*

WATER ACTIVITIES & TOURS

Boat Tours & Charters

Trilogy Oceansports Lāna'i. If you're staying in Lāna'i and want to play on the ocean, Trilogy is your outfitter.

A four-hour morning snorkel sail, with two different sites, includes lessons, equipment, and a hot BBQ lunch at the Trilogy Pavilion when you return to Mānele harbor. It's $132 for adults and $67 for kids 15 and under. These snorkel sails have a kayaking upgrade option. The upgrade costs an additional $27; it's an extra $14 for kids, who must be accompanied by an adult in a double kayak.

Two-tank dives with Trilogy explore two different dive sites; the location depends on the weather. It's $138 for certified adults; bring your certificate. Cinnamon rolls and coffee are included. Beginners (minimum age 12 years) can try the one-tank introductory dives for $75; you wade into Hulopo'e Bay with an instructor.

If that's not enough, sign up for a blue-water dolphin watch, whale-watching sail, or a sunset cruise. You can book trips through your hotel concierge, but try online first, where discounts are often available. ☎ *888/628–4800* ⊕ *www.sailtrilogy.com.*

Deep-Sea Fishing

Some of the best sportfishing grounds in Maui County are off the southwest shoreline of Lāna'i. Pry your eyes open and go deep-sea fishing in the early morning, with 6 or 6:30 AM departures from Mānele Harbor. Prime seasons are spring and summer, although good catches have been landed year-round. Mahimahi, ono, 'ahi, and marlin are prized catches, with mahi and ono (which means delicious in Hawaiian) preferred eating. The single sportfishing boat operating out of Mānele Harbor on Lāna'i is the luxurious *Kila Kila.*

Kila Kila. Jeff Menze, with 30 years' experience in Hawaiian waters, captains this elegant 53-foot Merritt, which has world records to its credit. If there are fish to find, Menze can find them. The sleek *Kila Kila* has a fly bridge, spacious cockpit, air-conditioned salon, showers, and two toilets. Menze and his crew clean your catch, cut fillets, and send them up to the Mānele chefs to be cooked to order. Or you can take the fillets for a picnic barbeque or dinner elsewhere. A four-hour trip with up to six passengers costs $825; a full-day run is $1,200. Pastries and soft drinks provided. A sunset sail or sightseeing along the coast are other options, but they do not allow snorkeling. Book with the concierge at the resort. ☎ *808/565–2387 or 808/565–4555.*

Kayaking

Lāna'i's northeast coast offers leisurely paddling inside the windward reef. Curious sea turtles and friendly manta rays may tag along for company. There are miles of scenic coastline with deserted beaches on the inside reef to haul up on for an informal picnic. When the wind comes from the southwest, the windward coast is tranquil. Kayaking along the leeward cliffs is more demanding with rougher seas and strong currents. No kayaking is permitted in the Marine Conservation District at Hulopoʻe Bay.

Early mornings tend to be calmer. The wind picks up as the day advances. ⚠ **Expect strong currents along all of the coasts.** Experience on the water is advised, and knowing how to swim is essential.

Unless you travel with your own kayak, you will have to book with Trilogy (⇨ *See* Boat Tours & Charters, above), the single purveyor of guided kayaking trips on Lānaʻi. There are no kayak rentals on Lānaʻi.

Scuba Diving

When you have a dive site such as Cathedrals—with eerie pinnacle formations and luminous caverns—it's no wonder that scuba-diving buffs consider exploring the waters off Lānaʻi akin to having a religious experience.

Just outside of Hulopʻe Bay, the boat dive site **Cathedrals** was named the best cavern dive site in the Pacific by *Skin Diver* magazine. Shimmering light makes the many openings in the caves look like the stained-glass windows in cathedrals. A current generally keeps the water crystal clear, even if it's turbid outside. In these unearthly chambers, large ulua and small reef shark add to the adventure. **Sergeant Major Reef**, off Kamaiki Point, is named for big schools of yellow- and black-striped manini (Sergeant Major fish) that turn the rocks silvery as they feed. The site

> Schools of manini feeding on the coral coat the rocks with flashing silver, and you can view kala, uhu, and papio in all their rainbow colors.

is made up of three parallel lava ridges, a cave, and an archway, with rippled sand valleys between the ridges. Depths range 15–50 feet.

Trilogy (⇨ *See* Boat Tours & Charters, above) is the only company running boat dives from Lānaʻi.

Snorkeling

Snorkeling is the easiest ocean sport available on the island, requiring nothing but a snorkel, mask, fins, and good sense. Purchase equipment in Lānaʻi City if you don't bring your own. The basic rules of snorkeling are: never turn your back on the ocean; wait to enter the water until you are sure no big sets are coming; and observe the activity of locals on the beach. If little kids are playing in the shore break, it's usually safe to enter (although little local kids are expert wave riders). Put your mask and fins on once you have passed the shore break, rather than trying to wade in with fins through the waves.

Hulopoʻe Beach is an outstanding snorkeling destination. The bay is a State of Hawaiʻi Marine Conservation District and no fishing or diving is allowed. Schools of manini feeding on the coral coat the rocks with flashing silver, and you can view kala, uhu, and papio in all their rainbow colors. Wade in from the sandy beach, the best snorkeling is toward the left. Beware of rocks and surging waves. When the resident spinner dolphins are in the bay, it's courteous to watch them from the shore. If swimmers and snorkelers go out, the dolphins may leave and be deprived of their necessary resting place. Another wade-in snorkel spot is just beyond the break wall at **Mānele Small Boat Harbor.** Enter over the rocks just past the boat ramp. ⚠ **It's dangerous to enter if waves are breaking.**

Book with Trilogy (⇨ *See* Boat Tours & Charters, above) for snorkel sails.

GOLF, HIKING & OUTDOOR ACTIVITIES

Biking
Many of the same red-dirt roads that invite hikers are excellent for biking, offering easy flat terrain and long clear views. There's only one hitch: you may have to bring your own bike, as there are no rentals or tours for nonresort guests available.

A favorite biking route is along the fairly flat red-dirt road northward from Lāna'i City through the old pineapple fields to Garden of the Gods. Start your trip on Keōmoko Highway in town. Take a left just before the Lodge's tennis courts, and then a right where the road ends at the fenced pasture, and continue on to the north end and the start of Polihua and Awalua dirt roads. If you're really hardy you could bike down to Polihua Beach and back, but it would be a serious all-day trip. In wet weather these roads turn to slurry and are not advisable. Go in the early morning or late afternoon because the sun gets hot in the middle of the day. Take plenty of water, spare parts, and snacks.

For the exceptionally fit, it's possible to bike from town down the Keōmoko Highway to the windward beaches and back or to bike the Munro Trail (⇨ *See* Hiking, below). Experienced bikers also bike up and down the Mānele Highway from Mānele Bay to town.

Camping
Camping isn't encouraged outside Lāna'i's one official campground at Hulopo'e: the island is privately owned; islanders are keen on privacy; and, unless you know about local conditions, camping on the beach can be hazardous.

Castle & Cooke Resorts Campground. The inviting, grassy campground at Hulopo'e Beach has shade trees, clean restrooms, BBQ grills, and beachside showers. Buy charcoal in Lāna'i City, as well as basic camping supplies and food. Cutting fire wood is not allowed and camping on the beach itself is reserved for residents only. Call in advance; it's $20 for a permit, plus a $5 fee per person per night (three-night limit). ☎ *808/ 565–3982 permits, 808/565–0415 advance reservations.*

Golf
Lāna'i has just three courses and a total of 45 holes (not counting an 18-hole putting course), but all three are good and offer very different environments and challenges. The two resort courses, especially, are so different, it's hard to believe that they're on the same island, let alone just 20 minutes apart by resort shuttle.

★ **The Challenge At Mānele.** Holes at the Challenge at Mānele, play across an ancient lava flow that rises abruptly from the sea. It's links-style, with few trees in sight. Jack Nicklaus takes advantage of the world's biggest water hazard: the par-3 12th plays along a 150-foot cliff above Hulupoʻe Bay and over the Pacific. Elevation change and distance is key on most holes. Greens here are Bermuda. ⊠ *Mānele Bay Hotel* ☎ *808/565–2222* ⊕ *www.islandoflanai.com* ⅃. *18 holes. 7039 yds. Par 72. Green Fee: $225* ☞ *Facilities. Driving range, putting green, golf carts, lessons, pro shop, restaurant, bar.*

Fodor'sChoice **The Experience At Kōʻele.** At the Experience at Kōʻele (1991), Ted Robin-
★ son took on a rookie architect named Greg Norman and taught him a bundle with two nines built on very different terrain. The front nine climbs up to 2,000 feet elevation, with the first seven holes winding across mountain ridges so high you can see ocean on two sides. The back nine plays across mostly flat land but cleverly incorporates mounding, bunkers, trees, and lakes. The 18th is one of the best closing holes in Hawaiʻi—a par-5 double dogleg that plays off an elevated tee and then uphill to a huge green, which is protected on the front and left by a lake and waterfall. Greens are bent grass. Kōʻele also has an 18-hole putting course. ⊠ *Lodge at Kōʻele* ☎ *808/ 565–4653* ⊕ *www.islandoflanai.com* ⅃. *18 holes. 7014 yds. Par 72. Green Fee: $225* ☞ *Facilities: Driving range, putting green, rental clubs, lessons, pro shop, restaurant, bar.*

> The two resort courses, especially, are so different, it's hard to believe that they're on the same island, let alone just 20 minutes apart by resort shuttle.

Hiking

Only 30 mi of Lānaʻi's roads are paved. But red-dirt roads and trails, ideal for hiking, will take you to sweeping overlooks, isolated beaches, and shady forests. Don't be afraid to leave the road to follow deer trails. Or take a self-guided walk through Kāne Puʻu, Hawaiʻi's largest native dryland forest. You can explore the Munro Trail over Lānaʻihale with views of plunging canyons, or participate in a guided hike along an old, coastal fisherman trail or across Koloiki Ridge. Wear hiking shoes, a hat, and sunscreen, and carry plenty of water.

BEST TRAILS **Koloiki Ridge** is a marked, moderate trail that starts behind the Lodge at Kōʻele takes you along the Munro Trail to overlook the windward side, with impressive views of Maui, Molokaʻi, Maunalei Valley, Naio Gulch, and, if you're lucky, dolphins. The average time for the 5 mi round-trip is three hours. Pick up a self-guided trail booklet at the Lodge. The Lodge also has a 2½ hour guided, interpretative hike for hotel guests; it costs $15 per person, snacks and drinks included.

Local fishermen still use the **Lānaʻi Fisherman Trail** to get to their favorite fishing spots. The trail takes about 1½ hours to hike and follows the rocky shoreline below the Mānele Bay Hotel, along cliffs bordering the golf course. Caves and tide pools beckon beneath you, but be careful climbing down. The marked trail entrance begins at the west end of Hulopoʻe Beach. The Mānele Bay Hotel offers early-morning guided coastal

4

fitness hikes that take approximately 1½ hours at a cost of $15 per person. Keep your eyes peeled for dolphins spinning offshore.

Pu‘u Pehe Trail begins to the left (facing the ocean) of Hulop‘i Beach, travels a short distance around the coastline, and then climbs up a sharp rise. At the top, you're level with the offshore stack of Pu‘u Pehe and can overlook miles of coastline in both directions. The trail is not difficult, but it's hot and steep. ⚠ **Never go next to the edge, as the cliff can easily give way.** The hiking is best in the early morning or late afternoon, and it's a perfect place to look for whales in season (December–April).

The **Munro Trail** is the real thing: a strenuous 9-mi trek that begins behind the Lodge and follows the ridge of Lāna‘ihale through the rain forest. The island's most demanding hike, it has an elevation gain of 1,400 feet and leads to a lookout at the island's highest point, Lāna‘ihale. It's also a narrow dirt road so watch out for careening jeeps that are as unfamiliar with the terrain as you are. The trail is named after George Munro, who supervised the planting of Cook pine trees and eucalyptus wind breaks. Mules used to wend their way up the mountain carrying the pine seedlings. Unless you arrange for someone to pick you up at the trail's end, you have a long boring hike back through the Palawai Basin to return to your starting point.

Horseback Riding

Stables at Kō‘ele. The subtle beauty of the high country slowly reveals itself to horseback riders. Sunset rides, private saunters, and two- to four-hour adventures traverse leafy trails with scenic overlooks. The Mahana Meal ride that overlooks the islands of Moloka‘i and Maui is enhanced with a gourmet meal from the Lodge at Kō‘ele. There's a fancy horse-drawn carriage for romantic couples and well-trained horses for riders of all ages and skill levels. Prices start at $60 for one hour. ☎ *808/565–4424.*

Sporting Clays & Archery

★ **Lāna‘i Pine Sporting Clays and Archery Range.** Outstanding rustic terrain, challenging targets, and a well-stocked pro shop make this sporting-clays course top-flight in the expert's eyes. Sharpshooters can complete the meandering 14-station solar-powered course in an hour, by golf cart. There are group tournaments, and even kids can enjoy skilled instruction at the archery range and compressed air rifle gallery. The $45 archery introduction includes an amusing "pineapple contest"—contestants are given five arrows with which to hit a pineapple. The winner takes home a crystal pineapple as a nostalgic souvenir of the old Dole Plantation days. ✉ *Just past Cemetery Rd. on windward side of island, first left off Keōmuku Hwy.* ☎ *808/559–4600.*

EXPLORING LĀNA‘I

Most of Lāna‘i's sights are out of the way—rent a four-wheel-drive vehicle, ask for a road map, be sure you have a full tank, and bring a snack. Don't stray from marked paths, and ask your hotel's concierge about road conditions before you set out.

Lānaʻi has an ideal climate year-round, hot and sunny at the sea and a few delicious degrees cooler Upcountry. In Lānaʻi City, the nights and mornings can be almost chilly when a mystic fog settles in.

The main road in Lānaʻi, Route 440, refers to both Kaumalapau Highway and Mānele Road. On the Islands, the directions *mauka* (toward the mountains) and *makai* (toward the ocean) are often used.

Lānaʻi City & Mānele Bay

Pineapples once blanketed the Pālāwai Basin, the flat area south of Lānaʻi City. Today it's primarily a wilderness traversed by hunters and botanists, and holds historic treasures. You'll need a four-wheel-drive vehicle to explore this rugged area.

4

a good drive

Start at the Lodge at Kōʻele to get a glimpse of early-ranching history. The lone **Norfolk Pine ❶** ☛ in front of the Lodge, planted in 1875, was the source of inspiration for the island's current watershed of pines. On the left stands **Ka Lokahi o Ka Mālamalama Church ❷**.

Pause in **Lānaʻi City ❸** for an espresso, and then drive south on Route 440 until you reach a major intersection. Turn left on Highway 440 East, and drive down the long, steep hill. At the bottom awaits **Mānele Bay ❹** and the island's only true swimming area, Hulopoʻe Beach. Backtrack up the hill. After about 5 mi you see a stop sign and a dirt road on the right, leading to the **Luʻahiwa Petroglyphs ❺**.

Most of Lānaʻi's sights are out of the way—rent a four-wheel-drive vehicle, ask for a road map, be sure you have a full tank, and bring a snack.

Return to the Highway 440 intersection. Follow Highway 440 past the airport to **Kaumalapau Harbor ❻**, the island's main seaport and a great sunset spot.

TIMING You could explore this small area in half a day, but if you like water sports, you may indulge in a few hours at Hulopoʻe Beach. The wind often picks up in the afternoon, so it's best to swim early. The south is sunny, clear, and warm, so wear sunscreen and find shade at midday.

What to See

❷ **Ka Lokahi o Ka Mālamalama Church.** This picturesque church was built in 1938 to provide Hawaiian services for Lānaʻi's growing population—for many people, the only other Hawaiian church, in coastal Keōmuku, was too far away. Typical of plantation days, the church had to be moved from its original Lānāi Ranch location when the Lodge at Kōʻele was built. Services are still held, in Hawaiian and English. ✉ *Left of entrance to Lodge at Kōʻele.*

❻ **Kaumalapau Harbor.** Built in 1926 by the Hawaiian Pineapple Company, which later became Dole, this is Lānaʻi's principal seaport. The cliffs that flank the western shore are as much as 1,000 feet tall. Water activities aren't allowed here, but it's a dramatic sunset spot. On Thursday you can witness the arrival of the barge: the island depends on its weekly

deliveries. ✉ *From Lāna'i City follow Hwy. 440 (Kaumalapau Hwy.)
west as far as it goes.*

❸ **Lāna'i City.** This tidy plantation town was built in 1924 by Jim Dole. It
reflects his wish to create a model plantation village: a simple grid of
roads lined with tall Cook pines and all the basic services a person might
need. Visit the **Lāna'i Arts & Cultural Center** to get a glimpse of this island's creative abundance. ✉ *339 7th Ave.*

❺ **Lu'ahiwa Petroglyphs.** On a steep slope overlooking the Pālāwai Basin
are 34 boulders with carvings. Drawn in a mixture of ancient and historic styles dating to the late 1700s and early 1800s, the simple stick-
figure illustrations depict life on Lāna'i. Some of the stones are believed
to possess the spiritual power of rain gods. ✉ *From Lāna'i City follow
Hwy. 440 (Mānele Rd.) south 2 mi to unmarked dirt road leading left
through fallow pineapple fields; at road's end, walk up unmarked trail
to petroglyphs.*

❹ **Mānele Bay.** The site of a Hawaiian village dating from AD 900, Mānele
Bay is flanked by lava cliffs that are hundreds of feet high. Though a
Marine Life Conservation District, it's the island's only public boat harbor and was the location of most post-contact shipping until Kaumalapau Harbor was built in 1926. The ferry to and from Maui also
pulls in here.

Just offshore you can catch a glimpse of **Pu'upehe.** Often called Sweetheart Rock, the isolated 80-foot-high islet carries a sad Hawaiian legend. The rock is named after Pehe, a woman so beautiful that her
husband, afraid that others would steal her away, kept her hidden in a
sea cave. One day, while Pehe was alone, the surf surged into the cave
and she drowned. With the help of the gods, her grief-stricken husband
buried her offshore on the summit of this rock and then jumped to his
own death. ✉ *From Lāna'i City follow Hwy. 440 (Mānele Rd.) south
to bottom of hill and look for harbor on your left.*

▶ ❶ **Norfolk Pine.** More than 100 feet high, this majestic pine tree was planted
here, at the former site of the manager's house, in 1875. Almost 30 years
later, George Munro, then the ranch manager, would observe how, in
foggy weather, water collected on its foliage, forming a natural rain. This
drip led to the planting of Cook pines along the ridge of Lāna'ihale and
across town. ✉ *Entrance of Lodge at Kō'ele.*

Garden of the Gods & Windward Lāna'i

The north and east sections of Lāna'i are wild and untouched. A ghost
town and deserted heiau are the only traces of civilization. Four-wheel
drive is a must to explore this side of the isle, and be prepared for hot,
rough conditions. Pack a picnic lunch and bring plenty of drinking water.

a good
drive

Set out north of the Lodge at Kō'ele on Keōmuku Highway: turn left
on the road between the Stables at Kō'ele and the tennis courts. Follow
the dirt road a couple of miles and turn right at the crossroads onto Polihua Road, which heads north through the dryland forest of **Kānepu'u
Preserve ❼** ▶ and, 1½ mi beyond, the **Garden of the Gods ❽**.

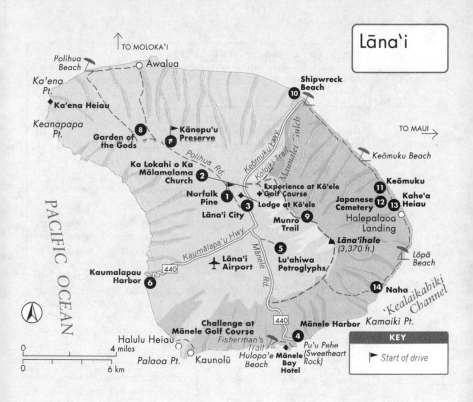

Return to Keōmuku Highway and head east. After about 1 mi, make a right onto the only road in sight, Cemetery Road, and you're on your way to the **Munro Trail ⑨**, a 9-mi route that runs over the top of Lāna'ihale, the mountain that rises above Lāna'i City.

Back on Keōmuku Highway, head makai—at an unofficial scenic point between mile markers 4 and 5 you'll find awesome views of Moloka'i, Maui, and Kaho'olawe and a first glimpse of the stranded World War II oiler at **Shipwreck Beach ⑩**.

If you feel adventurous, head southeast at the fork in the road where the beach starts, and follow the dirt road along the coast. During the rainy season the shoreline road may be impassable at places crossed by stream beds. Note that many of the spur roads leading to the windward beaches from the coastal dirt road cross private property and are closed off by chains. Look for open spur roads with recent tire marks (a fairly good sign that they are safe to drive on). It's best to park on firm ground and walk in to avoid getting your car mired in the sand.

The landscape changes from coastal dunes to *kiawe* forest (kiawe is a mesquite-type wood; watch for thorns!). Along the way, you'll come across abandoned Hawaiian homesteads. Five miles later, dozens of tall coconut trees announce the site of the old village **Keōmuku ⑪**, once a bustling sugar-

FODOR'S FIRST PERSON

Joana Varawa
Writer

I first came to Lāna'i in 1977 to study whales and dolphins. The Lāna'i Company allowed me to set up an observation camp on the cliff above the entrance to Mānele Harbor. My research station comprised a tent, which I never slept in, and an outside pallet with a mattress, which I did sleep on. Everything I owned fit in a big basket.

And so I began the best year of my entire life. I called my cliff-top aerie my million dollar condo (a million was worth more then), and each morning I would make my coffee, sit on the rocks overlooking the sea, and watch the dolphins in their early-morning resting ritual. They had a way of getting rid of whale-watching boats by sending out bow riders who would lead the boats away from the school, which would then resume its lazy circling in the deep water under the cliff. I would walk to the beach on a path unblemished by footprints, and enter the crystal water, pushing myself to go farther and longer until I was comfortable

in the ocean. One memorable time I swam out to the dolphins only to find a shark sculling peacefully beneath me. Panic was no option, so I followed him, thinking it better than turning my back and yelling, and he slowly melted into the distance. Admittedly, my return to shore was the best swim I ever made, in the shortest time.

One night I listened to the heart-stopping pounding of a whale smashing her tail against the water beneath me, a booming that seemed to rock the foundations of the land itself, and in the morning discovered the form of a creamy white-and-turquoise baby whale at her side, and understood I had heard a whale giving birth.

The island revealed itself to me in all its beauty. My companions were geckos, mice, and deer, and I knew the time by the moon's stately progress and the stars slowly turning above me. I was not an observer, but an equal participant in the great unfolding of life. I had come to learn about the whales and dolphins, but ultimately I learned the most about myself.

---

mill town. Pause at the **Japanese Cemetery** ⑫. Nearby are the ruins of a temple called **Kahe'a Heiau** ⑬, but you may need an experienced guide to find it. The road passes the often-deserted Lōpā Beach and ends 3 mi later at the remnants of an old Hawaiian fishpond at **Naha** ⑭.

TIMING   Give yourself a day to tour the island's northern and eastern reaches. Keep your eye on the sky: the highlands tend to attract heavy fog. If you're a hiker, you'll want a day just to enjoy the journey up to Lāna'ihale. Since many of the roads are bumpy, it takes more time to reach sights than it does to actually experience them. But getting there is half the fun.

What to See

❽ **Garden of the Gods.** This preternatural plateau is scattered with boulders of different sizes, shapes, and colors, the products of a million years of wind erosion. Time your visit for sunset, when the rocks begin to glow—

Fodor'sChoice ★

from rich red to purple—and the fiery globe sinks to the horizon. Magnificent views of the Pacific Ocean, Moloka'i, and, on clear days, O'ahu provide the perfect backdrop for photographs.

The ancient Hawaiians shunned Lāna'i for hundreds of years, believing the island was the inviolable home of spirits. Standing beside the oxide-red rock spires of this strange, raw landscape, you might be tempted to believe the same. This lunar savannah still has a decidedly eerie edge; but the shadows disappearing on the horizon are those of escaped game animals—mouflon sheep and axis deer—not the fearsome man-eating bird spirits of lore. According to tradition, the spirits were vanquished by Kā'ulula'au, a chief's son who was exiled here for destroying his father's prize breadfruit groves. The clever boy outwitted and exhausted the spirits, and announced the island's liberation with a giant bonfire. ⊠ *From Stables at Kō'ele, follow dirt road through hay fields 2 mi; turn right at crossroads and head through ironwood forest 1½ mi.*

⑫ **Japanese Cemetery.** In 1899, sugar came to this side of Lāna'i. A plantation took up about 2,400 acres and seemed a profitable proposition, but that same year, disease wiped out the labor force. This authentic Buddhist shrine commemorates the Japanese workers who died. ⊠ *6½ mi southeast from where Keōmuku Hwy. dead-ends at Shipwreck Beach, on dirt road running along north shore.*

⑬ **Kahe'a Heiau.** What was once a central place of worship for the people of Lāna'i may now be hard to find through the kiawe overgrowth. Equally hidden are the remaining stone platforms of the **Halepaloa Landing,** a wharf used by the Maunalei Sugar Company (1899) to ship cane. Some say that the company failed because attempted construction of a railroad disturbed the sacred stones of the heiau, which angered the gods, who then turned the drinking water salty, forcing closure in 1901. ⊠ *6½ mi southeast from where Keōmuku Hwy. dead-ends at Shipwreck Beach, on dirt road running along north shore.*

► ⑦ **Kānepu'u Preserve.** The 590 acres of this native dryland forest are under the stewardship of the Nature Conservancy of Hawai'i. Kānepu'u contains the largest remnant of this rare forest type. More than 45 native species of plants, including the endangered Hawaiian gardenia, grow in the shade of such rare trees as Hawaiian sandalwood, olive, and ebony. A short self-guided loop trail, with eight signs illustrated by local artist Wendell Kaho'ohalahala, reveals this ecosystem's beauty and the challenges it faces. ⊠ *Polihua Rd., 6 mi north of Lāna'i City* ☎ *808/537–4508* ☽ *Daily 9–4.*

⑪ **Keōmuku.** There's an eerie beauty about Keōmuku, with its crumbling, weed-choked stone walls and homes. During the late 19th century, this busy Lāna'i community of some 900 to 2,000 residents served as the headquarters of Maunalei Sugar Company. After the company failed, the land was used for ranching, but by 1954 the area lay abandoned. Its church, **Ka Lanakila O Ka Mālamalama,** the oldest on the island, was built in 1903. It has been partially restored by volunteers. Among the worn stone walls you may find a Portuguese beehive-shape communal bread oven, or the remains of a windmill. ⊠ *5 mi along unpaved road southeast of Shipwreck Beach.*

★ ⑨ **Munro Trail.** This 9-mi jeep trail along a pine-covered ridge was named after George Munro, manager of the Lāna'i Ranch Co., who began a reforestation program in the 1950s to provide a much-needed watershed. The trail climbs **Lāna'ihale** (House of Lāna'i), which, at 3,370 feet, is the island's highest point; on clear days you'll be treated to a panorama of canyons and almost all of the Hawaiian Islands. ⚠ **The roads get very muddy, and trade winds can be strong. Keep an eye out for hikers along the way.** You can also hike the Munro Trail (⇨ *See* Hiking *earlier in this chapter*), though it's a difficult trek: it's steep, the ground is uneven, and there is little shade. ⊠ *From Lodge at Kō'ele head north on Keōmuku Hwy. for 1¼ mi, then turn right onto dirt road; trailhead is ½ mi past cemetery on right.*

⑭ **Naha.** An ancient rock-walled fishpond—visible at low tide—lies here, where the sandy shorelines end and the cliffs begin their rise along the island's shores. The beach is a frequent resource for local fisherfolk. ⚠ **Treacherous tides make this a dangerous place for swimming.** ⊠ *East side of Lāna'i, at end of dirt road that runs from end of Keōmuku Hwy. along eastern shore.*

★ ⑩ **Shipwreck Beach.** The rusting World War II tanker may be a clue that the waters off this 8-mi stretch of sand aren't friendly. Strong trade winds have propelled innocent vessels onto the reef since at least 1824, when the first shipwreck was recorded. Some believe that the unknown oiler you see stranded today, however, was merely abandoned. ⚠ **The water is unsafe for swimming; stick to beachcombing.** ⊠ *End of Keōmuku Hwy. heading north.*

WHERE TO STAY

Though Lāna'i has few properties, it does have a range of price options. The Lodge at Kō'ele and Mānele Bay Hotel are a single luxury resort with beachside and upcountry locations. Although the room rates are different, guests can partake of all the resort amenities at both properties. If you're on a budget, seek out a friendly bed-and-breakfast or consider the Hotel Lāna'i. Vacation house rentals, a great option for families, give you a feel for everyday life on the island. In hunting seasons, from mid-February through mid-May, and from mid-July through mid-October, most of the private properties are booked way in advance.

WHAT IT COSTS				
$$$$	**$$$**	**$$**	**$**	**¢**
HOTELS	over $200	$150–$200	$100–$150	$60–$100	under $60

Hotel prices are for two people in a standard double room in high season, including tax and service.

Hotels & Resorts

$$$$
Fodor'sChoice
★
🏨 **Lodge at Kō'ele.** In the highlands edging Lāna'i City, this grand country estate exudes luxury and quiet romance. Secluded by old pines, 1½ mi of paths meander through formal gardens with a huge reflecting pond and an orchid greenhouse. Afternoon tea is served in front of the immense stone fireplaces beneath the high-beamed ceilings of the magnificent Great Hall. The music room lounge is a relaxing haven after a day on the Lodge's golf course or sporting clays range. A long veranda, furnished with wicker lounge chairs, looks out over rolling green pastures toward spectacular sunsets. ⌂ *Box 360310, Lāna'i City 96763* ☎ *808/ 565–7300 or 800/321–4666* 🖷 *808/565–3868* ⊕ *www.lodgeatkoele. com* ↪ *84 rooms, 12 suites* ♿ *2 restaurants, room service, fans, in-room safes, minibars, cable TV with movies and video games, 18-hole golf course, tennis courts, pool, gym, hot tub, massage, bike rentals, archery, croquet, hiking, horseback riding, lawn bowling, horseback riding, bar, library, children's programs (ages 5–12), Internet, laundry service, no-smoking rooms* ▭ *AE, DC, MC, V. $400–$575.*

★ $$$$
🏨 **Mānele Bay Hotel.** Reached by a sweeping circular driveway lined with rose bushes, this ornate property overlooking Hulopo'e Bay has spectacular views of Lāna'i's coastline and beyond. Courtyard gardens, breezeways, and bridges connect two-story guest-room buildings. The architecture combines Mediterranean and South Pacific elements; Chinese warrior robes, vases, and carved ivory tusks decorate the common areas. Hulopo'e Beach's white-sand crescent, with facilities for resort guests, is just below the pool terrace, and a *keiki* (children's) program focuses on the island's cultural and environmental heritage, with petroglyph walks, crab hunting, 'ukulele playing, and more. ⌂ *Box 630310, Lāna'i City 96763* ☎ *808/565–7700 or 800/321–4666* 🖷 *808/565–3868* ⊕ *www. manelebayhotel.com* ↪ *212 rooms, 22 suites* ♿ *3 restaurants, room service, A/C, in-room safes, minibars, cable TV with movies and video games, 18-hole golf course, 6 tennis courts, pool, health club, spa, billiards, bar, library, babysitting, children's programs (ages 5–13), Internet, laundry service, no-smoking rooms* ▭ *AE, DC, MC, V. $400–$800.*

In hunting seasons, from mid-February through mid-May, and from mid-July through mid-October, most of the private properties are booked way in advance.

$$–$$$
🏨 **Hotel Lāna'i.** Built in 1923 to house visiting pineapple executives, this 10-room inn was once the only accommodation on the island. The plantation-inspired rooms, with country quilts, light pine woods, and watercolors by a local artist, make it seem like you're staying in someone's home. Rooms with porches overlooking the pine trees and Lāna'i City are especially nice. The restaurant has a small bar. A self-serve continental breakfast with fresh-baked breads is served on the veranda and is included in the rate. ✉ *828 Lāna'i Ave., Lāna'i City 96763* ☎ *808/ 565–7211 or 800/795–7211* 🖷 *808/565–6450* ⊕ *www.hotellanai.com* ↪ *10 rooms, 1 cottage* ♿ *Restaurant; no A/C, no room TVs, no smoking* ▭ *AE, MC, V. $105–$175.*

B&Bs & Vacation Rentals

All vacation rentals are in Lāna'i City, where altitude and prevailing trade winds replace air-conditioning. During hunting seasons, rentals are booked months—possibly years—in advance.

$$–$$$ 🏠 **Sheila Black.** A log cabin cottage next to the Black's residence on "Haole Hill" is available as a vacation rental. This simply furnished, family-friendly two-bedroom, two-bath cottage offers a fully equipped kitchen with all appliances, linens, pine trees, and country peace. It can accommodate up to seven, with extra beds in the living room ($15 extra per night per additional person over four). ⌧ 656 Pu'ulani Pl., 96763 ☎808/565–6867 ⎙808/565–7695 ✉adblack@aloha.net ⏎2-bedroom cottage ⚘ Kitchen, cable TV; no A/C, no smoking ▤ No credit cards. 2-bedroom cottage $150.

$ 🏠 **Dreams Come True.** Michael and Susan Hunter rent out a four-bedroom, four-bathroom plantation home in the heart of Lānai City, available in its entirety or as individual guest rooms. Antiques gleaned from many trips through South Asia add to the atmosphere. Some rooms have canopy beds, and each has its own marble bath with whirlpool tub. The living room has a TV and VCR, and the kitchen is available for guest use. There's also a veranda and garden. Enjoy the Hunters' company and gather information about the island each morning, when a home-cooked full breakfast becomes a special occasion. They will arrange vehicle rental and book activities, too. ⌧ 1168 Lāna'i St., Lāna'i City 96763 ☎ 808/565–6961 or 800/566–6961 ⎙ 808/565–7056 ⊕ www.circumvista.com/dreamscometrue.html ⏎ 3 rooms ⚘ Laundry facilities; no A/C, no room phones, no room TVs, no smoking ▤ AE, D, MC, V. $99.

$ 🏠 **Hale Moe.** Momi Suzuki has turned her elegant esthetic into a peaceful Japanese-inspired retreat. This serenely furnished bed and breakfast has a well-tended garden with expansive views of the distant ocean. There's TV in the living room and a kitchen available for guest use. Help yourself to coffee and continental breakfast on the sunny deck. Momi will advise you on where to go and what to do on the island. Sometimes her jeep is available for rent as well. You can also rent the three-bedroom, three-bath house for $300 a night with a limit of seven people. ⌂ Box 630196, 96763 ☎ 808/565–9520 ⊕ staylanai.com ⏎ 3 rooms ⚘ No A/C, no phones in some rooms, no TVs in some rooms, no smoking ▤ No credit cards. $80–$90.

¢–$ 🏠 **McOmber Enterprises.** Five different houses in Lāna'i City are available as short-term economy vacation rentals. They can accommodate from two to eight persons. Kitchens are fully furnished and equipped, and linens are supplied. ⌂ Box 630646, 96763 ☎ 808/565–6071 ✉ mcomber@aloha.net ⏎ 5 houses ⚘ Kitchen, laundry facilities; no A/C, no room phones, no TV in some rooms, no smoking ▤ No credit cards. $35 per person per night.

WHERE TO SPA

If you're looking for rejuvenation, the whole island could be considered a spa, though the only spa facilities are at the Mānele Bay Hotel or the Health Center at the Lodge at Kō'ele. For a quick polish in town, try Neda at **Island Images** (☏ 808/565–7870) for haircuts, waxing, and eyebrow shaping with threads (an ancient technique); Kathy at **Highlights** (☏ 808/565–7207) for hair, nails, and makeup; or Nita at **Nita's In Style** (☏ 808/565–8082) for hair care and facials.

The Spa at Mānele. State-of-the-art pampering enlists a panoply of oils and unguents that would have pleased Cleopatra. The Spa After Hours Experience drenches you in private service including pineapple tea, neck and shoulder massage, and 50-minute treatment of your choice. Then melt down in the sauna or steam room, finish off with a scalp massage and light pūpū, and ooze out to your room. The *Ali'i* banana coconut scrub and pineapple citrus polish treatments have inspired their own cosmetic line. Massages in private *hale* (houses) in the courtyard gardens are available for singles or couples. A tropical fantasy mural, granite stone floors, eucalyptus steam rooms, and private cabanas overlooking the sea set the scene for indulgence. The on-site fitness center is a separate facility. ⊠ *Mānele Bay Hotel* ☏ *808/565–7700* ⊕ *www.manelebayhotel.com. $110–$120 50-min massage; $300 per person 2-hr Spa After Hours Experience (2-person minimum), $20 extra for use of facilities with a 50-min massage ⚭ Hair salon, sauna, steam room. Gym with: cardiovascular equipment, free weights. Services: aromatherapy, reflexology, body wraps, facials, hair care, waxing. Classes and programs: aquaerobics, hula classes, guided hikes, personal training.*

WHERE TO EAT

Lāna'i's own version of Hawai'i regional cuisine draws on the fresh bounty provided by local hunters and fishermen, combined with the skills of well-trained chefs. The upscale menus at the Lodge at Kō'ele and Mānele Bay Hotel encompass European inspired cuisine and innovative preparations of quail, 'ahi, wild deer, and boar. Lāna'i City's eclectic ethnic fare runs from construction-worker–sized local plate lunches to Cajun ribs and pesto pasta.

WHAT IT COSTS				
$$$$	**$$$**	**$$**	**$**	**¢**
RESTAURANTS over $30	$20–$30	$12–$20	$7–$12	under $7

Restaurant prices are for one main course at dinner.

Mānele Bay

★ **$$$$** ✕ **'Ihilani.** The Mānele Bay Hotel's dining room shimmers with crystal and silver as light filters through the glass ceiling. Executive chef Pierre

Bellon prepares fresh island ingredients in the tradition of the Mediterranean, in particular southern France. Sterling choices on the menu include herb-crusted 'ahi with goat cheese polenta or a scrumptious baked onaga in a sea salt crust. Service is nonintrusive but attentive. ⊠ *Mānele Bay Hotel* ☎ *808/565–7700* ⚑ *Reservations essential* ▤ *AE, DC, MC, V* ☯ *No lunch.*

$$–$$$$ ✕ **The Challenge At Mānele Clubhouse.** This terraced restaurant has a stunning view of the legendary Pu'u Pehe offshore island which only enhances its imaginative fare. Tuck into a Hulop'e Bay prawn BLT at lunch. At night, enjoy cocktails or a glass of chilled wine with pan-seared opakapaka or a Hawaiian seafood stew with coconut lobster broth and parsley pesto. ⊠ *Mānele Bay Hotel* ☎ *808/565–7700* ▤ *AE, DC, MC, V* ☯ *No dinner Tues. and Wed. $14–$33.*

Upcountry & Lāna'i City

$$$$
Fodor'sChoice
★
✕ **Formal Dining Room.** Reflecting the Lodge's country manor elegance, this romantic octagonal restaurant is one of the best in the state. Intimate tables sit close to a roaring fireplace with room between for private conversation. Expanding Hawai'i regional cuisine, the changing menu includes the signature crispy seared moi (a fish once reserved for Hawaiian chiefs). Start with roasted quail on baby greens and finish with a warm pear soufflé (ordered in advance). Expect visiting chefs as well as a master sommelier who provides exclusive wine pairings. Service is flawless. ⊠ *Lodge at Kō'ele* ☎ *808/565–7300* ⚑ *Reservations essential* 🏛 *Jacket required* ▤ *AE, DC, MC, V* ☯ *No lunch. $42–$46.*

$$–$$$$ ✕ **Henry Clay's Rotisserie.** With the only bar and comparatively fine dining in Lāna'i City, this is a lively spot, right at the Hotel Lāna'i. Louisiana-style ribs, Cajun-style shrimp, and gumbo add up to what chef Henry Clay Richardson calls "American country," but he brings it back home with island venison and locally caught fish. A fireplace and paintings by local artists add to the upcountry feel. Large parties can be accommodated and are sometimes quite noisy. ⊠ *Hotel Lāna'i, 828 Lāna'i Ave., Lāna'i City* ☎ *808/565–7211* ▤ *MC, V. $17–$35.*

$$–$$$$ ✕ **The Terrace.** Floor-to-ceiling glass doors open onto formal gardens and lovely vistas of the mist-clad mountains. Breakfast, lunch, and dinner are served in an informal atmosphere with attentive service. Try poached eggs on crab cakes to start the day and a free-range strip loin with pesto mashed potatoes to finish it. A complete wine list and the soothing sounds of the grand piano in the Great Hall in the evening complete the ambiance. ⊠ *Lodge at Kō'ele* ☎ *808/565–7300* ▤ *AE, DC, MC, V. $12–$35.*

$–$$$ ✕ **Pele's Other Garden.** Mark and Barbara Zigmond's colorful little eatery is a deli and bistro all in one. For lunch, deli sandwiches reward an arduous hike. You can also order picnic lunches served in a convenient cooler bag. At night, the tiny spot turns into an intimate tablecloth-dining bistro, complete with soft jazz music. Bring your own wine, start with bruschetta, then choose from a selection of pasta dishes or pizzas. ⊠ *811 Houston St., Lāna'i City* ☎ *808/565–9628 or 888/764–3354* ▤ *AE, DC, MC, V. $10–$22.*

$–$$ ✗ **The Experience at Koʻele Clubhouse.**
The clubhouse overlooks the emerald greens of the golf course. Sit inside and watch sports on the TV or on the terrace to enjoy the antics of lumbering wild turkey families. A grilled fresh-catch sandwich is accompanied by thick cottage fries, or try their succulent hamburgers, the best on the island. Salads and sandwiches, beer and wine, soft drinks, and some not very inspiring deserts complete the menu. ⊠ *Lodge at Kōʻele* ☎ *808/565–7300* ⊟ *AE, DC, MC, V* ☉ *No lunch. $9–$14.*

¢–$$ ✗ **Blue Ginger Café.** This cheery blue-and-white-painted eatery is a Lānaʻi City institution. The owners, Joe and Georgia Abilay, have made this place into one of the town's most popular hangouts with the most consistent, albeit simple, food. Locally inspired paintings and photos line the walls inside, while the town passes the outdoor tables in parade. For breakfast, try the Portuguese sausage omelet with rice or fresh pastries. Lunchtime selections range from burgers and pizza to Hawaiian staples such as saimin and *musubi* (fried Spam wrapped in rice and seaweed). Try a shrimp stir-fry for dinner. ⊠ *409 7th Ave., Lānaʻi City* ☎ *808/565–6363* ⊟ *No credit cards. $3–$14.*

¢–$ ✗ **565 Café.** Named after the only telephone prefix on Lānaʻi, this is a convenient stop for anything from pizza to a Palawai chicken breast sandwich on fresh-baked foccacia. Make a quick stop for plate lunches or try a picnic pūpū platter of chicken katsu to take along for the ride. If you need a helium balloon for a party, you can find that here, too. The patio and outdoor tables are kid friendly. ⊠ *408 8th St., Lānaʻi City* ☎ *808/565–6622* ⊟ *D, DC, MC, V. $3–$10.*

¢ ✗ **Lānaʻi Coffee.** A block off Dole Park, you can sit outside on the large deck, sip cappuccinos, and watch the slow-pace life of the town slip by. Bagels with lox, deli sandwiches, and pastries add to the caloric content, while blended espresso shakes and gourmet ice cream complete the old-world illusion. Caffeine-inspired specialty items make good gifts and souvenirs. ⊠ *604 Ilima St., Lānaʻi City* ☎ *808/565–6962* ☉ *Closed Sun. $3–$6.*

FOOD WITH A VIEW

Don't miss a meal at the Challenge at Mānele clubhouse, overlooking Hulopoʻe Bay. Day or night, the view is spectacular. Palm trees frame a vista of the curving white-sand beach with the rocky headland of Puʻu Pehe (Sweetheart Rock), punctuating the luminous sky. In the distance is Kahoʻolawe, recently rescued as a bombing target from the U.S. Navy, and in the foreground, the Challenge golf course with its scurrying golf carts adds visual interest. At night, with the full moon scattering sequins on the sea, it's enough to get you singing the whole score of *South Pacific*.

ENTERTAINMENT & NIGHTLIFE

Lānaʻi is certainly not known for its nightlife. Fewer than a handful of places stay open past 9 PM. At the resorts, excellent piano music or light live entertainment makes for a quiet, romantic evening. Another romantic alternative is star-watching from the beaches or watching the full moon rise in all its glory.

Hotel Lāna'i. A visit to the small, lively bar here is an opportunity to visit with locals. Last call is at 9. ☎ *808/565–7211.*

Lāna'i Theater and Playhouse. This 153-seat, '30s landmark presents first-run movies Friday through Tuesday, with showings at 6:30 and 8:30. This is also the venue that shows films from the Hawai'i Film Festival. ✉ *465 7th Ave., Lāna'i City* ☎ *808/565–7500.*

SHOPPING

A miniforest of Cook Pine trees in the center of Lāna'i City surrounded by small shops and restaurants, Dole Park is the closest thing to a mall on Lāna'i. Except for the high-end resort boutiques and pro shops, it provides the island's only shopping. A morning or afternoon stroll around the park offers an eclectic selection of gifts and clothing, plus a chance to chat with residents. Friendly general stores are straight out of the '20s, and new galleries and a boutique have original art and fashions for men, women, and children. The shops close on Sunday and after 5 PM, except for the general stores, which are open a bit later.

General Stores

Lāna'i City Service. In addition to being a gas station, auto parts store, and car-rental operation, this outfit sells Hawaiian gift items, sundries, T-shirts, beer, sodas, and bottled water in the **Plantation Store**. Open 7 to 7 daily for gas and sundries; auto parts store open weekdays 7–4. ✉ *1036 Lāna'i Ave., Lāna'i City* ☎ *808/565–7227.*

Richard's Shopping Center. Richard Tamashiro founded this store in 1946, and the Tamashiro clan continues to run the place. Along with groceries, the store has a fun selection of Lāna'i T-shirts. Richard's has a good selection of what they call "almost" fine wines, and a few gourmet food items. ✉ *434 8th St., Lāna'i City* ☎ *808/565–6047.*

Sergio's Oriental Store. Sergio's, the closest thing to a Costco on Lāna'i, has Filipino sweets and pastries, case loads of sodas, water, juices, family-size containers of condiments and frozen fish and meat. Open 8 to 8 daily. ✉ *831-D Houston St., Lāna'i City* ☎ *808/565–6900.*

Specialty Stores

Heart of Lāna'i. The bright yellow house behind the Hotel Lāna'i shows watercolors by Denise Hennig, oil paintings by Macario Pascual, and bowls and 'ukulele by Cyrus Keanini. Afternoon tea is served at the gallery Tuesday through Saturday from 2:30 to 4:30. ✉ *758 Queens St., Lāna'i City* ☎ *808/565–7815.*

Lāna'i Arts and Cultural Center. Local artists practice and display their crafts at this dynamic center. Workshops in the pottery, photography, woodworking, and painting studios welcome visitors, and individual instruction may be arranged. The center's gift shop sells original art and unique Lāna'i handicrafts. ✉ *337 7th Ave., Lāna'i City* ☎ *808/565–7503.*

Mike Carrol Gallery. The dreamy, soft-focus oil paintings of resident painter Mike Carroll are showcased along with wood bowls and koa 'ukulele by Warren Osako and fish-print paper tapestries by Joana

Varawa. Local photographer Ron Gingerich, island artists Cheryl McElfresh and Susan Hunter are also featured. ⌧ *443 7th St., Lāna'i City* 🕾 *808/565–7122.*

LĀNA'I ESSENTIALS

Transportation

BY AIR

You can reach Lāna'i from O'ahu's Honolulu International Airport via Island Air. Island Air offers several flights daily on 18-passenger Dash-6s and 37-seat Dash-8s; round-trip tickets start at $210. Traveling from other islands requires a stop in Honolulu and a transfer to Island Air and is booked through Aloha Airlines.

AIRPORT The airport has a federal agricultural inspection station so that guests departing to the mainland can check luggage directly.
🚩 **Lāna'i Airport** 🕾 *808/565–6757.*

TO & FROM Lāna'i Airport is a 10-minute drive from Lāna'i City. If you're staying
THE AIRPORT at the Hotel Lāna'i, the Lodge at Kō'ele, or the Mānele Bay Hotel, you'll be met by a shuttle for a $25 fee, which includes all transportation for the length of your stay. Day rates are $5 round-trip to town, and $10 round-trip to Mānele. See the resort receptionist at the airport. Dollar will pick you up if you're renting a car or jeep. Call from the red courtesy phone at the airport. See the resort shuttle driver.

BY CAR

There are only 30 mi of paved road on the island. Keōmuku Highway starts just past the Lodge at Kō'ele and runs north to Shipwreck Beach. Mānele Road (Highway 440) runs south down to Mānele Bay and Hulopo'e Beach. Kaumalapau Highway (also Highway 440) heads west to Kaumalapau Harbor. The rest of your driving takes place on bumpy, muddy, secondary roads, which generally aren't marked.

You'll never find yourself in a traffic jam, but it's easy to get lost on the unmarked dirt roads. Before heading out, ask for a map at your hotel desk and verify that you're headed in the right direction. Always remember mauka (toward the mountain) and makai (towards the sea) for basic directions. If you're traveling on dirt roads take water. People still drive slow here, wave, and pull over to give each other lots of room. The only gas station on the island is in Lāna'i City, at Lāna'i City Service (open 7 to 7 daily).

CAR RENTAL Renting a four-wheel-drive vehicle is expensive but almost essential. Make reservations far in advance of your trip, because Lāna'i's fleet of vehicles is limited. Lāna'i City Service, a subsidiary of Dollar Rent A Car, is open daily 7–7. Jeep Wranglers and minivans go for $130 a day, full-size cars are $80, and compact cars are about $60.
🚩 **Lāna'i City Service** ⌧ *Lāna'i Ave. at 11th St.* 🕾 *808/565–7227 or 800/533–7808.*

BY FERRY

Ferries cross the channel five times daily, departing from Lahaina on Maui and Mānele Bay Harbor on Lāna'i. The crossing takes 45 minutes and costs $25 each way.

🚢 **Expeditions** ☎ *808/661-3756 or 800/695-2624* ⊕ *www.go-lanai.com.*

TO & FROM Lāna'i City Service will shuttle you from the harbor to downtown for
THE HARBOR $10 one-way. However, the service is only available if they're already making the trip. The resort shuttle will bring you from the harbor to the Mānele Bay Hotel for a day fee of $5 round-trip or to town for a day fee of $10 round-trip. See the shuttle driver.

🚢 **Lāna'i City Service** ✉ *Lāna'i Ave. at 11th St.* ☎ *808/565-7227 or 800/533-7808.*

BY SHUTTLE

A shuttle transports hotel guests among the Hotel Lāna'i, the Lodge at Kō'ele, the Mānele Bay Hotel, and the airport. A $25 fee covers all transportation during the length of stay.

Contacts & Resources

EMERGENCIES

In an emergency, dial **911** to reach an ambulance, the police, or the fire department.

The Lāna'i Family Clinic, part of the Straub Clinic & Hospital, is the island's health-care center. It's open daily from 8 to 5 and closed on weekends. There's a limited pharmacy. In emergencies, call 911 or go to the emergency room of the hospital next door.

🚢 **Straub Clinic & Hospital** ✉ *628 7th St., Lāna'i City* ☎ *808/565-6423 clinic, 808/565-6411 hospital.*

VISITOR INFORMATION

Destination Lāna'i, the island's visitor bureau, is your best bet for general information and maps. Feel free to stop in, but be aware that opening hours are erratic. The Maui Visitors Bureau also has some information on the island.

🚢 **Destination Lāna'i** ✉ *730 Lāna'i Ave., Suite 102, Lāna'i City 96763* ☎ *808/565-7600.*
Maui Visitors Bureau ☎ *808/244-3530* ⊕ *www.visitmaui.com.*

The Big Island of Hawai'i

Pu'uhonua O Hōnaunau (Place of Refuge) Park

WORD OF MOUTH

"Probably the best snorkeling I've done yet [in Hawai'i] was adjacent to Pu'uhonua O Hōnaunau (Place of Refuge) National Park . . . looking up and seeing the little thatched heiaus of the park off in the distance is very cool—it creates an awesome sense of place."

—turn-it-on

WELCOME TO THE BIG ISLAND

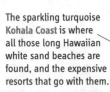

TOP 5
Reasons to Go

1 **Hawai'i Volcanoes National Park:** Catch the nighttime lava fireworks at the end of Chain of Craters Road.

2 **Waipi'o Valley:** Experience a real-life secret garden, the remote spot known as the Valley of the Kings.

3 **Kealakekua Bay Double Feature:** Kayak past spinner dolphins to the Captain Cook Monument, then go snorkeling along the fabulous coral reef.

4 **The Heavens:** Star-gaze through gigantic telescopes on snow-topped Mauna Kea.

5 **Hidden Beaches:** Discover one of the Kohala Coast's lesser-known gems.

■ **TIP→→** Directions on the island are often given as *mauka* (toward the mountains) and *makai* (toward the ocean).

The sparkling turquoise Kohala Coast is where all those long Hawaiian white sand beaches are found, and the expensive resorts that go with them.

Kailua-Kona is a seaside town bustling with tourists.

In South Kona, younger residents and transplants have turned defunct coffee farms into lively art communities overlooking beautiful Kealakekua Bay.

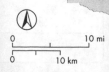

Getting Oriented

You could fit all of the other Hawaiian Islands onto the Big Island and still have a little room left over—hence the clever name. Locals refer to the island by side: Kona side to the west and Hilo side to the east. Most of the resorts, condos, and restaurants are crammed into 30 miles of the sunny Kona side, while the rainy, tropical Hilo side is much more local and residential.

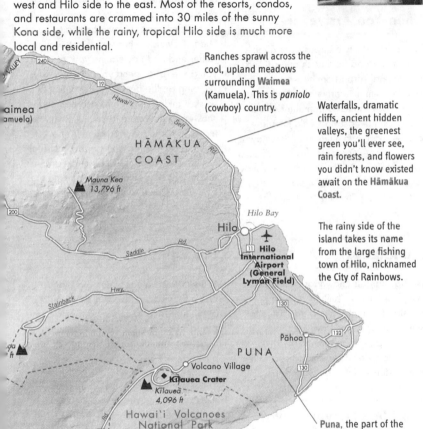

Ranches sprawl across the cool, upland meadows surrounding **Waimea** (Kamuela). This is *paniolo* (cowboy) country.

Waterfalls, dramatic cliffs, ancient hidden valleys, the greenest green you'll ever see, rain forests, and flowers you didn't know existed await on the **Hāmākua Coast**.

The rainy side of the island takes its name from the large fishing town of Hilo, nicknamed the City of Rainbows.

Puna, the part of the island most recently covered by lava, has brand-new, jet-black beaches punctuated with volcanically-heated hot springs.

Hawai'i Volcanoes National Park is growing, as active Kīlauea Volcano sends lava spilling into the ocean, creating new land. The nearest village is **Volcano**.

BIG ISLAND PLANNER

When You Arrive

The Big Island's two airports are directly across the island from each other. Kona International Airport on the west side is about a 10-minute drive from Kailua-Kona and 30 to 45 minutes from the Kohala Coast. On the east side, Hilo International Airport, two miles from downtown Hilo, is about 40 minutes from Volcanoes National Park. ■ **TIP**➔➔ The shortest, best route between Hilo and Kailua-Kona is the northern route, a 96-mi, two-and-a-half-hour drive.

Manta Rays

The Big Island is known for its scuba diving, and the visibility is amazing. The island's manta rays were scarce for awhile, but they are slowly returning. If you book a nighttime manta-ray dive, you will probably actually see some, and it's an experience not to be missed.

Will I See Flowing Lava?

You may or may not see flowing lava. Anyone who tries to tell you they can guarantee it or predict it is lying or trying to sell you something. No one knows when there will be a lava show. Your best bet is to call the Visitor's Center at the National Park before you head out; even at that you could be pleasantly surprised or utterly disappointed. Keep in mind that the volcano is a pretty amazing sight even if it's not spewing fire.

Fitting It All In

Yes, it's big, and yes, there's a lot to see. If you're short on time, consider flying into one airport and out of the other. That will give you the opportunity to see both sides of the island without ever having to go "back." Decide what sort of note you'd rather end on to determine your route—if you'd prefer to spend your last few days sleeping on the beach, go from east to west; if hiking through rain forests and showering in waterfalls sounds like a better way to end the trip, move from west to east. If you're short on time, head straight for Hawai'i Volcanoes National Park and briefly visit Hilo before traveling the Hāmākua Coast route and making your new base in Kailua-Kona.

Car Rentals

You will need a car on the Big Island. Get a four-wheel-drive vehicle if you're at all interested in exploring. Some of the island's best sights (and most beautiful beaches) are at the end of rough or unpaved roads.

TIPS➔➔

■ Talk to the agency in advance if you want to pick up a car at one airport and drop it off at the other. Though they allow this, most charge an additional fee of up to $50. If you arrange it ahead of time, they can often be talked into waiving the fee.

■ Most agencies make you sign an agreement that you won't drive on the Saddle Road, the path to Mauna Kea and its observatories. Though smoothly paved, the Saddle Road is remote, winding, unlit, and bereft of gas stations. Alamo, Budget, Dollar, and Harper Rentals let you drive it in their four-wheel-drive vehicles.

Timing is Everything

You can see humpback whales clearly off the western coast of the island from about January until May. Technically, whale season is from November to May, but the migration doesn't really get going until January. The few scattered sightings in November and December are usually young males showing off. The Merrie Monarch Festival brings a full week of hula, both ancient and modern, to Hilo, beginning the week after Easter. Fish stories abound in Kailua-Kona every August during the week-long Hawaiian International Billfish Tournament. The Ironman Triathlon takes place every October in Kailua-Kona. Consider volunteering—you'll be inspired, and it's a great party.

Will it Rain?

The Kona side of the Big Island is arid and hot, with mile upon mile of black lava fields lining a shimmering coastline. The Hilo side, on the other hand, gets roughly 130 inches of rain a year, so the chances of getting rained on while driving along the Hāmākua Coast to Hilo are pretty high. That said, it tends to rain in the morning on the Hilo side and clear up by afternoon, leaving a handful of rainbows behind.

5

Surfing

The Big Island is not known for its surf, but that doesn't mean that there isn't any, or that there aren't plenty of local surfers. Surf's up in winter, down in summer; the beautiful peaceful beach you went to last summer could be a rough and rowdy surfer beach in the winter.

Keep the Kids Happy

With a little advance planning, you can please your smallest critics. If you're renting a condo in Kailua-Kona, ask if they have a pool and, if so, how large it is. Many of the condo complexes have pools that are about the size of your bathtub. Make advance reservations for family favorites, like *Fair Winds* snorkel cruises to Kealakekua Bay (they've got a sweet slide off the back of the boat) or the *Atlantis VII* submarine (it can be a bit pricey, but you really do see things you couldn't otherwise see, plus submarines are just cool).

Guided Activities

The Kona Coast has long been famous for its deep-sea fishing, and late summer to early fall is peak season. The Big Island is also rapidly building a reputation as the golfers' island.

ACTIVITY	COST
Deep-Sea Fishing	$400–$800
Golf	$35–$195
Helicopter Tours	$115–$370
Kayak Tours	$100–$135
Lū'au	$65–$75
Snorkel Cruises	$80–$100
Surfing Lessons	$90–$125
Whale Watching	$60–$70

1-Day Itineraries

The following one-day itineraries will take you to our favorite spots on the island.

A Day (or Two) at Hawai'i Volcanoes National Park

The volcano is not to be missed. How often do you have the chance to see earth being formed? Call ahead of time to check the lava activity and plan your time accordingly. If the volcano is very active, go straight to the lava flow area. If it's less active, find out the best times of day for seeing what lava glow there is and head to the active flows at that time. And don't forget that there's a lot more to see in the park. Hike on the Kīlauea Iki trail, a 4-mile loop that takes you down through volcanic rain forests and then across the floor of a small vent, and check out the Thurston Lava Tube. Just before sunset, head down to the ocean via Chain of Craters Road; this is the best spot to see the nighttime lava show. Consider staying a night in Volcano Village, especially if your home base is on the Kona side. It will give you the time to explore, without having to rush off for the long (over 2 hours), dark drive back to Kona.

Waipi'o Valley

Completely off the grid today, it's hard to believe that Waipi'o Valley was once home to a thriving little village, not to mention early Hawaiian royalty. Waipi'o is a uniquely Big Island experience—untouched nature and a mystifying bit of island history. It's best to book a tour to see the valley either on horseback or from a jeep. Most tours last from two to four hours.

Hāmākua Coast

This jagged stretch of coastline along the eastern side of the island embodies all things tropical. There are waterfalls galore, and the trees and plants are thick and bright green. It's wet, but it tends to rain most in the mornings and clear up in the afternoons. Plan to spend some time driving down the tiny roads that dart off the main highway. Anywhere you see a gulch there's a waterfall waiting to be discovered. And keep your eyes peeled for rainbows.

Kohala Beach Day

Chances are that one of the main reasons you came to Hawai'i was to lie on the beach and work on your tan—do the whole island vacation thing. You will not be disappointed with the Kohala Coast. Hāpuna Beach has powdery soft white sand and crystal-clear blue water. Or get an early start and hike into one of the Kohala Coast's unmarked beaches, like Kua Bay or Makalawena. Either way, end the day at a seaside restaurant in Kawaihae or Kailua-Kona, watching the sunset and sipping a mai tai.

Paniolo Country

Upcountry Waimea is not what pops to mind when you think "Hawai'i"—rolling green hills, a chill in the morning, and ranches. Stop first at the old sugarcane town of Hāwī or at Pololū Valley. Then take Kohala Mountain Road (Highway 250) up the hill to Waimea, stopping along the way to snap pictures of the incredible view. There are several ranches in Waimea where you can go horseback or ATV riding. Plan on staying for dinner at one of Waimea's top-notch restaurants.

■ For more details on the destinations mentioned in these itineraries, see *Exploring the Big Island* in this chapter.

BEACHES

By Peter
Serafin & Amy
Westervelt

Don't believe anyone who tells you that the Big Island lacks beaches.

It's not so much that the Big Island has fewer than the other islands, just that there's more island so getting to the beaches can be slightly less convenient. That said, there are plenty of those perfect white beaches you think of when you hear "Hawai'i," and the added bonus of black-and green-sand beaches, thanks to the age of the island and its active volcanoes. New beaches appear—and disappear—regularly. In 1989 a black-sand beach, Kamoamoa, formed when molten lava shattered as it hit cold ocean waters; it was closed by new lava flows in 1992.

The bulk of the white sandy beaches are on the northwest part of the island, along the Kohala Coast. Black-sand beaches and the island's famous green-sand beaches are in the southern region, along the coast nearest the volcano. On the eastern side of the island, beaches tend to be of the rocky-coast–surging-surf variety, but there are still a few worth visiting, and this is where the Hawaiian shoreline is at its most picturesque.

Kohala Coast

This is where all those white sandy beaches are, and also, understandably, where all the resorts are on the island. The resorts are required to offer public access to at least part of their beach, so don't be frightened off by a guard shack and a fancy sign. The resort beaches aside, there are some real hidden gems on the Kohala coast accessible only by boat, four-wheel drive, or 15–20-minute hike. It's 100% worth the effort to get to at least one of these. The beaches here are listed in order from north (farthest from Kona) to south.

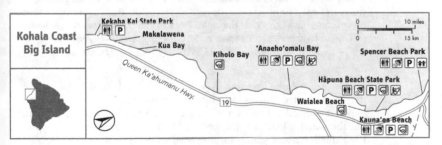

Pololū Beach. You should go to Pololū Valley for a variety of reasons. While you're there, leave time to hike down to Pololū Beach. Follow the trail at the end of Highway 270, the northernmost point of the island. The black-sand beach below is absolutely beautiful, surrounded by jagged green cliffs and huge black-sand dunes. ⚠ The surf is almost always rough here, and the currents strong, so it's not an ideal spot for swimming or snorkeling. The

BEACHES KEY

🚹	Restroom
🚿	Shower
🏄	Surfing
🤿	Snorkel/Scuba
🚻	Good for kids
🅿	Parking

KEEP IN MIND

Note that many beaches have dangerous undertows—rip currents and pounding shore breaks may cause serious risk anywhere at any time. The Kona side (west) tends to be calmer, but still the surf gets rough in winter. Few public beaches have lifeguards. To be safe, swim only when you see other swimmers in the area. Local surfers in the water are not an indication that the area is safe.

Here sunscreen is even more important than usual. The sun is intense, and everyone burns—even all you people who are reading this and saying, "whatever, I've never been sunburned in my life." Wear the sunscreen. Locals are very territorial about the unmarked, smaller beaches; they tend to go there on weekends, and they don't much like to see tourists. During the week, it's never a problem, but you may want to stick to the better-known spots on the weekends.

Finally, remember that black or green sand is not a souvenir. There's only so much, and we want everyone to be able to enjoy these spots for years to come. Plus, they are technically the remnants of lava, and everyone knows that Madame Pele will put a serious curse on the head of anyone who removes lava from the island.

hike's not easy going back up, but there are plenty of spots to stop for a rest. ⊠ *End of Hwy. 270* ᕼ *No facilities.*

Māhukona Beach Park. This used to be a fairly busy harbor when sugar was the economic staple of Kohala. Now it's a great swimming hole and an underwater museum of sorts. Remnants of shipping machinery and what looks like an old boat are easily visible in the clear water. No sandy beach here, but there's a ladder off the old dock that makes getting in the water easy. Snorkeling is decent as well, but it's only worth a visit on tranquil days. ⚠ **When the weather's bad and the seas are rough, heavy surf makes swimming here dangerous.** ⊠ *Off Hwy. 270, between mile markers 14 and 15, Māhukona* ☎ *808/961–8311* ᕼ *Toilets, showers, parking lot.*

🐾 **Spencer Beach Park.** This spot is popular with local families because of its reef-protected waters. It's safe for swimming year-round, which makes it an excellent spot for a lazy day at the beach. The water is clear, but there aren't loads of fish here, so it's not a great snorkeling spot. It's a smaller beach, gently sloping with white sand and a few pebbles. You can walk from here to the Pu'ukoholā and Mailekini heiaus. ⊠ *Entry road off Hwy. 270, uphill from Kawaihae Harbor* ☎ *808/961–8311* ᕼ *Lifeguard, toilets, showers, grills, parking lot.*

Fodor'sChoice ★ **Kauna'oa Beach at Mauna Kea Beach Hotel.** Hands-down one of the most beautiful beaches on the island, Kauna'oa unfolds like a white crescent, and it slopes very gradually. It's a great place for snorkeling. ⚠ **Currents can be strong, and powerful winter waves can be dangerous, so be careful.** Amenities are hotel-owned. Public parking places are limited (only 30), so it's best to arrive early (before 10). ⊠ *Entry through gate to Mauna Kea Beach Resort, off Hwy. 19* ᕼ *Lifeguard, toilets, showers, parking lot.*

Fodor'sChoice   **Hāpuna Beach State Recreation Area.** Guidebooks always say it's a toss-
★ up between Hāpuna and Kauna'oa for "best beach" on the island, but,
while Kauna'oa is indeed beautiful, most locals give the gold star to
Hāpuna. First of all, there's loads of parking so you don't have to get
here early. Second, though a tiny section of the beach was (grudgingly)
taken over by the Hāpuna Prince Hotel a few years back, it doesn't feel
like the hotel's property. The beach itself is a long (½-mi), white, perfect crescent, wide enough for half the island to show up on a holiday
and still not seem as crowded as any mainland beach. The water is
turquoise, clear, and very calm in summer, with just enough rolling
waves to make bodysurfing or boogie boarding fun. ⚠ In winter, surf
can be very rough, and there can be a strong current here year-round, so be
careful if you plan on venturing past the jagged rocks that border the beach on
either side. For strong swimmers, though, there's some excellent snorkeling to be found near and just past these rocks on particularly calm days.
The only downside to Hāpuna is that it tends to get a little windy in the
late afternoon; the upside is that the wind clears the beach just in time
for you to get your own private, perfect sunset. ⊠ *North of Kailua-Kona
near mile marker 69 on Hwy. 19 at Hāpuna Beach Prince Hotel* ☎ *808/
974–6200* ⚬ *Lifeguard, toilets, showers, food concession, picnic tables,
grills, firepits, parking lot.*

Waialea Beach (Beach 69). Just before Hāpuna if you're driving up the Kohala coast from Kona (off Puakō Road), Waialea is lesser known and not
as big, but it's a perfect white-sand beach all the same. The water's clear,
blue, and calm; the sand is white; and the snorkeling can be great (especially toward the reef on the right-hand side if you're looking out at the
ocean). It is not marked; park in Puakō, then walk down Puakō road toward
the houses (Neil Young has one along the shoreline). Find telephone pole
No. 71 (there's a little sign next to it); it used to be No. 69. Follow the
trail to the shore. ⊠ *Turn off Hwy. 19 at Puakō, follow trail at Telephone
No. 71* ⚬ *No facilities.*

★ **'Anaeho'omalu Beach (A-Bay), at Waikoloa Beach Marriott.** This expansive
beach, also known as A-Bay, is perfect for swimming, windsurfing,
snorkeling, and diving. It's a well-protected bay, so even when surf is
rough on the rest of the island, it's fairly calm here. Snorkel gear, kayaks,
and boogie boards are available for rent at the north end. Be sure to
wander around the ancient fishponds and petroglyph fields. There's also
a trail that runs along the shoreline between the Hilton Waikoloa and
the Marriott that passes by a few busy tide pools. Not a good barefoot
walk, though—between the lava rock and the coral, you'll regret leaving your shoes on the beach mat. ⊠ *Follow Waikoloa Beach Dr. to Kings'
Shops, then turn left at signs to park; parking lot and beach right-of-
way just south of Marriott* ⚬ *Toilets, showers, picnic tables, food concession, parking lot.*

Kīholo Bay. A new gravel road to the shoreline makes Kīholo an absolute must-see (previously you'd have to hike for 20 minutes over lava,
which would probably rule it out for some). What was once the site of
King Kamehameha's gigantic fish pond is now (thanks to Mauna Loa)

5

several freshwater ponds (some of them privately owned fish ponds off-limits to swimmers) encircling a beautiful little bay. The water's a bit cold and hazy because of the mix of fresh and ocean water, but there are tons of green sea turtles here, and the snorkeling is great. Follow the shoreline heading southwest (toward Kona), and just past the big yellow house is another piece of public beach near which sits a Queen's Bath (the name given to naturally occurring freshwater pools) inside a lava tube. It's open to the public, and yes, it's as cool as it sounds. ✉ *Hwy. 19, between mile markers 82 and 83, gravel road* ♿ *No facilities.*

Kua Bay. Locals are pretty unhappy about the dirt road leading to Kua Bay, the northernmost beach in the stretch of coast that comprises Kekaha Kai State Park. At one time you had to hike over a few miles of unmarked, rocky trail to get here, which kept many people out. It's easy to understand why the locals would be so protective. This is one of the most beautiful bays you will ever see—the water is crystal clear, deep aquamarine, and peaceful in summer. Rocky shores on either side keep the beach from getting too windy in the afternoon, ⚠ **but the surf here can get very rough in winter.** Still, it's always beautiful, and usually pretty quiet. Even with the new road, Kua Bay is a well-kept secret—it's unmarked, and amidst the lava fields it's still pretty hard to spot a dirt road, much less figure out where it leads. ✉ *Kekaha Kai, Kona Coast, State Park, Hwy. 19, just north of mile marker 88* ♿ *No facilities.*

Makalawena. Also a Kekaha Kai beach, Makalawena is a long white crescent, dotted with little coves and surrounded by dunes and trees—if it weren't so hard to get to, this would be the unanimous choice for best beach on the island. The sand is powdery fine, the water is perfect, and there's hardly ever anyone there, because of that whole "it's hard to get to" thing. You either have to rent a boat and anchor there, walk 20 minutes over a lava trail from Kekaha Kai, or take a pretty brutal four-wheel-drive jaunt over the lava, and then walk the rest of the way (5–10 minutes). But it's worth it. Makalawena is more than just a great beach—it's a truly magical place. An afternoon here is a recipe for delirious happiness. Sometimes people are so happy they just want to frolic around naked. Did we mention that there are wild goats hanging in the wings? Plus there's a freshwater pond that beats hosing off at one of those water-spigot showers at the marked public beaches hands-down. ✉ *Kekaha Kai, Kona Coast, State Park, Hwy 19, between mile markers 88 and 89; if you're walking, park in lot at Kekaha Kai and follow footpath along shoreline to north* ♿ *No facilities.*

Kekaha Kai (Kona Coast) State Park. Beyond the park's entrance, at the end of separate, unpaved roads, about 1½ mi each, you can find two sandy beaches, Mahai'ula to the south, and Ka'elehuluhulu to the north. In calm weather, they're great for swimming. You can hike along a historic 4½-mi trail from one to the other, but be prepared for the heat and bring lots of drinking water. ✉ *Sign about 2 mi north of Keāhole–Kona International Airport, off Hwy. 19, marks rough 1½-mi road to beach* ☎ *808/ 327–4958 or 808/974–6200* ♿ *Parking lot at entrance, Mahai'ula: Toilets, picnic area; Ka'elehuluhulu: No facilities.*

Kailua-Kona

Most of the coastline around Kona is rocky, so you won't find the white sandy beaches of Kohala here. What you will find, though, is excellent snorkeling and scuba diving, some super calm swimming spots, and decent surf conditions.

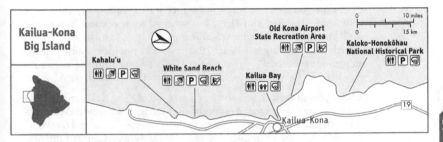

Kaloko–Honokōhau National Historical Park. This 1,160-acre park down the road from Honokōhau Harbor has three beaches, rich in archaeology and good for swimming. **'Ai'opio** (⚐ Toilets), a few yards north of the harbor, is a small beach with calm, protected swimming areas (good for kids) and great snorkeling in the water near Hale o Mono *heiau* (an ancient Hawaiian place of worship). **Honokōhau Beach** (⚐ No facilities) a ¾-mi stretch with ruins of ancient fishponds, is also north of the harbor. At the north end of the beach, a historic trail leads *mauka* (toward the mountain) across the lava to a pleasant freshwater pool also called Queen's Bath. A Hawaiian settlement until the 19th century, the park is being developed as a cultural and historical site. **'Alula** (⚐ No facilities) is a slip of white sand at the south end of the Harbor, a short walk over lava to the left of the harbor entrance. For information about the park, visit its headquarters, a 5- to 10-minute drive away. ⊠ *Park Headquarters and Main Gate, off Hwy. 19 opposite Kaloko Industrial Park between mile markers 96 and 97* ☎ *808/329–6881* ⊕ *www.nps. gov* ⊙ *Park road gate 8 AM–3:30 PM* ⚐ *Toilets, parking lot, food concession in harbor.*

Old Kona Airport State Recreation Area. The unused runway—great for jogging—is still visible above this palm-tree-lined beach at Kailua Park. The beach has a sheltered, sandy inlet with tide pools for children, but for adults it's better for snorkeling than swimming. An offshore surfing break known as Old Airport is popular with Kona surfers. ⊠ *North end of Kuakini Hwy., Kailua-Kona* ☎ *808/327–4958 or 808/974–6200* ⚐ *Toilets, showers, picnic tables, tennis courts, parking lot.*

🐚 **Kailua Bay & Kamakahonu Beach.** Right between the King Kamehameha Hotel and the Kona Harbor, this little square of white sand used to be King Kamehameha's and is now the only beach in downtown Kailua-Kona. Protected by the harbor, the calm of the water makes this a perfect spot for kids; for adults it's a great place for a swim and a lazy beach day. There's a stand with snorkeling and kayaking equipment rentals.

The water is surprisingly clear for being surrounded by an active pier and downtown Kona. Snorkeling can be really good, especially if you move south (toward the left) from the beach; ■ **TIP→→** there's a little family of sea turtles that likes to hang out next to the sea wall, so keep an eye out. ⊠ *Ali'i Dr., next to King Kamehameha hotel* ⟶ *Toilets.*

White Sands, Magic Sands, or Disappearing Sands Beach Park. Now you see it, now you don't. Overnight, winter waves wash away this small white-sand beach on Ali'i Drive just south of Kailua-Kona. In summer you'll know you've found it when you see the body- and board surfers. Though not really a great beach, this is a really popular summer hangout for young locals. ⊠ *4½ mi south of Kailua-Kona on Ali'i Dr.* ☎ *808/961–8311* ⟶ *Lifeguard, toilets, showers, food concession, parking lot.*

Kahalu'u Beach Park. This spot was a favorite of King Kalākaua, whose summer cottage is on the grounds of the Outrigger Keauhou Beach Resort next door. Kahalu'u is popular with commoners, too, and on weekends there are often too many people. This is, however, one of the best snorkeling spots on the island—it's a good place to see reef fish up close, as the fish are used to snorkelers. ⚠ **Beware–a strong riptide during high surf pulls swimmers away from shore.** A narrow path takes you directly to the resort's beach bar, which serves sandwiches and plate lunches. ⊠ *5½ mi south of Kailua-Kona on Ali'i Dr.* ☎ *808/961–8311* ⟶ *Lifeguard, toilets, showers, food concession, parking lot.*

South Kona & Ka'ū

You wouldn't expect to find sparkling white-sand beaches in the moonscape of South Kona and Ka'ū, and you won't. What you will find is something a bit more rare and well worth the visit: black- and green-sand beaches. Rent a four-wheel-drive vehicle if you plan on hitting the beach in this region. Beaches are listed here from north to south.

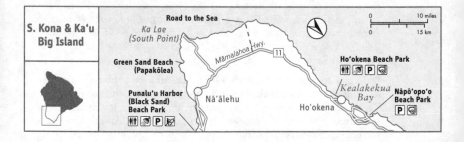

Nāpō'opo'o Beach Park. There's no real beach here, but don't let that deter you—this is a great spot. Kealakekua Bay is protected by impossibly high green cliffs, so the water's always very calm. It's a marine reserve, so the water is also super clean. Swimming is great here, but bring a mask if you come, as the snorkeling is amazing; your chances of seeing Hawaiian spinner dolphins are very high. This is also a great kayaking spot, and several stands along the road down rent kayaks, in addition to snorkel gear. You can enter the water fairly easily from the short pier at the left side of the parking lot; if you're snorkeling, you can see coral and fish almost immediately upon entry. Another great way to enjoy this marine preserve is to take a snorkel, scuba, or glass-bottom boat tour from Keauhou Bay. *Fair Winds* cruises is the only operation allowed to dock within the bay. ⊠ *End of Nāpō'opo'o Rd., off Hwy. 11, Kealakekua Bay* ☎ *808/961–8311* ⚭ *Parking lot.*

Ho'okena Beach Park. Driving south from Kealakekua Bay, you can see the sign for Ho'okena. The road down to the beach is narrow and steep, but the views are great, plus you feel like you're venturing off the beaten path. The white- and black-sand beach is on the small side and is mostly frequented by the people living in the village nearby; it's rarely crowded, except on weekends. By Hawaiian standards, Ho'okena's an average beach (water's nice for swimming, there's a bit of snorkeling but nothing amazing), but that still makes it great for the rest of us. Plus it's the only white-sand beach on this part of the island. ⊠ *2-mi drive down road bordered by ruins of stone wall off Hwy. 11, 23 mi south of Kailua-Kona* ☎ *808/961–8311* ⚭ *Toilets, showers, picnic tables, parking lot.*

Road to the Sea. Contrary to popular belief, Green Sand Beach is not the only green-sand beach on the island. There are two black- and green-sand beaches along this road, but you'll need four-wheel drive to get to them. The access road is about ¼ mi before mile marker 81 on Highway 11; the first beach is at the end of this road, and the second is at the end of a second, much rougher road that veers off just before the end of the access road (once you're on this second road, stay to the left to get to the beach). The second beach is more substantial, and swimming tends to be better there as well; it's also slightly more difficult to get there, so you have a decent chance of having the beach to yourself, especially if you go during the week. Swimming is pretty amazing at either beach on a calm day; ⚠ on windy or rough days, it can get treacherous far from shore, but is still decent close to land. ⊠ *Access road between mile markers 80 and 81 off Hwy. 11, just after Manuka State Wayside park if you're driving from Kona* ⚭ *No facilities.*

★ **Green Sand (Papakōlea) Beach.** You'll need good hiking shoes and a four-wheel-drive vehicle to get to this green crescent, one of the most unusual and prettiest beaches on the island. The beach lies at the base of Pu'u o Mahana, at Mahana Bay, where a cinder cone formed during an early eruption of Mauna Loa. The greenish tint is caused by an accumulation of olivine that forms in volcanic eruptions. ⚠ Swimming can be dangerous, and it's often windy here. In calm water close to the shore, however, the aquamarine surf feels great, and the landscape is totally surreal. Take the road toward the left at the end of the paved road to Ka Lae (South Point). Park at the end of the road and follow the trail 2 to 3 mi along the shoreline. Anyone trying to charge you for parking is running a scam. ⊠ *2½ mi northeast of South Point, off Hwy. 11* ⚭ *No facilities.*

★ **Punalu'u (Black Sand) Beach Park.** The endangered Hawaiian green sea turtle nests in the black sand of this beautiful and easily accessible beach. You can see the turtles feeding on the seaweed along the surfbreak. They're used to people, and will swim along right next to you; please resist the

5

urge to touch them, grab on to them, etc. Fishponds are just inland. At the northern end of the beach near the boat ramp lie the ruins of a heiau and a flat sacrificial stone. This used to be a sugar and army port until the tidal wave of 1946 destroyed the buildings. ⚠ **Offshore rip currents are extremely dangerous**, though you'll see a few local surfers riding the waves. Inland is a memorial to Henry 'Ōpūkaha'ia. In 1809, when he was 17, 'Ōpūkaha'ia swam out to a fur-trading ship in the harbor and asked to sail as a cabin boy. When he reached New England, he entered the Foreign Mission School in Connecticut, but he died of typhoid fever in 1818. His dream of bringing Christianity to the Islands inspired the American Board of Missionaries in 1820 to send the first Protestant missionaries to Hawai'i. ⊠ *Hwy. 11, 27 mi south of Hawai'i Volcanoes National Park* ☎ *808/961–8311* ⚭ *Showers, toilets across road, parking lot.*

Hilo

Hilo isn't exactly known for its beautiful white beaches. However, there are a few gems, and plenty of opportunities to dip into streams and waterfalls if the ocean is being uncooperative. Beaches here are listed from south to north (moving from Hilo toward the Hāmākua coast).

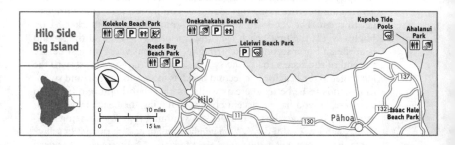

Leleiwi Beach Park and Richardson Ocean Park. There's hardly any sand here, but these two beaches, along Hilo's Keaukaha shoreline comprise one beautiful spot—laced with bays, inlets, lagoons, and pretty parks. The grassy area is ideal for picnics. Snorkeling can be great, though, as turtles and dolphins frequent this area. ⊠ *2349 Kalaniana'ole Ave.; follow Kalaniana'ole Ave. along the water about 4 mi east of Hilo* ☎ *808/ 961–8311* ⚭ *Lifeguard on weekends, picnic tables, parking lot.*

Onekahakaha Beach Park. A protected, white-sand beach with a shallow, enclosed tide pool makes this a favorite for Hilo families with small children. ⊠ *Follow Kalaniana'ole Ave. 3 mi east of Hilo* ☎ *808/961– 8311* ⚭ *Lifeguard, toilets, showers, picnic tables, parking lot.*

Reeds Bay Beach Park. Safe swimming, proximity to downtown Hilo, and a freshwater-fed swimming hole called "the Ice Pond" are the enticements of this cove. ⊠ *Banyan Dr. and Kalaniana'ole Ave., Hilo* ☎ *808/ 961–8311* ⚭ *Toilets, showers, parking lot.*

Hāmākua Coast

Kolekole Beach Park. The Kolekole river flows into the ocean at this small beach park off Highway 19 between 'Akaka and Umauma Falls. Though there's a rocky shoreline, the river is calm and great for swimming. There's even a rope swing tied to a banyan tree on the opposite side, and the river is deep enough to jump in off the swing. Local surfers like this spot in the winter. ⚠ **Where the river meets the ocean, surf can be rough and currents strong. Only very experienced swimmers should venture past the river's mouth.** ✉ *Off Hwy. 19* ☎ *808/961–8311* ✆ *Free* ☉ *Daily 7 AM–sunset* ♿ *Toilets, outdoor showers, picnic tables, grills, parking lot.*

Puna

As the region closest to Kīlauea, Puna's few beaches have some unique attributes—black sand, volcano-heated hotsprings, and a coastline that is beyond dramatic (sheer walls of black lava rock dropping off into the bluest ocean you've ever seen). Beaches here are listed in order from north to south along Highway 137 (from Kapoho to the Highway 130 junction near what used to be Kalapana).

Kapoho Tide Pools. Snorkelers will find tons of coral and the fish who feed off it in this network of tide pools at the end of Kapoho-Kai road. Take the road to the end, turn left and park. Some of the pools are on private property and have been incorporated into people's yards as swimming pools; the pools closest to the ocean, Waiʻōpae (ponds), are open to all. The pools are usually very calm, and some are volcanically heated. It's best to go during the week as it gets a little crowded on the weekend. ✉ *End of Kapoho-Kai road, off Hwy. 137* ♿ *No facilities.*

Ahalanui Park. This 3-acre beach park, also known as Pūʻālaʻa, has a ½-acre pond heated by volcanic steam. There's nothing like swimming in this warm pool, but the nearby ocean is rough. ⚠ **Since mid-2003, the thermal pool has had bacterial-contamination problems; check with the lifeguard–attendant on safety and heed all posted signs.** ✉ *Southeast of Pāhoa, 2½ mi south of junction of Hwys. 132 and 137* ☎ *808/961–8311* ♿ *Lifeguard, toilets, showers, picnic tables, grills.*

Isaac Hale Beach Park. Not really a beach, this is essentially a fishing dock dominated by locals who don't particularly want you there. However, there's a nice, volcano-heated pool right next to the park, surrounded by jungle and accessible via the trail next to the boat launch. ✉ *Off Hwy. 137, about 10 mi northeast of Kaimū* ☎ *808/961–8311* ♿ *No facilities.*

WATER ACTIVITIES & TOURS

The waters surrounding Hawaiʻi are some of the world's greatest natural playgrounds. The sailing, snorkeling, scuba diving, and deep-sea fishing are among the best anywhere, and the surfing isn't bad if you know where to go. As a general rule, waves are more gentle here than on other Islands, but here are a few things to be aware of before heading down to the shore:

We've all heard it a hundred times, but it bears repeating: Don't turn your back on the ocean. It's unlikely, but if conditions are right a rogue wave could come along and slam you face first into the sand or rocks, or drag you out to sea. Keep your eyes open. And now the big one: personal responsibility. Listen to the lifeguards and obey warning signs, but realize that ultimately you must keep yourself safe. Conditions can change quickly and are not always gentle. We strongly encourage you to obey the lifeguards and national park rangers wherever you are on the Big Island—it could save your trip, or even your life.

Boogie Boarding & Bodysurfing

According to the movies, in the Old West there was always friction between cattle ranchers and sheep ranchers. Some will say the same situation exists between surfers and boogie boarders. Sure, there's some good-natured trash-talking between the groups, but nothing more. The truth is, boogie boarding is a blast. The only surfers who don't (or haven't) done it are hardcore surfing purists, and almost none of that type live on this island.

Novice boogie boarders should use smooth-bottom boards, wear protective, microfiber rash guard shirts (or at least T-shirts), and catch shore waves only. You'll need a pair of short fins to get out to the bigger waves offshore (not recommended for newbies). As for bodysurfing, just catch a wave and make like Superman going faster than a speeding bullet.

Best Spots

When conditions are right, **Hāpuna Beach** (⊠ North of Kailua-Kona near mile marker 69 on Hwy. 19 at Hāpuna Beach Prince Hotel) is fabulous. ⚠ It's not known as the broken-neck capital for nothing. Take heed of the warning signs, and remember that if almost no one is in the water, there's a good reason for it. Exercise appropriate caution, however, and you'll have an absolutely terrific time.

Under normal tide cycles at **White Sands, Magic Sands, or Disappearing Sands Beach Park** (⊠ 4½ mi south of Kailua-Kona on Ali'i Dr.), much of the sand washes out to sea and forms a sandbar just offshore. This causes the waves to break in a way that's great for intermediate or advanced boogie boarding. This small beach can get pretty crowded and ⚠ there can be nasty rip currents at high tide. If you're not using fins, wear reef shoes because of the rocks. Ask about the **Magic Sands Bodysurfing Contest,** which brings out young, local hardcore bodysurfers to compete sometime each winter.

Honoli'i Cove (⊠ North of Hilo on Hwy. 19, access road just past mile marker 4) is the best boogie boarding–surfing spot on the east side of the island.

Equipment Rentals

Equipment rental shacks are all over the place. Boogie board rental rates are $5 to $8 per day or $15 to $20 per week.

Pacific Vibrations. ⊠ *75-5702 Likana La., at Ali'i Dr., Kailua-Kona* ☎ *808/329–4140.*

Orchid Land Surf Shop. ⊠ *262 Kamehameha Ave., Hilo* ☎ *808/935–1522.*

Deep-Sea Fishing

Along the Kona Coast you can find some of the world's most exciting "blue-water" fishing. Although July, August, and September are peak months, with the best fishing and a number of tournaments, charter fishing goes on year-round. You don't have to compete to experience the thrill of landing a big Pacific blue marlin or other big game fish. More than 60 charter boats, averaging 26 to 58 feet, are available for hire, most of them out of **Honokōhau Harbor,** just north of Kailua-Kona.

Prices vary but generally range $400–$500 for a half-day charter and $600–$800 for a full day. If fuel prices continue increasing, expect charter costs to also go up. Most boats are licensed to take up to six passengers per trip (plus crew). Tackle, bait, and ice are furnished, but you'll have to bring your own lunch. You won't be able to keep your catch although if you ask, many captains will send you home with a few fillets.

> **ON THE SIDELINES**
>
> Kona hosts quite a few fishing tournaments, but the Big Kahuna is the **Hawaiian International Bill-fish Tournament** (☎ 808/329-6155 ⊕ www.konabillfish.com/), held each first week of August since 1959. Billfish are marlin—the big boys. If you're in town, you'll find a number of tourney-related activities. Results are also a useful guide in choosing which boat to charter.

Big fish are weighed in daily at **Honokōhau Harbor's Fuel Dock.** Show up at 11 AM to watch the weigh-in of the day's catch from the morning charters, or 3:30 PM for the afternoon and all-day charters. If you're lucky you'll get to see a "grander" (1,000-plus pounds) on the scale, as a surprising number of these are caught just outside Kona Harbor. ■ TIP→→ On Kona's Waterfront Row look for the "Grander's Wall" of anglers with their prizes.

Booking Agencies
Before you sign up with anyone, think about the kind of trip you want. Looking for a romantic cruise? A rockin' good time with your buddies? Serious fishing in one of the "secret spots"? A family friendly excursion? Be sure to describe your expectations so your booking agent can match you with a captain and a boat that suits your style.

Honokōhau Harbor Charter Desk. With 50 boats to book, they can take care of almost anyone. You can make arrangements through your hotel activity desk, but we suggest you go down to the desk at the harbor and look things over for yourself. ✉ 74-381 Kealahe Pkwy., Kailua-Kona ☎ 808/329–5735 ⊕ www.charterdesk.com.

Boats & Charters
Pamela Big Game Fishing, Inc. This family-operated company has been in the business since 1967. *Pamela,* the 38-foot Bertram, is captained by either Peter Hoogs or his son. They've also got an informative Web site with great information on sportfishing. ☎ 808/329–3600 or 800/762–7546 ⊕ www.konabiggamefishing.com.

Charter Locker. This fleet of four boats (38–53 feet) is a good bet for both novices and experts. Operating since 1964, Charter Locker is one of the respected old-timers at Honokohau Harbor. ☎ 808/326–2553 ⊕ www. charterlocker.com.

Reel Action Light-Tackle Sportfishing. Attention fishing fanatics. They take only two people per trip on their 25-foot open-console boat, where you can bottom fish, reef fish, or fly-fish—as well as go after the big game fish. No Web site, no e-mail, no fax, and no nonsense. Call to make reservations. ☎ *808/325–6811.*

Jet Skiing

Kailua Bay in Kona has generally calm waters that are perfect for jet skiing.

Aloha Jet Ski Rentals. The only outfitter on the island charges $85 an hour (with an early-bird discount) for a ski that can take up to three passengers. Drivers must be at least 16, and Jet Skis are allowed to operate only in a designated area south of the pier. ⊠ *Kailua Pier across from King Kamehameha Hotel, Kailua-Kona* ☎ *808/329–2754* ⊕ *www.mauiwatersports. com.*

Kayaking

Kayaks are great for observing Hawai'i's diverse marine life and serene shores. When you venture out, however, be sure to respect Hawai'i's waters: 30% of marine mammals here are unique to the Big Island, and coral reefs are endangered; as a result, many bays are protected marine reserves. A reputable kayak shop can brief you on proper conduct and point out friendly locations, as currents can be dangerous.

Best Spots

Fabulous snorkeling and the likelihood of seeing dolphins makes **Kealakekua Bay** (⊠ South of Kailua-Kona at bottom of Nāpō'opo'o Rd.) one of the best and most popular kayak spots on the Big Island. The Kona side bay is usually calm, and the kayaking is not difficult—except during high surf. If you're there in the morning you're likely to see spinner dolphins. Depending on your strength and enthusiasm, you'll cross the bay in 30–60 minutes and put in at the ancient canoe landing about 50 yards to the left of the **Captain Cook Monument.** The monument marks the landfall of Captain James Cook in 1778, the first European to visit Hawai'i. The coral around the monument itself is too fragile to land a kayak, but it makes for fabulous snorkeling (⇨ *See* Snorkeling, *below*) and is the main reason people come here.

There are several rental outfitters on Highway 11 between mile markers 110 and 113, but none at the shore.

> **DOLPHINS AT REST**
>
> Kealakekua Bay is a designated marine refuge where the dolphins return to rest after nightly hunting. Occasionally kayakers aggressively pursue the dolphins. This is illegal and, because of the actions of a few, some environmental activists are working to close the bay to all kayakers. Those who charge after dolphins will probably be videotaped and could have complaints filed against them (as well as suffer the ephemeral but very real consequences of behaving without the aloha spirit). However, if you behave in a calm, nonthreatening manner, the dolphins are very likely to come to you.

After they've loaded your kayak onto the roof of your car, follow the 2-mi road down the steep-ish hill to an old cement landing. There are usually local guys who will set up your kayak and get you into (and out of) of the water; tips ($5–$10) are encouraged, expected, and appreciated.

Ōneo Bay (✉ Just south of Waterfront Row on Ali'i Dr.) just to the south of downtown Kailua-Kona, is usually quite a placid place to kayak. It's easy to get to and great for all levels. If you can't find a parking spot on Ali'i Drive (very likely), there is a parking lot across the street near the farmer's market.

On the Hilo Side, **Hilo Bay** is a favorite kayak spot. The best place to put in is at **Richardson's Ocean Beach Park** (✉ 2349 Kalaniana'ole Ave., follow Kalaniana'ole Ave. along the water about 4 mi east of Hilo). Most afternoons you can share the bay with local paddling clubs. Stay inside the breakwater unless the ocean is calm (or you're feeling unusually adventurous). Conditions can range from extremely calm to quite choppy.

Equipment Rentals & Tours

Flumin' Da Ditch. When King Sugar ruled this island, immigrant Japanese, Chinese, Portuguese, and Filipino plantation workers built irrigation ditches to bring water to the crops. Generations of adventurous plantation kids grabbed their inner tubes or anything else that floated, sneaked onto the plantations and went "flumin' da ditch"–gently floating through pitch-dark tunnels and emerging in an unspoiled rainforest. Today guides will take you on a kayak tour through the 22.5-mi irrigation system of the historic Kohala Sugar Plantation. This is a nonstrenuous activity appropriate to almost everyone and the guides are well-informed about local history—from the plantation economy to the story of King Kamehameha I, who was born nearby and went on to unify all the islands into a single kingdom. Rates are $98 for adults, $68 for children 5–18. ✉ 55-519 Hāwī Rd., Hwy. 250, Hāwī ☎ 808/889–6922 or 877/449–6922 ⊕ www.flumindaditch.com.

Kona Boys. On the highway above Kealakekua Bay, this full-service rental–sales outfitter handles kayaks, boogie boards, and related equipment. Single-seat kayaks are $27, doubles $47, clear bottoms $79. Dive kayaks with a well for an air tank are also available. They also provide guided trips to Kealakekua (½ day for $135 per person), as well as customized overnight camping–kayaking trips to Miloli'i, Pololū, or our favorite, Waipi'o Valley. ✉ 79-7539 Mamalahoa Hwy., Kealakekua ☎ 808/328–1234 ⊕ www.konaboys.com.

Ocean Safari's Kayak Adventures. There are two guided tours from Keauhou Bay with Ocean Safari's. A two-hour dolphin–whale tour ($30 per person) leaves at 7 AM on Tuesday. On the regular 3½-hour tours, you can see sea caves south of the bay, then anchor and swim ashore for cliff jumping and snacks. The kayaks are right on the beach so you don't have to hassle with transporting them. ✉ end of Kamehameha III Rd., Box 515, Keauhou, Kailua-Kona ☎ 808/326–4699 ⊕ www.oceansafariskayaks.com.

Kiteboarding

⇨ *See* Windsurfing & Kiteboarding, *below*.

Sailing

FodorsChoice   **Hawaiian Sailing Adventures.** Owner–builder Captain Casey Cho takes
★   you on a 2½-hour cruise off the Kohala Coast on the *Hahalua Lele*
(i.e., Flying Manta Ray), his traditional wooden double-hull Hawaiian
canoe. Sail, snorkel, or troll for deep-sea fish and talk story about
Hawaiian history and legends. Cruises depart from Pauoa Bay at the
Fairmont Orchid Hawai'i Hotel, cost $95 per person, and can be
booked through the hotel concierge. ☎ 808/885-2000 ⊕ *www.*
hawaiiankineadventures.com.

Maile Charters. Ralph Blancato and Kalia Potter offer unique around-
the-Islands sailing adventures that range from half-day trips to five-day
journeys to Maui, Moloka'i, or Lāna'i featuring custom-designed island-
style meals, itineraries, and activities. Private cabins and hot showers
keep you comfortable. Fees start at $590 for six passengers for a half-
day charter to $5,000 for five days. ⊠ *Kawaihae Harbor, Kawaihae*
☎ *808/326–5174 or 800/726–7245* ⊕ *www.adventuresailing.com.*

Scuba Diving

With the steep undersea drop-offs, the Big Island has some of the most
dramatic diving in the Hawaiian chain. Although they do dive on the
Hilo side, the Kona coast is much better. Kona-side dive operators are
helpful about suggesting dive sites from Kohala to as far south as
Pu'uhonua O Hōnaunau (Place of Refuge). Two-tank dives average
$100–$150 depending on whether you're already certified or not and
whether you're diving from a boat or from shore. Many dive outfitters
rent underwater cameras. Instruction with PADI, SDI, or TDI certification in three to five days costs $400–$650. Some companies also
teach surfing, and most rent out dive equipment, snorkel gear, and
other water toys. A few organize otherworldly manta-ray dives at night,
or whale-watching cruises in season.

Best Spots

Hāpuna Beach (⊠ Adjacent to and below Hāpuna Beach Prince Hotel,
off Hwy. 19) in Kohala can be a good shore dive. **Plane Wreck Point,** off
Keāhole Point, is for expert divers only. Damselfish, fantail, and filefish
hover around in the shadows.

Dive boats come to **Pu'uhonua O Hōnaunau (Place of Refuge)** (⊠ South
of Kailua-Kona on Rte. 160 ⊕ www.nps.gov/puho/) for the steep drop-
offs and dramatic views, but you can also get in from the shore on the
north end. **South Point** is for more experienced divers as the currents can
be tricky. ⚠ Only go in when the sea is calm—otherwise it's not recommended. You'll see lots of old fishing equipment on the sea floor.

Equipment Rentals & Guide Tours

There are quite a few good dive shops on the Kona coast. Most are happy
to take on all customers but a few offer specific strengths.

★ **Aloha Dive Company.** Native-born Hawaiian and PADI Master Dive Instructor Mike Nakamachi, together with wife Buffy (a registered nurse and PADI dive instructor) and PADI divemaster–videographer Earl Kam, have been in business 15 years. Although they'll take anybody, they are biased in favor of hardcore, experienced divers who want unique locations and know how to take care of themselves in deep water. Their boat is fast enough to take you places other companies can't reach. They're fun people with great attitudes and operate the only true kamāʻaina (Hawaiʻi born and raised) outfitter around. ☎ 800/708–5662 or 808/325–5560 ⊕ www.alohadive.com.

Body Glove Cruises. They offer primarily snorkel cruises but can accommodate several divers. It's a good choice for families where at least one member is a certified diver and the rest want to snorkel. A 55-foot catamaran sets off from the Kailua Pier daily for a 4½-hour dive and snorkel cruise, which includes breakfast and a buffet lunch. Snorkelers pay $94 per adult and $54 per child, plus an additional $53 per certified diver who needs equipment (you'll get a single tank). ✉ Kailua Pier, Kailua-Kona ☎ 808/326–7122 or 800/551–8911 ⊕ www.bodyglovehawaii.com.

Jack's Diving Locker. The best place for novice and intermediate divers (certified to 60 feet), Jack's has trained and certified tens of thousands of divers over the past 23 years. The company has two boats that can each take 12 divers. They do a good job looking out for customers and protecting the coral reef. Before each charter the divemaster briefs divers on various options and then everyone votes on where to go. Jack's also runs the biggest dive shop on the island, and they have classrooms and a dive pool for beginning instruction. ■ TIP➔➔ Kona's best dive bargain for newbies is their introductory shore dive from Kailua Pier for $55. ✉ 75-5813 Aliʻi Dr., Kailua-Kona ☎ 800/345–4807 or 808/329–7585 ⊕ www.jacksdivinglocker.com.

★ **Ocean Eco Tours.** Ecofriendly and full-service, this outfit is eager to share a wealth of knowledge. They're close to a number of good reefs and other prime locations. ✉ Honokōhau Harbor, 74-425 Kealakehe Pkwy., Kailua-Kona ☎ 808/324–7873 ⊕ www.oceanecotours.com.

Snorkeling

Although the snorkeling on the Hilo side is passable (except for the Kapoho tide pools, which are stunning), the real action is on the Kona side where colorful tropical fish frequent the lava outcroppings and coral reefs. It's easy to arrange a do-it-yourself snorkeling tour by renting masks and snorkels from any of the many diving outfits in Kailua-Kona or at the resorts.

Many snorkel cruises are also available. Shop for prices at kayak, scuba, and sailing outfitters; ask about the size of the boat, and be sure you know what equipment (and snacks) is included. Also find out what the extras (mask defogger, dry bags, underwater cameras, etc.) will cost.

Best Spots

Kealakekua Bay (✉ South of Kailua Kona, at bottom of Nāpōʻopoʻo Rd.) is, hands down, the best snorkel spot on the island, with fabulous coral reefs around the Captain Cook monument and generally calm waters. Besides, you'll probably get to swim with dolphins. Overland access is difficult, so you'll want to kayak across the bay to get to the monument. (⇨ *See* Kayaking, *above*). ■ **TIP→→** Be on the lookout for kayakers who might not see you swimming beneath them.

The snorkeling just north of the boat launch at **Pu'uhonua O Hōnaunau (Place of Refuge)** (⊠ South of Kailua-Kona on Rte. 160 ⊕ www.nps.gov/puho/) is almost as good as Kealakekua Bay, and it's much easier to reach. It's also a popular scuba diving spot.

Since ancient times, **Kahalu'u Bay** (⊠ 5½ mi south of Kailua-Kona on Ali'i Dr.) has been a traditional net fishing area. The swimming is good, and the snorkeling is even better. You'll see angelfish, parrotfish, needlefish, pufferfish, and a lot more. ⚠ Snorkeling is quite safe within the bay, but dangerous and unpredictable currents swirl just outside.

Kapoho Tidepools (⊠ End of Kapoho-Kai road in Puna, off Hwy. 137) has the best snorkeling on the Hilo side. Fingers of lava from the 1960 flow (that destroyed the town of Kapoho) jut into the sea to form a network of tide pools. Conditions near the shore are excellent for beginners, and challenging enough farther out for experienced snorkelers.

Cruises & Equipment Rentals

Captain Zodiac Raft Expedition. The exciting four-hour, 14-mi trip on an inflatable raft takes you along the Kona Coast to explore gaping lavatube caves, search for dolphins and turtles, and snorkel Kealakekua Bay. The cost is $80. ⊠ *Honokōhau Harbor, Kailua-Kona* ☎ *808/329–3199* ⊕ *www.captainzodiac.com.*

★ *Fair Wind* **Snorkel Adventures.** *Fair Wind* is a 60-foot double-decker catamaran with a 15-foot water slide and a dive tower. This outfit offers 4½-hour morning snorkeling and 3½-hour afternoon excursions to Kealakekua Bay. Snorkel gear included (ask about prescription masks), but bring your own towel. On morning cruises you'll get a continental breakfast and a barbecue lunch. These trips are great for families with small kids (lots of pint-size flotation equipment), and they provide underwater viewing devices for those who don't want to use a mask–snorkel setup. Morning snorkel cruises cost $99 for adults and $59 for kids— afternoons are cheaper, but you're less likely to see dolphins in the bay. ⊠ *78-7130 Kaleiopapa St., Keauhou Bay, Kailua-Kona* ☎ *808/322–2788 or 800/677–9461* ⊕ *www.fair-wind.com.*

Snorkel Bob's. You're likely to see his uniquely wacky ads in your airline inflight magazine. They actually do deliver what they promise, and you can make rental reservations online before beginning your trip. ⊠ *75-5831 Kahakai St., Kailua-Kona* ☎ *808/329–0770* ⊕ *www.snorkelbob.com.*

Snuba

Snuba—a cross between scuba and snorkeling—is a great choice for non-scuba divers who want to go a step beyond snorkeling. You, accompanied by an instructor, dive off a raft attached to a 25-foot hose and regulator; you can dive as deep as 20-feet or so. This is a good way for to explore reefs a bit deeper than you can get to by snorkeling.

Snuba Big Island. Rendezvous with your instructor across from the King Kamehameha Hotel in Kona for 30 minutes of instruction and a one-hour dive in Kailua Bay ($79). They offer both shore and boat dives. Boat dives leave from Honakahou Harbor (3 hours, 1–2 people, $120 each). You can also dive with them in Kealakekua Bay off the *Fair Winds* boat. ☎ *808/326–7446 ⊕ www.snubabigisland.com.*

Submarine Tours

Fodor'sChoice ★ **Atlantis VII Submarine.** Want to stay dry while exploring the undersea world? Climb aboard the 48-foot *Atlantis VII* submarine anchored off Kailua Pier, across from King Kamehameha's Kona Beach Hotel in Kailua-Kona. A large glass dome in the bow and 13 viewing ports on the sides allow clear views of the aquatic world 100–plus feet down, where you are the guest. This is a great trip for kids and nonswimmers. Each one-hour voyage (35 minutes underwater, plus transportation to and from shore) costs $79.99 for adults and $42 for children under 12 (kids must be at least 3 feet tall). The company also operates on O'ahu and Maui, and in the Caribbean. ☎ *808/329–6626 or 800/548–6262 ⊕ www.atlantisadventures.com.*

Surfing

You won't find the monster, world-class waves of O'ahu's North Shore or Maui on the Big Island, but there is decent surf and a thriving surf culture. Expect high surf in the winter and much calmer activity during summer. The surf scene is much more active on the Kona side.

Your best bet on the Kona side is **Kahalu'u Beach** (⊠ 5½ mi south of Kailua-Kona on Ali'i Dr.). On the east side, try **Honoli'i Cove** (⊠ North of Hilo on Hwy. 19, access road just past mile marker 4).

Surf Shops & Schools
Pacific Vibrations. ⊠ *75-5702 Linana La., at Ali'i Dr. a block south of Kailua Pier Kailua-Kona* ☎ *808/329–4140.*

Orchid Land Surf Shop. ⊠ *262 Kamehameha Ave., Hilo* ☎ *808/935–1522.*

Whale-Watching

Each winter humpback whales migrate from the waters off Alaska to the warm Hawaiian ocean to give birth and care for their newborns. Recent reports indicate that the whale population is on the upswing—a few years one even came to the mouth of Hilo Harbor, which marine biologists say is quite rare. Humpbacks are here from early December through the end of April, but other species live here year-round. Most ocean tour companies offer whale outings during the season, but two owner–operators do it full time. They are much more familiar with whale behavior and you're more likely to have a quality whale-watching experience. ■ TIP→→ If you take the morning cruise you're more likely to see dolphins as well.

Captain Dan McSweeney's Year-Round Whale Watching Adventures. This is probably the most experienced small operation on the island. Captain Dan McSweeney offers three-hour trips year-round for up to 42 passengers on his 40-foot boat. In addition to humpbacks in the winter, he'll show you some of the six other whale species that live off the Kona Coast year-round. Three-hour tours cost $59.50 per adult and $39.50 for kids under 12 (snacks and juices included). The Captain guarantees you'll see a whale or he'll take you out again free. ⊠ *Honokōhau Harbor, Kailua-Kona* ☎ *808/322–0028 or 888/942–5376* ⊕ *www.ilovewhales.com.*

Living Ocean Adventure. Captain Tom Bottrell provides whale-watching (combined with deep-sea fishing if desired) on *Spinner,* his 31-foot Bertram fishing boat, for up to six passengers. Standard 3½- hour tours cost $70 (bottled water included but bring your own snacks). Full- and half-day charters also available for families and small groups. ☎ *808/ 325–5556* ⊕ *www.livingoceanadventures.com.*

Windsurfing & Kiteboarding

Windsurfers trim their sails along the Big Island's Kohala Coast. In the new sport of kiteboarding (also know as kite surfing), you are pulled along by a kite attached to your surfboard. Great fun, but tougher to learn than windsurfing.

One of the best windsurfing–kiteboarding locations on the Big Island is at **'Anaeho'omalu Bay** (⊠ Follow Waikoloa Beach Dr. to Kings' Shops, then turn left at signs to park; parking lot and beach right-of-way just south of Marriott) in North Kohala.

Equipment Rentals & Lessons
Ocean Sports. This concession rents boards and teaches windsurfing on the beach. ⊠ *Waikaloa Beach Resort* ☎ *808/886–6666* ⊕ *www. hawaiioceansports.com.*

GOLF, HIKING & OUTDOOR ACTIVITIES

Aerial Tours

⇨ *See also* Hawai'i Volcanoes National Park, *later in this chapter.*

There's nothing quite like the aerial view of a waterfall that drops a couple thousand feet into multiple pools, or seeing lava flow to the ocean, where clouds of steam billow into the air. Most outfitters provide a worthwhile service, but a few unscrupulous operators have tarnished the image of the whole industry and earned the wrath of local communities. Rogue pilots will buzz communities in violation of FAA rules. How to get the best experience for your money? ■ TIP➔➔ Before you hire a company, be a savvy traveler and ask a the right questions. Do you have two-way headsets so passengers can talk with the pilot (very desirable)? Also, find out what kind of aircraft they fly. The best touring 'copters are Eco-Stars, Hughes, and AStars.

Blue Hawaiian Helicopters. Blue Hawaiian has a decent reputation in the community. Noise cancelling headphones for all passengers are an excellent touch. They offer group tours from Hilo (45 minutes for $180 per person) or from Waikaloa (2 hours for $370). Private tours are also available. Don't waste your precious time aloft looking through the viewfinder of your camcorder—for $20 they'll shoot a video of your trip. ⌧ *Hilo Airport or Waikoloa Helipad* ☎ *808/961–5600 or 800/ 786–2583* ⊕ *www.bluehawaiian.com.*

Mokulele Flight Service. For a fixed-wing air tour, contact Kawehi Inaba, a native Hawaiian who was bitten by the flight bug when she worked the counter at Aloha Airlines. She earned her commercial pilot's license and now her company offers 45-minute volcano–waterfall plane tours from Hilo; and two-hour Circle Isle tours from Kona (as well as interisland charters). ☎ *808/326–7070 or 866/260–7070* ⊕ *www.mokulele.com.*

Paradise Helicopters. Paradise also operates form Kona, but your best bet is flying out of Hilo on their 4-passenger MD-500 aircraft. Everyone has a window seat in these highly maneuverable helicopters, and you can even select the "doors off" option for best viewing. Communicate with the friendly and knowledgable pilots over 2-way headsets. ⌧ *Hilo Airport, Kona Airport* ☎ *808/969–7392* ⊕ *www.paradisecopters.com.*

ATV Tours

A different way to experience the Big Island's rugged coastline and wild ranch lands is through an off-road adventure. At higher elevations, weather can be nippy and rainy, but views can be awesome. You can ride in your own all-terrain vehicle or share a Hummer. Protective gear is provided. Prices range from $85 to $125 per person, depending on tour length and specifics.

Kahuā Ranch ATV Rides. ⌧ *Hwy. 250, 10 mi north of Waimea* ☎ *808/ 882–7954 or 808/882–4646* ⊕ *www.kahuaranch.com.*

Kukui ATV & Adventures. ⌧ *Pickup from Waipi'o Valley Artworks, Kukuihaele* ☎ *808/775–1701 or 877/757–1414* ⊕ *www.topofwaipio.com.*

Biking

The **Puna Beach Road** (⌧ Trailhead: Take Kaloli Rd. off Highway 130 to Beach Rd.) is a 10.5 mi (round trip) ride at sea level through the subtropical jungle in one of the island's most islolated areas. You'll start out on a cinder road which becomes a four-wheel-drive trail. If it's rained recently, you will have to deal with some puddles—the first few of which you'll gingerly avoid until you give in and go barreling through the rest of them for the sheer fun of it. This is a great ride for all abilities that takes about 90 minutes.

Fodor'sChoice ★ *Mountain Bike Magazine* voted **Kulani Trails** the best ride in the state. This is a technically demanding ride for advanced cyclists. ■ TIP→→ For other suggested rides see the Alternative Hawai'i (⊕ www.alternative-hawaii. com/activity/biecotrb.htm) Web site.

Guided Rides

Kona Coast Cycling Tours. Kona Coast leads a number of bike tours all over the Big Island. See the Big Island up close on a tour including the

Kohala Coast, Hāmākua Coast, historical Māmalahoa Highway, Kona coffee country, and backcountry Mauna Kea via the Mana Road. Custom tours are also available. Rates for standard tours range from $50 to $150. ⊠ *74-5588 Pawai Pl., Suite 1, Kailua-Kona 96740* ☎ *808/327–1133 or 877/592–2453* ⊕ *www.cyclekona.com.*

Mauna Kea Mountain Bikes, Inc. Daily tours down the upper slopes of Mauna Kea—chances are you'll start out in the snow—and downhill along the Kohala Mountains, as well as bike rentals are offered by this company. Tour prices range from $50 to $115. ⊡ *Box 44672, Kamuela 96743* ☎ *808/883–0130 or 888/682–8687* ⊕ *www.bikehawaii.com/maunakea.*

Bike Shops & Clubs

If you want to strike out on your own, there are several rental shops in Kailua-Kona and a couple in Waimea and Hilo. Resorts rent bicycles that can be used around the properties. Most outfitters listed can provide a bicycle rack for your car.

Big Island Mountain Bike Association (BIMBA). This nonprofit has tons of information on biking the Big Island. Their slogan is "Take only pictures and leave only your tracks." They provide maps and detailed descriptions of rides for for all ability levels. ⊕ *www.interpac.net/~mtbike/.*

B&L Bike and Sports. This shop rents various bikes, with prices for mountain bikes starting around $30 for 24 hours. ⊠ *75-5699 Kopiko Pl., Kailua-Kona* ☎ *808/329–3309.*

C&S Outfitters. Upcountry, close to trails that flank the slopes of Mauna Kea, this Waimea shop has both road and mountain bikes, accessories, and repair services. These folks have a wealth of knowledge about the island's biking trails. Plus they rent kayaks and can equip you for paintball and archery sports held at a nearby range. ⊠ *64-1066 Māmalahoa Hwy., Waimea 96743* ☎ *808/885–5005.*

Hawaiian Pedals. Road and mountain bike rentals start at $15 for five hours or $20 for the whole day. ⊠ *Kona Inn Shopping Village, 75-5744 Ali'i Dr., Kailua-Kona* ☎ *808/329–2294* ⊕ *www.hpbikeworks.com.*

Hilo Bike Hub. This shop caters to bike enthusiasts ready to explore Puna, Volcano, and the Hāmākua Coast. They don't rent bikes themselves, but they're a great connection to the mountain bike community on the Hilo side and can point you in the right direction. ⊠ *318 E. Kawili St., Hilo* ☎ *808/961–4452.*

Golf

For golfers, the Big Island is a big deal—starting with Mauna Kea, which opened in 1964 and remains one of the state's top courses. Black lava and deep blue sea are the predominant themes on the island. Most of the best courses are concentrated along the Kona Coast, statistically the sunniest spot in the Hawaiian archipelago.

★ **Big Island Country Club.** Set 2,000 feet above sea level on the slopes of Mauna Kea, the Big Island Country Club is rather out of the way but well worth the drive. Pete and Perry Dye (1997) created a gem that plays

CLOSE UP

Ironman & Friends

LIFE IN HAWAI'I has always been focused on the outdoors, but organized running really took off during the jogging boom of the 1970s.

Run annually since 1978, the Ironman Triathlon World Championship (☎ 808/329-0063 ⊕ www. ironmanlive.com) is the granddaddy of them all. For about a week prior to Race Day (the third Saturday of October), Kailua-Kona takes on the air of an Olympic Village as top athletes from across the globe arrive to compete for glory and $480,000 in prize money at the world's premiere swim/bike/run endurance event. To watch these 1,500 competitors push themselves to the ultimate in this grueling event is an inspiring testament to the human spirit. The competition starts at Kailua Pier with a 2.4 mi open-water swim, immediately followed by a 120-mi bicycle ride, then a 26.2-mi marathon. The Ironman wouldn't happen without the 7,000 doctors and nurses, aid station workers, cleanup-crews, and others who donate their time and services. To volunteer and be part of the action with these world-class athletes, register online at the Ironman Web site (the preferred method), or sign up at the temporary Ironman office at the King Kamehameha Hotel in Kona during race week.

The Honu Half-Ironman Triathlon (☎ 808/329-0063 ⊕ www. honuhalfironman.com), an Ironman "farm team event, " is held in early June. Thirty mainland and international participants (and 55 Hawai'i residents) can distance-qualify here for the Ironman. They swim at Hāpuna beach, bike the

Ironman course, and run on the Mauna Lani resort grounds.

Supermen/women do the Ironman. A few notches down on the difficulty scale, but still extremely challenging, is the Manna-Man Eco-Biathlon (☎ 808/989-3655 ⊕ www. bigislandraceschedule.com), held the last Sunday in March. The race starts with a 3.75-mi run from Pu'uhonua O Hōnaunau (Place of Refuge) to Nāpō'opo'o Beach, followed by a 1-mi swim across Kealakekua Bay to the Captain Cook monument. You're required to either wear or carry your shoes while swimming (points are given for creative ways to keep 'em with you, and you're penalized for leaving equipment or trash anywhere on the racecourse). The final leg of the race is a tough 2-mi run up to Nāpō'opo'o Road on a trail ascending from sea level to 1,288 feet. Everyone is invited to the post-race potluck dinner.

How about racing on an active volcano? No, you're not trying to outrun flowing lava (which is actually not much of a challenge, given the speed at which it usually travels). Approximately 1,000 runners from around the world compete in the Kīlauea Volcano Wilderness Runs (☎ 808/967-8222 ⊕ www. volcanoartcenter.org), either in the marathon, the 10-mi and 5-mi races, or the noncompetitive 5-mi run-walk. This event is held on the last Saturday of July completely within Hawai'i Volcanoes National Park.

For the most current race information, check out the Big Island Race Schedule (⊕ www. bigislandraceschedule.com/Race Links.html) for an islandwide listings.

5

through an upland woodlands—more than 2,500 trees line the fairways. On the par-5 15th, a giant tree in the middle of the fairway must be avoided with the second shot. Five lakes and a meandering natural mountain stream mean water comes into play on nine holes. The most dramatic is on the par-3 17th, where Dye creates a knockoff of his infamous 17th at the TPC at Sawgrass. ✉ *71-1420 Māmalahoa Hwy., Kailua-Kona* ☎ *808/325–5044* ⊕ *www.intrawest.com* ⅃ *18 holes. 7034 yds. Par 72. Green Fee: $99. Facilities: Driving range, putting green, rental clubs, golf carts, pro shop, lessons.*

★ **Hualālai Resort.** Named for the volcanic peak that is the target off the first tee, the Nicklaus Course at Hualālai is semiprivate, open only to guests of the adjacent Four Seasons. From the forward and resort tees, this is perhaps Jack Nicklaus' most friendly course in Hawai'i, but the back tees play a full mile longer. The par-3 17th plays across convoluted lava to a seaside green, and the view from the tee is so lovely, you may be tempted to just relax on the koa bench and enjoy the scenery. ✉ *100 Ka'ūpūlehu Dr., Kohala Coast* ☎ *808/325–8480* ⊕ *www.fourseasons. com/hualalai* ⅃ *18 holes. 7117 yds. Par 72. Green Fee: $185. Facilities: Driving range, putting green, pull carts, golf carts, rental clubs, lessons, pro shop, restaurant, bar.*

★ **Kona Country Club.** This venerable country club offers two very different tests with the aptly named Ocean and Ali'i Mountain courses. The Ocean Course (William F. Bell, 1967) is a bit like playing through a coconut plantation, with a few remarkable lava features—such as the "blow-hole" in front of the par-4 13th, where sea water propelled through a lava tube erupts like a geyser. The Ali'i Mountain Course (front nine, William F. Bell, 1983: back nine, Robin Nelson and Rodney Wright, 1992) plays a couple of strokes tougher than the Ocean and is the most delightful split personality you may ever encounter. Both nines share breathtaking views of Keauhou Bay, and elevation change is a factor in most shots. The most dramatic view on the front nine is from the tee of the par-3 fifth hole, one of the best golf vistas in Hawai'i. The green seems perched on the edge of the earth, with what only seems to be a sheer 500-foot drop just beyond the fringe. The back nine is links-style, with less elevation change—except for the par-3 14th, which drops 100 feet from tee to green, over a lake. The routing, the sight lines and framing of greens, and the risk-reward factors on each hole make this one of the single best nines in Hawai'i. ✉ *78-7000 Ali'i Dr., Kailua-Kona* ☎ *808/322–2595* ⊕ *www.konagolf.com* ⅃ *Ocean Course: 18 holes. 6806 yds. Par 72. Green Fee: $155. Mountain Course: 18 holes. 6673 yds. Par 72. Green Fee: $89. Facilities: Driving range, putting green, golf carts, rental clubs, lessons, restaurant, bar.*

Mākālei Country Club. Set on the slopes of Hualālai, at an elevation of 2,900 feet, Mākālei is one of the rare Hawai'i courses with bent grass putting greens, which means they're quick and without the grain associated with bermuda greens. Former PGA Tour official Dick Nugent (1994) designed holes that play through thick forest and open to provide wide ocean views. Elevation change is a factor on many holes, especially the par-3 15th, with the tee 80 feet above the green. ✉ *72-3890*

Hawai'i Belt Rd., Kailua-Kona ☎ *808/325–6625* ⚑ *18 holes. 7041 yds. Par 72. Green Fee: $110. Facilities: Driving range, putting green, golf carts, rental clubs, pro shop, lessons, restaurant.*

Fodor'sChoice ★ **Mauna Kea Beach Resort.** Mauna Kea Golf Course isn't just a golf course, it's a landmark, an icon, a national treasure. Robert Trent Jones Sr., who designed more than 500 courses around the world, rated Mauna Kea among his three best. Built on a 5,000-year-old lava flow, an essential part of Mauna Kea's greatness is the way Jones insinuated holes into the landscape. Only two fairways, holes five and six, are parallel. Mauna Kea is a classic championship design, somewhat forgiving off the tee but quite stern about approach shots. Although No. 3, which plays across a blue bay from rocky promontory to promontory, gets all the photo ops, the toughest par-3 is the 11th. Arnold Palmer and Ed Seay created the resort's second course, Hāpuna, in 1992. Unlike seaside Mauna Kea, Hāpuna is a links-style course that rises to 600 feet elevation, providing views of the ocean and elevation-change challenges. Trees are a factor on most holes at Mauna Kea, but they seldom are at Hāpuna. Palmer-Seay put a premium on accuracy off the tee, and are more forgiving with approaches. The two courses have separate clubhouses. **Hāpuna Golf Course:** ✉ *62-100 Kauna'oa Dr., Kohala Coast* ☎ *808/ 880–3000* ⊕ *www.hapunabeachprincehotel.com* ⚑ *18 holes. 6534 yds. Par 72. Green Fee: $145. Facilities: Driving range, putting green, golf carts, rental clubs, pro shop, lessons, restaurant, bar.* **Mauna Kea Golf Course:** ✉ *62-100 Mauna Kea Beach Dr., Kohala Coast* ☎ *808/ 882–5400* ⊕ *www.maunakearesort.com* ⚑ *18 holes. 6737 yds. Par 72. Green Fee: $195. Facilities: Driving range, putting green, golf carts, rental clubs, pro shop, lessons, restaurant, bar.*

Fodor'sChoice ★ **Mauna Lani Resort.** Black lava flows, lush green turf, white sand, and the Pacific's multihues of blue define the 36 holes at Mauna Lani. The South Course includes the "signature" par-3 15th across a turquoise bay, one of the most photographed holes in Hawai'i. But it shares "signature hole" honors with the seventh. A long par-3, it plays downhill

> ### LAVA HAZARDS
>
> Lava tends to be razor-sharp and not good for the life of golf balls, or golf shoes. If you hit a ball into the black stuff, consider it an offering to Madame Pele, goddess of lava, and drop another one.

over convoluted patches of black lava, with the Pacific immediately to the left and a dune to the right. The North Course plays a couple of shots tougher. Its most distinctive hole is the 17th, a par-3 with the green set in a lava pit 50 feet deep. The shot from an elevated tee must carry a pillar of lava that rises from the pit and partially blocks your view of the green. ✉ *68-1310 Mauna Lani Dr., Kohala Coast* ☎ *808/885– 6655* ⊕ *www.maunalani.com* ⚑ *North Course: 18 holes. 6601 yds. Par 72. Green Fee: $195. South Course: 18 holes. 6436 yds. Par 72. Green Fee: $195. Facilities: Driving range, putting green, golf carts, rental clubs, pro shop, lessons, restaurant, bar.*

Volcano Golf & Country Club. Located just outside Volcanoes National Park—and barely a stout drive from Halem'um'a Crater—Volcano is by far Hawaiʻi's highest course. At 4,200 feet elevation, shots tend to fly a bit farther than at sea level, even in the often cool, misty air. Because of the elevation and climate, Volcano is one of the few Hawaiʻi courses with bent grass putting greens. The course is mostly flat and holes play through stands of Norfolk pines, flowering lehua trees, and multitrunk hau trees. The uphill par-4 15th doglegs through a tangle of hau. ⊠ *Piʻi Mauna Dr., off Hwy. 11, Volcanoes National Park* ☎ *808/967–7331* ⊕ *www.volcanogolfshop.com* ⅃ *18 holes. 6106 yds. Par 72. Green Fee: $62. Facilities: Driving range, putting green, golf carts, rental clubs, restaurant, bar.*

FodorsChoice   **Waikoloa Beach Resort.** Robert Trent Jones Jr. built the Beach Course at
★   Waikoloa (1981) on an old flow of crinkly aʻā lava, which he used to create holes that are as artful as they are challenging. The third tee, for instance, is set at the base of a towering mound of lava. The par-5 12th plays through a chute of black lava to an oceanside green, the blue sea on the right coming into play on the second and third shots. At the King's Course at Waikoloa (1990), Tom Weiskopf and Jay Morrish built a very linksesque track. It turns out lava's natural humps and declivities remarkably replicate the contours of seaside Scotland. But there are a few island twists—such as seven lakes. This is "option golf" as Weiskopf and Morrish provide different risk-reward tactics on each hole. Beach and King's have separate clubhouses. **Waikoloa Beach Course:** ⊠ *1020 Keana Pl., Waikoloa* ☎ *808/886–6060* ⊕ *www.waikoloagolf.com* ⅃ *18 holes. 6566 yds. Par 70. Green Fee: $175. Facilities: Driving range, putting green, golf carts, rental clubs, lessons, restaurant, bar.* **Waikoloa Kings' Course:** ⊠ *600 Waikoloa Beach Dr., Waikoloa* ☎ *808/886–7888* ⊕ *www.waikoloagolf. com* ⅃ *18 holes. 6594 yds. Par 72. Green Fee: $175. Facilities: Driving range, putting green, golf carts, rental clubs, lessons, restaurant, bar.*

Waikoloa Village Golf Course. A 20-minute drive above Waikoloa Beach Resort, Waikoloa Village (Robert Trent Jones Jr., 1972) is not affiliated with the resort. It is, however, the site of the annual Waikoloa Open, one of the most prestigious tournaments in Hawaiʻi. Holes run across rolling hills with sweeping mountain and ocean views. ⊠ *68-1792 Melia St., Waikoloa* ☎ *808/883–9621* ⊕ *www.waikoloa.org* ⅃ *18 holes. 6230 yds. Par 72. Green Fee: $100. Facilities: Driving range, putting green, golf carts, rental clubs, lessons, restaurant, bar.*

Hiking

⇨ *See also* Hawaiʻi Volcanoes National Park, *later in this chapter.*

Meteorologists classify the world's weather into 23 climates. Twenty-one are here on the Big Island, and you can hike as many of them as you like. The ancient Hawaiians blazed many trails across their archipelago, and many of these paths can still be hiked today. Part of the King's Trail at ʻAnaehoʻomalu winds through a field of lava rocks covered with prehistoric carvings meant to communicate stories of births, deaths, marriages, and other family events. Plus, the serenity of remote beaches, such as the Green Sand (Papakōlea) Beach, is accessible only to hikers.

For information on all Big Island's state parks, contact the **Department of Land and Natural Resources, State Parks Division** (✉ 75 Aupuni St., Hilo 96720 ☎ 808/974–6200 ⊕ www.hawaii.gov/dlnr/dsp/hawaii.html).

Best Spots

The **Mauna Kea Trail** (✉ Trailhead at Onizuka Visitors Center) ascends from the visitor center (9,200-foot) to the 13,000-foot summit. The difficult, four-hour trek rewards the hardy with glimpses of endangered species, a stunning view of the primeval Lake Waiau, and fabulous views from the top of the world (you look down on the sunset). ⚠ Because of the difficulty of the trail and the low-oxygen environment, it's a very tough hike even for the most fit. At these altitudes, you must drink plenty of water. Also, wear warm clothes and sunglasses, and put on plenty of sunscreen. This is not recommended for children under 16, pregnant women, or those with respiratory problems.

At **Kekaha Kai (Kona Coast) State Park** (✉ Sign about 2 mi north of Keāhole–Kona International Airport, off Hwy. 19), separate, unpaved 1.5 mi access roads from the highway lead to Mahaiʻula Beach and to the Kua Bay sections of the park. Mahaiʻula has a sandy beach with a picnic area and great boogie boarding in moderate waves (but stay out in high surf). A 4.5-mi hike north (the ocean on your left) through this wilderness park on the Ala Kahakai historic coastal trail leads to Kua Bay and quality beach time. Midway, a hike to the summit of Puʻu Kuʻili, a 342-foot high cinder cone, offers an excellent view of the coastline. It's dry and hot with no drinking water, so be sure to pack sunscreen and bottled water.

Guided Hikes

To get to some of the best trails and places, it's worth going with a skilled guide. Costs range from $75 to $180, and hikes include picnic meals and gear such as binoculars, ponchos, and walking sticks. The outfitters mentioned here also offer customized adventure tours.

Hawaiʻi Forest and Trail. Expert naturalist guides take you to 500-foot Kalopa Falls in North Kohala and on bird-watching expeditions. They, as well as Hawaiʻi Volcanoes National Park rangers, also offer tours into lava tubes and through normally inaccessible areas of Hawaiʻi Volcanoes National Park and rain forests. ☎ *808/331–8505 or 800/464–1993* ⊕ *www.hawaii-forest.com.*

Hawaiian Walkways. Hawaiian Walkways conducts several tours—waterfall hikes, coastal adventures, flora and fauna explorations, and jaunts through Hawaiʻi Volcanoes National Park—as well as custom-designed trips. ☎ *808/775–0372 or 800/457–7759* ⊕ *www.hawaiianwalkways.com.*

Horseback Riding

With its *paniolo* (cowboy) heritage, the Big Island is a great place for equestrians. Riders can gallop through green Upcountry pastures, ride to Kealakekua Bay to see the Captain Cook Monument, or saunter into Waipiʻo Valley for a taste of old Hawaiʻi. In addition to the companies listed below, the Mauna Kea Beach Hotel maintains stables in Waimea.

King's Trail Rides O'Kona, Inc. Riders take a 4½-hour excursion to Captain Cook Monument in Kealakekua Bay for snorkeling (gear provided, except for own fins and reef walkers). The cost is $135 to $150 and custom rides are available. ⊠ *Hwy. 11, mile marker 111, Box 270, Kealakekua* ☎ *808/323-2388* ⊕ *www.konacowboy.com.*

Waipi'o on Horseback. Only two riding outfits venture into the green jungle of the valley floor. Waipi'o on Horseback takes you to an authentic taro farm. Rides depart twice daily from the Last Chance Store and cost $78. ⊠ *Last Chance Store, off Hwy. 240, Kukuihaele* ☎ *877/775-7291 or 808/775-7291.*

Waipi'o Ridge Stables. Two different rides around the rim of Waipi'o are offered—a 2½-hour trek for $75 and a 5-hour hidden-waterfall adventure for $145. Riders meet at Waipi'o Valley Artworks. ⊠ *Waipi'o Valley Artworks, off Hwy. 240, Kukuihaele* ☎ *808/775-1007, 877/757-1414 for information about trail rides, 808/775-0958 for Artworks* ⊕ *www.topofwaipio.com.*

Skiing

Where else but Hawai'i can you surf, snorkel, and snow ski on the same day? During winter, the 13,796-foot Mauna Kea (Hawaiian for "white mountain") has snow at higher elevations—and along with that, skiing. No lifts, no facilities, no faux-Alpine lodges, no manicured slopes, no après-ski nightlife—but the chance to ski some of the most remote (and let's face it, unlikely) runs on earth. Some even have been known to use boogie board as sleds, but we don't recommend it. As long as you're up there, fill your cooler with the white stuff for a snowball fight on the beach with local kids. ⚠ **Don't take children under 16 all the way to the summit as they can't handle the low-oxygen environment, but you'll often find snow at the Mauna Kea Visitor's Center (9,000 feet).**

Ski Guides Hawai'i. So you're an experienced skier but didn't pack your gear on a tropical Hawaiian vacation? Christopher Langan of Mauna Kea Ski Corporation is the only licensed outfitter providing transportation, guide services, and ski equipment on Mauna Kea. Snow can fall from Thanksgiving through June, but the most likely months are February and March. This isn't Sun Valley; the runs are fairly short, and hidden lava rocks and other dangers abound. Langan charges $450 per person for a daylong experience that includes refreshments, lunch, ski or snowboard equipment, guide service, transportation from Waimea, and four-wheel-drive shuttle back up the mountain after each ski run. He also offers a $250 mountain ski service without the frills and ski or snowboard rentals. ⊕ *Box 1954, Kamuela 96743* ☎ *808/885-4188, 808/884-5131 off-season* ⊕ *www.skihawaii.com.*

Tennis

School and park courts are free and open to anyone, though students have first priority during school hours at high school courts. Contact the **County of Hawai'i Department of Parks and Recreation** (⊠ 25 Aupuni

St., Hilo 96720 ☎ 808/961–8311 ⊕ www.hawaii-county.com/directory/ dir_parks.htm) information on all public Big Island tennis courts.

In Kailua-Kona, you can play for free at the **Kailua Playground** (✉ 75-5794 Kuakini Hwy., Kailua-Kona). Tennis courts are available at the **Old Kona Airport** (✉ North end of Kuakini Hwy., Kailua-Kona).

On the Hilo side, the eight courts (three lighted for night play) at **Hilo Tennis Stadium** (✉ Hoʻolulu County Park, Piʻilani and Kalanikoa Sts., Hilo ☎ 808/961–8720) require a small fee.

> ## ON THE SIDELINES
>
> The world's best players compete in January in the **USTA Challenger** (☎ 518/274-1674) on the courts of **Hilton Waikoloa Village** (☎ 808/886-1234).

EXPLORING THE BIG ISLAND

5

The first secret to enjoying the Big Island: rent a car (ideally one with four-wheel drive). The second: stay more than three days, or return again and again to really explore this fascinating place. With 266 mi of coastline made up of white coral, black lava, and a dusting of green-olivine beaches, interspersed with lava cliffs, emerald gorges, and splashing waterfalls, the Big Island can be overwhelming. Depending on the number of days you have available, it would be best to divide your time between the Hilo and Kona sides of the island in order to take in the attractions of each.

The Big Island is truly big; some areas are largely undeveloped and without amenities for miles on end. Each year, unmarked trails and dangerous currents claim the lives of unprepared adventurers. Swim and hike only in areas that are established and designated as safe. Take plenty of drinking water when hiking, along with proper footwear and clothing for the area. And always let someone know where you are going.

The Kohala District & Waimea

Along the roadside of Highway 19, brightly colored bougainvillea stands out in relief against chunky black-lava landscape that stretches as far as the eye can see. Most of the lava flows, spreading from the mountain to the sea, are from the last eruptions of Mt. Hualālai, in 1800–01. They are interrupted only by the green oases of irrigated golf courses surrounding the glamorous luxury resorts along the Kona-Kohala Coast. Kohala is a microcosm of the Big Island as a whole, both in terms of people—wealthy Mainlanders vacationing at the resorts, locals commuting in to work at the resorts from nearby villages and from the Upcountry, and both local and foreign artists reviving the old sugar towns—and land, from the arid coast to the lush valley of Pololū and the rolling hills of Waimea's farm country. The island's best beaches are here, as are the best restaurants, some excellent hiking, and the only destination spas on the island. During the winter months, glistening humpback whales cleave the waters just offshore. If you had only a weekend to spend on the Big Island, this is where you'd want to do it.

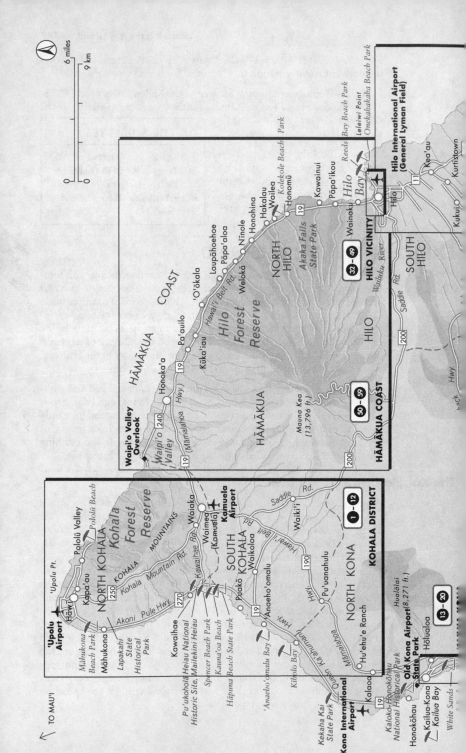

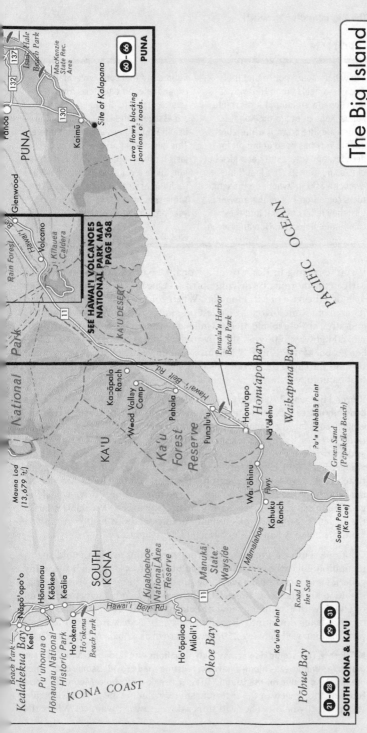

The Big Island of Hawai'i

Graffiti

You will no doubt notice that the black-lava fields lining Highway 19 from Kona International Airport into Kailua-Kona or out to the Kohala resorts are littered with white-coral graffiti. This has been going on for decades, and locals still get a kick out of it, as do tourists. The first thing everyone asks is "where do the white rocks come from?" and the answer is this: they're bits of coral and they come from the ocean. Now that we've

figured out that coral isn't totally expendable, no one starts from scratch anymore. If you want to write a message in the lava, you've got to use the coral that's already out there. This means that no one's message lasts for long, but that's all part of the fun. Some local couples even have a tradition of writing their names in the same spot on the lava fields every year on their anniversary.

a good drive

If you're staying in Kona or at a Kohala Coast resort, begin this tour early in the morning by driving north on Queen Ka'ahumanu Highway 19 along the base of Mt. Hualālai. When you get to the split in the road 33 mi from Kailua-Kona, turn left on Highway 270 toward Kawaihae and stop at **Pu'ukoholā Heiau National Historic Site ❶** ⌐. Go straight when Highway 270 veers sharply to the right to continue on to **Kawaihae Harbor ❷**. Here, in 1793, British captain George Vancouver brought on land the cattle that would proliferate beyond control and draw the first paniolo (cowboys).

Rejoin Highway 270 to drive north along the coast. ■ TIP→→ **Views are generally of lava rock and water from here, but the sweeping coastline is a good vantage point for whale spotting during the season (November–May).** Continue north for 7 or 8 mi to **Lapakahi State Historical Park ❸**. A 1-mi trail meanders through the site of once-prosperous Koai'e, an ancient fishing village. Back on the highway, past Māhukona Beach Park and Kapa'a Beach Park, turn left at the sign for the remote, old 'Upolu Airport. At the bottom of the paved road you'll need a four-wheel-drive vehicle or good hiking shoes to traverse a 1½-mi dirt lane to eerie **Mo'okini Heiau ❹**, the ancient site of numerous human sacrifices. About 1,000 yards away from the heiau is King Kamehameha I's birthplace.

Continue north on the highway. Your next stops are in the old sugar-plantation villages of **Hāwī and Kapa'au ❺**. Browse through the many galleries and gift shops, have some lunch, and be sure to visit the original **King Kamehameha Statue ❻**. Highway 270 ends farther east at an overlook with a stunning view of **Pololū Valley ❼**. A rugged, steep hiking trail leads down into the valley. Drive back toward Hāwī to complete the loop via Highway 250, better known as Kohala Mountain Road.

■ TIP→→ **This scenic ride across high elevations and through ironwood trees that act as windbreaks along a narrow, twisting road provides some of the most breathtaking views on the island.** Take a break at **Kohala Mountain Road Lookout ❽** for a view of the entire coastline, including the protective breakwater, directly below. The road slopes down toward Waimea. Where the road bumps into Highway 19, take a sharp right and turn into the first open gate on your left to visit **Kamuela Museum ❾**.

Next, head for Waimea, a bustling, affluent town with a paniolo cowboy heritage. Behind the shops of High Country Traders on your right on Highway 19, **Waimea Visitor Center ❿** offers detailed information on the cultural and historic sites of Kohala. On the other side of the traffic lights are the **Parker Ranch Visitor Center and Museum ⓫** and the recently renovated Parker Ranch Shopping Center. In the parking lot, there's a handsome sculpture of famous Parker Ranch cowboy, Ikua Purdy, roping a steer. Purdy won the roping event at a national rodeo years ago and brought fame to the Hawaiian paniolo. If you happen to hit Waimea around dinnertime, there are a handful of excellent restaurants waiting to feed you.

Drive northeast on Highway 19. On the left lies Church Lane—stop to peek into the cream-color '**Imiola Congregational Church ⓬** to see its unique koa-wood interior. Be sure to browse through Cook's Discoveries at the third traffic light for exquisite local-theme gifts.

Reverse directions and head west on Highway 19 to get back to the resorts along the coast or take Highway 190 to Kailua-Kona.

TIMING   This is an all-day excursion covering many miles over ground that ranges from lava-covered flatlands with glorious seaside views to lush mountain pastures. If you're short on time, head either straight for Waimea to shop and dine and to visit the Parker Ranch Museum or drive to Hāwī and Kapaʻau via Highway 270 to see beautiful Pololū Valley and to experience the dramatic history of these sugar towns. Allow a half day or more for the abbreviated trip.

What to See

❺ **Hāwī and Kapaʻau.** These two neighboring villages thrived during plantation days. There were hotels, saloons, and theaters—even a railroad. Today, both towns are blossoming once again, thanks to strong local communities and an influx of artists keen on honoring the towns' past. Old historic buildings have been restored and now hold shops, galleries, and eateries. In Kapaʻau, browse through the Hawaiian collection of **Kohala Book Shop** (⊠ 54-3885 Akoni Pule Hwy. ☎ 808/889–6400 ⊕ www. kohalabooks.com), the second-largest bookstore in the state. ⊠ *Hwy. 270, North Kohala.*

> **need a break?**   If you're looking for something sweet, **Tropical Dreams** (⊠ Hāwī ☎ 808/889–5577) makes *da kine* (translation: awesome, amazing, pick a superlative) ice cream.

⓬ '**Imiola Congregational Church.** Stop here to admire the dark koa interior and the unusual wooden calabashes hanging from the ceiling. Be careful not to walk in while a service is in progress, as the front entry of this church, which was established in 1832 and rebuilt in 1857, is behind the pulpit. ⊠ *Off Hwy. 19, along Waimea's famous "church row," Waimea* ☎ 808/885–4987.

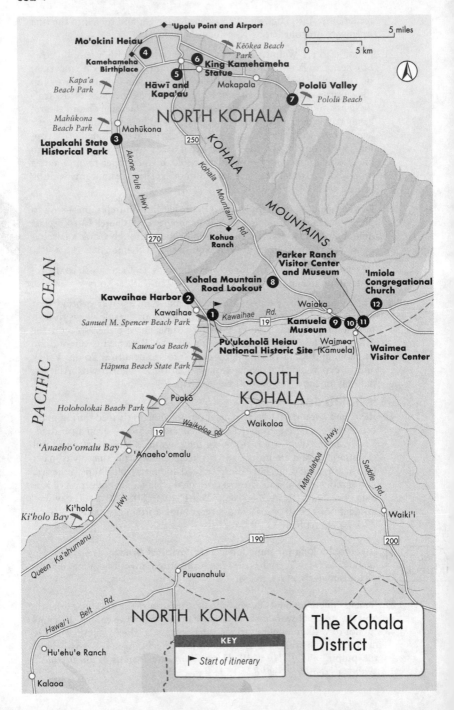

'Upolu Point and Airport

Mo'okini Heiau

4

Kamehameha
Birthplace

Kēōkea Beach
Park

6 King Kamehameha
Statue

5

Kapa'a
Beach Park

Hāwī and
Kapa'au

Makapala

Pololū Valley

7

Pololū Beach

Mahūkona
Beach Park

Mahūkona

NORTH KOHALA

3

Lapakahi State
Historical Park

250

KOHALA

Akone Pule Hwy.

Kohala Mountain Rd.

270

Kohua
Ranch

MOUNTAINS

Parker Ranch
Visitor Center
and Museum

8

'Imiola
Congregational
Church

12

PACIFIC OCEAN

Kohala Mountain
Road Lookout

Kawaihae Harbor **2**

1 Kawaihae
Kawaihae Rd.

Samuel M. Spencer Beach Park

Waiaka

19

Kamuela
Museum

9 **10** **11**

Waimea
Visitor Center

Kauna'oa Beach

Pu'ukoholā Heiau
National Historic Site

Waimea
(Kamuela)

Hāpuna Beach State Park

SOUTH
KOHALA

Holoholokai Beach Park

Puakō

19

Waikoloa Rd.

Waikoloa

Māmalahoa Hwy.

Saddle Rd.

'Anaeho'omalu Bay

'Anaeho'omalu

Ki'holo

Ki'holo Bay

Queen Ka'ahumanu Hwy.

190

Waiki'i

200

Puuanahulu

Hawai'i Belt Rd.

NORTH KONA

Hu'ehu'e Ranch

Kalaoa

The Kohala
District

KEY

⚑ Start of itinerary

0   5 miles
0   5 km

Fire House Gallery. Walk across the Parker Ranch Shopping Center parking lot to a historic 77-year-old fire station, now a gallery, to glimpse what the artists in Hāmākua and Kohala are up to. The Waimea Arts Council sponsors free *kaha ki'is* (one-person shows). ⊠ *Near main stoplight in Waimea, toward Kailua-Kona on Hwy. 190* ☎ *808/887–1052.*

❾ Kamuela Museum. This small private museum has a fascinating collection of artifacts from Hawai'i and around the world. The eclectic collection includes Hawaiian weapons and a satiny-smooth koa table that once graced 'Iolani Palace in Honolulu. There are also period furniture pieces, artwork, and military and war memorabilia. ⊠ *Hwys. 19 and 250, Waimea* ☎ *808/885–4724* ⊑ *$5* ☉ *Daily 8–4.*

❷ Kawaihae Harbor. This commercial harbor, where in 1793 the first cattle came on land, setting the course of the Big Island's ranching history, is a hub of activity, especially on weekends, when paddlers and local fishing boats float on the waves. Second in size only to Hilo Harbor on the east coast, the harbor is often home to the *Makali'i,* one of three Hawaiian sailing canoes. King Kamehameha I and his men launched their canoes from here when they set out to conquer the island chain. ■ **TIP→→** There are several restaurants with nice sunset views in Kawaihae should you be nearby at dinnertime. ⊠ *Kawaihae Harbor Rd. off Hwy. 270.*

❽ Kohala Mountain Road Lookout. The lookout here provides a splendid view of the Kohala Coast and Kawaihae Harbor far below. On clear days, you can see well beyond the resorts. It's one of the most scenic spots on the island and great for a picnic. Often, thick mists drift in, casting an eerie feeling. ⊠ *Kohala Mountain Rd., Hwy. 250.*

Kahuā Ranch. The verdant Kohala Mountains land stretches down to the sea from the rim of Pololū Valley high in the rain forest and holds legendary stories about King Kamehameha and his troops. Here, the owners of the 8,000-plus acres of Kahua Ranch—known for its lamb, beef, and hydroponic vegetables—provide horseback riding, operations tours, ATV adventures, mountain biking, hiking, and clay shooting. There's even a guesthouse. ⊠ *Kahuā Ranch, Hwy. 250* ☎ *808/882–4646* ⊕ *www.kahuaranch.com.*

❻ King Kamehameha Statue. This is the original of the statue in front of the Judiciary Building on King Street in Honolulu. It was cast in Florence in 1880 but lost at sea when the German ship transporting it sank near the Falkland Islands. A replica was shipped to Honolulu. Two years later an American sea captain found the original in a Port Stanley (Falkland Islands) junkyard and brought it to the Big Island. The legislature voted to erect it near Kamehameha's birthplace. Every year, on King Kamehameha Day (June 11), a magnificent abundance of floral lei adorns the image of Hawai'i's great king. It's in front of the old Kohala Courthouse next to the highway. ⊠ *Hwy. 270, Kapa'au.*

need a break? **Kohala Rainbow Cafe** (☎ 808/889–0099), across from the King Kamehameha statue in Kapa'au, serves wraps, salads, smoothies, and sandwiches all day long. Try the Kamehameha wrap—filled with Hawaiian-style kalua pork, organic greens, tomatoes, onions, cheeses and Maui onion dressing. Open weekdays, except Tuesday 10–6, weekends 11–5.

★ ❸ **Lapakahi State Historical Park.** A self-guided, 1-mi walking tour leads through the ruins of the once-prosperous fishing village Koai'e, which dates as far back as the 15th century. Displays illustrate early Hawaiian fishing, salt gathering, legends, games, shelters, and crops, and a park guide is often on-site to answer questions. Since the shores off Lapakahi are now mostly a Marine Life Conservation District, and part of the site itself is considered sacred, swimming is discouraged. For some reason they make a distinction between swimming and snorkeling, and allow the latter, which is fortunate because the snorkeling here is superb. ⌧ *Hwy. 270, between Kawaihae and Māhukona, North Kohala* ☎ *808/974–6200 or 808/882–6207* ☒ *Free* ☉ *Daily 8–4.*

★ ❹ **Mo'okini Heiau.** This National Historic Landmark, an isolated *luakini* (sacrificial) heiau, is so impressive in size it may give you goose bumps. Its foundations date to about AD 480, but the high priest Pa'ao from Tahiti built the heiau in earnest several centuries later to sacrifice people to please his gods. You can still see the lava slab that hundreds of people were sacrificed on, which gives this place a truly haunted feel. A nearby sign marks the place where Kamehameha I was born in 1758. The area is now part of the Kohala Historical Sites State Monument. ⌧ *Turn off Hwy. 270 at sign for 'Upolu Airport, near Hāwī, and hike or drive in a four-wheel-drive vehicle 1½ mi southwest* ☎ *808/974–6200.*

⓫ **Parker Ranch Visitor Center and Museum.** The center chronicles the life of John Palmer Parker (and his descendants), who founded Parker Ranch in 1847. Parker married the granddaughter of King Kamehameha and bought 2 acres of land from the king for the sum of $10. Purchase your tickets here for the **Parker Ranch Historic Homes,** a

> ### WAIMEA OR KAMUELA?
>
> Both, actually. The name of the Waimea post office is Kamuela, while the name of the town itself is Waimea. Some say the post office is named for the son of the founder of Parker Ranch.

couple of miles south of town. The original family residence, Māna, is built entirely from native koa-wood. Pu'ōpelu, added to the estate in 1879, was the residence of Richard Smart, a sixth-generation Parker who expanded the house to make room for his European art collection. On Friday, Hawaiian crafts demonstrations take place at the homes. A wagon ride allows you a comfortable, albeit old-fashioned, visit to the pastures. Also available are horseback rides and walking tours. ⌧ *Parker Ranch Shopping Center, 67-1185 Māmalahoa Hwy., Waimea* ☎ *808/885–7655, 808/885–5433, 800/262–7290 toll-free* ⊕ *www.parkerranch.com* ☒ *Museum $6.50, homes $8.50, both $14* ☉ *Museum daily 9–5, homes daily 10–5.*

❼ **Pololū Valley.** A steep trail leads into this lush green valley, and down to Pololū Beach, which edges a rugged coastline ribboned by silver waterfalls. The valleys beyond provide water for the Kohala Ditch, the ingenious project that used to bring water to the area's sugar plantations. Some of the former ditch trails have become inaccessible and dangerous. A kayak cruise through the old irrigation ditch, a mule ride, and a ditch-trail hike, offered by tour operators and outfitters, reveal more of this dramatic part of Kohala history. **Hawai'i Forest and Trail** (☎ 808/331–8505 or 800/464–1993 ⊕ www.hawaii-forest.com) leads half-day mule rides into the valley. ⊠ *End of Hwy. 270.*

★ ☞ ❶ **Pu'ukoholā Heiau National Historic Site.** In 1790 a prophet told King Kamehameha I to build a heiau on top of Pu'ukoholā (Hill of the Whale) and dedicate it to the war god Kūkā'ilimoku by sacrificing his principal Big Island rival, Keōua Kūahu'ula. By doing so the king would achieve his goal of conquering the Hawaiian Islands. The prophecy came true in 1810. A short walk over arid landscape leads from the visitor center to **Pu'ukoholā Heiau** and to **Mailekini Heiau,** a navigational heiau constructed about 1550. An even older temple, dedicated to the shark gods, lies submerged just offshore. The center organizes Hawaiian arts-and-crafts programs on a regular basis. ⊠ *Hwy. 270, Kawaihae* ☎ *808/882–7218* ⊕ *www.nps.gov* ☞ *Free* ⊙ *Daily 7:30–4.*

❿ **Waimea Visitor Center.** The old Lindsey House—a restored ranch cabin built in 1909 and now listed on the Hawai'i Register of Historic Places—serves as a visitor center. Part of the Waimea Preservation Association, it offers detailed information on Kohala's many historic and cultural sites. ⊠ *65-1291 Kawaihae Rd., behind High Country Traders, Waimea* ☎ *808/885–6707* ⊕ *www.northhawaii.net* ⊙ *Mon.–Sat. 9:30–4:30.*

> **need a break?**
>
> If you're in the mood for a steaming caffe latte and a warm pastry, stop by **Waimea Coffee & Company,** sit out on their veranda and try to believe you're in Hawai'i and not West Virginia (⊠ Parker Sq., 65-1279 Kawaihae Rd., Waimea ☎ 808/885–4472).

Kailua-Kona

The touristy seaside village of Kailua-Kona, at the base of the 8,271-foot Mt. Hualālai, has many historic sites tucked among the open-air shops and restaurants that line Ali'i Drive, its main oceanfront street. This is where King Kamehameha I died in 1819 and where his successor, Liholiho, broke the *kapu* (taboo) system, a rigid set of laws that had provided the framework for Hawaiian government. The following year, on April 4, 1820, the first Christian missionaries from New England came ashore at Kailua-Kona.

> **a good walk**
>
> This ½-mi walk follows Ali'i Drive south. Begin at **King Kamehameha's Kona Beach Hotel** ⓭ ☞ at the northern end of town. The hotel, which borders the last residency of King Kamehameha I, **Kamakahonu** ⓮, offers free tours of a replica of the king's temple, Ahu'ena Heiau. You can also wander around the two stone platforms at the ocean's edge to view the site on your own. Next, investigate **Kailua Pier** ⓯. Walk a short distance and take in **Hulihe'e Palace** ⓰, on your right, and **Moku'aikaua Church** ⓱, on your left. Tackle a maze of shops in the block-long **Kona Inn Shopping Village** ⓲. End your walk at **St. Michael's Church** ⓳, on your left, across the street from the wooden restaurant complex known as Wa-

terfront Row, or continue another block past the Ali'i Sunset Plaza to the Coconut Grove Marketplace.

If you have a car, return to it to complete your historical tour; drive to the end of Ali'i Drive past Disappearing Sands Beach Park, the tiny blue-and-white St. Peter's Catholic Church, the ruins of a heiau, and Kahalu'u Beach Park. There, a jagged lava lake on the edge of a bay outlines the **Kuamo'o Battlefield and Lekeleke Burial Grounds ⓩ**.

> ## WHERE DO I PARK?
>
> The easiest place to park your car (fee $3) is at King Kamehameha's Kona Beach Hotel. Some free parking is available: when you enter Kailua via Palani Road (Highway 190), turn left onto Kuakini Highway; drive for a half block, and turn right (into the small marked parking lot). Walk *makai* (toward the ocean) on Likana Lane a half block to Ali'i Drive and you'll be in the heart of Kailua-Kona town.

TIMING   You can walk the whole ½-mi length of "downtown" Kailua-Kona and back again in an hour, or else spend an entire day here, taking time to browse in the shops, do the historical tours, and have lunch. The drive to the Kuamo'o Battlefield and Lekeleke Burial Grounds takes less than 10 minutes. If you want to know more about Kailua's fascinating past, arrange for a guided tour by the Kona Historical Society.

Kailua-Kona enjoys year-round sunshine—except for the rare deluge. Mornings offer cooler weather, smaller crowds, and more birds singing in the banyan trees, but afternoon outings are great for cool drinks while gazing out over the ocean.

What to See

Astronaut Ellison S. Onizuka Space Center. This informative museum 7 mi north of Kailua-Kona, at the airport, was opened as a tribute to Hawai'i's first astronaut, who was killed in the 1986 *Challenger* disaster. The space center has computer-interactive exhibits. You can launch a miniature rocket and rendezvous with an object in space, feel the effects of gyroscopic stabilization, participate in hands-on science activities, and view educational films. ⊠ *Keāhole–Kona International Airport, Kailua-Kona* ☎ *808/329–3441* ⊕ *www.planet-hawaii.com/astronautonizuka* ⊠ *$3* ⊙ *Daily 8:30–4:30.*

off the beaten path

HŌLUALOA – A charming surprise hugging the hillside above Kealakekua Bay, the tiny village of Hōlualoa, just up Hualālai Road from Kailua-Kona, is a great place to find local art and wares that go beyond the tourist schlock you'll typically find downtown. Formerly coffee country, there are still quite a few coffee farms and an equal number of abandoned, colorful farmhouses, dotting the narrow winding road up to Hōlualoa from Kailua-Kona. These days the town itself is comprised almost entirely of galleries in which all types of artists, from woodworkers to jewelry-makers and more traditional painters, work in their studios in back and sell the finished product up front. Hōlualoa is also smack in the middle of coffee country, so there are plenty of farms nearby offering free tours and cups of joe. Alternatively you could stop by the only café in town, the cleverly

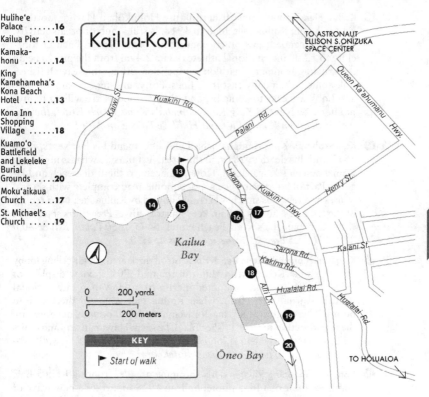

Hulihe'e Palace **16**

Kailua Pier ...**15**

Kamaka-honu **14**

King Kamehameha's Kona Beach Hotel **13**

Kona Inn Shopping Village **18**

Kuamo'o Battlefield and Lekeleke Burial Grounds **20**

Moku'aikaua Church **17**

St. Michael's Church **19**

Kailua-Kona

TO ASTRONAUT
ELLISON S. ONIZUKA
SPACE CENTER

Kailua Bay

0 ——— 200 yards
0 ——— 200 meters

KEY

▶ *Start of walk*

Ōneo Bay

TO HŌLUALOA

named **Hōluakoa Cafe** (✉ 76-5900 Mamalahoa Hwy. ☎ 808/322–2233) and grab a cup to sip while you stroll through town. Don't try to stay at the old pink hotel, but do stop by to say hello to the old-timers on their porch. People are full of aloha here, and locals tend to sit out in front of their houses or stores to shoot the breeze all day long.

★ **⑯** **Hulihe'e Palace.** Fronted by a wrought-iron gate decorated with the royal crest, Hulihe'e Palace is one of only three royal palaces in America. The two-story residence was built of lava, coral, koa wood, and 'ōhi'a timber in 1838 by the island's governor, John Adams Kuakini, a year after he completed Moku'aikaua Church. During the 1880s it served as King David Kalākaua's summer palace. The oversize doors and koa-wood furniture bear witness to the size of some of the Hawaiian people. On weekday afternoons hula schools rehearse on the grounds. The Palace is currently operated by The Daughters of Hawai'i, a nonprofit focused on maintaining Hawaiian heritage. ■ TIP→→ They offer free Hawaiian concerts fairly regularly and, for you crazy romantics planning a Hawai'i wedding, Hulihe'e Palace is available for receptions and dinners. ✉ *75-5718 Ali'i Dr.* ☎ *808/329–1877* ⊕ *www.huliheepalace.org* ✉ *$5* ⊙ *Weekdays 9–4, weekends 10–4.*

⑮ Kailua Pier. Though most fisherfolk use Honokōhau Harbor, north of Kailua-Kona, Kailua Pier, built in 1918, is still a hub of ocean activity. Outrigger canoe teams practice, and tour boats depart. Each October close to 1,500 international athletes swim 2.4 mi from the pier to begin the grueling Ironman Triathlon competition. Along the **seawall** fisherfolk and children daily cast their lines. For youngsters, a bamboo pole and hook are easy to come by, and plenty of locals are willing to give pointers. ☒ *Next to King Kamehameha's Kona Beach Hotel; the seawall is between Kailua Pier and Hulihe'e Palace on Ali'i Dr.*

★ **⑭ Kamakahonu.** King Kamehameha I chose to spend his last years, from 1812 until his death in 1819, in this area, just outside what is now King Kamehameha's Kona Beach Hotel, adjacent to the little beach and lagoon. Part of what was once a 4-acre homestead complete with several houses and religious sites has been swallowed by Kailua Pier, but a replica of the temple, **Ahu'ena Heiau,** keeps history alive. Free tours start from King Kamehameha's Kona Beach Hotel. ☒ *75-5660 Palani Rd.* ☎ *808/ 329–2911* ☒ *Free* ☉ *Tours weekdays at 1:30.*

▶ ⑬ King Kamehameha's Kona Beach Hotel. Stroll through the high-ceiling lobby of this Kailua-Kona fixture, built in the mid-'70s, to view displays of Hawaiian artifacts and mounted marlin from Hawaiian International Billfish tournaments (from when Kailua Pier was still the weigh-in point). These "granders," marlin weighing 1,000 pounds or more, are the big attraction for Kona fisherfolk. Classes in Hawaiian arts and crafts take place regularly. ☒ *75-5660 Palani Rd.* ☎ *808/329–2911, 800/367– 6060 toll-free* ⊕ *www.konabeachhotel.com.*

⑱ Kona Inn Shopping Village. This shopping arcade, fronting Kailua Bay, was once the Kona Inn, a hotel built in 1928 to attract a new wave of wealthy travelers. As new vacation condos and resorts opened along the Kona and Kohala coasts, the old Kona Inn lost much of its appeal and finally closed in 1976. The former hotel was renovated into a shopping complex with dozens of clothing boutiques, art stores, gift shops, and island-style eateries. Prior to the construction of the inn, the personal heiau of King Liholiho was on this shore. Today, shops and restaurants line the boardwalk. Broad lawns with coconut trees on the ocean side are lovely for afternoon picnics. ☒ *75-5744 Ali'i Dr.*

> **need a break?**
>
> If it's late afternoon, it's time to get one of those umbrella drinks and unwind. For cocktails at sunset head to the **Kona Inn Restaurant** (☒ 75-5744 Ali'i Dr. ☎ 808/329–4455), a traditional favorite.

⑳ Kuamo'o Battlefield and Lekeleke Burial Grounds. In 1819, an estimated 300 Hawaiians were killed on this vast, desolate black-lava field now filled with terraced graves. After the death of his father, King Kamehameha I, Liholiho became king; shortly thereafter King Liholiho ate at the table of women, thereby breaking an ancient kapu. Chief Kekuaokalani, vying for the throne and with radically different views about traditions and religion, unsuccessfully challenged King Liholiho in battle. In breaking the ancient kapu, Liholiho forced a final battle not just between him and his opponent but, more importantly, between traditional and new religious beliefs in Hawai'i. ✉ *South end of Ali'i Dr.*

★ **⑰ Moku'aikaua Church.** The earliest Christian church on the Islands was founded here as a thatch hut by Hawai'i's first missionaries in 1820. The present incarnation of the church was built in 1836 with black stone from an abandoned heiau. The stone was mortared with white coral and topped by an impressive steeple. Inside, at the back, behind a panel of gleaming koa wood, is a model of the brig *Thaddeus*. ✉ *75-5713 Ali'i Dr.* ☎ *808/329–0655.*

⑲ St. Michael's Church. The site of the first Catholic church built in Kona, in 1840, is marked by a small thatch structure to the left of the present church, which dates from 1850. In front of the church a coral grotto shrine holds 2,500 coral heads, harvested in 1940, when preservation was not yet an issue. ✉ *75-5769 Ali'i Dr.* ☎ *808/326–7771.*

> **need a break?**
>
> **Island Lava Java** (✉ 75-5799 Ali'i Dr. ☎ 808/327–2161), in the Ali' Sunset Plaza, this popular, laid-back café, has the best and biggest cinnamon rolls, bagels, and great coffee in the mornings, decent sandwiches, fresh fruit smoothies and ice cream in the afternoon. All that and a large outdoor seating area with a bird's-eye view of the ocean. Locals hang out here to read the paper, play board games, or just watch the surf. The café also has Internet access, both on the two desktops inside and on the laptops they rent out to folks who want to work outside.

South Kona & Kealakekua Bay

South of Kailua-Kona, Highway 11 hugs splendid coastlines, leaving busy streets behind. A detour along the winding narrow roads in the mountains above takes you straight to the heart of coffee country where lush plantations and jaw-dropping views offer a taste of what Hawai'i was like before resorts. Take a tour at one of the coffee farms to find out what the big deal is about Kona coffee, and snag a free sample while you're at it. A half-hour back on the highway will lead you to magical Kealakekua Bay, where Captain James Cook arrived in 1778, changing the Islands forever. Hawaiian spinner dolphins swim and play alongside kayakers and snorkelers in the bay, now a marine preserve nestled alongside impossibly high green cliffs more reminiscent of Ireland than posters of Hawai'i. The winding road above is home to a quaint little painted church, as well as several reasonable B&Bs with stunning views. The communities surrounding the bay (Kainaliu and Captain Cook) are brimming with local and transplanted artists, making them great places to stop for a meal, some unique gifts, or an afternoon stroll.

> **a good drive**

From Kailua-Kona, drive south on Highway 11, also known as Hawai'i Belt Road or Māmalahoa Highway, to the town of Captain Cook. Keep an eye out once you hit the town, as just past the main buildings is a junction where you'll need to turn right to follow the steep descent along Nāpō'opo'o Road to **Kealakekua Bay ㉑** ⌐. Park your car at the end of the road at rocky **Nāpō'opo'o Beach.** You could spend the whole day

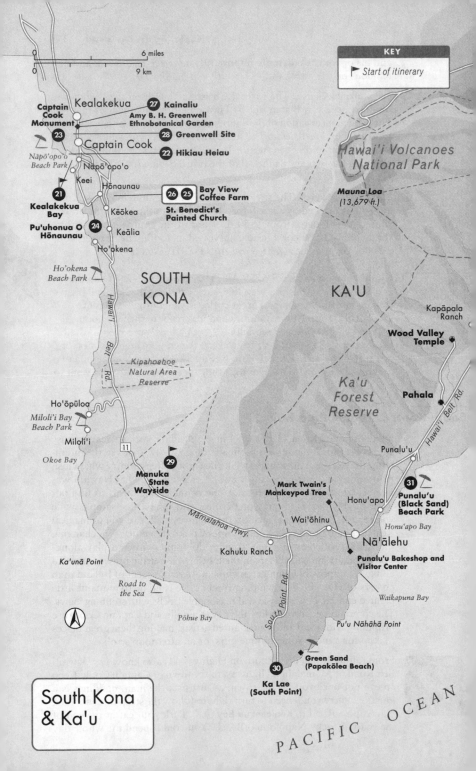

0 ————— 6 miles
0 ————— 9 km

Kealakekua

Captain Cook Monument

27 Kainaliu

Amy B. H. Greenwell
Ethnobotanical Garden

23

28 Greenwell Site

Captain Cook

22 Hikiau Heiau

Nāpō'opo'o Beach Park

Nāpō'opo'o

Keei

Hōnaunau

26 25 Bay View
Coffee Farm

St. Benedict's
Painted Church

21

Kealakekua Bay

Kēōkea

Pu'uhonua O Hōnaunau

24

Keālia

Ho'okena

Ho'okena Beach Park

SOUTH KONA

Hawai'i Belt Rd.

Kipahoehoe Natural Area Reserve

Ho'ōpūloa

Miloli'i Bay Beach Park

Miloli'i

Okoe Bay

11

29

Manuka State Wayside

Mamalahoa Hwy.

Ka'unā Point

Road to the Sea

Pōhue Bay

Kahuku Ranch

30

Ka Lae (South Point)

South Point Rd.

Green Sand
(Papakōlea Beach)

Hawai'i Volcanoes National Park

Mauna Loa
(13,679 ft.)

KA'U

Kapāpala Ranch

Wood Valley Temple

Ka'u Forest Reserve

Pahala

Hawai'i Belt Rd.

Punalu'u

31

Punalu'u (Black Sand) Beach Park

Mark Twain's
Monkeypod Tree

Honu'apo

Wai'ōhinu

Honu'apo Bay

Nā'ālehu

Punalu'u Bakeshop and
Visitor Center

Waikapuna Bay

Pu'u Nāhāhā Point

PACIFIC OCEAN

South Kona & Ka'u

here, and, if you do, be sure to pack a lunch and your snorkeling equipment (⇨ *See* Kayaking, Snorkeling *earlier in this chapter*).

When you can tear yourself away from the bay, walk to the nearby **Hikiau Heiau ㉒**. A moderately difficult three-hour hike on a rough trail from the top of Nāpōʻopoʻo Road takes you to **Captain Cook Monument ㉓**, which sits above some of the most populated coral reefs on the island.

Pulling out of the parking lot turn right onto Route 160, which hugs the coast, and follow the road to **Puʻuhonua O Hōnaunau ㉔**. Plan to spend some time walking around this ancient Hawaiian sanctuary. Visit the restored royal Hale-o-Keawe Heiau, built circa 1650, and wander to the tide pools south of the park. Back in your car, head mauka on Route 160 toward Kēōkea, and turn left at Painted Church Road to visit the whimsical **St. Benedict's Painted Church ㉕**. Java junkies should head ½ mi farther up Painted Church Road to **Bay View Coffee Farm ㉖**, which you can spot by its wooden gazebo.

Follow Painted Church Road back to Highway 11 to return to Kona, leaving time for food and/or shopping in historic **Kainaliu ㉗**. The **Greenwell Site ㉘**, just outside of Kainaliu, is headquarters of the Kona Historical Society. Stop in to learn more about everything you've just seen.

Signs in this part of the island about buying "cherries" are referring to "coffee cherries"—coffee beans grow with a cherrylike husk around them.

TIMING Start out early to make it to Kealakekua Bay before it gets too hot or the afternoon clouds roll in. Snorkeling is superb here, as it is a protected marine reserve, so you may want to bring your gear and spend an hour or so exploring the coral reefs. This is also a nice kayaking spot, as the bay is extremely calm, and kayaks are available for rent from a dozen or so vendors between Kailua-Kona and Nāpōʻopoʻo Beach.

What to See

Amy B. H. Greenwell Ethnobotanical Garden. Often overlooked, this garden fosters a wealth of Hawaiian cultural traditions. On 12 acres, it has 250 types of plants, including food and fiber crops, that were typical in an early Hawaiian *ahupuaʻa*, a pie-shape land division that ran from the mountains to the sea. Call to find out about guided tours or drop in between 8:30 AM and 5 PM. ✉ *82-6188 Māalahoa Hwy., Captain Cook* ☎ *808/323–3318* ⊕ *www.bishopmuseum.org/greenwell.*

㉖ **Bay View Coffee Farm.** Most of the coffee farms on the island offer tours, and Bay View's is one of the better ones—mostly because the coffee's really good. The tour lasts about an hour; it's interesting, even if you're not into coffee. Plus, it's fueled with a great cup of 100% Kona. ✉ *½ mi past St. Benedict's Painted Church, 83-5249 Painted Church Rd., Hōnaunau* ☎ *808/328–9658* ⊗ *Daily 9–5* ✆ *Free.*

㉓ Captain Cook Monument. No one knows for sure what happened on February 14, 1779, when English explorer Captain James Cook was killed here. He chose Kealakekua Bay as a landing place in November 1778 and initiated Hawai'i's dramatic change. Cook was welcomed at first, arriving during the celebration of Makahiki, the harvest season. Some Hawaiians saw him as an incarnation of the god Lono, and he was received with great reverence. Cook's party reprovisioned and sailed away in February 1779, but a freak storm off the Kona Coast forced him back to Kealakekua Bay for repairs. The Hawaiians were not so welcoming this time, and various confrontations arose between them and Cook's sailors. The theft of a longboat brought Cook and an armed party ashore to reclaim the boat. One thing led to another: shots were fired, daggers and spears were thrown, and Captain Cook fell, mortally wounded. Strangely enough, this didn't deter other Westerners from visiting the Islands; Captain James Cook and his party had effectively introduced the Hawaiian Islands to the world. Soon after, Western influences arrived on Hawai'i's shores: whalers, sailors, traders, missionaries, and more, and they brought with them crime, debauchery, alcohol, disease, and a world unknown to the Hawaiians. A 27-foot-high obelisk marks the spot where Captain Cook died on the shore of Kealakekua Bay. Locals like to point out that the land the monument sits on is technically British territory (to clarify: the British government owns the land that the monument sits on, but it's still technically U.S. territory). The three-hour 2½-mi hike to get to the monument begins at the trailhead 100 yards off Highway 11 on Nāpō'opo'o Road. Look for the downslope trail opposite three large royal palm trees.

㉘ Greenwell Site. Established in 1850, the homestead of Henry N. Greenwell served as cattle ranch, sheep station, post office, store complex, and family home all in one. Now, all that remains is the 1875 stone store, which is listed on the National Register of Historic Places. It's headquarters for the **Kona Historical Society,** which has a fascinating museum, including ranching and coffee-farming photographs and exhibits. ✉ *81-6551 Māmalahoa Hwy.* ☎ *808/323–3222* ⊕ *www.konahistorical.org* ✑ *Donations accepted* ⊙ *Weekdays 9–3.*

㉒ Hikiau Heiau. The remains you see of the stone platform and walls were once an impressive state temple, a large and sacred site enclosed by stone walls, dedicated to the god Lono. When Captain Cook arrived in 1778, ceremonies in his honor were held here. ✉ *Bottom of Nāpō'opo'o Rd.*

㉗ Kainaliu. Like many of the Big Island's old plantation towns, Kainaliu is experiencing a bit of a renaissance. In addition to a ribbon of funky old stores, many of them traditional Japanese family-operated shops, a handful of new galleries and eateries have sprung up in the last couple of years. Browse around Heritage Stores such as Oshima's, established in 1926, and Kimura's, established in 1927, to find authentic Japanese goods beyond tourist trinkets, then pop into Cafe Nasturtium for a tasty vegetarian snack. Cross the street to peek into Aloha Theatre, built in 1932, where community-theater actors might be practicing a Broadway revue. ✉ *Hwy. 11, mile markers 112–114.*

▶ **㉑** **Kealakekua Bay.** This is one of the most beautiful spots on the island.
Fodor'sChoice Dramatic cliffs surround crystal clear, turqoise water chock-full of stun-
★ ning coral and tropical fish. Before the arrival here of Captain Cook in
the late 18th century, this now tranquil state marine park and sanctuary lay at the center of Hawaiian life. Historians consider Kealakekua
Bay to be the birthing ground for the postcontact era.

The term "beach" is used a bit liberally for Nāpō'opo'o Beach (⊕ End
of Nāpō'opo'o Rd.), on the south side of the bay. There's no real beach
to speak of, but there are easy ways to enter the water. To the left of the
parking lot is an old cement pier that serves as a great ladder for swimmers coming in and out of the bay. This is a nice place to swim as it's
well protected from weather or currents, so the water is almost always
calm and clear. ⚠ **Be very careful entering the bay from the Captain Cook
Monument (north) side—stepping on either coral or a sea urchin can be extremely
painful to you and devastating to them. Remember that this is a protected marine reserve.** Snorkel cruises into the bay from Kailua-Kona are well worth
it and can be booked through *Fair Winds* Cruises (⇨ *See* Snorkeling *earlier in this chapter*), the only company allowed to dock in Kealakekua.
✉ *Bottom of Nāpō'opo'o Rd.*

need a break? Before or after winding down Nāpō'opo'o Road, treat yourself to
awesome views of Kealakekua Bay at the **Coffee Shack** (✉ 83-5799
Māmalahoa Hwy. ☎ 808/328–9555 ⊕ www.coffeeshack.com), a
deli and pizza place with just nine tables on an open, breezy lānai.
The bread is home-baked, the sandwiches are generous, and the staff
is friendly.

Kona Coffee Living History Farm (D. Uchida Farm). Known as the D. Uchida
Farm, this farm is unique in its heritage of coffee pioneers. The site, which
has been preserved and restored by the Kona Historical Society, includes
a 1913 farmhouse surrounded by coffee trees, a Japanese bathhouse,
Kuriba (coffee-processing mill), and Hoshidana (traditional drying platform). Tours of the farm are available by reservation only and cost $20.
✉ *Kona Historical Society, 81-6551 Māmalahoa Hwy., Kealakekua*
☎ *808/323–3222* ⊕ *www.konahistorical.org.*

★ **㉔** **Pu'uhonua O Hōnaunau (Place of Refuge).** This 180-acre National Historic
Park, about 20 mi south of Kailua-Kona, was, in early times, a place of
refuge and healing. It was a safe haven for women in times of war as
well as for *kapu* breakers (kapu roughly translates to "forbidden, " and
was the name for the early Hawaiian code of conduct), criminals, and
prisoners of war—anyone who could get inside the 1,000-foot-long
wall, which was 10 feet high and 17 feet thick, was safe and could avoid
punishment. **Hale-o-Keawe Heiau,** built in 1650 as the burial place of
King Kamehameha I's ancestor Keawe, has been restored. South of the
park, tide pools offer another delight. Demonstrations of Hawaiian
skills, games, poi pounding, canoe-making, and more are scheduled occasionally. ✉ *Rte. 160* ☎ *808/328–2288* ⊕ *www.nps.gov* ✆ *$3–$5*
☺ *Park grounds Mon.–Thurs. 6 AM–8 PM, Fri.–Sun. 6 AM–11 PM; visitor center daily 8 AM–4:30 PM.*

㉕ St. Benedict's Painted Church. Whimsical, bright, and creative, the ceiling, columns, and walls of this Roman Catholic church depict Bible scenes through the paintbrush of Belgian-born priest Father Velghe. Mass is still held every weekend. The view of Kealakekua Bay from the entrance is amazing. ⊠ *Painted Church Rd. off Hwy. 160, Hōnaunau* ☎ *808/ 328–2227.*

Ka`u & Ka Lae (South Point)

The most desolate region of the island, Ka`u is nonetheless home to some spectacular sights. Mark Twain wrote some of his finest prose here, where macadamia-nut farms, fine beaches, and tiny villages offer as-yet largely undiscovered beauty. The 50-mi drive from Kailua-Kona to windswept South Point, where the first Polynesians came ashore as early as AD 750, winds away from the ocean through a surreal moonscape of lava-covered forests. Past South Point, glimpses of the ocean return and a hidden Green Sand beach tempts hikers to stop awhile before the highway narrows and returns to the coast, passing verdant cattle pastures and sheer cliffs on the way to the black sand beach of Punalu`u, the nesting place of the Hawaiian sea turtle.

> **a good drive**

Take Highway 11 south from Kailua-Kona. Just past Captain Cook (about 30 mi outside of Kona), you'll pass the turnoff to Ho`okena Beach Park, a busy steamer port in the 19th century. About 12 mi farther south, at mile marker 88, the infamous Mauna Loa lava flow of 1926 destroyed an entire Hawaiian fishing village. Turn left here for a 2-mi scenic drive along the old Māmalahoa Highway; then take a break at **Manuka State Wayside ㉙** ►.

Drive another 12 mi on Māmalahoa Highway to reach the windswept South Point Road, which leads to the southernmost part of the United States, **Ka Lae (South Point) ㉚**. It's a 12-mi drive down the narrow road to the point, past a field of windmill turbines. Continue down the road (parts at the end are unpaved, but driveable), bear left when the road forks and park in the lot at the end; walk past the boat hoists toward the little lighthouse. South Point is just past the lighthouse at the southernmost cliff. No vehicles are allowed on the coastal trail beyond road's end to **Green Sand (Papakōlea) Beach.**

Drive back up South Point Road to Highway 11, and turn right, heading east. The highway hugs the coast again, providing a dramatic shift in scenery as lava forests are replaced by rolling green hills and cattle pastures on the left, and high cliffs and crashing surf on the right. For the last leg of this drive, continue east on Highway 11 to the wetter, windward towns of Wai`ōhinu and Nā`ālehu, small communities struggling in the aftermath of sugar-plantation closures. As you near Wai`ōhinu, keep an eye out for mile marker 64 and the Hawaiian warrior sign marking the spot where **Mark Twain's Monkeypod Tree** once grew. In Nā`ālehu, you'll see the large **Punalu`u Bakeshop and Visitor Center,** with its large parking lot. You can stop here, or at any of a number of other cafés in these towns for a snack or lunch.

After you've refueled, continue on to swim with the sea turtles at **Punalu`u (Black Sand) State Beach ㉛** and end your tour.

TIMING   This drive works as a longer jaunt starting from Kailua-Kona or as a shorter drive from one of the B&Bs overlooking Kealakekua Bay. Coming in the opposite direction, it's a short trip from the Volcano area B&Bs. If you're starting from Kailua-Kona, start your day early, as it takes 2½ hours from Kona just to get to the southern end of the island. From either Hawai'i Volcanoes National Park or Captain Cook the drive is shortened to about 45 minutes. Fill up on gasoline and pack some snacks, as there are few amenities along the way. If your homebase is Kailua-Kona, chances are it'll be close to dinnertime by the time you've completed this tour, but eateries in Kailua-Kona remain open late.

What to See

Green Sand (Papakōlea) Beach. It takes awhile to get down and even longer to get back, but where else are you going to see a green sand beach? Add to that the fact that the rock formations surrounding the beach are surreally beautiful, and this is a detour worth taking. ✛ *2 ½ mi northeast of South Point.*

★ ③⓪ **Ka Lae (South Point).** Windswept Ka Lae is the southernmost point of land in the United States. A few abandoned structures were used in the 19th and early 20th centuries to lower cattle and produce to ships anchored below the cliffs. It's thought that the first Polynesians came ashore here. Check out the old canoe-mooring holes that are carved through the rocks, possibly by settlers from Tahiti as early as AD 750. Some artifacts, thought to have been left by early voyagers who never settled here, date to AD 300. Driving down to the point, you pass Kama'oa Wind Farm; although the rows of windmill turbines are still fueled by the nearly constant winds sweeping across this coastal plain, the equipment and facilities are falling into disrepair due to neglect. Indeed, some of the windmills are no longer working at all. Continue down the road (parts at the end are unpaved, but driveable), bear left when the road forks and park in the lot at the end; walk past the boat hoists toward the little lighthouse. South Point is just past the lighthouse at the southernmost cliff. ■ **TIP→** Don't leave anything of value in your car, and you don't have to pay for parking. It's a free, public park, so anyone trying to charge you is running some sort of scam. ✉ *Turn right just past mile marker 70 on Māmalahoa Hwy. and drive for 12 mi down South Point Rd.*

▶ ②⑨ **Manuka State Wayside.** This is a dry, upland native forest spread across several lava flows. It has a well-maintained arboretum. A rugged trail follows a 2-mi loop past a pit crater and winds around ancient trees such as *hau* and *kukui*. This is an okay spot to stretch your legs, snap a shot of the eerie, desolate forest, and let the kids scramble around trees so large you can't get your arms around them, but we don't recommend spending too much time here, especially if you're planning on driving all the way down to South Point. Pathways are not well maintained, but restrooms, picnic areas, and telephones are available. ✉ *Hwy. 11, north of mile marker 81* ☎ *808/974–6200* ✉ *Free* ☉ *Daily 7–7.*

Mark Twain's Monkeypod Tree. The tree that Mark Twain, who gained inspiration for some of his writings during his travels in this area, planted here in 1866 has long since passed and been replaced by a new tree. Still, a Hawaiian warrior marker sign marks the spot that Twain once touched. ⊠ *Hwy. 11, just before mile marker 64, in Wai'ohinu.*

---

off the
beaten
path

PAHALA – About 16 mi east of Na'lehu, beyond Punalu'u Beach Park, Highway 11 flashes past this little town. You'll miss it if you blink. Pahala is a perfect example of a sugar-plantation town. Behind it, along a wide cane road, you enter Wood Valley, once a prosperous community, now a mere road heavily scented by night-blooming jasmine, coffee blossoms, and eucalyptus trees. Here you'll find **Wood Valley Temple** (☎ 808/928–8539), a quiet Tibetan Buddhist retreat that welcomes guests who seek serenity and solitude.

Punalu'u Bakeshop and Visitor Center. Granted, this place is a little tourist-trappy, but it's also a good spot to grab a snack before heading back out on the road. Try some Portuguese sweetbread, or a homemade ice cream sandwich, paired with some local Ka'u coffee (that's right, not Kona, but equally as tasty), then take a wander through their "botanical garden"—a quaint garden path planted with some local plants. ⊠ *Māmalahoa Hwy. at Kaalaiki Rd., Na'alehu* ☎ *808/929–7343* ⊙ *Daily 9–5.*

③① **Punalu'u (Black Sand) State Beach.** This easily accessed beach is well worth at least a short stop for two reasons: it's a beautiful black-sand beach, and it's where the Hawaiian sea turtles like to nest so the water's swarming with them. The turtles are very used to people by now, and have no problem swimming right along side you. ✛ *Turn right down driveway into beach off Hwy 11 south. Beach is very well marked off Hwy.*

Hilo

Hawai'i Volcanoes National Park   See Page 368

Hilo is a town of both modern and rustic buildings stretching from the banks of the Wailuku River to Hilo Bay, where a few hotels rim stately Banyan Drive. Nearby, the 30-acre Lili'uokalani Gardens, a formal Japanese garden with arched bridges and waterways, was created in the early 1900s to honor the area's Japanese sugar-plantation laborers. It also became a safety zone after a devastating tidal wave swept away businesses and homes on May 22, 1960, killing 60 people.

Though the center of government and commerce for the island, Hilo is primarily a residential town. Mansions with perfectly kept yards of lush tropical foliage surround older wooden houses with rusty corrugated roofs. It's a friendly community, populated primarily by descendants of the contract laborers—Japanese, Chinese, Filipino, Puerto Rican, and Portuguese—brought in to work the sugarcane fields during the 1800s. Bring your umbrella: the rainfall averages 130 inches per year.

FODOR'S FIRST PERSON

Amy Westervelt
Writer

I was fifteen when I went to End of the World for the first time, and I chickened out. The rocks looked too close, the surge looked too strong, and I was a little afraid of heights anyway. I was the only one who didn't jump, and afterward I wished I had. A few years later I tried to go back, but I'd only ever been there with other people, and I couldn't remember exactly where it was. Besides, who wants to go to a place called "End of the World" by themselves? Finally, 10 years after that first day, I went out on a snorkel cruise for an assignment, and was invited to go jump off a cliff. It's more friendly than it sounds. I agreed, and then asked what the place was called— "End of the World, do you know it?"

Despite my decade-long hankering to do this, it took me a good hour to work up the courage, and I still jumped from the slightly lower ledge. The high ledge looks like a cragged point you could just fall off onto the rocks below. Even from the lower (only by about a foot, I swear!) ledge, it's a pretty long jump—long enough to realize halfway down that you're still nowhere near hitting the water. It was a little surge-y that day, so a couple of veterans hung below in the water, ready to yell, "Go!" when it was calm enough to be safe. And when they did, I finally jumped. I think I hit the water in some sort of modified fetal position, but I made it back up the rocks okay, and my new friends gave me a cheer. Now I go back every year but have yet to make it up to the high ledge!

When the sun shines and the snow glistens on Mauna Kea, 25 mi in the distance, Hilo sparkles. In the rain the town takes on the look of an impressionist painting—greenery muted alongside weather-worn brown, red, and blue buildings. Several of these buildings have recently been spruced up to revitalize the downtown area. Often the rain blows away by noon and a colorful arch appears in the sky. One of Hilo's nicknames is the City of Rainbows.

The whole town has fewer than 1,000 hotel rooms, most of them strung along Banyan Drive. By contrast, the eight Kohala Coast resorts alone have more than 3,704 rooms combined. Nonetheless, Hilo, with a population of almost 50,000 in the entire district, is the fourth-largest city in the state and home to the University of Hawai'i at Hilo.

a good tour

Historic downtown Hilo is best explored on foot. Start your excursion in front of the public library, on Waiānuenue Avenue, four blocks from Kamehameha Avenue. Here, you'll find the ponderous **Naha and Pinao stones** ㉜ ▶, which legend says King Kamehameha I was able to lift as a teenager, thus foretelling that someday he would be a powerful king. Cross the road to walk southeast along Kapi'olani Street, and turn right on Haili Street to visit the historic **Lyman Mission House and Museum** ㉝. Back on Haili Street, follow this busy road toward the ocean; on your right you'll pass **Haili Church** ㉞.

Continued on page 377

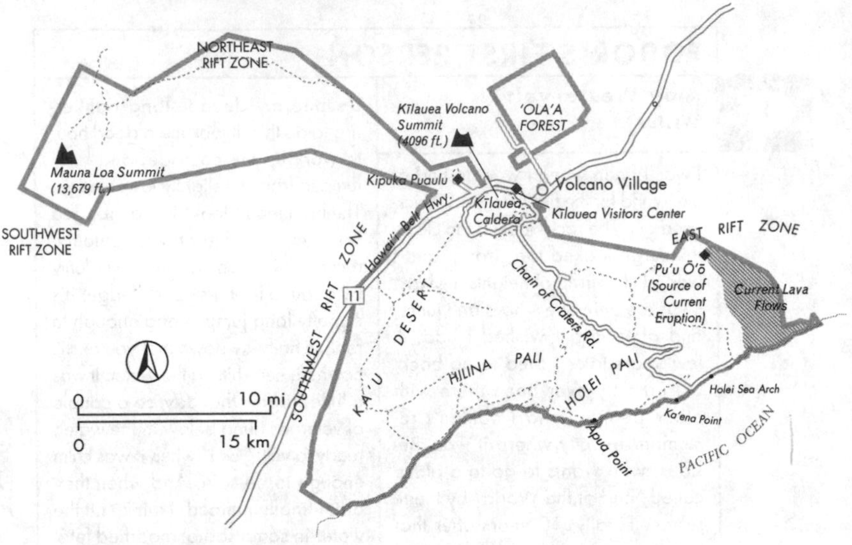

NORTHEAST RIFT ZONE

Kīlauea Volcano Summit (4096 ft.)

'OLA'A FOREST

Mauna Loa Summit (13,679 ft.)

Kīpuka Puaulu

Volcano Village

SOUTHWEST RIFT ZONE

Kīlauea Visitors Center

Kīlauea Caldera

EAST RIFT ZONE

Hawai'i Belt Hwy.

SOUTHWEST RIFT ZONE

Chain of Craters Rd.

Pu'u 'Ō'ō (Source of Current Eruption)

Current Lava Flows

11

KA'U DESERT

HILINA PALI

HOLEI PALI

Holei Sea Arch

Ka'ena Point

Āpua Point

PACIFIC OCEAN

0 10 mi

0 15 km

HAWAI'I VOLCANOES NATIONAL PARK

It's nothing short of miraculous. Kīlauea Volcano is adding new land to the Big Island. Not hundreds of thousands of years ago—today. Molten lava meets the ocean, cools, and solidifies into a brand-new stretch of coastline. It's fire and water, creation at its most elemental. What makes it even more amazing? You can watch it happen right in front of you. If you do nothing else on the Big Island, do the volcano.

Kīlauea, youngest and most rambunctious of the Hawaiian volcanoes, erupted at its summit from the 19th century through the 1950s. Since then, the top of the volcano has been more or less quiet, frequently shrouded in mists. Its eastern side, on the other hand, has been percolating, sending lava spilling into the ocean. The current eruption has been ongoing since January 3, 1983, primarily from Pu'u 'Ō'ō vent. The lava flows are generally steady and slow, appearing and disappearing from view. And the Volcano doesn't only create, it destroys. In 1990, a lava flow engulfed and demolished the coastal town of Kalapana.

Exploring the surface of the world's most active volcano—from the moonscape craters at the summit to the red lava flows on the coast—is the ultimate ecotour.

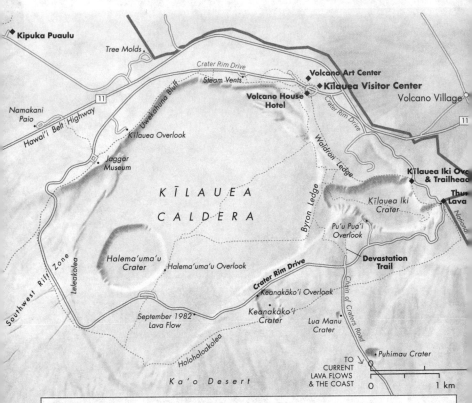

THE SUMMIT: CALDERA & CRATERS

At the summit of Kīlauea is a massive grey pit (2 mi long and 3 mi wide) encircled by plumes of sulfuric smoke. The size of this main caldera, not to mention its uncanny resemblance to those old Apollo moon photos, makes for an eerie, awe-inspiring spot. Within and around the caldera are several smaller craters. Although the summit does not currently have any active lava flows, signs of devastation—black fields of lava, dried in folds and ripples of rock, burnt-out forests; steaming sulfur vents—are everywhere, as are signs of rebirth—scrubby vegetation taking root, fern forests, and even the endangered nēnē.

Keep in Mind: As you explore Kīlauea, remember that it is dwarfed by neighboring

Mauna Loa, the National Park's other volcano and the world's most massive. Mauna Loa's last eruption was in 1984, and scientists believe another is due. The summit is difficult to reach, but you will most likely walk on some part of this volcano during your visit to the Big Island, as it encompasses nearly half of the island.

CAUTION

Yellow, acrid-smelling sulfur banks and gaping vents emitting warm steam are found throughout the cool environs of the park. Pregnant women and anyone with heart or respiratory problems should avoid both the sulfur banks and the noxious fumes.

EXPERIENCING THE SUMMIT

Wear comfortable shoes because the best way to experience the wonder of this place is to hike it. Even a short stroll can take you deep into a primeval landscape. The summit is easy to navigate; trailheads and overlooks are signposted off Crater Rim Drive.

1ST STOP: KĪLAUEA VISITOR CENTER
808/985–6010, Daily 7:45–5.

Always check the status of the current lava flows first. Don't get caught on the summit when the lava is bubbling on the coast. The summit is amazing, but as it's currently dormant, it will be there when you're ready for it. Plus rangers know the inside scoop on summit trails.

While you're there: Check out Volcano House (808/967–7321). This remarkable old lodge peers impudently down into Kīlauea from its perch on the caldera's rim. The 1941 building itself is sadly showing wear-and-tear, but there's usually a blaze in the stone fireplace. Skip the food, but don't miss the views.

Take a look at the work of Big Island photographers, artists, and craftspeople at the **Volcano Art Center** (808/967–7565, www.volcanoartcenter.org, Daily 9–5).

Kīlauea Iki Trail

DRIVING TOUR OF CRATER RIM DRIVE
Distance: 11 mi • Time: 1–3 hrs

Crater Rim Drive circles Kīlauea Caldera and Kīlauea Iki Crater, providing panoramic vistas of vast lava deserts, steam vents, and forests all along the way. The drive loops back to the visitor center. This is a must-do to get a sense of the size and scope of the caldera.

BEST TRAILS

Devastation Trail.
Distance: 1 mi • Time: 30 min. Difficulty: Easy.

The 1959 eruption of Kīlauea Iki spewed cinder onto an 'ōhi'a forest. This is a paved path through hundreds of stark tree skeletons protruding from the mounds of cinders and pumice. It's like a walk through an eerie abstract painting.

Thurston Lava Tube Trail.
Distance: 3 mi • Time: 45 min. Difficulty: Easy.

A lava tube is the tunnel formed when the surface of a lava flow cools and solidifies, and the still-molten interior drains away. A paved trail leads from the parking lot through the rainforest to the Thurston tube entrance, which resembles an old coal mine. A 15-minute walk inside takes you through narrow tunnels and fairly large rooms. Bring a flashlight for everyone in your group and hike the secondary cave that goes back another 330 yards.

Kīlauea Iki Trail.
Distance: 4 mi • Time: 2–3 hrs.
Difficulty: Moderate.
Elevation Change: 400 ft.

This could be the best hike on the Big Island. You descend from the lush rainforest, cross the hardened (and surprisingly flat) lava lake, then climb up the other side to the crater rim. If it seems quiet, consider that Kīlauea Iki was geysering lava as recently as 1959.

EXPLORING THE CURRENT LAVA FLOWS

Pu`u `Ō`ō Vent is the source of the current lava flows at Kīlauea Volcano. Lava has been flowing from this crater on the eastern face of the volcano since 1983. The eruption has created over 560 acres of land, covered 8.9 mi of coastal highway, and destroyed over 150 structures. The coastal town of Kalapana (in Puna) was engulfed in 1990. Lava flows have covered a vast swath of the mountainside and coast, leaving behind a stark, treeless plain.

The chance to see red–hot, flowing lava is most likely what you're here for. Plan to be on the coast at sunset to maximize your chances of catching the show. Chain of Craters Road is the only way into and out of this area of the park; trailheads and overlooks are signposted along its length.

1ST STOP: KĪLAUEA VISITOR CENTER
808/985–6010, Daily 7:45–5.

Make a quick stop here. It's a long drive down to the coast—make sure that that is where the action is before you set out.

DRIVING DOWN CHAIN OF CRATERS ROAD
Distance: 38 mi. Time: 3 hrs.
No food, water, or gasoline is available.

Chain of Craters Road descends 3,700 ft from the fern forests and thick stands of `ōhi`a at the steaming summit to the starkly barren, lava-covered beaches of the Kalapana Coast. The road passes by or near several small craters on the side of the volcano on its way down to the ocean. Lava flow from one of them, Mauna Ulu, forced the rerouting of this road back in 1974. You can still see steam rising occasionally from Mauna Ulu, so keep an eye out (on your left as you head down toward the coast). You can also see the path of lava from past eruptions zigzagging this way and that down the mountainside, as well as panoramic glimpses of the coast and ocean below. The road ends at the point where it was engulfed in a 1983 flow. The pavement disappears beneath folds and rolls of hardened lava. A NO PARKING sign sticks forlornly out of the tumbled rock. Rangers usually set up an information booth and portable toilets here.

THE LAVA HIKE
Distance: Variable. Time: Variable.

At the end of Chain of Craters Road, you can (with Madame Pele's consent) see flowing lava up close. If you've got a GPS, this is the place for it—there are no marked trails, the terrain is quite uneven, and you're on your own. Although you can hike any time of the day, the best time is just before dusk, so that you'll be on the flow to see the red glow of any lava flowing off the cliffs or into the ocean.

Park rangers man the mobile information shack at the end of the road until an hour or two after dark. Check with them before setting out about conditions and hazards. Because lava flows are unpredictable, it's impossible to say how long a hike to flowing lava will take, but if you leave at dusk figure to be back around midnight (give or take a couple of hours).

CAUTION

When lava enters the sea it produces huge clouds of white steam. Stay out of them. They contain (among other harmful gasses) hydrofluoric acid, which can etch glass (like camera lenses and eyeglasses, to say nothing of what it can do to your lungs). Do not get too close to the ocean. This is brand new land and unstable "lava benches" can (and do) break off and drop into the ocean.

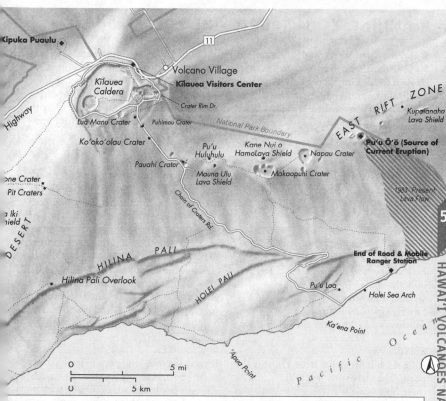

Kīpuka Puaulu

Volcano Village

Kīlauea Caldera

Kīlauea Visitors Center

11

Crater Rim Dr.

Highway

National Park Boundary

EAST RIFT ZONE

Kupaianaha Lava Shield

Lua Manu Crater

Puhimau Crater

Ko'oko'olau Crater

Pu'u Hulyhulu

Kane Nui o HamoLaya Shield

Napau Crater

Pu'u Ō'ō (Source of Current Eruption)

Pauahi Crater

Mauna Ulu Lava Shield

Makaopuhi Crater

1983–Present Lava Flow

one Crater

Pit Craters

Chain of Craters Rd.

a Iki hield

DESERT

HILINA PALI

HOLEI PALI

End of Road & Mobile Ranger Station

Hilina Pali Overlook

Pu'u Loa

Holei Sea Arch

Ka'ena Point

'Āpua Point

Pacific Ocean

0   5 mi
0   5 km

HAWAI'I VOLCANOES NATIONAL PARK

5

WILL I SEE FLOWING LAVA?

You may or may not see flowing lava. Conditions change daily. You might be able to see red lava from the end of Chain of Craters Road, or you might have to hike to it. If it's really gushing, you'll be able to see it during the day. If, however, as is typically the case, it's just sort of seeping, then the best time to see it is at night. Lava flows beneath the surface can shine through the crust in the dark of night.

PLANNING YOUR TRIP TO THE VOLCANO

■ **Stay the night.** We strongly recommend staying the night. There is more than enough to fill a day and a half. And you signficantly improve your chances of seeing red lava if you are there at night. (⇨ *See* Where to Stay *later in this chapter.*)

■ **Always stop in at Kīlauea Visitor Center first.**

■ **Go for at least two hikes or walks** (one on the summit and one on the coast).

Park Information

CONTACT:
Hawai'i Volcanoes National Park
P.O. Box 52
Hawai'i National Park, HI 96718
808/985–6000
www.nps.gov/havo
Hours: Open 24 hours a day
Admission: $10 per car for seven days

GETTING HERE:
It's a 45-minute drive from Hilo to the park. The drive from Kailua-Kona is three hours one way (another reason to stay the night); the southern route (via South Point) is quickest from the Kona Side.

WHAT TO BRING:
Dress in layers. Take a sweater (or a jacket in winter), as temperatures get nippy at the summit's 4,000-foot elevation, and maybe a poncho for the occasional downpour. It's much hotter and windier on the coast; wear sunscreen and a hat. Pack a lunch. Volcano Village is too far from the park to be convenient midday, and food at Volcano House is forgettable tour group fare.

If your hiking plans are more ambitious than a short walk, there's more to pack. Wear sturdy shoes. You can go in tennis shoes (though the lava will do a number on the soles), but hiking boots are much better. Forget about hiking in sandals or flip flops. Wear sunscreen and maybe a hat. Bring plenty of water (2–3 liters per person) and energy bars or other snacks. If you plan to hike to the shoreline lava flow at dusk or dawn, flashlights (with extra batteries) are mandatory for everyone in your group.

HEALTH & SAFETY:
With very few exceptions, the entire park is open to visitors, and, in the ever-changing eruption conditions, only the fool enters into closed areas or ignores posted warnings. The risk of injury from falling into a lava crack is real, as is the threat of becoming disoriented and lost due to volcanic fumes, smoke, and haze clouds. This is a dangerous place, and signs are posted for a reason. Be sure to follow all rules and posted signs and markers, and don't wander off by yourself.

GUIDED HIKES:
If you plan to do the park in a single day and if you are coming from the Kona side, consider booking your excursion with an outfitter.

National Park Ranger Programs. Tours vary; information is posted at the Visitors' Center by 9 each morning. Register a week in advance for the Wednesday wild cave hike.

Hawai'i Forest and Trail. 808/331–8505 or 800/464–1993, www.hawaii-forest.com.

Hawaiian Walkways. 808/775–0372 or 800/457–7759, www.hawaiianwalkways.com.

Airplane & Helicopter Tours

There's nothing quite like the aerial view of lava flowing into the ocean with clouds of steam billowing into the air. Aerial tours have unfortunately become a controversial subject. The park service requests that tour helicopters avoid flying directly over certain sites that are of religious significance to native Hawai-

Pu'u Ō'o Cone, Kīlauea Volcano

ians. A few unscrupulous operators, however, ignore these requests and even advertise better safety records than they've actually earned. Be smart when booking your tour, and ask the right questions: How close will I get to the surface of a lava flow? (FAA regulations mandate an altitude of 500 feet) Do you fly over Halema'uma'u or Kīlauea caldera? (Culturally sensitive areas to be avoided.) Do you have 2-way headsets so passengers can talk with the pilot? (Very desirable.) Book a tour from Hilo airport, if possible. It's much cheaper as you won't pay to fly from Kona over the relatively boring landscape on the way.

Blue Hawaiian Helicopters. Hilo Airport or Waikoloa Helipad, 808/961–5600 or 800/786–2583, www.bluehawaiian.com.

Mokulele Flight Service. 808/326–7070 or 866/260–7070, www.mokulele.com.

Sunshine Helicopters. Helipad at the Hāpuna Beach Prince Hotel and Hilo Airport, 808/882–1223, 808/969–7506, or 800/469–3000, www.sunshinehelicopters.com.

Tropical Helicopters. Hilo Airport, 808/961–6810, www.tropicalhelicopters.com.

Volcano Village

If you plan to stay the night or are just hungry for a good meal, Volcano Village is your destination. With two country stores, a couple of family-run restaurants, a post office, and a hardware store, this little village of a few thousand souls nestled at the edge of the volcano's summit is Mayberry in the rainforest. Stop by the Sunday morning farmer's market at Cooper Center on Wright Road, across from the firehouse (the community pitched in to build both structures).

ALSO NEAR THE PARK:

Akatsuka Orchid Gardens. Tour one of the largest orchid collections in Hawai'i. The cool Volcano climate provides the ideal conditions for cultivation. The shop sells plants and cut flowers and can ship to anywhere in the world. Hwy. 11, just past mile marker 22, 808/967–8234 or 888/967–6669, www.akatsukaorchid.com, Free, Daily 8:30–5.

Kīpuka Puaulu. A kīpuka is a forested island surrounded by a sea of lava. This 100-acre mesic forest is also known as Bird Park; native birds, such as the 'apapane and the 'elepaio, call from their hiding places in the thick canopy. Drive southwest on Highway 11 from the park to the next right and turn onto Mauna Loa Road. You'll see a sign marked TREE MOLDS. Each chimneylike formation was created when molten lava hardened around a tree, burning it away in the process. About 2 mi in, you can take a self-guided mile-long walk around Kīpuka Puaulu. Hawai'i Volcanoes National Park.

Volcano Winery. This unusual winery creates white table wines from Symphony grapes, as well as honey wines, a red Pele Delight, Guava or Passion Chablis, and Volcano Blush. Experiments with traditional varietals such as pinot noir are underway. 35 Pi'imauna Dr., 808/967–7772, www.volcanowinery.com, Daily 10–5:30.

5

HAWAI'I VOLCANOES NATIONAL PARK

YOUR HOST, MADAME PELE

Hawai'i is full of myths and legends that have been passed down from the ancients, but the Big Island is the only one with its own mercurial, vengeful, gin-guzzling goddess, Pele. Kīlauea, specifically Halema'uma'u Crater, is her home.

It's said that, before every eruption, Pele appears in human form as a wrinkled old woman walking along isolated back roads. Those who offer her a ride return home to find a river of boiling magma abruptly halted inches from their property or diverted around their houses. Those who pass her by find their homes devastated by molten lava.

And she doesn't just mess with the natives, so don't think you're off the hook. Madame Pele wreaks havoc on the lives of those who take lava rock from the island, and that includes green, black, or even white sand that came from lava. You can't help the bits that make it into your shoes and suits, but don't even think about taking any extra. People have been returning rocks and sand to the Big Island for years after suffering health problems, bizarre accidents, and any number of other problems thought to be the curse of Pele. Nine times out of 10 when they bring the lava back, their luck changes. If you see leis and gin bottles scattered on the ground around a crater, those are gifts for Pele.

Some forms of lava take their names from the goddess. **Pele's hair,** thin strands of volcanic glass drawn out from molten lava, resembles golden blond hair. Solidified, round, jet black bits of volcanic glass (molten lava that cools quickly) are known as **Pele's tears.** They are often found at the end of strands of as hair.

Tales of Pele also wind around many of the remarkable plants that flourish in her home. **Ohi'a Lehua,** the most common of the Park's native trees, has blossoms, called Lehua, that range from dark red to light yellow. Legends say that Pele fell in love with a local boy called Ohi'a, who was already in love with a beautiful young girl called Lehua. Pele asked Ohi'a to be her husband, but he refused and professed his undying love for Lehua. Angry, Pele turned Ohi'a into an ugly grey tree. The rest of the gods were unable to bring Ohi'a back to life, so they turned Lehua into a blossom on the same tree. It is still believed that picking a Lehua blossom will bring rain (tears from above for separating the lovers).

Of the several different varieties of **'ohelo** found around Kīlauea, the most common is a small bush with serrated leaves and juicy berries ranging from yellow to red. The 'ohelo is believed to be the embodiment of Hi'iaka, one of Pele's sisters. Its berries are sacred to Pele, and today there are those who will not eat the fruit and who will not even pass through the Kīlauea area without making an offering of 'ohelo to Pele.

Skylight, Kīlauea Volcano

Soon you'll reach **Keawe Street** ㉟ with its plantation-style architecture. Stop at the **Big Island Visitors Bureau** ㊱ on the right-hand corner for maps and brochures before taking a left. You'll bump into Kalākaua Street; for a quick respite turn left and rest on the benches in **Kalākaua Park** ㊲.

Continue makai on Kalākaua Street to visit the **Pacific Tsunami Museum** ㊳ on the corner of Kalākaua and Kamehameha Avenue. After heading three blocks east, you'll come across the **S. Hata Building** ㊴, which has interesting shops and restaurants and the **Mokupapapa: Discovery Center for Hawaii's Remote Coral Reefs Museum.** Just next door, on either side of Mamo Street, is the **Hilo Farmers' Market** ㊵.

Once you've fully explored Hilo, take a drive to some of the area's outlying sights. Begin this excursion driving southwest from the cluster of hotels along **Banyan Drive** ㊶. **Liliʻuokalani Gardens** ㊷, on the right, has Japanese gardens and an arched footbridge to **Coconut Island** ㊸. When you reach the intersection of Banyan Drive and Kamehameha Avenue at the bridge over the Waiakea Fish Pond–Wailoa River, turn right on Kamehameha and head toward downtown, then turn left at the traffic signal onto Pauahi Street, then left again into Wailoa State Park. Close to the Waiakea Fish Pond is the **Wailoa Center** ㊹.

From Wailoa State Park and Wailoa Center, go back to Pauahi Street, turn right back to Kamehameha Avenue and the bayfront, and take a left to downtown on Kamehameha Avenue. Follow Kamehameha Avenue as it passes along a block inland from the bayfront and winds into downtown. At the intersection of Kamehameha and Waiānuenue Avenue, turn left for a short ride to two popular sights a couple of miles outside town. When the road forks, after about a mile in a southwest direction, stay to the right to reach **Rainbow Falls** ㊺. Two miles farther up the road, also on the right, you'll come across the photogenic Boiling Pots at the base of **Peʻepeʻe Falls** ㊻.

Drive back to the Bayfront Highway and take a right. It intersects with Highway 11, Kanoelehua Avenue, which takes you directly to the volcano. Close to Hilo, however, are three more attractions. On the right, just past mile marker 4, you'll pass the sign for **Panaʻewa Rain Forest Zoo** ㊼. Five minutes up Stainback Highway, it's a great stop for children. Back on Highway 11, 5 to 6 mi south of Hilo, turn left when you reach the marker for **Mauna Loa Macadamia Factory** ㊽. On your return to Hilo, find serenity and tropical beauty at the **Nani Mau Gardens** ㊾ on Makalika Street off Route 11.

TIMING Rain is inevitable in Hilo; they get 130 inches a year, and it's distributed throughout the seasons. That said, it does tend to rain in the mornings and let up by afternoon. Plus, the rain is that nice Hawaiian warm rain. Allow a full day to explore Hilo if you want to take in all the sights, less if you skip the museums and have little interest in shopping. Remember that morning hours are generally cooler for walking the streets than late afternoon, when the humidity can soar. It's definitely worth timing a visit for a Wednesday or Saturday, when the farmers' market is in full swing. You could easily spend a night at one of the B&Bs on the Hāmākua Coast, then hit both the coast and Hilo while you're there.

What to See

★ **41 Banyan Drive.** The more than 50 leafy banyan trees with aerial roots dangling from their limbs were planted some 60 to 70 years ago by visiting celebrities. You'll find such names as Amelia Earhart and Franklin Delano Roosevelt on plaques on the trees. ⊠ *Begin at Hawai'i Naniloa Resort, 93 Banyan Dr.*

36 Big Island Visitors Bureau. Marked by a red-and-white Hawaiian warrior sign, the bureau is worth a visit for brochures, maps, and up-to-date, friendly insider advice. ⊠ *250 Keawe St., at Haili St.* ☎ *808/961–5797* ⊕ *www.bigisland.org* ☉ *Weekdays 8–4:30.*

★ **43 Coconut Island.** This small (approximately 1 acre) island, just offshore from Lili'uokalani Gardens, was a place of healing in ancient times. Today children play in the tide pools while fisherfolk try their luck. The island is accessible via a footbridge. ⊠ *Lili'uokalani Gardens, Banyan Dr.*

34 Haili Church. This church was originally constructed in 1859 by New England missionaries, but the church steeple was rebuilt in 1979 following a fire. Haili Church is known for its choir, which sings hymns in Hawaiian during services. ⊠ *211 Haili St.* ☎ *808/935–4847.*

★ **40 Hilo Farmers' Market.** An abundant and colorful market draws farmers and shoppers from all over the island. Two days a week, bright orchids, anthuriums, and birds-of-paradise create a feast for the eyes, while exotic vegetables, tropical fruits, and baked goods create a feast for the stomach. ⊠ *Mamo and Kamehameha Sts.* ☉ *Wed. and Sat. 6:30 AM–2:30 PM.*

37 Kalākaua Park. King Kalākaua, who revived the hula, was the inspiration for Hilo's Merrie Monarch Festival. The park is named in his honor. A bronze statue, sculpted in 1988, depicts the king with a taro leaf in his left hand to signify the Hawaiian peoples' bond with the land. In his right hand the king holds an *ipu,* a symbol of Hawaiian culture, chants, and hula. The park also features a huge spreading banyan tree and small fishponds, but no picnic or recreation facilities. In a local tradition, families that have held recent funerals for loved ones often set up leftover floral displays and funeral wreaths along the fishpond walkway as a way of honoring and celebrating the deceased. It makes for a unique and colorful display. ⊠ *Kalākaua and Kino'ole Sts.*

> **need a break?**
>
> For breads and sandwiches, mouthwatering apple pies, croissants, and biscotti, **O'Keefe & Sons Bread Bakers** (⊠ 374 Kino'ole St. ☎ 808/934–9334) is the place to go. Their tiny retail shop is filled with specialties such as five-grain sourdough, banana bread, and cinnamon toast.

35 Keawe Street. Buildings here have been restored to their original 1920s and '30s plantation styles. Although most shopping is along Kamehameha Avenue, the ambience on Keawe Street offers a nostalgic sampling of Hilo as it might have been 80 years ago.

★ **42 Lili'uokalani Gardens.** Fish-filled ponds, unique Japanese stone lanterns, half-moon bridges, pagodas, and a ceremonial teahouse make this 30-acre park a favorite Sunday destination for residents. It was designed

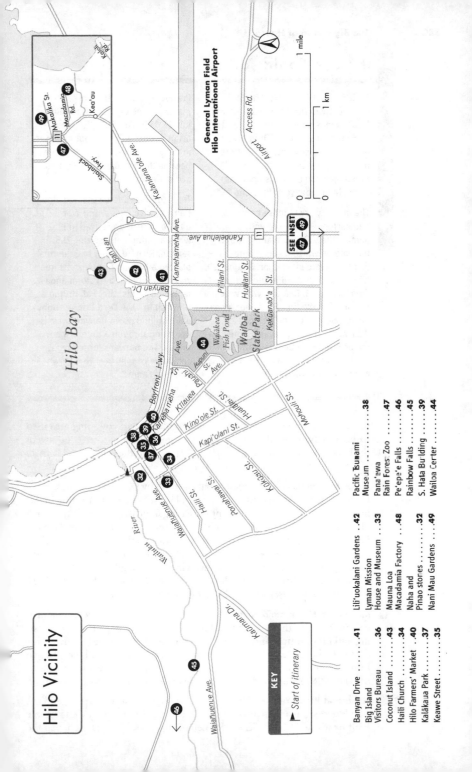

Hilo Vicinity

Hilo Bay

General Lyman Field
Hilo International Airport

KEY

▲ *Start of itinerary*

Banyan Drive **41**	Lili'uokalani Gardens . . **42**
Big Island	Lyman Mission
Visitors Bureau **36**	House and Museum . . **33**
Coconut Island **43**	Mauna Loa
Haili Church **34**	Macadamia Factory . . **48**
Hilo Farmers' Market . . **40**	Naha and
Kalākaua Park **37**	Pinao stores **32**
Keawe Street **35**	Nani Mau Gardens . . . **49**

Pacific Tsunami	
Museum **38**	
Pana'ewa	
Rain Forest Zoo **47**	
Pe'epe'e Falls **46**	
Rainbow Falls **45**	
S. Hata Building **39**	
Wailoa Center **44**	

CLOSE UP

If Trees Could Talk

THE HISTORY OF THE TREES lining Hilo's Banyan Drive is one of the Big Island's most interesting and least-known stories. Banyan Drive was named for these trees, which were planted by VIP visitors to Hilo. Altogether, some 50 or so banyans were planted between 1933 and 1972.

The majority are Chinese banyans, and each one is marked with a sign naming the VIP who planted it and the date on which it was planted. The first trees were planted on October 20, 1933, by a Hollywood group led by director Cecil B. DeMille, who was in Hilo making the film *Four Frightened People*. Soon after, on October 29, 1933, another banyan was planted by the one and only George Herman "Babe" Ruth, who was in town playing exhibition games.

President Franklin D. Roosevelt planted a tree on his visit to Hilo on July 25, 1934. And in 1935, famed aviatrix Amelia Earhart put a banyan in the ground just days before she became the first person to fly solo across the Pacific Ocean.

Trees continued to be planted along Banyan Drive until World War II. The tradition was then revived in 1952 when a young and aspiring U.S. senator, Richard Nixon of California, planted a banyan tree. Nixon's tree was later toppled by a storm and was replanted by his wife, Pat, during a Hilo visit in 1972. On a bright, sunny day, strolling down Banyan Drive is like going through a green, shady tunnel. The banyans form a regal protective canopy over Hilo's own "Walk of Fame."

---

to honor Hawai'i's first Japanese immigrants. The surrounding area used to be a busy residential neighborhood until a tsunami in 1960 swept the buildings away, taking the lives of 60 people in the process. ⊠ *Banyan Dr. at Lihiwai St.* ☎ *808/961–8311.*

㉝ Lyman Mission House and Museum. Built in 1839 by David and Sarah Lyman, Congregationalist missionaries, Lyman House is the oldest frame building on the island. In the adjacent museum, dedicated in 1973, the Earth Heritage Gallery includes a realistic magma chamber and displays the Earth's formation and the arrival of life, with a section on Hawaiian flora and fauna. You can view unique artifacts of Hawaiian and other major ethnic groups in the Island Heritage Gallery. The gift shop sells a map of the tsunami flows in the Hilo area. ⊠ *276 Haili St.* ☎ *808/935–5021* ⊕ *www.lymanmuseum.org* ⊠ *$10* ⊙ *Mon.–Sat. 9–4:30.*

㊽ Mauna Loa Macadamia Factory. Acres of macadamia trees lead to a processing plant with viewing windows. A videotape depicts the harvesting and preparation of the nuts, and there are free samples in the visitor center. Children can run off their energy on the nature trail. Feel free to bring your own picnic lunch. ⊠ *Macadamia Rd. off Hwy. 11, 5 mi south of Hilo* ☎ *808/966–8618* ⊕ *www.maunaloa.com* ⊙ *Daily 8:30–5:30.*

▶ ㉜ Naha and Pinao stones. These two huge, oblong stones are legendary. The Pinao stone is purportedly an entrance pillar of an ancient temple built near the Wailuku River. Kamehameha I is said to have moved the

5,000-pound Naha stone when he was still in his teens. Legend decreed that he who did so would become king of all the islands. The building they're in front of is the Hilo Public Library. ⌧ *300 Waiānuenue Ave.*

★ ㊾ **Nani Mau Gardens.** Theme gardens (a Hawaiian garden and a palm garden among them) are spread over 20 acres, showcasing several varieties of fruit trees and hundreds of varieties of ginger, orchids, anthuriums, and other exotic plants. A botanical museum details the history of Hawaiian flora. Guided tours by tram are available. ⌧ *421 Makalika St., off Hwy. 11* ☎ *808/959–3500* ⊕ *www.nanimau.com* ⌦ *$10, tram tour $15* ⊗ *Daily 8–5.*

㊳ **Pacific Tsunami Museum.** A memorial to all those who lost their lives in the tragedies that have struck this side of the island, this small museum offers a poignant history of tsunamis. In a 1931 C. W. Dickey–designed building—former home of the First Hawaiian Bank—you'll find an interactive computer center, a science room, a theater, a replica of Old Hilo Town, a *keiki* (children's) corner, and a knowledgeable, friendly staff. In the background, a striking quilt tells a silent story. ⌧ *130 Kamehameha Ave.* ☎ *808/935–0926* ⊕ *www.tsunami.org* ⌦ *$7* ⊗ *Mon.–Sat. 9–4.*

☺ ㊼ **Pana'ewa Rain Forest Zoo.** Children enjoy the monkeys and the white tiger in this quiet, often wet zoo, which also hosts native Hawaiian species such as the state bird—the nēnē. It's the only rain-forest zoo in the United States. Trails have been paved, but you should take an umbrella for protection from the frequent showers. ⌧ *Stainback Hwy. off Hwy. 11* ☎ *808/959–7224* ⊕ *www.hilozoo.com* ⌦ *Free* ⊗ *Daily 9–4.*

㊻ **Pe'epe'e Falls.** Four separate streams fall into a series of circular pools, forming the Pe'epe'e Falls. The resulting turbulent action—best seen after a good rain when the water is high—has earned this stretch of the Wailuku River the name Boiling Pots. ⚠ **There's no swimming allowed in these pools due to extremely hazardous currents.** ⌧ *3 mi northwest of Hilo on Waiānuenue Ave.; keep to right when road splits and look for green sign.*

★ ㊺ **Rainbow Falls.** After a Hilo rain, these falls thunder into Wailuku River gorge. If the sun peeks out in the morning hours, rainbows form above the mist. ⚠ **There's no swimming allowed anywhere in the Wailuku River due to dangerous currents and undertows.** ⌧ *Take Waiānuenue Ave. west of town 1 mi; when road forks, stay on right of Waiānuenue Ave.; look for Hawaiian warrior sign.*

㊴ **S. Hata Building.** Erected as a general store in 1912 by Sadanosuke Hata and his family, this historic structure now houses shops, restaurants, and offices. During World War II the Hatas were interned and the building confiscated by the U.S. government. When the war was over, a daughter repurchased it for $100,000. A beautiful example of Renaissance-revival architecture, it won an award from the state for the authenticity of its restoration. ⌧ *308 Kamehameha Ave., at Mamo St.*

㊹ **Wailoa Center.** This circular exhibition center, adjacent to Wailoa State Park, has shows by local artists that change monthly. There's also a photographic exhibit of the 1946 and 1960 tidal waves. Just in front of the center is a 12-foot-high bronze statue of King Kamehameha I, made in

Italy in the late 1980s. Check out his gold Roman sandals. ⊠ *Pi'opi'o St. off Kamehameha Ave.* ☎ *808/933–0416* ⊙ *Mon., Tues., Thurs., and Fri. 8:30–4:30, Wed. noon–4:30, Sat. 9:30–3.*

Hāmākua Coast

The Hilo–Hāmākua Heritage Coast leads past green cliffs and gorges, waterfalls, jungle vegetation, open emerald fields, and stunning ocean scenery along Highway 19, which runs north-northwest from Hilo. Brown signs featuring a sugarcane tassel point out this area's history: thousands of acres of sugar land are now idle, as the area's sugar mills all went out of business by the late 1990s. "King Sugar," which once dominated daily life here, is no longer the economic backbone of the Hāmākua Coast community. The 45-mi drive winds through little plantation towns—Pāpa'ikou, Laupāhoehoe, and Pa'auilo among them. It's a great place to wander off the main road and see "real" Hawai'i—untouched nature, overgrown banyan trees, tiny coastal villages. In particular, the "Heritage Drive," a 4-mi loop just off the main highway, is well worth the detour. Once back on Highway 19, you'll pass the road to Honoka'a, which leads to the end of the road bordering Waipi'o Valley. The isolated valley floor has maintained the ways of old Hawai'i, with taro patches, wild horses, and a handful of houses.

a good drive

Seven miles north of Hilo, turn right off Highway 19 onto a 4-mi scenic drive to reach **Hawai'i Tropical Botanical Garden** 50 ▶. After the scenic drive rejoins Highway 19, turn left toward **Honomū** 51. At Honomū, travel 4 mi inland to **'Akaka Falls State Park** 52. Continue north on Highway 19 and stop at **Kolekole Beach Park** 53: it's a nice place for a picnic, and it has facilities. Keep heading north on Highway 19 and turn left to visit the 300-acre, still-growing **World Botanical Gardens** 54. From here you see stunning views of triple-tiered **Umauma Falls,** one of the prettiest waterfalls on the isle.

Continue north on Highway 19 and enjoy the ride through sleepy little villages with music in their names: Wailea, Hakalau, Ni'nole, Pāpa'aloa, and Laupāhoehoe. The **Laupāhoehoe Train Museum** 55 takes you back to the time when sugar reigned along the Hāmākua Coast.

Just beyond the museum is **Laupāhoehoe Point Park** 56, which is good for fishing but not swimming. About 13 mi farther inland, hikers will enjoy the nature walk through the cool upland forest of **Kalōpā State Park** 57.

Next, you reach the turnoff to **Honoka'a** 58. Secondhand and antiques stores, with dusty dishes, fabrics, and crafts, line Honoka'a's main street along with a few cafés and island-style eateries.

Just before the road (Route 240) ends, 8 mi beyond Honoka'a, a sign directs you to the right to Kukuihaele, a small, quiet plantation village on a coastal loop with no name. Here, at the Last Chance building and Waipi'o Valley Artworks gallery, you can make arrangements for tours to explore the 6-mi-deep Waipi'o Valley. The once heavily populated valley is a tropical Eden bounded by 2,000-foot cliffs. There are spectacular views of the valley and coast from the **Waipi'o Valley Overlook** 59, located at the very end of Route 240.

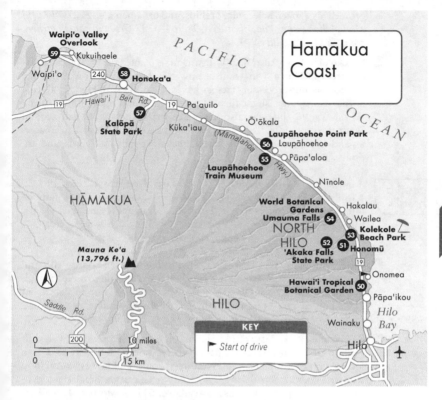

TIMING If you've stopped to explore the quiet little villages with wooden board-walks and dogs dozing in backyards, or if you've spent several hours in Waipi'o Valley, night will undoubtedly be falling by the time you complete this journey. Don't worry: the return to Hilo via Highway 19 only takes about an hour, or you can continue on the same road to stop for dinner in Waimea (30 minutes) and head to the Kohala Coast resorts (another 25 to 45 minutes).

What to See

★ **52** 'Akaka Falls State Park. A meandering 10-minute loop trail takes you to the best spots to see the two falls, **'Akaka** and **Kahuna**. The 400-foot Kahuna Falls is on the lower end of the trail. The majestic upper 'Akaka Falls drops more than 442 feet, tumbling far below into a pool drained by Kolekole Stream amid a profusion of fragrant white, yellow, and red torch ginger. ⊠ *4 mi inland off Hwy. 19, near Honomū* ☎ *808/974–6200* 🔁 *Free* ⊘ *Daily 7–7.*

★ ▶ **50** Hawai'i Tropical Botanical Garden. Eight miles north of Hilo, stunning coastline views appear around each curve of the 4-mi scenic jungle drive that accesses the privately owned, nonprofit, 17-acre nature preserve beside Onomea Bay. Paved pathways lead past waterfalls, ponds, and more than 2,000 species of plants and flowers, including palms, bromeliads, ginger, heleconia, orchids, and ornamentals. ⊠ 27-717 Old Māmalahoa Hwy., Pāpa'ikou ☎ 808/964–5233 ⊕ www.hawaiigarden. com ⊠ $15 ⊙ Daily 9–4.

⑤⑧ Honoka'a. In 1881 Australian William Purvis planted the first macadamia-nut trees in Hawai'i in what is now this funky little town. But the macadamia-nut-processing factory has long since closed. Honoka'a's true heyday came when sugar thrived, in the early and mid-1900s. During World War II, this was also the place for soldiers stationed around Waimea to cut loose. Its historic buildings are home today to little eateries and stores crammed with knickknacks, secondhand goods, and antiques. ⊠ Mamane St., Hwy. 240.

> **need a break?**
>
> A quick stop at **Tex Drive-In** (⊠ 45-690 Pakalana St. and Hwy. 19 ☎ 808/775–0598) will give you a chance to taste the snack it is famous for: *malasada,* a puffy, doughy Portuguese doughnut (sans hole), deep-fried and rolled in sugar and best eaten hot. They also come in cream-filled versions, including vanilla, chocolate, and coconut.

⑤① Honomū. A plantation past is reflected in the wooden boardwalks and tin-roof buildings of this small, struggling town. It's fun to poke through old, dusty shops such as Glass from the Past, where you find an assortment of old bottles. The Woodshop Gallery/Café showcases fine local art. ⊠ 2 mi inland from Hwy. 19 en route to 'Akaka Falls State Park.

★ ☺ ⑤⑦ Kalōpā State Park. Past the old plantation town of Pa'auilo, at a cool elevation of 2,000 feet, lies this 100-acre state park. There is a lush forested area with picnic tables and restrooms, and an easy ¾-mi loop trail with additional paths in the adjacent forest reserve. Small signs identify some of the plants. Cabins are available. ⊠ 12 mi north of Laupāhoehoe and 3 mi inland off Hwy. 19 ☎ 808/775–8852 ⊠ Free ⊙ Daily 7–7 or by permit.

⑤③ Kolekole Beach Park. This rocky beach at the mouth of the Kolekole River offers an idyllic setting for a barbecue or picnic. The river runs into the ocean just under an old train bridge. The beach is rocky next to the water, so it's a bit treacherous getting in, but once there it's a nice spot for a cool dip. ⚠ **Where the river meets the ocean, surf can be rough and currents strong. Only very experienced swimmers should venture past the river's mouth.** Back on the road, a scenic drive takes you from the top of the park through the old town of Wailea back to Highway 19. ⊠ Off Hwy. 19 ☎ 808/ 961–8311 ⊠ Free ⊙ Daily 7 AM–sunset.

⑤⑥ Laupāhoehoe Point Park. Come here to watch the surf pound the jagged black rocks at the base of the stunning point. ⚠ **This is not a safe place for swimming.** Still vivid in the minds of longtime area residents is the 1946 tragedy in which 21 schoolchildren and three teachers were swept to sea by a tidal wave. ⊠ On northeast coastline, Hwy. 19, makai side, north of Laupāhoehoe ☎ 808/961–8311 ⊠ Free ⊙ Daily 7 AM–sunset.

⑤⑤ Laupāhoehoe Train Museum. Behind the stone loading platform of the once-famous Hilo Railroad, constructed around the turn of the 20th century, the former manager's house is a poignant display of the era when sugar was king. The railroad, one of the most expensive built in its time, was washed away by the tidal wave of 1946. Today, one of the old engines is running again on a short Y-track at the museum. ⊠ *Hwy. 19, Laupāhoehoe, mauka side* ☏ *808/962–6300* 🖃 *$3* ☉ *Weekdays 9–4:30, weekends 10–2.*

Fodor'sChoice
★

Mauna Kea. Mauna Kea is the antithesis of the typical island experience. Freezing temperatures and arctic conditions are common at the summit, and snowstorms can occur year-round. It's also home to Lake Waiau, one of the highest lakes in the world. The summit—at 13,796 feet—is reputedly the clearest place in the world for viewing the night sky; it's also an outstanding place to see the sun rise and set. If you're driving to the summit on your own, stop in first at the **Onizuka Center for International Astronomy Visitor Information Station** (☏ 808/961–2180 ⊕ www.ifa.hawaii.edu/info/vis ☉ Daily 9–10), at a 9,300-foot elevation. (Technically it can be reached in a standard automobile, but you'll need four-wheel drive to get to the summit.) The observatory patio here is the best amateur observation site on Earth, with three telescopes and a knowledgeable staff. They host nightly stargazing sessions from 6 to 10. To reach the station from Hilo, which is about 34 mi away, take Highway 200 (Saddle Road), and turn right at mile marker 28 onto the John A. Burns Way, which is the access road to the summit.

Mauna Kea Summit Tours. On the weekend, the **Onizuka Center** offers a free, escorted summit tour, but you have to bring your own four-wheel-drive vehicle. Departure is at 1 PM, and reservations are not required. You must be 16 or older, in good health, and not pregnant.

If you haven't rented a four-wheel-drive vehicle, don't want to deal with driving up to the summit (it can be kind of a hassle), or want to stay and see the stars (the Onizuka tour gets everyone off the summit no later than a half hour after sunset), consider booking a tour. **Arnott's Lodge & Hiking Adventures** (☏ 808/969–7097 ⊕ www.arnottslodge.com) leaves from Hilo and is therefore a bit cheaper than the others. **Hawai'i Forest & Trail** (☏ 808/331–8505 or 800/464–1993 ⊕ www.hawaii-forest.com). and **Mauna Kea Summit Adventures** (☏ 808/322–2366 ⊕ http://maunakea.com) both pick people up along the West Coast. Mauna Kea only gives tours to the mountain, and they were the first ones to start doing it, so they generally have a bit more cred than the rest of the pack. All provide parkas, as well as telescopes, snacks, and meals; excursion fees range from about $90 to $165.

⚠ Whether you're hiking or driving to the summit, take the change in altitude seriously—don't overexert yourself, especially at the top. Note that scuba divers must wait at least 24 hours before attempting a trip to the summit to avoid getting the bends.

Waipi'o Valley. Though completely off the grid today, Waipi'o was once the center of Hawaiian life; somewhere between 4,000 and 20,000 people made it their home between the 13th and 17th centuries. In 1780 Kamehameha I was singled out here as a future ruler by reigning chiefs. In 1791 he fought Kahekili in his first naval battle at the mouth of the valley. In 1823 the first white visitors found 1,500 people living in this

Eden-like environment amid fruit trees, banana patches, taro fields, and fishponds. The 1946 tidal wave drove most residents to higher ground. Now, as then, waterfalls frame the landscape, but the valley has become one of the most isolated places in the state. To preserve this pristine part of the island, commercial transportation permits are limited—only four outfits offer organized valley trips—and Sunday the valley rests. The walk down into the valley is less than a mile—start at the four-wheel-drive road leading down from the lookout point—but keep in mind, the climb back up is strenuous in the hot sun.

If climbing back out of the valley is not an appealing prospect, or if your time is short, consider a guided tour. Costs range from about $40 to $145 depending on the tour. **Waipi'o on Horseback** (☎ 808/775–7291) and **Waipi'o (Na'alapa) Stables** (☎ 808/775–0419) offer horseback riding in the Valley. Other outfitters include **Waipi'o Rim Backroad Adventures** (☎ 808/775–1122 or 877/757–1414 ⊕ www.topofwaipio.com), **Waipi'o Valley Shuttle** (☎ 808/775–7121), and **Waipi'o Valley Wagon Tours** ☎ 808/775–9518.

★ ⓢ **Waipi'o Valley Overlook.** Bounded by 2,000-foot cliffs, the Valley of the Kings—Waipi'o—was once a favorite retreat of Hawaiian royalty. Waterfalls drop 1,200 feet from the Kohala Mountains to the valley floor. Sheer cliffs make access difficult. Only four-wheel-drive vehicles should attempt the steep road from the overlook. A handful of families still cultivate taro in the pastoral valley, a few residents find refuge here, and horses roam narrow trails and rocky streams. A crescent of black sand makes it a popular spot for surfers, but the beach is not safe for swimming due to strong currents and undertows. ⚠ **Continued overuse of the beach area and lack of sanitary facilities have caused serious unhealthy conditions to persist since mid-2003 at Waipi'o's beach.** Landowners and government officials are working to resolve the problem. ✉ *Follow Hwy. 240 8 mi northwest of Honoka'a.*

☺ ⓢ **World Botanical Gardens.** About 300 acres of former sugarcane land are slowly giving way to a botanical center, which includes native Hawaiian plants such as orchids, palms, gingers, hibiscus, heliconias, and more. In the 10-acre arboretum children love to wind their way through a maze of 5-foot shrubs. From within the gardens you have access to splendid views of one of the prettiest waterfalls on the isle, triple-tiered **Umauma Falls.** You may feel a little bit cheated, since it's $8 a person, but unfortunately this is the only place to see Umauma without some pretty rigorous hiking and scrambling. ✉ *Hwy. 19, from Hilo just past mile marker 16* ☎ *808/963–5427* ⊕ *www.wbgi.com* ✉ *$8* ☉ *Mon.–Sat. 9–5:30.*

Puna

The Puna District is a wild place in every sense of the word. The coast is relatively new and changing all the time; the trees are growing out of control to form canopies over the few paved roads; the land is dirt-cheap and there are no building codes; and the people, well, there's something about living in an area that could be destroyed by lava at any moment (as Kalapana was just a decade or so ago) that makes the laws of mod-

Puna

Kahakai Blvd.

**Cape Kumukahi
Lighthouse** 62

**Lava Tree
State Park** 61

Kapoho

Pāhoa 60

63

*Kapoho
Tide Pools*

132

132

137

PUNA

Pahoa

Pohoiki Rd.

**Ahalanui
Park** 64

*Isaac Hale
Beach Park*

65

**MacKenzie
State Recreation Area**

137

130

PACIFIC
OCEAN

5

Kehena Beach

**1986-1992
Lava Flows**

66

Kehena

Kaimū

**Star of the Sea
Painted Church**

KEY	
►	*Start of itinerary*

*Former Site of
Kalapana*

TO HAWAI'I VOLCANOES
NATIONAL PARK

0   5 miles

0   5 km

ern society seem silly. So it is that Puna has its well-deserved reputation as the "outlaw" region of the Big Island. That said, it's a unique place that's well worth a detour, especially if you're in this part of the island anyway. There are volcanically heated springs, and tide pools bursting with interesting sea life, a jagged black coastline, and some mighty fine people-watching opportunities in Pāhoa, a funky little old-west town that the outlaws call home. This is also farm country (yes, that kind of farm, too, but also the legal sort). Local farmers grow everything from orchids and anthuriums to papayas, bananas, and macadamia nuts. Several of the island's larger, rural residential subdivisions are between Kea'au and Pāhoa, including Hawaiian Paradise Park, Orchidland Estates, Hawaiian Acres, Hawaiian Beaches, and others.

**a good
drive**

Heading out from Hilo, turn left at Kea'au—or take the new bypass road (Highway 130) just south of this little town—and drive about 11 mi; then take the turnoff to **Pāhoa** 60 ►.

At the bypass intersection of Pāhoa, continue on Highway 132 in the direction of Kapoho. Take a break at **Lava Tree State Park** 61. Just south of the park entrance is the intersection of the highway and Pāhoa-Pohoiki Road. Continue southeast on Highway 132, passing papaya and orchid farms. As you near the coast, you pass through recent lava flows that cover the former town of Kapoho. The highway intersects with the coastal road, Highway 137, which turns south along the Kapoho–Opihikao coast, linking up with Highway 130 in the Kalapana area to complete the loop back to Pāhoa.

When it crosses Highway 137, Highway 132 terminates and becomes a gravel road that leads straight to the coast and **Cape Kumukahi Lighthouse** ⓺. After visiting the lighthouse, return to Highway 137 and go southwest along the coast, turning down Kapoho-Kai road to check out the **Kapoho Tide Pools** ⓺ before continuing on for a soak in the volcanically heated pond at **Ahalanui Park** ⓺.

From Ahalanui Park, continue driving southwest along Highway 137. This proves to be a narrow winding coastal road with some magnificent views of rugged coastline, plus relaxing stops at **MacKenzie State Recreation Area** ⓺ and **Kehena Beach.** After passing through the settlements of Pohoiki and Opihikao on the coast, the road links up with Highway 130 at the Kaimu-Kalapana area. This area marks the eastern expanse of lava flows of the early 1990s, which covered the Kalapana residential area and several fine black-sand beaches and parks. Take Highway 130 north back toward Pāhoa, stopping at **Star of the Sea Painted Church** ⓺, about a mile north of the intersection of Highways 130 and 137.

TIMING   The Pāhoa to Kapoho and Kalapana coast drive is a loop that's about 25 mi long; driving times are from two to three hours, depending on the number of stops you make and the length of time at each stop. There are long stretches of the road that may be completely isolated at any given point; this can be a little scary at night, but beautiful and tranquil during the day.

What to See

⓺ **Ahalanui Park.** This park was established with a federal grant in the mid-1990s to replace parks lost to the lava flows at Kalapana. It's 2½ mi south of the intersection of Highways 132 and 137 on the Kapoho Coast, southeast of Pāhoa town. There's a half-acre pond fed by thermal freshwater springs mixed with seawater, which makes for a relaxing warm-saltwater swim or soak. ⚠ However, there have been recent reports of occasional bacterial contamination; the health department has been monitoring the situation. Check with on-duty lifeguards and follow any posted advisory signs. Facilities include portable restrooms, outdoor showers, and picnic tables; no drinking water is available. ✉ *Hwy. 137, Puna District.*

⓺ **Cape Kumukahi Lighthouse.** The lighthouse, 1½ mi east of the intersection of Highways 132 and 137, was miraculously unharmed during the 1960 volcano eruption here that destroyed the town of Kapoho. The lava flowed directly up to the lighthouse's base but instead of pushing it over, actually flowed around it. According to Hawaiian legend, Pele, the volcano goddess, protected the Hawaiian fisherfolk by sparing the lighthouse. The lighthouse itself is a simple metal-frame structure with a light on top, similar to a tall electric-line transmission tower. Seeing the hardened lava flows skirting directly around the lighthouse is worth the visit. ✉ *Past intersection of Hwys. 132 and 137, Kapoho.*

63 Kapoho Tide Pools. This network of tide pools at the end of Kapoho-Kai Road are great for a swim or a snorkel, or even just a beautiful view of new coastline. Some of the pools are volcanically heated, so if your back's a little sore from exploring the island, stop for a 10-minute soak and you can feel better immediately. Take the road to the end, turn left and park. Some of the pools are on private property, but those closest to the ocean, Waiʻōpae (ponds), are open to all. ⊠ *End of Kapoho-Kai Rd., off Hwy. 137.*

61 Lava Tree State Park. Tree molds that rise like blackened smokestacks formed here in 1790 when a lava flow swept through the ʻōhiʻa forest. Some reach as high as 12 feet. The meandering trail provides close-up looks at some of Hawaii's tropical plants and trees. There are restrooms and a couple of picnic pavilions and tables. ■ TIP→→ Mosquitoes like to live here in abundance, so be sure to bring repellent. ⊠ *Hwy. 132, Puna District* ☎ *808/974–6200* 🄳 *Free* ⊘ *Daily 30 min before sunrise–30 min after sunset.*

65 MacKenzie State Recreation Area. This is a coastal park located on rocky shoreline cliffs in a breezy, cool ironwood grove. There are picnic tables, restrooms, and a tent-camping area; bring your own drinking water. The park is significant for the restored section of the old "King's Highway" trail system, which circled the island along the coast in the days before Hawaiʻi was discovered by the Western world. In those pre-Western-contact times, the Hawaiian tribal kings and chiefs used these trails to connect the coastal villages, allowing them to collect taxes and maintain control over the common people. Short hikes of an hour or less are possible along the existing sections of the rough rocky trail. There are views of rugged coast, rocky beach, and coastal dry forest. ⊠ *Hwy. 137, Puna District.*

▶ 60 Pāhoa. Sort of like an outlaw town from the Wild West, but with renegade Hawaiians instead of cowboys, this little town is all wooden boardwalks and rickety buildings. The secondhand stores, tie-dye clothing boutiques, and art galleries in quaint old buildings are fun to wander through, but Pahoa is not the best spot to go wandering around alone at night. Pāhoa's main street boasts several island eateries including **Luquin's Mexican Restaurant** and **The Godmother.** ■ TIP→→ Keep an ear open for the sound of the ubiquitous Kukio frogs; farmers consider them a pest both for the effect they have on crops and because they continuously let out the loudest, shrillest squeaks you've ever heard. ⊠ *Turn southeast onto Hwy. 130 at Keaʻau, drive 11 mi to right turn marked Pāhoa.*

66 Star of the Sea Painted Church. This historic church, now a community center, was moved to its present location in 1990 just ahead of the advancing lava flow that destroyed the Kalapana area. The church, which dates from the 1930s, was built by a Belgian Catholic missionary priest, Father Evarest Gielen, who also did the detailed paintings at St. Benedict's Painted Church in Hōnaunau. The building has several lovely stained-glass windows. ⊠ *Hwy. 130, 1 mi north of Kalapana.*

5

SIGHTSEEING TOURS

GUIDED TOURS ON THE ISLAND are great for specific things: seeing Mauna Kea, exploring Waipi'o Valley, maybe even touring Volcanoes National Park (especially if your time is short). Sticking to a guided tour the whole time, though, would not be a great idea. Half the fun of the island is in exploring it on your own. Plus, if you stick to a guided tour, you'll only see the major tourist attractions, none of the Big Island's many hidden treasures.

Local tour-bus operators conduct volcano tours and circle-island tours, with pickup at the major resorts.

Costs range from $38 to $68, depending on pickup location. The circle-island tour is a full 12-hour day, but Jack's and Polynesian Adventure Tours also offer half-day tours to the volcano, Mauna Kea observatory, and around Kailua-Kona.

Jack's Tours. ☎ 808/329-2555 in Kona, 808/961-6666 in Hilo, 800/442-5557 ⊕ www.jackstours.com.

Polynesian Adventure Tours. ☎ 808/329-8008 in Kona, 800/622-3011 ⊕ www.polyad.com.

Roberts Hawai'i. ☎ 808/329-1688 in Kona, 808/966-5483 in Hilo, 800/831-5541 ⊕ www.robertshawaii.com.

WHERE TO STAY

You'll almost always be able to find a room on the Big Island, but you might not get your first choice if you wait until the last minute. Make reservations six months to a year in advance if you're visiting during the winter season (December 15 through April 15). The week after Easter Sunday, when the Merrie Monarch Festival is in full swing, all of Hilo's rooms are taken. Kailua-Kona bursts at the seams in mid-October during the Ironman World Triathlon Championship. (Even tougher than trying to find a room at these times is trying to find a rental car.)

There are literally hundreds of vacation condo rentals in Kailua-Kona, and along the Kohala Coast, which is a good way to get more space at a lower cost and save some money by eating in (although it's easy to amass a huge bill at the grocery store, so you still have to be careful).

Hotel package deals are often available in all price categories and may include a rental car, meals, spa treatments, golf, and other activities. Children under 17 can sometimes stay for free. Check with a travel agent or visit the listed Web sites.

If you choose a B&B, inn, or an out-of-the-way hotel, explain your expectations fully and ask plenty of questions before booking. Be clear about your travel and location needs. Some places require stays of two or three days. When booking, ask about car-rental arrangements, as many B&B networks offer discounted rates. No matter where you stay, you'll want to rent a car—preferably one with four-wheel drive. This is imperative for getting to some of the best beaches and really seeing the island.

Members of the Big Island–based Hawai'i Island Bed and Breakfast Association are listed with phone numbers and rates in a comprehensive online brochure from the Hawai'i Island Bed and Breakfast umbrella organization. Or you can go with several network booking agencies that try to meet your needs on an individual basis.

Bed & Breakfast Honolulu (Statewide) (☎ 800/288–4666 🖷 808/595–7533 ⊕ www.hawaiibnb.com). **Hawai'i Island Bed and Breakfast Association** (⊕ www.stayhawaii.com). **Hawai'i's Best Bed and Breakfasts** (☎ 808/985–7488 or 800/262–9912 🖷 808/967–8610 ⊕ www.bestbnb.com).

For information on camping at county parks, including Spencer Beach Park, contact the **Department of Parks and Recreation** (⊠ 25 Aupuni St., Hilo 96720 ☎ 808/961–8311 ⊕ www.hawaii-county.com).

WHAT IT COSTS				
$$$$	**$$$**	**$$**	**$**	**¢**
HOTELS over $200	$150–$200	$100–$150	$60–$100	under $60

Hotel prices are for two people in a standard double room in high season, including tax and service.

Kohala Coast

Hotels & Resorts

$$$$ **🖼 The Fairmont Orchid Hawai'i.** The Fairmont is an elegant, old-school
Fodor'sChoice hotel—rooms are tasteful, the lobby is enormous with lots of marble and
★ sweeping ocean views, service is impeccable, and the restaurants are all top-notch. The grounds are expansive, lush, and well-maintained. This is one of the largest resorts, and its romantic botanical gardens and waterfall ponds stretch along 32 beachfront acres. Though they used to charge a "resort fee" for things like the morning paper and yoga classes, they now offer a $20 activity pass good for your entire stay that gets you access to all sorts of classes, equipment rentals, and various other amenities. The resort also offers 2½-hour voyages aboard an authentic Polynesian double-hull sailing canoe, the *Hahalua Lele*, or "Flying Manta Ray." Their new "Gold Floor" includes free breakfast and a daily wine and hors d'oeuvres hour. This can be especially useful for breakfast as there's nearly always a wait for a table at their breakfast restaurant. ⊠ *1 N. Kanikū Dr., Kohala Coast 96743* ☎ *808/885–2000 or 800/845–9905* 🖷 *808/885–8886* ⊕ *www.fairmont.com* 🛏 *486 rooms, 54 suites* ⚭ *4 restaurants, A/C, in-room broadband, in-room safes, minibars, cable TV with movies and video games, 2 18-hole golf courses, 10 tennis courts, pool, hair salon, health club, sauna, spa, beach, snorkeling, boating, basketball, volleyball, 4 bars, shop, children's programs (ages 5–12), business services; no smoking* ⊟ *AE, D, DC, MC, V. $309–$559.*

★ **$$$$** **🖼 Four Seasons Resort Hualālai.** Beautiful views everywhere, polished wood floors, warm earth and cool white tones, and Hawaiian artwork make Hualālai a peaceful retreat. Ground-level rooms have outdoor garden showers. Guest bungalows are large and cozy, with down comforters and spacious slate-floor bathrooms. One of the five pools, "King's Pond" is a brackish water pond housing loads of fish and two manta rays that guests have the opportunity to feed daily. The main infinity pool looks like something out of an ad for an expensive liquor—it's long and peace-

5

WHERE TO STAY: KOHALA COAST & WAIMEA

★ HOTEL NAME	Worth Noting	Cost $	Pools	Beach	Golf Course	Tennis Courts	Gym	Spa	Children Programs	Rooms	Restaurants	Other	Location
Hotels & Resorts													
★ 6 Fairmont Orchid Hawai'i	Impeccable Service	309–559	1	yes	yes	10	yes	yes	5–12	540	4		Kohala Coast
★ 1 Four Seasons Hualālai	Great Restaurants	560–775	5	yes	yes	8	yes	yes	5–11	274	3		Kohala Coast
★ 9 Hāpuna Beach Prince	Outstanding Beach	360–650	1	yes	yes	13	yes	yes	5–12	350	5	shops	Kohala Coast
★ 3 Hilton Waikoloa Village	Dolphin Quest	190–690	3	yes	yes	8	yes	yes	5–12	1,297	9	no A/C	Kohala Coast
★ 2 Kona Village Resort	Thatch-Roof Bungalows	530–940	2	yes	yes	3	yes		6–17	125	2	no A/C	Kohala Coast
★ 10 Mauna Kea Beach Hotel	Great lū'au	370–650	1	yes	yes	13	yes	yes	5–12	310	5		Kohala Coast
★ 7 Mauna Lani Bay Hotel	One-of-a-kind spa	395–850	1	yes	yes	16	yes	yes	5–12	350	6		Kohala Coast
4 Waikoloa Beach Marriott	Good deal	254–445	1	yes	yes	6	yes	yes	5–12	545	1		Kohala Coast
14 Waimea Country Lodge	Some kitchenettes	101–127								21		no A/C	Waimea
Condos													
5 Aston the Shores	Borders a golf course	285–400	1		yes	2				75		kitchens	Kohala Coast
8 Mauna Lani Point	Ocean front	325–650	1		priv.					61		kitchens	Kohala Coast
B&Bs & Vacation Rentals													
15 Cook's Discoveries Waimea	Private apartment	135								2		no A/C	Waimea
11 Hale Ho'onanea	Kitchenettes	100–130								3		no A/C	Kawaihae
12 Jacaranda Inn	1897 ranch house	159–350								9		no A/C	Waimea
13 Kamuela Inn	Good deal	59–85								31		no A/C	Waimea
15 Kohala Village Inn	Great for backpackers	65–95								17		no A/C	Hāwī
16 Kohala's Guest House	Near Pololū Valley	49–125								4		no A/C	Hāwī

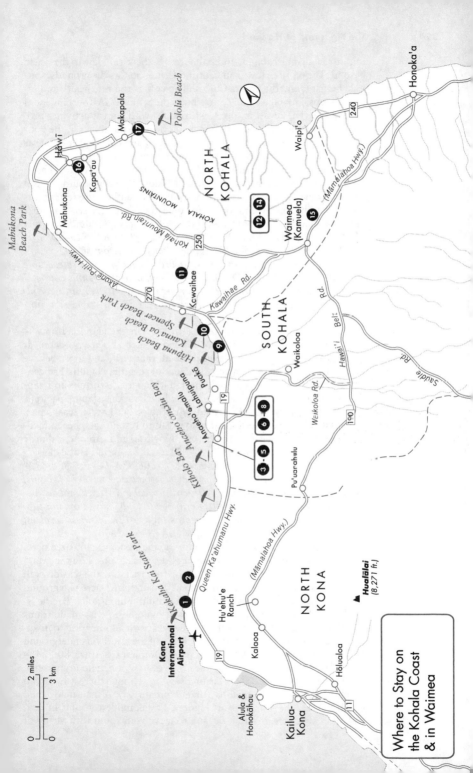

Where to Stay on the Kohala Coast & in Waimea

NORTH KOHALA

SOUTH KOHALA

NORTH KONA

Honoka'a

Pololū Beach

Makapala

Hāwī

Kapa'au

Māhukona

Mahukona Beach Park

KOHALA MOUNTAINS

Kawaihae

Kohala Mountain Rd.

Spencer Beach Park

Kauna'oa Beach

Hāpuna Beach

Puakō

Lahuipua'a

'Anaeho'omalu Bay

Kiholo Bay

Kekaha Kai State Park

Kona International Airport

Hu'ehu'e Ranch

Kalaoa

Alula & Honokōhau

Kailua-Kona

Hōlualoa

▲ *Hualālai* (8,271 ft.)

Waikoloa

Waikoloa Rd.

Pu'uanahulu

Waimea (Kamuela)

Kawaihae Rd.

Akoni Pule Hwy.

Queen Ka'ahumanu Hwy. (*Māmalahoa Hwy.*)

(*Māmalahoa Hwy.*)

Saddle Rd.

Waipi'o

(*Māmalahoa Hwy.*)

Hawai'i Belt Rd.

270

250

19

19

11

240

190

17

16

15

12 - 14

11

10

9

6 - 8

3 - 5

1

2

0   2 miles

0   3 km

ful, surrounded by cabanas and palm trees with a clear view to the ocean beyond. The on-site Hawaiian Cultural Center honors the grounds' spiritual heritage, and the Sports Club and Spa offers top-rate health and fitness options. Hualālai's golf course hosts the Senior PGA Tournament of Champions. The resort is super kid-friendly, with a great activities program. The downside is this: despite their efforts to the contrary, the Four Seasons doesn't feel much like Hawai'i; add to that the number of guests who will be squawking on their cell phones next to you at the pool (despite the posted "no cell phones" sign), and the too-good-to-be-true cheeriness of the staff with their near-constant "Aloha" greetings, and you can see why some folks avoid this place. Still, it's beautiful, the restaurants are perfect, the rooms are more than comfortable, and the service is definitely of Four Seasons quality. ⊠ *100 Ka'ūpūlehu Dr., Ka'ūpūlehu/Kona* ᴆ *Box 1269, Kailua-Kona 96745* ☎ *808/325–8000, 800/819–5053, or 888/340–5662* ᴃ *808/325–8200* ⊕ *www.fourseasons.com* ⬝ *243 rooms, 31 suites* ⬝ *3 restaurants, A/C, in-room broadband, in-room safes, cable TV with movies, in-room DVDs, 18-hole golf course, 8 tennis courts, 5 pools, health club, spa, beach, 2 bars, recreation room, babysitting, children's programs (ages 5–11), laundry service, business services, airport shuttle, no-smoking rooms* ▤ *AE, DC, MC, V. $560–$775.*

$$$$ ▣ **Hāpuna Beach Prince Hotel.** Locals love to hate the Hāpuna Prince— it's because of this hotel that you're no longer allowed to camp at Hāpuna Beach. The hotel's never done all that well, and most believe that its lack of success is karmic. Because of this, the Hāpuna Prince is often cheaper than its neighbors, though it's no less luxurious and happens to be sitting on a corner of the best beach on the island. Spacious, with marble bathrooms and private lānai, all rooms have at least a partial ocean view. Meandering pathways lead to restaurants, beach facilities, and a spectacular golf course. A hiking trail and a frequent shuttle connect Hāpuna with its partner, the Mauna Kea Beach Hotel. ⊠ *62- 100 Kauna'oa Dr., Kohala Coast 96743* ☎ *808/880–1111 or 800/882– 6060* ᴃ *808/880–3112* ⊕ *www.princeresortshawaii.com* ⬝ *314 rooms, 36 suites* ⬝ *5 restaurants, A/C, refrigerators, cable TV with movies, 18- hole golf course, 13 tennis courts, pool, health club, hair salon, hot tub, spa, beach, 2 bars, children's programs (age 5–12), business services, no-smoking rooms* ▤ *AE, D, DC, MC, V. $360–$650.*

$$$$
Fodor'sChoice
★
▣ **Hilton Waikoloa Village.** Dolphins chirp in the lagoon; a pint-sized daredevil zooms down the 175-foot water slide; a bride poses on the grand staircase; a fire-bearing runner lights the torches along the seaside path at sunset—these are the scenes that greet you at this 62-acre playground of a resort. Shaded pathways lined with a multimillion-dollar Pacific Island art collection connect the three tall buildings; Swiss-made trams and Disney-engineered boats shuttle the weary (in another nod to imagineering, employees access the various areas of the resort via underground tunnels, à la Disney World). The stars of **Dolphin Quest** (☎ 800/248– 3316 ⊕ www.dolphinquest.org) are the resort's pride and joy; reserve in advance for an interactive learning session. Though there is no ocean beach, there's a seaside trail to 'Anaeho'omalu Bay. A man-made sand beach borders the 4-acre resort lagoon. Large, modern rooms in neutral tones have private lānai. Be sure to leave your room with plenty of

time before any appointment, or you'll learn to appreciate the size of this place at top speed as you sprint past the tram. Brides-to-be take note: this is one-stop shopping; the resort has a wedding planning office, cakes, flowers, photography, and even fireworks and a "Just Married" boat ride. ⊠ *425 Waikoloa Beach Dr., Waikoloa 96738* ☎ *808/886–1234 or 800/445–8667* 🖷 *808/886–2900* ⊕ *www.hiltonwaikoloavillage.com* ↴ *1,240 rooms, 57 suites* ⟷ *10 restaurants, room service, A/C, in-room broadband, in-room safes, minibars, cable TV with movies, 2 18-hole golf courses, putting green, 8 tennis courts, 3 pools, health club, spa, beach, bike rentals, racquetball, snorkeling, volleyball, 9 bars, shops, babysitting, children's programs (ages 5–12), laundry service, laundry facilities, business services, car rental, no-smoking rooms* ▭ *AE, D, DC, MC, V. $199–$649.*

★ **$$$$** ⊞ **Kona Village Resort.** Without phones, TVs, or radios, the Kona Village is a time warp—the perfect place to completely get away from it all in your own thatch-roof *hale* (house) near the resort's sandy beach. Built on the grounds of an ancient Hawaiian village, the modern bungalows reflect styles of South Seas cultures—Tahitian, Samoan, Maori, Fijian, or Hawaiian. The extra large Royal rooms have private hot tubs. Rates include meals, an authentic Polynesian Friday-night lū'au, ground tours, tennis, sports activities, and rides in the resort's glass-bottom boat. ⊠ *Queen Ka'ahumanu Hwy., Box 1299, Kailua-Kona 96745* ☎ *808/ 325–5555 or 800/367–5290* 🖷 *808/325–5124* ⊕ *www.konavillage. com* ↴ *125 bungalows* ⟷ *2 restaurants, fans, 3 tennis courts, 2 pools, health club, hot tub, beach, boating, 3 bars, children's programs (ages 6–17; not available in May or Sept.), meeting room, airport shuttle; no A/C, no room phones, no room TVs* ▭ *AE, DC, MC, V. $530–$940.*

★ **$$$$** ⊞ **Mauna Kea Beach Hotel.** The Mauna Kea Beach Hotel is the grande dame of Kohala Coast hotels. Opened in 1965, it has long been regarded as one of the world's premier vacation resort hotels. It borders one of the islands' finest white-sand beaches, Kauna'oa. Rare works of art, such as a 7th-century Buddha, enhance walkways and open spaces. The rooms have a natural look with pastel tones and natural woods. Shuttles operate between the Mauna Kea and the adjacent Hāpuna Beach Prince Hotel, allowing guests to use the facilities at both hotels. ⊠ *62- 100 Mauna Kea Beach Dr., Kohala Coast 96743* ☎ *808/882–7222 or 800/882–6060* 🖷 *808/880–3112* ⊕ *www.princeresortshawaii.com* ↴ *300 rooms, 10 suites* ⟷ *5 restaurants, A/C, in-room safes, refrigerators, cable TV, 2 18-hole golf courses, 13 tennis courts, pool, health club, hair salon, spa, beach, children's programs (age 5–12), business services, no-smoking rooms* ▭ *AE, D, DC, MC, V. $370–$650.*

★ **$$$$** ⊞ **Mauna Lani Bay Hotel and Bungalows.** This is one of the oldest, and still one of the most beautiful, resorts on the island. The lobby is open-air with astronomically high ceilings and an old-money feel. Ninety percent of the spacious rooms have ocean views, and all have a large lānai; comfortable furnishings grace rooms with natural fabrics and teak. The resort is known for its two spectacular golf courses and their award-winning spa. The only downside here is the food—none of the restaurants would qualify as phenomenal (though the Canoe House is beautiful and has won awards at various points in its existence) and all are a bit

5

pricey. ⊠ *68-1400 Mauna Lani Dr., Kohala Coast 96743* ☎ *808/885–6622 or 800/367–2323* 🖷 *808/885–1484* ⊕ *www.maunalani.com* 🛏 *335 rooms, 10 suites, 5 bungalows* ♿ *6 restaurants, A/C, in-room data ports, in-room safes, refrigerators, minibars, cable TV, in-room VCRs, 2 18-hole golf courses, 16 tennis courts, pool, gym, spa, 5 bars, children's programs (ages 5–12), business services, no-smoking rooms* ▤ *AE, D, DC, MC, V. $395–$850.*

$$$$ 🏨 **Waikoloa Beach Marriott.** The most affordable of the Kohala Coast resorts, this hotel covers 15 acres, and encompasses ancient fishponds, historic trails, and petroglyph fields. All rooms have Hawaiian art and bamboo-type furnishings. The oversize cabana rooms overlook the lagoon. Reliable dining is available at the Hawai`i Calls restaurant. The Hawaiian Rainforest Salon & Spa offers a full range of treatments. Bordering the white-sand beach of `Anaeho`omalu Bay, the hotel has a range of ocean activities, including wedding-vow renewals on a catamaran. ⊠ *69-275 Waikoloa Beach Dr., Waikoloa 96738* ☎ *808/886–6789 or 800/688–7444* 🖷 *808/886–1554* ⊕ *www.marriott.com* 🛏 *524 rooms, 21 suites* ♿ *Restaurant, A/C, in-room broadband, refrigerators, cable TV with movies and video games, 2 18-hole golf courses, 6 tennis courts, pool, health club, hair salon, 2 hot tubs, sauna, spa, beach, 2 bars, children's programs (ages 5–12), laundry facilities, business services, no-smoking rooms* ▤ *AE, D, DC, MC, V. $254–$445.*

Condos

Along the Kohala Coast, most of the available condos are associated with the resorts and can be booked through the resort reservations desk.

$$$$ 🏨 **Aston the Shores at Waikoloa.** These red-tile-roof villas are set amid landscaped lagoons and waterfalls at the edge of the championship Waikoloa Village Golf Course. The spacious villas and condo units—the ground floor and upper floor are available separately—are privately owned, so all furnishings are different. Sliding glass doors open onto large lānai. Large picture windows look out on rolling green fairways. All units have complete kitchens with washer-dryer and come with maid service. Check their Web site for deals; separate rates are quoted for online booking. ⊠ *69-1035 Keana Pl., Waikoloa 96738* ☎ *808/886–5001 or 800/922–7866* 🖷 *808/922–8785* ⊕ *www.aston-hotels.com* 🛏 *75 1- and 2-bedroom units* ♿ *A/C, fans, kitchens, putting green, 2 tennis courts, pool, hot tub, laundry facilities, shop* ▤ *AE, D, DC, MC, V. 1-bedroom $285–$345, 2-bedroom $330–$400.*

$$$$ 🏨 **Mauna Lani Point Condominiums.** Surrounded by the emerald greens of a world-class oceanside golf course,

CONDO COMFORTS

There are fewer stores and takeout options on the Kohala coast, but, as the condos are all associated with resorts, most of your needs will be met. If you require anything not provided by the management, the **King's Shops at Waikoloa Village** (⊠ 250 Waikoloa Beach Dr., Waikoloa ☎ 808/886–8811) is the place to go. There's a small grocery store, a liquor store, and a couple of decent takeout options. It's not exactly cheap, but you're paying for the convenience of not having to drive into town.

spacious two-story suites offer a private, independent home away from home. The privately owned units, individually decorated according to the owners' tastes, have European cabinets and oversize soaking tubs in the main bedrooms. The pool has a little waterfall. You're just a few steps away from the Mauna Lani Bay Hotel and Bungalows, where you have access to golf, tennis, spa facilities, and restaurants. ⊠ *68-1050 Mauna Lani Point Dr., Kohala Coast 96743* ☎ *808/885–5022 or 800/642–6284* 🖷 *808/885–5015* ⊕ *www.classicresorts.com* 🗊 *24 1-bedroom units, 37 2-bedroom units* ♨ *BBQs, A/C, fans, some kitchens, some kitchenettes, TV, golf privileges, pool, hot tub, sauna* ☰ *AE, DC, MC, V. 1-bedroom $325–$445, 2-bedroom $425–$650, 3-night minimum stay.*

B&Bs & Vacation Rentals

$$ 🏨 **Hale Ho'onanea.** The Hawaiian translation of this comfortable home's name is "House of Relaxation." It sits on 3 acres in the Kohala Estates hills, above the ocean. From here you can watch the sun rise over Mauna Kea and set over the Pacific, and view the sparkling beauty of Hawai'i's night sky. It's minutes away from dining and shopping at Waimea and the attractions of the Kohala Coast resorts. Continental breakfast is included in the rates. There's a two-night minimum if you book less than a week in advance; $25 fee applied to single night bookings made within 7 days of arrival. ⊠ *Kohala Estates, 59-513 Ala Kahua Dr., Kawaihae 96743* ☎ *808/882–1653 or 877/882–1653* 🖷 *808/ 882–1653* ⊕ *www.houseofrelaxation.com* 🗊 *3 suites* ♨ *BBQs, kitchenettes, cable TV, library; no A/C* ☰ *No credit cards. $100–$130.*

¢–$$ 🏨 **Kohala's Guest House.** In rural North Kohala, the birthplace of King Kamehameha, contemporary comforts and the aloha style of old meet in the tropical orchard property of Don and Nani Svendsen. The cozy studio and three-bedroom rental house, adorned with Svendsen's flowers, are minutes away from Pololū Valley. It's just 30 minutes to the white-sand beaches of the resorts. Close to the shops, eateries, and activities in Hāwī and Kapa'au, but sheltered from heavy tourism, you can live like the locals here. The house can be rented for families or as separate room units. 🖆 *Box 172, Hāwī 96719* ☎ *808/889–5606* 🖷 *808/889–5572* 🗊 *1 studio, 1 three-bedroom house (for families or rented as separate room units)* ♨ *No A/C* ☰ *No credit cards. $49–$125.*

¢–$ 🏨 **Kohala Village Inn.** Located in the heart of Hāwī town in the rural far-north peninsula of the Big Island, this budget no-frills country lodge offers clean and simple rooms and continental breakfast. It's perfect for backpackers or those seeking the opposite of the resort experience. Some rooms accommodate up to six. It's steps away from Hāwī dining and shops. There's easy access to Pololū Valley, Kapa'au, Mo'okini Heiau, King Kamehameha's birthplace, and whale-watching spots. ⊠ *55-514 Hāwī Rd., Box 74, Hāwī 96719* ☎ *808/889–0404* ⊕ *www.kohalavillageinn. com* 🗊 *17 rooms* ♨ *Cable TV; no A/C* ☰ *MC, V. $65–$95.*

Waimea

Hotels & Resorts

$$ 🏨 **Waimea Country Lodge.** In the heart of cowboy country, next door to the Paniolo Country Inn, this quiet, modest lodge offers views of the green, rolling slopes of Mauna Kea yet is close to the activity of busy Waimea town. The rooms are adequate and clean, with Hawaiian quilts lending them a personal touch. There are rooms with kitchenettes available for $110. There's a continental breakfast included in the rate, and you can arrange to charge meals at Merriman's restaurant and the Paniolo Country Inn to your room. ⊠ *65-1210 Lindsey Rd., Waimea* ☏ *Box 2559, Kamuela 96743* ☎ *808/885–4100 or 800/367–5004* 🖷 *808/885–6711* ⊕ *www.castleresorts.com/WCL* ⌨ *21 rooms* △ *In-room data ports, some kitchenettes, cable TV with movies, no-smoking rooms; no A/C* ⊟ *AE, D, DC, MC, V. $101–$127.*

B&Bs & Vacation Rentals

$$$–$$$$ ▦ **Jacaranda Inn.** Built in 1897, this sprawling estate was once the home of the Parker Ranch manager. Charming inside and out, it's been completely restored in raspberry and lavender colors, with lots of koa wood and Upcountry Victorian elements, and most of the rooms have Jacuzzis. The units are booked under two separate plans. Plan A includes daily maid service, full breakfasts, and a bottle of wine; Plan B is simpler, with continental breakfast and less service. ⊠ *65-1444 Kawaihae Rd., Waimea 96743* ☎ *808/885–8813* 🖷 *808/885–6096* ⊕ *www. jacarandainn.com* ⌨ *8 suites, 1 cottage* △ *Some in-room hot tubs, billiards, recreation room; no A/C, no room phones, no room TVs, no smoking* ⊟ *MC, V. $159–$225, cottage $350.*

$$ ▦ **Cook's Discoveries Waimea Suite.** Patti Cook, owner of the well-known Cook's Discoveries arts-and-crafts shop in Waimea, has opened her elegant Waimea country home to guests. The Waimea Suite is a private lower apartment unit that opens onto an expansive lawn with beautiful trees framing views of Mauna Kea. The common living room has beautiful antique furniture and decorative artwork. The double and twin bedrooms are tastefully furnished. Make a direct booking and receive a $20 gift certificate to Cook's Discoveries; stay six nights and you get the seventh night free. ⊠ *64-5246 Lokua St., Hwy. 19 at Kamamalu St., Waimea 96743* ☎ *808/937–2833* 🖷 *808/885–9691* ⊕ *www.hawaii-island.com/cooks.htm* ⌨ *2 rooms* △ *Kitchen, cable TV, in-room VCR; no A/C, no smoking* ⊟ *AE, D, MC, V. $135, 2-night minimum.*

$ ▦ **Kamuela Inn.** The rooms in this unpretentious, peaceful inn, just 20 minutes from the island beaches, are basic but clean. Small lānai look out over the inn's gardens. Depending on your needs, you can choose anything from a no-nonsense single bedroom to two connecting penthouse suites with a lānai and full kitchen. ⊠ *65-1300 Kawaihae Rd., Box 1994, Waimea 96743* ☎ *808/885–4243 or 800/555–8968* 🖷 *808/ 885–8857* ⊕ *www.kamuelainn.com* ⌨ *20 rooms, 11 suites* △ *Some kitchenettes, cable TV; no A/C, no phones in some rooms* ⊟ *AE, D, DC, MC, V. $59–$85.*

Kailua-Kona

Hotels & Resorts

$$$$ ▦ **Royal Kona Resort.** This is a great option if you're on a budget, with the added bonus of being a nice place. The lobby and restaurants are right on the water, and rooms (all with lānai) are decked out in Hawai-

ian kitsch. The resort is within walking distance of Kailua-Kona and right across from shops and restaurants. Little artificial streams and a private lagoon with a sandy beach set the stage for carefree tropical living. The resort hosts a weekly lū'au with Polynesian entertainment. ⊠ *75-5852 Ali'i Dr., Kailua-Kona 96740* ☎ *808/329–3111 or 800/222–5642* 🖷 *808/329–9532* ⊕ *www.royalkona.com* ↩ *452 rooms, 8 suites* ♺ *Restaurant, A/C, in-room data ports, in-room safes, refrigerators, cable TV with movies, 4 tennis courts, pool, health club, hair salon, spa, beach, bar, laundry facilities, Internet room, no-smoking rooms* ▭ *AE, D, DC, MC, V. $210–$385.*

$$$$ ▦ **Sheraton Keauhou.** The Sheraton corporation took over the old Kona Surf hotel, which had been rotting away for a good many years at the edge of Keauhou Bay, and restored it to glory. Or at least they're trying—there are still some rusty pipes left from the good old days that cause some plumbing problems from time to time. To be fair, they only just opened, so they're still working out the kinks, and it's a huge improvement over what was there before. The lobby is particularly stunning, and well-designed Kai serves a limited but excellent menu. The pool, which can only be described as massive, is the coolest pool on the island, with a slide, waterfalls, and an ocean view. The rooms, though, are less impressive, and they seem to have scrimped on the details (rough sheets and bathrooms that don't look like they've changed at all from the Kona Surf). At this writing, they were still working on the spa, but it will be oceanfront, which is always a good start. ⊠ *78-128 Ehukai St., Kailua-Kona* ☎ *808/930-4900* ⊕ *www.sheratonkeauhou.com* ↩ *521 rooms and suites* ♺ *Restaurant, A/C, in-room data ports, Wi-Fi, in-room safes, refrigerators, cable TV with movies, 2 tennis courts, pool, health club, beach, volleyball, bar, playground, business services, no-smoking rooms* ▭ *AE, D, DC, MC, V. $335–$460.*

$$$-$$$$ ▦ **King Kamehameha's Kona Beach Hotel.** Rooms are not particularly special here (the fifth- and sixth-floor oceanfront rooms are best), but what you get instead of the luxury of upscale Kohala resorts is a great central Kailua-Kona location with a small white-sand family beach and a calm swimming bay, right next to Kailua Pier. Visitors can explore the grounds and Ahu'ena Heiau, which King Kamehameha I had reconstructed in the early 1800s. The hotel serves an ample champagne brunch every Sunday and hosts a fabulous beachfront Polynesian lū'au several nights a week. ⊠ *75-5660 Palani Rd., Kailua-Kona 96740* ☎ *808/329–2911 or 800/367–6060* 🖷 *808/329–4602* ⊕ *www.konabeachhotel.com* ↩ *455 rooms* ♺ *2 restaurants, A/C, in-room data ports, in-room safes, cable TV with movies, tennis courts, pool, hair salon, hot tub, sauna, beach, 2 bars, shops, laundry facilities, laundry service, travel services* ▭ *AE, D, DC, MC, V. $170–$250.*

$$-$$$$ ▦ **Outrigger Keauhou Beach Resort.** Though it has won awards for preservation of its unique history (its grounds include a heiau, a sacred fishpond, and a replica of the summer home of King David Kalākaua), the Keauhou is not doing such a hot job at preserving their guest accommodations. That said, if you can find a good rate, this is still a decent place to stay, mainly for its proximity to Kahalu'u, one of the best snorkeling beaches on the island. ⊠ *78-6740 Ali'i Dr., Kailua-Kona 96740*

WHERE TO STAY: KONA COAST & UPCOUNTRY

★ HOTEL NAME	Worth Noting	Cost $	Pools	Beach	Golf Course	Tennis Courts	Gym	Spa	Children Programs	Rooms	Restaurants	Other	Location
Hotels & Resorts													
13 King Kamehameha's Kona	Great lū'au	170–250	1	yes		1				455	2	shops	Kailua-Kona
12 Kona Seaside Hotel	Across from Kailua Bay	60–120	2				yes			224			Kailua-Kona
10 Kona Tiki Hotel	Oceanfront bargain	61–84	1							15		no A/C	Kailua-Kona
6 Outrigger Keauhou	Historic grounds	119–250	1	yes		6	yes			317	1		Kailua-Kona
11 Royal Kona Resort	Good deal	210–385	1	yes		4	yes	yes		460	1		Kailua-Kona
5 Sheraton Keauhou	Cool pool	335–460	1	yes		2	yes			521	1		Kailua-Kona
Condos													
9 Aston Kona by the Sea	On the ocean	270–445	1					yes		78		kitchens	Kailua-Kona
4 Kanaloa at Kona	Borders country club	169–315	3			2				166	1	kitchens	Kailua-Kona
8 Kona Bali Kai	Near beach and town	75–167	1							62		kitchens	Kailua-Kona
7 Kona Magic Sands	Ocean views	93–112	1							37	1	kitchens	Kailua-Kona
B&Bs & Vacation Rentals													
1 Bougainvillea B&B	Remote and secluded	70–75	1							3			South Point
14 Hōlualoa Inn	Artist colony	175–205	1							6		no A/C	Hōlualoa
2 Horizon Guest House	40 acres of grounds	250	1							4		no A/C	Hōnaunau
3 Manago Hotel	Old Hawai'i vibe	31–70								64	1	no A/C	Captain Cook

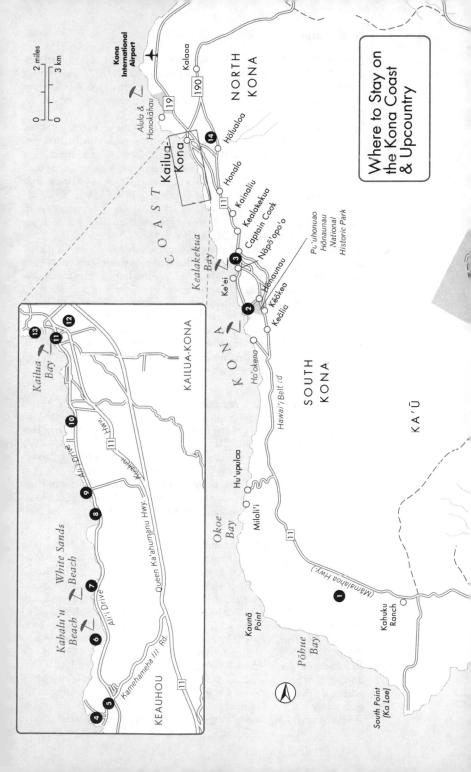

Where to Stay on the Kona Coast & Upcountry

☎ 808/322–3441 or 800/462–6262 🖷 808/322–3117 ⊕ www.outrigger. com ⬠ 311 rooms, 6 suites ☖ Restaurant, A/C, cable TV with movies and video games, 6 tennis courts, pool, health club, beach, bar, laundry facilities, laundry service, parking (fee), no-smoking rooms ▭ AE, D, DC, MC, V. $119–$250.

$–$$ ▥ **Kona Seaside Hotel.** If you're on a budget, want a central location, and don't need resort extras, spacious rooms, or lavish bathrooms, you'll feel at home in this casual hotel. It's on a busy intersection, right across the street from Kailua Bay. Rooms nearest the main street are built around a private pool. The staff is very friendly. ⊠ 75-5646 Palani Rd., Kailua-Kona 96740 ☎ 808/329–2455 or 800/560–5558 🖷 808/329–6157 ⊕ www.konaseasidehotel.com ⬠ 223 rooms, 1 suite ☖ A/C, fans, refrigerators, cable TV, 2 pools, gym, bar, laundry facilities, no-smoking rooms ▭ AE, D, DC, MC, V. $60–$120.

¢–$ ▥ **Kona Tiki Hotel.** The best thing about this three-story walk-up budget hotel, about a mile south of Kailua-Kona, is that all the units have lānai right next to the ocean. The rooms are modest but pleasantly decorated. You can sunbathe by the seaside pool, where a continental breakfast is also served. Some would call this place old-fashioned; others would say it's local and the best deal in town, with glorious sunsets no different from those at the resorts. ⊠ 75-5968 Ali'i Dr., Kailua-Kona 96745 ☎ 808/329–1425 🖷 808/327–9402 ⬠ 15 rooms ☖ BBQ, fans, refrigerators, pool, beach; no A/C, no room phones, no room TVs ▭ No credit cards. $61–$84.

Condos

When booking a condo, remember that most are individually owned and that most owners oursource the rental process. Renters make arrangements through property management companies. **Property Network** (🏠 75-5799 B-3 Ali'i Dr., Kailua-Kona 96740 ☎ 808/329–7977 🖷 808/329–1200 ⊕ www.hawaii-kona.com) looks after most of the vacation rentals on the Kona side of the island. With over 250 units in nearly every condo complex along Ali'i Drive, Property Network can find exactly what you're looking for, whether you're on a budget or looking to splurge on a deluxe oceanfront rental. You can also browse their Web site for photos of available units to find the perfect one.

$$$$ ▥ **Aston Kona by the Sea.** Complete modern kitchens, tile lānai, and a washer-dryer can be found in every suite of this comfortable oceanfront condo complex. Despite being near the bustling town of Kailua-Kona, this four-story place is quiet and relaxing. The nearest sandy beach is 2 mi away, but the pool is next to the ocean. ⊠ 75-6106 Ali'i Dr., Kailua-Kona 96740 ☎ 808/327–2300 or 800/922–7866 🖷 808/922–8785 ⊕ www.aston-hotels.com ⬠ 37 1-bedroom units, 41 2-bedroom units ☖ A/C, kitchens, cable TV, pool, hot tub, spa, no-smoking rooms ▭ AE, D, DC, MC, V. 1-bedroom $270–$385, 2-bedroom $335–$445.

$$$–$$$$ ▥ **Kanaloa at Kona.** The 16-acre grounds provide a peaceful, spacious, and verdant background for this low-rise condominium complex bordering the Keauhou-Kona Country Club. It's walking distance to the golf course but a five-minute drive to the nearest beaches (Kahalu'u and White Sands). Large one-, two-, and three-bedroom apartments have

koa-wood cabinetwork and washer-dryers; oceanfront villas have private hot tubs. Edward's at Kanaloa Restaurant serves excellent Mediterranean cuisine. ⊠ *78-261 Manukai St., Kailua-Kona 96740* ☎ *808/322–9625, 808/322–2272, or 800/688–7444* 🖷 *808/322–3818* ⊕ *www.outrigger.com* ⇩ *166 units* ⚲ *Restaurant, in-room safes, kitchenettes, 2 tennis courts, 3 pools, hot tub, bar, laundry facilities; no A/C in some units* ⊟ *AE, D, DC, MC, V. 1-bedroom $169–$265, 2-bedroom $185–$315, 2-night minimum.*

$–$$$ 🏨 **Kona Bali Kai.** Though slightly older, with rattan furnishings and a basic layout, these condominium units, spread out through three low-rises on the ocean side of Ali'i Drive, do have a pretty good location; they're just a couple of minutes from Kailua-Kona and walking-distance to popular White Sands beach. And they're great for families. Kitchens are fully equipped, and there's a little convenience store. If you can afford it, choose an oceanfront unit for the luxury of quiet sunsets. ⊠ *76-6246 Ali'i Dr., Kailua-Kona 96740* ☎ *808/329–9381 or 800/535–0085* 🖷 *808/326–6056* ⊕ *www.marcresorts.com* ⇩ *13 studios, 25 1-bedroom, 24 2-bedroom* ⚲ *BBQ, A/C in some rooms, fans, kitchens, in-room VCRs, pool, hair salon, hot tub, shop, laundry facilities* ⊟ *AE, D, DC, MC, V. Studios $75–$95, 1-bedroom $100–$125, 2-bedroom $135–$167.*

$–$$ 🏨 **Kona Magic Sands.** Cradled between two small beach parks, one of which is Magic Sands, this condo complex is great for swimmers and sunbathers in summer (the sand washes away in winter). Units vary because they're individually owned, but all are oceanfront, spacious, and light. Some units have enclosed lānai, and all have an ocean view. ⊠ *77-6452 Ali'i Dr., Kailua-Kona 96740* ☎ *808/329–9393 or 800/622–5348* 🖷 *808/326–4137* ⊕ *www.konahawaii.com* ⇩ *37 units* ⚲ *Restaurant, kitchens, kitchenettes, pool, bar; no A/C in some rooms* ⊟ *MC, V. Studios $93–$112.*

B&Bs & Vacation Rentals

$$$–$$$$ 🏨 **Hōlualoa Inn.** Six spacious rooms are available in this cedar home on a 40-acre Upcountry orchard estate with glorious coastal views, 4 mi above Kailua Bay. The artists' town of Hōlualoa is steps away. Each room has an island theme. The premium Balinese suite has wraparound windows with stunning views. A lavish breakfast includes estate-grown coffee as well as homemade breads and macadamia-nut butter. Rooftop gazebos inspire quiet, relaxing moments, and for stargazers there's a telescope. ⊠ *76-5932 Māmalahoa Hwy., Box 222, Hōlualoa 96725* ☎ *808/*

CONDO COMFORTS

Crossroads Shopping Center. The Safeway here is the cleanest, largest, and best-stocked store on the island. It's right next to Kona Natural Foods, so you can supplement what you find at Safeway with local organic produce and other tasty treats. There's also a Coldstone Creamery in this shopping center, so you've got dessert taken care of, too. ⊠ *75-1000 Henry St., Kailua-Kona.*

Pizza-wise, Kona Brewing Company is best if you're willing to go pick it up. Otherwise, Domino's (☎ 808/329–9500) is actually good here.

Blockbuster. ⊠ *Kona Coast Shopping Center, 74-5588 Palani Rd., Kailua-Kona* ☎ *808/326–7694.*

5

324–1121 or 800/392–1812 🖷 *808/322–2472* ⊕ *www.holualoainn.com* 🛏 *6 rooms* △ *Fans, pool, hot tub, billiards; no A/C, no room TVs, no kids under 13, no smoking* 🗀 *AE, D, DC, MC, V.* 🖴 *$175–$205, 2-night minimum.*

South Kona & Ka'u

$$$$ 🖽 **Horizon Guest House.** About 30 mi south of Kona, at an elevation of 1,100 feet on 40 acres overlooking the Kona Coast, this private luxury retreat offers tranquility, comfort, sweeping views, and a state-of-the-art solar-heated pool. Hawaiian quilts, collectibles, and antiques give personality and warmth to the four spacious suites, all with private lānai. Host Clem Classen's generous breakfast starts your day. The estate borders the native forests of the 15,000-acre McCandless Ranch. ⍟ *Box 268, Hōnaunau 96726* 🖀 *808/328–2540 or 888/328–8301* 🖷 *808/328–8707* ⊕ *www.horizonguesthouse.com* 🛏 *4 suites* △ *BBQ, refrigerators, pool, hot tub, library, laundry facilities, Internet; no A/C, no kids under 14, no smoking* 🗀 *MC, V. $250, 2-night minimum.*

$ 🖽 **Bougainvillea Bed & Breakfast.** This large country home is off Highway 11 at Ocean View Estates (between mile markers 77 and 78). The remote, quiet area is close to South Point and the rural charm of Ka'u District and within easy distance of Hawai'i Volcanoes National Park, hiking, and black- and green-sand beaches. Breakfast is served on the lānai. There are restaurants, a Laundromat, a grocery store, and a gas station nearby. ⍟ *Box 6045, Ocean View 96737* 🖀 *808/929–7089 or 800/688–1763* ⊕ *hi-inns.com/bouga* 🛏 *3 rooms* △ *A/C, in-room VCRs, pool, hot tub, massage, lounge* 🗀 *MC, V. $70–$75.*

¢–$ 🖽 **Manago Hotel.** This historic hotel is a great deal, and a good option if you want to escape the touristy thing but still be close to everything you'd want to see on the island. Don't let the front TV room creep you out—you have not just checked into an old folks' home. Rooms in the newer wing come with great ocean views high above the Kona Coast, and their restaurant is one of the best on the island. To honor his grandparents, Kinzo and Osame Manago, who built the main hotel in 1917, Dwight Manago has maintained one Japanese-style room with tatami mats and a *furo,* a traditional Japanese bath. The other rooms are nothing special, but the hotel has an authentic old Hawai'i vibe. ⊠ *81–6155 Māmalahoa Hwy., Box 145, Captain Cook 96704* 🖀 *808/323–2642* 🖷 *808/323–3451* ⊕ *www.managohotel.com* 🛏 *64 rooms, 42 with bath* △ *Restaurant, bar; no A/C, no room TVs* 🗀 *D, MC, V. $31–$70.*

Volcano

Hotels & Resorts

$–$$$$ 🖽 **Volcano House.** This is a hotel on the very rim of a volcano. Knockout views of Kīlauea Caldera are worth a visit even if you're not staying here. It's the only lodging (except for cabins or camping) within the National Park grounds. Alas that the 1941 hotel itself is looking so worn, with its tired carpets and '50s-era furnishings. Book a crater-view room as far from the busy dining room area as possible, and enjoy the views. ⊠ *Crater Rim Dr., Box 53, Hawai'i Volcanoes National Park, 96718*

☎ *808/967–7321* ▤ *808/967–8429* ⇦ *42 rooms* ♨ *Restaurant, snack bar, shop; no A/C* ▭ *AE, D, DC, MC, V. $95–$225.*

B&Bs & Vacation Rentals

$$–$$$$ 🏠 **Hydrangea Cottage & Mountain House.** You'll find this landscaped jungle estate about a mile from Hawai'i Volcanoes National Park. The private one-bedroom cottage has a wraparound covered deck and floor-to-ceiling windows looking out over giant tree ferns. The Mountain House has three bedrooms with antique furnishings, each with its own bath. Both units have a kitchen and breakfast fixings are provided. ℗ *Reservations: Pacific Islands Reservations, 571 Pauku St., Kailua-Kona 96734* ☎ *808/262–8133* ▤ *808/262–5030* ⊕ *www.aloha.com/~pir/ hydcott.html* ⇦ *1 3-bedroom house, 1 cottage* ♨ *Kitchen, cable TV, in-room VCRs, laundry facilities; no A/C* ▭ *No credit cards. 1-bedroom cottage $125-$150, 3-night minimum; 3-bedroom house $375–$450, 4-night minimum.*

¢–$$$$ 🏠 **Chalet Kīlauea Collection.** The Collection comprises five inns and lodges and five vacation houses in and around Volcano Village; the theme rooms, suites, and vacation homes range from no-frills dorm-style bedrooms in a funky old house to a plantation mansion with its own six-person Jacuzzi. Best known is the **Inn at Volcano,** a "boutique resort." Afternoon tea is served before a fireplace. A candlelit breakfast under a glittering chandelier adds a touch of elegance. Double occupancy rooms here are $139–$159. The Inn's two-story Treehouse Suite ($299), with wraparound windows, a marble wet bar, and a fireplace, gives one the impression of floating on the tops of the trees. Less well-known but more reasonably priced, **Volcano Bed and Breakfast** (☞ $49–$69 double occupancy room) has a communal kitchen and fireplace. ⊠ *Wright Rd., Volcano Village 96785* ☎ *808/967–7786 or 800/937–7786* ▤ *808/ 967–8660* ⇦ *11 rooms, 9 suites, 5 houses* ♨ *Some kitchens, some microwaves, cable TV with movies; no A/C, no phones in some rooms, no smoking* ▭ *AE, D, DC, MC, V. $49–$399.*

★ $$–$$$ 🏠 **Kīlauea Lodge.** A mile from the Hawai'i Volcanoes National Park entrance, this country inn is tastefully furnished and cozy, with fireplaces. The original building dates from the 1930s, and rooms have rich quilts, Hawaiian photographs, and European antiques, as well as their own wood-burning fireplaces. Two cottages off the main property include the two-bedroom Tutu's Place, and Pii Mauna House on the 6th fairway of the Volcano Golf Course. On property, a charming one-bedroom cottage with a gas fireplace and a deluxe honeymoon room with a private balcony are perfect for romance. Rates include breakfast. ⊠ *Old Volcano Hwy. about 1 mi northeast of Volcano Store* ℗ *Box 116, Volcano Village 96785* ☎ *808/967–7366* ▤ *808/967–7367* ⊕ *www.kilauealodge.com* ⇦ *11 rooms, 3 cottages* ♨ *Restaurant, dining room, hot tub, shop; no A/C, no TV in some rooms, no smoking* ▭ *AE, MC, V. $140–$165.*

$$ 🏠 **Carson's Volcano Cottages.** You can choose the privacy of a romantic hideaway with a full kitchen and a hot tub in the midst of hapu ferns; a deluxe oceanfront cottage down at Kapoho, an hour away; or the intimate rooms and cottages around the property itself. Each unit has its own theme decor, from country-style to Hawaiian. Elaborate breakfasts in the

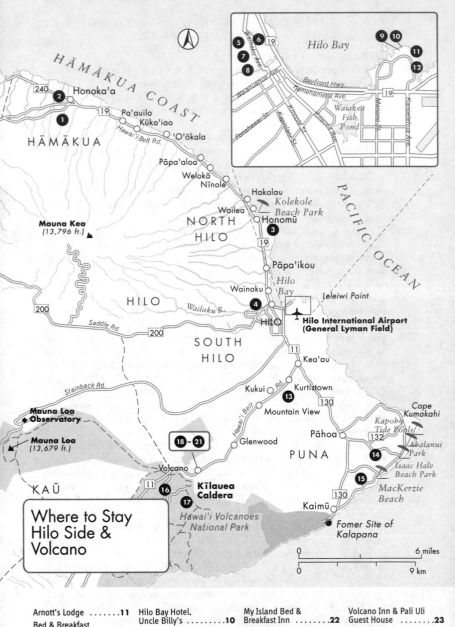

Where to Stay
Hilo Side &
Volcano

Arnott's Lodge **11**

Bed & Breakfast
Mountain View **13**

Carson's Volcano
Cottages **18**

Chalet Kīlauea
Collection **19**

Dolphin Bay Hotel **8**

Hale Kai **6**

Hilo Bay Hotel,
Uncle Billy's **10**

Hilo Hawaiian Hotel **9**

Hilo Seaside Hotel **12**

Hydrangea Cottage &
Mountain House **20**

Kalani Oceanside
Retreat **15**

Kīlauea Lodge **21**

My Island Bed &
Breakfast Inn **22**

Nāmakani Paio Cabins . **17**

Shipman House
Bed & Breakfast Inn **5**

The Inn at Kulaniapia . . **4**

The Palms Cliff
House Inn **3**

Volcano House **16**

Volcano Inn & Pali Uli
Guest House **23**

Waianuhea **1**

Waipi'o Wayside **2**

Waterfalls Inn
Bed & Breakfast **7**

Yoga Oasis **14**

main house's cozy dining room include home-baked breads and such dishes as spinach quiche and poi doughnuts. ⌂ *Box 503, Volcano 96785* 🖃 *808/ 967-7683 or 800/845-5282* 🖶 *808/967-8094* ⊕ *www.carsonscottage. com* ⋒ *5 rooms, 6 cottages* ⚭ *Dining room, hot tub, no-smoking room; no A/C, no phones in some rooms* 🖃 *AE, D, MC, V. $110–$125.*

$$ ▨ **Volcano Inn & Pali Uli Guest House.** Nestled among tree ferns within a rain forest, Volcano Inn offers a choice of four private rooms with enormous picture windows, one of three rooms in the main Pali Uli Guest House, or a separate studio with kitchenette (Sushi Guest House) adjacent to Pali Uli. Wherever you stay, the owners provide a breakfast every morning that includes fresh eggs and whole-grain breads. Guests have access to a pay phone. ⌂ *19-3820 Old Volcano Hwy., Volcano Village* ⌂ *Box 490, Volcano 96785* 🖃 *808/967-7293 or 800/997-2292* 🖶 *808/985-7349* ⊕ *www.volcanoinn.com* ⋒ *7 rooms, 1 one-room cottage* ⚭ *Some microwaves, cable TV with movies; no A/C, no room phones, no smoking* 🖃 *AE, D, DC, MC, V. $105–$136.*

$–$$ ▨ **My Island Bed & Breakfast Inn.** Gordon, Joann, and daughter Ki'i Morse opened their historic century-old home and 7-acre botanical estate to visitors in 1985. The house is the oldest in Volcano, built in 1886 by the Lyman missionary family. Three rooms, sharing two baths, are available in the main house. Scattered around the area are five fully equipped guesthouses and another three rooms in private garden apartments. You won't start the day hungry after a deluxe all-you-can-eat breakfast. ⌂ *19-3896 Old Volcano Hwy., Volcano Village* ⌂ *Box 100, Volcano 96785* 🖃 *808/967-7216 or 808/967-7110* 🖶 *808/967-7719* ⊕ *www.myislandinnhawaii.com* ⋒ *6 rooms, 3 with bath; 5 guesthouses* ⚭ *No A/C, no phones in some rooms, no TV in some rooms, no smoking* 🖃 *MC, V. $70–$105.*

Cabins

¢ ▨ **Nāmakani Paio Cabins.** These cabins, managed by Volcano House, a concession of the National Park Service, were just remodeled and are now open again. Be forewarned, though, this is still "roughing it." The cabins are at the end of a long, deserted road, and they are definitely simple. Inexpensive and clean, each has a double bed, two bunk beds, and electric lights. Bring extra blankets, as it gets cold in these basic units. Each cabin also has a grill outside, but you must bring your own firewood. ⌂ *Volcano House, Box 53, Hawai'i Volcanoes National Park, Volcano Village* 🖃 *808/967-7321* 🖶 *808/967-8429* ⋒ *10 cabins* ⚭ *No A/C, no phones, no TVs* 🖃 *MC, V. $45.*

Hilo

Hotels & Resorts

★ **$$–$$$$** ▨ **Hilo Hawaiian Hotel.** With large bay-front rooms offering spectacular views of Mauna Kea and Coconut Island, this is one of the most pleasant lodgings on Hilo Bay. Streetside rooms overlook the golf course. Most accommodations have private lānai, and kitchenettes are available in some one-bedroom suites. Views of the bay are showcased in the Queen's Court dining room, and the Wai'oli Lounge has entertainment Thursday through Saturday. ⌂ *71 Banyan Dr., 96720* 🖃 *808/935-9361, 800/367-5004*

5

from the mainland, 800/272–5275 interisland ⊟ *808/961–9642* ⊕ *www. hilohawaiian.com* ⬄ *286 rooms, 6 suites* ⚭ *Restaurant, A/C, in-room data ports, cable TV, some kitchenettes, refrigerators, pool, bar, laundry facilities, no-smoking rooms* ☰ *AE, D, DC, MC, V. $96–$385.*

★ **$–$$** 🏨 **Dolphin Bay Hotel.** A glowing lava flow sign marks the office and bespeaks owner John Alexander's passion for the volcano. Stunning lava pictures adorn the common area, and Alexander is a great source of information for visiting the park and for exploring the backroads of Hilo. Units in the 1950s-style motor lodge are modest, but they are clean and inexpensive. Coffee and fresh fruit are offered daily. Four blocks from Hilo Bay, in a residential area called Pu'ue'o, the hotel borders a verdant 2-acre Hawaiian garden with jungle trails and shady places to rest. Guests of the hotel return repeatedly, and it's ideal for families who seek a home base. ⊠ *333 'Iliahi St., 96720* ☎ *808/935–1466* ⊟ *808/935– 1523* ⊕ *www.dolphinbayhotel.com* ⬄ *13 rooms, 4 1-bedroom units, 1 2-bedroom unit* ⚭ *Fans, kitchens, kitchenettes, microwave; no A/C, no room phones, no room TVs* ☰ *MC, V. $66–$99.*

¢–**$$** 🏨 **Arnott's Lodge.** The best part about Arnott's are the activities—you can plan through them for way cheaper than any tour operator on the island. Lodging is budget, so it's simple, but pleasant and clean. You can choose to tent on the lawn or stay in dormitory-style bunk beds, semiprivate rooms, or private accommodations. Four rooms in an adjacent house have private tile bathrooms. There's a shared kitchen and a separate video gazebo for all. Arnott's latest addition is an Internet café. ⊠ *98 'Apapane Rd., 96720* ☎ *808/969–7097* ⊟ *808/961–9638* ⊕ *www.arnottslodge.com* ⬄ *12 semiprivate units, 6 private units, 36 bunks* ⚭ *Some microwaves, hair salon, bicycles, hiking, laundry facilities, Internet room, airport shuttle, travel services; no A/C in some rooms, no room phones, no room TVs* ☰ *AE, D, DC, MC, V. $9–$125.*

¢–**$$** 🏨 **Hilo Seaside Hotel.** This is as close to the airport as you can get, which means it can get noisy during the day. It's also a friendly, laidback, and otherwise peaceful place, with neutral rooms that have private lānai. The nicest ones overlook the koi-filled lagoon, or are around the pool. The staff is friendly, the restaurant serves local fare, and the tropical foliage around you gives you a sense of old Hawai'i. ⊠ *126 Banyan Way, 96720* ☎ *808/935–0821 or 800/560–5557* ⊟ *808/969– 9195* ⊕ *www.hiloseasidehotel.com* ⬄ *135 rooms* ⚭ *Restaurant, A/C, fans, some kitchenettes, refrigerators, cable TV, pool, laundry facilities, no-smoking rooms* ☰ *AE, D, DC, MC, V. $55–$110.*

$ 🏨 **Hilo Bay Hotel, Uncle Billy's.** Funky and cheap, 'nuf said. This is a popular stopover for Neighbor Islanders who enjoy proprietor Uncle Billy Kimo's Hawaiian hospitality. A nightly hula show and entertainment during dinner are part of the fun. ⊠ *87 Banyan Dr., 96720* ☎ *808/935– 0861, 800/367–5102 from the mainland, 800/442–5841 interisland* ⊟ *808/935–7903* ⊕ *www.unclebilly.com* ⬄ *145 rooms* ⚭ *Restaurant, A/C, some kitchenettes, refrigerators, pool, bar, laundry facilities, Internet room, no-smoking rooms* ☰ *AE, D, DC, MC, V. $84–$94.*

B&Bs & Vacation Rentals

★ **$$$–$$$$** 🏨 **Shipman House Bed & Breakfast Inn.** You'll have a choice between one of three rooms in the main house—a 100-year-old turreted "castle"—or one of two rooms in a separate cottage unit. The B&B is on 5½ verdant acres on Reed's Island; the house is furnished with antique koa and period pieces, some dating from the days when Queen Liliʻuokalani came to tea. On Tuesday night, an authentic hula school practices Hawaiʻi's ancient dances in the house. ⊠ *131 Kaiulani St., 96720* ☎ *808/934–8002 or 800/627–8447* 🖷 *808/934–8002* ⊕ *www.hilo-hawaii.com* ➾ *3 rooms, 2 cottage rooms* ⚹ *Fans, refrigerators, library; no A/C, no room phones, no room TVs, no kids, no smoking* ⊟ *AE, MC, V. $199–$219.*

$$ 🏨 **Hale Kai.** On a bluff above Hilo Bay, just 2 mi from downtown Hilo, this 5,400-square-foot modern home has four impeccable rooms with patios and a private loft that is ideal for families—all with grand ocean views and within earshot of lapping waves. Fresh flowers add a warm, European touch. The Norwegian-Hawaiian hosts, Evonne and Paul Bjornen, serve a delightful breakfast—fruits, breads, and special egg dishes—on an outdoor deck or in the kitchen's bay-window dining area. ⊠ *111 Honoliʻi Pali St., 96720* ☎ *808/935–6330* 🖷 *808/935–8439* ⊕ *www.halekaihawaii.com* ➾ *4 rooms, 1 suite* ⚹ *A/C, fans, cable TV, pool, hot tub, laundry service; no kids, no smoking* ⊟ *No credit cards. $115–$140, 2-night minimum.*

$–$$ 🏨 **Waterfalls Inn Bed & Breakfast.** This elegant old family home is in the exclusive Reed's Bay neighborhood, just a few blocks from downtown Hilo. Relaxation is the key here. Bounded on two sides by tropical streams and forest, there's no traffic and no noise except the gentle gurgle of the stream. The 1916-era home has been carefully restored, retaining the original light fixtures, fine ʻōhiʻa wood flooring, antique furniture, and some original bath fixtures. You'll find lots of room to unwind in the expansive glassed-in lānai; breakfast is served in the large dining room. Business travelers enjoy easy access to town, government offices, and the University of Hawaiʻi at Hilo. There's a $20 fee for one night stays. ⊠ *240 Kaiulani St., 96720* ☎ *808/969–3407* ⊕ *www.waterfallsinn.com* ➾ *4 suites* ⚹ *Refrigerators, Wi-Fi, cable TV, in-room DVDs/VCRs, meeting room; no A/C, no kids under 6* ⊟ *AE, MC, V. $130–$175, 2-night minimum.*

$ 🏨 **The Inn at Kulaniapia.** With an awesome view of Hilo Bay 4 mi below, as well as access to a magnificent 120-foot waterfall that tumbles into a 300-foot-wide swimming pond, this inn is an oasis of beauty and tranquillity. Trails meander to the river, and Hilo is just a 15-minute drive

---

BED & BREAKFAST, HAWAIIAN STYLE

Hōlualoa Inn (Kailua-Kona). Gorgeous wood floors, quiet location, beautiful coffee-country views, close to the quaint artist's community of Hōlualoa.

The Inn at Volcano (Volcano Village). Close to the Volcano, Jacuzzis, candlelighted breakfasts and unique themed suites.

Jacaranda Inn (Waimea). Charming, country-style, Jacuzzis, walking distance to all the best restaurants in Waimea.

Palms Cliff House Inn (Hāmākua Coast). Stunning views of the coast and a gourmet breakfast on the veranda.

Waterfalls Inn (Hilo). Quiet and stately, in the nicest neighborhood in Hilo, walking distance to downtown.

5

away over sugarcane roads. Hosts Jane and Len Sutton added Asian accents, koa, and eucalyptus wood floors to the inn. Complete breakfasts are served, and you can cook an informal dinner on the barbecue. ⌂ *Box 11338, 96721* ☎ *808/935–8088 or 888/838–6373* 🖶 *808/935–8088* ⊕ *www.waterfall.net* ➘ *4 rooms* ⚬ *No A/C, no smoking* ▤ *AE, MC, V. $109.*

Hāmākua Coast

Hotels

$$$–$$$$　📺 **The Palms Cliff House Inn.** This handsome Victorian-style mansion is
Fodor'sChoice　perched on the sea cliffs 150 feet above the crashing surf of the tropi-
★　cal Hāmākua Coast, 15 mi north of Hilo. You can pick tropical fruit and macadamia nuts from the gardens of the 3½-acre estate. Individually decorated rooms have private lānai. Suites include double Jacuzzi tubs (room 8's tub is in the window with a stunning view of the coast), but there's also a communal hot tub in the garden. The husband-and-wife owner–operators serve breakfast with pride on the veranda overlooking the cliffs; breakfasts generally include fresh-baked muffins, local fruit, a warm egg or meat dish (they always ask about guest food allergies or diets ahead of time) and, of course, fantastic local coffee. Dinner is available on request. They can help you plan activities, including hula lessons. ⊠ *28-3514 Māmalahoa Hwy., Honomū, 96728-0189* ☎ *808/963–6076* 🖶 *808/963–6316* ⊕ *www.palmscliffhouse.com* ➘ *2 rooms, 6 suites* ⚬ *Fans, in-room data ports, in-room safes, cable TV, in-room DVDs, hot tub; no A/C in some rooms, no kids under 12, no smoking* ▤ *AE, D, DC, MC, V. $175–$375.*

$$$–$$$$　📺 **Waianuhea.** Fully self-contained, this gorgeous country home in a forested pasture area upslope on the Hāmākua Coast has solar electric power. The four guest rooms and large suite are lavishly furnished with tasteful color schemes, and contemporary artwork throughout. The large common room and lava-rock fireplace are big attractions, especially at the wine tasting hour each evening. Stroll the flower garden and fruit orchards. Waianuhea defines Hawaiian country elegance. ⊠ *45-3503 Kahana Dr., Honoka'a, 96727* ☎ *888/775–2577 or 808/775–1118* 🖶 *888/296–6302* ⊕ *www.waianuhea.com* ➘ *5 rooms* ⚬ *Cable TV, in-room DVDs, Internet; no A/C, no smoking* ▤ *AE, D, MC, V. $170–$350.*

$–$$$　📺 **Waipi'o Wayside.** Nestled amid avocado and kukui trees, on a plantation estate, this serene inn provides a retreat close to Waipi'o Valley.

HAWAI'I ON A BUDGET

Arnott's Lodge (Hilo). Backpacker haven, camping available, clean private cabins, reasonable activity and tour rates.

Kona Tiki Hotel (Kailua-Kona). Oceanfront, all rooms have ocean views, walking distance to downtown.

Manago Hotel (South Kona). Historic, Japanese theme, clean, some oceanfront rooms, super reasonable, excellent restaurant.

Nāmakani Paio Cabins (Volcano Village). Close to the Volcano, cheap, clean, recently renovated

Royal Kona Resort (Kailua-Kona). Old-school Hawai'i, oceanfront, great bar, good package deals, close to downtown Kailua-Kona.

Hostess Jacqueline Horne has given each room its own character with, for example, rare Chinese antiques or patchwork quilts. A sprawling garden with an orchid-covered deck and a little gazebo has hammocks to help you indulge your lazy side. ✉ *Waipi'o Valley Rd., Hwy. 240, Honoka'a 96727* ☎ *808/775–0275 or 800/833–8849* 📠 *808/775–0275* ⊕ *www.waipiowayside.com* 🛏 *5 rooms* ⚭ *Snack bar, in-room data ports; no A/C, no room phones, no room TVs, no smoking* ▭ *MC, V. $95–$170.*

¢–$ 🏨 **Hotel Honoka'a Club.** This basic bargain hotel is 45 minutes from Hilo and close to Waipi'o Valley. Rustic rooms range from lower-level dormitory-style hostel units—bring your own sleeping bag—with shared bathrooms to upper story rooms with private bath, queen-size beds, an ocean view, and a complimentary Continental breakfast. ✉ *45-3480 Māmane St., Box 247, Honoka'a 96727* ☎ *808/775–0678 or 800/808–0678* ⊕ *www.hotelhono.com* 🛏 *13 rooms, 5 hostel rooms* ⚭ *Restaurant, Wi-Fi; no A/C, no room phones, no TV in some rooms, no smoking* ▭ *MC, V. Hostel rooms $18–$38, rooms $50–$75.*

Puna

$$–$$$$ 🏨 **Kalani Oceanside Retreat.** Kalani is not for everyone, but it might be the perfect spot for some. Even the driveway is beautiful, and the grounds are lush and well-kept. Food is good, too, but a bit pricey ($20 each for dinner, $10 each for lunch) considering it's cafeteria style. There's a thermal spring nearby, and they offer numerous yoga and meditation classes in addition to a revolving schedule of other classes like ecstatic dance, *watsu* (aquatic body therapy), and massage, as well as programs on Hawaiian culture, healing, and gay relationships. Accommodations include campsites; shared rooms; cottage units with shared kitchen; lodge rooms; and private, luxurious tree-house units. Bathing suits are optional both on the nearby beach and at the Olympic-size pool. Full meal plans are available at an additional charge. ✉ *Pāhoa-Beach Rd., Hwy. 137, R.R. 2, Box 4500, Pāhoa 96778* ☎ *808/965–7828 or 800/800–6886* 📠 *808/965–0527* ⊕ *www.kalani.com* 🛏 *24 rooms with shared bath, 9 cottages, 4 tree-house units, 3 guesthouse rooms* ⚭ *Fans, some refrigerators, tennis court, pool, hair salon, hot tub, sauna, laundry facilities, laundry service, no-smoking room; no A/C, no room TVs* ▭ *AE, D, MC, V. $110–$240.*

$–$$ 🏨 **Yoga Oasis.** This center, on 26 tropical acres, isn't your average vacation rental: with an expensive design of Mexican tiles, finished redwood, Balinese doorways, and imported art, it draws those who seek rejuvenation, and perhaps a free yoga lesson or two. You're close to hot springs and black-sand beaches; the volcano is a 45-minute drive away. Bathrooms are shared. A 1,600-square-foot state-of-the-art yoga and gymnastics space, with 18-foot ceilings, crowns this friendly retreat. ✉ *Pohoiki Rd., Box 1935, Pāhoa 96778* ☎ *808/965–8460 or 800/274–4446* ⊕ *www.yogaoasis.org* 🛏 *5 rooms with shared bath, 4 bungalows, 1 cottage* ⚭ *Some fans, massage, laundry service; no A/C, no room phones, no room TVs, no smoking* ▭ *MC, V. $75–$145.*

¢–$$ 🏨 **Bed & Breakfast Mountain View.** This modern home is surrounded by rolling forest and farmland. The secluded 4-acre estate has extensive floral gardens and a fishpond. Owners Linus and Jane Chao are longtime

Big Island art educators and have an art studio on the lower level, where they conduct ongoing classes. Inquire about special packages that include art lessons. The house itself is a virtual art gallery with varied displays in oil, acrylic, watercolor, and Oriental brush paintings. ⊠ *South Kulani Rd., Kurtistown 96760* ☎ *808/968–6868 or 888/698–9896* 🖷 *808/968–7017* ⊕ *www.bbmtview.com* ↝ *4 rooms, 2 with shared bath* ⟨ *Pond, fishing, billiards, laundry facilities; no A/C, no TV in some rooms, no kids under 5* ⊟ *MC, V. $55–$110.*

WHERE TO SPA

Hawaiian Rainforest Salon and Spa at the Waikoloa Marriott. The Marriott recently added a bunch of treatments to their spa services menu, which really adds to the value of this reasonable Kohala Coast resort. The additions were a good idea to round out the menu, but, though treatments like their Smooth and Sunkissed body treatment (an exfoliating scrub, followed by bronzer that will make sure you don't frighten anyone on the beach) are appealing, none are as spectacular as the standard oceanside massage. Their therapists are highly skilled, and their tables are right on one of the prettiest beaches on the coast. One caveat: this is not the place to get your hair cut on vacation. ⊠ *69-275 Waikoloa Beach Dr., Waikoloa* ☎ *808/886–7727* ⊕ *www.marriott.com. $80–$100, 50–80-min massage* ⟨ *Gym with: cardiovascular machines. Services: body scrubs and wraps, facials, massages. Classes and programs: aerobics, yoga.*

Kalona Salon and Spa at the Outrigger Keauhou. Kalona is a great place to get a massage or body treatment for a lot less than you'd likely pay at the big resorts without sacrificing quality. Though not quite as nice as the big boys, it's on the ocean, simple, clean, and staffed with well-trained therapists. They also do facials here, but they use their own line of products made from local island ingredients, which could be tricky for anyone with touchy skin. ⊠ *78-6740 Ali'i Dr., Kailua-Kona* ☎ *808/ 322–3441 or 800/462–6262* ⊕ *www.outrigger.com. $80 massage* ⟨ *Services: facials, massage.*

★ **Kohala Sports Club & Spa at the Hilton Waikoloa.** Orchids run riot in the rain forests of the Big Island and suffuse the signature treatments at the Kohala Spa. By the end of the Orchid Isle Wrap, you are completely immersed in the scent and in bone-deep relaxation. The island's volcanic character is also expressed in several treatments, as well as in the design of the lava rock soaking tubs. Locker rooms are outfitted with private changing rooms for the modest and a wealth of beauty and bath products for the adventurous. The extensive hair and nail salon could satisfy even Bridezilla with its updo consultations and luxe pedicure stations. The spa is right next to the tennis center; nearby oceanside cabanas are the venue for massage on the beach. The fitness center is well-equipped, but group classes that roam across the beautifully manicured resort grounds—like tai chi on the lawn or walking meditation at Buddha Point—are much more appealing. ⊠ *The Hilton Waikoloa, 425 Waikoloa Beach Dr., Kohala Coast* ☎ *808/886–2828 or 800/445– 8667* ⊕ *www.kohalaspa.com. $135–$145 50-min. massage, $180 body* *wrap, $145 facial ⚬ Hair salon, hot tubs (indoor and outdoor), sauna, steam room. Gym with: cardiovascular machines, free weights, weight-training equipment. Services: acupuncture, aromatherapy, body scrubs and wraps, facials, hydromassage, massage. Classes and programs: body sculpting, fitness analysis, personal training, Pilates, spinning, step aerobics, tai chi, yoga.*

Mauna Kea Beach Hotel. The spa at the Mauna Kea is not as flashy as its neighbors; it doesn't have a specific theme or high-end design concept. Massages are good but not great. The best thing going here is the body treatment menu, with unusual options like the aloe and herbal wrap, which combats cellulite, in addition to island standards like the Hawaiian Sea Salt Body Glow. ✉ *62-100 Mauna Kea Beach Dr., Kohala Coast* ☎ *808/882–7222* ⊕ *www.maunakeabeachhotel.com. $96–$100, 50-min massage, $55 body polish, $110 body treatment ⚬ Hair salon, sauna, steam room. Gym with: cardiovascular machines, weight-training equipment. Services: aromatherapy, body treatments, facials, massage. Classes and programs: aerobics.*

★ **Mauna Lani Spa.** If you're looking for a one-of-a-kind experience, this is your destination. Most treatments take place in outdoor, bamboo-floor hales surrounded by lava rock. Incredible therapists offer a mix of the old stand-bys (lomi lomi massage, moisturizing facial) and innovative treatments, many of which are heavily influenced by local tradition and incorporate local products. The outdoor lava sauna is an exfoliating body treatment that's self-administered in one of the outdoor saunas—a great choice for people who aren't too keen on strange massage therapists seeing them in their birthday suits. Watsu therapy takes place in the amazing lava tube pool. The pool is in a replicated lava tube; the water flows from the actual lava tube next door into the pool, and it's heated by solar panels. Meant to re-create the feeling of being in a womb, the therapy is essentially an hour-long massage in water. You feel totally weightless, thanks to some artfully applied weights and the buoyancy of the warm salt water. It's a great treatment for people with disabilities that keep them from enjoying a traditional massage. The spa also offers more Mainland-style procedures like Botox and Restylane injections, as well as a full regimen of fitness classes and a lap pool. ✉ *Mauna Lani Resort, 68-1400 Mauna Lani Dr., Kohala Coast* ☎ *808/885-6622* ⊕ *www.maunalani.com. $125, 50-min massage, $150–$265 facials, $60 lava sauna, $140–$190 watsu ⚬ Hair salon, hot tubs (indoor and outdoor), sauna, steam room. Gym with: cardiovascular machines, free weights, weight-training equipment. Services: facials, massage, Botox, Restylane, aquatic therapy, body wraps, baths, scrubs. Classes and programs: aerobics, kickboxing, personal training, pilates, Spinning, weight training, yoga.*

Paul Brown Salon and Spa at the Hāpuna Beach Prince Hotel. It's not unusual for people to drive an hour each way to get their hair cut here. Paul Brown has been in the business for 30 years, and he now has three locations in Hawai'i. Hair is still the specialty here, but it's not just a salon. The very well-run, full-service spa has an extensive menu of massages, facials, and body treatments, and the facility is nicely designed and clean, with lots of light. You feel safe having anything done here—

these people know their stuff. They even have a trained Oriental Medicine staff who administer expert acupuncture treatments. They're also the best place for waxing in case you didn't have time before you left home. ✉ *62-100 Kauna`oa Dr., Kohala* ☎ *808/880–1111 or 800/882–6060* ⊕ *www.princeresortshawaii.com. $100, 50-min massage; $85, 50-min facials; $100–$150 acupuncture* ♿ *Hair salon, sauna, steam room. Gym with: cardiovascular machines. Services: acupuncture, body wraps, facials, massage. Classes and programs: aerobics, yoga.*

Spa Without Walls at the Fairmont Orchid. This is possibly the best massage on the island, partially due to having the best setting. Massages at the Spa without Walls are either oceanside or waterfall-side. Though most people will probably opt for oceanside, the waterfall experience is equally relaxing, and both settings are absolutely peaceful. There are other great treatments available as well, including facials, fragrant herbal wraps, and Hawaiian-coffee and vanilla scrubs, but the massages are the best thing going. ✉ *The Fairmont Orchid, 1 N. Kanikū Dr., Kohala Coast* ☎ *808/885–2000* ⊕ *www.fairmont.com. $129, 50-min massage, $150 facial, $120 body treatment* ♿ *Sauna, steam room. Gym with: cardiovascular machines, free weights, weight-training equipment. Services: baths, body wraps, facials, massage, scrubs. Classes and programs: aquaerobics, guided walks, meditation, personal training, yoga.*

The Spa at Hualālai. The Spa is for the exclusive use of hotel guests, so you can sign everything to your room, and you'll never have a problem booking a treatment. Though there are outdoor massage hales that afford somewhat of a "Hawaiian" experience, this is essentially a New York spa dropped in the middle of a tropical island. That said, the therapists are top-notch, and the spa menu does take advantage of local produce, incorporating kokui nuts, coconut, and Thai honey into their body scrubs and massage oils. Aesthetic treatments are under separate management, so facials and salon services take place in the neighboring building. ✉ *100 Ka`ūpūlehu Dr., Ka`ūpūlehu/Kona* ☎ *808/325–8000* ⊕ *www.fourseasons.com. $120, 50-min massage, $145 body scrub, $120 facials* ♿ *Hair salon, outdoor hot tubs, sauna, steam room. Gym with: cardiovascular machines. Services: body treatments, facials, massage. Classes and programs: personal training, Pilates, Spinning, tai chi, yoga.*

WHERE TO EAT

Hotels along the Kohala Coast invest in top chefs to match their opulent settings; diners are rarely disappointed. Cutting-edge chefs cook with the freshest local produce, fish, and herbs, creating intriguing blends of flavors that reflect the island's varied cultural backgrounds, and the unique training of each chef. Events such as the Great Waikoloa Food, Wine and Music Fest at the Hilton Waikoloa Village, and Cuisines of the Sun at Mauna Lani Bay Hotel draw hundreds of guests to starlighted open-air dinners celebrating the bounty of the isle's land and waters.

As the bulk of Big Island tourism is on the Kona-side, the majority of restaurants are here as well, and they tend to be a bit pricey. In addition to the resorts, there are also some great choices in Upcountry

Waimea, North Kohala (in Kawaihae and Hāwī—both a short drive from the resort area) as well as on the east side of the island in Hilo. Less populated areas like Kaʻū, the Hāmākua Coast, and Puna offer limited choices for dinner, but usually at least one or two spots that do a decent plate lunch. A handful of excellent little eateries have recently cropped up in Kainaliu, near Kealakekua Bay. As more and more young people move into this area they are opening up their own businesses, from funky clothing boutiques to organic cafés.

WHAT IT COSTS				
$$$$	**$$$**	**$$**	**$**	**¢**
RESTAURANTS over $30	$20–$30	$12–$20	$7–$12	under $7

Restaurant prices are for one main course at dinner.

Kohala

American–Casual

$–$$$ ✕ **Café Pesto.** Both branches of Café Pesto—in the quaint harbor town of Kawaihae and in Hilo—are equally popular. Fresh local seafood, exotic pizzas (with chili-grilled shrimp, shiitake mushrooms, and cilantro crème fraîche, for example), and Asian-inspired pastas and risottos reflect the ethnic diversity of the island. Local microbrews and a full-service bar make this a good place to end the evening. ⊠ *Kawaihae Shopping Center, Kawaihae* ☎ *808/882–1071* ⊕ *www.cafepesto.com* ▤ *AE, D, DC, MC, V. $10–$29.*

$–$$$ ✕ **Kawaihae Harbor Grill and Seafood Bar.** This popular little restaurant is always packed—there's something about their crisp green and white, 1850s building that just catches the eye and draws people in. That and the fact that it smells way are too good to pass up if you're hungry. Food is not adventurous but very good; fresh island fish, chicken, and ribs are all in hearty portions. Inside, it's all vintage Hawaiana—old records, a surfboard, and hula skirts. The Seafood Bar is upstairs in a separate structure that also dates from the 1850s, and it has been a "hot spot" since it opened in 2003. The bar is a good place to wait until your table is ready, or to feast from the all-*pūpū* (Hawaiian appetizers) menu. ⊠ *Kawaihae Harbor, Hwy. 270, Kawaihae* ☎ *808/882–1368* ▤ *MC, V. $6–$24.*

Chinese

$–$$$$ ✕ **Grand Palace Chinese Restaurant.** A reasonable alternative in a land of high-price hotel dining, this restaurant offers dishes from most regions, including such standards as egg foo yung, wonton soup, chicken with snow peas, and beef with broccoli. More adventurous dishes include sautéed local seafood, lobster, and sizzling shrimp with garlic sauce. Etched-glass panels are a nice embellishment. ⊠ *King's Shops, Waikoloa Resort, 250 Waikoloa Beach Dr., Kohala Coast* ☎ *808/886–6668* ▤ *AE, DC, MC, V. $9–$40.*

Contemporary–Hawaiian

★ **$$$$** ✕ **The Batik at Mauna Kea Beach Hotel.** For the hotel's elegant signature restaurant—with its glass-enclosed, split-level waterfront dining room—

executive chef Thomas Woods combines French-Mediterranean elements with Indonesian influences to create dazzling dishes such as a macadamia-nut-crusted ono with lemongrass-coconut emulsion. Most of the staff has been here for 15 years, so the service is seamless. ⊠ *Mauna Kea Beach Hotel, 62-100 Mauna Kea Beach Dr., Kohala Coast* ☎ *808/882–5810* ▭ *AE, D, DC, MC, V* ⊘ *Closed nights vary. No lunch. $31–$48.*

$$$$
Fodor'sChoice
★
✕ **Brown's Beach House at the Fairmont Orchid.** Brown's is nearly perfect and well worth the splurge—waterfront, torch-light, inventive (but not too inventive) menu, excellent wine list. Though you can order steak here, the seafood is really where it's happening. Their crab-crusted ono is a little piece of heaven, sitting on clouds of wasabi mashed potatos. Leave room for the dessert; the menu changes regularly, but they're always worth the indulgence. Local Hawaiian musicians play nightly on the grassy knoll outside. ⊠ *Fairmont Orchid, 1 N. Kanikū Dr., Kohala Coast* ☎ *808/885–2000* ▭ *AE, D, DC, MC, V* ⊘ *No lunch. $30–$50.*

$$$$
✕ **Hale Samoa at Kona Village Resort.** Formal and romantic, this Kona Village restaurant has a magical atmosphere, especially at sunset. In a Samoan setting with tapa screens and candles, you can feast on five-course prix-fixe dinners that change daily. Specialties may include papaya-and-coconut bisque, duck stuffed with andouille sausage, or wok-charred prime strip loin. Reservations can be made only on the day you want to dine. ⊠ *Kona Village, 12 mi north of Kailua-Kona on Hwy. 19, North Kona Coast* ☎ *808/325–5555* ⚑ *Reservations essential* ▭ *AE, DC, MC, V* ⊘ *Closed Wed., Fri., and 1st wk in Dec. $65–$90.*

★ $$$–$$$$
✕ **Alan Wong's Hualalai Grille at Four Seasons Hualālai.** The menu changes regularly, depending on availability of local produce, fish, and meat, but expect the sort of "fusion" fare you'd find in a top-notch New York or San Francisco restaurant, with the added bonus of being able to sit outside to enjoy it on a balmy Hawaiian winter night. The food is surprisingly reasonable for what you get and where you're eating. You could easily make a meal out of a selection of pūpū. The wine list is extensive and well-chosen, and servers are extremely well-versed and helpful. ⊠ *Four Seasons Resort Hualālai, 100 Ka'ūpūlehu Dr., North Kona Coast* ⚑ *Reservations essential* ▭ *AE, DC, MC, V* ⊘ *Closed Wed., Fri., and 1st wk in Dec. $18–$90.*

$$$–$$$$
✕ **CanoeHouse at the Mauna Lani Bay Hotel and Bungalows.** Although the open-air, beachfront setting is stunning, overall the CanoeHouse does

---

BEST BREAKFAST

Bianelli's (Kailua-Kona). A good old-fashioned, straightforward breakfast.

Bubba Gump's (Kailua-Kona). A chain, but a chain with the best outdoor seating in Kailua-Kona and cream-cheese filled cinnamon-raisin French toast.

Café 100 (Hilo). Local destination for *loco moco* on the Hilo side.

Ken's House of Pancakes (Hilo). Like IHOP, but with Spam.

Sam Choy's Kaloko Restaurant (Kailua-Kona). Local destination for huge plates of *loco moco* on the Kona side.

Pahu i'a at Four Seasons Resort Hualālai (Kohala). Hands-down the best fancy brunch on the island, whether you go for the buffet or the menu.

not really live up to the hype surrounding it. The menu is Pacific Rim fusion, and options are standard—meat or seafood paired with sauces derived from local fruits and vegetables. Shanghai lobster is the big standout, but even it is not exactly amazing. That said, the wine list is great, and the location could almost make the price tag worth it, if there weren't better restaurants a few miles away. ⊠ *Mauna Lani Bay Hotel and Bungalows, 68-1400 Mauna Lani Dr., Kohala Coast* ☎ *808/885–6622* ▤ *AE, D, DC, MC, V. $27–$40.*

★ **$$$–$$$$** ✕ **Coast Grille at Hāpuna Beach Prince Hotel.** The Hāpuna Prince is sort of the red-headed step-child of the Kohala Coast resorts. Each of the other resorts has carved out a niche for themselves, but for some reason the Hāpuna Prince is just kind of there. That said, this restaurant is fantastic. It's beautiful, with high ceilings and a lānai overlooking the ocean, and they offer perhaps the best seafood menu on the island, including loads of fresh oysters and creative Pacific Rim dishes like pan-seared *opah* (moonfish) in cardamom sauce and, when available, delicate farm-raised moi, in ancient times enjoyed only by chiefs. Don't overlook the appetizer sampler with seared 'ahi and tempura sushi, and save room for warm Valrhona chocolate cake. ⊠ *Hāpuna Beach Prince Hotel, 62-100 Kauna'oa Dr., Kohala Coast* ☎ *808/880–3192* ▤ *AE, D, DC, MC, V* ⊘ *No lunch. $26–$36.*

$$$–$$$$ ✕ **Hawai'i Calls at Waikoloa Beach Marriott.** With its retro art, Hawai'i Calls offers a nostalgic taste of the past, from the '20s to the '50s. The menu, however, is contemporary and fresh, changing seasonally, with specialties such as moi, seared crispy and served with coconut rice, pickled ginger, and spicy cucumber salad. Don't miss the macadamia-chocolate tart with vanilla ice cream. The spacious outdoor setting is lovely—ask for a table near the koi pond and waterfall—and a great place to watch the sun set as tiki torches light up the gardens. The adjacent Clipper Lounge serves tropical drinks and features a bistro menu. ⊠ *Waikoloa Beach Marriott, 69-275 Waikoloa Beach Dr., Kohala Coast* ☎ *808/886–6789* ▤ *AE, D, DC, MC, V. $20–$42.*

$$$–$$$$ ✕ **Kamuela Provision Company at the Hilton Waikoloa Village.** Quiet guitar music, tables along a breezy lānai, and a sweeping view of the Kohala-Kona coastline are the perfect accompaniments to KPC's elegant yet down-to-earth Hawai'i regional cuisine. Popular are the bouillabaisse with *nori crostini* and the Parker Ranch rib-eye steak with green peppercorn sauce. KPC is a great place to sip cocktails—the adjacent Wine Bar makes for a romantic evening in itself, with an appetizer menu and more than 40 labels available by the glass. ⊠ *Hilton Waikoloa Village, 425 Waikoloa Beach Dr., Kohala Coast* ☎ *808/886–1234* ▤ *AE, D, DC, MC, V* ⊘ *No lunch. $28–$52.*

$$$–$$$$
Fodor$Choice
★ ✕ **Pahu i'a at Four Seasons Resort Hualālai.** *Pahu i'a* means "aquarium" in English, so it's fitting that a 9- by 4-foot aquarium in the entrance casts a dreamy light through this exquisite restaurant. Presentation is paramount—tables are beautifully set, with handblown glassware—and the food tastes as good as it looks. Asian-influenced dishes on the menu stand out for their layers of flavor. Don't miss the three sashimi and three caviar appetizers, or the crispy whole moi served with Asian slaw, black beans, and sweet chili-lime vinaigrette. Breakfast is also su-

perb; there's a buffet, but you can also order from the menu. Their lemon ricotta pancakes are so good they should be illegal. Reserve a table on the patio and you may be able to spot whales while dining. ⊠ *Four Seasons Resort Hualālai, 100 Ka'ūpūlehu Dr., North Kona Coast* ☏ *808/ 325–8000* ☰ *AE, D, DC, MC, V* ☉ *No lunch. $25–$48.*

$$–$$$ ✕ **Bamboo Restaurant.** It's out of the way, but the food at this spot in the heart of Hāwī is good and the service has a country flair. Creative entrées feature fresh island fish prepared several ways. Thai-style fish, for example, combines lemongrass, kaffir lime leaves, and coconut milk—best washed down with a passion-fruit margarita or passion-fruit iced tea. Bamboo finishes, bold artwork, and an old unfinished wooden floor make the restaurant cozy. Local musicians entertain on Friday and Saturday night. ⊠ *Old Takata Store, Hwy. 270, Hāwī* ☏ *808/889–5555* ☰ *MC, V* ☉ *Closed Mon. No dinner Sun. $15–$28.*

$$–$$$ ✕ **Roy's Waikoloa Bar and Grill.** You can easily fill up on the enormous selection of appetizers at Roy Yamaguchi's cool and classy place overlooking a golf course lake. If you want a full meal, try the blackened island 'ahi with spicy soy-mustard-butter sauce, or jade-pesto steamed Hawaiian whitefish with cilantro, ginger, garlic, and peanut oil. An extensive wines-by-the-glass list offers good pairing options. Be forewarned that the place tends to get noisy. ⊠ *King's Shops, Waikoloa Resort, 250 Waikoloa Beach Dr., Kohala Coast* ☏ *808/886–4321* ⊕ *www. roysrestaurant.com* ☰ *AE, D, DC, MC, V. $18–$29.*

Italian

★ **$$–$$$$** ✕ **Donatoni's at the Hilton Waikoloa Village.** This romantic restaurant overlooking the boat canal resembles an Italian villa and serves scrumptious dishes with the subtle sauces of northern Italy. From mahimahi with marinated artichokes to fettuccine with Hawaiian lobster, this intimate place sets out to please. Be sure to look over the Italian wine and champagne list. ⊠ *425 Waikoloa Beach Dr., Kohala Coast* ☏ *808/886– 1234* ☰ *AE, D, DC, MC, V* ☉ *No lunch. $18–$46.*

Japanese

$$$$ ✕ **Hakone Steakhouse and Sushi Bar at Hāpuna Beach Prince Hotel.** It's hard not to start whispering in this tranquil and graceful restaurant. Choose from exquisite Japanese sukiyaki, *shabu shabu* (thin slices of beef cooked in broth), and an elaborate sushi bar. The broad selection of sake (try a sakitini, a martini made with sake) is guaranteed to enliven your meal. ⊠ *Hāpuna Beach Prince Hotel, 62-100 Kauna'oa Dr., Kohala Coast* ☏ *808/880–3192* ☰ *AE, D, DC, MC, V* ☉ *No lunch. $34–$45.*

$$$$ ✕ **Imari at the Hilton Waikoloa Village.** This elegant restaurant, complete with waterfalls and a teahouse, serves sukiyaki and tempura aimed to please mainland tastes. Beyond the impressive display of Imari porcelain at the entrance, you can find *teppanyaki* (beef or shrimp cooked table-side), shabu shabu, and an outstanding sushi bar. Impeccable service by kimono-clad waitresses adds to the quiet refinement. ⊠ *425 Waikoloa Beach Dr., Kohala Coast* ☏ *808/886–1234* ☰ *AE, D, DC, MC, V* ☉ *No lunch. $25–$52.*

$$$ ✕ **Norio's Sushi Bar and Restaurant.** Cool grey tones and straight lines meet in a Zen-like vibe that meshes well with sushi master Norio's traditional Japanese fare. Freshness is key—mouthwatering 'ahi and abalone are not to be missed. Although not necessarily worth driving out to reach, if you're staying at the Orchid or nearby and are in the mood for sushi, Norio's is the way to go. ✉ *Fairmont Orchid, 1 N. Kaniku Dr., Kohala Coast* ☎ *808/885–2000* ▤ *AE, D, DC, MC, V* ✹ *Closed Tues. and Wed. No lunch. $20–$30.*

Mexican

$–$$ ✕ **Tres Hombres Beach Grill.** The food is decent, if a bit pricey for Mexican, but what you come here (or to the Kailua-Kona location) for are the margaritas. They're perfect and offered in all sorts of local island flavors, like *lillikoi* (aka passion fruit). Lunch is the usual Mexican combination plates (enchiladas, tacos, chiles rellenos) as well as burgers and sandwiches. Dinner items include bean-and-rice combinations, fresh fish, salads, and steaks. ✉ *Kawaihae Shopping Center, Kawaihae* ☎ *808/882–1031* ▤ *MC, V. $11–$20.*

Steak Houses

★ $$$$ ✕ **The Grill at the Fairmont Orchid.** Inside, set back from the beach, the Grill is a martini and filet mignon kind of place. The menu is heavier on meats (leaving the seafood to the resort's Brown's Beach House), and you'd be hard-pressed to find a better steak on the island. Service is impeccable, the wine list superb, and their version of macadamia-nut pie may just be the best dessert we've ever had. Open-air seating is available, and they're still close enough to the ocean to catch the breeze. ✉ *The Fairmont Orchid, 1 N. Kanikū Dr., Kohala Coast* ☎ *808/885–2000* ⚓ *Reservations essential* ▤ *AE, D, DC, MC, V. $36–$59.*

$$–$$$$ ✕ **Big Island Steak House.** A good old-fashioned steak house with a bit of Blue Hawai'i kitsch thrown in. This is always a safe bet if you're in the mood for a straightforward steak, and the portions are huge. Seafood is also on the menu, but why order fish at a steak house? There's also a bar and an outdoor dining area overlooking the golf course lake. ✉ *King's Shops, Waikoloa Resort, 250 Waikoloa Beach Dr., Kohala Coast* ☎ *808/886–8805* ▤ *AE, D, MC, V* ✹ *No lunch. $15–$43.*

$$–$$$ ✕ **The Village Steak House.** Sunset views overlooking the golf course and steaks are the highlights here. Start with pūpū like Togarashi skewered shrimp, crab cakes Kohala or, Hawaiian-Chinese mushrooms. Steaks come in all sizes and include filet, tenderloin shiitake, New York strip, T-bone, and porterhouse. Other features range from fresh island fish, to chicken Ka'u with orange sauce, baby back ribs with passion fruit–hoisin sauce, pork chops pineapple, curry coconut prawns, and more. There's a quiet, comfortable clubhouse atmosphere. Dress is casual, but reservations are recommended. ✉ *68-1792 Melia St., Waikoloa* ☎ *808/883–9644* ▤ *AE, D, MC, V* ✹ *Closed Mon. $15–$30.*

Waimea

American–Casual

$$–$$$ ✕ **Parker Ranch Grill.** With cowhides serving as wallpaper and riding boots as doorknobs, this popular restaurant is not shy about its paniolo identity and Parker Ranch heritage. In front of a blazing fire, the koa tables are a perfect setting for, of course, Parker Ranch beef entrées. A separate bar area offers a variety of pūpū. ⊠ *Parker Ranch Shopping Center, 67-1185 Māmalahoa Hwy.* ☎ *808/887–2624* 🖃 *AE, D, MC, V. $18–$25.*

Contemporary

$$$–$$$$ ✕ **Daniel Thiebaut.** Underneath 11-foot ceilings, the space once known as the historic Chock In Store (built in 1900) has been transformed into seven dining areas. Collectibles abound, such as antique porcelain, original bar stools, and a long redwood community dining table, once the store's countertop. Chef Daniel Thiebaut's French-Asian creations include an amazing appetizer of sweet-corn crab cake with a lemongrass, coconut, and lobster sauce. Other signature dishes include Hunan-style rack of lamb served with eggplant compote, and Big Island goat cheese. ⊠ *65-1259 Kawaihae Rd.* ☎ *808/887–2200* ⊕ *www.danielthiebaut.com* 🖃 *AE, D, DC, MC, V. $20–$40.*

★ $$$–$$$$ ✕ **Merriman's.** This is the signature restaurant of Peter Merriman, one of the pioneers of Hawai'i regional cuisine. Merriman's is the home of the original wok-charred 'ahi, usually served with buttery Wainaku corn. If you prefer meat, try the Kahuā Ranch lamb, raised to the restaurant's specifications, or opt for the prime Kansas City Cut steak, grilled to order. The wine list includes 22 selections poured by the glass, and the staff is refreshingly knowledgeable. ⊠ *'Opelo Plaza, Hwy. 19 and 'Opelo Rd., 65-1227 'Opelo Rd., Waimea* ☎ *808/885–6822* ⊕ *www. merrimanshawaii.com* ⚞ *Reservations essential* 🖃 *AE, MC, V. $20–$33.*

German

★ $$$–$$$$ ✕ **Edelweiss.** An authentic German *gasthaus* right in the middle of Hawai'i, Edelweiss is truly a great place. Fear not if you don't see anything on the menu that you want; they have 15 to 20 daily specials that your server will rattle off to you without batting an eye. No one can figure out how (or why) they do it. The rack of lamb is always good, anything ending in schitzel is a safe bet, as are items ending in brat or bratten. The chicken cordon bleu is large enough and rich enough for two. Soup (almost always what sounds like a weird combination turns out to be a real treat), salad, and coffee or tea are included in dinner prices. Wine list is decent, but c'mon, get the Hefeweizen. You won't have room for dessert with the size of their portions, but you're not missing much. ⊠ *Hwy. 19, entering Waimea* ☎ *808/885–6800* ⚞ *Reservations essential* 🖃 *MC, V* ☺ *Closed Sun. and Mon. and Sept. $21–$56.*

Kailua-Kona

American–Casual

$$$–$$$$ ✕ **Kona Inn Restaurant.** This historic open-air restaurant is the best place to have a mai tai and watch the sunset. They serve a limited menu of salads and sandwiches on the patio. A more formal menu is served in the main dining area, but it's a little pricey and not really worth the splurge. ⊠ *75-5744 Ali'i Dr., Kailua-Kona* ☎ *808/329–4455* 🖃 *AE, MC, V. $19–$36.*

$$$ ✕ **Jameson's by the Sea.** If you can't get a table outside, Jameson's is not really worth the trip, so call ahead and reserve one—the waves actually

splash your feet while you eat. Their traditional continental fare is decent but not amazing; fresh fish is always the best bet. ⊠ *77-6452 Ali'i Dr., Kailua-Kona* ☎ *808/329–3195* ▤ *AE, D, DC, MC, V* ☉ *No lunch weekends. $21–$27.*

$$–$$$ ✕ **Rooster's** Tucked away as it is behind some shops, a visitor information kiosk, and table-upon-table of trinkets, it's easy to see why Rooster's is still such a well-kept secret. The food is best described as "comfort food," but the chef adds plenty of inventive twists to old standbys like ribs and fried chicken. The dining room is small and cozy—it could even be described as romantic if Hawai'i's put you in that frame of mind. Their wine list is great, focusing on an assortment of well-chosen California varietals. They even have live jazz on Friday and Saturday that is surprisingly good and not at all invasive, despite the fact that the dining room is tiny. Once the secret's out it will probably be hard to get a table. ⊠ *Ali'i Dr., underneath Hula Cafe and tucked back* ☎ *808/327–9453* ▤ *MC, V, AE* ☉ *No lunch. $15–$25.*

$–$$ ✕ **Jackie Ray's Ohana Grill.** In the Pottery Terrace up the hill from downtown Kailua-Kona, this bright green open-air restaurant is a popular new lunch destination. The Huli Huli chicken sandwich with avocado and swiss is an excellent combination of flavors, and their fries are crisped to perfection. They're open for dinner, too, but the menu is a little blah. ⊠ *Pottery Terrace, 75-5995 Kuakini Hwy., Kailua-Kona* ▤ *MC, V. $7–$15.*

$–$$ ✕ **Kona Brewing Company and Brewpub** Probably the best addition to Kailua-Kona's food and bar scene in recent history, the Kona Brewpub has got three great things going for it: the food is excellent and varied (pulled kalua pork quesadillas, gourmet pizzas, spinach salad with Gorgonzola, mac nuts and strawberry dressing); the outdoor patio is huge and often has live music; their beer is seriously good. Go for their beer tasting menu—it's six of their eight beers in miniature glasses that adds up to roughly the equivalent of two regular-sized beers. They only distribute in Hawai'i. ⊠ *Kuakini Hwy. just past Palani intersection on right, tucked back a bit so keep an eye out once you pass light at Palani, Kailua-Kona* ☎ *808/329–2739* ▤ *MC, V. $9–$15.*

$–$$ ✕ **Quinn's Almost By the Sea.** Quinn's is directly across the street from the King Kamehameha Hotel, and, to be honest, it's a bit of a dive. That said, it does have a few things going for it—the best Ono sandwiches on the island, excellent calamari, low prices, a funky bar filled with fishermen, and good hours. They're open until 11 PM, later than any other restaurant in Kailua-Kona (with the exception of Denny's). If time gets away from you on a drive to South Point or the Volcano, Quinn's is awaiting your return with a cheap beer and a basket of fresh calamari. ⊠ *75-5655A Palani Rd.* ☎ *808/329-3822* ▤ *MC, V. $8–$15.*

¢–$ ✕ **Ocean View Inn.** To those on a tight budget, this local hangout facing the pier at Kailua Bay has been a lifesaver for breakfast, lunch, and dinner since the 1920s. Chinese and American food are on the plate-lunch menu, and you can get Hawaiian specialties à la carte. The atmosphere is pure old-time diner, with a funky full bar. Note that the "ocean view" is across the road. ⊠ *75-5683 Ali'i Dr., Kailua-Kona* ☎ *808/329–9998* ▤ *No credit cards* ☉ *Closed Mon. $5–$12.*

The Plate Lunch Tradition

TO EXPERIENCE ISLAND HISTORY FIRST-HAND, take a seat at one of Hawai'i's ubiquitous "plate lunch" eateries, and order a segmented Styrofoam plate piled with rice, macaroni salad, and maybe some fiery pickled vegetable condiment. On the sugar plantations, native Hawaiians and immigrant workers from many different countries ate together in the fields, sharing food from their "kaukau kits," the utilitarian version of the Japanese *bento* lunchbox. From this "melting pot" came the vibrant language of pidgin and its equivalent in food: the plate lunch.

At beaches and events, you can probably see a few tiny kitchens-on-wheels, another excellent venue for sampling plate lunch. These portable restaurants are descendants of "lunch wagons" that began selling food to plantation workers in the 1930s. Try the deep-fried chicken *katsu* (rolled in Japanese panko flour and spices). The marinated beef teriyaki is another good choice, as is miso butterfish. The noodle soup, *saimin*, with its Japanese fish stock and Chinese red-tinted barbecue pork, is a distinctly local medley. Koreans have contributed spicy barbecue *kal-bi* ribs, often served with chili-laden *kimchi* (pickled cabbage). Portuguese bean soup and tangy Filipino *adobo* stew are also favorites. The most popular Hawaiian contribution to the plate lunch is the *laulau*, a mix of meat and fish and young taro leaves, wrapped in more taro leaves and steamed.

¢ ✕ **Bubba's.** If you're hankering for a burger but don't want the chain variety, try Bubba's. Their specialty is old-fashioned burgers with a dozen toppings to choose from, and their milk shakes do a mean job of washing those burgers down. For something different, try the corn dog or local-style chili rice. The atmosphere is casual and fun, as shown by their slogan: "We cheat tourists, drunks and attorneys." ✉ *75-5705 Kuakini Hwy., Kailua-Kona* ☎ *808/329–2966* ⊕ *www.bubbaburger.com* ☰ *MC, V. $7 or less.*

¢ ✕ **Bubba Gump's.** Okay, it's a chain, and a chain that centers around a Tom Hanks movie, no less. Bubba Gump's has got some things going for it, though. For starters, they have the largest outdoor, oceanfront patio of any restaurant on the island for about ¹⁄₁₀ the price. And the food's not bad, if you can get over the silly names. Anything with popcorn shrimp in it is good, and their "Run Chicken Run" salad (a combination of greens, chicken, Gorgonzola cheese, walnuts, and cranberries) is the perfect size for lunch. They do a great breakfast, too, with strong coffee and plenty of options, from the cream-cheese stuffed French toast to standard bacon and eggs. ✉ *75-5776 Ali'i Dr., Kailua-Kona* ☎ *808/ 331–8442* ⊕ *www.bubbagump.com* ☰ *MC, V. $7 or less.*

Contemporary

$$$–$$$$ ✕ **Edward's at Kanaloa.** What is essentially a covered patio next to the pool of a condo complex also happens to be (weather permitting) a decent little restaurant overlooking the ocean. Real tablecloths, fresh flow-

ers, and candles on the tables make this a romantic spot as well. Offering an alternative to the regional cuisine, Edward's Mediterranean menu includes fresh fish, rack of lamb, pork tenderloin, and a 16-ounce T-bone steak. Edward's is discreetly tucked away inside a residential community just south of the Keahou Shopping Center; it's a good idea to call for directions. Reservations are recommended. ⊠ *Kanaloa at Kona, 78-261 Manukai St., Kailua-Kona* ☎ *808/324–1434* ▭ *MC, V. $19–$42.*

$$–$$$ ✕ **Huggo's.** This is the only restaurant in town that's comparable to the splurge restaurants at the Kohala-coast resorts. Open windows extend out over the rocks at the ocean's edge, and at night you can almost touch the manta rays drawn to the spotlights. Relax with a Kīlauea cocktail for two and feast on fresh local seafood; the catch changes daily, and the nightly chef's special is always a good bet. **Huggo's on the Rocks,** next door, is a great little outdoor bar literally on the rocks with a floor of sand; it's become Kailua-Kona's hot spot for drinks and live music on Friday nights. ⊠ *75-5828 Kahakai Rd., off Ali'i Dr., Kailua-Kona* ☎ *808/329–1493* ⊕ *www.huggos.com* ▭ *AE, D, DC, MC, V. $15–$30.*

$$–$$$ ✕ **Kai at Sheraton Keauhou.** Aside from the lobby, this is the best-looking part of the new Sheraton. Kai has a primo view of Keauhou Bay, and they smartly designed enormous windows along the ocean-side of the restaurant. The windows are left open most of the time, making it almost feel like an outdoor restaurant. The menu is limited, but everything on it is good, from the fresh local fish to Waimea-raised, hormone-free chicken. All is prepared with that fusion of Pacific Rim and continental that makes up Hawaiian cuisine. The seared 'ahi appetizer is not to be missed. Breakfast is a good bet as well; very reasonable, and the view during the daytime is just about perfect. ⊠ *78-128 Ehukai St., Kailua-Kona* ☎ *808/930–4900* ⊲ *Reservations recommended* ▭ *AE, MC, V. $13–$25.*

$$–$$$ ✕ **O's.** (Formerly Oodles of Noodles). Chef Amy Ferguson-Ota combines Southwestern flavors with Hawaiian regional cuisine and a touch of French cooking. There are noodles of all types, in all shapes, from all ethnic backgrounds—be they as delicate spring rolls, as a crisp garnish to an exquisite salad, or as orecchiette in Ota's tuna casserole with wok-seared spiced 'ahi and shiitake cream. ⊠ *Crossroads Shopping Center, 75-1129 Henry St., Kailua-Kona* ☎ *808/329–9222* ▭ *AE, D, DC, MC, V. $15–$22.*

$–$$$ ✕ **Tropics Café at Royal Kona Resort.** From the open-air dining room, you have a lovely view of boats bobbing in Kailua Bay, outlined by the sun. The restaurant serves daily breakfast buffets and is open nightly for à la carte dinners, but the place is best known for its ample seafood and prime-rib buffets on Tuesday, Friday, and Saturday nights—a good-value feast for big eaters. The resort is within walking distance of central Kailua-Kona. ⊠ *75-5852 Ali'i Dr., Kailua-Kona* ☎ *808/329–3111* ▭ *AE, D, DC, MC, V. $11–$30.*

French

$$$–$$$$ ✕ **La Bourgogne.** A genial husband-and-wife team owns this relaxing, country-style restaurant with dark-wood walls and private, romantic booths. The traditional French menu has classics such as beef fillet with

5

a cabernet sauvignon sauce, escargots, rack of lamb with roasted garlic and rosemary, and a less-traditional venison with a pomegranate glaze. ⊠ *Kuakini Plaza S on Hwy. 11, 77-6400 Nālani St., Kailua-Kona* ☏ *808/329–6711* ⟁ *Reservations essential* ⊟ *AE, D, DC, MC, V* ⊘ *Closed Sun. and Mon. No lunch. $20–$32.*

$–$$ ✕ **Peaberry and Galette.** This new creperie in the Keauhou shopping center, right next to the movie theater, is a welcome addition to the neighborhood. They serve Illy espresso, excellent sweet and savory crepes, and rich desserts like lemon cheesecake and chocolate mousse made fresh daily. It's got a cool, urban-café vibe, and it's a nice place to hang for a bit if you're waiting for your film to start, or just feel like taking a break from paradise to flip through the latest *W* and sip a decent espresso. ⊠ *Keauhou Shopping Center, 78-6740 Makolea St., Kailua-Kona* ☏ *808/322–6020* ⊟ *MC, V. $10–$15.*

Hawaiian Fast Food

¢–$ ✕ **Sam Choy's Kaloko Restaurant.** Low prices and huge portions make this a local favorite. Highlights include the huge *loco moco* breakfast (rice, gravy, and grilled onions topped with fried egg and 13 choices ranging from Spam to teriyaki chicken), and home-style plate lunches. The restaurant is cafeterialike and adorned with photos of celebrity visitors. It's in the Kaloka Light Industrial Park, off Highway 19, between Kona and the airport. ⊠ *73-5576 Kauhola St., Kailua-Kona* ☏ *808/326–1545* ⊟ *MC, V* ⊘ *No dinner. $5–$13.*

¢ ✕ **Ba-Le.** Comparable to Kona Mix Plate in terms of prices, food quality, and local cred, Ba-Le serves a great plate lunch. They also have tasty Vietnamese-influenced food, such as their popular croissant sandwiches stuffed with mint, lemongrass, sprouts, and your choice from a variety of Vietnamese-style meats. They've got a Hilo location, too, and about 20 other shops throughout the state, but they're Hawaiian-owned and operated, so they don't really feel like a chain. ⊠ *Kona Coast Shopping Center, 74-5588 Palani Rd., Kailua-Kona* ☏ *808/327–1212* ⊟ *No credit cards. $5–$7.*

¢ ✕ **Kona Mix Plate.** Don't be surprised if you find yourself rubbing elbows with lots of hungry locals at this inconspicuous Kona lunch spot. The antithesis of a tourist trap, this casual island favorite with fluorescent lighting and stark wooden tables is all about the food. Try the teriyaki chicken, shrimp tempura, or the *katsu*—a chicken breast fried with Japanese bread crumbs and served with a sweet, rich sauce. ⊠ *341 Palani St., Kailua-Kona* ☏ *808/329–8104* ⊟ *No credit cards* ⊘ *Closed Sun. $5–$7.*

Indonesian

$$ ✕ **Sibu.** This excellent and reasonable restaurant is inside a tiny shopping mall (and nearly hidden by a large stone fountain) close to the pier in central Kailua-Kona. Try one of their combo platters to get a little taste of everything, from Balinese chicken to the shrimp satay flavored with coconut milk and red chili. Opt for the Indonesian fried rice with raisins—it puts plain Basmati rice to shame. Be forewarned: the tasty Ayum Panggang Pedis (spicy grilled chicken fillets with black and red pepper) really packs a punch! ⊠ *75-5695 Ali`i Dr., Kailua-Kona* ☏ *808/329–1112* ⊟ *No credit cards. $12–$18.*

Italian

$$–$$$ ✗ **Michaelangelo's Italian & Seafood Restaurant.** This dining room has a lovely upstairs location, with great waterfront views, in the Waterfront Row complex of shops and eateries. The traditional Italian fare is prepared with creative local flavors. Favorite entrées include lasagna, chicken cacciatore, and macadamia-nut sea scallops. The crusted mozzarella planks or fried calamari are excellent appetizers. Dress is casual, but reservations are recommended. ✉ *75-5770 Ali'i Dr., Kailua-Kona* ☎ *808/329–4436* ▭ *AE, D, MC, V. $12–$30.*

$$ ✗ **Basil's.** This tiny traditional Italian spot is nothing special, really—the tablecloths are checkered, the candles are in chianti bottles, there's pizza and spaghetti on the menu, and it always feels a little hot and greasy inside. That said, the pizza is decent, the beer's cheap, and you can't beat the location. It's on Ali'i Drive in downtown Kailua-Kona, right across the street from an unobstructed ocean view. ✉ *75-5707 Ali'i Dr., Kailua-Kona* ☎ *808/326–7836* ▭ *MC, V. $12–$30.*

$$ ✗ **Bianelli's Gourmet Pizza.** Bianelli's is a local favorite for happy hour, which is no wonder, what with $2 Millers and $3 Kona microbrews, plus free pizza. Otherwise, dinner is not spectacular. Breakfast, on the other hand, is a good deal, and this is one of the few places in town to get what Mainlanders consider a traditional breakfast. ✉ *Kuakini Hwy., right side just before Palani, Kailua-Kona* ☎ *808/329–4436* ▭ *AE, D, MC, V $12–$30.*

Japanese

$–$$ ✗ **Kenichi Pacific.** With its black-lacquer tables and deep-red banquettes, Kenichi's seems a little out of place in this small strip mall, and its location has kept many tourists from finding it, though they've been open for a few years now. This is where everyone in Kailua-Kona goes when they feel like splurging on top-notch sushi. It's a little on the spendy side, but it's worth it. The sashimi is so fresh it melts in your mouth, and their signature rolls are inventive and tasty. For vegetarians, the Austin roll—tempura asparagus—is fish-free and delicious. ✉ *Keauhou Shopping Center, Kailua-Kona* ☎ *808/322–9140* ▭ *No credit cards. $17–$30.*

Mexican

$$ ✗ **Pancho & Lefty's.** Downtown, above the stores across the street from the Kona Village Shopping Center, Pancho & Lefty's is a typical Tex-Mex place—great for nachos and margaritas (watch out, they pour 'em strong on a lazy afternoon). Some of the items on their menu are expensive, and some of the combos are described exactly the same way in other sections of the menu for less, so read carefully. ✉ *75-5719 Ali'i Dr., Kailua-Kona* ☎ *808/326–2171* ▭ *MC, V. $12–$18.*

$$ ✗ **Tres Hombres.** The food's good, but a little overpriced. The real reason to come here is their assortment of margaritas, many mixed with fresh local fruit juice. They also have a location in Kawaihae. ✉ *75-5864 Walua Rd., Kailua-Kona* ☎ *808/329–1292* ▭ *MC, V. $11–$20.*

¢ ✗ **Tacos El Unico.** At last, Mexican food at the right price on the Big Island. You can find an array of soft-taco choices (beef, chicken, and more), burritos, *tortas*, great homemade tamales, quesadillas, and *taquitos*. Order at the counter, take a seat outside at one of a dozen yellow tables with

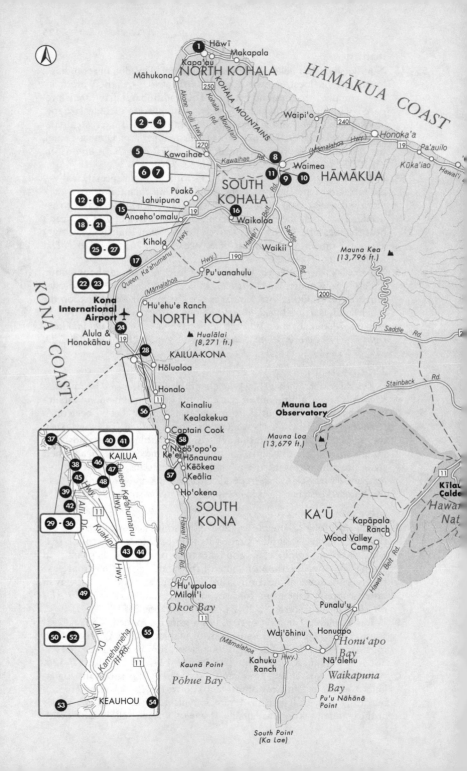

Kohala ▼

Alan Wong's Hualalai Grille at Four Seasons . **23**

Bamboo Restaurant **1**

The Batik at Mauna Kea Beach Hotel **5**

Big Island Steak House **26**

Brown's Beach House at the Fairmont Orchid . . . **10**

Café Pesto **3**

CanoeHouse at the Mauna Lani Bay Hotel and Bungalows . . **15**

Coast Grille at Hāpuna Beach Prince Hotel **6**

Donatoni's at the Hilton Waikoloa Village **20**

Grand Palace **25**

The Grill at the Fairmont Orchid **14**

Hakone at Hāpuna Beach Prince Hotel **7**

Hale Samoa at Kona Village Resort . . . **17**

Hawai'i Calls at Waikoloa Beach Marriott **21**

Imari at the Hilton Waikoloa Village **18**

Kamuela Compan Provision at the Hilton Waikoloa Village **19**

Kawaihae Harbor Grill and Seafood Bar **4**

Norio's Sushi Bar & Restaurant **12**

Pahu i'a at Four Seasons Resort Hualālai **22**

Roy's Waikoloa Bar and Grill **27**

The Village Steak House **16**

Waimea ▼

Daniel Thiebaut **9**

Edelweiss **11**

Merriman's **8**

Parker Ranch Grill **10**

Kailua-Kona ▼

Ba-Le **33**

Basil's **34**

Bianelli's Gourmet Pizza **35**

La Bourgogne **55**

Bubba's **43**

Edward's at Kanaloa . . . **50**

Huggo's **39**

Jackie Ray's Ohana Grill **44**

Jameson's by the Sea . . **49**

Kai at Sheraton Keauhou **53**

Kenichi Pacific **51**

Kona Brewing Company and Brewpub **31**

Kona Inn Restaurant . . . **30**

Kona Mix Plate **46**

Michaelangelo's **29**

Ocean View Inn **40**

Orchid Thai Cuisine . . . **28**

O's **47**

Pancho & Lefty's **36**

Peaberry & Galette . . . **52**

Quinn's Almost By the Sea **32**

Rooster's **38**

Sam Choy's **24**

Sibu **41**

Tacos El Unico **37**

Thai Rin Restaurant . . . **48**

Tres Hombres Beach Grill **2, 45**

Tropics Café at Royal Kona Resort **42**

South Kona ▼

Café Nasturtium **56**

Ke'ei Café **57**

Manago Hotel **58**

Teshima's **54**

Volcano ▼

Kīlauea Lodge **60**

Lava Rock Cafe **59**

Hilo ▼

Ba-Le **61**

Café 100 . . . . **64**

Café Pesto **69**

Harrington's **74**

Ken's House of Pancakes **63**

Kuhio Grille **75**

Naung Mai **66**

Nihon Restaurant **62**

Pescatore **67**

Queen's Court at Hilo Hawaiian Hotel . . . **71**

Retaurant Kaikodo . . . **68**

Royal Siam **65**

Seaside Restaurant **73**

Ting Hao **72**

Uncle Billy's Restaurant **70**

Where to Eat on the Big Island

blue umbrellas, and enjoy all the good flavors served up in those red plastic baskets. ⊠ *Kona Marketplace, 75-5729 Ali'i Dr., Kailua-Kona* ☎ *808/326–4033* ▤ *No credit cards. $3–$7.*

Thai

$–$$ ✕ **Orchid Thai Cuisine.** This reasonably priced, family-run restaurant is off the beaten track in a small strip mall in Kona's old industrial area. It's cheerfully decorated with purple-and-gold Thai fabrics, and orchids (real and fake) abound. Entrées range from barbecue hen with lemongrass and garlic to basic curries (red, green, yellow, and "evil"); don't miss the summer rolls. Top off your meal with mango and sticky rice. ⊠ *77-5563 Kaiwi St., Suite B 27–28, Kailua-Kona* ☎ *808/327–9437* ▤ *MC, V* ☉ *Closed Sun. $7–$14.*

$–$$ ✕ **Thai Rin Restaurant.** The Thai chef-owner at this old-timer in Ali'i Sunset Plaza is likely to take your order, cook it, and bring it to your table himself. The menu includes five curries, a green-papaya salad, and a popular Thai Rin platter, which combines spring rolls, satay, *tom yum* (lemongrass soup), and beef salad. ⊠ *75-5799 Ali'i Dr., Kailua-Kona* ☎ *808/329–2929* ▤ *AE, D, DC, MC, V. $9–$17.*

South Kona

American–Casual

$–$$ ✕ **Cafe Nasturtium.** This bright café is tucked into a happy little red-orange house in Kainaliu, about 10-minutes away from Kailua-Kona. They've got signs just before and after so you'll know when it's coming up and when you've passed it. They serve only organic food here, some of it vegan and all of it very good, from soups made fresh daily to the 'ahi tuna sandwiches to homemade *lilikoi* (passionfruit) sorbet. The back patio is sunny and green, with flowers and vines climbing the walls. The downside—service is painfully slow, and the hours are a little strange. Call ahead to make sure they're open. ⊠ *Hwy. 11, Kainaliu* ☎ *808/322–5083* ▤ *MC, V* ☉ *Closed weekends. $9–$15.*

$–$$ ✕ **Ke'ei Café.** This casual restaurant is in a plantation-style building 15 minutes south of Kona. Delicious dinners with Brazilian, Asian, and European flavors utilize fresh ingredients provided by local farmers. Try the Thai red curry or wok-seared 'ahi accompanied by a selection from the extensive wine list. ⊠ *Hwy. 11, ½ mi south of Kainaliu, Hōnaunau* ☎ *808/328–8451* ⌔ *Reservations essential* ▤ *No credit cards* ☉ *Closed Sun. $9–$19.*

★ $ ✕ **Manago Hotel.** About 20-minutes south of Kailua-Kona, Manago is a time-warp experience. A vintage neon sign identifies the hotel, and Formica tables, ceiling fans, and venetian blinds add to the flavor of this film-noir spot. Their T-shirts (which are totally wearable and not tacky if you need to bring back a gift for anyone) brag that they have the best pork chops in town, and it's not false advertising. Fresh fish is excellent as well, especially ono and butterfish. Unless you request something different, the fish is all sautéed with Manago's special butter-soy-sauce concoction (always good, don't worry). Meals come with an assortment of side dishes that change from time to time, and rice for everyone, served family style.

✉ *82-6155 Māmalahoa Hwy., Captain Cook* ☎ *808/323–2642* ⊕ *www. managohotel.com* ⊟ *D, DC, MC, V* ⊘ *Closed Mon.* *$7–$12.*

Japanese

$–$$ ✕ **Teshima's.** Locals show up at Teshima's whenever they're in the mood for sashimi, beef *hekka* (beef and vegetables cooked together in an iron pot), or puffy shrimp tempura at a reasonable price. You might also want to try a *teishoku* (tray) of assorted Japanese delicacies. Service is laid-back and friendly. The restaurant is 15-minutes south of Kailua-Kona. ✉ *Māmalahoa Hwy., Honalo* ☎ *808/322–9140* ⊟ *No credit cards.* *$8–$16.*

Volcano

American–Casual

$–$$ ✕ **Lava Rock Cafe.** For a decent meal, a drink, or Internet access, head to the Lava Rock, which serves breakfast and lunch daily and dinner Tuesday through Saturday in a breezy, pinewood-latice setting. Dishes range from chicken salad to New York steak, beverages from cappuccino to wine. ✉ *Old Volcano Hwy., behind Kimlauea General Store, Volcano* ☎ *808/967–8526* ⊘ *No dinner Sun.* ⊟ *MC, V.* *$7–$18.*

Contemporary

$$–$$$$ ✕ **Kīlauea Lodge.** Chef Albert Jeyte combines contemporary trends with traditional cooking styles from the mainland, France, and his native Hamburg, Germany. Entrées include venison, duck à l'orange with an apricot-mustard glaze, and authentic *hasenpfeffer* (braised rabbit served with Jeyte's signature sauerbraten). Built in 1937 as a YMCA camp, the restaurant still has the original "Friendship Fireplace" made from stones from around the world. The roaring fire, koa tables, and warm lighting create a lodge feel inside the sunny main building. ✉ *Old Volcano Hwy., Volcano Village* ☎ *808/967–7366* ⊕ *www.kilauealodge.com* ⊟ *AE, MC, V* ⊘ *No lunch.* *$17–$38.*

$–$$ ✕ **Thai Thai Restaurant.** The food is authentic, and the prices are reasonable at this little Volcano Village find. A steaming-hot curry or a dish of pad thai noodles is the perfect antidote to a chilly volcano day. A chicken satay is excellent—the peanut dipping sauce the perfect match of sweet and spicy. Service is warm and friendly. ✉ *19-4084 Old Volcano Rd.* ☎ *808/967–7969.* ⊘ *No Lunch.* ⊟ *MC, V.* *$9–$16.*

Hilo

American–Casual

$$$ ✕ **Queen's Court at Hilo Hawaiian Hotel.** Queen's Court is known for one thing: buffets. On the weekends they have Seafood (Friday and Saturday) and Hawaiian (Sunday), and during the week it's Prime Rib every night. The prime rib's not great, but their seafood specialties are, so both the Seafood and the Hawaiian buffets are recommended. ✉ *1730 Kamehameha Ave.* ☎ *808/935–8711* ⊟ *AE, D, DC, MC, V.* *$16–$25.*

$$–$$$ ✕ **Harrington's.** A great view and a daily happy hour make this steak-and-seafood restaurant on Reed's Bay a popular place. You can't go wrong with either the catch of the day served in a tangy citrus-wasabi beurre blanc or the New York peppercorn steak. The garlic-laced Slavic steak is a specialty. For lunch try the Harrington's Burger, served with cream cheese aioli. ⊠ *135 Kalaniana'ole Ave.* ☎ *808/961–4966* ⊟ *MC, V. $16–$25.*

$$–$$$ ✕ **Seaside Restaurant.** The Nakagawa family has been running this home-based eatery and aquafarm since the early 1920s. The decor is bare-bones, with plastic chairs and wooden tables, but Seaside serves some of the best and freshest fish on the island. Locals travel far for the fried *āholehole* (young Hawaiian flagtail). Not a fish eater? Try the grilled lamb chops, pasta, chicken, or prime rib. Arrive before sunset and request a table on the patio for a view of fishponds and egret roosting. ⊠ *1790 Kalaniana'ole Ave.* ☎ *808/935–8825* ⊟ *AE, DC, MC, V* ⊘ *Closed Mon. No lunch. $11–$27.*

$–$$$ ✕ **Café Pesto.** Both branches of Café Pesto—in the quaint harbor town of Kawaihae and in Hilo—are equally popular. Fresh local seafood, exotic pizzas (with chili grilled shrimp, shiitake mushrooms, and cilantro crème fraîche, for example), and Asian-inspired pastas and risottos reflect the ethnic diversity of the island. Local microbrews and a full-service bar make this a good place to end the evening. ⊠ *S. Hata Bldg., 308 Kamehameha Ave., Hilo* ☎ *808/969–6640* ⊕ *www.cafepesto.com* ⊟ *AE, D, DC, MC, V. $10–$29.*

$–$$$ ✕ **Uncle Billy's Restaurant.** Uncle Billy's is pure Hawaiian kitsch—right out of 1930s Hollywood—but the thatch roofs, tinkling Capiz-shell wind chimes, and Tahitian-print curtains add to the fun, as does a free nightly hula show. The show and the ambience are the reasons to come here; the experience is great fun, the food is so-so. Choose from mahimahi meunière, teriyaki chicken, pastas, soup and salad, and local specialties. ⊠ *Hilo Bay Hotel, 87 Banyan Dr.* ☎ *808/935–0861* ⊟ *AE, D, DC, MC, V* ⊘ *No lunch. $9–$25.*

$–$$ ✕ **Ken's House of Pancakes.** For years this 24-hour coffee shop between the airport and the Banyan Drive hotels has been a gathering place for Hilo residents. As its name implies, Ken's serves good pancakes but there are about 180 items to choose from on the menu. Wednesday is paniolo prime-rib night. ⊠ *1730 Kamehameha Ave.* ☎ *808/935–8711* ⊟ *AE, D, DC, MC, V. $8–$15.*

Chinese

¢–$$ ✕ **Ting Hao.** This Mandarin restaurant on the edge of Hilo Bay emphasizes fresh island fish with offerings that change daily. Entrées include spicy Szechuan and Hunan dishes and scrumptious specialties from Taiwan and Beijing. The special slow-roasted Peking duck, wrapped in a Mandarin pastry layer and served with plum sauce, must be ordered a day in advance. ⊠ *Hawai'i Naniloa Resort, 93 Banyan Dr.* ☎ *808/935–8888* ⊟ *AE, D, DC, MC, V* ⊘ *Closed Tues. $3–$15.*

Contemporary

★ **$$–$$$$** ✕ **Restaurant Kaikodo.** Hilo's newest upscale fine-dining room blends East-West cuisines and decor. For appetizers, try the Chinese dumplings, Big Island sushi roll, stir-fried Hawaiian peppers and mushrooms, or wok-seared crispy tofu. Seafood rules here, so sample the gomashio-seared 'ahi tuna, lemongrass-steamed *'ōpakapaka* (blue snapper), or shrimp with green-and-white pasta ribbons. There are lamb, beef, and chicken selections as well, and scrumptious desserts to top off the meal. A long Victorian bar graces the lounge area. ⊠ *60 Keawe St.* ☎ *808/961–2558* ▭ *AE, D, DC, MC, V. $16–$35.*

Hawaiian Fast Food

¢–$$ ✕ **Kūhiō Grille.** There's no ambience to speak of, and your water is served in unbreakable plastic, but if you're searching for local fare—that eclectic and undefinable fusion of ethnic cuisines—Kūhiō Grille is a must. Sam Araki serves a 1-pound *laulau* (a steamed bundle made with Waipi'o Valley–grown taro leaves and pork), alongside plate lunches and grilled meats. This diner at the edge of Hilo's largest shopping mall opens as early as 6 AM. ⊠ *Prince Kūhiō Shopping Plaza, 111 E. Puainako St., at Hwy. 11* ☎ *808/959–2336* ▭ *AE, MC, V. $5–$14.*

¢–$ ✕ **Café 100.** This popular local restaurant is famous for their huge and tasty *loco moco,* in over a dozen varieties, and their dirt cheap breakfast and lunch specials (you can stuff yourself for $3 if you order right). If you're looking for a salad, keep walking. ⊠ *969 Kilauea Ave* ☎ *808/935–8683* ▭ *No credit cards. $5–$10.*

¢ ✕ **Ba-Le.** Comparable to Café 100 in terms of prices, food quality, and local cred, Ba-Le serves a great plate lunch, but people come here more often for the Vietnamese-influenced sandwiches—tasty concoctions of mint, lemongrass, sprouts, and your choice of Vietnamese-style meats served on either a croissant or crusty french bread. They've got a Kailua-Kona location too, and about 20 other shops throughout the state, but they're Hawaiian-owned and operated, so they don't really feel like a chain. ⊠ *111 East Puainako Hilo* ☎ *808/959–1300* ▭ *No credit cards. $5–$7.*

Italian

$$–$$$ ✕ **Pescatore.** With dim lights, stately high-back chairs, and dark wood, Pescatore serves surprisingly authentic Italian cuisine. The menu features several types of pasta, pizza, and items like cioppino, lasagne, chicken marsala, eggplant, and chicken or veal Parmigiana. Lunch consists of Italian-style sandwiches; breakfast, on weekends only, features Italian omelettes and crepes. Families love the pastas made to please choosy children. ⊠ *235 Keawe St., at Haili St.* ☎ *808/969–9090* ▭ *AE, D, DC, MC, V. $15–$29.*

Japanese

$$–$$$ ✕ **Nihon Restaurant.** This open, airy dining room has a scenic view of Hilo Bay and is adjacent to the Lili'uokalani Gardens and the Banyan Drive hotels along the bayfront. Servers are dressed in colorful kimonos, and Japanese art and music add to the ambience. The menu offers a wide choice of authentic Japanese cuisine including beef, pork, chicken, and seafood. Try the soba noodles, *misoyaki* butterfish (marinated in a rich miso-soy blend, then grilled), and teriyaki steak. A sushi bar provides a full range of wonderful and varied sushi. ⊠ *123 Lihiwai St.* ☎ *808/969–1133* ▭ *AE, MC, V* ☺ *Closed Sun. $12–$30.*

Thai

$ ✕ **Naung Mai.** This restaurant in downtown Hilo is nothing more than five tables, three booths, and owner-chef Alisa Rung Khongnok hard at work in the visible kitchen. It's hard to find, but a colorful exterior, a cozy interior with mellow music and original art on the walls, and fresh, reasonably priced meals greet intrepid customers. It may be the best Thai food on the island. ✉ *86 Kīlauea Ave.* ☎ *808/934–7540* ▤ *MC, V* ☺ *Closed Sun. No lunch Wed. or Sat. $8–$11.*

$ ✕ **Royal Siam.** A downtown Hilo fixture, this authentic Thai eatery offers little ambience in its straightforward dining room. But you don't need a dramatic view when you can choose from a menu that includes five curries and plenty of stir-fry—the tangy stir-fried garlic shrimp with coconut milk and wild mushrooms is particularly good. ✉ *70 Mamo St.* ☎ *808/961–6100* ▤ *AE, D, DC, MC, V* ☺ *Closed Sun. $7–$12.*

ENTERTAINMENT & NIGHTLIFE

If you're the sort of person who doesn't come alive until after dark, you're going to be pretty lonely on the Big Island. Blame it on the plantation heritage. People did their cane-raising in the morning.

Entertainment

Hula

★ For hula lovers, the biggest show of the year and the largest event of its kind in the world is the annual **Merrie Monarch Hula Festival** (✉ Hawai'i Naniloa Resort, 93 Banyan Dr., Hilo 96720 ☎ 808/935–9168). Honoring the legacy of King David Kalākaua, Hawai'i's last king, the festival is staged in Hilo at the spacious Edith Kanaka'ole Stadium during the first week following Easter Sunday. Hula hālau compete in various classes of ancient and modern dance styles. You need to reserve accommodations and tickets up to a year in advance.

Lū'au & Polynesian Revues

KOHALA COAST & WAIKOLOA

Hilton Waikoloa Village. The Hilton seats 400 people outdoors at the Kamehameha Court, where the acclaimed Polynesian group Tihati performs a lively show. A buffet dinner provides samplings of Hawaiian food as well as fish, beef, and chicken to appeal to all tastes. ✉ 425 *Waikoloa Beach Dr., Waikoloa* ☎ 808/886–1234 ⊕ *www.hiltonwaikoloavillage. com* ✆ *$75* ☺ *Fri. at 6.*

Mauna Kea Beach Hotel. Once a week, on the gracious North Pointe Lū'au Grounds of the Mauna Kea Beach Hotel, you can sample the best of Hawaiian cuisine while listening to the enchanting songs of Nani Lim. Every Tuesday, chefs come together here to create a traditional Hawaiian *pa'ina* (dinner feast), which includes the classic *kālua* (roasted in an underground oven) pig. ✉ 62-100 *Mauna Kea Beach Dr., Kohala Coast* ☎ 808/882–7222 ⊕ *www.maunakeabeachhotel.com* ✆ *$76* ☺ *Tues. at 6.*

Waikoloa Beach Marriott. The Marriott offers a great-value lū'au at the Lū'au Grounds, where entertainment includes a Samoan fire dance as well as songs and dances of various Pacific cultures. Traditional Hawai-

Hawai'i's Hippy Hippy Shake

LEGENDS IMMORTALIZE LAKA as the goddess of hula, portraying her as a gentle deity who journeyed from island to island, sharing the dance with all who were willing to learn. Laka's graceful movements, spiritual and layered with meaning, brought to life the history, the traditions, and the genealogy of the islanders. Ultimately taught by parents to children and by *kumu* (teachers) to students, the hula preserved the culture of these ancient peoples without a written language.

Some legends trace the origins of hula to Moloka'i, where a family named La'ila'i was said to have established the dance at Ka'ana. Eventually the youngest sister of the fifth generation of La'ila'i was given the name Laka, and she carried the dance to all the Islands in the Hawaiian chain.

Another legend credits Hi'iaka, the volcano goddess Pele's youngest sister, as having danced the first hula in the *hala* groves of Puna on the Big Island. Hi'iaka and possibly even Pele were thought to have learned the dance from Hōpoe, a mortal and a poet also credited as the originator of the dance.

In any case, hula thrived until the arrival of puritanical New England missionaries, who with the support of Queen Ka'ahumanu, an early Christian convert, attempted to ban the dance as an immoral activity throughout the 19th century.

Though hula may not have been publicly performed, it remained a spiritual and poetic art form, as well as a lively celebration of life presented during special celebrations in many Hawaiian homes. David Kalākaua, the popular "Merrie Monarch" who was king from 1874 to 1891, revived the hula. Dancers were called to perform at official functions.

Gradually, ancient hula, called *kahiko*, was replaced with a lively, updated form of dance called *'auana* (modern). Modern costumes of fresh ti-leaf or raffia skirts replaced the voluminous *pa'u* skirts made of *kapa* (cloth made of beaten bark), and the music became more melodic, as opposed to earlier chanted routines accompanied by *pahu* (drums), *'ili 'ili* (rocks used as castanets), and other percussion instruments. Such tunes as "Lovely Hula Hands," "Little Grass Shack," and the "Hawaiian Wedding Song" are considered hula 'auana. Dancers might wear graceful *holomu'u* with short trains or ti-leaf skirts with coconut bra tops.

In 1963 the Merrie Monarch Festival was established in Hilo on the Big Island and has since become the most prestigious hula competition in the state. It's staged annually the weekend after Easter, and contestants of various *halau* (hula schools) from Hawai'i and the mainland compete in the categories of Miss Aloha Hula, hula *kahiko* (ancient), and hula *'auana* (modern). For more information, contact the **Merrie Monarch Hula Festival** (✉ Hawai'i Naniloa Resort, 93 Banyan Dr., Hilo 96720 ☎ 808/935–9168).

5

ian dishes are served alongside more familiar fare. ⊠ *69-275 Waikoloa Beach Dr., Waikoloa* ☎ *808/886–6789* ⊕ *www.outrigger.com* ⊠ *$67, including open bar* ⊙ *Wed. and Sun. 5–8:30.*

KAILUA-KONA **King Kamehameha's Kona Beach Hotel's Island Breeze Lū`au.** Witness the arrival of the Royal Court by canoe and have pictures taken at this beachfront event, which includes a 22-item buffet, an open bar, and a show. ⊠ *75-5660 Palani Rd.* ☎ *808/326–4969 or 808/329–8111* ⊕ *www. islandbreezeluau.com* ⊠ *$63* ⊙ *Tues.–Thurs. and Sun. 5:30–8:30.*

★ **Kona Village Resort.** In its utter isolation, the lū`au here is one of the most authentic and traditional on the Islands. As in other lū`au, activities include the steaming of a whole pig in the *imu* (ground oven). A Polynesian show on a stage over a lagoon is magical. ⊠ *6 mi north of Kona International Airport, off Queen Ka`ahumanu Hwy., Kailua-Kona* ☎ *808/325–5555 or 808/325–4273* ⊕ *www.konavillage.com* ⊠ *$84, including open bar* ⊙ *Fri. from 5; walking tour at 5:30, imu ceremony at 6:30, dinner at 7, show at 8.*

Royal Kona Resort. This resort lights lū`au torches for a full Polynesian show and a Hawaiian-style oceanfront buffet three times a week. ⊠ *75-5852 Ali`i Dr.* ☎ *808/329–3111 Ext. 4* ⊕ *www.konaluau.com* ⊠ *$59, including beer and wine* ⊙ *Mon., Wed., Fri., and Sat. at 5.*

Sunset Cruises

★ **Captain Beans' Polynesian Dinner Cruise.** This is the ever-popular standby in sunset dinner cruises. You can't miss it—as the sun sets in Kailua, look out over the water and you'll see a big gaudy boat with distinctive orange sails. This cruise is corny, and dinner is nothing great, but it's an experience, with unlimited drinks and a Hawaiian show. This is for adults only. ⊠ *Kailua Pier, Kailua-Kona* ☎ *808/329–2955 or 800/831–5541* ⊕ *www.robertshawaii.com* ⊠ *$55–$66, including dinner, entertainment, and open bar* ⊙ *Tues.–Sun. at 5:15.*

☾ **Island Grill Dinner Cruise.** The *Kona Dream*, a comfortable modern trimaran, takes you on a fabulous sunset cruise along the scenic Kona Coast from Kailua-Kona Pier. Enjoy tropical libations and indulge in a spectacular island grilled dinner served pūpū-style while relaxing to the sounds of contemporary island music. This two-hour cruise includes the best of Kona's famed beautiful blazing sunsets. ⊠ *Kailua-Kona Pier, Ali`i Dr. at Palani Rd., Kailua-Kona* ☎ *808/326–6000 or 800/400–7300* ⊕ *www.dream-cruises.com* ⊠ *$57* ⊙ *Daily 5:30–7:30.*

Film

KAILUA-KONA **Keauhou 7 Cinemas** (⊠ Keauhou Shopping Center, 78-6831 Ali`i Dr. ☎ 808/324–7200) is a splendid seven-theater complex. The 10-screen **Makalapua Stadium Cinemas** (⊠ Makalapua Ave. next to Big Kmart ☎ 808/327–0444) has stadium seating and digital surround sound. Alas, these two theaters frequently show the exact same films, albeit at slightly different times.

HILO **Kress Cinemas** (⊠ 174 Kamehameha Ave. ☎ 808/961–3456) screens selected art films. After decades of being closed, the historic **Palace Theatre** (⊠ 38 Haili St. ☎ 808/934–7010), built in 1925, now shows movies. First-run films are shown regularly at the state-of-the-art **Prince Kūhiō Stadium Cinemas** (✉ Prince Kūhiō Plaza, 111 E. Puainako St. ☎ 808/959–4595).

Bars & Clubs

Kohala District

Honu Bar. This elegant spot at the Mauna Lani Bay Hotel and Bungalows on the Kohala Coast has a nice dance floor for weekend revelers; the music varies, so call ahead. Regardless, appetizers, imported cigars, and fine cognacs make this a popular, upscale gathering spot. ✉ 68-1400 *Mauna Lani Dr., Kohala Coast* ☎ *808/885–6622.*

Polo Bar at the Fairmont. An old-school, wood-paneled watering hole, with a huge lānai and a great view. Bartenders are great, service is impeccable. The crowd's not rowdy, but it's a great place for a cocktail or an after-dinner port. ✉ *1 N. Kanikū Dr., Kohala Coast* ☎ *808/885–2000.*

Kailua-Kona

Huggo's. Jazz, country, and even rock bands perform at this popular restaurant, so call ahead of time to find out what's on. Outside, people often dance in the sand to Hawaiian songs. ✉ *75-5828 Kahakai Rd., at Aliʻi Dr., Kailua-Kona* ☎ *808/329–1493.*

Lulu's. A young crowd gyrates until 1:30 AM Friday and Saturday to hot dance music—hip-hop, R&B, and rock—spun by a professional DJ. ✉ *75-5819 Aliʻi Dr., Kailua-Kona* ☎ *808/331–2633.*

Oceans. This is the current hot spot in Kona—a sports bar in the back of the Coconut Grove Marketplace. There's a pool table and an outdoor patio, and this place really gets hopping on most weekend evenings. ✉ *Coconut Grove Marketplace, Aliʻi Dr., Kailua-Kona.*

Hilo

Hoʻomalimali Lounge. This lounge and dance club at the Hawaiʻi Naniloa Resort in Hilo competes with the crashing surf on Friday and Saturday night with live music from 9 to midnight. ✉ *93 Banyan Dr., Hilo* ☎ *808/969–3333.*

> ## BEST SUNSET MAI TAIS
>
> **Huggo's on the Rocks (Kailua-Kona).** Perched literally on the rocks above the ocean, with a sand-covered floor, live music Friday and Saturday, and strong drinks.
>
> **Kawaihae Harbor Grill (Kohala).** Views off the deck of the upstairs Seafood Bar, great food in the restaurant next door, and well-poured drinks.
>
> **Kona Inn (Kailua-Kona).** Wide, unobstructed view, in the middle of downtown, best Mai Tais on the island.
>
> **Waiʻoli Lounge in the Hilo Hawaiian Hotel (Hilo).** A nice view of Coconut Island, live music most nights and karaoke others.

5

SHOPPING

Residents like to complain that there isn't much to shop for on the Big Island, but unless you're searching for winter coats or high-tech toys, you can find plenty to deplete your pocketbook. Kailua-Kona has a range of souvenirs from far-flung corners of the globe. Resorts along the Kohala Coast have high-quality exclusive clothing, art, and accessories. Galleries and boutiques, many with the work of local artists, fill historic buildings in Waimea and North Kohala. Hotel shops generally offer the most attractive and original resort wear, but prices run higher than elsewhere.

In general, stores and shopping centers on the Big Island open at 9 or 10 AM and close by 6 PM. Hilo's Prince Kūhiō Shopping Plaza stays open until 9 weekdays. In Kona, most shops in shopping plazas that are geared to tourists remain open until 9. Big outlets such as KTA (a supermarket in Kona Coast Shopping Center) or Wal-Mart on Henry Street are open until midnight.

Kohala

Shopping Centers

Kawaihae Center. This harborside shopping plaza houses restaurants, a dive shop, a bathing-suit store, and art galleries, including the Harbor Gallery. ⊠ *Hwy. 270, Kawaihae.*

King's Shops. Here you can find fine stores such as Under the Koa Tree, with its upscale gift items by artisans, along with high-end outlets such as DFS Galleria and Louis Vuitton and several other specialty resort shops and boutiques. At the other end of the spectrum, there are a couple of convenience stores here, but the prices are stiff. ⊠ *250 Waikoloa Beach Dr., Waikoloa* ☎ *808/886–8811.*

Books & Maps

Kohala Book Shop. In the historic Old Nanbu Hotel, the largest used-book store in the state contains one of the most complete Hawaiian and Pacific collections in the nation plus rare first editions. ⊠ *54-3885 Akoni Pule Hwy., Kapa'au* ☎ *808/889–6400* ⊕ *www.abebooks.com/home/kohalawind.*

Clothing

As Hāwī Turns. This North Kohala shop, in the historic 1932 Toyama Building, adds a sophisticated touch to breezy resort wear, pareos, and hand-painted silk clothing. There are vintage and secondhand treasures, crafts, and gifts as well. ⊠ *Akoni Pule Hwy., Hāwī* ☎ *808/889–5023.*

Paradise Found. Upcountry on the one-street town of Kainaliu—and in Kailua-Kona's shopping centers—this reputable spot carries contemporary silk and rayon clothing. ⊠ *Māmalahoa Hwy. 11, Kainaliu* ☎ *808/322–2111* ⊠ *Lanihau Center, Kailua-Kona* ☎ *808/329–2221* ⊠ *Keauhou Shopping Center, Kailua-Kona* ☎ *808/324–1177.*

Hawaiian Arts & Crafts

Remote North Kohala has dozens of artists and hosts a remarkable number of galleries in its old restored plantation buildings.

Ackerman Gallery. Painter Gary Ackerman; his wife, Yesan; and their daughter, Camille, have a fine and varied collection of gifts for sale in two locations near the King Kamehameha statue. ⊠ *Akoni Pule Hwy., Kapa'au* ☎ *808/889–5971.*

Elements. Be sure to stop at the Old Nanbu Hotel, a historic building constructed in 1898. Here, working in the front window of his store, Elements, John Flynn creates exquisite jewelry such as delicate, silver-maile lei and gold waterfalls. The shop also showcases carefully chosen gifts, including unusual ceramics and glass. ⊠ *54-3885 Akoni Pule Hwy., Kapa'au* ☎ *808/889–0760.*

Gallery at Bamboo. Inside the Bamboo Restaurant in Hāwī, this gallery seduces visitors with koa-wood pieces such as rocking chairs and writing desks. It also has a wealth of gift items such as boxes, jewelry, and Hawaiian wrapping paper. ⊠ *Hāwī Rd., Hāwī* ☎ *808/889–1441.*

Nanbu Gallery. Here you can admire the paintings of owner Patrick Sweeney and other island artists. ⊠ *54-3885 Akoni Pule Hwy., Kapa'au* ☎ *808/889–0997.*

Rankin Gallery. Watercolorist and oil painter Patrick Louis Rankin runs this shop in the old Wo On Store, next to the Chinese community and social hall, the Tong Wo Society. ⊠ *53-4380 Akoni Pule Hwy., Kapa'au* ☎ *808/889–6849.*

Sue Swerdlow Art Gallery. It's worth a stop here to browse the tropically inspired artworks of resident artist Sue Swerdlow. ⊠ *54-3862 Akoni Pule Hwy., Kapa'au* ☎ *808/889–0002.*

Tropical Flowers

Na Pua O Kohala. At this North Kohala flower shop, you can order leis or let owner Johanna Bard help you create a memorable bouquet. She'll ship your selections for you. ⊠ *55-3413 Akoni Pule Hwy.* ☎ *808/889–5541 or 877/889–5571* ⊕ *www.kohalaflowers.com.*

Waimea

Shopping Centers

Parker Ranch Center. With a snazzy renovated ranch-style motif, this shopping hub's anchors include a Foodland supermarket, Starbucks, a natural foods store called Healthways II, and some clothing boutiques. The Parker Ranch Store and Parker Ranch Visitor Center and Museum are also here. ⊠ *67-1185 Māmalahoa Hwy., Waimea.*

Parker Square. Browse around boutiques here and in the adjacent **High Country Traders,** where you may find hand-stitched Hawaiian quilts. ⊠ *65-1279 Kawaihae Rd., Waimea* ☎ *808/331–1000.*

Waimea Center. Here you can find an eclectic mix of stores, including a large KTA supermarket, an unusual San Francisco–style gift shop, and a travel service, Without Boundaries. ⊠ *65-1158 Māmalahoa Hwy., Waimea.*

Clothing

Adasa. Proprietor and designer Donna Lore carries high-end couture, her own designs, and matching accessories. Custom design is also possible. ⊠ *3 Opelo Plaza, Waimea* ☎ *808/887–0997.*

Hawaiian Arts & Crafts

★ **Cook's Discoveries.** This is one of the best places in the state for high-end Hawaiian gifts. ⊠ *64-1066 Māmalahoa Hwy., Waimea* ☎ *808/885–3633.*

Gallery of Great Things. At this Parker Square shop, you might fall in love with the Ni'ihau shell leis ($150–$7,000). More affordable perhaps are koa mirrors and other high-quality artifacts from all around the Pacific basin. ✉ *65-1279 Kawaihae Rd., Waimea* ☎ *808/885-7706.*

Dan DeLuz's Woods, Inc. Master bowl-turner Dan DeLuz creates works of art from 50 types of exotic wood grown on the Big Island. The shop features fine woodwork crafts including bowls, carvings, picture frames, furniture, jewelry and jewelry boxes, and a variety of accessory items made from koa, monkeypod, mango, kiawe, and other fine local hardwoods. This country craftshop is the place to stop for handmade native Hawaiian hardwood crafts. Dan's wife, Mary Lou, operates the Koa Shop Kaffee restaurant next to the woodshop. There's a another branch south of Hilo in Mountain View. ✉ *64-1013 Māmalahoa Hwy., Waimea* ☎ *808/885-5856* ✉ *17-4003 Ahuahu Pl., Hwy. 11, at mile marker 12, Mountain View* ☎ *808/968-6607.*

Harbor Gallery. For fine art, furniture, and decorative pieces made with koa and other native woods, be sure to stop here. ✉ *Kawaihae Shopping Center, Kawaihae* ☎ *808/882-1510.*

Mauna Kea Galleries. The specialty here is rare vintage collectibles, including hula dolls, prints, and koa furniture. ✉ *65-1298 Kawaihae Rd., Waimea* ☎ *808/887-2244.*

Kailua-Kona

Shopping Centers

Coconut Grove Plaza. Just south of Kona Inn Shopping Village, this meandering labyrinth of airy buildings hides coffee shops, boutiques, ethnic restaurants, and an exquisite gallery. ✉ *75-5795–75-5825 Ali'i Dr.*

Crossroads Shopping Center. Shopping in Kailua-Kona has begun to go the way of mainland cities at this complex with Wal-Mart, a huge Safeway, Borders Books & Music, and an eclectic collection of restaurants. ✉ *75-1000 Henry St.*

Keauhou Shopping Center. About 5 mi south of Kailua-Kona town, the stores and boutiques here include KTA Superstore, Long's Drugs, and Alapaki's Hawaiian Gifts. ✉ *78-6831 Ali'i Dr.*

Kona Inn Shopping Village. On the makai side of Ali'i Drive in the heart of Kailua-Kona, extending for an entire block along Kailua Bay, the village is crammed with boutiques selling bright pareus (beach wraps) and knickknacks. **Island Salsa** (☎ 808/329–9279) has great tropical toppers and T-shirts. ✉ *75-5744 Ali'i Dr.* ☎ *808/329–6573.*

Makalapua Center. Just north of Kona, off Highway 19, islanders find bargains at Big Kmart at this prodigious mall. Of more interest might be the large Macy's; although a mainland chain, it keeps nice selections in apparel and gifts from local vendors. ✉ *Makalapua Ave.*

Books

Middle Earth Bookshoppe. This is a great independent bookstore with superb maps and an esoteric collection of literary works. ✉ *75-5719 Ali'i Dr., Kailua-Kona* ☎ *808/329–2123.*

Candies & Chocolates

Kailua Candy Company. The chocolate here is made with locally grown cacao beans from the Original Hawaiian Chocolate Factory. Of course, tasting is part of the fun. Through a glass wall you can watch the chocolate artists at work. ⊠ *74-5563 Kaiwi St., Kailua-Kona* ☎ *808/329–2522.*

Clothing

A'ama Surf & Sport. This boutique has some cool button-ups for men, along with unbelievably cute suits for women in a variety of unusual styles and fabrics. ⊠ *75-5741 Kuakini Hwy.* ☎ *808/326–7890.*

Coconut Willie. The only shop downtown to shun beachwear in favor of trendier threads for women, Coconut Willie sells mainland standards like Free People tops and dresses, Seven jeans, and Juicy sweats. ⊠ *Kona Inn Shopping Village, 75-5744 Ali'i Dr.* ☎ *808/329–6573.*

Flamingo's. Stop by to browse rare vintage clothing and authentic antique jewelry. ⊠ *Kona Inn Shopping Village, 75-5744 Ali'i Dr.* ☎ *808/ 329–4122.*

Honolua Surf Company. Locals have been complaining forever that you can't find "cool" clothes on the Big Island. That's finally changed in the last few years as stores like this one have updated their wares. Honolua has hip casual wear plus the more expected inventory of Roxie shorts and suits. ⊠ *Kona Inn Shopping Village* ☎ *808/329–1001.*

Sirena. Just outside of town in Kealakekua is the Big Island's first high-end designer boutique, carrying squeal-worthy contemporary clothing from designers like Carlos Miele, Barbara Bui, and Catherine Malandrino. If these names are familiar, we don't need to tell you to expect high price tags. ⊠ *79-7491 Mamalahoa Hwy., Kealakekua* ☎ *808/322–3900.*

Hawaiian Arts & Crafts

Alapaki's Hawaiian Gifts. For hula instruments, intricate feather headbands, and other original art, look no further than this popular shop. ⊠ *Keauhou Shopping Village, 78-6831 Ali'i Dr.* ☎ *808/322–2007.*

Hōlualoa Gallery. Upcountry of Kailua-Kona, in the little coffee town of Hōlualoa, this is one of several excellent galleries that crowd the narrow street. It carries stunning *raku* (Japanese lead-glazed pottery). ⊠ *76-5921 Māmalahoa Hwy., Hōlualoa* ☎ *808/322–8484.*

★ **Kimura's Lauhala Shop.** Men can pick up an authentic *lauhala* hat here for some top-level sun protection. ⊠ *Māmalahoa Hwy., Hōlualoa* ☎ *808/324–0053.*

Kona Arts Center. There's an entire community of artists at this complex; feel free to drop in if the doors are open. ⊠ *Māmalahoa Hwy., Hōlualoa.*

★ **Made on the Big Island.** This place is geared to cruise-ship passengers with little time. It's a one-stop shopping for traditional Big Island gifts. You can find quite a few treasures here, such as koa boxes and bonsai trees that may be exported. ⊠ *King Kamehameha's Kona Beach Hotel, 75-5660 Palani Rd., at Kailua Pier* ☎ *808/326–4949.*

Rift Zone. Owned by ceramist Robert Joiner and his wife, Kathy, this gallery not only carries ceramics but also exquisite jewelry, bowls, ornaments, and handblown glass. ⊠ *Coconut Plaza, 75-5801 Ali'i Dr.* ☎ *808/331–1100.*

Markets

Ali'i Gardens Market Place. Open Wednesday through Sunday, this compound of individual entrepreneurs sells everything from tropical flowers to Kona coffee, baskets, souvenirs, and crafts. It's more of a flea market than a farmers' market. ⊠ *75-6129 Ali'i Dr., 1½ mi south of Kona Inn Shopping Village, Kailua-Kona* ☎ *808/334–1381.*

Kona Inn Farmers' Market. The low-key market is filled with colorful tropical flowers and locally grown produce, including macadamia nuts and coffee. It takes place Wednesday and Saturday from 7 AM until 3 PM. ⊠ *75-7544 Ali'i Dr., Kona Inn Shopping Village parking lot, Kailua-Kona.*

Hilo

Shopping Centers

Prince Kūhiō Shopping Plaza. Hilo's most comprehensive mall, similar to mainland versions, is where you can find Macy's for fashion, Safeway for food, and Longs Drugs for just about everything else, along with several other shops and boutiques. ⊠ *111 E. Puainako St., at Hwy. 11.*

Hilo Shopping Center. This rather dated shopping plaza has several air-conditioned shops and restaurants. Great cookies, cakes, and baked goodies are at Lanky's Pastries. And there's plenty of free parking. ⊠ *Kekuanaoa St. at Kīlauea Ave.*

Waiakea Center. Here you can find a Borders Books & Music, Island Naturals, a food court, and a Wal-Mart. ⊠ *Maka'ala St. and Kanoelehua Ave., across from Prince Kūhiō Shopping Plaza, at Hwy. 11.*

Books & Magazines

Basically Books. This shop stocks one of Hawai'i's largest selections of maps and charts, including USGS, topographical, and raised relief maps. It also has Hawaiiana books, with great choices for children. ⊠ *160 Kamehameha Ave., Hilo* ☎ *808/961–0144 or 800/903–6277* ⊕ *www.basicallybooks.com.*

Candies & Chocolate

★ **Big Island Candies.** This chocolate factory lets you tour and taste before you buy. ⊠ *585 Hinano St., Hilo* ☎ *808/935–8890* ⊕ *www.bigislandcandies.com.*

Clothing

★ **Hilo Hattie.** The well-known clothier matches his-and-her aloha wear and carries a huge selection of casual clothes, slippers, jewelry, and souvenirs. Call for free transportation from selected hotels. ⊠ *Prince Kūhiō Plaza, 111 E. Puainako St., Hilo* ☎ *808/961–3077* ⊠ *75-5597 Palani Rd., Kopiko Plaza, Kailua-Kona* ☎ *808/329–7200.*

★ **Sig Zane Designs.** This acclaimed boutique sells distinctive island wearables with bold colors and motifs. ⊠ *122 Kamehameha Ave., Hilo* ☎ *808/935–7077.*

Gifts

Dragon Mama. Step into this spot to find authentic Japanese fabrics, futons, and antiques. ⊠ *266 Kamehameha Ave.* ☎ *808/934–9081* ⊕ *www.dragonmama.com.*

Ets'ko. You'll find exquisite ceramics, Japanese tea sets, and affordable bamboo ware here. ⊠ *35 Waiānuenue Ave.* ☎ *808/961–3778.*

Fuku-Bonsai Cultural Center. In addition to selling and shipping miniature *brassaia lava* plantings and other bonsai plants, this place on the way to

Volcano has free educational exhibits of different ethnic styles of pruning. ✉ *Ola'a Rd., Kurtistown* ☎ *808/982–9880* ⊕ *www.fukubonsai.com.*
Hoaloha. If you're driving north from Hilo, take time to browse through this shop and pick up a colorful pareu or accessory. ✉ *Last Chance Store, off Hwy. 240, Kukuihaele* ☎ *808/775–0502.*
Most Irresistible Shop. This place lives up to its name with unique gifts from the Pacific, be it coconut-flavored butter or a whimsical wind chime. ✉ *256 Kamehameha Ave.* ☎ *808/935–9644* ✉ *Prince Kūhiō Plaza, 111 E. Puainako St., at Hwy. 11* ☎ *808/959–6515.*
Waipi'o Valley Artworks. In this remote gallery you can find finely crafted wooden bowls, koa furniture, paintings, and jewelry—all made by local artists. ✉ *Off Hwy. 240, Kukuihaele* ☎ *808/775–0958.*

Markets
★ **Hilo Farmers Market.** The farmers here sell a profusion of tropical flowers, high-quality produce, and macadamia nuts. This colorful, open-air market—the most popular in the state—takes place on Wednesday and Saturday from 6:30 AM to 2:30 PM. ✉ *Kamehameha Ave. and Mamo St., Hilo.*

Hāmākua Coast

Shopping Centers
Kaloko Industrial Park. Developed for local consumers, this shopping plaza has outlets such as Costco Warehouse and Home Depot. It's useful for industrial shopping, off-the-beaten-path finds, and wholesale prices. ✉ *Off Hwy. 19 and Hina Lani St., near Keāhole-Kona International Airport.*

BIG ISLAND ESSENTIALS

Transportation

BY AIR
CARRIERS Several domestic and international airlines serve the Big Island's two airports from the mainland as well as from the other islands. Connections of airlines listed are direct, but keep in mind that you can fly from anywhere as long as you're willing to transfer on O'ahu or Maui. Hawaiian Airlines, for example, now serves San Diego, San Francisco, Portland, Phoenix, Las Vegas, Los Angeles, and Seattle from Honolulu. Aloha Airlines has daily trips connecting Oakland, Orange County, Burbank, Phoenix, Vancouver, and Las Vegas with the Islands. United offers daily direct and seasonal flights from San Francisco and Los Angeles to Kona International Airport.

Between the Neighbor Islands, Aloha and Hawaiian airlines offer frequent jet flights that take about 40 minutes from Honolulu to either Hilo or Kona. Fares are approximately $160 to $220. Charters around the Islands are available from any airport location through Pacific Wings, a charter and scheduled airline serving all airports in Hawai'i with twin-engine Cessna 402C-8 passenger aircraft.

Aloha Airline's sister commuter carrier Island Air provides frequent, direct flights from Kona to Hawai'i's resort and smaller community destinations, including Lāna'i, Moloka'i, and Kapalua.

⇨ *See* Smart Travel Tips A to Z *for airline contact information.*
🛦 Charter Information: Pacific Wings ☎ 888/575-4546 or 808/873-0877 ⊕ www.pacificwings.com

AIRPORTS   The Big Island has two main airports: Kona, near Kailua-Kona, and Hilo. If you're staying on the west side of the island, fly into Kona International Airport. If you're staying on the eastern side, in Hilo or near Volcano, fly into Hilo International Airport. Waimea-Kohala Airport, near Waimea, is a small airstrip that services private and chartered planes only. **🛦 Kona International Airport (KOA)** ☎ 808/329-3423 visitor information. **Hilo International Airport (ITO)** ⊠ General Lyman Field ☎ 808/934-5838 visitor information. **Waimea-Kohala Airport (MUE)** ☎ 808/887-8126.

TO & FROM KONA   Kona International Airport is about 7 mi (a 10-minute drive) from
INTERNATIONAL   Kailua-Kona. The Keauhou resort area stretches another 6 mi to the south
AIRPORT   beyond Kailua. It takes about 30 to 45 minutes by car to reach the upscale resorts along the North Kona-Kohala Coast.

If you have booked accommodations in the Waimea area, expect an hour's drive north from Kona.

Limousine service with a chauffeur who will act as your personal guide averages $100 and up an hour, with a two-hour minimum. A few have all the extras—TV, bar, and narrated tours, plus Japanese-speaking guides.

There's no regularly scheduled shuttle service from Kona, although private service is offered by the Kohala Coast resorts to the north of the airport. The rates for this service vary depending on the distance but are less than taxi fare. Check-in is at the Kohala Coast Resort Association counters at the Aloha and Hawaiian airlines arrival areas. **Speed-iShuttle** (☎ 808/329–5433) arranges shared rides from Kona International Airport for $10 per person each way, but you must call ahead of time.

If you're staying in Kailua or at the Keauhou resort area to the south of the airport, check with your hotel upon booking to see if shuttle service is available.

Taxi fares start at about $20 for transport to King Kamehameha's Kona Beach Hotel and are slightly more expensive for other Kailua-Kona hotels and condos. Taxi fares to Kohala Coast resorts range from $45 to $65. Several taxis offer guided tours.
🛦Aloha Taxi ☎808/325-5448. **Elsa Taxi** ☎808/887-6446. **Luana Limousine** ☎808/326-5466. **Kona Airport Taxi** ☎ 808/329-7779. **Paradise Taxi** ☎ 808/329-1234.

TO & FROM HILO   Hilo International Airport is just 2 mi from Hilo's Banyan Drive ho-
INTERNATIONAL   tels. If you have chosen a B&B closer to Hawai'i Volcanoes National
AIRPORT   Park, plan on a 40-minute drive south from Hilo International Airport.

If you have booked accommodations in the Waimea area, expect an hour's drive north from Hilo.

Limousine service with a chauffeur who will act as your personal guide averages $100 and up an hour, with a two-hour minimum. A few have all the extras—TV, bar, and narrated tours, plus Japanese-speaking guides.

There's no regularly scheduled shuttle service from Hilo.

Taxis from the airport to Hilo's Banyan Drive hotels charge about $10 to $12 for the 2-mi ride.

🚖 **A-1 Bob's Taxi** ☎ 808/959-4800. **Hilo Harry's Taxi** ☎ 808/935-7091.

BY BUS

Ali'i Shuttle operates a bus service in the Kona resort area between Keauhou Bay and Kailua-Kona town Monday through Saturday, 8:30 AM to 7 PM. The shuttle connects all major hotels, condos, attractions, and shopping centers along Ali'i Drive. The cost is $3.

Hele-On Bus operates Monday through Saturday between Hilo and Kailua-Kona, for $6 each way. The once-daily connection takes about three hours each way and stops in numerous locations. An additional $1 is charged for luggage and backpacks that do not fit under the seat. The Hele-On operates in the Hilo and Kailua-Kona town areas themselves for 75¢ and up; exact fare is required. The bus also services the regions of North Kohala, Waimea, and Ka'u. The county Web site shows complete schedules, additional services, and fees.

🚌 **Ali'i Shuttle** ☎ 808/938-1112. **Hele-On Bus** ☎ 808/961-8744 ⊕ www.hawaii-county. com/mass_transit/transit_main.htm

BY CAR

You need a car to see the sights of the Big Island in any reasonable amount of time. Even if you're solely interested in relaxing at your self-contained megaresort, you may still want to rent a car, simply to travel to Kailua-Kona or to the restaurants in Waimea.

Though there are several car-rental companies from which to choose, cars can be scarce during holiday weekends, special events (especially the Ironman Triathlon, the third week in October), and peak seasons—from mid December through mid-March. It's best to book well in advance.

CAR RENTAL Alamo, Avis, Budget, Dollar, Enterprise, Hertz, National, and Thrifty have offices on the Big Island, and all but Thrifty have locations at both Kona and Hilo airports. ■ TIP→→ Make sure you talk to them before planning on picking up a car at one location and dropping it off at the other. Though they allow this, most charge an additional fee of up to $50. If you arrange it with them ahead of time, though, they can often be talked into waiving the fee.

To get the best rate on a rental car, book it in conjunction with an interisland Hawaiian or Aloha Airlines flight, or ask your travel agent to check out room-and-car packages. Drivers must be 25 years or older.

Most agencies make you sign an agreement that you won't drive on Saddle Road between Hilo and Waimea. This is a holdover from when Saddle Road was actually dangerous. Now it's paved and not at all bumpy, although it's still a very windy road with no lighting, gas stations, or emergency phones that you don't particularly want to be driving on at night. If you're thinking about stargazing, you'll have to take the road up to Mauna Kea off Saddle Road for the clearest views. Alamo, Budget, Dollar, and Harper Rentals let you do this in their four-wheel-drive vehicles.

We highly recommend that you rent a four-wheel-drive vehicle anyway—there are several sights that are only reachable this way, and many of those that are accessible with regular cars are more easily reached with four-wheel-drive.

See Smart Travel Tips A to Z *for car rental company contact information.*

RV RENTAL Two companies on the island rent RVs. Island RV gives you a ready-to-go vacation that includes a complete itinerary, equipment rentals, and customized care. Harper Car and Truck Rental just gets you the RV as is. Linens are available at both outfits.

🚐 **Island RV** ☎ 808/334-0464 or 800/406-4555 ⊕ www.islandrv.com. **Harper Car and Truck Rental** ☎ 808/969-1478 or 800/852-9993 ⊕ www.harperhawaii.com.

BY MOTORCYCLE

Scooters and motorcycles can be rented in Hilo and Kailua-Kona. You must be 18 to rent from most operators. Some words of warning: Big Island roads often have narrow shoulders, and the drafts from oversize tour buses swooping by can unexpectedly double the excitement of a simple Sunday ride. Helmets are advised but not mandatory in Hawai'i.

🚐 **DJ's Rentals** ✉ 75-5563A Palani Rd., Kailua-Kona ☎ 808/329-1700 or 800/993-4647 ⊕ www.harleys.com. **Hilo Harley Davidson** ✉ 100 Kanoelehua Ave., Hilo ☎ 808/934-9090. **Kona Harley Davidson** ✉ 74-5615 Luhia St., Kailua-Kona ☎ 808/326-9887.

BY TAXI

To get from the airport to Kailua-Kona will cost you about $30 by taxi, and to get to the Kohala Coast resorts will be $15–$30 depending on which resort you're staying at (the Fairmont and the Mauna Lani are farther out, the Four Seasons is very close to the airport). It cost an average of $50 each way from the Kohala Coast into Kailua-Kona town by taxi. Several companies advertise guided tours by taxi, but it is an expensive way to travel, with a trip around the island totaling about $350.

Contacts & Resources

EMERGENCIES

Dial **911** in an emergency to reach the police, fire department, or an ambulance. Call one of the hospitals listed for a doctor or dentist close to you. The Volcano Update Hotline provides 24-hour recorded information.

🚑 Emergency Services: **Police** ☎ 808/935-3311. **Poison Control Center** ☎ 800/362-3585. **Volcano Update Hotline** ☎ 808/985-6000.

🚑 Hospitals: **Hilo Medical Center** ✉ 1190 Waiānuenue Ave., Hilo ☎ 808/974-4700. **Kona Community Hospital** ✉ Hwy. 11 at Hau Kapila St., Kealakekua ☎ 808/322-9311. **Kona-Kohala Medical Associates** ✉ 75-137 Hualalai Rd., Kailua-Kona ☎ 808/329-1346. **North Hawai'i Community Hospital** ✉ 67-1125 Māmalahoa Hwy., Waimea ☎ 808/885-4444.

VISITOR INFORMATION

🚐 **Big Island Visitors Bureau** ✉ 250 Keawe St., Hilo 96720 ☎ 808/961-5797 🖨 808/961-2126 ✉ 250 Waikoloa Beach Dr., B12, King's Shops, Waikoloa 96738 ☎ 808/

886–1655 ⊕ www.bigisland.org. **Destination Hilo** ⊠ 2109F Kaiwiki Rd., Hilo 96720 ☎ 808/935–5294. **Destination Kona Coast** ⬠ Box 2850, Kailua-Kona 96745 ☎ 808/ 329–6748 ⊕ www.destinationkonacoast.com. **Hawai'i Island's Magazine online** ⊕www.hawaii-island.com. **Hawai'i Visitors and Convention Bureau** ⊕www.gohawaii. com. **Kohala Coast Resort Association** ⊠ 69-275 Waikoloa Beach Dr., Waikoloa 96743 ☎ 808/886–4915 or 800/318–3637 ⊕ www.kkra.org. **Weather** ☎ 808/961–5582.

5

Kaua'i

Shipwreck Beach, South Shore (Poi'pū area)

6

WORD OF MOUTH

"We watched the Kaua'i North Shore surf from Princeville lookout yesterday morning. Absolutely awesome. Today's surf is down to 'only 18 to 25 feet,' but another swell is due here Friday. As those monster waves hit the reef, we can hear the BOOMS at our house and the sea mist nearly obscures all the cliffs surrounding Hanalei Bay."

—auntiemaria

WELCOME TO KAUA'I

TOP 5
Reasons to Go

1 **Nā Pali Coast:** On foot, by boat, or by air--explore what is unarguably one of the most beautiful stretches of coastline in all Hawai'i.

2 **Kalalau Trail:** Hawai'i's ultimate adventure hike will test your endurance but reward you with lush tropical vegetation, white-sand beaches, and unforgettable views.

3 **Kayaking:** Kaua'i is a mecca for kayakers, with four rivers plus the spectacular coastline to explore.

4 **Waimea Canyon:** Dramatic, colorful rock formations and frequent rainbows make this natural wonder one of Kaua'i's most stunning features.

5 **Wildlife:** Birds and wildlife thrive on Kaua'i, especially at the Kīlauea Point National Wildlife Refuge.

> ■ **TIP→→** On Kaua'i, the directions *mauka* (toward the mountains) and *makai* (toward the ocean) are often used. Locals tend to refer to highways by name rather than by number.

Dry, sunny, and sleepy, the **West Side** includes the historic towns of Hanapēpē, Waimea, and Kekaha. This area is ideal for outdoor adventurers because it's the entryway to the Waimea Canyon and Kōke'e State Park, and the departure point for most Nā Pali Coast boat trips.

NĀ PALI COAST

Kalalau Trail

Kōke'e State Park

550

WAIMEA CANYON

WEST SIDE

552

550

50

Kekaha

Kaulakahi Channel

Waimea

TO NI'IHAU

50

Hanapēpē

Hanap Bay

0   8 mi
0   8 km

Getting Oriented

Despite its small size—550 square mi—Kaua'i has four distinct regions, each with its own unique characteristics. The windward coast, which catches the prevailing trade winds, consists of the North Shore and East Side, while the drier leeward coast encompasses the South and West sides. One main road nearly encircles the island, except for a 15-mi stretch of sheer cliffs comprising Nā Pali Coast.

Dreamy beaches, green mountains, breathtaking scenery, and abundant rain, waterfalls, and rainbows characterize the North Shore, which includes the towns of Kīlauea, Princeville, and Hanalei.

The East Side is Kaua'i's commercial and residential hub, dominated by the island's largest town, Kapa'a. The airport, harbor, and government offices are found in the county seat of Līhu'e.

Peaceful landscapes, sunny weather, and beaches that rank among the best in the world make the South Side the resort capital of Kaua'i. The Po'ipū resort area is here along with the main towns of Kōloa, Lāwa'i, and Kalāheo.

KAUA'I PLANNER

Car Rentals

Unless you plan to stay strictly at a resort or do all of your sightseeing as part of guided tours, you'll need a rental car. You can take the bus, but they tend to be slow and don't go everywhere. ■ TIPS→→ You most likely won't need a four-wheel-drive vehicle anywhere on the island, so save yourself the money. And while convertibles look fun, the frequent, intermittent rain showers and intense tropical sun make hardtops a better (and cheaper) choice. ■ Reserve your vehicle in advance, especially during the Christmas holidays. This will not only ensure that you get a car, but also that you get the best rates. Kaua'i has the highest gas prices in the islands.

When You Arrive

All commercial flights land at Līhu'e Airport, about 3 mi east of Līhu'e town. A rental car is the best way to get to your hotel, though taxis and some hotel shuttles are available. From the airport it will take you about 15 to 25 minutes to drive to Wailua or Kapa'a, 30 to 40 minutes to reach Po'ipū, and 45 minutes to an hour to get to Princeville or Hanalei.

Timing is Everything

If you're a beach lover, keep in mind that big surf can make many North Shore beaches unswimmable during winter months, while the South Side gets its large swells in summer. If you want to see the humpback whales, February is the best month, though they arrive as early as December and a few may still be around in early April. In the winter, Nā Pali Coast boat tours are sometimes rerouted due to high seas, and the Kalalau Trail can become very wet and muddy or, at times, impassable. Kayaking Nā Pali during winter is simply not an option. If you have your heart set on visiting Kaua'i's famed coast you may want to visit in the drier, warmer months (May–September).

Will it Rain?

Kaua'i is beautiful in every season, but if you must have good beach weather you should plan to visit between June and October. The rainy season runs from November through February, with the windward or east and north areas of the island receiving most of the rainfall. Nights can be chilly from November through March. Rain is possible throughout the year, of course, but it rarely rains everywhere on the island at once. If it's raining where you are, the best thing to do is head to another side of the island, usually south or west.

Guided Activities

When it comes to kayaking, Kaua'i is the island of choice. It's the only island with navigable rivers. A boat tour along Nā Pali Coast is another unique-to-Kaua'i experience. This chart lists rough prices for Kaua'i's top guided activities.

ACTIVITY	COST
Boat tours	$80–$175
Deep Sea Fishing	$125–$575
Golf	$50–$300
Helicopter Tours	$179–$250
Lū'au	$50–$95
Kayaking Tours	$60–$185
Scuba Diving	$110–$255
Snorkel Cruises	$80–$175
Surfing Lessons	$50–$150
Whale-Watching	$40–$69

1-Day Itineraries

So much to do, so little time, is a common lament among visitors who think they can see Kaua'i in a day or two. To get a good sample of the highlights, try some of the following one-day itinerar-

Waimea Canyon & Kōke'e State Park.
Start early, pack a picnic, and head up the mountain for some of the loveliest scenery on the island. Stop at the scenic overlooks and peer into the colorful chasm of Waimea Canyon, then continue on to the cool forests of Kōke'e. Spend the afternoon hiking, then cruise down to Salt Pond Beach Park and watch the sunset.

Wailua River & Kapa'a.
Whether you rent a kayak, take a guided tour, or board one of the motor boats, spend the morning traversing the Wailua River. You'll pass through lush tropical foliage and wind up at the Fern Grotto. Afterward, drive up Kuamo'o Road to 'Ōpaeka'a Falls, then head into Kapa'a for lunch and a bit of shopping in one of the many boutiques and galleries on the northern edge of town.

Sweet History.
Start at the Kaua'i Museum in Līhu'e for an overview of island history, then tour Grove Farm Homestead to get a feel of country life in bygone days. As you head west on Kaumuali'i Highway, stop in at Kilohana Plantation and check out the mansion. Continue on to Kaumakani, the dusty little camp town on the west side, where you can take a guided tour of the island's last sugar plantation, owned by Gay & Robinson. After viewing the fields and seeing how cane is processed into granulated sugar, head east to Kōloa town, site of Kaua'i's first plantation. Browse the shops in the historic buildings that line the charming main street, or zip over to Po'ipū Beach, where you can wash off the dust with a refreshing swim before dinner.

Beaches & Birds.
Load up the kids and head for Lydgate State Park on the East Side, where they can enjoy Kamalani Playground and everyone can swim and snorkel. For lunch, grab a bite to eat as you drive north through Kapa'a. Relax and enjoy the scenery as you continue to the Kīlauea Point National Wildlife Refuge, where you can watch seabirds soar and perhaps spot whales and dolphins cavorting offshore. Continue north to Hanalei Bay, where you can swim, boogie board, or jog on the beach. If the waves are huge, stay out of the water and check out the surfing scene. As the sun sinks and the mountains turn rosy, pick up a pizza and drive back to your hotel while the kids snooze in the back seat.

■ *For details on any of the destinations mentioned in these itineraries, see* Exploring Kaua'i *in this chapter.*

Ways to Save

■ Save on produce and flowers by shopping at the farmers' markets held on different days of the week all around the island.

■ Stock up on gas and groceries in Kapa'a and Līhu'e if you're staying on the North Shore or South Side, as prices go up farther from town.

■ Book guided activities, such as Nā Pali Coast boat tours, on the Internet. Individual outfitters' Web sites usually offer discounts for those who book on-line.

■ Reserve the smallest car for your needs to save money on gas and rental fees.

6

BEACHES

By Joan
Conrow & Kim
Steutermann
Rogers

Kaua'i has more sandy beaches per mile of coastline than any other Hawaiian island, and if you've seen one, you certainly haven't seen them all. Each beach is unique unto itself, for that day, that hour. Conditions, scenery, and intrigue can change throughout the day and certainly throughout the year, transforming, say, a tranquil lakelike ocean setting in summer into monstrous waves drawing internationally ranked surfers from around the world in winter.

Kaua'i is encircled by a variety of beaches. There are sandy beaches, rocky beaches, wide beaches, narrow beaches, skinny beaches, and alcoves. Generally speaking, surf kicks up on the North Shore in winter and the South Side in summer, although summer's southern swells aren't nearly as frequent or big as the northern winter swells.

All beaches are public, but their accessibility varies greatly. Some require an easy half-mile stroll, some require a four-wheel-drive vehicle, others require boulder-hopping, and one takes an entire day of serious hiking. And then there are those "drive-in" beaches onto which you can literally pull up and park your car. ■ TIP➜➜ Kaua'i is not Disneyland, so don't expect much signage to help you along the way. One of the top-ranked beaches in all the world—Hanalei—doesn't have a single sign in town directing you to the beach.

We've divided the island's best beaches into four sections in clockwise order: North, East, South, and West. We'll take you from the road's end on the North Shore to the road's end on the West Side, and a bit beyond. If you think of the island as a clock, the North Shore beaches start at about 11; the East Side beaches start around 2, the South Side beaches at 5, and the West Side beaches around 7.

The North Shore

If you've ever dreamed of Hawai'i—and who hasn't—you've dreamed of Kaua'i's North Shore. Lush, tropical, abundant are just a few words to describe this rugged and dramatic area. And the views to sea aren't the only attraction—the inland views of velvety green valley folds and carved mountain peaks will take your breath away. Rain is the reason for all the greenery on the North Shore and winter is the rainy season. Not to worry though, it rarely rains *everywhere* on the island at one time. The rule of thumb is to head south or west when it rains in the north.

The waves on the North Shore can be big—and we mean huge—in winter, drawing crowds to witness nature's spectacle. By contrast, in

BEACH SAFETY

Some general rules of thumb when beach-going:

- Check with lifeguards regarding beach and surf conditions.
- Always swim or snorkel with a buddy.
- Never turn your back on the ocean.
- If the lava rock boulders you're about to go exploring are wet, that means a wave may wash in and knock you down.
- When in doubt, don't go out.

KEEP IN MIND

Kauaʻi's waters are beguiling. The Pacific Ocean, despite its tranquil-sounding name, is a *real* ocean deserving real respect. Dangerous conditions can occur at any time of the year at any beach, even in normal surf conditions and under clear, sunny skies. Remember, not all beaches have lifeguards—even those with lifeguard stands aren't necessarily staffed all day or even year-round.

The most frequent and dangerous hazards of Kauaʻi's waters are rip currents, especially in the shallower waters nearshore. A rip current develops at sand channels, river mouths, and other routes through which the water flowing in and over a reef escapes back out to sea. If you find yourself in a current, Kauaʻi Ocean Rescue Council recommends the following four-point response plan: 1) Remain calm; 2) Go with the flow, do not fight the current; 3) Wait until the current dissipates a bit before you even attempt to swim; 4) Swim parallel to shore and make your way in.

summer the waters can be completely serene. The beaches below are listed in order—west to east—from Hanakāpīʻai to Kalihi Wai. ■ TIP➜➜Remember to gear up before you head to the beach. Try one-stop shopping at Ching Young Village in Hanalei, which has several stores that will fill your trunk with goodies such as snorkel gear, surf and body boards, beach chairs, umbrellas, snacks, coolers, and more.

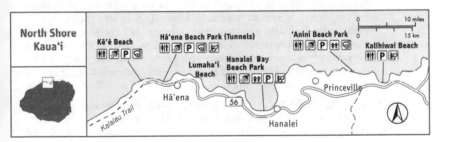

FodorśChoice **Hanakāpīʻai Beach.** *See the* Kalalau Trail *feature later in this chapter.*

Kēʻē Beach. Highway 560 on the North Shore literally dead ends at this beach, which is also the trailhead for the famous Kalalau Trail and the site of an ancient *heiau* (a stone platform used as a place of worship) dedicated to hula. The beach is protected by an offshore reef—except during high surf—creating a small, sandy bottom lagoon and making it a popular snorkel destination. If there's a current, it's usually found on the western edge of the beach as the incoming tide ebbs back out to sea. Makana (a prominent peak also known as Bali Hai after the blockbuster musical *South Pacific*) is so artfully arranged, it feels like a movie backdrop, so don't forget your camera. The popularity of this beach makes parking difficult; but, it's worth a stop. ■ TIP→→ Just start extra early or, better yet, arrive at the end of the day, in time to witness otherworldly sunsets sidelighting Nā Pali Coast. ⊠ *End of Rte. 560, 7 mi west of Hanalei* ⚑ *Toilets, showers, parking lot.*

★ **Hā'ena Beach Park.** This is a drive-up beach park popular with campers year-round. The wide bay here—named Mākua and commonly known as Tunnels—is bordered by two large reef systems creating quite favorable waves for surfing during peak winter conditions. In July and August this same beach is usually transformed into lakelike conditions and snorkelers enjoy the variety of fish life found in a hook-shape reef made up of underwater lava tubes, on the east end of the bay. ■ TIP→→ During the summer months only, this is the premier snorkel site on Kaua'i. ⊠ *Near end of Rte. 560, across from lava tube sea caves, after stream crossing* ⚑ *Lifeguard, toilets, showers, food concession, picnic tables, grills/firepits, parking lot, camping.*

Lumaha'i Beach. Famous because it's the beach where Nurse Nellie washed that man out of her hair in *South Pacific*, Lumaha'i Beach's setting is all you've ever dreamed Hawai'i to be. That's the drawing card; however, there are drawbacks. First, it's hard to find. Second, there's little parking. Third, there's a steep hike in. Most importantly, however, too many people misjudge the waves here, even those never intending to step foot in the water. There's a year-round surge of onshore waves, massive sand movements (especially around the river mouth), and a steep foreshore assaulted by strong currents. Like the mythical creature from the deep, rogue waves have actually washed up on lava rock outcroppings and pulled sightseers out to sea. ⚠ Lumaha'i Beach has the second highest drowning rate on Kaua'i, behind Hanakāpī'ai. Our advice: look from the safety of the scenic overlook and play at another beach. ⊠ *On winding section of Rte. 560 west of Hanalei, east of mile marker 5. Park on makai side of road and walk down steep path to beach* ⚑ *No facilities.*

🔄 **Hanalei Bay Beach Park.** This 2-mi, crescent-shape beach surrounds a spa-
Fodor'sChoice cious bay that is quintessential Hawai'i. After gazing out to sea and re-
★ alizing you have truly arrived in paradise, look landward. The site of the mountains, ribboned with waterfalls, will take your breath away. In winter, Hanalei Bay boasts some of the biggest onshore surf breaks in the state, attracting world-class caliber surfers. Luckily, the beach is wide enough to have safe real estate for your beach towel even in winter. In summer the bay is transformed—calm waters lap the beach, sailboats moor in the bay, and outrigger canoe paddlers ply the sea. Pack the cooler, haul out the beach umbrellas, and don't forget the beach toys, Hanalei Bay is definitely worth scheduling for an entire day, maybe two. ⊠ *In Hanalei, turn makai at Aku Rd. and drive 1 block to Weli Weli Rd. Parking areas are on makai side of Weli Weli Rd.* ⚑ *Lifeguard, toilets, showers, picnic tables, grills/firepits, parking lot, camping.*

🔄 **'Anini Beach Park.** A great family park, 'Anini is unique in that it features one of the longest and widest fringing reefs in all Hawai'i creating a shallow lagoon that is good for snorkeling and quite safe in all but the highest of winter surf. The reef follows the shoreline for some 2 mi and extends 1,600 feet offshore at its widest point. During times of low tide—usually occurring around the full moon of the summer months—much of the reef is exposed. 'Anini is unarguably the windsurfing mecca on Kaua'i, even for beginners, and it's also attracting the newest athletes of wave riding: kiteboarders. ■ **TIP→→** On Sunday afternoons in summer, polo matches in the fields behind the beach park draw a sizeable crowd. ✉ *Turn makai off Rte. 56 onto Kalihi Wai Rd., on Hanalei side of Kalihi Wai Bridge; follow road left to reach 'Anini Rd. and beach ♿ Toilets, showers, food concession, picnic tables, grills/firepits, parking lot, camping.*

★ **Kalihiwai Beach.** A winding road leads down a cliff face to this picture-perfect beach. A jewel of the North Shore, Kalihiwai Beach is on par with Hanalei, just without the waterfall-ribbon backdrop. It's another one of those drive-up beaches, so it's very accessible. Most people park on the sand under the grove of ironwood trees. Families set up camp for the day at the west end of the beach, near the stream, where young kids like to splash and older kids like to boogie board. This is also a good spot to disembark for a kayaking adventure up the stream. It's not a long paddle but it is calm, so it's perfect for beginning paddlers. (Haul in your own; there's none for rent on the beach.) On the eastern edge of the beach, from which the road descends, there's a locals' favorite surf spot during winter's high surf. The onshore break can be dangerous during this time. During the calmer months of summer, Kalihi Wai Beach is a good choice for beginning board riders and swimmers. ✉ *Turn makai off Rte. 56 onto Kalihi Wai Rd., on Kilauea side of Kalihi Wai Bridge ♿ Toilets, parking lot.*

The East Side

The East Side of the island is considered the "windward" side, a term you'll often hear in weather forecasts. It simply means the side of the island receiving onshore winds. The wind helps break down rock into sand, so there are plenty of beaches here. Unfortunately, only a few of those beaches are protected, so many are not ideal for beginning ocean-goers, though they are perfect for long sunrise ambles. On super windy days, kite boarders sail along the east shore, sometimes jumping waves and performing acrobatic maneuvers in the air.

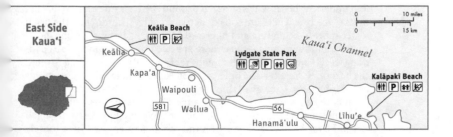

The beaches below are listed in order from 'Aliomanu in the north to Kalapakī in the south. ■ TIP➔➔ Fill your cooler with sandwiches and drinks at Safeway or Foodland in Kapa'a before you hit the sand. Snorkel and other beach gear is available at Seasport Divers, Snorkel Bob's, and Play Dirty, among others.

Keālia Beach. You can't miss this beach. A half-mile long and adjacent to the highway heading north out of Kapa'a, Keālia Beach attracts body boarders and surfers year-round (possibly because the local high school is just up the hill). Keālia is not generally a great beach for swimming or snorkeling, the waters are usually rough and the waves crumbly due to an onshore break (no protecting reef) and northeasterly trade winds. A scenic lookout on the southern end, accessed off the highway, is a superb location for saluting the morning sunrise or spotting whales during winter. A level dirt road follows the coastline north and is one of the most scenic coastal trails on the island for walking, running, and biking. ⊠ *At mile marker 10 on Rte. 56* ⚐ *Lifeguard, toilets, parking lot.*

⟳ **Lydgate State Park.** This is hands-down the best family beach park on Kaua'i. The waters off the beach are protected by a hand-built breakwater creating two boulder-enclosed saltwater pools for safe swimming and snorkeling just about year-round. The smaller of the two is perfect for *keiki* (children). Behind the beach is Kamalani Playground—designed by the children of Kaua'i and built by the community. Children of all ages, that includes you, enjoy the swings, lava-tube slides, tree house, and more. Picnic tables abound in the park and a large covered pavilion is available by permit for celebrations. Recently, Kamalani Bridge was built, again by the community and again based on the children's design, as a second playground south of the original. (The two are united by a walking path that will some day go all the way to Anahola Beach Park.) A second, smaller pavilion is the newest addition to the park—built near the bridge—and is surrounded by campsites, perfect for group outings. ■ TIP➔➔ This park is perennially popular; the quietest times to visit are early mornings and weekdays. ⊠ *Just south of Wailua River, turn makai off Rte. 56 onto Lehu Dr. and left onto Nalu Rd.* ⚐ *Lifeguard, toilets, showers, picnic tables, grills/firepits, playground, parking lot, camping.*

★ ⟳ **Kalapakī Beach.** Five minutes south of the airport in Līhu'e, you'll find this wide, sandy-bottom beach fronting the Kaua'i Marriott. One of the big attractions is that this beach is almost always safe from rip currents and undertow because it's situated around the backside of a peninsula, in its own cove. There are tons of activities here, including all the usual water sports—beginning and intermediate surfing, body boarding, body surfing, and swimming—plus, there are two outrigger canoe clubs paddling in the bay and the Nāwiliwili Yacht Club's boats sailing around the harbor. Kalapakī is the only place on Kaua'i where sailboats—in this case Hobe Cats—are available for rent (at Kaua'i Beach Boys, which fronts the beach next to Duke's Canoe Club restaurant). Visitors can also rent snorkel gear, surfboards, body boards, and kayaks from Kaua'i Beach Boys. A volleyball court on the beach is often used by a loosely organized group of local players; visitors are always welcome. ⊠ *Off*

Wapa'a Rd., which runs from Līhu'e to Nāwiliwili ☆ Toilets, food concession, picnic tables, grills/firepits, playground, parking lot.

The South Side

The South Side's primary access road is Highway 520, a tree-lined, two-lane, windy road. As you drive along it, there's a sense of tunneling down a rabbit hole into another world, à la Alice. And the South Side is certainly a wonderland. On average, it only rains 30 inches per year, so if you're looking for fun in the sun, this is a good place to start. The beaches with their powdery-fine sand are consistently good year-round, except during high surf, which, if it hits at all, will be in the summer. If you want solitude, this isn't it; if you want excitement—well, as much excitement as quiet Kaua'i offers—this is the place for you.

The beaches below are listed in order from Māhā'ulepū west to Po'ipū Beach Park. ■ TIP→→ The best places to gear up for the beach are Nukumoi Surf Co. across from Po'ipū Beach, and Seasport Divers at the junction to Spouting Horn on Po'ipū Road.

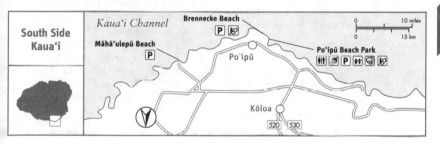

★ **Māhā'ulepū Beach.** This 2-mi stretch of coast with its sand dunes, limestone hills, sinkholes, and caves is unlike any other on Kaua'i. Remains of a large, ancient settlement, evidence of great battles, and the discovery of a now underwater petroglyph field indicate Hawaiians lived in this area as early as 700 AD. ⚠ Māhā'ulepū's coastline is unprotected and rocky, which makes venturing into the ocean hazardous. There are three beach areas with bits of sandy-bottom swimming; however, we think the best way to experience Māhā'ulepū is simply by roaming, especially at sunrise. ✉ *Continue on Po'ipū Rd. past Hyatt Regency, (it turns into dirt road) to T-intersection and turn makai; road ends at beach parking area* ☆ *Parking lot.*

Brennecke Beach. Pending surf and tides, there's little beach here on the eastern end of Po'ipū Beach Park; however, Brennecke Beach is synonymous on the island with board and body surfing, thanks to its shallow sand bar and reliable shore break. Because the beach is small and often congested, surf boards are prohibited near shore. The water on the rocky, eastern edge of the beach is a good place to see the endangered green sea turtles noshing on plants growing on the rocks. ✉ *Turn makai off Po'ipū Rd. onto Ho'owili Rd., then left onto Ho'one Rd.; beach is at intersection with Kuai Rd.* ☆ *Food concession, parking lot.*

CLOSE UP

Seal-Spotting on the South Side

WHEN STROLLING ON one of Kaua'i's lovely beaches, don't be surprised if you find yourself in the rare company of Hawaiian monk seals. These are among the most endangered of all marine mammals, with perhaps fewer than 1,500 remaining. They primarily inhabit the Northwestern Hawaiian Islands, although more are showing their sweet faces on the main Hawaiian islands, especially on Kaua'i. They're fond of hauling out on the beach for a long snooze in the sun, especially after a night of gorging themselves on fish. They need this time to rest and digest, safe from predators.

During the past several summers, female seals have birthed young in the calm waters of Kaua'i's Po'ipū Beach, where they have stayed to nurse their pups for upwards of six weeks. It seems the seals enjoy this

particular beach for the same reasons we do: it's shallow and partially protected.

If you're lucky enough to see a monk seal, keep your distance and let it be. Although they may haul out near people, they still want and need their space. Stay several hundred feet away, and forget photos unless you've got a zoom lens. It's illegal to do anything that causes a monk seal to change its behavior, with penalties that include big fines and even jail time. In the water, seals may appear to want to play. It's their curious nature. Don't try to play with them. They are wild animals—mammals, in fact, with teeth. If you have concerns about the health or safety of a seal, or just want more information, contact the **Kaua'i Monk Seal Watch Program** (☎ 808/246–2860 ⊕ www.kauaimonkseal.com).

🐚
Fodor's Choice
★

Po'ipū Beach Park. The most popular beach on the South Side, and perhaps on all of Kaua'i, is Po'ipū Beach Park. The snorkeling's good, the body boarding's good, the surfing's good, the swimming's good, and because the sun is almost always shining, that's good, too. The beach can be crowded at times, especially on weekends and holidays, but that just makes people-watching that much more fun. You'll see *keiki* (kids) experiencing the ocean for the first time; snorkelers trying to walk with their flippers on; 'ukulele players; birthday party revelers; young and old; visitors and locals. Even the endangered Hawaiian monk seal may make an appearance. ⊠ *From Po'ipū Rd., turn right on Ho'ōne Rd.* ⚓ *Lifeguard, toilets, showers, food, picnic tables, grills/firepits, parking lot.*

The West Side

While Kaua'i's North Shore is characterized by the color green, the West Side's coloring is red. When you look closer, you'll see the red is dirt, which happens to have a high iron content. With little vegetation on the West Side, the red dirt is everywhere—in the air, a thin layer on the car, even in the river. In fact, the only river on the West Side is named "Waimea" which means "reddish water." The West Side of the island receives hardly enough rainfall year-round to water a cactus, and because it's also the leeward side, there are hardly any tropical breezes.

That translates to sunny and hot with long, languourous, and practically deserted beaches. You'd think the leeward waters—untouched by wind—would be calm; but there's no offshore reef system, so the waters are not as inviting as one would like.

■ **TIP→→ The best place to gear up for the beaches on the West Side is on the south or east shores.** While there's some catering to visitors here, there's not much!

Salt Pond Beach Park. A great family spot, Salt Pond Beach Park features a naturally made, shallow swimming pond behind a curling finger of rock where *keiki* (children) splash and snorkel. This pool is generally safe except during a large south swell, which usually occurs in summer, if at all. The center and western edge of the beach is popular with body boarders and body surfers. On a cultural note, the flat stretch of land to the east of the beach is the last spot in Hawai'i where ponds are utilized to harvest salt in the dry heat of summer. The beach park is popular with locals and can get crowded on weekends and holidays. ⊠ *From Rte. 50 in Hanapēpē, turn makai onto Lele Rd., Rte. 543* ᗡ *Lifeguard, toilets, showers, picnic tables, grills/firepits, parking lot, camping.*

Fodor'sChoice **Polihale State Park.** The longest stretch of beach in Hawai'i starts in
★ Kekaha and ends about 15 mi away at the start of the Nā Pali Coast. The Nā Pali end of the beach is the 5-mi-long, 140-acre Polihale State Park. In addition to being long, this beach is 300-feet-wide in places and backed by sand dunes 50 to 100 feet tall. Polihale is a remote beach ■ **TIP→→ (be sure to start the day with a full tank of gas and a cooler filled with food and drink)** accessed via a 5-mi haul cane road (4WD preferred, not required) at the end of Route 50 in Kekaha. It's also a hot beach, so don't leave your shoes in the car. Many locals wheel their 4WD vehicles up and over the sand dunes right onto the beach; but don't try this in a rental car, you're sure to get stuck and found in violation of your rental car agreement.

On weekends and holidays Polihale is a popular locals' camping location, but even on "busy" days this beach is never crowded. On days of high surf, experts only surf the waves. In general, the water here is extremely rough and not recommended for recreation; however, there's one small fringing reef, called Queen's Pond, where swimming is usually safe. Neighboring Polihale Beach is the Pacific Missile Range Facility (PMRF), operated by the U.S. Navy. Since September 11, 2001, access to the beaches fronting PMRF is restricted to military personnel. ⊠ *Drive to end of Rte. 50 and continue on dirt road; several access points along the way* ᗡ *Toilets, showers, picnic tables, grills/firepits, parking lot, camping.*

WATER ACTIVITIES & TOURS

Boat Tours

Fodor'sChoice One of the best ways to experience Nā Pali Coast is by boat. There are
★ numerous boat tour operators to choose from, and, quite frankly, they all do a good job. The most important thing is to match you and your group's personality with the personality of the boat. If you like thrills

and adventure, the rubber, inflatable rafts—often called Zodiacs, which Jacques Cousteau made famous and which the U.S. Coast Guard uses—will entice you. They're fast and sure to leave you drenched. If you prefer a smoother, more leisurely ride, then the large catamarans are the way to go.

You'll also have to decide whether you want to go on the morning tour, which includes a deli lunch and a stop for snorkeling, or the afternoon tour, which does not stop to snorkel but does include a sunset over the ocean. The 5½-hour morning tour with snorkeling is more popular with families and those who love dolphins. (In summer, most tour operators run an afternoon snorkel cruise, in addition to the morning tour.) Hawaiian Spinner Dolphins are so prolific in the mornings that some tour companies guarantee you'll see them. The 3½-hour afternoon tour is more popular with non-snorkelers—obviously—and photographers interested in capturing the setting sunlight on the coast.

Most tour companies operate seven days a week, although schedules may vary by season, and offer both morning snorkeling and afternoon sightseeing tours of Nā Pali Coast.

> **WEATHER**
>
> If it's raining where you're staying, that doesn't mean it's raining over the water, so don't let a little rain scare you away from a boat tour. Besides, it's not the rain (unless it's really dumping) that should concern you, it's the wind. The wind creates surface chop and makes for rough riding. Typical northeast trade winds are not a concern. It's the due north and south winds that cause the problems. As for swells, the larger craft are designed to handle winter's ocean swells, so unless there are monster waves out there, your tour should depart without a hitch. If the water is too rough, your boat captain may reroute the tour to calmer waters.

Most companies do not allow pregnant women, people with bad backs or other serious health concerns, or children under four.

Catamaran Tours

Blue Dolphin Charters. This company operates 63-foot and 65-foot sailing (rarely raised and always motoring) catamarans designed with three decks of spacious seating with great visibility. ■ TIP→→ **The lower deck is best for shade-seekers.** Upgrades from snorkeling to scuba diving—no need for certification—are available, but the diving is really best for beginners or people who need a refresher course. On Tuesday and Friday a tour of Nā Pali Coast includes a detour across the channel to Ni'ihau for snorkeling and diving. Blue Dolphin recently implemented a two-drink maximum; probably because the mai tais are so good. Prices range from $99 to $175. ⊠ *In Port Allen Marina Center. Turn makai onto Rte. 541 off Rte. 50, at 'Ele'ele* ☎ *808/335–5553 or 877/511–1311* ⊕ *www.kauaiboats.com.*

Catamaran Kahanu. This Hawaiian-owned-and-operated company has been in business since 1985 and runs a 36-foot power catamaran with 18-passenger seating. The boat is smaller than most, and may feel a tad crowded, but the tour feels more personal, with a laid-back, 'ohana style.

Guests can learn the ancient cultural practice of weaving with ti leaves on board. There's no alcohol allowed. Prices range from $80 to $105. ✉ *From Rte. 50, turn left on Rte. 541 at 'Ele'ele, proceed just past Port Allen Marina Center, turn right at sign; check-in booth on left* ☎ *808/645-6176 or 888/213-7711* ⊕ *www.catamarankahanu.com.*

HoloHolo Charters. Choose between a 48-foot sailing (wind contingent and always motoring) catamaran trip to Nā Pali Coast, and a 65-foot powered catamaran trip to the island of Ni'ihau. Both boats have large cabins and little outside seating. Originators of the Ni'ihau tour, Holo-Holo Charters built their 65-foot powered catamaran with a wide beam to reduce side-to-side motion, and twin 425 HP turbo diesel engines specifically for the 17-mi channel crossing to Ni'ihau. Prices range from $89 to $169. ✉ *Check in at Port Allen Marina Center. Turn makai onto Rte. 541 off Rte. 50, at 'Ele'ele* ☎ *808/335-0815 or 800/848-6130* ⊕ *www. holoholocharters.com.*

Kaua'i Sea Tours. This company operates a 61-foot sailing catamaran designed almost identically to that of Blue Dolphin Charters—hence, with all the same benefits. They also have upgrades from snorkeling to intro-to-scuba-diving lessons. Snorkeling tours anchor at Nūalolo Kai (a great snorkeling spot); and in summer, guests are offered a shuttle ride to shore on an inflatable raft and a tour of an ancient fishing village—a unique cultural experience. Prices range from $95 to $149. ✉ *Turn makai off Rte. 50 onto Rte. 541 at 'Ele'ele and left at Aka Ula Rd. Office on right* ☎ *808/826-7254 or 800/733-7997* ⊕ *www.kauaiseatours.com.*

Inflatable Raft Tours

Nā Pali Explorer. Owned by a woman of Hawaiian descent, these tours are operated out of Waimea, a tad closer to Nā Pali Coast than most of the catamaran tours. The company operates two inflatable rubber rafts: a 48-foot, 35-passenger craft with an onboard toilet, freshwater shower, shade canopy, and seating in the stern, which is surprisingly smooth and comfortable; and a 26-foot, 16-passenger craft for the all-out fun and thrills of a white-knuckle ride in the bow. Both stop at Nūalolo Kai for snorkeling; in summer the smaller vessel ties up onshore for a tour of the ancient fishing village. Rates range from $79 to $125, and charters are available. ✉ *Follow Rte. 50 west to Waimea; office mauka after crossing river, 9935 Kaumuali'i Hwy., Waimea 96796* ☎ *808/338-9999 or 877/335-9909* ⊕ *www.napali-explorer.com.*

River Boat Tours to Fern Grotto

This 3-mi, upriver trip culminates at a yawning lava tube that is covered with enormous fishtail ferns. During the boat ride, guitar and 'ukulele players regale you with Hawaiian melodies and tell the history of the river. It's a kitschy bit of Hawaiiana; worth the little money ($20) and short time required. Flat-bottom, 150-passenger riverboats depart from Wailua Marina at the mouth of the Wailua River. Round-trip excursions take 1½ hours, including time to walk around the grotto and environs. Tours run every half hour from 9 AM to 3 PM daily. Reservations are not required. Contact **Smith's Motor Boat Services** (☎ 808/821-6892 ⊕ www.smithskauai.com) for more information.

Boogie Boarding & Bodysurfing

The most natural form of wave riding is bodysurfing, a popular sport on Kaua'i, because there are many shore breaks around the island. Wave riders of this style stand waist-deep in the water, facing shore, and swim madly as a wave picks them up and breaks. It's great fun and requires no special skills and absolutely no equipment other than a swimsuit. The next step up is boogie boarding, also called body boarding. In this case, wave riders lie with their upper body on a foam board about half the length of a traditional surf board and kick as the wave propels them toward shore. Again, this is easy to pick up, and there are many places around Kaua'i to practice. The locals wear short-finned flippers to help them catch waves, although they are not necessary for and even hamper beginners. It's worth spending a few minutes watching these experts as they spin, twirl, and flip—that's right—while they slip down the face of the wave. Of course, all beach safety precautions apply and just because you see wave riders of any kind in the water doesn't mean it's safe. Any snorkel gear outfitter (⇨ *see* Snorkeling) also rents body boards.

Best Spots

Some of our favorite body surfing and body boarding beaches are **Brennecke, Wailua, Keālia, Kalihi Wai,** and **Hanalei.** ⇨ *For directions, see* Beaches, *earlier in this chapter.*

Deep-Sea Fishing

Simply step aboard and cast your line for mahimahi, 'ahi, ono, and marlin. That's about how quickly the fishing—mostly trolling with lures—begins on Kaua'i. The water gets deep quickly here, so there's less cruising time to fishing grounds. Of course, your captain may elect to cruise to a hot location where he's had good luck lately.

There are oodles of charter fishermen around; most depart from Nāwiliwili Harbor in Līhu'e. Inquire about each boat's "fish policy," that is, what happens to the fish if any are caught. Some boats keep all; others will give you enough for a meal or two. On shared charters, ask about the maximum passenger count and about the fishing rotation; you'll want to make sure everyone gets a fair shot at reeling in the big one. Another option is to book a private charter. Shared and private charters run four, six, and eight hours in length.

> ### THE ROLLING & REELING OCEAN
>
> As anyone who's been on a boat in Kaua'i's waters knows, the Pacific Ocean isn't always so pacific. Even some lifelong Navy men have admitted to feeling queasy on board a Nā Pali boat tour. Some people think the bigger the boat the better, but in fact studies show the lowest incidence of seasickness occurs on the rubber inflatable rafts. It may have something to do with being closer to the water and moving in a more natural rhythm with the waves. The captains say seasickness is all in the head—if you think you're going to get sick, you probably will get sick. If this sounds like you, motion sickness tablets are probably a good idea.

Boats & Charters

Captain Don's Sport Fishing & Ocean Adventure. Captain Don is very flexible—he'll stop to snorkel or whale-watch if that's what the group (four to six) wants. Saltwater fly-fishermen (bring your own gear) are welcome. He'll even fish for bait and let you keep part of whatever you catch. Rates start at $125 for shared; $525 for private charters. ⊠ *Nāwiliwili Harbor* ☎ *808/639–3012* ⊕ *www.captaindonsfishing.com.*

Hana Pa'a. The advantage with Hana Pa'a is that they take fewer people (minimum two, maximum four), but you pay for it. Rates start at $200 for shared, $575 for private charters. Their fish policy is flexible. ⊠ *Nāwiliwili Harbor* ☎ *808/635–3474* ⊕ *www.fishkauai.com.*

North Shore Charters. This is a great choice for anyone staying on the North Shore, although conditions may get iffy in the winter. The owner-operator—there are no hired hands running the boat—will fish for live bait or bottom fish if passengers are interested. You'll get to keep a share of whatever you catch. The boat carries four to six passengers and is also available for narrated tours of Nā Pali Coast. ⊠ *'Anini Beach Boat Ramp* ☎ *808/828–1379 or 877/728–1379.*

Kayaking

★ Kaua'i is the only Hawaiian island with navigable rivers. As the oldest inhabited island in the chain, Kaua'i has had more time for wind and water erosion to deepen and widen cracks into streams and streams into rivers. Because this is a small island, the rivers aren't long, and there are no rapids; that makes them perfectly safe for kayakers of all levels, even beginners.

For more advanced paddlers, there aren't many places in the world more beautiful for sea kayaking than Nā Pali Coast. If this is your draw to Kaua'i, plan your vacation for the summer months when the seas are at their calmest.

■ **TIP→→** Tour and kayak rental reservations are recommended at least a week in advance during peak summer and holiday seasons. In general, tours and rentals are available year-round, Monday through Saturday. Pack a swimsuit, sunscreen, a hat, bug repellent, water shoes (sport sandals, aqua socks, old tennis shoes), and motion sickness medication if you're planning on sea kayaking.

Best Spots for River Kayaking

Tour outfitters operate on the Hulē'ia, Wailua, and Hanalei rivers with guided tours that combine hiking to waterfalls, as in the case of the first two, and snorkeling, as is the case of the third. Another option is renting kayaks and heading out on your own. There are advantages and disadvantages to each, but it boils down as follows:

If you want to swim at the base of a remote, 100-foot waterfall, sign up for a five-hour kayak (4 mi round-trip) and hiking (2 mi round-trip) tour of the **Wailua River**; it includes a dramatic waterfall that is best accessed with the aid of a guide, so you don't get lost. ⚠ Remember that it's dangerous to swim directly under waterfalls no matter how good a water massage may sound. Rocks and logs are known to plunge down, especially after heavy rains.

If you want to kayak on your own, choose the **Hanalei River**; it's the most scenic from the kayak itself—there are no trails to hike to hidden waterfalls. And better yet, a rental company is right on the river—no hauling kayaks on top of your car.

If you're not sure of your kayaking abilities, head to the **Hulē'ia River**; 3½-hour tours include easy paddling upriver, a nature walk through a rain forest with a cascading waterfall, a rope swing for playing Tarzan and Jane, and a ride back down river—into the wind—on a motorized, double-hull canoe.

As for the kayaks themselves, most companies use the two-person, sit-on-top style that are quite buoyant—no Eskimo rolls required. The only possible danger comes in the form of communication. The kayaks seat two people, which means you'll share the work (good) with a spouse, child, parent, friend, or guide (the potential danger part). On the river, the two-person kayaks are known as "divorce boats." Counseling is not included in the tour price.

Best Spots for Sea Kayaking
In its second year and second issue, *National Geographic Adventure* ranked kayaking **Nā Pali Coast** second on its list of "America's Best 100 Adventures," right behind rafting the Colorado River through the Grand Canyon. That pretty much says it all. It's the adventure of a lifetime in one day—involving eight hours of paddling. Although it's good to have some kayaking experience, feel comfortable on the water, and be reasonably fit, it doesn't require the preparation, stamina, or fortitude of, say, climbing Mt. Everest. Tours run May through September, ocean conditions permitting. In the winter months sea-kayaking tours operate on the **South Side**—beautiful, but not Nā Pali.

Kayak Rentals & Tours
Aloha Canoes and Kayaks. This group bills itself as the only Hawaiian-owned-and-operated kayak tour outfitter in the world. Kayak tours available include 3½-hour morning and afternoon tours on the Hulē'ia River, as well as a longer picnic lunch version. In addition to kayaking, river and ocean paddling adventures in a Hawaiian-style outrigger canoe are available. All tours leave from their mooring on the Hulē'ia River. Rates start at $82. ⊠ *Check-in office in Anchor Cove Shopping Center, 3416 Rice St., Līhu'e* ☎ *808/246–6804 or 877/473–5446* ⊕ *www.hawaiikayaks.com.*

Kayak Kaua'i. Based in Hanalei, this company offers guided tours on the Hanalei and Wailua rivers, and along Nā Pali Coast. They have a great shop right on the Hanalei River for kayak rentals and camping gear. The guided Hanalei River Kayak and Snorkel Tour starts at the shop and heads downriver, so there's not much to see of the scenic river valley. (For that, rent a kayak on your own.) Instead, this three-hour tour paddles down to the river mouth where the river meets the sea. Then, it's a short paddle around a point to snorkel at either Puʻu Poa Beach or, ocean conditions permitting, a bit farther at Hideaways Beach. This is a great choice if you want to try your paddle at a bit of ocean kayaking.

A second location in Kapaʻa (only open during check-in times) is the base for Wailua River guided tours and kayak rentals; it's not right on the river, however, so shuttling is involved. For rentals, the company provides the hauling gear necessary for your rental car. Guided tours range from $60 to $185. Kayak rentals range from $28 to $75. ⊠ *Hanalei: 1 mi past Hanalei bridge, on makai side.* ⊠ *Kapaʻa: south end of Coconut Marketplace near movie theaters* ☎ *808/826–9844 or 800/437–3507* ⊕ *www.kayakkauai.com.*

> **TIPPING**
>
> A word on gratuities: remember that you're not the only one paying extraordinary prices for basics such as milk and gasoline. Kamaʻāina (residents) pay those rates year-round, so gratuities are greatly appreciated. A good rule of thumb is 10% to 20%. There's one exception: helicopter pilots do not expect tips, although if you're inspired to share one, they'll willingly accept.

Nā Pali Kayak. A couple of longtime guides for Kayak Kauaʻi ventured out on their own a few years back to create this company that focuses solely on sea kayaking—Nā Pali Coast in summer and the South Side in winter. These guys are highly experienced and still highly enthusiastic about their livelihood. Prices start at $175. ⊠ *5-575 Kuhio Hwy., next to Postcards Cafe* ☎ *808/826–6900 or 866/977–6900* ⊕ *www.napalikayak.com.*

Outfitters Kauaʻi. This well-established tour outfitter operates year-round river-kayak tours on the Huleʻia and Wailua rivers; as well as sea-kayaking tours along Nā Pali Coast in summer and the South Side in winter. They're always coming up with new adventures and their latest is the **Kipu Safari.** This all-day adventure starts with kayaking up the Huleʻia River, and includes a rope swing by a swimming hole, a wagon ride through a working cattle ranch, a picnic lunch by a private waterfall, hiking, and a "zip" across the river (strap on a harness, clip into a cable and zip across the river). It ends with a ride on a motorized, double-hull canoe. It's a great tour for the family, because no one ever gets bored. The Kipu Safari costs $145; other guided tours range from $90 to $185. ⊠ *2827-A Poʻipū Rd., Poʻipū 96756* ☎ *808/742–9667 or 888/742–9886* ⊕ *www.outfitterskauai.com.*

Wailua Kayak & Canoe. This is the only purveyor of kayak rentals on the Wailua River, which means no hauling your kayak on top of your car (a definite plus). Rates are $37.50 per person (not per boat) and may increase during busier summer months. ⊠ *Across from Wailua Beach, turn mauka at Kuamoʻo Rd. and take first left, 169 Walua Rd., Kapaʻa* ☎ *808/821–1188.*

Kiteboarding

The latest wave-riding craze to hit the islands is **kiteboarding.** As the name implies, there's a kite and a board involved. The board you strap on your feet; the kite is attached to a harness around your waist. Steering is accomplished with a rod that's attached to the harness and the kite. Depending on conditions and the desires of the kiteboarder, the kite is played out some 30 to 100 feet in the air. The result is a cross between waterskiing—without the boat—and windsurfing. Speeds are fast and aerobatic maneuvers are involved. If you're a surfer of any kind, you might like to give this a try. (We highly recommend a lesson; besides, there's no rental gear available on the island.) Otherwise, you might find it more fun to watch. The most popular year-round spot for kiteboarding is **Kapa'a Beach Park** due to its reliable northeast trade winds.

'Anini Beach Windsurfing. The certified kiteboarding instructors here give five-hour lessons for $400 for one person or $600 for two. Lessons are usually held at Hanalei Bay and are only available when conditions allow. Call for reservations. ✉ *Meet at beach, Hanalei* ☎ *808/826–9463.*

■ TIP→→ **Many visitors come to Kaua'i dreaming of parasailing. If that's you, make a stop at Maui or the Big Island. There's no parasailing on Kaua'i.**

Scuba Diving

The majority of scuba diving on Kaua'i occurs on the South Side. Boat and shore dives are available, although boat sites surpass the shore sites for a couple of reasons. First, they're deeper and exhibit the complete symbiotic relationship of a reef system; and, second, the visibility is better a little farther off shore.

The dive operators below offer a full range of services, including certification dives, referral dives, boat dives, shore dives, night dives, and drift dives. As for certification, ■ TIP→→ **we recommend completing your confined-water training and classroom testing before arriving on island;** that way, you'll spend less time training and more time diving.

Best Spots

The best and safest scuba-diving sites are accessed by boat on the South Side of the island, right off the shores of Po'ipū. The captain selects the actual site based on ocean conditions of the day; **Sheraton Caverns, General Store,** and **Brennecke's Ledge** are good picks. Beginners may prefer shore dives, which are best at **Kōloa Landing** on the South Side year-round and **Mākua (Tunnels) Beach** on the North Shore in the calm summer months. Keep in mind though, you'll have to haul your gear quite a ways down the beach.

For the advanced diver, the island of Ni'ihau—across an open ocean channel in deep and crystal-clear waters—beckons and rewards, usually, with some big fish. Seasport Divers and Bubbles Below venture the 17 mi across the channel in summer when the crossing is smoothest. Divers can expect deep dives, walls, and strong currents at Ni'ihau where conditions can change rapidly. To make the long journey worthwhile, three dives and Nitrox are included.

Dive Tours & Equipment Rentals

Seasport Divers. Rated highly by readers of Rodale's *Scuba Diving* magazine, Seasport Divers' 48-foot *Anela Kai* tops the chart for dive-boat

HAWAI'I UNDERWATER

Hawai'i's isolation has allowed fish and other marine life to evolve over millennia into unique species. That means we have fish in Hawai'i that are found nowhere else on earth. Approximately 30% of our fish population is endemic. Cool, huh? And they're quite colorful. What's not always colorful is Hawai'i's coral—consider yourself warned. The most common form of coral found in the Hawaiian waters is Lobe Coral; it forms into large mounts and is rather blah in color. Some visitors think it's dead—it's not, so treat it with respect. Then, there's the second most common form of coral: Finger Coral. It's shaded hues of gray. Get the black-and-white picture? So, familiarize yourself with the fish instead. Local grocery stores, drug stores, and various other retail outlets sell fish identification cards. Some endemics that are easy to spot include the Bluestripe Butterflyfish, Lemon Butterflyfish, Belted Wrasse, Hawaiian Cleaner Wrasse, Saddle Wrasse, Hawaiian Convict Tang, Potters Angelfish, Hawaiian Pufferfish, and Chocolate Dip Damselfish. The state fish that gets all the attention is the Picasso Triggerfish, known in Hawai'i as the Humuhumunukunukuāpua'a. Strangely enough, though, it's not endemic to Hawai'i

6

luxury. The company does a brisk business, which means they won't cancel at the last minute because of a lack of reservations—like some other companies. They also run a good-sized dive shop for purchase and rentals. Ni'ihau trips are available in summer. All trips leave from Kukuiula Harbor in Po'ipū. Rates start at $120 for a two-tank boat dive; $20 extra for rental gear. ⊠ *Check-in office on Po'ipū Rd. just north of Lawa'i Rd. turnoff to Spouting Horn. Look for yellow submarine in parking lot, 2827 Po'ipū Rd., Po'ipū* ☎ *808/742–9303 or 800/685–5889* ⊕ *www.kauaiscubadiving.com.*

Bubbles Below. Marine ecology is the emphasis here. This company discovered some pristine dive sites on the West Side of the island where white-tip reef sharks are common—and other divers are not. In summer they offer Ni'ihau and Nā Pali dives. A bonus on these tours is the Grinds pizza serveed up between dives. There's a charge of $110 for a standard two-tank boat dive; up to $25 extra for rental gear. ⊠ *Port Allen Small Boat Harbor; turn makai onto Rte. 541 from Rte. 50 in 'Ele'ele* ☎ *808/332–7333 or 866/524–6268* ⊕ *www.bubblesbelowkauai.com.*

Snorkeling

Generally speaking, the calmest water and best snorkeling can be found on Kaua'i's North Shore in summer and South Side in winter. The eastern shore, known as the windward side, has year-round, prevalent northeast trade winds that make snorkeling unpredictable, although there are some good pockets. The best snorkeling on the West Side is accessible only by boat.

A word on feeding fish: don't. As Captain Ted with HoloHolo Charters says, fish have survived and populated reefs for much longer than we have been donning goggles and staring at them; they will continue to do so without our intervention. Besides, fish food messes up the reef and—one thing always leads to another—can eliminate a once-pristine reef environment.

Best Spots

Just because we say these are good places to snorkel doesn't mean the exact moment you arrive, the fish will flock—they are wild, after all. The beaches here are listed in clockwise fashion starting on the North Shore.

★ The search for **Tunnels (Mākua)** (⊠ At Hā'ena Beach Park, near end of Rte. 560, across from lava-tube sea caves, after stream crossing) is as tricky as the snorkeling. Park at Hā'ena Beach Park and walk east—away from Nā Pali Coast—until you see a sand channel entrance in the water, almost at the point. Once you get here,

---

TIPS ON SAFE SNORKELING

Mike Hopkins with SeaFun Kaua'i, a guided walk-in snorkel tour operator, suggests these tips for safe snorkeling:

- Snorkel with a buddy and stay together.
- Choose a location where lifeguards are present.
- Ask the lifeguard about conditions, especially currents, before getting in the water.
- Plan your entry and exit points prior to getting in the water.
- Swim into the current on entering and then ride the current back to your exit point.
- Look up periodically to gauge your location with a reference point on land.
- When in doubt, don't go without a snorkeling professional; try a guided tour.

---

the reward is fantastic. The name of this beach comes from the many underwater lava tubes, which always attract marine life. The shore is mostly beach rock interrupted by three sand channels. You'll want to enter and exit at one of these channels (or risk stepping on a sea urchin or scraping your stomach on the reef). Follow the sand channel to a drop-off; the snorkeling along here is always full of nice surprises. Expect a current running east to west. ⚠ Please note that snorkeling here in winter can be hazardous; summer is the best and safest time for snorkeling.

🐚 **Lydgate Beach Park** (⊠ Just south of Wailua River, turn makai off Rte. 56 onto Lehu Dr. and left onto Nalu Rd.) is the absolute safest place to snorkel on Kaua'i. With its lava-rock wall creating a protected swimming pool, this is the perfect spot for beginners, young and old. The fish are so tame here it's almost like swimming in a saltwater aquarium.

You'll generally find good, year-round snorkeling at **Po'ipū Beach Park** (⊠ From Po'ipū Rd., turn right on Ho'ōne Rd.), except during summer's south swells (which are not nearly as frequent as winter's north swells). The best snorkeling fronts the Marriott Waiohai Beach Club. Stay inside the crescent shape created by the sand bar and rocky point. The current runs east to west.

Don't pack the beach umbrella, beach mats, or cooler for snorkeling at **Beach House (Lāwa'i Beach)** (⊠ Makai side of Lāwa'i Rd.; park on road in front of Lāwaʻi Beach Resort). Just bring your snorkel gear. The beach—named after its neighbor the Beach House restaurant (yum)—is on the road to Spouting Horn. It's a small slip of sand during low tide and a rocky shoreline during high tide; however, it's right by the road's edge, and its rocky coastline and somewhat rocky bottom make it great for snorkeling. Enter and exit in the sand channel (not over the rocky reef) that lines up with the Lāwaʻi Beach Resort's center atrium. Stay within the rocky points anchoring each end of the beach. The current runs east to west.

FodorśChoice
★ **Nuʻalolo Kai** was once an ancient Hawaiian fish pond and is now the best snorkeling along Nā Pali Coast (and perhaps on all of Kauaʻi). The only way to access it is by boat, and only a few Nā Pali snorkel tour operators are permitted to do so. We recommend Nā Pali Explorer and Kauaʻi Sea Tours (⇨ *see* Boat Tours).

FodorśChoice
★ With little river runoff and hardly any boat traffic, the waters off the island of **Niʻihau** are some of the clearest in all Hawaiʻi, and that's good for snorkeling. Like Nuʻalolo Kai, the only way to snorkel here is to sign on with one of the two tour boats venturing across a sometimes rough open ocean channel: Blue Dolphin Charters and HoloHolo (⇨ *see* Boat Tours). Sammy the Monk Seal likes to hang out behind Lehua Rock off the north end of Niʻihau and swim with the snorkelers.

Guided Snorkel Tours

SeaFun Kauaʻi. This guided snorkel tour, for beginners and intermediates alike, is led by a marine expert, so not only is there excellent "how-to" instruction, but the guide actually gets in the water with you and identifies marine life. You're guaranteed to spot a plethora of critters you'd never see on your own. This is a land-based operation and the only one of its kind on Kauaʻi. (Don't think those snorkel cruises are guided snorkel tours, they are not. A member of the boat's crew serves as lifeguard, not a marine life *guide*.) A half-day tour includes all your snorkel gear—including a wetsuit to keep you warm—and stops at two snorkel locations, chosen based on ocean conditions. ⊠ *Check in at Kilohana Plantation in Puhi, next to Kauaʻi Community College* ☎ *808/245–6400 or 800/452–1113* ⊕ *www.alohakauaitours.com.*

Surfing

Good old stand-up surfing is alive and well on Kauaʻi, especially in winter's high surf season on the North Shore. If you're new to the sport, we highly recommend taking a lesson. Not only will this ensure you're up and riding waves in no time, instructors will provide the right board for your experience and size, help you time a wave, and give you a push to get your momentum going. If you're experienced and want to hit the waves on your own, most surf shops rent boards for all levels—from beginners to advanced.

Best Spots

Perennial-favorite beginning surf spots include **Poʻipū Beach** (the area fronting the Marriott Waiohai Beach Club); **Hanalei Bay** (the area next to the Hanalei Pier); and the stream end of **Kalapakī Beach**. More advanced surfers move down the beach in Hanalei to an area fronting a grove of pine trees known as **"Pine Trees, "** of course. When the trade winds die, the north ends of **Wailua** and **Keālia** beaches are teeming with surfers. Breaks off **Po'ipū** and **Beach House/Lāwa'i Beach** attract intermediates year-round. During high surf, the break on the cliff side of **Kalihi Wai** is for experts only. ⇨ *See* Beaches, *earlier in this chapter, for complete beach information and directions.*

Lessons

Blue Seas Surf School. Surfer and instructor Charlie Smith specializes in beginners (especially children) and will go anywhere on the island to find just the right surf. His soft-top, long boards are very stable, making it easier to stand up. Rates start at $50 for a two-hour lesson. ✉ *Meet at beach; location varies pending surf conditions* ☎ *808/634–6979* ⊕ *www.blueseassurfingschool.com.*

Margo Oberg Surfing School. Seven-time world surfing champion Margo Oberg runs a surf school that meets on the beach in front of the Sheraton Kaua'i in Po'ipū. Lessons are $48 for two hours, though she rarely teaches any more. ✉ *Po'ipū Beach* ☎ *808/332–6100.*

Titus Kinimaka. Famed as a pioneer of big-wave surfing, this Hawaiian just started his surf school in 2004. Beginning, intermediate, and "extreme" lessons, including tow-in, are available. If you want to learn to surf from a living legend, this is the man. Rates are $65 for a 90-minute group lesson; $100 to $120 per hour for a private lesson; $150 for a two-hour, tow-in lesson. A surf DVD is included with each lesson. ✉ *Meets at various beaches* ☎ *808/652–1116.*

Surf Board Rentals

Progressive Expressions. ✉ *On Kōloa Rd. in Old Kōloa Town* ☎ *808/742–6041.*

Tamba Surf Company. ✉ *Mauka on north end of Hwy. 56 in Kapa'a; across from Scotty's Beachside BBQ; 4-1543 Kūhiō Hwy., Kapa'a* ☎ *808/823–6943.*

Hanalei Surf Company. ✉ *Mauka at Hanalei Center, 5-5161 Kūhiō Hwy., Hanalei* ☎ *808/826–9000.*

Whale-Watching

Every winter North Pacific humpback whales swim some 3,000 mi over 30 days, give or take a few, from Alaska to Hawai'i. Whales arrive as early as November and sometimes stay through April; though they seem to be most populous in February and March. They come to Hawai'i to breed, calve, and nurse their young.

Although humpbacks spend more than 90% of their lives underwater, they can be very active above water while they're in Hawai'i. Here are a few maneuvers you may see: 1) Blow: the expulsion of air that looks like a geyser of water. 2) Spy hop: the raising of just the whale's head out of the water, as if to take a look around. 3) Tail slap: the repetitive slap of the tail, or fluke, on the surface of the water. 4) Pec slap: the repetitive slap of one or both fins on the surface of the water. 5) Fluke up dive: the waving of the tail above water as the whale slowly rolls under water to dive. 6) Breach: the launching of the entire whale's body out of the water.

Of course, nothing beats seeing a whale up close. During the season, any boat on the water is looking for whales; they're hard to avoid, whether the tour is labeled "whale-watching" or not. Several boat operators will add short, afternoon whale-watching tours during the season that run on the South Side (not Nā Pali). Operators include **Blue Dolphin, Catamaran Kahanu, HoloHolo,** and **Nā Pali Explorer** (⇨ *see* Boat Tours). There are a few lookout spots around the island with good land-based viewing: Kilauea Lighthouse on the North Shore, the Kapa'a Scenic Overlook just north of Kapa'a town on the East Side, and the cliffs to the east of Keoneloa (Shipwreck) Beach on the South Side.

> **KEEP IN MIND**
>
> If you book your activities through a concierge, don't just ask, "What's the best (fill-in-the-blank)?" Make sure you follow up with the question, "Why?" because what's perfect for one person may not be perfect for you. If you love adventure, for example, you can sign up for a rubber raft tour of Nā Pali Coast; whereas, if you respect (translation: fear) the ocean, you'll be much more comfortable on a 60-some foot sailing catamaran.

6

Windsurfing

Windsurfing on Kaua'i isn't nearly as popular as it is on Maui; however, 'Anini Beach Park is the place if you're going to windsurf or play the spectator. Rentals and lessons are available from **Windsurf Kaua'i** (☎ 808/828–6838). Lessons run $75 for three hours; rentals run $25 for one hour, and up to $75 for the day. The instructor will meet you on 'Anini Beach.

GOLF, HIKING & OUTDOOR ACTIVITIES

Aerial Tours

FodorsChoice From the air, the Garden Isle blossoms with views you cannot see by
★ land, on foot, or from the sea. In an hour you can see waterfalls, craters, and other places that are inaccessible even by hiking trails (some say that 70% of the island is inaccessible). The majority of flights depart from the Līhu'e airport and follow a clockwise pattern around the island. ■ TIP→→ **If you plan to take an aerial tour, it's a good idea to fly when you first arrive, rather than saving it for the end of your trip.** It will help you visualize what's where on the island and it may help you decide what you want to see from a closer vantage point during your stay.

Helicopter Tours

Inter-Island Helicopters. This company flies a four-seater Hughes 500 helicopter *with the doors off.* It can get chilly at higher elevations, so bring a sweater. They offer a spectacular tour that includes landing by a waterfall for a picnic and swim. Tours depart from Hanapēpē's Port Allen Airport. Prices range from $185 to $250 per person. ⊠ *From Rte. 50, turn makai onto Rte. 543 in Hanapēpē* ☎ *808/335–5009 or 800/656– 5009* ⊕ *www.interislandhelicopters.com.*

Island Helicopters. Family-owned and -operated, this company gives 60-minute tours out of the Līhu'e Airport. The pilots are generally bubbly and extremely knowledgeable, and headsets allow passengers to ask questions along the way. The chopper's movements are impressively choreographed to an eclectic soundtrack. A free video of the tour is included in the price. ⊠ *Līhu'e Airport, Līhu'e* ☎ *808/245–8588 or 800/829– 5999* ⊕ *www.islandhelicopters.com.*

■ **TIP→→** Many companies advertise a low-price 30- or 40-minute tour, which they rarely fly, so don't expect to book a flight at the advertised rate. The most popular flight is the 60-minute flight.

Safari Helicopters. This is the only company to include a video of your actual flight—the entire length. Two-way microphones allow passengers to converse with the pilot. Prices start at $179. ⊠ *3225 Akahi St., Līhu'e* ☎ *808/246–0136 or 800/326–3356* ⊕ *www.safariair.com.*

Will Squyres Helicopter Tours. The majority of this company's pilots were born and raised in Hawai'i, making them excellent tour guides. In an interesting move, Will Squyres removed its two-way microphones, eliminating the possibility of one passenger hogging the airwaves. Prices start at $199. ⊠ *3222 Kūhiō Hwy., Līhu'e* ☎ *808/245–8881 or 888/245– 4354* ⊕ *www.helicopters-hawaii.com.*

Plane Tours

Kaua'i Aero Tours. This tour is really a flying lesson in a Citabria tail dragger that was designed specifically for aerobatics. You can take the stick or let your pilot handle the controls. The aerobatics roll on until you say stop. The plane can only take one passenger at a time. Tours last 30 to 60 minutes; prices range from $125 to $165. ⊠ *Līhu'e Airport* ☎ *808/639–9893.*

Tropical Bi-Planes. This company flies a bright red Waco biplane, built in 2002 based on a 1936 design. An open cockpit and staggered wing design means there's nothing between you and the sights. The plane can carry two passengers in front and flies at an altitude of 1,000 feet, at about 85 mph. The hourly rate is $356 for two people. ⊠ *Līhu'e Airport Commuter Terminal* ☎ *808/246–9123* ⊕ *www.tropicalbiplanes.com.*

ATV Tours

Although all the beaches on the island are public, much of the interior land—once sugar and pineapple plantations—is privately owned. This is really a shame, because the valleys and mountains that make up the vast interior of the island easily rival the beaches in sheer beauty. The good news is some tour operators have agreements with landowners making exploration possible, albeit a bit bumpy, and unless you have back troubles, that's half the fun.

★ **Aloha Kaua'i Tours.** You get *way* off the beaten track on Aloha Kaua'i Tours' 4WD van excursions. There's the half-day Backroads Tour (which could also be called the Sugar Tour; it's a good primer on the sugar industry) covering 33 mi of what is mostly haul cane roads behind the locked gates of Grove Farm Plantation. The full-day Aloha Kaua'i Tour starts with the Backroads tour and then spends the other half of the day covering the public roads along the Waimea Canyon. These are roads you can traverse on your own; however, the tour will teach you a lot about the many rare and endangered plants and birds in the Waimea Canyon and Kōke'e State Park. Another half-day tour, the Rainforest Tour, follows the Wailua River to its source, Mt. Wai'ale'ale. This tour includes a 3-mi easy walk to the basin of the crater and the unofficial start of the river. We cannot say enough about the expert guides with Aloha Kaua'i Tours. They are some of the absolute best on the island. Rates are $63, $120, and $68, respectively. ✉ *Check in at Kilohana Plantation on Rte. 50 in Puhi, Līhu'e* ☎ *808/245–6400 or 800/452–1113* ⊕ *www.alohakauaitours.com.*

Kaua'i ATV Tours. This is *the* thing to do when it rains on Kaua'i. Consider it an extreme mud bath. Kaua'i ATV in Kōloa is the originator of the all-terrain-vehicle tours on Kaua'i. Their $99 three-hour jaunt takes you through a private sugar plantation and historic cane-haul tunnel. The $145 four-hour tour visits secluded waterfalls and includes a picnic lunch. The more popular longer excursion includes a hike through a bamboo forest and a swim in a freshwater pool at the base of the falls—to rinse off all that mud. You must be 16 or older to operate your own ATV, but Kaua'i ATV also offers its six-passenger, dune-buggy "Mud Hog" vehicle and its two-passenger "Mud Bug" to accommodate families with kids age five and older. ✉ *5330 Kōloa Rd., Kōloa* ☎ *808/742–2734 or 877/707–7088* ⊕ *www.kauaiatv.com.*

Kaua'i Backcountry Adventures. This ATV operator has a 3½-hour Hali'i Falls tour that traverses Līhu'e Plantation—land that just happens to be tucked beneath one of the wettest spots on earth, Mt. Wai'ale'ale, increasing the mud quotient. (Remember mud means fun on an ATV.) In winter the waterfall can rise to dangerous levels, meaning the usual dip in the waterfall pool is bypassed. You must be 16 or older to operate your own ATV; however, Kaua'i Backcountry Adventures offers its souped-up, golf-cart-looking "Ranger" for kids age five and older and nondrivers. Prices start at $145. ✉ *3–4131 Kūhiō Hwy., across from gas station, Hanamā'ulu* ☎ *808/245–2506 or 888/270–0555* ⊕ *www.kauaibackcountry.com.*

Biking

Kaua'i is a labyrinth of cane haul roads, which are fun for exploring on two wheels. The challenge is to find the roads where biking is allowed and then to not get lost in the maze. Maybe that explains why Kaua'i is not a hub for the sport . . . yet. Still, there are some epic rides for those who are interested—both the adrenaline-rushing and the mellower beach cruiser kinds. If you want to grind out some mileage, the main highway that skirts the coastal areas is perfectly safe, though there are only a few designated bike lanes. It's hilly, but you'll find that keeping your eyes on the road and not the scenery is the biggest challenge. You can rent bikes (with helmets) from the activities desks of certain hotels, but these are not the best quality. You're better off renting from either Kaua'i Cycle in Kapa'a, or Outfitters Kaua'i in Po'ipū (⇨ *see below*).

■ TIP→→ If you're headed for the dirt tracks, be sure your bike is in top condition, take plenty of water and energy bars, and let someone know when and where you're going. If you're venturing into the unknown, explain what you've got in mind to someone who knows the area and heed any advice offered. And be sure to get explicit directions; don't expect signage.

Best Spots

For the cruiser, **Keālia Coastal Road** (⊠ Trailhead: 1 mi north of Kapa'a; park at north end of Keālia Beach), a dirt haul cane road, is easy to follow along the coastline to Donkey Beach. From here, the trail splinters into numerous, narrower trails through fallow sugarcane fields where dirt bikers now roam, especially on weekends. It's easy to get lost here, but eventually all trails lead to Anahola Beach Park, some 4 mi from Keālia. If you're not sure how to find your way back the way you came, follow Anahola Road inland to Route 56 and return to Keālia via the highway.

For those wanting a road workout, climb **Waimea Canyon Road**, also known as Route 550 (⊠ Road turns mauka off Rte. 50 just after grocery store in downtown Waimea). After a 3,000-foot climb, the road tops out at mile 12 adjacent to the Waimea Canyon, which will pop in and out of view on your right as you ascend. From here it continues several miles (mostly level) past the Koke'e Museum and ends at the Kalalau Lookout. It's paved the entire way, uphill 100%, and curvy. ⚠ There's not much of a shoulder—sometimes none—so be extra cautious. The road gets busier as the day wears on, so you may want to consider a sunrise ride.

For the novice mountain biker, the **Wailua Forest Management Road** is an easy ride and is easy to find. From Route 56 in Wailua, turn mauka on Kuamo'o Road and continue 6 mi to the picnic area, known as Keāhua Arboretum; park here. The potholed 4WD road includes some stream crossings—⚠ stay away during heavy rains as the streams flood—and continues for 2 mi to a T-stop, where you should turn right. Stay on the road for about 3 mi until you reach a gate; this is the spot where the gates to the movie Jurassic Park were filmed, though it looks nothing like the movie. Go around the gate and down the road for another mile to a confluence of streams at the base of Mt. Wai'ale'ale. Be sure to bring your camera.

Advanced riders should try **Powerline Trail** (⊠ Trailhead is mauka just past stream crossing at Keāhua Arboretum; see directions for Wailua Forest Management Rd. above). The trail is actually a service road for the electric company that splits the island. It's 13 mi in length; the first 5 mi goes from 620 feet in elevation to almost 2,000. The remaining 8 mi is a gradual descent over a variety of terrain, some technical. Some sections will require carrying your bike. The views will stay with you forever.

Bike Rentals & Guided Tours

Kauaʻi Adventure Trek. This 4½-hour bike, hike, and beach adventure follows an old cane road through Grove Farm Plantation, stops for a tour of the island's first sugar mill, then heads for Māhāʻulepū Beach, where a picnic lunch is served. After lunch there's a short hike to a hidden beach. Trips are geared to novice and intermediate-level bikers and cost $96. ⊠ *Check in at Kilohana Plantation on Rte. 50, Puhi* ☎ *808/245–6400 or 808/635–8735* ⊕ *www.kauaiadventuretrek.com.*

Kauaʻi Cycle. This reliable, full-service bike shop rents, sells, and repairs bikes. Mountain bikes and road bikes are available for $20 to $35 per day and $95 to $150 per week with directions to trails. ⊠ *Across from Beezers Old Fashioned Ice Cream, 1379 Kūhiō Hwy., Kapaʻa* ☎ *808/ 821–2115* ⊕ *www.bikehawaii.com/kauaicycle.*

Outfitters Kauaʻi. Beach cruisers and mountain bikes are available at this shop in Poʻipū. You can ride right out the door to tour Poʻipū, or get information on how to do a self-guided tour of Kokeʻe State Park and Waimea Canyon. The company also leads sunrise coasting tours (under the name **Bicycle Downhill**) from Waimea Canyon (100 % downhill for 12 mi) to the island's West Side beaches. Rentals cost $20 to $45 per day. Tours cost $90. ⊠ *2827-A Poʻipū Rd., Poʻipū, Follow Poʻipū Rd. south from Kōloa town; shop is on right just before turn-off to Spouting Horn* ☎ *808/742–9667 or 888/742–9887* ⊕ *www.outfitterskauai.com.*

Pedal ʻnʼ Paddle. This company rents beach cruisers and mountain bicycles for $10 to $20 per day; $40 to $80 per week. ⊠ *Ching Young Village, Rte. 560, Hanalei* ☎ *808/826–9069* ⊕ *www.pedalnpaddle.com.*

Golf

For golfers, the Garden Isle might as well be known as the Robert Trent Jones Jr. Isle. Four of the island's nine courses, including Poʻipū Bay—home of the PGA Grand Slam of Golf—are the work of Jones, who maintains a home at Princeville. Combine these four courses with those from Jack Nicklaus, Robin Nelson, and local legend Toyo Shiraī, and you'll see that golf sets Kauaʻi apart from the other Islands as much as the Pacific Ocean does.

FodorsChoice
★

Kauaʻi Lagoons Golf Club. When Jack Nicklaus opened the Kiele (pronounced kee-EL-ay) Course here in 1989, it was immediately compared to Mauna Kea, Robert Trent Jones Sr.'s Big Island masterpiece. Depending on the rater, Kiele continues to be considered among the top three or four courses in the state. Nicklaus's design is like a symphony, starting nice and easy, and finishing with a rousing par-4 that plays deceptively uphill—into the trade winds—to an island green. The adjacent Mokihana Course (Nicklaus,

> **TIP!**
>
> In theory, you can play golf in Hawaiʻi 365 days a year. But there's a reason the Hawaiian islands are so green. Better to bring an umbrella and light jacket and not use them than to not bring them and get soaked.

1990) is flatter and doesn't have Kiele's oceanfront. According to handicap ratings it's supposed to play easier, but Nicklaus makes par a challenge with creative mounding, large waste areas, and false fronts for greens. The boomerang-shape par-5 18th is among the state's finest finales. ⊠ *3351 Ho'olaulea Way, Lihu'e* ☎ *808/241–6000* ⊕ *www. kauailagoonsgolf.com* ⅂ *Kiele Course: 18 holes. 6,637 yds. Par 72. Green Fee: $170. Mokihana Course: 18 holes. 6,545 yds. Par 72. Greens Fee: $120* ☞ *Facilities: Driving range, putting green, golf carts, rental clubs, lessons, restaurant, bar.*

Kiahuna Plantation Golf Course. A meandering creek, lava outcrops, and thickets of trees give Kiahuna its character. Robert Trent Jones Jr. (1983) was given a smallish piece of land just inland at Po'ipū, and defends par with smaller targets, awkward stances, and optical illusions. It's a fun course that looks easier than it plays. ⊠ *2545 Kiahuna Plantation Dr., Kōloa* ☎ *808/742–9595* ⊕ *www.kiahunagolf.com* ⅂ *18 holes. 6,366 yds. Par 70. Greens Fee: $90* ☞ *Facilities: Driving range, putting green, rental clubs, lessons, pro shop, restaurant, bar.*

Kukuiolono Golf Course. Local legend Toyo Shirai designed this fun, funky 9-holer where holes play across rolling, forested hills that afford views of the distant Pacific. Though Shirai has an eye for a good golf hole, Kukuiolono is out of the way and a bit rough, and probably not for everyone. But at $8 for the day, it's a deal. ⊠ *854 Pu'u Rd., Kalāheo* ☎ *808/332–9151* ⅂ *9 holes. 3,173 yds. Par 36. Greens Fee: $8* ☞ *Facilities: Driving range, putting green, golf carts, pull carts, rental clubs.*

Fodor'sChoice ★ **Po'ipū Bay Golf Course.** Po'ipū Bay has been called the Pebble Beach of Hawai'i, and comparisons are apt. Like Pebble Beach, Po'ipū is a links course built on headlands, not true links land. And as at Monterey Bay, there's wildlife galore. It's not unusual for golfers to see monk seals sunning on the beach below, sea turtles bobbing outside the shore break, and humpback whales leaping offshore. ⊠ *2250 Ainako St., Kōloa* ☎ *808/742–8711* ⊕ *www.kauai-hyatt.com* ⅂ *18 holes. 7,034 yds. Par 72. Greens Fee: $145* ☞ *Facilities: Driving range, putting green, rental clubs, golf carts, golf academy/lessons, restaurant, bar.*

Fodor'sChoice ★ **Princeville Resort.** Robert Trent Jones Jr. built two memorable courses overlooking Hanalei Bay, the 27-hole Princeville Makai Course (1971) and the Prince Course (1990). The three Makai nines—Woods, Lake, Ocean—offering varying degrees of each element, plus lush mountain views above. Three quick snapshots: the par-3 seventh on the Ocean nine drops 100 feet from tee to green, with blue Hanalei Bay just beyond. The Ocean's par-3 eighth plays across a small bay where dolphins often leap. On the Woods' par-3 eighth, two large lava rocks in Jones's infamous Zen Bunker really

> ## RENTAL CLUBS
>
> All resort courses and most daily fee courses provide rental clubs. In many cases, they're the latest lines from Titleist, Ping, Callaway, and the like. This is true for both men and women, as well as left-handers, which means you don't have to schlepp clubs across the Pacific.

are quite blissful, until you plant a tee shot behind one of them. The Prince is often rated Hawai'i's best course. It is certifiably rated Hawai'i's second toughest (behind O'ahu's Ko'olau). This is jungle golf with holes running through dense forest and over tangled ravines, out onto headlands for breathtaking ocean views, then back into the jungle. Makai Golf Course: ⊠ *4080 Lei O Papa Rd., Princeville* ☎ *808/826–3580* ⊕ *www.princeville.com* ⚑ *27 holes. 6,886 yds. Par 72. Greens Fee: $175* ☞ *Facilities: Driving range, putting green, rental clubs, golf carts, pro shop, golf academy/lessons, restaurant, bar.* Prince Golf Course: ⊠ *5-3900 Kūhiō Hwy., Princeville* ☎ *808/826–5001* ⊕ *www.princeville.com* ⚑ *18 holes. 7,309 yds. Par 72. Greens Fee: $125* ☞ *Facilities: Driving range, putting green, rental clubs, golf carts, pro shop, golf academy/lessons, restaurant, bar.*

Hiking

The best way to experience the 'āina—the land—on Kaua'i is to step off the beach and into the remote interior. The best way to do that is by hiking. The rewards are waterfalls so tall you'll strain your neck looking, pools of crystal cool water for swimming, tropical forests teeming with plant life, and ocean vistas that will make you wish you could stay forever.

⚠ **For your safety, wear sturdy shoes, bring plenty of water, never hike alone, stay on the trail, and avoid hiking when it's wet and slippery.** All hiking trails on Kaua'i are free, so far. There is a rumor that the Waimea Cayon and Koke'e state parks will some day charge an admission fee. Whatever it may be, it will be worth it.

Best Spots

Waimea Canyon and Kōke'e State Parks. The parks contain a 50-mi network of hiking trails of varying difficulty that take you through acres of native forests, across the highest-elevation swamp in the world, to the river at the base of the canyon, and onto pinnacles of land sticking their necks out over Nā Pali Coast. All hikers should register at Kōke'e Nat-

---

LEPTOSPIROSIS

The sparkling waters of those babbling brooks trickling around the island can be potentially life-threatening, and we're not talking about the dangers of drowning, although they, too, exist. Leptospirosis is a bacterial disease that is transmitted from animals to humans. It can survive for long periods of time in fresh water and mud contaminated by the urine of infected animals, such as mice, rats, and goats. The bacteria enter the body through the eyes, ears, nose, mouth, and broken skin. To avoid infection, do not drink untreated water from the island's streams; do not wade in waters above the chest or submerge skin with cuts and abrasions in island streams or rivers. Symptoms are often mild and resemble the flu—fever, diarrhea, chills, nausea, headache, vomiting, body pains. Symptoms may occur two to 20 days after exposure. If you think you have these symptoms, see a doctor right away.

ural History Museum, where you'll find trail maps, current trail information, and specific directions. All mileage mentioned here is one-way.

The **Kukui Trail** descends 2½ mi and 2,200 feet into Waimea Canyon to the edge of the Waimea River—it's a steep climb. The **Awa'awapuhi Trail,** with 1,600 feet of elevation gains and losses over 3¼ mi, feels more gentle than the Kukui Trail; but, it offers its own huffing-and-puffing sections in its descent along a spiny ridge to a perch overlooking the ocean.

The 3½-mi **Alaka'i Swamp Trail** is accessed via the **Pihea Trail** or a 4WD road. There's one strenuous valley section, otherwise, it's a pretty level trail—once you access it. This trail is a birder's delight and includes a painterly view of Wainiha and Hanalei valleys at the trail's end. The trail traverses the purported highest-elevation swamp in the world on a boardwalk so as not to disturb the fragile wildlife.

The **Canyon Trail** offers much in its short 2-mi trek: spectacular vistas of the canyon and the only dependable waterfall in Waimea Canyon. The easy, 2-mi hike can be cut in half if you have a 4WD vehicle. Outfitted with a head lamp, this would be a great hike at sunset as the sun's light sets the canyon walls awash in color. ⊠ *Kōke'e Natural History Museum: Kōke'e Rd., Rte. 550* ☎ *808/335–9975 for trail conditions.*

Hiking the Kalalau Trail See Page 479

Sleeping Giant Trail. An easy and easily accessible trail practically in the heart of Kapa'a, the Sleeping Giant Trail—or simply "Sleeping Giant"—gains 1,000 feet over 2 mi. We prefer an early-morning—say, sunrise—hike, with sparkling blue-water vistas, up the east-side trailhead. At the top you can see a grassy grove with a picnic table; don't stop here. Continue carefully along the narrow trail toward the Giant's nose and chin. From here there are 360-degree views of the island. ⊠ *In Wailua, turn mauka off Rte. 56 onto Haleilio Rd.; proceed 1 mi to small parking area on right.*

Horseback Riding

Most of the horseback riding tours on Kaua'i are primarily walking tours with very little trotting and no cantering or galloping, so there's no experience required. Zip. Zilch. Nada. If you're interested, most of the stables offer private lessons. The most popular tours are the ones including a picnic lunch by the water. Your only dilemma may be deciding what kind of water you want—waterfalls or ocean. You may want to make your decision based on where you're staying. The "waterfall picnic" tours are on the wetter North Shore, and the "beach picnic" tours take place on the South Side.

CJM Country Stables. Just past the Hyatt in Po'ipū, CJM Stables offers breakfast and lunch rides with noshing on the beach. Shorter rides are

Continued on page 484

HIKING THE KALALAU TRAIL

Kalalau Lookout (above).
Nā Pali Coast (below).

There are few places left on earth where only your feet can take you. But even a small horse would not fit on some stretches of Kaua'i's prized hike, the Kalalau Trail. This ancient path, blazed by early inhabitants, winds through one of the most beautiful stretches of coastline in all Hawai'i, if not the entire world, the famed Nā Pali Coast.

TRAIL OPTIONS

Easy	1 mi round-trip to half-mile mark for dramatic coastal views
Moderate	4 mi round-trip to Hanakāpī'ai Beach
Moderate/Advanced	8 mi round-trip to Hanakāpī'ai Falls
Advanced	22 mi round-trip, with camping at Kalalau Beach

The Kalalau Trail begins at the western end of Route 56 and proceeds 11 mi to Kalalau Beach. Folding sea cliffs thousands of feet high, sliced by deep valleys of tropical vegetation, tower over the narrow footpath. There are sea caves, arches, secluded beaches, waterfalls, and after it rains, rainbows. (Don't think a little rain spoils the views here.) And did we mention green? Every possible shade of green is revealed by the myriad plants growing along the coast.

Nā Pali Coast

Feral goats and wild pigs share the trails, while large marine and tiny forest birds soar on the wind currents above. Once, large settlements of Hawaiians lived in the valleys and terraced the land for taro cultivation. Many of the valleys still contain rock walls, housing platforms, and other remains of their communities.

In winter months the big surf is dramatic as seen—and heard—from the coastal trail, although heavy rains can cause flash floods at stream crossings and trail erosion in some places. Summers, the trail is dryer and, frankly, safer. It's also busier.

With hairpin turns and constant ups and downs, this hike is a true test of endurance and isn't tackled round-trip in one day, even by the fittest of the fit. Many people don't even make the 11 mi to Kalalau Beach in one day; actually, most don't event attempt it. Instead, most people hike the first 2 mi to Hanakāpī'ai Beach, a rewarding hike in itself.

There are small quarter-mile markers all along the trail (although some are missing). At the half-mile point, the wrinkles of the Nā Pali Coast unfold before you. Even if you go no further, make every attempt to reach this point, and after you look down the coastline, look back. You'll see a dramatic view of the beach you came from.

TO HANAKĀPĪ'AI BEACH
The trailhead is easy to find just before Kē'ē Beach. It starts at sea ̄ doesn't waste any time ga

HIKING TIPS

■ The trail is rocky and frequently muddy, so wear comfortable shoes and recognize that they may never be clean again. We suggest *amphibious* shoes versus waterproof mountaineering boots. With the various stream crossings and mud, a self-bailing sort of shoe is perfect.

■ Even if you plan to complete only the first 2 mi of the 11-mi trek, start early and bring mosquito repellant, lots of drinking water, and a hat, as it gets hot on the hike back. No concessions or drinking water are available past Haena.

■ If you need minute camp Wal-Mart in l Hardware in l Kayak Kaua'i Paddle, both elevation. Take heart. The uphill *only* lasts about a mile and tops out at about 400 feet; then it's downhill all the way to Hanakāpī'ai Beach.

This two-mile portion of the trail will take about 1½ hours one-way, possibly longer, depending on how often you stop to gawk at the scenic beauty of Nā Pali Coast along the way.

To reach Hanakāpī'ai Beach, you'll have to boulder-hop across a stream. During heavy rains or even just after, the stream can flood, stranding hikers on the wrong side. Don't cross unless the boulders are visibly exposed and easily hopped. The cats you'll most likely encounter here are feral, although quite friendly. With all the hikers tossing them crumbs, they tend to thrive.

Hanakāpī'ai Beach is a great spot for a picnic, but don't plan on cooling off with a refreshing swim. The waters here are what locals like to call "confused." The radical change in water depth and the sheer cliff walls create wicked rip currents, rogue waves, backwash, undertow, and cross waves. This is not water you want to mess with.

PERMITS:

Permits: Campers and anyone hiking past Hanakāpī'ai must obtain permits from the State Department of Land and Natural Resources in Līhu'e; there's a five-night limit in Na Pali State Park and rangers do check permits. Campsites are numbered, and requests are recommended up to a year in advance, especially for summer months.

Department of Land and Natural Resources
3060 Eiwa St., Līhu'e 96766
808/274-3444
www.kauai-hawaii.com

TO HANAKĀPĪ'AI FALLS

If you're prepared with water and food, continue another two miles *inland*, criss-crossing the rough, slippery stream trail numerous times (read: easy to lose) and scrambling over boulders in some places, to the 300-foot Hanakāpī'ai Falls. The water here can be cool—okay, cold—because it originates up in

6

HIKING THE KALALAU TRAIL

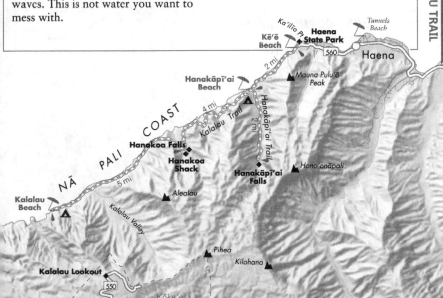

the mountains, but how many times will you have an opportunity to swim under a waterfall? (Just be careful, especially after a heavy rain, rocks and tree limbs do tumble over the falls.)

Keep in mind, round-trip to the waterfall is eight miles; start early if you don't want to risk getting lost in the dark on your return trip.

TO HANAKOA VALLEY

Backpackers and serious hikers with the proper state permits can continue on another 4 mi to Hanakoa Valley.

Climb the steep switchback trail out of Hanakāpīʻai and follow the narrow, winding trail through numerous lush and humid valleys. A primitive camp shelter on the trail and lovely falls ⅓ mi inland distinguish Hanakoa, which is well above sea level and offers no access to the ocean. Once camping was permitted at Hanakoa, and you may still see some campers here; but it is now illegal and we don't recommend it. We do recommend mosquito repellent—for this valley in particular and all other inland areas that are heavily foliaged.

TO KALALAU BEACH

The last 5 mi of the hike tend to be the most treacherous, as the trail is often eroded, and the crumbly, loose soil can make hiking quite dangerous. The terrain is more open here, offering sweeping coastal views as it slowly drops down to sea level.

This is the magnificent Kalalau Valley, anchored on one end by a year-round stream and on the other by a refreshing and spectacular waterfall—which makes for a perfect shower. In summer the beach is broad, and you can walk right into a dry sea cave beyond the waterfalls. A number of campsites are tucked behind the beach and protected by trees.

In the summer you'll certainly not lack for company, including some free spirits who have shed their clothes and are (illegally) on extended stays in nature. Winter is not as populated. Throughout the year there's a friendly, sharing atmosphere among campers of all sorts, with group campfires and even potluck dinners.

THOSE ZANY LOOKING TREES

While the vistas are indeed magnificent, and in winter the possibility of spotting whales will tempt your gaze, don't overlook the flora. Some fascinating indigenous plants grow along Nā Pali Coast. The zany-looking trees you'll see all along the trail with aerial roots and long, skinny, serrated leaves are known as hala. Early Hawaiians plaited their leaves to make mats, baskets, and canoe sails. The red blossoms of the ʻōhiʻa tree—which blankets the slope before the half-mile point—are known as Pele's (the volcano goddess's) favorite flower; they bloom in spring.

ōhiʻa trees

HEALTH AND SAFETY TIPS

■ If you are planning to hike all the way to Kalalau, train. Arrive fit and ready for such an adventure. The only legal camping is two miles in at Hanakāpīʻai and at the end of the 11-mile trail at Kalalau.

■ Note that swimming is extremely dangerous due to strong currents and surf conditions at all the beaches along Nā Pali, although you can cool off in the many streams that bisect the trail.

■ To find a parking space, arrive early and do not leave any valuables in the car. While overnight parking is allowed, rental cars are easy prey for vandals.

OTHER WAYS TO SEE NĀ PALI

Nā Pali Coast kayakers

If you don't have the time or inclination to hike the Kalalau Trail, there are other ways to experience the majesty of Nā Pali Coast.

■ For a truly up-close view, try **a Zodiac boat ride**. These inflatable rubber rafts are wet and wild. In summer months, many will dip into sea caves. Some tour operators have special permits to land at Nualolo Kai for a tour of the remains of an ancient fishing village. ⇨ *See* Boat Tours *earlier in this chapter.*

■ If you prefer enjoying a refreshing beverage—say, a mai tai—as you gaze upon the majesty of Nā Pali Coast, then the usually smooth, **leisurely sailing catamarans** are just the ticket. In calm waters, these boats are even known to back into a waterfall for a dip. ⇨ *See* Boat Tours *earlier in this chapter.*

■ For a once-in-a-lifetime adventure, consider **kayaking** Nā Pali Coast—summer months only. These day-long tours are definitely physical, but you don't need to train like Lance Armstrong to paddle out. ⇨ *See* Kayaking *earlier in this chapter.*

■ Somehow, only **a helicopter tour** gives a true perspective of the sheer enormity of the cliffs. Plus, there's nothing like zipping over a knife-edge cliff to truly understand how these cliffs are cut. ⇨ *See* Aerial Tours *earlier in this chapter.*

■ **Sunset at the Kalalau Lookout,** at the paved road's end in Kōkeʻe State Park, is the perfect end to a day in paradise. You'll take in views of the glorious Kalalau Valley with the sands of Kalalau Beach glimmering in the fading light. ⇨ *See* Exploring the West Side *later in this chapter.*

available. The landscapes here are rugged and beautiful, featuring sand dunes and limestone bluffs. Guides are real *paniolo*. CJM sponsors seasonal rodeo events that are free and open to the public. Prices range from $90 to $125. ✉ *1.6 mi from Hyatt Regency Kaua'i off Po'ipū Rd., Kōloa* 📞 *808/742–6096* ⊕ *www.cjmstables.com.*

Esprit de Corps. If you ride, this is the company for you. Esprit de Corps has two- to eight-hour rides and allows some trotting and cantering based on the rider's experience and comfort with the horse. There are also pony parties and half-day horse camps for kids. Weddings on horseback can be arranged, and custom rides for less-experienced and younger riders are available, as well as private lessons. Rates range from $120 to $350. ✉ *End of Kualapa Pl., Kapa'a* 📞 *808/822–4688* ⊕ *www.kauaihorses.com.*

★ **Princeville Ranch Stables.** A longtime *kama'āina* (resident) family operates Princeville Ranch. They originated the waterfall picnic tour, which runs three to four hours and includes a short but steep hike down to Kalihi Wai Falls, a dramatic three-tier waterfall, for swimming and picnicking. Princeville also has shorter, straight riding tours, and if they're moving cattle while you're visiting, you can sign up for a cattle drive. Prices range from $65 to $125. ✉ *Just west of Princeville Airport mauka between mile markers 27 and 28, Princeville* 📞 *808/826–6777* ⊕ *www.princevilleranch.com.*

Mountain Tubing Tours

Kaua'i Backcountry Adventures. Very popular with all ages, this laid-back adventure can book up two weeks in advance in busy summer months. Here's how it works: you recline in an inner tube and float down fern-lined irrigation ditches that were built more than a century ago—the engineering is impressive—to divert water from Mt. Wai'ale'ale to sugar and pineapple fields around the island. Simple as that. They'll even give you a headlamp so you can see as you float through one stretch of covered tunnel. The scenery from the island's interior at the base of Mt. Wai'ale'ale on Līhu'e Plantation land is superb. Ages five and up are welcome. The tour takes about three hours and includes a picnic lunch and a swim in a swimming hole. ■ TIP➔➔ **In winter or after the rain, the water can be chilly; some people wear a surfer's rash guard over their swimsuit.** You'll definitely want to pack water-friendly shoes (or rent some from the outfitter), sunscreen, a hat, bug repellent, and a beach towel. Tours cost $92 per person and are offered twice a day, Monday through Saturday. In summer, additional tours may be available. ✉ *3–4131 Kūhiō Hwy., across from gas station, Hanamā'ulu* 📞 *808/245–2506 or 888/270–0555* ⊕ *www.kauaibackcountry.com.*

Tennis

If you're interested in booking some court time on Kaua'i, there are public tennis courts in Waimea, Kekaha, Kōloa, Kalaheo, Līhu'e, Wailua Homesteads, Wailua Houselots, and Kapa'a New Park. For specific directions or more information, call the **County of Kaua'i Parks and Recreation Office** (📞 808/241–4463). Many hotels and resorts have tennis courts on property; even if you're not staying there, you can still rent court time. Rates range from $10 to $20 per person per hour. On the South Side, try the **Hyatt Regency Kaua'i Resort and Spa** (☎ 808/742–1234) and **Kiahuna Swim and Tennis Club** (☎ 808/742–9533). On the North Shore try the **Princeville Tennis Center** (☎ 808/826–1230).

Zipline Tours

The latest adventure on Kaua'i is "zipping" or "zip lining." It's so new that the vernacular is still catching up with it, but regardless of what you call it, chances are you'll scream like a rock star fan while trying it. Strap on a harness, clip onto a cable running from one side of a river or valley to the other, and zip across. The step off is the scariest part.

■ **TIP→→** Pack knee-length shorts or pants, athletic shoes, and courage for this adventure.

Outfitters Kaua'i. This company offers a half-day adventure of multiple zips, along with rope-swinging off a cliff adjacent to Kīpū Falls. There's only one zipline involved, so you'll be making the same crossing several times, but it's a Swiss Family Robinson–like setting with a tree-house launching pad and a swinging bridge. Outfitters Kaua'i also has a zipline stream crossing as part of their Kipu Safari tour (⇨ see Kayaking earlier in this chapter). ✉ 2827-A Po'ipū Rd., Po'ipū ☎ 808/742–9667 or 888/742–9887 ⊕ www.outfitterskauai.com.

Princeville Ranch Adventures. The North Shore's answer to ziplining is an eight zipline course with a bit of hiking, waterfall crossing, and swimming thrown in for a half-day adventure. This is as close as it gets to flying; just watch out for the albatross. Prices start at $115. ✉ Just west of Princeville Airport on Rte. 56., between mile markers 27 and 28, Princeville ☎ 808/826–7669 ⊕ www.adventureskauai.com.

EXPLORING KAUA'I

The main road tracing Kaua'i's perimeter takes you past much more scenery than would seem possible on one small island. Chiseled mountains, thundering waterfalls, misty hillsides, dreamy beaches, lush vegetation, and quaint small towns comprise the physical landscape. And there's plenty to do, as well as see: plantation villages, a historic lighthouse, wildlife refuges, a fern grotto, a colorful canyon, and deep rivers are all easily explored.

■ **TIP→→** While exploring the island, try to take advantage of the many roadside scenic overlooks to pull off and take in the constantly changing view. And don't try to pack too much into one day. Kaua'i is small, but travel is slow.

The North Shore

Traveling north from Līhu'e, the coastal highway crosses the Wailua River and the busy towns of Wailua and Kapa'a before emerging into a decidedly rural and scenic landscape, with expansive views of the island's rugged interior mountains. As the two-lane highway turns west and nar-

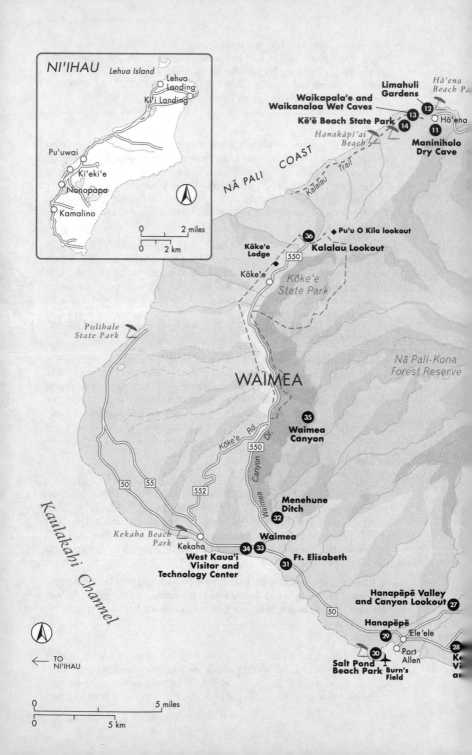

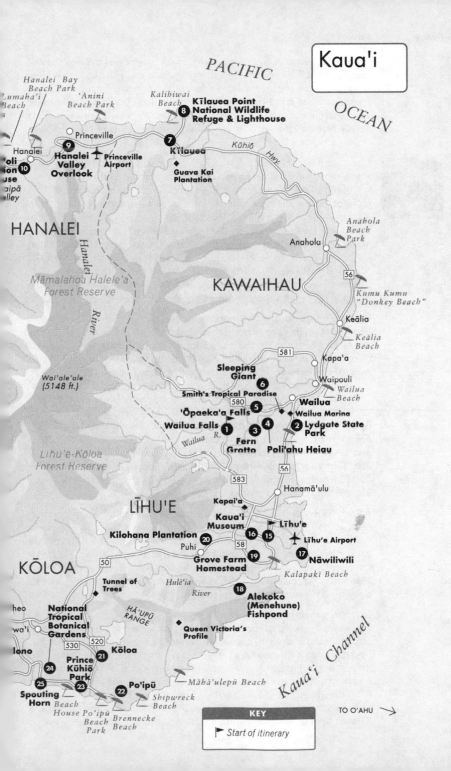

rows, it winds through spectacular scenery and passes the posh resort community of Princeville before dropping down into Hanalei Valley. Here it narrows further and becomes a federally recognized scenic roadway, replete with one-lane bridges (yield to drivers already waiting on the other side), hairpin turns, and heart-stopping coastal vistas. The road ends at Kē'ē, where the ethereal rain forests and fluted sea cliffs of Nā Pali Coast Wilderness State Park begin.

a good drive

Head north out of Līhu'e town on Kūhiō Highway (Route 56). This main artery mostly hugs Kaua'i's eastern coastline as it cuts through Kapa'a, the island's largest town, and meanders on into the scenic rural landscape of the North Shore. Shortly after leaving town, the road dips into Kapaia Valley. Turn left onto Mā'alo Road (Route 583) for a 4 mi sidetrip to view the dramatic cascade of **Wailua Falls ❶** ▷. Backtrack to Route 56 and continue north, through the old plantation town of Hanamā'ulu. When you reach the intersection of Route 51 and Route 56, turn left (this is still Route 56 north). After passing the public Wailua Golf Course on your right and the local jail on your left, you ll see a sign pointing the way to **Lydgate State Park ❷**.

Back on Route 56, the two northbound lanes split at the Wailua River, with the far right lane making the crossing on an old bridge, then converge again after the river crossing. Signs offer directions to Wailua Marina, where it's possible to join a boat ride up Hawai'i's only navigable river to **Fern Grotto ❸**. This region, favored by Kaua'i's monarchs and chiefs, is rich in culture and history. It has many well-preserved archaeological sites, including bellstones, royal birthing stones, and a series of heiau (pre-Christian temples). These were erected all along the river, and can be viewed by turning left onto Kuamo'o Road (Route 580) after crossing the bridge. Follow the road about 2 mi to **Poli'ahu Heiau ❹**, a complex with interpretive storyboards. Across the road is a scenic overlook for the spectacular **'Ōpaeka'a Falls ❺**. The falls and mighty Wailua River are fed by the 500-plus inches of rain that fall annually on Wai'ale'ale, whose table-flat summit can be viewed on clear days.

Return to Route 56, which heads north past the many shops, restaurants, condominiums, and resorts of Waipouli, Coconut Marketplace, and finally Kapa'a, a quaint town with many historical buildings that harken back to the days when pineapple reigned in these parts. It's now the population hub of the island, with most folks living mauka of the Nounou ridge, nicknamed the **Sleeping Giant ❻** for its resemblance to a mythical creature lying on its back.

Just north of Kapa'a the landscape opens up and traffic thins out as the highway takes you past the broad beach of Keālia and the dramatic mountain peaks that define the Hawaiian Homes community of Anahola. The next real town is **Kīlauea ❼**, a former sugar plantation camp that is mightily resisting urbanization. When you see a gas station and Menehune Foodmart, turn right on Kolo Road and then take the first left, across from the quaint stone Episcopal Church. This is Kīlauea Road, which ends in several miles at the **Kīlauea Point National Wildlife Refuge & Kīlauea Lighthouse ❽**, a seabird sanctuary with a historic lighthouse.

After Kīlauea, continue west on Route 56, which offers three distinct waterfall views while crossing the lovely Kalihiwai River valley. The road passes Princeville Airport and cuts through ranch lands before reaching the resort community of Princeville. Just beyond the Princeville Shopping Center, on the mauka side, pull into the **Hanalei Valley Overlook** ❾ for a sweeping view of the wetland taro fields that keep Honolulu folks supplied with poi while also offering safe haven to endangered water birds. From here the road descends into the valley, where it crosses the Hanalei River on a rustic, one-lane bridge built in 1912 (yield to cars already waiting on the other side when you arrive). It's the first of many historic narrow bridges you encounter as you follow this federally designated scenic roadway on to its end at Kē'ē Beach.

West of Hanalei town, with its touristy shops and 19th-century **Wai'oli Mission House** ❿, the highway (now labeled 560 on street signs) winds its way between the mountains and the sea and crosses numerous rivers. Lovely beaches are found around every corner, including Lumaha'i, made famous in the movie *South Pacific*.

As you head west past the tiny community of Wainiha and Hanalei Colony Resort, the farthest outpost of tourism on this side of the island, look on the mauka side for **Maniniholo Dry Cave** ⓫, then **Limahuli Garden** ⓬, and finally two more wet caves, **Waikapala'e and Waikanaloa** ⓭. The road dead-ends at a crowded parking lot that serves **Kē'ē Beach State Park** ⓮ and Nā Pali Coast Wilderness State Park, home of the famed Kalalau Trail.

TIMING Without stopping, you can drive the 40 mi from Līhu'e to Hā'ena in less than 90 minutes, but no one with a choice would want to. It's far more pleasant to schedule a full day, allowing plenty of time for slow traffic and frequent stops to eat, enjoy the scenery, swim, or hike.

What to See

❸ **Fern Grotto.** This yawning lava tube swathed in lush fishtail ferns is 3 mi upriver. Although it's part of a state park, the state leased the landing concession to two motorboat companies that offer rather campy tours. Recently, Sonny Waialeale lost his concession and the state confiscated his boats when he refused to pay his concession fees, claiming an inherent right as a Native Hawaiian to use the river. Smith's Motor Boat Services is now the only way to legally see the grotto, recently refurbished under a state tourism grant. You can access the entrance with a kayak, but if boats are there, you won't be allowed to land. ✉ *Depart from Wailua Marina on mauka side of Rte. 56* ☎ *808/821–6892.*

off the beaten path

GUAVA KAI PLANTATION – This 480-acre farm is one of the world's most productive guava plantations and a major player in the island's push toward diversified agriculture. You can wander around the orchard and then see how the fruit is processed into jellies, juices, marinades, and other goodies, all sold at the visitor center. ✉ *North of mile marker 23 on Rte. 56; turn mauka onto Kuawa Rd., near Kīlauea, and follow sign* ☎ *808/828–6121* 🎫 *Free* ☉ *Daily 9–5.*

★ **⑨ Hanalei Valley Overlook.** Dramatic mountains and a patchwork of neat taro farms bisected by the wide Hanalei River make this one of Hawai'i's most picturesque sights. The fertile Hanalei Valley has been planted in taro since perhaps 700 AD, save for a century-long foray into rice that ended in 1960. (The historic Haraguchi Rice Mill is all that remains of the era.) Many taro farmers lease land within the 900-acre Hanalei National Wildlife Refuge, helping to provide wetland habitat for four species of endangered Hawaiian water birds. ⊠ *Rte. 56, Princeville.*

★ **⑭ Kē'ē Beach State Park.** This stunning, and often overcrowded, beach marks the start of majestic Nā Pali Coast. The 11-mi **Kalalau Trail** begins near the parking lot, drawing day hikers and backpackers (⇨ *see* Hiking the Kalalau Trail *earlier in this chapter*). Another path leads from the sand to a stone hula platform dedicated to **Lohi'au,** which has been in use since ancient times. This is a sacred site that should be approached with respect; it's inappropriate for visitors to leave offerings at the altar tended by students in a local hula halau (school). Most folks head straight for the sandy beach and its idyllic lagoon, which is great for snorkeling when the sea is calm. ⊠ *Drive to western end of Rte. 560.*

⑦ Kīlauea. A former plantation town, Kīlauea is struggling to maintain its rural flavor in the midst of unrelenting gentrification. Especially noteworthy are its historic lava-rock buildings, including **Christ Memorial Episcopal Church** on Kolo Street and the Kong Lung Co. on Keneke Street, now an expensive shop. ⊠ *Rte. 56, 25 mi north of Līhu'e.*

⑧ Kīlauea Point National Wildlife Refuge & Kīlauea Lighthouse. A beacon for sea traffic since it was built in 1913, this National Historic Landmark has the largest clamshell lens of any lighthouse in the world. It's within a national wildlife refuge, where thousands of seabirds soar on the trade winds and nest on the steep ocean cliffs. Endangered nene geese, native plants, dolphins, humpback whales, huge winter surf, and gorgeous views of the North Shore add to the drama of this special place, making it well worth the modest entry fee. The gift shop has a great selection of books about the island's natural history and an array of unique merchandise, with all proceeds benefitting education and preservation efforts. ⊠ *Kīlauea Lighthouse Rd., Kīlauea* ☎ *808/828–0168* ⊕ *www.kilaueapoint.com* ⊡ *$3* ☉ *Daily 10–4.*

FodorsChoice ★

> **need a break?**

Banana Joe's Tropical Fruit Stand (⊠ 5-2719 Kūhiō Hwy., Kīlauea ☎ 808/828–1092) occupies a rustic yellow shelter on the mauka side of Route 56, past the turnoff to Kīlauea. Owners Joe and Cindy Halasey make refreshing frosties and smoothies from tropical fruits, including their own bananas. They also sell dried fruits, flower lei, and a very good selection of locally grown fruits and fresh vegetables. It's a great place to try seasonal specialties and things you likely won't find in the produce section back home.

⑫ Limahuli Garden. Narrow Limahuli Valley, with its fluted mountain peaks and ancient stone taro terraces, creates an unparalled setting for this botanical garden and nature preserve. Dedicated to protecting native plants and unusual varieties of taro, it represents the principles of

FodorsChoice ★

conservation and stewardship held by its founder, Charles "Chipper" Wichman. Limahuli's priomordial beauty and strong mana (spiritual power) eclipse the extensive botanical collection. It's one of the most gorgeous spots on Kaua'i and the crown jewel of the National Tropical Botanical Garden, which Wichman now heads. Call ahead to reserve a guided tour, or tour on your own. Be sure to check out the quality gift shop and revolutionary compost toilet. ⊠ *Rte. 560, Hā'ena* ☎ *808/826–1053* ⊕ *www.ntbg.org* ⚲ *Self-guided tour $10, guided tour $15* ☉ *Tues.–Fri. and Sun. 9:30–4.*

2 Lydgate State Park. The park, named for the Reverend J. M. Lydgate, founder of the Līhu'e English Union Church, has a large children-designed and community-built playground, pavilions, and campgrounds. It also houses the remains of an ancient site where commoners who broke a royal tabu could seek refuge from punishment. It's part of an extensive complex of sacred archaeological sites that runs from Wai'ale'ale to the sea, underscoring the significance of this region to the ancient Hawaiians. ⊠ *Before mouth of Wailua River turn makai off Rte. 56 onto Leho Dr. and left onto Nalu Rd.* ⚲ *Free* ☉ *Daily.*

⓫ Maniniholo Dry Cave. According to legend, Maniniholo was the head fisherman of the Menehune, the possibly real, possibly mythical first inhabitants of the island. As they were preparing to leave Kaua'i and return home (wherever that was), Maniniholo called some of his workers to Hā'ena to collect food from the reef. They gathered so much that they couldn't carry it all, and left some near the ocean cliffs with plans to retrieve it the following day. It all disappeared during the night, however, and Maniniholo realized that imps living in the rock fissures were the culprits. He and his men dug into the cliff to find and destroy the imps, leaving behind the cave that now bears his name. Across the highway from Maniniholo Dry Cave is **Hā'ena State Park,** a fine beach for swimming when there's no current. The well-protected **Makua (Tunnels)** Beach adjoins Hā'ena State Park. ⊠ *Rte. 560, Hā'ena.*

off the beaten path

NĀ PALI COAST WILDERNESS STATE PARK – This park contains Kaua'i's ultimate adventure hike: the Kalalau Trail. For more information, ⇨ *see* Hiking the Kalalau Trail *earlier in this chapter.*

★ 5 'Ōpaeka'a Falls. The mightly Wailua River produces many dramatic waterfalls, and 'Ōpaeka'a (pronounced oh-pie-kah-ah) is one of the best. It plunges hundreds of feet to the pool below and can be easily viewed from a scenic overlook with ample parking. 'Ōpaeka'a means "rolling shrimp," which refers to tasty native crustaceans that were once so abundant they could be seen tumbling in the falls. ⊠ *Rte. 580, Kuamo'o Rd., Wailua.*

4 Poli'ahu Heiau. Storyboards near this ancient heiau recount the significance of the many sacred structures found along the Wailua River. It's unknown exactly how the ancient Hawaiians used Poli'ahu Heiau—one of the largest pre-Christian temples on the island—but legend says it was built by the Menehune because of the unusual stonework found in its walled enclosures. From this site it's possible to walk downhill a short

6

way to **pōhaku hānau,** a two piece birthing stone said to confer special blessings on all children born there, and **pōhaku piko,** whose crevices were a repository for umbilical cords left by parents seeking a clue to their child's destiny, which reportedly was foretold by how his cord fared in the rock. Some Hawaiians feel these sacred stones shouldn't be viewed as "tourist attractions," so always treat them with respect. Never stand or sit on the rocks, or leave any offerings. ⊠ *Rte. 580 (Kuamo'o Rd.), Wailua.*

SUNSHINE MARKETS (County of Kaua'i farmers' markets; ☎ 808/241–6303 ⊕ www.kauaigov.org) – If you want to rub elbows with the locals and purchase fresh produce and flowers at very reasonable prices, head for one of Kaua'i's farmers' markets. These busy markets are held weekly, usually in the afternoon, at locations all around the island. They're good fun, and they support small, neighborhood farmers. Arrive a little early, bring dollar bills to speed up transactions and plastic shopping bags to carry your produce, and be prepared for some pushy shoppers. Farmers are usually happy to educate visitors about unfamiliar fruits and veggies, especially when the crowd thins. Call the county or check the local newspaper for exact locations and hours.

❻ **Sleeping Giant.** Although its true name is Nounou, this landmark mountain ridge is better known as the Sleeping Giant because of its resemblance to a very large man sleeping on his back. Legends differ on whether the giant is Puni, who was accidentally killed by rocks launched at invading canoes by the Menehune, or Nunui, a gentle creature who has not yet awakened from the nap he took centuries ago after building a massive temple and enjoying a big feast. ⊠ *Rte. 56, about 1 mi north of Wailua River.*

Ⓒ **Smith's Tropical Paradise.** Nestled up next to Wailua Marina along the mightly Wailua River, this 30-acre botanical and cultural garden offers a glimpse of exotic foliage, including fruit orchards, a bamboo rain forest, and tropical lagoons. Take the tram and enjoy a narrated tour or stroll along the mile-long pathways. It's a popular spot for wedding receptions and other large events, and its thrice-weekly lū'au is one of the island's oldest and best. ■ TIP➜➜ It's very difficult to make a northbound turn onto Kūhiō Highway from this road, so it's best to stop in when you're Līhu'e-bound. ⊠ *174 Wailua Rd., Kapa'a* ☎ *808/821–6895* ⊠ *$5.25* ⊘ *Daily 8:30–4.*

⓭ **Waikapala'e and Waikanaloa Wet Caves.** Said to have been dug by Pele, goddess of fire, these watering holes used to be clear, clean, and great for swimming. Now stagnant, they're nevertheless a photogenic example of the many haunting natural landmarks of Kaua'i's North Shore. Waikanaloa is visible right beside the highway. Across the road from a small parking area, a five-minute uphill walk leads to Waikapala'e. ⊠ *Western end of Rte. 560.*

Wailua. Wailua is more a community than a formal town. It's distinguished by a wide bay, broad beach, and Hawai'i's only navigable river, as well as small homes, a number of restaurants, and a few shops. Coconut palms abound, harking back to a failed foray into the copra industry. Wailua was one of Kaua'i's earliest inhabited areas, and favored by royalty and chiefs as a summer retreat. A complex of elaborate stone heiau (temples) running from the rainy summit of Wai'ale'ale–the river's source–to the sea offers evidence of the area's ancient cultural significance. Its name, Wailua, means "two waters." ⊠ *Rte. 56, 7 mi north of Līhu'e.*

need a break?
The jukebox at **Beezers** (⊠ 1380 Kūhiō Hwy., Kapa'a ☎ 808/822–4411) plays '50s songs you can sing to, and pictures of Marilyn and Elvis adorn the walls. On the way north to Wailua, stop in for a malt, root-beer float, or chocolate brownie topped with ice cream, hot fudge, whipped cream, and nuts.

▶ **❶ Wailua Falls.** You may recognize this impressive cascade from the opening sequences of the *Fantasy Island* television series. Kaua'i has plenty of noteworthy waterfalls, but this one is especially picturesque and easy to photograph. ⊠ *End of Rte. 583 (Ma'alo Rd.), 4 mi west of Rte. 56.*

❿
Fodor'sChoice
★
Wai'oli Mission House. This 1837 home was built by missionaries Lucy and Abner Wilcox. Its tidy New England architecture and formal koa-wood furnishings epitomize the prim and proper missionary influence, while the informative guided tours offer a fascinating peek into the private lives of the island's first white residents. Half-hour guided tours are available. ⊠ *Kūhiō Hwy., Hanalei* ☎ *808/245–3202* ⊠ *Donations accepted* ☉ *Tues., Thurs., and Sat. 9–3.*

Līhu'e & the South Side

As you follow the main road south from Līhu'e, the landscape becomes lush and densely vegetated before giving way to the decidedly dry and desertlike conditions that characterize Po'ipū, the South Side's major resort area. Po'ipū owes much of its popularity to a steady supply of sunshine and a string of sandy beaches. With its extensive selection of accommodations, services, and activities, it attracts more visitors than any other region on Kaua'i.

a good drive
Begin in **Līhu'e** ⓯ ▶ and visit the **Kaua'i Museum** ⓰. Head southeast on Rice Street, the town's main road, until it drops you off at **Nāwiliwili** ⓱, Kaua'i's major port. From Wa'apā Road, turn right onto Hulemalu Road and follow the Hulē'ia River to view **Alekoko (Menehune) Fishpond** ⓲. The majestic, rugged mountains of the Hā'upu range are the dominant feature in the Līhu'e landscape.

Return to Nāwiliwili, take a left on Nāwiliwili Road (Route 58), and look to your right for **Grove Farm Homestead** ⓳, where you can stop if you have reserved a tour. At the intersection of Nāwiliwili Road and Route 50, turn left and head west on Route 50, past Kukui Grove Shopping Center, the island's regional mall. About a mile farther, on the right, is the entrance to **Kilohana Plantation** ⓴, followed by the Kaua'i Community College campus, home to a modern Performing Arts Center that hosts quality theater, music, and film events.

6

Continue west on Route 50 to the intersection of Routes 50 and 520. On your left you can see the pass through the Hā'upu range known as Knudsen Gap, the gateway to the South Side. Turn left onto Route 520 (Maluhia Road), also known as the Tunnel of Trees because of the shady overhead canopy formed by eucalyptuses planted along the road.

Route 520 takes you to **Kōloa ㉑**, site of Kaua'i's first sugar mill, dating from 1830. Continue south on Route 520, which is also called Po'ipū Road once it leaves Kōloa town. At the fork stay to the left.

From here turn right onto Ho'owili Road, which takes you through the heart of the **Po'ipū ㉒** resort community. You pass Po'ipū Beach Park, Brennecke Beach, and Shipwreck Beach, all prime spots for sunbathers, snorkelers, and bodysurfers. Return to Po'ipū Road and follow it past the meandering Hyatt Regency Kaua'i, the island's largest hotel, and its equally expansive golf course. The road abruptly turns to dirt, but 2 mi farther awaits the dramatically scenic Māhā'ulepū coastline, the last stretch of wilderness beach in this area. It's privately owned, but open to the public daily from 7:30 AM to 6 PM; you need to sign in at the gate. Park at the end of the dirt road and take a short walk to the beach. (Note that there are no facilities and the water may be too rough for swimming during periods of big summer surf.)

Backtrack on Po'ipū Road, but instead of turning toward Kōloa, take a left onto Lāwa'i Road just after the bridge over Waikomo Stream. You soon come to tiny **Prince Kūhiō Park ㉓**, dubbed "PKs" by the board surfers who haunt this popular surf break. Beyond the park is the visitor center for the **National Tropical Botanical Gardens ㉔**. At the end of this beachfront road is **Spouting Horn ㉕**, where a plume of sea spray signals your drive's end.

TIMING   It's 14 mi from Līhu'e to Po'ipū, but the drive takes a good half hour—or more during the *pau hana* (end of work) traffic crawl. Since there's plenty to see, you can easily devote a day or two to this itinerary, especially if you want to log some serious beach time. If you have only a half day, make a point of catching the sunset from a South Side beach. The colors are dreamy, and the board and body surfers put on a mesmerizing show, especially when the waves are big.

What to See

⑲ Grove Farm Homestead. Guided tours of this carefully restored 80-acre
FodorsChoice   country estate offer a fascinating, and authentic, look at how upper-class
★   Caucasians experienced plantation life in the mid-19th century. The tour focuses on the original home, built by the Wilcox family in 1860 and filled with a quirky collection of classic Hawaiiana. You can also see the workers' quarters, farm animals, orchards, and gardens that reflect the practical, self-sufficient lifestyle of the island's earliest Western inhabitants. Tours of the homestead are conducted twice a day, three days per week. To protect the historic building and its furnishings, tours may be canceled on very wet days. ■ TIP➜➜ With a six-person limit per tour, reservations are essential and young children are not encouraged. ⊠ *Rte. 58, Nāwiliwili Rd., Līhu'e* ☎ *808/245–3202* ⊠ *$5* ☉ *Tours Mon., Wed., and Thurs. at 10 and 1.*

★ **⑯ Kaua'i Museum.** Maintaining a stately presence on Rice Street, the historic museum building is easy to find. It features a permanent display, "The Story of Kaua'i," which provides a competent overview of the Garden Island and Ni'ihau, tracing the islands' geology, mythology, and cultural history. Local artists are represented in changing exhibits in the second-floor Mezzanine Gallery. The gift shop alone is worth a visit, with a fine collection of authentic Ni'ihau shell lei, feather hatband lei, handturned wooden bowls, reference books, and other quality arts, crafts, and gifts, many of them locally made. ⊠ *4428 Rice St., Līhu'e* ☎ *808/245–6931* ⚏ *$5* ⊙ *Weekdays 9–4, Sat. 10–4.*

♨ **⑳ Kilohana Plantation.** This estate dates back to 1896, when plantation manager Albert Spencer Wilcox first developed it as a working cattle ranch. His nephew, Gaylord Parke Wilcox, took over in 1936, building Kaua'i's first mansion. Today the 16,000-square-foot, Tudor-style home houses specialty shops, art galleries, and Gaylord's, a pretty restaurant with courtyard seating. Nearly half the original furnishings remain, and the gardens and orchards were replanted according to the original plans. You can tour the grounds for free; children enjoy visiting the farm animals. Horse-drawn carriage rides are available, or you can tour the old Grove Farm Plantation in a sugarcane wagon pulled by Clydesdales. ⊠ *3-2087 Kaumuali'i Hwy., Rte. 50, Līhu'e* ☎ *808/245–5608* ⊙ *Mon.–Sat. 9:30–9:30, Sun. 9:30–5.*

㉑ Kōloa. Hawai'i's lucrative foray into sugar was born in this sleepy town, where the first sugar was milled back in 1830. You can still see the mill's old stone smokestack. Little else remains, save for the charming plantation-style buildings that have kept Kōloa from becoming a tacky tourist trap for Poipu-bound visitors. The original small-town ambience has been preserved by converting historic structures along the main street into boutiques, restaurants, and shops. Placards describe the original tenants and life in the old mill town. Look for Kōloa Fish Market, which offers poke and sashimi takeout, and Progressive Expressions, a popular local surf shop. ⊠ *Rte. 520.*

▶ **⑮ Līhu'e.** The commercial and political center of Kaua'i County, which includes the islands of Kaua'i and Ni'ihau, Līhu'e is home to the island's major airport, harbor, and hospital. This is where you can find the state and county offices that issue camping and hiking permits, and the same fast-food eateries and big-box stores that blight the mainland. Once your business is done, there's little reason to linger in lackluster Līhu'e. ⊠ *Rtes. 56 and 50.*

⑱ Alekoko (Menehune) Fishpond. No one knows just who built this intricate aquaculture structure in the Hule'ia River. Legend attributes it to the Menehune, a possibly real, possibly mythical ancient race of people known for their small stature, industrious nature, and superb stoneworking skills. Volcanic rock was cut and fit together into massive walls 4 feet thick and 5 feet high, forming an enclosure for raising mullet and other freshwater fish that has endured for centuries. ⊠ *Hulemalu Rd., Niumalu.*

FODOR'S FIRST PERSON

Joan Conrow
Writer

I'm accustomed to seeing rainbows on Kaua'i, where showers and sunshine frequently collide. But I discounted reports about moonbows—until I saw one myself. The full moon had just risen from the ocean, and it was shining over my shoulder when a shower blew in on the west wind. I bent down for a moment to pet my dog and when I looked up, there it was: a perfect arch, each band of color distinct and vibrant, clear and bright from end to end. And I was smack in the middle, at the crest of the bow, crowned by its magical shimmer. It stayed put for a long while, then slowly drifted northward, still intact, but growing ever fainter, until it finally disappeared, leaving me mesmerized, enchanted, and grateful, as always, for the priceless gifts of nature.

★ ㉔ **National Tropical Botanical Gardens** (NTBG). Tucked away in Lāwa'i Valley, these gardens include lands and a cottage once used by Hawai'i's Queen Emma for a summer retreat. Visitors can take a self-guided tour of the rambling 252-acre **McBryde Gardens** to see and learn about plants collected from throughout the tropics. The 100-acre **Allerton Gardens**, which can be visited only on a guided tour, artfully display statues and water features that were originally developed as part of a private estate. A secluded cove known as Lāwa'i Kai can be reached through Allerton Gardens; the beach is otherwise largely inaccessible to the public. Reservations are required for tours of Allerton Gardens, but not for the self-guided tours of McBryde Gardens. The visitor center has a high-quality gift shop with botany-theme merchandise.

Besides harboring and propagating rare and endangered plants from Hawai'i and elsewhere, NTBG functions as a scientific research and education center. The organization also operates gardens in Limahuli, on Kaua'i's north shore, and in Hāna, on Maui's east shore. ✉ *Lāwa'i Rd., across from Spouting Horn parking lot, Po'ipū* ☎ *808/742–2623* ⊕ *www.ntbg.org* ✉ *Self-guided tour (McBryde) $15, guided tour (Allerton) $30* ☉ *McBryde Gardens Mon.–Sat. 9:30–5, Allerton Gardens tours Mon.–Sat. at 9, 10, 1, and 2, Sun. at 10 and 1:30.*

⑰ **Nāwiliwili.** The commercial harbor at Nāwiliwili is a major port of call for container ships, U.S. Navy vessels, and passenger cruise lines. Anglers and recreational boaters use the nearby small boat harbor. This is the main departure point for deep-sea fishing charters, boat tours, and snorkeling and sightseeing adventures along the coast. There's protected swimming at Kalapakī Bay, fronting the Marriott resort, although the water quality is questionable at times. ✉ *Makai end of Wa'apā Rd., Līhu'e.*

㉒ **Po'ipū.** Po'ipū has emerged as Kaua'i's top visitor destination, thanks to its generally sunny weather and a string of golden-sand beaches dotted with oceanfront lodgings, including the Sheraton Kaua'i Resort and a half dozen condominium projects. Beaches are user-friendly, with protected waters for *keiki* (children) and novice snorkelers, lifeguards, clean restrooms, covered pavilions, and a sweet coastal promenade ideal for leisurely strolls. Some experts even rank Po'ipū Beach Park number one in the nation. That may be a bit of an overstatement, although it certainly does warrant high accolades. ⊠ *Rte. 520.*

㉓ **Prince Kūhiō Park.** A triangle of grass behind the Prince Kūhiō condominiums honors the birthplace of Kaua'i's beloved Prince Jonah Kūhiō Kalaniana'ole. Known for his kind nature and good deeds, he lost his chance at the throne when Americans staged an illegal overthrow of Queen Lili'uokalani in 1893 and toppled Hawai'i's constitutional monarchy. This is a great place to view wave riders surfing a popular break known as "PKs," and to watch the sun sink into the Pacific. ⊠ *Lāwa'i Rd., Po'ipū.*

★ ㉕ **Spouting Horn.** If the conditions are right, you can see a natural blowhole in the reef behaving like Old Faithful, shooting salt water high into the air. It's most dramatic during big summer swells, which force large quantities of water through an ancient lava tube with great force. ⚠ Stay on the paved walkways as rocks can be slippery and wave action unpredictable. Vendors hawk inexpensive souvenirs and other items in the parking lot. You may find good deals on shell jewelry, but ask for a certificate of authenticity to ensure its a genuine Ni'ihau shell lei before paying the higher price that these intricate creations command. ⊠ *Lāwa'i Bay, Lāwa'i Rd., Po'ipū.*

The West Side

Exploring the West Side is akin to visiting an entirely different world. The landscape is dramatic and colorful: a patchwork of green, blue, black, and orange. The weather is hot and dry, the beaches are long, the sand is dark. Ni'ihau, a private island where only Hawaiians may live, can be glimpsed offshore. This is rural Kaua'i, where sugar is making its last stand and taro is still cultivated in the fertile river valleys. The lifestyle is slow, easy, and traditional, with many folks fishing and hunting to supplement their diets. Here and there modern industry has intruded into this pastoral scene: huge generators turn oil into electricity at Port Allen; scientists cultivate experimental crops of genetically engineered plants in Kekaha; the Navy launches rockets at Mānā to test the "Star Wars" missile defense system; and NASA mans a tracking station in the wilds of Koke'e. It's a region of contrasts that simply shouldn't be missed.

Heading west from Kaua'i's South Side, you pass through a string of tiny towns, plantation camps, and historical sites, each with a story to tell of centuries past. There's Hanapēpē, whose coastal salt ponds have been harvested since ancient times; Kaumakani, where the sugar industry still clings to life; Fort Elisabeth, from which an enterprising Russian tried to take over the island in the early 1800s; and Waimea, where Captain Cook made his first landing in the Islands, forever changing the face of Hawai'i.

From Waimea town you can head up into the mountains, skirting the rim of magnificent Waimea Canyon and climbing higher still until you reach the cool, often-misty forests of Kōke'e State Park. From the vantage point at the top of this gemlike island, 3,200 to 4,200 feet above sea level, you can gaze into the deep verdant valleys of the North Shore and Nā Pali Coast. This is where the "real" Kaua'i can still be found: the native plants, insects, and birds that are found nowhere else on Earth.

a good drive

Start in Līhu'e and head west on Route 50, more commonly called Kaumuali'i Highway, past the turnoff to Kōloa. Blink and you might miss Lāwa'i, a former cannery town whose fortunes fell with the demise of pineapple. It's emerged as a bedroom community for Līhu'e and significant producer of tropical fruits and flowers. The next stop is Kalāheo, where you can turn left onto Pāpālina Road, at the town's sole traffic light, for a delightful side trip to hilltop **Kukuiolono Park** ㉖ ▶.

Return to the highway and continue west to the **Hanapēpē Valley and Canyon Lookout** ㉗, a scenic vista where warring chiefs launched their final, decisive battle to gain control of the island. On your return trip you can skip this site and instead visit the **Kaua'i Coffee Visitor Center and Museum** ㉘. Just look for Route 540 on your right shortly after leaving Hanapēpē. It's a loop road through acres of coffee trees that will deliver you back to the highway west of Kalāheo.

Hanapēpē ㉙ is a sleepy little town where the shifting light seems to appeal to a growing number of artists. They've opened a number of fine galleries along the dusty old main street, which juts off to the right from Route 50 at the entrance to town and then runs parallel to the highway. If you'd rather sunbathe, continue west on Route 50 to the outskirts of town, where you can turn left onto Lele Road. It leads through a scrubby landscape to **Salt Pond Beach Park** ㉚, the safest place to swim on the westside.

Return to Route 50 and turn left, again heading west. Watch the makai side of the road for the Hawaiian warrior sign, an image used statewide to identify points of interest for tourists. Here it marks the turnoff to **Fort Elisabeth** ㉛. The next point of interest is the Waimea River, whose waters have been diverted into taro fields for more than 1,000 years through a sophisticated aqueduct system. A section known as the **Menehune Ditch** ㉜ is visible about 2½ mi up Menehune Road, the first road on the right past the bridge. Continue on Route 50 into **Waimea** ㉝, the thriving hub of island life when Captain Cook came ashore in 1778. It's a pretty, peaceful town that is slowly rebuilding its economy around tourism and high-tech, which explains the rather unlikely presence of the modern **West Kaua'i Visitor and Technology Center** ㉞ on the outskirts of town.

Route 50 hugs a stretch of sandy coastline as it passes the fading sugar town of Kekaha and enters the Mānā, a vast wetland drained to grow sugar. Security fences enclose the Navy's Pacific Missile Range Facility on the makai side of the highway, which soon dead-ends at a sugarcane field, where a long, bumpy dirt road leads to Polihale State Park. The road can be passable or a nightmare of ruts and potholes, depending on weather and the state road crew's maintenance schedule. The park itself is well-appointed for camping and day use, although the sea is often too rough for swimming and the sand gets burning hot in summer. Still, if you're hanking for privacy and a long, long walk on a sandy beach, press on.

Kaua'i Sightseeing Tours

TOURS ARE GREAT WHEN YOU WANT TO RELAX and let someone else do the driving. You also benefit from the knowledge and experience of your guide, and gain a better sense of what it's like to actually live on this green gem in the Pacific.

Kaua'i Island Tours. A good general tour company, Kaua'i Island Tours will arrange charter tours around Kaua'i in anything from a passenger car to a 57-person bus. ☎ 808/245–4777 or 800/733–4777.

Roberts Hawai'i Tours. The Round-the-Island Tour, sometimes called the Wailua River/Waimea Canyon Tour, gives a good overview of the island including Fort Elisabeth, 'Ōpaeka'a Falls, and Alekoko (Menehune) Fishpond. Guests are transported in air-conditioned, 17-passenger minivans. The $59 trip includes a boat ride up the Wailua River to the Fern Grotto, and a visit to the lookouts above Waimea Canyon. ☎ 808/245–9101 or 800/831–5541 ⊕ www.robertshawaii.com.

Gay and Robinson Tours. Gay and Robinson, the island's last sugar grower, offers tours of its plantation and factory. You can go into the fields to hear about how cane is grown and processed into the white, granular stuff we eat so heartily, and you learn about the history of sugar in Hawai'i. One highlight is viewing scenic coastal areas otherwise closed to the public. Tours are offered weekdays at 8:45 and 12:45 for $35. ☎ 808/335–2824 ⊕ www.gandrtours-kauai.com.

Hawai'i Movie Tours. Hawai'i Movie Tours' minibuses with in-van TV monitors let you see the actual scenes of films while visiting the real locations used for the filming of *Jurassic Park, Raiders of the Lost Ark, South Pacific, Blue Hawaii, Gilligan's Island,* and other Hollywood hits. The standard land tour is $95. The four-wheel-drive Off Road Tour is $113 and takes you to film locations on private lands and rugged backcountry areas that are otherwise not easily visited. We recommend this tour primarily for serious movie buffs. ⊠ 4-885 Kūhiō Hwy., Kapa'a ☎ 808/822–1192 or 800/628–8432 ⊕ www.hawaiimovietour.com.

Kapa'a History Tour–Kaua'i's Historical Society. History buffs curious about Kapa'a's past during the World War II years and heyday of sugarcane and pineapple will enjoy this 90-minute walking tour past many historic buildings and interesting landmarks. It's an insider's look at what made Kapa'a into the island's biggest little town. Tours take place on Tuesday, Thursday, and Saturday at 10 AM and 4 PM and cost $15. ☎ 808/245–3373.

Plantation Lifestyles Walking Tour. To see a rapidly vanishing lifestyle that once dominated life in Hawai'i, take the fascinating and unique Plantation Lifestyles Walking Tour through the residential area of a real mill camp. In the shadow of an old sugar mill, the dirt lanes of the 70-year-old camp are shaded by fruit trees and tropical gardens. Sometimes elderly residents come out to say aloha to touring guests. Reservations are needed for the $10 1½-hour to 2-hour volunteer-led tours that begin at 9 AM every Tuesday, Thursday, and Saturday at Waimea Plantation Cottages. ☎ 808/335–2824 ⊕ www.gandrtours-kauai.com.

6

It's much easier to reach **Waimea Canyon** ㉟, which is served by two scenic routes. We like to go up the mountain on Kōke'e Road (Route 55), which starts in Kekaha, and back down on Waimea Canyon Drive (Route 550), which meets Route 50 at Waimea. Either way, the two routes soon converge and the ascent continues along the canyon rim. Take every opportunity to pull over or stop at a lookout, as each spot offers a different view of this scenic wonder dubbed the "Grand Canyon of the Pacific." At about the 4,000-foot-level, the road enters Kōke'e State Park, where a natural history museum and the rustic Kōke'e Lodge are the sole commercial enterprises.

Waimea Canyon Drive ends 4 mi above the park at the **Kalalau Lookout** ㊱, with its bird's-eye view into the legendary valley. A sweeping panorama of the North Shore rewards those who walk a bit farther to the Pu'u-o-Kila lookout.

TIMING   The 36-mi drive from Līhu'e to Waimea and Kōke'e can take 60 to 90 minutes without any stops, but that's pushing it. Realistically, it can take at least half a day; plan on a full day if you want to hike, eat, shop, or explore. ■ TIP→→ This is one part of the island where you'll be glad you brought a jacket and rain gear, as it can be cool and misty any time of the year, and downright nippy and wet in winter.

What to See

㉙ **Hanapēpē.** In the 1980s, Hanapēpē was fast becoming a ghost town, its farm-based economy mirroring the decline of agriculture. Today it's a burgeoning art colony, with galleries, craft studios, and a lively art-themed street fair on Friday nights. The main street has a new vibrancy enhanced by the restoration of several historic buildings. The emergence of Kaua'i Coffee as a major West Side crop and expanded activities at Port Allen, now the main departure point for tour boats, also gave the town's economy a boost. ⊠ *Rte. 50.*

> **need a break?**
>
> You can savor fresh baked goods and coffee drinks at the spiffy black-and-white bar, or dine on wholesome vegetarian fare and fish at **Hanapēpē Café and Espresso** (⊠ 3830 Hanapēpē Rd., Hanapēpē ☎ 808/335–5011).

㉘ **Hanapēpē Valley and Canyon Lookout.** This dramatic divide and fertile river valley once housed a thriving Hawaiian community of taro farmers, with some of the ancient fields still in cultivation today. From the lookout you can take in the farms on the valley floor with the majestic mountains as a backdrop. ⊠ *Rte. 50.*

★ ㊱ **Kalalau Lookout.** Near the end of the road, high above Waimea Canyon, Kalalau Lookout marks the start of a challenging one-hour, 2-mi (one-way) hike to **Pu'u o Kila lookout.** On a clear day at either spot you can look down at a dreamy landscape of gaping valleys, sawtooth ridges, waterfalls, and turquoise seas, where whales can be seen spouting and breaching during the winter months. If clouds obscure the spectacle, don't despair. They tend to blow through fast, giving you time to snap that photo of a lifetime before the next cloud bank drifts in. You may spot wild goats clambering on the sheer, rocky cliffs, and white tropic birds soaring gracefully on the thermals, their long tails streaming behind them. If it's very clear to the northwest, look for the shining sands of Kalalau Beach, gleaming like golden threads against the deep blue of the Pacific. ⊠ *Waimea Canyon Dr., 4 mi north of Kōke'e State Park.*

★ **Kōke'e State Park.** This 4,345-acre wilderness park is 4,000 feet above sea level, an elevation that affords you breathtaking views in all directions. You can gain a deeper appreciation of the island's rugged terrain and dramatic beauty from this vantage point. Large tracts of native 'ōhi'a and koa forest cover much of the terrain, along with many varieties of exotic plants. Hikers can follow a 45-mi network of trails through diverse landscapes that feel wonderfully remote—until the tour helicopters pass overhead. (⇨ *See* Hiking, *earlier in this chapter.*)

Fodor's Choice **Kōke'e Natural History Museum** is a great place to start your visit. The
★ friendly staff is knowledgeable about trail conditions and weather, while informative displays and a good selection of reference books can teach you more about the unique attributes of the native flora and fauna. You may also find that special memento or gift you've been looking for. ⊠ *Rte. 550* ☎ *808/335–9975* 💲 *Donations accepted* ☉ *Daily 10–4.*

6

> **need a break?**
>
> There's only one place to buy food and hot drinks, and that's the dining room of rustic **Kōke'e Lodge** (⊠ Kōke'e State Park, 3600 Kōke'e Rd., mile marker 15 ☎ 808/335–6061). Peruse the gift shop for T-shirts, postcards, or campy Kōke'e memorabilia.

▶ ㉖ **Kukuiolono Park.** Translated as "light of the god Lono," Kukuiolono has serene Japanese gardens, a display of significant Hawaiian stones, and spectacular panoramic views. This quiet hilltop park is one of Kaua'i's most scenic areas and an ideal picnic spot. There's also a small golf course. ⊠ *Pāpālina Rd., Kalāheo* ☎ *808/332–9151* 💲 *Free* ☉ *Daily 6:30–6:30.*

★ ㉚ **Salt Pond Beach Park.** This popular park lies just west of some privately owned salt ponds where Hawaiians continue the traditional practice of harvesting salt (valued for its culinary and medicinal properties). They let the sun evaporate the seawater in mud-lined drying beds, then gather the salt left behind. You can't visit the ponds, but the beach park's protected swimming cove and camp grounds are worth a stop. ⊠ *Lele Rd., Hanapēpē.*

㉝ **Waimea.** This serene, pretty town has played a major role in Hawaiian history since 1778, when Captain James Cook became the first European to set foot on the Hawaiian Islands. Waimea was also the place where Kaua'i's King Kaumuali'i acquiesced to King Kamehameha's unification drive in 1810, averting a bloody war. The town hosted the first Christian missionaries, who hauled in massive timbers and limestone blocks to build the sturdy Waimea Christian Hawaiian and Foreign Church in 1846. It's one of many lovely historic buildings preserved by residents who take great pride in their heritage and history. The town itself has the look of the Old West and the feel of Old Hawai'i, with a lifestyle that's decidedly laid-back. Waimea beaches are sunny and sandy, but near-shore waters are often murky with runoff from the Waimea River. It's an ideal place for a refreshment break while sightseeing on the West Side. ⊠ *Rte. 50.*

③⑤ Waimea Canyon. Carved over countless centuries by the mighty Waimea
FodorśChoice River and the forces of wind and rain, this dramatic gorge is aptly nick-
★ named the "Grand Canyon of the Pacific." Hiking and hunting trails wind through the canyon, which is 3,600 feet deep, 2 mi wide, and 10 mi long. The cliffsides have been sharply eroded, exposing swatches of colorful soil. The deep red, brown, and green hues are constantly changing in the sun, and frequent rainbows and waterfalls enhance the natural beauty. This is one of Kaua'i's prettiest spots, and it's worth stopping at both the **Pu'u ka Pele** and **Pu'u hinahina** lookouts to savor the views. Clean public restrooms are at both lookouts.

WHERE TO STAY

The Garden Isle has lodgings for every taste, from swanky resorts to rustic cabins, and from family-friendly condos to romantic B&Bs. When choosing a place to stay, location is an important consideration—Kaua'i may look small, but it takes more time than you might think to get around. If at all possible, stay close to your desired activities. ■ TIP→→ Prices are highest near the ocean and in resort communities like Princeville and Po'ipū.

As a rule, resorts offer a full roster of amenities and large, well-appointed rooms. They are all oceanfront properties that lean toward the luxurious. If you want to golf, play tennis, or hang at a spa, stay at a resort. The island's hotels tend to be smaller and older, with fewer on-site amenities.

Individual condominium units are equipped with all the comforts of home, but each property offers different services, so inquire if you want tennis courts, golf, and on-site restaurants. They're ideal for families, couples traveling together, and longer stays.

Vacation rentals run the gamut from fabulous luxury estates to scruffy little dives. It's buyer-beware in this unregulated sector of the visitor industry, so choose carefully. Many homes are in rural areas far from beaches, or in crowded neighborhoods that may be a bit too local-style for some tastes. ■ TIP→→ Condos and vacation rentals typically require a minimum stay of three nights to a week, along with a cleaning fee.

The island's bed-and-breakfasts allow you to meet local residents and more directly experience the aloha spirit. They tend to be among the more expensive types of lodging, though, and don't assume you get a lavish breakfast unless it's a featured attraction. You'll usually get a very comfortable room in a private house along with a morning meal; some properties have stand-alone units on-site.

If you need help choosing a property, **Bed and Breakfast Kaua'i** (⊠ 105 Melia St., Kapa'a 96746 🕿 808/822–1177 or 800/822–1176 🖶 808/826–9292 ⊕ www.bnb-kauai.com) may prove helpful. Liz Hay, a longtime island resident, maintains a network of more than 200 cottages, condos, and B&Bs that consider all lifestyles and budgets. Most large real estate companies also maintain a roster of vacation rentals.

	WHAT IT COSTS				
	$$$$	$$$	$$	$	¢
HOTELS	over $200	$150–$200	$100–$150	$60–$100	under $60

Hotel prices are for two people in a standard double room in high season, including tax and service.

The North Shore

The North Shore is mountainous and wet, which accounts for its rugged, lush landscape. Posh resorts and condominiums await you at Princeville, a community with dreamy views, excellent golf courses, and lovely sunsets. If you want to visit other parts of the island, be prepared for a long drive—that's very dark at night.

Hotels & Resorts

★ **$$$$** **Princeville Resort.** Built into the cliffs above Hanalei Bay, this sprawling resort offers expansive views of the mountains and sea. You'll surely recognize Makana, a landmark peak that Hollywood immortalized as mysterious "Bali Hai" island in the film South Pacific. Guest rooms are spacious and designed in primary colors to match those of Kaua'i's abundant yellow hibiscus, red 'ōhi'a flower, and dark green mokihana berry. Little details make a difference, like lighted closets, dimmer switches on all lamps, original artwork, and door chimes. Bathrooms feature height-adjustable showerheads and a privacy window—flip a switch and it goes from clear to opaque so you can see the sights without becoming an attraction yourself. Two restaurants serve excellent food in dining rooms that capitalize on the views, and the poolside lū'au is lavish. The Living Room is a swanky bar with nightly entertainment and big windows that showcase gorgeous sunsets. There's shuttle service to the resort's two top-ranked golf courses, spa, and tennis center, none of which are on the hotel grounds. ⊠ 5520 Ka Haku Rd., Princeville 96722 ☎ 808/826–9644 or 888/488–3535 🖷 808/826–1166 ⊕ www.starwood.com/hawaii ⇆ 201 rooms, 51 suites ⚙ 4 restaurants, room service, A/C, minibars, 2 18-hole golf courses, 8 tennis courts, pool, gym, health club, massage, spa, beach, 2 bars, children's programs (ages 5–12), dry cleaning, laundry service, concierge, business services, meeting rooms, travel services ⊟ AE, D, DC, MC, V. $350–$750.

Condos

$$$–$$$$ 🖼 **Hanalei Bay Resort.** This condominium resort has a lovely location overlooking Hanalei Bay and Nā Pali Coast. Three-story buildings angle down the cliffs, making for some steep walking paths. Units are extremely spacious, with high, sloping ceilings and large private lānai. Rattan furniture and island art add a casual feeling to rooms. Studios have small kitchenettes not meant for serious cooking, the larger units have full kitchens. The resort's upper-level pool is one of the nicest on the island, with authentic lava-rock waterfalls, an open-air hot tub, and a kid-friendly sand "beach." The restaurant is expensive, but the food and views are worth the price. The friendly tropical bar offers live music. The tennis courts are on-site, and guests have golf privileges at Princeville Resort.

More than half the units on this property are now dedicated to vacation ownership rentals. ✉ *5380 Honoiki Rd., Princeville 96722* ☎ *808/826–6522 or 800/827–4427* 🖷 *808/826–6680* 🌐 *www. hanaleibayresort.com* 🛏 *134 units* 🍴 *Restaurant, A/C, in-room safes, kitchenettes, refrigerators, cable TV, golf privileges, 8 tennis courts, 2 pools, hot tub, massage, beach, lobby lounge, shop, babysitting, children's programs (ages 5–12), laundry facilities* ▤ *AE, D, DC, MC, V. Studios $195–$205, 1-bedroom $225–$255, 2-bedroom $290–$310, 3-bedroom $335.*

> ### STOCKING UP
>
> Foodland, in the Princeville Shopping Center, has the best selection of groceries, sundries, and other items needed to supply the kitchen. It's open daily from 7 AM to 11 PM. Be sure to ask for a Maka'i discount card, as the prices may give you sticker shock.

B&Bs & Vacation Rentals

$$$$ 🏠 **Kīlauea Lakeside Estate.** The world revolves around you at this private island retreat, where the amenities and activities are custom-designed to create your dream vacation. The proprietors can arrange for personal chefs, windsurfing lessons, lakeside spa treatments, and on-site weddings. A private 20-acre freshwater lake teeming with bass and catfish awaits your fishing pole. You can also have your own par-3 golf hole and putting green and 3 acres of botanical gardens to stroll through. The modern three-bedroom house includes a romantic master suite and bath. ✉ *4613 Waiakalua Rd., Kīlauea 96754* ☎ *310/379–7842* 🖷 *310/379–0034* 🌐 *www.kauaihoneymoon.com* 🛏 *1 house* 🍴 *BBQ, fans, kitchen, cable TV, in-room VCRs, putting green, lake, beach, fishing, laundry facilities; no A/C* ▤ *AE, D, MC, V. $400–$650.*

$$$ 🏠 **Hanalei Colony Resort.** This 5-acre property is a laid-back, go-barefoot kind of place sandwiched between towering mountains and the sea. The only true beachfront resort on Kaua'i's North Shore, its charm is in its simplicity. There are no phones, TVs, or stereos in the rooms. Each of the two-bedroom units can sleep a family of four. The units are well maintained, with Hawaiian-style furnishings, full kitchens, and lānai. Amenities, like cocktail receptions and cultural activities, vary from season to season. There's an art gallery with coffee bar on-site. ✉ *5-7130 Kūhiō Hwy., Hā'ena 96714* ☎ *808/826–6235 or 800/628–3004* 🖷 *808/ 826–9893* 🌐 *www.hcr.com* 🛏 *48 units* 🍴 *BBQs, fans, kitchens, pool, hot tub, beach, shop, laundry facilities; no A/C, no room phones, no room TVs* ▤ *AE, MC, V. $185–$300.*

$$ 🏠 **North Country Farms.** These comfortable lodgings are tucked away
FodorśChoice on a tidy, 4-acre organic fruit, flower, and vegetable farm just east of
★ Kīlauea. Although simple, they're clean and provide everything a couple or family might need, including kitchenettes. Owner Lee Roversi and her children are warm, friendly, and creative. You'll enjoy the thoughtful selection of videos, games, puzzles, and reading material. The setting is rural and quiet, with lush tropical landscaping around the two units. Guests are welcome to pick fresh produce. Several nice beaches are just a few minutes' drive away. ✉ *Kahili Makai, Box 723, Kīlauea 96754* ☎ *808/828–1513* 🖷 *808/828–0899* 🌐 *www.northcountryfarms.*

Where to Stay on Kaua'i

See chart pp. 506–507

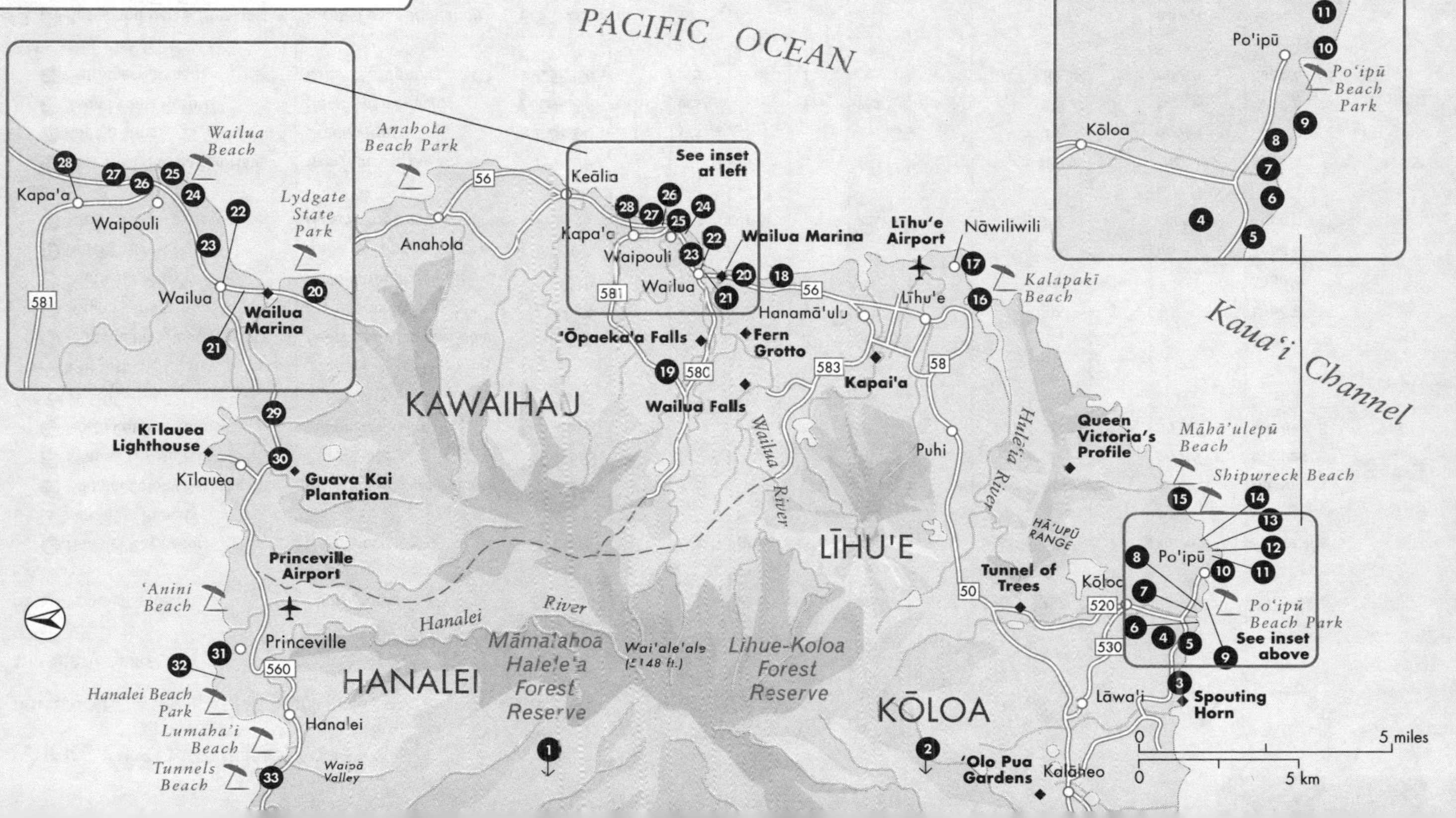

WHERE TO STAY ON KAUA'I

HOTEL NAME	Worth Noting	Cost $	Pools	Beach	Golf Course	Tennis Courts	Gym	Spa	Children programs	Rooms	Restaurants	Other	Location
THE NORTH SHORE													
Hotels & Resorts													
★ 31 Princeville Resort	Lavish poolside lū'au	350–750	1	yes	yes	8	yes	yes	5–12	252	4		Princeville
Condos													
32 Hanalei Bay Resort	Great views	195–335	2	yes	priv.	8	yes	yes	5–12	134	1	kitchen	Princeville
B&Bs & Vacation Rentals													
33 Hanalei Colony Resort	Go-barefoot kind of place	185–300	1	yes						48		no A/C	Hā'ena
30 Kīlauea Lakeside Estate	Private lake	400–650								1		no A/C	Kīlauea
★ 29 North Country Farms	Popular with families	120								2		no A/C	Kīlauea
THE EAST SIDE													
Hotels & Resorts													
20 Aloha Kaua'i Beach Resort	Beach cottages available	150–290	2			2	yes			214	1		Kapa'a
24 Aston Islander	Plantation-style design	120–160	1	yes		1				196	1		Kapa'a
27 Courtyard Kaua'i	Popular nightly lū'au	159–259	1	yes		3				311	1		Kapa'a
28 Hotel Coral Reef	Good location, low price	70–100		yes						26		no A/C	Kapa'a
23 Kaua'i Sands	Hawaiian-owned & operated	100–150	2	yes			yes			252		kitchen	Kapa'a
Condos													
26 Best West. Plantation Hale	Beach across the street	185–210	3							120		kitchens	Kapa'a
21 Kapa'a Sands	Ocean views	100–160	1	yes						20		no A/C	Kapa'a
25 Kaua'i Coast Resort	Uncrowded beach	190–295	2	yes		1	yes	yes		108	1	kitchen	Kapa'a
22 Outrigger Lae nani	Cultural programs	225–350	1	yes		1				84		no A/C	Kapa'a
B&Bs and Vacation Rentals													
19 Rosewood Bed & Breakfast	Located on a plantation	50–135								7		no A/C	Kapa'a

LIHU'E

Hotels & Resorts

#	Name	Comments	Price ($)						Ages	Rooms		Notes	Location
16	Garden Island Inn	Beach across the street	85–150	1	yes					24	2	kitchen	Kalapaki Beach
17	Kaua'i Marriott Resort	26,000-sq-ft pool	333–464	2	yes	7	yes	yes	5–12	599	2		Lihu'e
18	Radisson Kaua'i	Great pool area	139–289	2	yes	4	yes	yes	5–12	355			Lihu'e

THE SOUTH SIDE

Hotels & Resorts

#	Name	Comments	Price ($)						Ages	Rooms		Notes	Location
★ 15	Hyatt Regency Kaua'i	5 acres of swimming lagoons	395–600	1	yes	4	yes	yes	5–12	602	6	shops	Kōloa
11	Sheraton Kaua'i Resort	Ocean wing right on water	280–460	2	yes	3	yes	yes	5–12	413	4		Kōloa

Condos

#	Name	Comments	Price ($)						Ages	Rooms		Notes	Location
14	Makahuena at Po'ipū	Close to center of Po'ipū	170–375	1		1				79		no A/C	Po'ipū
9	Outrigger Kiahuna Plantation	Popular with families	200–450	1	yes	6				333	1	no A/C	Kōloa
8	Po'ipū Kapili	Deluxe PH suites available	220–575	1		2				60		no A/C	Kōloa
13	Po'ipū Shores	Excellent whale-watching	230–400	1						33		no A/C	Kōloa
10	Suite Paradise Po'ipū Kai	Short walk to beach	120–500	6		9				130	1	kitchen	Kōloa
6	Whalers Cove	Rocky beach	320–475	1	yes					30		no A/C	Kōloa

B&Bs & Vacation Rentals

#	Name	Comments	Price ($)						Ages	Rooms		Notes	Location
★ 5	Garden Isle Cottages	Beautiful ocean view	169–190							4		no A/C	Kōloa
★ 3	Gloria's Spouting Horn B&B	Romantic	325	1	yes					3		no A/C	Po'ipū
7	Kaua'i Cove Cottages	Excellent snorkeling	105–125							3		no A/C	Po'ipū
4	Kōloa Landing Cottages	Short walk to beach	95–175							8		no A/C	Kōloa
12	Po'ipū Plantation Resort	Cottages available	105–90							12		kitchen	Kōloa

THE WEST SIDE

Hotels & Resorts

#	Name	Comments	Price ($)						Ages	Rooms		Notes	Location
★ 2	Waimea Plantation Cottages	Good for large groups	140–675	1	yes			yes		48	1	no A/C	Waimea

Vacation Rentals

#	Name	Comments	Price ($)						Ages	Rooms		Notes	Location
★ 1	Kōke'e Lodge	Rustic wilderness cabins	35–45							12	1	no A/C	Kekaha

com ⟳ *2 cottages* ⚴ *Kitchenettes, cable TV, in-room VCRs; no A/C. $120.*

The East Side

The East Side, or Coconut Coast, is a good centralized home base if you want to see and do it all. It has a number of smaller, older properties that are modestly priced, but still comfortable. This region also has a wider choice of inexpensive restaurants and shops than the resort areas. The beaches here are so-so for swimming but nice for sunbathing, walking, and watching the sun and moon rise.

Hotels & Resorts

$$$–$$$$ 🏨 **Courtyard Kaua'i at Waipouli Beach.** Formerly known as the Kaua'i Coconut Beach Resort, this popular oceanfront hotel was bought and refurbished by Courtyard by Marriott in 2005. The bright, spacious rooms face the ocean or pool and have been outfitted with modern amenities, including free wireless high-speed Internet access. Each oceanfront room has a large lana'i. The 11-acre site has always been desirable, nestled as it is among ancient coconut groves and close to a coastal bike/walking path, shops, restaurants, and the airport. The new owners wisely kept the best of the old resort, including its sunset torch-lighting ceremony and nightly lū'au—one of the best and most authentic on the island. ✉ *4-484 Kūhiō Hwy., Kapa'a 96746* ☎*808/822–3455 or 800/760–8555* 🖷*808/822–1830* ⊕ *www.marriott.com* ⟳ *311 rooms* ⚴ *Restaurant, coffee shop, A/C, Wi-Fi, in-room safes, wet bars, 3 tennis courts, pro shop, oceanfront pool, beach, hot tub, shuffleboard, lobby lounge, meeting rooms, no-smoking rooms* ▤ *AE, D, DC, MC, V. $159–$259.*

$$–$$$$ 🏨 **Aloha Kaua'i Beach Resort.** Nestled between Wailua Bay and the Wailua River, this low-key, low-rise resort is an easy, convenient place to stay. Families will enjoy being within walking distance of Lydgate Beach Park. It's also close to shops and low-cost restaurants. Rooms are in two wings and have beach, mountain, or ocean views. The resort also offers one-bedroom beach cottages with kitchenettes. ✉ *3-5920 Kūhiō Hwy., Kapa'a 96746* ☎ *808/823–6000 or 888/823–5111* 🖷 *808/823–6666* ⊕ *www.abrkauai.com* ⟳ *188 rooms, 2 suites, 24 beach cottages* ⚴ *Restaurant, A/C, in-room safes, in-room data ports, 2 tennis courts, 2 pools, gym, hot tub, shuffleboard, volleyball, lobby lounge* ▤ *AE, D, DC, MC, V. $150–$290.*

$$–$$$ 🏨 **Aston Islander on the Beach.** A Hawai'i-plantation style design gives this 6-acre beachfront property a pleasant, low-key feeling. Rooms are spread over eight three-story buildings, with lānai that look out on lovely green lawns. Rooms have showers but not tubs. A free-form pool sits next to a golden-sand beach, and you can take the lounge chairs to the ocean's edge. ✉*4-484 Kūhiō Hwy., Kapa'a 96746* ☎ *808/822–7417 or 877/977–6667* 🖷 *808/822–1947* ⟳ *194 rooms, 2 suites* ⚴ *Restaurant, in-room safes, cable TV, tennis court, pool, beach, hair salon, hot tub, volleyball, bar, laundry facilities, meeting room* ▤*AE, D, DC, MC, V. $120–$160.*

$$ 🏨 **Kaua'i Sands.** Hawaiian-owned and operated, this oceanfront inn is an example of what island accommodations were like before the arrival of the megaresorts. This is basic, no-frills lodging. Furnishings are spare, simple, and clean. It's so retro it's unintentionally hip. A big grassy court-yard opens to the beach and there's plenty of dining and shopping at the Coconut Marketplace. ⊠ *420 Papaloa Rd., Kapa'a 96746* ☎ *808/822–4951 or 800/560–5553* 🖷 *808/822–0978* ⊕ *www.kauaisandshotel.com* ⤳ *250 rooms, 2 suites* ⚿ *A/C, some kitchenettes, cable TV, 2 pools, beach, gym, lobby lounge, laundry facilities, no-smoking rooms* ▭ *AE, D, DC, MC, V. $100–$150.*

$ 🏨 **Hotel Coral Reef.** Coral Reef has been in business since the 1960s and is something of a beachfront landmark. The location is better than the hotel, which is perfectly adequate and not much more, although a recent major renovation spruced it up quite a bit. Upper-floor units have carpeting, while ground-level rooms are done in terrazzo tile with patios that lead out to the beach and barbecue grills. Rooms have showers only, no tubs. The two two-room units are good for families. ⊠ *1516 Kūhiō Hwy., Kapa'a 96746* ☎ *808/822–4481 or 800/843–4659* 🖷 *808/822–7705* ⊕ *www.hotelcoralreef.com* ⤳ *24 rooms, 2 suites* ⚿ *Picnic area, some refrigerators, cable TV, beach, laundry facilities, free parking; no A/C, no room phones* ▭ *MC, V. $70–$100.*

Condos

Location, Location, Location. The Coconut Coast is the only resort area on Kaua'i where you can actually walk to the beach, restaurants, and stores from your condo. It's not only convenient, but comparatively cheap. You pay less for lodging, meals, services, merchandise, and gas here—all because the reefy coastline isn't as ideal as the sandy-bottomed bays that front the fancy resorts found elsewhere. We think the shoreline is just fine. There are pockets in the reef to swim in, and the coast is very scenic and uncrowded.

$$$ $$$$ 🏨 **Best Western Plantation Hale Suites.** These attractive plantation-style one-bedroom units have well-equipped kitchenettes and garden lānai. Rooms are clean and pretty, with white-rattan furnishings and pastel colors. You couldn't ask for a more convenient location for dining, shopping, and sightseeing: it's across from Waipouli Beach and near Coconut Marketplace. Request a unit on the makai side, away from noisy Kūhiō Highway. ⊠ *484 Kūhiō Hwy., Kapa'a 96746* ☎ *808/822–4941 or 800/775–4253* 🖷 *808/822–5599* ⊕ *www.plantation-hale.com* ⤳ *120 units* ⚿ *BBQs, A/C, in-room safes, kitchenettes, microwaves, cable TV with movies and video games, putting green, 3 pools, hot tub, shuffleboard, laundry facilities* ▭ *AE, D, DC, MC, V. 1-bedroom $185–$210.*

$$$–$$$$ 🏨 **Kaua'i Coast Resort at the Beachboy.** Fronting an uncrowded stretch of beach, this three-story primarily time-share resort is convenient, and a bit more upscale than nearby properties. The fully furnished one- and two-bedroom condo units, each with a private lānai and well-equipped kitchen, are housed in three buildings. They are decorated in rich woods, tropical prints, and Hawaiian-quilt designs. The 8-acre property looks out on the ocean and offers a heated pool with waterscapes, a day spa, a children's pool, a good restaurant, and an oceanside hot tub. ⊠ *520 Aleka Loop, Kapa'a 96746* ☎ *808/822–3441 or 877/977–4355* 🖷 *808/822–0843* ⊕ *www.shellhospitality.com* ⤳ *108 units* ⚿ *Restaurant, A/C, in-room safes, kitchens, microwaves, refrigerators, in-room data ports, tennis*

6

court, 2 pools, beach, gym, hot tub, spa, lobby lounge, concierge ⊟ *AE, D, DC, MC, V. 1-bedroom $190–$235, 2-bedroom $255–$295.*

$$$–$$$$ ☷ **Outrigger Lae nani.** Ruling Hawaiian chiefs once returned from ocean voyages to this spot, now host to condominiums comfortable enough for minor royalty. Hotel-sponsored Hawaiiana programs and a booklet for self-guided historical tours are nice extras. Units are all uniquely decorated, with bright, full kitchens and expansive lānai. Your view of landscaped grounds is interrupted only by a large pool before ending at a sandy, swimmable beach. You can find plenty of dining and shopping at the adjacent Coconut Marketplace. ⊠ *410 Papaloa Rd., Kapa'a 96746* ☎ *808/822–4938 or 800/688–7444* 🖷 *808/822–1022* ⊕ *www.outriggerlaenani.com* ➼ *84 condominiums* ♿ *Picnic area, BBQs, fans, in-room safes, kitchens, microwaves, cable TV, tennis court, pool, beach, laundry facilities; no A/C* ⊟ *AE, D, DC, MC, V. 1-bedroom $225–$270, 2-bedroom $260–$350.*

$$–$$$ ☷ **Kapa'a Sands.** An old rock etched with *kanji,* Japanese characters, reminds you that the site of this condominium gem was formerly occupied by a Shinto temple. Two-bedroom rentals—equipped with full kitchens and private lānai—are a fair deal. Studios feature pull-down Murphy beds to create more daytime space. Ask for an oceanfront room to get the breeze. ⊠ *380 Papaloa Rd., Kapa'a 96746* ☎ *808/822–4901 or 800/222–4901* 🖷 *808/822–1556* ⊕ *www.kapaasands.com* ➼ *20 units* ♿ *Fans, kitchens, microwaves, cable TV, in-room VCRs, pool, beach; no A/C* ⊟ *MC, V. Studios $100–$130, no 1-bedroom units, 2-bedroom $140–$160.*

B&Bs and Vacation Rentals

$–$$ ☷ **Rosewood Bed and Breakfast.** This charming B&B on a macadamia-nut plantation estate offers four separate styles of accommodations, including a two-bedroom Victorian cottage, a little one-bedroom grass-thatch cottage, a bunkhouse with three rooms and a shared bath, and the traditional main plantation home with two rooms, each with private bath. The bunkhouse and thatched cottage feature outside hot–cold private shower areas hidden from view by a riot of tropically scented foliage. ⊠ *872 Kamalu Rd., Kapa'a 96746* ☎ *808/822–5216* 🖷 *808/822–5478* ⊕ *www.rosewoodkauai.com* ➼ *2 cottages, 3 rooms in bunkhouse, 2 rooms in main house* ♿ *Kitchens, some cable TV; no A/C, no room phones, no smoking* ⊟ *No credit cards. $50–$135.*

Līhu'e

Hotels & Resorts

$$$$ ☷ **Kaua'i Marriott Resort & Beach Club.** An elaborate tropical garden, waterfalls right off the lobby, Greek statues and columns, and an enormous 26,000-square-foot swimming pool characterize the grand—and grandiose—scale of this resort on Kalapakī Bay, which looks out at the dramatic Hā'upu mountains. This resort has it all—fine dining, shopping, a spa, golf, tennis, and water activities of all kinds. Rooms have tropical decor, and most have expansive ocean views. It's comfortable and convenient, though the airport noise can be a turnoff. ⊠ *3610 Rice St., Kalapakī Beach, Līhu'e 96766* ☎ *808/245–5050 or 800/220–2925*

☎ *808/245–5148* ⊕ *www.marriotthotels.com* ⇨ *356 rooms, 11 suites, 232 time-share units* ♨ *2 restaurants, A/C, room service, minibars, 2 18-hole golf courses, 7 tennis courts, pool, health club, outdoor hot tub, spa, beach, boating, lobby lounge, children's programs (ages 5–12), airport shuttle* ▤ *AE, D, DC, MC, V. $339–$464.*

$$–$$$$ 🏨 **Radisson Kaua'i Beach Hotel.** A low-rise, horseshoe-shape hotel, the Radisson surrounds a pool complex with rock-sculpted slopes, waterfalls, tropical flowers, and a cave resembling the Fern Grotto. It's the best feature in this rather ho-hum hotel. Still, there are lots of little extras here, such as the complimentary mai tai happy hour, torch-lighting ceremony, and live Hawaiian music. Guest rooms are attractive in rich tones with maroon accents and dark wood. The lānai have views of mountains, gardens, or the sea. ⊠ *4331 Kaua'i Beach Dr., Līhu'e 96766* ☎ *808/245–1955 or 888/805–3843* 🖷 *808/246–9085* ⊕ *www. radissonkauai.com* ⇨ *347 rooms, 8 suites* ♨ *2 restaurants, room service, A/C, in-room safes, some refrigerators, cable TV, in-room VCRs, 18-hole golf course, 4 tennis courts, 2 pools, wading pool, health club, hot tub, beach, lobby lounge, pub, Internet, airport shuttle* ▤ *AE, D, DC, MC, V. $139–$289.*

$–$$ 🏨 **Garden Island Inn.** Bargain hunters will love this three-story inn near Kalapakī Bay and Anchor Cove shopping center. You can walk across the street and enjoy the majesty of Kalapakī Beach or check out the facilities and restaurants of the Marriott. It's clean and simple, and the innkeepers are friendly, sharing fruit and beach gear. ⊠ *3445 Wilcox Rd., Kalapakī Beach 96766* ☎ *808/245–7227 or 800/648–0154* 🖷 *808/ 245–7603* ⊕ *www.gardenislandinn.com* ⇨ *21 rooms, 2 suites, 1 condo* ♨ *A/C in some rooms, fans, some kitchens, some kitchenettes, microwaves, refrigerators, cable TV; no smoking* ▤ *AE, DC, MC, V. $85–$150.*

The South Side

Sunseekers usually head south to the condo-studded shores of Po'ipū, where three- and four-story complexes line the coast and the surf is ideal for swimming. Po'ipū has more condos than hotels, with prices in the moderate to expensive range. ■ **TIP→→** The area's beaches are the best on the island for families.

Hotels & Resorts

$$$$ 🏨 **Hyatt Regency Kaua'i Resort and Spa.** Dramatically handsome, this clas-

Fodor'sChoice sic Hawaiian low-rise is built into the cliffs overlooking an unspoiled

★ coastline. It's open, elegant, and very island-style, making it our favorite of the megaresorts. It has three very good restaurants, including Dondero's, the best on Kaua'i. Spacious rooms, two-thirds with ocean views, have a plantation theme with bamboo and wicker furnishings and island art. Five acres of meandering fresh- and saltwater-swimming lagoons—a big hit with kids—are beautifully set amid landscaped grounds. While adults enjoy treatments at the first-rate Anara Spa, kids can check out Camp Hyatt. ⊠ *1571 Po'ipū Rd., Kōloa 96756* ☎ *808/742–1234 or 800/633–7313* 🖷 *808/742–1557* ⊕ *www.kauai.hyatt.com* ⇨ *565 rooms, 37 suites* ♨ *6 restaurants, room service, A/C, in-room safes, mini-*

bars, refrigerators, cable TV with movies, in-room data ports, 18-hole golf course, 4 tennis courts, pro shop, pool, health club, hot tub, massage, spa, beach, horseback riding, 4 bars, 6 lounges, nightclub, shops, babysitting, children's programs (ages 5–12), concierge ⊟ AE, D, DC, MC, V. $395–$600.

$$$$ ⊞ **Sheraton Kaua'i Resort.** The ocean wing accommodations here are so close to the water you can practically feel the spray of the surf as it hits the rocks below. Beachfront rooms have muted sand and eggshell colors which complement the soothing atmosphere of this quiet, calm resort. Brighter palettes enliven the garden rooms. Dining rooms, king beds, and balconies differentiate the suites. Hawaiian artisans stage crafts demonstrations under a banyan tree in the central courtyard. The dining Galleria was designed so that all

> ### KIDS RULE
>
> Islanders love kids, and kids love the Islands, making for a good match. Kids are welcome most everywhere, but some places make a special effort to enhance their stay. The **Hyatt** has a great camp for kids, if you can pry them away from its swimming pool—the largest on the island and replete with cool stuff like a water slide and tunnels. The **Aloha Kaua'i Beach Resort** in Wailua is next door to a fabulous playground designed by kids, and a beach with a protected swimming lagoon perfect for small fry. At **North Country Farms** in Kīlauea, they'll feel right at home with the books, toys, videos, and games carefully selected for their entertainment.

restaurants take advantage of the endless ocean horizon. ⊠ *2440 Ho'onani Rd., Po'ipū Beach, Kōloa 96756* ☎ *808/742–1661 or 888/488–3535* ☐ *808/742–9777* ⊕ *www.starwood.com/hawaii* ⇨ *399 rooms, 14 suites* ⚭ *4 restaurants, room service, A/C, in-room safes, some minibars, refrigerators, cable TV, 3 tennis courts, 2 pools, 2 wading pools, gym, massage, beach, bar, babysitting, children's programs (ages 5–12), laundry facilities, concierge, Internet, meeting rooms* ⊟ *AE, D, DC, MC, V. $280–$460.*

Condos

$$$–$$$$ ⊞ **Outrigger Kiahuna Plantation.** Kaua'i's largest condo project is lackluster, though the location is excellent. Forty-two plantation-style, low-rise buildings arc around a large, grassy field leading to the beach. The individually decorated one- and two-bedroom units vary in style, but all are clean, have lānai, and get lots of ocean breezes. This is a popular destination for families who take advantage of the swimmable beach and lawn for picnics and games. Great sunset and ocean views are bonuses in some units. The Sheraton is next door, and there are facility-use agreements between the two locations. ⊠ *2253 Po'ipū Rd., Kōloa 96756* ☎ *808/742–6411 or 800/688–7444* ☐ *808/742–1698* ⊕ *www.outrigger. com* ⇨ *333 units* ⚭ *Restaurant, fans, some kitchens, some kitchenettes, microwaves, cable TV, in-room VCRs, in-room data ports, 18-hole golf course, 6 tennis courts, pool, beach; no A/C* ⊟ *AE, DC, MC, V. 1-bedroom $200–$325, 2-bedroom $300–$450.*

$$$$ ⊞ **Po'ipū Kapili.** Spacious one- and two-bedroom condo units are minutes from Po'ipū's restaurants and beaches. White-frame exteriors and double-pitched roofs complement the tropical landscaping. Interiors

include full kitchens and entertainment centers. There are garden and across-the-street ocean views to choose from. Three deluxe 2,600-square-foot penthouse suites have enormous lānai, private elevators, and cathedral ceilings. You can mingle at a weekly coffee hour held beside the ocean-view pool, or grab a good read from the resort library. Fresh seasonings are ready to be picked from the herb garden, and there's a BBQ located poolside. In winter you can whale-watch as you cook ✉ 2221 Kapili Rd., Kōloa 96756 ☎ 808/742–6449 or 800/443–7714 🖷 808/742–9162 ⊕ www.poipukapili.com 🛏 60 units ☝ Fans, kitchens, microwaves, cable TV, in-room VCRs, 2 tennis courts, pool, library; no A/C ☰ MC, V. 1-bedroom $220–$350, 2-bedroom $375–$575.

$$$$ 🏨 **Poʻipū Shores.** Sitting on a rocky point above pounding surf, this is a perfect spot for whale- or turtle-watching. Weddings are staged on a little lawn beside the ocean, and a sandy swimming beach is a 10-minute walk away. There are three low-rise buildings, with a pool in front of the middle one. Condo units are individually owned and decorated. All have large windows and many of them have bedrooms on the ocean side; each unit either shares a sundeck or has a lānai. ✉ 1775 Peʻe Rd., Kōloa 96756 ☎ 808/742–7700 or 800/367–5004 🖷 808/742–9720 ⊕ www.castleresorts.com/psc 🛏 33 units ☝ Fans, kitchens, kitchenettes, microwaves, cable TV, pool, laundry facilities; no A/C ☰ AE, MC, V. 1-bedroom $230–$255, 2-bedroom $260–$310, 3-bedroom $350–$400.

$$$$ 🏨 **Whalers Cove.** Perched about as close to the water's edge as they can get, these two-bedroom condos are the most luxurious on the south side. The rocky beach is good for snorkeling, and a short drive or brisk walk will get you to a sandy stretch. A handsome koa-bedecked reception area offers services for the plush units. Two barbecue areas, big picture windows, spacious living rooms, lānai, and modern kitchens with washer-dryers make this a home away from home. ✉ 2640 Puʻuholo Rd., Kōloa 96756 ☎ 808/742-7100 or 800/367–8020 🖷 808/742–9121 ⊕ www.suiteparadise.com 🛏 30 units ☝ Fans, some kitchens, some kitchenettes, microwave, cable TV with movies, in-room VCRs, in-room data ports, pool, beach, hot tub, laundry facilities; no A/C ☰ AE, MC, V. 2-bedroom $320–$475.

$$$–$$$$ 🏨 **Makahuena at Poʻipū.** Situated close to the center of Poʻipū, on a rocky point over the ocean, the Makahuena is near Shipwreck and Poʻipū beaches. It's a better deal for the price than some of the nearby properties. Large, tastefully decorated one-, two- and three-bedroom suites with white tile and sand-color carpets are housed in white-wood buildings on well-kept lawns. Each unit has a kitchen and washer and dryer; there's also a small pool and shared BBQ area on the property. ✉ 1661 Peʻe Rd., Poʻipū 96756 ☎ 808/742–2482 or 800/367–5004 🖷 808/742–2379 ⊕ www.castleresorts.com/mkh 🛏 79 units ☝ BBQs, fans, kitchenettes, in-room VCR, tennis court, pool, hot tub; no A/C ☰ AE, MC, V. 1-bedroom $170–$235, 2-bedroom $190–$340, 3-bedroom $300–$375.

$$–$$$$ 🏨 **Suite Paradise Poʻipū Kaī.** Condominiums, many with cathedral ceilings and all with big windows overlooking the lawns, give this property the feeling of a spacious, quiet retreat inside and out. Large furnished lānai have views to the ocean and across the 110-acre grounds. All the condos are furnished with modern kitchens. Some units are two-level; some have sleeping lofts. Three-, four-, and five-bedroom units are also available. A two-night minimum stay is required. Walking paths connect to both Brennecke and Shipwreck beaches. ✉ *1941 Po'ipū Rd., Kōloa 96756* ☎ *808/742–6464 or 800/367–8020* 📠 *808/742–9121* ⊕ *www.suite-paradise.com* ⤺ *130 units* ⚝ *Restaurant, A/C in some rooms, fans, in-room safes, kitchens, cable TV, in-room VCRs, in-room data ports, 9 tennis courts, 6 pools, hot tub* ⊟ *AE, D, DC, MC, V. 1-bedroom $120–$180, 2-bedroom $225–$300, 3-bedroom $325–$400, 4-bedroom $425, 5-bedroom $500.*

B&Bs & Vacation Rentals

★ **$$$$** 🏨 **Gloria's Spouting Horn Bed & Breakfast.** The most elegant oceanfront B&B on Kaua'i, this cedar home was built specifically for guests. The common room has a soaring A-frame ceiling and deck. Waves dash the black rocks below, while just above the ocean's edge a tiny beach invites sunbathers. All three bedrooms have four-poster beds with canopies created from koa, willow, or bamboo woods, oceanside lānai, and bathrooms with deep soaking tubs and separate showers. You will be treated to a full breakfast each morning, and in late afternoon there's an open bar with *pūpū*, timed to the setting of the sun. ✉ *4464 Lāwa'i Rd., Po'ipū* ☎ *808/742–6995* 📠 *808/742–6995* ⊕ *www.gloriasbedandbreakfast.com* ⤺ *3 rooms* ⚝ *Fans, refrigerators, cable TV, in-room VCRs, pool, beach; no A/C* ⊟ *No credit cards. $325.*

★ **$$$** 🏨 **Garden Isle Cottages.** Tropical fruit trees and flower gardens surround these spacious oceanside cottages. Contemporary Hawaiian furnishings include some rattan; amenities include kitchens with microwaves, ceiling fans, and washers and dryers. The restaurants of nearby Po'ipū are a five-minute walk away. The best part of staying here is the ocean view. ✉ *2660 Pu'uholo Rd., Kōloa 96756* ☎ *808/742–6717 or 800/742–6711* ⊕ *www.oceancottages.com* ⤺ *4 cottages* ⚝ *Fans, kitchens, microwaves, laundry facilities; no A/C* ⊟ *No credit cards. $169–$190.*

$$–$$$ 🏨 **Po'ipū Plantation Resort.** Plumeria, ti, and other tropical foliage create a lush landscape for this resort, which has one B&B-style plantation home and nine one- and two-bedroom cottage apartments. All cottage units have vaulted ceilings and full kitchens and are decorated in light, airy shades. The 1930s plantation home has three rooms with private baths and one suite. A full complimentary breakfast is served daily for those staying in the main house. A minimum three-night stay is required, but rates decrease with the length of stay. ✉ *1792 Pe'e Rd., Kōloa 96756* ☎ *808/742–6757 or 800/634–0263* 📠 *808/742–8681* ⊕ *www.poipubeach.com* ⤺ *3 rooms, 9 cottages* ⚝ *BBQs, fans, kitchens, in-room VCRs, hair salon, hot tub, laundry facilities* ⊟ *D, MC, V. $105–$190, 3-night minimum.*

$–$$$ 🏨 **Kōloa Landing Cottages.** You'll be treated like family at this small, homey lodging complex. The property consists of five cottages, a studio, and a two-bedroom home. The cottages are across the street from Kōloa Landing—a popular location for diving, snorkeling, and fishing—and about a five-minute walk to great swimming at Po'ipū Beach Park. Accommodations sleep two to eight; all cottages have showers only. Open-beam ceilings and fans keep the interiors cool. Book well in advance. ⊠ *2704-B Hoʻonani Rd., Kōloa 96756* ☎ *808/742–1470 or 800/779–8773* ⊕ *www.koloa-landing.com* ↘ *5 cottages, 1 studio, 2 rooms* ⚤ *BBQs, fans, some kitchens, some kitchenettes, laundry facilities; no A/C* ⊟ No *credit cards. $95–$175, 4-night minimum.*

$$ 🏠 **Kauaʻi Cove Cottages.** Three modern studio cottages sit side by side at the mouth of Waikomo Stream, beside an ocean cove that offers super snorkeling. The studios have airy tropical decor under cathedral ceilings; each has a complete kitchen. Private patios on the ocean side have gas barbecue grills. There's a $25 cleaning fee for stays of fewer than three nights. VCRs are available on request. ⊠ *2672 Puʻuholo Rd., Poʻipū 96756* ☎ *808/742–2562 or 800/624–9945* ⊕ *www.kauaicove.com* ↘ *3 cottages* ⚤ *BBQs, fans, kitchens, cable TV, snorkeling, laundry facilities; no A/C* ⊟ *D, MC, V. $105–$125.*

The West Side

If you want to do a lot of hiking or immerse yourself in the island's history, find a room in Waimea. A few very spartan cabins are rented in Kōkeʻe State Park.

Hotels & Resorts

$$–$$$$ 🏠 **Waimea Plantation Cottages.** History buffs will adore these reconstructed sugar-plantation cottages, which offer a vacation experience unique in all Hawaiʻi. The one- to five-bedroom cottages are tucked among coconut trees along a lovely stretch of coastline on the sunny West Side. (Note that swimming waters here are sometimes murky, depending on weather conditions.) ■ TIP➔➔ **It's a great property for family reunions or other large gatherings.** These cozy little homes, replete with porches, feature plantation-era furnishings, modern kitchens, and cable TV. BBQs, hammocks, porch swings, a gift shop, a spa, and a museum are on the property. Complimentary wireless Internet access is available in the main building; in-room data ports are available if requested in advance. ⊠ *9400 Kaumualiʻi Hwy., Box 367, Waimea 96796* ☎ *808/338–1625 or 800/992–4632* ☐ *808/338–2338* ⊕ *www.waimea-plantation.com* ↘ *48 cottages* ⚤ *Restaurant, fans, some kitchens, cable TV, pool, spa, beach, horseshoes, bar, concierge, Internet; no A/C* ⊟ *AE, D, DC, MC, V. $140–$675.*

Fodor'sChoice
★

Vacation Rentals

¢ 🏠 **Kōkeʻe Lodge.** If you're an outdoor enthusiast, you can appreciate Kauaʻi's mountain wilderness from the 12 rustic cabins that comprise this lodge. They are austere, to say the least, but more comfortable than a tent, and the mountain setting is grand. Wood-burning stoves ward off the chill and dampness (wood is a few dollars extra). If you aren't partial to dormitory-style sleeping, request the cabins with two bedrooms; both styles sleep six and have kitchenettes. The lodge restaurant serves a light breakfast and lunch between 9 and 3:30 daily. ⊠ *3600 Kōkeʻe Rd., at mile marker 15, Kekaha* ☐ *Box 819, Waimea 96796* ☎ *808/335–6061* ↘ *12 cabins* ⚤ *Restaurant, hiking, shops; no A/C, no room phones, no room TVs* ⊟ *D, DC, MC, V. $35–$45.*

6

WHERE TO SPA

Kaua'i is often touted as the healing island, and local spas try hard to fill that role. With the exception of the Hyatt's Anara Spa, the facilities aren't as posh as some might want. But it's in the human element that Kaua'i excels. Island residents are known for their warmth, kindness, and humility, and you can find all these attributes in the massage therapists and technicians who work long hours at the resort spas. These professionals take their therapeutic mission seriously; they genuinely want you to experience the island's relaxing, restorative qualities. Private massage services abound on the island—your spa therapist may offer the same services at a much lower price outside the resort—but if you're looking for a variety of health-and-beauty treatments, an exercise workout, or a full-day of pampering, a spa will prove most convenient. Though most spas on Kaua'i are associated with resorts, none are restricted to guests only.

Alexander Day Spa at the Kaua'i Marriott. This sister spa of Alexander Simson's Beverly Hills spa focuses on body care rather than exercise, so don't expect any fitness equipment or exercise classes. Tucked away in a free-standing building in a back corner of the Marriott, the spa doubles as a golf clubhouse. It has the same ambience of stilted formality as the rest of the resort, but is otherwise a sunny, pleasant facility. Massages in treatment rooms are more enjoyable than those offered beachside, where it's often windy and the calm is disrupted by the roar of jets using nearby Līhu'e Airport. Wedding-day and custom spa packages can be arranged. ⊠ *Kaua'i Marriott Resort & Beach Club, 3610 Rice St., Līhu'e* ☎ *808/246–4918* ⊕ *www.alexanderspa.com. $50–$125 massage* ⚲ *Services: Body wraps, facials, hair styling, manicures, beachside and in-spa massages, pedicures.*

Fodor'sChoice
★
Anara Spa. This luxurious facility is far and away the best on Kaua'i, setting a standard that no other spa has been able to meet. It has all the equipment and services you expect from a top resort spa, along with a pleasant, professional staff. Best of all, it has indoor and outdoor areas that capitalize on its tropical locale and balmy weather, further distinguishing it from the Marriott and Princeville spas. It's also big, covering 25,000 square feet of space, including a landscaped courtyard where you can relax or enjoy a healthful breakfast, lunch, or smoothie from adjacent Kupono Café. Relax and unwind with a single treatment or full day of luxurious pampering. Local ingredients are featured in some of the treatments, such as a coconut-mango facial and a body brush scrub that polishes your skin with a mix of ground coffee, orange peel, and vanilla bean. The open-air lava-rock showers are wonderful, introducing many guests to the delightful island practice of showering outdoors. The spa adjoins the Hyatt's legendary swimming pool. ⊠ *Hyatt Regency Kaua'i Resort and Spa, 1571 Po'ipū Rd., Po'ipū* ☎ *808/742–1234* ⊕ *www.anaraspa.com $75–$150 massage* ⚲ *Gym with: cardiovascular machines, free weights and weight-training equipment. Services: Body scrubs and polishes, body wraps, facials, manicures, massage, pedi-*

cures. Classes and Programs: *Aerobics, aquaerobics, body sculpting, fitness analysis, flexibility training, nutritional analysis and counseling, personal training, Pilates, step aerobics, weight training, and yoga.*

★ **Hart-Felt Massage & Day Spa.** This is the only full-service day spa on the laid-back West Side. It's in one of the restored plantation cottages that comprise the guest quarters at Waimea Plantation Cottages, creating a distinctive setting you won't find elsewhere. The overall feel is relaxed, casual, and friendly, as you'd expect in this quiet country town. The staff is informal, yet thoroughly professional. ⊠ *Waimea Plantation Cottages, 9400 Kaumuali'i Hwy., Waimea* ☎ *808/338–2240* ⊕ *www.waimea-plantation. com $50–$100 massage* ⋄ *Services: Body wraps and scrubs, facials, hydrotherapy, massage.*

Princeville Health Club & Spa. Inspiring views of mountains, sea, and sky provide a lovely distraction in the gym area of this spa, which is well equipped, but small and often overly air-conditioned. The treatment area is functional, but lacks charm and personality. Luckily the gorgeous setting helps to make up for it. This is the only facility of this kind on the North Shore, so it's well used, and has a generally well-heeled clientele that pays attention to gym attire. It's in the Princeville Clubhouse, at the Prince Golf Course, several miles from the Princeville Hotel. A room in the hotel or round of golf at a Princeville course entitles you to a complimentary admission to the spa, otherwise it's $20 for a day pass. ⊠ *Princeville Resort, 53-900 Kūhiō Hwy., Princeville* ☎ *808/826–5030* ⊕ *www.princeville.com $75–$150 massage* ⋄ *Gym with: cardiovascular machines, free weights and weight-training equipment. Services: Body polishes and wraps, facials, massages, skin scrubs. Classes and Programs: Aerobics, personal training, Pilates, step aerobics, yoga.*

6

WHERE TO EAT

Food is a big part of local culture, playing a prominent role at parties, celebrations, events, and even casual gatherings. The best grinds (food) are homemade, so if you're lucky enough to win an invitation to a potluck, baby lū'au, or beach party, accept. Dieters, picky eaters, and vegetarians are considered odd on Kaua'i, where folks are urged to eat until they're full, then rest, eat some more, and make a plate to take home, too. Small, neighborhood eateries are a good place to try local-style food, which bears little resemblance to the fancy Pacific Rim cuisine served in upscale restaurants. Expect plenty of meat—usually deep-fried or marinated in a teriyaki sauce and grilled pulehu-style over an open fire—and starches. Rice is ubiquitous, even for breakfast, and often served alongside potato-macaroni salad, another island specialty. Another local favorite is *poke,* made from chunks of raw tuna or octopus seasoned with sesame oil, soy sauce, onions, and pickled seaweed. It's a great *pūpū* (appetizer) when paired with a cold beer.

Kaua'i's cultural diversity is apparent in its restaurants, which offer authentic Vietnamese, Chinese, Korean, Japanese, Thai, Filipino, Mexican, Italian, and Hawaiian specialties. Less specialized restaurants cater

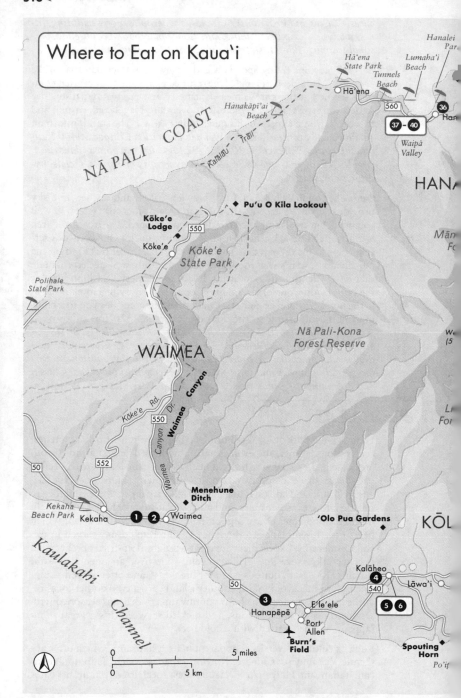

Where to Eat on Kaua'i

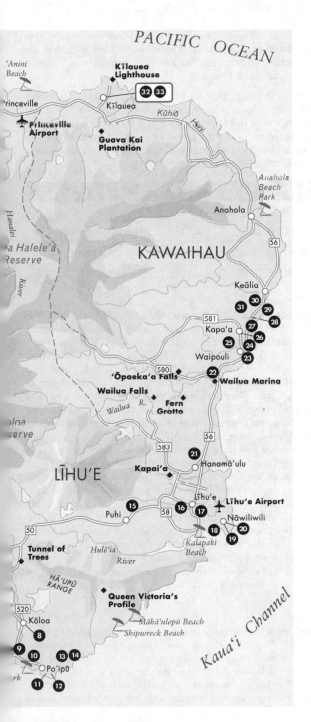

Bali Hai **35**
Bamboo Bamboo **40**
The Beach House **7**
Brennecke's Beach Broiler . . .**12**
Bull Shed **28**
Cafe Hanalei and Terrace **34**
Café Portofino **19**
Caffé Coco **25**
Camp House Grill **4**
Casa di Amici **13**
Dani's Restaurant **17**
Dondero's **14**
Duke's Canoe Club **20**
The Eggbert's **27**
Gaylord's **15**
Green Garden **3**
Hamura Saimin **16**
Hanalei Gourmet **37**
Hanamā'ulu Restaurant, ...**21**
JJ's Broiler **18**
Kalāheo Steak House **5**
Keoki's Paradise **9**
Kīlauea Bakery and
Pau Hana Pizza **33**
Kukui's Restaurant and Bar . . .**20**
La Cascata **34**
Lemongrass Grill,
Seafood and Sushi Bar **29**
Lighthouse Bistro **32**
Līhu'e Barbecue Inn **16**
Mema Thai
Chinese Cuisine **24**
Uno Family Restaurant **30**
Papaya's **31**
Plantation Gardens **10**
Pomodoro
Ristorante Italiano **6**
Postcards Cafe **36**
Restaurant Kintaro **26**
Roy's Po'ipū Bar & Grill **9**
Shells Steak and Seafood **11**
Sushi Blues **39**
Tidepools **14**
Tomkats Grille **8**
Wailua Family Restaurant **23**
Wailua Marina
Restaurant **22**
Waimea Brewing Company **1**
Wrangler's Steakhouse **2**
Zelo's Beach House **38**

to the tourist crowd, serving standard American fare—burgers, pizza, sandwiches, surf-and-turf combos, and so on. Kapa'a offers the best selection of restaurants, with options for a variety of tastes and budgets; most fast food joints are in Lihū'e.

Parents will be relieved to encounter a tolerant attitude toward children, even if they're noisy. Men can leave their jackets and ties at home; attire tends toward informal, but if you want to dress up, you can. Reservations are accepted in most places, and required at some of the top restaurants. ■ TIP➜➜ One cautionary note: most restaurants stop serving dinner at 8 or 9 PM, so plan to eat early.

WHAT IT COSTS				
$$$$	$$$	$$	$	¢
RESTAURANTS over $30	$20–$30	$12–$20	$7–$12	under $7

Restaurant prices are for one main course at dinner.

The North Shore

American–Casual

$–$$$ ✕ **Hanalei Gourmet.** In Hanalei's restored old school house, this North Shore spot offers diners dolphin-free tuna, low-sodium meats, fresh-baked breads, and homemade desserts as well as a casual atmosphere where both families and the sports-watching crowds can feel equally comfortable. Early birds can order coffee and toast or a hearty breakfast. Lunch and dinner menus feature sandwiches, burgers, filling salads, and nightly specials of fresh local fish. They also will prepare a picnic and give it to you in an insulated backpack. A full bar and frequent live entertainment keep things hopping even after the kitchen closes. ✉ *5-5161 Kūhiō Hwy., Hanalei* ☎ *808/826–2524* ▭ *D, DC, MC, V. $7–$24.*

¢–$$$ ✕ **Kīlauea Bakery and Pau Hana Pizza.** This bakery has garnered tons of well-deserved good press for its Hawaiian sourdough loaf made with guava starter, and its specialty pizzas topped with such yummy ingredients as smoked ono, Gorgonzola-rosemary sauce, barbecued chicken, goat cheese, or roasted onions. Open from 6:30 AM, the bakery serves coffee drinks, delicious fresh pastries, bagels, and breads in the morning. Late-risers beware: breads and pastries sell out quickly on weekends. Pizza, soup, and salads can be ordered for lunch or dinner. If you want to hang out or do the coffee shop bit in Kīlauea, this is the place. A pretty courtyard with covered tables is a pleasant place to linger. ✉ *Kong Lung Center, 2490 Keneke St., Kīlauea* ☎ *808/828–2020* ▭ *MC, V. $4–$26.*

Contemporary

$$–$$$$ ✕ **Cafe Hanalei and Terrace.** You're in for a very romantic evening here:
Fodor'sChoice the view from the Princeville Resort overlooking Hanalei Bay is mes-
★ merizing, and the food and service are superb. In all but the rainiest weather you'll want to be seated outside on the terrace. The Sunday brunch and daily breakfast buffet are enormous feasts, as is the Friday night seafood buffet. The Japanese specialties, fresh-fish specials, and Kaua'i

coffee rack of lamb are excellent choices for dinner. If you're on a budget, come for lunch when you can enjoy the fabulous views and a leisurely, relaxing meal—try the Cobb salad—for less than you'd spend at dinner. The pastry chef deserves praise for delicious, innovative desserts. Save room for the decadent "Tower of Passion," a chocolate tower filled with passion-fruit mousse. ✉ *Princeville Resort, 5520 Ka Haku Rd., Princeville* ☎ *808/826–2760* ⌚ *Reservations recommended* 🖃 *AE, D, DC, MC, V. $16–$35.*

★ **$$–$$$** ✕ **Postcards Cafe.** With its postcard artwork, beamed ceilings, and light interiors, this plantation-cottage restaurant has a menu consisting mostly of organic, additive-free vegetarian foods. But don't get the wrong idea—this isn't simple cooking: specials might include carrot-ginger soup, fish tacos, taro fritters, or fresh fish served with peppered pineapple-sage sauce. Their signature breakfast is a seven-grain English muffin topped with sautéed greens, tempeh strips, and hollandaise—all dairy free. Desserts are made without refined sugar. This is probably your best bet for dinner in Hanalei town. ✉ *5-5075A Kūhiō Hwy., Hanalei* ☎ *808/826–1191* 🖃 *AE, MC, V* ☯ *No lunch. $12–$23.*

$ $$$ ✕ **Lighthouse Bistro.** Tucked into the heart of Kīlauea, next to the Kong Lung store (and miles from Kīlauea Lighthouse), this North Shore bistro has terra-cotta floors, bamboo chairs, and open-air dining, reminiscent of the plantation era. The atmosphere is far better than the food, and the service can be a little rough around the edges. The lunch menu is minimal, with soup, fish tacos, and sandwiches. Some dinner entrées, like seafood linguine or tortellini, have an Italian flair. Others, such as stuffed shrimp in phyllo or mango-cherry chicken, are more Pacific Rim. There's live music Sunday through Wednesday evenings. ✉ *2484 Keneke St., at Lighthouse Rd., Kīlauea* ☎ *808/828–0480* 🖃 *MC, V. $10–$27.*

$–$$$ ✕ **Bamboo Bamboo.** Locally grown produce, island fish, and homemade desserts are served in this restaurant, which also features a cappuccino bar. It's quite pleasant to sit outdoors in the bamboo garden overlooking Hanalei's lush green taro fields and dramatic mountains. Choose from 'ahi (tuna) spring rolls, potato-crusted mahimahi, and Kīlauea goat-cheese salad, among other items. The food is good, if not especially inspired. It's reasonably priced for the area and the diverse menu will please diners with varied tastes. ✉ *Hanalei Center, 5-5161 Kūhiō Hwy., Hanalei* ☎ *808/826–1177* 🖃 *AE, MC, V. $8–$25.*

Eclectic

$–$$$ ✕ **Zelo's Beach House.** When you're traveling with a family or group and everyone wants to eat something different, a restaurant like Zelo's comes in handy. The menu is extensive and eclectic, borrowing from Hawaiian, American, Thai, and Mexican cuisines. The portions are huge and the prices moderate. The tropical decor, relaxed family atmosphere, and outdoor seating add to its appeal, as does its prime location on Hanalei's main drag. The one drawback is the inconsistent quality of the food. As is often the case in restaurants with such wide-ranging menus, the food is not always as tasty as it sounds. ✉ *5-5156 Kūhiō Hwy., Hanalei* ☎ *808/826–9700* 🖃 *MC, V. $10–$26.*

Italian

★ $$$–$$$$ ✕ La Cascata. Terra-cotta floors, hand-painted murals, and trompe-l'oeil paintings give La Cascata a Tuscan-villa flair that makes it ideal for cozy, romantic dining. Picture windows offer dazzling views of Hanalei Bay, though you'll have to come before sunset to enjoy them. Local ingredients figure prominently on a fairly standard menu of pasta, fresh seafood, beef, and lamb prepared with competence and creativity. Savor *Brodetto di Pesce* (Kaua'i prawns, snapper, scallops, and clams with *Arrabbiata* sauce served over linguine), or seared 'ahi with artichoke cannelloni, carmelized onion broth, and toasted pine nuts. The service is professional and efficient. This is one of two excellent—though pricey—restaurants at the luxurious Princeville Resort. ⊠ *Princeville Resort, 5520 Ka Haku Rd., Princeville* ☎ *808/826–2761* ⚔ *Reservations essential* ▭ *AE, D, DC, MC, V* ✆ *No lunch. $24–$38.*

Steak & Seafood

$$$–$$$$ ✕ Bali Hai. Sweeping views of Hanalei Bay and Nā Pali Coast are the highlight at this open-air restaurant—though it can be a bit too exposed to winter winds and rain (bring a jacket). Specialties include the Kaua'i-onion soup topped with melted provolone cheese; the "Namolokama Platter," a combo of watermelon-barbecued pork ribs, chicken skewers, and tiger prawns with sweet chili sauce; and pan-seared fresh fish served over a crispy crab cake. Breakfast includes poi pancakes, fried taro, and eggs; lunch is a mix of salads and sandwiches. The menu descriptions sound good, but the food lacks refinement, making it hard to justify prices that are among the highest on the island. If you arrive before sunset, however, the view makes it worth it. ⊠ *Hanalei Bay Resort, 5380 Honoiki Rd., Princeville* ☎ *808/826–6522* ▭ *AE, D, DC, MC, V. $22–$38.*

$$–$$$ ✕ Sushi Blues. If you've tried and liked Zelo's, you'll like this second-story restaurant and sushi bar, which is owned by the same folks. It has a nice ambience, with copper table tops, lovely views of mountains streaked with waterfalls, and photos of international jazz greats lining the staircase. Regular entertainment, a full bar, and a sake menu add to its appeal. Choose from steaks, seafood dishes, and specialty sushi items such as the Las Vegas Roll, which is filled with tuna, yellowtail, and avocado and fried in a tempura batter. ⊠ *Ching Young Village, 5-5190 Kūhiō Hwy., Hanalei* ☎ *808/826–9701* ▭ *AE, D, DC, MC, V. $18–$25.*

The East Side

American–Casual

¢–$$ ✕ The Eggbert's. If you're big on breakfasts, try Eggbert's, in the Coconut Marketplace, which serves breakfast items until 3 PM daily. This family-friendly restaurant, with a sunny soft-yellow interior, lots of windows, and lānai seating, is a great spot for omelets, banana pancakes, and eggs Benedict in five styles. Lunch and dinner selections include club sandwiches, stir-fry, pot roast, and fresh fish. Take-out orders are also available. ⊠ *Coconut Marketplace, 4-484 Kūhiō Hwy., Kapa'a* ☎ *808/ 822–3787* ▭ *MC, V. $6–$18.*

Contemporary

$-$$$ ✕ **Caffé Coco.** A restored plantation cottage set back off the highway and surrounded by tropical foliage is the setting for this island café. You'll know it by its bright lime-green storefront. An attached black-light art gallery and a vintage apparel shop called Bambulei make this a fun stop for any meal. Outdoor seating in the vine-covered garden is pleasant during nice weather. Acoustic music is offered regularly, attracting a laid-back local crowd. Pot stickers filled with tofu and chutney, 'ahi wraps, Greek and organic salads, fresh fish and soups, and a daily list of specials are complemented by a full espresso bar and wonderful desserts. Allow plenty of time, because the tiny kitchen can't turn out meals quickly. ✉ 4-369 *Kūhiō Hwy., Wailua* ☎ 808/822–7990 ▭ *MC, V* ⊙ *Closed Mon. $8–$23.*

Eclectic

¢-$$ ✕ **Wailua Family Restaurant.** Catering to families, seniors, and folks on a budget, this restaurant offers basic food in a basic setting. Hearty eaters will appreciate the self-serve, all-you-can-eat, hot-and-cold salad bar; tostada, taco, and pasta bar; sushi bar; and dessert bar. Steaks, chops, and seafood fill out the menu. Breakfast buffets on weekend mornings include eggs Benedict, a mahimahi and eggs combo, fresh tropical fruit, and cornbread muffins, among other things. It gets crowded after church on Sunday mornings. ✉ *4-361 Kūhiō Hwy., Kapa'a* ☎ *808/822–3325* ▭ *AE, D, MC, V. $5–$16.*

¢-$ ✕ **Ono Family Restaurant.** It's not always easy to grab a table at Ono, especially on weekend mornings. Dependable food and efficient service account for its popularity with locals and tourists alike. The decor is country diner, with wooden booths and tables, local antiques, and old-fashioned fixtures. The menu has a touch of Hawaiian style, with local favorites like kim chee, banana macadamia-nut pancakes, breakfast burritos, Portuguese sausage, and fried rice offered alongside such all-American offerings as eggs Canterbury (poached eggs, ham, turkey, jack cheese, tomato, hollandaise sauce, and mushrooms on an English muffin). Lunch is less interesting, with the usual burgers, sandwiches, salads, and soups. You have a choice of indoor or outdoor seating in this downtown Kapa'a eatery. ✉ 4-1292 *Kūhiō Hwy., Kapa'a* ☎ *808/822–1710* ▭ *AE, D, DC, MC, V* ⊙ *No dinner. $5–$10.*

Japanese

$$-$$$ ✕ **Restaurant Kintaro.** If you want to eat someplace that's a favorite with locals, visit Kintaro's. But be prepared to wait, because the dining room and sushi bar are always busy. Try the Bali Hai, a roll of eel and smoked salmon, baked and topped

6

BUDGET-FRIENDLY EATS ON THE EAST SIDE

At these small, local-style eateries, two people can generally eat dinner for under $20.

- **Korean BBQ.** ✉ *4-356 Kūhiō Hwy., Wailua* ☎ *808/823-6744.*
- **Waipouli Restaurant.** ✉ *Waipouli Town Centre, Kūhiō Hwy., Wailua* ☎ *808/822-9311.*
- **Papaya's.** ✉ *4-831 Kūhiō Hwy., Kapa'a* ☎ *808/823-0190.*
- **Garden Island BBQ and Chinese Restaurant.** ✉ *4252-A Rice St., Līhu'e,* ☎ *808/245-8868.*
- **Hamura's Saimen.** ✉ *2956 Kress St., Līhu'e,* ☎ *808/245-3271.*

with wasabi mayonnaise. For an "all-in-one-dish" meal, consider the *Nabemono*, a single pot filled with a healthy variety of seafood and vegetables. We like the *teppanyaki* dinners, with meat, seafood, and vegetables flash-cooked on tabletop grills in an entertaining display. Tatami-mat seating is available behind shoji screens that provide privacy for groups. The restaurant was recently remodeled, making the dining room feel less cramped and hectic than it did in the past. ⊠ *4-370 Kūhiō Hwy., Kapa'a* ☎ *808/822–3341* ⊟ *AE, D, DC, MC, V* ⊗ *Closed Sun. No lunch. $12–$25.*

Pan-Asian

$$–$$$ ✕ **Lemongrass Grill, Seafood and Sushi Bar.** Don't be put off by the exterior of this two-story restaurant with its odd mix of Western and Asian design elements. The dining room is much more pleasing with Asian art, sculptures, and fresh orchids. The menu is intriguing and reflects the culinary experience of its Chinese owner, who was raised in Laos. His food is inventive and exciting, combining elements of Burmese, Chinese, Laotian, Thai, and Japanese cuisines. As the name implies, seafood stars in many roles, including salmon grilled with lemongrass and ginger; fresh fish of the day on Thai spiced eggplant; and fried Kaua'i prawns. Sushi orders arrive on tiny surfboards via a waterway that surrounds the bar. ⊠ *4-885 Kūhiō Hwy., Kapa'a* ☎ *808/821–2888* ⊟ *AE, D, DC, MC, V* ⊗ *No lunch. $13–$21.*

Steak & Seafood

$$–$$$ ✕ **Bull Shed.** The A-frame exterior of this popular restaurant imparts a distinctly rustic feel. Inside, light-color walls and a full wall of glass highlight an ocean view that is one of the best on Kaua'i. Ask for a window seat, where you can watch surf crashing on the rocks while you study the menu. The food is simple and basic—think white bread and iceberg lettuce—but they know how to do "surf and turf." You can try both in one of several combo dinner platters, or order fresh island fish and thick steaks individually. The restaurant is best known for its prime rib and Australian rack of lamb. Residents love this place, which hasn't changed much in 20 years. Arrive by 5:30 for early-bird specials and your best shot at a window seat. ⊠ *796 Kūhiō Hwy., Kapa'a* ☎ *808/822–3791 or 808/822–1655* ⊟ *AE, D, DC, MC, V* ⊗ *No lunch. $12–$21.*

★ $–$$$ ✕ **Wailua Marina Restaurant.** Offering the island's only river view, this marina restaurant is a good spot to stop after a boat ride up the Wailua River to the Fern Grotto. The menu is a mix of comfort food and more sophisticated dishes; portions are gigantic. The chef is fond of stuffing: you'll find stuffed baked pork chops, stuffed chicken baked in plum sauce, and 'ahi stuffed with crab. The steamed mullet is a classic island dish. ⊠ *Wailua River State Park, Wailua Rd., Wailua* ☎ *808/822–4311* ⊟ *AE, DC, MC, V* ⊗ *Closed Mon. $10–$21.*

Thai

$–$$ ✕ **Mema Thai Chinese Cuisine.** Refined and intimate, Mema Thai serves its dishes on crisp white linens accented by tabletop orchid sprays. Menu items such as broccoli with oyster sauce and cashew chicken reveal Chinese origins, but the emphasis is on Thai dishes. A host of curries—red, green, yellow, and house—made with coconut milk and kaffir lime leaves run from mild to mouth-searing. The traditional green-papaya salad adds a cool touch for the palate. ✉ *Wailua Shopping Plaza, 369 Kūhiō Hwy., Kapaʻa* ☎ *808/823–0899* ▤ *AE, D, DC, MC, V* ⊘ *No lunch weekends. $7–$19.*

Vegetarian

¢–$ ✕ **Papaya's.** Kauaʻi's largest natural foods market dedicates a corner area to its café, which serves breakfast, lunch, and dinner. The good food and low prices make it a popular place. Begin your day with a tofu scrambler, fruit smoothie, or fresh-baked muffin. Lunch and dinner specialties run the gamut from tempeh sushi and baked tofu to spinach lasagna and fish tacos. No chicken or meat is served. You can order takeout, or eat at a covered table in the courtyard. ✉ *Kauaʻi Village Shopping Center, 4-831 Kūhiō Hwy., Kapaʻa* ☎ *808/823–0190* ▤ *AE, D, MC, V* ⊘ *Closed Sun. $5–$10.*

Līhuʻe

American–Casual

$–$$ ✕ **JJ's Broiler.** This spacious, low-key restaurant is almost like two eateries in one. Hearty American fare, including burgers and 2-pound buckets of steamer clams bathed in white wine, garlic, and herbs, is served in the bar and dining room downstairs. On sunny days, ask for a table on the lānai overlooking Kalapakī Bay. Upstairs you can feast on fancier Pacific Rim dishes, including sugarcane shrimp and Peking chicken tacos in a garlic oyster sauce. The house specialty is Slavonic steak, a broiled sliced tenderloin dipped in a buttery wine sauce. ■ **TIP→** **The restaurant is open until 11 PM, making it one of the few places on Kauaʻi where you can eat late.** ✉ *Anchor Cove, 3146 Rice St., Nāwiliwili* ☎ *808/246–4422* ▤ *D, MC, V. $9–$20.*

★ $–$$ ✕ **Līhuʻe Barbecue Inn.** Few Kauaʻi restaurants are more beloved than this family-owned eatery, a mainstay of island dining since 1940. The menu runs from traditional American fare to Asian. Try the baby back ribs, macadamia-nut chicken, or Cajun seafood medley with king crab. Or choose a full Japanese dinner from the other side of the menu. If you can't make up your mind, the Inn's tri-sampler is a good compromise. Choose the fruit cup—fresh, not canned—instead of the soup or salad, and save room for a hefty slice of homemade cream pie, available in all your favorite flavors. ✉ *2982 Kress St., Lihuʻe* ☎ *808/245–2921* ▤ *No credit cards. $9–$19.*

Eclectic

$$$–$$$$ ✕ **Gaylord's.** Located in what was at one time Kauaʻi's most expensive plantation estate, Gaylord's pays tribute to the elegant dining rooms of 1930s high society. Tables with candlelight sit on a cobblestone patio surrounding a fountain and overlooking a wide lawn. The innovative menu features classic American cooking with an island twist. Try wonton-wrapped prawns with a wasabi plum sauce, New Zealand venison, blackened prime rib, or fresh-fish specials. Lunches are a mix of salads, sandwiches, and pasta, enjoyed in a leisurely fashion. The lavish Sunday brunch may include such specialties as sweet-potato hash and Cajun

6

'ahi in addition to the standard omelets and pancakes. Before or after dining you can wander around the estate grounds or take a horse-drawn carriage ride. ⊠ *Kilohana Plantation, 3-2087 Kaumuali'i Rd., Līhu'e* ☎ *808/245–9593* ⊟ *AE, D, DC, MC, V. $20–$32.*

$$–$$$$ ✕ **Kukui's Restaurant and Bar.** The healthy choices and cross-cultural flavors on Kukui's menu are well matched with its casual, open-air setting. The meals are imaginative and intriguing, with hints of Hawaiian, Asian, and contemporary American cuisines. Blackened Pacific salmon with grilled-pineapple-scallion salsa, *kālua* (roasted) pork quesadillas, and Thai-chicken pizza are representative of the diverse fare. A shrimp boat buffet, served from a real island canoe, is an unusual attraction at dinner. A prime rib and king crab buffet is served on Friday and Saturday nights in addition to the regular menu. An extensive breakfast buffet is offered every morning, or choose from the à la carte menu. This is the best place to eat at the Marriott. ⊠ *Kaua'i Marriott Resort & Beach Club, 3610 Rice St., Līhu'e* ☎ *808/245–5050* ⊟ *AE, D, DC, MC, V. $19–$36.*

Hawaiian

¢–$ ✕ **Dani's Restaurant.** Kaua'i residents frequent this big, sparsely furnished eatery near the Līhu'e Fire Station for hearty, local-style food at breakfast and lunch. Dani's is a good place to try lū'au food without commercial lū'au prices. You can order Hawaiian-style *laulau* (pork and taro leaves wrapped in ti leaves and steamed) or kālua pig, slow-roasted in an underground oven. Other island-style dishes include Japanese-prepared *tonkatsu* (pork cutlet) and teriyaki beef, and there's always the all-American New York steak. Omelets are whipped up with fish cake, kālua pig, or seafood; everything is served with rice. ⊠ *4201 Rice St., Līhu'e* ☎ *808/245–4991* ⊟ *No credit cards* ☉ *Closed Sun. No dinner. $6–$9.*

★ ¢ ✕ **Hamura Saimin.** Folks just love this funky old plantation-style diner. Locals and tourists stream in and out all day long, and neighbor islanders stop in on their way to the airport to pick up take-out orders for friends and family back home. *Saimen* is the big draw, and each day the Hiraoka family dishes up about 1,000 bowls of steaming broth and homemade noodles, topped with a variety of garnishes. We love the barbecued chicken and meat sticks, which adopt a smoky flavor during grilling. The landmark eatery is also famous for its *liliko'i* (passion fruit) chiffon pie. ■ TIP→➤ As one of the few island eateries open until 11 PM on week nights and midnight on weekends, it's favored by night owls. ⊠ *2956 Kress St., Līhu'e* ☎ *808/245–3271* ⊟ *No credit cards. $4–$7.*

Italian

★ $$–$$$ ✕ **Café Portofino.** The menu at this authentic northern Italian restaurant is as inspired as the view of Kalapakī Bay and Hā'upu range. Owner Giuseppe Avocadi's flawless dishes have garnered a host of culinary awards and raves from dining critics. The fresh 'ahi carpaccio is a signature dish, while pasta, scampi, and veal are enhanced by sauces "with an Italian soul" that soar like Avocadi's imagination. Excellent service and a soothing, dignified ambience complete the delightful dining experience. ⊠ *Kaua'i Marriott & Beach Club, 3610 Rice St., Līhu'e* ☎ *808/245–2121* ⊟ *AE, D, DC, MC, V* ☉ *No lunch. $14–$27.*

Japanese

$–$$ ✕ **Hanamā'ulu Restaurant, Tea House, Sushi Bar, and Robatayaki.** Business is brisk at this landmark Kaua'i eatery. The food is a mix of Japanese, Chinese, and local-style cooking, served up in hearty portions. The ginger chicken and fried shrimp are wildly popular, as are the fresh sashimi and sushi. Other choices include tempura, chicken *katsu*, beef broccoli, and *robatayaki* (grilled seafood and meat). The main dining room is rather unattractive, but the private rooms in back look out on the Japanese garden and fish ponds and feature traditional seating on tatami mats at low tables. These tearooms can be reserved, and are favored for family events and celebrations. ⊠ *1-4291 Kuhiō Hwy., Rte. 56, Hanamā'ulu* ☎ *808/245–2511* ▭ *MC, V* ☺ *Closed Mon. $8–$16.*

Seafood

$–$$$$ ✕ **Duke's Canoe Club.** Surf legend Duke Kahanamoku is immortalized at this casual bi-level restaurant set on Kalapakī Bay. Guests can admire surfboards, photos, and other memorabilia marking his long tenure as a waterman. It's an interesting collection, and an indoor garden and waterfall add to the pleasing ambience. Duke's claims to have the biggest salad bar on the island, though given the lack of competition that isn't saying much. You can find simple fare ranging from fish tacos and stir-fried cashew chicken to hamburgers. At dinner, when prices increase, fresh fish prepared in a variety of styles is the best choice. A bar menu is available at the high-energy Barefoot Bar. A happy-hour drink and appetizer is a less expensive way to enjoy the moonrises and ocean views here—though it can get pretty crowded. ⊠ *Kaua'i Marriott & Beach Club, Līhu'e* ☎ *808/246–9599* ▭ *AE, D, DC, MC, V. $10–$32.*

The South & West Sides

American–Casual

$–$$ ✕ **Camp House Grill.** A plantation-style camp house with squeaky wooden floors has become a simple, down-home restaurant. The food is equally basic: hamburgers, chicken, pork ribs, and fresh fish aimed to please families. Barbecue specialties include chicken marinated in a blend of Chinese, Cajun, and Hawaiian spices. Huge sandwiches are served at lunchtime. Large breakfasts are available, and pies are baked fresh daily; you can eat a slice on the premises or take home an entire pie for a late-night craving. As you enter Kalāheo heading west toward Waimea Canyon, look for the blue building on the right. The food and setting at the Kalāheo branch are superior to the Kapa'a eatery. ⊠ *Kaumuali'i Hwy., Rte. 50, Kalāheo* ☎ *808/332–9755* ⊠ *Kaua'i Village, Kūhiō Hwy., Kapa'a* ☎ *808/822–2442* ▭ *AE, D, MC, V. $6–$19.*

Contemporary

$$$–$$$$ ✕ **The Beach House.** This restaurant is one of our favorites, with a dreamy
Fodor'sChoice ocean view and impressive cuisine. Few Kaua'i experiences are more de-
★ lightful than sitting at one of the outside tables and savoring a delectable meal while the sun sinks into the glassy blue Pacific. It's the epitome of tropical dining, and no other restaurant on Kaua'i can offer anything quite like it. The menu changes often, but the food is consistently cre-

6

ative and delicious. A few trademark dishes appear regularly, such as the Local Boy paella and fire-roasted 'ahi. Seared macadamia-nut-crusted mahimahi, a dish ubiquitous on island menus, gets a refreshing new twist when served with a citrus *aki* miso sauce. The excellent desserts must not be skipped; either the hot chocolate mousse or coconut-butter *mochi* (doughy Japanese rice cake) sundae are worthy finales of a meal at this pleasing and deservedly popular restaurant. ⊠ *5022 Lāwa'i Rd., Kōloa* ☎ *808/742–1424* ⚑ *Reservations essential* ▤ *AE, D, DC, MC, V* ⊘ *No lunch. $18–$34.*

$–$$$ ✕ **Tomkats Grille.** Tropical ponds, a waterfall, a large bar area, and a porch overlooking an inner court-yard give this grill a casual island am-bience. Try the blackened "katch of the day" with tropical salsa, or the homemade chili and burger. Wash it down with a glass of wine or one of 35 ales, stouts, ports, and lagers. Plenty of Tomkats' Nibblers—buf-falo wings, stuffed mushrooms, sautéed shrimp—enliven happy hour from 3 to 6 PM. ⊠ *Old Kōloa Town, 5402 Kōloa Rd., Kōloa* ☎ *808/742–8887* ▤ *DC, MC, V. $8–$26.*

> **BUDGET-FRIENDLY EATS ON THE SOUTH & WEST SIDES**
>
> ■ **Taqueria Nortenos.**
> ⊠ *2827-A Po'ipū Rd., Kōloa*
> ☎ *808/742-7222.*
>
> ■ **Grind's Cafe and Espresso.**
> ⊠ *Rte. 50, 'Ele'ele*
> ☎ *808/335-6027.*
>
> ■ **Wong's Chinese Restaurant.**
> ⊠ *Kaumuali'i Hwy., Hanapēpē*
> ☎ *808/335-5066.*

$$ ✕ **Waimea Brewing Company.** Housed within the Waimea Plantation Cottages, this brewpub-restaurant is spa-cious, with hardwood floors and open-air decks. Dine indoors amid rat-tan furnishings or at a bar decorated with petroglyphs and colored with Kaua'i red dirt. Smoked-chicken quesadillas, grilled portobellos, ham-burgers, *kal-bi* beef short ribs, and fresh fish are highlights. Entrées come in two sizes (small and big!) and are reasonably priced. It's a good place for a snack or appetizer while traveling to or from Waimea Canyon, but you can find better choices for dinner if you push on to Kalāheo or Po'ipū. ⊠ *9400 Kaumuali'i Hwy., Waimea* ☎ *808/338–9733* ▤ *MC, V. $14–$20.*

Eclectic

$$$–$$$$ ✕ **Roy's Po'ipū Bar & Grill.** Hawai'i's culinary superstar Roy Yamaguchi is fond of sharing his signature "Hawaiian Fusion" cuisine by open-ing clones of the successful Honolulu restaurant where he got his start. One of these copycat eateries can be found on Kaua'i's South Side, in a shopping-center locale that feels too small and ordinary for the exotic food. The menu changes daily, with the hardworking kitchen staff dreaming up 15 to 20 (or more) new specials each night—an impres-sive feat. The food reflects the imaginative pairings and quality ingre-dients that characterized the original Roy's, and the presentation is spectacular, but the atmosphere is a little different. As with most restau-rant branches, it just doesn't have the same kind of heart and soul as the original. The visitors who fill this celebrity restaurant each night don't seem to mind, but those looking for authenticity may prefer the Beach House, just a little way down the road. ⊠ *Po'ipū Shopping Village, 2360*

Kiahuna Plantation Dr., Poʻipū Beach ☎ *808/742–5000* ▤ *AE, D, DC, MC, V* ☾ *No lunch. $20–$36.*

$$–$$$ ✗ **Green Garden.** Once a family plantation manager's home, this historic building was transformed into a restaurant at about the same time Hawaiʻi was transformed from a U.S. territory into a state. This restaurant is like Old Faithful: enduring, dependable, and popular with tourists. Surrounded by tropical greenery that seems to hug its very foundation, Green Garden is very low-key: servers treat you like longtime friends, and the food is solid, no-frills fare. Hawaiian, Asian, and American influences are reflected in the 30-plus items on the dinner menu. Mahimahi, scallops, oysters, and shrimp are key ingredients along with kiawe-broiled rack of lamb and steak. The homemade desserts are the best part of a meal here, particularly the *likoʻi* (passion fruit) chiffon pie. ⊠ *Hwy. 50, Hanapēpē* ☎ *808/335–5422* ▤ *AE, MC, V* ☾ *Closed Tues. $13–$25.*

Italian

$$$–$$$$ ✗ **Dondero's.** The inlaid marble floors, ornate tile work, and Italianate
FodorsChoice murals that comprise the elegant decor at this restaurant compete with
★ a stunning ocean view. And in addition to the beautiful setting, Dondero's offers outstanding food, a remarkable wine list, and impeccable service, making this Kauaʻi's best restaurant. Chef Vincent Pecoraro combines old-world techniques with new energy to create menu selections as enticing as the surroundings. Porcini-mushroom crêpes with Parmesan sauce, fresh tomato salad topped with his flavorful homemade mozzarella cheese, and lobster piccata on a bed of fettuccine blackened with squid ink thrill the palate and delight the eye. Order a light, traditional tiramisu or chocolate crème brûlée with fresh raspberries so you can linger over coffee. The waitstaff deserves special praise for its thoughtful, discrete service. ⊠ *Hyatt Regency Kauaʻi Resort and Spa, 1571 Poʻipū Rd., Poʻipū Beach* ☎ *808/742–1234* ▤ *AE, D, DC, MC, V* ☾ *No lunch. $24–$42.*

$$–$$$ ✗ **Casa di Amici.** Tucked away in a quiet neighborhood above Poʻipū Beach, this "House of Friends" has live classical piano music on weekends and an outside deck open to sweeping ocean views. Entrées from the internationally eclectic menu include a saffron-vanilla paella risotto made with black tiger prawns, fresh fish, chicken breast, and homemade Italian sausage. For local flavor, try a *laulau Borsettino* (spinach pasta purses stuffed with kālua pork and served with a smoked portobello sauce). For dessert, take the plunge with a baked Hawaiʻi: a chocolate-macadamia-nut brownie topped with coconut and passion-fruit sorbet and flambéed Italian meringue. The food and setting are pleasant, but service can be maddeningly slow, especially when you're really hungry. ⊠ *2301 Nalo Rd., Poʻipū* ☎ *808/742–1555* ▤ *AE, D, DC, MC, V* ☾ *No lunch. $19–$28.*

★ **$$–$$$** ✗ **Plantation Gardens.** A historic plantation manager's home has been converted to a restaurant that serves Italian food in a Polynesian atmosphere—an interesting mix with good results. You'll walk through a tropical setting of torch-lighted orchid gardens and lotus-studded koi ponds to a cozy, European-feeling dining room with cherrywood floors and veranda dining. The menu is based on fresh, local foods: fish right off

6

the boat, herbs and produce picked from the plantation's gardens, fruit delivered by neighborhood farmers. The result is Italian cuisine with an island flair—shrimp and wasabi ravioli, seafood *laulau* (seafood wrapped in ti leaves and steamed) served with mango chutney—served alongside traditional classics like osso buco served with saffron risotto. ✉ *Kiahuna Plantation, 2253 Po'ipū Rd., Kōloa* ☎ *808/742–2216* ▤ *AE, DC, MC, V* ⊘ *No lunch. $14–$29.*

★ **$–$$$** ✗ **Pomodoro Ristorante Italiano.** Begin with prosciutto and melon, then proceed directly to the multilayer meat lasagna, a favorite of the chefs—two Italian-born brothers. Other highlights include eggplant or veal parmigiana, chicken saltimbocca, and scampi in a garlic, caper, and white wine sauce. Two walls of windows brighten this intimate second-story restaurant in the heart of Kalāheo, where you'll find good food at reasonable prices. ✉ *Upstairs at Rainbow Plaza, Kaumuali'i Hwy., Rte. 50, Kalāheo* ☎ *808/332–5945* ▤ *MC, V* ⊘ *No lunch. $11–$25.*

Steak & Seafood

$$$–$$$$ ✗ **Tidepools.** The Hyatt Regency Kaua'i is notable for its excellent restau-
Fodor'sChoice rants, which differ widely in their settings and cuisine. This one is def-
★ initely the most tropical and campy, sure to appeal to folks seeking a bit of island-style romance and adventure. You'll dine in your own private grass-thatch hut, which seems to float on a koi-filled pond beneath starry skies while torches flicker in the lushly landscaped grounds nearby. The food is equally distinctive, with an island flavor that comes from the chef's advocacy of Hawai'i regional cuisine and extensive use of Kaua'i-grown products. You won't go wrong ordering the fresh-fish specials or one of the signature dishes, such as macadamia-crusted mahimahi, prime rib, or filet mignon. Start with Kimo's crab cake to wake up your taste buds, and if you're still hungry at the end of the meal, the ginger crème brûlée is sure to satisfy. ✉ *Hyatt Regency Kaua'i Resort and Spa, 1571 Po'ipū Rd., Po'ipū Beach* ☎ *808/742–1234 Ext. 4260* ▤ *AE, D, DC, MC, V* ⊘ *No lunch. $25–$42.*

$$–$$$$ ✗ **Shells Steak and Seafood.** Chandeliers made from shells light the dining room and give this restaurant its name. The menu is upscale surf-and-turf, with prime cuts of steak and fresh fish enhanced by tropical spices and sauces. On Friday evenings take advantage of a bountiful seafood buffet. Shells is one of three signature restaurants in the Sheraton's Oceanfront Galleria. Each of these restaurants has been designed to embrace the view of the Pacific Ocean from sunrise to starlight. ✉ *Sheraton Kaua'i Resort, 2440 Ho'onani Rd., Po'ipū Beach, Kōloa* ☎ *808/742–1661* ▤ *AE, D, DC, MC, V* ⊘ *No lunch. $15–$32.*

$$–$$$ ✗ **Kalāheo Steak House.** Prime rib, tender top sirloin, Cornish game hen in citrus marinade, Kalāheo shrimp, Alaskan king crab legs, and Portuguese bean soup are competently prepared and served up in hearty portions at this cozy, country-ranch-house style restaurant. Weathered wood furnishings and artifacts pay tribute to Hawai'i's *paniolo* (cowboys), who can still be found in these parts. Fresh-baked rum cake comes with Lappert's ice cream (made at a factory up the road). Wines range from $8 to $25 a bottle. ✉ *4444 Pāpālina Rd., Kalāheo* ☎ *808/ 332–9780* ▤ *D, MC, V* ⚑ *Reservations not accepted* ⊘ *No lunch. $17–$26.*

$$–$$$ ✕ **Keoki's Paradise.** Built to resemble a dockside boathouse, this is an active, boisterous place that fills up quickly on weekend nights because of live music. Seafood appetizers span the tide from sashimi to Thai shrimp sticks. The day's fresh catch is available in half a dozen styles and sauces. And there's a sampling of beef, chicken, and pork-rib entrées for the committed carnivore. A lighter menu is available at the bar. ⊠ *Po'ipū Shopping Village, 2360 Kiahuna Plantation Dr., Po'ipū Beach* ☎ *AE, D, DC, MC, V. $12–$28.*

$$–$$$ ✕ **Wrangler's Steakhouse.** Denim-cover seating, decorative saddles, and a stagecoach in a loft helped to transform the historic Ako General Store in Waimea into a West Side steak house. You can eat under the stars on the deck out back or inside the old-fashioned, wood-panel dining room. The 16-ounce steak comes sizzling with either garlic, capers, peppers, or teriyaki. Those with smaller appetites might consider the vegetable tempura or the 'ahi served on penne pasta. Local folks love the special lunch: soup, rice, beef teriyaki, and shrimp tempura served in a three-tier *kaukau* tin, or lunch pail, just like the ones sugar-plantation workers once carried. A gift shop has local crafts (and sometimes a craftsperson doing demonstrations). ⊠ *9852 Kaumuali'i Hwy., Waimea* ☎ *808/338–1218* ☐ *AE, MC, V* ⊙ *Closed Sun. $12–$30.*

$–$$$ ✕ **Brennecke's Beach Broiler.** Brennecke's is decidedly casual and fun, with a busy bar, windows overlooking the beach, and a cheery blue-and-white interior. It specializes in big portions of kiawe-broiled foods such as New York steak, spiny lobster, and the fresh catch of the day. Seafood kebabs, jumbo shrimp skewers, New Zealand green-lip mussels, pasta, and deluxe fish sandwiches are other options, although we recommend sticking with the kiawe-broiled specialties. There's a take-out deli downstairs. ⊠ *2100 Ho'ōne Rd., Po'ipū* ☎ *808/742–7588* ☐ *AE, D, DC, MC, V. $11–$30.*

> **TOP SPOTS FOR ROMANCE**
>
> Whether you're already feeling sparks or trying to fan banked embers into flame, there's nothing like a romantic meal to help things along. Fortunately, Kaua'i has a number of restaurants that are conducive to love. Be sure to make reservations, though, and plan to drop a wad of cash. Romance doesn't come cheap in the Islands, unless you opt for a bottle of champagne on the beach.
> Our Top 5 picks for romantic restaurants are: The Beach House, Cafe Hanalei and Terrace, Dondero's, Gaylord's, and La Cascata.

6

ENTERTAINMENT & NIGHTLIFE

Kaua'i has never been known for its nightlife. It's a rural island, where folks tend to retire early, and the streets are dark and deserted well before midnight. The island does have its nightspots, though, and the after-dark entertainment scene is expanding, especially in areas frequented by tourists.

Most of the island's dinner and lū'au shows are held at hotels and resorts. Hotel lounges are a good source of live music, often with no cover charge, as are a few bars and restaurants around the island.

Check the local newspaper, the *Garden Island Times*, for listings of weekly happenings, or tune in to community radio station KKCR—found at 90.9 and 91.9 on the FM dial—at 5:30 PM for the arts and entertainment calendar. Free publications such as *Kaua'i Gold, This Week on Kaua'i,* and *Kaua'i Beach Press* also list entertainment events. You can pick them up at Līhu'e Airport near the baggage claim area.

Entertainment

Lū'au

Although the commercial lū'au experience is a far cry from the backyard lū'au thrown by local residents to celebrate a wedding, graduation, or baby's first birthday, they're nonetheless entertaining and a good introduction to the Hawaiian food that isn't widely sold in restaurants. Besides the feast, there's often an exciting dinner show with Polynesian-style music and dancing. It all makes for a fun evening that's suitable for couples, families, and groups, and the informal setting is conducive to meeting other people. Every lū'au is different, reflecting the cuisine and tenor of the host facility, so compare prices, menus, and entertainment before making your reservation. Most lū'au on Kaua'i are offered only on a limited number of nights each week, so plan ahead to get the lū'au you want.

Drums of Paradise Lū'au. More than just music and dance, the Hyatt lū'au also displays Hawaiian artwork and crafts. Entertainment includes the dances of Polynesia and a traditional fire dance, while a mixed menu of traditional and contemporary dishes suits all tastes. ⊠ *Hyatt Regency Kaua'i Resort and Spa, 1571 Po'ipū Rd., Po'ipū Beach* ☎ *808/742–1234* ⊠ *$65* ☉ *Thurs. and Sun. 6–8:30.*

Kaua'i Aloha Lū'au. Performers from the celebrated "Rohotu" dance company take the stage at these lū'au festivities held each Monday evening on the grounds of the Radisson Kaua'i Beach Resort while guests dine on traditional lū'au foods. ⊠ *4331 Kau'ai Beach Dr., Līhu'e* ☎ *808/335–5828* ⊠ *$60* ☉ *Mon. 5:15–8:30.*

Fodor'sChoice
★ **Courtyard Kaua'i at Waipouli Beach Lū'au.** The event begins with a traditional *imu* (underground oven) ceremony where the oven is opened and the roast pig is removed. A giant buffet includes all the traditional favorites, such as poi, raw and cooked fish, sweet potatoes, and *haupia* (coconut pudding). Entertainment starts after dark, with time-honored dances from nearly all of the Polynesian islands, including the dramatic Samoan fire dance. This is one of the best lū'au on the island, especially for the price. ⊠ *4-484 Kūhiō Hwy., Kapa'a* ☎ *808/822–3455 Ext. 651* ⊠ *$57* ☉ *Mon.–Sat. 6–9.*

Lū'au Kilohana. This lū'au—on a former sugar plantation manager's estate—has a twist: all guests arrive at the feast by horse-drawn carriage (reservations are staggered to prevent lines). Families especially seem to enjoy the food and fun here, although it lacks authenticity—sugar plantations are a decidedly Western affair. The evening's theme is the history of sugar on the Islands. ⊠ *3-2087 Kaumuali'i St., Līhu'e* ☎ *808/*

The Forbidden Isle

SEVENTEEN MILES from Kaua'i, across the Kaulakahi Channel, lies the privately owned island of Ni'ihau. It's known as the "Forbidden Isle" because access is limited to the Robinson family, which owns it, and the 200 or so Native Hawaiians who were born there.

Ni'ihau was bought from King Kamehameha in 1864 by a Scottish widow, Eliza Sinclair. Sinclair was introduced to the island after an unusually wet winter; she saw nothing but green pastures and thought it would be an ideal place to raise cattle. The cost was $10,000. It was a real deal, or so Sinclair thought.

Unfortunately, Ni'ihau's usual rainfall is about 12 inches a year, and the land soon returned to its normal desertlike state. Regardless, Sinclair did not

abandon her venture and today the island and ranching operation are owned by Bruce Robinson, Eliza Sinclair's great-great-grandson.

Visits to the island are restricted to custom hunting expeditions and flightseeing tours through Ni'ihau Helicopter. Tours depart from Kaumakani and avoid the western coastline, especially the village of Pu'uwai. There's a four-passenger minimum for each flight, and reservations are essential. A picnic lunch on a secluded Ni'ihau beach is included, with time for swimming, beachcombing, and snorkeling. The half-day tour is $280 per person.

For more information contact **Ni'ihau Tours** (🖃 Box 690370, Makaweli 96769 ☎ 808/335-3500 or 877/441-3500 ⊕ www.niihau.us)

245-9593 🖃 $61 ⊘ *Tues. and Thurs. wagon rides begin at 5:15, dinner at 6, show at 6:30.*

Pa'ina o Hanalei. A conch shell is blown in the traditional way to signal the start of this gourmet lū'au feast held on the shore of Hanalei Bay. It's lavish, as one might expect from the Princeville Hotel, with a buffet line that's heavy on upscale, Pacific Rim cuisine and light on traditional lū'au fare. The event includes entertainment that celebrates the songs and dances of the South Pacific. 🖃 *Princeville Resort, 5520 Ka Haku Rd.* ☎ 808/826-2788 🖃 $68 ⊘ *Mon. and Thurs. at 6.*

★ **Smith's Tropical Paradise Lū'au.** A 30-acre tropical garden provides the lovely setting for this popular lū'au, which begins with the traditional blowing of the conch shell and imu ceremony, followed by cocktails, an island feast, and an international show in the amphitheater overlooking a torch-lighted lagoon. It's fairly authentic and a better deal than the pricier resort events. 🖃 *174 Wailua Rd., Kapa'a* ☎ 808/821-6895 🖃 $58 ⊘ *Mon., Wed., and Fri. 6-9:15.*

Tahiti Nui Lū'au. This venerable—and decidely funky—institution in sleepy Hanalei is a welcome change from the standard commercial lū'au. It's intimate (about 40 guests), casual, and put on by an island family that really knows how to throw a party. The all-you-can-eat buffet includes kālua pig that has been slow-roasted in an imu, and the show has plenty of dancing, music, and laughs. ☒ *Kūhiō Hwy., Hanalei* ☎ *808/826–6277* 🍴 *$62* ⊙ *Wed. at 5.*

Music

Check the local papers for outdoor reggae and Hawaiian-music shows, or one of the numbers listed below for more formal performances.

Kaua'i Community College Performing Arts Center (☒ 3-1901 Kaumuali'i Hwy., Līhu'e ☎ 808/245–8270) is the main venue for island entertainment, hosting a concert music series, visiting musicians, dramatic productions, and special events such as the International Film Festival. **Kaua'i Concert Association** (☒ 3-1901 Kaumuali'i Hwy., Līhu'e ☎ 808/245–7464) offers a seasonal program at the arts center.

Film & Theater

The **Kaua'i Community Players** (☒ Līhu'e Parish Hall, 4340 Nāwiliwili Rd., Līhu'e ☎ 808/245–7700) is a talented local group that presents plays throughout the year.

The venerable **Kīlauea Theater and Community Event Center** (☒ 2490 Keneke St., Kīlauea ☎ 808/828–0438) is the site of North Shore live concert events, first-run movies, and art films.

Bars & Clubs

Nightclubs that stay open to the wee hours are rare on Kaua'i, and the bar scene is pretty limited. The major resorts generally host their own live entertainment and happy hours. All bars and clubs that serve alcohol must close at 2 AM, except those with a cabaret license, which allows them to close at 4 AM.

The North Shore

Hanalei Gourmet. The sleepy North Shore stays awake—until 10:30, that is—each evening in this small, convivial setting inside Hanalei's restored old school building. The emphasis here is on local live jazz, rock, and folk music. ☒ *5-5161 Kūhiō Hwy., Hanalei Center, Hanalei* ☎ *808/826–2524.*

★ **Happy Talk Lounge.** Hawaiian entertainment takes center stage Monday through Saturday evenings in this lounge at the Hanalei Bay Resort. Come Sunday, this joint is swinging to the sounds of jazz in jam sessions that run from 3 PM to 7 PM. ☒ *5380 Honoiki Rd., Princeville* ☎ *808/826–6522.*

Līhu'e & the East Side

Duke's Barefoot Bar. This is one of the liveliest bars on Kalapakī Beach. Contemporary Hawaiian music is performed in the beachside bar on Thursday and Friday, and upstairs a traditional Hawaiian trio plays nightly for diners. The bar closes at 11 most nights. ☒ *Kalapakī Beach, Līhu'e* ☎ *808/246–9599.*

Rob's Good Times Grill. Let loose at this sports bar, which also houses Kaua'i's hottest DJs spinning Thursday through Saturday from 9 PM to

2 AM. Wednesday you can kick up your heels with country line dancing from 7:30 PM to midnight. Sunday, Monday and Tuesday evenings are open mike for karaoke enthusiasts. ⊠ *4303 Rice St., Līhuʻe* ☎ *808/ 246–0311.*

The Shack. The live music offered several nights a week draws a crowd to this combination sports bar and burger joint on the north end of Kapaʻa. It stays open until 2 AM if there's a crowd ⊠ *4-139 Kūhiō Hwy, Kapaʻa* ☎ *808/823–0200.*

The South & West Sides

Keoki's Paradise. A young, energetic crowd makes this a lively spot on Friday and Saturday nights. After 9 PM, when the dining room clears out, there's live music for dancing and a bit of a bar scene for singles. ⊠ *2360 Kiahuna Plantation Dr., Poʻipū* ☎ *808/742–7354.*

SHOPPING

Along with one major shopping mall, a few shopping centers, and a growing number of big-box retailers, Kauaʻi has some delightful mom-and-pop shops and specialty boutiques with lots of character.

The Garden Isle also has a large and talented community of artisans and fine artists, with galleries all around the island showcasing their creations. You can find many unique island-made arts and crafts in the small shops, and it's worthwhile to stop in at craft fairs and outdoor markets to look for bargains and mingle with island residents.

If you're looking for a special memento of your trip that is unique to Kauaʻi County, check out the distinctive Niʻihau shell leis. The tiny shells are collected from beaches on Kauaʻi and Niʻihau, pierced, and strung into beautiful necklaces, chokers, and earrings It's a time-consuming and exacting craft, and these items are much in demand, so don't be surprised by the high price tags. Those made by Niʻihau residents will have certificates of authenticity and are worth collecting. You often can find cheaper versions made by non-Hawaiians at craft fairs.

Stores are typically open daily from 9 or 10 AM to 5 PM, although some stay open until 9 PM, especially those near resorts. Don't be surprised if the posted hours don't match the actual hours of operation at the smaller shops, where owners may be fairly casual about keeping to a regular schedule.

The North Shore

Shopping Centers

Ching Young Village. This popular shopping center looks a bit worn, despite a recent face lift, but that doesn't deter business. The town's only grocery store, **Big Save,** is here along with a number of other shops useful to locals and visitors. These include **Hanalei Natural Foods,** with its supply of fresh organic produce; **Hanalei Music and Video,** where you can buy Hawaiian sheet music, compact discs, and handmade instruments; **Village Variety,** which has a bit of everything; **Village Bake Shop;**

and several restaurants. A few steps away is **Evolve Love Artists Gallery,** a good place to find quality work by local artisans; and **On The Road to Hanalei,** a neat boutique with gifts, clothing, jewelry, housewares, and collectibles from Indonesia. ⊠ *5-1590 Kūhiō Hwy., Hanalei* ☎ *808/ 826–7222.*

Hanalei Center. Listed on the Historic Register, the old Hanalei school has been refurbished and rented out to boutiques and restaurants. You can dig through '40s and '50s vintage clothing and memorabilia in the **Yellow Fish Trading Company,** search for that unusual gift at **Sand People,** or buy beach gear at the classic **Hanalei Surf Company.** You can even catch a class at the **Hanalei Yoga studio** in the two-story modern addition to the center. ⊠ *5-5161 Kūhiō Hwy., Hanalei* ☎ *808/826–7677.*

Princeville Shopping Center. Foodland, a full-service grocery store, and **Island Ace Hardware** are the big draws at this small center. This is the last stop for gas and banking on the North Shore. You'll also find two restaurants, a mail service center, post office, ice-cream shop, toy and hobby shop, and clothing stores. ⊠ *5-4280 Kūhiō Hwy., Princeville* ☎ *808/826–7513.*

Shops & Stores

Kong Lung Co. Sometimes called the Gump's of Kaua'i, this gift store sells elegant clothing, exotic glassware, ethnic books, gifts, and artwork— all very lovely and expensive. The shop is housed in a beautiful 1892 stone structure right in the heart of Kīlauea. It's the showpiece of the pretty little Kong Lung Center, our favorite retail area on the North Shore. You can find distinctive jewelry, handmade soaps and candles, hammocks, plants, excellent pizza and baked goods, art work, and consignment clothing, among other items. Next door are the classic Kīlauea Theater and the Farmers Market, a good place to buy natural and gourmet foods, wines, and sandwiches. ⊠ *2490 Keneke St., Kīlauea* ☎ *808/828–1822.*

Village Variety Store. How about a fun beach towel for the folks back home? That's just one of the gifts you can find here, along with shell leis, Kaua'i T-shirts, macadamia nuts, and other great souvenirs at low prices. The store also has many small, useful items like envelopes, housewares, and toiletries. ⊠ *Ching Young Village, Kūhiō Hwy., Hanalei* ☎ *808/826–6077.*

East Side

Shopping Centers

Coconut Marketplace. This visitor-oriented complex is on the busy Coconut Coast near resort hotels and condominiums. Sixty shops sell everything from snacks and slippers (as locals call flip-flop sandals) to scrimshaw. There are also two movie theaters with first-run features, restaurants open from breakfast to evening, and a free nightly Polynesian show at 5 PM. ⊠ *4-484 Kūhiō Hwy., Kapa'a* ☎ *808/822–3641.*

Kaua'i Village Shopping Center. The buildings of this Kapa'a shopping village are in the style of a 19th-century plantation town. **ABC Discount Store** sells sundries; **Safeway** carries groceries and alcoholic beverages; **Long's Drugs** has a pharmacy, health and beauty products, and a good selection of Hawaiian merchandise; **Papaya's** has health foods; and other shops sell jewelry, gift items, children's clothes and toys, and art. Worth a look is the **Kaua'i Heritage Center,** which sponsors cultural workshops and displays authentic crafts for sale. For children, there's the **Kaua'i Children's Discovery Museum** which, in addition to interactive exhibits, offers children's day-camp programs. ⊠ *4-831 Kūhiō Hwy., Po'ipū Beach* ☎ *808/822–4904.*

Kinipopo Shopping Village. Kinipopo is a tiny little center on Kūhiō Highway in Wailua. **Korean Barbeque** fronts the highway, as does **Goldsmith's Gallery,** which sells handcrafted Hawaiian-style gold jewelry. Worth a stop is **Tin Can Mailman,** with its eclectic collection of used books, stamps and coins, rare prints, vintage maps, and collectibles. ⊠ *4-356 Kūhiō Hwy., Kapa'a* ☎ *No phone.*

Waipouli Town Center. **Foodland** is the focus of this small retail plaza, one of three shopping centers anchored by a grocery store in Kapa'a. You' can also find a **Blockbuster** video outlet, **McDonald's, Pizza Hut,** and **Fun Factory** video arcade, along with a local-style restaurant and a bar. ⊠ *4-901 Kūhiō Hwy., Kapa'a* ☎ *808/524–2023.*

Shops & Galleries

★ **Bambulei.** Two 1930s-style plantation homes have been transformed into this unique boutique featuring vintage and contemporary clothing, antiques, jewelry, and accessories. ⊠ *4-369 Kūhiō Hwy., Wailua* ☎ *808/ 823–8641.*

Jim Saylor Jewelers. Jim Saylor has been designing beautiful keepsakes for more than 20 years on Kaua'i. Gems from around the world appear in his unique settings, including black pearls and diamonds. ⊠ *1318 Kūhiō Hwy., Kapa'a* ☎ *808/822–3591.*

Kahn Galleries. You can purchase the works of many local artists—including seascapes by George Sumner and Roy Tabora—at this gallery's many locations. ⊠ *Coconut Marketplace, 4-484 Kūhiō Hwy., Kapa'a* ☎ *808/822–3636* ⊠ *Kilohana Plantation, 3-2087 Kaumuali'i Hwy., Līhu'e* ☎ *808/246–4454* ⊠ *Kaua'i Village Shopping Center, 4-831 Kūhiō Hwy., Kapa'a* ☎ *808/822–4277* ⊠ *Kōloa Rd., Old Kōloa Town* ☎ *808/742–2277* ⊠ *Hanalei Center, 5-5161 Kūhiō Hwy., Hanalei* ☎ *808/826–6677.*

Kaua'i Gold. A wonderful selection of rare Ni'ihau shell leis ranges in price from $20 to $200. Ask about how these remarkable necklaces are made to appreciate the craftsmanship, understand the sometimes high prices, and learn to care for and preserve them. The store also sells a selection of 14-karat gold jewelry. ⊠ *Coconut Marketplace, 4-484 Kūhiō Hwy., Kapa'a* ☎ *808/822–9361.*

FodorśChoice **Kaua'i Heritage Center.** Authentic reproductions of old Hawaiian crafts
★ by Kaua'i artisans are displayed here: feather hatbands, nose flutes, *konane* (a Hawaiian game similar to checkers) boards and playing pieces, calabashes, and woven *lau hala* hats and pocketbooks. Sales help to support the center's cultural workshops and programs, which sometimes take place in the courtyard by the clock tower. ⊠ *Kaua'i Village, 4-831 Kūhiō Hwy., No. 838, Kapa'a* ☎ *808/821–2070.*

Kaua'i Products Fair. Open weekends, this outdoor market features fresh produce, tropical plants and flowers, aloha wear, and collectibles along with craftspeople, artisans, and wellness practitioners who will give you a massage right on the spot. ⊠ *Outside next to 4-1621 Kūhiō Hwy., in Kapa'a* ☎ *808/246–0988.*

Fodor$Choice **Kebanu Gallery.** A stunning collection of original wood sculptures,
★ whimsical ceramics, beaded jewelry, colorful glassware, and other creations—many of them by Hawai'i artists—make this contemporary shop a pleasure to visit. ⊠ *Hee Fat Marketplace, 4-1354 Kūhiō Hwy., Kapa'a* ☎ *808/823–6820* ⊕ *www.aloha.net/~kebanu.*

M. Miura Store. This mom-and-pop operation has a great assortment of surfware and clothes for outdoor fanatics, including tank tops, visors, swimwear, and Kaua'i-style T-shirts at low prices. ⊠ *4-1419 Kūhiō Hwy., Kapa'a* ☎ *808/822–4401.*

Tin Can Mailman Books and Curiosities. Both new and used books can be found here, along with an extensive collection of Hawaiian and South Pacific literature. The shop also sells maps, tapa cloth from Fiji, and specialty gift items. ⊠ *Kinipopo Shopping Village, 4-356 Kūhiō Hwy., Kapa'a* ☎ *808/822–3009.*

Ye Olde Ship Store & Port of Kaua'i. Scrimshaw-decorated pocket and army knives, boxes, and other gift items are available at this store in the Coconut Marketplace. The shop carries the work of nearly 40 scrimshaw artists and sponsors an annual contest celebrating the art form. ⊠ *Coconut Marketplace, 4-484 Kūhiō Hwy., Kapa'a* ☎ *808/822–1401.*

Līhu'e

Shopping Centers

Kilohana Plantation. This 16,000-square-foot Tudor mansion contains five art galleries and Gaylord's restaurant. The restored outbuildings house a craft shop and a Hawaiian-style clothing shop. The house itself is filled with antiques from its original owner and is worth a look. Horse-drawn carriage rides are available, with knowledgeable guides reciting the history of sugar on Kaua'i. ⊠ *3-2087 Kaumuali'i Hwy., 1 mi west of Līhu'e* ☎ *808/245–7818.*

Kukui Grove Center. This is Kaua'i's only true mall. Besides **Sears Roebuck** and **Kmart,** anchor tenants are **Longs Drugs, Macy's,** and **Star Market,** a local grocery store. **Borders Books & Music,** and its coffee shop, is one of the island's most popular stores. **Starbucks** recently opened its first outlet on Kaua'i here. The mall's various stores offer women's clothing, surf wear, art, toys, athletic shoes, jewelry, and locally made crafts. Restaurants range from fast food and sandwiches to Mexican and Chinese. The center stage often has entertainment. ⊠ *3-2600 Kaumuali'i Hwy., west of Līhu'e* ☎ *808/245–7784.*

Shops & Galleries

Art Shop. This intimate gallery in Līhu'e sells original oils, photos, and sculptures. ⊠ *3196 'Akahi St., Līhu'e* ☎ *808/245–3810.*

Hilo Hattie Fashion Factory. This is the big name in aloha wear for tourists throughout the Islands. You can visit the factory, a mile from Līhu'e Airport, to pick up cool, comfortable aloha shirts and mu'umu'us in bright floral prints, as well as other souvenirs. While there, check out the line of Hawaiian-inspired home furnishings. ✉ *3252 Kūhiō Hwy., Līhuʻe* ☎ *808/245–3404.*

FodorsChoice ★ **Kapaia Stitchery.** Hawaiian quilts made by hand and machine, a beautiful selection of fabrics, quilting kits, and fabric arts fill this cute little red plantation-style structure. The staff is friendly and helpful, even though a steady stream of customers keeps them busy. ✉ *Kūhiō Hwy., ½ mi north of Līhuʻe* ☎ *808/245–2281.*

Kauaʻi Fruit and Flower Company. At this shop near Līhuʻe you can buy fresh sugarloaf pineapple, sugarcane, ginger, coconuts, local jams, jellies, and honey, plus Kauaʻi-grown papayas, bananas, and mangos in season. Stop by on your way to the airport (although it's hard to make a left turn back onto Kūhiō Highway) to buy fruit that's been inspected and approved for shipment to the mainland. ✉ *3-4684 Kūhiō Hwy., Kapaʻa* ☎ *808/245–1814 or 800/943–3108.*

★ **Kauaʻi Museum.** The gift shop at the museum sells some fascinating books, maps, and prints, as well as lovely feather lei hatbands, Niʻihau shell jewelry, handwoven *lau hala* hats, and other quality local crafts at reasonable prices. ✉ *4428 Rice St., Līhuʻe* ☎ *808/245–6931.*

Kauaʻi Products Store. Every seed lei, every finely crafted koa-wood box, every pair of tropical-flower earrings; indeed, every item in this boutique is handcrafted on Kauaʻi. Other gift options include koa oil lamps, pottery, hand-painted silk clothing, sculpture, and homemade fudge. Although some of the merchandise isn't all that appealing, it's nice to support local talent when you can. ✉ *Kukui Grove Center, 3-2600 Kaumualiʻi Hwy., Līhuʻe* ☎ *808/246–6753.*

Kilohana Clothing Company. This store in the guest cottage by Gaylord's restaurant offers vintage Hawaiian clothing as well as contemporary styles using traditional Hawaiian designs. The store also features a wide selection of home products in vintage fabrics. ✉ *Kilohana Plantation, 3-2087 Kaumualiʻi Hwy., Līhuʻe* ☎ *808/246–6911.*

★ **Piece of Paradise Gallery.** Fine art, koa-wood clocks and sushi platters, carved island tikis, handblown glass, and unique jewelry—all designed by talented Kauaʻi-based artisans—are available here. ✉ *Radisson Kauaʻi Beach Hotel, 4331 Kauaʻi Beach Dr., Līhuʻe* ☎ *808/246–2834* ⊕ *www.apieceofparadise.org.*

Remember Kauaʻi. Pick up a memento of your trip in the form of jewelry, Niʻihau shell necklaces, or other gift items here. The shop also runs a booth at Poʻipū Spouting Horn. ✉ *Radisson Kauaʻi Beach Hotel, 4331 Kauaʻi Beach Dr., Līhuʻe* ☎ *808/639–9622.*

The South & West Sides

Shopping Centers

ʻEleʻele Shopping Center. Kauaʻi's West Side has a scattering of stores, including those at this no-frills strip-mall shopping center where several tour-boat companies have offices. It's a good place to rub elbows with local folk or to grab a quick bite to eat at the casual **Grinds Cafe** or McDonald's. ✉ *Rte. 50 near Hanapēpē, ʻEleʻele* ☎ *808/246–0634.*

Poʻipū Shopping Village. Convenient to nearby hotels and condos on the South Side, the two-dozen shops here sell resort wear, gifts, souvenirs, and art. The upscale **Black Pearl Kaua'i** shop and the **Hale Manu** store, with "gifts for the spirited," are particularly appealing. Restaurants include **Keoki's Pardise, Roy's, Po'ipū Tropical Burgers,** and **Pattaya Asian Cafe.** A Polynesian Revue performs in the open-air courtyard Tuesday and Thursday at 5 PM. ⊠ *2360 Kiahuna Plantation Dr., Po'ipū Beach* ☎ *808/742–2831.*

Waimea Canyon Plaza. As Kekaha's retail hub and the last stop for supplies before heading up to Waimea Canyon, this tiny, tidy complex of shops is surprisingly busy. Look for local foods, souvenirs, and island-made gifts for all ages. ⊠ *Kōke'e Rd. at Rte. 50, Kekaha* ☎ *No phone.*

Stores & Shops

Coconut Republic. Come here for the beautiful clothing embroidered by local artists. There's also a selection of the island's unique "red dirt" T-shirts. ⊠ *Po'ipū Shopping Village, 2360 Kiahuna Plantation Dr., Po'ipū Beach* ☎ *808/742–6691.*

Kaua'i Coffee Visitor Center and Museum. Kaua'i produces more coffee than any other island in the state. The local product can be purchased from grocery stores or here at the source. ⊠ *870 Halawili Rd., off Rte. 50, west of Kalāheo* ☎ *808/335–0813 or 800/545–8605.*

Kaua'i Tropicals. You can have this company ship heliconia, anthuriums, ginger, and other tropicals in 5-foot-long boxes directly from its flower farm. ⊠ *3870 Waha Rd., Kalāheo* ☎ *808/332–9071 or 800/303–4385.*

Lee Sands' Eelskin. Eel-skin handbags and other accessories are sold at wholesale prices at this shop in the Hawaiian Trading Post building. It's an unusual store, with other skin lines such as sea snake, chicken feet, and frog. A lizard card case is available for about $12. ⊠ *Rte. 50 at Kōloa Rd., Lāwa'i* ☎ *808/332–7404.*

Paradise Sportswear. This is the retail outlet of the folks who invented Kaua'i's popular "red dirt" shirts, which are dyed and printed with the characteristic local soil. Ask the salesperson to tell you the charming story behind these shirts. Sizes from infants up to 5X are available. ⊠ *4350 Waialo Rd., Port Allen* ☎ *808/335–5670.*

KAUA'I ESSENTIALS

Transportation

BY AIR

Regular air service from Honolulu, and a few direct flights from Maui, the Big Island, and select West Coast cities make for convenient, if not quick, travel to the Garden Island.

CARRIERS Two Hawaii-based carriers, Aloha Airlines and Hawaiian Airlines, offer daily round-trip flights from Honolulu and Neighbor Islands to Līhu'e Airport. Rates vary widely from $63 to $170 one-way. It's generally a 20- to 40-minute flight, depending on where you start. Aloha and Hawaiian airlines also provide a few direct flights from select West Coast cities, as do United Airlines and American Airlines. ⇨ *See* Smart Travel Tips *at the front of this book for airline contact information.*

AIRPORTS The Līhuʻe Airport is 3 mi east of the town of Līhuʻe. All commercial and cargo flights use this modern airport. It has just two baggage-claim areas, each with a Visitor Information Center. There's a heliport that serves tour helicopters nearby.

Used only by a tour helicopter company and a few private planes, the Princeville Airport is a tiny strip on the North Shore, set within rolling ranches and sugarcane fields. It's a five-minute drive from the Princeville Resort and condo development, and a 10-minute drive from the shops and accommodations of Hanalei.

🗺 **Līhuʻe Airport** ☎ 888/697–7813 for visitor information center. **Princeville Airport** ☎ 808/826–3040.

TO & FROM THE Līhuʻe Airport is a five-minute drive from Līhuʻe. If you're staying in Wailua
AIRPORT or Kapaʻa, your driving time from Līhuʻe is 15 to 25 minutes; to Princeville and Hanalei it's about 45 to 60 minutes.

To the south, it's a 30- or 40-minute drive from Līhuʻe to Poʻipū, the major resort area. To Waimea, the drive takes a little more than an hour; to the mountains of Kōkeʻe, allow a good two hours driving time from Līhuʻe.

Check with your hotel or condo to see if there's free shuttle service from the airport.

For luxurious transportation between the airport and your accommodations, contact **Custom Limousine Service** (808/246–6318). Rates are $75 per hour, with a two-hour minimum. They also have packages that include lei greetings, wedding arrangements, and tours. **North Shore Limousine** (808/826–6189) specializes in service in the Hanalei and Princeville areas, including transport to Līhuʻe Airport.

Taxi fares around the island are $2 at the meter drop plus $2 per mile. That means a taxicab from Līhuʻe Airport to Līhuʻe town runs about $6 and to Poʻipū about $32, excluding tip. **Akiko's Taxi** (808/822–7588) offers its services from the east side of the island. **Poʻipū Taxi** (808/639–2042 or 808/639–2044) will take you to Līhuʻe and Poʻipū. **Scotty Taxi** (808/245–7888 or 808/639–9807) provides quick service around the airport and Līhuʻe.

BY CAR

CAR RENTAL Unless you plan to stay strictly at a resort or do all of your sightseeing as part of guided tours, you will need a rental car. You can hitchhike or take the bus, but both are slow modes of travel that don't take you everywhere you might want to go. You can easily walk to the rental-car counters, directly across the street from the baggage claim at Līhuʻe Airport. They'll shuttle you to their nearby lot to pick up your car. All the major companies have offices at the Līhuʻe Airport. Several companies operate small reservation desks at major hotels, but spur-of-the-moment rentals will cost you more than pre-arranged ones.

CAR TRAVEL Although Kauaʻi is relatively small, its sights stretch across the island and its narrow, often busy roads are not especially conducive to walking or bicycling. You may be able to walk to beaches, stores, and restaurants in your resort area, but major attractions are not usually within walking distance.

It's easy to get around on Kaua'i, but be prepared for slow travel and high gas prices. A two-lane highway that widens to three lanes in several places nearly encircles the island. It's essentially one road, called Kūhiō Highway on its northwest course and Kaumuali'i Highway when it turns to the southwest. Līhu'e serves as the juncture point. Your rental-car company will supply you with a pretty decent map, and others can be found in the free tourist magazines.

Traffic is a major source of irritation for residents, who encounter it at unpredictable times and the usual rush-hour periods. It's thickest between Līhu'e and the South Side, and all around Kapa'a. Residents know the tight spots, so don't worry, they'll let you into the line of traffic or stop so you can make your left turn. Be sure to acknowledge them with a wave and repeat the kindness when you can. It's also the local practice to let in drivers from a side street or closed lane one at a time, alternating with cars on the through road. Aggressive driving is not appreciated. And if you're gawking at the sights and holding up traffic, pull over and let cars go by.

⚠ **Although Kaua'i looks like paradise, it does have crime, and much of it is directed at tourists and their property. Lock your car (but forget that annoying alarm) whenever you park and never leave valuables in your rental car, even for a short time, and especially not in the trunk. Pay attention to parking signs and speed limits. And be sure to buckle up, as seat-belt citations carry hefty fines.**

BY TAXI

Cabs are costly on Kaua'i and must be called for service. Each mile is $2, after a $2 meter drop; from Līhu'e to Po'ipū the price is $32; from Līhu'e to Princeville it's $60, excluding tip. It's best to use a cab for short distances only (to a restaurant, for instance).

Akiko's Taxi operates from Kapa'a and has minivans in its fleet. City Cab is a reliable taxi company with island-wide services; it uses Līhu'e as a home base. North Shore Cab Company, based in Princeville, caters to the north and east sections of the island.

🚖 **Akiko's Taxi** ☎ 808/822-7588 or 808/634-6018. **City Cab** ☎ 808/245-3227 or 808/639-7932. **North Shore Cab Company** ☎ *808/826-4118 or 808/639-7829.*

Contacts & Resources

EMERGENCIES

To reach the police, ambulance, or fire department in case of any emergency, dial **911**.

Kaua'i's Wilcox Memorial Hospital in Līhu'e has x-ray facilities, physical therapy, a pharmacy, and an emergency room. It's linked to Kaua'i Medical Clinic (KMC), with physicians trained in many different specialties, and clinics all around the island. Major emergency cases are airlifted to O'ahu. West Kaua'i Medical Center serves the area from Po'ipū to Kekaha.

Most pharmacies close around 5 PM, though Longs Drugs, Safeway, and Wal-Mart stay open a few hours later.

🚹 Doctors: **Kaua'i Medical Clinic** ✉ 3420-B Kūhiō Hwy., Līhu'e ☎ 808/245-1500, 808/245-2471 for pharmacy, 808/245-1831 for 24-hr on-call physicians, 808/338-9431 for after-hours emergencies ✉ North Shore Clinic, Kīlauea and Oka Rds., Kīlauea ☎ 808/828-1418 ✉ 4392 Waialo Rd., 'Ele'ele ☎ 808/335-0499 ✉ 5371 Kōloa Rd., Kōloa ☎ 808/742-1621 ✉ 4-1105 Kūhiō Hwy., Kapa'a ☎ 808/822-3431.

🚹 Hospitals: **West Kaua'i Medical Center** ✉ 4643 Waimea Canyon Dr., Waimea ☎ 808/338-9431. **Wilcox Memorial Hospital** ✉ 3420 Kūhiō Hwy., Līhu'e ☎ 808/245-1010.

🚹 Pharmacies: **Longs Drugs** ✉ Kukui Grove Center, Rte. 50, Līhu'e ☎ 808/245-8871. **Safeway Food and Drug** ✉ Kaua'i Village Shopping Center, 4-831 Kūhiō Hwy., Kapa'a ☎ 808/822-2191. **Shoreview Pharmacy** ✉ 4-1177 Kūhiō Hwy., Suite 113, Kapa'a ☎ 808/822-1447. **Westside Pharmacy** ✉ 1-3845 Kaumuali'i Hwy., Hanapēpē ☎ 808/335-5342.

VISITOR INFORMATION

The Kaua'i Visitors Bureau—the local chapter of the Hawai'i Visitors and Convention Bureau—has an office at 4334 Rice Street, Līhu'e's main thoroughfare, near the Kaua'i Museum.

You'll find plenty of kiosk-type activity centers that can help you book tours, schedule activities, and rent recreational gear, convertibles, mopeds, and motorcycles all over the island. Beware, some of them are linked to timeshare projects, and you may have to sit through a sales pitch to get those great deals.

Po'ipū Beach Resort Association is the central source of information about the South Side. You can make online reservations through the organization's Web site, find out about activities and attractions, and request maps and brochures.

The many free visitor magazines are also helpful, offering maps, descriptions of activities, discount coupons, sightseeing and shopping tips, and other tidbits of advice and information.

🚹 **Kaua'i Visitors Bureau** ✉ 4334 Rice St., Suite 101, Līhu'e 96766 ☎ 808/245-3971 or 800/262-1400 🖨 808/246-9235 ⊕ www.kauaivisitorsbureau.com.

Po'ipū Beach Resort Association 🏠 Box 730, Kōloa 96756 ☎ 808/742-7444 or 888/744-0888 🖨 808/742-7887 ⊕ www.poipu-beach.org.

UNDERSTANDING HAWAI'I

**The Aloha Shirt:
A Colorful Swatch
of Island History**

These Volcanic Isles

Hawai'i At a Glance

Hawaiian Vocabulary

THE ALOHA SHIRT: A COLORFUL SWATCH OF ISLAND HISTORY

ELVIS PRESLEY had an entire wardrobe of them in the '60s films *Blue Hawaii* and *Paradise, Hawaiian Style*. During the '50s, entertainer Arthur Godfrey and bandleader Harry Owens often sported them on television shows. John Wayne loved to lounge around in them. Mick Jagger felt compelled to buy one on a visit to Hawai'i in the 1970s. Dustin Hoffman, Steven Spielberg, and Bill Cosby avidly collect them.

The roots of the aloha shirt go back to the early 1930s, when Hawai'i's garment industry was just beginning to develop its own unique style. Although locally made clothes did exist, they were almost exclusively for plantation workers and were constructed of durable palaka or plain cotton material.

Out of this came the first stirrings of fashion: Beachboys and schoolchildren started having sport shirts made from colorful Japanese kimono fabric. The favored type of cloth was the kind used for children's kimonos—bright pink and orange floral prints for girls; masculine motifs in browns and blues for boys. In Japan, such flamboyant patterns were considered unsuitable for adult clothing, but in the Islands such rules didn't apply, and it seemed the flashier the shirt, the better—for either sex. Thus, the aloha shirt was born.

It was easy and inexpensive in those days to have garments tailored to order; the next step was moving to mass production and marketing. In June 1935 Honolulu's best-known tailoring establishment, Musa-Shiya, advertised the availability of "Aloha shirts—well tailored, beautiful designs and radiant colors. Ready-made or made to order . . . 95¢ and up." This is the first known printed use of the term that would soon refer to an entire industry. By the following year, several local manufacturers had begun full-scale production of "aloha wear." One of them, Ellery Chun of King-Smith, registered as local trademarks the terms "Aloha Sportswear" and "Aloha Shirt" in 1936 and 1937, respectively.

These early entrepreneurs were the first to create uniquely Hawaiian designs for fabric as well—splashy patterns that would forever symbolize the Islands. A 1939 *Honolulu Advertiser* story described them as a "delightful confusion [of] tropical fish and palm trees, Diamond Head and the Aloha Tower, surfboards and leis, 'ukuleles and Waikīkī beach scenes."

The aloha wear of the late 1930s was intended for—and mostly worn by—tourists, and interestingly, a great deal of it was exported to the mainland and even Europe and Australia. By the end of the decade, for example, only 5% of the output of one local firm, the Kamehameha Garment Company, was sold in Hawai'i.

World War II brought this trend to a halt, and during the postwar period aloha wear really came into its own in Hawai'i itself. A strong push to support local industry gradually nudged island garb into the workplace, and kama'āina began to wear the clothing that previously had been seen as attire for visitors.

In 1947, for example, male employees of the City and County of Honolulu were first allowed to wear aloha shirts "in plain shades" during the summer months. Later that year, the first observance of Aloha Week started the tradition of "bankers and bellhops . . . mix[ing] colorfully in multihued and tapa-designed Aloha shirts every day," as a local newspaper's Sunday

"The Aloha Shirt: A Colorful Swatch of Island History" first appeared in ALOHA *magazine. Reprinted with permission of Davick Publications.*

magazine supplement noted in 1948. By the 1960s, "Aloha Friday," set aside specifically for the wearing of aloha attire, had become a tradition. In the following decade the suit and tie practically disappeared as work attire in Hawai'i, even for executives.

Most of the Hawaiian-theme fabric used in manufacturing aloha wear was designed in the Islands, then printed on the mainland or in Japan. The glowingly vibrant rayons of the late '40s and early '50s (a period now seen as aloha wear's heyday) were at first printed on the East Coast, but manufacturers there usually required such large orders that local firms eventually found it impossible to continue using them. By 1964, 90% of Hawaiian fabric was being manufactured in Japan—a situation that still exists today.

Fashion trends usually move in cycles, and aloha wear is no exception. By the 1960s the "chop suey print" with its "tired clichés of Diamond Head, Aloha Tower, outrigger canoes [and] stereotyped leis" was seen as corny and garish, according to an article published in the *Honolulu Star-Bulletin*. But it was just that outdated aspect that began to appeal to the younger crowd, who began searching out old-fashioned aloha shirts at the Salvation Army and Goodwill thrift stores. These shirts were dubbed "silkies," a name by which they're still known, even though most of them were actually made of rayon.

Before long, what had been 50¢ shirts began escalating in price, and a customer who had balked at paying $5 for a shirt that someone had already worn soon found the same item selling for $10—and more. By the late 1970s, aloha-wear designers were copying the prints of yesteryear for their new creations.

The days of bargain silkies are now gone. The few choice aloha shirts from decades past that still remain are offered today by specialized dealers for hundreds of dollars apiece, causing many to look back to the time when such treasures were foolishly worn to the beach until they fell apart. The best examples of vintage aloha shirts are now rightly seen as art objects, worthy of preservation for the lovely depictions they offer of Hawai'i's colorful and unique scene.

— DeSoto Brown

THESE VOLCANIC ISLES

DAWN AT THE CRATER ON HORSE-BACK. It's cold at 10,023 feet above the warm Pacific—maybe 45°F. The horses' breath condenses into smoky clouds, and the riders cling to their saddles. It's eerily quiet except for the creak of straining leather and the crunch of volcanic cinders underfoot, sounds that are absurdly magnified in the vast empty space that yawns below.

This is Haleakalā, the "house of the sun." It's the crown of east Maui and the largest dormant volcanic depression in the world. The park encompasses 28,665 acres, and the valley itself is 21 mi in circumference and 19 square mi in area. At its deepest, it measures 3,000 feet from the summit, and could accommodate all of Manhattan. What you see here isn't actually a crater at all but something called a caldera, formed by the collapsing of the main cone, the result of eons of wind and rain wearing down what was once a small dip at the original summit peak. The small hills within the valley are volcanic cinder cones, each the site of an eruption.

Every year thousands of visitors drive the world's steepest auto route to the summit of Haleakalā National Park. Sunrise is extraordinary here. Mark Twain called it "the sublimest spectacle" he had ever witnessed.

But sunrise is only the beginning.

Hiking Haleakalā is like walking on the moon, with thirty-two miles of trails weaving around volcanic rubble, crater cones, frozen lava flows, vents, and tubes. The colors are muted yet dramatic—black, yellow, russet, orange, lavender, brown, even a pinkish blue—and change throughout the day.

This ecosystem sustains the surefooted mountain goat; the rare nēnē goose (no webbing between its toes, the better to negotiate this rugged terrain); and the strange, delicate silversword. A spiny, metallic-leaf plant, the silversword once grew abundantly on Haleakalā's slopes. Today it survives in small numbers at Haleakalā and at high elevations on the Big Island of Hawai'i. The plants live up to 40 years, bloom only once, scatter their seeds, and die.

It's not difficult to see this place as a bubbling, sulfurous cauldron, a direct connection to the core of the earth. Haleakalā's last—and probably final—eruption occurred in 1790, a few years after a Frenchman named Jean-François de Galaup, Comte de La Pérouse, became the first European to set foot on Maui. The rocky area on the southwest side of east Maui known as La Pérouse Bay is the result of that flow.

Large and small, awake or sleeping, volcanoes are Hawai'i's history and heritage. Behind their beauty is the story of the flames that created this ethereal island chain. The islands in the Hawaiian archipelago are actually the upper bodies of immense mountains rising from the bottom of the sea. Formed by molten rock known as magma, the islands have slowly grown from the earth's volatile mantle, lava forced through a "hot spot" in the thin crust of the ocean floor. The first ancient eruptions cooled and formed pools on the Pacific bottom. Then as magma spilled from the vents over millions of years, the pools became ridges and grew into crests. The latter built upon themselves over the eons, until finally they towered above the surface of the sea. This type of volcano, with its slowly formed, gently sloping sides, is known as a shield volcano. All of the Hawaiian Islands were created this way.

As the Islands cooled in the Pacific waters, the lava slopes slowly bloomed, over centuries, with colorful flora. About once every 35,000 years a seed, spore, bird, or insect arrived here on the winds or waves. They found a fertile, sun-and-rain–drenched home, free of predators. Over time, these migrants developed into highly specialized organisms. A land with no predatory species breeds a population of plants and animals devoid of biological protections, making them especially fragile and vulnerable to foreign species and human development. Today Hawai'i suffers from one of the world's highest species extinction rates; eighty percent of native Hawaiian birds are now gone.

But for all the talk of geology, Hawaiian myth casts a different history of the islands. Pele, the beautiful and tempestuous daughter of Haumea, the Earth Mother, and Wakea, the Sky Father, is the Hawaiian goddess of fire, the maker of mountains, melter of rock, eater of forests—a creator and a destroyer. Legend has it that Pele came to the Islands long ago to flee from her cruel older sister, Na Maka o Kahai, goddess of the sea. Pele ran first to the small island of Ni'ihau, making a crater home there with her digging stick. But Na Maka found her and destroyed her hideaway, so Pele again had to flee. On Kaua'i she delved deeper, but Na Maka chased her from that home as well. Pele ran on—from O'ahu to Moloka'i, Lāna'i to Kaho'olawe, Molokini to Maui—but always Na Maka pursued her.

Pele came at last to Halema'uma'u, the vast fire-pit crater of Kīlauea, and there, on the Big Island, she dug deepest of all. There she is said to remain, all-powerful, quick to rage, and often unpredictable; the mountain is her impenetrable fortress and domain—a safe refuge, at least for a time, from Na Maka o Kahai.

The chronology of the old tales of Pele's flight from isle to isle closely matches the reckonings of modern volcanologists regarding the ages of the various craters. Today, the Big Island's Kīlauea and Mauna Loa retain the closest links with the earth's

superheated core and are active and volatile. The other volcanoes have been carried beyond their magma supply by the movement of the Pacific Plate. Those on Kaua'i, O'ahu, and Moloka'i are completely extinct. Those at the southeasterly end of the island chain—Haleakalā, Mauna Ke'a, and Hualālai—are dormant and slipping away, so that the implacable process of volcanic death has begun. As erosion continues, the islands will someday melt back into the sea.

The largest island of the archipelago, the Big Island of Hawai'i rises some 13,796 feet above sea level at the summit of Mauna Ke'a. Mauna Loa is nearly as high at 13,667 feet. Geologists believe it required more than 3 million years of steady volcanic activity to raise these peaks up above the waters of the Pacific. From their bases on the ocean floor, these shield volcanoes are the largest mountain masses on the planet.

Mauna Loa's little sister, Kīlauea, at about 4,077 feet, is the most active volcano in the world. Between the two volcanoes, they have covered nearly 200,000 acres of land with their red-hot lava flows over the past 200 years. In the process, they have ravished trees, fields, meadows, villages, and more than a few unlucky humans. For generations, Kīlauea, in a continually eruptive state, has pushed molten lava up from the earth's magma at 1,800°F and more. But as active as she and Mauna Loa are, their eruptions are comparatively safe and gentle, producing continuous small flows rather than large bursts of fire and ash. The exceptions were two explosive displays during recorded history—one in 1790, the other in 1924. During these eruptions, Pele came close to destroying the Big Island's largest city, Hilo.

It is around these major volcanoes that the island's Hawai'i Volcanoes National Park was created. A sprawling natural preserve, the park attracts visitors from around the world for the unparalleled opportunity to view lava up-close and personal. Geology experts and vulcanologists have been coming for a century or more to study and to improve methods for predicting the times and sites of eruptions.

Thomas Augustus Jaggar, preeminent vulcanologist and student of Kīlauea, built his home on stilts wedged into cracks in the volcanic rock of the crater rim. Harvard-trained and universally respected, he was the driving force behind the establishment of the Hawaiian Volcano Observatory at Kīlauea in 1912. When he couldn't raise research funds from donations, public and private, he raised pigs to keep the scientific work going. After Jaggar's death, his wife scattered his ashes over the great fiery abyss.

The park is on the Big Island's southeastern flank, about 30 minutes out of Hilo on the aptly named Volcano Highway. Wear sturdy walking shoes and carry a warm sweater. It can be a long hike across the lava flats to see Pele in action, and at 4,000 feet above sea level temperatures can be brisk, however hot the volcanic activity. So much can be seen at close range along the road circling the crater that Kīlauea has been dubbed the "drive-in volcano."

At the park's visitor center sits a large display case. It contains dozens of lava-rock "souvenirs"—removed from Pele's grasp and then returned, accompanied by letters of apology. They are sent back by visitors who say they regret having broken the *kapu* (taboo) against removing even the smallest grain of native volcanic rock from Hawai'i. A typical letter might say: "I never thought Pele would miss just one little rock, but she did, and now I've wrecked two cars . . . I lost my job, my health is poor, and I know it's because I took this stone." The letters can be humorous, or poignant and remorseful, requesting Pele's forgiveness.

It is surprisingly safe at the crater's lip. Unlike Japan's Mount Fuji or Washington State's Mount St. Helens, Hawai'i's shield volcanoes spew their lava downhill, along the sides of the mountain. Still, the clouds of sulfur gas and fumes produced during volcanic eruptions are noxious and heady and can make breathing unpleasant, if not difficult. It has been pointed out that the chemistry of volcanoes—sulfur, hydrogen, oxygen, carbon dioxide—closely resembles the chemistry of the egg.

It's an 11-mi drive around the Kīlauea crater via the Crater Rim Road, and the trip takes about an hour. But it's better to walk a bit. There are at least eight major trails in the park, ranging from short 15-minute strolls to the three-day, 18-mi (one way) Mauna Loa Trail. An easy, comfortable walk is Sulfur Banks, with its many steaming vents creating halos of clouds around the rim of Kīlauea. The route passes through a forest of sandalwood, flowers, and ferns.

Just ahead is the main attraction: the center of Pele's power, Halema'uma'u. This yawning pit of flame and burning rock measures some 3,000 feet wide and is a breathtaking sight. When Pele is in full fury, visitors come in droves, on foot and by helicopter, to see her crimson expulsions coloring the dark earth and smoky sky. Kīlauea's most recent violent activity has occurred at mountainside vents instead of at the summit crater. Known as rift zones, they are lateral conduits that often open in shield volcanoes.

Kīlauea has two rift zones, one extending from the summit crater toward the southwest, through Kau, the other to the east-northeast through Puna, past Cape Kumakahi, into the sea. In the last two decades, repeated eruptions in the east rift zone have blocked off 12 mi of coastal road—some under more than 300 feet of rock—and have covered a total of 10,000 acres with lava. Where the flows entered the ocean, roughly 200 acres have been added to the Big Island.

Farther along the Crater Rim Road is the Thurston Lava Tube, an example of a strangely beautiful volcanic phenomenon common on the Islands. Lava tubes form when lava flows rapidly downhill. The sides and top of this river of molten rock cool, while the fluid center flows on. Most formations are short and shallow, but some measure 30 to 50 feet high and hundreds of yards long. Lava tubes were often used to store remains of the ancient Hawaiian royalty—the *ali'i*. The Thurston Lava Tube sits in a beautiful prehistoric fern forest.

Throughout the park, new lava formations are continually being created. These volcanic deposits exhibit the different types of lava produced by Hawai'i's volcanoes: *'a'ā*, the dark, rough lava that solidifies as cinders of rock; and the more common *pāhoehoe*, the smooth, satiny lava that forms the vast plains of black rock in ropy swirls known as lava flats, which in some areas go on for miles. Other terms that help identify what may be seen in the park include *caldera*, which are the open, bowl-like lips of a volcano summit; *ejecta*, the cinders and ash that float through the air around an eruption; and *olivine*, the semiprecious chrysolite (greenish in color) found in volcanic ash.

But this volcanic landscape isn't all fire and flash, cinders, and devastation. Hawai'i Volcanoes National Park is also the home of some of the most beautiful of the state's black-sand beaches; forest glens full of lacy butterflies and colorful birds such as the dainty flycatcher, called the *'elepaio*; and exquisite grottoes sparked with bright wild orchid sprays and crashing waterfalls.

Even as the lava cools, still bearing a golden, glassy skin, lush, green native ferns—*ama'uma'u, kupukupu,* and *'ōkupukupu*—spring up in the midst of Pele's fallout, as if defying her destructiveness or simply confirming the fact that after fire she brings life.

Some 12 centuries ago, in fact, Pele brought humans to her verdant islands: the fiery explosions that lit Kīlauea and Mauna Loa probably guided the first explorers to Pele's side from the Marquesas Islands, some 2,400 mi away across the ocean.

Once settled, they worshiped her from a distance. Great numbers of religious *heiau* (outdoor stone platforms) dot the landscapes near the many older and extinct craters scattered throughout Hawai'i, demonstrating the reverence the native islanders have always held for Pele and her creations. But the ruins of only two heiau are to be found near the very active crater at Halema'uma'u. There, at the center of the capricious Pele's power, native Hawaiians caution one even today to "step lightly, for you are on holy ground."

In future ages, when mighty Kīlauea is no more, this area will still be a volcanic isle. Beneath the blue Pacific waters, fiery magma flows and new mountains form and grow. Off the south coast of the Big Island, a new island is forming. Still ½ mi below the water's surface, it won't be making an appearance any time soon, but already has a name: Lōihi.

— Gary Diedrichs

HAWAI'I AT A GLANCE

Fast Facts

Nickname: Aloha State
Capital: Honolulu
State song: "Hawai'i Pono'i"
State bird: The nēnē, an endangered land bird and variety of goose
State flower: Yellow Hibiscus Brackenridgii
State tree: Kukui (or candlenut), a Polynesian-introduced tree
Administrative divisions: There are four counties with mayors and councils: City and County of Honolulu (island of O'ahu), Hawai'i County (Hawai'i Island), Maui County (islands of Maui, Moloka'i, Lāna'i and Kahoolawe), and Kaua'i County (islands of Kaua'i and Ni'ihau)
Entered the Union: August 21, 1959, as the 50th state
Population: 1,334,023
Life expectancy: Female 82, male 76
Literacy: 81%

Ethnic groups: Hawaiian/part Hawaiian 22.1% Caucasian 20.5% Japanese 18.3% Filipino 12.3% Chinese 4.1%
Religion: Roman Catholic 22%; Buddhist, Shinto and other East Asian religions 15%; Mormon 10%; Church of Christ 8%; Assembly of God and Baptist 6% each; Episcopal, Jehovah's Witness and Methodist 5% each
Language: English is the first language of the majority of residents; Hawaiian is the native language of the indigenous Hawaiian people and an official language of the state; other languages spoken include Samoan, Chinese, Japanese, Korean, Spanish, Portuguese, Filipino, and Vietnamese

The loveliest fleet of islands that lies anchored in any ocean.

—Mark Twain

Geography & Environment

Land area: An archipelago of 137 islands encompassing a land area of 6,422.6 square mi in the north-central Pacific Ocean (about 2,400 mi from the west coast of the continental U.S.).
Coastline: 750 mi
Terrain: Volcanic mountains, tropical rain forests, verdant valleys, sea cliffs, canyons, deserts, coral reefs, sand dunes, sandy beaches
Natural resources: Dimension limestone, crushed stone, sand and gravel, gemstones
Natural hazards: Hurricanes, earthquakes, tsunamis
Flora: More than 2,500 species of native and introduced plants throughout the islands.
Fauna: Native mammals include the hoary bat, Hawaiian monk seal, and Polynesian rat. The humpback whale migrates to Hawaiian waters every winter to mate and calve. More than 650 fish and 40 different species of shark live in Hawaiian waters. Freshwater streams are home to hundreds of native and alien species. The humuhumunukunukuāpua'a (Hawaiian triggerfish) is the unofficial state fish.
Environmental issues: Plant and animal species threatened and endangered due to hunting, overfishing, overgrazing by wild and introduced animals, and invasive alien plants

Hawai'i is not a state of mind, but a state of grace.

—Paul Theroux

Economy

Tourism and federal defense spending continue to drive the state's economy. Efforts to diversify in the areas of science and technology, film and television production, sports, ocean research and development, health and education, tourism, agriculture, and floral and specialty food products are ongoing.

GSP: $40.1 billion
Per capita income: $30,000
Inflation: 1%
Unemployment: 4.3%
Work force: 595,450
Debt: $7.3 billion
Major industries: Tourism, Federal government (defense and other agencies)
Agricultural products: Sugar, pineapple, papayas, guavas, flower and nursery products, asparagus, alfalfa hay, macadamia nuts, coffee, milk, cattle, eggs, shellfish, algae
Exports: $616 million
Major export products: Aircraft and parts, naphthas, medical equipment and supplies, fruit, steel scrap, electronic components, unleaded gasoline, artwork, cocoa, coffee, flowers, macadamia nuts
Imports: $2.6 billion
Major import products: Crude oil, electronic and digital equipment, coal, passenger motor vehicles

In what other land save this one is the commonest form of greeting not "Good day," or How d'ye do," but "Love?" That greeting is "Aloha"–love, I love, my love to you . . .It is a positive affirmation of the warmth of one's own heart, giving.
—Jack London

Debate has waxed and waned for more than a century over how and when to return to native Hawaiians more than 1 million acres of land and other assets seized when American business interests overthrew the island monarchy in 1893. Certain native factions still advocate a return to independent nationhood. Sovereignty gained new momentum in the 1990s with the passage of a federal law formally apologizing for the overthrow and urging reconciliation. Momentum has since fizzled. Hawaii's current governor has renewed efforts to have Congress recognize Hawaiians as an indigenous people, much like Native Americans and Alaskans. The governor also has pledged to support continued funding of health care, language, and other cultural programs, and to achieve state and federal obligations to distribute homestead lands to qualified Hawaiians.

Did You Know?

- Hawai'i is home to the world's most active volcano: Kīlauea, on the Big Island.

- 'Iolani Palace had electricity and telephones installed several years before the White House, and is the only palace on U.S. soil.

- Hawai'i has about 12% of all endangered plants and animals in the U.S.; 75% of the country's extinct plants and birds were Hawaiian.

- The Royal Hawaiian Band is the only intact organization from the time of Hawaiian monarchy that is fully functional and still preserves Hawai'i's musical history.

HAWAIIAN VOCABULARY

Although an understanding of Hawaiian is by no means required on a trip to the Aloha State, a *malihini*, or newcomer, will find plenty of opportunities to pick up a few of the local words and phrases. Traditional names and expressions are widely used in the Islands, thanks in part to legislation enacted in the early '90s to encourage the use of the Hawaiian language. You're likely to read or hear at least a few words each day of your stay. Such exposure enriches a trip to Hawai'i.

With a basic understanding and some uninhibited practice, anyone can have enough command of the local tongue to ask for directions and to order from a restaurant menu. One visitor announced she would not leave until she could pronounce the name of the state fish, the *humuhumunukunukuāpua'a*. Luckily, she had scheduled a nine-day stay.

Simplifying the learning process is the fact that the Hawaiian language contains only eight consonants—H, K, L, M, N, P, W, and the silent *'okina*, or glottal stop, written '—plus one or more of the five vowels. All syllables, and therefore all words, end in a vowel. Each vowel, with the exception of a few diphthongized double vowels such as *au* (pronounced "ow") or *ai* (pronounced "eye"), is pronounced separately. Thus *'Iolani* is four syllables (ee-oh-la-nee), not three (yo-la-nee). Although some Hawaiian words have only vowels, most also contain some consonants, but consonants are never doubled.

Pronunciation is simple. Pronounce *A* "ah" as father; *E* "ay" as in weigh; *I* "ee" as in marine; *O* "oh" as in no; *U* "oo" as in true.

Consonants mirror their English equivalents, with the exception of W. When the letter begins any syllable other than the first one in a word, it is usually pronounced as a *V. 'Awa*, the Polynesian drink, is pronounced "ava," *'ewa* is pronounced "eva."

Nearly all long Hawaiian words are combinations of shorter words; they are not difficult to pronounce if you segment them into shorter words. *Kalaniana'ole*, the highway running east from Honolulu, is easily understood as *Kalani ana 'ole*. Apply the standard pronunciation rules—the stress falls on the next-to-last syllable of most two- or three-syllable Hawaiian words—and Kalaniana'ole Highway is as easy to say as Main Street.

Now about that fish. Try *humu-humu nuku-nuku āpu a'a*.

The other unusual element in Hawaiian language is the *kahakō*, or macron, written as a short line (ˉ) placed over a vowel. Like the accent (´) in Spanish, the kahakō puts emphasis on a syllable that would normally not be stressed. The most familiar example is probably *Waikīkī*. With no macrons, the stress would fall on the middle syllable; with only one macron, on the last syllable, the stress would fall on the first and last syllables. Some words become plural with the addition of a macron, often on a syllable that would have been stressed anyway. No Hawaiian word becomes plural with the addition of an *S*, since that letter does not exist in the *'ōlelo Hawai'i* (which is Hawaiian for "Hawaiian language").

What follows is a glossary of some of the most commonly used Hawaiian words. Don't be afraid to give them a try. Hawaiian residents appreciate visitors who at least try to pick up the local language.

'a'ā: rough, crumbling lava, contrasting with *pāhoehoe*, which is smooth.
'ae: yes.
aikane: friend.
āina: land.
akamai: smart, clever, possessing savoir faire.
akua: god.
ala: a road, path, or trail.

ali'i: a Hawaiian chief, a member of the chiefly class.

aloha: love, affection, kindness; also a salutation meaning both greetings and farewell.

'ānuenue: rainbow.

'a'ole: no.

'apōpō: tomorrow.

'auwai: a ditch.

auwē: alas, woe is me!

'ehu: a red-haired Hawaiian.

'ewa: in the direction of 'Ewa plantation, west of Honolulu.

hala: the pandanus tree, whose leaves (*lau hala*) are used to make baskets and plaited mats.

hālau: school.

hale: a house.

hale pule: church, house of worship.

ha mea iki or **ha mea 'ole:** you're welcome.

hana: to work.

haole: ghost. Since the first foreigners were Caucasian, *haole* now means a Caucasian person.

hapa: a part, sometimes a half; often used as a short form of *hapa haole,* to mean a person who is part-Caucasian; thus, the name of a popular local band, whose members represent a variety of ethnicities.

hau'oli: to rejoice. *Hau'oli Makahiki Hou* means Happy New Year. *Hau'oli lā hānau* means Happy Birthday.

heiau: an outdoor stone platform; an ancient Hawaiian place of worship.

holo: to run.

holoholo: to go for a walk, ride, or sail.

holokū: a long Hawaiian dress, somewhat fitted, with a yoke and a train. Influenced by European fashion, it was worn at court, and at least one local translates the word as "expensive mu'umu'u."

holomū: a post–World War II cross between a *holokū* and a mu'umu'u, less fitted than the former but less voluminous than the latter, and having no train.

honi: to kiss; a kiss. A phrase that some tourists may find useful, quoted from a popular hula, is *Honi Ka'ua Wikiwiki:* Kiss me quick!

honu: turtle.

ho'omalimali: flattery, a deceptive "line," bunk, baloney, hooey.

huhū: angry.

hui: a group, club, or assembly. A church may refer to its congregation as a *hui* and a social club may be called a *hui.*

hukilau: a seine; a communal fishing party in which everyone helps to drive the fish into a huge net, pull it in, and divide the catch.

hula: the dance of Hawai'i.

iki: little.

ipo: sweetheart.

ka: the. This is the definite article for most singular words; for plural nouns, the definite article is usually *nā.* Since there is no *S* in Hawaiian, the article may be your only clue that a noun is plural.

kahuna: a priest, doctor, or other trained person of old Hawai'i, endowed with special professional skills that often included the gift of prophecy or other supernatural powers; the plural form is kāhuna.

kai: the sea, saltwater.

kalo: the taro plant from whose root poi is made.

kama'āina: literally, a child of the soil; it refers to people who were born in the Islands or have lived there for a long time.

kanaka: originally a man or humanity in general, it is now used to denote a male Hawaiian or part-Hawaiian, but is occasionally taken as a slur when used by non-Hawaiians. *Kanaka maoli,* originally a full-blooded Hawaiian person, is used by some native Hawaiian rights activists to embrace part-Hawaiians as well.

kāne: a man, a husband. If you see this word on a door, it's the men's room. If you see *kane* on a door, it's probably a misspelling; that is the Hawaiian name for the skin fungus tinea.

kapa: also called by its Tahitian name, *tapa,* a cloth made of beaten bark and usually dyed and stamped with a repeat design.

kapakahi: crooked, cockeyed, uneven. You've got your hat on *kapakahi.*

kapu: keep out, prohibited. This is the Hawaiian version of the more widely known Tongan word *tabu* (taboo).

kapuna: grandparent; elder.

kēia lā: today.

keiki: a child; *keikikāne* is a boy, *keikiwahine* a girl.

kona: the leeward side of the Islands, the direction (south) from which the *kona* wind and *kona* rain come.

kula: upland.

kuleana: a homestead or small plot of ground on which a family has been installed for some generations without necessarily owning it. By extension, *kuleana* is used to denote any area or department in which one has a special interest or prerogative. You'll hear it used this way: If you want to hire a surfboard, see Moki; that's his *kuleana*. And conversely: I can't help you with that; that's not my *kuleana*.

lā: sun.

lamalama: to fish with a torch.

lānai: a porch, a balcony, an outdoor living room. Almost every house in Hawai'i has one. Don't confuse this two-syllable word with the three-syllable name of the island, Lāna'i.

lani: heaven, the sky.

lau hala: the leaf of the *hala,* or pandanus tree, widely used in Hawaiian handicrafts.

lei: a garland of flowers.

limu: sun.

lolo: stupid.

luna: a plantation overseer or foreman.

mahalo: thank you.

makai: toward the ocean.

malihini: a newcomer to the Islands.

mana: the spiritual power that the Hawaiian believed inhabited all things and creatures.

manō: shark.

manuwahi: free, gratis.

mauka: toward the mountains.

mauna: mountain.

mele: a Hawaiian song or chant, often of epic proportions.

Mele Kalikimaka: Merry Christmas (a transliteration from the English phrase).

Menehune: a Hawaiian pixie. The *Menehune* were a legendary race of little people who accomplished prodigious work, such as building fishponds and temples in the course of a single night.

moana: the ocean.

mu'umu'u: the voluminous dress in which the missionaries enveloped Hawaiian women. Now made in bright printed cottons and silks, it is an indispensable garment in a Hawaiian woman's wardrobe. Culturally sensitive locals have embraced the Hawaiian spelling but often shorten the spoken word to "mu'u." Most English dictionaries include the spelling "muumuu," and that version is a part of many apparel companies' names.

nani: beautiful.

nui: big.

ohana: family.

'ono: delicious.

pāhoehoe: smooth, unbroken, satiny lava.

Pākē: Chinese. This *Pākē* carver makes beautiful things.

palapala: document, printed matter.

pali: a cliff, precipice.

pānini: prickly pear cactus.

paniolo: a Hawaiian cowboy, a rough transliteration of *español,* the language of the Islands' earliest cowboys.

pau: finished, done.

pilikia: trouble. The Hawaiian word is much more widely used here than its English equivalent.

puka: a hole.

pupule: crazy, like the celebrated Princess Pupule. This word has replaced its English equivalent in local usage.

pu'u: volcanic cinder cone.

waha: mouth.

wahine: a female, a woman, a wife, and a sign on the ladies' room door; the plural form is *wāhine*.

wai: freshwater, as opposed to saltwater, which is *kai*.

wailele: waterfall.

wikiwiki: to hurry, hurry up (since this is a reduplication of *wiki,* quick, neither W is pronounced as a V).

INDEX

A

Ahalanui Park (Big Island), 329, 388
'Āhihi-Kīna'u (Maui), 153
Ahu'ena Heiau (Big Island), 358
'Aiea Loop Trail (O'ahu), 28
'Ai'opio Beach (Big Island), 325
'Akaka Falls State Park (Big Island), 382, 383
Akatsuka Orchid Gardens (Big Island), 375
Ala Moana Beach Park (O'ahu), 7, 34
Ala Moana Shopping Center, 125
Ala Wai Yacht Harbor (O'ahu), 35, 39–40
Alaki'i Swamp Trail (Kaua'i), 478
Alan Wong's (Honolulu) ✕, 109
Alan Wong's Hualalai Grille at Four Seasons Hualālai (Big Island) ✕, 416
Ālau islet (Maui), 204
Alekoko (Menehune) Fishpond (Kaua'i), 493, 495
Alexander & Baldwin Sugar Museum (Maui), 179, 180
Ali'i Kula Lavender (Maui), 186, 193
Aloha Cottages ☷ (Maui), 222
Aloha Dive Company (Big Island), 335
Aloha Kaua'i Tours, 473
Aloha shirts, 546–547
Aloha Tower Marketplace (O'ahu), 48, 51
'Alula Beach (Big Island), 325
Amy B.H. Greenwell Ethnobotanical Garden (Big Island), 361
'Anaeho'omalu Bay (Big Island), 338
'Anaeho'omalu Beach, at Waikoloa Beach Marriott (Big Island), 323
Anara Spa (Kaua'i), 516–517
'Anini Beach Park (Kaua'i), 454–455
Ann Fielding's Snorkel Maui, 154
Anne Namba Designs (O'ahu), 126
Aquariums, 47, 66, 186
Arboretums, 200, 365
Archery, 300
Arizona Memorial (O'ahu), 57, 59

Art Night (Lahaina), 172
Aston Waikīkī Circle Hotel ☷, 86–87
Astronaut Ellison S. Onizuka Space Center (Big Island), 356, 385
Atlantis Cruises, 116
Atlantis Submarines, 23–24, 41, 337
ATV tours, 160, 273, 339, 472–473
Awa'awapuhi Trail (Kaua'i), 478

B

Ba Le (Maui) ✕, 239
Bailey House (Maui), 180, 182
Baldwin Beach (Maui), 143–144
Baldwin Home, 173
Bambulei (Kaua'i boutique), 537
Banyan Drive (Hilo), 377–378, 380
Banyan Tree (Lahaina), 173
Banyan Tree, The (Maui) ✕, 233
Banzai Pipeline (O'ahu), 13, 67, 69, 71
Batik at Mauna Kea Beach Hotel, The ✕, 415–416
Bay View Coffee Farm (Big Island), 361
Beach House Beach (Kaua'i), 468–469, 470
Beach House, The (Kaua'i) ✕, 527–528
Beach 69 (Big Island), 323
Bed and Breakfast, Traditional Style, (O'ahu), 90–91
Bellows Beach (O'ahu), 19, 61
Big Island, 315–445
  Hāmākua Coast, 328–329, 382–386, 410–411, 441
  Hawai'i Volcanoes National Park, 368–376, 404–407, 427
  Ka'u, 326–328, 364–366, 404
  Puna, 329, 386–389, 411–412
Big Island Candies, 440
Big Island Country Club, 340, 342
Big Island Visitors Bureau (Hilo), 367, 378
Bishop Museum (O'ahu), 41, 51
Black Rock (Maui), 153
Black Sand Beach (Big Island), 327–328
Boat tours & charters, 15–16, 296, 331–332, 459–461
Bottomless Pit (Haleakalā), 191
Bowfin Memorial (O'ahu), 59

Brenneckes Beach (Kaua'i), 457
Brennecke's Ledge (Kaua'i), 466
Brick Palace (Maui), 173
Brocken Specter phenomenon, 189–190
Brown's Beach House at the Fairmont Orchid (Big Island) ✕, 416
Buffalo's Annual Big Board Surfing Classic (O'ahu), 72
Byodo-In Temple (O'ahu), 67, 68

C

C&K Beach Service (O'ahu), 25
Cafe Hanalei and Terrace (Kaua'i) ✕, 520–521
Café Portofino (Kaua'i) ✕, 526
Camping, 192, 298, 481, 482
Canyon Trail (Kaua'i), 478
Cape Kumukhi Lighthouse (Puna), 388
Capische (Maui) ✕, 241
Captain Beans' Polynesian Dinner Cruise (Big Island), 434
Captain Cook Monument (Big Island), 332, 361, 362
Castle Waikīkī Shores ☷, 89
Cathedrals dive site (Lāna'i), 116, 297
Chain of Craters Road (Big Island), 372
Challenge At Manele golf course (Lāna'i), 299
Chef Mavro (Honolulu) ✕, 109
Chez Paul (Maui) ✕, 232
Children, attractions for, F26
Big Island, 319, 322, 325–326, 328, 356, 381, 384, 386, 434
Kaua'i, 454–455, 456–457, 458, 459, 465, 468, 469, 470, 491, 492, 495
Maui, 140–141, 142, 143–144, 155, 168, 178, 182–183, 184, 185, 186, 247
O'ahu, 7, 8–10, 11, 25, 33–34, 45, 47, 51, 52, 64, 66, 73–74, 117
Chinatown (Honolulu), 46, 48, 51–52, 104–108
Christ Memorial Episcopal Church (Kaua'i), 490
Church Row (Moloka'i), 275
Church of St. Joseph's (Moloka'i), 280
Coast Grille at Hāpuna Beach Prince Hotel (Big Island) ✕, 417

Cobalt Lounge (O'ahu nightclub), *120*
Cocktail and dinner cruises, *15–16, 115–116*
Cocktail and dinner shows, *116–119*
Coconut Island (Hilo), *377, 378*
Converse Hawaiian Open Surfing Championships (O'ahu), *72*
Cook's Discoveries (Big Island), *437*
Coral Creek Golf Course (O'ahu), *28–29*
Court House (Lahaina), *173, 177*
Courtyard Kaua'i at Waipouli Beach Lū'au (Kaua'i), *532*
Cove Park (Maui), *156*
Crater Rim Drive (Big Island), *371*
Crouching Lion rock formation (O'ahu), *67*

D

D. T. Fleming Beach (Maui), *139*
David Paul's Lahaina Grill (Maui) ✕, *233*
Devastation Trail (Big Island), *371*
Diamond Head, *10, 35, 44–45, 47, 108–111*
Diamond Head State Monument and Park, *45*
Dinner and sunset cruises, *115–116, 246*
Disappearing Sands Beach Park (Big Island), *326, 330*
Doctors. ⇨ *See* Emergencies
Dole Plantation (O'ahu), *74*
Dolphin Bay Hotel (Hilo) 🏨, *408*
Donatoni's at the Hilton Waikoloa Village (Big Island) ✕, *418*
Dondero's (Kaua'i) ✕, *529*
Duke Kahanamoku Beach (O'ahu), *8*
Duke Kahanamoku Statue, *39, 40*
Duke's Canoe Club (O'ahu nightclub), *120*
Dunes at Maui Lani, The (golf course), *162*

E

East End Trails (Moloka'i), *269–270*
Ed Robinson's Diving Adventures (Maui), *151–152*
Edelweiss (Big Island) ✕, *420*

'Ehukai Beach Park (O'ahu), *13, 67*
Electric Beach (O'ahu), *23*
Experience At Kō'ele golf course (Lāna'i), *299*

F

Fair Wind Snorkel Adventures (Big Island), *336*
Fairmont Kea Lani Hotel Suites & Villas (Maui) 🏨, *214, 221*
Fairmont Orchid Hawai'i, The 🏨, *391*
Falls of Clyde (historic ship, O'ahu), *52*
Feast at Lele, The (Lahaina), *245*
Fern Grotto (Kaua'i), *488, 489*
Finest Kind, Inc. (Maui), *147*
Fire House Gallery (Big Island), *353*
First Hawaiian Bank (O'ahu), *38, 40*
505 Front Street (Lahaina), *172, 177*
Flea market, *251*
Flora and fauna, *167*
Formal Dining Room, Lodge at Kō'ele (Lāna'i) ✕, *310*
Fort (Lahaina), *173, 177*
Ft. DeRussy Beach (Waikīkī, *8–9*
Fort Elisabeth (Kaua'i), *498*
Four Seasons Resort (Maui) 🏨, *211, 214*
Four Seasons Resort Hualālai (Big Island) 🏨, *391, 394*
Friendly Isle Coffee plantation (Moloka'i), *274, 277*

G

Garden of the Gods (Lāna'i), *302, 304–305*
Garden Isle Cottages (Kaua'i) 🏨, *514*
Gardens
Big Island, 361, 375, 378, 381, 383–384, 386
Kaua'i, 490–491, 492, 496
Maui, 182–183, 194, 202
O'ahu, 73, 74–75
General Store dive spot (Kaua'i), *466*
Gerard's (Maui) ✕, *233*
Gloria's Spouting Horn Bed & Breakfast (Kaua'i) 🏨, *514*
Goofy Foot surf shop (Maui), *157*
Gray's Beach (O'ahu), *9*
Green Sand (Papakōlea) **Beach** (Big Island), *327, 364, 365*
Greenwell Site (Big Island), *361, 362*

Grill at the Fairmont Orchid, The (Big Island) ✕, *419*
Groceries
Kaua'i, 492
Lāna'i, 312
Maui, 212, 220, 223, 224, 253–254
Moloka'i, 280, 285, 287–288
Grove Farm Homestead (Kaua'i), *493, 494*
Guava Kai Plantation (Kaua'i), *489*
Gump Building (O'ahu), *38, 40*

H

Hā'ena Beach Park (Kaua'i), *454, 491*
Ha'ikū (Maui), *193*
Haili Church (Big Island), *367, 378*
Hālawa Beach Park (Moloka'i), *265*
Hālawa Valley (Moloka'i), *278–279*
Hale O Lono Harbor (Moloka'i), *267*
Hale Pa'ahao (Old Prison, Maui), *172, 177*
Hale Pa'i (printing shop, Maui), *172, 177*
Hale-o-Keawe Heiau (Big Island), *363*
Haleakalā Crater (Maui), *165, 187*
Haleakalā Highway, *F16, 189*
Haleakalā National Park, *165–166, 187–192*
Haleakalā Visitor Center, *190*
Hale'iwa (O'ahu), *67, 68, 113–114*
Hale'iwa Beach, *14, 67, 69, 70*
Haleki'i Pihana Heiau State Monument (Maui), *180, 182*
Halekūlani (O'ahu) 🏨, *F17, 39, 40, 76*
Halemau'u Trail (Haleakalā), *191*
Hāli'imaile General Store (Maui) ✕, *244*
Hālona Blowhole (O'ahu), *61, 64*
Hālona Cove (O'ahu), *10*
Hāmākua Coast (Big Island), *328–329, 382–386, 410–411, 441*
Hamoa Bay House & Bungalow (Maui) 🏨, *227*
Hāmoa Beach (Maui), *145, 204*
Hamura Saimin (Kaua'i) ✕, *526*
Hāna (Maui), *144–145, 203, 225, 227–228, 253*
Hāna Coast Gallery, *253*

Hāna Cultural Center Museum, 203

Hāna Hale Malamalama (Bamboo Inn) ⌂, 227

Hāna Highway, 197–205

Hanakao'o Beach Park (Maui), 153

Hanakāpī'ai Beach (Kalalau), 480–481

Hanakāpī'ai Falls, 481–482

Hanakoa Valley (Kaua'i), 482

Hanalei Bay Beach Park (Kaua'i), 454, 469

Hanalei River, 464

Hanalei Valley Overlook, 489, 490

Hanapēpē (Kaua'i), 498, 500

Hanapēpē Valley and Canyon Lookout, 498, 500

Hanauma Bay Nature Preserve (O'ahu), 10, 22, 61, 64

Happy Talk Lounge (Kaua'i nightclub), 534

Hāpuna Beach State Recreation Area (Big Island), F17, 323, 330, 334

Hart-Felt Massage & Day Spa (Kaua'i), 517

Hawai'i (Big Island). ⇨ See Big Island

Hawai'i Kai (O'ahu), 111–112

Hawai'i Maritime Center (O'ahu), 48, 52

Hawai'i Nature Center (Maui), 168

Hawai'i Prince Golf Course (O'ahu), 29

Hawai'i State Art Museum (O'ahu), 48, 52

Hawai'i State Capitol, 50, 52

Hawai'i State Library, 50, 52

Hawai'i Theatre (O'ahu), 48, 52–53

Hawai'i Tropical Botanical Garden (Big Island), 382, 383–384

Hawai'i Volcanoes National Park (Big Island), 368–376

Hawaiian International Billfish Tournament (Big Island), 331

Hawaiian Sailing Adventures (Big Island), 334

Hāwī and Kapa'au (Big Island), 350, 351

Heiaus (sacred places of worship)
Big Island, 354, 355, 358, 362, 363
Kaua'i, 491–492
Lāna'i, 305
Maui, 182, 202
Moloka'i, 279
O'ahu, 66, 73

HI Humpback Whale Sanctuary, 184, 185

Hike Maui, 168

Hikiau Heiau (Big Island), 361, 362

Hilo (Big Island), 328, 366–367, 377–381, 407–410, 427–429, 432, 440–441

Hilo Bay, 333

Hilo Farmers Market, 377, 378, 441

Hilo Hattie, 440

Hilo Hawaiian Hotel ⌂, 407–408

Hilton Hawaiian Village Beach Resort and Spa (O'ahu) ⌂, 35, 41, 77

Hilton Waikoloa Village ⌂, 394–395

Hirohachi (Maui) ✕, 242

Hoapili Trail (Maui), 166

Hoku's at the Kāhala Mandarin Oriental (O'ahu) ✕, 109

Hōlua cabin (Haleakalā), 192

Honaka'a (Big Island), 382, 384

Honokōhau Beach (Big Island), 325

Honokōhau Harbor (Big Island), 331

Honoli'i Cove (Big Island), 330, 337

Honolua Bay (Maui), 151, 152–153

Honolulu, 7, 48–60, 91–92, 101–111, 121–123, 125–128. ⇨ Also Waikīkī

Honolulu Academy of Arts, 50, 53

Honolulu Hale (City Hall), 50, 53

Honolulu Zoo, 44, 45, 119

Honomanū Valley (Maui), 200

Honomū (Big Island), 382, 384

Honouliwai Taro Patch Farm, 278, 279

Ho'oilo House ⌂, 213

Ho'okena Beach Park (Big Island), 327

Ho'okipa Beach (Maui), 144, 156–158, 193

Ho'omau Congregational Church (Maui), 188, 191

Hosmer Grove (Haleakalā), 188, 191

Hot Island Glassblowing Studio & Gallery, 253

Hotel Hāna-Maui ⌂, 203, 225

Hotel Moloka'i ⌂, 284

Hotels. ⇨ See Lodging

Hualālai Resort Golf Course (Big Island), 342

Huelo (Maui), 198

Hui No'eau Visual Arts Center (Maui), 193, 194

Hula dancing, 432, 433

Hulē'ia River (Kaua'i), 464

Hulihe'e Palace (Big Island), 355–357

Hulopo'e Beach (Lāna'i), F17, 295, 297–298

Hyatt Regency Kaua'i Resort and Spa (Kaua'i) ⌂, F17, 511–512

I

'Īao Needle, 166, 182

'Īao Valley State Park (Maui), 166, 168, 180, 182

'Ihilani (Lāna'i) ✕, 309–310

'Ili'ili'ōpae Heiau (Moloka'i), 278, 279

'Ili'ili'ōpae Heiau Hike, 270–271

'Imiola Congregational Church (Big Island), 351

I'o (Maui) ✕, 233

'Iolani Palace (O'ahu), 48, 53

Ironman Triathlon (Big Island), 341

Isaac Hale Beach Park (Puna), 329

Island Treasures (gift shop), 128

Izakaya (Japanese pub-restaurants), 106

J

J. W. Marriott 'Ihilani Resort & Spa (O'ahu) ⌂, 94

Japanese Cemetery (Lana'i), 304, 305

Japanese pub-restaurants (izakaya), 106

Jet Skiing, 332

Jogging, 34

K

Ka Lae (South Point, Big Island), 334, 364, 365

Ka Lanakila O Ka Mālamalama (Lāna'i), 305

Ka Lokahi o Ka Mālamalama Church (Lāna'i), 301

Kā'anapali (Maui), 172, 177–178

Kā'anapali Beach, 140–141

Kāanapali Resort Golf Course, 162

Ka'eleku Caverns (Maui), 201

Kāena Point Trail (O'ahu), 28

Kahakuloa (Maui), 172, 178

Kāhala (O'ahu), 64, 65

Kāhala Mandarin Oriental Hawai'i ⌂, 91–92

Kahaloa Beach (O'ahu), 9
Kahalu'u Bay (Big Island), 336
Kahalu'u Beach Park, 326, 337
Kahana River (O'ahu), 19
Kahanu Garden (Maui), 202
Kahe'a Heiau (Lāna'i), 304, 305
Kahua Ranch (Big Island), 353
Kahuna (Wizard) Stones of Waikīkī, 39, 41
Kai (Maui) ✕, 237
Kailua (Maui), 198–199
Kailua (O'ahu), 112–113
Kailua Bay (Big Island), 325–326
Kailua Beach Park (O'ahu), F17, 12, 61
Kailua Pier (Big Island), 355, 358
Kailua-Kona (Big Island), 325–328, 355–359, 398–400, 402–404, 420–426, 438–440
Kainaliu (Big Island), 361, 362
Kakāako Kitchen (O'ahu) ✕, 108
Kalahaku Overlook (Haleakalā), 190
Kalākaua Park (Hilo), 367, 378
Kalalau Beach, 482
Kalalau Lookout, 483, 500–501
Kalalau Trail (Kaua'i), 479–483, 490
Kalapakī Beach (Kaua'i), 456–457, 469
Kalaupapa (Moloka'i), 274, 275
Kalaupapa Lookout, 277
Kalaupapa National Historical Park, 271
Kalaupapa Trail, 271
Kalepolepo Beach (Maui), 158
Kalihiwai Beach (Kaua'i), 455, 470
Kaloko'eli Fishpond (Moloka'i), 278, 279
Kaloko-Honokōhau National Historical Park (Kailua–Kona), 325
Kalōpā State Park (Big Island), 382, 384
Kaluakoi Golf Course (Moloka'i), 270
Kaluako'i Hotel and Golf Club, 273, 274
Kamakahonu (Big Island), 355, 358
Kamakahonu Beach, 325–326
Kamakou Preserve (Moloka'i), 271–272, 279–280
Kamalō (Moloka'i), 278, 280
Kama'ole I, II, and III (Maui), 141, 146

Kamehameha I, statue of, 48, 50, 60
Kamuela Museum (Big Island), 351, 353
Kanahā Beach (Maui), 143, 158
Kanemitsu Bakery and Restaurant (Moloka'i) ✕, 282
Kāne'ohe (O'ahu), 113
Kānepu'u Preserve (Lāna'i), 302, 305
Kapa'a Beach Park (Kaua'i), 466
Kapaia Stitchery (Kaua'i), 539
Kapala'oa (Haleakalā), 192
Kapalua (Maui), 172, 178
Kapalua Bay, 153
Kapalua Beach, 139–140
Kapalua Resort Golf Course, 162–163
Kapalua Wine & Food Festival, 241
Kapi'olani Bandstand, 44, 47
Kapi'olani Park (O'ahu), 34, 44–45, 47
Kapoho Tide Pools (Big Island), 329, 336, 388, 389
Kapolei Golf Course (O'ahu), 29
Kapuāiwa Coconut Grove (Moloka'i), 275
Kapukahehu Bay (Moloka'i), 264
Ka'u (Big Island), 326–328, 364–366, 404
Kaua'i, 447–543
Kalalau Trail & Nā Pali Coast, F16, 459–460, 464, 479–483, 491
Lihu'e, 493–497, 510–511, 525–527, 534–535, 538–539
Kaua'i Coffee Visitor Center and Museum, 498
Kaua'i Community College Performing Arts Center, 534
Kaua'i Community Players, 534
Kaua'i Concert Association, 534
Kaua'i Heritage Center, 537
Kaua'i Lagoons Golf Club, 475–476
Kaua'i Museum, 493, 495, 539
Kaumahina State Wayside Park (Maui), 199
Kaumalapau Harbor (Lāna'i), 301–302
Kaunakakai (Moloka'i), 275, 277
Kaunakakai Wharf, 275, 277
Kauna'oa Beach at Mauna Kea Beach Hotel, 322
Kaupō Road (Maui), 205
Kaupoa Beach Village (Moloka'i) 🏨, 283

Kawaiaha'o Church (O'ahu), 50, 60
Kawaihae Harbor (Big Island), 350, 353
Kawākiu Beach (Moloka'i), 263
Kawela Cul-de-Sacs trail heads (Moloka'i), 272
Kealakekua Bay (Big Island), F16, 332, 335–336, 359, 363
Keālia Beach (Kaua'i), 456, 470
Keālia Coastal Road, 474
Ke'anae Arboretum (Maui), 200
Ke'anae Overlook (Maui), 200
Keawakapu Beach (Maui), 160
Keawe Street (Hilo), 367, 378
Kebanu Gallery (Kaua'i), 538
Kē'e Beach State Park (Kaua'i), 453–454, 489, 490
Kehena Beach (Puna), 388
Kekaha Kai (Kona Coast) State Park, 324, 345
Kēōkea (Maui), 193, 194
Keōmuku (Lāna'i), 303, 305–306
Keōpūolani Park (Maui), 182
Kepaniwai Park & Heritage Gardens (Maui), 180, 182–183
Kepuhi Beach (Moloka'i), 263–264, 268
Kīhei (Maui), 184, 185
Kīholo Bay (Kohala), 323–324
Kīlauea (Kaua'i), 488, 490
Kīlauea Caldera (Big Island), 370
Kīlauea Iki Crater (Big Island), 371
Kīlauea Lighthouse and Kīlauea Point National Wildlife Refuge (Kaua'i), 488, 490
Kīlauea Lodge (Big Island) 🏨, 405
Kīlauea Theater and Community Event Center (Kaua'i), 534
Kīlauea Visitor Center (Big Island), 371, 372
Kilohana Plantation (Kaua'i), 493, 495
Kimura's Lauhala Shop (Big Island), 439
King Kamehameha Statue (Big Island), 350, 353
King Kamehameha's Kona Beach Hotel 🏨, 355, 358
Kīpuka Puaulu (Big Island), 375
Kiteboarding, 26–27, 149, 338, 465–466
Ko Olina Golf Club (O'ahu), 30

Kohala Mountain Road Lookout, 350, 353
Kohala Sports Club & Spa at the Hilton Waikoloa, 412–413
Kōke'e Natural History Museum, 501
Kōke'e State Park (Kaua'i), 477–478, 501
Kāilī Beach (Maui), 145, 204
Kolekole Beach Park (Big Island), 328–329, 382, 384
Kōloa (Kaua'i), 494, 495
Kōloa Landing, 466
Koloiki Ridge (Lāna'i), 299
Kona Coffee Living History Farm, 363
Kona Country Club, 342
Kona Inn Shopping Village, 355, 358
Kona Village Resort ⊞, 395, 434
Kōolau Golf Club (O'ahu), 30
Kua Bay (Big Island), 324
Kualoa Regional Park (O'ahu), 12
Kuamo'o Battlefield and Lekeleke Burial Grounds (Big Island), 356, 358–359
Kūhiō Beach Park (O'ahu), 9, 17
Kūkaniloko Birthstone State Monument (O'ahu), 74
Kukui Trail (Kaua'i), 478
Kukuiolono Park (Kau'i), 498, 501
Kula Botanical Gardens (Maui), 186, 194
Kulani Trails (Big Island), 339

L

La Cascata (Kaua'i) ✕, 522
La Mer (Waikīkī) ✕, 101
La Pérouse Bay (Maui), 185
Lahaina (Maui), 172–173, 177, 178–179
Lahaina Coolers ✕, 232
Lahaina Inn ⊞, 211
Lahaina-Kā'anapali & Pacific Railroad, 178
Lāna'i, 291–314
Lāna'i City, 301, 302, 310–311
Mānele Bay, 301, 302, 309–310
Windward Lāna'i, 302–306
Lāna'i Arts & Cultural Center, 302
Lāna'i City, 301, 302, 310–311
Lāna'i Fisherman Trail, 299–300
Lāna'i Pine Sporting Clays and Archery Range, 300
Lāna'ihale (Lāna'i), 306
Lanikai Beach Park (O'ahu), F17, 11–12, 19
Lapakahi State Historical Park (Big Island), 350, 354

Launiupoko State Wayside (Maui), 156
Laupāhoehoe Point Park (Big Island), 382, 384
Laupāhoehoe Train Museum, 382, 384–385
Lava Tree State Park (Puna), 387, 389
Lāwa'i Beach (Kaua'i), 468–469, 470
Leleiwi Beach Park and Richardson Ocean Park (Big Island), 328
Leleiwi Overlook (Haleakalā), 189–190
Lighthouses
Big Island, 388
Kaua'i, 490
O'ahu, 65
Līhu'e (Kaua'i), 493–497, 510–511, 525–527, 534–535, 538–539
Līhu'e Barbecue Inn ✕, 525
Lili'uokalani Gardens (Hilo), 377, 378
Lili'uokalani Protestant Church (O'ahu), 68
Limahuli Garden (Kaua'i), 489, 490–491
Lindbergh, Charles, grave of, 205
Little Beach (Maui), 146
Little Village Noodle House (O'ahu) ✕, 107
Lodge at Kō'ele (Lāna'i) ⊞, F17, 307
Lodge at Moloka'i Ranch, The ⊞, 283
Lōpā Beach (Moloka'i), 295
Lu'ahiwa Petroglyphs (Lāna'i), 301, 302
Lū'aus & Polynesian revues
Big Island, 432, 434
Kaua'i, 532–534
Maui, 245–246
O'ahu, 114–115
Lumaha'i Beach (Kaua'i), 454
Lydgate State Beach Park (Kaua'i), 456, 468, 488, 491
Lyman Mission House and Museum (Big Island), 367, 380

M

Mā'alaea Small Boat Harbor (Maui), 184, 185
MacKenzie State Recreation Area (Puna), 388, 389
Made on the Big Island, 439
Magic Sands Beach Park (Big Island), 326, 330
Magic Sands Bodysurfing Contest, 330

Magic Sportfishing (O'ahu), 18
Māhā'ulepū Beach (Kaua'i), 457
Mahi Waīanae sunken ship, 21
Māhukona Beach Park (Big Island), 322
Mai Tai Bar at Ala Moana Center (O'ahu), 122
Mailekini Heiau (Kohala District), 355
Ma'kaha Beach Park (O'ahu), 14, 24–25, 72
Ma'kaha Resort Golf Club, 31
Makalawena (Big Island), 324
Makapu'u Beach (O'ahu), 11, 17, 61
Makapu'u Lighthouse, 65
Makapu'u Point, 61, 65
Makawao (Maui), 193, 194
Mākena (Big) Beach State Park (Maui), F17, 142–143, 184, 185–186
Makena Landing, 148
Makena Resort Golf Course, 163–164
Mākua Beach (Kaua'i), 466, 468, 491
Mālaekahana Beach Park (O'ahu), 12
Mama's Fish House (Maui) ✕, 244–245
Mana Kai Maui ⊞, 218
Manago Hotel (Big Island) ✕, 426–427
Manana Island (Rabbit Island), 65
Mandara Spa at the Hilton Hawaiian Village (O'ahu), 96
Mānele Bay (Lāna'i), 301, 302, 309–310
Mānele Bay Hotel ⊞, 307
Mānele Small Boat Harbor, 298
Maniniholo Dry Cave (Kaua'i), 489, 491
Ma'noa Falls (O'ahu), 33
Manuka State Wayside (Big Island), 364, 365
Mark Twain's Monkeypod Tree (Big Island), 364, 365–366
Market Street (Wailuku), 180, 183
Master's Reading Room (Maui), 173, 178
Maui, 133–258
Haleakalā National Park, 165–166, 187–192
Hāna, 144–145, 225, 227–228, 253
Road to Hāna, 197–205
Maui Academy of Performing Arts, 247
Maui Arts & Cultural Center, 180, 183, 245

Maui Community Theatre, 247
Maui Crafts Guild, 253
Maui Film Festival, 246–247
Maui Girl, 253
Maui Hands, 253
Maui Ocean Center, 184, 186
Maui Onion ✕, 239–240
Maui Prince ⬛, 215
Maui Stables, 170
Maui Tropical Plantation &
  Country Store, 184
Maui's Best Tamales ✕, 243
Mauna Kea (Big Island), 385
Mauna Kea Beach Hotel ⬛,
  395
Mauna Kea Beach Resort Golf
  Course, 343
Mauna Kea Summit Tours, 385
Mauna Kea Trail, 345
Mauna Lani Bay Hotel and
  Bungalows (Big Island) ⬛,
  F17, 395–396
Mauna Lani Resort Golf Course
  (Big Island), 343
Mauna Lani Spa (Big Island),
  413
Mauna Loa Macadamia Factory
  (Hilo), 377, 380
Maunaloa (Moloka'i), 273,
  274
Maunaloa Room (Moloka'i) ✕,
  280–281
Maunalua Bay (O'ahu), 21
Maunawili Falls (O'ahu), 33
McGregor Point Lookout (Maui),
  160
Menehune Ditch (Kaua'i), 498
Merrie Monarch Hula Festival
  (Big Island), 432, 433
Merriman's (Big Island) ✕,
  420
Mission Houses Museum
  (O'ahu), 50, 60
Missouri (battleship, O'ahu),
  58, 59
Moanalua Gardens (O'ahu),
  74–75
Mōkapu Beach (Maui), 142,
  153
Mokoli'i Island, 67
Moku'aikaua Church (Big
  Island), 355, 359
Mokuleia Beach (Maui), 139
Mokulē'ia Beach Park (O'ahu),
  14, 19
Mokupapapa: Discovery Center
  for Hawaii's Remote Coral
  Reefs Museum (Big Island),
  377
Moloka'i, 259–290
Moloka'i Mule Ride, 274, 277
Moloka'i Ranch bicycling,
  269

Molokini Crater (Maui), 151
Mo'okini Heiau (Big Island),
  351, 354
Mopeds and motorcycles
  Big Island, 444
  Maui, 256
  O'ahu, 131–132
Mountain tubing tours, 484
Mule rides (Moloka'i), 274,
  277
Mulligan's on the Blue (Maui
  nightclub), 248
Munro Trail (Lāna'i), 300, 303,
  306

N

Na Hoku II Catamaran (O'ahu),
  20
Nā Pali Coast Wilderness State
  Park (Kaua'i), F16,
  459–460, 464, 479–483,
  491
Naha (Lāna'i), 304, 306
Naha and Pinao stones (Big
  Island), 367, 380
Nahiku (Maui), 201
Na'iwa Mountain Trails
  (Moloka'i), 269
Nani Mau Gardens (Hilo), 377,
  381
Nāpili Beach (Maui), 140
Nāpili Kai Beach Club (Maui)
  ⬛, 212–213
Nāpō'opo'o Beach Park
  (Big Island), 326–327, 359,
  363
National Memorial Cemetery of
  the Pacific (NTBG) (O'ahu),
  60, 65
National Tropical Botanical
  Gardens (Kaua'i), 494, 496
Nāwiliwili (Kaua'i), 493, 496
Ni'ihau (Kaua'i), 469, 533
Norfolk Pine (Lāna'i), 301,
  302
North Country Farms (Kaua'i)
  ⬛, 504
North Shore Surf and Cultural
  Museum (O'ahu), 67, 68, 73
Nu'alolo Kai (Kaua'i), 469
Nu'uanu Pali Lookout (O'ahu),
  61, 65

O

O'ahu, 1–132
  Pearl Harbor, 54–59
  Waikīkī, 7–8, 35–44, 76–77,
    81–91, 100–104, 119–121,
    123–125
Ocean Club, The (O'ahu
  nightclub), 122–123
Ocean Eco Tours (Big Island),
  335

'Ohe'o Gulch (Maui), 166,
  204–205
Old Kona Airport State
  Recreation Area, 325
Old Lahaina Lū'u, 246
Old Wailuku Inn (Maui) ⬛,
  221
Olowalu (Maui), 153
Olowalu Beach (Maui), 148
One Ali'i Beach Park
  (Moloka'i), 264
Onekahakaha Beach Park (Big
  Island), 328
Ōneo Bay (Big Island), 333
Onizuka Center (Big Island),
  356, 385
'Ōpaeka'a Falls (Kaua'i), 488,
  491
Opium Den & Champagne Bar at
  Indigo's (O'ahu nightclub),
  123
Original Glider Rides, The
  (O'ahu), 27
Our Lady of Fatima Shrine
  (Maui), 201
Outrigger Waikīkī on the Beach
  ⬛, 84

P

Pacific Tsunami Museum (Big
  Island), 377, 381
Pacific Whale Foundation
  (Maui), 155, 160
Pacific Whaling Museum
  (O'ahu), 66
Pacific'O (Maui) ✕, 237
Pahala (Big Island), 366
Pāhoa (Puna), 387, 389
Pahui'a at Four Seasons Resort
  Hualālai (Big Island) ✕,
  417–418
Pā'ia (Maui), 193, 194, 196,
  198
Pāia Bay (Maui), 146
Pālā'au State Park (Moloka'i),
  274, 277
Palikū cabin (Haleakalā),
  192
Palms Cliff House Inn, The (Big
  Island) ⬛, 410
Pana'ewa Rain Forest Zoo
  (Hilo), 377, 381
Paniolo Hale (Moloka'i) ⬛,
  283
Pāpōhaku Beach (Moloka'i),
  264, 273, 274
Paradice Bluz (Maui
  nightclub), 248
Paradise Cove Lū'au (O'ahu),
  115
Parker Ranch Visitor Center and
  Museum (Big Island), 351,
  354

Parks, national, *F38–F39*
Big Island, 325, 368–376
Kaua'i, 490
Maui, 165–166, 187–192
Moloka'i, 271
Pearl Harbor, 54–59
Pe'epe'e Falls (Hilo), 377, 381
Pele's Paint Pot (Haleakalā), *191*
Petroglyphs, 302
Phallic Rock (Moloka'i), 277
Piece of Paradise Gallery (Kaua'i), 539
Pihea Trail (Kaua'i), 478
Pi'ilanihale Heiau (Maui), 202
"Pine Trees" surfing area (Kaua'i), 470
Plane Wreck Point (Big Island), 334
Plantation Gardens (Kaua'i) ✕, 529–530
Plantation Inn (Maui) ⊞, 210–211
Pōhaku hānau (Kaua'i), 492
Pōhaku piko (Kaua'i), 492
Pōhaku-ho'ohānau (Kaua'i), 492
Po'ipū (Kaua'i), *F17, 494, 496–497*
Po'ipū Bay Golf Course, 476
Po'ipū Beach Park, 458, 468, 469, 470
Poli'ahu Heiau (Kaua'i), 488, 491–492
Polihale State Park (Kaua'i), 459
Polihua Beach (Moloka'i), 295
Polipoli Forest (Maui), 161, 166
Polo Beach (Maui), 142, 153
Pololū Beach (Big Island), 321–322
Pololū Valley (Big Island), 350, 354–355
Polynesian Cultural Center (O'ahu), 67, 73, 115, 117
Polynesian revues, 114–115, 245–246, 434, 532–534
Pomodoro Ristorante Italiano (Kaua'i) ✕, 530
Postcards Cafe (Kaua'i) ✕, 521
Powerline Trail (Kaua'i), 474
Prince Kūhiō Park (Kaua'i), 494, 497
Princeville Ranch Stables (Kaua'i), 484
Princeville Resort (Kaua'i) ⊞, 503
Princevile Resort Golf Courses, 476–477
Puahokamoa Stream (Maui), 199

Puna (Big Island), 329, 386–389, 411–412
Puna Beach Road, 339
Punalu'u Bakeshop and Visitor Center (Big Island), 364, 366
Punalu'u (Black Sand) Beach Park (Big Island), 327–328, 364, 366
Punchbowl Crater (O'ahu), 65
Purdy's Macadamia Nut Farm (Moloka'i), 274, 277
Pu'u hinahina Lookout (Kaua'i), 502
Pu'u ka Pele Lookout (Kaua'i), 502
Pu'u O Hoku Ranch (Moloka'i), 272–273, 278, 280
Pu'u o Kila Lookout (Kaua'i), 500
Pu'u Pehe Trail (Lāna'i), 300
Pu'u 'Ula'ula Overlook (Haleakalā), 190
Pu'uhonua O Hōnaunau (Place of Refuge) (Big Island), 334, 336, 361, 363
Pu'ukoholā Heiau National Historic Site (Kohala District), 350, 355
Pu'uomahuka Heiau (O'ahu), 73
Pu'upehe (Sweetheart Rock) (Lāna'i), 302

Q

Queen Emma Summer Palace (O'ahu), 61, 65–66
Queen's Surf beach (O'ahu), 9, 22, 72
Quicksilver in Memory of Eddie Aikau Big Wave Invitational (O'ahu), 72

R

R. W. Meyer Sugar Mill and Moloka'i Museum, 274, 277–278
Rabbit Island, 65
Rainbow Falls (Hilo), 377, 381
Red Sand Beach (Maui), 144–145
Reeds Bay Beach Park (Big Island), 328
Restaurant Kaikodo (Big Island) ✕, 428–429
Richardson's Ocean Beach Park (Big Island), 333
Ritz-Carlton (Kapalua) ⊞, 207
Road to Hāna, 197–205
Road to the Sea (Big Island), 327
Rodeos, 169

Royal Hawaiian Hotel (O'ahu) ⊞, 39, 41
Royal Kunia Country Club (O'ahu), 32
Roy's (O'ahu) ✕, 111–112
Roy's Kahana Bar & Grill (Maui) ✕, 233
RV rental, 444

S

S. Hata Building (Big Island), 377, 381
Saigon Café, A (Maui) ✕, 239
St. Benedict's Painted Church (Big Island), 361, 364
St. Michael's Church (Big Island), 355, 359
Salt Pond Beach Park (Kaua'i), 459, 498, 501
Sandy Beach (O'ahu), 10–11, 17, 61
Sans Souci beach (O'ahu), 9–10
Sansei (Maui) ✕, 237
Sansei Seafood Restaurant & Sushi Bar (O'ahu) ✕, 102–103
Science City (Haleakalā), 190
Sea Life Park (O'ahu), 61, 66
Seamen's Hospital (Maui), 173, 178
Senator Fong's Plantation and Gardens (O'ahu), 67, 73
Sergeant Major Reef dive site (Lāna'i), F16, 297
Shark's Cove (O'ahu), F16, 21, 23
Sheraton Caverns (Kaua'i), 466
Sheraton Maui ⊞, 210
Sheraton Moana Surfrider (O'ahu) ⊞, 39, 41
Shipman House Bed & Breakfast Inn (Big Island) ⊞, 408–409
Shipwreck Beach (Lāna'i), 295–296, 303, 306
Shuttle service
Lāna'i, 314
Maui, 256–257
Side Street Inn (O'ahu) ✕, 104, 106
Sierra Club, 168
Sig Zane Designs (Big Island), 440
Skiing, snow, 346
"Slaughterhouse" Beach (Maui), 139
Sleeping Giant rock formation (Kaua'i), 488, 492
Sleeping Giant Trail, 478
Sliding Sands Trail (Haleakalā), 191

Smith's Tropical Paradise
(Kaua'i), *492, 533*
Snow skiing, *346*
South Pacific Kayaks (Maui),
148
South Point (Big Island), *334,
364, 365*
South Shore Reef (Moloka'i),
266–267
Spa Grande, Grand Wailea
(Maui), *F17, 229*
Spa at Hotel Hāna Maui, *229*
Spa Olakino at the Waikīkī
Beach Marriott, *97–98*
Spa Suites at the Kāhala
Mandarin Oriental, *98*
Spa at the Westin Maui, The,
231
Spago (Maui) ✕, *240*
Spencer Beach Park (Kohala),
322
Spouting Horn blowhole
(Kaua'i), *494, 497*
Star of the Sea Painted Church
(Puna), *388, 389*
Stargazing, *245*
Submarine Museum & Park
(O'ahu), *59*
Submarine tours, *23–24, 337*
Sunset on the Beach
entertainment events (O'ahu),
117
Sunset Beach (O'ahu), *13, 25,
67, 69, 70*
Sunset cruises, *434*
Symbols, *F7*

T

Tamarind Park (O'ahu), *48*
Tastings (Maui) ✕, *240, 241*
Tedeschi Vineyards and Winery
(Maui), *193, 196*
Thai Cuisine (Maui) ✕, *243*
Theater
Kaua'i, 534
Maui, 247
O'ahu, 52–53
3660 on the Rise (Honolulu)
✕, *109*
Thompson Road (Maui), *161*
Three Tables reefs (O'ahu), *F16,
21*
Thurston Lava Tube (Big Island),
371
Tidepools (Kaua'i) ✕, *530*
Triathlons, *341*
Triple Crown of Surfing, *69–72*
Trolley travel, *130*
Tunnels Beach (Kaua'i), *466,
468, 491*
Turtle Bay Resort (O'ahu) 🏨,
32
Twin Falls (Maui), *198*

U

Ukumehame Beach (Maui),
148, 156
"'Ulalena" at Maui Theater, *247*
Ulua Beach (Maui), *142, 153*
Ulukou Beach (O'ahu), *9, 25*
Ulupō Heiau (O'ahu), *61, 66*
Umauma Falls (Big Island),
382, 386
Urasenke Foundation, The, *35,
41, 44*
U.S. Army Museum (O'ahu), *35,
44*
USS *Arizona* Memorial, *57, 59*
USS *Bowfin* Memorial, *59*
USS *Missouri*, *58, 59*

V

Vans Triple Crown of Surfing
(O'ahu's North Shore),
69–72
Victoria Ward Centers, *126*
Volcano Art Center, *371*
Volcano House, *371*
Volcano Village (Big Island),
375, 404–407, 427
Volcano Winery, *375*

W

Waialea Beach (Big Island),
323
Waialua Beach Park
(Moloka'i), *265, 268*
Wai'ānapanapa State Park
(Maui), *144, 202–203*
Waihī Falls (O'ahu), *73*
Waihikuli Wayside Park (Maui),
153
Waikamoi Nature Trail (Maui),
199
Waikāni Falls (Maui), *201*
Waikapala'e and Waikanaloa
Wet Caves (Kaua'i), *489,
492*
Waikele Premium Outlets, *129*
Waikīkī, *7–8, 35–44, 76–77,
81–91, 100–104, 119–121,
123–125*
Waikīkī Aquarium, *45, 47*
Waikīkī Beach Marriott Resort
🏨, *85*
Waikīkī Historic Trail, *39, 44*
Waikīkī Parc (O'ahu) 🏨,
82–83
Waikīkī Shell (concert arena),
44, 47
Waikīkī War Memorial
Natatorium, *45, 47*
Waikoloa (Big Island), *432,
434*
Waikoloa Beach Resort Golf
Course, *344*

Wailea (Maui), *184, 186*
Wailea Beach (Maui), *142,
153*
Wailea Resort golf courses
(Maui), *164–165*
Wailea Villas 🏨, *219*
Wailoa Center (Hilo), *377, 381*
Wailua (Kaua'i), *470, 492–493*
Wailua Falls, *488, 493*
Wailua Forest Management
Road, *474*
Wailua Marina Restaurant
(Kaua'i) ✕, *524*
Wailua Overlook (Maui),
200–201
Wailua River, *463–464*
Waimānalo (O'ahu), *61, 66*
Waimānalo Beach Park (O'ahu),
11, 61
Waimea (Big Island), *347,
350–355, 397–398,
419–420, 437–438*
Waimea (Kaua'i), *498,
501–502*
Waimea Bay (O'ahu), *13, 67,
72*
Waimea Canyon (Kaua'i), *500,
502*
Waimea Canyon Road, *474*
Waimea Canyon State Park,
477–478
Waimea Christian Hawaiian and
Foreign Church (Kaua'i), *501*
Waimea Plantation Cottages
(Kaua'i) 🏨, *515*
Waimea Valley Audubon Center
(O'ahu), *67, 73–74*
Waimea Visitor Center (Big
Island), *351, 355*
Waimoku Falls (Maui), *166,
205*
Waiola Church and Cemetery
(Maui), *173, 179*
Wai'oli Mission House (Kauai),
489, 493
Waipi'o Valley (Big Island),
385–386
Waipi'o Valley Overlook, *382,
386*
Warren & Annabelle's (Maui
nightclub), *247*
Waterfalls
Big Island, 381, 383, 386
Kaua'i, 481–482, 491, 493
Maui, 166, 198, 201, 205
O'ahu, 33, 73
West Kaua'i Visitor and
Technology Center, *498*
West Kaunala Trail (O'ahu), *28*
Whale-watching, *26, 158–160,
269, 337–338, 470–471*
Whaling Museum (Maui),
177–178

White Plains Beach (Oʻahu), 25
White Sands Beach Park (Big
   Island), 326, 330
Wildlife preserves
Big Island, 332
Kauaʻi, 490
Lānaʻi, 305
Molokaʻi, 271–272, 279–280
Oʻahu, 10, 22, 64

Wine & wineries, F31, 196,
   241, 375
Wo Hing Museum (Maui), 173,
   179
Wood Valley Temple (Big
   Island), 366
World Botanical Gardens (Big
   Island), 382, 386

Y
Yokohama Bay (Oʻahu), 14–15

Z
"Ziplining," 485
Zoos
Big Island, 381
Oʻahu, 45, 119

PHOTO CREDITS

Introduction: F8, Walter Bibikow/www.viestiphoto.com. F9 (left), Corbis. F9 (right), Walter Bibikow/www. viestiphoto.com. F10, Molokai Ranch. F11, Douglas Peebles/age fotostock. F12, SuperStock/age fotostock. F13 (left), Walter Bibikow/www.viestiphoto.com. F13 (right), J. Luke/PhotoLink/Photodisc/Getty Images. **Chapter 1: Oahu:** 1, Polynesian Cultural Center. 2 (top), Ken Ross/www.viestiphoto.com. 2 (bottom left), Michael S. Nolan/age fotostock. 2 (bottom right), SuperStock/age fotostock. 3 (top), Oahu Visitors Bureau. 3 (bottom left), Corbis. 3 (bottom right), Oahu Visitors Bureau. 4, SuperStock/age fotostock. 5, Oahu Visitors Bureau. 6, Andre Seale/age fotostock. 55, U.S. National Archives . 57 (top), Corbis. 57 (bottom), NPS/ USS Arizona Memorial Photo Collection . 58, Army Signal Corps Collection in the U.S. National Archives. 58 (inset), USS Missouri Memorial Association. 59, USS Bowfin Submarine Museum & Park. 69, ASP Tostee. 70, ASP Tostee. 71, ASP Tostee. 72, Carol Cunningham/cunninghamphotos.com. **Chapter 2: Maui:** 133, Michael S. Nolan/age fotostock. 134 (top), S. Alden/PhotoLink/Photodisc/Getty Images. 134 (bottom left), Douglas Peebles/age fotostock. 134 (bottom right), Walter Bibikow/www.viestiphoto.com. 135 (top), Ron Dahlquist/Maui Visitors Bureau . 135 (bottom left), Walter Bibikow/www.viestiphoto.com. 135 (bottom right), Chris Hammond/www.viestiphoto.com. 137, Maui Visitors Bureau. 187, National Park Service. 190, Maui Visitors Bureau. 191, Karl Weatherly/Photodisc/Getty Images. 192, Maui Visitors Bureau. 197, Chris Hammond/www.viestiphoto.com. 199, Ron Dahlquist/Maui Visitors Bureau. 200, Chris Hammond/www. viestiphoto.com. 203, Richard Genova/www.viestiphoto.com. 204, SuperStock/age fotostock. 205, Chris Hammond/www.viestiphoto.com. **Chapter 3: Molokai:** 259, Molokai Visitors Association. 260 (top), Walter Bibikow/www.viestiphoto.com. 260 (bottom left), Molokai Visitors Association. 260 (bottom right), Molokai Visitors Association. 261 (top), Molokai Ranch. 261 (center), Walter Bibikow/www.viestiphoto.com. 261 (bottom left), Douglas Peebles/age fotostock. 261 (bottom right), Walter Bibikow/www.viestiphoto.com. **Chapter 4: Lanai:** 291, Lanai Image Library. 292 (top), Walter Bibikow/www.viestiphoto.com. 292 (bottom left), Lanai Visitors Bureau. 292 (bottom right), Walter Bibikow/www.viestiphoto.com. 293 (top), Michael S. Nolan/age fotostock. 293 (bottom left), Lanai Image Library. 293 (bottom right), Lanai Image Library. 294, Lanai Image Library. **Chapter 5: The Big Island of Hawaii:** 315, Walter Bibikow/www.viestiphoto.com. 316 (top), Big Island Visitors Bureau. 316 (bottom left), Big Island Visitors Bureau. 316 (bottom right), S. Alden/PhotoLink/Photodisc/Getty Images. 317 (top), Big Island Visitors Bureau. 317 (bottom left), Big Island Visitors Bureau. 317 (bottom right), Big Island Visitors Bureau. 319, Big Island Visitors Bureau. 320, Big Island Visitors Bureau. 369, Big Island Visitors Bureau. 371, Russ Bishop/age fotostock. 373 (left), R. Hoblitt/U.S. Department of Interior, U.S. Geological Survey. 373 (right), G. Brad Lewis/age fotostock. 375, R. Hoblitt/U.S. Department of Interior, U.S. Geological Survey. 376, J. Kauahikaua/U.S. Department of Interior, U.S. Geological Survey. **Chapter 6: Kauai:** 447, Karl Weatherly/age fotostock. 448 (top), Kauai Visitors Bureau. 448 (bottom left), Kauai Visitors Bureau. 448 (bottom right), Kauai Visitors Bureau. 449 (top), Kauai Visitors Bureau. 449 (center), Kauai Visitors Bureau. 449 (bottom), Kauai Visitors Bureau. 451 (left), Corbis. 451 (right), SuperStock/age fotostock. 479 (top), Kauai Visitors Bureau. 479 (bottom), SuperStock/age fotostock. 480, Andre Seale/age fotostock. 482, Karen Shigematsu/Lyon Arboretum. 483, Kauai Visitors Bureau. **Color Section:** Surfers walking along Waikiki Beach, Oahu: Allan Seiden/Oahu Visitors Bureau. Catching a wave: SuperStock/age fotostock. Garden of the Gods, Lanai: Walter Bibikow/www.viestiphoto.com. Fire eater: SuperStock/age fotostock. Children with haku (head) lei: SuperStock/age fotostock. Waikiki, Oahu: J.D.Heaton/Picture Finders/age fotostock. Hula dancers: Hawaii Visitors & Convention Bureau. Hawaii Volcanoes National Park, Big Island: G. Brad Lewis/age fotostock. Waianapanapa State Park, Maui: SuperStock/age fotostock. Surfers, North Shore, Oahu: Ken Ross/www. viestiphoto.com. Lava flow, Hawaii Volcanoes National Park, Big Island: Larry Carver/www.viestiphoto.com. Golf Course at Mauna Lani Resort, Kohala Coast: Big Island Visitors Bureau. Haleakala National Park, Maui: Maui Visitors Bureau. Na Pali Coast, Kauai: Scott West/www.viestiphoto.com. Coffee picking contest, Kona, Big Island: Joe Viesti/www.viestiphoto.com. Cyclists overlooking Kalaupapa peninsula, Molokai: Molokai Visitors Association. Green Sea Turtles: HVCB/Na Pali Explorer.

ABOUT OUR WRITERS

Wanda A. Adams was born and raised on Maui and now makes her home on O'ahu. She has been a newspaper reporter for more than 25 years, specializing in food, dining, and travel.

Don Chapman is the editor of the award-winning *MidWeek*, Hawai'i's largest-circulation newspaper. The golf writer for this guide, Don has played 88 golf courses in Hawai'i and writes about golf for a variety of national publications. He is also the author of four books.

Joan Conrow has lived on Kaua'i since 1987. She writes frequently about Hawai'i's natural world—and any other subject that strikes her fancy—for a number of national and regional publications.

Chad Pata has been covering the beaches and sports of Hawai'i for *MidWeek* and *The Honolulu Advertiser* for six years. Originally from Atlanta, Georgia, he moved to O'ahu in 1993, married a local girl, and now lives for his two kids, Honu and Calogero.

Peter Serafin lives on the Big Island, where he writes for the *Hawaii Island Journal*, the Associated Press, and the *Honolulu Star-Bulletin*. Before coming to Hawai'i, Peter lived in Tokyo for many years, writing for the *Japan Times*. He continues to spend part of the year in Asia.

Kim Steutermann Rogers is a freelance journalist living on Kaua'i, where she hikes the mountains in her backyard, and paddles the ocean's waters in her front yard. She drags her dog and husband along on her adventures and in between writes about them for regional and national travel and outdoor magazines.

Life-long O'ahu resident **Lance Tominaga** has been writing about the Aloha State for more than 15 years. His work has been published in *ALOHA Magazine*, *Hawaii Business*, *Hawaii Magazine*, *Spirit of Aloha*, *Downtown Planet*, and *Island Scene*.

Joana Varawa has lived on Lāna'i for 30 years and is editor of *The Lāna'i Times*. She writes for Hawaiian and Aloha airlines' magazines, has authored three books, and—along with her beloved dog—could lead you around "her" island blindfolded, investigating deer trails and supervising sunsets.

Travel writer **Amy Westervelt** has been dividing her time between Kona and San Francisco for more than fifteen years. When she's not hanging out at the beach or hiking the Hilo valleys, Amy writes about travel, food, and culture for publications like *Travel +Leisure*, *Modern Bride*, and the *San Francisco Chronicle*.

Shannon Wianecki was raised on Maui and loves divulging its secrets. With over a decade of experience in the travel industry, she splits her time between writing and conservation. She is the food editor for *Maui nō ka 'oi* magazine and the outreach coordinator for a high-school science curriculum based on the ecosystems of Haleakalā.

Paul Wood, an independent writer and writing teacher—and long-time resident of Maui—contributes regularly to publications interested in Hawai'i-based topics. His recent work includes a collection of humorous stories called *False Confessions* (Flying Rabbit Press) and a series of picture guides about the botany of Hawai'i (Island Heritage).

After 20 years as a Hawai'i hotel executive, **Maggie Wunsch** now covers Hawai'i for a variety of radio, print, and broadcast media. She is an unabashed fan of room service, sandy beaches, and the delicious scents of her state—from pikake jasmine to teriyaki barbeque.

Hawai'i resident **Katie Young** has spent five years as a writer, columnist, and editor for *MidWeek*, covering everything from entertainment to island living. Her work has also appeared in *Makai* magazine and the *Honolulu Star-Bulletin*. She enjoys dancing hula and watching the sunset with her dog, Pono.